Rum & Reggae's Caribbean

Caribbean

FIFTH EDITION

written and edited by

Jonathan Runge

Rum & Reggae Guidebooks, Inc.
Boston, Massachusetts • December 2006

Fifth Edition

ISBN: 1-893675-14-9
ISSN: 1529-2495

Edited by Jonathan Runge
Co-edited by Joe Shapiro

Book design by Valerie Brewster, Scribe Typography
Cover design by Jonathan Runge and Valerie Brewster
Cover Illustration by Eric Orner
Illustrations by Eric Orner
Back cover photo by Jupiterimages
Author photo by Vincent-louis Apruzzese of behemothmedia.com
Maps by Shane Matthews of Full View Mapping

Printed in the United States

For Lynn

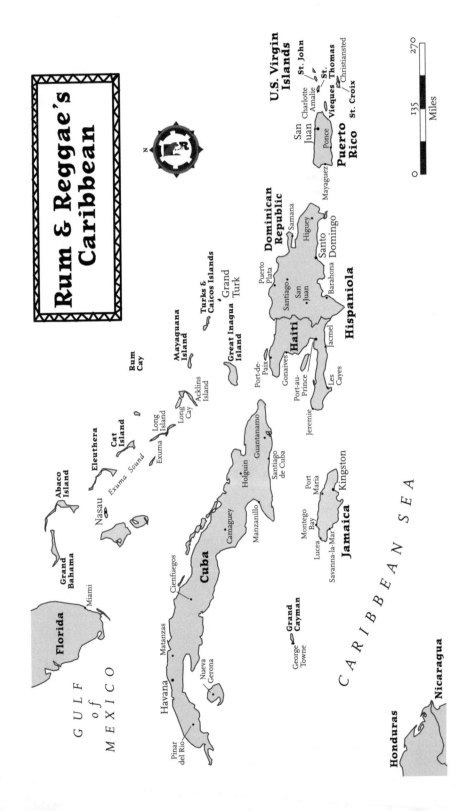

Rum & Reggae's Caribbean

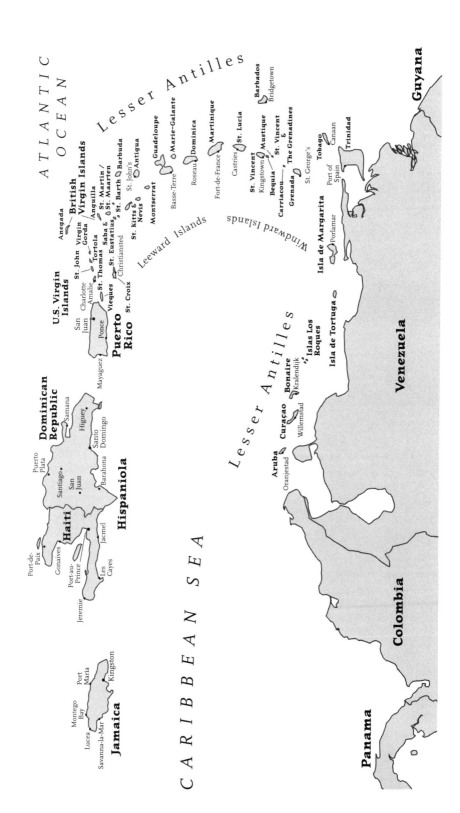

CONTENTS

Before You Go 3

Anguilla 21

Antigua and Barbuda 37

Aruba 63

Barbados 75

Bonaire 91

INDEX OF MAPS

Lodging and Restaurant Key

Note: We have used a number of symbols and terms to indicate prices and ambiance. Here are the code breakers.

Lodging Symbols

(C) telephone number

(fax symbol) fax number

(computer symbol) Web site URL and/or e-mail address

($) room rates

(meal symbol) meal plan

(CC) major credit cards
Be sure to ask if your credit card is accepted when making reservations.

(★) This is a Rum & Reggae "best of category" establishment.

Lodging Rates

- Prices are rack rates for the least expensive double (two people) in high season — generally mid-December through mid-April — unless otherwise noted. Off-season rates are often as much as 50 percent cheaper. Unless otherwise noted, prices for singles are the same or slightly less.

- Expect a service and tax charge of at least 15 percent added to your bill. Some countries can reach 25 percent! Ouch! Be sure to ask

Dirt Cheap	under $50
Cheap	$51–$100
Not So Cheap	$101–$150
Pricey	$151–$200
Very Pricey	$201–$300
Wicked Pricey	$301–$400
Ridiculous	$401–$500
Beyond Belief	$501–$600
Stratospheric	$601 and up!

ahead of time to avoid going into shock. On the French islands, tax and service is generally included in the quoted rates, although there are exceptions. (Ask at the front desk how the service charge will be distributed to employees — usually you are not expected to leave any additional tips.)

- Be sure to ask about credit cards when making your reservations if you intend to use them for payment. A few places, even expensive ones, do not accept credit cards.

- Hotels in *Rum & Reggae's Caribbean* are listed in order of what we recommend most to what we recommend least (within each town), regardless of rates. By doing this, we avoid the practice of listing hotels solely in order of rates, which often serves to bury the lower-priced hotels at the bottom of the list.

Lodging and Meal Codes 🍴

All hotel prices are assigned a corresponding code that relates to the meals that are included in the rates.

EP	**European Plan** — No meals included.
CP	**Continental Plan** — Continental breakfast (bread, cereal, juice, coffee) included.
BP	**Breakfast Plan** — Full hot breakfast included.
MAP	**Modified American Plan** — Full breakfast and dinner included.
FAP	**Full American Plan** — Full breakfast, lunch, and dinner included (sometimes with an afternoon "tea" or snack as well).
All-Inclusive	All meals, beer, wine, and well drinks (house brands) are included, most or all on-site activities, and usually tax and service charges.

Restaurant Prices

Prices represent per-person cost for the average meal, from soup to nuts. Restaurants are separated by neighborhood (where applicable) and are listed alphabetically.

$	Under $15
$$	$15–$25
$$$	$26–$35
$$$$	$36–$50
$$$$$	Over $50

Touristo Scale 💀

You'll find the key to our Touristo Scale on the last page of the book.

PREFACE

The fifth edition of *Rum & Reggae's Caribbean* is the 13th book to be published by Rum & Reggae Guidebooks, Inc. Writing these books is now a team effort, and for this guide, David Swanson, Adam Carter, and Sam Logan were all contributors.

David Swanson is a San Diego–based freelance writer who has been traveling to the Caribbean for two decades. Although he appreciates all of the islands to various degrees, he has particularly enjoyed discovering the region's more exotic corners, including Haiti, Cuba (in 1989, just as the Soviet Union was dropping aid), and the summit of Montserrat's smoldering volcano. Swanson's work has appeared in more than 50 North American newspapers and in assorted magazines, including *Caribbean Travel and Life, American Way*, and *National Geographic Traveler*.

Adam Carter is a Chicago-based Cubs fan who spends his summers vending beer at the ballpark. While waiting for the Cubs to finally win the big one, he obtained a master's degree in International Relations. Merging this background with journalism, Adam served as the cultural arts reporter for a Washington, D.C., paper, *The Hatchet*, and while working for the UN he traveled to Colombia to write articles about its internal refugees. His articles have been published in *Worldview Magazine* and the *San Francisco Chronicle*. He currently writes for *Filosophy Magazine* as he works on his first novel, which is set in Brazil. Adam has an unchallenged thirst for travel and has seen just about every corner, nook, and cranny of the globe. Adam was the co-author of *Rum & Reggae's Costa Rica* and was also a major contributor to *Rum & Reggae's Brazil*.

Sam Logan hails from New Orleans but is usually based in Rio de Janeiro, Brazil. When not in Rio, he is muckraking for freelance assignments in just about every forest, slum, city, or beach in Latin America. "Mr. Everything," as we like to call him, has done it all, from having founded two marketing consulting firms to working for Outward Bound and leading white-water kayaking tours. In addition to working as an investigative reporter for a number of news publications and a Texas-based private intelligence organization (shhhhh), Sam finds time to surf and hurtle off raging waterfalls. Oh, and he also holds an M.A. in International Policy Studies. Sam was a major contributor to *Rum & Reggae's Brazil*.

We hope you enjoy the book. Please be sure to visit our Web site at www.rumreggae.com.

ACKNOWLEDGMENTS

Contrary to what you might think, writing a book on the Caribbean is not very glamorous. The most glamorous part about doing it is answering the "So what do you do?" question at cocktail parties. It's all uphill from there. We did not spend our days on the beach or by the pool sipping a piña colada. Well, okay, sometimes we did. But most of the time we were running around checking out this or that and complaining about the heat. Just when we started to get comfortable on an island, it was time to uproot ourselves and start all over again. Try doing that at least 30 times and you'll begin to know what we mean.

Fortunately, some wonderful people helped us out along the way. We'd like to take this opportunity to sincerely thank those who did. In no particular order, they are Suzanne Adams, Linda and Burr Vail, Concepción Cano, Leana and Enrique Ducournau, Celia Ross, Gaia Peri, Simonique Jack, Harold Davies and Kingsley Wratten, Wilhelm Sack, Mark Browne, Andres Branger, Diane Lulek, Laura Davidson, Kim Greiner, Luana Wheatley, Cheryl Andrews, Margie Benziger, Lisa Blau, Molly Tichy, Gerald Hill, Roberta Garzaroli, Muriel Wiltord, Guy-Claude Germain, Glenn C. Holm, Roland Lopes, Elise Magras, Helen Kidd, Cristina Rivas, Marilyn Marx, Angela Sinto, Leslie Cohen, Marie Kephart, Melanie Brandman and Associates, Jodie Diamond, Janelle James, Kara Barbakoff, Marie Rosa, Cathy Preece, Melissa Lukis, Shantini Ramakrishnan, Barbara Walker and Shireen Aga, Matthew Snow, Erika Vives, Andria Mitsakos, Katie Rogers, and Gay Myers. If we overlooked your name, sorry, but thanks for your help!

Rum & Reggae's Caribbean is the flagship publication of Rum & Reggae Guidebooks, Inc., which translates to a helluva lot more work for our staff. We have many helpers, and all deserve hearty thanks. First and foremost, a lot of credit for this latest edition goes to David Swanson, our chief Caribbean writer and editor and general bon vivant of the West Coast. He did the lion's share of updating and revising. Thanks, too, to our other contributors: Adam Carter and Sam Logan. Our warmest gratitude goes to the following: our fabulous and wonderfully easygoing book designer, Valerie Brewster of Scribe Typography; our very talented Web designer, Michael Carlson; our corporate illustrator and Disney animation megastar, Eric Orner; our cartographer, Shane Matthews of Full View Mapping; our very supportive distributor, Independent Publishers Group—its chief, Curt Matthews, the tireless

Mary Rowles, and the rest of its great staff; our legal team at Sheehan, Phinney, Bass & Green of Maria Recalde and Doug Verge; our printer, McNaughton & Gunn; and our patient copy editor and indexer, Judith Antonelli.

There were several people who helped in other ways. Many thanks to Lynn Clark, Dorothy Shapiro, Jordan Shapiro, Gail Shapiro, Andy Shapiro, Ruth Bonsignore, Kevin Moore, Duncan Donahue and Tom Fortier, Nan Garland, Elvis Jiménez-Chávez and Chris Lawrence, Bucky Parker, Brendan Hickey and Judith Wright, Martin Merle, Matt Wilhelm, Megan McElheran, Nicole Riddle and the rest of the Stanford gang, and Tony Lulek.

Finally, a wicked thanks to Rum & Reggae Guidebooks' president, Joe Shapiro, whose enthusiasm, dedication, and hard work helped push this edition to completion.

As always, a can of dolphin-safe tuna to my cat and guardian angel, Jada. To all who helped, many thanks—YAH MON!

Jonathan Runge
Author, Editor, Publisher
Rum & Reggae Guidebooks, Inc.
Boston, Massachusetts
September 1, 2006

WRITE TO RUM & REGGAE

Dear *Rum & Reggae's Caribbean* Readers,

We really do appreciate and value your comments, suggestions, or information about anything new or exciting in the Caribbean. We'd love to hear about your experiences, good and bad, while you were in the Caribbean. Your feedback will help us to shape the next edition. So please let us hear from you.

Visit our Web site at www.rumreggae.com,
e-mail us at yahmon@rumreggae.com, or write to:

Mr. Yah Mon
Rum & Reggae Guidebooks
P.O. Box 130153
Boston, MA 02113

Sincerely,

Jonathan Runge

P.S. We often mention cocktails, drinking, and other things in this book. We certainly do not mean to upset any nondrinkers or those in recovery. Please don't take offense — rum and its relatives are not a requirement for a successful vacation in the Caribbean.

INTRODUCTION

Travel with an Opinion®. That's how we describe our distinct point of view. *Rum & Reggae's Caribbean* is not your typical tourist guide to these beautiful and exotic pearls. We like to say that the Rum & Reggae series is written for people who want more out of a vacation than the standard tourist fare. This is not for the cruise-ship crowd. Our reader is sophisticated and independent. He's also more lively — be it exploring, beaching, hiking, sailing, windsurfing, golfing, scuba diving, festivities-seeking, or just pure partying. Or she's more particular, in search of places that are secluded, cerebral, or spiritual.

This book differs from other guidebooks in another way. Instead of telling you that everything is "nice" — nice, that is, for the average Joe and Jane — *Rum & Reggae's Caribbean* offers definitive opinions. We will tell you what's fantastic and what's not, from the point of view of someone who loathes the tourist label and the other bland and tired travel books whose names we won't mention.

We'll take you throughout the Caribbean and share our recommendations of where to go (and where not to go). More important, we filter out all the crap for you so you can have fun reading the book and enjoy your vacation and keep the decision making to a minimum.

So mix yourself a stiff rum punch (don't forget the bitters and freshly grated nutmeg), put on some Bob Marley, *mon,* and sit back and let *Rum & Reggae's Caribbean* take you on your own private Caribbean adventure.

Rum & Reggae's Caribbean

Before You Go

Calling the Caribbean

In planning your trip, you're likely to make a few phone calls to the destinations you'll be visiting. Fortunately, international dialing codes are easy to decipher. To call most Caribbean islands you'll simply dial 1, a three-digit area (island) code, and a seven-digit local number, the same as you would when calling from one state to another in the United States. However, some islands utilize the 011 prefix for international dialing, as you find for the rest of the world:

- The French islands (Guadeloupe, Martinique, St. Martin, St. Barth)
- The Dutch islands (Aruba, Bonaire, Curacao, Saba, St. Eustatius, St. Maarten)
- The Venezuelan islands (Los Roques, Margarita)
- Cuba

For these islands, you'll dial 011, a country code, and a local number. Dialing instructions for each island are detailed in the Key Facts in each chapter.

English Spoken Here?

Some visitors are concerned about languages, but rest assured, English is widely spoken throughout most of the islands, particularly within establishments like hotels and restaurants that cater to tourists. You may find a French-language handbook useful if you plan to visit Les Saintes, Marie-Galante, or the remote parts of Martinique or Guadeloupe. Similarly, a Spanish language handbook might be useful for exploring off the beaten track in Cuba, the Dominican Republic, or the Venezuelan islands. Otherwise, a few key phrases in French or Spanish—as a courtesy—is all you'll need for these islands. More specific information is contained in each of the chapters mentioned above.

Passport Formalities for U.S. Citizens

As we go to press, a number of Caribbean destinations do not require American citizens to provide a passport on entry—a birth certificate and picture

ID is sufficient. Specific entry requirements at the time of publication for every island are detailed in the Key Facts section of each chapter. However, U.S. Customs is planning to require passports to re-enter the United States, even for American citizens, effective January 1, 2007. The passport rules will *not* apply to those traveling to Puerto Rico or the U.S. Virgin Islands. If you are considering traveling outside the United States without a passport, check with the U.S. Department of State Web site to verify re-entry requirements before you go: www.travel.state.gov. If you hold a non-U.S. passport and will be traveling from the Caribbean to the United States, make sure you are familiar with the latest requirements that the U.S. Department of State requires for your country of origin.

About Money

Unlike typical overseas travel, throughout most of the Caribbean the U.S. dollar is widely accepted. This is due to the fact that on most islands the exchange rate of the local currency is tied to the greenback, and with the bulk of tourists coming from America, shops, restaurants, and hotels are ready to accept U.S. dollars, as well as traveler's checks and major credit cards (Visa, Master Card, and — usually — American Express). It's not necessary to exchange U.S. dollars into the local currency on these islands. If you get change in the local currency, try to spend it before you come home, because it will be difficult (and costly) to exchange it at your local bank.

Exceptions are Jamaica, the Dominican Republic, and Cuba, where the local currency fluctuates with the U.S. dollar on a daily basis; and the French islands, which use the euro. In the chapters for these islands we've addressed any money issues you'll need to know.

Laundry

Doing laundry in the Caribbean can be incredibly expensive and inconvenient, especially in the French West Indies (about $20 a load). The reason is the dryer — it uses a lot of energy, which is costly down here. Laundromats as we know them don't exist, except in Puerto Rico, the U.S. Virgin Islands, and a few other islands with big cities. So if you're traveling for long periods, try to bring mostly hand-washables.

A Note to Our Gay and Lesbian Readers

Travel to the Caribbean should be a relaxing and wonderful experience for all, and it usually is. However, please be advised that many of the islands — especially the former and current British colonies — are not as socially accepting of gay and lesbian relationships as in certain enlightened parts of the United States, and in Canada and Britain. In fact, some islands, especially Jamaica, are very homophobic (see www.glaad.org for more information), with a very conservative Christian value system. The most tolerant island in the Caribbean is St. Barth, followed by Martinique and Guadeloupe. We've found the U.S. Virgin Islands, Puerto Rico, Vieques, and Culebra to be somewhat relaxed, too (although San Juan can have the big city safety issues, like anywhere else). We've always thought that Aruba, Bonaire, Curaçao, and Saba are also very mellow. That said, many gay and lesbian travelers go anywhere and everywhere, and we would never discourage anyone from seeking adventure and fun.

Most gays and lesbians never encounter problems related to homophobia in their travels around the Caribbean, but we have been informed of a few incidents that give us pause and warrant this alert. So when in unfamiliar environments, please use good judgment and common sense. We value everyone's safety more than making political or social statements in a foreign land, where your rights are not as secure or guaranteed. Reserve that energy for helping to achieve policy changes at home.

Climates of the Caribbean

The weather in the Caribbean is about as close to perfect as anywhere on Earth. The temperature rarely dips below 70°F or scales to above 90°F (at sea level). It can get cooler at night in the mountains of some of the islands, making it ideal for sleeping. The sun shines almost every day. Rainfall comes in the form of brief, intense cloudbursts, quickly followed by sunshine. It's pretty hard not to get a tan.

The reasons for this ideal climate are the constant temperature of the ocean—about 80°F year-round—and the steady trade winds from Africa. The Caribbean is not susceptible to the harsh weather patterns of the middle latitudes. The only weather peril of a Caribbean vacation is an occasional summer tropical depression or hurricane, which can make life very exciting.

On the individual islands you'll find three basic climate categories: arid (hot and slightly humid), lush (hot, very humid, with lots of rainfall), and a little of both (the windward side being the wetter and greener) or something in the middle. The larger, mountainous islands almost always fall in the latter two categories. Conversely, the flatter, smaller ones are more arid. Trade winds can usually be relied on throughout the region to keep things from getting too sticky. Summer, while only about 5°F hotter than winter, feels much warmer due to the increased humidity and decreased wind. The one constant is the sun. It is always strong and will swiftly fry unprotected pale faces—and bodies—to a glowing shade of lobster red.

There is also another climate down here, which we measure by what we call the Friendliness Barometer. This reflects the attitude of the local people toward tourists. Some of the island nations of the Caribbean are wonderfully warm and positive, whereas others are fairly antagonistic. The determining factor is often the amount of tourist traffic and the degree to which the local government has educated the populace about the economic importance of tourism. For example, both St. Thomas and Barbados are flooded with tourists every season, yet the atmosphere of the former is hostile, whereas the latter is remarkably warm — thanks to education. Other islands, because tourism is a recent phenomenon, are more open and friendly.

How do you find which "climates" are best for you? Simple — check out the chart below. Note that some islands might appear in more than one friendliness climate.

Friendliness Barometer and Climates Chart

	ARID	LUSH	BOTH
Very friendly	Bonaire Aruba Los Roques Margarita Mayreau	Tobago Puerto Rico Saba Jamaica	Montserrat Cuba
Warm	Anegada Bequia Carriacou Culebra Jost Van Dyke Vieques Virgin Gorda	Dominica Grenada Jamaica Trinidad	Barbados Dominican Republic
Neutral	Anguilla Curaçao Barbuda St. Eustatius	Jamaica	Nevis Tortola
Cool	Antigua Mustique St. Barth St. Martin/ St. Maarten Cayman Islands	Guadeloupe Jamaica Martinique St. Lucia St. Vincent	St. John St. Kitts St. Croix
Nasty		Jamaica	St. Thomas

What to Wear and Take Along

Less is more. That is always the motto to remember when packing to go to the Caribbean. Bring only what you can carry for 10 minutes at a good clip, because you'll often be schlepping your luggage for at least that time, and it's hot. Rollerboards—that is, luggage with wheels—are handy, although you'll still have to check (or gate-check) them on many of the smaller planes.

What you really need to take along are a bathing suit, shorts, T-shirts or tanks, a cotton sweater, a pair of sandals, sunglasses, and a Discman or an iPod. After all, you are on vacation. However, this is the new millennium and people are dressing up for no reason, so you might want to bring some extra togs to look presentable at the dinner table. To help you be totally prepared (and to make your packing a lot easier), we've assembled a list of essentials for a week.

The Packing List

Clothes

- [ ] bathing suit (or two)
- [ ] T-shirts (4)—you'll end up buying at least one
- [ ] tank tops (2)—they're cooler, show off your muscles or curves, and even out T-shirt tan lines
- [ ] polo shirts (2)
- [ ] shorts (2)
- [ ] nice, compatible lightweight pants (also good for the plane)
- [ ] sandals—those that can get wet, like Tevas, are best
- [ ] cotton sweater or sweatshirt (if traveling in the winter)
- [ ] undergarments
- [ ] sneakers (or good walking shoes) or topsiders (for boaters)
- [ ] Women: lightweight dress (most women prefer to bring a couple of dresses for evening)
- [ ] Men: if you must have a lightweight sport coat wear it (with appropriate shoes) on the plane

Essentials

- [ ] toiletries and any necessary meds
- [ ] sunscreen (SPF 15+, 8, 4 [oil], and lip protector)
- [ ] moisturizer
- [ ] pure aloe gel for sunburn

- ☐ some good books — don't count on finding a worthwhile read there
- ☐ Cutter's or Woodsman's insect repellent, or Skin So Soft (oh, those nasty bugs)
- ☐ sunglasses (we bring two pairs!)
- ☐ hat or visor
- ☐ iPod
- ☐ camcorder, digital camera, or pocket camera (disposables are great for the beach, and underwater disposables for snorkeling)

Sports Accessories (where applicable)

- ☐ tennis racket
- ☐ golf clubs
- ☐ hiking shoes
- ☐ fins, mask, snorkel, regulator/BC, and C-card (certification card)

Documents

- ☐ ATM card and credit cards
- ☐ valid passport (keep in hotel safe and carry around a photocopy in your wallet)
- ☐ driver's license

Flying the Caribbean Way

If you are traveling only to one of the major islands for your vacation, you'll probably be flying on a major carrier to and from your destination. However, if you are traveling between islands in the region (as we always seem to be), chances are you'll be flying on one or more of the regional carriers. Although we've had many faultless experiences, we've also had a few hiccups along the way. Having flown local island carriers extensively, we've developed some golden rules for stress-free flying when in the friendly but sometimes tricky skies of the Caribbean:

- Always have a reservation.

- Reconfirm 72 hours before departure.

- Get to the airport at least an hour before departure — overbooking can be a problem.

- Never fly standby, especially during peak periods — you won't get on.

- Go immediately to the gate once you've checked in. We were left behind once when the plane arrived early and took off early without us.

- Avoid itinerary changes when flying on Sunday. Everything, including reservation lines and ticket counters, closes down on some islands.

- Keep luggage to a minimum. Carrying a lot in the heat is unpleasant.

- Carry all valuables with you — don't check them! Guard your passport with your life (especially if you're connecting in Miami — we had one stolen there)! A U.S. passport is worth thousands of dollars on the black market.

The main regional airlines, their hubs, and contact info are as follows:

Air Caraïbes (Guadeloupe and Martinique): 877-772-1005, www.aircaraibes.com

Air Jamaica (Montego Bay and Kingston): 800-523-5585, www.airjamaica.com

BWIA (Trinidad): 800-538-2942, www.bwee.com. Note that BWIA will be replaced by a new airline, **Caribbean Airline**, starting in early 2007.

Caribbean Star and **Caribbean Sun Airlines** (Antigua and San Juan): 866-864-6272, www.flycaribbeanstar.com, www.flycsa.com

Dutch Antilles Express (Bonaire): 011-599-717-0808, www.flydae.com.

LIAT (Antigua): 866-549-5428 or 268-462-0700, www.liatairline.com

Mustique Airways (St. Vincent): 800-526-4789 or 784-458-4380, www.mustiqueairways.com

SVG Air (St. Vincent): 784-457-5124, www.svgair.com

Trans Island Air (TIA) (St. Vincent): 246-418-1654, www.tia2000.com

Winair (St. Maarten): 011-599-545-4237, www.fly-winair.com

Although Air Jamaica and BWIA fly both jets and smaller planes, the other island airlines all fly small planes, from the 19-seat DeHavilland Twin Otter to the 44-seat Dash 8.

Other Airfare Tips

Be sure to check the Internet; deals are always available there. Always shop around and ask for the lowest fare, not just a discount fare. If you're adventurous, call again as your departure date draws nearer — additional low-cost seats may have become available. You can also investigate the major travel tour companies for a charter flight.

Island-Activities Matchup

Looking for the best island for diving, golf, restaurants, or gay nightlife? This chart will give you some suggestions.

BEACHES
Anegada
Anguilla
Antigua
Barbuda
Culebra
Dominican Republic
Los Roques
St. Barth
St. John

PRIVACY
Anguilla
The Grenadines
Nevis
Vieques

SCUBA
Bonaire
Cayman Islands
Dominica
Saba

SNORKELING
British Virgin Islands
Culebra
St. John

HEDONISM & NIGHTLIFE
Barbados
Cuba (Havana)
Dominican Republic
   (Santo Domingo)
Jamaica (Negril)
Puerto Rico (San Juan)
St. Martin/St. Maarten
Trinidad (during Carnival)

GAY NIGHTLIFE
Dominican Republic
   (Santo Domingo)
Puerto Rico (San Juan)

SAILING
Antiqua
British Virgin Islands
The Grenadines

CULTURE
Cuba
Curaçao
Jamaica
Martinique
Trinidad

COOKIE-CUTTER MEGA-RESORTS
Aruba
Grand Cayman
Dominican Republic
Jamaica
Puerto Rico
St. Thomas

FOOD
Anguilla
Guadeloupe
Martinique
Puerto Rico
St. Barth
St. Martin
St. Thomas

GOLF
Barbados
Dominican Republic
Jamaica
Puerto Rico

NATURE

Bonaire
Dominica
Guadeloupe
Martinique
Saba
St. John
Trinidad and Tobago

QUIET

Anguilla
Bonaire
Culebra
The Grenadines
Montserrat
Nevis
Saba
St. Eustatius
Tobago
Vieques

WINDSURFING

Aruba
Barbados
Bonaire
Dominican Republic (Cabarete)
Guadeloupe
Puerto Rico (Rincón)

LUXURY

Anguilla
Barbados
The British Virgin Islands
The Grenadines (Canouan,
	Mustique, Petit St. Vincent)
Nevis
St. Barth

NUDE BEACHES

Bonaire
Guadeloupe
Jamaica
St. Martin

SUN

Anegada
Anguilla
Aruba
Barbuda
Bonaire
Curaçao
Los Roques
Margarita

Caribbean Superlatives

Best Beach — Playa Flamenco, Culebra

Best Island for Beaches — Anguilla

Best Place for Sun — Aruba; Bonaire

Best New Destination — Isabela, Puerto Rico; Vieques

Best Large Luxury Resort (over 100 rooms) — Four Seasons Resort, Nevis

Best Small Luxury Resort (under 100 rooms) — Hotel Le Toiny, St. Barth;
	Cap Est Lagoon Resort & Spa, Martinique

Best Romantic Hotel — Goldeneye, Jamaica; Villa Serena, Samaná, Domini-
	can Republic

Best Inn — Montpelier Plantation, Nevis

Best Guesthouse — Posada La Cigala, Los Roques, Venezuela

Best Value Hotel — Rockhouse, Jamaica

Best Eco-Friendly Hotel — Concordia Eco-Tents and Estate Concordia Studios, St. John

Best Mountain Lodging — Strawberry Hill, Jamaica

Best Gay-Friendly Accommodation — Numero Uno, San Juan, Puerto Rico

Sexiest Hotel — Bravo!, Vieques

Best City Hideout Hotel — Kura Hulanda, Curaçao

Best Beach House Accommodation — Casa Isleña, Rincón, Puerto Rico

Best Room with a View — Ladera Resort, St. Lucia

Best Spa — Raffles Resort Canouan Island, Canouan

Best Creole Restaurant — Le Karacoli, Guadeloupe

Best Continental Restaurant — Le Belem, Martinique

Best Lunch Spot — Harmony Hall, Antigua

Best Lobster — Big Bamboo, Anegada

Best Pizza — Mac's Pizzeria, Bequia

Best Island for Food — St. Barth; Martinique; St. Martin

Best Restaurant Row — Grand Case, St. Martin

Best Sushi — Sake, Old San Juan

Best Romantic Seaside Restaurant — The Cliff, Barbados

Best Vegetarian Restaurant — Café Berlin, Old San Juan, Puerto Rico

Best Beer — Red Stripe; Presidente

Best Rum — Mount Gay

Best Rum Punch — Golden Rock Plantation, Nevis

Best Place for a Sunset Cocktail — Uncle Ernie's, Anguilla

Best Nightclub — Ku Lounge/Kudetá, Puerto Rico

Best Gay Nightclub — Eros, San Juan, Puerto Rico

Best Place for Nightlife — San Juan, Puerto Rico

Best Place to Get High — Negril, Jamaica

Best Place to Be for New Year's — Foxy's, Jost Van Dyke

Best Monthly Party — The Full Moon Party at Bomba's Shack, Tortola

Best Carnival — Port of Spain, Trinidad

Best Reggae Music — Reggae SumFest, Montego Bay, Jamaica

Best Calypso Music — Port of Spain, Trinidad

Best Pan Music — Port of Spain, Trinidad

Best Salsa — Havana, Cuba

Best Merengue — Santo Domingo, Dominican Republic

Best Beachside Party Spot — Tamboo, Rincón, Puerto Rico

Best Place for Live Music — Nuyorican Café, San Juan, Puerto Rico

Best Diving — Bonaire; Little Cayman

Best Dive Site — Third Encounter, Saba

Best Snorkeling — British Virgin Islands; St. John

Best Camping — St. John

Best Sailing — British Virgin Islands

Best Mountain Biking — Bonaire

Best Golf Course — The Green Monkey, Sandy Lane, Barbados

Best Port of Call — Port Elizabeth, Bequia

Best Museum — Museum Kura Hulanda, Curaçao

Best Historical Site — Castillo de San Felipe del Morro, Old San Juan, Puerto Rico

Best Hike — The Boiling Lake, Dominica

Best Hiking — Martinique

Best Bird-Watching — Asa Wright Nature Centre, Trinidad

Best Tennis — Four Seasons, Nevis

Best Windsurfing — Cabarete, Dominican Republic

Best Shopping — St. Martin/St. Maarten

Best T-Shirt — Jack Iron Strong Rum, Carriacou

Best Bargain Island — Los Roques, Venezuela

Best Value Destination — Dominican Republic

Best-Kept Secret — Mayreau, the Grenadines

The 12 Best Beaches in the Caribbean

(in alphabetical order)

Anse du Gouverneur, St. Barth
Here the swells meet the swells. This is a very pretty and private beach.

Cayo de Agua, Los Roques
This is the prettiest and one of the longest stretches of deserted white sand in an archipelago of sandy islets.

Coco Point, Barbuda
This achingly beautiful stretch of white sand with a pinkish hue is a very tony place to take in the sun.

Englishman's Bay, Tobago
This beautiful crescent of golden sand with a greenish hue is framed by two rocky points and offers great snorkeling.

Maunday's Bay, Anguilla

This is a beautiful arc of bright, talcum-powder sand and turquoise water that is usually calm and inviting. Despite the fact that it is often filled with guests of Cap Juluca, it is still the quintessential Caribbean beach.

Meads Bay, Anguilla

We love this stunning stretch of white sand and crystal-clear water. The rocky bluff on the eastern end adds appeal to the setting. It's also a great location from which to watch the sunset.

Negril Beach, Jamaica

This is an experience in itself.

Playa El Agua, Margarita

This might not be the prettiest beach, but the great restaurants, waiter service at your chaise, and all those sexy Venezuelans make it an exceptional experience.

Playa Flamenco, Culebra

This almost perfect crescent of blindingly white sand often has body-surfable waves in the wintertime.

Playa Rincón, Samaná, Dominican Republic

A deserted crescent tucked away at the elbow of Bahia de Rincón, this is the most scenic beach in a country filled with gorgeous beaches.

Saltwhistle Bay, Mayreau, the Grenadines

This is a beautiful and quiet crescent of white sand, palm trees, and tranquil, clear turquoise water on a sleepy island.

Trunk Bay, St. John

Despite the crowds, this is still the prettiest beach in the U.S. Virgins.

Nude Beaches in the Caribbean

You might expect the Caribbean to be a paradise for nudists, or "naturists," as they prefer to be called. In fact, there are surprisingly few official buff options — the proper British heritage and the strict religious conservatism of most islands (as bad as any "religious right" dogma in the United States) make for a dim view of such "uncivilized" habits. Fortunately, most of the French and Dutch islands are more lenient. It's best to use your discretion at the more deserted beaches — keep your clothes close at hand in case of disapproving visitors. Women would be well advised not to sunbathe topless or nude alone.

Another option is to stay at a resort with its own private beach — many have sections that are clothes-optional (don't be too shy to ask when making reservations). Consult Lee Baxandall's *World Guide to Nude Beaches* or check out www.naturist.com.

The following are some of the better-known nude beaches. In many cases, nude beaches exist without the blessing of local laws, so please remember to check out the scene with reliable local sources (like your hotel) before shedding your clothes and cares.

Anse des Grande Salines, St. Barth

You'll feel weird if you don't take your clothes off here. This is one of St. Barth's best.

Anse Trabaud, Martinique

The nicest beach on Martinique, located in the southeast corner of the island, is also quite "free" during the week.

Bloody Bay Beach, Negril, Jamaica

Negril is the home of Hedonism II and is the land of anything goes. The buff area is in Bloody Bay, just east of Hedonism II.

Hawksbill Beach, Antigua

A lovely beach and Antigua's only buff beach, it's located next to the Hawksbill Beach Resort.

Los Roques (several)

With so many islets, your *posada* hosts can take you to a spot that's totally private.

Orient Beach, St. Martin

One of the first "official" clothes-optional beaches in the Caribbean, it is also the home of Club Orient, a naturist resort.

Plage Crawen, Les Saintes, Guadeloupe

A secluded, private beach with lots of shade and a great lunch spot over the hill at Bois Joli.

Plage Tarare, Guadeloupe

This is the primary buff beach on an island that put the *N* in *nudité*.

Salomon Beach, St. John

Although there is a "No Nudity" sign posted here, and we hear park rangers occasionally issue citations, this has been a nude hangout since the 1960s. The trail to the beach is a little more than 1/2 mile north of Cruz Bay, on the left.

Sorobon, Lac Bay, Bonaire

The home of the pink flamingo also has the Sorobon Resort, a naturist resort. Nonresort guests can use the beach for a fee.

What About Tennis?

Just about every large hotel in the Caribbean has a tennis court or access to one. However, if you're a tennis freak, be warned that the smaller islands will have fewer courts or courts in questionable condition. So be sure to ask when making reservations at some remote destination. The following will particularly appeal to tennis buffs.

Anguilla Tennis Pavilion, Anguilla

Opened in 2005, the $3 million Anguilla Tennis Pavilion boasts seven pristine courts with the same specifications of the U.S. Open facility in Flushing Meadows, New York, and a facility designed by acclaimed architect Myron Goldfinger (of Covecastles).

The Buccaneer, St. Croix

This has eight Laykold courts — two lit for night play — and a tennis director on the job since 1978, organizing regular matches.

Caneel Bay, St. John

Eleven courts are surrounded by lush National Park lands and managed by Peter Burwash.

Casa de Campo, Dominican Republic

There are 13 clay courts (10 lit) and a staff of more than 70 (counting landscaping and maintenance), plus plenty of ball boys from the local junior program.

Curtain Bluff, Antigua

There are four hard-surface courts, a tournament in May, and three resident tennis pros on staff.

Four Seasons Resort, Nevis

There are 10 courts of two different surfaces (six all-weather and four red clay); three are lit for night play. The Peter Burwash staff makes tennis another reason to stay here.

Half Moon Resort, Jamaica

There are 13 hard-surface courts (all lit for night-play) and four squash courts.

Rawlins Plantation Inn, St. Kitts
This is a rare, beautifully maintained grass court on the slopes of the island's slumbering volcano.

The 12 Most Luxurious Resorts

We've been lucky enough to tour (and occasionally stay at) some of the world's most sumptuous hotels. Here are the ones that top our list for a dream vacation (again, in alphabetical order).

Cap Juluca, Maunday's Bay, Anguilla
On the best beach in Anguilla, this Moorish-style resort is a major celeb hangout.

Carlisle Bay, Antigua
Uber-modern and looking like a slice of New York more than the Caribbean, this is nonetheless a seriously luxe resort with superb dining and a splendid spa complex.

Cotton House, Mustique
This small hotel on this rich and fabulous island pulls in a diverse and interesting clientele, and we love the pillow menu.

Four Seasons Resort, Pinney's Beach, Nevis
The Four Seasons has achieved a level of service unparalleled in the Caribbean. It has every imaginable amenity, service, and facility. Come here to pamper yourself.

Hôtel Carl Gustaf, Gustavia, St. Barth
With incredible views of the sunset and the Caribbean's most scenic harbor, this tony and tasteful hotel has sumptuous guest rooms.

Hôtel Le Toiny, St. Barth
This very chichi small resort has fabulous villas, each with its own pool.

La Samanna, St. Martin
Restored to its original magnificence, this classic hotel on a beautiful stretch of beach is an oasis on crowded St. Martin.

Little Dix Bay, Virgin Gorda, British Virgin Islands
Originally a RockResort and now owned by Rosewood Hotels, Little Dix is the pinnacle of old-money, subtle luxury in a beautiful setting.

Malliouhana, Meads Bay, Anguilla
Still a bastion of luxury and taste, Malliouhana's service is great, and the Haitian paintings even match the upholstery!

Petit St. Vincent Resort, Petit St. Vincent, the Grenadines
This remote, deluxe cottage-colony resort is on its own island in the southern Grenadines. It is home of the flag-signal system for room service. Privacy rules here.

Round Hill Hotel & Villas, Montego Bay, Jamaica
This is a celeb hangout, where Ralph Lauren hangs his polo cap. The 27 wonderful WASPy bungalows and the lush vegetation maintain your privacy on a 98-acre peninsula.

Sandy Lane, Barbados
Over-the-top in almost every way, the re-created Sandy Lane can't be beat for its wealth of lavish touches. The property has a mammoth spa that sets jaws agape, as well as the Green Monkey, which is one of the region's top two or three golf courses.

About Haiti

The very name *Haiti* conjures imagery both bold and evanescent. Voodoo ceremonies, the bloody reign of Papa Doc, Graham Greene's *The Comedians*, desperate boat refugees, colorful folk art, the American military occupation — all of these get top billing. Although each of these themes is indeed part of the country's dynamic tapestry, they all just skim the surface of a very complicated and difficult picture. The only way to get a handle on what Haiti is about is to travel there — and even then, the country will get under your skin, rattle your senses and leave you with far more questions than when you arrived. Of course, almost no Americans are currently making the trek to Haiti. More than anyplace else in the Caribbean, it is the very definition of "third world" in the Americas, and its future is one that no one can see clearly.

During our last visit to Haiti, in 1998, things were looking up somewhat, and the government was starting to invest in rebuilding tourism. It proved to be an evanescent moment, however. Shortly after our visit, the Club Med Magic Isle — long the country's best link to tourists — closed for lack of business. The elections of 2000 were condemned as flawed by international observers, and the pervading economic uncertainty caused the value of Haiti's currency to dwindle. The election of Rene Preval in 2006 might be a sign of better times, but he is regarded by many as a puppet of former President Jean-Bertrand Aristide, who fled to South Africa when he could not turn the country around. Haiti has become a haven for drug traffickers, who use the country as the primary funnel for cocaine flowing from Colombia to the United States. There is evidence of trafficking complicity within the Haitian government, although no one really knows how high the involvement in the drug trade by Haiti's elected officials reaches. Perhaps most problematic is that the country recently surpassed Colombia as the world's kidnapping capital, with 8–10 abductions occurring every day. At least 28 U.S. citizens were reported kidnapped in Haiti during the last eight months of 2005.

Everyone hopes that Haiti has seen its worst days, but it has a long way to go to be embraced by adventurous travelers. We hope that by the time the next edition of *Rum and Reggae's Caribbean* appears, a more positive picture will be emerging and we'll be able to make some concrete travel recommendations.

Hissing

Don't be startled or offended if someone hisses at you; that's just the Caribbean way of saying "Hey, you." It's very effective — a woman once got our attention clear across the airline terminal in Guadeloupe (she wanted to tell us that the plane was boarding). It seems that the hiss can be directionally controlled; no one but us turned around — a true Caribbean phenomenon.

Rum & Reggae's Caribbean Cocktails

Rum & Reggae's Punch

Are you dreaming about Carnival, but it's the middle of July? Don't worry, you can create your own festivity with this recipe.

Ingredients

1 lime
4 oz. water
2–3 oz. good dark rum (the stronger, the better)
2 oz. sugar syrup*
bitters
ice
freshly grated nutmeg

Directions

Squeeze the lime and add the juice and water to the rum and sugar syrup in a tall glass. Shake bitters into the glass four times. Add the rocks, then sprinkle with freshly grated nutmeg (it must be fresh!). Yum! Serves one.

*To make sugar syrup, combine 1 lb. of sugar and 2 cups of water in a saucepan. Boil for about two minutes for sugar to dissolve. Let cool. Keep handy for quick and easy rum punches.

Rum & Reggae's Canchanchara

The *canchanchara* is one of the oldest drinks in the Caribbean and one you will be happy to make at home.

Ingredients

> 2 oz. white rum
> juice of one lemon
> 2 tsp. of honey
> ice (half a glass)
> cold water (about half a glass)

Directions

Mix lemon juice, honey, and white rum in a glass, add ice, and fill with water. Enjoy!!

Rum & Reggae's Mojito

The *mojito* is Cuba's national drink — the Cuba Libre (rum & Coke) is a close second.

Ingredients

> 2 oz. good white rum
> 2 tsp. sugar
> juice of half a lime
> fresh mint leaves
> club soda
> ice (half a glass)

Directions

Mix sugar and lime juice in a glass. Crush a few fresh mint leaves into the sugar–lime juice mixture. Pour in the rum and add the ice cubes. Stir. Fill to top with soda water. Garnish with a sprig of mint. Enjoy!!

Rum & Reggae's Piña Colada

Ingredients

> 1 oz. Coco López (or any coconut cream)
> 1 oz. heavy cream (yes, this is a fattening drink!)
> 2 oz. light rum (preferably Bacardi or Don Q)
> 2 oz. unsweetened pineapple juice (fresh is best)

Directions

Mix with 2/3 cup crushed ice in blender until creamy smooth.
Garnish with a slice of fresh pineapple and a cherry (the latter just for the visual). Enjoy!

Anguilla

TOURISTO SCALE:

👤👤👤👤👤 (6)

On the *scala di fabula* (the fabulousness scale), Anguilla is right up there with the likes of St. Barth and Mustique. Its white-sand-gilded shores and mega-expensive resorts rival any in the West Indies. Yet it doesn't throw, or should we say hurl, the attitude that the other two islands do. It is surprisingly mellow for someplace so chic. We like Anguilla's refreshingly down-to-earth tone, even if we have to pay through the nose for it.

Our first impression of Anguilla, which seems like light-years ago now, was that the island reminded us of Cape Cod gone West Indian. Its dunes, scrubby vegetation, gentle terrain, and beautiful beaches were reminiscent of that sandy hook on the 42nd parallel. Of course, the water temperature and color vanquished that illusion, for the better. In the shadow of bustling St. Martin, Anguilla seemed like a sleepy island, with a handful of places to stay and only the Malliouhana to beckon the rich and fab. Time has changed all that. The word got out that Anguilla has the best collection of beaches in the Caribbean — more than 30 talcum-soft strands framing the island's snakelike coastline. The super-deluxe resorts multiplied like rabbits, and so did the well-heeled on this little corner of idyll.

Fortunately, and defying conventional wisdom, development has been relatively low scale. Despite intense pressure to build, none of the resorts is larger than 100 rooms, and high-rises are not allowed here. We arrived with

Anguilla

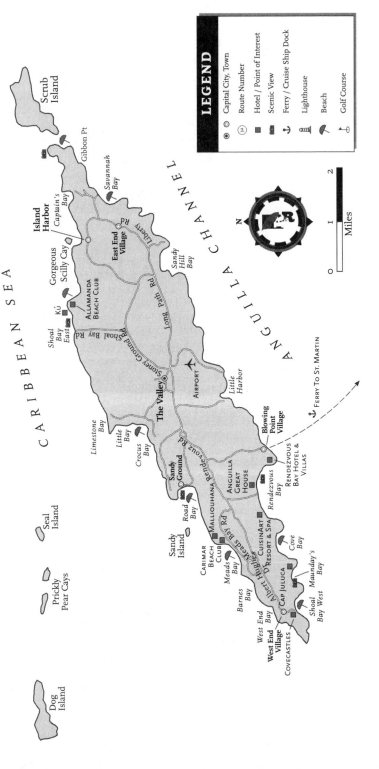

Anguilla: Key Facts

Location	18°N by 64°W 9 miles/15 kilometers north of St. Martin/St. Maarten 1,675 miles/2,695 kilometers southeast of New York
Size	35 square miles/91 square kilometers
Highest point	Crocus Hill (213 feet/65 meters)
Population	11,561
Language	English
Time	Atlantic Standard Time (1 hour ahead of EST, same as EDT)
Area code	264
Electricity	110 volts AC
Currency	The Eastern Caribbean dollar, EC$ (EC$2.68 = US$1); however, U.S. dollars are more commonly used everywhere.
Driving	On the left; you'll need a temporary permit — $20 with a valid license.
Documents	Valid passport; Americans can enter just with proof of nationality with photo.
Departure tax	$20 by air, $3 by ferry
Beer to drink	Heineken
Rum to drink	Pyrat
Music to hear	Dancehall
Tourism info	800-553-4939 www.anguilla-vacation.com

great trepidation for our most recent visit, knowing that several major projects were in various stages of construction, but the three main hotel projects are actually rebuilds of existing properties and will do little to increase the total number of rooms on the island from what it was in 2000 (when the last big resort arrived).

Every now and then, the concept of bringing cruise ships to Anguilla comes up as a potential revenue booster, but they're not in the picture for now, because cruise ships go against the grain of what makes this island special. Besides, Anguilla isn't for everyone: Life crawls along at a languid pace, there's little in the way of shopping or touring or activities, and the topography is undramatic (actually, it's fairly boring). Nevertheless, the island is satisfying for those who really want to unwind and decompress, especially top-drawer celebs, who use Anguilla as a low-profile escape in the winter (although even its fabled tranquillity couldn't keep Brad and Jen from pulling out their prenup after their vacation here). Anguilla's people are sweet and good-natured, and we like the informality of this place.

Fortunately, the sheer quantity of sandy shores is such that Anguilla never feels crowded, even during high season — that is, until you try to snag a last-minute dinner reservation in high season at one of Anguilla's clutch of surprisingly polished restaurants. Perhaps spurred on by the culinary fire-works showcased across the channel on St. Martin, Anguilla works hard to keep up appearances. The island benefits greatly from the importing of fine produce, cheese, wine, and other items through St. Martin, and its restau-rants serve a variety of cuisines with a kind of flair rarely seen in the Caribbean. All of this comes at a price, and the food-and-bed bill on Anguilla rivals St. Barth as the costliest in the Caribbean. Nevertheless, Anguilla is a perfect place to spend about five days vacationing your mind and body in surf and sun. Don't expect much else: There's the beach, a good book, laz-ing about, and wallowing in trendy resorts and snazzy dining. For some, that's just what the doctor ordered.

The Briefest History

The Ciboney first settled this dry, flat island well before the first century A.D. Then the Arawaks arrived about A.D. 200 and were left undisturbed until the Carib invasion about 900 years later. The Caribs named it Malliouhana. Anguilla, which is Spanish for "eel" (in deference to the island's slender out-line), was one of the few islands not "discovered" by Columbus or even men-tioned in any of his expeditions. The British first colonized the island in 1650, and it remained under the Union Jack until 1967, despite attempts by the Caribs and the French to dislodge them. That is a rarity in the Caribbean: one government for 300 years. In 1967 the island gained its independence from Britain as a part of the new Associated State of St. Kitts–Nevis–Anguilla. This did not go well with the Anguillians, and unrest on the island became so bad that in 1969 a British peacekeeping force parachuted in to es-tablish order. Then the London police took over and remained for three years until Anguilla formed its own police force. Finally, in 1980, Anguilla for-mally became a self-governing British possession.

Getting There

Anguilla's Wallblake Airport is not big enough for jets, so you'll want to consider the two primary routings. St. Maarten is the closest gateway to Anguilla, with direct and nonstop flights from the States on American, Con-tinental, Delta, United, and US Airways, and from Canada on Air Canada. From St. Maarten, Winair, LIAT, and TransAnguilla fly the seven-minute trip throughout the day. The other gateway for Anguilla is San Juan, which is reached by a number of carriers; American Eagle flies to Anguilla two or three times daily from San Juan. There is limited service from other nearby Caribbean islands on Caribbean Star, LIAT, and Winair.

A fun and sometimes cheaper alternative to flying in from St. Maarten is to take the ferry. From Juliana, grab a cab (about $20) and head for Marigot, where you can enjoy a delicious French repast in one of several restaurants on the waterfront. Then hop a ferry to Blowing Point, Anguilla. There are several boats that do the 20-minute trip. The fare is $12 one way, and departures are about every half hour, beginning at 8 a.m., with the last scheduled boat leaving St. Martin at 7 p.m.; (later service is usually available on weekends and holidays, for which the fare is $15. No reservations are necessary.

Recently, there have been a few other ferry services popping up that offer a direct jaunt between Anguilla's Blowing Point and St. Maarten's Juliana International Airport. These services generally use smaller yet faster boats and, despite the higher price, can be quite convenient for those who are in a time crunch and need to go directly to the St. Maarten airport from Anguilla. Contact your hotel's concierge for details about these ferry services.

Getting Around

A rental car is a good idea if you want to explore this island's fine beaches and leave your place of residence every once in a while. Of the international agencies, Avis and Hertz both have affiliates here, with rates that average about $45 per day in winter; summer rates are about 20 percent less. Avis works with Apex (264-497-2642), and Hertz with Triple K (264-497-5934). If you want the car for the whole week, it's best to reserve in advance. For Avis and Hertz, just call their toll-free numbers: 800-331-1084 and 800-654-3131, respectively. There are several local agencies, including Connor's (800-633-7411 or 264-497-6433) and Island Car Rentals (264-497-2723), with which we've had good experiences. All provide free drop-off and pickup at your hotel — a good thing, since the agencies are not conveniently located for the airport or ferry terminal. A local driver's license will set you back $20.

Focus on Anguilla: The Beaches

Of the more than 30 beaches, there are 10 outstanding ones scattered throughout Anguilla. You're never far from one. All have some of the whitest sand in the Caribbean, a creamy mixture of ground-up shells and coral. It's quite lovely. Heck, even the ferry dock at Blowing Point has a beach — below average by Anguilla standards, but fine enough to make a few other islands cry with envy. So starting from the west end of the island and working our way to Windward Point, here are the best:

Shoal Bay West

Located at the western end of a paved road, this beach is the home of Covecastles, the futuristic white structures made famous by *Architectural Digest*. The beach, however, is quite nice, and it's often empty if you walk to the eastern end (to the left, as you face St. Martin/St. Maarten and spiky Saba), just past the pink house (which belongs to the ex-wife of Chuck Norris). The snorkeling is good at the west end, near the last of the Covecastles villas.

Maunday's Bay

On our first visit 20 years ago there was nothing here except a half-moon arc of beach culminating in dunes and a sand wall on the western end — one of the most beautiful deserted beaches of the islands. Now there's a blinding-white arabesque resort called Cap Juluca tucked into the dunes between groups of sea grape trees. Maunday's is still pretty, particularly when the resort isn't full, and the water is typically quite calm. Follow the signs for Cap Juluca.

Cove Bay

Just to the east of Maunday's, this long sweep of beach is too rough and exposed on the western end, but the other side is calmer and often vacant until it intersects the St. Regis project. A nice touch is the palm trees on the far side of the dunes, giving the illusion of tiny trees on top. Follow the signs for Cap Juluca, but don't turn right at the resort; go straight ahead and park.

Barnes Bay

This is another nice stretch of beach that has had to endure development. Most unfortunate was the Coccoloba complex, which has been torn down and is being rebuilt as a new resort as we write. You can escape much of this, however, if you walk as far as possible in the opposite direction. Follow the signs for the Viceroy Anguilla.

Meads Bay

Malliouhana, a chichi resort, sits on a bluff on the eastern end of the beach. This is a beautiful beach, with great views at sunset. Meads is also where Anguilla's colorful boat race is held each year in August. Follow signs for Carimar Beach Club.

Rendezvous Bay

Now here's a superb and very long (more than 2 miles) stretch of beach. There's plenty of room despite the addition of the 93-room CuisinArt Resort. So the best way to access this beach is from either the Anguilla Great House or the Rendezvous Bay resort. Neither of these are big hotels, so you won't have to fight to locate a piece of the pearl-white sand to call your own. Immediately west of CuisinArt is a funky beach bar called The Dune Preserve, run by local reggae star Bankie Banx.

Little Bay

This is Anguilla's tiniest beach — it's little more than a pocket of sand tucked into a bend in the cliff. You might be the only one here, and there's good snorkeling under the cliff to the east. To get here, drive up the hill out of The Valley toward Crocus Hill. Just as the road heads down toward Crocus Bay and the hospital, take a right on the obvious paved road — you'll come to another rise, then you'll see some unmarked turnouts. From here, you should be able to spot Little Bay through the vegetation at the base of the sheer cliff. A short trail heads left (west) around the cliff and to a rope that can be used to help climb down to the beach. The rope isn't always in great shape, so don't put your weight on it. Alternatively, hire a boat from Calvin Rogers at Crocus Bay to drop you off at Little Bay. The cost is $12 per person, round-trip. Calvin can be reached at 264-772-1332.

Limestone Bay

This small, sandy cove is a local favorite. It is reached by heading up toward Crocus Hill and taking a right turn just before the Cottage Hospital. Follow the road about 2 miles — just after it turns into a dirt road, it heads downhill and ends at Limestone.

Shoal Bay East

Calm water, fine snorkeling right off the reef, and a collection of perky beach bars make Shoal Bay, more than a mile in length, a favorite of day-trippers from St. Martin/St. Maarten. A villa development and a few smaller hotels don't help the crowding matters any, but the trade-off is good people-watching. Your best bet here is to pull into the parking lot at ✪ **Uncle Ernie's** and go all the way down to either end of the beach — our preference is the eastern end (to your right). The "corner" — where the sand makes a right turn to the south (and becomes Upper Shoal Bay) — is a great spot at which to watch the sunset and fiddle about with a cheap rum punch or Cape Codder carried from Uncle Ernie's. Uncle Ernie's is also a lovely spot for live jazz on a late Sunday afternoon.

Savannah Bay

This is a very pretty, long, and deserted beach on the still undeveloped, quiet East End. It serves up some good surf and a steady onshore breeze. For calmer water, the coconut-tree-studded left side is best. The only drawback to this beach is that during heavy trade winds, the turbulent water tends to wash up debris that must have come all the way from Africa. However, it's peaceful, and the snorkeling is good near Palm Grove Beach Bar, which serves light seafood and beer.

To get to Savannah Bay, take the main road north out of The Valley to Island Harbour. The road passes through this town along the shore and then takes a right up the hill — after going half a mile, you will see on the left a turnoff onto a dirt road. The road here is not always in good shape, but a standard rental car will make it (maybe with a few scrapes and loud thuds — don't worry, it's a rental). You will bump down to a fork — the left eventually takes you to Captains Bay (a pretty but rough spot); the right leads to half-moon-shaped Savannah Bay.

Where to Stay

Major changes are underway for Anguilla, but we hope they won't substantially alter the laid-back character of this island. At the site of the former Sonesta hotel (razed in 2003) on Merrywing Bay, the 97-room Temenos Anguilla St. Regis Resort and a collection of villas is under construction and slated to open in 2008; the resort's 18-hole Greg Norman golf course should be open by the time you read this. The Cocoloba Resort was torn down in 2005 and is being replaced by the Viceroy Anguilla resort, also opening in 2008. There are also big plans for Rendezvous Bay Hotel, which is the island's first guesthouse (see below).

Don't expect Anguilla's sleepy image to be matched by sleepy prices. It's very expensive to stay here, and don't forget that a 10 percent government tax will be added to your bill, plus 10 percent for service. All the accommodations recommended are on the water. Some have kitchens, which is an advantage given the high cost of eating out every night. Also note that many of the island's hotels (and restaurants) are closed for six or eight weeks in late summer or early fall. This is when Anguilla sinks beyond its usual sleepy demeanor to become near comatose!

Covecastles, P.O. Box 248, Shoal Bay West, Anguilla, BWI. ✆ 800-223-1108 or 264-497-6801, ✉ 264-497-6051, 🖳 www.covecastles.com, covecastles@anguillanet.com

$ Stratospheric ▥ EP ⒸⒸ 16 units

When we were researching the first edition of *Rum & Reggae's Caribbean*, we drove up to the then-new Covecastles and just hated it because the highly contemporary structures overwhelmed the delicate setting. This made us angry—hence our decision to exclude it. We eventually warmed up to this most un-Caribbean place, however, mostly because of what goes on inside the villas. What a great space!

Covecastles is a series of futuristic white structures that sit on Anguilla's quiet, westernmost beach amid wild and natural landscaping. The villas range from two to five bedrooms, each with two or more baths. They all have a fully equipped gourmet kitchen, dining room, living room, and terra-cotta tile veranda. They are furnished simply but beautifully in custom rattan, with plush white cushions and raw silk décor right out of *Architectural Digest* (in which the property was twice featured). All are designed to ensure maximum privacy. One complaint: Although master bathrooms are appropriately luxurious throughout, additional bathrooms in each villa are surprisingly small, with cramped plastic shower installations!

The trade winds provide ample ventilation, and the views are of the sublime water and the profile of St. Martin/St. Maarten in the distance. Amenities include your own housekeeper (who does everything but cook), cable TV, VCR, CD players, beach chairs and umbrellas, snorkeling gear, Sunfish sailboats, fishing gear, bikes, tennis rackets, and a lighted tennis court. There is an intimate, sophisticated restaurant, but no bar. There's also no pool (other than private ones for the larger villas), but the beach is fabulous. Other activities and services can be arranged by the management. Closed late August through mid-October.

Cap Juluca, P.O. Box 240, Maunday's Bay, Anguilla, BWI. ✆ 888-858-5822 or 264-497-6666, ✉ 264-497-6617, 🖥 www.capjuluca.com, capjuluca@anguillanet.com

💲 **Stratospheric** ⑪ **CP** ⒸⒸ 98 rooms

Situated on the prettiest beach in Anguilla, with the whitest sand you'll ever see, this Moorish extravaganza of stucco and domed turrets is an unusual architectural statement in the West Indies. From the paisley wall coverings, tapestries, and exotically upholstered furniture of the main building to the curves and columned arches of the guest accommodations, the effect is startling—a little out of place but striking nonetheless.

The rooms, of various degrees of size and luxury, are found in a series of 18 two-story villas strung along this gorgeous beach. Unlike the Covecastles setup, here the villas are shared with other guests (unless you rent the whole thing). Not to fear: Each room has its own private entrance and private patio or balcony, so you might not even encounter other guests sharing your villa. Each villa also has its own manager, who acts like a concierge for those rooms, plus a housekeeper who prepares and delivers continental breakfast to your terrace. The rooms are fully equipped, with a/c and ceiling fans, hammocks, Italian tile floors, voluptuous marble baths, and so on. You can also rent suites with their own plunge pools. There are three tennis courts, two lighted for night play, and an 1,800-square-foot pool with private tanning areas separated by hedges, with attendants available at the summons of a bell. A variety of water sports is available, and cups of icy sorbet are doled out on the beach each day at 3 p.m.

On the eastern end of the beach is Pimm's, a superb French-Caribbean restaurant in a quite romantic setting on a peninsula facing the cresent of Maundays. An adjoining lounge, Kemia's, serves impressive hors d'oeuvres and tapas; in the center of the beach is George's, a very pleasant venue for lunch and a weekly barbecue; and 24-hour room service is also available. A menu of spa services, handled in guest rooms, features a variety of Asian- and Indonesian-influenced treatments, including a Jamu Massage, a Rice and Spice Ritual, and a Sea and Flower Scrub. Mmmm.

Rates drop by half when summer rolls around, and packages can save even more. Closed September through October.

Malliouhana, P.O. Box 173, Meads Bay, Anguilla, BWI. ℂ 800-835-0796 or 264-497-6111, ✉ 264-497-6011, 💻 www.malliouhana.com

💲 **Stratospheric** ⓨ **EP** ⓒⓒ 56 rooms

Like a celebrity traveling incognito, Malliouhana doesn't disclose its whereabouts. You won't find many signs pointing the way — usually a good tip-off to an ultra-chic resort, and this is one of the Caribbean's poshest. Promising to "replenish the spirit of living," it will also most assuredly deplete your bank account. But if you have the money and want sumptuous and tranquil surroundings, with nothing and no one to harass you, then why not?

Conceived and still managed by the Roydon family, who built it in 1984, everything at Malliouhana is carefully considered, from the tasteful color scheme of earth reds, forest greens, and sandy beiges to the multitiered layout of the many public loggias and alcoves. Throughout, there is a feeling of intimacy. You expect to see Beyoncé or Gwyneth sipping a lime squash under one of the countless oversize (and color-coordinated, of course) Haitian or West Indian paintings. The bar is particularly sexy, with very comfortable sofas, piles of pillows, muted tones, and a terrific sound system.

Outside, there are two free-form pools and an oversize Jacuzzi. The pools are at different levels, so that one spills into the next by means of a man-made stone waterfall. But far more appealing for swimming is the little-used, spectacular ocean down a series of steps from the pool. Some more steps and a landing have been carved into the rock. This allows you to dive into the crystal clear water and swim to the resort's private beach, about 100 yards to the right (another set of stairs accesses the beach directly). All water-sports activities and equipment (snorkeling, fishing gear, waterskiing, out-island cruises, windsurfing, and sailing) are complimentary, which is the least the resort can do, considering the price you pay for a room!

The excellent and *très cher* open-air restaurant overlooks the water; the wine list here is possibly the Caribbean's most extravagant, with 30,000 bottles cellared. There's even more: a lavish spa that opened in 2002, a fine fitness room with wonderful water views, and a children's pool with a pirate-themed play area that is set aside from the rest of the resort. Four tennis courts (two lighted for night play) and another restaurant down on Meads Bay round out the facilities. Oh yes, and the rooms — suffice it to say that they uphold the elegance of the rest of the resort. Each one has a terrace and ceiling fan, bamboo platform beds, and the same tasteful design scheme and furnishings. Rates drop considerably in the summer; closed September and October.

Carimar Beach Club, P.O. Box 327, Meads Bay, Anguilla, BWI. ✆ 800-235-8667 or 264-497-6881, ✉ 264-497-6071, 💻 www.carimar.com, carimar@anguillanet.com

💲 **Wicked Pricey** ⑪ EP ⒸⒸ 24 units

Down the hill from Malliouhana is Carimar Beach Club. This is a friendly and charming little resort that rents one-, two- and three-bedroom apartments, each with a fully equipped kitchen, living and dining room, and a spacious patio and balcony overlooking the nicely tended gardens or the beach. Run by an accommodating Anguillian, this is a good pick for families who need space and cooking facilities. The atmosphere is very low-key and, though not cheap, it can work out to be a decent value when four are sharing a two-bedroom unit. (Summer rates are a steal, at more than 50 percent off winter prices.) There is a great beach out front (Meads Bay, the same one Malliouhana's guests pay much more for) and a western exposure for sunset-watching. There is a tennis court, and water sports are available, but there's no bar or dining; however, three of the island's finest restaurants are within walking distance. Closed September through October.

CuisinArt Resort & Spa, P.O. Box 2000, Rendezvous Bay, Anguilla, BWI. ✆ 800-943-3210, 212-972-0880, or 264-498-2000, ✉ 264-498-2010, 💻 www.cuisinartresort.com

💲 **Stratospheric** ⑪ CP ⒸⒸ 93 rooms

Yes, you read correctly—it's not a typo. Anguilla is home to what is probably the first hotel anywhere named after a kitchen appliance. The 93-room CuisinArt resort sits near the middle of Rendezvous Bay, a long, beautiful beach that escaped major development for a number of years; not anymore. Now a series of 10 three-story structures dominate the beach, housing most of the oversize guest rooms. The architecture is pretty (think Mykonos, or perhaps Cap Juluca?), but it's hardly discreet: This place does have an air of New Money and, accordingly, the level of taste involved wavers wildly. On the positive side is a swank entryway that leads to striking reflecting pools and unusually green (for dry Anguilla) gardens. There is an excellent spa in an odd but appealing three-story facility (love those wide, blue glass bowls for pedicures), and except for two smaller, less-expensive units, the rooms are huge. Most are minimally furnished Junior Suites with great beach views and vast, plush marble bathrooms.

The CuisinArt prides itself on its cuisine. We'd have to agree that the food is very good, but the art, well, it's not so good—one might say it's a bit louder than your average food processor. The art in the lobby and the rooms features a series of gaudy (not Gaudi) oils from contemporary Italian artists. Getting back to the cuisine: Most of our meal was very good, and the lobster buffet on Tuesday night is not to be missed. The resort also has its own hydroponics farm for growing veggies and herbs.

CuisinArt will please the clientele who prefer that their resorts display some opulence, but we generally prefer chic with a little more soul. Regardless of your style preferences, the personal service and extremely friendly staff who will bend over backwards for their guests definitely help to make for a very comfortable and enjoyable stay. Closed September through October.

Kú, P.O. Box 51, Shoal Bay East, Anguilla, BWI. ℂ 800-869-5827 or 264-497-2011, ✎ 264-497-3355, 🖳 www.kuanguilla.com

💲 **Very Pricey** 🍴 **EP** ⓒⓒ 27 rooms

Now overseen by the management team behind Cap Juluca, Kú is a 2005 reincarnation of the old Shoal Bay Hotel. The style is South Beach minimalist chic — white on white — and all the rooms are very tasteful suites in two- and three-story buildings set a little back from the sand. Each of these 775-square-foot units is identical except for view. All are well appointed — stocked with CD and DVD player and Balinese bath amenities — and have a full kitchen, an alternative to the island's pricey restaurants (there is also a small convenience store on the property that sells imported cheeses, pate, etc.). The tones of white, pale cool blue, and lavender are quite soothing.

However — and this is a big caveat — in revamping the resort, the new management added a 75-foot-long outdoor bar and restaurant that sits between most of the rooms and the sand. The attempt was to create something like the Nikki Beach scene over on St. Barth — beautiful people listening to cool music while sipping colorful drinks — but to us, the people staying at Kú lose out. Although the hotel probably needed a bigger dining facility, the new restaurant has a canvas canopy overhead that blocks much of the sea view for lower level rooms, and the bar manages to block the view from most of the dining tables. Ah... excuse us, but we came to this island to enjoy the ambiance of sea and sand, not to have our panorama limited to dinnerware and dining companions! That said, Kú *is* a fresh infusion of energy and style for Anguilla, and it will probably launch a number of new projects on this silky strand. Although Kú has little on the surface in common with the Cap Juluca experience, it provides a decent alternative for those not on the Cap Juluca budget.

Rendezvous Bay Hotel and Villas, P.O. Box 31, Rendezvous Bay, Anguilla, BWI. ℂ 800-274-4893 or 264-497-6549, ✎ 264-497-6026, 🖳 www.rendezvousbay.com

💲 **Not So Cheap** for standard rooms; **Very Pricey** for villas 🍴 **EP** ⓒⓒ 19 rooms and 24 villas

The late Jeremiah Gumbs, leader of one of Anguilla's dynasties, created the island's original beach resort. Located on a 50-acre site at the end of one of Anguilla's most splendid beaches (and by now, you know that's saying a lot), it was built in 1962 as a 5-room guesthouse and eventually grew to 40-something units. Gumbs passed away in 2003, and his family has developed a plan to substantially redevelop the property. The original buildings are scheduled to be torn down in summer 2007 and rebuilt in high style. Prices will no doubt increase substantially for the resort's reopening at the end of 2007. Until then, you can stay in one of the pleasingly simple but comfortable standard rooms, or in the cluster of 24 low-key villas that dapple the beach. There's no pool or a/c, and the restaurant doesn't mess about with fancy French cuisine, but this is a place with character, and we hope the family is able to maintain that integrity as the resort moves on to its next incarnation.

Anguilla Great House, P.O. Box 157, Rendezvous Bay, Anguilla, BWI.
℃ 800-583-9247 or 264-497-6061, ✉ 264-497-6019,
🖳 www.anguillagreathouse.com, flemingw@anguillanet.com

💲 Very Pricey ⑪ EP ⒸⒸ 31 rooms

Located midway on the long stretch of sand at Rendezvous Bay, this is a small, locally owned resort with a nice, casual ambiance and attractive rooms. If you're priced out of Rendezvous Bay Hotel (or locked out during its reconstruction), this is a fine alternative. The grounds could use some water and a manicure, but there is a great beach in front and you'll rarely see many people on it. The style is refreshingly West Indian, with white Antillean roofs and gingerbread trim. The original rooms are comfortably furnished with mahogany repros and chintz upholstery—simple but tasteful. The baths are marble and a good size; ceiling fans keep the rooms cool. There are four newer rooms on the second floor of a building near the office; these are priced the same but are set back from the beach. There are some comfy chaises on the long veranda outside the rooms. A pool is adjacent to the Old Caribe bar and restaurant, and there are water sports available on the beach. It's a little rustic, perhaps, but charming.

Allamanda Beach Club, P.O. Box 662, Shoal Bay East, Anguilla, BWI.
℃ 264-497-5217, ✉ 264-497-5216, 🖳 www.allamanda.ai,
allamanda@offshore.com.ai

💲 Not So Cheap ⑪ EP ⒸⒸ 16 units

You've heard all about the great beach resorts on Anguilla, but by now you've noticed that they all come with a steep price tag. Well, not all: Alamanda sits just off one of the island's loveliest stretches of sand, Shoal Bay East. This is nothing fancy—just a 16-unit, three-story apartment complex with a pool and restaurant that is otherwise pretty much devoid of the glamour found at the tonier places. The least expensive rooms are a pair of studios with a kitchen and a pullout sofa; other units have a separate bedroom and queen bed, as well as a kitchen. The beach is a two-minute walk from your room.

Where to Eat

The dining choices are superb on Anguilla, and with more than 70 restaurants, you'll have your hands full trying to decide where to go. At the big resorts, the restaurants at Malliouhana (264-497-6111), Cap Juluca (264-497-6666), Covecastles (264-497-6801), and CuisinArt (264-498-2000) are excellent (and expensive). Even if you aren't staying at one of these spots, you should splurge one night and dine at one of them. Reservations are a must. Here are some others to try.

$$$$ Barrel Stay, Sandy Ground, 264-497-2831

This is a French Créole restaurant that sits beside the beach. Fresh seafood is the specialty here — the fish bouillabaisse is famous (order ahead). Lunch and dinner are served daily. Reservations are recommended.

$$$ Fat Cat Gourmet, George Hill, 264-497-2307

Not to be missed, particularly for those with kitchens, is the Fat Cat Gourmet. It features excellent packaged and frozen homemade dishes, such as chicken marbella, conch stew (guaranteed tender), and lobster quiche, that can be reheated whenever. Thus you are relieved of shopping and cooking, which would otherwise take up precious beach time. Fat Cat makes lots of desserts and will custom-bake a birthday cake or your favorite pie. Also available are pasta salads and daily specials for beach picnics, as well as a catering service for any cocktail parties or dinner parties you decide to throw. Fat Cat also delivers. Closed Sunday.

$$$$$ Gorgeous Scilly Cay, Island Harbour, 264-235-5000

A legendary hangout for celebs (who are known to helicopter over from St. Martin/St. Maarten and St. Barth), this restaurant sits on a tiny islet off Island Harbour — a water taxi appears when you flag him down for the two-minute shuttle over to the cay. Grilled lobster and a fierce rum punch are the focus, but other barbecued items are available, along with lounge chairs for sunning. Open Wednesday, Friday, and Sunday only, until 5 p.m., with live music (sometimes by an ancient scratch band) on Wednesday and Sunday.

$$$$$ Hibernia, Island Harbour, 264-497-4290

This small, highly respected restaurant offers one of the most creative cuisines to be found on this or any other island, an exotic mix of French and Asian flavors. Chef Raoul Rodriguez and his wife, Mary Pat, take extended vacations each year to exotic corners of the world and bring back new ideas each time. It's definitely worth the long trip out to Island Harbour, but there are just 11 tables, so reservations are required. Closed Monday.

$$ **Johnno's**, Sandy Ground, 264-497-2728

Johnno's has good local-style food, late-night dining, and great live music on Friday night and Sunday and Wednesday afternoons. Closed Monday.

$$$$$ **Koal Keel**, The Valley, 264-497-2930

The cuisine here is best described as nouvelle West Indian, but the atmosphere is pure lust. The restaurant is in one of the oldest houses on the island and is decorated with a collection of 19th-century island antiques, capped by a bed that sits in the middle of the whole thing. We can't explain it, but we like it. The wine cellar houses 25,000 bottles. Reservations are recommended.

$$$$$ **Mango's**, Barnes Bay, 264-497-6479

This is an American California grill with a West Indian flair. The food is fresh, simple, and very good, and the beachfront setting is perfect. Although some Anguilla regulars told us that the kitchen was not at its best (despite the sky-high prices), our meal was excellent. Dinner is served daily. Reservations are recommended.

$$$$ **Oliver's Seaside Grill**, Long Bay, 264-497-8780

In a simple yet stylish space perched above the shoreline of Long Bay, Oliver's is our idea of a perfect romantic Caribbean setting. The food is right up there with the ambiance. The menu presents a dynamic array of superbly prepared meats, pastas, and seafood. The marinated sting ray is a must-have appetizer, and, although we're partial toward the crayfish or the Caribbean lobster, any dish that follows will be sure to please. Open nightly from 7 p.m.

$$$ **Ripples**, Sandy Ground, 264-497-3380

Expat Jacquie Ruan and her husband, "Chocolate," are the congenial hosts at this reliable institution favored by residents. The food is quite international, but with roots in pub fare. It's a good late-night choice. Saturday night happy hour (5 to 7 p.m.) features $10 entrees.

$$$ **Roy's Bayside Grill**, Sandy Ground, 264-497-2470

This English pub and grill is a fave among the yachty set because of its fresh seafood and good value. Happy hour on Friday (5 to 7 p.m.)

is a big hit here, too, due to half-price meals. Open for lunch and dinner daily.

$$$$ **Straw Hat**, Forest Bay, 264-497-8300
Situated on pilings over the water, facing the twinkling lights of St. Martin, this is one of Anguilla's most romantic dinner landings, with attentive service, generous portions, and great presentation. Don't miss the delicious conch spring rolls. Closed Sunday.

$$$ **Tasty's**, above Sandy Ground, 264-497-2737
Chef and owner Dale got his training at Malliouhana. He's aiming for something less lofty (but still appealing), and island flavors rule at his informal eatery. This means lots of fresh seafood, like steamed potfish with mushrooms and local provisions.

$$$$ **Trattoria Tramonto**, Shoal Bay West, 264-497-8819
This is one of the few real Italian restaurants on the island (maybe the only one) — northern Italian, to be specific, with bellinis and brothy seafood soups, all served just off the sand. Open for lunch and dinner; closed Monday.

Don't Miss

The Dune Preserve

Formerly known as Dune, this is local reggae star Bankie Banx's beach bar, with a new moniker to protest the development of the CuisinArt Resort next door. It's mostly a collection of washed-up flotsam and jetsam, centered around a beached boat that serves as the bar. Bankie is always adding to his artistic compound and is an amiable host. Stop by for a beer or a chat — it's an essential Anguillian experience. Come for the annual (usually in March) Moonsplash, held right on the beach, showcasing Caribbean and international music.

The Heritage Collection

Local historian (and memorabilia collector) Colville Petty runs a small museum dedicated to the history of Anguilla out of his home in Pond Ground near Island Harbour. There are a few choice Amerindian artifacts from way back, but more interesting are the items that document Anguilla's bloodless revolution of 1967, such as the flag that was flown for only a few hours, or currency and car license plates that refer to "CN," for St. Christopher and Nevis — Anguilla wasn't even recognized as part of the tri-island alliance (no wonder they rebelled!). Open daily except Sunday by appointment; admission $5; call 264-497-4440.

Antigua and Barbuda

TOURISTO SCALE:

ANTIGUA 👤👤👤👤👤👤👤👤 (8)

BARBUDA 👤👤👤 (3)

The country of Antigua and Barbuda comprises two islands that are separated by just 27 miles, but their contrasting character would suggest that they are worlds apart. Whereas Antigua is a well-established presence in the Caribbean tourism scene, Barbuda is one of the region's most off-the-beaten-track destinations, "boasting" just a trio of very expensive resorts that combine for a total of fewer than 100 rooms. Barbuda presents some of the finest deserted beaches we've ever seen, and since it is reachable only through Antigua, some would suggest (and that would include us) that Barbuda is the best reason to come to Antigua. That being said, at least Antigua is loaded with attractive beaches, so travelers might still see it as a worthwhile option.

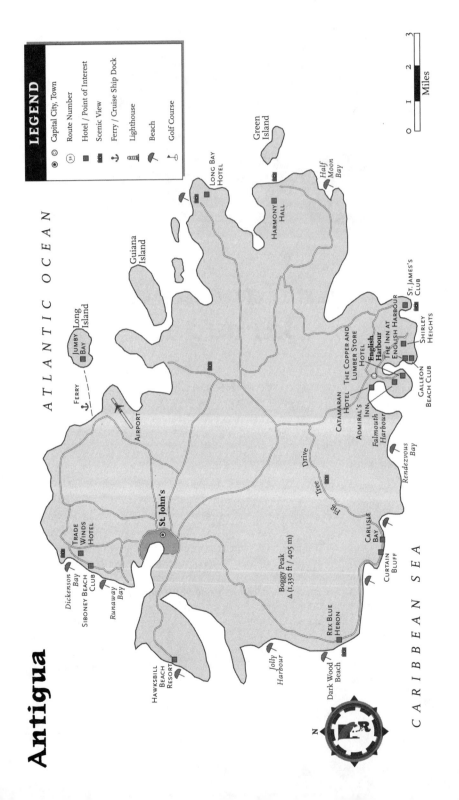

Antigua

ON THE ISLAND OF ANTIGUA (PRONOUNCED "AN-TEE-GA"), you'll find beautiful talcum-soft beaches, swaying palm trees, scenic sailing anchorages, and a spectrum of hotels and resorts — all of which implies that you've found the quintessential tropical paradise. Well, as the old saying goes, "You can't judge a book by its cover." Despite the initial appeal, if it weren't for the annual Sailing Week and a collection of superb beaches, Antigua wouldn't be among our first picks for a Caribbean holiday. Why, you ask? It all starts at the V.C. Bird International Airport's Immigration counter, where an always frosty officer looks at us the way one ponders a cockroach, and he never utters a hello or welcome. Shades of things to come? Unfortunately it is, for there is a deliberate coolness about Antiguans. Despite tourism being the island's bread and butter, many residents are brusque and unwelcoming toward visitors. Although this is not a new phenomenon (Parisians perfected this kind of kiss-off years ago), it's a tad unsettling when you're on vacation on a small Third World island. There's definitely an attitude problem here, which is strange, considering that more than 70 percent of the island's revenue is derived from tourism (the balance largely comes from Internet gambling businesses and offshore banking).

Antigua does have its merits, however. There are many wonderful beaches (the tourist office claims 365 — does the mud in St. John's Harbour count as one?), some rather nice resorts, including a good array of moderately priced beachfront hotel options, a dry climate with constant trade winds, a happening yachting scene, great British historic sights, and an international airport that serves as a hub for two airlines flying the eastern Caribbean. Antigua is also the largest of the Leeward Islands, covering an area of about 108 square miles. It's just that with all the other choices in the Caribbean, why deal with attitude, lots of tourists, bad roads, and an island that really isn't all that pretty? Unless, of course, it's Sailing Week (see below).

Being a major hub in the Caribbean transportation wheel and a big resort destination, Antigua attracts all kinds of travelers. Americans, Brits, Canadians, and Germans pour in on jumbo jets. Once on the island, most of them head to the resorts on the western and southern coasts, and the yachty set heads for English Harbour, one of the primary boating centers in the Caribbean. A select few with bulging wallets hop over to Barbuda, where a trio of extravagantly priced resorts and long deserted beaches (and little else)

Antigua: Key Facts

Location	17°N by 61°W
	38 miles/61 kilometers north of Guadeloupe
	27 miles/43 kilometers south of Barbuda
	1,800/2,896 kilometers miles southeast of New York
Size	108 square miles/280 square kilometers
Highest point	Boggy Peak (1,330 feet/405 meters)
Population	71,068
Language	English
Time	Atlantic Standard Time (1 hour ahead of EST, same as EDT)
Area code	268
Electricity	Most of the island's electricity is 220 volts AC, 60 cycles; however, some hotels have 110 volts AC, 60 cycles.
Currency	The Eastern Caribbean dollar, EC$ (EC$2.68 = U.S.$1)
Driving	On the left; you'll need a temporary permit, which is obtained by presenting your valid U.S. or Canadian driver's license and $20.
Documents	U.S. and Canadian citizens need a passport or proof of nationality with a photo; British citizens need a passport; all visitors must present a return or an ongoing ticket.
Departure tax	$20
Beer to drink	Wadadli
Rum to drink	Cavalier
Music to hear	Dancehall
Tourism info	888-268-4227 or 212-541-4117
	www.antigua-barbuda.org

are found. Antigua's modern cruise-ship dock lures big ships almost daily, and the swarms descend into St. John's, creating a shopping frenzy that overwhelms the little town and trickles into Nelson's Dockyard at English Harbour. With all of this commotion, there are a lot of options for the visitor, and Antigua may appeal to those who, if they are not sailors, like the activity and variety the island offers.

The Briefest History

Antigua has been inhabited for more than 4,000 years, starting with the Ciboney in 2400 B.C., followed by the Arawaks from the first century A.D. until about A.D. 1100, when the Caribs took over. Columbus sighted and named the island after Santa Maria de la Antigua on his second voyage, in

1493. The Caribs and the lack of fresh springwater kept out the Europeans until 1632, when the English landed a party from St. Kitts and eventually conquered the Caribs. Sugar planting (by African slaves) was quite successful, and there were over 150 mills in operation at one time (the plantations also deforested the island, from which it has never recovered). Antigua played an important role in British hegemony in the West Indies, as the "landlocked" and incognito port of English Harbour was the key naval base for Lord Nelson in the Caribbean (palm fronds on the masts of English ships in the harbor hid them from the French). When slavery was abolished in 1834, the economy slid downhill, and conditions for the former slaves were deplorable (this might also help to explain today's Antiguan demeanor). This led to unrest and violence in the early part of the 20th century; in the 1930s the average workers in the sugar-based economy earned less than their counterparts on other islands.

In 1939, Vere Cornwall Bird became a co-founder of the Antigua Trades and Labour Union; soon after, the Antigua Labour Party was formed and Bird led strikes for better pay with strident anticolonial rhetoric. In 1967, England granted Antigua and Barbuda self-rule, and V.C. Bird became the island's first premier. Sugarcane was phased out in the early 1970s, and Bird looked to tourism as the next primary economy for the island. The Bird government had more success squelching opposition than it did creating employment, however, and when the island was granted full independence by Britain in 1981, V.C. Bird became prime minister. He controlled Antigua and Barbuda until his retirement in 1994, when his son, Lester Bird, took over. Scandal repeatedly rocked the governments of both men — arms smuggling for both apartheid-era South Africa and the Medellin drug cartel in Colombia, drug smuggling by Lester's brother Ivan, money-laundering schemes, and so on. Much of the $400 million in foreign debt that Antigua had rung up since independence is said to have wound up in the Bird family's pockets. V.C. died in 1998, but it wasn't until 2004 that the Bird family's rule — lasting most of four decades — came to an ignominious close, in resounding elections with a turnout of more than 90 percent of the voters. Today, longtime opposition leader Baldwin Spencer holds the office of prime minister.

Getting There

Antigua is centrally located and a major hub for neighboring Caribbean islands. Its airport, V.C. Bird International, handles jumbo jets and has non-stop service on American from San Juan; Continental from Newark; Delta from Atlanta; and on US Airways from Charlotte and Philadelphia. Air Canada and BWIA serve the island from Toronto; British Airways, BWIA and Virgin Atlantic fly from London. Antigua is also home to LIAT and Caribbean Star, with daily flights to most destinations in the Eastern Caribbean. BWIA has flights from Barbados; Kingston, Jamaica; and Trinidad. Winair flies in from St. Maarten.

Getting Around

To really explore Antigua, you'll need a rental car. The roads here have traditionally been among the region's worst, but elections usually provide the
impetus to make improvements. There are plenty of agencies located at the airport, to your right as you walk out of Customs. Competition is fierce, so go
to each counter and ask for its best price (the agency will show you its rate
on a piece of paper so the competitors don't shout out a lower one). You can
get a decent economy car for about $40 a day; weekly rentals will yield a bet-
ter rate. Among the international car-rental agencies are Budget (800-527-
0700 or 268-462-3009), Dollar (800-800-4000 or 268-462-0362), Hertz
(800-654-3131 or 268-481-4440), National (800-227-3876 or 268-462-2113),
and Thrifty (800-847-4389 or 268-462-9532).

If you loathe driving, there are plenty of taxis available, but be advised that
if this is your method of seeing the island, you'll spend a lot during your
visit. Rates from the airport to all major destinations are posted in the Customs area, and your hotel will also advise you to be sure to agree on the price
before you get in the cab.

Focus on Antigua: Sailing Week

If there is one time in yachting when socializing is just as important as racing (if not more so), it is Sailing Week (or, more corporately, the Rolex Antigua Sailing Week). Having survived four decades of festive inebriation, it's
still going strong as the premier yachting event in the Caribbean and has
emerged as one of the top five regattas in the world. Since Sailing Week
starts each year at the end of April, this ritual puts the final wrap on the winter season. Afterward, most boats head north to the United States or east to
the Mediterranean for the summer.

Race Week also attracts a large crowd of nonracers. This is because of the
range of activities that happens onshore. In fact, most people participating
in Race Week don't give a damn about the races and can't tell the difference
between a shroud and a stay. What they want is to have a good time while
rubbing elbows with the sailing set. On weekend nights, a good part of the
younger Antiguan population will be there, too, because this is one of two
major events on the island (the other being Carnival in August).

People get pretty toasted during this celebration (boating people are notorious drinkers, putting Nick and Nora Charles to shame). Despite the
alcohol, there is order, due to what seems to be a policeman every 20 feet —
a sobering effect; the presence of the police also reflects the political unease
with a sport as white and wealthy as yachting on an island that is predominantly black and poor. Since Race Week is a major tourist draw, the Hotel
Association and the government want to ensure that all goes smoothly —
hence the cops. In the official programs, there is a plea to "please help us
keep Antigua Sailing Week a happy, carefree, but controlled experience for
the benefit of all."

Most of the activity during Race Week is focused on **Nelson's Dockyard**, a restored complex of historic Georgian brick buildings and warehouses that sits in the middle of English Harbour. Now it's a national park and major tourist attraction, and some of the buildings are stunning — especially the Admiral's Inn (see Where to Stay). The daily parties happen at various beaches and resorts all around the island.

In any given year, some 200 boats from roughly 25 countries compete, with an equal split between racing and cruising classes. Just so you will know for future cocktail conversation, there are five days of races taking place on the west and south coasts of the island. There are two divisions: Division A encompasses Racing, Big Boat, and Racer/Cruiser (with spinnaker) classes; Division B consists of Performance Cruiser, Cruiser, and Bareboat classes. Each boat carries a minimum four-person team. The Racers are semipros, traveling around the seas on the racing circuit. The Cruisers are more mellow — many of their boats are available for a crewed charter any other week but this one. The Cruisers also drink a lot more during the event — beer and rum consumption goes through the roof during Race Week. Now you know all the essentials to hold your own at the numerous cocktail parties affiliated with Sailing Week.

Leading up to Sailing Week is the **Guadeloupe Race**, typically held the Thursday before the start of Sailing Week. This is a 42-mile race from Deshaies, Guadeloupe, to English Harbour. There are three classes of boats in this race: Multihulls, Racers, and Cruisers. The cocktail party hosted by Les Amis de Voile de Point-à-Pitre is fabulous (usually at the Admiral's Inn).

Sunday is the day of the first yacht race, the first leg of the Round the Island Race. It's a 35-mile course for Racers (Division A) and a 21-mile course for Cruisers (Division B), between Falmouth Harbour (next to English Harbour) and Dickenson Bay on the northwest coast of Antigua. Racers do the route counterclockwise; Cruisers do the course clockwise. It's near the finish line that the real fun begins — some claim this is the best party of the week. The combination of hundreds of boats in the bay, a pretty beach, a large local turnout, and tourist-clogged resorts creates a highly festive atmosphere. A traveling band of vendors sets up on the beach, offering chicken and chips, ice cold beer, and an endless array of mediocre T-shirts. A reggae band provides the pulsating beat for the huge crowd on the beach. If you ever wanted to dance barefoot in the sand, this is the ideal opportunity to do so. The action actually begins around noon as the nonmariners arrive at the beach for sun, fun, and watching the boats come in — so plan to spend the day. You'll never be far from the bar or a bathroom.

The second race is held Monday in the same area. It consists of an Olympic-type course, most of which is too far out to sea to see. After the races, it's pretty much a rerun of the night before, if not quite as much fun or as crowded, and is held at a different resort and beach. It's back to Nelson's Dockyard for the third race, on Tuesday, the return leg of the Round the Island Race. The course runs south along the west coast, and after the race, another party kicks off in English Harbour. This is a major drinking event because the following day is **Lay Day**—that is, no races. A must-not-miss is Limey's Bar on the second floor overlooking the action. This is the place to rendezvous and talk about plans for the summer or for the delivery north.

Lay Day is lots of fun for landlubbers, too. All the festivities are held at the Antigua Yacht Club, just down the road from Nelson's Dockyard, about a 12-minute walk, on Falmouth Harbor. The action starts in the early afternoon with a rubber-raft race, tug-of-war, boardsailing races, a beer-drinking contest, and other "what-the-hell" games. A new one we heard about called Carry-On Camping involves couples racing into little tents to exchange clothes, the winner being the pair that emerges first. There is also a single-handed yacht race for boats 45 feet and under, and team racing in Lasers by country or territory, which can be fun.

After Lay Day, the fourth event is the **South Coast Race**, which begins at Falmouth Harbour. Once again, there is a party with a band in front of a hotel—the party starts around 6 p.m. and goes until your walking hangover says "enough already." The fifth race, the **Ocean Race**, is held off the south coast again, and the *après* scene shifts back to Nelson's Dockyard for the last of the Race Day sailing parties. By now, you'll be feeling just a little weary and will probably want to venture over to one of the local bars outside the Dockyard.

The most social of the local bars is undoubtedly **Abracadabra's**, located just across from the Dockyard parking lot. This is the place to go if you want to hook up. The deck will be jammed with the sailing set—count on 20 minutes to get from end to end. Don't even think of trying to get through when the management shows video highlights of the day's races on the big screen. The crowd here is very attractive, generally bleached out, and horny. In the garden, a reggae band sets up and gets to really jammin' later in the evening. The partying here sometimes doesn't end until daybreak.

Probably the prettiest spot for having a drink or listening to music is the **Admiral's Inn**, located in the Dockyard. The grounds are beautiful, particularly the huge stone columns that line a narrow slipway and are the only remnants of the old boathouse. The canopy created by some very old trees, combined with the elegance of the inn, makes a quietly grand and stately sight. The bar inside is comfortable and very nautical, with large French doors opening out onto the terrace and grounds. The live music here can be surprisingly good—one night we heard one of the best pan bands outside Trinidad.

With the main races over and the final standings posted, the atmosphere the next day becomes quite festive. Even while crews scurry around readying their boats for imminent departure, all seem to find time for a few pops here and there. Indeed, for many it's a liquid diet from the beginning, starting with breakfast. So by the time things start happening, a lot of people are juiced up and ready to go—not that there's really all that much going on, except for the greased-pole contest where local boys (the only ones daring enough) try to walk a machine-greased wooden pole over the water. The goal is to touch a red flag before falling in. Winners get a bottle of rum and a pat on the back. It's amusing to watch for about 20 minutes.

Around 3 p.m., the much-heralded **Non-Mariner's Race** takes place at the ramp in front of the Officer's Quarters. The requirements of the race are that the vessel be homemade, cost no more than $100 to build, and never have been in the water. The best part of the race is the start, when the contestants plunge into the water with their vessels. Their destination is the dock at the Admiral's Inn, where a crowd with cocktails awaits and cheers on the participants. Unfortunately, the race is over too soon, and that's that. The milling around on the waterfront continues while a band kicks up to keep everyone going until the evening and Lord Nelson's Ball.

Lord Nelson's Ball is supposedly the culmination of social events during Sailing Week, but in reality the first night at Dickenson's or the deck at Abracadabra's is much more fun. The ball is a throwback to the days when yachting was exclusively WASPy. The crowd (when we attended) was almost entirely white, thanks to the jacket-and-tie dress code and the fact that admission is $45 in advance, $55 at the door. It just doesn't seem right in the here and now, not that it ever was. We were embarrassed for the governor-general, who spoke at the ball to an audience that was hardly his constituency, which was not invited. That said, the ball is enjoyable for all the alcohol flowing freely from the open bar. Also amusing is how women manage to stow away their best taffetas in their duffel bags and then throw them on for this formal occasion. Some of the men come up with black tie, although most are dressed in natty blue blazers, tie, and button-downs with wrinkled khakis or Lilly Pulitzers; cocktail dresses are the prerequisite for ladies. The setting of the Admiral's Inn and grounds is quite handsome and colonial. When you've had enough, go over to Abracadabra's for reggae and a much more civilized environment.

For more information on this year's event, call 268-462-8872 or visit www.sailingweek.com. Another good resource for sailing events is www.antiguayachtclub.com, and note that Sailing Week isn't the only big event on Antigua's yachting calendar. The **Antigua Charter Yacht Show** draws dozens of the toniest yachts in the world each December. In April, immediately prior to Sailing Week, the **Antigua Classic Yacht Regatta** takes place—it invites classic tall ships with acres of canvas on three island races.

Where to Stay

Antigua is loaded with hotels, virtually all of which are on the beach. As with the other Leeward Islands, it's not cheap to stay here, but a few bargains can be found. Investigate package deals—significant discounts will be offered on both airfare and accommodations. Also note that Antigua is home to several all-inclusive properties, where your meals, drinks, and some (or most) activities are included in one set price. We don't particularly care for this setup, because it tends to limit one's exploration of the island, and all-inclusives are often fairly pricey compared to comparable accommodations. There are, however, two included below—both of which vie for the title of the island's premier resort.

The West Coast

There is a grand stretch of beach that begins just north of St. John's. The two main sections are Runaway Bay and Dickenson Bay, separated only by a marina channel, and on this strand there are no fewer than eight hotels, resorts, and condo villages.

Siboney Beach Club, P.O. Box 222, St. John's, Antigua, WI.
📞 800-533-0234 or 268-462-0806, 🖂 268-462-3356,
🖳 www.siboneybeachclub.com

💲 **Pricey** 🍽 **EP** CC 13 rooms

Dickenson Bay is a pretty busy spot, but Siboney is an intimate oasis amid the larger resorts. All but one of the rooms here are in a three-story structure that overlooks a festive tangle of greenery wrapping around a pool. Each of the rooms is really a suite with a kitchenette, furnished in rattan, with a/c in the bedrooms. We love the nice heavy sliding glass doors on the first-floor units. There's a romantic seaside restaurant (Coconut Grove), and a variety of water sports are available nearby. Aussie Tony Johnson, Siboney's builder and its warm and gracious owner, knows what an Antiguan vacation is all about and does his best to secure it for every guest.

Trade Winds Hotel, P.O. Box 1390, St. John's, Dickenson Bay, Antigua, WI. 📞 268-462-1223, 🖂 268-462-5007,
🖳 www.antiguatradewindshotel.com, twhotel@candw.ag

💲 **Very Pricey** 🍽 **EP** CC 50 rooms

Perched on top of a hill overlooking Dickenson Bay, this is a great option for view and breeze aficionados and for those who aren't particularly keen on lying on the beach—it draws a number of visiting businesspeople but doesn't suffer from a business-y environment. A small but attractive free-form pool lies at the center of a terrace with lots of shade and a bar—it's a pleasant spot at which to hang out, and so is the restaurant, which serves three meals a day. The rooms are clean and simply yet handsomely furnished. Each one has an ocean view, a minifridge, a/c, a phone, and a lanai. There are three types: a two-bedroom apartment with kitchen, a studio with kitchen, and a standard room with kitchen. It's a five-minute walk down the hill to the beach, and a shuttle is available on request.

Hawksbill Beach Resort, P.O. Box 108, St. John's, Five Islands, Antigua, WI. ℂ 800-255-5859 or 268-462-0301, ✎ 268-462-1515, 🖥 www.hawksbill.com, hawksbill@candw.ag

💲 **Wicked Pricey** 🍽 **All-Inclusive** CC 107 rooms

Set on 37 acres on an isolated peninsula west of St. John's, this resort —acquired by the English Rex Resorts chain in 2004—boasts four of its own beaches, including one that is reserved for nude sunbathing. Most of the original rooms are centered around a Great House. They don't have a/c, but they are well ventilated, and all offer sea views. Newer Beach Club rooms have a/c and a balcony or patio. Two restaurants, two bars, a swimming pool, a tennis court, and water sports round out the facilities. The food wasn't great when we last dined here, but that was before Rex Resorts took over the hotel. The all-inclusive rates include tennis and nonmotorized water sports, but there's a fee for scuba, waterskiing, and off-site activities. We're told that Hawksbill continues to cater more to Europeans, and if you like beaches, especially a nude one, and a resort setting, this just might be the place.

The Southwest Coast

Some of Antigua's most beautiful beaches, as well as the island's only real mountains, are found on the long southwest coast between Jolly Harbour and Carlisle Bay. Fortunately, most of these beaches have not sprouted resorts. There's a large development at Jolly Harbour, but it really caters more to the mass-market audience, so you won't find it listed below.

Curtain Bluff, P.O. Box 288, St. John's, Old Road, Antigua, WI. ℂ 888-289-9898 or 268-462-8400, ✎ 268-462-8409, 🖥 www.curtainbluff.com

💲 **Stratospheric** 🍽 **All-Inclusive** CC 72 rooms

Curtain Bluff is almost the opposite of the typical all-inclusive resort. Yes, the rates include all meals, drinks, and activities, but that's where the similarities end. This is a family-owned beach club where the emphasis is on genuine service and luxury, and the wine cellar holds 30,000 bottles with 500 labels represented. The guy in charge of this concept is Howard Hulford, a crusty old Caribbean legend of sorts, and although the day-to-day operation has been passed on to younger souls, Howard still plies the grounds daily, showing off his orchids and palms to all who express the slightest interest.

Located on a striking promontory jutting off the remote south coast, framed by two beaches, Curtain Bluff has been the grande dame of luxury hotels on Antigua since 1961, when Hulford built it. Run on the "old school" approach to deluxe vacations, it's quiet and elegant, if still slightly formal. The clientele is predominantly older, with the occasional honeymooners thrown in for ogling, but of late Curtain Bluff is actively soliciting a younger clientele by adding a lavish gym. The food here — much of it personally imported to the island by Hulford — is well beyond the norm for an all-inclusive (and note that the fine wines cost extra). The rooms are furnished in tropical décor, and all have lanais, water views, and Italian marble baths. In 2006, a/c was finally added to all the rooms in 2006 (this was perhaps spurred on by the debut of Carlisle Bay — see below). Rates include *all* water sports — including snorkeling trips, diving, water-skiing, and deep-sea fishing (now that's something we haven't seen at other all-inclusives) — and complimentary room service for meals and drinks until 11 p.m. Curtain Bluff has the best tennis facility on Antigua, including a resident pro, and is the site of a tennis challenge in May. Recently, a pool with lap lanes was added, and, last but not least, 2006 also saw the addition of a new spa (the treatments are not included in the rates, but we're always psyched about a spa). Closed late May through October.

Carlisle Bay, Carlisle Bay, Old Road, Antigua, WI. ℂ 800-628-8929 or 268-484-0002, ✉ 268-484-0003, 🖳 www.carlisle-bay.com

🔳 **Stratospheric** 🍽 **BP** and afternoon tea ⓒⓒ 88 rooms

In contrast to Curtain Bluff, Carlisle Bay (which opened in 2003) is a striking, utterly contemporary resort by the creator of the esteemed London hotel, One Aldwych. Located just a stone's throw from Curtain Bluff, the two are arch-rivals — not that they need to be, they cater to completely different clientele. In contrast to the usual tropical color scheme that filters into most Caribbean resorts of any class, Carlisle Bay sticks to white walls with a lavender-hued gray trim; the little color provided is from splays of purple orchids or the tray of blood-red cherries that were sitting in our room at check-in. This modernist look is quite bold, and we liked it, but it's a turnoff to anyone who prefers more floral tropical color schemes. All the rooms are suites, and most boast sea views from Frette-wrapped beds. The airy suites are stark but comfortable. They are well outfitted with nifty niceties: Gaggia coffeemaker, proper bedside reading lights, flat-screen TV, chic bath products, and a deep bathtub with a view into the mangrove lagoon that backs the resort.

There's a 17,000-square-foot spa and a 45-seat screening room that plays two movies nightly — *Rear Window* or *Private Benjamin*, anyone? There's a well-equipped water-sports center, and the beach is pretty and fine for swimming, although it doesn't enjoy the iridescent, tourmaline glow of which Antigua's most beautiful beaches can brag. During our visit, we saw more people hanging by the garden-wrapped pool than on the sand. Most of these guests are British, and there's a noticeable reserve to their temperament, but the largely Antiguan staff is cheerful and gracious. The meals are quite good; one restaurant serves a pan-Asian menu that is surprisingly authentic, and an open-air dining room with a grill has many organic items. On the other hand, we didn't appreciate the omnipresent, sterile buzz of fans and air conditioners everywhere, particularly in the restaurants and bathrooms, obscuring the natural island sounds of lapping waves and fussing birds. Nonetheless, Carlisle Bay is a serious addition to the Caribbean's collection of ultra-plush berths, and despite winter room rates hovering at $1,000 a night, we think it will be a trendsetter for years to come. Closed September through mid-October.

Rex Blue Heron, P.O. Box 1715, Johnson's Point, Antigua, WI. ✆ 800-255-5859 or 268-462-8564, ✉ 268-462-8005, 🖥 www.rexresorts.com

💲 **Pricey** 🍴 **EP** CC 64 rooms

This resort on the quiet southwest coast of the island is a little worn at the edges but generally offers good value for beach lovers. Because there are few other hotels or restaurants nearby, having a rental car is a good idea — taxis to other parts of the island aren't cheap. The hotel is situated on a spectacular, uncrowded beach. The least expensive rooms do not have a/c, TV, or sea views — you'll pay a little more for these amenities in the Superior category. There is a restaurant, and all-inclusive packages are available, but we don't particularly recommend this option. Otherwise, this is a cheerful little hideaway on a great beach.

English Harbour

If you want to be at the hub of activity during Sailing Week, then we strongly suggest that you stay in this area. Keep in mind that there will be a lot of noise from bands and people during this fiesta. English Harbour doesn't have the island's best beaches, but it is the hub of the island's history.

Admiral's Inn, P.O. Box 713, St. John's, English Harbour, Antigua, WI. ✆ 800-223-5695 or 268-460-1027, ✉ 268-460-1153, 🖥 www.admiralsantigua.com, admirals@candw.ag

💲 **Not So Cheap** 🍴 **EP** CC 14 rooms

A singular and historic inn set on the waterfront amid stately trees and old columns, this 220-year-old, weathered brick and shuttered Georgian building is also the site of Lord Nelson's Ball during Sailing Week. Originally an engineer's quarters, today it has 13 twin-bedded, character-filled rooms of various sizes — some with a/c, others with ceiling fans. There's also a two-bedroom apartment, known as the Joiner's Loft, that's right on the water. The Admiral's Bar is festooned with tasteful nautical memorabilia, and the terrace is a grand place for sipping rum punch while comparing the virtues of various winches.

In choosing to stay at Admiral's Inn (or Copper and Lumber Store, below), be aware that your hotel is situated next to the island's most popular tourist attraction and that visitors are frequent throughout the day.

Copper and Lumber Store Hotel, P.O. Box 184, St. John's, Nelson's Dockyard, English Harbour, Antigua, WI. ✆ 268-460-1058, 🖂 268-460-1529, 🖳 www.copperandlumberhotel.com, clhotel@candw.ag

💲 **Very Pricey** 🍴 EP CC 14 rooms

This is a wonderfully elegant hotel set in an old Georgian building in the heart of Nelson's Dockyard. Unfortunately, the operation has been up and down for the last several years, so we include it here with the hope that a steady hand will be guiding it in the near future. (At this writing, the local National Park is running the show.)

Like the Admiral's Inn next door, it has a weathered brick and shuttered or louvered exterior with suites and studios — all named after Lord Nelson's ships — and the same brick and wood décor throughout. It is the interior that makes the Copper and Lumber one of the more interesting hotels on Antigua. The restorer's detailing is evident in the Honduran mahogany woodwork, the hand-stenciled wallpaper, and the numerous and elegant antique furnishings. Even the bathrooms are cool — the showers are paneled with mahogany. The best rooms are the four suites, which are deluxe. All the rooms have kitchenettes and a/c. There is a restaurant and pub on the premises. During Sailing Week, this place is in the middle of the action, fronting the main plaza on the bay where the bands play.

Catamaran Hotel, Falmouth Harbour, Antigua, WI. ✆ 268-460-1036, 🖂 268-460-1339, 🖳 www.catamaran-antigua.com

💲 **Not So Cheap** 🍴 EP CC 14 rooms

If you're in the market for a budget hangout, we recommend this inn, family-run since 1968 and situated on Falmouth Harbour (next door to English Harbour). The hotel faces a marina and small beach (one that would rank very low on Antigua's purported list of 365). Standard rooms are small apartments with kitchens, most of which have a water view from the shared balcony. The rooms don't have phones, but cell phones can be rented for $10 a day. There's a pool, and basic water sports are offered from the beach. There's a restaurant next door, and many more are within a 10-minute drive at English Harbour. Manager-owner Fiona Bailey is attentive and goes out of her way to share the best of Antigua with her guests.

The Inn at English Harbour, P.O. Box 187, St. John's, English Harbour, Antigua, WI. ✆ 800-970-2123 or 268-460-1014, 🖂 268-460-1603, 🖳 www.theinn.ag

💲 **Very Pricey** ⑪ **EP** CC 35 rooms

We've always liked the 45-year-old inn for its slightly stuffy yet moderately priced air of British formality, and the location — just across the bay from Nelson's Dockyard, overlooking the entrance to English Harbour — is lovely. Acquired in 1999 by an Italian family, it still has a modicum of charm and character that lures a mostly British clientele. It also has a decent beach, water sports, and a fab view of the Dockyard from the inn's Terrace Restaurant and Bar.

The original and cheapest rooms are on top of the hill, with views across the channel to Montserrat; these are fine, as long as you don't mind a five-minute walk down the hill to the sand (a shuttle is also available on request). The original beachfront cottages were torn down and replaced with a trio of colonial-style buildings set well back from the beach. The rooms are sprawling and handsome, with jalousie windows, four-poster beds draped in mosquito netting, hardwood floors, and balconies that overlook a broad lawn, an infinity-lipped pool, and the beach beyond. There's a fitness center and tennis court, and water sports include snorkel equipment, windsurfers, and kayaks. The Inn runs a frequent boat launch to and from the dockyard, where there are numerous restaurant options. Closed mid-September through mid-October.

Galleon Beach Club, P.O. Box 1003, St. John's, Freeman's Bay, English Harbour, Antigua, WI. ☏ 268-460-1024, ✇ 268-460-1450, 🖥 www.galleonbeach.com, galleonbeach@candw.ag

💲 **Very Pricey** ⑪ **EP** CC 27 cottages, 7 villas

Located right next door to The Inn, on a bay facing the entrance to English Harbour, this is a pleasant time-share property, and with a nice beach, too. There are one- and two-bedroom cottages and three- and four-bedroom villas, all of which have living rooms, fully equipped kitchens, and lanais. Each of the units is individually decorated. Two tennis courts, water sports, and a mediocre restaurant round out the amenities. It's a great spot for families. Closed in September.

The East Coast

The eastern part of Antigua is less developed for tourism and therefore quieter.

St. James's Club, P.O. Box 63, St. John's, Mamora Bay, Antigua, WI. ☏ 800-858-4618 or 268-460-5000, ✇ 268-460-3015, 🖥 www.eliteislandresorts.com

💲 **Wicked Pricey** ⑪ **EP** CC 250 rooms and villas

Formerly affiliated with the St. James's in London, this resort attempted to put the *p* in pretentious — it had an "honorary committee" of Sirs and Ladies. You'd think that Aga Khan built the place out of marble and gold; in reality, it used to be a Holiday Inn! Several years of middling business apparently brought its owners down to earth, and in 1997 the hotel was taken over by Elite Island Resorts. Standard (or Club) rooms are fine, if expensive, but only a few have a partial ocean view. The two-bedroom villas here, though interesting in design, are jammed together — hardly worth the lofty price tag. There are two beaches, three restaurants, and a casino, and an array of activities is available, including water sports, fitness center, and tennis. An all-inclusive plan is also available, and during the Christmas period you'll be bullied into it.

Long Bay Hotel, P.O. Box 442, St. John's, Long Bay, Antigua, WI.
☏ 800-291-2005 or 268-463-2005, ✆ 268-463-2439,
🖳 www.longbayhotel.com

🛍 **Wicked Pricey** 🍴 **MAP** CC 18 rooms, 5 cottages

Owned and operated by the Lafaurie family since 1966, this intimate inn has a nice, casual ambiance about it and sits just off a pretty beach on the rather remote east coast. It offers rooms and cottages and a villa, each simply and attractively furnished. Rooms do not have a/c (the breezes at this spot are good) or TVs. All water sports are available, and a protected bay on one side of the property allows for waterskiing and sailing; a tennis court is on the premises (bring your own racket). There are two restaurants and two bars, and the hotel shares the busy beach with the Pineapple Beach Club. Closed July through October.

Jumby Bay Resort, P.O. Box 243, St. John's, Antigua, WI. ☏ 888-767-3966 or 268-462-6000, ✆ 268-462-6020, 🖳 www.jumbybayresort.com

🛍 **Stratospheric** 🍴 **All-Inclusive** CC 40 rooms and 11 villas

This is an unusual, 300-acre private outpost found 2 miles off Antigua, albeit one with a history of ups and downs, courtesy of management and ownership changes. In 2003, the resort was acquired by Rosewood Hotels and Resorts (of Little Dix Bay and Caneel Bay in the Virgins), and the hotel might finally have found an owner to make it all work. Jumby Bay is built upon a flat, scrubby islet located just northwest of Antigua's runway (yes, it's in the flight path), reached by a 10-minute ferry crossing. The original development concept called for a small resort combined with sleek villas for the rich and famous (or in one case, the corpulent and infamous).

There are various types of accommodation, the most charming of which are rondavels that dapple a grassy hillside, with octagonal bedrooms and four-poster beds; these are a one- to two-minute walk from the sand. There are also sprawling suites in a two-story Spanish mission–style structure overlooking the water, and elegant two- and three-bedroom villas seemingly designed for first-rate house parties (we like the showers in these, fringed by indoor gardens and topped with a vast skylight). Jumby's main beach is a quarter-mile-long stretch of brilliant white sand. Pasture Bay is a nesting ground for endangered hawksbill turtles. Activities include nonmotorized water sports, tennis, and walking or bicycling on the island's 3-mile path (there are no cars on the island—only a fleet of golf carts). Returning guests will not see major physical changes, although a/c, phones, and minibars have been added, and there is now a fitness center and a lap pool.

Our only real hesitation staying here is that Jumby Bay could be anywhere—it lacks any sense of place. On the other hand, it's the Caribbean boiled down to the essentials: sun, sea, and (fabulous) sand, with a high-amenity resort at your beck and call. If you want a vacation from the real world, and the locale is irrelevant, and you don't mind an ambiance as stimulating as white noise (with the occasional jet overhead), this could be the ideal place to park your bags for a few days. Besides, you may be able to crash a game of croquet with one of the homeowners. We were taught how to play by one Robin Leach (the *Lifestyles of the Rich and Famous* guy), who crowed—erroneously—about how the resort was flying in Maine lobster daily and was working with British Airways to alter the flight plan for 747 takeoffs.

Where to Eat

Given the quantity of hotel rooms on this island, it's not surprising that there are plenty of options for dining. Listed below are some of the best and/or most interesting.

$ **Big Banana Holding Company**, Redcliffe Quay, St. John's, 268-462-2621

This is a lively place, where $4 for a slice of plain pizza is ridiculously expensive (the proceeds probably go to the mortgage payment on the bitchin' stereo system and the collection of reggae CDs). Prices for a whole pie are better, and there are also pastas and salads. It's worth a stop just to have a drink and listen to the tunes. There's also a location at the airport, and we've enjoyed many a bowl of pumpkin soup while waiting for a delayed LIAT flight. Open late; closed Sunday.

$$ **Catherine's Café**, English Harbour, 268-460-5050

This is a simple dockside bistro on the opposite side of the harbor from the Dockyard and run by a delightful Frenchwoman, Catherine Ricard. She oversees a bustling kitchen and a solid wine list. We particularly recommend her ti punch, the drink of the French Antilles. Catherine's serves breakfast, lunch, and dinner.

$$$$ Coconut Grove, Dickenson Bay, 268-462-1538

This is a classic romantic nook located at the south end of Dickenson Bay, in front of Siboney Beach Club. Prices are above moderate and the food is good but not great. Nevertheless, the setting — underneath a thatched roof and palm trees with the waves rippling across the sand — is perfect. Reservations are advised.

$$$$$ Curtain Bluff, Old Road, 268-462-8400

If you can't stay here, at least you can eat here. True, you'll have to dress up (guys will need a jacket), but for one night, why not? The cuisine is continental, and guests rave about it. The restaurant also has one of the most extensive wine lists in the Caribbean (some 30,000 bottles in the cellar). Reservations are a must. Closed late May through October.

$$$$ ⊛ Harmony Hall, Brown's Bay (near Freetown), 268-460-4120

The best way to find this spot is to stumble across it accidentally — it's like an unexpected oasis on the remote and undeveloped east coast. Since that's unlikely, come out anyway and sample the great Italian cuisine. Before you order lunch, have the staff take you (by boat) to a great beach and snorkeling spot. Then come back and dine on the delicious Italian food prepared with island flair. It's all served alfresco, under a restored mill. Dinner is also available. The spot has a respectable art gallery that showcases regional artists, with opening receptions generally the first Sunday of each month. Reservations are advised, especially for Sunday. Closed June through October.

$$$ Hemingway's, St. Mary's Street, St. John's, 268-462-2763

This is a cool place for Caribbean cuisine overlooking Heritage Quay. It is situated on the second floor of an old wooden building and has a wraparound veranda with comfortable, unique booths along the rail. It's bright, airy, and attractive in a real West Indian style. The staff is friendly and attentive. Each booth is curiously equipped with a phone jack — shades of Polo Lounge on Antigua? It's also romantic due to the lighting outside. Be sure to try the pumpkin soup. Open for breakfast, lunch, and dinner.

$$$$$ Le Bistro, Hodges Bay, 268-462-3881

One of the most famous restaurants on Antigua and written up in many international mags, this is French country cuisine served in a wonderful bistro setting. Reservations are recommended. Closed Monday and in June and July.

$$ OJ's, Crab Hill Beach, 268-460-0184

This is a basic beach barbecue restaurant, but when the beach is this beautiful and the food is this delicious, *basic* is probably the last word that should come to mind.

$$ **Trappas**, Falmouth Harbour, 268-562-3534

Trappas offers inexpensive chicken curry, fish curry, steaks, and well-prepared fresh catch of the day, served in a shacklike house in the center of the action. It's very popular with the budget-conscious expats. Open for dinner only; closed Sunday and Monday; reservations are essential.

Going Out

Between the locals and the visitors, this island manages to kick up some action on weekends; **18 Carat** on Market Street in St. John's is popular for dancing and draws a mostly Antiguan, mostly young crowd (cover charge on weekends); **Miller's by the Sea** is popular for beach lunches and live music Thursday through Sunday afternoon and evening (lots of cruise-ship passengers during the day). On Sunday afternoon (and usually until well after dusk), **Shirley Heights** is the place for live music, inexpensive barbecue, and fine sunsets. There are also casinos — at Heritage Quay in St. John's, and at the St. James's Club and Royal Antiguan hotels — none of which strike us as a particularly rich experience.

Don't Miss

The Beaches

We don't count anywhere near the island's claim of 365 beaches, but there are indeed dozens on Antigua, and many of them are among the Caribbean's finest. Here are a few that are particularly worth visiting, starting from the west coast: Fryes Beach, Dark Wood Beach, Crab Hill Bay, Rendezvous Bay, and Half Moon Bay.

Nelson's Dockyard National Park

Admiral Horatio Nelson became northern division commander of Britain's Leeward Islands Station at the age of 25. Very impressive. However, his stint on Antigua at the superb hurricane hole of English Harbour — before he performed the military heroics for which he became famous — was not exactly a happy one. (He referred to the island as a "vile place.") Still, the region's only intact Georgian-era shipyard is rife with history, providing a fascinating glimpse into British naval history, with officer's quarters, the admiral's house, and the careening facilities looking ready for inspection.

Lunch at Harmony Hall

This beloved restaurant and art gallery, run by Riccardo and Marilisa Parisi of Naples, Italy, is set below the 1843-era sugar mill on Antigua's east coast.

It's a rough, 40-minute drive from either St. John's or English Harbour, but you won't regret it.

Sunset at Shirley Heights Lookout

The fort at the top of Shirley Heights, above English Harbour, is one of the most scenic lookouts in the Caribbean. It affords views stretching to Guadeloupe and Montserrat to the south and west, and down to the harbors of Antigua. It's a fine spot whenever the weather's clear (crowded on busy cruise-ship days), but we prefer coming here for sunset, especially on Sunday, when a steel pan band strikes up around 4 p.m. and the barbecue grills fire up an inexpensive early dinner. For more information, call 268-460-1785.

A Day Trip to Montserrat

The island of Montserrat is just a 20-minute flight from Antigua. A day trip to this volcano-ravaged island is a fascinating glimpse at Mother Nature's fury.

Barbuda

LITTLE MORE THAN A STARK FLAT OF CORAL LOCATED 27 MILES north of Antigua, Barbuda (pronounced bar-BEW-da) is a strange outpost that is little seen, even by Caribbean regulars. You won't find nightlife, shopping, a restaurant scene, diving, or most other traditional island activities. There's virtually no natural vegetation taller than your knees, and the highest point is just 125 feet above sea level.

What you do find are staggeringly beautiful beaches—long carpets of blinding white sand that unroll for miles around much of the perimeter of this 62-square-mile island. You will also find real solitude, since Barbuda has a population of just 1,500 and there are essentially only three small resorts, posting rate cards that could make a Swiss banker reach for the smelling salts. Such a package was what lured the late Princess Diana, who stayed at the K Club three times in the two years prior to her death—the resort delivered an escape from the paparazzi who otherwise plagued her daily.

Getting There

Barbuda's small landing strip is served by two scheduled flights per day from Antigua on Carib Aviation (268-481-2400). One flight leaves in the morning, the other leaves in the late afternoon. There are no flights from any other islands. The Coco Point Lodge has its own private airstrip and plane— it arranges transfers for its guests only.

Focus on Barbuda: Day-Tripping

Although many of our readers are no doubt royalty of some kind, most of us don't have the $695 and up a night (low season) that it takes to stay here. So here are a few tips for those of you who might want to consider a day trip to Barbuda.

As mentioned above, Carib Aviation has two daily flights from Antigua to Barbuda. The eight or so hours between the morning and late afternoon flights is enough to see all of the island's highlights. The airport is at the edge of Codrington, the only village on Barbuda; there's not much to see here, and no one will tell you otherwise. The first place to head is **Codrington Lagoon** and the frigate bird sanctuary. Barbuda is one of the few places

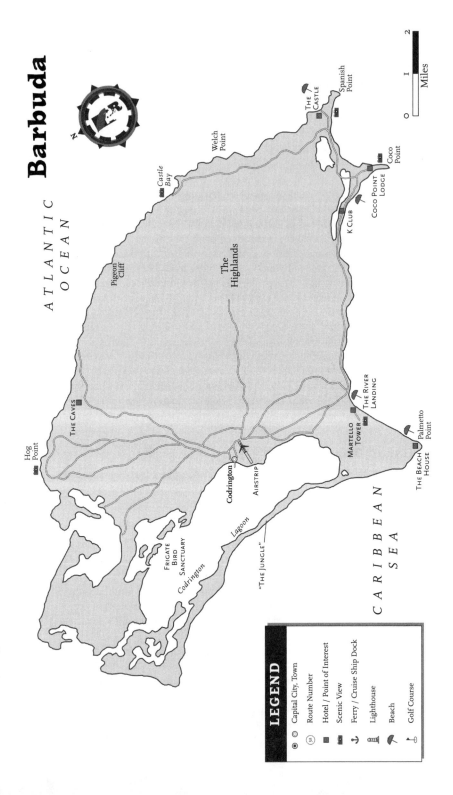

in the world where the magnificent frigate bird nests — in mangrove stands at the north end of the vast lagoon. The birds have 8-foot wingspans and can soar at speeds of up to 100 miles per hour. The best time to visit is during mating season, August through November, when the males guard the nests and puff out a bright red pouch under their beaks as a means of attracting females. A boatman will motor you up to the sanctuary for about $10 per person (ask at the boat dock at the edge of the village). On the way back, ask your boatman to take you by the "jungle," a grove of a dozen or so palm trees at the west side of the lagoon. You can walk across the sandbar separating the lagoon from the sea, where you'll find one of Barbuda's trademark deserted beaches, stretching unbroken for miles in each direction, and with a pink hue (the color of the coral that creates the sand).

To see other parts of the island, you'll need to rent a car, which runs about $65 a day from Junie Walker (268-773-6414) or Bryon Askie (268-562-3134), or hire a driver — again, ask around in Codrington and someone will hook you up. Devon Warner (268-772-7440) does snorkel and beach trips for $150 per person including lunch, transfers, and snorkel gear. Other Barbuda highlights include **Spanish Point**, at the southern tip of the island, where the Atlantic meets the Caribbean. You can explore **Dark Cave**, which has an underground chamber containing deep pools and blind shrimp. Also situated here is a 300-foot-wide sinkhole called **Darby Sink Cave**, which has a "rainforest" 70 feet below the ground. On the east coast, there's a pretty beach called **Two Foot Bay**. There's excellent snorkeling along the coast between Coco Point and Spanish Point, as well as at **Tuson Rock**, a reef located 3 miles west of Codrington Lagoon. Of course, there are also miles of beaches to loll on — the nicest of which are near Coco Point, where Coco Point Lodge and K Club are located. For food, you're limited to a couple of snack bars in Codrington or the exorbitant restaurants at the resorts (reservations required).

Where to Stay

Alas, there are limited lodging options here, none of them cheap.

The Beach House, Palmetto Point, Barbuda, WI. ℭ 888-776-0333 or 516-944-6057; local: 268-725-4042, ✆ 516-767-6529, 🖳 www.thebeachhousebarbuda.com

🛍 **Stratospheric** ⍟ **MAP** ⓒⓒ 21 rooms

Finally, Barbuda has a hotel we can get behind with enthusiasm. Created from the bones of the old Palmetto Beach Hotel, the Beach House sits at a remarkable site. At Palmetto Point, the sand gathers into a 90-degree corner that points toward the sea, with the hotel in the middle. The huge sweep of sand is dramatic — indeed, if there's an objection to be made, it's that the beach is *too* big (it's a walk of several hundred feet from the hotel to the water's edge). How many hotels can complain of too large a beach? The understated lobby and restaurant are in a lovely whitewashed building, with large wooden shutters that open on all sides to the breeze. The backdrop is an unusually large pool, the beach, and the sea, all of which are unfettered by palm trees, cabanas, or watersports equipment. The hotel staff, referred to here as service ambassadors, wear attractive uniforms of flowing white linens, and one ambassador is assigned to each room. Like personal butlers, they unpack luggage, coordinate your welcome massage (in-room or on the beach), and arrange activities, which include most water sports, yoga lessons, and horseback riding.

The rooms are of generous size, with a bed positioned in the middle of the space, bulging with a goose-down featherbed and Fili d'Oro linens. Like the common areas, the surfaces are all white, with occasional deep blue accents. Amenities include a cell phone, espresso machine, and chichi bath products by Essential Elements. Not to carp, but the minimalist bathroom is a little underwhelming for a high-end resort. Each room has a deck facing a man-made, foot-deep pond, backed by the beach—at night the lagoon sparkles with blue lights. Depending on your mood, the effect could be magical, or it might feel a little like a deserted airport runway at night. The hotel's cuisine was overly ambitious, but some items were right on the mark. The Beach House is not for everyone: People who want flashy décor and buzzy social scenes will be put off by the minimalist scene here. However, we thought it was terrific, and—though very expensive—great for those seeking a real escape.

No children under 16; closed October through mid-November.

Coco Point Lodge, Coco Point, Barbuda, WI. ✆ 212-986-1416 or 268-462-3816, ✉ 268-464-8334, 💻 www.cocopoint.com

💲 **Stratospheric** 🍴 **All-Inclusive** CC 38 cottages

The best thing about Coco Point Lodge is its location, on a sensational, 164-acre finger of sand that protrudes into the sea, embellished with palms and other vegetation. The setting looks like a mirage, but the lodge has been here since 1961, built by the late Bill Kelly, and has weathered several hurricanes handily. It even has its own airstrip to fly guests in from Antigua. The resort consists of 38 cottages, some of them individual, some duplex, that overlook the fine beach. The exteriors have a nice bungalow quality—simple without being rustic. Inside, furnishings are surprisingly passé, with average-size rooms and amenities that belie the stiff rate card. Activities that are included in the price are deep-sea fishing (the area is noted for bone fishing), waterskiing, windsurfing, bird hunting (not our thing), and tennis. The meals are well rounded—we had the single best lobster salad of our life here. Still owned by the Kelly family, Coco Point has a clubby feel that might leave some guests feeling left out. Closed May through mid-November. Rates include transportation from Antigua.

K Club, Coco Beach, Barbuda, WI. ℰ 800-223-6800 or 268-460-0300, ℰ 268-460-0305, 🖵 www.kclubbarbuda.com, k-club@candw.ag

🛍 **Stratospheric** ⑪ **FAP** ⒸⒸ 44 rooms

This stylish hideaway is the cogitation of Milanese fashion designer Krizia, who dumped a small fortune into this impulsive creation. Legend has it that the Mandellis (Krizia's owners) were onetime regulars at Coco Point but had a falling-out with the Kellys. What do you do when you're wealthy and unwelcome at your favorite desert island retreat? Build your own next door—on the same beach, if possible. Although the 230-acre K Club has a similar bungalow-style setup for its 44 rooms, the similarities end there, for the interior is minimalist chic, adorned with classy amenities. It's even more overpriced than Coco Point, with most activities (like waterskiing, fishing, and golf at the moribund nine-hole course) costing additional bucks. The food is grand and Italian (beverages are extra), but the service and revolving door management often leave much to be desired. If you need to escape the paparazzi, however, this is a good choice. Closed September through mid-November.

Don't Miss

Art Café

Just about everyone makes a stop at this tiny shop run by English transplant Claire Frank, who moved here and married a Barbudan in 1993. Here are some of the items that are for sale: palmetto reed brooms, Antiguan coffee and tea, and Frank's own paintings on silk. She's also a Barbuda booster and runs a helpful Web site, www.barbudaful.net.

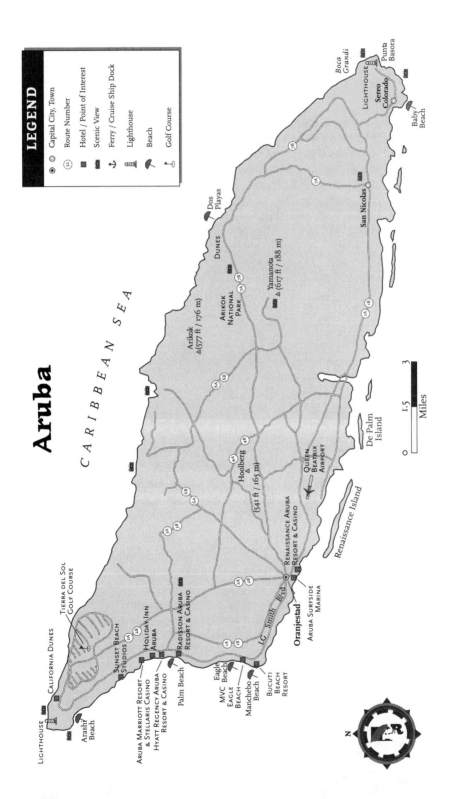

Aruba

CARIBBEAN SEA

LEGEND

- ⊙ Capital City, Town
- ㉟ Route Number
- ▣ Hotel / Point of Interest
- ▣ Scenic View
- ⚓ Ferry / Cruise Ship Dock
- ♁ Lighthouse
- ♀ Beach
- ⚑ Golf Course

LIGHTHOUSE
California Dunes
Tierra del Sol Golf Course
Sunset Beach Studios
Holiday Inn Aruba
Arashi Beach
Aruba Marriott Resort & Stellaris Casino
Hyatt Regency Aruba Resort & Casino
Radisson Aruba Resort & Casino
Palm Beach
MVC Eagle Beach
Eagle Beach
Manchebo Beach
Bucuti Beach Resort
L.G. Smith Blvd
Oranjestad
Aruba Surfside Marina
Renaissance Aruba Resort & Casino
Queen Beatrix Airport
Renaissance Island
De Palm Island

Hooiberg
△ (541 ft / 165 m)

Arikok
△ (577 ft / 176 m)

Arikok National Park

Yamanota
△ (617 ft / 188 m)

Dunes

Dos Playas

San Nicolas

Boca Grandi
Punta Basora
LIGHTHOUSE
Sereo Colorado
Baby Beach

Miles
0   1.5   3

N

Aruba

TOURISTO SCALE:

🎭🎭🎭🎭🎭🎭🎭🎭🎭🎭 (10)

If all you want to do on your vacation is ensconce yourself at a deluxe resort, take in the sun, and stick close to the swim-up bar, then you will love Aruba. This small desert island (not deserted, but arid, with less than 20 inches of rain annually) can pretty much guarantee sunny, breezy, hot days. Tourism is big business on Aruba, attracting more than 700,000 visitors a year, many of whom check into their time-shares year after year. Beyond the sun worshiping and water sports, shopping and casinos are major recreational activities. The island has more than 100 restaurants and 6,800 hotel rooms, and virtually all are located on Aruba's west coast, along the two best beaches. Are you getting the picture?

Now, we've seen a lot of islands. We have our personal favorite Caribbean destinations, and Aruba is not one of them. This is an island that tries hard to be the quintessential Caribbean escape, but it has less personality than boiled potatoes. Granted, the sea does have a year-round temperature of 82°F, and constantly blowing trade winds keep the tropical heat to a comfortable slow roast—in fact, we're told that the thermometer has not once dropped below 66°F during the last three decades! It's not a particularly pretty island, however. Most of the resorts have interesting landscaping inside their gates, but if you drive around the island, you'll see that it's mostly a dust bowl with cactus and the oddly bent divi-divi trees. Actually, we've

Aruba: Key Facts

Location	12°N by 70°W
	15 miles/24 kilometers north of Venezuela
	2,090 miles/3,365 kilometers southeast of New York
Size	70 square miles/181 square kilometers
Highest point	Mount Yamanota — 617 feet/188 meters
Population	95,300
Language	Papiamento plus Dutch (the official language); English and Spanish widely spoken
Time	Atlantic Standard Time (1 hour ahead of EST, same as EDT)
Area code	Dial 011 (the international access code), then 297 (the country code), plus the seven-digit local number.
Electricity	110 volts AC, 60 cycles
Currency	Aruban florin, AFL (AFL1.80 = US$1)
Driving	On the right; a valid U.S. or Canadian driver's license is accepted.
Documents	Passport or proof of citizenship with photo for U.S. and Canadian citizens, plus an ongoing or a return ticket.
Departure tax	$36.75 (included when airline ticket is issued)
Beer to drink	Polar
Rum to drink	Mount Gay
Music to hear	Salsa
Tourism info	800-TO-ARUBA or 201-330-0800
	www.aruba.com

never seen so much cactus in our lives. If you drive or horseback-ride on the undeveloped windward side, where waves crash along the craggy coast, there are jungles of it. We like dense lush tropical foliage, and Aruba just doesn't have it.

In Aruba's favor is that everything runs smoothly and the visitor infrastructure is polished — it's a convenient, fairly easy island. There is abundant air access from the east coast, and the local bus system serves tourists as well as locals, minimizing the need for a pricey rental car. We like the fact that service is consistent. Aruba *is* a good spot for travel neophytes who are leery of their first trip abroad and for families who want easy access to babysitting services and a variety of activities suitable for children.

However, with little local culture in evidence, visitors are left with (a) a couple of great beaches lined with big resorts and littered with time-share salespeople, (b) a thoroughly Americanized veneer that runs the gamut from Outback to Hooters to Hard Rock, and (c) miserable sightseeing excursions in — your choice — big tour buses or caravans of jeeps, which tour the featureless countryside in search of a view. Nor is this a cheap island — eating out, in particular, will cost you a wad of greenbacks. Aruba is a major package-tour destination for Americans and Canadians who fancy high-rise resorts, casinos, and duty-free shopping. It's like one huge cruise ship anchored 15 miles off the coast of Venezuela — all that's missing is Kathie Lee. Aruba is a major cruise-ship port, with several behemoths parked and disgorging their passengers every day in high season. If what you want is to burn up some hotel points and get pampered at a deluxe resort — say, the Marriott or the Radisson — then you'll be quite content, and you'll sport a great tan by the end of the week.

One cool thing about Aruba is the people. The license plates say "One Happy Island," and for once a marketing slogan rings true. It's a cosmopolitan culture with 80 nationalities represented on the island, and the people are friendly and helpful — except in the casinos, where a Vegas glaze settles over the workers. You'll also overhear a strange language that sounds a lot like Spanish but is not. It's Papiamento, a native dialect that is a combination of Spanish, Dutch, and Portuguese, with some African and Arawak words thrown in. If you understand Spanish, you should get the gist of it — not that you'll need to. Most Arubans speak three other languages: Dutch (Aruba's official language), English, and Spanish. Oh, one other bonus: Aruba lies completely outside the Caribbean's hurricane belt, making August through October visits — peak hurricane season for most of the region — a safe vacation investment.

A Missing Teen and Aruba Tourism

We agree that the disappearance of Alabama teen Natalee Holloway from Aruba on May 30, 2005, is a heartbreaking tragedy. We empathize with her parents and applaud them for successfully utilizing the news media to raise awareness of their daughter's plight. However, we still believe that Aruba is a relatively safe vacation destination. Although the island government *was* slow to investigate the teen's disappearance and has (so far) failed to prosecute the culprit(s) involved, we don't think that the boycott of Aruba initiated by the governor of Alabama is justified. So far, it appears that travelers would agree — tourism numbers for the island have by and large remained the same.

The Briefest History

The Arawak peoples first settled Aruba and were still on the island when the Spanish claimed it in 1499. The Spanish thought that the land was useless (they didn't see high-rise hotels in their future) and left it to the Arawaks for more than a century. The Dutch seized the island in 1636, near the end of the 80-year war between Holland and Spain, and began to settle Aruba in the late 1600s at Oranjestad, which later became the island's capital. The English were in control here between 1805 and 1816, during the Napoleonic wars; when they departed, the Dutch returned. The discovery of gold in 1824 brought new waves of immigration from Europe and Venezuela. When the gold mines were exhausted, aloe production kept up the economy until the Lago oil refinery (a subsidiary of Standard Oil) was built on the southeastern tip of the island in 1924. That brought a new wave of prosperity to Aruba; at one time the oil industry employed 8,000 people.

Aruba got into the tourism game early on. A tourism commission started in 1953, and untouched Palm Beach was the area eyed for development. The arrival in 1959 of the first high-rise hotel, the Golden Tulip (now the Radisson), marked the island's entry of tourism. It was helped along greatly by America's trade embargo with Cuba, which started in 1961. Aruba's refinery shut down in 1985, causing widespread unemployment. Tourism quickly replaced oil as the largest employer with the construction of more high-rise resorts along Palm Beach (the refinery reopened six years later). In 1986 Aruba became a separate entity within the Kingdom of the Netherlands under a political arrangement called Status Aparte. Although there are extensive business and family ties with neighboring Curaçao, when it comes to politics, Aruba deals directly with Holland.

Getting There

Aruba's Queen Beatrix International Airport is one of the region's best facilities, and it's well connected from the United States, especially by charter operators from major cities in the northeast. American Airlines serves Aruba from Boston, Miami, New York–JFK, and San Juan; Continental from Houston and Newark; Delta from Atlanta; US Airways from Boston, Charlotte, New York–La Guardia, and Philadelphia; and United from Chicago and Washington-Dulles. Air Canada has flights from Toronto. Dutch Caribbean Airways serves Aruba from Bonaire, Curaçao, Jamaica, the Dominican Republic, St. Maarten, and Trinidad. When you leave the island for the U.S., you'll clear U.S. Customs in Aruba.

Getting Around

If you're just going to stay at your hotel and never leave, take a cab from the airport to the hotel (about a 20-minute ride at most). If you want mobility and want to see what desert vegetation is really like, then drive — driving is easy and the roads are good and well marked. All the major rental-car players are represented, including Avis (800-331-1084 or 297-582-5496), Hertz (800-654-3001 or 297-588-7577), Budget (800-527-0700 or 297-582-8600), National (800-227-3876 or 297-582-5451), and Thrifty (800-367-2277 or 297-583-5335), plus several local outfits, including Amigo Rent-a-Car (297-583-8833; www.amigocar.com) and Courtesy Car Rental (297-582-4129; www.courtesyaruba.com). Make winter reservations in advance to ensure availability and the best rate.

Renting a car isn't really necessary, however — a reliable bus service connects all the main hotel areas to the capital and even to the airport. Major bus routes run between Oranjestad and Palm Beach as frequently as every 20 minutes, until as late as midnight, and the fare is just $1.15. Getting out to the east end of the island is a little more complicated, but it's not hard if you examine the schedules at the bus terminal in Oranjestad.

Focus on Aruba: Pampering Yourself

The sun
The sea
The beach
A chaise
A good book
A piña colada (or two)
A spa treatment
For seven days

Where to Stay

Almost all the hotels are found on two beaches, Palm Beach — a.k.a. the "high-rise beach" — and Eagle Beach. Whereas the bigger resorts are found on Palm, we prefer the ambiance of Eagle, where Waverunners and speed boats are less an issue, and finding a stretch of sand to call your own is rarely a problem. There's one terrific, moderately priced hotel on Eagle, as well as a few smaller options, but since the object here is to pamper yourself, you'll probably be parking your bags at the local Marriott, the Hyatt Regency, or the Radisson. Package deals are common, especially in the summer, and can often save you up to 50 percent off regular rack rates.

Bucuti Beach Resort, P.O. Box 1299, 55 L. G. Smith Boulevard, Eagle Beach, Aruba, WI. ☏ 800-223-1108 or 297-583-1100, ✉ 297-582-5272, 💻 www.bucuti.com, bucuti@setarnet.aw

🔳 **Wicked Pricey** ⑪ **CP** 🆑 102 rooms

Family-owned and catering to an international and adult clientele, this intimate resort snared the choice spot on the widest part of Eagle

Beach. The beach here is as broad and sugary white as they come, and there's a *palapa* for every room. The best reason to stay here is the 39 suites in the three-story Tara wing that were added in 2004 — they offer a handsome boutique approach to resort living, they have a soothing Zen ambiance, and all face the sea. The 63 original rooms were upgraded in similar style in 2006; all have minibar, microwave, fridge, iron and board, and coffeemaker. There's also a new spa. A replica of an old Dutch galleon serves as the hotel's beachfront restaurant (dubbed The Pirate's Nest), and it's our one complaint about Bucuti: A hotel of this quality deserves a better dining venue. Still, you can arrange for a candlelight dinner on the beach, and that's a good way to spend the sunset.

Radisson Aruba Resort and Casino, 81 J. E. Irausquin Boulevard, Palm Beach, Aruba, WI. ✆ 800-333-3333 or 297-586-6555, 🖂 297-586-3260, 🖳 www.radisson.com/aruba, rd.arub@radisson.com

💲 **Ridiculous** 🍽 **EP** **CC** 358 rooms

After catering to regulars like Liberace and Jack Benny in the 1960s, Aruba's oldest resort underwent a two-year, $55 million renovation in 2000, and the resulting Radisson gives the competing Marriott and Hyatt Regency properties a run for their money. Originally designed by architect Morris Lapidus (of Miami's Hilton Fontainbleau), the 14-acre resort sits on the island's premier parcel and now features a lush pool area with a pair of "zero entry" swimming pools (wheelchairs can just roll in), tropical birds, waterfalls, whirlpools, and a beach bar that salutes sunset each evening with a flag lowering and cannon blast. The fries served at happy hour are scrumptious.

The rooms are found in three separate towers and feature colonial West Indian furnishings, rich colors and lots of pillows, minibars, marble baths, balconies with ocean views, and 24-hour room service. There is an Arabian-theme casino, a 15,000-square-foot meeting and convention facility, and three restaurants. The resort's signature dining room is the Sunset Grill, which offers a menu of Angus beef and sirloin and Porterhouse steaks, all served from an open kitchen. A $5.2-million, 15,000-square-foot oceanfront spa, with Swiss shower rooms, a couples room, and fitness center, was added in 2006.

Hyatt Regency Aruba Resort & Casino, 85 J. E. Irausquin Boulevard, Palm Beach, Aruba, WI. ✆ 800-233-1234 or 297-586-1234, 🖂 297-586-1682, 🖳 www.aruba.hyatt.com

💲 **Ridiculous** 🍽 **EP** **CC** 360 rooms

The Hyatt Regency is one of Aruba's most attractive resorts. Unlike the creators of the other monster hotels, the Hyatt's architect actually looked at the site and at the island and designed a handsome building with Spanish, Dutch, and Caribbean flourishes. It's set on 12 acres

in the middle of Palm Beach; its 360 guest rooms are tastefully decorated and feature all the deluxe amenities, including 24-hour room
service, minibar, and coffeemaker.

There is an 8,000-square-foot ruins-theme pool complex with waterfalls, two whirlpools, and a two-story waterslide — kids love it. Adjacent to the pool is a 5,000-square-foot lagoon teeming with tropical
fish. Black and white swans make the lagoon their home. Tropical
gardens surround the restaurant, built to resemble the ruins of an old
plantation. The beach in front is very pleasant, with all water sports
available from Red Sail Sports. There are two lighted tennis courts as
well. The complex also has a carnival-theme casino, five restaurants
(our meal was so-so at Ruinas del Mar), four bars, and a health and
fitness center with sauna, steam, and massage.

Aruba Marriott Resort & Stellaris Casino, 101 L. G. Smith Boulevard, Palm
Beach, Aruba, WI. 🕿 800-223-6388 or 297-586-9000, 📠 297-586-
0649, 🖳 www.marriotthotels.com, marriott@setarnet.aw

💲 **Wicked Pricey** 🍴 **EP** CC 413 rooms and suites

Located at the far end of the high-rise section of Palm Beach, closest
to prime waters for windsurfing, this eight-story resort was originally
intended as condominiums. The resulting plus for guests is the
largest standard rooms on the island, with 100-square-foot balconies facing the sea. If you're a health nut, book this place, which
has the island's largest and best-equipped health club, with free
weights and Universal machines, sauna, and whirlpool. It also has a
free-form pool with swim-up bar, rock grotto waterfalls, tennis, a
10,700-square-foot casino, and on-site shopping. There's also a huge
Mandara spa with 12 treatment rooms; spa cuisine is even on the
room service menu. Otherwise Tuscany's, a northern Italian restaurant, boasts fine, expensive meals produced by one of the island's
best chefs. Beware: There are lots of meeting and incentive groups
here.

Aruba Surfside Marina, 7 L. G. Smith Boulevard, Aruba, WI. 🕿 297-583-
0300, 📠 297-583-0444, 🖳 www.arubasurfsidemarina.com

💲 **Pricey** 🍴 **EP** CC 5 rooms

Located a few minutes east of Oranjestad, near the airport and with
no other hotels nearby, this unique inn has just five rooms on the second floor of a conference facility, two of which are spacious suites. All
are smartly designed in a contemporary style, featuring teak furniture, a/c, plush bedding, a wet bar, microwave, TV, and phone; they
share a balcony that overlooks a courtyard and a small beach. The
restaurant on the pier serves meals and cocktails against a sunset
backdrop, and a short walk east is Havana Beach Bar, one of the island's
best hangouts. The major advantage of staying here is privacy and

personalized attention; the drawback is noise from incoming planes, but we found the rooms to be surprisingly well insulated from both airplane noise and the major thoroughfare at the entrance.

Renaissance Aruba Resort & Casino, 82 L. G. Smith Boulevard, Oranjestad, Aruba, WI. ✆ 800-468-3571 or 297-583-6000, ✆ 297-583-4389, 🖥 www.renaissancearuba.com, sonesta.sales@setarnet.aw

💰 **Very Pricey** 🍴 **EP** (CC) 558 rooms and suites

Shopaholics favor this sprawling resort, formerly Sonesta-managed and situated in the heart of Oranjestad, Aruba's beachless capital. As the biggest resort complex on the island, it has two casinos (one is open 24 hours a day), three pools, two shopping malls next door, a multiplex cinema, eateries fronting a marina marketplace, and fine dining venues. The guest rooms sprawl on both sides of the main drag through Oranjestad and include 15 suites and 250 one-bedroom suites with kitchenettes. One bummer is that the Renaissance doesn't have a beach. However, boats leave from the lagoon in the lobby—you read that right—every 20 minutes for the resort's own 40-acre private island, 10 minutes away, which has tennis courts, a fitness center, a water-sports center operated by Red Sail Sports, and the Spa Cove, featuring an open-air massage hut. Fronted by breakwaters, the two man-made beaches aren't terribly plush—the sand is quite well packed—but it's a nice escape, and one of the beaches is designated for topless sunbathing.

Sunset Beach Studios, 486 L. G. Smith Boulevard, Malmok, Aruba, WI. ✆ 800-813-6540 or 297-586-3940, ✆ same, 🖥 www.arubasunset blvds.com

💰 **Not So Cheap** 🍴 **EP** (CC) 11 units

This is a fine and friendly value that sits a mile north of busy Palm Beach, where all the high-rise resorts are located. The rooms face a sunny garden, just behind an oceanfront home; each is bright and has a fully equipped kitchenette, a/c, and TV. One studio is located in front and offers ocean and sunset views; another is oversize and great for families. You can also rent part or all of the four-bedroom main house. There is a small, attractive pool, and the beach is a 10-minute walk. The owners have children and a menagerie of pets (you have been warned!); they also run a nearby windsurfing shop. A six-night minimum applies during high season.

MVC Eagle Beach, P.O. Box 1279, Eagle Beach, Aruba, WI. ✆ 297-587-0113, ✆ 297-587-0117, 🖥 www.mvceaglebeach.com

💰 **Cheap** 🍴 **EP** (CC) 19 rooms

Until recently, this was a marine recreational camp. Now the local MVC serves as an upbeat, budget, beach-facing inn, with the uncrowded

Eagle Beach immediately across the street. Accommodations are in a two-story lodge facility and are small and simply decorated—each has two twin beds, a private shower and bathroom, and a/c, no TVs or phones. There are three "family rooms" that are double the size. There's an informal restaurant that serves the largely Dutch crowd, a tennis court, and a shallow pool that's ideal for children.

Holiday Inn Aruba, 230 J. E. Irausquin Boulevard, Palm Beach, Aruba, WI. ✆ 800-465-4329 or 297-586-3600, 🖂 297-586-5165, 🖥 www.aruba.sunspreeresorts.com

💰 **Very Pricey** 🍴 **EP** CC 600 rooms

A big part of the Aruba experience is its high-rise resorts, but most of them are expensive. It would be a shame to not uncover one moderate option, and good old Holiday Inn delivers the goods. You know it as part of the chain that seals toilets with protective wrappers, but this one avoids such nonsense and instead keeps guests focused on a prime asset: its location on Palm Beach, next to the Marriott. The 38-year-old hotel—Aruba's second largest—has plenty to keep you busy: a casino, an arcade, a health club, shops, tennis courts, and a water-sports center with PADI five-star dive shop. It may not be a glamour-puss—parts of the property look downright dowdy—but with rates starting at just $150 in summer months, it's a solid off-season deal and popular with families.

Where to Eat

Because so many nationalities are present on the island, finding a good restaurant isn't a problem here, unlike on some other Caribbean islands. Finding a reasonably priced place presents a challenge, however, and outrageous import taxes on wine render it virtually impossible to get a decent bottle without paying sky-high prices. Although some of the best restaurants are at the hotels, several places are worth a taxi ride.

If you arrive with a hankering for fine dining, you'll want to investigate the dine-around program put together by the Aruba Gastronomic Association (297-586-1266; www.arubadining.com). The alliance sells packages redeemable for meals at 21 of the island's restaurants, starting at $109 for three full dinners (appetizer, entrée, dessert, coffee or tea, and service charge). It shaves a few dollars off pricey meals at midpriced restaurants. Note that many of these restaurants also offer discount coupons in the local tourist publications (pick them up at the airport). Many of the best restaurants are located at the resorts, but there are a few others worth checking.

$$ **Brisas del Mar**, Savaneta, 297-584-7718

Located 7 miles east of Oranjestag, this spot has an ideal waterside location and down-home ambiance, but middling food. The specialty is fish, prepared Aruba style, and the pan-broiled catch, fish kebabs, fish cakes, and other dishes are inexpensive; so are the daily lunch specials. Weekends feature live music and lots of local color. Also open for dinner; closed on Monday.

$$$ Charlie's Bar, 56 Main Street, San Nicolas, 297-587-1517

For a simple, tasty lunch on the day you head to Baby Beach, stop by this atmospheric bar, in operation since 1941. Tourists and locals while away the afternoons amid walls cluttered with oddities left behind over the years. The food is a little overpriced, but the ambiance is pretty unique.

$$$$$ Chez Mathilde, 23 Havenstraat, Oranjestad, 297-583-4968

One of the best restaurants on the island has French cuisine in an elegant house built in the 1800s. It's somewhat dressier than other places, and definitely more expensive. Lunch and dinner are served nightly; reservations are a must.

$$$$ The Flying Fishbone, Savaneta, 297-584-2506

Sitting on a handful of sand just big enough for a couple dozen tables, this off-the-beaten track restaurant has simple but romantic décor for barefoot dinners under a star-filled sky. It serves delicious food that's well worth the trip out to the east end (it's a $25 cab ride each way from Palm Beach); get precise directions if you're driving. Dinner is served nightly from 5:30 p.m.; reservations are essential.

$$$ Gasparito, 3 Gasparito, Gasparito, 297-586-7044

Across from the high-rise district, housed in a traditional country house, this restaurant and art gallery turns out some of the best local cuisine around. Try the *keshi yena*—Dutch cheese filled with seafood, spiced chicken, or beef. Closed on Sunday.

$$$ Madame Janette, Cunucu Abao (south of Bubali), 297-587-0184

Named after the spicy native pepper, this is a local favorite that serves reasonably priced international cuisine at the edge of a well-lit garden festooned with tiki torches. It serves dinner only; closed on Tuesday.

$$$$ Marandi, Surfside Beach, 297-582-0157

This is a smart casual seaside restaurant under a big *palapa* with tables on the sand or on wood decks. The Dutch chef has a flair for continental cuisine that's so good, even the plane landings won't disturb your meal. Come early and enjoy the island's best sunset, but note that Arubans party on this beach a lot on Sunday and it can be pretty noisy until after dark. Closed on Monday; reservations are advised.

$$ MooMba Beach Bar, Palm Beach, 297-586-5365

This popular spot is located under a pair of giant *palapas* sandwiched between the Marriott and Holiday Inn resorts — one *palapa* focuses on breakfast, lunch, and dinner, the other specializes in drinks; tucked behind is an Internet café. You'll find live Latin jams — and lots of locals — on Sunday at sunset.

$$$ **Papiamento**, 61 Washington, Oranjestad, 297-586-4544

Lenie and Eduardo Ellis design their own nightly changing menus, garnish their continental dishes with homegrown herbs, and serve wondrous meals in the beautiful gardens surrounding their antiques-filled private home. Request a table poolside or ask for the honeymoon table. Closed on Monday.

$$ **Que Pasa**, 2 Wilhelminastraat, Oranjestad, 297-583-4888

This little gem, in an old Cunucu-style (small plantation–style) house in town, is a find for anyone willing to forego water views for modestly priced continental cuisine.

Don't Miss

Beaches

Aruba's beaches are world-class — your only task is deciding where to land. If you want to play on a busy one with dining and water sports nearby, try Palm, Eagle, and Manchebo — home to all of the island's resorts. For a more remote spot, try Baby Beach at the east end, which is great for families (owing to its shallow, calm water), or, for snorkeling, head to intimate Arashi at the west end, below the picturesque California Lighthouse (check out the ice cones from the van in the parking lot).

Another option is to spend the day at a fantasy island, and there are two to choose from. **Renaissance Island** is located just off Oranjestad and is served by ferry every 20 minutes from the Renaissance Resort; a $50 package sold at the concierge desk buys the boat transfer, lunch, and a drink, plus use of the beach chairs. Water sports, including diving, are available. A destination designed for the cruise-ship trade, **De Palm Island** is reached by regular ferry from Spanish Lagoon, 4 miles east of Oranjestad; the ferry ride and a drink are $8; meals are offered at several restaurants. On De Palm, there's not much of a beach, but you'll find snuba (a relaxed introduction to scuba that is sort of a combination of snorkeling and scuba), which takes beginners down to a depth of 20 feet.

Golf

Designed by Robert Trent Jones II, the breezy Tierra del Sol (297-586-0978) is an 18-hole, par-71 course in a rugged, desert setting below the California Lighthouse. Greens fees are expensive ($145 in winter) but are discounted after noon and in summer. The golf clinic is a good deal — $45 for 90 minutes of training along with a tasty lunch at the pretty Ventanas del Mar restaurant.

The Divi Resort has its own nine-hole course, The Links (297-581-GOLF), with a nine-hole rate of $75 for nonguests (the second round is half-price).

The Butterfly Farm

This odd little attraction is home to 32 species from around the world, with 600 to 700 butterflies fluttering through the small aviary. A brief tour explains how the creatures are raised from egg to caterpillar to chrysalis to butterfly — the life span ranges from 24 hours to as long as nine months. It's located across the street from the Aruba Phoenix and Wyndham resorts.

Havana Beach Bar

Overlooked by most first-time visitors, this is a scene worth discovering. The bar sits almost at the water's edge next to the incoming flight path for the airport, and a snack shack serves cheap Indonesian cuisine. Movies are shown on Monday night, and there's a full moon party with a DJ booth in the water on the Friday or Saturday closest to the full moon. Call 297-592-6584 for more info.

Windsurfing and Kitesurfing

With its steady, strong winds, Aruba is a natural for windsurfing. Most activity occurs at Hadicurari and Malmok beaches, north of the Marriott. You can usually count on 15-knot winds. Both Sailboard Vacations (800-252-1070 or 297-586-2527) and Kitesurfing Aruba (297-733-1515) sell windsurfing and accommodations packages; they have fully equipped shops and offer instruction. Aruba is also the site of the annual Hi-Winds Amateur World Challenge, a 10-day competition held in June.

Diving or Snorkeling the Antilla

Aruba is a top wreck-dive destination, primarily for this hulking relic, an obscure slice of World War II history sunk just a few hundred yards off Boca Catalina Beach (near the lighthouse). Built to supply German U-boats, the *Antilla* was scuttled in 1940 to keep it out of the hands of Dutch marines, subsequently creating Aruba's future star tourist attraction. The 400-foot wreck has been down long enough to evolve into a giant aquarium for all types of fishes. With a maximum depth of just 60 feet, divers can take in the entire wreck in one swift trip, but because the *Antilla* is so large and at a shallow depth, it can be enjoyed by snorkelers; a few feet of bow mast even extend above the surface. Several tour operators do half- and full-day trips to the site; try Red Sail Sports (297-586-1603; www.redsailaruba.com).

Horseback Riding

The countryside is perfect for exploring by horseback. Take a sunset gallop along the beach or through the countryside to the Natural Pool. Try Rancho Del Campo (297-585-0290), Rancho Notorious (297-586-0508), or Gold Mine Ranch (297-585-9870).

Barbados

B arbados is the Florida of the West Indies, albeit with distinctly Caribbean and British accents. It is highly developed, crowded (along the south coast), and gets lots of tourists on packages — it's not a get-away-from-it-all kind of place. Barbados also caters to upper-crust types who like their lodging in primped suites with voluptuous balconies and don't mind dressing smartly for dinner — it's certainly not a cheap destination. In fact, the island is home to the single most expensive resort in the Caribbean. Sandy Lane is a hotel that draws a somewhat snobby crowd but does have fabulous accommodations, a jaw-dropping spa, and one of the Caribbean's finest golf courses, the Green Monkey (Tiger Woods got married here, so you know these links are up to snuff). Barbados does have some fine beaches, especially on the southeast and east coasts, which are less crowded and far less developed than the south coast.

The mood here is definitely more hectic — or, should we say, faster paced — than other islands nearby (Barbados is the third most densely populated island in the Caribbean). Actually, it's light-years away from a Grenada or Tobago, both of which lie to the south, or from one of the Grenadines. Visitors come here for beaches, first-class resorts, and diversions such as nightlife, restaurants, shopping, and golf — basically the comforts of home in the West Indies. They also come to windsurf. They don't come for privacy — there are

Barbados

LEGEND

- ◉ ◎ Capital City, Town
- ⑫ Route Number
- ■ Hotel / Point of Interest
- Scenic View
- ⚓ Ferry / Cruise Ship Dock
- Lighthouse
- Beach
- Golf Course

North Point

ATLANTIC OCEAN

1C

2

Speightstown

Cobbler's Cove

1

Lone Star Hotel

Cattlewash

The Edgewater Inn

Bathsheba

Fairmount Royal Pavilion

Atlantis Hotel

3

Coral Reef Club

Holetown

St. John's Parish Church

Sandy Lane

Harrison's Cave

3b

2

3

Mt Gay Distillery

Crane Beach

Bridgetown

Barbados Museum

Rockley Resort (Golf)

Lighthouse

7

Airport

Abbeville Hotel

Butterfly Beach Hotel

Sea Foam Haciendas

Salt Ash Apt Hotel

Fairholme

Club Mistral

Silver Sands

Peach and Quiet

Allamanda Beach Hotel

Lighthouse

South Point

CARIBBEAN SEA

N

0 1 2 3 4 5
Miles

Barbados: Key Facts

Location	13°N by 59°W 100 miles/161 kilometers east of St. Vincent 2,200 miles/3,540 kilometers southeast of New York
Size	166 square miles/430 square kilometers
Highest point	Mt. Hillaby (1,116 feet/340 meters)
Population	279,254
Language	English
Time	Atlantic Standard Time year-round (1 hour ahead of EST, same as EDT)
Area code	246
Electricity	110 volts AC, 60 cycles
Currency	The Barbados dollar, Bds (Bds$1.98 = US$1)
Driving	On the left; a temporary permit is needed if you do not have an international driver's license; there is a $5 fee for the permit.
Documents	Proof of citizenship with photo for U.S. and Canadian citizens and an ongoing or a return ticket; British citizens need a valid passport.
Departure tax	$12.50
Beer to drink	Banks
Rum to drink	⊛ Mount Gay; Cockspur
Music to hear	Calypso
Tourism info	800–221–9831 www.barbados.org

many more private places on other islands. The ease of reaching Barbados, especially nonstop from England on jumbo jets, makes the package tourist the mainstay of the economy.

Tourism is the business of Barbados, and the industry is more highly developed here than on almost any other Caribbean island. The government makes a point of educating its citizens on the value of the tourist dollar. A banner we once saw strung across a major access road into Bridgetown, the capital, said it all: "Tourism is our business. Let's do our part." Bajans (as the locals call themselves) are surprisingly friendly despite the hordes of tourists who stream through Barbados (about 550,000 overnight arrivals a year). British visitors outnumber Americans by a wide margin, and quite a few Canadians vacation here as well. All are treated well by the Bajans; one gets the feeling that they view visitors as they do rain—a necessity to keep the island growing.

Because of this emphasis on tourists, there are tons of tourist attractions from which to choose. Most are not worth it. They are designed to cater primarily to the standard tourist crowd — that is, the ones who prefer to be led around the island by the nose rather than getting out and seeing it for themselves. After all, you might get *lost!* Actually, getting lost in the maze of roads, especially on the less-populated east coast, is one of our favorite pastimes here — it doesn't take long for a friendly Bajan to spot us perusing our map, engine idling, and to ask us, "Can I help you find the way?" There are nevertheless a few tourist attractions worth your while.

One is **Harrison's Cave**, in the parish of St. Thomas (246-438-6640; www.harrisoncave.com). An electric trolley runs on a paved road down through these fascinating caverns of stalactites, stalagmites, and running, dripping water, all to the accompaniment of a schoolmarmish guide reciting a rote speech that must have been written for morons. We couldn't help but get the feeling that we were on a ride at a third-rate Disney World. Yet the caves are real, and if you can get past the tourist BS, it's very interesting. We recommend you avoid the caves on heavy cruise-ship days, or come first thing in the morning or late afternoon (the last tour is at 4 p.m.). Admission is $16 for adults.

Another attraction is the **Atlantis II** (246-436-8929; www.atlantisadventures.com), a submarine that takes you down 150 feet to view marine flora and fauna. The vessel holds 28 people and has sixteen 2-foot viewports (eight on each side) and one 52-inch window on the bow. Due to decades of environmental damage and overfishing along Barbados's coast, there's not a lot to be seen in terms of fish life or coral formations, but with a group of friends and a few cocktails, it can be fun. The cost is $84 per person for the 50-minute ride; the tours operate from morning till late afternoon.

Another activity of interest is **cricket** (the Bahan national sport). Matches are held at the Kensington Oval in Bridgetown. The season usually runs from October through March, but cricket is played locally year-round. In March and April 2007, the ICC Cricket World Cup will be held in the Caribbean for the first time — the 47-day, multi-island World Cup will climax in Bridgetown (the Final has previously been hosted by only five cities in the world, making Barbados a member of a very elite club). Polo is also popular, and regular matches are held December through April. Check the local papers for upcoming matches, or ask the Tourist Board for a schedule.

The **Barbados Jazz Festival** is held in January and features two days of open-air concerts held at the very scenic Farley Hill National Park. Even bigger is the monthlong Holders Season, held in March on the grounds of the 18th-century Holders Plantation House; opera, classical music, dramatic performances, and Latin and Caribbean music are among the highlights. Crop Over, held in July and early August, celebrates the completion of the annual sugarcane harvest. This is the Barbados version of Carnival, with calypso bands, tons of food, and a grand finale called Kadooment Day. Several days a month, between January and April, there are tours of Bajan Great Houses, sponsored by the Barbados National Trust, featuring weekly "open houses" of private estates that are not normally open to the public. Every Sunday, the Trust also sponsors free hikes to interesting parts of the island. For more information call the Trust at 246-426-2421, or visit http://trust.funbarbados .com.

In fact, the Barbados National Trust oversees nine sites of historical or scenic significance. Among them are the following: The **Morgan Lewis Sugar Mill**, the largest and only complete sugar windmill extant in the Caribbean; the **Gun Hill Signal Station**, one of a chain of signal towers that were used for semaphore communication from one end of the island to the other in the early 19th century; the **Andromeda Gardens**, a beautifully arranged 6-acre garden in Bathsheba; and the **Tyrol Cot Heritage Village**, a carefully restored 1854 mansion and chattel house village. Since admission fees can add up, consider a Heritage Passport, which provides discounted admission to the sites.

Barbados, unlike many other islands its size, has a robust nightlife scene. Currently, the hottest place to go for live music and dancing is **Harbour Lights** (246-436-7225; www.harbourlightsbarbados.com), located in an old converted house on the beach in Christ Church. Open Monday, Wednesday, and Friday at about 9 p.m., it draws a great mix of both locals and tourists, and the cover charge of $20 includes all your drinks. **The Boatyard** (246-436-2622), on the beach south of Bridgetown, is also quite popular—it stays open past midnight daily, with live music on Tuesday starting about 11 p.m. For a publike atmosphere that's hardly mellow, you can crawl into the **St. Lawrence Gap** and slug down a few Banks beers at the **Ship Inn** (246-420-7447). Next door is **McBride's** (246-420-7646), an Irish pub that has a dance floor that kicks up around 10:30 p.m., with live bands several nights a week. Right in Bridgetown overlooking the Carenage is the **Waterfront Café** (246-427-0093; www.waterfrontcafe.com.bb), which has live steel pan on Tuesday night and jazz most other nights. It's also fun to visit the eateries on **Baxter Road** in the wee hours of the morning. There are always people awake, and their antics will keep you in stitches.

The Briefest History

Originally settled by Amerindians from South America, the island was uninhabited when the Portuguese discovered it in the early 16th century (the name comes from the Portuguese *os barbados*, "the bearded ones"—the explorers found bearded fig trees on the shore). The first settlers were British, who arrived in 1627. Probably Barbados's location, about 90 miles east of the chain, and its flatness (making it hard for navigators to sight), saved it from the typical power struggles of other Caribbean islands. Due to its agreeable terrain, sugar plantations blossomed and prospered into this century. The island remained British until it achieved independence in 1966. Barbados is now a sovereign state within the British Commonwealth of Nations. It is the highest-ranked Caribbean island on the UN Human Development Index, which ranks countries based on life expectancy, income, and education levels.

Getting There

You know Barbados loves tourists when you arrive at the Grantley Adams International Airport — it's one of the best in the region, and the object of a 2006 overhaul. A number of carriers fly nonstop or direct to Barbados: Air Jamaica from Montego Bay and New York–JFK; American from Miami, New York–JFK, and San Juan; BWIA from Miami, New York–JFK, and Washington, D.C.; Delta from Atlanta; and US Airways from Charlotte, North Carolina, and Richmond, Virginia. BWIA, Caribbean Star, and LIAT provide service from neighboring islands, and Air Caraïbes flies in from St. Lucia and the French islands. BWIA and Air Canada fly in from Toronto; BMI, British Airways, BWIA, and Virgin Atlantic fly nonstop from London.

Getting Around

There are excellent roads throughout the island, so there's no reason not to rent a car, although driving is on the left and prices start at about $60 for a one-day rental (the rates drop substantially for weekly rentals). There are no major international car-rental agencies on the island (perhaps the government is protecting local businesses); try National (246-422-0603; www.carhire.tv — not affiliated with the one operating in the U.S.), Sunny Isle Motors (246-435-7979), and P&S (246-424-2052). Courtesy (246-431-4160; www.courtesyrentacar.com) is the only one with a desk at the airport, although prices seem to be higher here. There is also excellent bus service running along the west and south coasts, to and from Bridgetown. The fare is under $1; service is quite regular along these routes and runs well into the evening. There is more limited service to the interior of the island and the east coast.

Focus on Barbados: Windsurfing

With everything else that Barbados has to offer, the fact that the island is also one of the windsurfing capitals of the Caribbean is almost lost in the shuffle. Strong, steady winds for most of the year and fine surf conditions on the southern coast of the island combine to make optimal boardsailing. Add sunny skies, warm water, and Barbados's other amenities, and it's easy to understand why so many vacation here, or even spend a season hanging 10.

Most activity centers around **Club Mistral** in Oistins, (246-428-7277; www.club-mistral.com), open November through July when the winds are at their peak. The beach here has some coral cobble and reefs to dodge and is not the best sunbathing that Barbados has to offer. However, the Barbados Windsurfing Club's bar next door is a fun place to hang out and watch the action. If you're not on your board, you're at the bar. If the Bajan bartender has his way, and he usually does, some kind of island music is on the stereo. The bar is open to the ocean on two sides, providing the best vantage point for viewing the action on the high seas. There is always a breeze to ventilate the accommodations and wiggle the bar glasses from the overhead rack to a crashing demise. People come and go constantly, yet it's very common just to hang out all day and not even bother getting wet.

Club Mistral is an offshoot of Mistral of Switzerland, one of the leading manufacturers of equipment, providing state-of-the-art gear and top-notch instruction for beginners and experts alike. For serious windsurfers, being able to rent equipment solves logistical problems in regard to transport, Customs officials, and spare parts. Mistral has also designed its equipment to meet the challenge of the local wind and surf conditions. (Club Mistral has an outfit in Cabarete, too, which is mentioned in the Dominican Republic chapter.)

Mistral has two facilities on the south coast of Barbados. Suitable for beginners to advanced, the operation at Oistins offers several different kinds of boards and many different sail rigs. The staff can tailor a board and rig to accommodate both your abilities and the day's weather. The conditions at the Mistral's Silver Sands facility (located on the southern tip of the island and the site of the Barbados Waterman Festival held each February) are strictly for experts (the equipment provided reflects that). Here you'll find shorter boards that are big on speed, surf jumping, and wave riding. The instruction offered at the Sands focuses on improving the highly developed skills of boardsailors who want to make the leap to expert.

For the majority of windsurfers who want to improve, the Mistral shop at Oistins is the best place to get instruction. Lessons for tacking and use of the harness are available on request; so is private instruction. The rates are by no means cheap, starting at $65 for one hour, but you can buy as much as five hours of instruction for $290 and spread the training out over a week or more. If all you want to do is rent a board, there are many combinations that will suit individual abilities and current conditions (you won't be stuck with a light-air sail when it's blowing a gale). Rates are as follows: one hour, $35; half day, $60; full day, $75; one week, $285. There is a rescue boat poised at the ready should any equipment — or you — break down.

For those with a competitive spirit, Club Mistral will set up races for any group that is interested. With Club Mistral's encouragement, resident experts often give advice or on-the-spot seminars almost anytime. So don't be surprised if someone approaches you with helpful hints. There is usually someone around to offer repair and breakdown tips should you bring your own board. Note that things get pretty quiet here in late summer and early fall, when the winds aren't so great.

Where to Stay

With just a couple of exceptions, virtually all accommodations are on the south and west coasts. All of the high-end resorts are on the west side, which has the calmest water and is nicknamed the Platinum Coast, probably by some real estate agent. Better value (and more nightlife) is found on the south coast. With more than 75 hotels, 55 apartment-hotels and 14 guesthouses on the island, there is a terrific variety of places to stay. Try to book a land or air package that includes one of our recommended establishments — it will save you a lot of money. A traditional resort isn't the only way to go: One third of the island's 6,000 bedrooms are actually in villas that can be rented; check with Bajan Services for options (246-422-2618; www.bajanservices.com).

The West Coast

Sandy Lane, St. James, Barbados, WI. ✆ 866-444-4080 or 246-444-2000, ✉ 246-444-2222, 🖥 www.sandylane.com

💲 **Stratospheric** ⑪ BP ⒸⒸ 112 rooms

Almost since it first opened in 1961, Sandy Lane was *the* hoity-toity check-in for the Caribbean, drawing a fairly dazzling crowd, ranging from Fidel Castro to Mick Jagger to Luciano Pavarotti. In 1998, a trio of Scottish investors bought it, planning a quick nip-and-tuck on the already polished resort and its golf course. Their plans got bigger and more posh, however, with an eye to making Sandy Lane the region's *ne plus ultra* in luxury. Halfway through the renovation, they decided it wasn't enough, so the entire hotel was leveled and rebuilt, reopening in 2001. Today, although it looks pretty much like the old Sandy Lane from the outside, only the name, location, and some graceful old trees remain the same. The cost of the redo — initially budgeted at $153 million before overruns (but widely thought to be at least twice as much) — makes it, with just 112 rooms, the most costly resort ever built in the region (on a per-unit basis). Small wonder that Sandy Lane has gone from being the most expensive hotel stay in the Caribbean to — well, even more. The cheapest room now starts at an eye-popping $1,100 a night in high season.

At first, the hotel looks much the same as it did before. For example, it has the same portico, which leads to the same circular terrace-cum-dance floor. Then you start to notice subtle differences — the ground floor is a couple feet taller, and the wings with the rooms off to the side of the main building are bigger and more imposing. The rooms are, of course, sumptuous. The Orchid Suites (the least expensive berths on offer) encompass a sprawling 779 square feet, and have 21-by-14-foot marble bathrooms. The rooms come with plasma widescreen TVs and DVD player, a stereo system, a private bar, a fax machine, and personalized butler service. For $1,100 a night, however, you get only a garden view; the same room with a sea view is $400 more. The beach is still gorgeous, one of the best on the island, although several other hotels share this same stretch of sand. The other thing that really sets Sandy Lane apart is the facilities, starting with the 47,000-square-foot spa. It ranks as the most impressive such facility we've ever encountered in the islands — there are no less than 14 treatment rooms (several with their own private plunge pool and waterfall), a meditation room, a gym (with more flat screen TVs), and an oasis-like, somewhat Disneyish pool. The original golf course has been remade, while a new course, the Green Monkey, is spectacular, with deep gulleys and long shots.

Our big complaint is that this whole operation is a little too slick, particularly with all the high-tech gizmos installed to improve efficiency. It lacks soul. The service, which is friendly and upbeat, was also unpolished and somewhat disorganized during one of our visits. We found Sandy Lane to be a tad too stuffy for us.

Lone Star Hotel, Mt. Standfast, St. James, Barbados, WI. ✆ 246-419-0599, ✉ 246-419-0597, 🖥 www.thelonestar.com, lonestargarage@caribsurf.com

💲 **Stratospheric** 🍴 **BP** CC 4 suites

At last, the Caribbean's first hotel, restaurant, *and* garage. Yes, you read correctly — garage. Although this place is almost as exclusive as Sandy Lane, it has nearly the opposite temperament and ambiance. The establishment started out as a chic beach eatery situated behind a '40s-era, art deco filling station near Speightstown that somehow escaped a wrecking ball. The restaurant is owned by a team responsible for trendy London hot spots (including Prego on Kew Road), and in 1999 they opened four smashing suites to create a hip, boutique hotel designed to appeal to world-weary types secure enough in their standing that they don't need a Sandy Lane to tell them they're wonderful (John Cleese and Prince Albert of Monaco among them). Each suite—named Cord, Studebaker, Lincoln, and Buick—is filled out by Italian-origin modernist furniture and beds you can really sink your bones into. Each has a broad balcony framed by billowy white curtains and a bathroom outfitted in Philip Stark accoutrements along with big bottles of Molton Brown products.

Our verdict: The rooms are a glam fix of London style that offer a fresh minimalist alternative to the marble and chintz glory of Barbados's standard bearers. The beach is great and quiet, and no more than a seven-second stroll from your suite, with a full-length mirror propped provocatively against a palm. We believe in always looking our best, so we love this accessory. Then again, we also love the fact that meals from the restaurant can be chauffeured to your balcony for a no-primp evening.

Coral Reef Club, St. James Beach, St. James, Barbados, WI. ℂ 800-223-1108 or 246-422-2372, ✆ 246-422-1776, 💻 www.coralreefbarbados.com, coral@caribsurf.com

💲 **Beyond Belief** but with noteworthy discounts for singles ℗ **EP** Ⓒ Ⓒ 88 rooms

Run by the O'Hara family for almost five decades, Coral Reef Club is one of Barbados's most flawless and consistent operations. Over the last few years, virtually the entire 12-acre property has been rebuilt, but it still has its graceful airs intact — primped, but not as stuffy as Sandy Lane. There are spacious cottages scattered about the 12 acres — all vary in size and location (a few, in fact, are smallish and designated for singles only). There is a two-story wing that holds sumptuous junior suites with expansive bathrooms. The oldest rooms are closest to the beach and lobby and have rough-hewn coral walls and sea views through the casuarina pines (the lower level suffers from noise of footsteps above). The latest addition is a quintet of third-floor Plantation Suites, decorated by Helen Green of Lifestyles Interiors in London. (Go Helen!) These elegant colonial-style abodes are decked out with modern conveniences (CD players, fax machine), walk-in closets, wraparound decks, and a plunge pool on the terrace. Sweet!

The family's sister hotel, The Sandpiper, is nearby and is equally appealing (246-422-2251; www.sandpiperbarbados.com).

Fairmount Royal Pavilion, Porters, St. James, Barbados, WI. ℂ 800-257-7544 or 246-422-5555, ✆ 246-422-0188, 💻 www.royalpavilion.com, royalpavilion@fairmont.com

💲 **Stratospheric** ℗ **EP** Ⓒ Ⓒ 72 rooms

This stucco Spanish mission-style luxury resort, though a tad out of character with Bajan architecture, is still a very posh place to stay should comfort and service be your first priority. The resort is owned by Canadian hotelier Fairmont Hotels and is on the grounds of the former Cunard estate (the Great House is now the reception and administration area), with archways and pergolas that are colorfully framed in hibiscus and bougainvillea. The oversize rooms are in a pair of three-story buildings that hug the sand, and every room has a broad balcony overlooking the sea. The beach-pool-bar area is terrific, and dining is polished, as is the service. Two night-lit tennis courts, two pools (one for children), and complimentary water sports complete the facilities, and the Royal Westmoreland Golf Course is across the street.

Cobblers Cove, Road View, St. Peter, Barbados, WI. ℂ 800-890-6060 or 246-422-2291, ✆ 246-422-1460, 💻 www.cobblerscove.com, reservations@cobblerscove.com

💲 **Stratospheric** but with noteworthy discounts for singles 🍴 **BP** CC
42 rooms

Tucked into an indolent bay at the quieter north end of Barbados's
west coast, this intimate inn provides a proper dollop of relaxed English country living. The operation is described as "a restaurant with
rooms," which explains why the hotel is a member of the prestigious
Relais & Chateax organization. The food is reliably delicious, served
on an open terrace above the sea. The standard rooms are actually
suites and, though far from posh, are quite comfortable—most overlook
the lush garden, and eight face the ocean. The apex of this inn is a
pair of elegant suites, named Colleton and Camelot, that occupy the
second floor of the castlelike edifice that serves as the hub of the
property. These unique units are large and adorned in "English style,"
with rich fabrics in bold colors, marble floors, and potted orchids that
are always in bloom; each unit has a private plunge pool on a rooftop
terrace. The rates include waterskiing, tennis, and preferred tee times
at the Royal Westmoreland.

The South and East Coasts

Peach and Quiet, Inch Marlow, Christ Church, Barbados, WI. ✆ 246-428-
5682, 📧 246-428-2467, 🖳 www.peachandquiet.com

💲 **Cheap** 🍴 **EP** CC 22 rooms

This small hotel is located in charmingly named Inch Marlow, a residential area a half mile south of the Barbados airport. The spot is a
world away from the hustle and noise of the island's busier districts,
and you won't hear planes landing. The seaside inn's secret is a minimalist approach to infrastructure, but the reception is unstinting. So
although there's no bartender, the installation of an honor bar
means that drinks cost under $2; and although Inch Marlow is not
near dining, taxi vans sponsored by several fine restaurants shuttle
guests two nights a week, minimizing the need for a rental car. Rooms
are basic but have quality bedding, plus a tea and coffee kettle and an
ice crest; do note that there's no a/c, TV, or phones. The owners serve
tasty meals, there's a deep pool, and the beach is a five-minute walk.
Walking tours of the island are a specialty. The hotel is usually closed
for a few months in the summer.

The Edgewater Inn, Bathsheba Beach, St. John, Barbados, WI. ✆ 246-433-
9900, 📧 246-433-9902, 🖳 www.newedgewater.com,
resedgewater@caribsurf.com

💲 **Not So Cheap** 🍴 **CP** CC 20 rooms

Barbados's most dramatic scenery is found on the east coast, particularly around Bathsheba, but few accommodations are found here.

Of several guesthouses, the Edgewater is the best. It's a quaint inn refurbished in 2005 that draws an eclectic mix of travelers who want to avoid the bustle of the other coasts, as well as surfers who ply the Atlantic rollers below (we like a sign we once saw at the check-in counter: "No surfing stickers in room, please"). The rooms are outfitted with heavy, old-fashioned wood furniture; all have sea views, and some have a soundtrack provided by a nearby river that is frequented by green monkeys each morning. There is a modest restaurant, a nice pool (the beach is iffy for swimming), and nightlife sometimes at the nearby Round House.

Butterfly Beach Hotel, Maxwell Main Road, Christ Church, Barbados, WI. ℂ 246-428-9095, ℘ 246-418-0502, 🖳 www.butterflybeach.com, reservations@butterflybeach.com

💲 **Cheap** 🍴 **EP** 🆑 94 rooms

Located at windswept Oistins Bay, Butterfly Beach is the nicer of two side-by-side facilities that cater to windsurfers from around the world. The recently refurbished hotel sits on a good beach; there is also a pool and basic restaurant. There are smallish but cheap standard rooms, or you can spring for a studio with kitchenette or a superior studio with a/c. Next door, studios with kitchenette and balcony are small and simple at the 24-room Windsurf Beach Hotel (246-420-5862; www.windsurfbeach.com), and cheaper still. Club Mistral (see Focus on Barbados, above) is the affiliated windsurf shop, and U.K. Sailing Academy students are frequent guests.

Sea Foam Haciendas, Worthing, Christ Church, Barbados, WI. ℂ 246-435-7380, ℘ 246-435-7384, 🖳 www.seafoamhaciendas.com

💲 **Very Pricey** for four persons 🍴 **EP** 🆑 12 rooms

You won't find a lot of hotel services at the Sea Foam Haciendas, but these 12 two-bedroom units provide everything you need for a housekeeping setup, including a full, smartly equipped kitchen; cable TV, direct-dial phones, a/c and full maid services are part of the package. Every unit has a sea view through almond and casuarina trees from a wide balcony. The beach is decent, and restaurants are within walking distance. Note that during high season the units are rented only as a quad, whereas in May through October they can be rented as an inexpensive double as well.

Allamanda Beach Hotel, Rockley, Barbados, WI. ℂ 246-438-8888, ℘ 246-426-9566, 🖳 www.allamandabeach.com

💲 **Pricey** 🍴 **EP** 🆑 50 rooms

The tidy oceanfront accommodations here range from hotel-type rooms to studios with full, if small, kitchens; to one- and two-bedroom units; all in three-story apartment-style buildings. The beach is often more coral than sand, but there is a decent pool and sunning terrace, plus a restaurant and bar — Rockley Beach is a five-minute walk, and plenty of restaurants are close by.

Salt Ash Apartment Hotel, Dover, Christ Church, Barbados, WI. ✆ 246-428-8753, ✆ 246-428-2845, 🖥 www.candoo.com/saltash

🛍 **Cheap** 🍴 **EP** Ⓒ🅒 9 rooms

For rock-bottom beachfront prices, head to this worn but clean, three-story apartment complex that provides oversize units with kitchen and a/c — all are light and tidy. The furnishings won't win any style awards, but the upper units have a private balcony overlooking the beach, which is uncrowded and very appealing. The restaurant and bar operates on request.

The Fairholme, Maxwell, Christ Church, Barbados, WI. ✆ 246-428-9425, ✆ 246-420-2309

🛍 **Dirt Cheap** 🍴 **EP** 20 rooms

A five-minute walk from Club Mistral, the Fairholme is a clean, quiet, and cheap alternative. The common rooms are very spartan in their faded fabulous-'50s furnishings, but the rooms in the main house are surprisingly comfortable and attractive. All have private baths, ceiling fans, and firm double or twin beds. There are newer efficiency apartments in a separate wing, but they lack the main house's character and style. The garden and pool in the back are pleasant when kept up. The Fairholme is very popular with Europeans, especially the Dutch and Germans, who don't mind the no-frills aura. No credit cards are accepted.

Where to Eat

The more upscale hotels and restaurants of Barbados offer gourmet international dishes, but the native Bajan cuisine provides an entirely different dining experience. Don't miss the flying fish while you're here — it's an island specialty.

$$ **Atlantis Hotel**, Tent Bay, St. Joseph, 246-433-9445

This is a Bajan institution and a great and funky place to stop for lunch en route to Cattlewash Beach. Although the restaurant is open daily, the buffet lunch on Wednesday and Sunday has everything Bajan (and otherwise) that you would ever want to eat.

$$$$$ **Bagatelle Great House**, Highway 2A, St. Thomas, 246-421-6767

Set in a beautiful 300-year-old Bajan plantation house a 15-minute drive north of Bridgetown, the cuisine here is Bajan continental, served in a three-course meal that runs $42. Reservations are recommended.

$$ **The Boatyard**, Bay Street, Bridgetown, 246-436-2622

This popular spot offers a globe-girdling menu on the beach, including pasta dishes and fish entrees. The Boatyard is also a good place for nightlife—on Tuesday from 8 p.m. until 3 a.m., a $17.50 cover buys all the beer and house drinks on offer and live music to boot.

$$$ **Brown Sugar**, Aquatic Gap, St. Michael, 246-426-7684

This is a very popular lunch place because of its fixed-price Planters Buffet of Bajan cuisine (about $24). It's also open for dinner. Reservations are recommended.

$$$$$ ⊛ **The Cliff**, Derricks, St. James, 246-432-1922

Offering one of the Caribbean's most spectacular settings for any restaurant, The Cliff has equally outstanding French-accented cuisine and is quite romantic, especially on moon-drenched nights. The seating is arranged like a stage of sorts, and many people desire the front row, closest to the water; we rather like the rear tables, where you can survey the cooing and preening. Prices are quite dear—you'll need to budget $100 per person for food alone—but this is one special occasion place that's worth the splurge. Reservations are always a must.

$$$$ **David's Place**, St. Lawrence Main Road, Worthington, Christ Church, 246-435-9755

David's serves Bajan cuisine (fried chicken, flying fish, pepperpot, curried lamb) with a sophisticated twist. Reservations are suggested. Closed on Monday.

$ **Kitchen Korner**, Holetown, 246-432-1684

This is a well-liked lunch spot, with reasonably priced gourmet sandwiches, salads, and pastas.

$$$$$ **Lone Star**, Mt. Standfast, 246-419-0599

Our experiences here have not always lived up to the hype and prices, but it is a splendid setting, right on the beach, and when the food and service are good, it's a great time. The menu covers a lot of ground: highlights include the lobster, a king prawn green curry, and the "three-course traditional English roast"; and many diners are happy with the oyster and caviar bar. We suggest coming for lunch or for prepandial cocktails and appetizers.

$$$ **Naniki**, Suriname, 246-433-1300

This small new restaurant in the scenic bluffs above Bathsheba is hard to find (easiest coming from Bathsheba), but it's worth a special trip. The menu celebrates island cuisine with wonderful coastal views, and after lunch you can stroll through the owner's anthurium farm. A 10-cottage eco-lodge and spa, Lush Life Nature Resort, is due to open in March 2007. Reservations are advised particularly for Sunday lunch; closed on Monday.

$$ **Ragamuffins**, Holetown, 246-432-1295

Located in an authentic chattel house, this is an unpretentious, roots-style (rasta and reggae) restaurant and bar with an eclectic menu. The options range from vegetarian to T-bone and from pasta to rasta. There are just a few tables, so reservations are advised.

$$ **Ship Inn**, St. Lawrence Gap, 246-420-7447

Situated in a 250-year-old plantation house, this pub isn't known for great food, but it's usually a great scene, with sandwiches, prime rib, and home-baked pies heading the menu. It has dart boards and live music nightly, but the place really jumps on Thursday. For more info, visit www.shipinnbarbados.com.

$$$ **Waterfront Café**, The Carenage, Bridgetown, 246-427-0093

The Bajan continental food here is quite good, and the setting by the fishing boats is very apropos. The Caribbean buffet is accompanied by live steel pan music on Tuesday, and live jazz accompanies dinner most other nights (no cover).

$$$$ **Zen**, The Crane, St. Philip, 246-423-6220

Barbados's oldest hotel, the Crane, opened this sushi-plus restaurant in 2005. You can choose from either a Thai or a Japanese menu, or mix-and-match—items are prepared by a four-man team of Thai and Japanese chefs. The atmosphere is complete with a koi pond, Asian architecture, a tatami room, and a 12-seat sushi bar. It serves dinner only, but come before sunset to enjoy the view of one of the Caribbean's prettiest beaches. Reservations are suggested.

Don't Miss

The Mount Gay Distillery Tour

Located about five minutes from downtown Bridgetown, this tour allows you to finally see where the Mt. Gay of your Mt. Gay–and–tonics comes from. It is open Monday through Friday from 9 a.m. to 5 p.m. Admission is $6. Call 246-425-8757 for more information.

The Barbados National Trust

This offers open houses of historic Bajan estates in winter and free Sunday hikes. Call 246-436-9033 for additional information and to obtain meeting locations for the hikes.

A Drink at the Sandy Lane

Be fabulous for one drink at this incredibly expensive but renowned hotel. Call 246-444-2000.

⊛ A Round at the Green Monkey

Sandy Lane's premier golf course is carved from a former quarry that includes stimulating elevation changes. Named after the island's wild monkeys, the 7,200-yard course was designed by Tom Fazio. We hear that the Green Monkey is currently open to the resort's guests only, and greens fees run $350 (yikes!). Call 246-444-2000 for more info.

A Bike Hike

Rent a bike and explore the back roads of this relatively flat terrain. To make arrangements, contact Highland Adventure Centre, which does hiking, biking, and horseback-riding tours; reservations are required (246-438-8069).

Crane Beach

Gorgeous turquoise water, great bodysurfing waves, and a pretty beach make this a must stop.

Jolly Roger

Yes, it's a tourist thing, but people have a great time on their sunset cruises and get blotto at the open bar while they're at it. Prices start at $52.50. For information, call 436-6424.

Baxter Road (late at night on a weekend)

This is a fun scene of still-too-awake-to-go-to-bed-Bajans and good cheap food, too.

Bonaire

An arid climate and scorching sun balances with the beautiful undulating reality you will find beneath the calm waters that surround this island and cover its well-preserved reefs. Bonaire is an island that offers visitors much more by way of underwater exploration than topside activity. The relaxed locals and slow atmosphere are a perfect complement to the explosion of life, color, and movement you'll find on the other side of your mask 60 feet beneath the surface.

Bonaire is one of the top dive destinations in the Caribbean and in the world, thanks to forward-thinking pioneers who started the movement to protect the island's fringing reefs back in 1971. This culminated in all the reefs surrounding Bonaire — and a small, uninhabited offshore isle, Klein Bonaire — being declared the Bonaire National Marine Park in 1979. These waters are teeming with marine life: queen angelfish, rock beauties, parrot fish, blue tangs, grouper, tarpon, octopus, sea turtles, coral, sponges, sea anemones, urchins, eels, and more. Bonaire's corals are relatively pristine, although surveys have shown some bleaching, attributed to an unusual warming of the seawaters in 1995. However, Bonaire's license plates declare it a "diver's paradise," and we strongly agree.

Like the other islands in the Lesser Antilles, Bonaire is arid. It has a few nice beaches on the southern end of the island, a nice beach in Lac Bay, and

Bonaire

Boca Coolish

C A R I B B E A N   S E A

Playa
Chiquito

△ Brandars
Hill
(784 ft / 239 m)

PARK
ENTRANCE

GOTOMEER

GAS
STATION

Playa
Grand

FLAMINGO
SANCTUARY

OBSERVATION
POINT

Rincon

Playa
Frans

LIGHTHOUSE

CAPTAIN
DON'S
HABITAT

Playa
Lech

△ Seroe
Largu

SAND DOLLAR
CONDOMINIUM
RESORT

Klein
Bonaire

Seroe
△ Grande

GAS
STATION

Kralendijk

PLAZA RESORT
BONAIRE

DIVI FLAMINGO
BEACH RESORT

AIRPORT

Lac
Bay

THE
KONTIKI

Sorobon
Beach

SOROBON
BEACH
RESORT

Pink
Beach

LIGHTHOUSE

LEGEND

◉ ◎   Capital City, Town

㉜   Route Number

◼   Hotel / Point of Interest

📷   Scenic View

⚓   Ferry / Cruise Ship Dock

🗼   Lighthouse

🏖   Beach

⛳   Golf Course

0   1.5   3

Miles

Bonaire: Key Facts

Location	12°N by 68°W 50 miles north of Venezuela 1,720 miles southeast of New York
Size	112 square miles
Highest point	Brandaris Hill (784 feet/239 meters)
Population	15,000
Language	Papiamento plus Dutch (the offcial language); English and Spanish widely spoken
Time	Atlantic Standard Time (1 hour ahead of EST, same as EDT)
Area code	To call Bonaire from the U.S., dial 011 (the international code), plus 599 (country code), plus the seven-digit local number.
Electricity	127/220 volts, 50 cycles. Adapters are necessary in some cases.
Currency	Netherlands Antilles florin or guilder NAf 1.78 = US$1; dollars are widely accepted
Driving	Valid U.S. driver's licenses are accepted. Driving is on the right, and the absence of traffic lights makes driving around the island easy and unhurried.
Documents	Passport or proof of citizenship with photo for U.S. and Canadian citizens, plus an ongoing or a return ticket
Departure tax	$20
Beer to drink	Amstel
Rum to drink	Mount Gay
Music to hear	Salsa and Merengue
Tourism info	800-BONAIRE (800-266-2473) www.infobonaire.com www.bonairediving.org www.bonaireislandmap.com

one on the northern tip. Washington-Slagbaai National Park occupies about one-fifth of the island above sea level and has become a draw for eco-travelers. Prehistoric-looking iguanas and rare green parrots are frequently encountered on walks or bike rides on this small island. You'll also find lots of cactus and huge salt ponds. Bonaire lies outside the hurricane belt and gets only a few showers a year, which helps explain the crystal-clear waters that offer visibility up to 160 feet. The constantly blowing winds make the heat bearable and can even give you a chill at night.

Even without the western side's incredible reefs and those ringing Klein Bonaire, this place would be a pleasant, low-key, quiet escape. Bonaire's ambiance is wonderfully laid-back. Locals—typically a mix of European, African, and distant Arawak descent—are hospitable and accommodating. The diving elevates this place to heaven for those of us who go down, and the addition of several guided snorkeling sites makes it terrific for nondivers, too. The relatively easy nature of Bonaire's diving—including the mellow current, high visibility, and professional care—makes it ideal for beginners.

You'll notice a strange language being spoken here that sounds a lot like Spanish. Papiamento is a native dialect that combines Spanish, Dutch, and Portuguese with some African and Arawak words thrown in. (It's spoken on Aruba, too.) If you understand Spanish or Portuguese, you should get the gist of it. Most locals speak at least four languages: Papiamento, Dutch (the official language), English, and Spanish.

The Briefest History

Amerindians from nearby Venezuela first settled on Bonaire (the name is Amerindian for "low country") hundreds of years before its "discovery" by Amerigo Vespucci in 1499. The Spanish were the first Europeans to settle here, and they established a colony in 1527. They remained for almost a century, until a war with the Netherlands caused the Dutch to seize control of the island in 1636 from their base on Curaçao. They set up shop and began producing salt from the vast salt ponds, which became big business. Slaves, who occupied tiny stucco huts by the salt ponds, were imported to work the salt trade. In the early 1800s, British and French pirates periodically seized the island, but the Dutch regained final control in 1816. The striking slave huts have been restored. The settlers kept the slaves there, hoping that the pirates would seize the slaves first during their attacks.

When slavery was abolished by the Dutch in 1863 (29 years after the British!), salt's profitability plummeted, and the island sank into a 60-year depression. The advent of oil refineries on Aruba and Curaçao in the 1920s caused many residents to move to those neighboring islands to work; they would then send the money back to their families. The beginning of tourism in the 1950s helped to boost the economy. The union and autonomy of the Netherland Antilles (NA) within the Kingdom of the Netherlands yielded much-needed outside aid. Not until early 1962, when the first divers arrived and discovered the beauty below the sea, did Bonaireans learn that their greatest asset was just beneath the surface of the impossibly blue waters. Although the island produces 400,000 tons of salt a year, diving is now the big business.

Getting There

Bonaire's Flamingo International Airport receives one nonstop flight weekly (Saturday) from Miami on Air ALM. The airline also has daily service to

Curaçao from Miami and makes connections onward to Bonaire. Air Jamaica has service three times a week from Montego Bay, Jamaica, to Bonaire and makes connections from a variety of North American cities. In 2001, American Eagle started flying to Bonaire from San Juan, Puerto Rico; American Airlines and others serve San Juan from many North American gateways.

Getting Around

You should definitely rent a car to explore the island, because a big attraction on Bonaire is the diving freedom afforded by easy shore dives, available 24 hours a day. The roads are good, fairly well marked, and easy to drive. A few of the major companies are here, including Avis (800-331-4084), Budget (800-527-0700), Hertz (800-654-3001), and National (800-227-3876). Make reservations in advance to ensure availability and the best rate. Divers might consider a jeep or van to haul their gear. Bonaire even has a drive-in dive shop where you can quickly fill your dive tanks and be on your way.

You might also want to rent a mountain bike, because the island has almost 200 miles of flat coastal roadways and goat paths — not to mention off-road mountainous adventures — to explore. Combine the trip with kayaking or snorkeling in the mangrove swamp, which serves as a nursery for barracuda and red snapper. **Cycle Bonaire** (599-717-7558) maintains top-notch equipment with great service and offers packages of biking with scuba diving, snorkeling, and/or ocean kayaking. **Discover Bonaire** (599-717-5252), which specializes in Friday nature tours, has bike rentals, and offers guided excursions. **Outdoor Bonaire** (599-791-6272, hans@outdoor bonaire.com) offers tours in the mangroves on sit-on-top kayaks, rock climbing, caving, and other alternative daytime activities. Call or e-mail Hans ahead of time to set up a tour.

Focus on Bonaire: The Diving Experience

Always breathe. It sounds obvious, but that's the first rule of diving. Even when there is a 15-foot white shark swimming straight toward you, maintain your composure and breathe regularly. If you don't, your lungs could explode, which could ruin your vacation. Besides, air costs about $1 for every minute you're underwater, so you're paying for it anyway!

Never rise faster than your bubbles. That is cardinal rule number two. If you do, you could very likely experience the bends, which is not at all pleasant — not to mention that it can also paralyze and kill you.

In Bonaire, you will become a scuba addict. With 80°F water, visibility up to 140 feet, and an abundance of exotic tropical marine life to contemplate (197 species of reef fish and 84 species of coral have been identified), chances are that once you start, diving here will become an addiction. It'll be as essential as your therapist and the Sunday *Times*. It is an equipment-intensive sport, much like skiing, so soon you'll be shelling out tons of money for the latest in BCs, regulators, and fog-free face masks, but once you deflate your BC and start heading down, you'll realize the investment is worth it. Even a small amount of time living under the surface is enough to relax you for weeks. A week of diving in Bonaire will take months of stress off your shoulders.

You'll find some of the best diving in the world here, and it's certainly the most accessible for divers from the East Coast, the Midwest, and Canada. Hundreds of programs and packages are available for all levels of divers — from total neophyte to dive master and instructor.

What is it like to sink slowly to the bottom, look up, and see the surface 60 feet above your head? It's wild — like being in a giant aquarium. What do you feel when you're neutrally buoyant and floating past fabulously colored fish and coral? Fantastic. It's another dimension, like being in a 3-D movie. The best word to describe the experience is *nirvana*. Visit *Skin Diver* magazine's Web site at www.skin-diver.com for a taste of the sport.

For those in search of a real mind-blowing experience, try diving at night. Imagine the thrill of jumping into total darkness with only the glow rings on the other divers' tanks and flashlights to guide you. Turn around, and it's pitch black. Is the Great White lurking somewhere behind you? Strict imagination control is in order. Once you get to the bottom (which won't take long, because night dives normally don't go beyond a depth of 40 feet), you will observe the ocean asleep. Fish are so docile you could touch them — although that's a major no-no in these protected waters. Coral comes alive, sending out delicate feelers to feed on plankton. Shine a light on a coral head, and you'll see it close up within seconds. Colors become more brilliant than during the day, because the artificial white light brings out reds and yellows you can't see in sunlight. (As the water gets deeper, it "eats" the red and yellow light waves, giving everything a bluish cast.)

The island offers attractive options for novices. The **Resort Course** allows you to get your feet wet, so to speak, by completing a shallow dive (to 40 feet) in one day without any previous experience. This will cost around $100 and is available through most dive operations. After this sample, you'll know whether you want more, which is likely. Then you can sign up for certification — about five full days (four or five dives) — or just take more Resort Courses in between trips to the beach and windsurfing at Lac Bay.

Those interested in serious diving must be certified or have completed classwork for certification. In order to get tanks filled with air (or to rent scuba equipment), you must be a card-carrying (with photo) diver. Your certification is like your underwater driver's license — you must have it to dive. However, if you wait to take the classes on your vacation, you'll end up paying lots of money to sit in a room for five days listening to lectures while the sun and sea beckon. There are certification courses back home that will prepare you to take the final plunge and do your open-water dives in Bonaire

— far preferable to the wet suits, cold water, and limited visibility of the Atlantic or some murky lake. Any dive shop in your area will be able to tell you about certification courses (usually given by PADI or NAUI, the two largest professional diving organizations) and where to find them. Many local YMCAs also offer a course that is recognized by most dive operators.

There are four reasons we think diving on Bonaire is superb. The first is the reef profile of the island — Bonaire is not part of the continental shelf of South America, so the reef wall starts only 100 feet or so from the beach. Dozens of the island's dive sites are accessible from shore — that is, you wade in, rather than dive from a boat (you could dive two or three different sites a day for at least two weeks without ever entering a boat). The shore dives are marked by cute yellow-painted stones that you'll spot along the road (there's even a flamingo pink "dive bus" that parks at a different shore dive marker each day to provide lockers, drinks, and dive briefings). At the start of the reef, the depth is about 20 to 30 feet. The wall plunges to a depth of about 130 to 150 feet, where there is a kind of broad ledge, and then it drops again to about 600 feet. Shore and boat dive sites combined, there are 86 different dive sites, all along Bonaire's west coast and around Klein Bonaire. Be sure to take the time to check out the dive sites on the far end of Klein Bonaire. Carl's Hill is especially photogenic, and Leonora's Reef boasts 75-year-old coral.

The second reason is the marine life here and its protection. Because the entire coastline of Bonaire and Klein Bonaire is a marine park, nothing — dead or alive — can be touched or moved. Stiff fines await the diver who takes even a sand dollar from below the surface. Although that may be bad news for your shell collection, it's great news for the incredible hard and soft corals and, of course, the animals. It's great news for your viewing pleasure, as well! On our first dive on Bonaire, we saw two mammoth moray eels, a huge grouper, an octopus, and schools and schools of all kinds of colorful fish. We had been in the water for only 15 minutes!

Number three on the list of Bonaire superlatives is the visibility of the water. Lying outside the hurricane belt, Bonaire gets little rainfall to wash sand and silt into the sea, leaving the waters startlingly clear, with visibility that ranges between 60 and 140 feet. Water temperatures average 80°F, making only a light wet-suit skin or top necessary. It doesn't get better than this.

The final reason that diving is so fabulous here is the facilities. More than a dozen full-service dive operations are on the island, offering every conceivable kind of dive, instruction, certification, equipment, and accommodation-and-dive package. To be able to jump off the dock, go down, and know that your dive outfit is close at hand is a great convenience and an assurance for the novice. The island has a state-of-the-art decompression chamber in case you become a dive cowboy and make a mistake.

With all of these options, how do you decide which outfit to use? The grandfather of the lot is **Captain Don's Habitat** (Captain Don was the guy who was going underwater here way back in 1962; 599-717-8290). On our visits we have dived with **Sand Dollar** (599-717-8738) and a smaller operator, **Bon Bini Divers** (599-717-5425), and were impressed with both outfits' professionalism and service. We highly recommend them. Others that score high on reader surveys by *Rodale's Scuba Diving* magazine are **Buddy Dive** (599-717-5080) and the **Plaza Resort** (599-717-2500).

Bonaire now holds an **annual dive festival** in June. Sponsored by the Coral Reef Alliance, the focus is on conservation and cleanup of the reefs as well as fun in the sun. Highlights are the underwater photography workshops taught by some of the world's best photographers and the presentations by noted marine biologists.

Where to Stay

Deciding where to stay on Bonaire is complicated by the fact that dive operations are typically affiliated with or actually own the hotels where they are located, so when you choose a hotel, you're also choosing the outfit with which you'll be diving. That means you'll need to investigate a bit more up front. However, terrific dive-and-stay packages are abundant, and they lower your cost and simplify your life on the island. Even if you don't dive, any of the hotels below would love to have you. One of them has nothing to do with diving — it's a nudist resort.

Plaza Resort Bonaire, 80 J. A. Abraham Boulevard, Kralendijk, Bonaire, NA. ✆ 800-766-6016 or 599-717-2500, ✒ 599-717-7133, 🖳 www.plazaresortbonaire.com, info@plazaresortbonaire.com

💲 **Very Pricey** 🍴 **EP** CC 200 rooms

Sprawled out across a dozen acres of land, this mammoth resort boasts its own private beach and lagoon. We nearly got lost wandering around the compound! Although it's possible to slip into the water with your gear just beyond the sliding glass doors of your room, we recommend that you venture out of the resort's immediate area. Truthfully, if there is one place you could stay in Bonaire and never leave the grounds, the Plaza would be it. The resort opened in 1995 and offers an upscale option on the island as well as the most rooms. The Plaza has suites and one- or two-bedroom villas. This multifaceted resort also has a terrific dive operation and all the other amenities you'd expect, from a pool to a workout room plus a relaxing bar scene and a marina.

Sand Dollar Condominium Resort, P.O. Box 262, 79 Kaya Gobernador N. Debrot, Bonaire, NA. ✆ 800-288-4773 or 5997-8738, ✒ 5997-8760, 🖳 www.sanddollarbonaire.com, info@sanddollarbonaire.com

💲 **Pricey** 🍴 **EP** CC 85 apartments

The dive shop here is top-notch: A full-service five-star PADI operation offers every scuba course known to humanity as well as photo and video courses. It also offers kayaking and snorkeling trips. The accommodations are condos that come in studios and one-, two-, and three-bedroom configurations. Though not at all fancy, the units are spacious and comfortable. The style of each apartment is distinct; each has a different owner who decorates the apartment to his or her individual taste. All have balconies where you can hang your wet suit out to dry, as well as a/c, fully equipped kitchens, and cable TV. A small market is on the property for those who like to cook. A fresh-water pool and a tennis court round out the facilities. The tiny beach is strollable only during low tide.

Sand Dollar was voted one of the top 10 dive resorts in the world by readers of *Rodale's Scuba Diving*. In January 2006, Sand Dollar implemented a new program dedicated to the production of artificial reefs. In conjunction with Bonaire National Marine Park, it constructed twenty 600-pound reef balls (artificial reef modules made from concrete poured into a fiberglass mold), many of which were placed in the waters off Sand Dollar and near the Bari Reef.

Captain Don's Habitat, P.O. Box 88, 103 Kaya Gobernador N. Debrot, Bonaire, NA. © 800-327-6709 or 599-717-8290, ✆ 599-717-8240, 💻 www.habitatbonaire.com, bonaire@habitatdiveresorts.com

💲 **Pricey** ⑪ **EP** ⒸⒸ 93 rooms

Captain Don, who has now retired, was the original dive pioneer and dive operator on Bonaire. He often stops by on Tuesday nights to chat with guests and reminisce about the early days. The theme at this resort is dive freedom, reflecting the Captain's maverick style. There is a full-service, five-star PADI facility, and certification for NAUI and SSI is available. The villas are an attractive Mediterranean stucco style and come in all sizes and costs. Some at seaside have king-size beds and private balconies. Some have a rooftop solarium. All 93 units have a/c, and many have kitchens. The most recent addition is a Japanese garden–style area with two-bedroom apartments that look as if they were lifted from the set of *The Last Samurai*. This part of the Habitat is very relaxing and quiet, ideal for a romantic vacation. Just beyond the reception area, where you will find wireless Internet, there is a pretty pool area and a cool restaurant and bar right on the water.

Divi Flamingo Beach Resort & Casino, 40 J. A. Abraham Boulevard, Kralendijk, Bonaire, NA. © 800-367-3484 or 599-717-8285, ✆ 599-717-8238, 💻 www.diviflamingo.com, info@divibonaire.com

💲 **Not So Cheap** ⑪ **EP** ⒸⒸ 129 rooms

Divi Flamingo is home of Divi Dive Bonaire, located at the opposite end of a tiny beachfront. A full-service facility, it offers all levels of certification, and Photo Bonaire provides underwater photo and video courses as well as camera rental. A new airline, Divi Divi, is connected to this resort; it offers shuttle services from Curaçao and Aruba.

The hotel is one of the oldest on the island and has quite a history: It served as a German prisoner-of-war camp. These days, you'll find a friendly and helpful staff and 129 guest rooms, all with lanais, a/c, ceiling fans, tropical décor, phones, and cable TV. Avoid the rooms down the steps just past the reception area to the left. They seem a little stuffy and have a moldy motel feeling. There are two pools with Jacuzzis, several lighted tennis courts, and all manner of water sports. We complained that the Divi was overdue for a renovation, and in 2000 a major overhaul was completed. However, the new bright colors can get a little loud after a couple of minutes on the grounds. The Green Parrot Restaurant has been replaced by a four-level oceanfront eatery, the Chibi Chibi, our favorite waterfront bar and restaurant. January 2006 also saw the construction of the Flamingo Balashi Beach Bar, situated right over the water, next to the Calabas pier. The lobby, garden and pool area, and the 89 hotel rooms have all been remodeled. There's even a life-size chess board!

Kontiki, 64 Kaminda Sorobon, Bonaire, NA. © 599-717-5369, ✆ 599-717-5368, 🖳 www.kontikibonaire.com, info@kontikibonaire.com

💲 **Not So Cheap** 🍴 **EP** 🆑 13 rooms and 1 villa

If you want a remote place, away from the rest of the tourists and close to the only real beach on Bonaire, Kontiki is the place for you. There are four studio apartments, seven one-bedroom, three two-bedroom, and a villa. The natural setting around this resort is relaxing and far from the concrete, highly fabricated feeling you might find at other resorts on the island. Bonaire is becoming more of a windsurfing destination, with all the activity focused around Lac Bay. For a windsurf-heavy experience on Bonaire, the Kontiki is a perfect option due to its proximity to Lac Bay, the island's windsurfing center. All other resorts are located relatively far away, wheras the Kontiki is just a short walk. You could even walk home for lunch after a morning session, then return for a sunset surf after a long, relaxing siesta.

Sorobon Beach Resort, P.O. Box 14, Lac Bay, Bonaire, NA. © 599-717-8080, ✆ 599-717-5363, 🖳 www.sorobonbeach.com, info@sorobonbeachresort.com

💲 **Very Pricey** 🍴 **EP** 🆑 30 rooms

Bonaire has one "clothing-optional" (read: nude) resort. After all, the Dutch are known for being open-minded. Situated on a pretty, shallow, protected bay open to the trade winds, this pleasant, rather simple establishment has a fine private beach. Next door to the resort is Jibe City, the windsurf operation (Bonaire's best spot for windsurfing). Accommodations consist of 30 one-bedroom chalets. There is a bar, a restaurant, a library, water sports, and a dive affiliation with the Dive Inn.

Where to Eat

Local specialties are fresh-caught fish, an occasional *rijsttafel* (a traditional feast that includes rice, veggies, and chicken or beef), and traditional Dutch dishes like *keshi yena* (a Gouda cheese stuffed with spices and chicken or beef). Your best bet is to rent a villa or an efficiency with kitchen facilities, because food prices reflect the fact that everything must be flown in to the island. If you don't feel like cooking, however, you won't go hungry. Indeed, most of these places understand that divers are usually ravenous after their adventures and serve generous portions accordingly.

$$$ **Beefeater Garden**, 12 Kaya Grandi, Kralendijk, 717-7776

Dine in the large tropical garden behind a typical Bonairean house. Local art decorates the walls, and on Saturday you can listen to live music at this pleasant spot. A specialty is *cabrito stoba* (goat stew), but you can also get vegetarian dishes, fresh fish, steak, and curry dishes. It serves breakfast, lunch, and dinner. Closed Sunday.

$$$ **Blue Moon**, 5 Kaya C.E.B. Hellmund, 717-8617

Situated on a pleasant waterfront terrace overlooking the South Pier, this spot has a varied menu that offers New Zealand lamb, the fish catch of the day in a white wine and lemon sauce, and a chicken filet topped with mango in a spicy coconut sauce. There is also a five-course meal for $33. Blue Moon offers a happy hour from 5:30 to 7 p.m. Keep in mind that the kitchen closes at 10 p.m. The restaurant is closed on Wednesday.

$$$$ **Den Laman**, 77 Kaya Gobernador N. Debrot, 717-8955

This open-air seafood restaurant beside the Sand Dollar is notable for its live lobster tank and live music on Saturday night. From a state-of-the-art open kitchen, the chef offers four types of fish daily, besides conch and grouper. Patrons can even get an American-style bacon cheeseburger if they're really hungry, and the french fries alone are worth a stop. Open for breakfast, lunch, and dinner.

$$ **Mi Poron**, 1 Kaya Caracas, Kralendijk, 717-5199

The only spot on the island that turns out traditional Bonairean food is located in a historic Bonairean home and is run by locals. It features a small museum inside, along with a tiny gift shop. Dine on the patio and try the *keshi yena* or go for the conch. Closed Monday.

$$$ **Mona Lisa Bar & Restaurant**, 15 Kaya Grandi, 717-8718

On Main Street in Kralendijk, this popular watering hole and restaurant is decorated with local knickknacks and attracts locals eager to swap diving tales. Copious snacks are served at the bar. The diverse menu ranges from classic French to Dutch, with a touch of Asian for good measure.

$$$$ **Richard's Waterfront Dining**, 60 J. A. Abraham Boulevard, 717-5263

Owned by Richard Beaty, a transplanted Bostonian, this terrific restaurant is known for its spanking-fresh seafood. The menu is written on a chalkboard and changes daily. Its coral bar is a good place from which to watch the sunset.

Don't Miss

Washington-Slagbaai National Park

Occupying 13,500 acres, this wildlife sanctuary — formerly an aloe and divi-divi tree plantation — was established in 1978 and is the first of its kind in the Netherland Antilles. Two routes are laid through the park. One fork takes you to Playa Funchi, one of the best snorkeling spots on the island, the other to the deserted black-sand beach called Boca CoColishi. Bonaire's place in the migration path between North and South America, and the variety of vegetation from freshwater lakes and dry salt flats, makes it a bird-watcher's paradise. Early birds see the colorful flamingos, yellow orioles, and 150 other species of birds that populate the park's lowland forests, lakes, and salt flats. Take a four-wheel-drive and binoculars. Pack a picnic lunch and plenty of water.

Jibe City

This is located next to the Sorobon Resort at Lac Bay, a perfect bay for windsurfing. It has thigh-deep water with a sandy bottom (no knees scraped by corals) and has an onshore breeze, so you won't be blown out to sea. There is a little bar where you can down a few while you rest or watch. Rent boards or get lessons from Bonaire Windsurf Palace (717-2288), Jibe City (717-5233), or Bonaire Windsurfing School at the Plaza Resort (717-2500). Windsurfing in Bonaire is starting to rival windsurfing in El Yaque on Margarita Island. Stopping by to take a lesson at Jibe City is a good alternative to scuba diving if you want to take a break from swimming around underwater all day.

Slave Huts

The surreal sight of three 30-foot-high gleaming white obelisks on a beautiful strand called Pink Beach, surrounded by tiny whitewashed, thatch-roofed stone huts that look like something out of the computer game Myst, is puzzling until you learn that the obelisks were constructed in 1838 to guide salt ships to their moorings. The huts, built around 1850, housed the slaves who worked the salt ponds. Crawl into one of the huts and look back at the ocean — it's quite a view.

The Flamingos

These stunning pink birds — which have made a remarkable comeback to 40,000 in number from near extinction at 1,500 in the early 1900s — hang out at the flamingo sanctuary located in the southern salt ponds and at the Gotomeer pond in the north by the park. Driving or biking past the Gotomeer is perhaps the best way to get close to the flamingos. They are a skittish lot, so consider making your approach on foot without sudden movement or loud noises.

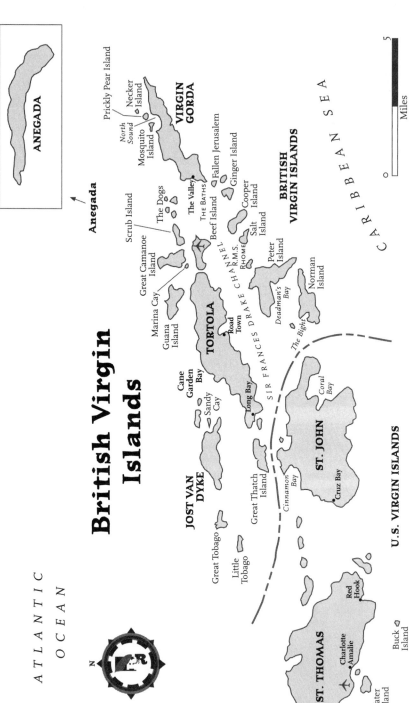

British Virgin Islands

ATLANTIC
OCEAN

ANEGADA

Anegada

CARIBBEAN SEA

Prickly Pear Island
Necker Island
VIRGIN GORDA
North Sound
Mosquito Island
Fallen Jerusalem
Ginger Island
The Valley
THE BATHS
Cooper Island
Scrub Island
The Dogs
Beef Island
Salt Island
Great Camanoe Island
Peter Island
Marina Cay
R.M.S. RHONE
BRITISH VIRGIN ISLANDS
Guana Island
Deadman's Bay
Norman Island
Road Town
TORTOLA
SIR FRANCES DRAKE CHANNEL
The Bight
Cane Garden Bay
Coral Bay
Sandy Cay
Long Bay
JOST VAN DYKE
ST. JOHN
Great Thatch Island
Cinnamon Bay
Cruz Bay
Great Tobago
Little Tobago
U.S. VIRGIN ISLANDS
Red Hook
ST. THOMAS
Charlotte Amalie
Buck Island
Water Island
ST. CROIX

N

Miles

The British
Virgin Islands

TOURISTO SCALE:

TORTOLA 👹👹👹👹👹👹👹 (7)

VIRGIN GORDA 👹👹👹👹👹 (5)

OTHER BVI 👹👹👹 (3)

The small harbor is squeezed with hundreds of yachts. There is a non-stop arrival of ferries from neighboring islands (some as far as St. Croix) that disgorge revelers by the boatload and go back to pick up more. The entire beach is literally jammin'. Soca music rocks the crowd from every gin joint, rum and beer flow like Niagara, faces smile and laugh, feet tap, legs wobble. Whoops, someone just did another face plant in the sand, much to the amusement of his or her companions. Now this is a party!

It is also New Year's Eve on Jost Van Dyke, one of the jewels of the British Virgin Islands necklace, and a primary port-of-call in this sailor's paradise. For decades a yachting destination, these islands offer some of the finest sailing waters in the world. They rival the Mediterranean and the South Pacific for steady winds and warm, clear water, providing superb opportunities for swimming and snorkeling around every bend as well as eyeball navigation for those unfamiliar with the waters.

British Virgin Islands: Key Facts

Location	18°N by 64°W
	1,650 miles/2,655 kilometers southeast of New York
Size	Tortola: 10 square miles/26 square kilometers
	Virgin Gorda: 8 square miles/21 square kilometers
	Anegada: 15 square miles/39 square kilometers
	Jost Van Dyke: 3 square miles/8 square kilometers
Highest point	Tortola: Mt. Sage (1,780 feet/543 meters)
	Virgin Gorda: Gorda Peak (1,370 feet/418 meters)
Population	26,000
Language	English
Time	Atlantic Standard Time (1 hour ahead of EST, same as EDT)
Area code	284
Electricity	110 volts AC, 60 cycles — same as the U.S. and Canada
Currency	U.S. dollar
Driving	On the left; a Canadian or American driver's license is accepted, but in addition you must pay $10 for a temporary BVI permit, valid for three months.
Documents	Passport or proof of nationality with photo is acceptable for U.S. or Canadian citizens up to six months; an ongoing or a return ticket or boat charter is also required.
Departure tax	$20 by air, $5 by sea
Beer to drink	Heineken
Rum to drink	Pusser's
Music to hear	Dancehall, calypso, fungi (traditional music unique to the BVI — a rythmic combination of rudimentary string percussion and wind instruments)
Tourism info	800-835-8530, www.bvitourism.com

There are more than 50 British Virgin Islands, or BVI—from the relatively large (24-square-mile) island of Tortola to teensy Sandy Cay, which is just large enough for a picnic with a dozen of your closest friends. Most are uninhabited. If you're not into sailing—after all, sailing can be torturous to the nonnautical—there are many islands where you can stay and never have to set foot on a boat. Landlubbers can visit Tortola, reached by lots of flights from San Juan, plus Virgin Gorda, Jost Van Dyke, Peter Island, Guana Island, Cooper Island, Anegada, and the incredibly expensive Necker Island (you rent the whole thing). Of course, a boat is the ultimate waterfront accommodation, and you can see so much more. A boat will also help you to access some of the many snorkeling spots that are hard to reach from shore — the BVI have perhaps the best variety of locations in the Caribbean. If you've never snorkeled before, you'll be spoiled for life. With such great sailing territory, most visitors to the BVI are sailors on a weeklong charter (this explains why 3-square-mile Jost Van Dyke, with a population of fewer than 300 people, has almost 20 bars). Tortola is the charter-boat headquarters and where most of the outfits in the BVI are based. These people are obviously mobile and migrate daily to different anchorages. Resort mavens have plenty of options, however. Tomatoes for some are tomahtoes to others, so you have your choice.

The Briefest History

Like the U.S. Virgins next door, the British Virgin Islands were first populated by Amerindians from South America. First came the Arawaks and the Caribs, then Columbus sighted these islands on his second voyage, in 1493. The Dutch were the first Europeans to settle the islands, yet it was Britain that took control in 1666 and has ruled the islands ever since. The first settlements were established on Virgin Gorda, but in 1741 the capital was moved to Fat Hogs Bay on Tortola, and eventually — in the mid-18th century — to Road Town. Until the recent tourist boom, sugar and fishing were the economic mainstays. Today, the BVI are still a Crown Colony of the British Commonwealth, although they are fairly self-governing and, conveniently, the U.S. dollar is the official currency. (We love these uncomplicated histories.)

Getting There

Tortola, or rather Beef Island (which is connected to Tortola by a short bridge), is the main gateway for the BVI. The small Beef Island airstrip does not accommodate jets, so most visitors fly into San Juan and connect to American Eagle, which offers up to eight flights a day, or to Air St. Thomas (340-776-2722), Air Sunshine (800-327-8900 or 284-495-8900), Cape Air (800-352-0714 or 284-495-2100), LIAT, or Caribbean Sun. You can also reach Tortola from other neighboring islands, including St. Thomas on Air Sunshine, Cape Air, Clair Aero Services (284-495-2271), or LIAT; and from Antigua and St. Maarten on Caribbean Sun or LIAT. For our friends across the pond, there are also weekly charters from Gatwick-London to St. Thomas, in the U.S. Virgins.

Another option that is frequently cheaper than flying direct to Beef Island is to fly into St. Thomas and ferry over to Tortola using Native Son (284-495-4617), Nubian Princess (284-495-4999), Road Town Fast Ferry (284-494-2323), Smith's Ferry (284-495-4495), or Speedy's (284-495-5240), all of which operate daily out of Charlotte Amalie and/or Red Hook in St. Thomas. They arrive at West End, Tortola, to clear Customs; some (not all) continue on to Road Town. Round-trip fare is $40 for adults. Inter-Island Boat Services (284-495-4166) has three ferries daily out of St. John to West End, Tortola, with additional service to Jost Van Dyke and Virgin Gorda several days a week. For current ferry schedules to all the BVI, visit www .bviwelcome.com.

Virgin Gorda has a small airstrip, with scheduled and charter flights on Air Sunshine and Air St. Thomas from San Juan and St. Thomas. However, most people reach Virgin Gorda via ferry. Smith's and Speedy's each make several runs daily between Road Town and The Valley (a.k.a. Spanish Town), and both also link Virgin Gorda with St. Thomas. North Sound Express (284-495-2138) runs throughout the day between Beef Island (a dock conveniently close to Tortola's airport) to The Valley, Leverick Bay, and Bitter End Yacht Club. Anegada is reached by Clair Aero several times a week each from Tortola and St. Thomas; there is no ferry service to Anegada. Jost Van Dyke is reached by ferry several times daily from Tortola via New Horizon (284-495-4495); there is no airport on Jost.

The other islands are reached only by private resort ferries or charter service. For Peter Island, Cooper Island, Guana Island, or Marina Cay service, contact the respective hotels. Note that Little Dix Bay, Biras Creek, and Bitter End Yacht Club also maintain their own ferry links to and from Tortola and Beef Island.

Getting Around

Well, *we* think the best way to get around is by sailboat (see Focus on the BVI, below). If you're a landlubber, only four islands — Tortola, Virgin Gorda, Anegada, and Jost Van Dyke — are big enough to have rental cars; the other islands are small enough that you can walk everywhere. Avis (800-331-1084 or 284-494-3322), Dollar (284-494-6093), Hertz (www.hertzbvi.com; 800-654-3001 or 284-495-4405), and National (800-227-3876 or 284-494-9387) all have offices on Tortola; expect to spend about $40 to $50 a day. On our last visit we were treated well by Itgo Car Rental (284-494-5150), based in Tortola. On Virgin Gorda, contact L&S Jeep Rental (284-495-5297); on Anegada, try D.W. Jeep Rentals (284-495-9677); and on Jost Van Dyke you can rent from Paradise Jeep (284-495-9477), but this island is so small that exploring on foot makes a lot more sense. Rentals on the outer islands run about $50 to $60 a day.

Focus on the BVI: The Sail Charter Experience

If the notion of occupying a sailboat for a week makes you anxious, relax. You can do it. Sailing is definitely more rigorous than cruising on an ocean liner. A word of caution here: Pay careful attention to the personalities being assembled — a sailboat provides little refuge from others. There are three primary types of sailing experiences you'll want to consider, and they each come with a variety of price levels, ranging from surprisingly moderate to all-out staggering.

The Crewed Boat Option

So you want the easy way out? No problem. If you just enjoy lying on the deck and having someone else do the work, or if your sailing experience was a Sunfish at summer camp, then a crewed boat is for you. Although the (typically) two- or three-man crew will usually welcome your assistance, they aren't looking for it. In this situation, the degree of your participation, from hoisting the sail to simply hoisting a drink, is up to you. The daily agenda, be it snorkeling, lazing on a deserted beach, or racing with the wind, is more or less up to you.

A fully provisioned, crewed boat accommodating two couples starts at about $5,500 a week in the winter season but can range much higher, depending on the boat size and the type of amenities offered. Rates drop considerably in summer, and the sheer quantity of yachts in the BVI means that there are often price wars during slack periods, even in high season (a broker will help you find the best deal). Of course, there are also the "mega" boats, such as the *Douce France*, a gorgeous 138-foot catamaran that sleeps 12 —yours to love for the base price of $85,000 a week. Once you've decided your budget, the field of options narrows substantially.

How does one get set up with one's dreamboat? As with just about everything else in life, you call a broker — and we all know how we feel about brokers, they're pretty far down the list. Where there's money to be made, there's a broker. However, there are some who are very good and reliable. They are as follows.

Swift Yacht Charters, 209 South Main Street, Sherborn, MA 01770, USA.
℃ 800-866-8340 or 508-647-1554, ℃ 508-647-1556,
🖳 www.swiftyachts.com

Hope Swift represents various boats through the Caribbean, as well as the Mediterranean and other popular areas. As a broker, she will walk you through the booking process from its earliest stage, send you brochures on the boats in your price range, and follow through with airline and hotel reservations as needed. She will also help you to make captain contact. We grew up with Hope, know her personally, and trust her. So we always recommend Swift Yacht Charters first.

Since you will be spending a week with captain and crew in very close quarters, it is crucial to establish a relationship by phone before laying out cash. Don't be shy about asking pertinent questions like "Do you mind more than two unmarried people sleeping together?" or "Is it okay to sunbathe topless or *au naturel*?" Bad chemistry between captain and guests can ruin your vacation. Using the cruising recommendations outlined later in the chapter, hash out an itinerary with the captain before you embark. Because the captain is more familiar with the waters and because he or she is the captain, you should be flexible and defer to his or her judgment. What might be a serene little harbor one day will look like Coney Island the next due to the migratory habits of bareboaters. The captain will know these things.

The Moorings, 19345 U.S. Highway 19 North, #4, Clearwater, FL 33764, USA. ✆ 888-952-8420 or 727-535-1446, 🖳 www.moorings.com

The worldwide reach and reputation of this company is renowned. With almost 900 monohulls and catamarans (from 32 feet to 62 feet) of their own, they should be able to match you up just right.

Ed Hamilton & Company, 37 Washington Street, Wiscasset, ME 04578, USA. ✆ 800-621-7855 or 207-882-7855, ✆ 207-882-7851, 🖳 www.ed-hamilton.com

This full-service outfit knows more than 900 bareboats and crewed boats, can package flights with charters, and has 35 years of experience.

Nicholson Yacht Charters, Inc., 29 Sherman Street, Cambridge, MA 02138, USA. ✆ 800-662-6066 or 617-661-0555, ✆ 617-661-0554, 🖳 www.yachtvacations.com

This venerable family company has been in the business for generations and specializes in crewed charters.

The Bareboat Option

Although the bareboat doesn't have all the amenities of the crewed yacht, it still has some significant advantages. The privacy (among friends) is hard to beat, the freedom to go wherever your charter agreement permits will allow you the spontaneity that makes good vacations great, and it's a helluva lot cheaper. You'll have to work harder, but you will get off on the accomplishment, and deservedly so. However, there must be at least one person on board who has a thorough understanding of, and experience in, big-boat sailing. He or she should be somewhat mechanical and very patient with those who don't comprehend the arcane language of sailing. That person will also have to pass a proficiency test before you set sail — and failure could be very embarrassing to all involved (not to mention inconvenient). It is also a good idea to have a first mate who has sailed before and can absorb unfamiliar maneuvers and territory very quickly. The rest of those aboard can learn through osmosis.

Chartering a bareboat is different from booking a crewed boat in that more emphasis should be placed on the composition of the crew and the size of the boat. With no objective authority figure like a professional captain, some friends become unnerved when a peer commands them to do something. When you're sailing, there often is not enough time to follow Miss Manners rules of asking nicely. So use extra care in the crew selection — these are people you will be intimate with for at least a week. Directly related to the success of this fragile coexistence is the size of the boat. Since most charter operations have a wide range of boats available, consider the amount of privacy you'll need (from your friends), and don't be cheap here — the additional space is worth it. We recommend a center-cockpit boat, generally 35 feet or longer, because it creates two distinct staterooms fore and aft, each with its own head (bathroom). There's nothing worse than listening to a couple go at it all night long (especially when you're not able to) because all that separates you from them is a wafer-thin, louvered door. There is a general rule: under 30 feet — one couple; 30 to 40 feet — two couples; more than 40 feet — five or more.

Once you've sized up your crew and boat, you're ready to contact a broker. Due to the intense competition among bareboat charter companies, especially in the Virgins, most boats are comparably equipped. Many boats used are designed for the charter business and have options available for more money, such as a sailboard or an inflatable dinghy with an outboard on it.

Call or e-mail for brochures and then compare the pros and cons of the specific designs and features of the boats available and weigh them with the cost. Also check out packages: Some include hefty discounts on airfare, provide ground transportation to the dock, strap a windsurfer on the deck, and have options for fully or partially provisioned (food and booze) boats. If you like eating ashore, then the latter is recommended. A bareboat runs about $2,600 to $5,400 per week during the winter season, depending on the size; catamarans are generally about double. Costs are up to 50 percent less in low season. Plan on $25 to $30 per day per person for full provisioning, which can be ordered before you even arrive. If you're unsure about your sailing expertise, an additional $100 per day will give you the services (sailing-related only) of a professional skipper.

The Stateroom Charter Option

Stateroom charters are another option for sailing the BVI. Typically, these boats will accommodate up to four couples (plus crew), and have preset departure dates throughout the year. Although they do not offer the privacy of a bareboat or quite the degree of personalized attention of a crewed yacht, with the right mix of crew and guests they can be a perfectly enjoyable experience — far better than a cruise ship. In general, you will have your own private stateroom with bath and will share the common areas with two or three other couples and a crew of two or three. However, one bad apple (or horse's ass) could ruin your trip. We'd be very apprehensive about this option (think of the last time you sat next to someone annoying on a packed trans-Atlantic flight — get the idea?). That said, a stateroom charter costs less

Cruising Guide to ⊛ Snorkel Spots

The Baths, Virgin Gorda; go in the morning; visibility sometimes murky

The Dogs; sea turtles

Long Bay, Mosquito Island; Cousteau's students used to come here; tricky access

The Indians, Norman Island; lots of fish; nice wall

The Bight, Norman Island; good snorkeling in the middle by the shore

Sandy Spit, off Jost Van Dyke; nudie snorkeling

White Bay, Jost Van Dyke; excellent Elkhorn coral

White Bay, Guana Island; lovely reefs at the south end

Brewer's Bay, Tortola; several reefs in harbor

Smuggler's Cove, Tortola; calm snorkeling on the reef 100 feet offshore

Loblolly Bay, Anegada; the island is a huge reef and is great for lobster

---

than a comparable crewed boat. Before confirming the exact week you wish to charter a room, check with the outfit personally to find out what type of guests will be sharing the boat. One such operator is below.

Endless Summer II, Box 823, Road Town, Tortola, BVI. ✆ 800-479-7904 or 284-494-3656, ✉ 284-494-4731, 🖥 www.endlesssummer.com, info@endlesssummer.com

This outfit operates a 72-foot ketch with four double cabins for six-night trips in the BVI, priced $4,500 per couple, all-inclusive. Certain themed weeks include clothes-optional charters.

Sailing the BVI

The British Virgin Islands are the best suited region for sailing in the Caribbean. The archipelago's well-protected waters, abundance of sheltered harbors, and short distances between islands will show off sailing's best side. You will also find a surprising number of seasoned sailors who relish the relative calm of the waters and the immense variety of sailboat options available. Unfortunately, the near-perfect conditions contribute to a less-than-perfect overpopularity. Crowded anchorages are the norm. Virgins they once were, but alas, the past three decades have taken their toll on them.

Even for well-versed old salts, these islands are among the favorite sailing waters in the world. The **Sir Francis Drake Channel** that cuts through the Virgins creates a sheltered passage 35 miles long by 10 miles wide — and still magnificent despite the explosion of cruising boats. Typically, charters begin in either St. Thomas (the USVI are just a few miles west of the BVI) or

Tortola, the major gateways, and both are within easy distance of the choice spots to visit. Plan to arrive on the island at least one day before your charter begins — this will be a godsend in the event of flight delays and will ensure some time to provision your boat.

If you are starting out from St. Thomas in the U.S. Virgins, the name of the game is to get out as fast as you can. St. Thomas, especially the main port, **Charlotte Amalie**, is overcrowded with cruise-ship tourists on a bargain-shopping frenzy. The roads around town resemble Los Angeles at rush hour all day long, but especially in the late afternoon, when cruise-ship passengers are headed back to their behemoths and bumper-to-bumper traffic ensues. St. Thomas does have some redeeming qualities (see the USVI chapter for highlights), but where you're headed is much better.

Alas, **Tortola** used to be a ramshackle little hub for the BVI, but in the last decade development has proceeded unbridled, and mass tourism — especially cruise ships — has invaded. This is largely thanks to the island's all-powerful taxi drivers, who look to St. Thomas as a role model (you think we're joking, but we're not; taxi drivers are the most powerful lobby on the island, and if they want more cruise-ship tourists, then no politician will dare stand in their way). So cruise-ship visitors have grown dramatically, from about 200,000 in 2001 to almost 500,000 today. If you're starting out from Tortola, you'll probably at least pass through Road Town (also known as Hot Town because the mountains block cooling breezes); there are some places worth checking out before you leave. Right in the town is **Pusser's Rum Shop**. This savory-sounding rum is the "Official Drink of the British Royal Navy." Some people think it tastes like it sounds, but we think it's worth a shot. The shop has some great souvenirs with the Pusser's name on them, including mugs, hats, and a wristwatch that spells out Pusser's Rum in code flags. Nearby is **Sunny Caribbee**, which sells some terrific spices in tasteful gift packs that make great treats for friends back home. For provisioning, there is a well-stocked supermarket called **Bobby's Market** (284-494-2189, fax 284-494-1121; www.bobbysmarketplace.com). It has a gourmet section and a great selection of wines. It will deliver to your boat at no extra charge — in fact, you can shop by Internet before you arrive, and your provisions will be waiting for you when you board your boat. Another option is **Rite Way** (284-494-2263, fax 284-494-2222), which also stocks gourmet items and wine.

Otherwise, uncharismatic **Road Town** — which might be more aptly named Reclaimed Landville — is probably the least pretty corner of the BVI, made even less so by the daily infestation of massive cruise ships. Before you escape this overtaxed isle, for an incredible view of the channel and the islands you'll be sailing to, head up to **Skyworld**, which is a great spot for sunset cocktails. On the hair-raising ride up the mountain, observant passengers will notice a beautiful fungus growing in the cow patties along the roadside. This can be obtained from any Rasta on the beach in Cane Garden Bay or at Bomba's Shack. Once at the summit, sop up a soursop daiquiri, a Skyworld specialty (soursop is a local fruit that is kind of a cross between a mango and a pineapple). Assuming you're overnighting before your sail out, go for dinner at Brandywine Bay outside Road Town, probably the best restaurant on Tortola.

Once you've left the hustle-bustle of the major home ports, plan to sail windward (east, in this instance) as much as possible during the first day out. This will allow for leisurely exploration of the islands worth seeing, with the winds in your favor. Start with North Sound, Virgin Gorda, and work your way west through the southern string of islands and the fringes of Tortola and Jost Van Dyke. If you elect to head over to St. John, you will have to deal with U.S. Customs, and then again upon your return. In the BVI, this means it will take forever to wait in line and fill out forms. To minimize this inconvenience, stay in the BVI until you leave them for good. Besides, an advantage of the British Virgins is that there are moorings everywhere. These not only make your stops easier but also help to protect the reefs from anchor damage.

One of the nicest places on **Virgin Gorda** is the **North Sound**, a splendidly protected harbor near the northeast end of the island. The mountains surrounding the Sound are relatively pristine — **Gorda Peak** to the southwest is part of a national park, whereas the eastern wing of Virgin Gorda is uninhabited except for two resorts (Biras Creek and the Bitter End Yacht Club), which can be reached only by sea. There are also several small islands to the north. When you enter the Sound, there is a massive reef to the right that boats are always hitting. There are markers, so just be prudent and leave plenty of room to starboard (the right). That reef, called Colquhoun Reef, offers super snorkeling when sea conditions are calm. Most people head for a mooring ball at Bitter End. It really isn't a yacht club in the proper sense — rather, it's a popular resort with a busy marina and launch service. We prefer a mooring near **Biras Creek**, a pretty inlet with a posh resort sitting on an isthmus between the Atlantic and the Sound.

If you can, take a hike out to the real **Bitter End** along the trail, and be sure to bring your camera. It's a healthy hike, so wear appropriate footwear. There's also a good reef for snorkeling off Prickly Pear Island. On land, the Bitter End's Quarterdeck Bar has some high-octane cocktails and a very "You watch me, I'll watch you" crowd. **The Dining Room** is a standard stop, perhaps the most popular on Virgin Gorda. The Caribbean lobster is good here, and it's only slightly more than the *prix fixe* for dinner, so you might as well have it, especially if you're splitting the bill. There are free movies shown in the **Sand Palace** outdoor pavilion, and popcorn is served. In front of the main pavilion, there is a shark pen with a startlingly low fence around it (someone is eventually going to fall in or get thrown in) with real-enough-looking sharks lurking in the water. Two hundred yards offshore from the Bitter End is **Saba Rock**, an island just a few hundred feet wide with a bar, restaurant, and "resort." Although the resort's eight rooms are well done, this is just too small a private island for us to stay overnight. Still, it's a great place to get smashed and watch the sunset. Careful getting back into your dinghy — those drinks are strong.

Across the Sound is the privately owned **Mosquito Island**, a 125-acre outpost with a now-closed resort called Drake's Anchorage. This is really too bad; it used to be a romantic place for a Crusoe-like escape. You may also moor here to avoid the Bitter End hubbub. The island is worth exploring, with trails all over its hilly terrain. Wear sneakers and hike to the eastern end, just beyond the last cottages of the hotel. There are underwater caves on Rocky Beach for snorkeling. Over to the west is **Honeymoon Beach**, a cozy cove that is just right for two people (wink, wink). On the other end of the island is **Long Beach**, a great snorkeling location. Getting to the reef, however, can be rather tricky. Rumor has it that a mogul has purchased Mosquito, but we weren't able to nail down his exact plans — drop us a line and let us know if you pick up some scuttlebutt.

When leaving North Sound, get out the binoculars and check out the palace of Richard Branson (the founder of Virgin Records and Virgin Atlantic Airways) on 74-acre **Necker Island**. You, too, can stay here — rates to rent the island and its 14-bedroom villa (with a staff of 50) start at $32,500 per night. Call 800-557-4255 for more information, or check Mr. Branson's Web site: www.neckerisland.com.

The **Virgin Gorda Yacht Harbor**, in The Valley (a.k.a. Spanish Town) on the southern wing of Virgin Gorda, is a good port to call on if you want to disembark at will. It's a cramped but well-run and clean marina, and the **Bath & Turtle** is a good bar to hang out in and sip a cold beer. On Wednesday night you'll find a jump-up party with live music.

Early the next morning, stop for a swim and snorkel at the world-famous **Baths**, just south of The Valley. By land, an easy trail leads from the parking area down to a small patch of sand and to a stretch of gigantic boulders along the shore that create dozens of caves and caverns with cool, clear saltwater pools — The Baths. Because it's one of the BVI must-stops, an armada of boats descends to its shore and it gets really crowded here, particularly in the afternoon. So come early before lines develop along the trail (before 9 a.m. is best). A fun pathway leads through the boulders to Devil's Bay, a small idyllic cove, and just beyond are Atlantic-facing beaches that offer more privacy. In calm water, the snorkeling is fantastic around the boulders and can be accessed from the beaches on either side. If you're comfortable swimming in deep (20-foot) open water, the best thing to do is take the trail through the boulders one way and snorkel on the way back. Unfortunately, the surge (swells) usually prevents comfortable overnight anchoring near The Baths.

After Virgin Gorda, there's a fork in "the road." You can head over to **Marina Cay** (just off Tortola) with its well-protected but not overly scenic anchorage. By all means, avoid **Trellis Bay** and **The Last Resort**. Trellis Bay is noisy due to the Beef Island airport it borders, but there is **De Loose Mongoose**, a ramshackle bar and grill east of the dock, plus an Internet café. On the other hand, The Last Resort puts on a painful comedy routine that only your grandparents would appreciate. For a better plan, you can take the southern route through the Sir Francis Drake Channel. First, stop for another swim and explore **Fallen Jerusalem** — a rarely visited jumble of rocks named because it reminded someone of Jerusalem after the Roman sacking. There's a small private beach and lots of rocks to scramble over and under (not unlike The Baths). Continuing, you can really only sail past **Ginger Island** and wave; there is no suitable anchorage, and it has often served as a haven for drug runners. If the authorities see you've stopped there, chances are you'll be searched. Next stop, **Cooper Island**, has snorkeling, a dive shop, and good dining at the Cooper Island Beach Club. Moorings are available.

The next island west, **Salt Island**, has a protected spot on the south for throwing out the hook. About 200 people worked here gathering salt from the ponds in the 19th century. Until very recently, the island's last inhabitant sat on the beach and bartered bags of sea salt for anything you might have: a bottle of rum or, of course, cold hard cash. He passed away, but rumor has it that a wealthy investor has acquired Salt, so its future is difficult to predict. On the west side of the island is the site of the wreck of the **Royal Mail Steamship Rhone**, lost in the hurricane of 1867. The wreck — one of the Caribbean's most accessible (and beautifully encrusted with coral) — is best suited for exploration by scuba divers because it lies between depths of 20 and 85 feet. When there are divers (and there usually are), snorkelers will find that the air bubbles create shimmering columns that are almost as interesting to look at from the surface as the wreck itself.

The story of the *Rhone*'s demise is worth mentioning. In its day, the *Rhone* was a sleek, modern, speedy 310-foot steamship that carried passengers, cargo, and mail across the Atlantic for the British Empire. Apparently, while docked at Peter Island, Captain Frederick Woolly knew the weather was going to turn really bad, so he threw out both anchors and successfully rode out the first half of the tempest by running the engines at full throttle, sheltered from the sea by the island. The eye of the hurricane passed, and it became dead calm, so he decided to hightail it for open water, but the anchor snagged amid the coral and snapped the cable's wrought-iron links, leaving the ship adrift. The wind and seas roared in, slammed the *Rhone* onto the reef off Salt Island, demolished the boat, and took more than 125 lives — only 20 survived. One last piece of lore: This is the wreck that Jacqueline Bisset swam around in *that* T-shirt in the film *The Deep*.

Next down the chain is **Peter Island**, home of an impressively expensive resort and a jaw-dropping spa complex. There is a fine beach and a very good, if pricey, restaurant if you've been craving gourmet (you'll need nice clothes), plus a beach bar that serves excellent salads and sandwiches at less lofty prices.

From Peter Island, head directly west for the **Bight** off **Norman Island**. This is one of the finest protected harbors in the Virgins, and one of the prettiest, too. Although the family that owns Guana Island has purchased Norman and has plans for villas here, at the time of this writing there are no man-made structures on the island other than a small beach bar. There are some caves at the western entrance to the Bight, reputed to have held major treasure troves and provided Robert Louis Stevenson with the inspiration to write *Treasure Island*. We don't know about that, but you can pilot your dinghy right inside one of the caves — now that's inspiration. When you've had enough, go for a snorkel at the cave entrance or around the reef off the center shore in the Bight. Then hit the floating bar, the **Willie T**, for a Nelson's Blood (grapefruit juice, orange juice, cranberry juice, and Thornton's rum), named for the man who designed the U.S. Capitol building in 1792 (seriously!). The original William Thornton, a former Baltic Sea trader, went to sleep with the fishes a few years back (no one seems to be able to tell us how or why). The "new" William Thornton II serves simple sustenance but is best noted for the wild scene that starts to unfold by late afternoon. Patrons are encouraged — and plied with drinks — to launch their sunburned bodies from the bridge deck into the sea. The less clothing, the better, so things can get interesting (free T-shirt for divers in their birthday suit). The Willie T stays open "until the lights go out."

Now it's time for some sailing as you head across the Sir Francis Drake and around the West End of Tortola to **Jost Van Dyke**. The island is named after some quasi-legend of a Dutch pirate, although we think that Jost Van Dyke means "cheers" in Dutch. Jost is rather an unusual place, kept afloat almost solely by the yachting scene. There's no airport, and electricity and a single road arrived here only in the 1990s. There are just 272 people living on the island, yet there are close to 20 bars. Obviously, such a situation demands a fitting response — that is, time to do some serious drinking. Keep those islanders in business, that kind of thing.

Great Harbour is most notably the home of **Foxy's**. Now, this used to be the kind of dive you'd see in deepest Appalachia, with sand floors and a rainbow of local color — you had to be careful not to trip over the chickens. As the legend of owner Foxy Callwood has spread, however, the bar has become a sailor's mecca. Today the place is called **Tamarind Bar and Grill** (but everyone still calls it Foxy's). It has wood floors and a second story, seats well over 100, seems professionally managed, and has a slick-looking gift shop (with the name Tabootique, so how can you resist?). Yikes! Has Foxy gone uptown on us? Not quite — last time we visited, it was just before noon and Mr. Callwood already appeared — well, er... lubricated for the day's agenda, which is to entertain his far-flung following with some tunes on his guitar. He'll ask you your name and where you're from and, next thing you know, you'll be the focus of some ditty he dreams up on the spot. Now that's a neat bar trick! Foxy's also has a DJ who spins reggae, calypso, and dancehall. There are some well-worn hammocks on which to lounge and sway. The real attraction is the crowd and the **Painkiller Punch** — a rum, coconut, and pineapple concoction. Friday and Saturday nights feature barbecue and live music, and in addition to *Olde* Year's Eve (Foxy's name for December 31, when more than 4,000 people and hundreds of yachts descend on Jost), Foxy puts on a fine music festival in March, the **Wooden Boat Regatta** in May, and a "cat fight" party at Halloween; check 'em out at the Web site: www.foxysbar.com. To the west of the Customs House is **Club Paradise**, and down past the church is **Rudy's Rendezvous**, which is actually quite nice. Here you'll find jump-up to the reggae beat until 2 a.m., if you haven't already passed out. Both have dance floors with disco balls.

Over at **Little Harbour**, a healthy and very beautiful couple of miles along the high road, is **Sidney's Peace and Love**, a bar where you're on the honor system to make your own drinks and write down how many you've had (if you can remember). Like his neighbor Foxy, Sidney collects business cards; the walls are covered with them. Next door is **Harris' Place**, a cute little hangout with live music, gusto-guzzling ice cold beers, and lobstermania on Monday. Across the harbor is **Abe's**, more of the same with a tiny marina. Before leaving Jost, **White Bay** to the west offers a quiet, secluded spot with a gorgeous beach to help ease you out of your hangover (then again, there's another bar here at the **Sandcastle**, in case you're still wanting). The same goes for **Sandy Cay**, a 14-acre deserted island off Little Harbour that's owned by the Rockefellers. It has trails and plenty of privacy for nude sunbathing (if there are no other boats — alas, a real rarity these days). Just beyond is **Sandy Spit**, which is little more than a, well, spit of sand toothpicked into place by a couple of palm trees — but you'll find great snorkeling on the east side.

East of Jost Van Dyke is **Cane Garden Bay** on Tortola, with its picture-perfect palm-lined beach. Unfortunately, this is the scene of daily (or almost daily, in summer) cruise-ship passenger gridlock, so we don't recommend spending much time here during the day. In fact, on our last visit, we saw more sunblocked-lathered skin than actual sand, and the guys handling beach chair rentals seemed better suited for a series called *The Sopranos Go Caribbean*. The day-trippers head out before sundown, then another party mobilizes, especially around the **Rhymer** complex and **Quito's**, which feature excellent live music five nights a week. Both have happy-hour specials. Keep an eye out for Rastas selling "magic" mushrooms (read: the trippy kind) to help you laugh the night away.

The Sailing Trousseau

Although the emphasis for sailing is "less is more," there are a few items that the wise crew member will stow away in his or her duffel bag before leaving home. Generally, a bathing suit (at times optional) and a T-shirt are all you'll need. But there are a few other things you should think about packing. Periodically, sunny skies become mean, and ominous-looking clouds can drop a torrent of cool water on you after you've just lotioned up. For these occasions, and for when the seas are sizable and the going gets wet and rough, the items below will be much appreciated.

Foul-Weather Jacket

Even though the water temperature hovers around 80°F/27°C year-round, the combination of cool rain, constant spray, and gusty winds can be bone-chilling. Foul-weather gear—the lighter the weight, the better—keeps you dry, doubles as a windbreaker, and looks great in pictures. Some boats provide this, so ask ahead of time.

Waterproof Sunscreen

You'll be in and out of the water so much that this will save you a lot of effort. Don't use suntan oils—they get all over the boat, smudging and smearing everything in sight.

Transderm (Scopolamine)

This anti-seasickness medicine is a miracle of modern science. Worn like a small, circular band-aid behind your ear, it releases a drug through the skin that essentially dulls the nerve endings in the inner ear—the area that motion affects. It doesn't make you as drowsy as Dramamine and other oral medications, and it lasts for three days. Better living through chemistry.

Two Pairs of Boat Shoes

One pair of shoes will inevitable become wet, so if you like dry feet, bring an extra pair of shoes. A pair of Tevas, or something similar with nonslip soles, can get wet and still help you negotiate sharp rocks or splintery docks.

Music

Almost all of the crewed boats have decent sound systems (usually with CD players) but not a preferred selection of good party music. Some of the smaller bareboats don't even have a sound system. Dancing on the deck can be great fun, so a boom box, an iPod, a CD or an MP3 player with portable speakers will do the trick. Bring a copy of the *Jaws* soundtrack and play it loud while others are having a late-night skinny dip.

Camcorder

A DVD or video memory of your cruise will be treasured forever. The antics of a loved one struggling with the winch or helm will provide infinite pleasure.

Waterproof Tropical Reef Guide

This is a laminated card or small book attached to your suit that allows you to know what those pretty fish are called.

A Hat and/or Visor

Do we really need to mention this?

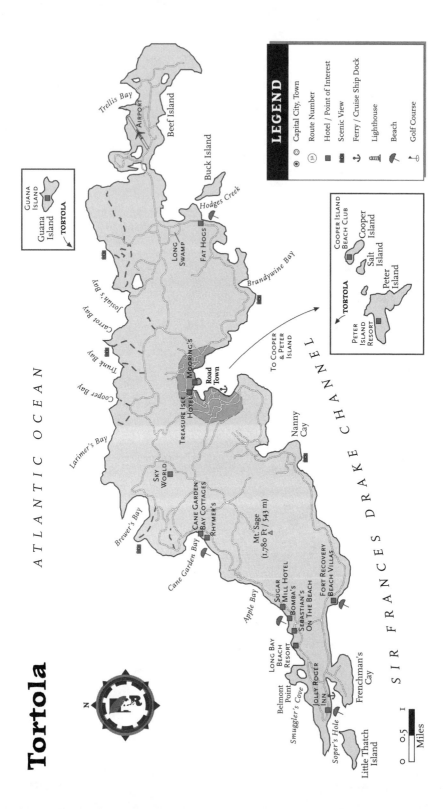

Tortola

ATLANTIC OCEAN

SIR FRANCES DRAKE CHANNEL

LEGEND

◎ Capital City, Town
⑬ Route Number
■ Hotel / Point of Interest
Scenic View
⚓ Ferry / Cruise Ship Dock
Lighthouse
Beach
Golf Course

Inset (top left):
GUANA ISLAND
Guana Island
TORTOLA

Inset (right):
Cooper Island Beach Club
Cooper Island
Salt Island
Peter Island
TORTOLA
Peter Island Resort

N
0 0.5 1
Miles

Trellis Bay
Airport
Beef Island
Buck Island
Hodges Creek
Long Swamp
Fat Hogs
Brandywine Bay
Josiah's Bay
Carrot Bay
Trunk Bay
Cooper Bay
Larimer's Bay
Brewer's Bay
Moorings
Treasure Isle Hotel
Road Town
To Cooper & Peter Island
Nanny Cay
Sky World
Cane Garden Bay Cottages
Rhymer's
Cane Garden Bay
Mt. Sage (1,780 Ft / 543 m)
Fort Recovery Beach Villas
Sugar Mill Hotel
Bomba's
Sebastian's On The Beach
Apple Bay
Long Bay Beach Resort
Belmont Point
Smuggler's Cove
Jolly Roger Inn
Frenchman's Cay
Soper's Hole
Little Thatch Island

Tortola

THE BIGGEST ISLAND IN THE BRITISH VIRGINS IS MOUNTAINOUS
Tortola. Situated imposingly over the Sir Francis Drake Channel like a
monarch presiding over her realm, Tortola is the commercial and political
hub of the BVI. Road Town, the BVI capital, is the only "city" in these islands
and the only port here capable of handling cruise ships. Unfortunately, the
government seems to believe the more ships, the better, with no concern for
island infrastructure (like toilets or roads) to accommodate the crush of visitors. The taxi drivers, however, are very happy about the daily cruise-ship
invasion. In fact, Road Town is starting to look more and more like Charlotte
Amalie in St. Thomas, although the ambiance is still a bit friendlier.

The advantage of this island is that there are a fair number of moderate
and inexpensive accommodations, allowing you to use Tortola as a base from
which to visit the other (more expensive) islands on day trips. The choice
accommodations are over the hills and mountains from Road Town on the
gorgeous beaches of the western shore. Driving around this island can be
rather hair-raising; the narrow, mountainous roads are loaded with twists,
turns, and hairpins. The vistas from these byways are stunning, however,
and there is life after sunset, too. The Full Moon Parties at Bomba's Shack
are legendary.

Where to Stay

Although a yacht is the best place from which to appreciate the BVI, if you
don't plan to tour by boat, there are plenty of options for you. Most accommodations are found right here on Tortola, where a decent variety of mid-
priced rooms is on offer (there aren't many cheap digs in the outer BVI).
Oddly enough, the best beaches are found on the north coast of the island,
whereas most hotel rooms are on the west and south coasts. The most interesting BVI accommodations are located on the other islands, often with
steep price tags, but note that Tortola is the hub for most activities.

Long Bay Beach Resort, Long Bay, Tortola, BVI. ✆ 800-943-4699 or
284-495-4252, ✆ 284-495-4677, 🖳 www.longbay.com,
reservations@longbay.com
🔹 **Wicked Pricey** 🍴 **EP** ⒸⒸ 152 rooms and villas

This resort is Tortola's premier establishment, and its best asset is its splendid location—it sits on a striking mile-long beach at the west end of the island, on a 52-acre estate secluded from most other distractions. Although the hotel has grown considerably since we first visited, it's still a good operation that caters to a wide range of interests. You'll find a variety of choices: hillside rooms, beachfront rooms, two- and three-bedroom villas, and best of all, slightly rustic cabanas built on stilts at the edge of the sand. These latter units have a full-length deck and private hammock—very romantic, though expensive. All have a/c, fridge and coffeemaker, modern tropical fabrics, and ocean views. There are two restaurants, two pools, tennis courts, and a good array of services (e.g., car rental, island tours).

Sugar Mill Hotel, P.O. Box 425, Road Town, Tortola, BVI. ✆ 800-462-8834 or 284-495-4355, ✉ 284-495-4696,
🖳 www.sugarmillhotel.com, sugmill@surfbvi.com

$ **Wicked Pricey** ⑪ **EP** **CC** 23 rooms

This sweet little spot is located in Carrot Bay, a seaside residential area on the north coast. The inn is made up of bungalows surrounding the ruins of an old plantation. Furnishings are low-key but comfortable, with a/c in most rooms and balconies offering sea views. Also available is a two-bedroom villa with a full kitchen. There's a small pool, and across the street from the hotel is a beach bar and a postage stamp of a beach (better ones are nearby). The restaurant here is one of the island's best, and the atmosphere on the terraces surrounding the bar is quite nice. It's closed in August and September; no children under 12 are allowed in high season.

Cane Garden Bay Cottages, Cane Garden Bay, Tortola, BVI. ✆ 284-495-9649, ✉ 284-495-3100, 🖳 www.canegardenbaycottages.com, info@virginislandsholiday.com

$ **Pricey** (three-night minimum) ⑪ **EP** **CC** 4 units

These cottages are situated in one of Tortola's most magical settings, a tranquil curl of bright white sand backed by steep hills. We'd avoid it in high season, when it's plagued by hundreds (if not thousands) of cruise-ship visitors daily, but if you like a busy, party-hearty scene, it might be your cup of tea. Otherwise, the duplex cottages (each sleeping two) are located about 100 feet from the beach, surrounded by gardens and coconut palms—each of the units has a small but full kitchen and a wide patio; a CD player, a/c, and ceiling fans round out the amenities. Water sports, six restaurants, and the lively Cane Garden bar scene are a short stroll away. Fortunately, these cottages are just far enough away from the bars that nighttime music noise shouldn't be too distracting.

The Cane Garden Bay cottages are represented by Purple Pineapple Villa Rentals, which also manages three dozen villa properties on Tortola — many of them quite a bit more expensive than this complex — plus another 50 on Virgin Gorda, Jost Van Dyke, and Anegada. If the villa vacation might be your style, call 866-867-8652 or 904-415-1231, or go to www.purplepineapple.com.

Treasure Isle Hotel, P.O. Box 68, Road Town, Tortola, BVI.
ℂ 800-233-1108 or 284-494-2501, ✆ 284-494-2507,
🖥 www.treasureislehotel.net

💲 **Pricey** 🍴 **EP** [CC] 40 rooms

If you're on Tortola only a night or two before heading out on a yacht (or to another island), this is the best option in Road Town. The 40 rooms, renovated in 2006, are found in several long two-story buildings that sit at the base of a hillside overlooking the marina. The décor is straightforward but agreeable, and there are three suites. A nice pool (with underwater portholes!), a restaurant, and lots of greenery round out the facilities. There's no beach, but the hotel provides a daily shuttle to the north coast coves, and it's a short walk into town for shopping and dining.

Fort Recovery Beach Villas, P.O. Box 239, Road Town, Tortola, BVI.
ℂ 800-367-8455 or 284-495-4354, ✆ 284-495-4036,
🖥 www.fortrecovery.com, ftrhotel@surfbvi.com

💲 **Very Pricey** 🍴 **CP** [CC] 30 rooms

This low-key inn has a casual ambiance that works nicely for undemanding types. The rooms surround the remains of a 17th-century Dutch fort and its surviving tower — all are found in one- and two-story villas. Most of the units make good use of pickled pine and have kitchenettes and balconies. You can also rent a four-bedroom villa that is stocked with contemporary art. There's a large pool and a very small beach, plus a dock where you can take yoga lessons in the morning. In 2005, it added rooms and a restaurant (for dinner only).

Sebastian's on the Beach, P.O. Box 441, Road Town, Tortola, BVI.
ℂ 800-336-4870 or 284-495-4212, ✆ 284-495-4466,
🖥 www.sebastiansbvi.com, info@sebastiansbvi.com

💲 **Not So Cheap** for the Tropical Yard units to **Very Pricey** for the beachfront rooms 🍴 **EP** [CC] 26 rooms

This is an appealing surferish hangout on Apple Bay with some lower-priced rooms that will get you within spitting distance of the sand. The furnishings are worn and dated in the Tropical Yard view rooms, which nevertheless represent a fair value on Tortola. The eight beachfront units are in better shape and have balconies and a/c, but they cost almost double—they're overpriced. There's a decent restaurant and bar that can get quite lively, and Bomba's Shack is almost next door. The beach is usually good, though often narrow when rough seas pummel the north coast.

Jolly Roger Inn, P.O. Box 21, West End, Tortola, BVI. ✆ 284-495-4559, ✆ 284-495-4184, ⌨ www.jollyrogerbvi.com, info@jollyrogerbvi.com

🟦 **Cheap** ($10 less for the shared bath units) ⑪ **EP** ⓒⓒ 6 rooms

This is the best cheap spot in the BVI, with a friendly atmosphere. The six rooms are simple and basic (and a bit dark), but clean and freshly painted. Two of the units share a bath (and are a few bucks less). The Jolly Roger has a well-liked restaurant, and a Hertz car rental is next door. The West End ferry dock (serving Road Town, Jost Van Dyke, St. Thomas, and St. John) is a short walk, whereas the nearest beach is about 2 miles away and is reached via a very scenic dirt road.

Where to Eat

$$$$$ **Brandywine Bay**, east of Road Town, 284-495-2301

Brandywine offers international, Florentine-influenced cuisine, a wonderful setting on a bluff, and Tortola's best, most romantic dining. Reservations are recommended; closed Sunday.

$$$ **Capriccio di Mare**, Road Town, 284-494-5369

A sister to Brandywine, this is the more casual (cheaper!) Italian spot in Road Town. It's not just pasta and pizza: you'll find tasty salads, pastries, and espresso in the morning, and be sure to try the mango Bellini for sunset. Reservations are recommended; closed Sunday.

$$ **C&F**, Road Town, 284-494-4941

Tucked just outside town (just past Riteway) is this distinctly local and usually busy place for barbecued chicken, fish, and pork, along with curried dishes. No reservations; dinner only.

$$$$$ **The Dove**, Road Town, 284-494-0313

Our new favorite in the BVI is a 2004 arrival located in an old house, hidden on the old part of Main Street. You'll find a nightly champagne happy hour under a mango tree, and fine French-Asian fusion cuisine inside the house. The wine list is excellent, up to and including a jeroboam of Opus One. Reservations are strongly recommended.

$$$$ **Eclipse**, Penn's Landing, East End, 284-495-1646

Eclipse has a lovely setting overlooking a marina. It has an eclectic menu with lots of seafood. Reservations are recommended.

$$$ **Fat Hog Bob's**, Hodge's Creek, 284-495-1010

Although the big-screen TV is tuned to whatever major sporting event is available, this place sees few tourists but lots of locals, and it is good for steaks, burgers, and (as might be expected from a place named "Fat Hog") large-portion barbecue dinners.

$$$ **Skyworld**, Ridge Road, 284-494-3567

The continental food here is spotty, but the view delivers whenever the clouds cooperate. The view goes great with the faboo soursop daiquiri. Reservations are recommended.

$$$ **Spaghetti Junction**, just east of Road Town, 284-494-4880

Although it's a little large and boisterous, replete with a "Bat Cave" for air-conditioned lunches, this place serves surprisingly decent Italian food at fair prices (with a West Indian menu, to boot). It's a popular spot with locals and visitors alike. Closed on Sunday.

$$$$ **Sugar Mill**, Apple Bay, 284-495-4355

The selections are few but flavorful at this atmospheric hotel restaurant that's situated in a restored mill. The service is graceful and efficient. Reservations are recommended.

Don't Miss

A drink at Skyworld

This is a great spot for sunset cocktails.

The R.M.S. Rhone

This is the Caribbean's most beautiful wreck dive.

The Indians

This is a wonderful snorkeling site near uninhabited (for now) Norman Island.

⊛ A Full Moon Party at Bomba's Shack

Located in Cappoon's Bay, this is Tortola's most famous reggae club and the site of the monthly Full Moon Party, an event that draws people from as far as Antigua. It starts at 6 p.m. and ends around 6 a.m. the next day. Purported "magic mushroom" tea is served around midnight from a big kettle on the fire. Our first time here, we each had five cups, with no change in perception, so we're not quite sure just how "magic" it is. Since that time, Bomba's has upped the price to $10 a cup, but you get to keep the plastic souvenir mug. Bomba has learned a thing or two about marketing over the years: He also charges $25 to take his photo. Call 284-495-4148 for more details.

Quito's Gazebo

This beautiful spot in Cane Garden Bay is the unexpected hub of nightlife for Tortola, with live entertainment and dancing spilling out onto the sand five nights a week. Call 284-495-4837 for the week's activities.

Virgin Gorda

VIRGIN GORDA ("FAT VIRGIN") WAS NAMED BY CHRISTOPHER
Columbus. From a distance, the island looked like a pregnant woman lying
on her back. Obviously, the long voyage must have clouded his judgment, as
a pregnant virgin is an oxymoron (unless, of course, he was thinking in the
realm of the Divine — although *fat* is not a word we would use in that context).

In the present, Virgin Gorda is known by sailors for its wonderfully protected North Sound and its famous Bitter End Yacht Club; for the marina pit
stop at which to replenish water, fuel, and liquor; and, of course, for the
striking boulders and beach configuration called The Baths. With a population of just 3,600, Virgin Gorda offers an away-from-it-all ambiance that
many visitors prefer. Only at The Baths will you find throngs of tourists and
beautiful and uncrowded beaches that lace much of the northwest shore.
Also tucked away on a fabulous bay is one of the Caribbean's finest resorts,
Little Dix Bay, built by the late Laurance Rockefeller as one of the original
RockResort playgrounds for the top-drawer crowd.

Ferries dock at The Valley, the island's hub (which is also referred to as
Spanish Town), and the North Sound Express from Beef Island makes stops
at Leverick Bay and Bitter End Yacht Club. The first ferry of the day into The
Valley usually unloads a batch of day-trippers who head straight to The
Baths. Our suggestion (if you're not staying for the night): Tour the rest of
Virgin Gorda first and come to The Baths as late in the afternoon as you can.

Where to Stay

There are three main areas of the island where visitors can stay: the North
Sound; the beautiful beaches and bays along the northwestern coast in the
middle of the island; and the area generally known as The Valley, which
leads down to The Baths. Note that several of the lodgings here and on the
other BVI include a meal plan in their rates (MAP = breakfast and dinner;
FAP = three meals daily; drinks are usually not included).

Little Dix Bay, P.O. Box 70, Virgin Gorda, BVI. ☎ 888-767-3966 or
284-495-5555, ✉ 284-495-5661, 🖳 www.littledixbay.com,
littledixbay@rosewoodhotels.com

Virgin Gorda

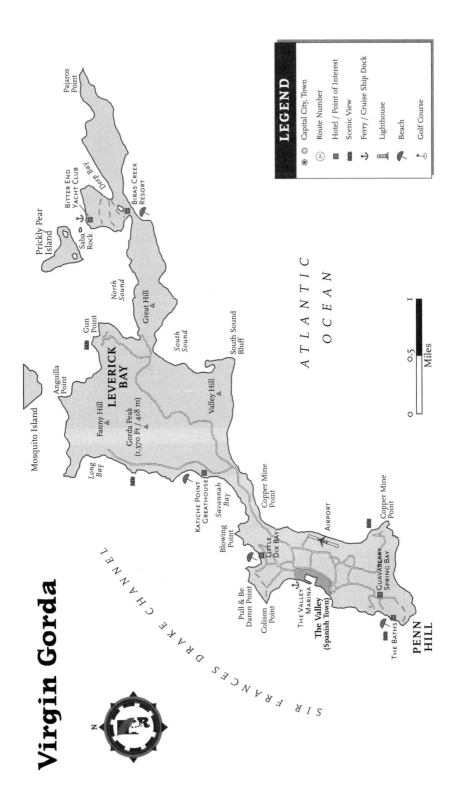

LEGEND

- Capital City, Town
- Route Number
- Hotel / Point of Interest
- Scenic View
- Ferry / Cruise Ship Dock
- Lighthouse
- Beach
- Golf Course

Pajaros Point

Deep Bay

Bitter End Yacht Club

Biras Creek Resort

Prickly Pear Island

Saba Rock

North Sound

Great Hill

South Sound

South Sound Bluff

Gun Point

Mosquito Island

Anguilla Point

LEVERICK BAY

Fanny Hill

Gorda Peak (1,370 Ft / 418 m)

Valley Hill

Long Bay

Katiche Point Greathouse

Savannah Bay

Copper Mine Point

Blowing Point

Little Dix Bay

Airport

Copper Mine Point

Pull & Be Damn Point

Colison Point

The Valley Marina

The Valley (Spanish Town)

Guavaberry Spring Bay

The Baths

PENN HILL

ATLANTIC OCEAN

SIR FRANCES DRAKE CHANNEL

N

0   0.5   1
Miles

💲 **Stratospheric** 🍴 **EP** CC 110 rooms and villas

This resort offers subtle elegance and high style similar to Caneel Bay, its larger sister property on St. John in the U.S. Virgins. Although it is nearly half a century old, the resort does not feel dated or out of fashion. This is largely due to the smart and down-to-earth architecture that Laurance Rockefeller used to create a true island retreat for the monied set — it's "roughing it" for the upper crust. There are several room styles, including wood-frame cottages on stilts, hexagonal hillside bungalows, or beach bungalows with fieldstone walls. All are beautifully decorated in tropical colors and tasteful prints, with wicker chairs, jalousie windows, refrigerators, and a/c.

There are two restaurants — one serving refined cuisine by candlelight. Water sports are extensive, and the half-mile-long beach is a great place to laze away; you'll also find tennis, a fitness center, a library, and a large children's activity center. The beautiful spa facility offers fabulous views of uninhabited islets. Guests also have the option of being whisked away by Boston Whaler water taxi to a hidden cove nearby (amazingly, there's no surcharge for this, and you can bring along a picnic basket, too). When on site, hang out at the new two-tiered pool that is wrapped with giant boulders (à la The Baths). It's all quite expensive, but a fine splurge for the romantically inclined — a Caribbean classic. Among the packages available is one that combines a stay at Caneel Bay, using a boat shuttle between the resorts.

Biras Creek Resort, P.O. Box 54, Virgin Gorda, BVI. 📞 800-223-1108 or 284-494-3555, 📠 284-494-3557, 🖥 www.biras.com, caribisles@aol.com

💲 **Stratospheric** 🍴 **FAP** CC 32 rooms

Now here's a special refuge for world-weary types. Biras Creek is located on a private 140-acre peninsula in the North Sound — the only way to reach it is via a five-minute boat ride from Gun Creek (or a 30-minute transfer from Tortola's Beef Island airport), so you know that seclusion is virtually guaranteed at this small resort. Duplex cottages house the rooms, each actually a suite with colorful décor and open-air showers, minibars, a/c, and large lanais. There are no locks or keys here, and it will take you all of about five minutes to get used to it. The hotel is surrounded by water, but the beach is a quarter mile or so down the path, so bikes are provided for tooling around (gourmet beach barbecues are scheduled several times a week). Dinners in the restaurant can be romantic, with views that encompass the North Sound below and the stars above. The food is outstanding.

Consider the hotel's unique Sailaway package: five nights in a room plus two nights aboard Biras's fully crewed 40-foot yacht, the unfortunately christened *Mary Irene* (her name sounds like a lobster boat to us). The cost is just a few dollars higher than the usual nightly rate, making this a great way to sample a top resort and the BVI sailing experience. Incidentally, Biras Creek is affiliated with the Relais & Chateaux organization, and it remains quite relaxed and informal. Closed September and October.

Bitter End Yacht Club, P.O. Box 46, Virgin Gorda, BVI. © 800-872-2392 or 284-494-2746, ✆ 284-494-4756, 🖳 www.beyc.com, binfo@beyc.com

$ **Stratospheric**; stays of seven nights or longer earn add-ons like snorkeling trips and dinner cruises. ⑪ **FAP** **CC** 95 rooms

This remote, full-service resort is also located on North Sound and is reached only by boat, but the atmosphere is more casual than at Little Dix or Biras Creek. The slap of sails and the clanging of rigging are a big part of the scene here, so for those who couldn't quite commit to a sailing vacation, read on. Bitter End has more than 100 watercraft —they are available to all guests of the hotel for unlimited use. If you're a yachting neophyte, Nick Trotter's Sailing 101 is also free for guests aboard a Rhodes 19 (more advanced lessons are available for an additional fee). Hobie cats, kayaks, and Boston Whalers are available to guests for tooling around the sound, and bigger boats are rented at fair prices. The rooms come in three different categories. Estate House Suites are bungalows located well up on the hillside and have a/c, fridge, and private verandas. There are also Beachfront and Hillside Villas connected by a series of boardwalks. These rooms have lots of beachcomber ambiance. Another option is to stay aboard a Freedom 30 live-aboard (docked at the yacht club).

We've had a couple of mediocre lunches here over the years, but dinner during our last visit was pretty satisfying. One drawback: The beach in front is mostly coral, although it's just a five- or ten-minute trip by water to Prickly Pear Island, which is quite sweet. For sailing buffs, this place is a tradition.

Guavaberry Spring Bay, P.O. Box 20, Virgin Gorda, BVI. © 284-495-5227, ✆ 284-495-5283, 🖳 www.guavaberryspringbay.com, gsbhomes@surfbvi.com

$ **Very Pricey** ⑪ **EP** 19 rooms

The southwest tip of Virgin Gorda has the island's main village, Spanish Town, and a few small hotels interspersed among private residences. Guavaberry is the best. Sprinkled between foliage and giant boulders (the same ones that form The Baths a short distance away), the hotel is a series of hexagonal cottages with one- and two-bedroom units. Each has a full kitchen and dining area, deck, and modern bath; each is perched on stilts to maximize the view and privacy. There's a commissary for rudimentary meals (frozen pizzas and chicken, beer, and wine), and the beach is a five-minute walk. It might be a bit rustic for some, but it's a bed, it's quiet, and the grounds are lovely. No credit cards are accepted.

Katiche Point Greathouse, Plum Bay Road, The Valley, Virgin Gorda, BVI. Ⓒ Germany: 49-761-55-62-004, or 284-495-5672, 🖂 284-495-5674, 🖳 www.katitchepoint.com

💲 **Stratospheric** (specifically, $2,190 a night for four suites, or $2,985 including master suite; seven-night minimum) Ⓨ **EP** (catering or a chef is available) ⒸⒸ 5 suites

Katiche Point is a stunning villa perched on an equally stunning point above the turquoise water of the Sir Francis Drake Channel. Also stunning is the price to stay here. However, Katiche Point could be the ticket for a splurge and is less of a bank-breaker for a group of eight to ten. The weekly rate is $15,330 in winter as a four-bedroom, or $20,895 with a fifth, master suite. Built as a second home by a German couple and designed by British architect Michael Helm, it has four suites in the great house and a master suite that can be used when all four equal-size suites are already full. The very tasteful décor is all *Architectural Digest* caliber and should please even the most jaded New Yorker. All suites have sumptuous baths and private lanais. The master suite has a bath with a koi pond terrace, an open-air shower, and a coral-stone soaking tub for two. There is daily maid service, and, with prior arrangement and an added fee, the maid will cook breakfasts and snacks.

The great house has a pyramid-shaped roof that is 34 feet high and is the social gathering spot of this place. Off the great house is a fabulous infinity pool, which mirrors the turquoise of the sea below. We couldn't think of anything better than a poolside chaise with a good book and a rum punch. Those who love the beach (that would be us) will be happy to know that Mango Bay is a five-minute walk down the hill. Katiche Point is affiliated with the Mango Bay Resort at the base of the point, which adds lots of options for services. Also at the base of the hill on the beach is Giorgio's Table, Virgin Gorda's only Italian restaurant.

Where to Eat

$$$$$ **Biras Creek**, Gun Creek, 284-494-3555

The international menu reveals superb dining, albeit at top dollar ($85 per person, last time we checked). The menu changes daily but finishes with a signature post-dessert plate of Stilton and port. The sea views and sunsets are wonderful. Biras maintains a formal ambiance — no jeans or T-shirts. Reservations are required.

$$$$ Bitter End Yacht Club, Gun Creek, 284-494-2745

Although our last lunch here was resolvedly middling, the weekly barbecue dinner that same night was a happy experience. This club is in a nice setting next to the water, and the yachty crowd often stays up late. Reservations are strongly suggested.

$$$$ Chez Bamboo, Spanish Town, 284-495-5752

This highly regarded and elegant restaurant serves French Creole cuisine with a New Orleans Creole rather than a Caribbean Creole slant. Reservations are recommended.

$$$$ Giorgio's Table, Mahoe Bay, The Valley, 284-495-5684

This is the only Italian restaurant on Virgin Gorda, and it's one of the better spots for Italian cuisine in all the islands. This covered lanai on the water is a great spot to dine on Giorgio's fresh fish and veal entrées, as well as on good pastas, risotto, and pizzas.

$$$ The Mine Shaft Café, Coppermine Road, 284-495-5260

With faboo views of Fallen Jerusalem, Ginger Island, and the distant isles of the Drake Channel, the Mine Shaft serves very good West Indian fare and is a nice alternative to the pricey resort restaurants. The chicken rôti is especially good. It offers a great barbecue buffet on Tuesday and an eggs benedict special on Sunday. Open for lunch and dinner.

$$$$$ The Pavilion, Little Dix Bay, 284-495-5555

This attracts a well-heeled crowd sans heels; dine and hobnob with the elite under Polynesian-style pavilions. The Mediterranean-accented menu features pastas and grilled items by and candlelight. Reservations are recommended.

$$ Thelma's Hideout, The Valley, 284-495-5646

Finally, a good West Indian restaurant and local hangout that serves as a nice contrast to the break-the-bank resort restaurants. Located on the access road to Little Dix Bay, the restaurant's décor is best described as local style, embellished by the fun locals who eat, hang out, and play darts here. Open for breakfast, lunch, and dinner. No credit cards.

$$ Top of the Baths, The Baths, 284-495-5497

This is an ideally situated lunch spot above the famous Baths (it's also open for breakfast and dinner), with a menu leaning to West Indian specialties. There's a pool, a great view, and a well-stocked bar — what more could one ask for?

Don't Miss

A drink at The Bath & Turtle

This is a great place to enjoy Happy Hour.

The Baths

One of the region's most unusual swimming locales, located at the western tip of Virgin Gorda. Come early in the morning or late in the afternoon to avoid the crowds.

Anegada

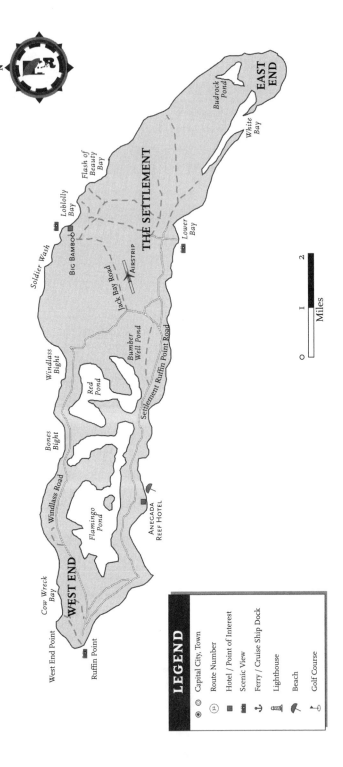

ATLANTIC
OCEAN

West End Point

Cow Wreck Bay

Ruffin Point

WEST END

Windlass Road

Flamingo Pond

Bones Bight

Red Pond

Windlass Bight

ANEGADA REEF HOTEL

Bumber Well Pond

Settlement Ruffin Point Road

Soldier Wash

BIG BAMBOO

Loblolly Bay

Jack Bay Road

AIRSTRIP

THE SETTLEMENT

Flash of Beauty Bay

Lower Bay

White Bay

Budrock Pond

EAST END

N

0   1   2
Miles

LEGEND

- Capital City, Town
- Route Number
- Hotel / Point of Interest
- Scenic View
- Ferry / Cruise Ship Dock
- Lighthouse
- Beach
- Golf Course

Other BVI

Where to Stay

There are some terrific away-from-it-all places to stay just beyond Tortola and Virgin Gorda. Some are privately owned islands with a single resort, but on Anegada and Jost Van Dyke you'll find small properties integrated into the simple lifestyle. Only Anegada is reached by plane; the others are served by ferry (see Getting There, in the BVI introduction).

Sandcastle, Jost Van Dyke, BVI. 🕾 284-495-9888, 📠 284-495-9999, 🖳 www.sandcastle-bvi.com, relax@sandcastle-bvi.com

💲 **Very Pricey** 🍴 **EP** (**MAP** also available) 🆑 6 rooms

You know you're heading someplace away from it all when electricity arrived there only in 1996. Sandcastle is on the *un*populated end of the *under*populated Jost Van Dyke, at beautiful White Bay, which is reached by a 20-minute walk from Great Harbour. There are just six rooms here—they are quite simple and rustic, but with sun-heated showers and electricity (most of the time). The newer rooms have a/c. You won't spend many waking hours in your room, though, as the hammock-laced beach delivers perfect relaxation. A small, informal restaurant serves meals to guests and the yachties who drop anchor—the aptly named Soggy Dollar Bar offers Painkillers throughout the day (the drink was invented here, they say). Otherwise, you can check in here with little more than a bathing suit and a change of clothes—it's a real barefoot holiday. A ferry serves Jost Van Dyke several times daily from West End, Tortola.

White Bay Campground, Jost Van Dyke, BVI. 🕾 284-495-9358

💲 **Cheap** for cabins, **Dirt Cheap** for tents 🍴 **EP** 15 cabins and 15 tents

Looking for a cheap seat on a fabulous beach? You need look no farther than this campground, situated on brilliant White Bay. Ivan and his daughter Darlene are the owner and manager, respectively, of this seriously laid-back spot, popular with students, Californians, and other free spirits. There are 15 very basic wood cabins, each with a fan and a light but without running water. There's a sun shower (that's a solar-heated plastic bag), located just outside each room, and shared bathroom facilities. You can also opt for one of 15 tents, which run just

Jost Van Dyke

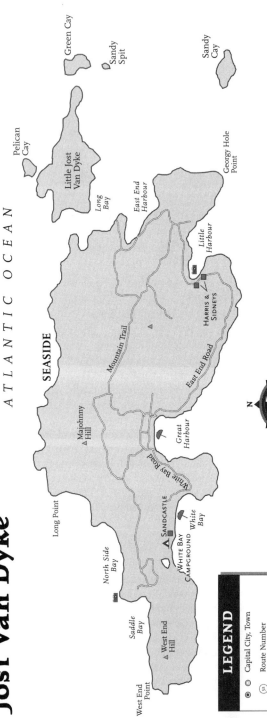

ATLANTIC OCEAN

Green Cay

Sandy Spit

Sandy Cay

Pelican Cay

Little Jost Van Dyke

Long Bay

East End Harbour

Georgy Hole Point

Little Harbour

SEASIDE

Mountain Trail

East End Road

HARRIS & SIDNEYS

Majohnny Hill

Great Harbour

White Bay Road

Long Point

SANDCASTLE

White Bay

White Bay Campground

North Side Bay

Saddle Bay

West End Hill

West End Point

SIR FRANCES DRAKE CHANNEL

N

LEGEND

- ◉ Capital City, Town
- ㉑ Route Number
- ■ Hotel / Point of Interest
- ⊿ Scenic View
- ⚓ Ferry / Cruise Ship Dock
- 🏛 Lighthouse
- ⛱ Beach
- ⛳ Golf Course

0   0.5   1
Miles

$40 a night in winter (or pitch your own for even less). There's a mix-your-own honor bar, and a Thursday night barbecue with live music; otherwise you'll need to traipse into Great Harbour for meals, about 15 minutes away on foot. This spot is not for everyone, but we love the informality of this friendly hideout (and the price is right).

Anegada Reef Hotel, Anegada, BVI. ☎ 284-495-8002, 🖂 284-495-9362, 🖳 www.anegadareef.com, info@anegadareef.com

💲 **Very Pricey** 🍴 **FAP** (an **EP** rate is also available) CC 20 rooms

Renowned for its lobster and the most remote island of the BVI, Anegada is a low-lying coral backwater with phenomenal, undeveloped beaches and a population approaching 300 — it's the most "virgin" spot remaining in the BVI. It has a pleasant and isolated feel, but this hotel delivers a dose of civility. It's not particularly attractive — a motel-like structure with little vegetation — but it offers a real change of pace from most of the Caribbean (it feels more like the out islands of the Bahamas). The rooms are tasteful and comfortable — some have ocean views, and a/c was recently added to all. The hotel has a small selection of low-key activities: bicycling, kayaking, snorkeling. The beach in front is not great, but superb beaches are a few miles away. Rates include three meals daily — there's a small surcharge for lobster, but none for picnic lunches packed for your beach explorations. Access to Anegada is via plane from Tortola.

Peter Island Resort, P.O. Box 211, Road Town, Tortola, BVI. ☎ 800-346-4451 or 284-495-2000, 🖂 284-495-2500, 🖳 www.peterisland.com, reservations@peterisland.com

💲 **Stratospheric** 🍴 **FAP** CC 54 rooms

Located 4 miles south of Tortola, this 1,800-acre island is home to a deluxe resort and nothing else. There are no parking lots, TVs, casinos, discos, or malls to remind you of home. The resort has undergone various refurbishments in recent years that brought the décor up-to-date and redesigned some of the common areas with an avocado and teak color scheme. It's physically more appealing now. The rooms are lush and seductive and range from beachfront junior suites, with large balconies and lots of amenities like minibar, CD player, and walk-in closets, to ocean- and garden-view rooms (the former have cathedral ceilings, the latter are larger in size). All are quite handsome, and service (from a staff of 175) is excellent and personalized. There are five beaches, one of which, Deadman's Bay, is among the BVI's finest. You'll find plenty of activities: Hobie cats and Sunfish, kayaks, bicycles, tennis courts, and a fitness center. Diving and deep-sea fishing can be arranged at an additional cost, and a dramatic full-service spa facility — unexpectedly large for a resort of this size — was added in 2003. There are two restaurants — the one on

Deadman's Bay is a terrific, casual lunch spot, even if you're lodging on Tortola (reservations required). A ferry provides transfers to Road Town about 10 times daily.

Cooper Island Beach Club, P.O. Box 859, Road Town, Tortola, BVI.
ⓒ 800-542-4624 or 413-863-3162, ✎ 413-863-3662,
🖥 www.cooper-island.com, info@cooper-island.com

💲 **Pricey** 🍽 EP ⒸⒸ 12 rooms

Located between Peter Island and Virgin Gorda is this 1.5-mile-long outpost called Cooper Island. It's a popular sailing anchorage—many of the yachts heading down the Sir Frances Drake Channel stop here overnight, and the sailors have dinner at this small hotel. There are a dozen rooms, all found in small but likable duplex cottages. They have simple amenities like radio-cassette player, outdoor (private) showers, and ceiling fans rather than a/c, but they are cute and colorful. The beach is decent, and snorkeling is excellent—a dive shop is right on the property (the wreck of the *Rhone* is just 10 minutes away). Food at Cooper is good and reasonably priced (most entrees are under $20). Although most of the island is private property, there are only a dozen or so permanent residents. There are no other businesses here, so someone staying more than a couple days needs to be content with the sea, sun, and sand, and definitely a good book. The hotel arranges the 35-minute boat transfers from Tortola.

Guana Island, Guana Island, BVI. ⓒ 800-223-1108 or 284-494-2354,
✎ 914-967-8048, 🖥 www.guana.com, guana@cyburban.com

💲 **Stratospheric** 🍽 FAP ⒸⒸ 15 rooms

We've saved the best hideaway for last: Guana Island, a choice medium between rustic and upscale. The inn on this 850-acre island was originally built in the 1930s, and its 15 whitewashed, stone-walled rooms sit on a saddle several hundred feet above sea level. The furnishings are modest but attractive, and each room has a terrace—some utterly private—furnished with wicker rockers. Each room has its own view and personality. A great pick is the stand-alone cottage named Eleuthera, which has a sweeping view that exceeds 180 degrees. Other prime units are Dominica 4, with its totally private sun perch, and the intimate Barbados. Although solitude is cherished, a well-stocked honor bar is a gathering place at sunset. Meals are unfussy yet satisfying, but be advised that they are shared with other guests around group tables.

However, it's really the island that attracts the guests. Guana has a 1/3-mile-long beach that is as ravishing as they come, and others are tucked into hidden coves (the managers will "maroon" you on a deserted beach with a picnic, if you like). There are miles of trails, including one to the island's 806-foot summit, plus tennis, snorkeling, and kayaks. There are also 100 reclusive rock iguanas (an endangered species that was reintroduced here in 1984 with great success) and a flock of flamingos that putters around in a salt pond. A team of naturalists studies here annually and publishes a natural history guide. If you want lodgings immersed in the natural Caribbean rather than filtered through posh superfluities, Guana is a great place to relax in peaceful, glitz-free comfort.

Where to Eat

$$$$ ⊛ **Big Bamboo**, Loblolly Bay, Anegada, 284-495-2019
The name may bring back memories to some. Remember the rolling papers? The name of the restaurant bears no relation, but this is one of tiny Anegada's best dining choices. Lobster is plucked fresh from the ocean, barbecued, and served at a beach bar next to the sea grape trees. If you're nice, Mr. Bamboo will share some of his sea grape wine. The beach is simply amazing, and the premeal snorkeling ain't bad, either. Reservations are recommended.

$$$ **Cooper Island Beach Club**, Cooper Island, 284-494-3111
The menu is mostly grilled items with a West Indian accent, but there's a tasty ratatouille to satiate the mostly yachting crowd. Although Ted Kennedy signed the guest book, this is a decidedly informal landing. Reservations are a good idea when the moorings are full.

$$$$ **Cow Wreck Beach Bar**, Anegada, 284-495-9461
A ship loaded with cow bones (destined to be buttons) wrecked off this stunning spot in the early 1800s. The awkward name is the only quirk to a perfect beach experience. The menu more or less duplicates Big Bamboo's for a few bucks more — the grilled lobster is a must (but is $45 a pop). Reservations are recommended.

$$$ ⊛ **Foxy's Tamarind Bar**, Great Harbour, Jost Van Dyke, 284-495-9258
Foxy Callwood's legend precedes him around the world, but the little shack on the beach has grown into a full-fledged restaurant with decent food. It's worth a stop, especially if Foxy is on stage (usually only during the day). Friday and Saturday are beach barbecue nights. Reservations are recommended.

$$ **Harris' Place**, Little Harbour, Jost Van Dyke, 284-495-9302
Harris' Place serves a great barbecue with live music and lobster mania on Monday and tasty pig roasts on other nights. Reservations are recommended.

$$$ **Peter Island Resort**, Peter Island, 284-495-2000

Lunch at the fab **Deadman's Beach Bar and Grill** is surprisingly good and not too expensive—definitely worth a day trip on the resort's ferry from Road Town (don't miss the hefty chocolate chip cookies). Dinner at **Tradewinds ($$$$$)** is more formal, and usually engorged with honeymooners. Reservations are recommended.

$$$ **Saba Rock Resort**, off the Bitter End, Virgin Gorda, 284-495-7711

This rock outcrop is just a 10-minute swim from Bitter End. It was purchased in 1999 and now sports nine rooms. They're nicely decorated, but we can't imagine spending a holiday in something smaller than our own backyard, even if it is surrounded by the sea. We would, however, pop over for a drink—and the menu offers decent pub grub. For those who can't kick their Internet addiction, Saba Rock offers free Wi-Fi.

$$$ **Sidney's Peace and Love**, Little Harbour, Jost Van Dyke, 284-495-9271

How could you not like this place, with a name like Sidney's Peace and Love? A favorite among the yachty set, Sidney's serves up delicious barbecued ribs, lobster, and fresh local seafood, including conch. We love the honor bar, Sidney's business card décor, and the groovy souvy T-shirts and tote bags. Reservations are recommended.

$$ **Willie T**, The Bight, Norman Island, 284-494-0183

Perhaps the BVI's most unique restaurant, this 98-foot schooner is parked off an uninhabited isle. The West Indian cuisine is basic (conch fritters and rôti); the scene is not. A supply boat, the Wet Willie, will carry landlubbers, and it heads to the island from Nanny Cay around 5 p.m., returning "whenever" (call to confirm).

Don't Miss

✭ New Year's Eve on Jost Van Dyke

Radiating from the nucleus of Foxy's, this is one of the most fun and happy drunks you'll ever experience. Like Bomba's Full Moon Parties, this particular evening attracts people from all of the neighbor islands (ferries run all night). So there is a huge crowd, but everyone is polite, forgiving, and up. Of course, it doesn't hurt that the average income of the participants is probably in the six figures (it's the tony, yachty set). Great Harbour becomes a sea of mast and anchor lights—a once-a-year galaxy. Occasional celeb sightings add to the fun. Information: www.foxysbar.com.

Anegada

Because it's more remote, it's not served by ferry, and you can't even really see the damn thing from a distance, Anegada is the most easily overlooked island of the BVI — but don't miss it. The second largest island of the chain rises to no more than 28 feet above sea level, is surrounded by one of the world's largest coral reefs riddled with lobsters, and is lined (on its north coast) with gorgeous beaches. For now, there are just 300 or so residents, but on our last visit we could tell that this island is in the process of being discovered — the old vibe won't last long. If you're pressed for time, Anegada is an easy day trip from Tortola or St. Thomas; call Clair Aero (284-495-2271) for reservations and ask about hiring a guide or renting a car (it's a long, hot walk from the airport to anything of note).

A drink at —

The Willie T on Norman Island, Foxy's on Jost Van Dyke, and Saba Rock Resort in North Sound.

The Indians

This is a wonderful snorkeling site near uninhabited (for now) Norman Island. Most snorkel trips leave from Tortola, but other islands also offer tours to this site.

The Cayman Islands

TOURISTO SCALE:

GRAND CAYMAN 🎎🎎🎎🎎🎎🎎🎎🎎🎎🎎 (10)

LITTLE CAYMAN 🎎🎎🎎 (3)

CAYMAN BRAC 🎎🎎🎎 (3)

Our first visit to Erma Eldemire's Guest House said more about Grand Cayman than we ever could have expected. We had heard that Mrs. Eldemire provided the best low-cost lodging option on this unusually expensive isle. So at 9 a.m. one day, we roamed about the grounds of the informal inn, looking for someone to show us around and provide rates. Not a soul was stirring, including any guests. In back, we happened upon a young woman in curlers with a toothbrush in her mouth. Her smile said she didn't seem to mind our intrusion, so we asked to see a room when she had a free moment. She replied: "It doesn't work today. Getting ready for church."

The three Cayman Islands are home to a very religious people, as we were told repeatedly during our first visit some years ago. This explains why bars must close at midnight Saturday night and cannot reopen until 1 p.m. on Sunday. Until recently, cruise ships—a major industry here—weren't allowed to dock on Sunday, and live music was also a no-no. It also explains in part the fracas that developed in 1998, when the minister of tourism abruptly

Cayman Islands: Key Facts

Location	19°N by 81°W 480 miles/772 kilometers south of Miami 180 miles/290 kilometers northwest of Jamaica Cayman Brac is 89 miles/143 kilometers northeast of Grand Cayman. Little Cayman is 7 miles/11 kilometers west of the Brac.
Size	Grand Cayman: 76 square miles/197 square kilometers Cayman Brac: 14 square miles/36 square kilometers Little Cayman: 10 square miles/16 square kilometers
Highest point	144 feet/44 meters (the bluff on Cayman Brac) Grand Cayman and Little Cayman are almost totally flat.
Population	Grand Cayman: 37,000 Cayman Brac: 1,200 Little Cayman: 170
Language	English
Area code	345
Electricity	110 volts, 60 cycle (same as in U.S.)
Time	Eastern Standard Time (same as New York)
Currency	The Cayman Islands dollar, CI$ (CI$.83=US$1)
Driving	On the left; a valid U.S. or Canadian driver's license is okay with a local permit ($7.50, issued by car rental firms).
Documents	Passport or proof of nationality with photo ID and an ongoing or a return ticket
Departure tax	$12.50, usually added to the price of airline ticket at purchase
Beer to drink	Red Stripe
Rum to drink	Tortuga Gold
Music to hear	Gospel (which we do love)
Tourism info	800-346-3313 www.caymanislands.ky www.divecayman.ky

canceled a scheduled visit by a gay cruise ship. Since then, Cayman has been a pariah in the gay travel industry.

There's been another kind of trouble in paradise, however. For Caymanians, the term "9/11" carries a different resonance than it does for Americans. That was the date—in 2004—that monstrous Hurricane Ivan took aim at Grand Cayman. Storm surges and winds gusting at over 200 mph rendered more than half the island's homes uninhabitable, causing more than $3 billion in damage. All the piers, including those of neighboring Cayman Brac and Little

Cayman, were taken out by the storm, and tony yachts and dive boats — the heart of the islands' tourism industry — were strewn about Grand Cayman's flat landscape like a child's toys.

A year after the storm, Grand Cayman was well along on the path to recovery, and the sister islands appeared remarkably untarnished. Cayman's capital, George Town, bustles again with cruise ships and commerce, having resolidified its position as a major banking center. Seven Mile Beach has been tidied and gleams radiantly once more, and the stingrays are back in force at Stingray City and the adjacent Sandbar, feeding from the hands of giddy, squealing waders and divers. With the debut of a mammoth Ritz-Carlton Resort, Grand Cayman finally had its full, pre-Ivan complement of rooms and the island's first true five-star resort. In 2006, the Cayman government allowed a visit by 3,200 passengers aboard a gay cruise ship, a sign that — from the government's perspective, at least — the welcome mat is out for all.

The Cayman Islands are famous for two things: diving and offshore banking. The diving, particularly on Grand Cayman's east end and Little Cayman's Bloody Bay Wall, is among the Caribbean's finest, and you can also play with flocks of stingrays that create an unparalleled undersea animal encounter (see Focus below). What surprised us about the banking industry is that it's practically invisible to the average visitor. Stroll around George Town and you'll be hard-pressed to identify that this is the world's fifth largest financial center, holding more than $500 billion in assets.

Of course, the dirty little secret is that the primary reason the industry exists is to launder ill-gained money or for non-Caymanians to avoid taxes at home — or both. John Grisham's espionage thriller *The Firm* was a big hit as a novel and a Tom Cruise movie, but at the center of the story was the theme of illicit money flowing through the Caymans. Don't assume the book was some trumped-up exaggeration: In the months following Enron's stunning 2001 collapse, it was revealed that the company had 881 subsidiaries in offshore tax havens, conceived for the purpose of sheltering money from the tax man. A whopping 692 of Enron's subsidiaries were in the Cayman Islands. Now, Cayman isn't the Caribbean's only offshore tax haven, but it's the richest, thanks to America's arcane tax laws that allow big-name corporations and small-time drug dealers alike to shield income from the IRS. So, although Caymanians are "very religious," they seem comfortable turning a blind eye to the wicked methods used to land some of the billions hoarded here.

What is more noticeable to visitors from all walks of life is the cost of staying in the Caymans. Simply put, you will get more vacation for your greenback on virtually any other island in the Caribbean. This is due primarily to the fact that essentially nothing is produced locally other than bankbooks. Almost everything has to be shipped in (take a look at the Cayman environment and you'll notice that most of the ground is harsh coral stone that receives minimal rainfall). The importing ranges from all the food on your table to the labor that cleans your rooms and washes your dishes. Although some other arid islands face similar shipping expenses, the Cayman government tacks on an unusually exorbitant duty tax for even basic imports like food (20 percent of the original cost) and charges $750 and up for foreign work visas (the bulk of the tourist industry labor force is non-Caymanian) — all factors that contribute to an unusually high cost of living.

Nowhere is this more noticeable than with liquor prices. Walk down Seven Mile Beach and try to locate a tropical drink for less than $8. Want to mix your own drinks? Go into a liquor store and try to find a liter of rum for less than $28 (we couldn't). The same bottle costs about $15 in the United States, and no more than $9 at Cayman's airport duty-free shops (but only after you've checked in for your flight home). Don't think that buying the local beer or rum (the latter is actually bottled in Jamaica) will get you a break. When Stingray Brewery started bottling beer on the island and selling it for below import beer prices, the government slapped a hefty duty onto hops, the beer's principal ingredient. The enormous duty assigned to liquor is little more than a "sin tax," encouraged by the pious Cayman elders.

Where does all the money go? Simply put: the infrastructure. Five government ministers each earn a salary that approaches that of a U.S. president, and islanders are very proud of their high standard of living. The roads are in good shape, there's little unemployment, and the tiny outpost even has its own (heavily subsidized) airline.

Grand Cayman is a highly polished, mass-market vacation destination — too burnished for our taste, really, with about 1.8 million cruise-ship passengers annually. Along with the influx of tourists and workers comes traffic, which clogs the main roads in and out of the capital every morning and evening, and crime, which is on the rise. Because virtually all the accommodations are concentrated along Seven Mile Beach, visitors have to make a real effort to escape the tourist fray and find something authentically Caymanian. Seven Mile Beach — which is quite attractive, if heavily developed and only 5.5 miles in length — is the only major stretch of sand on the island. Grand Cayman has worked hard to develop a few attractions for non-divers, including the Botanical Garden, golf courses, shopping, and some small pricey museums. If you manage to escape the tourism hub, you'll find a local population that is quite friendly. That's why, for our money, the more interesting part of the Caymans lies just east, on Little Cayman and Cayman Brac, which are discussed in separate chapters.

The Briefest History

The Cayman Islands were spotted by Columbus in 1503 on his last voyage to the Americas. He named them Las Tortugas, after the abundant turtle population. At some point, they were renamed Las Caymanas, the Carib word for *crocodiles* (which lived here at one time), but they are thought to have remained uninhabited through the early 1600s, when they served as a supply stop for European sailing ships. When Jamaica was captured by Oliver Cromwell in 1655, the English took an interest in the nearby Caymans. In

1670, they were recognized as British in the Treaty of Madrid, and Cayman was governed from Kingston. England began settling Cayman with loggers, planters, and Cromwell's soldiers, along with a comparatively small number of slaves from Africa. The principal 18th-century exports were turtle meat, cotton, and ropes made from the local silver thatch palm — the difficult and dry terrain was not suitable for sugarcane. There were attempts to settle Little Cayman and the Brac in the late 1600s, but persistent pirate problems forced the settlers to abandon the sister islands — the Brac was not settled for good until 1833, when the Foster family set up shop. Caymanian men became sailors, a tradition that has continued for more than a century (many elders today have stories of their days in the merchant marines). The Cayman Islands remained a dependency of Jamaica until 1962. When Jamaica declared its independence from Great Britain, Cayman chose to become a British Crown Colony (which it remains today). In 1970, Cayman's population was 10,249, but after tourism started in earnest, the island's population mushroomed to more than 38,000 — more than half of whom are not Caymanian by birth.

Getting There

Grand Cayman is well connected to the United States by a variety of carriers. American Airlines flies in from Miami; Cayman Airways from Boston, Fort Lauderdale, Havana, Houston, Kingston, Miami (with continuing service to Cayman Brac several times a week), Montego Bay, and Tampa; Continental Airlines from Newark; Delta Airlines from Atlanta; Spirit Airlines from Fort Lauderdale; US Airways from Charlotte, North Carolina; and Northwest Airlines from Detroit and Minneapolis (winter only). Air Canada flies to Grand Cayman from Toronto; Air Jamaica from Kingston and Montego Bay; and British Airways from London-Heathrow and Nassau.

Cayman Brac is served daily by Cayman Airways. Cayman Express, a smaller plane service, serves both the Brac and Little Cayman four times daily.

Getting Around

Car rental starts at about $32 per day in the summer and $50 in the winter, and a variety of U.S. chains operate here: Avis (800-331-1212 or 345-949-2468, with the best rates found online at www.aviscayman.com), Budget (800-472-3325 or 345-949-5605), Dollar (800-800-3665 or 345-949-4790), and Thrifty (800-367-2277 or 345-949-6640). If you're staying at a centrally located hotel on Seven Mile Beach and want to save a few bucks, you can probably get away with renting for just a day or two for island sightseeing. Otherwise, taxis are expensive and fares add up quickly. There's a public bus service that operates every 15 minutes between George Town and West Bay (along Seven Mile Beach), with less frequent service out to Bodden Town, East End, and North Side; the main routes operate daily until 11 p.m., and Friday and Saturday until midnight. The fare is $2. It's also possible to rent a scooter; try Scooters and Wheels (345-949-0064).

Focus on Cayman: Diving

By far the best reason to visit Cayman is its world-famous diving. Diving was "discovered" here by Bob Soto in 1957, but it wasn't until the 1970s and the introduction of BCs and PADI training that the sport really took off. Today, no other Caribbean destination takes as many divers into the deep as Grand Cayman, which is surrounded on four sides by spectacular walls that drop to 6,000 feet or more. Yes, Grand Cayman is truly grand, but most locals will tell you that the best diving is found on Little Cayman, at **Bloody Bay Wall**, where the sea floor plunges from a 20-foot depth to thousands in one extraordinary steep drop. The Brac doesn't specialize in such high drama but has lovely, diverse reefs and an impressive wreck, a 330-foot Russian destroyer nicknamed the **Tibbetts**. More information about diving on the sister islands is described in their respective sections.

On Grand Cayman, the sites can be divided into roughly four areas. The **West Reef** parallels Seven Mile Beach, is the most accessible to hotels, and usually has the best visibility. It is also the most frequented, which explains why there are fewer fish. At each end of the West Reef (immediately south of George Town, and off Boatswain's Beach to the north) are excellent, less crowded sites, some of which can be reached as a shore dive. The huge, shallow **North Sound** is breeding ground (some of which is off-limits), but at low tide, the bay flushes out and the **North Wall** becomes attractive to bigger fish. Diving is more advanced here, and visibility can be reduced (due to the rich effluent), but this is where the hammerheads and manta rays hang out.

The rugged **East End** is considered Cayman's dive frontier — this is where you'll find the most pristine, least visited sites, with lots of exciting tunnels and caves. At **Jack McKinney's Canyons**, reef sharks are regular visitors. The only problem is that this wall is farthest from most dive shops (the West End is a one-hour drive), but there are three dive shops located on the East End. There is also the **South Side**, which has a barrier reef that kisses the surface and offers predominantly shallow dives and sometimes more demanding conditions. You'll also find a few interesting wrecks scattered around Grand Cayman (including the **Oro Verde**, which lies at a depth of 50 feet and is located in front of the Courtyard by Marriott), but sunken-ship fans are best advised to head to the Tibbetts. Snorkeling is found around the island, but particularly along the ironshore on either end of Seven Mile Beach.

Grand Cayman has one particularly unique site, **Stingray City**, sometimes called the world's greatest 12-foot dive. Let's just say that it is undoubtedly the single most visited dive locale in the Caribbean, and even the most jaded divers can be seduced by this open-water petting zoo. Stingray City is a sandbank in the North Sound that local fishermen used to clean their catch, much to the delight of the rays. In 1986, a pair of dive instructors discovered the scene, and today it is frequented by more than 100 southern Atlantic stingrays, who have become accustomed to human interaction (and hand feedings throughout the day). Despite the plethora of rays, it's not unusual to see them outnumbered by divers, who can pet, feed, and frolic with the animals. There are actually two sites: the one described above, and another just east called **Sandbar**, where the floor comes within a foot of the surface and is suitable for nondivers (increasingly, they are both called Stingray City). If you do tackle either site, be sure to do so on a day that cruise ships are not in port so that you'll be sharing the interaction with dozens, rather than hundreds, of others—Tuesday through Thursday is busiest, and morning is more crowded than afternoon. For snorkeling trips we like **Native Way Watersports** (345-916-5027; www.nativewaywatersports.com.), which limits groups to 25 and offers a two-and-a-half-hour tour with a secondary snorkeling stop at a site called Coral Gardens—the price is $35 including snorkel gear. It also offers a five-hour Rays, Reef, and Rum Point Tour, which includes a grilled lunch and beach visit for $60. Of the larger operators, try **Captain Marvin's**: 345-945-4590; www.captainmarvins.com.

If you want to dive on Grand Cayman, there are more than two dozen dive shops from which to choose. Unfortunately, one bit of fallout from Hurricane Ivan is that, in the contraction of tourism, a number of smaller operations were squeezed out—dive prices immediately shot up at the remaining shops. Inexpensive diving is no longer the silver lining to the otherwise high price of a Cayman vacation (a two-tank dive averages about $100, but package deals for multiple dives will bring the costs down). Note that most of the operators along Seven Mile Beach cater to cruise-ship (and other) visitors, so groups of about 40 at a time are not unusual.

A few of the Grand Cayman operators to check out include **DiveTech** (888-946-5656 or 345-946-5658; www.divetech.com) and **Sunset Divers** (800-854-4767 or 345-949-7111; www.sunsethouse.com), both based at well-liked dive lodges; **Red Sail Sports** (877-733-7245 or 345-945-5965; www.redsailcayman.com), which has locations at the major resorts; **Don Foster's Cayman Ltd.** (800-833-4837 or 345-945-5132; www.donfosters.com), which primarily handles cruise-ship passengers; and **Ocean Frontiers** (800-348-6096 or 345-947-7500; www.oceanfrontiers.com), which is out on Grand Cayman's East End and specializes in "shark awareness dives." This list is by no means comprehensive, and you are encouraged to research Cayman dive shops through the frequent coverage appearing in *Scuba Diving* and other dive publications.

Alternatively, there is an easy way to take in the best diving on all three islands—by using a live-aboard boat. The **Cayman Aggressor IV** (800-348-2628 or 985-385-2628, or check www.aggressor.com.) does seven-night trips out of George Town every Saturday. You spend each night on the boat and dive all day—a boon for dive enthusiasts. Weather permitting, the 18-passenger boat stays a couple days on Grand Cayman, three on Little Cayman, and one on the Brac at the wreck of the Tibbetts. The price starts at $2,095 per person and includes accommodations, all meals, drinks, and dives.

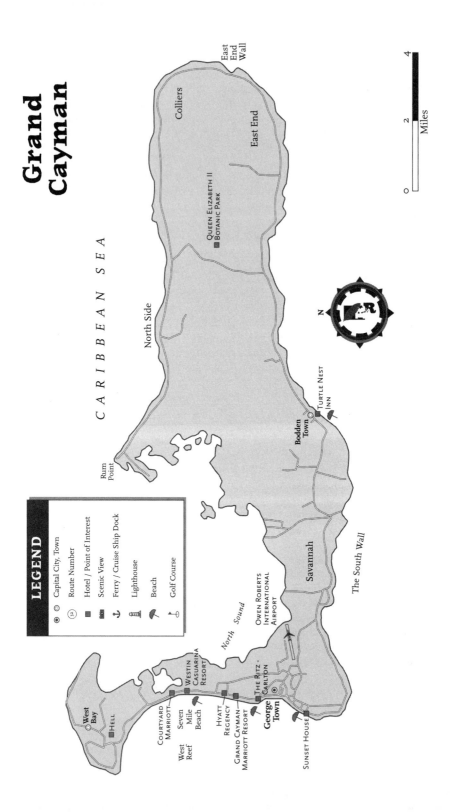

Grand Cayman

CARIBBEAN SEA

LEGEND

- ◉ Capital City, Town
- ⓐ Route Number
- ■ Hotel / Point of Interest
- ⚓ Scenic View
- ⚓ Ferry / Cruise Ship Dock
- 🗼 Lighthouse
- 🏖 Beach
- 🏌 Golf Course

North Side

Rum Point

Colliers

East End Wall

East End

Queen Elizabeth II Botanic Park

North Sound

Bodden Town

Turtle Nest Inn

Savannah

The South Wall

Owen Roberts International Airport

West Bay

Hell

Courtyard Marriott

West Reef

Seven Mile Beach

Westin Casuarina Resort

Hyatt Regency

Grand Cayman Marriott Resort

The Ritz-Carlton

George Town

Sunset House

N

0   2   4

Miles

Grand Cayman

UNLESS YOU'VE HAD YOUR HEAD UNDERWATER, YOU'VE probably read by now that it's all about the diving and the banking here in the Cayman Islands. And in terms of quantity (the quality ain't too shabby, either), Grand Cayman leads the way. As for banking, Grand Cayman boasts the greatest concentration of banks anywhere — at last count, more than 570 are found on the island to take care of all your offshore banking (or money laundering) needs. Yes indeed, that equals one bank for every 65 residents. Hmm... something's fishy here. Speaking of fish, like the banking industry, diving is a big business here, and every hotel has a dive shop or affiliate. Dive shops are popping up everywhere — no wonder some refer to Grand Cayman as the "McDonald's of dive destinations!" Call it Grand *McCayman* or whatever you want, but the diving here is spectacular, and once you're "below," you won't care about banking or McDonalds. (For specifics on Grand Cayman's diving, refer to the Focus section in the introduction.)

Where to Stay

Several big-name American hotel brands provide the top digs on the island (watch out for conventions), whereas a few smaller inns located away from Seven Mile Beach offer less expensive accommodations. If you are on a budget, we strongly suggest visiting in the off-season, and check out the summer promotion, which saves an additional 10 to 25 percent off hotels, restaurants, water sports, and more, with additional discounts for families with kids (check with the Department of Tourism for details).

Ritz-Carlton, Grand Cayman, P.O. Box 32348, Seven Mile Beach, Grand Cayman, BWI. (C) 800-241-3333 or 345-943-9000, 345-943-9001, www.ritzcarlton.com

🔹 **Stratospheric** 🍽 **EP** CC 365 rooms

Delayed by Hurricane Ivan's visit, the Ritz-Carlton finally opened in early 2006. The 144-acre facility sits along Seven Mile Beach and is dominated by an eight-story, bracket-shaped building the color of rinsed sand. Because the island is so flat, the structure can be seen from many miles away, a sight that displeases some islanders. They're not unhappy with the economic shot-in-the-arm that the Ritz-Carlton provides Cayman, however, especially given a crew of 750 employees. Directly overlooking the beach are the Residences — 69 individually owned condos with price tags running from $2.9 million to $40 million — and ocean-view hotel rooms lie just behind. These are of decent size, with the gilded Ritz-Carlton touches we expect from this brand; beach view rates start at a none-too-subtle $879 a night in winter. Actually, the bulk of the facility lies on the other side of the road, off the beach, with views facing water channels leading to the North Sound. Half the hotel rooms are located here, along with meeting spaces, a nine-hole Greg Norman–designed golf course, four restaurants — two of them by top New York chef Eric Ripert (of Le Bernardin) — and an extravagant, 20,000-square-foot La Prarie Spa (the first outside the United States).

The resort's children's program is noteworthy, helmed by Jean-Michel Cousteau of the Ocean Futures Society, who created a program designed to turn rich tykes into environmental ambassadors by immersing them in the natural Cayman environment. The resort also has a director of Culture, Environment, and Destination Services "to make sure guests have authentic Caymanian experiences," we're told — a position unique within the Ritz-Carlton company. We're not so sure this whopping facility provides the authentic Caribbean island experience we've grown to love, but we suspect that if we were invited to attend a convention here, we'd sign up in a jiffy and wallow in the authenticity of a Ritz-Carlton.

Westin Casuarina Resort Grand Cayman, P.O. Box 30620, Seven Mile Beach, Grand Cayman, BWI. ✆ 800-228-3000 or 345-945-3800, ✉ 345-949-5825, 🖳 www.westin.com

🛍 **Ridiculous** ⑪ **EP** ©© 343 rooms

For our money, the Westin is the best buy for an upscale resort on Grand Cayman. Built in 1995, the hotel sits to the north of most other beachfront properties, so the sand isn't as busy — in fact, the hotel's north side is bordered by the calm Governor's House (and the Gov likes to keep things subdued). The accommodations are positioned in a single, five-story building that surrounds an attractive tropical pool with a swim-up bar and Jacuzzis. Rooms are larger than most, with straightforward Westin furnishings; all have the same layout — the only price difference is based on view. As with all Westin properties, in 2006 the resort became 100 percent nonsmoking. There are three restaurants, including Casa Havana, serving *comida latina nueva*; the Sunday brunch is famous islandwide. There is a dive shop and tennis, and across the road is the 18-hole Links at Safehaven golf course.

A drawback: The resort's fitness room is small and under-equipped. Also, does the hotel really need a battleship-gray coat of paint? Otherwise, compared to most of the other resorts, you'll find larger rooms here, all of them just a few steps from the sand, an appealing pool area, and beachfront property that is easily twice as wide and less trafficked, too.

Hyatt Regency Grand Cayman, Seven Mile Beach, Grand Cayman, BWI.
  📞 800-55-HYATT or 345-949-1234, ✎ 345-949-8528,
  🖥 www.grandcayman.hyatt.com

💲 **Stratospheric** 🍽 **EP** Ⓒ⒞ 289 rooms

This property is in a state of flux as we go to press. Like the Ritz-Carlton, the original entrance to the Hyatt and the majority of its rooms are located on the inland side of the road running along Seven Mile Beach. Alas, Hurricane Ivan did a real number on these buildings, and Hyatt has not resolved outstanding issues with insurers; two years after the storm there was no date for the 236 rooms on this side of the hotel to reopen. That's okay, for in 1999 Hyatt expanded with a five-story, L-shaped wing on a narrow oceanfront lot across the street from the original hotel, right on Seven Mile Beach. The 53 suites here are very appealing (if quite expensive), with a concierge setup on the ground floor, deluxe appointments, a wet bar, a rich color scheme, and marble baths. The front units (which face north) have only a minuscule balcony; rear units (which face the beach to the west) are graced with a full balcony. You can also spring for the two-bedroom suites, which have balconies big enough to throw a party on them.

The Hyatt has one noteworthy problem: The hotel's frontage on the beach is surprisingly narrow, and cruise-ship passengers are frequently camped immediately next door. No quiet day at the beach here—if you want one, you'll need to spring $15 for the ferry ride to Rum Point, which Hyatt owns (although the ferry was not operational as we went to press). The resort has a well-appointed health club and two restaurants, one of which is a very popular sushi bar. We also like the Hyatt ministrations, like mimosas served on arrival and attentive service.

Turtle Nest Inn, P.O. Box 187BT, Bodden Town, Grand Cayman, BWI.
  📞 345-947-8665, ✎ 345-947-6379, 🖥 www.turtlenestinn.com,
  vacation@turtlenestinn.com

💲 **Not So Cheap** for the smaller room; **Pricey** for others 🍽 **EP** Ⓒ⒞
8 rooms

This Spanish-style charmer is located in Bodden Town, about 10 miles east of George Town. Though not close to most of the island's attractions (you'll want a rental car), this family-run inn is a good spot for those who want to experience the quiet side of Cayman, beyond the tourist sights. The tidy apartments have a full kitchen and an ocean view; each has a DVD player (a lending library is free to guests), and Wi-Fi is available throughout. There's also a lower priced, smaller, island-facing unit without a kitchen. The beach in front is rocky and not ideal for wading, but snorkeling is good and the pool is fine. The Canadian owners Marleine and Alain host West Indian dinners on Thursday evening for their guests ($34 per person).

Sunset House, P.O. Box 479, George Town, Grand Cayman, BWI. ✆ 800-854-4767 or 345-949-7111, ✉ 345-438-4220, ⌨ www.sunsethouse.com, sunsethouse@sunsethouse.com

💲 **Pricey** 🍴 **EP** Ⓒ️Ⓒ️ 59 rooms

Sunset House is the place to nest if you want a bargain Cayman dive package. This family-owned inn is set right on the water, in a residential area about a mile south of George Town. The rooms are straightforward and attractive and well designed; standard rooms are smallish, but the ocean-view category is quite a bit larger, with 15-foot ceilings and patio or balcony. All have digital cable TV, a dive-gear locker, and a queen-, a king-, or two queen-size beds. Be advised: Sunset House lies directly in the landing path for the Grand Cayman airport — but you'll be out diving during the day, when arrivals are most frequent. You can shore-dive from the rocks immediately in front, although there's no beach. A pool, *palapa*-topped bar, and restaurant overlooking the ironshore round out the amenities. Also on-site is Cathy Church's Underwater Photo Centre, which offers excellent photography classes, rents equipment, and has an E-6 lab for film processing (345-949-7415; www.cathychurch.com).

Grand Cayman Marriott Beach Resort, 389 West Bay Road, Seven Mile Beach, Grand Cayman, BWI. ✆ 800-228-9290 or 345-949-0088, ✉ 345- 949-0288, ⌨ www.marriott.com/gcmgc

💲 **Wicked Pricey** 🍴 **EP** Ⓒ️Ⓒ️ 307 rooms

Another big American chain hotel is located at the south end of Seven Mile Beach, 1 mile north of George Town. The beach here is narrower than in other places, but a beachside pool area helps to keep the crowding to a minimum. The 309-room, five-story resort benefits from a $15 million renovation completed in 2005 and features a big convention space on the second floor. The rooms are standard-issue Marriott and are priced based on view (which might be of a parking lot next door). All have high-speed wireless, balconies, and marble bathrooms.

Behind the oversize lobby is a plant-filled courtyard with a stream that flows toward the ocean. Overlooking the beach is the pool area, which is adequate, though nothing special. We're told the snorkeling just off the beach is actually pretty good. You'll find two restaurants, a small exercise room, a dive shop, concierge service, and an expanded spa.

Courtyard Hotel by Marriott, 590 West Bay Road, Seven Mile Beach,
 Grand Cayman, BWI. ℂ 800-228-9290 or 345-946-4433,
 ✎ 345-946-4434, 🖥 www.marriott.com/gcmcy

 💲 **Very Pricey** 🍴 **EP** CC 232 rooms

 This five-story chain hotel is short on personality, but it's the most affordable option on Seven Mile Beach. All the expected Marriott
 amenities are in place, and the rooms were upgraded post-Ivan with
 quality beds, minifridge, and oversize TV. All rooms are identical, but
 half face the beach and half face the pool and Governor's Harbour.
 There's free Wi-Fi in the lobby, and room service is available from
 morning until late in the evening. The hotel is actually situated across
 the street from Seven Mile, but there's a beach bar-restaurant and full
 water-sports facility.

Where to Eat

There are lots of good restaurants on Grand Cayman — alas, they're all *priced*
like excellent ones (note that almost all menus are in CI$). Here are the best
of the bunch, in all price ranges.

$ **Al La Kebab**, West Bay Road, 345-943-4343

 This is more of a takeout joint, but with outdoor seating, so you can
 come here for tasty gyro sandwiches, Greek salads, and more. It's located outside the island's two-screen cinema.

$$$ **Bamboo**, Seven Mile Beach, 345-949-1234

 Located at the Hyatt Regency, this is a swank sushi bar. It's a great
 place for a late meal and also for meeting the local expats (open un-
 til midnight or 1 a.m. daily). It has live jazz on Saturday; closed Sunday;
 no reservations are accepted.

$$$$$ **Casa Havana**, West Bay Road, 345-945-3800

 Awarded Four Diamonds by AAA, this is an unusually good hotel
 (Westin) restaurant, serving Latin fusion cuisine. The Sunday
 brunch is big, and it's $46 per person; otherwise it offers dinner only.
 Reservations are recommended.

$$ **Chicken! Chicken!**, West Bay Road, 345-945-2290

 Serving roast chicken (surprised?) and sides, this is fast food — but
 tasty. It's located at West Shore Center mall on Seven Mile Beach.
 Open for lunch and dinner.

$$ **Cimbocco**, West Bay Road, 345-94-PASTA (72782)

 Cimbocco is a colorful spot for Italian with a few island accents — we
 like the linguini with grilled shrimp and pesto, and we like not blowing
 the bank. Open daily for lunch and dinner.

$$$$ **Copper Falls Steakhouse**, West Bay Road (at Canal Point Road), 345-945-4755
A post-Ivan arrival, this steakhouse has an ambiance that's more Sedona than New York (or Cayman, for that matter), with Douglas fir, copper accents, and waterfalls filling the room. The steaks are fairly priced, especially because they come with sides and include one martini or well drink of your choice.

$$$ **Cracked Conch by the Sea**, West Bay Road, 345-945-5217
This is a local favorite, run by Suzy Soto (wife of Bob, who discovered Cayman diving). Island cooking, starring the titular treat, dominates the menu: conch prepared more than a dozen ways, turtle steaks, and pan-fried snapper. Old diving helmets and other artifacts make for a kitschy setting on the ironshore just north of Seven Mile Beach.

$$ **Eats**, West Bay Road, 345-945-1950
This diner is just across the street from Westin and is loved by locals for cheap breakfast; it's also fine for lunch and dinner.

$$$$ **Grand Old House**, South Church Street, 345-949-3333
A former plantation home in South Sound with a sweeping ocean view, the Grand Old House has excellent steak and seafood and live entertainment several nights a week. It's located about a mile south of George Town. Lunch is served Monday through Friday; dinner is served nightly.

$$ **Lone Star Bar & Grill**, West Bay Road, 345-945-5175
The menu offers little more than fajitas and burgers, and the sports bar setting (16 TVs, they brag) is less than posh — but it can be fun, and it's cheap. There are daily happy-hour specials on food and booze. It's situated across the street from the Hyatt Regency.

$$$$ **Mezza**, West Bay Road, 345-949-8511
Popular with local businesspeople looking to escape George Town when the unwashed hordes descend on cruise-ship days, the lunch menu leans to simple salads, wraps, and pastas. At dinner, you'll find delicious seafood, Moroccan spiced rack of lamb, and a lemon lobster gnocchi.

$$$$ **Pappagallo's**, West Bay, 345-949-1119
Northern Italian cooking meets thatched-roof Mexican Riviera ambiance. Pappagallo sits in a very romantic setting amid a 14-acre bird sanctuary and lagoon at the north end of North Sound. Reservations are advised.

$$$$ **Portofino Wreck View**, Gun Bay, 345-947-2700
Located out on the East End, this attractive spot looks out over the

Wreck of the Ten Sails and serves decent pastas, steak, and seafood Italian style. It's a good spot for lunch when you're exploring this end of the island; it's also open for dinner.

$ **Ye Olde English Bakery**, West Bay Road, 345-945-2420

Breakfast and lunch is served daily at this simple café, including sweet and savory pastries, salads, and sandwiches.

Don't Miss

Stingray City

This and its sister site Sandbar are major tourist attractions, but they afford a one-of-a-kind experience. Avoid this place (and the next two) on heavy cruise-ship days.

Queen Elizabeth II Botanic Park

This 65-acre garden opened in 1997 and is our favorite out-of-water experience on Grand Cayman, although it was roughed up during Hurricane Ivan. Within the park is a Caymanian garden with traditional crops and medicinal plants, a 2.5 acre color garden (arranged by colors of flower), and an iguana pen. The Woodland Trail is the best way to see the native habitat, including the striking local banana orchid (there's an annual orchid show around Valentine's Day). It's a must for the botanically inclined. For more info, call 345-947-9462.

Boatswain's Beach

Formerly known as the Turtle Farm, this site has been the island's most visited attraction for the sunburned masses for a number of years. It's the world's only green turtle farm — that is, a place the endangered turtles are raised from eggs to adults. Some are released into the wild, but most are butchered and sold to restaurants for soup and steaks. You'll learn lots of exotic factoids about turtles (such as that they mate for up to six days). In 2006 the entire facility was moved across the road, and a snorkeling lagoon and predator tank were added — a mini-SeaWorld for cruise visitors. It's located just past the north tip of Seven Mile Beach. For more info: 345-949-3894; www.boatswainsbeach.com.

Pedro St. James

This is Grand Cayman's big historic site. The Great House was constructed in 1780, and in 1831 it served as the meeting place for islanders when they formed the first democratically elected legislative assembly. As the birthplace of democracy in the Caymans, it means a lot to the locals, less to us. Still, it's a way of burning up an hour or so if you're curious about native history. Admission buys you a slick 20-minute multimedia presentation. For more info: 345-947-3329; www.pedrostjames.ky.

Black Pearl Skate & Surf Park

Grand Cayman has the largest outdoor concrete skate park in the world, designed by Mike McIntyre, who built champion Tony Hawk's private skate park. The 62,000 square feet of terrain includes concrete bowls, half and quarter pipes, and a 13-foot-high vert ramp, with courses ranging from beginner to advanced. Next door, there's a self-contained 11-foot wave flowing from a Waveloch Surf Machine. Lessons are available, and the adjacent shop rents and sells boards, wheels, and bearings — plus trendy skate- and surf-wear. Even if you don't skate, it's pretty entertaining to watch the local kids tackling the park, with peak crowds after 3 p.m., and if you're visiting the island with teens, this is a must. For more info: 345-947-4161; www.blackpearl.ky.

Hell

Stop here, and you can say you've been to Hell on earth. This odd tourist attraction is where the ironshore is particularly spiky and forbidding. Someone came up with the brilliant idea of naming it Hell and building a post office and gift shop. You can guess the rest.

Pure Art Gallery and Gifts

Debbie van der Bol is an American who has lived on Cayman since 1980. She set up this gift shop with an eye toward showcasing local crafts and art. As such, it's one of the better art galleries we've come across in the region. It's located on Church Street, a mile south of George Town.

Smith's Cove

Just past Pure Art is this tiny but pretty cove of sand. If you're lucky enough to arrive when few are here, it's as idyllic a spot as you'll find on Grand Cayman.

Rum Point

The Hyatt folks own this remote site overlooking Grand Cayman's North Sound. There is a fair beach, a restaurant and bar, and water sports. It's a long drive (more than an hour from Seven Mile Beach) since, unfortunately, you can no longer get there via Hyatt's ferry — it has not been operating the route across the Sound since Ivan.

Cayman Brac

KNOWN LOCALLY AS THE SISTER ISLANDS, CAYMAN BRAC (and Little Cayman, for that matter) are much more in keeping with what Rum & Reggae is about: away from it all, relaxing, and unique. Don't come to either of these outposts looking for McDonald's, nightlife, or organized tours. Do come if your idea of an afternoon's entertainment is lazing in a hammock with a book or stalking the rare Brac parrot or Little Cayman's iguana. Oh, and diving — these two islands have great diving and snorkeling, which is why virtually all the visitors are underwater enthusiasts.

Positioned 89 miles east of Grand Cayman and 7 miles east of Little Cayman, the Brac has a population of about 1,200. The number of residents is dwindling because there's essentially no economy here beyond dive tourism (which lies in the shadow of Little Cayman's), and the minimal number of visitors employs only a small percentage of the local workforce. So the Brac receives a good deal of government assistance — its jet airstrip and terminal are far grander than an island of this size needs (compare it with the miscellaneous rinky-dink, but adequate, airfields in the Grenadines). The twice-a-day service to the Brac via Cayman Airways jet is often nearly empty. Locals also get breaks on imported goods, which means that food costs are lower here than on Grand Cayman. It's an island in decline, but fortunately that fact doesn't make it less appealing. We think decline is actually good for the tourist scale.

The history of the Brac is tied largely to turtling — only three Brackers have licenses to hunt turtles today, but you will find it on local menus (we strongly object to any turtle items on any menus, because most sea turtles are endangered species). Many of the old-timers have an odd Scottish accent, and most are light-skinned. It's a curious culture that has developed on the Brac — they're tied to one of the Caribbean's richest communities, yet most Brackers are unemployed. On Sunday, the hamlet of Stake Bay feels like a ghost town. Most of the homes are found along the north shore and have carefully raked "lawns" of sand.

Though not as dramatic as Little Cayman's, the diving is quite good on the Brac, and fairly diverse. The star of the show is a world-class wreck: the 330-foot *356*, a Russian destroyer purchased from Cuba, renamed the *MV Captain Keith Tibbetts,* and sunk in 1996 as a dive site. It lies 600 or so feet from the coast and can be done as a shore dive. If you swim to the wreck from shore as we did, you'll never forget seeing this still-intact ship materialize from the inky blue depths — at first glance it looks as though it might have gone down yesterday. The bow of the ship lies in 100 feet of water; the stern sits 60 feet down. The radar mount rises to within 25 feet of the surface. Much of the wreck has been opened for interior exploration, and the marine life that has adopted the site includes eagle rays, a moray eel, and a 300-pound jewfish.

Elsewhere, the wall starts at about 50–60 feet, and tunnels and crevices are found at many of the Brac sites. Winter winds from the northwest can sometimes churn things up, but otherwise visibility is generally comparable to that found on the sister islands. The Brac dive shops make regular trips over to Little Cayman sites, so you can stay here and not miss out on Little Cayman's spectacle (the Brac is a cheaper base, but note that Brac dive shops charge extra for trips to Little Cayman). Snorkeling is easy from shore at several locations: The best are **Handcuff Reef** (in front of the police station on the north shore) and **Radar Reef** (at Stake Bay).

An outlandish project underway here is the underwater "Atlantis," conceived and built by an odd transplant named Foots. Foots told us that he had dreamed of creating an Atlantis since he was a boy, and the ruined city and its inhabitants are being molded and carved in cement, near-life size, and then positioned on a sandy floor just off Stake Bay, 50 feet below the surface. In position in 2006 were columns, a sundial, and figures resembling notable Caymanians; future phases will include a 16-foot-high pyramid with swim-through tunnels. You can check out Foots's progress at www.diveatlantis.com.

The Brac also has a day's worth of topside exploration to ponder. The word *brac* is Gaelic for "bluff," and this physical characteristic is a sort of spine to the cigar-shaped island, rising to a height of 144 feet on the eastern tip, where cliffs dive to the sea (some rock-climbing routes have even been put up here). Around the base of the cliff are numerous caves, most of them marked and accessible from the road; check out **Great Cave**, which has active stalactites and stalagmites. Bird lovers should definitely take the short hike at the center of the island through the 180-acre **Parrot Reserve**. There's a subspecies of the Cuban parrot in residence here, and it's fairly easy to spot in the early morning and late afternoon. You might see the local iguana (although Brackers have eaten most of them). There's a small museum in Stake Bay with photos and records of the island's history, plus artifacts like ship-building tools and cooking utensils.

Car or bike rental for at least part of your stay is a good idea. B&S Motor Ventures rents both and will meet you at the airport or at your hotel; cars are about $40 a day, slightly less in summer (345-948-1646; www.bandsmv.com). There's also Brac Rent-a-Car (345-948-1515) and CB Rent-a-Car (345-948-2424).

Where to Stay

There are just two resorts here — both of which have professional dive shops — and a smaller inn.

Brac Reef Beach Resort, P.O. Box 56, West End, Cayman Brac, BWI. ✆ 800-594-0843, 727-323-8727, or 345-948-1323, ✉ 345-948-1207, 💻 www.bracreef.com, brac@reefseas.com

💰 **Pricey** (including service charges and tax) 🍴 EP CC 40 rooms

This locally owned inn is probably the best option on the Brac. The rooms are found in a two-story, apartment-style building that sits well behind the nice beach. The building has wood floors and thin walls, so the sound of your neighbor's footsteps is unavoidable. There's a pleasant pool area with a Jacuzzi. The dive shop offers Nitrox and a full-service photo shop. Because the resort is a little smaller than its main competition, attention tends to be more personalized. The restaurant serves a cafeteria-style dinner nightly. Various dive packages are available.

Divi Tiara Beach Resort, P.O. Box 238, Cayman Brac, BWI. ✆ 800-661-3483, 305-451-1130, or 345-948-1553, ✉ 345-948-1316, 💻 www.divitiara.com

💰 **Pricey** 🍴 EP CC 71 rooms

This resort is the island's largest and is set just south of the airstrip on a fair beach. It is aggressively marketed in dive magazines and stays busy. Rooms are a bit bare-bones, given the "tiara" in the resort's name, but comfortable, with dive lockers outside each unit and a/c. Deluxe rooms are slightly larger, with TV and a balcony; there's also a luxury category, which adds a Jacuzzi bathtub. There's a pool, but with little greenery around the grounds. The hotel restaurant is overpriced for what looked pretty marginal to us. Divi has a fleet of five dive boats and a personable staff that assembles three or four different dives daily; there is also a complete photo-video shop on site offering same-day E-6 processing. Though still far from a luxury property, it was renovated in 2005. Meal and dive packages are also available.

Walton's Mango Manor, P.O. Box 56, Stake Bay, Cayman Brac, BWI. ✆ 345-948-0518, ✉ same, 💻 www.waltonsmangomanor.com

💰 **Cheap** for the bedrooms, **Pricey** for the villa 🍴 BP CC 6 units

Walt's is a sweet, five-room bed-and-breakfast, located near the middle of the north coast, away from the other hotels. The three-acre property is set a few hundred feet back from the shore (which is rough coral), in a 1930s-era sea captain's home. Each of the rooms has a/c and private bath. There's also a charming two-bedroom, two-bath villa, closer to the water. The B&B is named after the huge mango tree outside—in May, it is filled with local parrots that dine on the luscious fruit. Although you'll find excellent diving and snorkeling right in front, there's no dive operation, but Walt will hook you up with one of the shops if you like. In another Brac quirk, you'll find a beautiful little synagogue—the only one in the Caymans—tucked away behind the guesthouse. Designed by a Swiss architect, the intimate building was built by Walt for his wife for private use, but services are conducted on Friday evening, and all are welcome (call ahead to confirm).

Where to Eat

The Brac doesn't exactly have a hopping culinary scene. The two main resorts have adequate, if totally unspectacular, food, but they are overpriced (**Brac Reef** charges $31 for a mediocre buffet). There are several small diners that offer reasonably priced local food, including the **Tropical Delight** (345-948-1272); **Aunt Sha's Kitchen** (345-948-1581), found behind a Pepto pink bar named Coral Isle, just east of the airport on the south coast; and **La Esperanza** (345-948-0513), where you'll find excellent jerk on Wednesday, Friday, and Saturday.

Little Cayman

FROM THE AIR, LITTLE CAYMAN LOOKS LIKE LITTLE MORE than a 10-mile-long sandbar, but this topographical surface blip anchors what is probably the Caribbean's most spectacular wall. The formation starts at just 20–25 feet below the surface and plunges a pulse-quickening 1,200 feet, sometimes at a dead-vertical, or even inverse, angle. The 3-mile-long formation is actually divided into two areas: **Bloody Bay Wall**, the west side, is the sheer drop, and **Jackson Bay Wall** is more typical of the spur-and-groove structure found on Grand Cayman. Philippe Cousteau has called Little Cayman's wall one of the world's three finest dive locales. Who are we to argue?

Above the water, there's little else to see or do on Little Cayman, so the island is really geared to divers (and snorkelers). With a year-round population in the dozens, it's a pristine escape, particularly if you visit the east end of the island, where a beach — called **Point of Sand** — will indulge your best desert island fantasies. It's often devoid of people, but watch out for the painful stickers that lurk in the innocent-looking brush next to the sand. The native iguana is easy to locate — the one in "town" is tame enough to be fed bananas. Just don't speed down the road and drive over one (the fine is steep for assaulting this endangered species). The interior of the island is mostly a latte-colored soup of brackish water, some of which has been turned into a bird sanctuary — among the species present on the island are boobies, egrets, and frigate birds.

Getting around is limited to the bicycles conveniently provided by all the main hotels. You can also rent one of the couple dozen cars on the island through McLaughlin Rentals, but note that rates run $75 a day (345-948-1000).

Where to Stay

All of the lodging is found on the island's West End, near the airport and a pseudo-village named Blossom. All three of the following have their own dive operation, and all make regular trips to the Brac to dive the Tibbetts. There is no place that's remotely inexpensive to stay on Little Cayman, but nondivers will find slightly lower rates at all three of these spots. Note that all Little Cayman rates listed below are for double occupancy, but they are sold "per person" by the resorts.

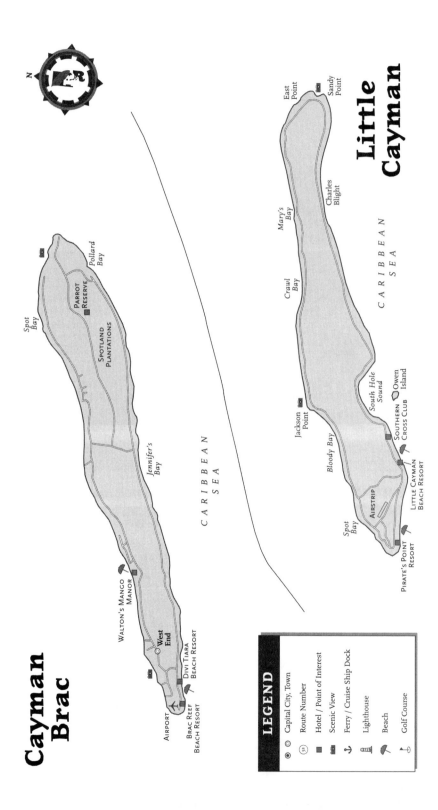

Cayman
Brac

Little
Cayman

Spot Bay

Pollard Bay

PARROT RESERVE

SPOTLAND PLANTATIONS

Jennifer's Bay

WALTON'S MANGO MANOR

West End

AIRPORT

BRAC REEF BEACH RESORT

DIVI TIARA BEACH RESORT

CARIBBEAN SEA

East Point

Sandy Point

Charles Blight

Mary's Bay

Crawl Bay

CARIBBEAN SEA

Jackson Point

South Hole Sound

Owen Island

SOUTHERN CROSS CLUB

Bloody Bay

LITTLE CAYMAN BEACH RESORT

AIRSTRIP

Spot Bay

PIRATE'S POINT RESORT

Pirate's Point Resort, P.O. Box 43LC, Little Cayman, Cayman Islands, BWI. ✆ 345-948-1010, 🖨 345-948-1011, 🖳 www.piratespointresort.com, piratept@candw.ky

💲 **Beyond Belief** including two daily boat dives 🍴 **FAP** including wine with dinner 🆑 10 rooms

Our favorite place to stay on Little Cayman is this very friendly, utterly unpretentious dive lodge run by an indefatigable Texan, Gladys Howard, a resident since 1986. Gladys is also a trained Cordon Bleu chef, so the meals are robust and satisfying, with a greater variety of tastes than is found at your typical backwoods outpost (we love being greeted with cookies when clambering off dive boats). The accommodations, in octagonal cottages, are nothing spectacular, but they're perfectly adequate for such an outpost: spacious, very clean, and well kept. Some have better sea views, others have a/c, but all are priced the same, and you can't be too fussy, anyway—this place stays full almost year-round. Phone and TV are limited to the lobby and bar area. In front is a pool and Jacuzzi, and the sandy ground is a beach of sorts (the water in front is rocky); huge sea grape trees dapple the property with shade. The resort has six dive instructors on staff (a high guest-to-instructor ratio), and the Bloody Bay Wall is just 2 miles from the resort dock. Probably the single biggest reason people return year after year is Gladys, who works tirelessly to make sure her guests are happy and well fed. Be sure to join her on the Sunday morning nature walk. It's closed from mid-September to early October.

Southern Cross Club, P.O. Box 44LC, Little Cayman, Cayman Islands, BWI. ✆ 800-899-2582, 619-563-0017, or 345-948-1099, 🖨 619-563-1665, 🖳 www.southerncrossclub.com, info@southerncrossclub.com

💲 **Stratospheric** including service charge, tax, and two daily boat dives 🍴 **FAP** 🆑 11 cottages

This is the oldest and most attractive of the resorts on the island, having been acquired and gradually upgraded since 1995, when Peter Hillenbrand took over the operation. Southern Cross started in 1959 as a private fishing club (the bonefishing in front is outstanding). It's fairly upscale but still has a relaxed quality that doesn't betray the backwater spirit of Little Cayman; the place gets by with an honor bar by day and tiki torches by night. There are 11 generously sized cottages overlooking the sea, all with a/c and muted pastels, but without TV and phone. The resort has a pool next to the lovely beach, and you can kayak over to deserted Owens Island, a few hundred feet offshore. The dive shop specializes in Nitrox diving and keeps boats to groups of no more than eight divers. Southern Cross is regularly ranked as one of the top dive resorts in the world by readers of *Scuba Diving* magazine.

Little Cayman Beach Resort, P.O. Box 51LC, Little Cayman, Cayman Islands, BWI. ℂ 800-327-3835, 727-323-8727, or 345-948-1033, ✉ 345-948-1040, 💻 www.littlecayman.com, bestdiving@reefseas.com

📦 **Beyond Belief** including service charge, tax, and three daily boat dives ⑪ **FAP**, but **MAP** and nondiver rates are also available ⒸⒸ 40 rooms

Owned by the same local family as Brac Reef, this 40-room resort is a polished and well-run operation, with slightly cheaper rates than the other inns. The two-story buildings offer two room categories. The standard room has a pool view, a/c, TV, and coffeemaker; it's pleasant but lacks much of any view; most face inward and don't offer much privacy. The oceanfront units add a microwave and wet bar with minifridge, and most have a balcony or patio; the décor in these units is very feminine. The resort has a spa and salon, a small gym, bikes, a tennis court, a pool, a Jacuzzi, a white-sand beach with yawning hammocks, and on-site E-6 photo processing and camera rental. The full-service dive center is well regarded, and there is a variety of water sports available, including kayaks and windsurfing equipment. MAP and nondiver rates are also available.

Where to Eat

There is only one place to dine and drink outside the inns: **Hungry Iguana** (345-948-0007). Located along the beach, this fun restaurant and bar serves simple American fare and some local dishes. Chomp down a burger and Red Stripe while you wait for the plane.

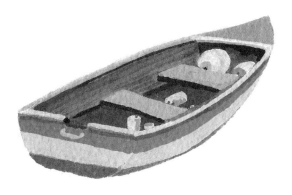

Cuba

TOURISTO SCALE:
👜👜👜👜👜 (5)

"Lucy, I'm home!" When we think of Cuba, we prefer the melodic accent of the endearing Ricky Ricardo to the Evil Santa–beard of the imposing Fidel Castro. To many of us, Cuba evokes a host of other thoughts: cigars, missiles, Che, communism, baseball, old American cars, salsa, merengue, the Buena Vista Social Club, little Elián, and, of course, Guantanamo Bay. Many others think of Cuba's economic and ideological isolation with a sigh, a deep breath, and slow exhale that inspires hope for a better future. Nevertheless, this time-locked land is a charismatic, quick-talking soothsayer that lures tourists by the droves with colorful culture and an illustrative past. Indeed, this country still harbors one of the richest cultures in the world. Despite the nightmares that many Cubans live and some tourists come home to tell, we will continue to visit Cuba because the Cuban charm outweighs any negative bump in the road that one might encounter while touring this wonderful island.

Time has not been friendly to Cuba. Over the years, the limitations imposed by a communist society and its heavy government taxes on private enterprise have begun to strain tourism. Hotels, restaurants, nightclubs, and service suffer from lapses in attention to detail in ways that one might find surprising. Five-star hotels will rent you a room with broken furniture or an empty refrigerator. Tuxedo-wearing waitstaff rarely smile and sometimes pretend to ignore their guests. Embroidered tablecloths are dirty, and antique

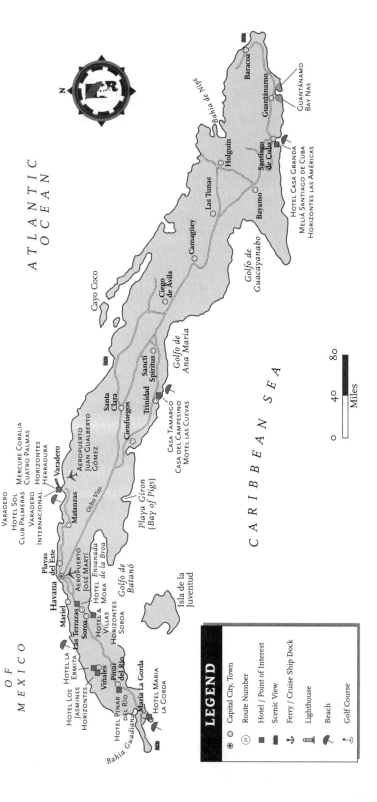

Cuba: Key Facts

Location	23°N by 82°W (Havana)
	90 miles south of Key West
	69 miles east of Haiti
	88 miles north of Jamaica
	132 miles west of the Yucatan Peninsula in Mexico
Size	About 66,666 square miles
	777 miles long by 119 miles at its widest point
Highest point	Pico Real del Turquino (6,573 feet)
Population	11,350,000
Language	Spanish
Time	Atlantic Standard Time (1 hour ahead of EST, same as EDT)
Area code	53 (the city code for Havana is 7)
Electricity	110 volts AC, 60 cycles (though not consistent in hotels); blackouts and brownouts are frequent.
Currency	Convertible peso and the Cuban peso. The convertible peso is 1 to 1 with the Euro and about 1 peso to US$1.12. An automatic surcharge of 10 percent is added to any dollar–convertible peso exchange. The Cuban peso is only for use by Cubans, although tourists are allowed to make purchases with it. No American bank–issued credit cards or traveler's checks are accepted anywhere. Canadian and European cards are OK.
Driving	On the right; for experienced and alert drivers only (risky night driving)
Documents	A tourist visa can be purchased for about $25 at the counter of airlines flying to Cuba. Please refer to Warning for U.S. Citizens (below).
Departure tax	U.S. $20
Beer to drink	Cristal or Bucanero
Rum to drink	Havana Club Anejo (5–7 years old)
Music to hear	Salsa, *reggaetón*, and bolero, of course
Tourism info	www.cuba.com; www.gocuba.ca (Canadian Web site)

silverware is missing tines and lacks shine. Although these are all minor details, when enough are strung together, it can make for a challenging trip.

Considering that tourism is Cuba's key to a brighter future, private enterprise on the entrepreneurial level inspired us to spend more time in the places that the Cuban government has a hard time controlling. Private houses called *casas particulares*, with restaurants called *paladares*, have experienced a small renaissance. Although these are a bit limited in Havana because of the pervasiveness of government control, we found that in tourist centers such as Trinidad, private families have made the necessary investment to welcome tourists into their homes with the level of service, food quality, and room comfort that you might expect from a four- or even five-star hotel. We encourage you to seek this alternative route, with caution, whenever the opportunity presents itself.

Tourism in Cuba offers two options. Most people join the ranks of the large swarm of tourists with sun-fried arms and legs and shoulder-slung cameras who choose multilingual tour guides. These are the beloved groups we call *packettes*. Others choose to go it alone, armed with as much Spanish as they can muster, a map, and some idea of where they want to go and stay and what they want to do. We definitely suggest that you choose the latter option. It can be more rewarding because you face and surmount the various challenges that Cuba presents to the unconventional traveler. You also have more opportunity to interact with Cubans — undoubtedly still the number one reason to visit Cuba.

It seems like light-years since Fidel Castro and Che Guevara rolled into Havana atop a tank in early 1959 to begin their revolution. The country's 30-year bout with Soviet-backed Marxist-Leninism ended in the early 1990s, leaving Cubans to ask themselves, "What now?" In the face of a collapsed economy, a huge part of the answer lies in tourism. Although most of those who come to savor the island's attractions these days arrive from Canada, Europe, and Latin America, there is little doubt that Cuba will again be a destination of choice for Americans visiting the Caribbean once relations between the two countries normalize. Americans will come as much for the country's beautiful beaches and the colonial and modern architecture as they will for its very special people.

Much has changed in the 17 years since our first visit to the island. As foreign journalists, on previous visits we were constantly accompanied by a government "facilitator." The sight of a gringo walking down the street attracted many inquisitive looks then. Soviet-style food rationing was the norm. Empty shelves lined supermarket aisles. If they were filled, it was mostly with endless rows of one product, like Bulgarian plum jam. When speaking with visitors, Cubans were nervous and paranoid lest someone report their "inappropriate contact" with foreigners. The streets were empty, and fashion was at least 20 years behind the times. Most young Cubans had also never seen a dollar. Visit Cuba today and you'll think you've landed in some poor capitalist tropical country. Fashion is still in the dark ages, but the food is marginally better, and many Cubans have seen a dollar. Whereas the possession of dollars a few years back was considered a criminal offense, today everyone is out to make a buck, only this time they're after *pesos convertibles*, not dollars or euros. For better or worse, the liberating power of the dollar has been unleashed and made more proximate by the new exchange program. What's more, Cubans are beginning to know what's out there, and what that dollar may buy them in an air-conditioned shopping mall in the United States, just 90 miles north. Government-subsidized food is still rationed and somewhat scarce for Cubans, and there isn't much in the way of merchandise in the pharmacies or peso stores (as opposed to the *peso convertible* stores, for tourists). Some of our *casa particular* hosts had not eaten meat for months. Milk was scarce. And you can forget about finding chicken breasts. We asked for chicken breasts all over the island, only to learn that there are none available. Where the hell did all the chicken breasts in Cuba go? Does Castro horde them?

The good news is that the people remain friendly, sensuous, and seductive, despite what seems to many foreigners like deplorable living conditions. The beaches are still as white and beautiful as ever, and Havana's colonial architecture, though quite decrepit, is still the richest in all the Caribbean.

Change is in the air, and Cuba is no longer the place it was even a few years ago. Some people claim, in whispers with shifty eyes, that Castro will be dead soon. Witness Havana's airport, with its new multimillion-dollar terminal, where gypsy cab rattletraps compete with spanking new taxis for your business. The cell phone company that caters to European, Canadian, and Latin American businessmen is open late and doing brisk business these days. Plush air-conditioned buses constantly pull up to the terminal's curb to ferry Canadian, German, Spanish, and French tourists to the most recently restored hotels in the districts of Old Havana, Vedado, and Miramar.

Although the number of tourists traveling to Cuba each year continues to rise (from nearly 1.4 million in 1998 to an expected 5 million in 2007), the purposes of their visits have changed. For one, Cuba's socialism is no longer an attraction for left-wing sympathizers. Cuba's "great socialist adventure" has been put on hold while pressing economic changes take its society in a more capitalist direction. Gone are the days when every Cuban had his or her job, food, vacation, medicine—even wedding gift and honeymoon sojourn—ensured by the state. Although the country's bankrupt economy has relied on joint ventures with other countries to expand its tourism industry, it has also forced individuals to find within themselves the strength and the wherewithal to survive in a world that increasingly resembles other less developed countries.

Yet, against all odds, Cubans have survived the changes. Small-scale entrepreneurs have changed the face of the economy. From the *paladares* to the *botero* ("gypsy") taxis and owners of *casas particulares*, Cubans are making money and learning the basics of capitalism. In addition to paying exorbitantly high taxes, the *paladares* are strictly regulated by the state and are officially not allowed to serve shrimp or lobster, because these items are reserved for state-run restaurants only. Despite this disadvantage, the food and service at the *paladares* are almost always superior to that of the state-run establishments —and at a fraction of the price!

Nevertheless, the freedom granted to the people by the state has also taken its toll on society. For one, there are the *jineteras* (female hustlers who are usually prostitutes) and *jineteros* (male hustlers who are sometimes prostitutes), the cornerstone of Cuba's "sexual tourism," the fastest-growing face of tourism on the island. *Jinetero* literally means a rider, as on horseback. If you are male, *jinetera* will be one of the first words you'll hear upon landing in Havana. It refers to the young women — often they are students, salaried workers, or professionals, like teachers or lawyers — who have sexual relations with foreigners for money or goods. For straight women and gay male tourists, *jineteros* are everywhere, too. In any other language they'd be "prostitutes." Like the Dominican Republic, Cuba has increasingly become a destination of choice for "sexual tourists." The Cuban government cracked down on this at the end of 1998, forcing many to retreat from the Malecón (Havana's waterfront) to more discreet locations. Please note that besides selling themselves, the *jineteros* will sell you a bottle of PPG — a "miraculous" sugarcane-based concoction that will supposedly reduce your cholesterol while working wonders on your libido (take that, Viagra!) — and a box of cigars. (Beware! Many of these cigars are fakes. Even if you pay full price, it's best to buy them at the cigar stores and in the upscale hotels). *Jineteros* will also sell their own sisters and are heavily involved in money scams.

In tourism, commission drives private enterprise around the world. Cuba is no exception, only here you will find that just about anyone will come up to you and start a conversation that usually begins with, "Whey u fron?"

Cubans are a very warm, charismatic people. Many of them speak English, Italian, German, or even some Chinese or Russian, so don't be surprised if you find yourself in conversation with a random Cuban who has approached you on the street.

Cubans are likely to offer you some type of guide service, tell you some history, or even suggest places to stay or things to do. If you decide to go along with them, know that any price they quote to you includes not only the price of the tour, hotel, or plate of food but also a 10 or 15 percent commission that they charge for their "services."

If you're approached on the street by a Cuban who begins to talk to you about making an exchange, be wary. Don't ever listen to or accept an exchange from anybody who offers you *pesos cubanos*. They are not the same as *pesos convertibles* — the true currency that you'll want to use. Although many Cubans are good-natured and will not seek to take advantage of unsuspecting tourists, there are a few who will take advantage of you. We have heard stories of tourists losing up to 1,000 euros (about $1,300) in slick exchange scams. Therefore, we advise that you exchange your currency in banks or hotels only.

With a population starved of American culture for the past four decades, Cuba will metamorphose overnight once the floodgates between the two countries open. Fast food, consumer consumption, billboards, neon, glass, and steel will replace Havana's grand but presently forlorn state. (A friend who is responsible for much of the restoration in Old Havana told us that parking areas are now being included in the urban renewal plans for the Old City, getting ready for the tide of cars that will roll off the ferries from Florida in the future.) For now, however, it's Cuba — catch it while you can.

Your point of entry for the country will most likely be Havana. A number of snapshots will become etched in your mind: the political billboards lining the roadways exhorting the people to stay the course; groups of Cubans crowded on corners or at major intersections looking for a ride; the dry staccato sound of dominoes smacking the Formica tables set up on the sidewalks in Old Havana; the "Detroit dinosaurs" rumbling by on a wing and a prayer and getting lost in a cloud of mauve-bluish exhaust; the silhouette of the city's skyline at sunset as you drive down the Malecón; the waves battering the low-slung wall along the Malecón during the stormy months of fall and winter; the *jineteras* lining Avenida 5ta or the Malecón after dark, waiting for a lift or a tourist who will take them out to dinner at La Cecilia or to dance at El Palacio de la Salsa; and the crumbling facades of the grand old buildings and villas in the districts of Vedado, Old Havana, and Miramar.

If you have the time, plan to travel around the country, because there's a lot to see outside the capital. For one thing, you'll get a glimpse of what Cuba used to be like before the country shifted to a more market-oriented economic system in the early 1990s. You'll find that most Cubans, other than the city dwellers, have had very little contact with Americans. Believe it or not, you'll also find that many people still believe in Marxism, Che Guevara, and Fidel.

There is also the dancing and the music. Whether it's salsa, merengue, conga, cha-cha-cha, *guaracha, guaguanco,* bolero, rumba, mambo, *sucu suco,* or *muerte-en-cuero,* Cubans love to dance and to listen to music, most often at a ridiculously loud volume. There is seldom any need for an excuse to join a fiesta in progress or to start dancing in the street if your favorite tune is playing on some stranger's stereo. Once, several years ago, while traveling around the island, we stopped in a small town to ask for directions at the only house that showed any sign of life in the oppressive noon heat. A Willy Chirinos's salsa tune was blaring inside the house, where two young women and a guy were dancing and drinking beer. Within 30 seconds we were dancing and drinking beer with our newfound friends.

A Not-So-Brief History (A Complicated Past)

In 1492, two weeks after landing in the New World (San Salvador in the Bahamas), Christopher Columbus "discovered" the coast of an island whose geography reminded him of Sicily. No doubt he thought he'd reached the elusive paradise of his quest. He christened the island Juana ("Jane"). Fortunately, this name did not stick, because the island had already been named Cuba (derived from the Taíno word *cubanacán,* which means "a central place") by the indigenous Taíno population. Although Columbus described the island as "the most beautiful land eyes have ever seen," he was searching for gold and there was none to be found here. So onward he went.

The Taíno people greeted the Spanish conquistadors with great hospitality and taught them to smoke rolled-up dried leaves that made them dizzy (tobacco). As in other nations conquered by the Spanish, the local population was evangelized while being stripped of its freedom and possessions. The Taíno rebelled. Among their leaders was Hatuey, who headed the island's first guerrilla movement. (Centuries late, a Cuban brew would bear his silhouette.) Hatuey was finally taken prisoner and burned at the stake after a three-month standoff. There were an estimated 100,000 natives living in Cuba in 1512. By the late 1570s they were almost all gone.

The conquistadors established the economy of Cuba with the introduction of sugarcane and slave trafficking (the first shipment took place in 1524); the island also functioned as a way station in the transport of gold from the Americas back to the Old World. It is estimated that some 200 million ducats worth of gold, silver, and precious stones traveled through Cuba between 1540 and 1600. Sunk by pirates and hurricanes, some of these riches still lie at the bottom of the sea off the Cuban coast.

Thanks to sugar, tobacco, and rum, Cuba's economy boomed well into the 18th century, much to the delight of the Spanish Crown and the Catholic Church, who together held a trade monopoly over the island. The British, eager to expand their commerce in the West Indies, demanded that Cuba be allowed to trade freely with other powers. In 1762 the English navy lay siege to Havana, and after two months it secured the capitulation of the city. After occupying Cuba for nine months, Britain agreed to exchange Florida for Cuba, and so the island was returned to Spain.

The United States had had its eye on the island since the days of Thomas Jefferson, who in 1809 wrote to President James Madison, saying, "Cuba [is] the most interesting addition that can be made to our system of States." Cuba, with its thirst for slaves to work the sugarcane fields, was a necessary addition to the Southern states' plan to spread slavery to new territories and counterbalance the abolitionist trend in the North. President James Polk, a Southerner, unsuccessfully offered to buy Cuba from Spain in 1848. The South's interest in Cuba increased in the 1850s, when France and England ended their West Indian slave system, making the island the only one in the Caribbean still supporting slavery. In 1857 and 1859, the abolitionist North had to step in to prevent Congress from seizing Cuba outright.

Although the importation of African slaves (nearly a million) ceased in 1865 with the end of the U.S. Civil War, slavery was not officially abolished in Cuba until 1886. Chinese and Mexican Indians were brought over to Cuba as indentured servants to fill the need for slave labor to work the sugarcane fields. An estimated 150,000 Cantonese found their way to Cuba between 1853 and 1871, when the import of indentured laborers from China ended.

By 1870 much of the island's sugar production had fallen into the hands of American investors. Cuba became a crucial link in America's "triangular" trade. It provided sugar to the United States, which sent rum to Africa, which in turn furnished Cuba with the slaves it needed to feed the booming sugar industry. By 1880, 83 percent of Cuba's exports went to the United States. Only 6 percent went to Spain.

It was the dawn of the "American century," as Henry Robinson Luce called it, and Cuba's small economy became the testing ground for America's rising economic and foreign dominance in the 1890s. By opening its market to Cuban sugar early in the decade, the United States managed to make the island wholly dependent on its demand. However, in 1894, a Democratic Congress favored Hawaiian sugar and increased import tariffs on Cuba, making its sugar more expensive and thus less competitive on the U.S. market. Within a year the island's economy had caved in, unemployment soared, and rebellions erupted all across the island. By changing its tariff rates, the United States had flexed its new economic muscles and injured Cuba's pride, helping to unleash a nationalist wave that stoked the embers of the Cuban revolution.

Enter José Martí, the father of Cuban independence. Imprisoned and then exiled for his seditious activity, he moved to the United States, where he founded a newspaper and the Cuban Revolutionary Party (Partido Revolucionario Cubano, or PRC), an independence movement. As the leader of the PRC, Martí launched the final war of independence with a proclamation from his New York headquarters on January 29, 1895. The apostle of Cuban independence, as he came to be known, joined the rebels fighting the Spaniards on April 2. He didn't last long. Martí died in battle, riding his white horse near Dos Rios, on May 19, 1895. His martyrdom was ensured forever.

The big bang of Martí's (and the seeds of Fidel Castro's) revolution occurred in the still waters of Havana's harbor on the night of February 15, 1898. Most of the sailors on the U.S. battleship *Maine*, lying peaceably at anchor in the deep harbor, had already turned in when a powerful explosion ripped through the ship's ammunition hold, killing 266 of its 354-man crew. The sinking of the *Maine* was the pretext that the United States had long been awaiting. Accounts written in Cuba state that the explosion was "considered to be a self-inflicted aggression to facilitate U.S. involvement in the Spanish-Cuban war." Cuba was being torn apart by the *independentistas'* revolution against Spanish colonial rule, but after three murderous years, the war was now at a stalemate. War fever broke out across the United States within days of the *Maine*'s sinking. Images of emaciated women and children forcibly relocated in camps and in the cities by the Spaniards appeared daily in the press and underscored the urgency of ending the carnage. Congress and the public urged the president to join the war and kick the Spanish out of Cuba once and for all. "The president has no more backbone than a chocolate éclair," taunted a young and hawkish Teddy Roosevelt.

The so-called yellow press had a stake in the warmongering effort. "Remember the *Maine!*" read the newspaper banners. The day after the *Maine* disaster, a drawing on the front page of William Randolph Hearst's newspaper, the *World*, showed the battleship at anchor in Havana's harbor atop an underwater mine connected by wires to a detonator in Morro Castle, the Spanish fortress at the harbor's mouth. Although an official investigation failed to conclusively blame Spain for the sinking, the United States nonetheless declared war by launching a blockade of the island in April. American military intervention in the war began with a brash Teddy Roosevelt, then assistant secretary of the Navy, leading the attack on San Juan Hill in Santiago de Cuba with his Rough Riders. Spain was quickly defeated after weak and haphazard resistance on the part of the exhausted colonial troops.

With American participation in Cuba's struggle for independence, the brutal and slow war between the rebels and Spain finally drew to an end in August 1898. Of a population of 1.5 million, some 300,000 Cubans would be dead by the end of the war. With this defeat, the Spanish crown effectively lost its last foothold in the New World, along with the Philippines, Guam, and Puerto Rico.

The economic boom of the 1920s fueled yet another wave of Chinese immigration, this time leading to the influx of some 30,000 Chinese men. Wilfredo Lam, perhaps Cuba's most famous living painter, is the perfect example of the racial integration that has been the hallmark of Cuban society: He is part Chinese, Spanish, and African. What's left of the once thriving Chinatown can be found in the two-block area of Centro Habana bounded by Zanja and Avenida Reina, behind the Capitol.

Cuba endured the tutelage of the United States for most of the first half of the 20th century, a domination that affected Cubans socially, politically, and economically. As a result, up until the 1950s, the U.S. ambassador was often perceived as being more powerful than the Cuban president himself. It is against this backdrop that a young, charismatic, hot-tempered, and fiercely nationalistic Fidel Castro emerged.

Fidel was born in 1926, the son of a moderately well-off Spanish immigrant landowner in the Oriente province. He studied law at the university in Havana and distinguished himself as a passionate and well-spoken attorney, full of *brio* and *chispa*. Hoping to spark a revolution that would overthrow the corrupt rule of dictator Fulgencio Batista, Fidel launched an unsuccessful attack on the Moncada army barracks, which landed him in prison in July 1953. After defending himself brilliantly in a much-publicized trial, he was exiled to Mexico by Batista.

With a group that included his brother Raúl and an Argentine doctor named Ernesto "Che" Guevara (nicknamed for his habit of interjecting the Argentine slang *che* into every sentence, meaning "hey" in English), Castro trained a small invasion force that eventually sailed back to Cuba in a leaky tub called the *Granma* (now on display at the Museo de la Revolucion) in 1956. From the hardscrabble peaks of the Sierra Maestra, Castro perfected his guerrilla war tactics, which led, two years later, to the downfall of the Batista regime.

Batista fled Havana in the early morning hours of January 1, 1959. A few days later, Fidel Castro rode triumphantly into the capital to herald the beginning of a new era in his country's history. Very quickly, however, his reforms—which included the expropriation and nationalization of foreign properties and the ruthless routing of his adversaries (including long prison terms or summary executions) — won him few friends at home and abroad. His increasingly communist sympathies and policies eventually led to a mass exodus of rich and middle-class Cubans and dramatically increased tensions with the United States.

These tensions culminated in the infamous and disastrous (for Cuban exiles and the United States) Bay of Pigs (Playa Giron) invasion in 1961 and the frightening missile crisis in the fall of 1962, when the world was on the brink of nuclear war. Castro's alignment with the Soviet Union forever alienated him from conservative American politicians. A trade embargo was implemented in June 1961 and, with the addition of the more restrictive Helms-Burton Act of 1996, is still in place today. Even more intense than the embargo, however, is the utter hatred of Castro by most Cuban exiles, who will be satisfied only when his head is served up on a platter. These exiles constitute a formidable power base in New Jersey and especially in Miami and other districts in South Florida. Who could forget the furor over Elián Gonzalez, who was shamefully made a cause célèbre and poster child for Cuban exiles? Of course, any attempts to lift the embargo are stifled by both Republicans and Democrats fearful of alienating such an influential group in these two important presidential-election states.

Before You Go

Warning for U.S. Citizens

Technically it is not illegal for U.S. citizens to travel to Cuba, but under the Trading with the Enemy Act, U.S. citizens and other people under the jurisdiction of the United States are legally forbidden to spend money — dollars or any other currency — in Cuba. This includes any payment for accommodations, food, airline tickets, taxis, goods, and services. Criminal penalties for violating the sanctions can range from 10 years in prison and up to $250,000 in fines. Exceptions do exist.

The U.S. Department of the Treasury may issue licenses to journalists, researchers, government officials, humanitarian aid workers, and Cuban Americans with relatives in Cuba, for academic excursions and religious missions. U.S. citizens who are fully hosted or sponsored by people not subject to U.S. jurisdiction are permitted to travel to Cuba but must still travel through a third country (i.e., Canada, Mexico, Jamaica, or the Bahamas). The Treasury Department puts the burden of proof of sponsorship on the individual traveler. The traveler will be considered in violation of the sanctions unless he or she can provide proper documentation of full sponsorship, including visa and proof of payment of the entry and exit tax. For more details, contact the Office of Foreign Assets Control (OFAC), U.S. Department of the Treasury, 1500 Pennsylvania Avenue NW, Annex Building 2nd floor, Washington, DC 20220, telephone 202-622-2480, info-by-fax at 202-622-0077, or on the Internet at www.treas.gov/ofac.

There is a legitimate way for U.S. citizens who do not have family in Cuba to visit the country. Cultural exchange-study programs are authorized by the U.S. Department of the Treasury, and there are several companies that are licensed by OFAC. These educational programs focus on Cuba's history and culture, and trips will have themes like architecture, music, African heritage, dance, the people of Cuba, language study, even Hemingway's Cuba. We recommend them for those Americans who want to see Cuba without Uncle Sam breathing down their neck, and hey, ya might learn something, too! Here are some of the licensed cultural exchange-study organizations that conduct Americans to Cuba tours:

Worldguest Travel Services 800-873-9691 or 201-861-5059
(www.worldguest.com)

Maruzul Tours, Inc. 800-223-5334 or 201-840-6711
(www.marazultours.com)

Cross-Cultural Solutions 800-380-4777 or 914-632-0022
(www.traveltocubanow.org)

Thousands of Americans made trips to Cuba in 2006, most of them authorized as nontourists who obtained visas from the Treasury Department. The Treasury Department tells us that 25,304 Americans legally traveled to Cuba to visit family in 2005. Most Americans who travel to Cuba, however, are unauthorized, entering through Canada, Mexico, the Bahamas, or Jamaica rather than via the scheduled charter flights operating out of Miami, New York, and Los Angeles. Most people who get in trouble for unauthorized travel to Cuba do so because they tell federal agents at customs that they went to Cuba. We don't advocate telling half-truths to federal agents, but if you went to Cuba illegally, keep it to yourself, unless you want to cough up more than your taxes to Uncle Sam. We checked the Treasury Department's files for 2005, and Big Brother fined an average of five people a month, at an average rate of $5,000 per person. Penalties range from a warning letter to a $65,000 fine, but fines are normally much lower—between $7,250 and $7,500, we're told. They are also negotiable, and one can request an administrative hearing to contest them. Alas, the department that handles these hearings is so backlogged that a new administration might well be in place by the time all these cases are heard (hint, hint). Remember, it is not illegal for Americans to visit the country—freedom to travel is protected under the Constitution—but it is against Treasury Department regulations to spend money while on Cuban soil, effectively preventing Americans from legally exploring the country.

Before traveling to Cuba, you will be required to purchase a visa at the counter of whatever airlines you are flying. The visa should not cost more than $25. When you arrive, don't be intimidated by all the people wandering around in green fatigues, or the German shepherds in muzzles. They're just walking around to make sure that sketchy characters don't enter the country with drugs, guns, warm body parts, or other contraband.

When you line up for passport control, the wall of opaque doors might be a bit intimidating. Make sure you have a hotel reservation in hand. If you made one over the Internet, just print out the receipt. The officers might ask you for proof of registration. They will also ask you some questions, such as the purpose of your visit, length of stay, and where you plan to visit. Be honest, be nice, and smile. You will be through in no time.

And don't worry, your U.S. passport—or any passport, for that matter—will not be stamped. The stamp goes on your travel visa, which you must present to officials when you leave the country. Upon departure, officials will stamp the same piece of paper and will hand back your passport, which will hold no proof of your Cuban experience—so take pictures!

Currency, Cash, Commission, and Exchange

There are two distinct currencies that circulate in Cuba. Cubans live and work within the system of the Cuban peso (*peso cubano*), whereas tourists use the convertible peso (*peso convertible*). The *peso convertible* is referred to as *un dolar* in Cuba, whereas the *peso cubano* is referred to as *un peso*. The conversion rate from the U.S. dollar to a *peso convertible* is around US$1 to *peso convertible* $.90. The euro exchanges a little better at EU$1 to *peso convertible* $1. The *peso convertible* to Cuban peso rate is around $1 *peso convertible* to some $23 *pesos cubanos*. Although both the *peso cubano* and the *peso convertible* have similar colors and designs, they can be clearly distinguished by the words *peso convertible* on the front and back of the convertible peso.

The *peso convertible* will work anywhere that tourists are expected to go: restaurants, taxis, hotels, discos, Internet centers, international telephones. *Pesos convertibles* will buy you the services, food, and other items that are a normal part of your trip to Cuba.

The *peso cubano* will most likely not be accepted by state-licensed tour operators; it is the currency of Cubans. *Pesos cubanos* will not buy you what Cubans consider luxuries and what tourists come to expect—a cold bottle of water, milk, a *mojito*, or fresh meat.

Everything you can buy with *pesos convertibles* is stratospherically priced for Cubans. Since Cubans are paid in *pesos cubanos*, the price of one *peso convertible* for a bottle of water is like you paying $23 for a bottle of water. Way too expensive! However, if you decide to use *pesos cubanos* while in Cuba, the reward is beyond economy; it allows you to interact with Cubans—the island's real treasure.

Non-Americans who decide to visit Cuba should make sure to bring three important items: cash, cash, and cash (this is obviously the case for Americans, too). Taxes for using anything but cash in Cuba are so high that you'll think the meager sales tax you pay at home is a luxury. Using a European

Union–based credit card, we withdrew money from an ATM at the base of Havana's FOCSA building (see La Torre in Where to Eat), paying a bank fee of 11 euros for every 100 withdrawn. But it doesn't stop there. Hotels that do accept credit cards will charge you up to 11 percent of the bill's balance, which can amount to paying for one extra night, depending on where you stay.

Credit cards that draw on the U.S. financial system do not work in Cuba, so your only option as a U.S. citizen is to bring cash. Think twice before you bring dollars, however. U.S. dollars are not frowned upon in Cuba, but the government requires that all state-licensed exchange booths levy a 10 percent tax on conversions from the dollar to the *peso convertible*.

For example, if you exchange $500 for *pesos convertibles*, you will be charged $50. By using euros instead of dollars, you can avoid the $50, or 10 percent, penalty.

Do make sure to exchange at least some money at the airport to pay the taxi for the ride from the airport to your hotel. Otherwise you'll not be able to leave the airport. You will most likely be told that the ride will cost 20 *pesos convertibles*. The driver receives only what is counted on his taxi meter (under 10 *pesos convertibles*, in most cases), and the rest goes to a commission for the officials at the airport. If you feel the need, it might be possible to reduce this fee through haggling.

Health Issues

The Center for Disease Control will prepare a Travax report for you through your doctor's office, with information regarding required AIDS testing (for those who stay longer than 90 days), recommended immunizations, and general information.

Don't drink the water or anything with ice cubes. Salad is suspect, as it is generally washed in tap water. Even the Cubans boil their drinking water. Bottled water is available everywhere, in small markets, ice cream stands, bars and restaurants, and the minibars in the hotel rooms. We even brushed our teeth with it.

There are no mosquitoes in Havana, but inland areas, away from ocean breezes, have enough to warrant packing bug spray.

Climate

The weather in Cuba varies, depending on what part of the country you are in. The northwestern section, including Havana, often has weather similar to the very southern tip of Florida (it lies barely south of the Tropic of Cancer). Cold fronts from the United States do make it here, resulting in some cooler days and nights during the winter. The southeastern part of the island is more tropical. Here, the temperature rarely dips below 70°F or scales to above 90°F (at sea level). It gets cooler at night in the country's three mountain ranges (the Sierra Maestra to the southeast, the Sierra del Escambray in the central region, and the Cordillera de los Organos in the west), making it ideal for sleeping. The sun shines almost every day. Rainfall comes in the form of brief, intense cloudbursts, quickly followed by sunshine. It's pretty hard not to get a tan. The only weather peril on a Cuban vacation is an occasional summer tropical depression or hurricane, which can make life very exciting. Many a marriage was ignited when visitors were stranded in a tempest.

There are two basic climate categories in Cuba: lush (very green, hot, somewhat humid, with lots of rainfall) and arid (brown with cactus and very dry). The windward side (the north and east coasts) is the lush, wetter, and greener side. The mountains that traverse the island from southeast to northwest block most of the typical rainfall that comes with the prevailing trade winds. This makes much of the southern coast in the lee of the mountains semi-arid to arid. Vegetation tends to be scrubby with cactus, although there certainly are enough palm trees around to keep palm tree lovers happy. The western end of Cuba is fairly lush because the mountains on this end of the island are too low to stop the rain.

Both lush and arid climes are warm to hot, depending on the season and the extent of the trade winds. Summer, while only about 5°–10° hotter than winter, feels much hotter due to the dramatically increased humidity and decreased wind. The one constant is the sun. It is always strong and will swiftly fry unprotected pale faces — and bodies — to a glowing shade of lobster red.

Telephones

Cuba is divided into provinces, each with its own area code. Within a province there are often towns or cities with the same name, but the area codes cover all the other towns within the province. The phone numbers have varying arrangements of numbers — sometimes a one-, two-, or three-digit area code and sometimes a five- or six-digit main number. If this is all too confusing for you, take advantage of the front desk, the concierge service, or the travel agency desk in your hotel to make the calls for you. The country code is 53, not necessary within the country. Keep in mind that phones and frustration go hand in hand in Cuba. Many phone numbers just don't work, and those that do work often take about five tries.

Here is a list of the area codes by province:

Havana	7	Cienfuegos	432
(and add an 8 to the prefix		Villa Clara	422
of all Havana city numbers)		Sancti Spiritus	41
Pinar del Río	82	Trinidad	419
Matanzas	52	Topes de Collantes	42
Varadero	5	Ciego de Avila	33
Playa Larga	59	Camaguey	32

Las Tunas	31	Santiago de Cuba	226
Holguìn	24	Guantánamo	21
Granma	23	Isla de Juventud	61

Calling internationally is a bit less confusing. Most of the fancier hotels have direct dialing from the room, but with surcharges. For a bit cheaper alternative, there are ETASCA phone centers, conveniently located in popular locations, where in air-conditioned comfort you can buy a phone card (in denominations of $10) and chat to your heart's content 24 hours a day. These centers are clean, brightly lit, and staffed, the phones look normal, and there are little partitions between the four or five phones. There are also phone booths on the streets, but we had no use for them (even if they were clean).

The People

Cubans have some unmistakable, if not always endearing, qualities: They are happy, loud, passionate, animated, and vigorous in their communication, and they make direct eye contact. Dramatic to the core, they'll often shout, regardless of whether they are inches away or down the block. Cubans are generous and effusive and will swear to die for you after a few drinks. People often try to engage in conversation on the street, to tell you about family members in the United States, to take you to a *paladar*, to sell you cigars made by their father, or whatever. Not everyone is a hustler, and many will befriend you to practice their English. Take the opportunity to ask for guidance in finding local places of interest, because as they themselves say, it's the neighborhoods and the people that will show you the real Cuba.

Because they spend as much time outside as they do indoors, life always spills over onto the street, turning sidewalks into extensions of the living room, and often late into the evening.

Getting There

There are two main ports of entry to Cuba: José Martí International Airport in Havana and Juan Alberto Gomez Airport in Varadero. Both are located about 9 miles outside the main urban areas. Flights are frequent to both destinations and arrive principally from Canada, Spain, France, Italy, Mexico, Jamaica, the Bahamas, and various other Latin American capitals. The airports are notable for the conspicuous absence of the familiar logos of American carriers. You will also immediately notice the abundance of military and police personnel. Many have Labrador retrievers, German Shepards, or cocker spaniels. Well fed and groomed, playful and well-behaved (not at all like the mangy mutts that roam Havana), they are trained to sniff out anything suspicious, and they race around (often unleashed) inspecting luggage and trash cans.

There are regular charter flights from Miami, New York, and Los Angeles, with tickets sold to approved travelers by agencies licensed by the U.S. Treasury Department. Potential travelers are screened for visa qualification. The preferred route, if you're traveling from the United States, is via Mexico City, Cancún, Toronto, Montreal, the Bahamas (Nassau), or Jamaica. Mexicana and Air Jamaica are reliable carriers. Because you cannot purchase a ticket to Cuba in the United States even through a third country's airline, you must pick up and pay for the last leg of the trip at the service counter at your stopover. It is there that you must also purchase a tourist visa ($25 to $30). Consider buying an air-hotel package when you book your flight, because it is required to have a hotel reservation at Customs upon entering the country (for at least a night or two), and this may substantially reduce your costs. To avoid suspicion from U.S. Customs, it is better to go through Customs in the third-party country on your way home. This means not checking your luggage straight through, and perhaps making a night or two stopover. Expect to find U.S. Customs agents in Jamaica or Cancun giving passengers a careful eye as they deplane. It is not uncommon for individuals to be stopped and questioned.

Getting Around

Upon exiting Customs, the visitor will be greeted by the din of animated conversation, honking taxis, and excited families waiting to meet relatives they haven't seen in 25 years. What really is shocking, however, are the old cars that are often available as taxis. Rather than hop into a spanking new Nissan taxi with a/c that will turn Havana into Anchorage, many choose something like a shiny black and sweet-looking 1956 Roadmaster. For 15 to 20 convertible pesos, the owner will take you to your hotel or for a tour of the town. Any taxi driver, or car owner, for that matter, will happily work as a tour guide if the price is right.

Cuba is about the size of Florida. Public transportation—whether it be train or bus—is very unreliable and not always comfortable, so being independent is definitely the way to go. If you're going to do Cuba outside Havana or Varadero, the best way is in a rental car. You'll get to see the country, meet people, and make friends. However, a few words of caution are in order.

There is only one highway in Cuba. It's called the Ocho Vias and stretches from Pinar del Río to a bit past Sancti Spiritus, about midway through the country. Although it is not heavily used—mostly because there are so few cars in Cuba—it can be hazardous. This highway is not I-95. There are no barriers to keep cattle from straying onto the (unmarked) roadway. Trucks often don't pull over to the shoulder when they break down. Drivers often use their horn in place of signals or brakes. After Sancti Spiritus, if you're going down to Santiago de Cuba, you'll have to drive on the busy two-lane Carretera Central.

Be sure to ask for a map before you go. Although the tourist maps you'll receive will not be as exact as a AAA guide, they will help you find your way around the country. There are relatively few signs on Cuban roadways, especially once you turn off the main highways. Be prepared to ask Cubans for directions, and remember that the intersection where there are dozens of Cubans waiting for a ride is probably the best spot to stop and ask for directions. Otherwise you might find a Cuban who has never left the province staring at you blank eyed.

In the city, be extra careful with the many bicycle riders with whom you'll share the streets. Bicycle riders are often distracted, and they don't have front or rear lights at night.

Car-Rental Services

Bear in mind that there is no competition for car-rental services in Cuba because government agencies — Havanautos, Cubacar, Transautos, Transtur, and Gaviota — hold the monopoly, so prices tend to be the same. For example, the per-day cost for two to six days for an economy car is $45, for a tourist car $55, and for a luxury car $80. Because American credit cards are not accepted, you'll have to leave a cash deposit ($200 to $500, depending on the type of car and length of rental). The distances between important cities can be great, so go for the unlimited mileage option on the contract. Before you leave the lot, make certain that you go over all the bumps and scratches on the car. Car rental agents can be found in every airport, many gas stations, and in almost every hotel in the country. Gas stations (Servi CU-PET and Oro Negro) can be found on the major roads, so fill up, because finding roadside service could be next to impossible.

Private Cars (Boteros)

Every Cuban with a car is a potential *botero* ("gypsy cab"). A trip from, say, Old Havana to Miramar can set you back $6. An official (state) taxi costs about $10. These are metered, generally newer models, ranging from Mercedes to Ford Escort, and the fares are consistent, so no need to negotiate. The Panataxis with 55-5555 on the sides are easy to spot, metered, and fairly reliable (the drivers know the city well). *Boteros* are illegal (thus cheaper), and the driver — often a well-educated professional with a low-paying government job — can be fined if he's caught moonlighting. Always ask the fare before you enter the car; negotiate if you feel it is too high. There are also taxis *particulares* (check the license plate), or private taxis. These are usually the owners of cars who pay the state a monthly fee that enables them to function as taxis. Again, ask the fare first. There are also numerous bicycle taxis in Old Havana, called *pedicabs*. If you're not in a hurry and prefer an open-air ride, hire a bicycle taxi to give you a spin around Old Havana. Be sure to pick a driver who's not too old, because some of the older guys will ask you to get off and meet them at the top of the hill. These bikes have no gears! The CocoTaxis (coconut-shaped, little scooter-powered, open-air, two-passenger coupes, in bright yellow or white) are fun, too.

If you're going to stick to Havana, you could negotiate with someone who has a car and arrange for him or her to pick you up and drop you off at your convenience. Beware of long-distance trips in hired cars, which tend to break down often. By the way, there are no tow trucks in Cuba (at least we never saw one!), and certainly no AAA.

If you're really on a budget, you can almost always hire a Cuban with a car for a day, to take you to the beach or to tour around a site (about $25). You might also be able to negotiate a weekly rate, which can run you about $400 for two weeks, gas included.

Flights

The other way to travel around the island is by flying, especially if you're going all the way to Santiago from Havana. Cubana (45-3133) flies from Havana to the Isla de la Juventud, Cienfuegos, Villa Clara, Camaguey, Holguin, Santiago de Cuba, Guantanamo, Matanzas, Las Tunas, and Baracoa. There are no intraprovincial flights. Note that flight times and dates vary widely among different routes. Aerocaribbean (33-4543) also flies between Havana and other provincial capitals, though not as frequently as Cubana.

Focus on Cuba: Hemingway's Havana, Walking Havana, and Afro-Cuban Culture

Hemingway's Havana

Ernest Hemingway was Cuba's most famous American. They'd shout "Papa!" as he strolled from his room in the Ambos Mundos hotel in Old Havana to the Bodeguita del Medio, just a few blocks away, for his first *mojito* of the day. A winning number on any given day, this refreshing cocktail was supposedly Hemingway's favorite drink. It's made with white rum, raw sugar, crushed mint leaves, lime juice, bitters, and club soda. Later, after he'd won the Nobel Prize (in gratitude for his award, he offered the medal to the shrine of La Virgen de la Caridad del Cobre, Cuba's patron saint), he lived in Finca Vigia, just outside Havana. He kept his fishing boat in Cojimar, a short drive from his farm, where Gregorio Fuentes, a local fisherman, looked after it. Sadly, Fuentes passed away on January 13, 2002, at the great age of 104. We had lunch with him a few years back and were astounded by his lucidity and the strength with which he pounded the table when he wanted to emphasize a point. Gregorio was Hemingway's inspiration for the character in *The Old Man and the Sea*.

The best place to start learning about Papa's Cuba is the **Museo Ernest Hemingway** at Finca Vigia, at the corner of Steinberts, in San Francisco de Paula (91-0809). It's open every day except Tuesday from 9 a.m. to 4 p.m., and

Sunday from 9 a.m. to noon. The house has barely changed since Hemingway left Cuba shortly after the revolution. The fine colonial-style house is surrounded by century-old trees. It is here that he wrote *The Old Man and the Sea*. His books, desk, and trophies are all still here. Outside, his ship, *Pilar*, built in Brooklyn, lies forever docked near the pool. Notice the rows of little mounds with crosses. They are all burial mounds for Hemingway's cats. Anyone who's been to the Hemingway house in Key West will immediately understand his affinity for cats — there are a dizzying number all over the house and grounds.

Next, head to Cojimar and have lunch and a cold drink at **Restaurante La Terraza** on Avenida Central. We like Cojimar a lot, and there is no greater pleasure than to sit down for lunch in La Terraza's dining room overlooking the cove after a day at the beach. Here ceiling fans cool as a well-dressed waitstaff in tan suits glide over tile floors. You can just have a beer and watch the spectacular sunsets. It is in this sleepy fishermen's village that Hemingway kept his *Pilar* moored. A bust of the writer adorns a modest monument near the old Spanish fort. Sadly, we will not be running into Gregorio having lunch at La Terraza anymore. The government considered him a national monument. He replaced Spencer Tracy in a couple of scenes in the movie *The Old Man and the Sea* directed by Fred Zinnemann.

Finally, take a look at the **Marina Hemingway**, at Avenida 5ta and Calle 248 in Santa Fe, 15 minutes from downtown Havana. Although Hemingway never visited this rather modern marina with its multiple canals, it is here that the International Blue Marlin Fishing Tournament is held every summer. If you happen to be here during the tournament, you're likely to come across a number of wealthy American yachtsmen who have flaunted the U.S. embargo and sailed to Cuba to participate in the fishing extravaganza. The competition was originally sponsored by Papa Hemingway, who was gracious enough to invite Fidel Castro to participate in 1960. Of course, Castro, the luckiest man in Latin America, won the trophy.

Walking Havana

Havana (Habana or La Habana, to Cubans) is made for exploration on foot, and it's easy to do. Our initial hotel reservation included a city tour with Gaviota Tours. Before we set out on our own, this was a great way to find our bearings and put an order to all the landmarks. First the van tour passes the important Government Ministry Buildings and Monuments. These include the **Plaza de la Revolución**, with sculptures of Marti and Ché, the **Capitol**, the **Museo de la Revolución** (with the tanks, planes and weaponry of Fidel's army, and the centerpiece — his boat *Granma*, replete with guards and an eternal flame) and the **Malecón**.

In **Old Havana** (Habana Vieja or La Habana Vieja), we disembarked and walked, linking together the plazas along the narrow streets. The Gaviota tour lasted more than four hours and included a running dialogue full of history, trivia, and suggestions for all sorts of interests. Walking through Old Havana you will find churches, museums, galleries, and workshops opening onto the streets, all welcoming tourists (with a rare admission charge of $1, but usually free). Cafes, bars, and restaurants abound, as do shaded benches in tiny parks. Many of the streets are closed to traffic.

Cuba isn't really much of a shopping destination like Paris, but there are certainly things to see and buy. In Vedado, Calle 23 has shops and a small open-air market. A film developing and supply store on the corner of Calle O and Calle 23 had the specialty batteries for our camera, at a better price than at home! The large hotels have shops and galleries. For diehard mall rats, the **Plaza Carlos III** on Avenida Salvador Allende between Retiro and Arbol Seco in Habana Centro (phone 33-8635) is an experience. Reminiscent of the Guggenheim Museum in New York, the building spirals up five levels, with a food court in the middle. Stores on every level include hardware, furniture, appliances, toys, clothes, electronics, and individual stores with items for $1, $2, and so on. The place is jammed on the weekends, and it is required to check bags before entering any of the stores.

In Havana Vieja, **Obispo** is the street with all the shops. You might not find anything to buy, but it is fun to look. Coffee shops and bakeries beckon. Some of the window displays could be described as *The Twilight Zone* meets Dada. At the end of Obispo (near the Floridita Restaurant) is a wonderful bookstore, **La Moderna Poesia**. Travel books and maps and picture books of Cuba are great if you plan to travel through the rest of the country. Reference books, fiction, children's books, political biographies, and philosophies can all be found. Posters, postcards, and lots of CDs (they will let you listen if you plan to buy) can all be had for extremely reasonable prices. For those who seek to impress the folks at home, cigars and rum can be bought at **La Taberna del Galeon**, on Calle Baratillo, at the corner of the Plaza de Armas, next to the Hotel Santa Isabel. There is a rum-tasting bar, with bottles for sale (about $8 and up). The back room is the place to buy cigars. Full boxes can cost you in the hundreds, but you can buy individual cigars, creating your own sampler. Cohibas, Partagas, and Monte Cristos range in price from about $5 to $10. Next door at the Casa del Café you can buy coffee (a kilogram, or 2.2 pounds, of beans is about $20), related gift items (espresso makers, cups, kits), and rum singles. If you venture out to the plaza on a sunny day, you will find a secondhand book market with shelves of old books for sale; textbooks, political tomes, fiction, poetry, whatever. People also sell old stamps and money, anything with the face of the always photogenic Che. Browsers and booksellers alike will engage you in conversation. Cross the plaza diagonally and check out the street cobbled with wood on the other side. The wife of one of the *capitan generales* who lived in the building there thought the sound of horseshoes on stone would keep her awake—hence the wood. Continue on Oficios to Tacon, where you will find the outdoor crafts market. Che berets, jewelry, sculpture, clothes, maracas, and the like are yours for the bargaining. It is crowded and hot, so hold on to your wallet.

Alongside, up on the sidewalk, are a great variety of paintings, prints, and drawings for sale at equally great prices — anything from landscapes to religious inspiration, realism to folk art, great variety and great prices. Be sure to ask for a receipt to avoid Customs declarations hassles.

The **Necropolis Cristobal Colón** (also called the Cementario) in Vedado is a beautiful place to walk. With nearly a million inhabitants, this city of the dead is neatly laid out in a grid with alphabetic streets and numbered avenues. Chapels, statuary, memorials, and ornate marble headstones of the famous and the unknown extend as far as the eye can see. Admission is about a buck. It's open from 9 a.m. to 5 p.m. daily. A guidebook with photos, listings, and a map (in English and Spanish) is available at the entrance for $5. See if you can find Papa Geraldo, the old guide. He gives the best tours.

Across the mouth of the bay, accessible by taxi through the underwater tunnel, lie the forts **Castillo de los Tres Reyes del Morro** and the **Forteleza de San Carlos de la Cabana**. From up on the hill at the **Morro Castle** you get a panoramic view of the city, from the Nacional Hotel on the right to the piers in the harbor on the left. There are a few small museums up there, but it is hot, and the guy selling sugarcane juice has only two cups and no running water. (Always carry your own water.) Farther down the road lies the Fortaleza, a much larger complex with a restaurant, gift shop, and nightclub. There is a cannon-firing ceremony nightly at 9 p.m., complete with people dressed as soldiers in old-style military uniforms. This is a good late afternoon trip, to see both forts and tour the museums (the museum at the Fortaleza is bigger and has many historical artifacts, including some from the revolution). Then you can find a good place to watch the ceremony before the crowds form (in nice weather).

Afro-Cuban Culture

The slave trade flourished in Cuba between the 16th and 19th centuries, as people were brought from West Africa to work the sugarcane. They brought with them their music, dance, and animistic religion. You'll notice a green and yellow beaded bracelet, worn on the right wrist, as the sign of Cuba's animists. Naturally, the missionary slave owners tried to impose their Catholic beliefs on the Africans. Not to be swayed from their own practices, the slaves used the images of the Catholic saints to represent their own deities and ancestral spirits (*orishas*). The largest Afro-Cuban religion is a combination of Catholic and Yoruba beliefs called Santeria. Yemaya, the goddess of the ocean and the mother of all *orishas*, is identified with the color blue and represented by Nuestra Senora de la Regla, the patron saint of sailors. Chango, the Yoruba god of fire and war, is identified by the color red and is associated with Santa Barbara. Ochun, the wife of Chango and friend of Yemaya, is the goddess of love and rivers. Her color is yellow, and she is associated with the patron saint of Cuba, the Virgin de la Caridad del Cobre. These are only part of the family of *orishas*, which are represented by Catholic statuary, draped in colored beads, and featured in shrines and rituals (some involving sacrifice of small animals).

Cubans are very open about Santeria, and beaded necklaces and representative paintings are sold at the craft markets. Santeria priestesses, dressed all in white and smoking cigars, can be found in the big plazas and will tell your fortune (by reading coconuts) for a small fee. You will also have to pay to photograph them.

There are several places to get a closer look at, or even participate in, the Santeria culture. In Central Havana, artist and Santeria priest (*babalawo*) Salvador Gonzales Escalona has taken over the entire block-long street **Callejon de Hamel** (between Aramburu and Hospital off San Lazaro). Found-art sculpture; decorated bathtubs sunken into the walls; Santeria shrines; a pit with small alligators and a turtle; poems, sayings, and philosophies painted in, on, and around walls, windows, furniture, street posts, every imaginable surface in every color; and abstract, figurative, and imaginative styles are here. The artist's studio is at Number 1054 (phone 78-1661), where paintings are on display and for sale. On sunny Sundays the street is host to a big rumba *peña*, live bands and people dancing in the streets. It gets very crowded and becomes wilder as more rum is consumed. All are welcome, but hopefully it won't turn into a big tourist attraction. Visit on a weekday when you can enjoy the place in relative peace and photograph to your heart's content.

For the very curious, there is a ferry to **Regla**, a small town across the bay from Habana Vieja. Regla is the center for Afro-Cuban religions and home to several Santeria priests. The **Iglesia de Nuestra Senora de Regla** (directly in front of the ferry landing) is where you will find La Santisima Virgen de Regla on the main altar. This black Madonna represents Yemaya, the *orisha* of the ocean and the patron saint of Havana Bay. The pilgrimage and procession with the statue (brought from Spain in 1664) takes place on September 7.

The **Museo Municipal de Regla** has a branch next to the church, but the main section of the museum is housed at 158 Marti, just up the street from the ferry dock. The histories of Regla and Afro-Cuban religions are told through exhibits and artifacts. Admission is $3, and the hours are 9 a.m. to 5:30 p.m. Monday through Saturday, and 9 a.m. to 12:30 p.m. on Sunday. The passenger ferry to Regla departs every 10 minutes from Muelle Luz, across from the intersection of San Pedro and Santa Clara in Habana Vieja (a small pier just beyond the three huge ones that dock the cruise ships and house the Customs Department, with the multicolored face of Che). The fare is about 10 cents.

HAVANA (LA HABANA)

Where to Stay

"Cuba is Havana; the rest is just scenery," proud Habaneros (citizens of Havana) like to say. Our first impression is that the city urgently needs a coat of paint and some pothole repair work. Covered by decades of grime and exhaust,

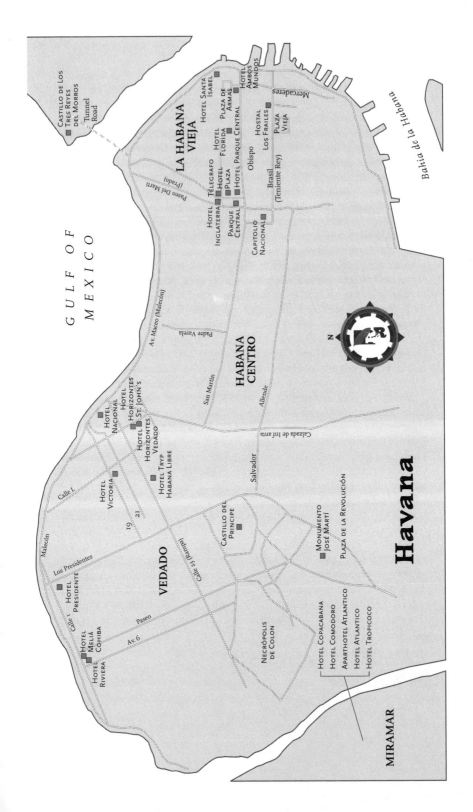

many crumbling facades are also in desperate need of repair. Everything seems abandoned, old, and distressed. Driving in from the airport, you'll see signs that distinguish Havana from any other Caribbean capital. For one, the billboards that read "Patria o Muerte" ("Homeland or Death") or "En cada barrio, Revolucion" ("In each neighborhood, Revolution") will be a clear indication that you're not in your average tourist destination. The platoons of Habaneros cycling everywhere (à la Miss Gulch) are a telltale sign of the country's energy woes. (Although things have gotten better in recent years, frequent outages and brownouts have wreaked havoc on home appliances.) The mass transport "camels" (semi trucks hauling cattle car–like trailers full of people) are a claustrophobe's nightmare.

While in Havana you'll be spending most of your time in the neighborhoods that run along the waterfront boulevard called the Malecón (sea wall). From east to west, the neighborhoods are Habana Vieja (Old Havana), at the entrance to the city's port, Centro Habana (Central Havana), Vedado, and Miramar. With their palacelike tenements, Habana Vieja and Centro Habana have been the city's poorest neighborhoods since the beginning of the century; Vedado has the faded glamour of the 1950s; Miramar, with its opulent villas and gardens, remains one of the city's choicest areas. It is also the preferred neighborhood of foreigners and home to consulates and embassies. The city's streets are clean, with workers sweeping late into the night. Neighborhood revitalization is ongoing throughout (be careful walking under rickety wooden scaffolding and around piles of rubble), especially in Habana Vieja. Due to planning decisions that favored industrial growth in the provinces and rural areas early in the revolution, Havana has been spared the sad fate of other capitals in developing countries — that is, the razing of its historical center in favor of modern glass and steel construction. As a result, Havana's skyline looks very much as it did in 1959 — an added bonus for Havana's retro look, what with the old rumbling cars and all. Whether it be the Morro Castle, the top of the FOSCA building, the Habana Libre, or the Malecón, the one thing we like most about Havana is that the city still looks grand, regardless of vantage point.

Attracted by the narrow and teeming streets, Europeans favor staying in the hotels located in or around Habana Vieja. Among the preferred are the Inglaterra, the Plaza, and the nicely appointed Santa Isabel, across from the Plaza de Armas, smack in the heart of Old Havana. Our absolute favorite in Habana Vieja is the NH Parque Central, located in the middle of the action on Neptuno, between Prado and Zulueta, right on José Martí Central Park.

Our hotel of choice in the Vedado district is still the Nacional. Located on a hill overlooking a great part of the city, it is reminiscent of The Breakers in Florida. The Vedado distict, with its high-rise hotels, grand old houses, and apartment building towers, is probably as central as it gets. The nightlife in the neighborhood is good and Calle 23 (La Rampa), lined with businesses and shops, is bustling during the day.

For a more sedate and out-of-the-way location, try one of the hotels in the tiny Miramar district, although you might find that you miss the proximity of the busy downtown. The upside is that the Miramar hotels have some of the best discos in town — not a negligible fact in a dance-oriented culture.

For those who are on a budget, Cubans are allowed to host foreigners in their homes (*casas particulares*). It is now possible to view and reserve accommodations online — our friend Luiz (in Centro Habana) is creating a Web site complete with pictures and descriptions at www.viajescuba.com. Another Web site we've found helpful is www.casaparticularcuba.org. Costs are usually very low compared to hotel rates, and amenities (a/c, private bath, etc.) vary. Take note that *casas particulares* in Cuba are required to post a sign on their door that lets anyone know that the people inside rent rooms. The sign is a triangle, bordered in forest green with white in the middle.

One last but important note on lodging conditions in Cuba: Bear in mind that this country is only just emerging from the grips of a non–service-oriented socialist economy. The fact that a certain establishment is rated as a five-star hotel does not necessarily mean that it would meet such standards in places with an entrenched and competitive tourism culture. Unless a hotel is run by an international chain (such as Spain's Tryp and Sol Meliá or France's ACCOR), the Cuban government runs all hotels. These are divided into groups and sorted by ratings, quality, and price. At the top are Cubanacan, Gran Carib, and Habaguanex, followed on the next tier by the Horizontes Group, Islazul, and Gaviota. All of the hotels have travel agency desks where agents can book you into other hotels in their chain throughout Cuba, as well as arrange tours, transportation, tickets, or reservations. Their markup is slight — only a couple of dollars.

Also, remember that *American bank-issued credit cards are not accepted in any hotel — or anywhere in Cuba*, for that matter.

Oh, by the way, Cubans are not allowed as "overnight guests" in hotel rooms in the city. Now, that's a real bummer! However, we have heard of stories where this rule has been flouted. Your Cuban guest will know how.

Old Havana — Habana Vieja

Hotel NH Parque Central, Neptuno between Prado and Zulueta, La Habana Vieja, Cuba. ☎ 537-860-6627, ✆ 537-860-6630, ⌨ www.nh-hotels.cu, nhparcen@nh-hoteles.cu

💲 **Very Pricey** and up 🍴 **CP** ⒸⒸ 277 rooms and suites

What used to be the Golden Tulip has been taken over by the NH management team, which has given a boost to service and presentation. This luxury hotel sits on the eastern side of Parque Central, between the Hotel Ingleterra and the Hotel Plaza. Built in detailed neocolonial style, 277 carpeted, tastefully decorated rooms and suites offer a/c, TV, minibar, safe, direct-dial telephone, and bathrooms with separate shower and bath. Dry cleaning and laundry services are available. The rooftop Greek-style swimming pool has a sweeping view of the ocean and Old Havana, along with the Nuevo Mundo pool bar. There is also a dome-roof Jacuzzi, a sport and fitness center with instructors, and a massage salon. The plant-filled multilevel lobby, with its double-sided central staircase leading to the mezzanine, has a very international feel, with conversations overheard in several languages. The hotel also boasts the moderately priced Restaurante El Paseo, the gourmet Restaurante Mediterraneo, and the Alameda lounge, where live Cuban music can be heard nightly. If it weren't for the wonderful Cuban nightlife, we could spend our whole vacation lounging by the pool or meeting new friends in the expansive lobby. The elegance, location, and excellent service provided by the NH team makes this hotel our new favorite in Habana Vieja.

Hostal Los Frailes, Calle Teniente Rey between Oficios and Mercaderes, La Habana Vieja, Cuba. ✆ 537-862-9383, ✆ 537-862-9718, 🖥 www.cuba.tc/habaguanex_hotels.html

💼 **Cheap** for rooms and **Not So Cheap** for suites 🍴 **CP** cc
18 rooms, 4 suites

Formerly the mansion of Marques Pedro Claudio Duqesne, captain of the French Armada in the early 1790s, Hostal Los Frailes is located only a few doors down from the Plaza de San Francisco de Asis. The theme is "Franciscan Monk." From the life-size bronze-hooded monk statues at the entrance and in the atrium to the background music of Gregorian-type chanting, from the frescos to the monk outfits and sandals worn by the staff, General Manager Ariel Fuachet has seen to every detail. With two floors of rooms and suites around the plant-, sculpture- and fountain-filled atrium, Los Frailes is small and intimate. The rooms are spacious and feature a well-lit sink and vanity separate from the bath, toilet, and bidet room. There is TV with cable, direct-access telephone, a safe, a refrigerator with a minibar, and in-room heat and a/c controls. Laundry services are available, but as with most places here, it takes 24 hours. There are wrought-iron candleholders that match the electric light fixtures; once again, every detail has been addressed. What really endeared us to Los Frailes is the staff. Friendly and energetic, helpful, thoughtful, and kind, they all really complement the experience — that and our free copy of the nationalist newspaper *Granma* (in English). Because it is so small, Los Frailes only has a lobby bar serving drinks and snacks. Breakfast is served in a little restaurant at the corner, included in the plan.

Hotel Ambos Mundos, 153 Calle Obispo, at the corner of Mercaderes, La Habana Vieja, Cuba. ✆ 537-860-9530, ✆ 537-860-9532, 🖥 www.cuba.tc/habaguanex_hotels.html

📷 **Not So Cheap** 🍴 **CP** (CC) 52 rooms

Located a few blocks away from the Plaza de Armas and Parque Central in the Old City, this tastefully restored hotel is a good choice for its location, its history, and the excellent view from its rooftop garden. Tall enough to dominate the neighboring buildings, the rooftop terrace (Bar Parrillada Hemingway) is a fantastic vantage point from which to watch the harbor's shipping traffic and the hustle and bustle of the neighborhood residents in the afternoon. It's also a great place for that afternoon *mojito*. The lobby is large, airy, and comfortable, with a beautiful bar for coffee or cocktails. A small establishment, Restaurante Plaza de Armas, seats 24 and serves Creole as well as international dishes. There are 49 standard rooms and 3 minisuites, all with a/c, minibar, cable TV, direct-dial telephones, irons, and safes. The business center has phone, fax, and e-mail capabilities but no direct Internet access. The hotel was Hemingway's home in the years before he won the Nobel Prize, and it was here, in a smallish bare room that's been preserved pretty much the way it was, that he penned *For Whom the Bell Tolls*.

Hotel Plaza, 267 Ignacio Agramonte, La Habana Vieja, Cuba. 𝄢 537-860-8583, -8584, -8585, -8586, -8587, -8588, or -8589, ✆ 537- 860-8869, 🖥 www.hotelplazacuba.com, comercial@hotelplazacuba.com

📷 **Not So Cheap** 🍴 **CP** (CC) 188 rooms

Diagonally across from the ever lively Parque Central, along with the neighboring Inglaterra and the NH Parque Central, the Plaza, built in 1909 and restored in 1991, holds its own in stature and elegance. Between 11 a.m. and 1 p.m. the four circular stained-glass skylights cast beautiful designs on the lobby's patio. Enrico Caruso, Anna Pavlova, and Isadora Duncan stayed here in their day. The fifth-floor terrace offers a great view of Old Havana's rooftops and of the ornate facade of the Bacardi building across the street. There are 188 rooms, and although this is rated a four-star hotel (remember, that's Cuban stars), the 15-year-old renovation is showing its age. There is no pool. The front desk has fax and e-mail service, but no Internet access. Dance lessons are offered in the charming lobby bar.

Hotel Florida, 252 Calle Obispo at Calle Cuba, La Habana Vieja, Cuba. 𝄢 537-862-4127, ✆ 537-862-4117, 🖥 www.cuba.tc/habaguanex_hotels.html, comercial@habaguanexhflorida.co.cu

📷 **Pricey** 🍴 **EP** (CC) 21 rooms 4 suites

Built in 1885, this beautifully and recently renovated hotel has an elegant lobby, with comfortable sofas and ornate chandeliers. Just beyond is an open-air arch-roofed atrium; clean, quiet, elegant, and full of plants. The marble floor around it leads to a gallery, piano bar, and the Restaurante La Floridiana, which serves Italian food. The Bar Café Maragato features live Cuban music. The beautiful and well-appointed rooms open onto the atrium, three stories high. Colonial class is this hotel's style.

Hotel Santa Isabel, 9 Calle Baratillo, between Obispo and Narciso Lopez, Plaza de Armas, La Habana Vieja, Cuba. ☎ 537-860-8201, ✆ 537-860-8391, 💻 www.cuba.tc/habaguanex_hotels.html, comercial@habaguanex hsisabel.co.cu

💲 **Pricey** and up 🍽 **CP** 🆑 27 rooms

Like many of the hotels in Habana Vieja, the Santa Isbel is a former mansion. Its location, on the east end of the Plaza de Armas, is well situated in one of the busiest corners of Habana Vieja. After years of endless renovations, this cool, if a bit forgotten, hotel is one of the most tastefully decorated in all of Havana. The lobby is understated elegance, with plush couches, beautiful dark wood furniture, and a blue beam ceiling with large wood window shutters painted to match. The open atrium has a marble floor, a fountain, and beautiful plants in the center. Metal cage elevators carry patrons to three floors of rooms, which open onto the atrium. Most of the rooms open out to the Plaza de Armas. Side rooms have disappointing views and should be avoided. This is where NBC chose to broadcast from during its coverage of John Paul II's visit. Use of the parking lot is included.

Hotel Inglaterra, 416 Prado, at the corner of San Rafael, La Habana Vieja, Cuba. ☎ 537-860- 8594, -8595, -8596, -8597, ✆ 537-860-8254, 💻 www.hotelinglaterracuba.com

💲 **Cheap** and up 🍽 **CP** 🆑 83 rooms

Despite its dark and dank interior and its not-quite-up-to-snuff service, we still have a weak spot for the baroque Inglaterra and its Old World charm. This hotel is one of the oldest in Havana and is a national monument. It's located across from the Parque Central and next to the National Theatre. The Cabaret Nacional ($5 cover, with live Cuban music and dance DJs), with its doorway on the side of the theatre leading downstairs, spills music and club-goers close to the sidewalk tables, where patrons may sometimes be accosted by neighborhood hustlers ready to sell cigars, sex, whatever. Best rooms are numbers 115, 315, 111, 211, 107, and 207 (the last four have large bathrooms). The Restaurante Colonial serves breakfast, lunch and dinner, and the Sevillana Snack Bar is open 24 hours. The Terraza Bar on the rooftop of this hotel is also a unique experience. It is here that reporters working for William Randolph Hearst and Joseph Pulitzer would gather during the Spanish-American War to conjure up some of the best (and often fantastic) accounts of Spanish atrocities.

Not long after, José Martí gave a famous independence speech here in 1879.

Hotel Telégrafo, 408 Prado, at the corner of Neptuno, La Habana Vieja, Cuba. ✆ 537- 861-1010, ✎ 537-861-4741, 🖳 www.cuba.tc/habaguanex_hotels.html

💲 **Pricey** ⑪ **CP** ©© 66 rooms

The Telégrafo shares frontage on the Parque Central José Martí with the Ingleterra, the Plaza, and the NH Parque Central. The eclectic façade of the lower two floors (the second was added in 1888) has been preserved and topped with two more contemporary stories. The upper three floors have a view of the Prado Promenade and the Parque Central and house the guest rooms. The 66 spacious and high-ceilinged rooms comprise 6 suites, 6 junior suites, and 54 doubles, all beautifully and discreetly decorated with modern furnishings. This hotel is part of Habaguanex chain, along with Hotel Florida, Hotel Santa Isabel, Hotel Los Frailes, and Hotel Ambos Mundos, so all of the rooms are tastefully and comfortably appointed with high-quality amenities.

The ground floor lobby is stunning, with large interior stained-glass windows, a huge ceramic mural collage, water fountains, and a sunroof. A brick and stone arcade houses boutiques, a coffee shop, a snack bar, and a gourmet restaurant serving international cuisine.

Vedado

Hotel Nacional, Calle P at the corner of Calle 21, Vedado, La Habana, Cuba. ✆ 537-873-3564, reservations: 537-55-0294, ✎ 537-33-5054, 🖳 www.hotelnacionaldecuba.com, reservas@gcnacio.gca.tur.cu

💲 **Pricey** ⑪ **EP** ©© 472 rooms and a presidential suite

Everyone knows "el Nacional." It's like saying "the Plaza" in New York. We have stayed in the Nacional for months on end and never tired of it. A late afternoon drink on the hotel's veranda has got to be the highlight of any trip to Cuba. Seen from the hotel's gardens, the view of the Malecón, the facades of the buildings along the waterfront, and the Morro Castle makes one feel privileged and serene. First opened in 1930, refurbished in the late '50s, and restored in 1992, this Spanish-style hotel has hosted innumerable celebrities, including Sir Winston Churchill, Edward VII, Johnny Weissmuller, Buster Keaton, Frank Sinatra, Ava Gardner, Marlon Brando, and others. In this very large building (eight floors), the 457 rooms, 15 suites, and the presidential suite offer a/c, safe, radio, cable TV, minibar, direct-access telephone, and hairdryer. For business travelers, the hotel offers an entire floor with an executive floor manager and his staff, an exclusive front desk, fax service around the clock, a bilingual secretary, translation and interpretation service, cellular phone rental, personal computers, car rentals, audiovisual service, DHL Worldwide, and breakfast, lunch, and dinner served from the snack bar. There are elegant halls for dinners, parties, and cocktails. Apart from the executive floor is a business center on the second floor providing phone and fax services, with e-mail but no Internet access. The little business center has its own bar. A gourmet restaurant, Comedor de Aguiar; a buffet service, Restaurante La Veranda; and a breakfast spot, the Desayunador; along with six bars and a Hall of Fame with traditional Cuban music in the evenings make this hotel self-contained enough to offer a bit of sometimes necessary respite from the city. Two pools, the larger featuring a bar and grill with occasional live entertainment, landscaped grounds with tennis courts, and the Salon Parisien (a huge production in several parts featuring costumes, lights, music, and dance, representing the past and present influences of Spain, Latin America, and Cuba) round out the amenities.

Hotel Tryp Habana Libre, Calle L between Calles 23 and 25, Vedado, La Habana, Cuba. © 537-834-6100, ✎ 537-834-6366, 🖳 tryp.habana.libre@solmelia.com, www.tryphabanalibre.solmelia.com

💰 **Not So Cheap** and up 🍴 **EP** CC 572 rooms

A former Hilton hotel, the last and tallest (25 floors) built before the revolution and inaugurated by Liz Taylor in 1958, the Habana Libre was taken by Castro in 1959 as the revolution's headquarters. A suite on one of the top floors housed its offices. Now run by the Spanish hotel chain Sol Meliá, this "luxury" hotel has a very frozen-in-time feel. The lobby is dominated by an open dark wood staircase to the mezzanine, which spirals over an amoeba-shaped turquoise pool with vertical jets of water. Frosted glass lights hang by thin cords from the second-floor ceiling. It is easy to picture slick-haired men in big-shouldered suits escorting bob-coiffed women in slender sheath dresses and spike-heeled shoes. Following the '50s theme are the restaurants: Polinesio (Chinese cuisine), El Barracon (Cuban Creole cuisine), and the rooftop Sierra Maestra, which shares the 25th floor with the Turquino Cabaret, a disco with live music and DJs. The restaurants share the distinction of providing mediocre food. (Fidel was almost poisoned by a would-be assassin in the cafeteria in 1959. Some things never change!) One of the best-known hotels, the Habana Libre was completely turned over to the press for the pope's visit. The 572 rooms feature balconies, cable TV, the occasional refrigerator (our friends had to climb the chain of command to the general manager to get the promised refrigerator moved into their room). The rooms are large and well lit, with beautiful views. There is a pool on the second floor, renovated in 2000. The business center (open 9:30 a.m. to 5:30 p.m.) on the mezzanine has Internet access with four computers in private little rooms that rent for $3 for 15 minutes, $5 for a half hour, and $10 for an hour. The arcade surrounding the entrance is convenient, but the shops are overpriced. One would do better to explore the busy streets of Vedado for more variety and better bargains. Situated near the very center of town, on the edge of La Rampa district, the hotel is very well located. Be sure to check out the ice cream parlor in the park, less than a block from the hotel.

Hotel Presidente, 110 Calle Calzada, at the corner of Avenida de los Presidentes, Vedado, La Habana, Cuba. ℂ 537-55-1801 or 537-55-1804, ✆ 537-33-3753, 🖳 (reservations) comerc@hpdte.gca.tur.cu

💲 **Cheap** and up 🍴 **CP** Ⓒ Ⓒ 160 rooms

Built between 1925 and 1927 and one of the first "skyscrapers" in the city, the Presidente has been lovingly restored by the Gran Carib Group to its original splendor. The lobby, all cream and black, with marble, silk, velvet, flowers, and brass, just breathes elegance. All the facilities have been updated in the 160 rooms, including two presidential suites, two junior suites, and two adapted for the physically handicapped. The rooms include fully equipped bathrooms, a/c, safe, direct-line telephone, satellite TV, minibar, and an audio system. Only two blocks from the Malecón, many of the rooms have an ocean view. The gourmet restaurant Chez Merito is, of course, expensive, and you would feel out of place unless dressed for dinner. There is also a buffet restaurant, a grill–snack bar, a lobby bar-terrace overlooking the street, and a shaded Gran Café terrace out by the ground-level pool.

Hotel Victoria, Calle 19 at the corner of Calle M, Vedado, La Habana, Cuba. ℂ 537-33-2625 or 537-33-3510, ✆ 537-33-3109, 🖳 www.hotelvictoriacuba.com

💲 **Not So Cheap** 🍴 **CP** Ⓒ Ⓒ 31 rooms

This well-located hotel was built in 1928 (renovated in 1987) and retains its classy feel. Though small, the rooms are well appointed, and there is a small swimming pool. Restaurants and discos share the corner, but the hotel is quiet — maybe too quiet. We found that room service lacks the luster of the hotel's name and past charm. The refrigerator is known to be empty, if working, and the breakfast buffet is nothing spectacular. The staff at the front desk, however, are very patient and easygoing. We even found the bellhop to be quite charming and a bit of a tour guide. From the steps of the Victoria, he gave us a concise overview of the surrounding area.

Hotel Meliá Cohiba, Avenida Paseo between 1a and 3era, Vedado, La Habana, Cuba. ℂ 537-833-3636, ✆ 537-833-4555, 🖳 www.meliacohiba.solmelia.com, melia.cohiba@solmelia.com

💲 **Pricey** and up 🍴 **EP** Ⓒ Ⓒ 462 rooms and suites

Managed by Sol Meliá, a Spanish hotel consortium, this modern, austere marble and glass tower opened in 1994 and is one of Havana's most expensive constructions. Located right off the Malecón and a stone's throw from the Foreign Ministry, the five-star Cohiba is preferred by businessmen (the 20th is the executive floor) and other fat cats. All rooms have a/c and most have ocean views. The rooms are standard big-hotel décor and come with satellite TV and pay TV, radio, minibar, hairdryer, direct-dial telephone and Internet access, 24-hour room service and a pillow menu (a plus). No-smoking rooms and disability-friendly rooms are available. Restaurant Abanico (gourmet), El Cedrano (international cuisine), Habana Café, Labrasa Parrillada (grill), and La Piazza (Italian) provide a classy dining experience, and numerous bars offer respite. Other facilities include a swimming pool, a fitness center, a shopping arcade, and an art gallery. The Ache Disco is definitely worth a visit, even if you stay elsewhere.

Hotel Riviera, Avenida Paseo and Malecón, Vedado, La Habana, Cuba.
℃ 537-33-3733 or 537-33-4051, ✆ 537-33-3738 or 3739

🛍 **Pricey** and up 🍴 EP CC 330 rooms

If ever a movie of gangsters and other savory characters were to be shot again in Havana, it would have to be here, where arch-racketeer Meyer Lansky had the run of the place back in the '50s. The décor is cool and totally in keeping with the tawdriness of the hotel's history. The cabaret used to be Lansky's casino, inaugurated by Ginger Rogers in 1957. The hotel's disco, El Palacio de la Salsa, always hosts the best salsa orchestras. The other Riviera venue, Cabaret Copa Room, is a bit smaller. Although it's removed from the commercial areas of Vedado, the hotel is right on the Malecón. The Riviera was renovated in 1997 and boasts 17 stories of fully appointed rooms. It features international cuisine in its four restaurants (L'Aiglon, Mirador Habana, and Salon Primavera) along with a 24-hour coffee shop near the pool.

Hotel Horizontes St. John's, Calle O between Calles 23 and 25, Vedado, La Habana, Cuba. ℃ 537-833- 3740 or 834-4187, ✆ 537-33-3561, 🖥 reserva@stjohns.gca.tur.cu

Hotel Horizontes Vedado, 244 Calle O between Calles 23 and 25, Vedado, Havana, Cuba. ℃ 537-33-4072 or -4073, ✆ 537-33-4186

🛍 **Dirt Cheap** and up 🍴 CP CC St. John's: 77 rooms; Vedado: 203 rooms

These two hotels are now run by the Gran Caribe group, which has improved service and some décor. However, they are still pretty basic and similar. Foam mattresses, views of the alleys and airshafts, noisy a/c, TV with Cuban channels, hot water in the shower but not in the sink, and no water pressure to speak of (the toilets barely flush!), and the occasional loss of power are de rigueur here. A buffet breakfast is included. Our favorite-looking dish was the spaghetti with bologna, and although we lacked the intestinal fortitude to try it, it was part of the charm. The fresh towels folded like swans added a lovely classy touch (not!). Both have small pools, bars, and nightclubs. You get what you pay for, perfect for those on a budget who need only a place to sleep and shower. Perhaps the best aspect of these hotels is location. Calle O is a hustle-bustle spot and comes to an end at the Malecón, just three blocks from these hotels. You will find, across the street, a cigar shop and, just a little farther down, a reliable ATM machine.

Miramar

Hotel Copacabana, 4404 Avenida 1, between Calles 44 and 46, Miramar, La Habana, Cuba. ⓒ 537-204-1037, 📧 537-204-2846, 🖥 www.grancaribe.cu

🛍 **Not So Cheap** and up 🍽 **EP** CC 168 rooms

Run by the Gran Carib group, this five-story hotel, with red clay roof tiles, balconies, and tan stucco walls, is fairly standard looking from the outside. The Hotel Copacabana was first opened in 1957 and refurbished in 1992. It's directly on the water, so most of the 164 rooms and suites (large and comfortable though nondescript) have an ocean view and feature a/c, safe, and satellite TV. The hotel also offers a business center, a gym, tennis, a freshwater pool with sculptures and a bridge, a poolside snack bar with thatched umbrellas, and a saltwater "natural" pool (no beach) created and protected by the sea wall—perhaps the hotel's most interesting feature. A woman rolling cigars in the lobby seems a little out of place among the bar and lounge areas and the noise they create. There are restaurants, a juice bar, a pizza parlor, and a conference room. The Ipanema Disco completes the experience.

Hotel Comodoro, Avenida 1a at Calle 84, Miramar, La Habana, Cuba. ⓒ 537-833-5551, 📧 537-833-2028

🛍 **Not So Cheap** and up 🍽 **EP** CC 432 rooms and bungalows

This used to be the old Yacht Club frequented by Cuba's social elite in pre-Castro days. It was a dormitory for Revolutionary Armed Forces (FAR) cadets in one of its multiple incarnations. This hotel's disadvantage is that it is rather far from the city's main attractions. However, the hotel's disco is still the den of iniquity that attracts the most beautiful *jineteras* in the city and the (foreign) men who "love" them. Decadence reigns here. The main four-story building, built before the revolution, houses 104 rooms, all equipped with private baths, satellite TV—the usual amenities. The complex was expanded in 1990 and again in 1996 to include 328 two-story tile-roof bungalows, with kitchenette and refrigerator, sitting room with TV, and bedrooms upstairs in single, double, or triple bedroom configurations. Due to its great distance from the center of the city, the Comodoro provides a resortlike atmosphere with its small protected sandy beach, shopping mall, tennis court, karaoke club, and Havana Club Disco.

Where to Eat

Despite the hype that surrounds Cuban cuisine in New York, Miami, and other cosmopolitan cities, you won't be blown away by the food in Cuban restaurants and hotels. You might stand a chance of tasting some authentic Cuban home cooking in the low-key *paladares*, the small (12 seats max) restaurants that have sprung up in the homes of citizens trying to earn a little extra to make ends meet. The food here is often better than in most state-owned restaurants and costs a fraction as much, between $15 and $25. The cuisine in most state-owned restaurants is often considered "international," whereas the *paladares* offer mostly *comida criolla*, typical local food including rice and black beans (called Morros y Cristianos, meaning "blacks and whites") with chicken, pork, or fish (lobster and beef are reserved for the state-run restaurants) and *tostones* (salty fried plantains). There are no sushi bars, Thai restaurants, Tex-Mex, or anything of the sort on the island. A few Italian expatriates have opened up restaurants here and there, and what's left of the once thriving Chinese community still serves up Chino (Cantonese)–Latino cuisine in its vastly reduced neighborhood behind the Capitol. Don't think you'll be able to go on a diet while in Cuba. Cuban cuisine is the product of a Spanish, African, and Chinese cultural combination. The food is well seasoned with garlic and onions, but not spicy, contrary to the cuisine of neighboring countries, and often fried (because much of the food is cooked on a griddle or cooktop — many people don't have ovens). Vegetarians complain that they have a difficult time finding dishes to suit their diet, especially as good fresh produce is hard to find.

The buffet-style meals in hotels are a good alternative to restaurant hunting, and if you choose to make this your big meal of the day, you can do pretty well for about $12 for lunch. For slightly over a buck you can take your chances with a burger and a soda in a Rapid, the Cuban equivalent of Mickey D's. Remember, no American bank–issued credit cards are accepted!

Restaurants

$$$ **Don Cangrejo**, 1606 Avenida 1a, between Calles 16 and 18, Miramar, 204-4169

Built as a 1950s-style residence, this restaurant by the water is owned and managed by Cuba's Ministry of Fisheries. The seafood is therefore good and varied, if a bit pricey. For a fraction of the cost of eating in the formal dining area, you can have lunch outside on a sunny day (highly recommended) and watch the Caribbean lap up to your table.

$$$ **El Aljibe**, Avenida 7 between Calles 24 and 26, Miramar, 204-1583 or 204-1584

This is the place everyone goes to when in Havana. The specialty, Pollo Aljibe, is basic: white rice, excellent black beans, french-fried potatoes and fried plantains, and a deliciously roasted chicken served with a secret citrus-based sauce called *mojo* (pronounced "MO-ho"). They do serve other dishes, but it seems that everyone goes for the signature meal. The restaurant, with its open-air thatched-roof design (complete with cats on the roof), is best for lazy summer lunches. It's very popular with tourist groups; off-hours are best for avoiding the noise and cigarette smoke. Find a hammock and a cool breeze after a meal here.

$$$ **El Floridita**, 557 Calle Obispo, at the corner of Monserrate, La Habana Vieja, 867-1299 or 867-1300

In the same vein as La Bodeguita (below), this erstwhile Hemingway haunt hasn't changed its décor since Papa had his last drink here. It's still cool, and it still makes the best daiquiris (Hemingway's favorite here) in town.

$$$ **El Patio Colonial**, Plaza de la Catedral, La Habana Vieja, 861-8504

This old mansion with stained-glass windows and a beautiful fountain in the courtyard might be a bit expensive, but the food is consistently good and the ambiance is always happening (and romantic). Lively music bands. Good for lunch and dinner.

$$$ **La Bodeguita del Medio**, 205 Calle Empedrado, between Avenidas Cuba and San Ignacio, La Habana Vieja, 862-4498

Immortalized by its "discoverer," Ernest Hemingway, this is probably Havana's best-known restaurant. The trademark scribbling on the wall and the claim to fame invention of the *mojito* bring the tourists in by droves. The food is hearty home-style Cuban, and overpriced. La Bodeguita charges for everything, including bread and butter. "A great place to get drunk," said Errol Flynn. If you just want a *mojito*, you'll be herded into the front room, where small stools are never available. Expect a crowd, decent Cuban music, and a gaggle of loitering street vendors just beyond the doorstep.

$$$$ **La Cecilia**, Avenida 5ta and Calle 110, Miramar, 204-1562

Another mainstay in the upper category of restaurants in Havana, this out-of-the-way but excellent surf-and-turf restaurant has a good salsa club. Dinner and a dance?

$$ **La Taberna**, corners of Mercaderes and Tienente de los Reyes (Brasil), La Habana Vieja 861-1637

This classy high-ceiling room on the ground floor of a 1772 building is filled with beautifully set tables, brass ceiling fans, and a massive dark mahogany bar. It hosts live music (several bands take shifts) through most of the day and night—some popular tunes, some boleros (ballads), and sometimes the audience sings along. It's a very pleasant place to ride out the heat of the day or a thundershower (common in the spring). It serves Cuban cuisine (lunches and dinners) and *mojito* after *mojito* (check the bill, the place charges for everything). Renovated in 2001, La Taberna now enjoys a much needed face-lift.

$$$ **La Torre**, Calle M at the corner of Calle 17, Edificio FOSCA, Vedado, 832-5650

This restaurant with adjoining bar is located in the tower of a bunker-like apartment complex and has the best view of Havana. It has good food and an unusually large selection of wines.

$$$ **La Zaragozana**, 352 Monserrate, between Calle Obispo and Obrapia, La Habana Vieja, 867-1040

Just around the corner next to El Floridita, this restaurant features Spanish cuisine, with an emphasis on seafood. It's elegant and expensive, with a very attentive waitstaff. Flamenco music can be heard nightly.

$$$$$ **Le Select**, Calle 28 between Avenidas 5 and 7, Miramar, 204-7410

Located in an air-conditioned mansion that was once home to Che Guevara, this restaurant is the top of the line and the most expensive. The service is impeccable, as is the food (old-style French). Dine indoors or at poolside in back. Come here to celebrate some extravaganza and forget about how much it costs.

$–$$$ **Tourist-Cultural Complex dos Gardenias**, Avenida 7 between Calles 24 and 26, Miramar

Right next door to El Aljibe, this large tile-roof and stucco building houses several restaurants, serving Chinese, Italian, and Cuban cuisines. A nightclub (live music, different bands, open every night, $10 cover), a French bakery, and an ice cream parlor round out the offerings. This is a convenient stop while walking through Miramar, admiring the parks, the architecture, and the embassies.

Paladares

$$ **Aires**, Calle L, near Universidad (near the University), Vedado

Everyone knows the Aires—we had countless offers from people walking around Vedado (surely they get a little kickback?) to show us there. By then, however, we had already found it ourselves and had enjoyed a wonderful dinner there. In an old Victorian-style house, customers wait in the entryway on old red velvet couches, listening to the parrot chatter away in Spanish. Dinners feature (when available, no surprise here) roast chicken or pork, grilled pork or fish, and stewed beef (*ropa vieja* — meaning "old clothes," for its appearance) and include salad and rice and beans. Appetizers (à la carte) include the very wonderful *tostones* (salty fried plantains) for $1. Aires is open noon to midnight, but it gets very busy at lunch and dinner. Try to stop in earlier to make a reservation if you are pressed for time; otherwise, expect a wait.

$$ **Calle 12**, Calle 12 between Avenidas 5ta and 3era, Miramar, no phone

This *paladar* is good for its food and for the elegant decor of the turn-of-the-century mansion: black-and-white-checkered tile floor, stained-glass windows, marble staircase. Calle 12 is a favorite with the foreign press crowd.

$$ **Dona Blanquilla**, 158 Paseo de Marti Prado, between Colon and Refugio, La Habana Vieja, 867-4958

Sitting on a balcony, overlooking the Prado, which connects the Malecón with the José Martí Central Park, is the best spot for people-watching in Cuba. We spotted this *paladar* while walking down the Prado at lunchtime. It was the only place we found black bean soup in a city that had all but run out of beans. The other food we tried was fine but not so great. The mixture of interesting decorations, from Mardi Gras beads to the Portuguese flag, seemed more a collection of the owner's memories than an astute eye for décor. The view alone is worth the short trip up a narrow staircase. Note: This *paladar* keeps interesting hours, open from noon to 3 a.m.

$$ **Huron Azul**, 153 Humboldt Street, Vedado, La Habana, 879-1691

Surrounded by a hive of Cubans looking for a commission, this *paladar* appears to be closed. Don't listen to the crowing; they're all liars. They'll tell you the place is closed because this *paladar* doesn't pay commission. Pass by the crowd, have a seat, and order a *mojito* and a plate of bombay curry chicken. You'll probably manage another *mojito*, a dessert, and a side dish before breaking $10.

$$ **La Esperanza**, 105 Calle 16, between Avenidas 1a and 3era, Miramar, 822-4361

This is the best *paladar* in Havana and attracts a rather sophisticated and independent clientele. It's run by Hubert and Manolo, a gay couple who have managed to turn their exquisitely decorated 1940s house into a warm and inviting place appropriate for intimate dinners or larger parties. Hubert, a former maitre d' in a Havana hotel, will fix you a fierce drink while you relax in the living room listening to old boleros. The décor is exquisite. A gilt mirror and elegant fireplace in a mint green and ivory parlor complement colonial-style rocking chairs and an eclectic collection of furniture and objets d'art. Reservations suggested. Closed on Thursday. Dinner for two is about $40 plus tip.

$$ **Restaurant Capitolio**, 1159 Calle 13, between Calles 16 and 18, Vedado, 863-4947

Another professional-turned-restaurateur, this time a lawyer, has converted his 1925 southern California–style home into a profitable business, serving close to 100 people a day. The food is simple, the portions generous, and the whole house clean. The menu changes every day and contains diverse selections, such as shrimp, barbecued lamb, and rabbit. However, as is the case in a *paladar*, not all items are always available. Open noon to midnight.

$$ **Restaurant Gringo Viejo**, 454e Calle 21, between E and F, Vedado, 832-6150

Gregory Peck, the Old Gringo himself, holds court in this tiny restaurant from his place on the wall in the big movie poster. Behind an iron gate sits this funky place with great food. Little tables and a little bar, movie posters old and new, stained glass, and plastic vines lend the place its charm. Open noon to 11 p.m.

$$$ **Restaurante La Guarida**, 418 Concordia, between Gervasio and Escobar, Centro Habana, 862-4940 or 863-7351

Fresa y Chocolate was filmed on location here in this beautiful (and well-worn, housing apartments on its four floors) mansion once owned by a well-known doctor in the pre-revolution era—you'll even find the old apple green refrigerator. Serving traditional Cuban food—fish, chicken, pork (and the ubiquitous black beans and rice), along with some surprises like red snapper seviche and gazpacho—it has lots of atmosphere. Photos of famous clients (Jack Nicholson and the queen of Spain, though not together) and movie stills line the entryway. Excellent for a tête-à-tête dinner. Reservations suggested. Open 7 p.m. to midnight.

Going Out

Most of the heavy-duty nightlife takes place in the discos of a handful of hotels; most places stay open until 4 a.m. Gone are the old days when couples would spend the evening in a cabaret or at the hotel casino. Gambling is prohibited under Cuban law. Gone also are the days of the high rollers in town to watch the wild sex acts on stage. Although "dancing and a bottle of rum" are every Cuban's raison d'être, you'll find that the discos are filled with a wide array of characters, chief among them single foreign men with their pockets full of Viagra. Keep in mind that Cubans have a very open and healthy attitude toward sex and that not every Cuban is there to pick up a john or find a sugar daddy.

If you're looking for gay and lesbian nightlife, check with Hubert and Manolo at La Esperanza (see above and plan to have dinner); they know the best private clubs catering to the scene. Officially, gay and lesbian clubs are outlawed. Hangouts for cruising have been at the Yara Cinema (Calle 23 at Calle L) and on the Malecón near the Fiat dealership, but the hot spots are always changing. Even if you don't dance and you're not interested in the meat-market scene, everyone should visit a disco once, if only for the people-watching and the human comedy. Jackets are not required anywhere, but a well-dressed foreigner will be appreciated. Some of the most outrageous places are listed below.

Clubs

Ache Disco, Hotel Meliá Cohiba, Avenidas Paseo and Malecón, Vedado, 833-3636

Just to watch the people — how do they move like that? — is worth the $10 admission. We love the name.

Club La Red and Discotheque Scherazada, Calle M between Calles 17 and 19, Vedado

These two small clubs are located diagonally across Calle M from one another. Both have live music and DJs, both cater to a mostly Cuban crowd, and both have about a $6 cover charge. La Red has a bit more staid atmosphere and an older clientele, but a great mix of salsa, merengue, and popular dance music. Scherazada is popular with a younger crowd, with disco lights, a tightly packed dance floor, and louder and more techno music. Scherazada has "matinees" — a $4 cover charge in the afternoon for the students from the university.

Havana Club, Hotel Comodoro, Avenida 3a at the corner of Calle 86, Miramar, 204-5551

Cuban women are not allowed in alone, so gorgeous women might stop men at the entrance and ask for an escort inside. Once inside, everything is literally up for grabs. The music is more on the techno and pop side. Havana Club remains the ultimate den of iniquity. Cover is about $10.

Palacio de la Salsa, Hotel Riviera, Avenidas Paseo and Malecón, Vedado, 833-3733

The hottest bands play here, and the club is consequently almost always full. Things don't get rocking till late. It's a favorite hangout of

Havana's *jineteros* and *jineteras*. Open from 10 p.m. to 4 a.m., with a cover charge of $10 to $20, depending on the band.

Music-Oriented Venues

Casa de la Música, at the corner of Calles 20 and 31, Miramar, 7-204-0447

The cover is $10 to $15, depending on the band playing—and there's always a band playing. The Casa de la Musica is frequented by Cuban musicians, artists, and families and friends of the musicians, who come to take in the salsa vibes.

El Gato Tuerto, Calle O between Calles 17 and 19, Vedado, 855-2696

Right down the street from the Hotel Nacional, this gated little stand-alone building houses a club that is popular with a more mature crowd. There is a dance floor, and the music featured ranges from jazz to salsa, live every night and filled in with a DJ between sets. The bar is well stocked and the bartenders are kept busy.

La Tropical, Salon Rosado, Calle 41 between Calles 44 and 46, Marianao

This place might be considered sketchy in some books, but Havana's proletarian youth love its weeknight (9 p.m. to 2 a.m.) live salsa and merengue bands. You'll probably stand out here as a foreigner, so be prepared to get hit on.

La Zorra y El Cuervo, Calle 23 at the corner of Calle O, Vedado

This smoky basement (with the colonial maple furniture recognizable to anyone who grew up in the '50s and '60s) is the coolest jazz bar in Havana. Open late. Cover charges vary widely (between $5 and $15), depending on the artists featured and the day of the week.

Sala Macumba-Habana, Tourist Complex La Giraldilla, Calle 222 at the corner of Calle 37, La Coronela, La Lisa, 833-3564, -3565, -3566, or -3567

This huge multipurpose hall hosts big blowouts, very popular with the locals. Saturday, Tuesday, Wednesday, and Friday nights feature a cabaret show. Monday night is the fashion and variety show. Thursday is Salsa Night, and hugely popular, featuring the "biggest groups of the moment." Recordings from Salsa Night can be heard constantly throughout Havana (we bought the CD, so it can be heard constantly from our place, too). Sunday night is Macumba en Carnaval, with a show and surprises. Open every day from 9 p.m. to 5 a.m. It's a bit of a long taxi ride, but the complex includes restaurants and shopping, so you could easily make an evening of it. Call first for the schedule and reservations, or ask at the tourist desk at any hotel. The tourist agencies often run tour buses out to clubs outside Vedado and Miramar for the evening, and these can be cheaper than a cab, but you are at their scheduling mercy.

Other Options

If you want to peer into the past, check out the review at the **Tropicana** (833-7507), where you'll witness some excellent dancing. Note the special number with the dancers wearing chandeliers for headgear! This is the most famous of the cabarets, and the most expensive. With one drink included, tickets (which must be reserved) will cost you about $100, depending on seat location. The club (open air) opens at 8:30 p.m., and the show starts at 10 p.m. Performances are canceled due to rain, and money is refunded relative to the percentage of the show performed. Other cabaret shows of note are presented at the **Nacional, Capri, Riviera**, and **Havana Libre** hotels. Any hotel tourist desk can arrange a reservation and transportation to any of these.

If you're really in the mood for something more adventurous and impromptu, you can always hang at the different but well-known *peñas* around town. Listings for some of the more organized *peñas* are in the free tourist magazine *Cartelera*, found in hotel lobbies, featuring music and dancing of all types — popular, folk, salsa, rumba, and bolero, to name a few. These are held at such venues as the **Teatro Nacional** at Paseo and Calle 39, near the **Plaza de la Revolución**, Centro Habana; phone 33-5713, and at the **Palacio de la Artesenia** at 64 Calle Cuba, at the corner of Peña Pobre and Cuarteles, Habana Vieja. Cubans sometimes get together informally in homes or restaurants for *el descargue*, a sort of poetry and music jam. Someone inevitably has a guitar, and you'll be welcome to join in by tapping on a bottle with a spoon. You'll be more than welcome if you bring a bottle of rum along with you!

Last but not least — and free — is the **Malecón**, otherwise known in Havana as *la sofa*, which describes its function perfectly. Built in 1901 during the American administration, the 5-mile-long sea wall runs from Miramar, along Avenida de Maceo skirting Vedado and Central Havana, to the mouth of the bay in Old Havana. The best place to sit is down by the Nacional or off Central Havana, where you can while away endless hours watching life go by. At night you're likely to find a fisherman, a group of teenagers with a bottle and a guitar, a couple kissing under the starry dome, or a grandmother selling *cerveza y mani* ("beer and peanuts"). Anything can happen on the Malecón.

BEACHES NEAR HAVANA — PLAYAS DEL ESTE

The closest beaches to Havana are those to be found in Playas del Este, which the Cubans call the Costa Azul, about 20 miles east of Havana. (Santa Maria del Mar, midway down the coastal district, is 30 minutes from Old Havana and 40 minutes from Vedado — about a $30 cab fare.) The roads are reasonable and the route is straight and well marked, so renting a car would be a reasonable choice. Habaneros will do anything to get out to any one of these seven beaches during the summer months. Of the seven, Bacuranao is the closest to Havana and Tropico the farthest. Between these two you'll find the beaches of Megano, Santa Maria del Mar, Boca Ciega, Guanabo, and Jibacoa. You'll find bungalows, villas, hotels, apartments (all for rent) and restaurants all along the Playas del Este. Santa Maria del Mar is the best of the beaches and probably the most popular. As in parts of Havana, the buildings are pretty worn, but many are undergoing extensive renovation. The water is warm and a beautiful turquoise. The beaches are relatively clean but not groomed, with lots of organic stuff like washed-up seaweed, coral, and wood. There's some trash, but it's not too bad. Nor are the beaches too crowded, even during school vacation. There are plenty of families, couples, joggers, fishermen (who ply their wares at the restaurants right there at the beach), an entrepreneurial soul giving massages and doing reflexology under a thatched roof to salsa music, and police in uniform, on foot or in four-wheel sand buggies, patrolling for thieves and U.S.-bound émigrés. There are small markets along the main street, Avenida de las Terrazas, for snacks, drinks, groceries, and assorted little items; ETASCA phone booths; a health clinic; sports facilities for tennis, basketball, and volleyball (well worn but functional—bring your own balls and rackets); and bars, restaurants, and open-air cafes under thatched roofs. Be advised that there is fumigation at night for mosquitos, as well as huge conflagrations of birds at the landfills.

Where to Stay

Aparthotel Atlantico, Avenida Las Terrazas between Calles 11 and 12, Santa Maria del Mar, La Habana, Cuba. ✆ 537-97-1494, 🖳 concuba@enet.cu

🏷 **Dirt Cheap** ⑪ EP 🆑 180 rooms

One block (one parking lot, really) from the beach, this place would be ideal for a group of friends. Lots of families, mostly Cuban, hang out by the pool (complete with bar and snack shop). There is a decent restaurant within (the entire meal, fish or chicken with rice and beans, is about $3, and a can of beer is $1), tennis and volleyball courts next door, and basketball courts across the street. There are 180 apartments in one-, two-, and three bedroom arrangements in three four-story buildings. For $40, we got a top-floor apartment, with three bedrooms (sleeps six), two bathrooms, kitchen, dining room, living room with TV (no reception, but it looked nice there on the stand), and balconies on two sides overlooking the ocean and the countryside. The windows and balcony doors had only louvered wood —no glass, no screens. There's no a/c, but with all the louvers open there is a fantastic sea breeze. The kitchen had a little cube fridge and a sink. The bathrooms had toilets with great water pressure. (They flushed! This was a big thrill after some of the places we stayed in Havana.) We had to ask them to turn on the lights at dusk, and there was no hope of hot water in the shower. It was a little like camping out, but much better. Camping is torture!

Hotel Atlantico, Avenida Las Terrazas at Calle 11, Santa Maria del Mar, La Habana, Cuba. ✆ 537-97-1085 or 537-97-1087, 📠 537-96-1532, 🖥 www.club-atlantico.com, vitudes@complejo.gca.tur.cu

💲 **Not So Cheap** 🍴 AP (CC) 192 rooms

Across the street from the aforementioned Aparthotel Atlantico and right on the beach sits this Gran Carib four-story, gated, pink cement block. Many Canadian and European tour companies book here for a relatively affordable all-inclusive vacation alternative to Varadero. We spoke to one Canadian guest who was very disappointed with the place and who informed us that it had just been downgraded from three stars to two. The place is falling into disrepair (notably the a/c and the bathrooms) — it looks shabby and has less than stellar service. Facilities include a swimming pool, tennis court, disco, buffet restaurant (serving all the meals included in the plan), and car rental and travel agency desk.

Hotel Tropicoco, Avenida Las Terrazas at Calle 7, Santa Maria del Mar, La Habana, Cuba. ✆ 537-97-1371 or 537-97-1389. 🖥 recepcion@htropicoco.hor.tur.cu

💲 **Dirt Cheap** to **Cheap** (depending upon the meal plan) (CC) 188 rooms

The last time we visited this place, it was full of Venezuelans on a state-sponsored retreat, and would be open to tourists only during the Christmas–New Year's high season. From what we can tell, renovations have been completed. The paint job is the envy of this area, and the furniture is relatively new. Even the bar area seems redesigned and more comfortable. The hotel's entrance opens immediately into a refreshing atrium, which is packed with greenery and relatively comfortable furniture. Since renovations, the hotel has shifted to an all-inclusive package — a pattern that is gaining popularity all over the island. The package includes all meals, a room, and an open bar.

WEST OF HAVANA

Most of Cuba's tourist destinations undoubtedly lie east of Havana, but we're convinced that you can spend just as much time in the less developed western reaches of the island. The scenery in this part of Cuba is rocky. It's home to dozens of rivers, numerous species of birds, world-class snorkeling and diving, and a set of flora not often found on a Caribbean island. Pine trees and deciduous swaths of forest mix regularly with tall, regal palms. Small mountains roll along in the distance. In western Cuba you can find corners of relaxation where you will forget you're even in Cuba. In the mountains, you can enjoy a break from the heat while taking in the best of what Cuba has to offer inland. In short, western Cuba should not be overlooked. Although this section of the island is lacking in size, it more than makes up for that in natural beauty.

If you're traveling west, take the desolate but picturesque north coast road (Costa Norte). Just outside Havana, you'll drive past the port of Mariel, which lent its name to the famous early '80s boat lift.

Pinar del Río is the third largest province in Cuba. Mountains, valleys, rivers, caves, plains, and beaches make for a varied landscape. The best tobacco in Cuba is grown here, and sugarcane plantations, rice paddies, citrus groves, cattle ranches, and copper mining provide for the people (via the government).

The town of Pinar del Río is a crossroads that travelers must pass through on their way to Maria la Gorda, Viñales, or beaches that sit on the northwestern end of Cuba. The town itself is a testimony to how long beautiful architecture lasts over the years even when it is not properly maintained. We were disappointed with Pinar del Río's surly residents. Also, its dense concentration of *jineteros* left us with a bad taste in our mouths. Although there are a few sections of the town that were much more beautiful than even Old Havana, we recommend that you spend the night here only if necessary. Stay away from the private houses (which seem to exist only to take advantage of tourists), and eat elsewhere.

Pine forests to the west, semi-deciduous forests to the east, and a swampy and marshy coastline are home to hundreds of species of birds, both endemic and migratory. It's paradise for bird-watchers. **Las Terrazas**, in the Sierra del Rosario, is a planned settlement that originated as a reforestation project and has been designated as a UNESCO biosphere reserve. Las Terrazas is also home to a gated tourist resort, with a hotel built in 1994, art galleries and workshops, an abandoned coffee plantation from the 19th century with a restaurant, many hiking trails, and the **Ecotourism Center**, where you can plan your adventures in the province. The mountain resorts of the **Hotel Moka** at Candelária and the **Villas Soroa** just to the south are among the finest in the area.

Next to the Villas Soroa is the **Orquidareo** (established in 1943), which houses 350 species of orchid easily grown in this area of rainforest. It's open daily, 9 a.m. to 4 p.m., but closed for an hour at noon; $3 admission. Across the street is a beautiful waterfall where you can swim in the pool at the base of the falls. Up the hill from the hotel, above the falls is the bar **Castillo de la Nubes**, with an excellent view of both the valley and the coastal plains. It's open daily, 8 a.m. to 5 p.m.

Heading farther west, the hot springs at **San Diego de los Banos** is a great place to rest and rejuvenate. The **Balneario San Diego** offers baths (communal and private) as well as beauty and massage services. The sulfurous waters are hot (85°F to 105°F) and potent, and only 15 minutes of immersion per day is allowed.

In the city of Pinar del Río, the provincial capital, check out the **Museo de Ciencias Naturales**, at 202 Martí, located in the old (1914) Palacio Guasch, a formidably eclectic piece of architecture. The **Fabrica de Bebedas Casa Garay**, at 189 Isabel Rubio, between Ceferino Fernandes and Frank Pais, is famous for its Guayabita del Pinar brandy made from guavas, and it has a tasting room and sells bottles of the sweet or dry versions for about $6. It's open Monday through Friday, 8:30 a.m. to 4:30 p.m. A visit to the **Fabrica de Tobacos Francisco Donatien** at 157 Maceo Oeste demonstrates the area's most famous industry as workers continuously roll cigars, which you can buy in their shop, open Monday through Friday from 7:30 a.m. to 4 p.m. and Saturday until 11:30 a.m. Visit the cathedrals and art galleries along and around Martí, then relax on a ride through the city streets in a *coche*, the popular old-fashioned horse-drawn carriage.

Just north of the city of Pinar del Río is the village of **Viñales**, known for its valleys in the Sierra de los Organos. Limestone hills (*mogotes*) rise from the green plains, and the geological effect known as karst (the irregular erosion of limestone, usually by water, resulting in irregular landforms, sinkholes, and caverns), give this valley its unique landscape. The hiking is fantastic, and for the intrepid, there are caves to explore, miles long, some with underground rivers. One such cave, the **Cueva del Indio** (once home to Indians) in the northern area of the valley, offers hiking and boat tours through the cave (lit by electric lights). For about $4, you can hike into the cave, navigate by rowboat, and emerge by a small waterfall at the other end. The area is quite touristy, very well publicized in the brochures, bringing busloads from Havana (about a four-hour trip) for day trips. **El Mural de la Prehistoria** is a yawn, and one of the first stops for the buses. The Horizontes Group runs both La Ermita and Los Jazmines in the town of Viñales, so if you stay in the area, you can plan your time around the tour groups and enjoy the landscape in relative peace.

It is said that Che Guevara headed the revolutionary strike force from a secret underground bunker in one of the area's mountains. Most of the Soviet nuclear missiles, which led to the missile crisis in the early '60s, were deployed in the Pinar del Río region.

Where to Stay

Pinar del Río

Hotel Pinar del Río, Islazul, Martí Final, at Autopista, Pinar del Río, Cuba.
🕿 82-5070

💲 **Dirt Cheap** 🍽 CP 136 rooms

Coming around the last curve before hitting Pinar del Río, this hotel grabs your attention as the only large building in the area with lights, just behind the Saiz Brothers monument. The entrance is usually populated with the usual fare of commission seekers, people asking for a ride to the next town, and the random old man begging for food. Apart from what can be a shocking entrance, the interior is neat, if a bit unkempt around the edges. A bar and sitting area, located in the back of the room beneath a canopy of flowering vines, allows guests to take a load off and simply people-watch—the ebb and flow of Cubans who populate the area is worth a beer or two. The open-air design is at least refreshing. The rooms are nothing special; they have a terrace, a small TV, and a decent shower. We've seen truck stops with more amenities, but for one night in Pinar del Río, you could do much worse. Note that this is the destination hotel for those Cubans who have won a state-sponsored vacation for loyalty to neighborhood Communist Party committees. At any given time, this hotel might be packed with a steady flow of Cubans on a free vacation. If you hit one of those periods, prepare to party, 'cause you're not gonna sleep! No credit cards.

Viñales

Hotel Los Jasmines Horizontes, Carretera at Viñales, km 25, Viñales, Cuba. ℂ 893-6205, ✆ 893-6215, ▭ gerencia@jazmines.esipr.cu

🛍 **Cheap** ⑪ **EP** ⒸⒸ 88 rooms

This is a good place to set up a base camp if you're going to tour the region. There are 72 rooms with TV and baths in two three-story buildings on either side of the pool, plus 16 slightly cheaper rooms called cabanas in a low building facing the valley. Niño Vera, who used to own the hotel, now runs the gift shop and will regale you with gossip about famous visitors. Stay in one of the cabanas if you can. The view is spectacular, and the pool area is often overrun with sightseers.

Hotel La Ermita, Carretera at La Ermita, km 1.5, Viñales, Cuba. ℂ 893-6071 or 893-6072, ✆ 893-6069, ▭ laermita@laermita.co.cu

🛍 **Cheap** ⑪ **EP** ⒸⒸ 62 rooms

On a hilltop east of the village of Viñales, this modern hotel has 62 rooms with balconies and bath, in either a one-story building facing the pool or in the two-story buildings facing the valley. The best rooms at this simple lodging are 51, 52, 61, and 64. The hotel offers tennis courts and horseback riding (for about $5 an hour) and is within walking distance of the village.

Soroa, Las Terrazas, Candelária

Hotel & Villas Horizontes Soroa, Carretera de Soroa, km 8, Candelária, Cuba. ℂ 80-2122 or 85-2041

💲 **Dirt Cheap** and up 🍴 EP CC 24 cabanas

In this resort of green hills and tall trees sit 24 cabanas (in four-unit, single-story buildings) with comfortable beds, baths, and refrigerators. There is a grubby pool with a loud bar; ask for a room on the other side. Staying at the Villa allows you guest privileges at the park across the street (free admission). It's next to the Orquidero and down the hill from the Castillo de la Nubes. What more could you ask for in a basic mountain resort?

Hotel Moka, Gran Carib, Autopista Nacional, km 51, Candelária, Cuba.
🕾 82-77-8600, 🖂 82-77-8605, 🖳 hmoka@terraz.co.cu

💲 **Cheap** 🍴 EP CC 26 rooms

This four-star hotel, brought to you by the same group managing the Nacional in Havana, is nestled in the woods. A two-story building houses 26 rooms, each with satellite TV, refrigerator, and bath. There is a swimming pool, a tennis court, rowboat and rod rental (black bass in the reservoir), mountain bike rental, and horseback riding available.

Maria la Gorda

We regret never having met the infamous Maria, the Venezuelan woman who brought hospitality to this section of Cuba. She must have been quite a personality! Judging from the artist's relief of this woman, she was a buxom brigand who made the best of a marooned situation by gathering enough swagger and charisma to firmly plant one of the best tourist destinations in Cuba on the very tip of this island's most western point. This is one of our favorite spots in Cuba, apart from Trinidad, to spend a few days of rest, relaxation, and, well, more relaxation. This area is very remote, extremely chill, and anchored by one hotel that sets the standard for service in Cuba.

The entire peninsula west of the town of La Bajada was declared a biosphere reserve in 1987 by UNESCO. The Coast Guard checks permits to enter the Parque Nacional Peninsula de Guanacahabibes, which are available for $10 at the Hotel Maria la Gorda. Beautiful but rough seas (the Caribbean Current becomes one with the Gulf of Mexico through the Estrecho de Yucatán) hide the ruins of a "lost city" that sits at a depth of 2,100 feet. The city is believed to have been built as long as 6,000 years ago. Swampy along the north coast and rocky along the south, this area is a bird-watcher's paradise.

Hotel Maria la Gorda is home to the country's best dive center. The snorkeling here is also excellent. Crystal-clear water allows you to see from top to bottom, up to 40 feet or more. The constant sunshine reflects its rays off the bottom, making for hours of easy visibility for snorkeling. Those who feel like taking a simple 300-yard walk down the beach will be treated to an isolated snorkeling experience—just you and the fish.

Maria la Gorda is a scuba diving mecca. Some divers consider this the best diving in the world (of course, we admit that there are tons of locations throughout the world that are given that distinction by somebody). At Hotel Maria la Gorda, there are more than 30 dive sites near shore. Rare black coral lives in this area, and the abundance of marine life is something we rarely see in Cuba. Because this is Cuba, certified divers will want to bring their own gear (including BC and regulator). Resort-course dives (beginners without certification) are available at your own risk. It costs $35 for one dive, $55 for two dives, and $70 for a full day's outing. There are many other packages available (including night dives) — some include as many as 20 dives for $400. Because diving certification is not required or available, the liability is yours, so we advise all divers to use caution (which we assume you would, anyway).

Hotel Maria la Gorda, 8.6 miles/14 kilometers southwest of the guardpost at La Bajada on the highway, Maria la Gorda, Cuba. ✆ 82-778-131, 82-773-072, or 82-773-075, 🖋 82-778-077 🖳 mlagorda@enet.cu

💲 **Dirt Cheap** and up 🍴 **FAP** ($15 per person per day) CC 40 rooms
Operating like a scuba camp, this diving resort is more functional than posh. However, it's certainly comfortable enough, and it's the only game in town. This three-star resort offers better rooms, service, food, and overall experience than some of the top five-star hotels we found in Varadero. The small gated resort is wonderfully isolated at the end of a long road made of patches of old pavement and crushed coral. Make a reservation in advance to get a room facing the ocean in the buildings closest to the reception area. The patch of palm trees in front of these buildings provides much-needed shade from the constant sunshine. The quintessential Caribbean water — in both color and temperature — is less than 20 yards from your door. Rooms come with TV, bath, and a/c. They are simple but comfortable. Refrigerators are available in some of the rooms. Breakfast is included, and a buffet dinner at the restaurant next to the dive center is optional. The other restaurant, located next to the bar in the same building as the reception area, serves the best (and cheapest) pizza we've found in Cuba. This is a great spot to enjoy dinner and a *mojito* while listening to live salsa. The band starts around 9 p.m. Free salsa lessons are available.

Where to Eat

Cueva del Indio, Carretera de Puerto Esperanza, km 38, Viñales, phone 82-93202. Located at the entrance of the cave, it serves baked chicken and manioc cakes at long tables, family style. There is also a bar-cabaret in the cave. **Casa del Marisco**, across the street from the Cueva del Indio, is serving — what else? — seafood specialties. For an evening of all-out gaudiness, go to the government-run **Cabaret Rumayor**, the city's largest restaurant-cabaret and disco. Its specialty is *pollo ahumado* ("smoked chicken"). Two miles on the road to the valley, Rumayor is open daily (except Thursday), noon to 10 p.m., at Carretera Viñales, km. 10, Viñales, phone 82-63007.

EAST OF HAVANA

Heading east, you might want to consider a four- or five-day trip. Starting from Havana, you can stop for a day or two in Varadero, the primary tourist area in the Matanzas province, for a swim and some sun. Expect to be sequestered away in a resort with lots of European tourists — not really the real Cuba. Then move on to Santa Clara, where Che Guevara's remains were finally laid to rest in 1997; and check out Remedios, Sancti Spiritus, and especially Trinidad, three of the seven colonial towns founded by the Spanish *conquistadores*. These three towns are beautiful examples of the way life used to flow in Cuba's interior provinces. Don't miss the activity around the main square at night, when the locals gather to chat, play dominoes, discuss baseball, or just stroll. On your way back, stop by Cienfuegos and Playa Giron, the infamous Bay of Pigs. The diving there is excellent.

Varadero

About 90 miles from Havana along the Via Blanca highway — about the same distance that separates Cuba from the United States — you'll come to the port city of Matanzas and Varadero Beach shortly thereafter.

If by chance your plane landed in Varadero, you'll wonder if the pilot didn't mistakenly land in Cancún or Jamaica. The new postmodern hotels lining the waterfront have meticulously well-tended lawns. The pavement is smooth and the people are service oriented. The sound of the gentle surf is barely muffled by the hum of the a/c that cools the hotel rooms in the noon heat.

What is there to say about these 10 miles of powdery white sand and clear turquoise water that hasn't been said before? A photo of Varadero hangs on the wall of every European or Canadian travel agency "selling" Cuba. The thing about Varadero is that although you're in Cuba — you're not. Everything is geared toward the sea-and-surf tourists, which makes it very difficult to distinguish Varadero from any other Caribbean sun destination. We recommend a brief stay here, if any.

One cultural site worth seeing to offset all the commercialism is the DuPont Mansion on the Avenida las Americas. Designed by Evelio Govantes and Partners Architects before the revolution, the house and surrounding gardens are still in pristine condition. Tours are available and are a nice respite from the endless beaches.

There are literally thousands of hotel rooms in Varadero, and chances are that finicky travelers will be able to find a few that are suitable to their taste.

In addition to the Web sites mentioned earlier in this chapter, check out these Web sites for more info on hotels and other facts regarding Varadero: www.cuba.tc/varadero and www.cubanacan.cu.

All the larger high-end hotels that cater exclusively to foreigners offer pretty much the same services: a/c, bars, restaurants, gift shops, pools, and water sports. Most were built in this decade, and the architectural style is somewhere between postmodern and neo-tropical Spanish.

Where to Stay

Hotel Meliá Varadero, Avenida Las Americas, Varadero, Cuba. ✆ 66-7013,
    ✆ 66-7012, ▫ www.solmeliá.com,
    jefe.ventas.mva@solmeliacuba.com

   📋 **Pricey** and up ⑪ **EP** ⒸⒸ 490 rooms

   Built in 1991 by the same Spanish corporation as the Meliá Cohiba in Havana in a joint venture with the government, this luxury 490-room star-shaped compound is where Havana's diplomatic corps likes to come for naughty weekends. The hotel has all the amenities you might possibly need, including five different bars, four restaurants, a disco, water sports, two swimming pools, a fitness center, and tennis courts. It is also conveniently located next to the golf course, for which packages are available through the hotel. All rooms have minibars, satellite TV, and balconies facing either the sea or gardens. The hotel sits on a rocky ledge with the beach a five-minute walk away.

Hotel Sol Club Palmeras, Autopista del Sur, Varadero, Cuba. ✆ 66-7009,
    ✆ 66-7008, ▫ www.solmeliá.com,
    jefe.ventas.sep@solmeliacuba.com

   📋 **Pricey** and up ⑪ **EP** ⒸⒸ 400 rooms

   This horseshoe-shaped luxury hotel was inaugurated by The Man himself in 1990 as part of another joint venture between the Cuban government group Cubanacan and the Spanish hotel group Sol Meliá. The 400-room hotel is built around a large swimming pool, which in turn opens up to a vast expanse of powdery sand beach. There are two lit tennis courts and a 24-hour pharmacy on the premises. Much like its cousin down the road, all the rooms in the Sol Palmeras have baths, minifridges, satellite TV, and balconies. About 200 rooms are available in the more independently styled bungalows —they are perfect for extended groups or families. However, we think that the stretch of beach near the main building is better than the one near the bungalows. The luxurious and labyrinthine lobby with restaurants, bars, and practically a rainforest of plants complete with caged birds is worth a look.

Varadero Internacional, Avenida Las Americas, Varadero, Cuba. ℂ 66-
7038 or 66-7039, ✺ 66-7045, ▢ reserva@gcinter.gca.tur.cu

💰 **Not So Cheap** and up ⑪ **EP** ⒸⒸ 163 rooms

This is probably Varadero's best-known hotel. Built in 1950 as a sister property to the Fontainebleau in Miami Beach, the four-story Internacional is a perfect example of an "international style" architecture that made its distinctive mark in Cuba in the last decade before
the revolution. This hotel is right on the beach, and, although it is
smaller and not as luxurious as many others in the region, it is an excellent value. The décor in the cabaret and the main restaurant will
make you dream of the "good old days" back in the 1950s. All rooms
are equipped with showers, balconies, and satellite TV. The hotel also
has a swimming pool, tennis courts, and water sports.

Mecure Coralia Cuatro Palmas, Avenida 1ra between Calles 60 and 61,
Varadero, Cuba. ℂ 66-8101, ✺ 66-7208,
▢ gerente@gcpalho.gca.cma.net

💰 **Not So Cheap** ⑪ **EP** ⒸⒸ 200 rooms

This hotel has 200 rooms, all with bath and satellite TV, in a Spanish-
style complex scattered in two- and three-story building blocks
arranged around the swimming pool. Make sure you're not booked in
the hotel annex across the street, which is a block back from the beach.
This has been under French (ACCOR) management since 1996.

Horizontes Herradura, Avenida de la Playa between Calles 35 and 36,
Varadero, Cuba. ℂ 61-3703, ✺ 66-7496,
▢ crh@horizontes.hor.tur.cu

💰 **Cheap** ⑪ **EP** ⒸⒸ 78 rooms

A more downscale but decent property, the 78-room Herradura is yet
another horseshoe-shaped hotel (what is it with these architects?) on
the beach in town. Make sure you get a private bathroom. This spot
is popular with Cubans, few of whom can afford the hip properties
mentioned above.

Where to Eat

Varadero has more than 100 restaurants, most of which offer the same in-
ternational cuisine. *Paladares* are not allowed to operate in this tourist town.
Reservations here are an unheard-of concept (except for the Universal and
Las Americas). The following are among the notable restaurants.

$ **Castel Nuovo**, Avenida 1ra and Calle 11, 66-7786

This Italian-style restaurant serves chicken, beef, and seafood as well
as your basic pastas and pizzas. Located opposite Villa Barlovento.

$$ **Chino Chong Kwok**, Complejo Mediterraneo, Avenida 1ra and Calle 54, 61-2460

We like this place, in part, because it's fun to say its name. Also, you can't beat its shrimp fried rice or steamed broccoli. (Well, OK, you *can* beat it, but it's pretty good for Cuba.)

$$ **El Bodegon Criollo**, Avenida Playa with Calle 40, 66-7784

This is quintessential *criollo* food, and probably the best place in town to find a bowl of steaming black bean soup.

$ **Lai-Lai**, Avenida 1ra and Calle 18, 66-7793

This serves "Chino-Latino" fare like you might find in New York or Miami.

$$$ **Las Americas**, Avenida Las Americas, 63-415

This restaurant is worth seeing if only because it is located in the library of the old DuPont mansion. In its prime, the spread boasted its own golf course, gardens, and private dock. The wine cellar and the majestic organ in the upstairs dining room are two of the charming details that only the out-of-sight rich could afford. Too bad the international cuisine does not match the décor.

$$$ **Universal**, Hotel Internacional, Avenida Las Americas, 63-011

Reservations are often required in this old-style restaurant. It's a nice environment punctuated by crystal chandeliers and Lalique décor. The house speciality is the Chateaubriand.

Trinidad

Pirates, brigands, Spanish royalty, rebellious slaves, and Cuban revolutionaries have populated the hills around Trinidad for centuries. Over the years, Trinidad has shifted from pirate pleasure center and sugar production powerhouse to prestigious outpost for Spanish gentry and, finally, music treasure trove. A colorful colonial history and rich music tradition are what bring tourists to Trinidad. A relatively short distance from Havana ensures easy travel time. The beauty of cobblestone streets, colonial facades, and seemingly constant music will keep you there longer than expected. It is one of our favorite spots in Cuba and one of the most charming colonial towns in the Caribbean.

Backed by the Sierra del Escambray and facing the sea, Trinidad was the third settlement founded by the Spanish *conquistadores*, in 1514. Sugar money bankrolled beautiful houses and buildings in the late 18th century, but as the plantation era ended, Trinidad became a quiet little village again. The railroad didn't reach here until 1919, and the highway not until the 1950s.

This isolation has made Trinidad the best preserved colonial town in Cuba. It is so unique in its conservation that UNESCO designated Trinidad part of its World Heritage program in 1988. Protected by law, old buildings and neighborhoods are being lovingly restored. Here the chickens, horses, and children all seem to have emerged from a turn-of-the-century silver gelatin photo plate (never mind the roaring air-conditioned buses that pull up to disgorge hordes of German and French tourists).

Many of the sights are located near the slanting **Plaza Mayor**, the city's neatly designed square. The church is the **Santisima Trinidad**, of course, and the most recognized landmark is the tower of the former **Convent of San Francisco**. Four museums, containing bits and pieces of the city's past, can be visited near the square: the Guamuhaya Archeological Museum, the Municipal Historical Museum, the Trinitarian Architecture Museum, and the Romanticism Museum.

All the museums are located within a block or two of the Plaza Mayor. The **Museo de Arqueologia Guamuhaya** (457 Bolivar) is open Sunday to Friday, 9 a.m. to 5 p.m.; admission is $1. The **Museo Historico Municipal** (423 Bolivar) is open Monday to Saturday, 9 a.m. to 6 p.m.). The **Museo de Arquitectura Trinitaria** (southeast side of Plaza Mayor), is open daily between 8 a.m. and 5 p.m.; admission is $1. The **Museo Romantico** (52 Echerri) is open Tuesday to Sunday, 8 a.m. to 5 p.m.; admission is $2.

The special cultural events in Trinidad are the **Fiestas Sanjuaneras**, a carnival from June 20–24, and the Semana de la Cultura Trinitaria, which occurs in the second half of November.

If ever you were curious to check out a *casa particular*, Trinidad is perhaps the best place to find a good fit. The limited number of local hotels forces most tourists to stay in private homes, which have a maximum capacity of two bedrooms. This translates into very personal service, some privacy, and a full-time, full service mini-hotel where you will find all your meals home cooked, your beer ice cold, and your nights peacefully calm.

Although the private restaurants are a little harder to find than the private houses, there is no limit to the number of people stopping you in the street to offer a plate of shrimp (*caramones*) or lobster (*langosta*). These meals can be had for about four times cheaper than the same dish in government-run establishments.

Where to Stay

Casa Tamargo, 266 Calle Rosario, Trinidad, Cuba. ☎ 419-6669, 🖳 www.pension-in-trinidad.de, felixmaltide@yahoo.com

💲 **Dirt Cheap** 🍴 EP 2 rooms

Just around the corner from Trinidad's Brunet Theatre, this private colonial house is the best Trinidad has to offer. It has been recently restored to its prior prestige and has smoothly extended itself with a patio and eating area. The two rooms are comfortable, with simple décor and colonial furniture. Both have private bathrooms with hot water and (not to be overlooked) good showers. A beautiful hardwood table, which easily seats 12, is at the center of the eating area. This is where our friend and owner, Matilde, serves a range of unique *criollo* dishes. For less than $30 a night, you will not find a more comfortable bed, better service, or more perfect food. The roof deck offers a view of both the sea and the mountains. It is a perfect place for watching the sun set, deepening your tan, or simply forgetting about time and letting the days slip by. No credit cards are accepted (only Cuban convertible pesos).

Casa del Campesino, Finca Maria Dolores, Trinidad, Cuba. ℂ 419-6481, 419-6394, and 419-6395

 💲 **Cheap** 🍴 **EP** 18 rooms

Twelve miles down the road toward Cienfuegos is this tiny and unbelievably cheap (think back to those youth hostel days) lodging option. The rooms are located in duplex cabanas, in single, double, and triple configurations. When musical groups stop by the restaurant, there are *fiestas campesinas* with Cuban folk music and dancing. Admission is $4 but free for diners. Casa del Campesino also offers horseback riding for a nominal fee.

Motel Las Cuevas, Finca Santa Ana, Trinidad, Cuba. ℂ 419-4013, ✉ 419-6161, 💻 jose@cuevas.co.cu

 💲 **Dirt Cheap** 🍴 **EP** 🆑 112 rooms

Less than a mile northeast of town, this uninteresting hotel is frequented by tourists in buses. The simple rooms (all include a private bath) are divided into several buildings, but be sure to avoid the building by the pool—it appears to be the favorite of the noisy tourists. One of the motel's draws is its on-premise cave (Cueva La Maravillosa). It is easily accessible—just look for the huge tree growing up out of the cave through a large pit nearby. The cave is OK, but we found the best part of this place to be the commanding view from the front deck—not a bad spot from which to catch a sunset.

Where to Eat

$ **Paladar Ania Noriega**, 306 Pablo Pisch Giron, Trinidad, 419-4463

Half a block south of Trinidad's famous Canchanchara bar, you will find a simple wooden door between two stalls that sell hand-embroidered tablecloths and napkins. Knock on the door and ask for our friend Ania. Specializing in traditional and *criollo* cuisine, this young cook prepared the best lobster dish we've had in years. Also, her warm manner was quite a relief from the often frosty attitudes of waiters at some of the government-run restaurants. Ania's cooking is certainly worth the effort required to find this place. She accepts patrons just about any time of day.

$ **Restaurante El Marino**, Cienfuegos and Frank Pais

This favorite with the locals turns into a disco on Saturday from 9:30 p.m. to 2 a.m. and on Sunday from 9:30 p.m. to midnight.

$ **Taberna La Canchachara**, Ruben Martinez Villena at Ciro Redondo

Local musicians play to a crowd of tourists and locals in this 17th-century building. Things can get quite lively when you're drinking the bar's signature cocktail, the *canchachara*, made with rum, honey, lemons, and water.

Santiago de Cuba

Santiago de Cuba is the island's second largest city. It has a lot more in common with the rest of the Caribbean than with its rival, Havana. Sort of like a New York City vs. Los Angeles thing, this competition goes back a long way. Santiago was the island's first seat of power. The revolution began in Santiago and ended in Havana. Santiago's racial composition is principally black, whereas Havana's is mostly white. Santiagueros speak in a singsong fashion; Habaneros don't. Santiago has an unquestionable and unique tropical flavor.

One thing both cities have in common is crime. Habaneros will tell you that there is more crime in Santiago de Cuba than anywhere else on the island. We were skeptical of that claim until we asked more Cubans in Pinar del Río, Trinidad, Cienfuegos, and other spots along the way. They all agreed. Some even claimed that members of their family had left the town. If you choose to visit this town, be aware of your wallet and personal belongings at all times.

There is plenty to see in Santiago de Cuba, including **San Juan Hill** (Teddy Roosevelt and his Rough Riders' triumph, although notice how the inscriptions have been removed from the bronze statue), the **Bacardí Rum factory** (Emelio Bacardí y Moreau was the first mayor of Santiago de Cuba), **Pico Turquino** (the highest point in Cuba), and the music. **The Festival of Caribbean Culture** is held in early June or July, the **Bolero de Oro** is in August. *Son*, the precursor of salsa, was invented here. The best places to catch folk music are at the **Casa de la Trova** (208 Heredia) and the **Patio Los Dos Arboles** (5 Francisco Perez Carbo, on the east side of the Plaza de Marte) where groups play for tips. The **Ballet Folklorico Cutumba** (170 Saco, upstairs, between Corona and Padre Pico, phone: 2-5860) is the place for Afro-Cuban folk dancing. Sunday morning at 10:30 a.m. is a dance show not to be missed, for a mere $4.

Most of the city's action, day and night, can be found around the downtown **Parque Cespedes**. On one side of the square is the mansion of Diego Velazquez, the island's first governor, currently the seat of the Colonial Art Museum. Overlooking Parque Cespedes, the Hotel Casa Granda, on the other side of the square, was the meeting point of the city's bourgeoisie in the olden days. Take a stroll down Calle Heredia, off Parque Cespedes, where you'll get a good feel for the people of Santiago as they go about their business.

Where to Stay

Hotel Casa Granda, 201 Calle Heredia, at the corner of San Pedro, Santiago de Cuba, Cuba. ✆ 226-86-600, ✆ 226-86-035, ⌨ reserva@casagran.gca.tur.cu

💲 **Not So Cheap** and up ⑪ **EP** ⒸⒸ 58 rooms

The dean of hotels in Santiago, the Casa Granda, run by Gran Carib, is equivalent in stature to the Nacional or the Inglaterra in Havana. The hotel and Parque Cespedes, located across the street, are the focal point for Santiago's social life. The view from the rooftop deck is excellent, and the restaurant Roof Garden hosts live music regularly.

Meliá Santiago de Cuba, Avenida de las Americas between Avenidas 4ta and Manduley, Santiago de Cuba, Cuba. ✆ 226-87-070, ✆ 226-87-170, ⌨ www.meliasantiagodecuba.solmelia.com, melia.santiago.de.cuba@solmelia.com

💲 **Not So Cheap** and up ⑪ **EP** ⒸⒸ 268 rooms and 34 suites

This five-star luxury hotel completed construction back in 1991, but it is now run by the Meliá chain (of the Cohiba in Havana) in partnership with Cubanacán. Thus you can count on good service. This modern hotel boasts 268 double rooms (88 of which are connected), 30 junior suites, 3 master suites, and 1 presidential suite with a private office, a Jacuzzi, and a lounge. All rooms are equipped with satellite TV, minibar, radio, safe, and 24-hour room service—a rarity on this island! Four restaurants, two bars, including a pool bar in one of the three swimming pools, and two cafes will keep your palate occupied on a constant basis. We recommend that you stay here if you're in need of guaranteed cleanliness and good service. However, the Cuban cultural feeling is somewhat lacking.

Horizontes Las Américas, Avenida de las Américas and General Cebreco, Santiago de Cuba, Cuba. ✆ 226-87-255, ✆ 226-87-075, ⌨ crh@horizontes.hor.tur.cu

💲 **Cheap** ⑪ **EP** ⒸⒸ 68 rooms

Built in 1991, this postmodern structure is painted in a screaming red, white, and blue. It is basic, comfortable, and standard for a Horizontes property. Of the 68 rooms, 50 come with a balcony, so make sure to request one those rooms so that you can get a bird's-eye view of the action below. If you want a minibar in your room, which is a great reservoir for midnight water runs, make sure you request it — only 15 of the rooms come with a minibar. The property has two restaurants, two bars, a cafeteria, a pool, and a disco.

Where to Eat

$$ **1900**, 354 San Basilio, 226-23-507

This former Bacardi spread is the best-known restaurant in Santiago today. The restaurant is also the training ground for the gastronomical school. It has an international and Cuban menu. Open Tuesday to Sunday, 1 to 3 p.m. and 6 p.m. to midnight.

$ **Restaurante El Morro**, Carretera del Morro, km 9, 226-91-576

Located 6 miles out of town, next to the Morro fortress at the mouth of Santiago Bay, this is good for a no-frills lunch.

Don't Miss

Cayo Coco Key

Unfortunately, overdevelopment of these tourist resorts has resulted in both omnipresent construction and the destruction of natural waterways. The opening of an international airport will only hasten the demise of the delicate balance of the marine ecology.

Baracoa

Toward the eastern tip of the island in the Guantanamo province you can visit Baracoa, a delicious little seaside town that's forgotten by everyone and retains an imaginary, otherworldly feel. Stay in the fortress El Castillo de Seboruco (now the Hotel Le Castillo) on the top of the hill overlooking the town. You can't miss it.

Santa Clara

The city of Santa Clara might not appeal to everyone. It is close to neither beaches nor mountains, but this midsize provincial town seems perfectly happy and oblivious to the outside world. We love hanging out in Parque Vidal late in the afternoon, when old-timers and lovers gather and children in their homemade carts careen around the park's pathways. Buy some ice cream and take a seat on one of the concrete benches across from the Hotel Santa Clara Libre (6 Parque Vidal, between Trista and Padre Chao, phone:

42-20-7548) and just watch life go by. The rooftop terrace has a great view of the city. Santa Clara is hallowed ground for Che Guevara buffs. The town is the site of his most famous battle (check out the well-preserved pockmarks on the Santa Clara Libre's facade and the Museo and Monumento del Tren Blindado) and the resting place of his recently discovered and much revered bones. The Museo Memorial Ernesto Che Guevara in the Plaza de la Revolution Che Guevara on the Carretera Central ties it together, with all you could ever want to know about this popular revolutionary.

Culebra

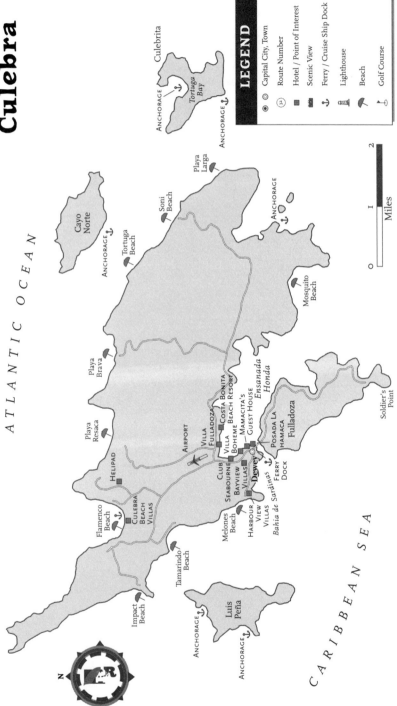

ATLANTIC OCEAN

CARIBBEAN SEA

Culebrita

ANCHORAGE
Tortuga Bay
ANCHORAGE

Playa Larga

Soni Beach

Cayo Norte

ANCHORAGE
Tortuga Beach

Playa Brava

Mosquito Beach

Playa Resaca

HELIPAD

AIRPORT

VILLA FULLADOZA

Ensanada Honda

VILLA COSTA BONITA RESORT

MAMACITA'S

BOHEME

GUEST HOUSE

POSADA LA HAMACA

ANCHORAGE

Soldier's Point

Fulladoza

Flamenco Beach

CULEBRA BEACH VILLAS

CLUB SEABOURNE

BAYVIEW VILLAS

Dewey

Sardinas

FERRY DOCK

Bahía de Sardinas

Tamarindo Beach

Melones Beach

HARBOUR VIEW VILLAS

Impact Beach

Luis Peña

ANCHORAGE

ANCHORAGE

LEGEND

- ◉ Capital City, Town
- ⊙ Route Number
- 🏨 Hotel / Point of Interest
- 📷 Scenic View
- ⚓ Ferry / Cruise Ship Dock
- 🗼 Lighthouse
- 🏖 Beach
- ⛳ Golf Course

Miles

0   1   2

N

Culebra

TOURISTO SCALE:

👤👤👤 (3)

Welcome to Culebra — the land of the very laid-back. Perhaps more than any other island in the Caribbean, Culebra is dominated by its natural wonders. Tourism here is not focused on fancy restaurants or five-star hotels. Instead, the major attraction here is the beaches, which are scattered around this island gem. Culebra is actually a collection of tiny islands and cays, and most of it is a national wildlife refuge, home to large colonies of migratory birds and marine life such as endangered sea turtles. Don't expect much, however — Culebra is a small and simple place. Although politically it is part of the Commonwealth of Puerto Rico, it is light-years away from the fast pace of San Juan. Spanish is the primary language here, but English is spoken everywhere. The main village on the island is Dewey, named for Admiral George Dewey, an American officer in the Spanish-American War. This is where the ferry, the post office, and most of the commerce are located. There are only a few hundred hotel rooms on the island — which has only about 3,000 inhabitants — a few good restaurants, and no real nightclubs, discos, or casinos. The pace is slow, slow, slow! Overall, one gets the impression that this is what the Caribbean used to be like. Indeed, Culebrenses — as residents are called — are very covetous of their way of life and are very suspect of any change or "progress." Their attitude is "leave us alone." So far, they've been successful. Actually, Hurricanes Hugo (1989), Luís

227

Culebra: Key Facts

Location	18°N by 65°W
	17 miles east of Fajardo, Puerto Rico
	12 miles west of St. Thomas
	1,660 miles southeast of New York
Size	7 miles long by 3 miles wide
Highest point	Mt. Resaca (650 feet)
Population	About 2,000
Language	Spanish, English
Time	Atlantic Standard Time (1 hour ahead of EST, same as EDT)
Area code	787 (must be dialed with all calls locally)
Electricity	110 volts AC, 60 cycles
Currency	The U.S. dollar
Driving	On the right; valid driver's license okay
Documents	U.S. citizens do not have to have a passport or visa. Canadians should have a passport or proof of citizenship with ID; British visitors need a passport and visa.
Departure tax	None
Beer to drink	Medalla
Rum to drink	Don Q or Bacardi
Music to hear	Rock, reggae, salsa, and *reggaetón*
Tourism info	800-223-6530
	www.culebra-island.com
	www.culebra.org

(1995), and Georges (1998) have helped their cause tremendously by hurting the flourishing tourist trade with both damaged accommodations and bad publicity.

Culebra is not a lush, verdant island. Rather, it's very arid. However, its star attraction, besides its isolation, is its beaches. Despite its beautiful beaches, Culebra is not for everyone. It's rustic, and if you expect to be pampered or entertained, forget it, it's not for you. But if you don't mind simple accommodations, cooking for yourself a lot or eating at mostly simple restaurants, and tons of quiet, then you'll love it. Probably the best analogy is that of a Cinderella who doesn't want to go to the ball. She purposely stays out of the spotlight cast on her star stepsisters, Puerto Rico and St. Thomas, loving the solitude. She is one of the Caribbean's best-kept secrets — an island where the pace is that of yesteryear, the beaches are gorgeous, and attitude nonexistent.

The Briefest History

Culebra was not inhabited by Europeans until the very late date of 1886, when it was settled by the Spanish (it was part of the Spanish Virgin Islands). It was ceded to the United States as part of the settlement of the Spanish-American War. The United States incorporated it into the Commonwealth of Puerto Rico, where it has remained ever since. In 1909 President Theodore Roosevelt designated the former Spanish Crown lands (2,800 acres) a national wildlife refuge, to protect the native seabird colonies. Nevertheless, the U.S. Navy used it for bombing practice from World War II until 1975. Today this area is administered by the U.S. Fish and Wildlife Service.

Getting There

San Juan is the primary gateway to the Caribbean and is reached by most major U.S. carriers. From San Juan and Fajardo, Vieques Air Link (888-901-9247 stateside, 787-741-8331 in Isla Verde and San Juan, 787-742-0254 in Culebra, and 787-863-3020 in Fajardo) has regularly scheduled service. Air Flamenco (787-724-6464 in San Juan, 787-742-1040 in Culebra), a new player on the scene, offers daily flights as well. Isla Nena (787-742-0972) also has scheduled service from San Juan's Luis Muñoz Marín International Airport and hourly trips to Fajardo. It also occasionally flies from Vieques if there is demand. For those who don't want to fly, there is passenger and car ferry service from Fajardo daily, with at least three ferries a day going back and forth; call the Fajardo Port Authority at 787-742-3161 or 787-863-0705 for the current schedules. Also, there is a seasonal Fast Ferry service available from Old San Juan to Culebra that takes under two hours. The one-way cost is $42; the round-trip fare is $69. Contact Island Hi-Speed Ferry at 877-899-3993 or www.islandhispeedferry.com more information.

Getting Around

Although there is good minivan taxi service (*públicos*) between Dewey and Playa Flamenco, a jeep or car is a good idea for getting to other beaches, the grocery store, and just general mobility. There are several outfits who rent cars, including Prestige Car Rental (787-742-3242), Jerry's Jeeps (787-742-0587), R & W Jeep Rental (787-742-0563), Carlos Jeep Rental (787-742-3514), Coral Reef Car Rental (787-742-0055), Dick & Cathy (787-742-0062), and Tamarindo Car Rental (787-742-3343). For scooters, try JM Rental (742-0521). There is a full-service bike shop in Dewey called Culebra Bikes Shop (787-742-2209), which rents mountain bikes. Dick & Cathy (787-742-0062) also rents bikes.

Focus on Culebra: The Beaches

For such a small island, there are some amazing beaches here. The lack of development has saved most of them from the usual Caribbean resort blight. Two of the beaches, **Resaca** and **Brava**, are nesting sites for leatherback turtles and are off-limits from April 1 to August 30. They are also hard to get to (the best way is by boat), but they are great for hikers. Since shade is minimal at all Culebra beaches, be sure to bring a beach umbrella so you don't get burned to a crisp.

We vacillate between which is the best beach on the island, Soni or Flamenco. In a previous edition of *Rum & Reggae's Caribbean*, we decided it was **Soni** (also spelled Zoni), at the eastern end of the island, with its wide stretch of white sand, calm surf, and no people. There are great views of the islets of Culebrita and Cayo Norte across the bay, and far in the distance you can see St. Thomas. To get to Soni, take the eastern road as far as it will go. You will see cars parked where the road gets really bad. Park there and walk the remaining 100 yards down to the beach. There are no facilities and no shade at the beach, so be sure to bring water and an umbrella.

We changed our minds in the last edition of *Rum & Reggae's Caribbean*. We're still mad for Flamenco, Culebra's most popular strand and again our favorite. In fact, for this edition, we are rating ⊛ **Playa Flamenco** as our best beach in the Caribbean (if it is even fair to do such a thing). A mile-long arc of totally white, powdery sand set in a large cove, this is truly a beautiful beach. Its exposure to the northern Atlantic allows for good bodysurfing, especially in the winter months. It can get busy on summer weekends and during Puerto Rican holidays. At the parking area there are restrooms and picnic tables. If you walk to the left, you'll come to a very secluded part of the beach, especially if you go around the rocky coral point. On the western end of the beach is Culebra Beach Villas & Resort, a camp lodge–like place with a beach bar that's popular with Puerto Rican families. To get to Flamenco, take the road that passes the airport (the runway will be on your right) and follow it to the end.

Other beaches to explore on the island are **Soldado** (great for scuba or snorkeling), **Tamarindo** (known for its brain coral and parrotfish), **Impact** (great snorkeling), and **Tortuga** (very private). **Carlos Rosario Beach** is probably the best snorkeling spot, whereas Brava Beach has the best waves. There is also a wonderful little beach on the islet of Luis Peña, and there are two gorgeous beaches on Culebrita. The latter can easily be reached by hiring a boat: **Muff the Magic Fun Boat** — talk to Jack or Pat (787-397-7497).

Where to Stay

Accommodations are much more basic in Culebra than on most Caribbean islands, but a few newcomers to the scene have injected some style into this small-island scene. Even the bigger resorts have started to arrive, such as the Costa Bonita Resort Villas. We like Club Seabourne and some of the guesthouses in Dewey, such as Villa Boheme, Posada La Hamaca, and Mamacita's. There are also several condos or villa properties, which may be the best way to go because they come with a kitchen.

Club Seabourne, P.O. Box 357, Calle Fulladoza, Culebra, PR. ✆ 787-742-3169, ✇ 787-742-0210, 🖳 www.clubseabourne.com

🏷 **Not So Cheap** 🍴 **CP** 12 rooms

We simply adore this inn because of its intimacy and subtle style. A few minutes out of town on Ensenada Bay is this small hotel, which welcomes guests who need to "press the restart button in life." We must admit that this is the ideal place for invigoration. We love the privacy here; rooms are housed in Old World plantation-style villas set amid tropical gardens designed by a prominent landscape artist. The fertile grounds include ginger and flamboyan trees and are blooming with color. The villas are done up in refined style with four-poster queen-size beds. They also have a/c and terraces with wondrous vistas. For those traveling with children (or two couples), the Family Villas with two bedrooms are ideal. The recently remodeled main building, done up in tasteful Caribbean style, includes a library and living room with huge TV for movie viewing. The pool has a wonderful view, and the gazebo bar and café offers tasty eats. However, the real attraction, when it comes to food, is the White Sands Restaurant. Its creative Caribbean cuisine makes this one of our favorite spots on the island. Once we tasted the delicious food, we realized that if there is one spot in Puerto Rico in which to partake in an all-inclusive package — which is available — this is it. With its exotic and intimate setting, Club Seabourne ranks as one of our favorites.

Villa Boheme, 368 Calle Fulladoza, Culebra, PR. ✆ and ✇ 787-742-3508, 🖳 www.villaboheme.com, villaboheme@yahoo.com

🏷 **Cheap** and up 🍴 **EP** 🆑 11 rooms

Set in a nice, breezy location right on Ensenada Bay, this guesthouse is a great place to get an authentic feel for Culebra. It's also within easy walking distance of town and restaurants. A symphony of beige and mauve, all rooms are simple and comfortable and feature a/c, ceiling fans, and private baths. A communal kitchen is available for guests. There are also efficiency apartments with fully equipped kitchens and private lanais. The Villa has a large lanai with chaises and chairs, a great place for a cocktail. This is great choice for windsurfers, who can sail right off the dock in front. This would make a good 007 getaway!

Costa Bonita Beach Resort, P.O. Box 147, Punta Carenero, Culebra, PR.
ⓒ 787-742-3000, ✆ 787-742-3003, 💻 www.costabonitaresort.com,
info@costabonitaresort.com

💰 **Wicked Pricey** 🍴 **EP** 164 rooms

Yep, it's official—even little Culebra has fallen prey to the big resorts.
Culebra's first high-luxury hotel has arrived. This seaside complex of
villas is by far the island's largest and most expensive hotel, and even
though we prefer some of the more intimate guesthouses—which reflect the true ambiance of Culebra, in our opinion—we must admit
that this hotel is quite beautiful. Half the villas are studios, the others
are one-bedrooms, and all are elegantly outfitted with fine craftsmanship and plush furniture. One-bedroom suites have dining
room tables, queen-size beds, and sofas that fold out into queen beds.
All villas have a/c, hairdryer, iron, and exquisite ocean views. The
kitchens are super—brand-new and well equipped with toaster, coffeemaker, fridge, stove, and microwave. Most guests seem to eat all
their meals at the two restaurants here. There's a Caribbean restaurant called El Yola, as well as a fine dining spot, El Pirata, that is open
only on weekends. For those venturing off-site, nearby Dewey also
has some lively little restaurants. The free-form swimming pool has
a swim-up bar and kids have their own pool. It's a little out of step
with the Culebra scene, but as far as big resorts go, the Costa Bonita is
indeed beautiful.

Posada La Hamaca, P.O. Box 388, 68 Calle Castelar, Dewey, Culebra, PR.
ⓒ 787-435-0028, ✆ 787-742-3516, 💻 www.posada.com,
ginny@posada.com

💰 **Cheap** 🍴 **EP** ⒸⒸ 10 rooms

Located right in Dewey on the canal by the drawbridge, Posada La
Hamaca was one of the original guesthouses on the island. This wonderfully clean and comfortable place is still a good choice for in-town
accommodation, especially since the efficiencies have recently been
remodeled. Situated in a simple Spanish-style house are six double
rooms and three efficiency units (i.e., with kitchenettes or kitchens).
Each room has a private bath, a/c, and ceiling fan. The Posada provides free ice, coolers, and towels for the beach. The new owners are
very friendly and helpful as well.

Mamacita's Guest House, P.O. Box 818, 66 Calle Castelar, Dewey, Culebra,
PR. ⓒ 787-742-0090, ✆ 787-742-0301, 💻 www.mamacitaspr.com,
info@mamacitaspr.com

💰 **Cheap** 🍴 **EP** ⒸⒸ 6 rooms

This is a small, brightly colored guest house located right next door to

Posada La Hamaca. Mamacita's also has a pretty, colorful patio on the canal, where breakfast, lunch, and dinner are served. There are only six rooms, located above the restaurant in decked spaces. The room on the top floor has the best views, including a sweeping vista of the harbor. All rooms have a/c, private baths, lanais, and ceiling fans and have recently been outfitted with satellite TV. The Caribbean Bar is a great place for a cocktail at sunset (or sunrise, if the urge arises).

Villa Fulladoza, P.O. Box 162, Culebra, PR. 📞 and 📠 787-742-3576

💲 **Cheap** 🍴 **EP** CC 7 rooms

Situated right on the water with nice views of Ensenada Honda, this is a popular, interesting, and somewhat eclectically decorated (*home-made* is the word they used to describe the décor) complex within a 10-minute walk of town. Each of the seven units has a fully equipped kitchenette, ceiling and/or floor fans, and private bath. There is a boat dock and moorings available to those who have boats. It's located bay-side, so there is no beach, but there are great views and a personal dock.

Bayview Villas, Culebra, PR. 📞 787-742-3392 or 787-783-2961

💲 **Pricey** and up 🍴 **EP** CC 3 units

Situated on a hill overlooking Ensenada Honda and within walking distance of town, these are good villa accommodations on the island. Owner Rafael welcomes guests to the three units (one has two bed-rooms and two baths, one has two bedrooms and one and a half baths, and the other has one bedroom and one bath). All are multi-leveled, with lots of Brazilian hardwood, sloped ceilings, large windows, tile floors, and a/c. The fully equipped kitchens have a dishwasher, a gas grill, and a washing machine. The baths are spacious and tiled, and ceiling fans keep the breeze moving in case the trade winds die down. Each unit has a large deck with hammocks and chaises. The units are available for weekly rentals only.

Harbour View Villas, P.O. Box 216, Culebra, PR. 📞 stateside: 800-440-0070, local: 787-742-3855, 📠 787-742-3171, 🖥 www.culebrahotel.com, info@culebrahotel.com

💲 **Not So Cheap** and up 🍴 **EP** 3 villas and 3 suites

These rather space age–looking villas on stilts sit just outside Dewey on the road to Melones Beach. Large lanais, lots of wood, 12-foot-high ceilings, big windows, and French doors with views of Bahia de Sardinas are the main features. The three villas, a one-bedroom and a two-bedroom, come with fully equipped kitchens, ceiling fans, and a living room. There are also three suites with kitchens, tile baths, and air-conditioned bedrooms at the top of the 5-acre property. You'll want to have a four-wheel-drive vehicle or a lot of nerve to negotiate the steep and treacherous driveway. We find these rustic accommodations to be a lot like a Vermont cabin — with mosquito netting over the beds for pioneer-like protection against the bugs. Nevertheless, the harbor views are spectacular! The restaurant here, Bonita Banana's, is also top-notch. It's run by the owner's daughter and open for dinner. The dishes are well prepared with fresh fruits and vegetables from the garden. No credit cards.

Culebra Beach Villas, Playa Flamenco, Culebra, PR. ✆ stateside: 877-767-7575, local: 787-754-6236, ✆ 787-281-6975, 🖥 www.culebrabeachrental.com, cbrental@prtc.com

💲 **Not So Cheap** and up 🍴 **EP** ⒸⒸ 33 units

The best thing about Culebra Beach Villas is the location — right on Playa Flamenco. It looks somewhat like a ski lodge with satellite cabins and is popular with Puerto Rican families. Don't expect much, as *rustic* is the buzzword here. However, the management is friendly, and there's that gorgeous beach in front. The units (18 in concrete villas, 15 in a multistory hotel) come with basic amenities like a fridge, microwave, stove, a/c, barbecue, TV, and private bath.

Where to Eat

There aren't many choices, and don't expect haute cuisine. Here's what we recommend.

$$ **Club Seabourne**, Calle Fulladoza, 742-3169

Just past Bayview Villas overlooking the Ensenada Honda is this jewel of a restaurant, located in the hotel of the same name. Chef Joan cooks up creative Caribbean cuisine. With tables out on the porch, this is a great place for dinner or happy hour.

$$ **Coconut's Beach Grill**, outside Dewey, toward Playa Flamenco

True to Culebra style, this restaurant has a relaxed feel. Although the cuisine is not fancy by any means, the location makes this a prime eating spot. Burgers and seafood are most popular, but it's the beachside location that draws us in.

$ **Culebra Deli**, 26 Calle Pedro Marquez, 742-3277

This is more of a cafeteria than a restaurant, but its tasty *criollo* food attracts crowds. Its chicken plates are popular, as are the *empanadillas* and breakfast options.

$$$ **Dinghy Dock**, on the road to Ensenada Honda in Dewey, 742-0581

Culebra's most popular restaurant for breakfast and dinner sits on the water and features grilled local seafood (lobster, grouper, yellowtail, and tuna). Its hearty pasta plates are a tasty cheap option. Open

Monday through Wednesday, 11:30 a.m. to 12:30 p.m. for lunch and 6:30 to 9 p.m. for dinner; open Thursday through Sunday, 8:30 a.m. to 11:30 p.m.

$ **El Batey**, on the airport road by the baseball field, 742-3828

Culebrenses rave about El Batey's sandwiches. Open from 8 a.m. to 2 p.m., it also opens later for drinks and dancing.

$ **El Caobo (Tina's)**, Barriada Clark, 742-0505

In the neighborhood between Dewey and the airport, this small, funky place serves good, cheap Puerto Rican cuisine. Open daily.

$$$ **Mamacita's**, 66 Calle Castelar, Dewey, 742-0090

This colorful and pleasant patio by the canal is the setting for affordable lunch and dinner (and Ben & Jerry's ice cream). It's also a great place for a cocktail. Open 10:30 a.m. to 4 p.m. for lunch ($$) and 6 to 9 p.m. for dinner. Reservations suggested on weekends.

Going Out

Culebra certainly isn't Ibiza, but nightlife on the island has slowly improved. Faced with the challenging task, we have compiled the best places — actually, the only places!

El Batey, 742-3828

Though a restaurant by day, El Batey turns into a late-night Culebra spot (which around here is not so late). It's not South Beach by any means, but dancing definitely ensues when the DJ spins mostly Latin tunes. Drinks are cheap, especially during happy hour.

El Oasis, 742-3175

This centrally located hangout offers cheap drinks and tasty pizza. Mixed with super-friendly staff and a lively happy hour, it's no wonder so many seem to pass the time here.

Happy Landing, 742-0135

For those who can't decide if they want to party or go to the airport, Happy Landing is the perfect match. Yes, it is located at the end of the airstrip, thus the clever name. A relaxed air pervades here, as cheap beer and pool tables dominate. Beware of stumbling pilots (hopefully post-flight!).

Mamacita's, 742-0090

Though not open very late, Mamacita's has live drummers and attracts people for its happy-hour specials. It has some great original recipe cocktails as well.

Don't Miss

Paradise Gift Shop

A great place for groovy souvies, this shop, located right next to Mamacita's on Calle Castelar in Dewey (742-3569), is a must stop. Open daily from 9 a.m. to 2 p.m. and 5 to 8 p.m.

Isla de Culebra Tourist Guide

For $2.50, this is a good thing to buy when you arrive. It's available at most shops, including Paradise.

La Loma Gift Shop

Owned by Bruce and Kathie Goble, creators of the Culebra Island Web site, www.culebra-island.com, this shop is located in downtown Dewey just steps from the bridge leading to the fire station. Bruce and Kathie are a wealth of information on the island. You can also pick up a copy of the *Isla de Culebra Tourist Guide* at their store.

The Culebra Calendar

This local monthly newspaper is a good source of Culebra happenings.

Water Sports

All these beautiful beaches (and no streams or rivers to cloud the water) —get thee out on them! For diving (depths range up to 100 feet, and the reefs are in great shape), call the Culebra Dive Shop (787-507-4656), Culebra Divers (787-742-0566), or Spa Ventures (787-742-0581). We have gotten positive feedback about a new dive shop that recently opened called Aquatic Adventures (209-3494), run by Captain Taz Hamrick, former military man. Anglers should contact Flamenco Fishing (787-742-3144). Kayaks can be rented at Villa Boheme.

Curaçao

You know that stuff that makes all those blue drinks blue? It's Blue Cu-raçao, the orange-flavored liqueur that makes your lips turn blue, too. Although we generally loathe drinks with food coloring in them (green beer on St. Patrick's Day is another one of those weird things that people do), we don't loathe Curaçao, a little island sharing the name (minus the Blue) and known heretofore mainly to cruise-ship shoppers and Europeans. Part of the Dutch Lesser Antilles and hovering only 35 miles north of the Venezuelan coast, Curaçao is becoming a hot spot for architecture and culture freaks on expedition, as well as divers looking for new territory to explore. Curaçao will also please the sophisticate who likes going to a Caribbean island where there's little risk of tangling with the tattooed, gold-chain party crowd that lives for happy hours and all-inclusives.

They say you can't judge a book by its cover, so don't get discouraged by the airport, which rates as one of the Caribbean's most desolate, surrounded by scrub cactus and down-at-the-heel motels. One of them, in fact, is the local brothel, Campo Alegre, luring Venezuelan businessmen for a night of in-dulgence (it's also the cleanest den o' sin we've ever seen, with about 150 pros-titutes and run by a very professional madam, although we passed on her services). The scenery improves as you head to town. Like its neighbors Aruba and Bonaire, Curaçao is arid (read: like a desert), getting barely 20

Curaçao

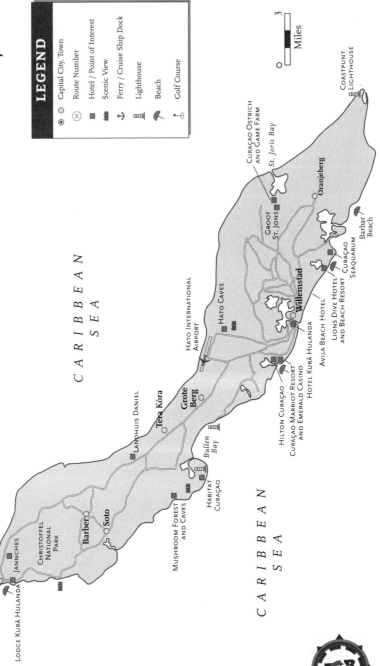

LEGEND

◉ ○	Capital City, Town
⓪	Route Number
■	Hotel / Point of Interest
⚓	Scenic View
⚓	Ferry / Cruise Ship Dock
🗼	Lighthouse
⛱	Beach
⛳	Golf Course

CARIBBEAN SEA

CARIBBEAN SEA

Coastpunt Lighthouse

Curaçao Ostrich and Game Farm

St. Joris Bay

Oranjeberg

Groot St. Jons

Barbar Beach

Willemstad

Curaçao Seaquarum

Lions Dive Hotel and Beach Resort

Hato Caves

Hato International Airport

Avila Beach Hotel

Hilton Curaçao

Curaçao Marriot Resort and Emerald Casino

Hotel Kurá Hulanda

Landhuis Daniel

Tera Kóra

Grote Berg

Bullen Bay

Habitat Curaçao

Mushroom Forest and Caves

Soto

Barber

Christoffel National Park

Westpunt

Jannches

Lodge Kurá Hulanda

Miles

3

N

Curaçao: Key Facts

Location	12°N by 68°W
	42 miles/68 kilometers east of Aruba
	1,250 miles/2,011 kilometers southeast of Miami
	1,710 miles/2,751 kilometers southeast of New York
Size	182 square miles/471 square kilometers
Highest point	Mount Christoffel (1,239 feet/378 meters)
Population	130,000
Language	Papiamento plus Dutch (the official language); English and Spanish widely spoken
Time	Atlantic Standard Time (1 hour ahead of EST, same as EDT)
Area code	To call Curaçao from the U.S., dial 011 (the international code), plus 5999 plus the seven-digit local number.
Electricity	110–130 volts, 50 cycles, which is similar to the U.S. standard but not identical. Adapters are necessary in some cases, and hairdryers and curling irons may overheat.
Currency	The Netherlands Antilles guilder, also called the florin, NAf (1.78 NAf = US$1). U.S. dollars are widely accepted, but large bills might be difficult to cash.
Driving	On the right; valid U.S. and Canadian driver's licenses are accepted.
Documents	Valid passport or original copy of birth certificate with proof of citizenship and photo, for U.S. and Canadian citizens, plus an ongoing or a return ticket
Departure tax	$22.50 (usually included in price of ticket), or $12.50 to the Netherlands Antilles
Beer to drink	Amstel, brewed from desalinated seawater
Liquor to drink	Curaçao
Music to hear	*Tumba*
Tourism info	800-3-CURAÇAO or 305-792-7102
	www.curacao.com

inches of rain annually and situated well outside the hurricane belt. In fact, in some spots the island looks like a set for a John Wayne western. However, the constantly blowing winds make the 85°F-plus heat bearable.

Curaçao is full of surprises, from its amazing diving to the charming waterfront city of **Willemstad** (which looks like a mini Amsterdam) to **Christoffel Park** with herds of small native deer, to the **Curaçao Ostrich and Game Farm**, run by an ornery South African (and fortunately, he'll likely be the only cranky person you meet in Curaçao). In addition, there are great restaurants and an active nightlife. Although the island is starting to catch on with Americans looking for a new twist to their annual Caribbean holiday, the number of South Americans and Europeans vacationing here means that you'll see more people dressing up at dinner and that the evenings tend to start later and rock until the wee hours. Almost every hotel has the word *casino* attached to its name, but most of these casinos still have a long way to go before they are glittering hot spots worth more than an evening of your time.

With its forts guarding the entrance to the harbor, its *landhuizen* (plantation houses dating back to the colonial era), and the 17th-century Dutch buildings in Willemstad, Curaçao boasts some of the most interesting architecture in the Caribbean. About a dozen of the *landhuizen* are open to the public. Landhuis Daniel, which dates to 1634 and is now a restaurant and guesthouse, served as a convenient rest stop for travelers going the east-west route or vice versa. In fact, Willemstad, which in 1999 celebrated its 500th year, was named a UNESCO World Heritage Site — joining the Taj Mahal and the Great Wall of China on the esteemed list.

The city is split in two by the **Santa Anna Bay**; the two parts are connected by a pedestrian pontoon bridge — the **Queen Emma**, which swings open for shipping traffic — or a free, two-minute ferry ride. Curaçao is one of the busiest ports in the region, and its long history as a major trade center is still apparent in the array of shops housed in historic buildings. On the eastern, **Punda** ("point") side of the harbor you'll find a colorful, iconic waterfront façade that looks like an Amsterdam in the tropics. Willemstad has good shopping for jewelry, electronics, and such. Nearby is a quaint old floating market with schooners from Venezuela and Colombia selling fruits and vegetables. The west side of the harbor is called **Otrobanda** (literally, "other side"), and this part of the city has seen the greatest revitalization in the last decade. An important museum, the Kurá Hulanda (and an accompanying fine hotel, restaurant, and conference center), has spurred the refurbishment of neglected historic buildings. At sunset, the deck of **Bistro Le Clochard**, a restaurant tucked into the corner of the Riffort, is the place to watch the oil tankers and boats slip by while enjoying a rum punch.

Perhaps due to a fiercely industrial oil refinery that hogs the skyline surrounding the island's large natural harbor, one of the misconceptions about Curaçao is that its natural wonders are limited, including its beaches. Actually, there are 38 of the latter to choose from, so beach lovers should be happy, although you won't find many resorts on them. Several come fully equipped with showers, snack bars, water-sports shops, and plenty of shade (very necessary at these latitudes); a small admission fee helps to keep these facilities up to snuff. One of the most popular is **Barbara Beach**, with calm water and wide stretches of sand. Snorkelers and divers love this island, which has water visibility up to 150 feet, with its abundance of great corals and marine life easily viewed at more than 60 marked dive sites (see Focus on Curaçao, below). At Christoffel Park, a 4,500-acre nature preserve, eight marked hiking trails lead you past rabbits, wild goats, divi-divi trees, cacti, and orchids. Late in the day, special bird- and deer-watching expeditions can be arranged, as can horseback rides through the park. Cave freaks will like **Hato Caves**—an underground cavern that features fossils, active stalagmites and stalactites, an underground waterfall, and bats. But if spelunking isn't your deal, skip it. The stench from the bat guano makes for a funky side trip that only diehards truly enjoy.

The Briefest History

One of Columbus's lieutenants, Alonso de Ojeda, "discovered" Curaçao in 1499. One legend claims that scurvy-stricken Spanish sailors were abandoned on the island, ate indigenous citrus fruit, and were miraculously cured. Thus they called the island Corazon, meaning "heart," which later became Curaçao. The island remained under Spanish rule until 1634, when the Dutch conquered it. The island then became one of the largest depots for the Caribbean slave trade as the Dutch West India Company purchased enslaved Africans and transported them to Curaçao and Brazil. Few slaves actually remained on Curaçao because agriculture wasn't an important part of its economy. For the next two centuries the Dutch and British played tug-of-war with the island. Even the French attempted a takeover. However, the Dutch solidified their hold by 1815, and slavery was finally abolished in 1863. It remained a Dutch colony until 1954, when Curaçao became self-governing within the Kingdom of the Netherlands. A sanctuary for Jews during the Spanish Inquisition and later for runaway slaves, Curaçao is known today for its tolerance.

Getting There

Curaçao is easily accessible from several major hubs. American Airlines flies to Curaçao from Miami and San Juan; Air Jamaica flies from Kingston; and Continental flies from Newark. All make connections to flights from major U.S. cities. There are also several flights daily from Aruba, Bonaire, and St. Maarten on Dutch Antilles Express, and daily flights from Bonaire on Divi Divi Air.

Getting Around

You should rent a car to explore the island. The roads are good, fairly well marked, and easy to drive, and you'll appreciate the mobility—rates average $30 to $40 per day. A few of the majors are here, including Avis (800-331-1084), Budget (800-527-0700 or 5999-868-3420), Hertz (800-654-3001), and National (800-227-3876). Make reservations in advance to ensure availability and the best rate. There's decent-scheduled public bus transportation in and out of Willemstad, and affordable organized tours of the island will get you to remote sights and the best beaches and still leave a few guilders in your wallet for the casinos.

Focus on Curaçao: Diving

Curaçao as a dive destination is a relatively new phenomenon, but experienced divers are increasingly choosing Curaçao over Bonaire, its neighbor and top dive spot, for its greater variety of topside attractions. Curaçao has wonderful coral formations, an abundance of marine life, and excellent shore dive opportunities that rival Bonaire, which is a pretty quiet island when it comes to nightlife and nonwater activities.

Curaçao is surrounded by a fringing reef located only 50 to 200 yards offshore. The drop-off starts at roughly 20 feet and falls off at angles varying from 45 to 90 degrees to depths well beyond the limit of recreational scuba. The richest coral formations are found between 20 and 70 feet, thus enabling lengthy bottom times using a multilevel dive profile. Water temperatures range from 77°F in the winter to 82°F in the summer. Visibility is a consistent 80 to 150 feet, with little or no current.

Curaçao has more than 60 identified dive sites along 40 miles of its protected coastline. Not to be missed is the **Mushroom Forest and Cave**, one of the most unique dive sites in the world. The "forest" gets its name from the large numbers of mountainous star corals that have been bio-eroded at their bases, giving them a pronounced mushroom shape. Abundant marine life includes white and purple cleaning shrimp that service snappers under overhangs, pufferfish hiding in the soft corals, spotted drums, lazy turtles, and maybe even an eagle ray. Adjacent to the Mushroom Forest is the Mushroom Cave, which is actually within snorkel range, at a depth of only 15 feet. This enormous grotto is filled with silversides, glassy sweepers, soldierfish, and walls lined with bright orange cup corals. Along the floor of the cave are peacock flounders and spiny lobsters.

A special happening for night divers occurs twice in the fall, when the corals spawn according to the lunar cycle—locally they call it "Sex on the Reef." The corals release their eggs and sperm separately in a half-hour display. Both float in the seawater for an undetermined time (generally up to a week) before "hooking up." In this part of the Caribbean, spawning occurs six to eight days after the full moons of September and October.

There are more than 20 dive operations on Curaçao, including **Habitat Curaçao** (5999-864-8205); **Ocean Encounters** (5999-461-8131; www.ocean encounters.com), with locations at Lion's Dive Beach Resort, Avila Beach Hotel, and the Lodge Kurá Hulanda; and **Caribbean Sea Sports** at the Marriott (5999-462-2620). Habitat offers 24-hour "dive freedom" with tanks readily available at all times, which means that you and your dive buddy can grab tanks and do a night shore dive at 2 a.m. if the spirit moves you.

Where to Stay

Curaçao has long had a number of big resorts, but in the last couple years there has been a major evolution as tourism shifted into high gear, name-brand hotel chains came to the island, and other developments unfolded. Marriott took over the Sonesta, the Curaçao Resort is now a Hilton, and the Princess Beach became a Breezes all-inclusive property (skip the latter). In the pipeline: Hyatt is building a $104 million, 350-room resort to open in 2007, including a marina and an 18-hole Pete Dye golf course; a 240-room Renaissance next to the cruise port in Willemstad is scheduled to debut in 2008. To us, the most interesting concepts are the Kurá Hulanda luxury boutiques. Most Curaçao properties are located in or near Willemstad, and many have casinos.

⊛ **Hotel Kurá Hulanda**, 8 Langestraat, Otrobanda, Willemstad, Curaçao, NA. ☏ 877-264-3106 or 5999-434-7700, ✆ 5999-434-7701, ⌨ www.kurahulanda.com, reservations@kurahulanda.com

💲 **Very Pricey** 🍴 **EP** ᴄᴄ 100 rooms

The Kurá Hulanda (which is Papiamento for *courtyard*) is Curaçao's top hotel — indeed it's one of the finest hotels in the Caribbean. The only thing it "lacks" (in the eyes of some) is a beach, but that caveat is part of what makes this place so special — it's more like a visit to a boutique hotel in Europe, yet beaches and other tropical diversions are not far away. In the winter, it's not as expensive as others of this quality on Curaçao — because Kurá Hulanda is in the heart of Otrobanda, not on a beach. The project has an interesting history, which starts with Willemstad being designated a World Heritage Site in 1997 for its historic, distinctly Dutch architecture. About the same time, Jacob Gelt Dekker, a Dutch entrepreneur, visited and fell in love with the island, and he bought and began to renovate a mansion in the derelict Otrobanda district. During the renovation, he discovered that the home was built atop the former hub of the Netherlands' slave-trading business. Dekker adapted his plans and began buying up the neighborhood — literally — spending $35 million to acquire and restore 16 acres and 65 buildings. One group of buildings became the outstanding Museum Kurá Hulanda (see Don't Miss, below), and other parts were adapted to create a unique hotel.

Accommodations are sprinkled around the property in various buildings, linked by cobblestone walkways and courtyards. No two rooms are alike, but most are filled with antiques and well-chosen replicas — hand-carved mahogany and teak furniture, hand-woven linens from India, and walls hand-painted by local artisans. There's also an Indian Bridal Suite that is fit for a maharani, with a suspended bed and furniture made with hammered sterling silver (now this is the place for a memorable honeymoon!). Cobblestone walk-ways lead through sculpture gardens and shopping boutiques, and the hotel also has four excellent restaurants (don't miss the Thursday night Indian buffet at Jaipur), three bars, a plush fitness center and spa, a business center, a casino, and two swimming pools. The conference facility is adorned by not one but two original Peter Paul Reubens paintings.

The luxurious rooms are matched by primped service that aims for European standards and by a high-tech infrastructure. The Kurá Hulanda caters particularly to businesspeople, but a complimentary shuttle links the hotel to a private beach club and an 18-hole golf course. The color, history, and architecture of Willemstad is within walking distance.

Lodge Kurá Hulanda, Westpunt, Curaçao, NA. ✆ 877-264-3106 or 5999-434-7700, ✆ 5999-839-3601, 🖳 www.kurahulanda.com, reservations@kurahulanda.com

💲 **Pricey** 🍽 **EP** CC 74 rooms

No, you're not seeing double. After successfully fashioning one of the Caribbean's most unique hotels from the dilapidated buildings of Willemstad (see above), Jacob Gelt Dekker acquired a 350-acre spread on the west end of the island to create a companion property that, while providing a completely different experience from his city hotel, is equally unique and appealing. In fact, we think splitting your stay between both properties is the ideal Curaçao vacation. The Lodge is perched along 30-foot coral cliffs abutting sapphire seas, and a short swim out from the narrow beach brings snorkelers and divers to some of the island's best sightseeing.

There are two basic types of accommodation. The Ocean Front wing is a series of two-story villas, each with four units — these have a balcony or large patio, kitchenette, and CD/DVD player. Upstairs suites have a nifty outdoor shower and sea views. Just inland are the Eco Garden View rooms in two-story rondavals; downstairs are the cheapest rooms, but we prefer the octagonal suites upstairs, with full kitchens and open-air living rooms that look out over a canopy of native mondi trees (no water views). All are supplied with 300-thread Egyptian cotton sheets, high-speed Internet access, and safes. One restaurant under a thatch-roof pavilion, another down on the beach, a pool, and the sea are the star attractions. There are also facilities for diving and nonmotorized watersports, mountain biking, a fitness center, and spa treatments. It's a 40-minute drive into Willemstad (and a $50 taxi trip), but there's a complimentary shuttle for guests; still, we think a rental car is a good idea for staying out here. It's very quiet out at this end of the island.

Avila Beach Hotel, 130 Penstraat, Willemstad, Curaçao, NA. ☎ 800-747-8162 or 5999-461-4377, ✆ 5999-461-1493, 🖳 www.avilahotel.com, info@avilahotel.com

💰 **Not So Cheap** 🍴 **EP** CC 108 rooms

This historic hotel is built around the 1780s governor's mansion and is favored by Dutch royalty—Queen Beatrix still pops down to Curaçao every few years and bunks here. It lies on the outskirts of Willemstad, in a neighborhood that is in a state of transition, but it's one of the few hotels in town that fronts a beach, albeit a small one. Although the lobby reeks of stuffy, overdone formality (under the watchful gaze of a portrait of the Queen), evenings attract a colorful mixture of South Americans dressed to the nines, chic Europeans, and a handful of in-the-know Americans (yes, we do exist). On Thursday and Saturday nights, Blues—a nightclub on a pier at the rear of the hotel—is one of the most happening spots on the island.

In 2006, the hotel added 68 new rooms and a new pool area (under construction during our visit). We still like the Blues section of the hotel, with its light, airy rooms built out over the water and decorated with prints of jazz greats. You'll get your own Jacuzzi, and some are equipped with kitchenettes. Room 291, at the end of the wing, is especially romantic. There are also deluxe rooms and suites in another wing, as well as the rooms in the original mansion, which has been operated as a hotel since 1949. These latter units are smaller and less attractive, and they don't have hot water (just what comes through "sun warmed" pipes)—but they are quite a bit less expensive. Restaurants on site are top-notch and pricey but deliver plenty of atmosphere, with dining on the terrace under moonlight, surrounded by flowers and flickering candles.

Habitat Curaçao, Rif St. Marie, Curaçao, NA. ☎ 800-327-6709 or 5999-864-8304, ✆ 5999-864-8464, 🖳 www.habitatcuracaoresort.com, reservations@habitatcuracaoresort.com

💰 **Pricey** 🍴 **EP** CC 70 rooms

Catering to divers, this stunning resort—painted brick red and butter yellow with turquoise accents—features Southwestern-style two-bedroom adobe cottages and junior suites with kitchenettes. A good 20-minute drive from Willemstad, the main attraction at Habitat is the dive freedom afforded by its location on one of Curaçao's most stunning reefs. Dubbed *nos kas*, which means "our house" in Dutch, the reef is right off Habitat's dock. The fantastic dive operation boasts a full-service five-star PADI facility with an underwater photography pro on call in addition to NAUI and SSI certification. Habitat has gear lockers and rinse tanks on the dock, separate docks for shore diving and boat diving, 24-hour tank availability, and the opportunity to do two-tank boat dives both morning and afternoon. On the days when you can't dive, or if a nondiver is along, the snorkeling; it ranks among some of the Caribbean's best. Elusive seahorses have been spotted in 12 feet of water within sight of the hotel.

In addition to having a horizon pool that gives the illusion of dropping off into the sea, the resort rents mountain bikes and offers guided hiking tours that are perfect for exploring the surrounding desert, abandoned plantation houses, and the nearby salt ponds inhabited by flamingos. There's a free shuttle service to Willemstad three times a day. Sharky's Restaurant & Bar, the resort's open-air eatery overlooking the sea, is a good place to trade dive stories with an eclectic group of travelers from all over the world.

Curaçao Marriott Beach Resort & Emerald Casino, Piscadera Bay, Curaçao, NA. ☎ 800-223-6388 or 5999-736-8800, ✆ 5999-462-7502, 🖥 www.offshoreresorts.com

💲 **Wicked Pricey** ⑪ **EP** (CC) 248 rooms

This stylish 248-room resort, five minutes from Willemstad, is designed in traditional Dutch architectural style and manages a delicate balancing act of appealing to both vacationers and business travelers. Even when a convention is in the house, guests won't feel that they're drowning in a sea of name tags. In addition, lush landscaping coupled with a terrific collection of island art help to give this place more of an island identity than the standard Marriott fare. It also has one of the better pools in the neighborhood and a small man-made beach that's perfect for sunning. Workout amenities are decent, too, for fitness buffs. Lovers and honeymooners will want to book the terrace rooms that boast private Jacuzzis and private rooftop decks for sunbathing (in the buff, if you're so inclined).

Hilton Curaçao, P.O. Box 2133, John F. Kennedy Boulevard, Piscadera Bay, Curaçao, NA. ☎ 877-GO-HILTON or 5999-462-5000, ✆ 5999-462-5846, 🖥 www.hiltoncaribbean.com/curacao

💲 **Very Pricey** ⑪ **EP** (CC) 196 rooms

Originally opened in 1967, this is one of Curaçao's original hotels, but it got a makeover in 1999 that revitalized the prime location, and it now operates under the Hilton banner. Located at the site of historic Fort Piscadera, five minutes from Willemstad, it has a smallish beach set within coral cliffs (pretty, except when the hotel is full), a full range of water sports, and a 6,000-square-foot free-form infinity pool. The six-story hotel is decorated in a by-the-book tropical motif, and the rooms feature coffeemaker, iron, and hairdryer. You'll find three restaurants, serving a range of food, and three bars. Other amenities include a fitness center, two tennis courts, an 18-hole miniature golf course, and a busy casino. There's a free shuttle bus into town twice daily (except Sunday).

Lion's Dive Hotel & Beach Resort, Bapor Kibra, Curaçao, NA. ✆ 866-546-6734 or 5999-434-8888, ✉ 5999-434-8889, 🖳 www.lionsdive.com, info@lionsdive.com

💰 **Pricey** ⑪ **CP** 🆒 72 rooms

Set on one of the island's best beaches about 2 miles southeast of Willemstad and next to the Sea Aquarium complex, this busy hotel, set in rustic Dutch Caribbean buildings, caters to water lovers and the active set. This is also singles central (there are three open-air bars in a row next door, with consecutive happy hours—hey, three strikes and you're out, bub). On the upside, it has a good gym, Body Beach Wellness Club, which is replete with organized classes and guests who actually make good use of the space, as well as Ocean Encounters, one of the top dive operators on the island. One of the best meals we had on the island was at the hotel's restaurant. Lion's is a good choice if one partner doesn't dive and the other does. The rooms are trim, with queen-size beds, a/c, minifridge, sea views, private balconies or patios, and wireless Internet. Guests get to visit the Sea Aquarium for free and have the use of a twice-daily shuttle to town.

Landhuis Daniel, Weg Naar Westpunt, Curaçao, NA. ✆ and ✉ 5999-864-8400, 🖳 www.landhuisdaniel.com, daniellh@cura.net

💰 **Dirt Cheap** ⑪ **EP** 🆒 8 rooms

Located near the center of the island, a couple miles west of the airport, Landhuis Daniel is a country home with its roots in a plantation established in the 1700s. It was converted into an informal inn in 1997 and is popular with bargain-seeking Dutch visitors. There are four rooms in the main house, two of these with a/c. Four more are found in a row house—former slave quarters—near the pool; these are smaller and darker, with odd, semi-outdoor showers. There are no restaurants nearby, so Daniel's shady terrace dining room is a nice haven, stoked by an organic garden and the foodie owner (cookbooks line the walls of the library). We found the common areas to be a bit unkempt, but otherwise this is a friendly spot for independent types.

Where to Eat

Reflecting the island's international population, Curaçao's restaurants offer terrific Dutch, Antillean, French, Créole, South American, Swiss, and Italian food. The local dish is *keshi yena*, which came about when Dutch slave owners gave the leftover rind of gouda cheese to their slaves; the slaves would stuff it with chicken and other meats and bake it. The best version of it we've tasted is at Belle Terrace, at the Avila Beach Hotel, where it is served under a sprawling flamboyant tree. For romance and great food, choose either Bistro Le Clochard, a cozy restaurant tucked away into the corner of the 18th-century Riffort, or Astrolab, at the Kurá Hulanda Hotel.

$$$$$ Astrolab Observatory Restaurant, Otrobanda, 5999-434-7700

The signature dining room at the island's finest hotel has as its backdrop various antique astrolabes on display. You can dine in the warm, leafy courtyard accompanied by the trickle of delicate marble fountains, or inside in air-conditioned comfort. You won't go wrong, especially when you ponder the choices: sea bass in tomato-lemongrass marmalade, grilled lobster in vanilla butter, or rack of lamb with garlic confit. Reservations are recommended for dinner; it's also open for breakfast.

$$$$ Bistro Le Clochard, Riffort, Willemstad, 5999-462-5666

Native Curaçaoan Freddy Berends, who studied at one of Switzerland's most famous hotel schools, presides over this cozy restaurant, one of the few in the Caribbean to earn the prestigious Relais et Châteaux Award. Tucked into the corner of the fort, it makes you feel as if you've stepped into an Old World, European restaurant. While the flowers are regrettably plastic — that's right, plastic! — everything else, from the service to the fine mix of French and Swiss cuisine, is top-notch. Vegetarians won't find this place appealing at all, however, because red meat is the main event here. Reservations are a must.

$$$ Café Gouverneur de Rouville, Otrobanda, 5999-462-5999

This is a great hangout — for lunch or dinner, or for a sunset cocktail when Willemstad's colorful waterfront takes on an amber glow. Burgers, salads, and sandwiches are offered for lunch, but a more international menu takes the stage at dinner.

$$ De Groente Boerr, 6 Scheveningenstraat, Willemstad, 5999-461-5300

Just south of Punda, this endearing restaurant is run out of a house in a residential neighborhood near Avila Beach. The quirky fusion menu changes daily and includes such items as a Greek salad with jalapeno-spiked feta cheese, escargot, and Argentine mixed grill. Large portions, small tables; closed Sunday.

$$ Jaanchie's, Westpunt, 5999-864-0126

On the day you explore the beaches around Westpunt, drop by this family-owned beach bar and restaurant for fresh seafood favorites like grouper, conch, wahoo, and shrimp and simple local food like fried fish, peas and rice, and fresh fruit. Open since 1936, its specialties include *rijsttafel* (a traditional feast that includes rice, veggies, chicken, and beef) and traditional Dutch dishes like *keshi yena*. Bananaquits and hummingbirds flit all around the open-air restaurant, attracted by the sugar that's put out for them. It's open only for lunch.

$$ **Playa Perla Kanoa**, Santa Catharina, 5999-560-5401

This is an unconventional and very local hangout that overlooks a tranquil, hidden lagoon on the north coast. Mixed seafood stew is a highlight; conch, oyster, tenderloin, and stewed goat are also inexpensive. There's live music on Sunday, and Thursday is lobster night. It's closed Monday — ask for directions.

$$$ **Rysttafel**, 13–15 Mercuriusstraat, Willemstad, 5999-461-2606

Save your appetite and reserve ahead for this traditional Indonesian feast, which features a mind-boggling 16 to 25 dishes with tasty chicken and beef, vegetables, rice, and special sauces (some extremely hot) for dipping. If you can put together a group of friends to go, the evening is more fun — this banquet spread is perfect for eating in a communal setting. Although you can order for two, you won't get as large a sampling of the Indonesian food. If you're traveling solo, opt for another restaurant.

$ **Sea Side Terrace**, Dr. Martin Luther King Boulevard, 5999-461-8361

Located next to the Breezes all-inclusive resort, this doesn't look like much from a distance — a shipping container with a neon sign attached to it — but you don't dine inside. Instead, you'll enjoy delicious fresh fish at informal tables next to the beach. It's a great deal when the guilders are running low. Closed on Monday.

Don't Miss

⊛ Museum Kurá Hulanda

Built on the site of a former slave yard and occupying 12 restored 19th-century buildings, the museum traces Curaçao's role as the main port through which African slaves were transported. This incredibly moving and well-done anthropological museum is definitely worth an afternoon — the 4,600-year-old collection of Mesopotamian pottery and Benin bronze pieces alone are worth the trip. It's open Monday through Saturday; admission is $6. For more info, call 5999-434-7765 or visit www.kurahulanda.com.

Sailing Aboard the Insulinde

Docked along the historic buildings of Punda, the 120-foot, 1931-era Belgian sailing ship *Insulinde* offers a classy route for landlubbers to explore Curaçao's remote beaches. A half-day cruise leaves Wednesday and Friday at 1:30 p.m., and the $40 price includes punch, snacks, and snorkel equipment for the stop at Barbara Beach (undeveloped and accessible only by sea). On Sunday, an all-day cruise to uninhabited Klein Curaçao boards at 6:30 a.m.; the sailing trip includes a buffet breakfast, a barbecue lunch of steak and salad, and snorkeling gear. This is quite a bargain at $65 per person. Information: 5999-560-1340; www.insulinde.com.

Curaçao Sea Aquarium

An above-average aquarium for the Caribbean, this attraction showcases more than 400 species of fish and creatures from local waters in tanks with seawater pumped in to support miniature reefs. It sounds cheesy, but get yourself on video here: A staff underwater videographer and dive master accompanies you on a 45-minute dive adjacent to the aquarium. In the large open-water pool, snorkelers and divers swim freely with the stingrays, angelfish, tarpon, and groupers. After feeding the rays, you'll move on to another enclosure to hand-feed reef sharks through holes in a Plexiglas wall; another section allows you to feed giant turtles. There's also a dolphin lagoon and, in contrast to many of these facilities, this one seems genuinely educational in nature.

Admission ($15) also gets you a day at the Sea Aquarium Beach, one of the island's best and busiest (three bars at one end offer consecutive happy hours at the day's end). The Animal Encounter is $54 for divers, $34 for snorkelers (reserve 24 hours in advance). The dolphin encounter is $69, whereas a swim with the dolphins runs $149. For more information, call 5999-461-6666 or visit www.curacao-sea-aquarium.com.

Maritime Museum

Across the bay from the Kurá Hulanda Museum, the Maritime provides great insight into Willemstad's fascinating history. Admission is $6; closed on Sunday. Information: 5999-465-2327.

Curaçao's Jewish History

The island's most exotic *un*natural attraction is Beth Haim, the 350-year-old Jewish cemetery located at Schottegatweg Nord, on the northwest side of Curaçao's harbor. By turns disturbing and moving, the resting place is bizarrely situated cheek by jowl with the 20th-century oil refinery, against a backdrop of towering smokestacks that spit fire and brimstone. As a result, the tombstones are quietly deteriorating from the toxic exhaust. Less exotic, but worth a visit in Willemstad is the Mikve Israel-Emanuel synagogue — dating back to 1732, it's the Western Hemisphere's oldest continuously operating synagogue, with a sand floor and 600-year-old chandeliers (there's a small, tantalizing museum). Check out the island's rich Jewish history at www.snoa.com.

Blues

On Thursday and Saturday nights, head to the Avila Beach Hotel's Blues Restaurant. It's built out over the water and has a feverish club featuring live jazz. The food is nothing special, but munching on a plate of appetizers with the hot tunes here is our idea of a good time.

Curaçao Ostrich and Game Farm

This is the largest working farm of its kind outside Africa. You'll see first-hand how an ostrich develops from an egg to the largest and fastest bird in the world. At the Zambesi Restaurant you can chow down on ostrich, too. Admission is $7. Closed on Monday. Call 5999-747-2777 or visit www.ostrichfarm.net for more info.

Curaçao Liqueur Factory (This is actually a "Do Miss")

Skip it: The wisdom obtained at the underwhelming Curaçao Liqueur Factory wouldn't fill a shot glass. Instead, purchase the liqueur — made from the peel of a locally grown bitter orange — at the airport duty-free shops, where it is cheaper and available in identically flavored orange, green, red, clear, and the more customary blue colors.

Dominica

DOMINICA PASSAGE

Cape Melville

Point Baptiste

Portsmouth

Picard Beach Cottages

ATLANTIC OCEAN

Syndicate

Melville Hall Airport

Marigot

Dublanc

Northern Forest Reserve

Mt Diablotins
(4,747 ft / 1,447 m)

Colihaut

Carib Reserve

Central Forest Reserve

Central Forest Reserve

Emerald Pool

Pont Casse

CARIBBEAN SEA

Morne Trois Pitons
(4,550 ft / 1,387 m)

Morne Macaque

Boeri Lake

Beori Valley

Fresh Water Lake

Laudat

NATIONAL PARK

Canefield Airport

Trafalgar

Titou Gorge

Papillote

Boiling Lake

Humming Bird Inn

Fort Young Hotel

Trafalgar Falls

Papillote Wilderness Resort

Valley of Desolation

Watt Mtn
(4,017 ft / 1,224 m)

Roseau

Evergreen Hotel

Jungle Bay Resort & Spa

Dive Dominica

Castle Comfort Lodge

Exotica

Morne Anglais
(3,683 ft / 1,123 m)

Zandoli Inn

Scott's Head

LEGEND

- ◉ ◎ Capital City, Town
- ⑫ Route Number
- ▪ Hotel / Point of Interest
- 📷 Scenic View
- ⚓ Ferry / Cruise Ship Dock
- 🗼 Lighthouse
- 🏖 Beach
- ⛳ Golf Course

0   1   2   3   4   5
Miles

Dominica

TOURISTO SCALE:
👤👤👤👤👤 (5)

Think green, very green. Add real lush vegetation and rainforest, vulcan mountains, a rugged black-sand coastline, and some very friendly locals. Got the image yet? If you do, then you've got Dominica, the true emerald of the West Indies.

Much of Dominica (pronounced "do-mi-NEE-ka") is rainforest. Its volcanic, mountainous topography traps moisture from the trade winds and converts it into as much as 300 inches of rain a year in the interior. The color green takes on a whole new meaning here, with so many shades it puts even Ireland to shame. Dominica has a few beaches, but this is not an island for beach freaks. The coves here are mostly of the black-sand variety, and the prettiest are on the windward side and have dangerous undertows. A few undeveloped, tawny-colored strands curl around Calibishie on the north coast, but quite frankly, there are better beaches on most other islands. Dominica's unique beauty is in its mountains. This is where the rainforest thrives, where waterfalls and thermal springs abound — where adventuring into the bush is the best in the Caribbean.

Dominica is for nature lovers, for those who like being in the rainforest, who enjoy hiking in wilderness areas, or who love the idea of lush, leafy thickets, raging rivers, waterfalls, hot springs, and so on. If you want big resorts, forget Dominica — you won't find them. The people who come here

Dominica: Key Facts

Location	15°N by 61°W
	30 miles/48 kilometers south of Guadeloupe
	23 miles/37 kilometers north of Martinique
	1,924 miles/3,098 kilometers southeast of New York
Size	290 square miles/751 square kilometers
	29 miles/47 kilometers long by 16 miles/26 kilometers wide
Highest point	Morne Diablotin (4,747 feet/1,447 meters)
Population	71,000
Language	English
Time	Atlantic Standard Time (1 hour ahead of EST, same as EDT)
Area code	767
Electricity	220 to 240 volts AC, 50 cycles; both adapters and transformers are needed for U.S.-made appliances
Currency	Eastern Caribbean dollar, EC$ (EC$2.68 = US $1)
Driving	On the left; a local permit is needed with your valid driver's license ($12).
Documents	U.S. and Canadian citizens must have proof of citizenship, such as a passport or a voter registration card or birth certificate with a photo ID, plus an ongoing or a return ticket
Departure tax	$20
Beer to drink	Kubuli
Rum to drink	D Special
Music to hear	Dancehall
Tourism info	212-949-1711 or 767-448-2045
	www.dominica.dm

like nature and simple things. Room service is not the MO here; splashing around in the sulfur pools is. Get the picture?

Although Dominica is rich in natural assets, it is relatively poor in economic terms. Per capita standards are below average for the Caribbean—fortunately, between the sea's bounty and the abundant crops, all have plenty to eat, and living conditions have been steadily improving since the mid-1980s. Otherwise, Dominica is quintessentially West Indian, with a style and charm that has all but vanished on most other islands. Unlike the forests, Roseau, the capital, has had a harder time enduring hurricanes and contemporary development—only a few of the interesting older buildings have survived. The remaining architecture is more modern and functional than attractive, and the town is hot and crowded. But it is still distinctly Caribbean, particularly when compared with the Americanized ports of other islands, like St. Maarten or St. Thomas. Even with the almost daily cruise-ship blight in high season, Roseau is very much market oriented, geared to satisfy the needs of islanders more than tourists. This is particularly refreshing, like the friendliness and openness of its people, especially those in the small mountain villages.

Since the 1990s, Dominica has sold itself as the Nature Island of the Caribbean. Although the region's natural assets are on display here in greater profusion than almost anywhere else, not everyone in the government has been on the same track, leading to a conflicted resolve by Dominica's leaders in the green vs. greenback debate. For instance, one of Dominica's key attractions is **whale-watching**—it is one of the best places in the Caribbean for viewing sperm whales and others, often remarkably close to the shore. The island is also one of six Caribbean countries with a vote on the International Whaling Commission. Not coincidentally, Dominica also benefits from significant financial aid from Japan, the nation that is trying hardest to overturn the ban on whaling established in 1982. The result: Year after year Dominica votes in favor of overturning the moratorium. Are there plans to change the island's "Nature Island" tag line? Don't bet on it. Dominica wants to have it both ways: maximize the financial aid it receives from other nations *and* profit from the ecotourism ventures it has become famous for.

As awareness of Dominica's special nature has spread beyond its shores, the government has also directed a major effort toward the cruise-ship business as a way of boosting tourism revenue. About 300,000 cruise-ship passengers dock here annually now, and it has taken its toll on the backwater ambiance of this island. Cruise-ship passengers seem to come here to buy T-shirts and ice cream cones and to use the bathrooms, most of them never experiencing Mother Nature in the raw, the island's chief asset. Visit the beautiful Emerald Pool on any day when a cruise ship is at port and you'll see what was once a national treasure overrun by people wearing Bermuda shorts and black socks. To appease the interest of nonhikers in exploring the island's higher volcanic peaks, a cable car was constructed to ferry cruise-ship passengers high up the slopes into formerly virgin forests. In attempting to sanitize and Disnefy the island, Dominica's government, it would seem, is content to sell its soul for some fast cash. In its defense, it does have an island to feed, and with empires like Chiquita forcing trade agreements to make the European Union buy their bananas in the cheaper-labor countries of Central and South America (which—surprise!—Chiquita happens to have a vested interest in), Dominica has little choice but to throw its energy behind tourism.

In spite of all this, we still think that Dominica is a very special island and well worth visiting for those who don't mind trading their swimsuit for hiking shoes and their luxury resort for a rustic inn. In 1997, Morne Trois Pitons

National Park, the portion of Dominica boasting some of the most spectacular scenery, was added to UNESCO's World Heritage List for encompassing the "richest biodiversity in the Lesser Antilles." In 2004, Dominica was the first country to receive benchmark designation from Green Globe 21. In sum, you won't find a better showcase for the Caribbean's natural assets than what is offered on Dominica.

The Briefest History

Dominica was first settled by Indians from South America in 3000 B.C.; later came the Arawaks, and finally the Caribs. The Caribs gave the island its best name, Wai'tukubuli, or "Tall Is Her Body." Columbus sighted the island in 1493 on his second voyage and christened it Dominica (Spanish for "Sunday Island"). Unfortunately, his brother Bartolomeo gave the same name to part of the island of Hispaniola at about the same time (no faxes or cell phones available then to avoid such a snafu), so there has been 500 years of confusion ever since. Officially, Dominica is called the Commonwealth of Dominica, whereas the Spanish country on Hispaniola is called the Dominican Republic. Mail is always getting mixed up, as well as the true identity of those who call themselves Dominican, but we digress. After Columbus, the British took theoretical possession of the island (without actually settling here) while the French turned it into a de facto colony and imported slaves from West Africa. In 1660, in an unusual arrangement, the French and the British agreed to leave the Caribs in undisturbed possession of the island. However, after recurring skirmishes in the 18th century, the French eventually ceded the island to the British, who gained full control by 1805. Independence was granted in 1978, and today Dominica is a member of the Commonwealth of Nations and governed by a prime minister.

Getting There

Dominica is not the easiest place to reach, but connections can be made easily from major eastern U.S. cities to American Eagle in San Juan. Dominica has two airports, neither of which can accommodate jets. American Eagle flies to Melville Hall, a runway located 32 miles from the capital on the island's northeast coast, a little over one hour from Roseau. Canefield Airport is the smaller, more convenient runway, just 3 miles north of Roseau. LIAT flies to both airports from neighboring islands; Caribbean Sun serves Melville Hall from neighboring islands; and Air Caraïbes flies in from the French islands. The nearest islands offering scheduled jet service from the US are Antigua, Barbados, and St. Lucia. Budget about $50 for a private taxi ride from Melville Hall to the Roseau area; alternatively, you can use a shared taxi for about $20 per person.

For island hoppers, there is a high-speed catamaran ferry from Dominica to Guadeloupe to Martinique called the Emeraude Express, operated by

L'Express des Isles. It brings you to Roseau from Pointe-à-Pitre, Guadeloupe, or from Fort-de-France, Martinique (it is helpful to *parle français* when choosing this option); 767-448-2181. The round-trip fare from either Martinique or Guadeloupe to Dominica is $101.

Getting Around

If you want to really explore the island, you should rent a car. Roads are often steep, very narrow, and winding, but generally in decent shape. There are a number of locally owned outfits on the island; we were happy with Courtesy Car Rental (767-448-7763), which included airport transfers in our $39-a-day rate. There's also a Budget affiliate (800-527-0700 or 767-449-2080). Word to the wise: Avoid driving at night—rampant potholes, unmarked gutters, scampering dogs and goats, lack of signs, and oncoming high-beams combine to challenge the most steel-nerved motorist. If you don't feel like driving, you can hire a van to take you around. As always, be sure to agree on a price, inclusive of everything, before you go. One outfit that definitely has it together is Ken's Hinterland Adventure Tours (866-880-0508 or 767-448-4850; www.kenshinterlandtours.com), with trips to all points on the island and hiking expeditions as well.

Focus on Dominica: Nature

There are several ways to enjoy the natural splendor of Dominica. If you aren't terribly mobile on foot, you can circuit the island by car in a day and get a sense of the rainforest, particularly by driving through the middle of the island and the **Central Forest Reserve**. You can hang out at **Papillote Wilderness Retreat** (see Where to Stay, below) and sip Cuthbert's killer rum punch while you soak up the gardens and hot springs around you. You can also hike, which for us is the only way to really experience Dominica. It's simple, it doesn't cost much (a taxi ride to the trailhead and a guide, if necessary) and brings you up close and personal with the natural forces of the island. So bring a good pair of hiking sneakers or shoes (ones that can and will get muddy and wet), and choose among the following adventures.

Trafalgar Falls

Located about 20 minutes due east from Roseau, up a fairly rough road and virtually next door to Papillote, Trafalgar Falls is a series of huge narrow waterfalls. A 20-minute walk and a moderately easy rock scramble will bring you to the base of **"Papa"** falls (**"Mama"** is the medium-size one on the right, and **"Baby"** is the smallest one way up on the left). You'll need to ford the river once, which at the right place is wet but not difficult. (If it starts raining in the mountains above, the river rises swiftly, so be advised.) Once at the base of "Papa," you can carefully slip into a pool of cool mountain water and work your way against a slight current to the left of the falls. Here you'll see mustard-orange-colored rocks, which is where the hot springs flow into the stream. Maneuver your way under this water — it's not too hot — and enjoy a natural Jacuzzi. The farther up you climb, the hotter it gets. As you bask in hot water while tons of cool water gush and tumble by 5 feet away, you'll think you've found a bit of heaven.

Before you start on the trail, you will be asked a dozen times if you want a guide to the falls. If you are reasonably sure-footed, you don't need one for this short hike. There is a trail leading up to the falls, although you will come to the stream first and think you've come to a dead end. You haven't — just ford the stream and follow the rocks and "path" to the left. You'll have to climb a little, but it's not very hard. Unfortunately, the beauty of the falls and their proximity to Roseau and Papillote's restaurant have made this destination popular with cruise ship tourists. Best advice: Go early in the morning or late in the afternoon (the light's best then, too) for more solitude and privacy.

⊛ The Boiling Lake

Trafalgar Falls is actually just kid stuff. The real hiking is farther up the valley. Here you'll find Caribbean wilderness in the **Morne Trois Pitons National Park**. There are several adventures that should appeal to serious walkers, but the best is the hike over the mountains, down through the **Valley of Desolation** to the Boiling Lake. It sounds Dante-esque, and indeed there are places along the way that seem right out of *The Inferno*; but there are also intensely green mountains, a lush rainforest, and fabulous vistas; you'll travel through several climate zones in one day. If you have only one hike in you, do this one. It's very strenuous — you'll be walking for at least six hours at a fast pace — but if you are in decent shape, you can do it and you'll never forget the hike. There aren't cliff faces to climb — just several mountains to go up and down. The trail is very narrow and can get very muddy, so the going can be tricky. You won't recognize your Reeboks after this one — hiking boots are better.

You will need a guide for the Boiling Lake hike. Although the trail can be followed, it's just too long and isolated to risk getting disoriented. A local guide can be found in the villages of Laudat and Trafalgar. Papillote (see below) can make recommendations, or you can go with Ken's Hinterland Tours (866-880-0508 or 767-448-4850; www.kenshinterlandtours.com), which charges $40 per person (minimum four) for the Boiling Lake hike.

You must bring plenty of water. We recommend at least one 1.5-liter plastic container of Loubiere spring water (available at any store in Dominica) per person. Also take along some high-energy food to replace the thousands of calories that it feels like you're burning (wishful thinking). The starting point for the Boiling Lake hike is the village of **Laudat**, at about 2,000 feet above sea level. This is about as high and as close to the park as you can go by car.

From here you will have stunning views of Trafalgar all the way down to Roseau and the sea. It's a scenic twist-and-shout drive up to this pretty little spot, and you'll want to be driven so as to save your strength for the walk ahead. Park at Titou Gorge (leave no valuables in the car, of course) or be dropped off here by the taxi (make sure to arrange a pickup time — about six to seven hours later; your guide will be the best judge, so defer to his or her wisdom).

Once you leave the gorge it's a very steady uphill climb, but not terribly difficult. At this point, the trail is in good shape and fairly clear — there are some roots and rocks to step over, but it's obvious it has been well trodden. After about 45 minutes of this you will arrive at what is called the **Breakfast River** by the locals (so named because it's a good place to rest and fuel up before the hard stuff begins on the other side). Here is where you will hear the siffleur montagne — one of the most exotic-sounding birds we've ever heard, which lives only at these elevations. A tiny grayish-blue bird that's almost impossible to see, it trills a beautiful, symphonic five-note song that ends on a high note.

After the pit stop, get ready to climb stairs for the next hour. It's a very steep trek up a narrow trail to the airy ridge that you must cross to get to the valley. This ascent and descent is the real kicker — and you'll do it twice! You arrive on top of the ridge dripping with sweat only to almost suffer hypothermia from the stiff breeze. On a clear day, the view is reminiscent of vistas afforded by the Rockies or Cascades, except that the ocean in the distance is an incredible light blue. Now you're ready to go down into the Valley of Desolation (sounds like a Joni Mitchell song). The descent is slow, muddy, and slippery, but when you look up, the view is unbelievable: a massive green sweep of valley with high, jagged mountain peaks and thermal vents sending wisps of steam into the air. Off in the distance and hidden by a peak, the Boiling Lake's giant cauldron bubbles away, sending a huge plume of white vapor several hundred feet into the air. The wonderfully fragrant smell of sulfur is everywhere. Talk about sensory overload!

Once in the valley, you'll go along a rocky riverbed with a hot-water stream flowing down it. The color of the water will change as you get farther into the valley (due to the mineral content and how it has stained the rock below). You'll see water that's black, gray, white, green, and light blue. Where the terrain is open to the sky and elements, it's cool and breezy, but at the bottom the vegetation is dense and the air is hot and humid.

When you finally reach the Boiling Lake — after a few more ups, downs, and across a rock-strewn slope — you will feel very remote and isolated. You are. The lake itself is situated in the crater of an extinct volcano. It's fairly large, about 100 yards across, and very round. It is the second largest of its type in the world (the biggest is in New Zealand, but since you can virtually park your car at the edge of that one, Dominica's is a much more distinctive experience). The water is usually milky gray and boiling. The rising steam combines with the cool ocean breeze to create a warm mist that envelops you. This is a good spot to rest and eat lunch, but don't get too comfortable, because it's an equally long and arduous hike back. It's worth noting that in early 2005, the Boiling Lake stopped simmering. Locals panicked that one of the island's key attractions might have been lost (or that the inactivity was a precursor to something dramatic), but it turned out to be a regular part of the caldera's cycle, and after a few weeks it started churning again.

To cool off once you've begun the return journey, take a dip in the first stream you encounter (check with your guide first). Upstream there are several warm-water pools of light blue water (from the mix of minerals), with little waterfalls and other touches of nature's kitsch that make swimming very pleasant. Since it's unlikely that you'll encounter anyone, feel free to whip off your clothes for a fun skinny-dip and splash around.

You return to Laudat the same way you came, but the different perspective allows you to see things you might have missed before. One thing you will definitely notice is the fatigue in your legs, so take it slow and hit the brakes. The descent down the muddy trails can be treacherous, but you have the Titou Gorge to look forward to—a wonderful reward for a hard day's work.

The **Titou Gorge** lies at the base of the trail and used to go almost unnoticed before they paved paradise and put up a parking lot (we're huge Joni fans!). Progress marches on. Far worse is the tampering with water levels in the gorge by the hydroelectric company in order to power the turbines. It used to be a guaranteed beautiful experience. Now it all depends on the whims of the company. That said, hopefully you will encounter something wonderful. Assuming this, jump into the cool but oh-so-very-refreshing-after-walking-and-sweating-for-seven-hours water and swim into the gorge. What you see at water level is truly beautiful: deep-light-blue or medium-green water (depending on the amount of sunlight), rock walls that rise up at least 50 feet, creating natural halls and chambers, and a roaring waterfall at the gorge's end. Unfortunately, the falls are hard to photograph unless you have a waterproof camera or play water polo and are used to propelling yourself upright with your feet. The waterfall does create a strong current, particularly as you get closer to it. Once you enter the waterfall room, it's fun to walk up the right side of it about 5 feet—it's not at all difficult—and sit behind the fall in the space Mother Nature has thoughtfully provided. The vantage point here is one of total hydration—memorize it for the next time you're stuck on a rush-hour subway in mid-July. Swimming out is anticlimactic, so we turned around and made a second approach—it's pretty difficult to get tired of this one.

Other Options

There are several other hikes in the National Park as well as in the Northern Forest Reserve in the north of the island. In the National Park, an easier walk than the Boiling Lake hike will take you along a road to the **Fresh Water**

Lake, a pristine and very tranquil lake that used to be swimmable but is now a reservoir. For those who would rather let their fingers do the walking, a four-wheel-drive vehicle like a Suzuki Samurai can take you right up to the lake. A little more remote is the **Boeri Lake**, where the water is very heavy and hard to swim in. The **Boeri Valley**, downstream from the lake, is still an essentially uninhabited wilderness area that's ideal for orienteering and bushwhacking. Before attempting it, check with the Forestry Department to make sure you won't get lost for days. Fortunately, there is nothing poisonous on Dominica to worry about. The Boeri Valley can be reached by a 45-minute climb from the **Middleham Falls** to **Stinking Hole**. This window to the Boeri Valley is located about halfway between the junction of the Laudat–Trafalgar road and Laudat. It is now well marked and maintained.

In the north of the island, the Northern Forest Reserve offers hiking up Dominica's highest mountain, **Morne Diablotin** (4,747 feet). The trailhead begins in Syndicate, which is also the place to view the imperial parrot (also known as the sisserou) and the red-necked parrot (or jaco). There aren't many of these species left (about 350 sisserou and 1,500 jaco, at last count), but they are protected and under study by a team of British birders. Fortunately, their efforts are helping — the parrots seem to be on the rebound. The birders have built a viewing platform over a gorge that should be scaled only by those with no fear of heights (it's precariously perched on a tree that leans several hundred feet over the gorge). The best time to see the birds is early in the morning or around dusk. They are loud squawkers, so you will be able to tell them from other large birds. To reach the viewing area and the trail to Morne Diablotin, take the west coast road north from Roseau. Go 4 miles north of the town of Colihaut. After you pass a school on your left and then, just around a bend, a white house with red trim, take a sharp right and follow this road until you come to a grapefruit orchard on your right (there will be a small house on the left). Turn left on the dirt road and right again at the next junction. You are now on a banana plantation road that borders the National Forest Reserve. Go for about half a mile until you pass a tiny concrete bridge and a little banana shed on the left just beyond the bridge. Park your car before the bridge and well out of the way of the occasional banana trucks. Walk past the shed for about 300 yards until the road bends to the left. At this point you will notice a trail on the right through banana trees. This will lead you to the parrot viewpoint and the trail to Morne Diablotin. When you've been on this trail for about 10 minutes, you will notice a trail on the right — this is the trailhead to Morne Diablotin. Continuing straight for another 10 minutes, you will reach the gorge and the viewing platform. It's both a good idea and island etiquette to contact the Forestry Department before venturing inland. It also has detailed maps and information that is very helpful. It can be reached by phoning 767-448-2401 or stopping by its headquarters in the Roseau Botanical Gardens.

Finally, there are the sulfur springs at **Wotten Waven** (sounds like Baba

Wawa). These are a short taxi ride from either Papillote or Roseau and an equally short (30 minutes, if that) walk to the springs. They can be muddy, so be prepared, and remember that sulfur smells a lot like rotten eggs.

Where to Stay

Dominica's tourist industry started to blossom in the 1990s with the steady addition of new hotels, guesthouses, and lodging compounds. The island possesses no high-amenity hotels. Most places to stay are along the west coast around the two major towns, Roseau and Portsmouth. Our recommendation is still the same — stay in the forests, which is what makes this island unique — but there are a few decent options in Roseau, a place on the beach near Plymouth, and a delightful inn on the east coast.

Papillote Wilderness Retreat, P.O. Box 2287, Trafalgar Falls Road, Morne Macaque, Roseau, Dominica, WI. ℂ 767-448-2287, ✆ 767-448-2285, 🖥 www.papillote.dm, papillot@cwdom.dm

💲 **Not So Cheap** 🍽 **EP** (or optional **MAP**) Ⓒ 7 rooms

This is a great choice for those who want to be at one with Nature. Papillote is geared to the outdoors, located high up in the mountains where the air is noticeably cooler. It combines the island's natural beauty with the warmth and friendliness of the locals. Sitting suspensefully under the perfect cone of a dormant volcano known as Morne Macaque, 1,000 feet above sea level, it is truly integrated into its surroundings, from the hot-water springs running through the compound and the painstakingly planned and cultivated botanic gardens to the exotic fowl and the ever-present residents of Trafalgar (the village down the road). The rooms are rustic but comfortable, decorated with local crafts. With the sound of rushing water everywhere, time here is meant to be spent outdoors. Two hot-water pools constructed by a Canadian artist out of indigenous stone feature sculptures of iguanas and fish that spew hot mineral water, which feels orgasmic after a day of hiking. Staying here will also give you a good chance to meet Dominicans from all walks of life, as the owners, the Jean-Baptistes, are popular among the locals. Papillote is conveniently located next to a vast wilderness area, the island's best hikes (Trafalgar Falls is a short 20-minute walk away), and Anne Jno Baptiste is very enthusiastic about showing plant lovers around. She has also built a separate restaurant and center at the base of the property to steer the day-tourist traffic away from the hotel so it won't interfere with the guests' privacy, a definite plus. Since you are miles away from the nearest restaurant, the MAP plan ($35 per day, per person) makes sense. The food is very good West Indian fare, featuring lots of fresh local produce.

Jungle Bay Resort & Spa, P.O. Box 2352, Point Mulatre, Roseau, Dominica, WI. © 767-446-1789, ✆ 767-446-1090, 💻 www.junglebaydominica.com, info@junglebaydominica.com

💲 **Pricey** 🍴 **EP** CC 35 cottages

Take a cleansing breath and find your inner chi at this yoga-themed eco-resort built in 2005. The 55-acre Jungle Bay Resort is situated on a seaside cliff overlooking the Atlantic Ocean and was built to minimize adverse impacts on the environment. The romantic cottages are tucked into the rainforest and elevated on stilts and include king-size platform beds, sitting areas, ceiling fans, safes, and private patios. All of the cottages boast semi-outdoor showers where you (and a loved one?) can commune with nature. The resort has a volcanic stone swimming pool and a beach bar and sundeck (located on the rocky beach below the property), but the main focus here is the Yoga Center. When it's time to get your om on, there's no better place in the Caribbean to practice than in these two gigantic studios with sweeping ocean views. The Yoga Center offers daily yoga, tai chi, and other wellness sessions for guests of the resort and will soon offer week-long holistic retreats. Once you've worked up a sweat, grab a healthy bite at the open-air Pavilion restaurant, which features organic local products with a gourmet Caribbean flair. The resort's Spa du Soleil will have you close to inner peace with five semi-open treatment rooms and a host of services ranging from the simple (manis and pedis) to the sublime (aromatherapy massage). When you're thoroughly rejuvenated, kick back at the Coconut Bar and play some pool or darts or get your groove on at the Beach Bar's Friday night reggae party — that is, if you haven't fallen asleep by then!

Exotica, P.O. Box 109, Morne Anglais, Roseau, Dominica, WI. © 800-822-3274 or 767-448-8839, ✆ 767-448-8829, 💻 www.exotica-cottages.com, exotica@cwdom.dm

💲 **Not So Cheap** 🍴 **EP** CC 8 cottages

Looking for a mountain hideaway where no one will find you? Perched on terraced slopes at the 1,200-foot elevation above Roseau, Exotica offers a hamlet of eight one-bedroom wooden cottages, each with full kitchen. The view from the veranda soars down the lush valley to the sea below — stupendous. There is a small restaurant, the Shade House, which uses fruits and vegetables from Exotica's organic farm. The proprietors are Fae and Athie Martin — he is the president of the Dominica Conservation Association and knows well the challenges and rewards of protecting this unique environment.

Zandoli Inn, P.O. Box 2099, Roche Cassee, Stowe, Dominica, WI. © 767-446-3161, ✆ 767-446-3344, 💻 www.zandoli.com

🔒 **Not So Cheap** 🍴 EP CC 5 rooms

More remote, more exotic still, Zandoli Inn clings to a cliff close to the water on the southeast coast of Dominica. The chief asset is isolation—it's a 30-minute, winding drive from Roseau—but there's also a charming Canadian innkeeper, Linda, who looks after guests graciously. The rooms are simple but pleasantly furnished, and a restaurant serves delicious breakfasts, dinners, and light lunches on request. There's a small pool, fine snorkeling for confident swimmers down below when the seas are calm, and views that extend for miles down the coast. We're not sure we'd want to stay a whole week here—there's no other business within a couple miles—but it's definitely an escape into a forgotten (but very beautiful) corner of the Caribbean. It's fun to knock back a few beers with the locals in the adjacent fishing village.

Fort Young Hotel, P.O. Box 519, Victoria Street, Roseau, Dominica, WI. 𝒞 800-581-2034 or 767-448-5000, ✎ 767-448-5006, 💻 www.fortyounghotel.com, fortyoung@cwdom.dm

🔒 **Cheap** 🍴 EP CC 73 rooms

This is the largest and most deluxe accommodation on Dominica, and even though it's not really a luxury property, it will do for those who need a modicum of service attached to their Caribbean vacation. It grew from the ruins of Fort Young, which is right in the heart of Roseau, above the water. Businesspeople use this hotel because of its proximity to government offices and other commercial establishments, and because it has a decent array of amenities—room service, a/c, cable TV, and direct-dial phones in each room. The location—a stone's throw from the cruise-ship dock—is a plus or minus, depending on your perspective (sometimes "ocean view" translates literally to "side-of-a-mammoth-ship view"). New rooms were added in 2005 that are comfortable and nicely appointed, and the original standard rooms are a good value at $95 a night in high season. Although there is no beach, there is a nice outdoor pool and a good restaurant and bar on the premises (but beware of the steep menu prices).

Humming Bird Inn, P.O. Box 20, Roseau, Dominica, WI. 𝒞 and ✎ 767-449-1042, 💻 www.thehummingbirdinn.com, hummingbird@cwdom.dm

🔒 **Cheap** 🍴 EP CC 10 rooms

Situated conveniently close to Canefield Airport and Roseau (just five minutes away), this charming establishment sits up on a hill called Morne Daniel and has wonderful views and a quiet, private setting. It's pleasant, still fresh, and very reasonably priced, and the rooms share a balcony and hammocks; there's also a nice honeymoon suite with a four-poster bed and a veranda. The delightful owner, Jeane James-Finucahe, is someone who actively embraces the ecotourism concept that makes Dominica so special. We love that she spends much of her day keeping the hummingbirds and iguanas happy.

Castle Comfort Lodge, P.O. Box 63, Roseau, Castle Comfort, Dominica, WI. ✆ 888-414-7626 or 767-448-2188, ✆ 767-448-6088, 💻 www.castlecomfortdivelodge.com, dive@cwdom.dm

💲 **Wicked Pricey** ⑪ **MAP** including two dives daily ⓒⓒ 15 rooms

Popular with divers because it offers several scuba packages, this is also the home of Dive Dominica, which started the underwater exploration of this island. It is very informal and spare but a great place for diver camaraderie. Located on the water south of Roseau, the 15 rooms are basic and air-conditioned, and some have TV — a few of the newer rooms are a little nicer. One week packages with two dives daily are the norm. It's closed in September.

Pointe Baptiste, c/o Elizabeth Edgerton, Calibishi, Dominica, WI. ✆ and ✆ 767-445-7368, 💻 www.pointebaptiste.com, manager@pointebaptiste.com

💲 **Cheap** for the cottage, **Very Pricey** for the house (sleeps 8) ⑪ **EP** ⓒⓒ 2 villas

A restored house and smaller cottage on the north coast just east of Calibishi, this has both a black- and a white-sand beach. The cottage sleeps two; the house sleeps six or more and is a good alternative for a large group that wants to be on the sea and still have access to the mountains (it comes with a maid and cook). You will need a car and should fly into Melville Hall Airport, not Canefield.

Picard Beach Cottages, P.O. Box 34, Portsmouth, Roseau, Dominica, WI. ✆ 800-448-8355 or 767-445-5131, ✆ 767-445-5599, 💻 www.avirtualdominica.com/picard.htm, pbh@cwdom.dm

💲 **Pricey** ⑪ **EP** ⓒⓒ 18 rooms

Located on the black-sand beach just south of Portsmouth on 16 acres of an old coconut plantation, these are nicely furnished Caribbean-style cottages with kitchen, veranda, bedroom, bath, and living and dining area. This is a great place to be away from it all, on a decent beach and yet accessible to the rainforest, which climbs up the slopes of Morne Diablotin above the cottages. There is also a restaurant on the grounds, and guests can use the pool next door at the medical school apartment complex.

Evergreen Hotel, P.O. Box 309, Castle Comfort, Dominica, WI. ✆ 767-448-3276, ✆ 767-448-6800, 💻 www.avirtualdominica/evergreen.htm, evergreen@cwdom.dm

💼 **Not So Cheap** 🍴 **BP** CC 16 rooms

Situated on the ocean just south of Roseau, this is nice lodging for those who want to be on the water and to have friendly service, clean and comfortable rooms, a swimming pool, and diving nearby. Rooms have a/c, cable TV, private bath, and phone. The newer waterfront units are polished and offer sea views. The Evergreen's restaurant serves tasty West Indian cuisine. Packages with Dive Dominica (located next door) are also available.

Where to Eat

Dominica isn't a "fine dining" kind of island, but local food is often good and generally highlights the island's fresh produce and seafood. Most people eat the majority of their meals at their hotel, but you might want a night out in Roseau, so here are the best choices.

$ **Corner House**, Roseau, 767-449-9000

We particularly like this place for breakfast, when $5 buys a plate of delicious banana pancakes. It's also an Internet café. Open for lunch and dinner; closed on Saturday and Sunday.

$ **Guiyave**, 15 Cork Street, Roseau, 767-448-2930

This is another typical West Indian–Creole restaurant, set on the second floor of an old wood-frame house. It's popular with the business-lunch set, so you know it's good. Guiyave serves a mean rum punch, as well as fresh tropical juices. Also open for breakfast and dinner.

$$$ **La Robe Creole**, 3 Victoria Street, Roseau, 767-448-2896

Still probably the best restaurant on the island, it is also Dominica's most famous. It's in a cozy and attractive 75-year-old stone house. The specialties include shrimp in coconut, "mountain chicken" (frog) in beer batter, lobster in coconut curry, fresh fish, local squash and pumpkin soups, and a fine rum punch. Service can be slow, but who's in a rush? Open for lunch and dinner; closed on Sunday.

$ **Mousehole Snackette**, 3 Victoria Street, Roseau, 767-448-2896

Located downstairs from La Robe Creole (and under the same management), this is a great place for West Indian takeout or a quick lunch.

$ **Pearl's Cuisine**, Roseau, 767-448-8707

Pearl's offers a fresh catch of the day with all the sides for under $15 in a charming old house—what more could you ask for? Closed on Sunday.

$ **World of Food**, Vena's Hotel, 48 Cork Street, Roseau, 767-448-3286

This restaurant should actually be called the World of Creole because of its excellent West Indian cuisine and atmosphere. If you want real local-style specialties — curried goat, rôti, crab backs, conch, and tee-tee-ree (tiny freshly spawned fish) — this is the place to go. No credit cards accepted.

Don't Miss

The Boiling Lake

It is probably the finest trek in the Caribbean, and one of the most challenging.

Diving and Snorkeling

Dominica is one of the Caribbean's top three dive destinations, per the readers of *Scuba Diving* magazine, which extols the island's healthy marine environment and the plethora of smaller exotic species like seahorses, frogfish, and crinoids (it's a great scene for macro photographers). You'll also find underwater tunnels with schooling fish that lead to soaring lava pinnacles. The shoreline of Soufriere Bay wraps around a 2,000-foot-deep submerged volcanic crater lined with vertical walls covered in sea life. Snorkelers aren't left out: At one spot, named Champagne Reef and just 12 feet deep, the island's volcanic activity creates a place where hot water and bubbles filter out of underground vents — parrotfish, octopus, and squid swarm around the barrel sponges, vase sponges, brain coral, and finger coral. There are several dive and snorkel tour operators, including Anchorage Hotel and Dive Center (767-448-2638; www.anchoragehotel.dm) and Dive Dominica (888-414-7626 or 767-448-2188; www.castlecomfortdivelodge.com).

Whale-Watching

Dominica is perhaps the whale-watching capital of the Caribbean, and boat operators boast a 90 percent success rate at spotting some of the 22 different whale species off the coast of the island — 70-foot sperm whales are the star of the show. Three- to four-hour trips are $50 per person; check with Anchorage Dive or Dive Dominica (see above).

Rainforest Aerial Tram

Okay, we admit, the first time we heard about this project we were — well, appalled. The tram was built, it opened in 2003, and although it caters primarily to the cruise-ship crowd, it *does* provide a pretty special immersion into the heart of Dominica's forests. The trams glide for almost a mile, slowly and silently along the canopy, while a guide narrates the excursion, which climaxes with a traverse of the sheer, waterfall-lined Breakfast River Gorge. You can disembark at the top to examine the spectacular chasm from an airy suspension bridge. It's expensive, but if you don't have the time (or stamina) for the Boiling Lake trek, this is a fair substitute. It offers limited operation in the summer. For more information, call 866-759-8726 or 767-448-8775, or visit www.rainforestram.com.

Indian River

It's touristy, but a canoe trip up the Indian River outside Portsmouth is un-deniably romantic — choose a hand-paddled boat rather than the sputtering motor-powered boats for a truly relaxing trip. The one-hour excursion is just $12 per person. Allow a little time for the unexpected oasis that emerges around the last bend: Radjah's Club, a bar playing hot *zouk* tunes that drift over the airwaves from neighboring Guadeloupe.

The Dominican Republic

The Dominican Republic attracts a wide range of tourists, from those who choose to bask in an all-inclusive resort to those who prefer more hands-on travel. Although we are not as enthused with the all-inclusive hotels — mainly because we feel this experience lacks any real cultural value — we must admit that the D.R. (as it is often called) is the cheapest place in the Caribbean to arrange these package deals. We are also fully aware that after 50 weeks of hard work, many tourists desire nothing more than vegging out on a beach with all their meals and drinks included. That being said, we urge readers to at least get a taste of the real D.R. that lies outside the resort walls. Even a two-day visit to the capital city, Santo Domingo, will provide some insight into this culturally rich Caribbean country. The Colonial Zone (Zona Colonial) of the city is full of monuments, forts, and churches dating back 500 years. All of this is interspersed among open plazas and cobblestone streets with posh new hotels and sophisticated bars and restaurants.

This is a poor country, and we mean *very* poor (second only to Haiti in the Western Hemisphere), so keep that in mind upon arrival. The extent of the poverty is shocking at first. Our hosts kept saying, "You'll get used to it." To a certain extent you do — like the way some become inured to the sight of

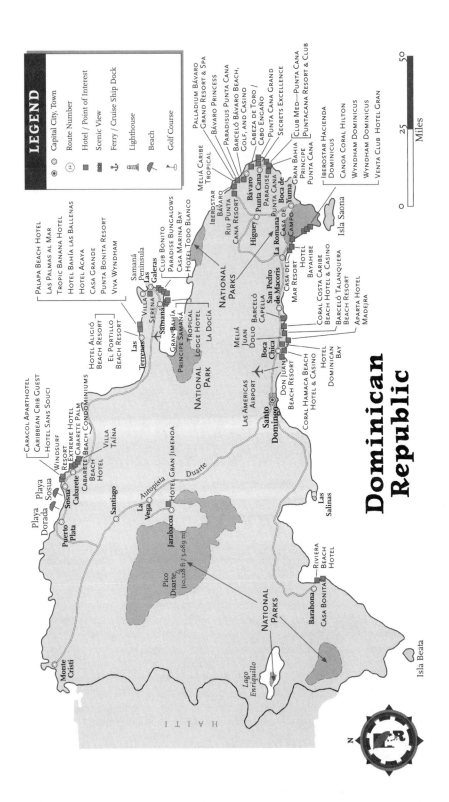

Dominican Republic

LEGEND

- ◎ Capital City, Town
- (11) Route Number
- ■ Hotel / Point of Interest
- ◫ Scenic View
- ⚓ Ferry / Cruise Ship Dock
- 🗼 Lighthouse
- Beach
- ⛳ Golf Course

CARACOL APARTHOTEL
CARIBBEAN CRIB GUEST
HOTEL SANS SOUCI

WINDSURF
RESORT
EXTREME HOTEL
CABARETE PALM
CABARETE BEACH CONDOMINIUMS
BEACH
HOTEL
VILLA
TAINA

Playa
Dorada

Playa
Sosua

Puerto
Plata

Sosua
Cabarete

Santiago

La
Vega

Autopista
Duarte

HOTEL GRAN JIMENOA

Monte
Cristi

Santo
Domingo

Jarabacoa

Pico
Duarte
(10,128 ft / 3,089 m)

NATIONAL
PARKS

Las
Salinas

Lago
Enriquillo

Barahona
CASA BONITA

RIVIERA
BEACH
HOTEL

HAITI

Isla Beata

PALAPA BEACH HOTEL
LAS PALMAS AL MAR
TROPIC BANANA HOTEL
HOTEL BAHÍA LAS BALLENAS
HOTEL ACAYA
CASA GRANDE
PUNTA BONITA RESORT
VIVA WYNDHAM

HOTEL ALICIÓ
BEACH RESORT
EL PORTILLO
BEACH RESORT

Las
Terrenas

VILLA
SERENA

Samaná
Peninsula
Las
Galeras

CLUB BONITO
PARADISE BUNGALOWS
CASA MARINA BAY
HOTEL TODO BLANCO

Samaná

GRAN BAHÍA
PRINCIPE SAMANÁ

TROPICAL
LODGE HOTEL
LA DOCÍA

NATIONAL
PARK

MELIÁ CARIBE
TROPICAL

PALLADIUM BÁVARO
GRAND RESORT & SPA
BÁVARO PRINCESS
PARADISUS PUNTA CANA
BARCELÓ BÁVARO BEACH,
GOLF, AND CASINO
CABEZA DE TORO /
CABO ENGAÑO
SECRETS EXCELLENCE

IBEROSTAR
BÁVARO
RIU PUNTA
CANA RESORT

Bávaro
Punta Cana
PARADISE
PUNTA CANA

GRAN BAHIA
PRINCIPE
PUNTA CANA

CLUB MED—PUNTA CANA
PUNTACANA RESORT & CLUB

IBEROSTAR HACIENDA
DOMINICUS
CANOA CORAL HILTON
WYNDHAM DOMINICUS
WYNDHAM DOMINICUS
VENTA CLUB HOTEL GRAN

Higüey

La Romana

CASA DE
CAMPO
Boca de
Yuma

Isla Saona

NATIONAL
PARKS

San Pedro
de Macorís

CASA DEL
MAR RESORT

CORAL COSTA CARIBE
BEACH HOTEL & CASINO
BARCELÓ TALANQUERA
BEACH RESORT
APARTA HOTEL
MADEIRA

MELIÁ
JUAN
DOLIO
Boca
Chica

BARCELÓ
CAPELLA

HOTEL
BAYAHIBE

DON JUAN
BEACH RESORT

CORAL HAMACA BEACH
HOTEL & CASINO

HOTEL
DOMINICAN
BAY

LAS AMERICAS
AIRPORT

N

0   25   50

Miles

Dominican Republic: Key Facts

Location	19°N by 70°W (at its center) 50 miles west of Puerto Rico 1,600 miles southeast of New York
Size	18,712 square miles
Highest point	Pico Duarte (10,128 feet/3,089 meters)
Population	8,000,000 (approximately)
Language	Spanish
Time	Atlantic Standard Time (1 hour ahead of EST, same as EDT)
Area code	809
Electricity	110 volts AC, 60 cycles (in most places)
Currency	The Dominican peso, RD$ (approximately RD$33 = US$1). Be sure to use the bank at the Customs area to change your currency so you'll have some RD$ when you leave Customs. You must have pesos; it is illegal to deal in dollars (although people and hotels do it).
Driving	Only for the experienced, assured driver. On the right; a valid American or Canadian driver's license and a valid credit card or a substantial cash deposit are required to rent a car.
Documents	U.S. and Canadian citizens need a passport or proof of citizenship; a tourist card ($10) must be purchased at the airport when you arrive (don't lose it), or you can purchase it at the airport counter at your point of embarkation.
Departure tax	$10
Beer to drink	⊛ Presidente
Rum to drink	Barcelo Gold
Music to hear	Merengue
Tourism info	800-723-6138 (brochure requests) 888-374-6361 (general info) www.godominicanrepublic.com www.dominicanrepublic.com/Tourism www.dr1.com www.hispaniola.com

homeless people on big-city streets in the United States. Here it's really a slap in the face, but after a while you see so much of it that you realize this is just the way it is. Not that it doesn't bother you—you just steel yourself to it.

It is also a country of striking contrasts. You can be in a car next to a man and a donkey laden down with wares and then walk into a very nice restaurant that would be at home in Manhattan. You see differences like this all the time. As you are driving to a resort, you might see incredibly poor people living in hovels just outside the entrance and then find yourself in a sumptuous hotel with buffet tables loaded with food. It blows you away.

The D.R. (don't call it the "Dominican"!) is a big country for the Caribbean, second only to Cuba in size. At 18,712 square miles, it's about as big as New Hampshire and Vermont combined. It occupies about two-thirds of the island of Hispaniola, which again is second in size only to Cuba. (The other third is occupied by Haiti, which is physically and culturally very different.) There are incredibly beautiful beaches along the D.R.'s 870 miles of coastline, high mountains (Pico Duarte reaches 10,128 feet — the highest in the Caribbean), lush vegetation, desert, and the urban sprawl of the capital, Santo Domingo. Throughout it all there are about 8 million people.

These people are very friendly, courteous, and polite, which is most refreshing and wonderful. For instance, the man at the car-rental desk, whose name was Francisco, shook our hands, which threw us a bit. We Americans are not used to such intimate contact from service people. We encountered this throughout our stay. Dominicans always shake hands before speaking to you. It's just done.

Dominicans are a mix of races. The majority of the ruling class is Latino white and, at least in the capital, heavy (a status symbol — it shows you have plenty to eat). Most Dominicans are shades of brown, a mixture of Latino, Indian, and African. Santiago, the commercial center of the country, is much whiter and more Latino than other parts of the country. The darkest people are from the southwest, closest to Haiti. One thing you notice about all Dominicans is that even though most people are very poor by our standards, they are surprisingly well dressed. Also, men always wear trousers, not shorts, everywhere in the country except at the beach, even when it's scorching outside.

The Dominican Republic attracts lots of European tourists, particularly French, Germans, and Italians. Although American have increased quite a bit in the last few years, gringos are still a rare breed here, except in Puerto Plata, Casa de Campo, and increasingly in Punta Cana. Most Dominicans thought we were Italians, which was a change from feeling that we had *American* stenciled on our foreheads. Most people who come here will stay in a resort and won't leave the grounds. If they do leave, they will most likely be on a tour bus. This is fine for those who just want to go someplace that has what they want and then stay put. However, if you are intrepid (which our readers are, we hope) and want to explore this fascinating and beautiful country, you should. If you don't speak Spanish, we'd recommend hiring a guide, because few people speak English outside the hotels. Arrangements can be made through your hotel or, if you know someone who lives here, through that person. It's easy and cheap (between $30 and $50 per day), and your guide will take you places you normally wouldn't see. This is big money to these people, so you should be able to get the best.

Your introduction to the Dominican road trip begins after exiting the airport. Driving into Santo Domingo on the Avenida de las Americas is a trip,

Safety

As in any country, there are precautions travelers should take when traveling through the Dominican Republic. Marching around with a Rolex and $2,000 camera is not too wise. In general, we found the D.R. to be quite safe. For those staying at all-inclusive resorts, *do not listen* to the tour desks that scare people from exploring the countryside on their own. We know of many travelers who were discouraged from taking their rental car out to explore. This is just a cheap sales ploy, because these same tour agencies that operate inside the hotels turn around and sell day trips to the tourists they have scared. Don't be afraid to leave the hotel grounds — the Dominicans are a very friendly lot, and some solo exploring will yield more than an organized trip, anyway.

too, and we're not talking about the 18-mile distance. A wave of vulnerability hits when you realize that this is a very foreign land, with different language, customs, and laws. It's a tad unsettling. What if you got into an accident or thrown in jail for no reason? Who will help you? At this point, you squelch the paranoia and focus on the task at hand, which is driving. The road is a four-lane parkway, with the Caribbean Sea to the left. By itself, it is pretty and could be anywhere. However, once you look to the right, you see the difference: men herding cattle along the side of the road, people walking everywhere, umpteen billboards, and that pervasive poverty. This contrast of modern versus primitive, rich versus poor, will hit you again and again as you experience the Dominican Republic. The story of this road is a classic example: The much-despised former dictator, Rafael Trujillo, built this parkway for his son so he could have a place to race his sports car.

Closer to the city, the Third World scenario gets more intense. Traffic lights might not work, and driver anarchy reigns when they don't. There are people everywhere, on foot, on bikes and mopeds, all headed for the bridge into town. On our first trip, we arrived at rush hour. Fortunately, in town a brigade of traffic cops somehow keeps traffic moving. Be sure you have your directions down before you leave the airport. With all that requires your attention, the last thing you'll need to do is try to figure out where you're going. You must be very alert behind the wheel. Three lanes will often be created where only two exist. Are you getting the picture? Hire a guide.

The Briefest History (A Complicated Past)

The island of Hispaniola was first settled by Amerindians who gradually migrated up the island chain from South America. There were several branches of the Arawak tribe on the island when Columbus landed on his first voyage in 1492, including the Taíno. They called the island Quisqueya, "Mother Earth." With the discovery of gold (gifts from the Arawaks), Columbus sent his brother Bartolomeo to establish a settlement, which he did. Founded in 1496, Santo Domingo became the capital of the Spanish colonies. From here expeditions (and conquests) were launched to Puerto Rico, Cuba, and Mexico.

However, the Spanish were never able to get a grip on the island they named Hispaniola ("Little Spain"). Sir Francis Drake and the British sacked the capital in 1586. Then the French laid claim to the western part of the island (what was eventually to become Haiti); by 1795 they had control of the entire island. The Haitian slave uprisings of the early 1800s caused major instability. As a result, France lost possession of the western portion of the island to the slaves, who established the Republic of Haiti. In 1809, France returned the eastern portion of the island (the part that became the D.R.) to Spain. Spain largely ignored its part of the island. This neglect triggered the Ephemeral Independence led by José Nuñez de Caceres, who proclaimed the eastern part of the island to be an independent state in 1821. However, Haiti objected to the idea of two countries on one island, and therefore invaded and ruled the island for the next 22 years. It was at this time that the seeds of the deep animosity between Haitians and Dominicans were planted. Rafael Trujillo's killing of about 10,000 Haitians in the next century certainly fanned the flames.

The 19th century was really a mess for the Dominicans. After the founding fathers of Dominican independence — Juan Pablo Duarte, Francisco del Rosario Sanchez, and Ramon Matias Mella — formed the new country of the Dominican Republic, there were long periods of instability and uncertainty. Factional bickering and territorial and economic fighting within the ruling class led to many civil wars. More invasions by Haiti and a four-year occupation by Spain didn't help matters at all.

In 1916 the United States entered the island and the Marines occupied the country until 1924. When the United States left, it had established a formidable army under the command of Rafael Leonidas Trujillo Molina. Six years later, he overthrew the president and began one of the most corrupt and evil dictatorships in the history of the Americas. It lasted until his assassination in 1961. The bumpy ride wasn't over, however, and a succession of brief presidencies and military coups caused tremendous instability. Civil war broke out again in 1965, and with Castro now entrenched in Cuba and threatening to become involved, the United States again quickly dispatched troops. Democracy was restored in 1966 under the leadership of President Joaquin Balaguer, who served off and on until 1996 (he was well into his 80s and blind but still going strong when a constitutional amendment for term limits forced him out). Free elections were held and won by Leonel Fernandez Reyna, whose four-year term as president ended in 2000. Reyna was born in the Dominican Republic but raised in New York City. Balaguer ran again in 2000 (Reyna could not run again, by law, because no president can hold office for consecutive terms). Balaguer was defeated by the current president, Rafael Hipolito Mejia. And the beat goes on.

On September 23, 1998, Hurricane Georges hit the unprepared southern coast of the Dominican Republic, including Santo Domingo, with up to 150 mph winds. It hugged the coast until finally turning inland and crossing the island into northern Haiti. One of the country's most destructive storms, it killed 270 and left more than 70,000 people homeless.

More recently, after pledging early support for the Iraq War, the Dominican government followed the Spanish lead in pulling its troops out of the coalition forces in April 2004. Leonel Fernandez Reyna, who had previously served as president, was reelected in May 2004 in the midst of nationwide economic turmoil. He undertook austerity measures and cut federal spending, and in 2005 the country was awarded a much-sought-after $664 million loan from the International Monetary Fund. The country is slowly putting its economy back together while dealing with continual labor protests.

Getting There

There are two major international airports in the Dominican Republic — Las Americas International in Santo Domingo and Puerto Plata's La Unión International Airport. In addition, there are four smaller international airports, including Punta Cana, which mainly handles charters from Europe; La Romana (Casa de Campo), which handles smaller commercial jets; Barahona's María Montez International Airport, which serves the southwestern part of the country; and Samaná–Arroyo Barril, the newest airport, serving the beautiful Samaná peninsula. American and Continental have nonstops to the D.R. from New York or Newark. American offers nonstop service to Puerto Plata and Santo Domingo and Punta Cana. Continental does as well, but only from Newark. American has nonstops from Miami and San Juan to Puerto Plata and La Romana. US Air flies nonstop from Philadelphia to Santo Domingo. American Eagle flies from San Juan to La Romana and Santiago. Beginning in mid-December 2006, Delta will launch service from Atlanta to Puerto Plata.

Getting Around

The D.R. is a big country, with more than 10,000 miles of roads. The best way to see it is by car. For those who choose to take public transportation, proper bus service is limited. Caribe Tours (221-4422) is the only real company. Its newly remodeled station in Santo Domingo is at Avenida 27 de Febrero and Leopoldo Navarro. More information is available on the Web site, www.caribetours.com.do. Caribe Tours operates daily buses to Barahona at 6:15 and 9:45 a.m; Rio San Juan (for Cabarete) at 7:30 and 9 a.m; Samaná at 7, 8:30, and 10 a.m.; and Sosúa (for Cabarete also) at 6, 7, 8, 9, and 10 a.m.

Besides the buses, *guaguas*, which are minivans that speed from town to town, make cross-country travel cheap, although piling in with 20 others is hardly comfortable. Most visitors choose to rent a car. However, driving in this country is a white-knuckle experience and is feasible only for confident, aggressive drivers with great reflexes. This is not a place for the meek—you will become a basket case before you even leave the airport. Roads, especially secondary ones, are often in bad shape, some with crater-size potholes to surprise you at 50 mph. Male drivers are aggressive and usually employ the macho rules of driving (e.g., tailgating, passing in no passing zones). Cars are not inspected here. You expect some to fall apart before your very eyes; many are without doors, fenders, windows, or lights and are carrying about three times as many people as was intended by the designer. Motorcycles and scooters abound, especially in the cities. The most passengers we've seen on a typical scooter here was a family of five. That's right, five! Three grown men on a scooter is very common. Of course, they don't move as fast, so there is a constant stream of them on the side of a two-lane road (which is shared with 18-wheelers). Directional signs, especially outside Santo Domingo, are few if existent at all. A route will end at a city plaza, and it's your guess as to where to go next to continue your journey. There's also the language issue: If you don't speak Spanish, getting comprehensible directions can be tough. Often the only mode of communication is elementary Spanish and lots of hand gestures. Then there are the police (see "¡Pero Señor Policia!" on the next page).

If you arrive in Santo Domingo, the first task is to find the car-rental desk area. As you walk out of Customs, you can't miss it.

Renting a car is very expensive in the Dominican Republic. It will cost you at least $300 per week, likely more. This is because cars cost twice as much here as in the United States (import duties double the price) and because the accident rate is so high. One look at your rental car will tell the tale. It will have several dents, broken lenses on the lights, ripped interior, and so on. Both of our college cars were in better condition than the one we were renting (and one of ours had been used by his mother and two brothers before him)! They make Rent-a-Wreck cars look brand-new.

Most of the major international players are here, including Budget (809-566-6666), Avis (809-535-7191), Thrifty (809-549-0717), Dollar (809-221-7368), Hertz (809-221-5333), and National (809-562-1444). We also had good luck with some local firms, which tend to be cheaper, like Honda Rent-a-Car (809-567-1015) and Nelly Rent-a-Car (809-687-7997). Be sure to make an advance reservation in the United States before you arrive—you will get a better rate. In addition, be sure to check with your credit card company for a collision damage waiver. Some may not provide you with coverage here. Understand all your liabilities before you hit the road, Jack.

¡Pero Señor Policia! (But Officer!)

When driving anywhere in the country, and especially on major routes, be prepared to be stopped by the police. They hang out at the side of the road and will flag you down. Then they will tell you that you were speeding, even though you weren't (and despite the fact that most don't have radar). What they want is a payoff — 40 pesos (about $3.50) will do. We were warned by some friends in Santo Domingo to expect this, and indeed it happened, several times. Don't get high and mighty unless you like the interior of a jail cell. Just pull out the money, pay the bribe, and be on your way. It's just the way it is here.

If you decide to drive on secondary roads, be sure to ask about the road's condition before you go (unless you have a jeep). It's easy to get stuck in the middle of nowhere, which can be a scary experience here. We drove from Sosua (on the north coast near Puerto Plata) to Santiago on a secondary road over the mountains. The primary roads are in surprisingly good shape, but the secondary ones can be horrific. Some are being improved, but most are not. On our drive, we hit the bad roads. We drove very slowly, the bottom of our loaded-down, old Honda Accord scraping the rocks, through tiny mountain towns where people looked at us as if they had never seen a tourist before in their lives. Then they would smile and wave. It was fascinating.

Driving Alert: Avoid driving at night outside urban areas. Many cars don't have taillights, and some cars and trucks don't even have headlights! The roads are narrow (mostly two-lane), trucks pass uphill and sometimes don't have lights, and there are pedestrians on the sides of the roads. 'Nuff said.

Focus on the Dominican Republic: Merengue

You hear it everywhere — on the car radio, at the corner bodega, from loudspeakers on the sidewalk, at the airport, at the baseball stadium, at the hotel clerk's desk, and in the nightclubs. There's no escaping the national pride of the Dominican Republic: merengue. Just as baseball is the national passion of the D.R., merengue is the pulse of the country, and it's a racing (and racy) one at that. As the tempos of the popular merengues get faster and faster every year, the lyrics become more loaded with naughty double entendres — all about sex, of course — so much so that some can't get airplay here. Unlike rap, which can be very explicit and vulgar, merengue prides itself in masking risqué ideas in the lyrics. The result makes you gasp and laugh and is definitely part of the fun of this music. An example of this can be heard in Jossie Esteban y La Patrulla 15's classic hit "El Tigeron," about a man called "the tiger" who seduces the narrator's wife while he is at work (the refrain *fue a la nevera y se comió mi salchichón* literally means "He ate my sausage in the fridge" but figuratively means "He screwed my wife"). Who knew? Another example comes from the first Miami Band CD and the song "Ponte el Sombrero"—which literally means "Put on Your Hat" but figuratively means "Put on Your Condom." It's about a girl who spurns the sexual advances of her date because he won't wear a condom (it's not macho). The refrain goes, *Ponte, ponte, ponte el sombrero, papi—ponte el sombrero*. Another song of theirs, "El Bigote," is a great example of the double entendre. The singer opens the song by stating, "They come in all sizes and colors; big and fat, small and thin, black or white," and then she reveals that she is speaking of mustaches (*bigotes*, in Spanish) and not the male sex organ.

Dominicans rule merengue. Several bands from this country top the Billboard Latin charts. One exception is the hottest merengue artist of the moment, Elvis Crespo, who was actually born in Puerto Rico. However, many others are very popular, including La Banda Gorda, Los Toros Band, Sergio Vargas, and Fulanito (a New York–based Dominican band). The kingpin of merengue and Dominican music is Juan Luis Guerra and his band 440. Other bands of note are Johnny Ventura, Wilfrido Vargas, the Hermanos Rosarios, Tono Rosario, and the Puerto Rican bands Cana Brava and Zona Roja. Although this genre is dominated by men, female artists have made their mark, including Giselle and Olga Tañon (who is Puerto Rican). One of the oldest "girl groups" is Las Chicas del Can, "The Fun Girls," who have been very successful and popular both in and out of the country.

All Dominicans seem to be born knowing how to dance to this music. We marveled at the way they move. Fortunately, merengue is much easier for non-Latinos to dance to than salsa, which seems to be a Latino genetic trait and is impossible for Anglos to master. With merengue, you have to feel the music deep down in your hips. It's a very fast-paced but erotic dance, with lots of hip-grinding body contact—swing meets the slow dance of the '60s, but at warp speed. My advice to novices: Watch the Dominicans dance it for a while; venture onto the dance floor with a Dominican or other Latino only when it's crowded; try to feel the music deep "down there"; follow your partner's lead, and then gaze into his or her eyes—it'll come to you.

For those who are interested in seeing and hearing merengue performed live, there is a **Merengue Festival** in Santo Domingo during the last week of July and the first week in August. This takes place in conjunction with the celebration of the founding of Santo Domingo on August 4, 1496. There is also a smaller festival in Puerto Plata every October. If you live in a major metro area with a Latino population (such as Miami, New York, Chicago, or Boston), check your local listings—these bands tour all the time. Most major CD stores and Internet sites have Latino music sections where you can find the artists mentioned here. Or try www.latinmusica.com.

SANTO DOMINGO

Where to Stay

Santo Domingo is a sprawling city of almost 3 million people. When you first arrive, one breath will indicate that pollution controls are nonexistent. Diesel engines are the norm, and the amount of exhaust (and dust) on the road will prompt you to turn on the a/c and push the lever over to "recirculate." The city core is the Colonial Zone, the site of the original settlement and of some of the oldest buildings in the hemisphere. Located at the western juncture of the Caribbean and the Rio Ozama, this will be the focus of your stay in "the Capital," as Santo Domingo is called by everyone who lives here. You don't live in Santo Domingo, you live in the Capital. The area between the Colonial Zone and the Avenida Máximo Gómez to the west is the best residential area of the city. This is where many of the good hotels are: the Jaragua, the Meliá, the Hotel V Centenario, the Hispaniola, and the Hotel Santo Domingo. Many of these hotels are on the Malecón (the waterfront drive) and offer ocean views. It is also the district where most of the government buildings, the Presidential Palace, the U.S. Embassy, many neoclassical public buildings built by various dictators, and the political party headquarters are located (even the Communist Party is in this fashionable neighborhood). Because most tourists who stay in Santo Domingo focus their time around the Zona Colonial, many prefer staying close to the sights. With the recent completion of the two Sofitels here, and a handful of other options, there are plenty of choices.

Sofitel Nicolas de Ovando, Calle Las Damas, Zona Colonial, Santo
Domingo, DR. ✆ 809-685-9955, 🖂 809-686-6590,
💻 www.sofitel.com, H2975@accor.com

💲 **Very Pricey** 🍽 **BP** 26 rooms

It's inconceivable to imagine a hotel more in tune with the original surroundings than this Sofitel creation, located in the spacious colonial house of the third governor of the Americas. In all of our travels, we have yet to find a hotel that incorporates a swimming pool and an ancient fort with such grace. We love the fact that each of the 26 rooms is different; all of them are scattered throughout this grand four-story old *casa*. Better yet is the way the rooms open out onto patios with fountains, palm trees, and gardens. The Hernando Cortes Patio is a wonderful space to have an alfresco meal, and the pool (with a view of the river) is a perfect respite from the oppressive city heat. The lobby bar leads to an open room with a pool table, and comfortable tables and chairs are scattered throughout, giving guests an opportunity to commune with the wonderful surroundings. There is also a gym and even a cigar bar. The rooms are what we would expect from Sofitel—elegantly decked out with every amenity and decorated

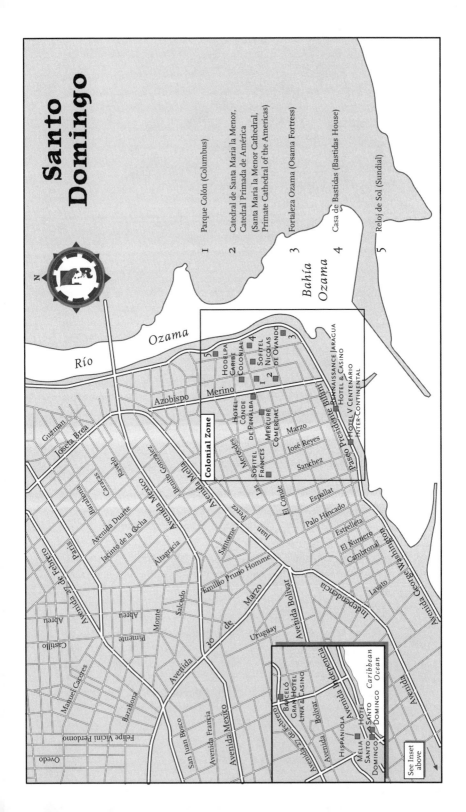

Santo Domingo

N

Río Ozama

Bahía Ozama

Colonial Zone

1 Parque Colón (Columbus)

2 Catedral de Santa María la Menor, Catedral Primada de América (Santa María la Menor Cathedral, Primate Cathedral of the Americas)

3 Fortaleza Ozama (Osama Forttress)

4 Casa de Bastidas (Bastidas House)

5 Reloj de Sol (Sundial)

HODELPA CARIBE COLONIAL

SOFITEL NICOLÁS DE OVANDO

HOTEL CONDE DE PEÑALBA

MERCURE COMERCIAL

SOFITEL FRANCÉS

RENAISSANCE JARAGUA HOTEL & CASINO

HOTEL V CENTENARIO INTER-CONTINENTAL

Paseo Presidente Billini

Azobispo

Merino

Mercedes

El Conde

Marzo

José Reyes

Sánchez

Espallat

Palo Hincado

Estrelleta

El Numero

Cambronal

Laviato

Independencia

Avenida Bolívar

Uruguay

20 de. Marzo

Emilio Pruno Homme

Salcedo

Abreu

Monte

Pimente

Avenida

San Juan Bosco

Avenida Francia

Avenida México

Avenida Bolívar

Avenida Independencia

Avenida 27 de Febrero

BARCELÓ GRAN HOTEL LINA & CASINO

HISPANIOLA HOTEL

MELIÁ SANTO DOMINGO

HOTEL SANTO DOMINGO

Caribbean Ocean

See Inset above

Avenida George Washington

Avenida Washington

Felipe Vicini Perdomo

Oyedo

Castillo

Manuel Cáceres

Barahona

Abreu

Avenida 25 de Febrero

París

Josefa Brea

Guzmán

Caracol

Barahona

Restauro

Delino González

Avenida México

Avenida Duarte

Jacinto de la Cocha

Altagracia

Avenida McElla

Santome

Pérez

1as.

Jueni

with special attention to maintain the style of this historically important residence. Although we are a little weary of seeing historical landmarks being turned into commercial establishments, we are confident that the Sofitel has at least applied integrity to this fine hotel.

Sofitel Frances, Calle Las Mercedes, Zona Colonial, Santo Domingo, DR. ℂ 809-685-9331, ✆ 809-685-1289, ⌨ www.sofitel.com, H2137@accor-hotels.com

💲 **Pricey** 🍽 **BP** 19 rooms

Wow! Sofitel has done it again. Located in a colonial house dating back to the 16th century, the Frances was converted to a hotel about five years ago. However, walking amid the period pieces that grace the house, we felt as if we had stepped back in time. What makes this hotel so special is its intimacy — with only 19 rooms, it's no wonder one guest commented to us, "We didn't feel like we were in a hotel, but in a well-tended house with extraordinary food." High-ceilinged rooms maintain the feel of the colonial house, with wooden furniture and fabrics that evoke eras long past. Rooms are well appointed, with climate control, cable TV, phone, and Internet connection. We love the rooms with the original little wrought-iron verandas that look out onto the central patio. The restaurant here is exceptional, and the patio inside is the perfect setting in which to read the morning paper over breakfast or stare into the fountain and imagine that the 18th century is still in the near future.

Renaissance Jaragua Hotel & Casino, 367 Avenida George Washington, Santo Domingo, DR. ℂ 800-331-3542, local: 809-221-2222, ✆ 809-686-0528, ⌨ www. renaissancehotels.com

💲 **Very Pricey** and up 🍽 **EP** 🆑 355 rooms and suites

Built on the site of the old hotel of the same name and opened in 1988, this massive yellow and white property on 40 acres of landscaped gardens is a modern deco mélange of design and décor. It's not in our taste, but many look at it as the premier place to stay in Santo Domingo. It has a great location adjacent to the Colonial Zone, yet the spacious grounds offer an oasis of retreat from the hustle and bustle of the city. The rooms and suites are luxurious, all with the accoutrements you'd expect from a good hotel. It also offers garden suites with a complete kitchen, although we cannot imagine cooking in a place like this. Best of all are the huge pool with cabanas and the health club with steam and sauna. Twenty-four-hour room service is a nice perk, as well. Add to this tennis courts, a casino, a nightclub, the Champions sports bar, and three restaurants, and you'll find the whole shebang is here.

Hodelpa Caribe Colonial, 159 Calle Isabel La Catolica, Zona Colonial, Santo Domingo, DR. ℂ 809-688-7799, ✺ 809-685-8128, 🖥 www.hodelpa.com, elcolonial@hotelhodelpa.com

💰 Cheap 🍴 EP ⒸⒸ 54 rooms

South Beach meets Santo Domingo in this art deco gem. It's the perfect antidote to the traditionally large hotels in Santo Domingo. Located in the heart of the Colonial Zone, it has tile floors and a very tasteful décor that exudes sensibility, cleanliness, and comfort. All the rooms include new wood furnishings, a/c, phone, refrigerator, cable TV, and small balcony. The two presidential suites are equipped with Jacuzzi and larger outdoor terraces. The hotel lobby includes a bar with small restaurant.

Hotel Santo Domingo, Avenida Independencia & Avenida Abraham Lincoln, Santo Domingo, DR. ℂ stateside: 800-877-3643, local: 809-221-1511, ✺ 809-535-4050, 🖥 www.hotelsantodomingo.com.do, reservaciones@hotelsantodomingo.com.do

💰 Not So Cheap and up 🍴 BP ⒸⒸ 215 rooms

With its recently renovated lobby, this is one of the most stylish and elegant hotels in the Capital, although it's certainly not the most lively (that's the Jaragua). The décor of the rooms is not in keeping with the new lobby. The rambling, modern stucco and tile-roofed complex set on 14 acres of gardens is located next to the Centro de los Héroes and the Malecón. The rooms and suites were decorated by Oscar de la Renta (a Dominican native), and many have lanais and ocean views. The rooms have recently been upgraded with new carpet and furniture, and many are embellished with TVs and Nintendo units for those who cannot get enough video games. It also offers a new Excel Club, which is a private club floor with more amenities like champagne cocktail at reception (big whoop!) and private elevators (whatever), newspapers delivered to the rooms, cocktail hour (this we'll take), and — our favorite — shoeshines for everybody! All the amenities of a good hotel are here, including 24-hour room service, Olympic-size swimming pool, three lighted tennis courts, a spa, three restaurants, and a piano bar. You'll need to cab it to the Colonial Zone from here, because who wants to scuff up those well-polished shoes?

Hispaniola Hotel and Casino, Avenida Independencia & Avenida Abraham Lincoln, Santo Domingo, DR. ℂ 800-877-3643 or 809-221-7111, ✺ 809-535-4050, 🖥 www.hotelhispaniola.com, reservation@hotelhispaniola.com

💰 Not So Cheap 🍴 BP ⒸⒸ 165 rooms

Though once associated with the Hotel Santo Domingo across the street, the Hispaniola has recently proclaimed its independence, but it is still a good value and actually more lively (casinos seem to have this effect). The rooms are standard big-hotel fare, with a/c and cable TV. With room service and a big new pool and spa, the Hispaniola has everything you need for an affordable stay in the Capital. You'll need to cab it to the Colonial Zone from here.

Mercure Comercial, Calle Hostos & Calle Conde, Zona Colonial, Santo Domingo, DR. ✆ 809-688-5500, ✎ 809-688-5522, ⌨ www.mercure.com, H2974@accor-hotels.com

💲 **Cheap** ⑪ **BP** 96 rooms

True to the Mercure's philosophy, the Comercial offers well-appointed rooms for affordable prices, without many of the amenities of the larger hotels. It's a self-service kind of place, which is quite easy, given its location right on the pedestrian promenade of Calle Conde. Just steps from the Zona Colonial, the Mercure is housed in a four-story building with rooms looking out over the shopping street below. Rooms have a/c, satellite TV, and minibar, as well as reading lamps and heavy curtains to block out the hot sun. Its street-side Le Colonial café is a good spot for people-watching.

Hotel V Centenario Inter-Continental, 218 Avenida George Washington, Santo Domingo, DR. ✆ 809-221-0000, ✎ 809-221-2020, ⌨ www.santo-domingo.interconti.com, santodomingo@interconti.com

💲 **Wicked Pricey** ⑪ **EP** 🆑 233 rooms

This rather sterile high-rise deluxe hotel was opened in 1992 for the 500th anniversary of Columbus's landing. It has 200 rooms with marble baths, all facing the Malecón and the water. All the amenities you'd expect from a deluxe hotel are here, including 24-hour room service, business services, pool, tennis, bar, and casino. There's not much in terms of local flavor, though; we forgot if we were in Santo Domingo or Frankfurt (luckily, we were still in Santo Domingo).

Meliá Santo Domingo Hotel and Casino, 365 Avenida George Washington, Santo Domingo, DR. ✆ 800-33-MELIA, 809-221-6666, or 809-688-0823, ✎ 809-687-8150, ⌨ www.solmelia.es, melia.santo.domingo@solmelia.com

💲 **Pricey** ⑪ **EP** 🆑 260 rooms

Formerly a Sheraton, the Meliá is a big complex with a high-rise tower located right on the Malecón and adjacent to the Colonial Zone —a great location. It's a hubbub of activity but is geared towards the business traveler. The comfortably refurbished rooms, many with lanais overlooking the sea and all with 24-hour room service, now have satellite TVs and marble bathtubs. A pool, two lighted tennis courts, three restaurants, a casino, a nightclub, and a bar round out the facilities. The new top-of-the-line spa and health center includes gym, sauna, steam room, and massage. There are two on-site restaurants and a lobby bar with nightly live music.

Barceló Gran Hotel Lina & Casino, P.O. Box 1915, Avenida Máximo Gómez & Avenida 27 de Febrero, Santo Domingo, DR. ✆ 809-563-5000, ✉ 809-686-5521, 🖥 www.barcelolina.com

💰 **Not So Cheap** 🍴 EP CC 202 rooms, 15 suites

Located near the American Embassy, this modern high-rise hotel is another good value when staying in the Capital. It has everything: two swimming pools (one for adults and one for kids), casino, gym and sauna, piano bar, gift shop, and 24-hour room service. Renovated in 1997, the rooms are standard big-hotel fare, with a/c, cable TV, and some with lanais. The Lina also has one of Santo Domingo's best restaurants (also called Lina). You'll need to cab it to the Colonial Zone from here.

Hotel Conde de Peñalba, Calle El Conde & Arzobispo Meriño, Zona Colonial, Santo Domingo, DR. ✆ 809-688-7121, ✉ 809-688-7375, 🖥 www.condepenalba.com, condepenalba@codetel.net.do

💰 **Cheap** 🍴 EP 24 rooms

Sure, this old-school, four-story hotel is a little on the drab side, but its history and location are impressive. For decades, this has been one of the most prominent hotels in the city, and its location in Columbus Park is ideal for those exploring the colonial city. The rooms have a/c, cable TV, and phone, and the décor is colonial, although we call it "outdated." The restaurant downstairs is always a hotbed of activity. Many of the rooms have tiny terraces with great views of the park below. Keep in mind that this is not the most quiet of spots.

Where to Eat

Santo Domingo has a surprisingly sophisticated restaurant scene. There are some excellent restaurants serving delicious and exotic cuisine, with attentive and courteous service. All the hotels recommended have at least one restaurant. These tend to be good but overpriced. If you're in the mood, it's best to venture out and discover how interesting the dining is.

$ **Cafe Los Flores**, 366 Calle Conde Peatonal, 689-1898

This happening spot, right on the pedestrian mall, is a great place to stop for a cold drink or a meal. With brightly painted murals and good local music, there is always activity here. It offers a range of pasta and meat dishes. However, for many, the cocktails are the main draw. Open 8 a.m. to 10 p.m.

$$$ **Costelao Grand Rodizio**, 21 Calle La Atarazana, Plaza de la
Hispanidad, Zona Colonial, 688-2773

The Brazilians have arrived! This brand-new *rodizio* steak house is
reminiscent of our favorites in Brazil, offering 20 cuts of meat from
its charcoal grill, including quail, veal, and our favorite: garlic beef
brisket. It's all-you-can-eat, which includes side dishes and salads.
Women eat for half price and kids under 10 eat for free, so bring the
whole omnivorous family. The décor is stylish, with upstairs, down-
stairs, and outdoor seating. There's live music on Thursday and Sunday.

$$$$ **El Mesón de la Cava**, 1 Avenida Mirador del Sur, 533-2818

This is an institution in the Capital, since it's the only restaurant set
up in a real underground cave. Although the food is not exceptional,
there's nightly entertainment and dancing to merengue, so why not?
Reservations are a must. Dress up.

$$$$$ **Fellini Restaurante & Bar**, 504 Avenida Roberto Pastoriza, 540-5330

Great nouvelle Italian and international cuisine is created by chef Ciro
Casola in an elegant environment. Dress up. Reservations suggested.

$$ **La Creperie**, 11 Calle La Atarazana, Plaza de la Hispanidad, Zona
Colonial, 221-4734

We cannot forget that the French fought for control of Santo Domingo,
and although the populace speaks Spanish (evidence of an Iberian
victory), crêpes are still served here in the colonial plaza. The dining
room is a bit bleak, but the shaded outdoor seating is ideal for weary
sightseers. Crêpes range from savory to sweet. Try the Caribbean
seafood crêpe and the dessert crêpe with caramelized apples, almonds,
and vanilla ice cream. Open 11:30 a.m. to 11 p.m.; closed Tuesday.

$$$ **La Résidence**, in Sofitel Frances, 685-1289

Inventive French dining is on the menu here at this elegant restau-
rant in this restored colonial house that is now home to the Sofitel
Frances. Diners can sit in the well-appointed dining room or on the
patio with Sevillan fountain. Be ready for excellent cuisine. The
nightly ambient music is a nice touch. Open for lunch from noon to
3 p.m. and for dinner from 7 to 11:30 p.m.

$$$ **Le Patio**, in Sofitel Nicolas de Ovando, Zona Colonial, 685-9955

This offers fine cuisine in a less elegant setting than the other Sofitel
restaurant (at the Sofitel Frances). Although there is an air-conditioned
dining room with all of the accoutrements, we prefer sitting on the
Patio Hernando Cortes and dreaming of centuries past. The smoked
salmon appetizer is recommended, and we loved the mushroom flan
with fresh herb cream sauce. The entrees reflect a French flair, such

as pork tenderloin with mushroom cream sauce. Open from 6 a.m. to 11:30 p.m.

$$$$ **Lina,** Gran Hotel Lina, Avenida Máximo Gómez, 563-5000

This is recognized as one of the best restaurants in the city. We didn't get too far sampling the extensive menu, but we can attest that the paella is the best in Santo Domingo. Reservations are a must. Dress up.

$$ **Mesón La Quintana,** 13 Calle La Atarazana, Plaza de la Hispanidad, Zona Colonial, 687-2646

We love sitting out on the Plaza de la Hispanidad for lunch or dinner at this Spanish restaurant. We can't think of a better place to sample authentic Spanish cuisine than in the heart of the Spanish Colonial Zone here in Santo Domingo. Maria, a native Spaniard, offers all of our favorite Spanish dishes, including tortilla omelettes, and even delicacies such as Pamplona spicy sausage and hot chili bull tail. Open noon to midnight; closed Monday.

$$$ **Porterhouse,** 918 Avenida Abraham Lincoln, 542-6000

Judging from the armada of Mercedeses out front, this new high-priced steak house would seem to be doing just fine, thank you very much. It offers a full range of carnivorous delights, and the sirloin in particular is highly recommended. The dress is formal, the crowd is swanky. Open from noon to 1 a.m.

$$$$ **Restaurante David Crockett,** 34 Avenida Gustavo Mejía Ricart, 547-2999

Why a restaurant in Santo Domingo is named after Davy Crockett baffles us, but it is a great steak house, so we won't ask. It's popular with businesspeople at lunch, so reservations are suggested.

$ **Restaurant El Conde,** Calle Esconde & Calle Arzobispo Meriño, Zona Colonial, 688-7121

Located right on the Parque Cristobal Colón, this packed restaurant is always humming with activity. The food is fair, but the location is what draws people to sit on the shady patio to people-watch. It has a cheap daily lunch special, but many prefer to sit back with a cold drink. Open all day, every day.

$$ **Restaurante El Conuco,** 152 Calle Casimiro de Moya, 686-0129

Good Dominican cuisine is served here. This is a popular tourist spot to sample local criollo cuisine.

$$$$ **Restaurante Juan Carlos,** 7 Avenida Gustavo Mejía Ricart, 562-6444

This is an attractive place that serves delicious Spanish and international cuisine by chef Doña Leda. The service is excellent, too. Dress up. Reservations are suggested.

$$$$ **Restaurante La Briciola**, Arzobispo Meriño 152-A, 688-5055

It's housed in a Spanish *casa* in the Colonial Zone, but this place is pure Italiano. La Briciola has a sister restaurant in Milan—hence the authentic Italian cuisine. We love the romantically lit central courtyard and candlelit tables. In addition, the service and food are excellent. Dress up.

$$$$ **Restaurante Rancho Steak House**, Fería Ganadera, Autopista 30 de Mayo, 532-9803

This is a good steak house next to the horse shows located at the Fería Ganadera (Ganadera Fair Grounds) in the 30 de Mayo neighborhood. It also makes a good paella. Reservations are suggested.

$$$$$ **Scheerezade**, 226 Avenida Roberto Pastoriza, Naco, 227-2323.

Mediterranean and Middle Eastern cuisine is served here in a formal setting decorated like the interior of a sultan's palace. It's a great choice for your Dominican Republic wedding reception! For those without a special ceremony, the lunch buffet (from Monday through Saturday) is a great spread.

$$$$$ **Season's**, 14 Avenida Robert Pastoriza, Ensanche Naco, 412-2655

Dark and imposing woodwork create a very continental decor and mood for fine and formal dining. It has a nouvelle cuisine and an extensive wine list.

$$$$$ **Spaghettissimo**, 13 Paseo de los Locutores, 547-2650

Superb Italian cuisine is served in a former residence converted into a brightly colored, upscale restaurant. It has super-attentive service and is a great choice for lunch or dinner. Closed Monday.

$$$$ **Vesuvio**, 521 Avenida George Washington, 221-1954

This is a very good Italian continental restaurant that is popular with locals. Seafood is Vesuvio's specialty. Dress up.

A Leftover Solution. If you go out to a restaurant in a major city and have food left over, have it wrapped and give it to some child on the street who looks hungry (you won't have a hard time finding one). Often these kids, mostly boys, have a little shoeshine kit. We picked out a kid and were rewarded with a big smile. Try it.

Going Out

It's a big city, so there are a number of choices for dancing the night away with merengue or the latest disco, as well as fun cafés and pubs. Please note that most of the clubs require jackets for men and dressy clothes for women. Jeans are iffy here, unless you're gorgeous. Among the best are the following.

Ataraza 9, 21 Calle La Atarazana, Plaza de la Hispanidad, Zona Colonial, 688-0969

This old colonial building might once have been the site of quiet candlelit dinners, but these days it thumps with club music. This is our favorite club within the Zona Colonial—beautiful people and good tunes, ranging from salsa, merengue, electronic, and *reggaetón*. Open 8 p.m. to dawn.

Bar Marrekesh, Hotel Santo Domingo, Avenida Independencia & Avenida Abraham Lincoln, 221-1511

This chill spot is a low-key place to enjoy a nightcap. On Monday, Marrekesh features live jazz. It also has a piano player Tuesday through Friday nights. Open 4 p.m. to midnight.

Camelot and **Monte Cristo**, 952 Avenida Abraham Lincoln, 683-9222

These two places right next to each other are hopping bars that cater to a young and middle-age crowd. Camelot often features live music on Wednesday, and Monte Cristo does the same on Wednesday and Sunday. Music ranges among salsa, merengue, electronic, and *reggaetón* and gets loud. Camelot has a small dance floor. Dress is formal. Camelot is closed on Monday. Open from 6 p.m. to dawn.

Champion Bar, Renaissance Jaragua Hotel & Casino, 221-2222

Yes, your dreams have been answered: an American sports bar.

Discoteca Bella Blu, 165 Avenida George Washington, Malecón, 622-5452

This is a popular disco playing a good mix of music.

Guacara Taína, Mirador Park, 533-0671

This is a fun place, located in a real cave, featuring live music, disco, and shows. Many claim it's the best place to go out in Santo Domingo, but it has become a little touristy in recent years. Still, it is a pretty cool sight to behold, and how many can claim they partied in a cave?

Il Grappolo Enoteca Bar, 17-A Avenida Abraham Lincoln, Plaza Castilla, 472-2469

This is a lively wine bar.

Jubilee Disco, Rennaisance Jaragua Hotel & Casino, 221-2222

For years, this hotel disco was popular with a young crowd. These days it's open only on Thursday.

Merengue Bar, Rennaissance Jaragua Hotel & Casino, 367 Avenida George Washington, 221-2222

This is a popular spot for live music. Keep in mind that here in the casino, it offers live music (mostly merengue) every night.

Pat e Palo Café, 25 Atarazana, Zona Colonial, 687-8089

Located in the Colonial Zone with great views of the Alcazar de Colón, this place is very popular and serves good food, too.

Segafredo Café, 54 Calle El Conde, Zona Colonial, 685-9569

This chic Italian café chain has just arrived in Santo Domingo, and its location in Zona Colonial, sleek design, and lounge music make it a wonderful place to relax after sightseeing or to sit outside and enjoy drinks in the evening. It serves salads and *panini* sandwiches and offers happy-hour drinks from 5 to 8 p.m. There are a few more cafés lining this quiet pedestrian street as well.

Trio Café, 6171 Avenida Abraham Lincoln, 412-1722

Recently refurbished, the only thing "café" about this place is its name. It's smaller than some of the bigger clubs, but music thumps as videos are simultaneously shown on big-screen TVs. The interior is so well designed that music videos have been filmed here. Music ranges among merengue, *reggaetón*, and everything in between. This place gets going at about 1 a.m. Open from 9 p.m. to dawn.

Gay Bars and Clubs

Arena & Punto, 313 Calle de las Mercedes, Zona Colonial, 689-4163

What was once Santo Domingo's hottest gay club, Aire, has been remodeled and recently reopened as Arena. This large, cavernous club is actually two clubs in one. Upstairs is dancing and downstairs is Punto, which has a more sophisticated, loungy feel. They play all the best music, especially house and *electronica*. This is the big dance club to go to in the Capital.

Bar Friends 10 Calle Polvorin, Zona Colonial, 689-7572

What was once the hustler bar, Phoenix, is now Friends, which has been revamped in appearance and clientele. With a much more distinguished crowd and shows to boot, this spot can now be recommended without any warnings.

Jay-Dees, 10 Jose Reyes, Zona Colonial, 333-5905

This is the most popular gay bar in town and gets hot and crowded on weekend nights. There is a drag show and strippers on Friday and Saturday. The American owner, Jerry, welcomes the patrons with a smile. Open Wednesday through Sunday, 9 p.m. till whenever.

Pario's, 51 Arzobispo Nouel, 803-5100

This place is right near Jay-Dee's and is a popular place to grab an early drink. It is open seven days a week and has shows, projection TVs, and good tunes.

Note: There is now a gay-run hotel in Santo Domingo called **La Hacienda**, by the owners of the gay club Arena. It is located at 68 Calle Santo Rodriguez in the Zona Colonial and offers four luxury studios and eight suites, all with cable TV, a/c, minibar, and kitchenette. The rooms share a terrace and have nice artwork inside. Rates include continental breakfast. For more information, see the Web site, www.grupoarena.com/lahaciendasantodomingo, or send an e-mail to lahacienda@arenalatino.com. The phone number is 809-333-5605.

THE SOUTHEAST

Boca Chica and Juan Dolio

These two beach towns are only 10 and 20 minutes east of Las Americas International Airport, respectively, and are very popular with German tourists. Boca Chica is closer to the airport and only 30 minutes from Santo Domingo.

Boca Chica was the site of a massive sugar mill in the early 20th century, but in the 1940s it became a playground for Santo Domingo's wealthy families, who bought summer houses on the beach. Soon the government built a hotel, and in time Boca Chica became the trendy place to be seen. It was frequented by celebrities and foreign dignitaries, such as Argentine ruler Juan Perón. Today, this is where *capitaliños* go to the beach, particularly on weekends (except the really wealthy ones—they have villas at Casa de Campo). The beach here is wide and pleasant, with all kinds of activity both at the beach (water sports, volleyball) and away from it (restaurants, bars, shops). If you're single and want to meet others, particularly Dominicans, this is a reasonably priced destination. We find the resorts in Boca Chica to be of higher quality and value than in Juan Dolio.

The beach town of Juan Dolio, once funky, small, and cheap, has mushroomed in size over the last decade. Because of its convenience to the airport, most of the dominant hotel chains (Barceló, AMHSA, Coral, Allegró, Occidental, Meliá) have built all-inclusive resorts here, overwhelming the nice but rather narrow beach. Rum & Reggae veterans know how we feel about all-inclusives—the bane of the Caribbean. Although there are still a lot of little eateries, shops, and beach bars (the latter to get "shif-fahst" at) in the village of Juan Dolio, there are prettier and longer beaches elsewhere in the country (Punta Cana and Bávaro) that can better handle the influx of tourists these hotel chains have brought.

Where to Stay

Hotel Dominican Bay, Boca Chica, DR. ✆ 809-412-2001, ✆ 809-523-6310, 🖳 www.hotetur.com, booking@hoteur.com

💼 **Not So Cheap** 🍽 **All-Inclusive** CC 437 rooms

This big boy sits across the road from the beach on a hill and is connected to the beach by a cement walkway. It offers larger rooms and ample common areas with a less crowded feeling than the hotels right on the water. Facilities include two pools. Rooms are equipped with cable TV, a/c, phone, balcony or terrace, and safe. The grounds are attractively manicured. Parking is limited. Guests can choose from the buffet or any of three à la carte restaurants.

Don Juan Beach Resort, Boca Chica Beach, DR. ✆ 800-820-1639, local: 809-687-9157, 🖂 809-523-6422, 🖥 www.donjuanbeachresort.com, h.donjuan@codetel.net.do

💼 **Cheap** 🍽 **All-Inclusive** CC 225 rooms

With a good location right on the main beach and a casual, relaxed ambiance about it, this Dominican-owned all-inclusive looks like an aging European housing project painted in pastels. It is a good choice when staying in Boca Chica, however, because it's easy to leave the grounds and mingle. It's also easy to zip into Santo Domingo from here. There are 225 rooms, all with a/c, TV, safes, and phones. There is a pool, a beach bar, tennis courts, water sports, a disco, and a restaurant. The Don Juan is popular with German, French, Italian, and Canadian tourists.

Barceló Capella, Villas de Mar, Juan Dolio, Santo Domingo, DR. ✆ 809-526-1080, 🖂 809-526-1088, 🖥 www.barcelo.com, capella.dh@barcelohotels.com.do

💼 **Not So Cheap** 🍽 **All-Inclusive** CC 522 rooms

Among the all-inclusive resorts here along this beach, this is one of the best. For starters, it is located right on a beautiful stretch of beach, set amid sprawling grounds full of tropical plants, pools, and even flamingos. As is the case with most of these all-inclusive hotels, this resort is not for those looking for much privacy—crowds are the norm, and so are the annoying activities such as "fun pool games." For those who want to stay on a resort for 24 hours a day, the Capella offers nightly music and dance shows in a mini amphitheater and also has a disco that is open every night, and yes, the drinks here are included in the all-inclusive price. Rooms are loaded with a/c, coffeemaker, minibar, iron, cable TV, and hairdryer. There is a complex of pools, our favorite being the swim-up pool bar with a view of the sea. Although there are more than 500 rooms, there are no big hotel blocks—the rooms are housed in yellow three-story structures that are well-placed among the hotel's lush grounds. Athletes will love the beach volleyball and soccer courts as well as the tennis courts and minigolf. The Chez Fontaine French Restaurant is the best of many restaurants here, and the breakfast buffet is quite a spread.

Coral Hamaca Beach Hotel and Casino, Boca Chica, DR.
ℂ 877-GO-HILTON or 809-523-4611, ✆ 809-523-6767,
🖳 www.coralbyhilton.com, hamaca@coralhotels.com

💲 Not So Cheap 🍴 All-Inclusive ©© 630 rooms

An imposing stucco structure (painted in a way-wrong mustard color) on the edge of town, this was the first deluxe resort built in the area. Now it's an all-inclusive; all rooms include a/c, cable TV, and phones. Some rooms have lanais. Hamaca has five restaurants, a disco and casino, a spacious lobby and several sitting areas, a beach, water sports, two adult pools, two children's pools, gym and sauna, and three lighted tennis courts. All water sports are available or can be arranged. The resort's Chocolate Friends (yes, that's what the entertainment staff is called) run the activities, which are popular with Québecois and German couples and families. We are most displeased that they have blocked off the beach here in a dastardly example of privatization. Boo.

Coral Costa Caribe Beach Hotel & Casino, Juan Dolio, DR. ℂ 877-GO-HILTON or 809-526-2244, ✆ 809-526-3141 or 305-599-1946, 🖳 www.coralbyhilton.com, costacaribe@coralhotels.com

💲 Not So Cheap 🍴 All-Inclusive ©© 520 rooms

Yep—another Hilton. This one is a pink and green resort that sprawls out over a good portion of a calm and protected beach. The rooms have tile floors, pink walls, rattan furniture, floral print upholstery, and a/c. The suites have super-high ceilings and a sitting room. Everything but the kitchen sink is available at this all-inclusive, including three restaurants, three pools, two hot tubs, a gym and sauna, a fresh fruit hut and pizza hut, a 24-hour sports bar, a disco, and a casino. All water sports are available or can be arranged. The resort's Chocolate Friends (yes, again, that's what the entertainment staff is called) run the activities. Of all the Juan Dolio resorts, this would be our preference, although the a/c in the rooms was noisy and we overheard more than one guest complaining to the staff about scalding hot water and poor service. We recommend that you avoid the Juan Dolio resorts on holiday weekends, especially the most popular one, Dia de Restauración, August 20.

Barceló Talanquera Beach Resort, Villas de Mar, Juan Dolio, Santo Domingo, DR. ℂ 809-526-1510, ✆ 809-526-2408, 🖳 www.barcelo.com, barcelotalanquadh@barcelohotels.com.do

💲 Not So Cheap 🍴 All-Inclusive ©© 433 rooms

Although it offers the usual array of amenities, this hotel is still near the bottom of our list. Our main gripe is that the resort is bisected by a road — as a result, the vast majority of the rooms are far removed from the sea. In addition to the rooms, the main pool and restaurants are also a hike from the beach. When we stay at a beach resort, we don't like to have to put on our shoes and walk across a road to reach the sea (and the beach here is not too appealing, anyway). The rooms are housed in magenta and amber buildings spread out among the tropical grounds and feature small patios with plastic furniture. Breakfast and lunch are served buffet style, but there are two other restaurants as well. The resort has its own dive shop, spa, tennis courts, beach volleyball court, and disco.

Aparta Hotel Madejra, 1 Calle Abraham Núnez, Boca Chica, Santo Domingo, DR. ☎ 809-523-4434, ✆ 809-523-4532, 🖥 www.hotel-madejra.com, madejra@verizon.net.do

💰 **Dirt Cheap** 🍴 **CP** 8 rooms

We have included this hotel for tourists who are turned off by the all-inclusive resorts. Unfortunately, there is not much to offer among the in-town nonresort hotels. Sandwiched between the main road and the beachfront restaurants, this Italian-owned hotel offers clean rooms with fan and cable TV for cheap prices. The hotel has a few computers for Internet access and a small restaurant, and guests are just steps away from all the restaurants lined along the beach here. Some of the top-floor (third-floor) rooms offer sea views, and all rooms have little balconies that face the ocean.

Meliá Juan Dolio, Playa de Juan Dolio, DR. ☎ stateside: 800-33-MELIA, local: 809-526-1521, ✆ 809-526-2184, 🖥 www.solmelia.es

💰 **Not So Cheap** 🍴 **All-Inclusive** CC 270 rooms

We can't find anything attractive about this all-inclusive resort. With rooms housed in three buildings, this is a more medium-size resort than some of the other behemoths in the area. The rooms are standard all-inclusive fare and have been refurbished either when Meliá bought the resort in 1997 or after the wrath of Hurricane Georges in 1998. Whichever is the case, the hotel appears to be on a downward slide. The brochure boasts a "magnificent spa-fitness center" that in reality is a horror show of filth in which you wouldn't even want to remove your shoes. The Jacuzzis appeared to be abandoned, stagnant pools. Overall, we found the hotel's tattered decor dreary, dark, and depressing. Facilities include a lagoon swimming pool, a gym with sauna and steam rooms, six Jacuzzis, four restaurants, two bars, a kid's playground, a miniclub, entertainment, and an activities staff — even a karaoke pub. All water sports are available or can be arranged.

Where to Eat and Go Out

Boca Chica is designed around all-inclusive resorts, but there is a variety of restaurants and bars in "town" and along the beachfront. To be honest, there aren't any restaurants that stand out — most feature the same menus, with fried fish being the most popular dish. Prices are a bit high for the quality of food, which explains why most take advantage of the meals offered through their all-inclusive plans. For those strolling the beach, there are countless spots at which to grab a drink and soak up some local color. When night descends on Boca Chica, **Calle Duarte**, the main road that runs parallel with the beach, is blocked off to traffic to create a small pedestrian zone. Restaurants and bars place tables and chairs out front as tourists and locals mingle. For night owls, there is a bar on the beach called **Boca Chica Beach Club**, with waitresses dressed in matching nautical costumes, and also a decent bar next to Coral Hamaca called **Neptune's**. The real action takes place at the slew of discos a few miles west of town. **Plaza Mundo**, **Osignio**, and **Mundo Center** are the most popular and are easily reached by taxi or moto-taxi for a few bucks. The action here goes well into the night — often until dawn. A word of warning: Much of the commerce here in Boca Chica revolves around prostitution. Single men will be accosted, and couples may not feel comfortable, either, there are throngs of "working girls." Although it is a bit revolting to see so many local women in the business, there is obviously a demand, as the presence of older (smiling) European men attests. In addition, there is a slew of raunchy strip clubs in town. As Boca Chica becomes more and more like Puerto Plata in terms of sleaze, we find ourselves getting repulsed by the scene here.

La Romana

La Romana is the home of Casa de Campo, the 7,000-acre resort that is the biggest (in area) and most renowned resort in the Dominican Republic. The resort is huge, rich, and pretty, but the town of La Romana is something that you want to get through quickly. Again, this is the land of contrasts. This is where one of 41 tariff-free zones is located. These are assembly factories that churn out lots of consumer goods for foreign companies, including some of the clothing you might be wearing. Many workers are transported to and from work in fenced-in flatbed trucks, where they are jammed in like sardines (and you thought the subway was bad!). If you don't take the Casa de Campo bypass road, you'll end up driving through muddy side streets with goats, donkeys, and barefoot people — it screams p-o-v-e-r-t-y — and then, a few miles away at Casa de Campo, you can ensconce yourself at a sumptuous patio bar with servants left and right, so you wonder, "What's wrong with this picture?" Our consciences were uncomfortable here. Yet the pragmatist among us wondered what would happen to these people without even these low-paying jobs?

Where to Stay

Casa de Campo, P.O. Box 140, La Romana, DR. ✆ 800-877-3643, 305-856-5405, or 809-523-3333, 🖳 809-523-8548,
🖳 www.casadecampo.com.do, reserva@ccampo.com.do

💰 **Very Pricey** and up for *casitas*, **Beyond Belief** for villas 🍽 **EP** 𝖢𝖢
300 rooms, 150 villas

We can describe this famed resort in five words: big and for the rich. However, there's a lot more to say about Casa de Campo even though it truly is a case study in the lifestyles of the rich and famous. The cream of the crop of its guests includes Elizabeth Taylor, Gloria Estefan, and Mikhail Gorbachev. Don't plan on landing your own private jet here, though. The resort's airstrip is being converted into more villas — which, by the way, come with maid and butler service if you prefer. The glitterati now fly into the new International Airport in Romana, which opened in December 2000.

Besides the impressive guest list and tremendous service, the third most impressive feature is the size of the resort: 7,000 acres! It is sprawling, with acres and acres of one- and two-story stucco and red corrugated tin-roofed villas, *casitas*, and hotel condo–looking buildings. It has 300 rooms (called *casitas* here) and 150 two- to four-bedroom villas; two Championship Pete Dye 18-hole golf courses, including The Teeth of the Dog, which is ranked number one in the Caribbean (number 23 in the world) by *Golf Magazine* and has seven oceanfront holes (the third most impressive feature); two polo fields and polo ponies; a complete equestrian center with 150 horses; 15 swimming pools; 13 clay tennis courts (10 lighted) and 4 lighted Laykold courts, all with ball boys (!); a Shooting Center (no, this is not where you bring your ex, it's where you can shoot trap, skeet, and sporting clays — and pretend that they are your ex!); nine restaurants; a small health and fitness center; its own private beach; a marina; and Altos de Chavón (see below). The only thing small about Casa de Campo is the fitness center, which surprisingly lacks a sauna, steam room, or Jacuzzi. We're told the original fitness center was destroyed by Hurricane Georges, but we remember that it was too small.

Casa de Campo was belted by Hurricane Georges in September 1998. The resort closed down for several months while an army of workers rebuilt and restored. Now all the rooms at the resort are newly redone, from new furnishings and décor to retiled baths. Dining facilities have been upgraded and expanded. Even the entrance and lobby area are new and redesigned. A third golf course, designed by Pete Dye, has just opened.

The atmosphere here is surprisingly casual. This is also one of the few Dominican resorts where Americans are a significant part of the clientele. The redesigned main lobby is a series of covered walkways in coral rock and mahogany connecting the various hotel desks with the patio bar, main pool, boutiques, and more. A big convenience is the American Airlines ticket counter in the lobby. The main pool is fairly large and has an in-water pool bar. There are three types of rooms: standard, deluxe, and luxury, with amenities and views making the difference (e.g., the deluxe category provides bathrobes — for your stay only — and Bose Wave radios with 31 channels of commercial-free music; the luxury category has the above plus Serta pillow-top mattresses and views of the golf course).

Golf seems to be what makes Casa de Campo a major destination. Golfers come from all over to play The Teeth. One of the times we were there, we saw many Japanese people on the course, which, given their fanaticism about the game, is testimony to the fame of these links. For more about it, see the Don't Miss section.

There is another attraction at Casa de Campo, though, while contrived, is certainly unique. Called **Altos de Chavón**, this is a very thorough reproduction of a 16th-century Tuscan village. The site is perched on a promontory overlooking the Río Chavón. The attention to detail — columns that look like the remnants of a Roman temple and stucco with a weathered look — is almost convincing and probably does convince some tourists. This is an artists' colony that features an art school affiliated with the Parsons School of Design in New York and galleries that exhibit the resident artists' work. There are several high-priced restaurants and boutiques. There is also the **Regional Archeology Museum** (open daily) with a good collection of Taíno artifacts. Although parts of Altos de Chavón are pretty, we couldn't help but wonder, why create a Tuscan village in the Dominican Republic? What were they thinking (or what were they on — let us have some!)? Well, it's here, and if you're in the area, you should see it. It's interesting, period. Also part of the complex is a 5,000-seat amphitheater, modeled after the Greek ruins at Epidaurus and dedicated by The Voice himself, the late Frank Sinatra.

Punta Cana and Bávaro

Legend has it that a big-shot American investor spotted the turquoise waters and white sands of Bávaro beach from an airplane. Although there was nothing here on what was the isolated southeastern tip of the island, he teamed up with other investors and built the region's first hotel in 1978. With an unbroken 20-mile strand of white sand, this area has one of the longest and nicest beaches in the Caribbean. So it comes as little surprise that so many hotel chains have followed suit, building resorts of their own. Punta Cana (which includes Bávaro) has experienced a frightening rate of development over the last 20 years. The completion of an international airport in 1984 increased the flow of tourists considerably, and even though the region was hit hard by Hurricane Georges in 1998, everything has been rebuilt and is more developed than ever. Most of the Spanish and Dominican hotel consortiums —Barceló, Meliá, Paradisus, Iberostar, Allegro, Fiesta, Hodelpa, and Riu—have built huge 500-(or more) room all-inclusive cluster hotels (on the same property and sharing many facilities but offering different levels of amenities, depending on the pocketbook) that are geared to European and South American package tourists. There is also a Club Med (one of the original resorts in the area) and a smattering of smaller resorts strung out along the beaches. An international airport services mostly jumbo jets from Europe (American flies here from Miami and New York; United flies from Miami). Even with this explosive growth, the beach is still extraordinary. If you want to do the all-inclusive thing (which makes sense for families and some singles), this is the area we would recommend.

Visitors should keep in mind that Punta Cana is not a city but rather a collection of beach resorts. Those seeking a Dominican experience or any cross-cultural experience whatsoever will be disappointed, unless saying *Buenos dias* to the pool boy or *Una cerveza, por favor* to the bartender qualifies as a cross-cultural exchange. The closest town is Higüey, about 30 miles away, home of the Basilica of Higüey, the site of a series of miracles by Our Lady of Altagracia, the patron saint of the Dominican Republic. There is a huge modern shrine in her honor in the center of town, and it is a major pilgrimage destination. There is also a neat little village called La Otra Banda, just east of town on the road to Punta Cana. Here you'll find lots of brilliantly painted, well-tended houses, which provide ample photo ops.

Outside the resorts there is little to do, especially at night. If you long to break away from the monotony of the shows and boring discos of the hotels, check out Mangu in the Hotel Flamingo, a popular club with the locals. For more insight and pointers on local restaurants and nightlife, stop by the TropiCALL Internet Cafe, directly across from the Plaza Bávaro. Charlie, the German owner, can tell you what's hot and what's not for local nightlife.

Where to Stay

Paradisus Punta Cana, Playa de Bávaro, Punta Cana, Higüey, DR.
    ✆ 800-33-MELIA or 809-687-9923, ✎ 809-687-0752,
    🖥 www.paradisuspuntacana.solmelia.com,
    paradisus.punta.cana@solmelia.com

  💰 **Very Pricey** 🍽 **All-Inclusive** CC 580 rooms
    This is our favorite all-inclusive resort in the area, with a winning combination of a stunning lobby, comfortable rooms, great service, lots of amenities, and the best location on Bávaro's beach (the beach

here is wide and the sand is blindingly white). Most rooms are junior suites in 37 two-story buildings (the latter look more like they belong in Boca Raton than the D.R., but that's minor). The two-level rooms (the sleeping area is elevated) have glazed terra-cotta tile floors, rattan furnishings, and brightly colored walls, fabrics, and furniture. All rooms have a/c, ceiling fans, satellite TV, safes, room service for continental breakfast, good-size lanais, and marble baths with separate loo.

The facilities are extensive and spread out, so bring your walking shoes, because we found the motorized cart service totally underwhelming in frequency. Guests are invited to use the nearby Cocotal Golf Club. Your hotel rate includes green fees. The pool here is the biggest in the area, with a swim-up bar and concrete "beaches" that are great for kids. Also for kids is a babysitting service, a miniclub, and a minidisco for ages 4 to 14. There are 10 restaurants, 7 bars, and a casino. We love the 24-hour room service for obvious reasons. A slew of activities, including tennis (four lighted courts), a new spinning room, horseback riding (full-moon rides are a must), archery, nature walks, and all water sports (even scuba) are in the package. Unlike most all-inclusives, where only national brands are included or available to drink (read: rum), the unlimited drinks at Paradisus include the brands you know and love (we must have our Absolut — and lots of it). Maybe that's why we like this place so much!

Paradisus also features an ecological park that has some hiking trails through the mangrove forest — a pleasant change of pace for an all-inclusive (a glimpse into the future, perhaps?). The new royal service option is a bit silly, though. These rooms have been recently renovated, but we can live without the pillow menu and the private breakfast lounge.

Secrets Excellence, Playa Uvero Alto, Punta Cana, DR. ✆ 809-685-9880, 🖂 809-687-9990, 🖳 www.secretsresorts.com, info@secretsexcellence.com.do

💲 **Pricey** 🍴 **All-Inclusive** CC 446 rooms

Unlike the U.S. federal schooling program, this resort embraces an "all children left behind" rule. For those couples seeking a romance-based resort, the no-children-allowed Secrets is the place. Formerly the Royal Resort Uvero Alto, it has taken on a new identity and has gotten rave reviews as Secrets. Situated on 1.5 miles of sugary white beach, this four-star resort is secluded from everything, including loose cannons (i.e., single people). The palm tree forest and deserted beach guarantee seclusion, as long as the presence of a few hundred other couples doesn't prove to be a distraction (or nauseating). In addition to the usual amenities, every room has its own Jacuzzi, and we also like the poolside candlelit dinners under *palapa*-style huts. The two pools cater to different moods. The main pool seems to stretch along the whole resort and has a lively swim-up bar; the second pool is more secluded, offering a little privacy. The resort also arranges romantic excursions like moonlit horseback rides. All rooms are suites. We loved our swim-up garden suite because we opened our back door to find ourselves a foot from the pool that reaches toward the beach side of the resort. Four-poster beds are the norm, and the rooms are decked out with flowers and candles. The verandas have comfy furniture and hammocks — a welcome addition. The food here is above average — especially popular is the Mexican restaurant. Also we could order food until late — that 2 a.m. pizza sure hits the spot! It's not a great pickup spot, but Secrets is super for couples and honeymooners (if you like that kind of thing).

Bávaro Princess, Playa de Bávaro, Punta Cana, DR. ℂ 809-221-2311, ℅ 809-686-5427, 🖳 www.princesshotelsandresorts.com, bavaro@bavaroprincess.om.do

💲 **Pricey** 🍴 **BP** ☐ 935 rooms

Although we like the Bali-inspired motif that the Spanish architect created here, we are not crazy about the resort itself. The only resort in the D.R. to be designated an "ecological hotel," it is set on 96 acres of forest and swamp (which the developers preserved, hence the designation). The problem is that the resort is so spread out that the beach is almost half a mile from the lobby. There is a tram system to transport guests, but some may find the distance annoying. We hate trams! The rooms are decorated in a tropical motif with glazed terracotta tile floors, rattan furnishings, and bright pastels. Sleeping areas are on a separate level, partitioned with a stepped wall and columns, and have firm mattresses. All the rooms have a/c, ceiling fans, minibar and fridge, satellite TV, lanais, and safes. We prefer the 86 bungalows — they lend a tropical theme instead looking like of a generic hotel room.

The Bávaro Princess has a small fitness center, two pools, six bars, seven restaurants (including the newest, El Goucho, featuring Argentine cuisine), a host of activities, and water sports, and it shares a casino with the adjacent Paradisus Punta Cana. The best thing about this place, however, is the beautiful beach in front. Look for package deals.

Barceló Bávaro Beach, Golf, and Casino Resort, Apartado Postal 1, Playa de Bávaro, Punta Cana, DR. ℂ 800-BARCELO or 809-686-5797, ℅ 809-221-9492, 🖳 www.barcelo.com

💲 **Not So Cheap** and up 🍴 **All-Inclusive** ☐ 1,921 rooms

The complex of five interconnected all-inclusive hotels — the Bávaro Palace, the Bávaro Beach, the Bávaro Garden, the Bávaro Casino, and the Bávaro Golf — sprawls along the beach for almost a mile. With thousands of rooms, 15 restaurants, 18 bars, 3 discos, 2 theaters, and a shopping center, the five provide an option for most people's budgets and needs. The top of the line is the recently completed Palace, with the most comfortable rooms and suites (644 of them, to be exact), a huge pool and hot tub, and the best food of the bunch. Thirty-six suites were added to the Palace in 2001. The management also plans to open a second 18-hole golf course and build two 5-star luxury hotels, with another 1,000 rooms, right on the beach.

All the rooms here have white tile floors, wicker furnishings, safes, and a pale-toned décor. Standard amenities include a/c, phone, TV, refrigerator, and private balcony or terrace. There are seven pools, six tennis courts, volleyball, an 18-hole golf course, and all water sports. A new 24-hour casino is perfect for gamblers. The beach here is exquisite. A tram provides transit between hotels. Look for package deals.

Mélia Caribe Tropical, Playa de Bávaro, Higüey-Altagracia, DR. ⓒ 800-33-MELIA or 809-221-1290, ✆ 809-221-6638, 💻 www.solmelia.com, melia.caribe.tropical@solmelia.com

💰 **Very Pricey** ⓜ **All-Inclusive** (except golf) CC 1,044 rooms

This brand new family-oriented all-inclusive resort (opened in 1999) has by far the most attractive landscaping of any we visited in Punta Cana. The lush grounds make it a true tropical paradise, and the low-slung buildings perfectly disguise the fact that the property has more than 1,000 rooms, 7 pools, 11 restaurants, and 2 fully equipped spas with the best marble steam rooms we've seen in the D.R. The huge white pagoda with statuary is popular for outdoor weddings. The main pool is absolutely huge, with lots of shade. The beach is not the widest, but the rest of the hotel makes up for it. The rooms feature marble baths, terrace, a/c, safe, minibar, satellite TV, and they can connect to suites. Golfers will love the nearby Cocotel Golf Course. There is also an on-site casino, eight tennis courts, and a climbing wall. That should keep you busy. Twenty-four-hour snacks are available for late-night munchies. Look for package deals.

Puntacana Resort & Club, P.O. Box 1083, Punta Cana, Higüey, DR. ⓒ 888-442-2262 or 809-959-2262, ✆ 809-959-3951, 💻 www.puntacana.com, reservations@puntacana.com

💰 **Pricey** and up ⓜ **All-Inclusive** CC 432 rooms

Located on 105 acres on a nice-size beach (though not the area's prettiest), this Dominican-owned establishment has a very pleasant and relaxed atmosphere pervading its coconut palm–studded grounds. It's bigger than it looks, with rooms dispersed throughout the property in three- and four-story buildings and Bermuda-style bungalows. Recent expansion includes an 18-hole Pete Dye–designed beachfront golf course with villas, but the resort still manages to have a very intimate feeling throughout, setting it apart from the other all-inclusive resorts in the area. The concerted effort to use Dominican materials and artisans in the construction and décor of the resort gives a definite local feel to the place. Although it offers superior deluxe rooms and villas, we were quite comfortable in the Cocotal, which is the standard room — most of these have a sea view, and all embody a Caribbean flair. Both rooms and villas are comfortable and offer all the amenities. There are five restaurants, five bars, a pool (which needs more shade), a disco, a "ranch" with mountable horses, four lighted clay tennis courts, and all water sports. Most of the guests who vacation here are European, especially German. Julio Iglesias and Oscar de la Renta are part owners and have homes here. The Clintons vacationed here in 2001.

Note that the all-inclusive rates do not include golf, spa, or diving. There is also a MAP that is sometimes available, depending on the season. Look for package deals.

Palladium Bávaro Grand Resort and Spa, Playa Bávaro, Punta Cana, DR.
☏ 809-221-8149, ✆ 809-221-8149, 🖳 www.fiestahotelgroup.com, reservas.bavaro@fiestahotelgroup.com

💲 **Pricey** ⑪ **All-Inclusive** ⒸⒸ 636 rooms

Built on 79 acres of tropical paradise, the Palladium is the shining star of the complex of Fiesta Hotels here on Bávaro Beach. It would be hard to find something that this hotel didn't have; it boasts a casino, a disco, 11 restaurants, and 17 bars, 3 of which are lobby bars. This begs the question: Why three lobby bars? As for swim-up bars, we counted four, although there might be a few more. We love the beachside spa with gym and massage right on the *playa*. As can be expected, there is a range of rooms available, but all include the usual amenities. The junior suites have recently been rehabbed and include huge bathrooms with his and her vanity sinks, hydromassage bathtubs, and separate showers. The Romance Suites (also recently redone) are worth the upgrade. They are perched beachside and have a Mayan shower and hammock on the big terrace and feature canopy beds.

Alas, the food here is just average, but the buffet restaurant is air-conditioned — a plus for some who sweat at other resorts' buffets. As with most resorts, the buffet is themed each night. However, à la carte restaurants do not live up to the four-star rating, in our opinion — and the Mexican restaurant is to be avoided. Another complaint is that the minibars are restocked only once every two days, which was a pain when we wanted more drinking water. We do love the fact that the sports bar is open late. It's a great spot for a bite for night owls who want refreshment until 6 a.m.

Riu Punta Cana Resort, Playa Arena Gorda, Punta Cana, DR. ℂ 809-221-7171, ✆ 809-682-1645, 💻 www.riuhotels.com, palace.macao@riu.com

💲 **Not So Cheap** and up 🍽 **All-Inclusive** CC 1,900 rooms

Another behemoth cluster of all-inclusive hotels, the Riu complex has five different hotels and its own "Caribbean Street" full of shops and services (a contrivance). You never have to leave the grounds, which is unfortunate. There are the Club Hotel Riu Bambu, the Hotel Riu Melao, the Hotel Riu Naiboa, the Hotel Riu Palace Macao, and the Hotel Riu Taíno. Got all those names straight? The most deluxe are the Bambu and the Palace. Both are on the beach, as is the Taíno. The four-story Palace tries to resemble a palace in architecture and décor, down to the pool with four fountains and statuary. However, the asphalt tiles in the pool areas and the terraces are *muy caliente* on bare feet. The beach is very pretty, though not the best of the area. The rooms run the gamut from the over-appointed Palace rooms to the more standard fare of the Naiboa. Tennis, water sports, a casino, the Pacha disco, and lots of activities are available. Mostly Germans and Brits are found here. We prefer the colonial-style Hotel Riu Palace Macao of the five. It offers a wonderful hotel feeling, albeit with an ambiance of over-the-top elegance. However, everything feels intimate (perhaps because it has *only* 356 rooms) and accessible in the multistory Gingerbread Key West design of the building. The Jacuzzi suites here are excellent, especially for lovebirds. The quiet atmosphere was free of screaming kids and stroller-pushing families. The crowd here is well heeled and savvy (if you can be well heeled and barefoot). Look for package deals.

Punta Cana Grand, Cabeza de Toro, Punta Cana, DR. ℂ 809-686-9898, ✆ 809-686-9699, 💻 www.globalia-hotels.com, reservations@puntacanagrand.com.do

💲 **Not So Cheap** 🍽 **All-Inclusive** CC 364 rooms

We enjoyed our stay at this Globalia establishment, which is located next to the Nautical Fishing Club (where world-class fishing tournaments are held). The architecture is described as English Caribbean but more resembled "Caribbean all-inclusive" to us. The superior rooms are very spacious, with pastel-colored walls and a big terrace — a great place to relax with a sea view. We love the open-air candlelit dinners at the beachside restaurant. The hotel's size is a little more manageable than some of the mega-resorts, so we wonder why the occupancy rates aren't higher. The hotel has just been taken over by a Spanish company called Travelplan, so expect some changes. Hopefully, upgrades will be made in the dining department; there is plenty of room for improvement. Unlike many other similarly priced hotels, it has many rooms with views of the water. The beach here is also better than at the adjacent Allegro. As usual, the buffet has a theme every day. The Thursday night beach parties are very popular, and so is the 24-hour access to food and drinks. We applaud the well-stocked minibars. For bow-and-arrow fans or medieval battle historians, archery is offered as one of the many activities. The on-site disco was not all that happening, but with more guests the scene could change.

Iberostar Bávaro Resort Complex (Iberostar Bávaro, Iberostar Dominicana, and Iberostar Punta Cana), Playa Bávaro, Higüey, DR. 🕐 800-923-2722 or 809-221-6500, 🖂 809-688-9888, 🖳 www.iberostar.com, reservaspuj@iberostar.com

🛑 **Not So Cheap** 🍴 **All-Inclusive** ⓒⓒ 1, 541 rooms

Located next to the Riu complex, this complex of three hotels — the Bávaro (588 rooms), the mirror-image Dominicana (526 rooms), and the Punta Cana (427 rooms) — are all-inclusives. As with the other chains, there are tons of activities and sports available, and some motorized sports are even included (jet ski, banana boat). A casino has been added to the property. This is probably a good bet for families on a budget. Guests of the three hotels share privileges, so they can "travel" freely among the three. The clientele is predominantly German. Look for package deals.

Club Med — Punta Cana, Apartado Postal 106, Punta Cana, Higüey, DR. 🕐 800-CLUBMED, 212-750-1670, or 809-686-5500, 🖂 809-685-5287, 🖳 www.clubmed.com

🛑 **Pricey** and up 🍴 **All-Inclusive** (except drinks) ⓒⓒ 534 rooms

This is one of the few resorts outside Puerto Plata where there is a sizable American contingent (about 50 percent of the guests). It's a Club Med, so it's all-inclusive. The physical campus (534 spartan rooms on 74 acres) looks just like a college campus in, say, Florida. The beach is pretty, however, and there are all those water sports and activities that have made Club Med famous. This resort has the added benefit for families of being very kid-focused. Teenagers have their own hangout called The Ramp. We tried to check it out but were turned away by a stoic 14-year-old with acne who pointed to the "Teens Only" sign. Child care is included along with all nonmotorized water sports (kayaking, windsurfing, and snorkeling). The rooms have all the amenities, but many are a tad small. There are also 14 tennis courts (6 lighted) and circus training (trampoline and trapeze) as well as an in-line skating center, a basketball court, and a large gym with up-to-date equipment. The resort was slammed by Hurricane Georges and has since been renovated, with the addition of 200 rooms and a new restaurant. The breakfast crêpes are excellent, but the talk of the town is the chocolate bread baked fresh daily. Look for package deals.

Gran Bahia Principe Punta Cana, Punta Cana, Higüey, DR.
📞 809-552-1444, 🖥 www.bahia-principe.com,
info.puntacana@bahia-principe.com

🛍 **Very Pricey** 🍽 **All-Inclusive** 💳 600 rooms

This five-star hotel falls short for a few reasons. Sure, the rooms themselves are comfortable, with hydromassage bathtubs, a sofa, minibar, and terrace. The problem is that they are distributed among villas that cascade back from the beachfront, where the pool is located. The result is that most of the rooms are far from the beach and pool, without views or breezes. We loathe hotels that require a shuttle to the water; we like to walk to the sea. For dining, there are Italian, Mexican, Japanese, and grill restaurants, as well as an international buffet. There is not much nightlife, and the entertainment show is not up to par (the bars also close early, except for the disco, which is pretty dead). However, we must admit that the stretch of beach here is divine.

Bayahibe

We felt compelled to include this quaint seaside spot, although we long for the days before the wave of tourism hit it. Bayahibe is a fishing village that is being quickly introduced to tourism, known first and foremost as an excellent place to scuba dive. There is a plethora of amazing dive sites around here, including some shipwrecks and sheer walls with amazing drop-offs. This little town with about 1,000 inhabitants was once home to just a few cheap hotels, but its proximity to La Romana and Boca Chica has spurred expansion. There are hotels popping up all over, including a tidal wave of all-inclusive resorts. Casa del Mar, the first to arrive, has blocked off half of the beautiful beach, in an act of selfish privatization. Shame on them!

For those seeking to head off on their own, there are reasonable alternatives and enough restaurants and activities to keep one busy. In addition to the hotels listed below, there is a handful of cheap hotels — calling themselves cabanas — with rooms for as low as $15 a night. **Hotel Llave del Mar** and **Hotel Boca Yate** are two such options. Keep in mind that Bayahibe is quite close to Playa Dominicus and Boca Chica, which makes it an easy day trip. The beach here is pleasant, especially after the dive boats have left in the morning. For those interested in diving, **Casa Daniel** (833-0050) is by far the best place in town. It is right on the main road next to Hotel Bayahibe, but it offers a free shuttle to and from local hotels and better trips and prices than those offered through the big hotels' tour desks. Check out the Web site for more info: www.casa-daniel.com. There are tour agencies that arrange cata-maran trips as well, but we recommend consulting with Casa Daniel first. This is also the place to purchase entrance tickets to Parque National del Este, which can be accessed by sea or by land. Because there is not much of a land entrance or abundance of wildlife (or guides, for that matter), we rec-ommend a day trip (including lunch) to Isla Saona—known for its white-sand beaches and crystal waters.

The town still retains a fishing-village ambiance, with little shacks serving up down-home Dominican food. The restaurants in Bayahibe are right on the gravel path—as close to a Main Street as Bayahibe has. There are a few shacks on the water that serve up great cheap plates of seafood daily. For full-scale restaurants, we recommend La Bahia. The disco in town was de-stroyed in Hurricane Georges. A few bars stay open late, but this is not nightlife central by any means.

Where to Stay

Casa del Mar Resort, Playa Bayahibe, DR. ✆ 809-221-8880,
✉ 809-221-2776, 🖳 www.sunscaperesorts.com,
info@sunscapecasadelmar.com.do

💲 **Very Pricey** 🍴 **All-Inclusive** CC 563 rooms

This was the first all-inclusive built here on Playa Bayahibe, and al-though we are still pissed that it closed off half of this beautiful beach for its exclusive use, its close proximity to the actual town of Bayahibe catapults the Casa del Mar to the top of our list. Although the resort mirrors the others here in amenities, we found a little more refined style here—displayed in the classy colonial-style furniture in the rooms. The rooms have either a king-size bed or two doubles, as well as a/c, hairdryer, coffeemaker, and satellite TV. The minibars are stocked daily—a nice touch—and all rooms have balconies, most with ocean views. We found the Sunscape Club upgrade to be a little over-the-top, but for those who want a DVD player, a $5 bottle of rum upon arrival, and Gatorade, chocolate, and potato chips in their mini-bar, go for it. Personally, we can live without the upgrade, even if it does mean that we have to bring our own bathrobe and snacks. The wide beach is spacious, but it does get crowded.

Whereas the sunsets from here are simply fabulous, the food is just decent. The Sanoa Grill is perched right above the ocean; in ad-dition to its grilled meat and seafood specialties, it also offers a great pizza. The Asian restaurant should be avoided. The hotel's proximity to Bayahibe allows guests to stroll into town for a cheap bite, which is usually better than standard resort fare.

Iberostar Hacienda Dominicus, Playa Dominicus, Bayahibe, DR. ✆ 809-688-3600, ✆ 809-686-8585, 🖥 www.iberostarcaribe.com, info@iberostarcaribe.com

💲 **Wicked Pricey** 🍽 **All-Inclusive** 𝖢𝖢 503 rooms

Besides the Casa del Mar, this five-star Spanish giant is our other favorite. It's refreshing to see an all-inclusive resort injected with such elegant style. Just being in the lobby reminded us of a European palace, somehow supplanted into the tropical paradise of the D.R. Imagine a palace without walls, with immense chandeliers hanging from the cathedral ceilings. Huge vases and flower bouquets adorn the surroundings. Since there are no walls, this grand open lobby seems to float on water. This stylish space not only houses the reception area and the lobby bar, it sets the tone for the whole resort. These elegantly tiled walkways lead through the waterway that links the restaurants, bars, shops, and disco of the hotel. One feature that sets the Iberostar apart from its competitors is the restaurants. La Geisha, the Japanese steak house, offers guests sushi and teppanyaki-style dining done right at the table on an iron grill. Its sleek design seems to be right out of Tokyo, New York, or Miami. The same goes for La Hacienda, the Mexican restaurant, and La Scala, the super-elegant French dining room. Unlike in the other places, we got the feeling here that we were actually "going out" for dinner, instead of filling up at another buffet. To mix things up, it also puts on barbecues and paella dinners on the beach at least once a week. The water theme runs throughout, with ducks and flamingos frolicking in the central pond. The pool area here is so expansive that it has been nicknamed *el lago*—a worthy name, for we have definitely seen ponds smaller than this winding, curved pool. In the middle is a small island with a Jacuzzi, which makes us ponder: Why can't all islands be like this? The swim-up pool bar is huge, and we love the separate pool for water sports, such as basketball and water polo. Yes, this is a huge hotel, with more than 500 rooms. However, we did not feel overwhelmed here—the rooms are housed in seven haciendas, staying true to the layout and style of an old Spanish estate. Each three-story hacienda is built around a central courtyard with a garden and fountain.

The rooms themselves are very spacious, with a/c, cable TV, fan, and king- or queen-size beds (or two doubles) as well as a sofa with pillows. The bathtub, accented with flowers, is a nice touch as well, and each room has a veranda with chairs and often a pool view. We were pleased to see the on-site artist sketching by the pool or painting on the beach, and we also liked the gym and spa services. For nightlife, nightly shows in the cabaret-style theater precede the late-night action in the submarine-theme Captain Nemo disco. The crowd here is a mix of European and American, but the resort is well laid out, so although it is usually at more than 90 percent capacity, it doesn't feel overcrowded.

Canoa Coral Hilton, Playa Dominicus, Bayahibe, DR. ✆ 809-682-2662, ✆ 809-688-6371, 🖳 www.coralbyhilton.com, canoa@coralhotels.com

🛎 **Wicked Pricey** 🍴 **All-Inclusive** CC 532 rooms

Second in line here on Playa Dominicus is this Hilton creation, which injects some Southwestern style into the mix — adobe, exposed wood, and pastel colors evocative of New Mexico. Although the beach is not as expansive as at some of the neighboring resorts, the sprawling pool area here is quite pleasant with its bridged walkways and swim-up bar. The rooms are set back a little from the beach and are housed in three-story pueblo-style units. They are done up in pastel-colored stucco and thatched grass, which is a bit of desert-meets-tropics eclectic, but OK. For big spenders, the villas are pretty cool — they loom over the lagoon that winds through the resort. Each has a veranda overlooking the water and is soothed by the sound of nearby fountains. Being at the center of the resort, the villas do not offer too much solitude, but each has a hidden second veranda with Jacuzzi. The facilities here are what can be expected from a four-star resort, with a full spa and themed restaurants — Italian, Mexican, and Dominican — as well as beach bars and giant buffets. There is a sports bar as well as nightly shows and a disco. The rooms have a/c, cable TV, iron, hairdryer, and minibar. Each also has a balcony, but what are we supposed to do with just a single plastic chair? Dear Hilton, please advise...

Wyndham Dominicus Palace, Playa Dominicus, Bayahibe, DR. ✆ 809-686-8583, ✆ 809-687-8583, 🖳 www.vivaresorts.com, viva.dominicuspalace@vivaresorts.com

🛎 **Very Pricey** 🍴 **All-Inclusive** CC 330 rooms

Of the two Wyndham resorts on this beach, we prefer this one — the younger sister, if you will. For starters, with "only" 330 rooms, it is less crowded than its next-door neighbor, and the slight difference in price seems to be warranted in quality. In short, the palace was built to provide a more relaxed atmosphere. As a result, its design is a little more elegant and exclusive. The rooms are colonial style, which seems to mean that the three-story blocks are adorned with a few columns here and a few arches there. There are nearly 100 rooms with ocean views, many of which are junior suites or superior rooms. The resort offers the same amenities as its sister, but it has a few advantages: the on-site spa and better restaurants, such as La Scala (an elegant Italian eatery). We like Bambu, the Asian restaurant, despite its politically incorrect "Oriental" cuisine tag (someone

please clue them in). Another difference is the more tranquil atmosphere here; as one staff member told us in reference to the more hectic
Wyndham Dominicus Beach, "Here you can actually sleep." Ah, what
a luxury.

Wyndham Dominicus Beach, Playa Dominicus, Bayahibe, DR. ✆ 809-
686-5658, ✆ 809-687-8583, 🖳 www.vivaresorts.com,
reservas.dompalace@vivaresorts.com

💰 **Very Pricey** 🍽 **All-Inclusive** ⒸⒸ 530 rooms

This was the first hotel built along this beach and is still the largest.
Although we cannot complain about the layout of the hotel, we must
admit that it was way too crowded for us to enjoy ourselves. In short,
it resembled an attraction park more than a laid-back resort. This is
a great party spot for those seeking lots of action, but for those craving some solitude, the beach is packed, there are crowds waiting for
a drink at the beach bar, and there are people everywhere! We do like
the bungalows, which are styled as thatched grass huts with coral
stone walls, but the units are a little cramped, and many look out onto
the sidewalk with its passing crowds. For those interested, the beachfront bungalows are best; the hotel rooms here are in blocks and lack
any flair. Standard rooms have a garden view, queen-size beds, and
the expected amenities, but we weren't crazy about the plastic chairs
on the decks. Guests are free to use the facilities (such as the spa) at
the more elegant Wyndham Palace next door, but they need to pay
$10 per person to eat at the better restaurants there. The disco here
gets rocking, which can be expected when a few hundred people go to
the Caribbean and drink for free.

Venta Club Hotel Gran Dominicus, Playa Dominicus, Bayahibe, DR.
✆ 809-221-6767, ✆ 809-221-5894, 🖳 www.grandominicus
.com.do, info@grandominicus.com

💰 **Very Pricey** 🍽 **All-Inclusive** ⒸⒸ 404 rooms

Stylistically, this hotel ranks up there with the best, but non-Italians
may feel a little left out—this Italian-owned resort is swarming with
Etruscans, Romans, and the like! It has a lot going for it, with refined
style, spacious grounds, and a gorgeous stretch of beach. The spacious rooms are housed in two-story colonial villas with red tile roofs
and roughly brushed stucco walls. There are queen-size beds, cable
TV, and terra-cotta floors. The style is simple, not extravagant, and the
wooden furniture on the patio is a welcome upgrade from the white
plastic chairs that remind us of a barbecue at Grandpa's. We also like
the presence of a ceiling fan in addition to a/c. The larger suites, located on the second floor (many with a sea view), are $20 extra, when
available. The pool area is comfortable, but the beach here is the real
attraction, with white sand and overhanging palms. As can be ex-

pected, there is no shortage of Italian food, but we weren't too pleased to discover that we had to pay extra to dine at the nicest restaurant, La Jacaranda, which makes us wonder just what "all-inclusive" means.

Hotel Bayahibe, Bayahibe, La Romana, DR. ☎ 809-833-0159, 📧 809-833-0159, 🖳 hotelbayahibe@hotmail.com

🏷 **Dirt Cheap** 🍽 **BP** 31 rooms

Although we are a tad puzzled by its motto, "A fascinating challenge," we found this basic hotel to be adequate for a no-frills spot like Bayahibe. Located just 10 steps from our favorite dive shop and the row of restaurants in town, this hotel has clean comfortable rooms with a/c, TV, minibar, and a small patio. It also offers free transfers to La Romana and has a little golf cart that whisks guests to the nearby beach. This Dominican-owned hotel was the first in town and seems to be handling the competition materializing all around it. It's by no means fascinating, nor is it a challenge, but if we only wanted a bed at a bargain, we could be comfortable here. No credit cards.

THE NORTH COAST

If you're heading to the North Coast from Santo Domingo (or vice versa), keep in mind that the road between Santo Domingo and Puerto Plata is the most heavily traveled in the country. Even with the fairly new Autopista Duarte connecting Santo Domingo and Santiago, it is not an easy drive. This is due to grade crossings with no stop lights or merge controls as well as to pedestrians who love to cross four-lane highways, dodging the speeding cars. There are lots of trucks, spewing out their diesel fumes and dust, along with all kinds of moving objects with two or more wheels. Be sure your car has air-conditioning (and that it works). On one trip, we had the windows down and the half of the face of the passenger next to the open window looked as if it had been blasted with black charcoal dust. Our skin and lungs felt as if we had been sitting in the Lincoln Tunnel for hours. Along the way, there are several pit stops (called *paradas*) that cater exclusively to the north-to-south travelers, particularly when you are about halfway. You can't miss them. For some reason, the good ones are on the west side of the road and are worth the stop, if only to use the bathroom (but be careful getting on and off the highway). There are rows of food stalls, most hawking fried food — there goes your no-fat diet — and beer, as well as merengue music and a general hubbub around mealtime. These are a genuine Dominican experience.

Puerto Plata and Sosúa

We loathe Puerto Plata and strongly recommend avoiding this area — especially since there are much nicer beaches and accommodations elsewhere.

Unfortunately, this is the area most Americans and Canadians visit — often to disappointment. It's just too touristy and not really very attractive. That's being kind. Let's face it, it's ugly. Puerto Plata is really a cruise-ship stop, an ugly town with several resorts, huddled mostly in one place, and a cable car. (Regarding the latter, if you ski, what's the big deal about a cable car — the view from the top? We'd rather be on the beach.)

As little as 15 years ago, Sosúa was magical. It has a very pretty beach with a variety of things: chaises, little shops, and tiny restaurants offering all sorts of cuisine — Italian, German, Québecois, French, and Dominican. Nevertheless, this little town has been overwhelmed with tourism to the point where its magic is gone, at least for us. It's heavily patronized by Germans; signs for German beer are everywhere. We prefer to keep moving down the road about 6 miles east to Cabarete.

Hey, where are the hotel recommendations? There aren't any. Stay somewhere else in this beautiful country!

⊛ Cabarete

This is the **windsurfing** capital of the Dominican Republic and one of the top windsurfing destinations in the Caribbean. The curving beach is more than 2 miles long, and the trade winds blow directly onshore, so you won't get blown out to sea. When the trades rage in the winter, the surf gets really big, because the beach becomes totally exposed to swells coming in from North Atlantic winter storms. During the summer, the trades blow, but the seas are calmer. Prime sailing season is from December through April and June through September. That said, overall conditions are so good here that even during our last visit, in May, there were plenty of happy windsurfers riding brisk winds. Cabarete Race Week, held in June, is an amateur event that anyone can enter.

All of the major board companies have operations here. These include **CaribBic Center** (809-571-0640), **Vela/Spinout** (809-571-0805), **Club Nathalie Simon** (809-571-0848), **Fanatic Board Center** (809-571-0861), **Club Mistral** (809-571-0770), and **Happy Surfpool** (809-571-0784). Given the international appeal of both windsurfing and the D.R., these outfits have devised a fairly simple way to divvy up the business: Each caters to a different language. Although you can use any of the operations we've mentioned (and rates are pretty competitive), English speakers will find like minds at Carib-Bic and Vela/Spinout. All of these companies can be contacted through the nifty Cabarete-focused Web site: www.hispaniola.com.

We recommend Vela, which is an international company that specializes in arranging windsurfing and kitesurfing vacations. It offers rentals and lessons, and it works in association with Dare2Fly Kitesurfing School. For those coming to enjoy these sports, Vela can arrange vacations, including accommodations, lessons, and rentals for affordable prices. The rates include insurance, in case of injury or inclement weather. See the Web site, www .velawindsurf.com, or call toll-free at 800-223-5443 for more information.

Given the nature of windsurfing, the crowd here is not only multilingual but also young and athletic. There are lots of lean, tan bodies and a California quotient of bleached hair. Cabarete is a laid-back town that has grown from an unheralded blip on the map only a decade ago to a thriving destination that caters not only to windsurfers but also "soft adventure" travelers (more on that below). In response to the boom, the number of resorts, inns, guesthouses, restaurants, and bars has multiplied faster than rabbits, providing a number of decent and cheap options. Getting to Cabarete is easy: Puerto Plata's La Unión International Airport is only a 20-minute drive away.

Although windsurfing remains the key draw, Cabarete is a hub of sorts for soft adventure options. Some of these are found on other islands, such as mountain-biking tours and horseback riding. Since the D.R. is so large and mountainous, a couple other notable activities are found here that aren't available anywhere else in the region: a multiday hike to Pico Duarte, the highest point in the Caribbean, and white-water rafting trips on the Rió Yaque del Norte.

The best way to experience the country surrounding Cabarete (and, in many ways, the D.R. itself) is with **Iguana Mama** (800-849-4720 or 809-571-0908; www.iguanamama.com), a company started by Patricia Thorndike de Suriel. She's a Coloradoan who traveled the globe and in 1993 chose the D.R. as a place to settle down, start a business, and raise a family. The business she founded is principally a mountain-bike tour operator, but it packages a variety of experiences. In fact, we would trust Iguana and its staff to construct an excellent, weeklong adventure in the D.R. —and although it predominantly works with singles and couples, some of its itineraries would make excellent family experiences.

The mainstay of Iguana's business is the **mountain-bike tours**, and we did the all-day downhill cruise, which starts at an elevation of 3,000 feet. The trip can be accomplished on paved, lightly traveled roads, but the itinerary allows for a couple off-road excursions that are highly recommended for riders comfortable on moderately steep dirt roads. The second of these off-roads includes two river crossings, and there's a swim in a freshwater pool. Then you move on to lunch at Blue Moon, an improbable countryside restaurant with a pool and delicious Indian food. There is a variety of other tours available for more experienced riders. There are also rentals.

Although it's possible to climb 10,128-foot **Pico Duarte** on your own, doing it with Iguana Mama makes this epic, 30-mile (round-trip) hike much easier. The trailhead starts at an elevation of about 4,000 feet and climbs steadily through bamboo forests, along lush streams and past tiny villages that can be reached only on foot or mule. Iguana and its guides routinely make contact with villagers, which adds tremendously to the experience; you will probably have at least one meal in a Dominican home—simple but tasty food. The terrain is more alpine than one expects in the Caribbean—it will remind you more of Colorado than of the tropics. In fact, the summit of Pico Duarte is said to receive light dustings of snow in December and January! Iguana Mama does the trek with mules to carry gear and often tired hikers (bring a pillow). Obviously, Pico Duarte is not done every day (or even every week), so if you're interested, contact Iguana Mama ahead of your trip. The friendly staff will also help to arrange accommodations and other activities, like the whale-watching trips out of Samana (January through March).

We were very surprised to discover **white-water rafting** down class III and IV rapids in the Caribbean. The **Yaque del Norte River** was established as a navigable option in the early 1990s. The all-day trip starts with buffet breakfast and then a drive to the tiny village of **Los Callabasos**, the put-in. The location is spectacular: a pine-dotted mountain valley on the slopes of Pico Duarte (where the Yaque del Norte originates). After a brief safety lecture, you'll be in the raft and on your way. The first half of the river is relatively easy but fun, which is a boon for the inexperienced. After a rest stop, you'll head down the second half, which has several class III rapids, and two decent class IVs, named **Mother-in-Law** and **Mike Tyson**. These are wicked fun. You can also book trips through Iguana Mama. The number of small tour operators operating in Cabarete has blossomed in recent years. Most offer the same excursions, such as catamaran charters and trips to Samaná Peninsula and Los Haitises National Park. They also offer deep-sea fishing, jeep safaris, horseback riding, helicopter tours, and white-water rafting. They are all located on the main road. We had a good experience with **Hurra Travel** (571-0005).

Where to Stay

Windsurf Resort, Cabarete, DR. ℂ 809-571-0718, ✆ 809-571-0710, 🖳 www.windsurfcabarete.com, windsurf@sunsetresorts.com

🛄 **Cheap** 🍴 **EP** [CC] 60 rooms

The second largest resort in Cabarete (and on its way to becoming the largest, with a major expansion on the way), this is a 60-unit Canadian timeshare property that rents apartments that come with or without a kitchen and as one- or two-bedroom units. The living rooms have a futon-like sofa but are not embellished with much style. Sliding glass doors open onto a small balcony or patio facing the garden and pool; a TV and phone are standard. The restaurant is decent, and the cascading pool area is a necessity—the resort is across the main road from the beach. Guests have free use of windsurf equipment, surfboards, kayaks, and sailboats on the beach just across the street.

Extreme Hotel, Cabarete, Sosúa, DR. ℂ 809-571-0880, ✎ 809-571-0727,
　💻 www.extremehotels.com, info@extremehotels.com

💰 **Cheap** 🍴 **BP** 32 rooms

Owned by natives of California, this hotel is brand-new, having taken over what was once the Playa de Oro. The result is an "extreme sports boutique hotel" catering to those who require boards to have a good time. For the surfers, windsurfers, and kiteboarders, the beach out front is the ideal spot on which to practice (or learn, for lessons are offered here, often for free). For skateboarders, this is home to the country's only sunken half-pipe, built into the ground so the entrance is at ground level. The rooms are housed in a three-story gray building and are basic, with wicker furniture, Serta beds, a/c, and fans. Kiteboard lockers are offered for free as well. Some of the staff are world-class kitesurfers, so there is always plenty of wave talk, especially by the pool bar and beach. There is also an on-site restaurant that serves three meals a day of tasty grub, mostly tapas and Mexican. The lounge bar has nine TVs and a projection TV, which is fun — it has movie night on Sunday. Happy hour runs from 5 p.m. till closing every night. The pool table and free Internet are nice perks as well. We love the young, energetic vibe here and definitely recommend it to anyone who is coming to enjoy the waves. Monthly rates and meal plans are also available.

Home Key Management, Cabarete, DR. ℂ 809-571-0370, ✎ 809-571-0523,
　💻 www.cabaretevillas.com, info@cabaretevillas.com

💰 **Cheap** for one-bedroom with full kitchen, **Not So Cheap** for two- or three-bedroom 🍴 **EP** 🆑

This condo agency merits attention, particularly for families or small groups. Home Key rents condos around the area, most of them at a site called Bahia de Arena, less than a mile west of town. The prices provide great value — we like an attractive three-bedroom, two-bath villa with full kitchen, its own pool, right on the beach, which rents for $1,100 a week in high season. The quartet of Americans staying at this home during our visit was astonished by the quality of the find (a comparable villa on St. Barth would rent for at least four times the price). The villas come with daily maid service, and you can hire a cook for about $20 a day. This is a super-tranquil spot for those who are seeking some peace and quiet.

Cabarete Beach Hotel, Cabarete, DR. ℂ 809-571-0755, ✎ 809-571-0831,
　💻 www.hispaniola.com/CBH, beach.hotel@codetel.net.do

💰 **Dirt Cheap** and up 🍴 **EP** or **MAP** for extra $18 per person per day
🆑 24 rooms

Perfectly located in the middle of Cabarete's long arcing beach, this 24-room hotel is what a laid-back, low-key beach place should be — where being barefoot and in a bathing suit is de rigueur. The rooms are simple yet comfortably furnished, with ceiling fans and/or a/c. We recommend the beachfront or ocean-view Superior rooms, which face the waves and trades, have lanais, and are away from the noisy street. For around $100 a night, including service and tax, why not!

A restaurant and two bars are on the property. A very good breakfast buffet is served on the panoramic second-floor terrace. Guests are provided with beach chairs and one hour per day of either kayaks, surfboards, boogie boards, snorkeling gear, Sunfish, beginner windsurfers, or beginner group instruction (all at the neighboring BIC Windsurf Center). Not a bad deal, and the staff is friendly, to boot!

Cabarete Palm Beach Condominiums, Cabarete, DR. ℂ 877-240-5605 or 809-571-0758, ✆ 809-571-0752, 🖥 www.cabaretecondos.com, info@cabaretecondos.com

💲 **Not So Cheap** 🍴 **EP** ⓒⓒ 16 rooms

This very attractive 16-unit complex is a wonderful place for those who want an efficiency setup. It's located right on the beach, with well-tended grounds and a small round swimming pool. Each spacious unit has two bedrooms (one with a queen bed and one with two twin beds), two baths, lanai, fully equipped kitchen, tropical wood furnishings, ceiling fans, white marble or tile floors, and phone (décor varies from one unit to another). Nanny services and cooks are available at an additional charge. The Palm Beach has a board-storage and grass-rigging area on the grounds. We love the location here under the swaying palms.

Villa Taína, Cabarete, DR. ℂ 809-571-0722, ✆ 809-571-0883, 🖥 www.villataina.com, info@villataina.com

💲 **Cheap** 🍴 **BP** ⓒⓒ 32 rooms

Though not on the beach (it's 30 yards away), this is a well-run, clean, and cheerful hotel. A new wing opened in 2000, and these rooms are colorful and chic (for the price) with attractive wicker furnishings. Housed in a three-story yellow building, all rooms have cable TV, a/c, high-speed Internet connection, lanais, minibars, and fridges. Their pool is complemented by an oceanside bar.

Caracol Aparthotel, Cabarete, Sosúa, DR. ℂ 809-571-0680, ✆ 809-571-0665, 🖥 www.hotelcaracol.com, info@hotelcaracol.com

💲 **Cheap** 🍴 **EP** 20 rooms

Located a short stroll down the beach, the Caracol offers well-equipped one- or two-bedroom apartments. The location is a bit out of the way, though, which is a pain when we want to hit a bar or restaurant, but it's merely a 75-cent motorcycle-taxi ride (yikes!). The apartments are well furnished with a/c and a queen or two twin beds. The living room has a foldout sofa, as well as a kitchenette and balcony. In addition, there are massage services, a TV room, two pools, and beach chairs on the beach. For those who are interested in kitesurfing (or learning to do it), the Caracol is ideal, because it has an on-site school run by a world champion. The Bozo Bar at the pool is a great hangout, especially once happy hour kicks in, from 5 to 7 p.m. The Tropicoco Restaurant is independently run and gets good reviews.

Caribbean Crib Guest House, Cabarete, Sosúa, DR. ☏ 809-571-0335, 🖥 www.caribbeancrib.com, trickster9369@aol.com

💲 **Cheap** 🍴 **BP** 6 rooms

Americans Mark and Sharon took over what was once a lesbian-only B&B, and, with the help of an ebullient Jersey surfer dude, Patrick, they have turned this into a great beach pad. Actually, this beach house has an intimate feel for those who want to avoid crowds or kids (it's adult only). Our only complaint is the fact that it's a few miles from town, which makes a rental car (or taxis) a must. However, for those who want solitude, the house has its own pool, beach, and sound system. Patrick cooks meals as well. Bring your iPod to plug into the stereo and jam tunes by the pool. The rooms are no-frill, but all have a/c and fans. The cabana with pool table is another perk. This place would be ideal for a group looking for its own space. Six couples could rent the whole place and have a really good time. No credit cards are accepted at the Crib, but it offers a payment system through its Web site, which does accept credit cards.

Hotel Sans Souci, Cabarete, Sosúa, DR. ☏ 809-571-0755, ✆ 809-571-1542, 🖥 www.hotel-sans-souci.com, sanssouci@verizon.net.do

💲 **Dirt Cheap** 🍴 **EP** 📷 74 rooms

It's pretty confusing to figure this place out. It's a complex of hotels and apartments with similar names, but what it boils down to is this: cheap, super-basic, beachside apartments. We like the Surf de Sans Souci because all the rooms are right on the beach. The apartments have a minibar, two double beds, little decoration, and a tiny TV mounted in the far corner. So for those television hounds, don't forget your binoculars! The terraces have plastic furniture, and the beach is steps away. The Beach Hotel rooms have a/c as well. The Villa Sans Souci is more "elegant" but to be avoided; the villas look out onto a gravel driveway — not so chic.

Where to Eat

Since the town is entirely beach focused, all nonwater activity is also along the beach. Contrary to what you might expect, there are a surprising number of different cuisines and commendable, reasonably priced small restaurants here.

$$ Bambu, 873-6565

For an informal bite, Bambu offers a little of everything, from pizza and pasta to Mexican and burgers. Prices are cheaper than at many places along the beach, and after dinner the music gets turned up.

$$$ Cabarete Blu, 571-9714

The "sense-awakening cuisine" moniker might be a stretch, but the fettucini with shrimp, zucchini, and herb cream sauce did pique our attention. There is a sizable selection of seafood, such as seabass in wine sauce and shrimp scampi.

$$$ Casa del Pescador, 571-0760

This offers fresh seafood on the beach. Try the seafood salad for a cool treat. The surfer's plate with *langostinos*, shrimp, and fish is a great spread, but most surfers cannot afford it. The seafood pasta is popular as well. This place consistently draws crowds, which is a good sign.

$$ D'Hot, 457-9268

Simon, a Bombay native, has brought Indian cuisine to Cabarete and has a nice perch up above the street. The food is vegetarian and incorporates all our favorite Indian spices. We like the inclusion of real basmati rice, and the spinach paneer is pretty darn close to the real thing. Open Monday through Saturday, 6 to 10 p.m.

$$ Ho-La-La Cafe and Bar, 571-0806

This colorful French-influenced beachside spot specializes in lobster and other seafood specialties. It's a great spot for a midday refueling lunch. We aren't sure why it is not more crowded, but our meals here have always been excellent.

$$$ José O'Shay's, 571-0775

Although we never imagined we would be hanging out at an Irish pub on the beach—itself a paradox—we must admit that the kitchen here is excellent! We found the best burgers in the D.R. and we love the Irish platters, such as corned beef and cabbage and fish 'n' chips. The Irish-American owners make sure everything is legit. The nachos are the best in Cabarete. They always celebrate the holidays here as well.

$$ **La Casita**, no phone
This offers fabulous fish, lobster, and the best shrimp on the island, and it's right on the beach.

$$ **Onno's**, 571-0461
One of the most popular spots in Cabarete, Onno's seems to cater to everyone. European couples sample the big seafood plates, whereas surfers (and struggling guidebook writers) love the affordable lunch specials. The Sunday beach barbeque is great as well. The kitchen is open late.

$$ **Pitú Café**, 571-0861
We love this colorful shack for its extensive breakfast options, fresh milk shakes, excellent pizza, and consistently high-quality tunes. Wednesday is two-for-one pizza night, and Tuesday is reggae and pasta night, which should be called Pastaman Live Up.

$ **Restaurante Chino**, 571-0572
Chino offers Chinese and Indonesian—take a chance. The problem here is that it is right on the main street, so the car exhaust can often be a problem. However, there is a huge array of choices on the menu.

$ **Sandro's Cafeteria**, 571-0723
This streetside restaurant is a local favorite, as the crowds indicate. Tourists have recently caught on and grab dependable *criollo* cuisine for cheap prices. Open until 10 p.m.

$ **Tipico Mercedes**, 571-0247
This is another great cheap Dominican-cuisine option.

Going Out

Cabarete has great nightlife, with lots of young people partying on the beach. Starting at 5 p.m., there is a variety of happy-hour specials. Our favorite hangout is **Lax**, which plays chill-out tunes all day. We love sitting in the swings here as Café del Mar–like music soothes us. Later, the pace picks up, and on weekends there are deejays. The Dominican Republic needs more places like this! For those who favor rock, **José O'Shays** has live music Wednesday through Sunday from 9:30 p.m. until 1:30 a.m. At other times it features a classic rock soundtrack. It also shows all-important sports events on projection TVs. These places close at 1 a.m. and the action shifts a few doors down the beach. **Tiki Bar** (571-0977) is a pleasant place to have a few drinks as well. Once the night gets cooking, **Onno's** and **Bambu** (conveniently located next to each other) dominate. Bambu (873-6565) plays more hip-hop, whereas Onno's (571-0461) favors electronic. Both are open till dawn.

Samaná Peninsula

One of the most beautiful and least developed coastal areas of the D.R. — and our favorite region of the country — is Samaná, a peninsula that juts out into the Atlantic like an arm thrust out to catch a baseball. What was once the haven of freed American slaves is turning into the country's hottest destination. The Samaná Peninsula is blessed with sensational beaches, lush hills, and a laid-back friendly vibe we cannot get enough of. What's more, the peninsula is also popular with whales that come down here from northern waters for three months a year to give birth to their young. The completion of the Samaná–Arroyo Barril International Airport means that tourists, most of whom come from France, can fly in directly from Europe. Before real estate values rise too high, foreigners are buying seafront property and rushing to build inns, and the big hotel chains — never to be outdone — are jumping into the mix as well in a race to grab the new tourist dollars. Samaná has yet to be exploited by the mega all-inclusive chains that have swallowed up much of the other prime beach areas, but this will probably change with the passage of time. As the saying goes, some things are inevitable: death, taxes, and the arrival of all-inclusives. Which is worse?

Mildly mountainous (the highest peak is just over 1,600 feet) and dotted with coves of sandy beaches within a rocky coastline, the peninsula is dominated by a spine of small mountains and big hills. There are three parts of Samaná that offer facilities for tourists: **Las Terrenas, Samaná** (including **Cayo Levantado**), and **Las Galeras**. Las Terrenas, a fishing village tucked at the end of a long, hilly, winding road on the arm's north side, is especially popular with the French and Italians, who thrive in these kinds of remote, out-of-the-way places of the Caribbean. We were amazed to see how many French-owned hotels, bars, and restaurants have popped up in the last five years. Little did we know that we would be called on to use our French language skills in the D.R. The area around Cayo Levantado is well known among Puerto Plata tourists day-tripping on bus excursions. Las Galeras is a small sleepy fishing village literally at the end of the road. It is also the home of Villa Serena, one of our favorite places to stay in the D.R. Hopefully, the peace, tranquillity, and natural beauty of this area will escape the developer's wrath. However, if what has happened in the rest of the country is an example, we had better enjoy this while it lasts.

The peninsula offers everything for travelers who are looking for an alternative to all-inclusive hotels. There is a variety of inns and B&Bs set on tranquil beaches — perfect for real rest and relaxation; but for folks looking for adventure, this peninsula is packed with options. Some who stay at major hotels will have tours available; for those with a choice, the best local agency is MS Tours (538-2499). We recommend requesting its tours from your hotel—it offers a very popular Jeep safari trip, as well as trips to the **Limon Waterfall** and **Los Haitises National Park**. For independent travelers, there are many agencies that offer similar trips. Perhaps the most popular excursion here is to the white-sand beach of Cayo Levantado. Unfortunately, this paradise is being ruined because a big resort is set to open, and half of the island's beaches have been privatized. The onslaught of vendors selling arts and crafts is a bit over-the-top as well, but the beach is so pretty that tourists flock here. On the days that cruise-ship groups are brought into town, the other half of the beach is reserved for them, which is a shame, because this is a magical beach that should have been protected more. After all, it is part of the national park system. Alas, we weren't hired as park wardens. It is extremely easy to set up a day trip to the isle, especially from the dock in Samaná—round-trip on a motorboat is usually about $10. There are seafood restaurants on the Cayo that are perfect for lunch. For those in Samaná who are looking for adventure trips, we recommend **Motomarina Tours** (538-2302, located on the Málecon, next to Bambú Restaurant). In Las Galeras, there is a very reputable dive company called **Punta Bellena Diving** (538-0247) that offers one- or two-tank dives all over the region. For excursions, **Adventure Tropical** (538-0046), across from Paradise Bungalows, offers everything from 4 × 4 trips to horseback riding to happy hour cruises. Unique to this area are the whale-watching excursions. Whale season is January to March, and these whale trips are not like some we have been on in other parts of the world where you *hope* to maybe see one; here they are everywhere.

This peninsula is the ideal place to get off the beaten track, and there are several desolate beaches that are simply divine. Be sure to check out **Playa Rincon**, **Playa Fronton**, and **Jackson Beach** before the development inevitably arrives.

Where to Stay

Las Galeras

⊛ **Villa Serena**, Apdo. Postal 51-1, Las Galeras, Samaná, DR. ✆ 809-538-0000, ✉ 809-538-0009, 🖳 www.villaserena.com, vserena@codetel.net.do

🔲 **Not So Cheap** and up 🍽 BP ⓒⓒ 21 rooms

Villa Serena is our favorite place to stay in the D.R. Tucked away, literally, at the end of the long road from Puerto Plata in the tiny fishing village of Las Galeras, this small, pretty 21-room hotel is one of the most romantic hotels in the Caribbean. It just oozes quiet sophistication and respect for privacy without attitude and outrageous expense—a hard combination to find. Well-tended grounds unfold to the sea and offer fabulous views of the bay and a tiny deserted islet with a handful of palm trees. Mountains frame the islet on the other side of the bay. The breezy lobby has rocking chairs and several nooks where you can read a book or play Scrabble. The waves crash against the rocky coast in front (there is a small beach to the side of the property and several beautiful strands nearby). Snorkeling is excellent right in front of the hotel. An attractive kidney-shaped white coral-stone decked pool sits in front for refreshment from your chaise. Palm trees around part of the pool provide shade.

There are four rooms on the ground floor and seven on the second floor. Each room is furnished differently (reflecting a different theme or mood); all have tile floors, ocean-view lanais, and private baths. Our room had bamboo beds and rattan furnishings and was simple yet elegant (we're not sure what the intended theme or mood was, but it made us feel calm—tropical Zen, perhaps?). We loved the rocking chairs on the lanai, where we sat and pondered everything from the beauty in front of us to what we needed to discuss in our next therapy session.

The Villa's restaurant is a fusion of Creole with European flourishes. The small and charming dining pavilion has been replaced by a larger one in front of the pool (completed in September 1999) to accommodate more guests. Ten more rooms were added where the old dining pavilion was located. We were apprehensive about this expansion but relieved to see that it hasn't upset the delicate balance that makes Villa Serena so serene (serene Serena—get it?). Three little flaws are still apparent and need attention: more water pressure (and hot water) for the shower; stronger vanity lights in the bath (our Burt's Bees regimen demands light); and a cozy bar (with bartender) in the lobby area so we can have a cocktail and drape over a barstool if we'd like.

The hotel can arrange many activities for guests, including trips to Playa Colorado or Playa Rincón (one of the Caribbean's best beaches) on horseback or by boat, scuba diving, golfing, hiking, fishing, and whale watches. However, one of our favorite activities was reading, sunning on a chaise, and being with someone special.

Hotel Todo Blanco, Las Galeras, Samaná, DR. ✆ 809-538-0201, ✉ 809-538-0064, 🖳 todoblanco@hotmail.com

🏷 **Cheap** 🍴 **CP** ⒸⒸ 8 rooms

Ever wonder what it would be like if Victorian style and minimalist design were combined in a tropical beach setting? We always dreamed of the possibilities (this is the sorry reality that we guidebook writers live with), and here we see the result. Todo Blanco, for those who know a few words of Spanish or Italian (or Latin), means All White, which is the underlying theme of this super-comfortable B&B on the gorgeous beach of Las Galeras. The rooms are located in a two-story Victorian house built by its Italian owners 13 years ago, and they are simply decorated with four-poster beds, white curtains, and periwinkle trim. Double French doors open onto spacious verandas, and each room is cooled by a fan (a/c is $20 extra due to the unusual electricity situation in Las Galeras). Although the hotel does not have a pool, we hardly noticed — the beach out front is barren and beautiful. The grounds here are well tended, and the views from the adjoining gazebo are as spectacular as the refreshing breezes. The common room has TV, chess, and cool wicker sofas. Whether it was the super views, the feeling of space, or the friendly staff, from the moment we arrived here, we felt at ease. Isn't that what it's all about?

Club Bonito, Las Galeras, Samaná, DR. ✆ 809-538-0203, 🕾 809-696-0082, 🖳 www.club-bonito.com, club.bonito@codetel.net.do

💲 **Cheap** and up 🍴 **CP** 🅲🅲 21 rooms

Set in the heart of the fishing village on Playa Las Galeras, this eclectic hotel is a mélange of Southwestern, Japanese, and tropical styles. The soaring lobby boasts earth-tone stucco, lots of native woods, terracotta tile floors, and 15-foot-long Naguchi-style lamps, all housed in a Spanish-style building with red stucco roof tiles. Yet the surrounding structures have thatched roofs and look like huts. There's even a Japanese fish pond. This clash made us a little disoriented, but we must admit it makes for conversation. An Itchycoo Park design concept, perhaps? Anyway, the rooms are comfortable with lots of wood, tile floors, ceiling fans, and a/c. We love the oriental carpets and well-crafted bamboo furniture. There are also 10 suites (bedroom, living room, fridge), which sleep up to four, in the Pelican Suites complex a short distance from the club. There is a nice bar and pool table and a brand-new pool with sundeck and thatched hut *palapa*. The Club is next to the public boat landing area, which can be noisy with motorbikes and locals partying at the public pavilion. The restaurant is excellent and features international cuisine prepared by an Austrian chef.

Paradise Bungalows, Las Galeras, Samaná, DR. ✆ 809-342-6955, 🖳 ruby@playarincon.com

💲 **Dirt Cheap** 🍴 **EP** 7 rooms

Run by a Swiss-Dominican couple, Paradise offers seven centrally located bungalows built around a garden. Though situated in the center of town, things don't get too noisy here–the other places listed above are obviously more peaceful. The bungalows are very well maintained and are nicely decorated with local art and matching curtains. The beds are a little small, but the windows have screens, and the fans are strong. Each has a veranda with rocking chairs and a hammock — not bad for $25 a night!

Casa Marina Bay, 7 Los Pinos, Samaná, La Julia, Santo Domingo, DR.
☎ stateside: 800-472-3985, local: 809-538-0020, ✆ 809-538-0040,
🖥 www.amhsamarina.com, infocmbay@amhsamarina.com

💲 **Cheap** and up 🍴 **All-Inclusive** CC 200 rooms, 50 bungalows

This all-inclusive resort—a rarity in Samaná—is nicely situated on Casa Marina Bay, but it has the typical feel and look of an all-inclusive, which clashes with Samaná's intimate, laid-back atmosphere. The commanding bay with its 2-mile-long beach, however, redeems the property's overall lack of distinction. The hotel offers standard and superior rooms and bungalow suites. Standard rooms come with two double beds; the bungalows have a queen-size bed along with two twins. All rooms feature a/c, cable TV, and telephone. The bungalows are equipped with a refrigerator and kitchenette but are rather dark inside. The rooms are more preferable, and most have ocean views. There are three restaurants and three bars, but the food is on par with other all-inclusives (i.e., not that great). Snacks are available until 1 a.m., drinks until 2:30 a.m.

Las Terrenas and El Portillo

El Portillo Beach Resort, Las Terrenas, Samaná, DR. ☎ 809-240-6100,
✆ 809-240-6104, 🖥 www.portillo-resort.com,
portillo@codatel.net.co

💲 **Cheap** and up 🍴 **All-Inclusive** CC 227 rooms

This resort was started decades ago and has evolved from a primitive 10-bungalow outpost connected to the world by an airstrip (and now by a potholed road) to a full-fledged resort with 227 rooms. Popular with Europeans (especially Germans and Italians), El Portillo sits on a lonely, windy point with miles of unspoiled beaches on either side. The main building is casual and comfortable, with plenty of places to sit and read or sip a drink. For obvious reasons, this is an all-inclusive resort.

The 11 bungalows, our choice because they're so rustic and close to the beach, sit on sand in a palm grove. There are two units in each, which can be combined to make a two-bedroom, two-bath configuration. Knotty pine (or some kind of knotty light wood) dominates the interior, and there is a kitchenette and air-conditioning. Best of all are the porches in front and the privacy afforded by the generous spacing. The newer rooms lack the character of the bungalows and are more standard resort fare and farther from the water. El Portillo has two clay tennis courts, a pool and Jacuzzi, horseback riding, and water sports.

Las Palmas al Mar, Calle Portillo, Las Terrenas, Samaná, DR. ✆ 809-240-6292, 🕾 809-240-6089, 🖳 www.lapalmasalmar.com, info@laspalmasalmar.com

💰 **Not So Cheap** 🍴 **EP** 12 rooms

This complex of well-appointed and affordable houses is a perfect place for families looking to enjoy the beaches of Samaná. Each two-story house includes a fully furnished kitchen, complete with stove, toaster, juicer (finally!), blender, and coffeemaker, and a terrace with table and chairs that's ideal for alfresco meals. The upper level is a mezzanine loft with two beds (or one double), and the downstairs area has plenty of living space. The sofa folds out into a bed, and the TV with CD/DVD player is a wonderful feature. The pool is not huge, but it's ample, given the small number of houses. Although these houses (complete with wooden shingles and fancy trim) don't match the tropical vibe of Samaná, the size and comfort of the houses make this a great fit for those who are seeking independence or family fun. Daily, weekly, and monthly rates are available.

Hotel Aligió Beach Resort, Las Terrenas, DR. ✆ 809-240-6255, 🕾 809-240-6169, 🖳 www.renthotel-online.com, resaligio@codatel.net.do

💰 **Cheap** 🍴 **All-Inclusive** 🆑 80 rooms

Although this place was once a big Italian hangout, new owners have come in and shaken things up a bit. Now the clientele seems to be mostly older European couples. Located across the road from the beach, this low-key place has two pools, a dive center, and a central thatched-roof pavilion where the bar and restaurant (Italian cuisine) are located. The rooms are white walled and tiled and adorned with colorful prints, rattan furnishings, and pastel fabrics. All rooms have fans, safes, phones, and bidets. There is no air-conditioning or gym. The rooms have a terrace with wicker furniture out front.

Note that the all-inclusive rate does not include drinks. There is a **MAP** for D.R. residents only.

Palapa Beach Hotel, 12 Calle Portillo, Las Terrenas, Samaná, DR. ✆ and 🕾 809-240-6797, 🖳 www.palapabeach.com, hotel@palapabeach.com

💰 **Cheap** 🍴 **EP** 🆑 16 rooms

On the surface, this stylish hotel is the most chic place in town, but despite all the money the French owners have poured into the design here, the Palapa comes up a bit short, in our opinion. Don't get us wrong—the style is impeccable. Using all natural materials, a giant two-story thatched roof *palapa* stands in front, housing a bar on the second floor with expansive views of the sea. Below, a sandy path leads to the lobby area, which is outfitted in eco-art using sticks and stones. Through an arch lies the lagoon, which, though artificial, is bedecked with lily pads. Surrounding the lagoon are the bungalows, which maintain the eco-art theme. Our major gripe is the layout of the bungalows. They have two floors, but it seems that much of this is a waste of space because the double bed is housed on the cramped upstairs loft, where the ceiling is pretty low. Meanwhile, the first floor is home to a tiny little single bed, placed in the middle of the floor, and the only bathroom. We got sick of going up and down the stairs when the whole first floor was wasted space. The verandas face the lagoons, but we weren't comfortable sitting at the dining room tables in plain view of the world. The décor is subtle, with lots of grays and earth tones, and the pool in back is pleasant, but overall we were not so comfortable here. With its sand volleyball court and upper deck bar, this is indeed a great hangout spot, so be sure to check it out for a sunset drink.

Tropic Banana Hotel, Las Terrenas, Samaná, DR. ⓒ 809-240-6110, ✆ 809-240-6112, 🖳 www.tropicbanana.com, hotel.tropic@verizon.net.do

💲 **Not So Cheap** ⑪ **BP** ⓒⓒ 134 rooms

We really enjoy this beachside hotel, but we are worried that the completion of the massive apartment and villa complex next door will spell doom for the laid-back charm of the Tropic Banana. The rooms are housed in two-story blocks adorned with wood latticework and are set back off the beach. They have a veranda with furniture on the outside and cable TV, a/c, and queen-size beds on the inside. The pool is suitable and the restaurant food tasty, but the addition of 112 rooms next door, to be administered by the owners here, will undoubtedly detract from the lazy vibe here. The upscale apartments will be for rent as well, but they will be in the Very Pricey range, which doesn't fit with Las Terrenas. Rooms 4 and 5 are our favorites — they have the best sea views and are far enough from the apartments to maintain some peace.

Playa Bonita

This beach is one of the laid-back options we alluded to in these pages. The beach is a long stretch of hanging palms, and there is plenty of open beach to explore in either direction, for all those beach bums like us who want to chart their own course. There is a little road that runs between the hotels and the beach, but it is more of a sandy trail that occasionally sees a motorcycle or home owner's car pass by. All of the hotels listed are right on the beach but located pretty close to one another. The clientele and proprietors are primarily French — we must credit them for having discovered this amazing spot before we did. They actually speak more English than the Dominicans around here, so don't be afraid.

Hotel Bahía Las Ballenas, Playa Bonita, Las Terrenas, Samaná, DR. ℭ 809-240-6066, ✆ 809-240-6107, 🖥 www.las-terrenas-hotels.com, b.lasballenas@verizon.net.do

💲 **Not So Cheap** 🍴 **BP** CC 32 rooms

Welcome to a completely stress-free environment! This six-year-old French-run hotel was the perfect respite for our weary souls. First of all, this place is more a collection of villas than an actual hotel. The villas are spread around the lush grounds, some with sea views, others facing the pools, and still others with garden views. We recommend the first two options; those toward the back of the property do not enjoy the caressing sea breezes we covet. Although all rooms are the same size, they differ in décor. Some have a Mexican motif, others a Moroccan theme, and for those who crave some Mediterranean role-play, the Southern France rooms are ideal. The color scheme and artwork creates a somewhat believable motif. Air-conditioning is not necessary here because the rooms are loaded with screened windows and fans. What's more, the monstrous thatched roof is constructed in such a manner that breeze actually passes through—we call it a breathing roof. The rooms are super-spacious, with colored tile floors and adobe walls with a keen design. The bathrooms are of the in-and-out variety, with vanity sinks inside and open-air showers outside, separated from the room itself. The free-form pool is complemented by lots of shady spots with comfy deck chairs, and in the front is a breezy gazebo with rocking chairs and hammocks. This place has everything—pool, beach, style, great restaurant, and a chill atmosphere. As we said, this zone is strictly stress free.

Hotel Acaya, Playa Bonita, Las Terrenas, Samaná, DR. ℭ 809-240-6161, ✆ 809-240-6166, 🖥 www.hotelacaya.com, contact@hotelacaya.com

💲 **Cheap** 🍴 **BP** 16 rooms

"Ze French, zey know a good spot when zey see one." Francophobes beware—we are in French territory. This is the kind of place the French love—natural beauty combined with a little sophistication, and, yes, great French cuisine. Now that new management has arrived on the scene, we are big fans of this hotel; the changes are already quite obvious. The rooms have been spruced up considerably—the handmade brazilwood furniture and fine fabric pillows make that evident. Housed in a white Victorian-style structure, all rooms possess sea views. The superior rooms with high ceilings and sea view (13–16) are fabulous. Each is equipped with a queen or two double beds, screened windows, and mosquito nets for us hopeless romantics who love crawling into our little love lair. The bathrooms have step-in showers and two vanity sinks. Rooms are not extravagant but are tastefully finished. The emphasis here is on serenity, not luxury, and there is plenty to go around. Air-conditioning is $10 extra and, in our opinion, unnecessary—we slept quite well with the fan and breeze. The high-quality restaurant, with a wonderful terrace along the beach, offers excellent French-Creole fusion, with such favorites as vanilla lobster and curry shrimp. Best of all, the Acaya is very reasonably priced.

Casa Grande, Playa Bonita, Las Terrenas, Samaná, DR. ℂ 809-240-6349, ▣ www.casagrandebeachhotel.com, casagrandebeachhotel@yahoo.es

🛍 **Cheap** ⑪ **BP** ⒸⒸ 10 rooms

It's only fitting that this place bills itself as a Gourmet Restaurant Hotel, because our dinner was more expensive than our room! Actually, we're not complaining—the food was excellent and the bed pretty cheap. The owners here (from Andorra) have recently rehabbed all the rooms, giving them different themes, such as Moroccan, Japanese, or Indian. Although we applaud the creative idea, the execution falls a little short; we were left guessing which was which. "Let's see, this one has orange trim—India, perhaps?" A little more art or regional décor would certainly provide more flair. The rooms have two doubles or one king-size bed, minibar, and fan (no a/c). Small (but not useful) sofas are built into the adobe walls. There is a well-tended lawn (insert image of favorite golf course here), but we wish we could trade some of the straight-backed chairs for a hammock or two—basking in the sun at a dining room table is not what we had in mind. The restaurant here is definitely worth a visit, for guests and nonguests alike. The open-air ambiance is elegant yet casual—if that isn't an oxymoron—and the Asian-Latino fusion cuisine is delicious and very well presented.

Punta Bonita Resort, Playa Bonita, Las Terrenas, Samaná, DR. ℂ and ✆ 809-240-5367, ▣ www.samana.net/puntabonitaresort/, hotelpuntabonita@hotmail.com

🛍 **Cheap** ⑪ **BP** ⒸⒸ 90 rooms

This German-owned hotel is not nearly as stylish as the other hotels along this beach, and its recent renovation has not completely hidden its signs of age. However, it does have a large pool, which is more than can be said about most hotels in this area. The rooms are housed in two-story blocks with tacky paint jobs inside and out. The TV is so tiny that we had to strain our eyes, and the a/c unit is quite aged—we may like our wine aged, but not our a/c. For those with back problems, beware the beds (or sleep on the beach). The rooms have a terrace with bamboo rocking chairs. There are two restaurants: a three-meal-a-day buffet and an à la carte spot closer to the beach. Punta Bonita has an all-inclusive meal plan available, but the food is better farther down the beach at the hotels listed above. We do like the disco here, which has glittery white walls and colored furniture. With enough people, it could make for fun times.

Viva Wyndham, Playa Cosson, Las Terrenas, Samaná, DR.
 ☎ 800-WYNDHAM or 809-240-5050, ✆ 809-240-5536,
 🖳 www.vivaresorts.com, viva.samana@vivaresorts.com
 💲 **Pricey** 🍴 **All-Inclusive** Ⓒⓒ 218 rooms

After staying at all of the tasteful inns here on Playa Bonito, arriving at the security gate of this disappointing resort was a letdown. Frankly, it's a shame that the Viva has even arrived here, because this beach, Playa Cosson, was once an idyllic stretch of white sand. Now there is another huge Wyndham going up next door—it seems as though another paradise has been lost. There is a buffet and à la carte restaurants, but the food here is not good. Many of the rooms are small and face the parking lot. For those who want an all-inclusive, we recommend another region of the country.

Samaná

Samaná was founded by the French in 1756 to protect the port they had established. Although this is obviously Dominican territory today, the French influence is still felt, and there are many French and Italian tourists here. Not long ago, Samaná was merely a jumping-off point for the rest of the peninsula. This is no longer the case; hotels are springing up here. The Spanish-owned Bahia hotel group is investing heavily around here. What was once the Cayacoa Hotel will soon be the Bahia Principe Cayacoa and will include a new casino. On the nearby island of Cayo Levantado, a natural paradise will turn into a hotel zone as Bahia opens a five-star resort with fancy villas that include butler service.

Gran Bahia Principe Samaná, Playa Los Cacaos, Samaná, DR. ☎ 34-971-221-310 (temporary phone in Spain), 🖳 www.grupo-pinero.com
 💲 **Pricey** 🍴 **All-Inclusive** Ⓒⓒ 103 rooms

This former Occidental Resorts hotel was taken over by the Spanish chain Grupo Piñero in August 2005. At press time, this gem of a hotel, located on the southeastern tip of the peninsula, right across from the enchanting Isla Levantado, was due to reopen in November 2006. Perched above the sea on a scraggly cliff, the Gran Bahia Principe resembles a cross between *Gone with the Wind* and *Robinson Crusoe*. Upon arriving at the circular driveway, we could tell that this hotel has more of the feeling of an inn, not a mega-resort—a welcome respite! Just one look at this stately mansion—its bright white and soft pink set against the blue sea and green hills—is enough to make any guest swoon.

All rooms are loaded with amenities. The only thing that puzzles us is the presence of fireplaces. We are speechless. Anyway, all the rooms are quite large. Junior suite beachfront rooms are the same as the superior rooms, except that they have a ridiculous terrace view right over the sea! These rooms are literally breathtaking. Guests can choose from the open-air buffet restaurant, Las Flechas, or the Italian restaurant, Anadel, which offers alfresco dining on the mansion porch with fans overhead. Although some people might be used to more variety from an all-inclusive, it's a good trade-off because there are no crowds here and hence there is a much more laid-back feeling. We also love eating off white linen.

There is a pool bar and a lobby bar that closes at 11 p.m. The suites have two big beds and are tastefully decorated with subtle floral prints and include a fan and a/c. The adjoining living room area has two comfortable wicker sofas and an elegant dining room table, but best of all is the rounded alcove with mini-cathedral ceiling and round turret-style lookout. The superior rooms usually have great terraces with wicker table and chairs—ideal for lazy breakfast eaters. The bathrooms could use a little sprucing, but they suited us fine. The pool is by no means a sprawling tropical lagoon, nor does it try to be, but it offers a beautiful view and reflects the style of the resort. The eight villas have their own pool area—they provide great seclusion for guests. The views from the pool decks are sensational. There is a private beach, which means that no vendors will bother us. The resort does offer free transport to and from Cayo Levantado as well. Keep in mind that this hotel is not known for its nightlife, so those craving the party scene might want to check out some of the industrial-size resorts listed below. Built in 1991, the hotel seems to be aging gracefully and is classier than most resorts here in the D.R.

Tropical Lodge Hotel, Apdo. Postal 14-2, Avenida La Marina, La Aguada, Samaná, DR. © 809-538-2480, ✆ 809-538-2068, 🖥 www.samana-hotel.com, juan.felipe@verizon.net.do

💲 **Cheap** 🍽 **BP** 17 rooms

This hilltop hotel, opened in 1987, is weathering well. Run by an affable Parisian couple, the Tropical Lodge is perfectly situated on the Málecon about two blocks from the city center. As a result, it is close to the action but remote enough to ensure peaceful mornings without much noise. The rooms are housed in a white-column building built into the hill and are equipped with a queen-size bed or two double beds, cable TV, a/c, and fan. Although all rooms face the bay, they don't offer much of a view, but the pool area and restaurant most certainly do. We just love the sunny terrace with a large pool and Jacuzzi. It's a great place for a hearty breakfast, sunbathing, or sunset cocktails. For a taste of "city life" in a tranquil atmosphere, come join Jean-Philippe and Brigitte here at the Tropical Lodge.

La Docía, Calle Teodoro Chacerreaux & Calle Duarte, Samaná, DR.

   $©$ 809-538-2041

   $ Dirt Cheap 🍴 **EP** 10 rooms

   For budget-hounds, this centrally located two-story hotel offers great value. Perched on a little hill across from a big church, the upper-floor rooms here at La Docía share a balcony with an airy vista of the sea beyond. The rooms won't win any awards for style, but the beds are comfortable, and the strong fan, coupled with the breezes that caress this lofty spot, makes for good sleep. The only problem is that in the morning there is plenty of action on the streets below that will awaken even the heartiest of sleepers (earplugs required). Because of the church hymns projected through a speaker and the honking motorcycles, we quickly discovered it was necessary to forgo a night on the town in order to get our sleep before the morning madness. However, for $15 per room, we cannot ask for the world. No breakfast is offered, but there is fresh coffee for guests. Lots of young guests end up hanging out on the balcony, drinking beer, and yes, listening to the church hymns. No credit cards.

Where to Eat and Go Out

The Samaná Peninsula is not nearly as sophisticated as many other Caribbean destinations, for there is an emphasis on laid-back natural fun. Although this region is renowned for that laid-back style, there is still action to be found. The restaurant scene is not too diverse, but each town invariably has a French and an Italian restaurant, because these nations represent the bulk of the region's tourism. In Samaná, there are a number of restaurants along the Málecon, which runs parallel with the coast — try **La Mata Rosada** for daily specials or **Le France** for French-influenced cuisine.

For true local flavor, there is a bunch of *pica pollo* stands on the Málecon, which are basically trailers with fried chicken, cold beer, and blasting merengue music. For those who have yet to experience this Dominican mainstay, this may be the perfect spot. Late at night, the **Naomi Disco** (next to the recently renovated Bambú Restaurant) is a popular spot. On the western end of the Málecon is a place we love called the **Car Wash**. Why do we love it, you ask? Because by day it's a car wash and by night a disco. This is a more chill spot for those who don't want as much thump.

In Las Galeras, there are some tasty options. For lunch, we recommend the little complex at the beach, where local women compete with each other (all in good fun) for business. These señoras cook up fresh seafood, such as conch (*lambí*), lobster, shrimp, and fish for cheap prices. Right off the beach, the best restaurants in town are **Chez Denise** (French cuisine and crepes), **Ruby's Playa** (Italian and grilled specialties), and **Club Bonito** (international). The bar on the beach is a popular spot for cold beers, $2 piña coladas (made in the pineapple), and loud merengue. This bar closes around 10 p.m., but there is a variety of bars on this main street that stay open late, the most popular being the **VIP Disco**.

In Las Terrenas, the **Café Atlantico** represents the new generation of up-scale dining. With its sleek blue and white, marine-theme style, the kitchen cooks up top-notch steak and seafood, served under a high-top white canopy. Across the street is the **Mosquito Art Bar**, a bohemian kind of place on the beach—it's perfect for a relaxing evening soiree. **Brasserie Tropico Latino** right in the center of town is a bit of a cultural mecca, mainly due to its location (and the presence of Häagen-Dazs ice cream). It also offers salads, sandwiches, and great milk shakes. Our favorite eatery, though, is the **Yucca Rojo**, which is a Spanish restaurant that features only the most authentic Iberian recipes. It was out of *torta* when we visited, but due to its pleasant tunes and airy seating, this place still "takes the cake" in our book. Since it attracts mostly European lovers, Las Terrenas is not known for its thumping nightlife. That being said, there is usually some degree of nocturnal activity. Our favorite spot is **La Bodega**, which is right at the main intersection. This open-air bar has comfortable seating as well as a dance floor and features live music three nights a week. The action gets cooking around 10 p.m. and continues until late. For those who want to burn the midnight oil, there is a bigger disco frequented by the locals, which is a $1 motorcycle taxi out of town. There is also a big disco in Limon called **Disco Nursandy**—it throws huge weekend parties that are a favorite with the locals. Ask any motorcycle taxi for info.

Along Playa Bonito, the restaurants are all run by the hotels, but the food here is leagues better than the all-inclusives throughout the rest of the country. **Casa Grande** has alfresco dining on the lawn and terrace, as well as seating in its airy and stylish dining room. The menu is diverse—from sashimi to coconut shrimp tempura to salmon crepes with melted goat cheese. **Bahía Las Bellanas** is another of our favorites—its tropical-French cuisine is top-notch. Try the stuffed crab or Tahitian-style fish tartar. The chef at **Acaya** is a master at using the local ingredients to create a fusion of French and local cuisine. Everything here is excellent.

THE INTERIOR

Jarabacoa

If you are exploring the Dominican Republic by car and are headed into the interior, check out Jarabacoa. We like a basic but appealing mountain lodge called Hotel Gran Jimenoa, located about 12 miles southwest of La Vega. If you are driving between the north coast and Santo Domingo, this is a great way to break up the often tedious journey.

Where to Stay

Hotel Gran Jimenoa, Jarabacoa, DR. © 809-574-6304, 🖂 809-574-4177, 🖥 www.granjimenoa.com, hotel.jimenoa@codetel.net.do

💲 **Cheap** 🍴 **EP** CC 60 rooms

This lodge comprises a pair of modern three-story buildings that sit alongside the beautiful, tumbling Rio Gran Jimenoa. The rooms are nothing to write home about, except that several have balconies that overlook the lush river scene, which is surrounded by pine trees and occasional villages. There is a likable pool, and a restaurant serves what is at best fair cuisine. The Gran Jimenoa is not worth a special trip, but if you have an interest in the unique Caribbean mountain life found only in the Dominican Republic, the hotel makes a worthwhile stop.

THE SOUTHWEST AND BARAHONA

The southwestern part of the D.R. has been heralded as the "undiscovered" part of the country. So we ventured south out of curiosity (natch!) in our rental car — for a road trip close to hell. From Santo Domingo, construction slowed us to a crawl as we approached the city limits and Haina, where many of the "drive-in *cabañas*" are located. These are places where men take their mistresses (or whomever) to have sex, supposedly out of sight of the wife (each unit has a drive-in garage with a door so that the philanderer's car is not in view). However, there were more than a few wives (and hookers) lurking by the gates. Once you are past that phenomenon, the heavily traveled Carreterra Sanchez, a two-lane road, dumps you at the central plazas of the cities of San Cristobal and then Baní. We saw no road signs, or else the legions of mopeds, bikes, and pedestrians made us miss them if they were there. It took guesswork and stopping to ask directions in our version of Spanish. After Baní, the traffic lightens considerably and the climate changes from lush to desert (it reminded us of interior southern California minus the freeways). We were parched and zooming through very poor villages of decrepit houses, and our expectations began to sink. However, through some fluke of nature, the landscape greened as we approached Barahona—nicknamed the Pearl of the South. It is also the home of the Magnetic Pole, where cars actually roll uphill (they do, but don't ask us why). The drive will take you at least three and a half hours from Santo Domingo's Malecón. Barahona does have an international airport, which is served by charter and periodically by commercial air service (check with your travel agent).

The city of Barahona was founded by the Haitan freedom fighter Toussaint Louverture in 1802, but its economy didn't develop until the arrival of coffee and sugar plantations in the 20th century. Barahona is a marginally interesting small city untouched by tourism, although there are hotels there. Is it worth the trip? We think not, considering other parts of the D.R. like Samaná. However, intrepid travelers and adventurers might find it interesting because there is a fairly large national park and an inland saltwater lake —**Lago Enriquillo**, which is 144 feet below sea level—in the region. The beaches to the south of Barahona are pretty but pebbly.

Barahona is a region dominated by a rural and mountainous landscape. The presence of the **Bahoruco Mountains** ("high protected place," in the indigenous language) and the extraordinary Enriquillo Lake (named in honor of the man who carried out the first indigenous uprising in the Americas) bestows the area with a historical and geographic appeal that is just beginning to be recognized by the public and private sectors. The lovely Caribbean coastline is home to towns such as Los Patos (The Ducks), Paraiso (Paradise), Enriquillo, and Oviedo, as well as the Jaragua Natural Reserve, which is named after another of the main indigenous leaders. Beach lovers will want to visit Bahoruco, San Rafael, Paraíso, La Ciénaga, or Saladilla. Rivers empty into the sea at most of these beaches, so they are perfect for rinsing off the salt. Naturalists will enjoy the crocodile tours in the salty Lago Enriquillo, which happens to be the Caribbean's largest lake. The island of Cabritos (within the lake) is the nesting spot for different alligator species.

Santa Cruz de Barahona is the "big city" around here, with a whopping 60,000 inhabitants, but it retains a Dominican charm. It is built around a central park, with lots of local restaurants and a public market close by. There are a few places to stay, two of which are listed below: the Riviera Beach Hotel (which is right in Barahona) and Casa Bonita (about a 20-minute drive south of Barahona in Bahoruco).

Where to Stay

Riviera Beach Hotel, Barahona, DR. ℂ 809-524-5111, ✆ 809-524-5798, 🖥 www.amhsa.com

    💲 **Cheap** 🍴 **All-Inclusive** 🆑 108 rooms

This all-inclusive resort is located on a protected mangrove lagoon. The water is very calm, but when we visited the beach we were swarmed by sand flies. We ran back to the hotel, which consists of two five-story buildings with a small noisy pool and a restaurant and function area in between. Rooms are standard hotel fare, with tile floors, a/c, ceiling fans, and safes. If you stay here, be sure to ask for a room away from the pool area. Expect buffets for all meals. Water sports and tennis are available.

Casa Bonita, Bahoruco, DR. ℂ 809-696-0215, 🕾 809-223-0548 or 809-472-2163 in Santo Domingo, 🖳 casabonita@hotmail.com

💼 Cheap 🍽 CP ⒸⒸ 12 rooms

We drove past Casa Bonita several times and finally had to ask where it was (no signs again). A woman waiting for a bus pointed inland and upward. All we could see was a house on a hill and a conspicuous (at least for these parts) pool slide. There it sat, high on a hill about a quarter of a mile from the beach. The access road passes several rudimentary houses on the steep drive up.

Did you ever have the feeling that you've arrived at a place where you will be counting the minutes until you leave? That's how we felt once we looked around. A 20-minute drive south of Barahona, this is an outpost with pretty views, a tattered look, and a friendly and courteous staff that seemed amazed that there were any guests at all, including us. There is a pavilion with a few sofas and chairs and a dining area. The sofas looked comfortable and inviting but had been staked out by a German couple (the only other guests) who gave no sign that they would ever give them up. We resigned ourselves to sitting at the bar and asked for a Stoli and tonic (no Absolut here). The bartender seemed hesitant to open the bottle of Stoli, as if it were being held for some special sacrifice or something. We persisted. After a drink, we strolled over to the pool, which was in disrepair (forget going on the pool slide). The rooms are small, the furnishings threadbare, and the bathrooms much too narrow. However, the view from our window of the mountains behind was stunning. Crowing roosters woke us up, and we were on the road before breakfast and before getting a chance to visit the Karaoke Kiosko, which we assume was for the better.

Don't Miss

The Colonial Zone (Zona Colonial), Santo Domingo

This is the oldest city in the Western Hemisphere, and the Zone is the oldest part of the city. The architecture and the buildings themselves are wonderful to see and were restored for the Columbus Quincentennial. This is the original part of Santo Domingo, founded by Bartolome Columbus,

Christopher's bro', in 1496. As we said earlier, some of the oldest colonial buildings in the Western Hemisphere are here, including the oldest church in North and South America: La Catedral de Santa María La Menor, Primada de América. This was the first cathedral of the New World, begun in 1514 and completed in 1540. There's plenty more to see, including El Alcázar de Colón (Diego Columbus's palace), El Convento de los Dominicos, the Torre del Homenaje, the Casa del Cordon, the Puerta de la Misericordia, the Casa de Nicolás de Ovando, and the Iglesia del Carmen. Just that partial list of history will keep you busy! The entire Colonial Zone is about the size of Central Park. So, once there, you can walk everywhere. One of the pleasures of the Colonial Zone is walking around in the evening. Residents leave windows and doors open for the breeze and are all sitting around watching TV. Families, friends, all gathered around the tube and chatting — we found it a real glimpse into the day-to-day lives of Dominicans.

El Faro a Colón

Built at a cost of hundreds of millions of dollars (which certainly could have been used for better purposes — like food and housing for the poor), this coffinlike behemoth is former President Joaquin Balaguer's tribute to Christopher Columbus (and himself). Here, underneath the beacon and under military guard, rest the remains of Columbus. It takes so much power to operate the lights that there are blackouts and brownouts in other neighborhoods while it's turned on. (It is something to see at night. The hundreds of lights along the edifice project a cross into the sky along with the superpowered beacon, which is visible for 100 miles at sea.)

The Teeth of the Dog, La Romana

Rated the toughest and best golf course in the Caribbean by *Golf Magazine*, this 6,888-yard links experience has seven oceanfront holes, is rated 74.1, and has a slope rating of 140. There are four par-5s of more than 500 yards.

Dominican Divorces

Remember on *Dynasty* (some of you might not be old enough) when Fallon flew to Santo Domingo to get her divorce from Jeff because it takes only 24 hours there? With a legal separation of mutual consent, one spouse can come to the Dominican Republic, hire a Dominican attorney to present the case to court, and be on his or her way the following day — a single person again.

Samaná

The still rather undeveloped peninsula on the northeast coast, this is where some of the nicest beaches in the country are located. The drive from Cabarete to Samaná is a great trip along the coast, with lots of beaches to explore on the way.

Baseball

This is a national obsession. There are ballparks in every town, but the capital of Dominican baseball is San Pedro de Macoris. It produces more Major Leaguers (including Sammy Sosa and Alfonso Soriano) than any other town in the world. Catch a game at the stadium here. The action heats up in December when the Major Leaguers return from the United States to play for their hometown teams. The biggest stadium is Quisqueya, right in Santo Domingo.

Merengue

Just listen, you'll hear it. Turn on the car radio and hit the clubs and experience the rhythm.

Aquatic Sports

The D.R. is a fabulous place to engage in some maritime pleasures. Certified divers will love the scuba diving on the Samaná Peninsula and along the eastern coast, especially around Bayahibe. Most big resorts offer diving, but there are plenty of independent dive shops as well. Cabarete, along the northern coast, is perhaps the best spot in the Caribbean for windsurfing and is also ideal for beginners. There are several schools from which to choose. This also happens to be the best kitesurfing spot.

Grenada

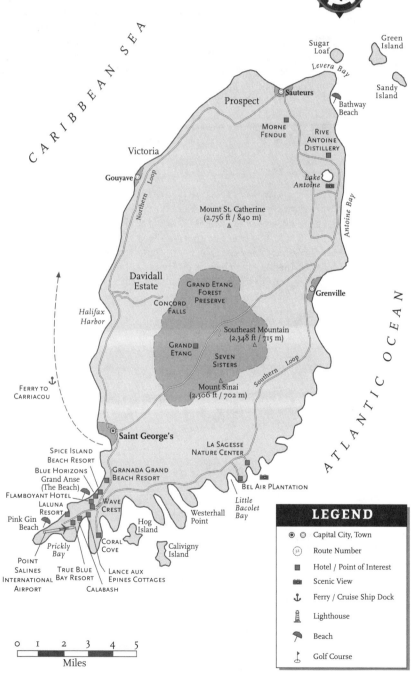

N

CARIBBEAN SEA

Sugar Loaf

Green Island

Levera Bay

Sandy Island

Prospect

Sauteurs

Bathway Beach

MORNE FENDUE

RIVE ANTOINE DISTILLERY

Victoria

Gouyave

Northern Loop

Lake Antoine

Antoine Bay

Mount St. Catherine
(2,756 ft / 840 m)

Davidall Estate

GRAND ETANG FOREST PRESERVE

CONCORD FALLS

Grenville

Halifax Harbor

Southeast Mountain
(2,348 ft / 715 m)

GRAND ETANG

SEVEN SISTERS

Southern Loop

FERRY TO CARRIACOU

Mount Sinai
(2,306 ft / 702 m)

Saint George's

LA SAGESSE NATURE CENTER

SPICE ISLAND BEACH RESORT

BLUE HORIZONS

Grand Anse (The Beach)

GRANADA GRAND BEACH RESORT

FLAMBOYANT HOTEL

LALUNA RESORT

WAVE CREST

Pink Gin Beach

Hog Island

Westerhall Point

BEL AIR PLANTATION

Little Bacolet Bay

Prickly Bay

CORAL COVE

Calivigny Island

POINT SALINES INTERNATIONAL AIRPORT

TRUE BLUE BAY RESORT

LANCE AUX EPINES COTTAGES

CALABASH

ATLANTIC OCEAN

LEGEND

◉ ◎ Capital City, Town

⑫ Route Number

■ Hotel / Point of Interest

📷 Scenic View

⚓ Ferry / Cruise Ship Dock

🗼 Lighthouse

⛱ Beach

🏌 Golf Course

0 1 2 3 4 5
Miles

Grenada

TOURISTO SCALE:
👤👤👤👤👤 (6)

The Grenada we know is wonderfully evocative. Nicknamed the Isle of Spice, the land is redolent with cloves, allspice, cinnamon, and especially nutmeg, which grow throughout its hillsides. The island's tranquil natural assets of lush tropical vegetation, gushing rivers, scenic mountains, and coastline are powerful and do much to overcome the memory of political turmoil and a brash American invasion in 1983.

Twenty-one years later, Grenada suffered an invasion of a different sort when "Ivan the Terrible," a category 5 hurricane, pounded Grenada on its way to Grand Cayman, Jamaica, and Florida. Hurricane Ivan was one of the most powerful Caribbean storms on record, and in the hours leading up to September 7, 2004, the government dallied with preparations while radio announcers blithely announced, "God is a Grenadian."

No Caribbean island is completely immune from tropical storms, but Grenada lies just far enough outside the traditional hurricane belt that the island had not taken a direct hit from a tempest since 1955. As Ivan spun toward the island, most Grenadians counted on the storm heading north, as storms usually do. Instead the hurricane plundered the southern tip of the island, where most of the population and almost all of Grenada's hotels are located, and the devastation was significant, compounded by a government completely unprepared for the calamity. An estimated 28,000 homes — roughly

Grenada: Key Facts

Location	12°N by 61°W
	90 miles/144 kilometers north of Trinidad
	2,200 miles/3,546 kilometers southeast of New York
Size	133 square miles/344 square kilometers
	21 miles/34 kilometers long, 12 miles/19 kilometers wide
Highest point	Mt. St. Catherine (2,756 feet/840 meters)
Population	92,100
Language	English
Time	Atlantic Standard Time (1 hour ahead of EST, same as EDT)
Area code	473
Electricity	220 volts AC, 50 cycles; transformers and adapters are necessary for U.S.-made appliances.
Currency	The Eastern Caribbean dollar, EC$ (EC$2.68 = US$1)
Driving	On the left; a valid U.S. or Canadian driver's license with a local permit ($12, issued by car-rental firms) is necessary.
Documents	Valid passport (recommended), or proof of nationality with photo ID and an ongoing or a return ticket
Departure tax	$20
Beer to drink	Carib
Rum to drink	Rivers
Music to hear	Dancehall
Tourism info	800-927-9554 or 473-440-2279
	www.grenadagrenadines.com

90 percent of those on the island — were badly damaged or destroyed. Little was spared: The Prime Minister's official residence was plundered, and almost every church on the island lost its roof, allowing visitors to walk the hills of St. George's and peer straight down at the pews.

We visited Grenada eight months after Ivan as the island was in the middle of a full-scale rebuilding campaign. Anyone who could wield a hammer, it seemed, was employed, with efforts underway to have the island in the best possible shape for the coming winter season. The beaches were back to their former beauty, and dive sites had recovered. The northern part of Grenada was starting to look like its former self again, although in the center of the island the forests of Grand Etang will take some years to fully recover — the trees, like fallen matchsticks, appear like remnants of a nuclear winter, a breathtaking post-traumatic vision of the storm's power. An even bigger setback was to the nutmeg industry, which lost more than 90 percent of its trees (prior to Ivan, the island supplied a third of the world's nutmeg). We feel confident, as we go to press, that Grenada is ready for tourism again, and we strongly encourage a visit to the island — not out of charity, but because it remains one of our favorites.

This is a great place to visit if you want to hike and immerse yourself in the people and the past. The country still has a bantam, out-of-the-way disposition, which makes Grenada a good choice for vacationers who don't care to follow in the footsteps of a million cruise-ship passengers (the island debuted a large cruise-ship dock in 2005, but fortunately — for us — there haven't been more than one or two a day, and only in high season). There is one excellent beach (**Grand Anse**) and a smattering of smaller coves, and the island's rugged interior beckons with hiking opportunities. Outside the primary tourist areas of Grand Anse, L'Anse aux Epines, and St. George's (the capital), you begin to experience the real Grenada. Vivid images come to mind of women washing clothes in a river, potholed roads, spice stations, rich hues of green, and the ever watchful eyes of the people, who are among the region's friendliest hosts.

The country (which includes the neighboring islands of Carriacou and Petite Martinique to the north, covered in the Grenadines section) is a popular destination for Europeans, particularly Brits, but Americans are increasingly discovering this special island. Tourists who visit here rarely venture into the interior of the island or dally in the fishing villages along the northern coast, which is a shame. Grenada appeals to adventurous travelers (our readers, we hope) as they discover so much more than what they'll see around the hotels.

The Briefest History

Grenada was first settled by Amerindians from South America. First came the Arawaks, and then the Caribs. By the time Columbus sighted the island on his third voyage, in 1498, the Caribs were firmly entrenched, thus inhibiting European settlement until the 17th century, when the French defeated the Caribs in 1651. This is a famous battle: Rather than be conquered, the last band of Carib warriors tossed the women and children into the sea and then, in a suicide leap, plunged to their own deaths off Leapers' Hill (Le Morne de Sauteur) onto a rocky beach below.

After this conquest, Grenada, like so many other islands in the West Indies, became a pawn in the constant tug-of-war between the two chief rivals of the region, France and Britain. The island changed hands several times. Finally, in 1783, the Treaty of Paris deeded the rights to Britain. Independence was granted almost 200 years later, when Grenada, Carriacou, and Petite Martinique became an independent state in 1974, with Sir Eric Gairy at the helm.

Now, Sir Eric was a weird fellow (he believed in extraterrestrials and said he communicated with them) and a demagogue. In 1979 Maurice Bishop, his chief rival both politically and ideologically, staged a coup d'etat while Sir Eric was out of the country. Bishop was a Marxist who wanted closer relations with both Castro (his mentor) and the Soviet Union. Bishop ruled for four years, trying to institute socialist reforms in the country. It was when Bishop started making overtures to the United States that a rival faction in his New JEWEL (Joint Endeavor for Welfare, Education, and Liberation) Movement, led by Bernard Coard, staged another coup d'etat in 1983 and had Bishop and his close advisers arrested and executed.

The country reeled as news of this event spread throughout St. George's, and unrest was widespread and sudden. The United States and the leaders of several Caribbean island nations—led by the late Eugenia Charles of Dominica—viewed the alliance of Grenada and Cuba with great suspicion; both felt that Castro wanted to use Grenada as a military base (indeed, he was building an airport large enough to receive jet aircraft). So under the pretext of rescuing about 100 American students at the island's medical school, the United States invaded Grenada, expelled the Cubans (who put up armed resistance), and restored order. As a whole, Grenadians were very happy that the "troubles" were over, and appreciative of the American effort and especially of all the aid money that poured in afterward (there were a lot of new cars around a year after the intervention). Elections were held in 1984 to choose a new government, and since then things have been more peaceful on the Isle of Spice. The Point Salines Airport was completed and subsequently provided Grenada an advantage over neighboring islands with smaller, less modern facilities. The government is expanding the tourist infrastructure and has particularly emphasized cruise ships (booo, hiss), although the expected onslaught has not arrived—yet. The medical university that was at the crux of the American invasion moved away from Grand Anse and has a spiffy new facility at True Blue, near L'Anse aux Epines. That, along with 3,000 students from around the world, lends a pleasing international air to the island. As for Castro, the Cuban leader made a goodwill visit to the country in 1998, with barely a peep of protest from Washington, D.C.

Getting There

The Point Salines International Airport is conveniently close to most tourist accommodations on the island (thanks, Fidel). Service to Grenada is available on Air Jamaica from New York and Montego Bay, American Eagle from San Juan, and on BWIA via Barbados and Trinidad, connecting to flights out of Miami, New York, and Washington, D.C. Air Canada Vacations flies in from Toronto; British Airways flies in from London. LIAT and Caribbean Star fly to Grenada from major destinations in the eastern Caribbean, and SVG Air connects Grenada with Carriacou, St. Vincent, and Union islands.

Getting Around

There are plenty of taxis at the airport. A taxi to the Grand Anse or L'Anse aux Epines area will cost about $12, officially. Be prepared to be ambushed by cabbies when the Customs door slides open. Do haggle — the competition is fierce and you should win, although there are official rates posted. Don't let anyone grab your luggage until all financial matters are settled. There are also minivans or minibuses, which charge a dollar or two for trips between points in the southern part of the island. They ply the major roads from Grand Anse into St. George's and provide easy and fun transport. The vans blast dancehall music and bear names like "Ruff Xample," "Oo-La-La," "Log On," "Out-ah-Order" or "Tight Clothes." It's a great way to meet Grenadians.

There are plenty of rental cars available, too, although the roads outside the tourist area aren't always well paved and directions are poorly marked. Avis/Spice Isle Rentals (800-331-1084 or 473-440-3936) and Dollar (800-421-6868 or 473-444-4786) have outposts here. Be sure to make your reservations well in advance to ensure the best rates.

There is a twice-daily ferry to the neighboring islands of Carriacou and Petite Martinique; see those chapters in the Grenadines section for details.

Focus on Grenada: Grenada Photo Safari

Grenada's physical beauty makes it a natural for the camera, but getting to your subject matter can prove difficult. There are several ways to photograph the island beyond the boundaries of your hotel. If you're comfortable with left-side driving, you can rent a car, and touring the southern part of Grenada (the most populated and touristed area) is easy. As you head north on either side of the island, however, you'll find that the roads are narrower, winding, and sometimes rutted (but actual road conditions have been steadily improving for the last few years). Worse yet, you'll find few directional signs to point your way, although as you get lost you may stumble across some interesting sights. For those with a sense of adventure, there is the bus system — an experience in itself. This is a fine way to get to know Grenadians (to whom you'll be squeezed close) as you careen rapidly down the roads, dancehall music blaring.

If these options aren't what you had in mind, look no further than Dennis Henry. **Henry's Safari Tours** (473-444-5313; www.spiceisle.com/safari) will take you for a six-hour tour, leaving at 9 a.m. from your hotel or guesthouse for $80 for one person, $35 each for three or more. Half-day tours are $60 for one or $25 each for three persons. Dennis, who goes by at least five names, will design a photo safari that will let you put the best of Grenada on film. You'll have frequent stops for photo ops, as well as a tasty lunch. The vehicle is a comfortable van with good visibility and height to let you take in as much as you can. Dennis is also an avid hiker and conducts mountain walking tours. One of his best is to **Seven Sisters Falls**. It's a three-and-a-half hour hike along freshwater streams that cascade into pristine swimming holes (don't forget your swimsuit). Dennis leads a number of other "safaris," too.

Camera Etiquette

Like some celebrities, many islanders get irritated when you snap a picture of them without their permission. To show courtesy and to avoid unpleasantness, ask before clicking the shutter. Sometimes a friendly gesture and a smile will do the trick. With group shots, use your judgment. A group of women washing clothes in a river might not mind a photo from a distance, whereas a group of Rastas toking on a spliff might feel that their personal space has been invaded and thus take the film — and maybe your camera — from you.

Photo Safari 1: St. George's

Photogenic St. George's is best seen on foot. The town, built on steep hills around a cozy harbor, has many stair accesses and roads too narrow for cars. It's easy to get to St. George's from your hotel; you are never more than a few miles away by taxi, minibus, or thumb. Avoid this tour on a day when a cruise ship is calling on the island — you don't need couples in matching black socks cluttering your pictures.

Plan on doing the walk in the morning, because it gets too hot by lunchtime. Also, bright midday light bleaches the color and life out of your subjects. The hour or two before sunset warms up the color. The best place to start is at the **Carenage**. You'll find a Grentel office for overseas calls, a LIAT office to reconfirm your return flight, a tourist board where you can buy a good map, and even FedEx — all in a row. Across the street to the right, mail boats depart on alternate days for Carriacou. These wooden boats with sails, mast, and so on might not inspire much confidence as a form of public transportation or especially as pleasure craft. (The more modern high-speed catamaran **Osprey Express** departs for Carriacou twice daily.)

Moving along, turn right on Young Street, and you'll pass the **National Museum** on the left. Admission is $2, and you can scour the island's history (including the 1983 intervention) in 20 to 30 minutes.

When you're ready to move on, just past the museum on the opposite side of Young Street is the **Yellow Poui Art Gallery** (473-440-3001). This is a legitimate gallery, not a tourist joint, with the work of 85 artists from around the world on display, including a number of Grenadian and West Indian painters. Prices are not too high, and it's worth a look. Owner Jim Rudin is very knowledgeable and will show you the latest from Caliste (a primitive painter from Carriacou who is much in favor). Yellow Poui is located just upstairs from Art Fabrik, a store that sells attractive batik pieces.

At Church Street, take a right and follow it all the way past several good examples of both English- and French-influenced island architecture — including the Anglican church and the cathedral — that dominates the top of the hill. These lost their roofs during the hurricane but are slowly being repaired. Then cruise down Market Hill to **Market Square**, where tables are set up and anyone can come in and sell their wares. This very picturesque area can be mobbed on cruise-ship days, but it's a good place to strike up a conversation, especially in one of the surrounding rum shops.

You're on the homestretch now. Take a left on Church Street, right on Simmons, and down the steps to Scott Street and the Carenage. That should put you right at the Nutmeg for lunch (and a much-needed rum punch).

Photo Safari 2: Northern Grenada

For this expedition, a guide is very helpful. The roads aren't marked and can be in bad shape — your AAA card won't work here. The guide will show you places you could never find on your own. Alternatively, have a good navigator with a copy of a recent map to help steer your way.

This is an all-day affair. From St. George's, head up the western road. As soon as you leave the capital you'll be on your way into the real Grenada. Some of the photographic highlights you should encounter are described below.

Laundry

Never did laundry look so photogenic. Along the west coast you will often encounter women doing laundry in the rivers. The light is muted from the green canopy, and the subjects are almost always interesting from any angle.

Concord Falls

A one-lane road snakes up the hill past countless nutmeg trees to the falls. Get out of the car and walk up to the Fontainebleu Falls (which takes about 30 minutes) — it's much prettier. There are lush greens with peaked hills as background.

Rum Shops

One thing becomes clear as you drive around Grenada (and most other West Indian islands): It seems as though every other house has a liquor license. These shops sell sundries as well as drinks, so you can have a rum punch while looking at the eggs and crackers. Now that's progress.

Douglaston Estate

This is a spice-processing station near Concord. Outside, there are several drying racks on rollers. Should it start to rain, they are swiftly pushed into the workhouse, to be rolled out when the sun shines again. Inside, women separate the mace from the nutmeg seed as well as prepare cocoa and coffee beans, cinnamon, and bay leaves. The faces of the workers alone are worth the trip. Although most of the island's nutmeg trees were lost in the hurricane, there are hopes to revive the industry.

Gouyave

Pronounced "guave," this is Grenada's nutmeg-processing station (the next stop after Douglaston). Gouyave is notorious for its loony citizens, who seem to burn the midnight oil more here than anywhere else on the island. There is also a sizable fishing community, whose odd hours may add to the general wackiness. Every Sunday evening there is a festive jump-up in the street with dancehall music.

Women with Things Balanced on Their Heads

You won't see this on the streets of New York. These women have strong necks. It's astonishing what they can balance. Bonus points if you can snap a woman carrying a case of Coke or Carib on her head.

Prospect

If the bridge is out, or just for the fun of it, take the road through this area. It's real Grenadian backcountry, with fine examples of rural dwellings.

Sauteurs

After Prospect, the road will suddenly end on a beach with a commanding view of Sauteurs and its cathedral on top of Leapers' Hill (Le Morne de Sauteur). The town itself is quaint and worth a brief tour with camera in hand. The drive up to the cathedral will bring you to Leapers' Hill, where the last remaining Carib Indians leaped to their deaths rather than be captured by their French pursuers. At the church, a busy workshop of the Young Grenadians United Crafts Workers Association produces candles and batik that can be bought on the spot. These are teenagers trying to make a cooperative succeed—a worthy effort. In front of the workshop is an old cemetery, and beyond that is an excellent view of Carriacou.

Morne Fendue

This is the home of the Morne Fendue Plantation Great House, where you should plan on having lunch. The charming great house was built of gray stone and wrought iron in 1908. There are several varieties of brilliant flowering shrubs and the biggest red poinsettias we've ever seen.

River Antoine

Several miles outside Morne Fendue, the road will emerge from the hinterland onto a windswept, palm-studded beach called **Bathaway** that curves around to some gigantic cliffs to the north. This is a good place to sit, cool off, and enjoy the view. If you swim, beware of the undertow (there's a natural "swimming hole" formed in the coral).

Right up the road from the beach is the River Antoine rum distillery. After driving through fields of sugarcane—many charred from the annual harvest burning—you'll arrive at some old stone buildings and the distillery's huge waterwheel. This is one of the few remaining distilleries that looks and operates the way it did more than 150 years ago.

There are four stages in the River Antoine distilling process. The first is the crushing station, where a big waterwheel squishes the juice from the cane stalks, then sluices the liquid into the next stage — the boiling room. In this cavernous barn, five tanks bubble the juice at different temperatures while birds and bats fly in and out around the rafters, adding their "seasoning" to the batch. It is then sluiced off again to the fermenting and storage room. After aging, it goes to the still to be boiled to its clear white state. Unfortunately, you can't sample it here due to strict Grenada laws regarding liquor taxes. Only the Customs man has the key. However, it's sold in just about any rum shop by the glass and in a few liquor stores in St. George's under the Rivers label.

Pearl's Airport

This rock-strewn strip with cattle grazing on the side used to be the international airport. See if you can spot the burned-out remains of an Aeroflot and a Cubana Airways airplane. It's a reminder of what used to be.

Grenville

This is a fishing and boat-building center with good waterfront and boat photo potential. Get out of the car and check it out. Then head south through the basket-weaving district. It seems as if everyone is weaving. Stop and ask about the craft, perhaps buy something, and ask to take a picture.

Grand Etang National Park

It's been a long, hot day, but you're almost home. Don't worry, you won't be hiking (save that for another day), just driving through Grenada's rainforest. Alas, most of the trees were felled by Hurricane Ivan in 2004, but when you come up to the main viewpoint, above a crater lake, the vista is awesome — as if a giant hand had smeared the forest into the hills in a series of violent sweeps. It's a true testament to Mother Nature's fury. As you crest the ridge there will be points along the snaking road back to the south with nice vistas of both the forest vegetation as it comes back and St. George's in the distance.

Where to Stay

Almost all of Grenada's accommodations are found on the southwestern corner of the island, from St. George's to the tip of L'Anse aux Epines and down to the airport. Many of the hotels are on or within walking distance of Grenada's most popular beach, Grand Anse. Some good news: Grenada has a wide variety of rooms in the moderate to low-budget range, as well as several nice luxury properties.

Laluna Resort, P.O. Box 1500, Morne Rouge, St. George's, Grenada, WI.
Ⓒ 866-452-5862 or 473-439-0001, ✆ 473-439-0600,
🖳 www.laluna.com, info@laluna.com

💲 **Stratospheric** ⑪ **EP** ⒸⒸ 16 rooms

If Laluna looks like it just stepped out of some swanky fashion magazine, it's not by accident. The owner and developer is an Italian fashion maven, Bernardo Bertucci (with backing from Benetton and Zegna), and it seems he is aiming for the Grenadian equivalent of world beat-chic, with the lofty prices one expects from a Milanese hot spot. Situated in a heretofore undeveloped cove just south of Grand Anse, Laluna is designed with a Moorish sensibility, with lots of richly painted cement; sienna, violet, and amber hues dominate. Each of the 16 cottages is identical (only one is next to the sand), with king-size beds facing the view and adorned with mosquito nets. Straw mats, lots of pillows, and very attractive Indonesian furniture like day beds fill the space. Amenities include CD player, TV/VCR, minibar, coffeemaker, and a/c. The bathrooms have an outdoor shower, and on the terrace is your own plunge pool. The main area has a thatched-roof restaurant (again, with lots of sexy Indonesian accents), and there is a large common-area pool. The beach is small but wonderful and uncrowded. Although there's a lot of high style, there's not much attitude — the place sells a laid-back vibe.

The restaurant — which blends Italian, Caribbean, and Asian elements in its menu — is quite expensive, but we had a very enjoyable meal here. For the moment, this is Grenada's exclusive encounter with the glam sensibilities found in places like St. Barth.

Spice Island Beach Resort, P.O. Box 6, Grand Anse Beach, St. George's, Grenada, WI. Ⓒ 800-742-4276 or 473-444-4258, ✆ 473-444-4807, 🖳 www.spicebeachresort.com, spiceisl@caribsurf.com

💲 **Stratospheric** ⑪ **All-Inclusive** (spa, motorized watersports and diving extra) ⒸⒸ 64 rooms

Situated on the south end of beautiful Grande Anse , this resort used the ransacking from Hurricane Ivan to completely upgrade the property, to the tune of $12 million, reopening in early 2006. Beachfront rooms were torn down and rebuilt at 720 square feet (50 percent larger than before). As before, the resort offers a variety of suites with private pools, whirlpools, saunas, and beachfront views; the amenities have been upgraded to include Philippe Starck fixtures, Frette linens, and Molton Brown products. All rooms have minibars, hairdryers, a/c, ceiling fans, radios, telephones, safes, coffeemakers, beach towels, chaise lounges, and a patio or balcony. There are pool suites that have a semiprivate pool (somewhat larger than a plunge pool) and a terrace for sunning — sweet! If you stay in one of the beach suites, your chaise lounge will be brought out to the beach for you each morning.

Meals are served in the open-air beachfront restaurant (you might have to do a Tippi Hedren at breakfast to keep the birds from stealing your food). The food is standard continental fare along with a nice touch of local dishes, including a Grenadian Night (Wednesday), when a buffet of wonderful local foods and live entertainment are provided. There's a small fitness center and spa and an appealing free-form pool. You'll also find Spice Island Divers, a complete dive and water-sports facility. The clientele tends to be a bit older (like, over 50), although there's even a wedding package complete with cake, photos, and a best man or maid of honor. How about offering a bride or groom, too?

Bel Air Plantation, St. David's, Grenada, WI. ✆ 473-444-6305, 📧 473-444-6316, 🖥 www.belairplantation.com, belair@caribsurf.com

💰 **Wicked Pricey** 🍴 **EP** ⒸⒸ 11 rooms

Overlooking St. David's Harbour, a small marina, this intimate resort opened in 2003 on the site of Grenada's first European settlement, where the French landed in 1650. American developer Susan Fisher chose the lush, 18-acre, Atlantic-facing peninsula—located just south of La Sagesse—as a refuge from busy beachfront resorts and named it after her mother's one-time plantation in Guyana. The 11 cottages and villas are fringed in gingerbread and vibrant colors, equipped with kitchens, locally crafted furniture, original island art, and bathrooms replete with Jacuzzi tubs and tiles from Italy and Portugal. Each unit is positioned to maximize both privacy and the panorama of the bay from a veranda. The pathways are made from nutmeg shells, and considerable attention has been paid to landscaping—20 different varieties of hibiscus for starters, and the nursery grows sugar apples, Surinam cherries, and herbs and vegetables for the restaurant. Activities include a swimming pool, day sails, and snorkeling (when the water is calm); there's a restaurant serving delicious meals. There's no beach per se, and although it's a bit quiet for our tastes, it's still lovely.

Calabash, P.O. Box 382, L'Anse aux Epines, St. George's, Grenada, WI. ✆ 800-528-5835 or 473-444-4334, 📧 473-444-5050, 🖥 www.calabashhotel.com, calabash@caribsurf.com

💰 **Ridiculous** 🍴 **BP** ⒸⒸ 30 rooms

Calabash is perhaps Grenada's most deluxe digs, and the resort underwent a complete refurbishment in 2005. The two-story cottages house spacious suites, decorated with tropical prints and white tile floors—eight have a totally private plunge pool in back. Full breakfast is included in the rates, prepared and served by a maid in your room each morning. Located on 8 acres on tranquil L'Anse aux Epines Beach, the atmosphere here is casually English, and the grounds and beach are quite pleasant. There's a pool, a lighted tennis court, a full dive shop, an aromatherapy room, and a small gym, and afternoon tea is served daily. The restaurant is possibly the best on the island, with a top-flight wine cellar. The staff is attentive and upbeat; however, they're not much up on the "real" Grenada—another reason to ring Dennis Henry for island explorations. It's closed from September through mid-October.

La Sagesse Nature Centre, P.O. Box 44, St. David's, Grenada, WI. © 473-444-6458, ✉ 473-444-6458, 🖥 www.lasagesse.com, lsnature@caribsurf.com

💰 **Not So Cheap** 🍽 **EP** ©© 12 rooms

If you're looking for a quiet place to stay that's off the beaten track, La Sagesse might be for you. Located well away from the commotion of Grand Anse, La Sagesse is an informal country house next to a tranquil Atlantic-facing beach. The rebuilt Manor House contains the five original rooms, just 30 feet from the sand; one has a/c. There's a two-room cottage, and a new building has five additional spacious rooms, all facing the sea. All have minibars, and hairdryers and teakettles are available on request. There's a solid restaurant serving breakfast, lunch, and dinner. The swimming is decent, and there are kayaks, miles of nature trails, and 77 acres of banana fields and cow pastures to contemplate.

True Blue Bay Resort, P.O. Box 1414, Prickly Bay, Grenada, WI. © 888-883-2482 or 473-443-8783, ✉ 473-444-5929, 🖥 www.truebluebay.com, mail@truebluebay.com

💰 **Not So Cheap** 🍽 **CP** ©© 31 rooms

If you don't mind the absence of a beach, this spot is a worthy option overlooking Prickly Bay, near the medical school and airport. Least expensive of the 31 rooms are bay view units or "tree top" rooms wrapped by almond and mahogany trees; all have kitchen or kitchenette, a/c, and balconies, and all are well appointed in teak and bright tropical colors. Hobie cats and kayaks are free to guests, and two pools, a children's playground, a marina, a dive shop, and a popular restaurant and bar round out the facilities. It's a well-run operation.

Lance aux Epines Cottages, P.O. Box 1187, St. George's, Grenada, WI. © 877-444-4565 or 473-444-4565, ✉ 473-444-2802, 🖥 www.laecottages.com, reservations@laecottages.com

💰 **Pricey** 🍽 **EP** ©© 11 units

We're not sure why they choose to spell L'Anse the way they do, but we like the beautiful coconut palm-studded grounds and the nice beach out front that offers lots of shade (shared with Calabash). This property features attractive stone and wrought-iron cottages with green tin roofs — behind them is a two-story block of apartments. All are screened and have fully equipped kitchens, ceiling fans, one or two air-conditioned bedrooms, and TV. Also included is full maid service — she'll clean, cook, and do light laundry, a definite plus. There's little on-site beyond the front desk, but the friendly family management will make any arrangements you need; six restaurants and a dive shop are within walking distance.

Blue Horizons Cottage Hotel, P.O. Box 41, St. George's, Grenada, WI.
   © 473-444-4316, ✎ 473-444-2815,
   🖳 www.grenadabluehorizons.com, blue@caribsurf.com
  💲 **Pricey** ⑪ **EP** Ⓒ🄲 32 rooms

Nestled within 6 acres of lawns and gardens and with a private aviary featuring 21 species of tropical birds, Blue Horizon is a good value. The cottage-style rooms are set a few hundred feet behind Grand Anse — 6 are studio units and 26 are one-bedroom suites. All have a/c, ceiling fan, color TV, hairdryer, telephone, clock radio, and kitchenette featuring a refrigerator, stove, and ample counter space. You can partake in various beach activities offered at its sister property, Spice Island Beach Resort (an added bonus). The hotel has a renowned restaurant, La Belle Creole, which features nouvelle West Indian cuisine.

The Flamboyant Hotel, P.O. Box 214, St. George's, Grenada, WI.
   © 800-223-9815 or 473-444-4247, ✎ 473-444-1234,
   🖳 www.flamboyant.com, flambo@caribsurf.com
  💲 **Pricey** ⑪ **EP** Ⓒ🄲 61 cottages and apartments

The name alone is reason to stay here (it's actually the name of a brilliant flowering tree found in these parts). The Flamboyant is a complex of 61 cottages and apartments on a hill, with a terrific view of Grand Anse and St. George's in the distance. They are functional in design (but nothing more), and come with one or two bedrooms, kitchenette, living and dining room, and front porch from which to enjoy the view. The grounds are nicely landscaped, and a footpath offers a three-minute walk down to the beach. There's a restaurant, bar, and pool, along with a full-service dive shop. Watch for Web specials.

Grenada Grand Beach Resort, P.O. Box 441, Grand Anse Beach, Grenada, WI. © 473-444-4371, ✎ 473-444-4800, 🖳 www.grenadagrand.com, paradise@grenadagrand.com
  💲 **Very Pricey** ⑪ **EP** Ⓒ🄲 245 rooms

If you want a big, comfortable, no-surprises resort, this is a good choice. Located in the middle of Grand Anse Beach — the best spot on the best beach in Grenada — this hotel delivers ample tropical setting, and as big resorts go, it's not bad-looking, particularly since the addition of a huge free-form swimming pool with waterfalls and greenery touches. The 185 original rooms, situated in two-story wings, are a decent size and attractive, with a/c, balcony or veranda, phone, satellite TV, and room service. An expansion of the resort in 2002 added 60 new rooms in an adjacent four-story building overlooking the beach; we wish they had done something less lofty, but the view is nice. There are two lighted tennis courts, all water sports, and an activities desk, plus two restaurants and three bars. The clientele here tends to be younger than at some of the neighboring resorts, except when a convention rolls into town and takes over the resort's copious meeting facilities.

Coral Cove Cottages and Apartments, P.O. Box 487, L'Anse aux Epines, St. George's, Grenada, WI. © 473-444-4422, ✆ 473-444-4718, 💻 www.coralcovecottages.com, coralcv@spiceisle.com

💲 **Not So Cheap** 🍽 **EP** CC 11 cottages and apartments

This is a nice little place on the water, located in a quiet residential area punctuated by foreign embassies. The guests have a choice of 11 simple but comfortable cottages or apartments, all with fully equipped kitchens, lanais, maid service, and ceiling fans. There are one- and two-bedroom units available, making this a great family option. The beach is not much, and in early summer the grounds tend to look a little dried out, but it is private and the snorkeling is good. There is also a tennis court and pool for your leisure.

Wave Crest Holiday Apartments, P.O. Box 278, St. George's, Grenada, WI. © and ✆ 473-444-4116, 💻 www.grenadawavecrest.com, wavecrest@caribsurf.com

💲 **Cheap** 🍽 **EP** CC 18 units

Situated on a residential hillside behind Grand Anse, Wave Crest is a good deal, with attentive managers. The rooms have a/c, verandas, and basic kitchens. Furnishings are a little tired but adequate for anyone on a no-frills vacation. The beach is a 10-minute walk, and grocery stores and restaurants are nearby; note that there's a fair amount of road traffic during the day.

Where to Eat

There is not a huge selection of great restaurants, but there are a few good places.

$$$$ **Aquarium**, Pink Gin Beach, 473-444-1410

This is one of our favorite hangouts in the Caribbean. A driveway heads down a gully to a parking lot and path, leading into a grottolike setting trimmed by a waterfall on one side and a gorgeous beach on the other. Lunch is the perfect time to experience it all, when you can arrange for a kayak or snorkeling spin before your meal; on Sunday there's a lobster barbecue. The food is satisfying and dependable, if a bit expensive, but the ambiance, replete with great music, is perfect. Closed on Monday.

$$$ **Coconut Beach**, Grand Anse, 473-444-4644

Located on the beach in a wonderful old funky house (scalped by Ivan), this establishment features good Creole cuisine and quite a number of lobster dishes in a romantic yet casual setting. Reservations are suggested. Closed on Tuesday.

$$ **De Big Fish**, True Blue, 473-439-4401

Here, you'll find a nice open-air ambiance on a waterfront dock at the Spice Island Marina with a menu encompassing grilled fish, entrée salads, and outstanding cheeseburgers.

$$$$ **La Belle Creole**, Blue Horizon Cottage Hotel, Grand Anse, 473-444-4316

This spot in Grand Anse features heavy, rich West Indian food (local dishes with a Continental flourish). We think it's expensive for what you get, and the service is a bit stuffy. Reservations are required.

$$ **La Sagesse**, La Sagesse Nature Centre, 473-444-6458

The restaurant at this hideaway tenders delicious seafood and sandwiches at modest prices. La Sagesse offers a smart day-trip package: round-trip transportation from any island hotel, a guided nature walk, and lunch (or dinner), all for $28 per person.

$$$$$ **Laluna**, Morne Rouge, 473-439-0001

Intimate, romantic, and pricey. If you've got a few extra bucks, Laluna's worth a splurge. It's Italian-meets-island with Asian accents and a great wine list.

$$ **Little Dipper**, Woburn, 473-444-5136

The Little Dipper faces Hog Island on the way to La Sagesse. We haven't tried it yet, but we hear this is a terrific local restaurant for seafood. It has just four tables, so reservations are advised.

$$ **Morne Fendue Plantation Great House**, St. Patrick's Parish, 473-442-9330

A classic old plantation house, Morne Fendue is located in the heart of Grenada's northern hills. The house is made of gray stone with wrought-iron grillwork and huge poinsettias in the circular driveway. When you arrive for lunch, you are greeted and sent to the washroom to freshen up. The cuisine is traditional West Indian: callaloo soup, oxtail and cow tongue, seasoned rice, chicken, christophene, and papaya custard and cream are typical fare. Morne Fendue was the home of Betty Mascol for most of the 20th century, but she passed away in 1998. The home was purchased by Jean Thompson, who carries on the tradition of this time-honored establishment. Lunch is about $15; reservations are required. No credit cards.

$$ **The Nutmeg**, on the Carenage, St. George's, 473-440-2539

The rum punch is fantastic, which might be the best reason to come here. The food is decent, the place is clean, and the second floor offers commendable views of the harbor. The fish specials and *lambi* (conch) are recommended, and be sure to check out the nutmeg ice cream. This is a great spot for breakfast and lunch in town; dinner is also available.

$$$$ **Rhodes**, Calabash Hotel, L'Anse aux Epines, 473-444-4344

With a seasonally inspired menu developed by London-based celebrity chef Gary Rhodes, this posh new spot serves possibly the island's finest food — its seafood is the freshest around. Reservations are required.

$$$ **True Blue**, True Blue Bay, 473-443-8783

Set on a dock over the water at the hotel of the same name, this spot is a terrific addition to the island's culinary scene. Meals like *lambi* linguini and tamarind shrimp have a decidedly Caribbean accent but Euro polish. It's popular for Sunday brunch, too. Reservations are advised.

Going Out

There are some fun things to do here at night. **Bananas in True Blue**, by the marina, has a popular Friday night party with a local DJ from about 11 p.m. **Fantazia Disco**, at the Gem Apartments on Morne Rouge Beach (473-444-1189), is the island's hot dance palace and is very popular with locals (no shorts). Wednesday is '70s disco music. For some old-fashioned fun, the local med heads frequent **Beachside Terrace** at the Flamboyant Hotel — on Monday there are crab races, whereas Wednesday, Saturday, and Sunday feature live music.

Don't Miss

Henry's Safari Tours
You won't be disappointed.

Foodland
If you have an efficiency, this is a great supermarket located in the Grand Anse Shopping Center.

Carriacou

Grenada's sister island is easy to visit on a day trip by ferry—or spend the night (for more info, see the Carriacou chapter in the Grenadines section).

Dive Grenada

This is the island's oldest dive shop, located on Grand Anse at the Flamboyant Hotel. It does trips to the *Bianca C*, the largest shipwreck in the Caribbean (a 584-foot Italian cruise-ship that went down in 1961 after a boiler explosion), and it is suitable for advanced divers. Easier sites, as well as daily snorkel excursions, are available for $25; two-tank dives are $80. Call 473-444-1092 or check out www.divegrenada.com for more info.

Grand Etang

This is an extinct volcanic crater nestled in the mountains above St. George's. On a clear day, this is a splendid sight, and a lovely trail circuits the lake. An eclectic mix of wildlife hangs out here, including mona monkeys, freshwater crayfish, and a variety of birds.

Saturday Marketplace in St. George's

Although the market is in place daily, the Saturday open-air market becomes a wonderful venue for glimpsing classic West Indian life. It's colorful, it's lively, it's tasty, and it's real. It's also a great place to shop (and bargain) for souvenirs. Go early, before the heat of the day saps your energy.

The Grenadines

TOURISTO SCALE:

BEQUIA 👤👤👤👤 (4)

CANOUAN 👤👤👤👤👤 (5)

CARRIACOU 👤👤👤 (3)

MUSTIQUE 👤👤👤👤 (4)

MAYREAU 👤👤 (2)

PALM ISLAND 👤👤 (2)

PETIT ST. VINCENT 👤 (1)

PETITE MARTINIQUE 👤 (1)

UNION ISLAND 👤👤 (2)

The 75-mile-long chain of islands strung between St. Vincent and Grenada, the Grenadines, is a yachters' dream — second only to the British Virgin Islands as the Caribbean's prime sailing destination. There are several dozen islands in the archipelago; most of them are uninhabited and can be explored on day trips, providing great opportunities for snorkeling, scuba diving, beachcombing, and picnics.

The islands belong to two countries: St. Vincent and the Grenadines are one (and often called SVG), and Grenada is the other. Several of the islands are home to some of the most amazing resorts in the Caribbean. The first of the major islands encountered heading south from St. Vincent is Bequia, the second most populated of the Grenadines and perhaps the most captivating. Next is Mustique, home of the rich, famous, and fabulous; Canouan, the location of the first mega-resort in the Grenadines; Mayreau, still a real gem and another favorite; Union Island, spectacular from a distance, a bit boring up close, but a good base for exploring the neighboring islands without blowing the bank; Palm Island, where a classic hideaway has been revitalized; and Petit St. Vincent, or PSV, a truly private old-money getaway. Just beyond PSV is a popular stop on the cruising circuit, the unpopulated Tobago Cays, a mini-archipelago of five tiny islets with great beaches and snorkeling (lots of boats will be anchored offshore). The Tobago Cays can be reached on a memorable day trip from any of the Grenadines, set up by the resorts or using charter companies like Captain Yannis out of Union Island. As you continue south, the Grenadian border is crossed upon reaching Petite Martinique (perhaps an old flame of Petit St. Vincent?), the reputed smuggling capital of the West Indies. Next is Carriacou, the largest of the Grenadines but a true step back in time. Finally, there is the island of Grenada, signaling the southern conclusion of the chain. (St. Vincent and Grenada, the much bigger "anchor" islands and the two governing bodies of this archipelago, each has its own chapter in this book.)

Getting to the Grenadines

The Grenadines are small islands and have small airports (if any at all), and therefore you'll have to reach them via connecting flights from their larger neighbors. This inconvenience has a payoff: Development in the Grenadines has stayed small and low-scale, whereas many other Caribbean islands have sold their souls to cement mixers and back hoes. So yes, you'll spend a little more time getting to the Grenadines, but we think the extra effort has a payoff.

At present, Carriacou and Petite Martinique are reached only via Grenada, which is served by American Eagle and Air Jamaica. Most people reach St. Vincent's Grenadines via Barbados, about 100 miles/160 kilometers to the east. Barbados is served by Air Jamaica, American, American Eagle, BWIA, and US Airways from the United States; by Air Canada and BWIA from Toronto; and by British Airways, BWIA, and Virgin Atlantic from London. The three carriers flying from Barbados to Bequia, Canouan, Mustique, and Union islands are Mustique Airways, SVG Air, and TIA, which operate under the banner Grenadine Airways (www.grenadineairways.com). Round-trip fare from Barbados is currently about $330, with Mustique being somewhat higher. The government of St. Vincent and the Grenadines maintains a small tourism desk at the Barbados airport that is open from about 1 p.m. until the last flight to the Grenadines departs. The staff at the desk can assist with connections and hotel reservations. Alas, many North American residents cannot make it to the Grenadines in one day, so an overnight in Barbados may be necessary (see the Barbados chapter for lodging options). It's also possible to fly from San Juan to Canouan on American Eagle.

There are also ferry services that run from St. Vincent south to Union (with stops along the way in Bequia, Canouan, and Mayreau), and from Grenada north to Carriacou and Petite Martinique. Details on the ferries are listed in each chapter. Crossing the border between the two countries is most easily accomplished using the smaller airlines listed above, although water taxis can be hired on both Union and Carriacou.

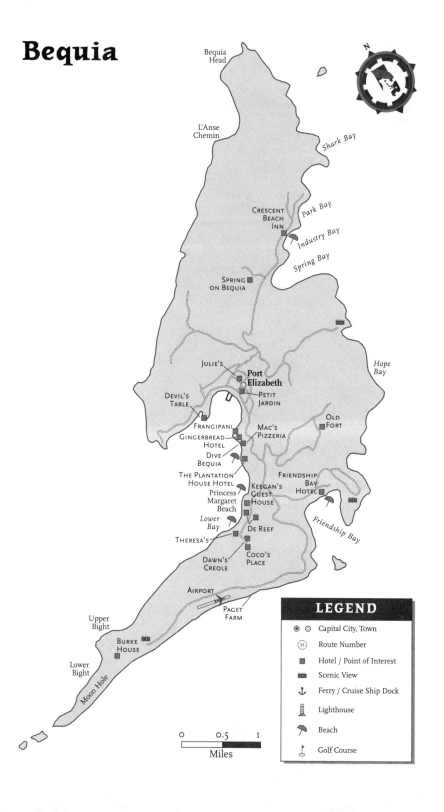

Bequia

Bequia
Head

L'Anse
Chemin

Shark Bay

CRESCENT
BEACH
INN

Park Bay

Industry Bay

Spring Bay

SPRING
ON BEQUIA

Hope
Bay

JULIE'S

**Port
Elizabeth**

DEVIL'S
TABLE

PETIT
JARDIN

OLD
FORT

FRANGIPANI

MAC'S
PIZZERIA

GINGERBREAD
HOTEL

DIVE
BEQUIA

THE PLANTATION
HOUSE HOTEL

FRIENDSHIP
BAY
HOTEL

KEEGAN'S
GUEST
HOUSE

Princess
Margaret
Beach

Lower
Bay

DE REEF

Friendship Bay

THERESA'S

DAWN'S
CREOLE

COCO'S
PLACE

AIRPORT

PAGET
FARM

Upper
Bight

BURKE
HOUSE

Lower
Bight

Moon Hole

0   0.5   I

Miles

LEGEND

◉ ◎	Capital City, Town
⑫	Route Number
■	Hotel / Point of Interest
📷	Scenic View
⚓	Ferry / Cruise Ship Dock
🗼	Lighthouse
⛱	Beach
⛳	Golf Course

Bequia

SITTING AT THE BAR AT THE FRANGIPANI ENJOYING A "HAPPY" Hairoun, the Vincentian brew, on our first visit to Bequia (pronounced "BECK-wee") back in 1987, we unwittingly revealed to the woman next to us that we were travel writers. She stiffened and brusquely requested that we not write anything about Bequia. "We don't need or want any more tourists," she said with conviction. It's the typical response of a seasonal resident who wants to slam the door in the face of any new arrival, but as we got to know Bequia, the northernmost of the Grenadines, we began to agree with her. This island is extraordinary—we would hate to see it spoiled. So it was with great reluctance and profuse apologies that we brought Bequia to light in the first edition of *Rum & Reggae's Caribbean*. After all these years, it is still relatively unspoiled and has managed to retain its magical charm.

The best way to describe Bequia is as the quintessential Caribbean experience—a harmony of all the elements that make the islands special. It is pretty, clean, and small enough to get to know intimately. The local residents are very friendly and responsive. There are handsome beaches, good restaurants, lots of bars and shops, and accommodations that are very reasonably priced. A sea orientation and a yachty element add the perfect touch to the island's ambiance.

For such a small place, Bequia is surprisingly lively. It's easy to spend a week here and not be bored. The action revolves around the waterfront of **Port Elizabeth**, starting at the ferry dock and winding around the **Belmont Walkway** to **Princess Margaret Beach** (also known as Tony Gibbons Beach). Here you can browse in a small but intelligent bookshop, buy fresh fruit and vegetables from Rastas, have a few drinks, check out the brown coral jewelry displayed by sidewalk vendors, dance to pan music, eat lobster pizza, go scuba diving, buy T-shirts and other clothes, have more drinks, and go for a swim at a pretty beach—all in a half-mile stretch.

Bequia has a great mix of people, too. In addition to the welcoming locals, there are all kinds of interesting visitors. The island has always attracted an artsy element. The late Sanford Meisner, the famed acting teacher, maintained a house here and often conducted classes and seminars on Bequia. Many artists spend the winter here, finding more than enough inspiration from the surroundings. There are many Europeans, especially Germans,

Bequia: Key Facts

Location	13°N by 60°W 9 miles/15 kilometers south of St. Vincent 2,050 miles/3,299 kilometers southeast of New York
Size	7 square miles/11 square kilometers 5 miles/8 kilometers long by 3 miles/5 kilometers wide
Highest point	Belle Pointe, 881 feet/269 meters
Population	4,861
Language	English
Time	Atlantic Standard Time (1 hour ahead of EST, same as EDT)
Area code	784
Electricity	220 volts AC, 50 cycles, so you'll need an adapter and transformer
Currency	The Eastern Caribbean dollar, EC$ (EC$2.68 = US$1)
Driving	On the left; you'll need a temporary permit, which costs $28 — just present your valid U.S. or Canadian driver's license and pay the fee.
Documents	All U.S. and Canadian citizens must have a valid passport and a return or an ongoing ticket.
Departure tax	$15
Beer to drink	Hairoun
Rum to drink	Any Vincentian brand
Music to hear	Dancehall
Tourism info	On-island: 784-458-3286; in New York: 800-729-1726 www.bequiatourism.com

who seem to love the island's mellow pace. The North Americans who visit tend to be more sophisticated (if less demanding) than, say, the average tourists who go to Aruba. Bequia appeals to independent travelers (that's you) who are looking for a low-key yet stimulating environment to shake off and forget whatever pressures they have in their everyday worlds. Finally, there are the boat people — the cocktail cruisers who come in on their yachts or charter boats and love to have a good time. They add a little zip and glamour to the mix.

There have been a few changes on Bequia since our first visit. The most anticipated was the opening of the airport in 1992. Built with a grant from the European Community, it made getting here in one day possible from both North America and Europe. Thankfully, the fear of hordes of tourists overrunning the island never materialized. Cruise ships arrive these days, but they're of the smaller variety — fewer than 200 passengers, for the most part — and they tend not to overwhelm the island's modest infrastructure. Other changes here include the reclamation of the Belmont Walkway, which winds along Admiralty Bay and connects the waterfront shops, restaurants, and hotels from the center of town to the Plantation House Hotel. Where once ocean surge and boat wake used to pelt the protective seawall, there are now a few feet of beach. The walkway makes for a great stroll along the bay at sunset (cocktail in hand, of course). Bequia's old ferry schooner, *Friendship Rose*, was refurbished and now makes wonderful day excursions to Mustique, the Tobago Cays, and St. Vincent. There's even a FedEx office — albeit a tiny one!

The Briefest History

Not much is known about Amerindian settlements on Bequia until the 1600s, when the Caribs inhabited an island they called Becouya, which means "Island of the Clouds" (a strange name for this rather dry island — perhaps it was rainy on the day it was named). There is no record of Columbus sighting the island on any of his voyages. Bequia was left in peace by the warring European navies in the region. Then in 1675, the slave ship *Palmira* sank off the island, and some of the slaves on board escaped and were welcomed by the Caribs. As a result of the intermarriage of Caribs and runaway African slaves, the tribe became known as Black Caribs. They used Bequia as a staging port for attacks on the Yellow Caribs of St. Vincent. The French soon claimed the settlement and all of the Grenadines. The French also imported slaves, many of whom escaped and went into St. Vincent's mountains and joined the Black Caribs. The result for the French was too many headaches and battles with the Black Caribs, so the islands were declared neutral between France and Britain in the Treaty of Aix-la-Chapelle in 1748. Of course, treaties were meant to be broken, and the two battled it out until finally, in 1783, the Treaty of Versailles deeded the islands to the British. One last gasp by the allied forces of the Black Caribs and the French failed to dislodge the British, and most of the Black Caribs were shipped off to Roatan (near Honduras). In 1871 the islands became a part of the British Windward Islands, and in 1979 St. Vincent and the Grenadines achieved independent statehood within the British Commonwealth.

Getting There

Bequia's major gateway is Barbados, which lies about 100 miles to the east (see Getting to the Grenadines at the beginning of this chapter). Once in Barbados, connect to TIA, Mustique Airways, or SVG Air for the 55-minute flight to Bequia. You can also fly from St. Vincent on these airlines, or, you can take a short taxi ride from the St. Vincent airport to the ferry dock in Kingstown and ride over on one of the small ships that ply the Grenadines. There are up to eight ferries a day making the trip (fewer on weekends), the fare is a bargain $8 ($13 round-trip), and the one-hour crossing is just long enough to be enjoyable but not so long as to induce seasickness. Departure times change, so check with the tourist office for exact schedules (784-458-3286).

Getting Around

Bequia is a small island, and you can walk everywhere if you enjoy getting out on foot. However, there are some hills to climb and descend to get to the other side, so you may want to take a taxi on your first day to get oriented; your hotel can call one for you. Other options are the public minivans that ply the main roads (fares are $1 almost anywhere), or your thumb. There are three car-rental agencies on the island: B&G Jeep Rental (784-458-3760), Phil's Car Rental (784-458-3304), and Sunset Rentals (784-458-3782). Prices are a bit steep — averaging about $50 for a day, and you'll have to pay $28 for a local driver's license — but lower rates are available for longer rentals, and you can sometimes wheel and deal in the off-season. Water taxis will take you from town or the Frangipani dock to Princess Margaret Beach or Lower Bay for $5.

Focus on Bequia: Exploring the Magic

It's easy to become possessive about Bequia because it is a small island that can become very familiar in a week. After discovering the magic of the island, you begin to feel that it's your own. So definitely get out and see it. There are walks that will take you to just about anywhere on Bequia in an hour or less. Port Elizabeth, where most of the hotels are, is not only the island's hub but its center as well — all roads lead to town. The walks are fairly easy, up over the hills to the other side.

Our favorite walk is to **Industry**, although the name is a misnomer if ever there was one. Leaving town on the road to Spring, you will climb over the hill and come upon an old sugar mill ruin, overgrown with hibiscus and bougainvillea, on the left — a good photo op. It is then a pleasant walk through tall coconut trees, acres of them, with the usually deserted Spring beach off to the right. The road follows the curve of a bluff, offering terrific views of Petit Nevis and Mustique. It quietly descends into more coconut groves and Industry Beach. There is a bar at the Crescent Beach Inn where you can quaff a rum punch before heading back, and the swimming here is also good.

Continue a little farther to **Orton "Brother" King's Oldhegg Turtle Sanctuary** in Park Bay. King started the sanctuary in 1995 to raise endangered hawksbill hatchlings brought to him from neighboring islands. His facility houses turtles until they are three years old, when they are released into the sea — more than 500 to date. A $5 donation is suggested. For the industrious, there is a hike from here to Bequia Head on cow paths. This should be attempted only with ample daylight. People get lost, so be sure of the way back and wear good walking shoes.

Another area worth exploring is **Moonhole**, an innovative development on the western end of Bequia. Designed and built by the late Tom Johnston starting in the 1960s, it strives to blend with its natural surroundings, and to a great degree it succeeds. The stone used in the walls matches the cliffs and gullies where they are built, and a lot of the construction is actually poured concrete. At first sight it looks as though the developer ran out of money. The complex looks unfinished; there is no glass in the window, no color except for gray stone and metal. Yet that is the architect's intention — to achieve harmony with the striking natural setting. The centerpiece of this creation is Moonhole, a huge natural arch that, it is said, frames the full moon. Underneath the arch is a terrace and a wood and stone house that hasn't been used in many years (due to falling rocks from the arch). It is weather-beaten and dilapidated but still adorned with relics from when Tom Johnston and his wife lived there (it is the first house they built). It's a bit odd but still stunning. To get to Moonhole, take the road to Friendship, and at the top of the hill follow the right fork (the left takes you down to the Friendship Bay Hotel). The road will hug the coast through La Pompe and Paget Farm. You'll pass Bequia's airport. Keep going and you'll eventually reach the entrance to Moonhole. Be as discreet as the designers were — this is not meant to be a tourist attraction.

A third walk takes you to **Hope Bay** and a totally deserted beach that is perfect for nude sunbathing. For this one, you'll want to take a taxi to the Old Fort — at one time an inn and now a private villa — and arrange for a pickup later. Bring water and other refreshment, for it is a long way down the mountain and a hot way back up. The friendly folks at the Old Fort will direct you to the path. The trail is not difficult, but you will sweat a little. Once at the beach, use caution swimming, because the water can be rough. If you want privacy, there is the ruin of an old mill on the north side of the beach, which is perfect for some hanky-panky if you are so inclined. When you return, be sure to have a rum punch as your reward for a job well done.

If you want to explore what's under the water, there is **Dive Bequia** (800-525-3833 or 784-458-3504; www.bequiadive.com). This is a very laid-back operation in the most "for sure" southern California style. Run by Bob Sachs, Dive Bequia offers anything from snorkel trips, resort courses, and PADI certification to night dives and underwater videos of yourself doing a Lloyd Bridges imitation. Bob has great T-shirts for sale, too. The other dive shop on the island is **Bequia Dive Adventures** (784-458-3286; www.bequiadiveadventures.com), which also offers boat dives, equipment rental, NAUI or PADI certification, snorkeling, and sailing trips. Certainly one of them will satisfy any *Sea Hunt* urges.

Where to Stay

There are a few more options for staying on Bequia these days. Most are very reasonably priced and quite satisfactory. Prices on Bequia are still lower than on the more resort-oriented Grenadines to the south. So who's complaining?

The Frangipani, P.O. Box 1, Bequia, St. Vincent and the Grenadines, WI. © 784-458-3255, ❦ 784-458-3824, ▣ www.frangipanibequia.com, frangi@caribsurf.com

🛍 **Cheap** for the main house, **Not So Cheap** for the Garden Units, and **Pricey** for the Deluxe rooms ⑪ **EP** 🆑 15 rooms

Always a favorite place of ours, the Frangi (as it is affectionately called) is our first choice for accommodations on Bequia. Owned by the former prime minister of St. Vincent and The Grenadines, Sir James ("Son") Mitchell, and well run and maintained by manager Sabrina Mitchell, the Frangipani sits on a point in the middle of the Belmont Walkway and seems to be the hub of the island. Because it is the center of attention, especially with the yachty set, there are people either marching by or sitting at its busy bar all day long. It's just a social kind of place. The old main house, with its trademark red roof, has several rooms with shared cold-water bathrooms and furnished with mahogany antiques (room 1 is where Sir Mitchell was born). The newer Garden Units are made of stone and wood; though set back from the water, they are much larger, more spacious and private, and have sundecks. The Deluxe rooms are bigger, with a/c, and have terrific views of the harbor. On Thursday night, there is a barbecue and buffet with decent pan bands for jump-up. Get there early because the music stops around 11 p.m., as does most activity on Bequia. The Frangi also has a 44-foot cutter (sailboat) called the *Pelangi*, which is available for day or multiday charters ($240 per day for up to four).

Spring on Bequia, Spring Bay, Bequia, St. Vincent and the Grenadines, WI. © 612-823-1202 or 784-458-3414, ❦ 784-457-3305, ▣ www.springonbequia.com, springonbequia@caribsurf.com

🛍 **Not So Cheap** with good discounts for singles ⑪ **EP** 🆑 9 rooms

If you want real quiet (i.e., seclusion) with extraordinary views, stay at Spring. Situated on a hillside amid the ruins of an old sugar mill and acres of coconut palms, this is one of the most peaceful (some might call it dead) places to stay anywhere. The airy design of stone and wood blends wonderfully with the surroundings. This is a reader's and meditator's heaven. The rooms are simple and minimally furnished, yet they're comfortable and consistent with the tranquillity of this inn. Most have views of the uninhabited islands of Baliceaux and Battowia from their lanais. There is a restaurant serving all meals, including a very popular Sunday curry brunch (reservations necessary). A pretty pool and a clay tennis court are on the grounds for your leisure, and the wonderful walks and beaches of Spring and Industry are steps away. A **MAP** plan is available for an additional $45 per day per person. Closed from mid-June through October.

The Gingerbread Hotel, P.O. Box 191, Bequia, St. Vincent and the Grenadines, WI. ℂ 784-458-3800, ✆ 784-458-3907, 🖥 www.gingerbreadhotel.com, ginger@caribsurf.com

💰 **Pricey** 🍴 **EP** 🆑 9 rooms

Right next to the Frangipani on Admiralty Bay and the Belmont Walkway is the Gingerbread. Long a popular restaurant with a few apartments for rent, the Gingerbread added its Bequia Suites in 1998. Like its namesake, it has abundant quaintness, with ginger-bread-style buildings and manicured gardens surrounded by a stone wall. The latter provides a welcome sense of seclusion from the harbor hubbub. Suites come with a fully equipped kitchen, bath, adjoining salon, and large lanai. The upper-level suites have king-size beds smack dab in the middle of the room. The bed as the focal point of your vacation? Hey, not such a bad idea! The ground-level suites feature twin beds, and a third bed is available in each room ("Honey, do we have to bring the kids?"). The hotel has a beachside cafe, great for ice cream or java jive, and the main restaurant is upstairs.

The Plantation House Hotel, P.O. Box 16, Admiralty Bay, Bequia, St. Vincent and the Grenadines, WI. ℂ 784-458-3425, ✆ 784-458-3612, 🖥 www.hotel-plantation.com, info@hotel-plantation.net

💰 **Very Pricey** 🍴 **CP** 🆑 27 rooms

Ideally situated between a stellar beach and the diversion of the waterfront, this is the most expensive place to stay on Bequia and caters to the French and Italian market. The establishment, a symphony of pink and turquoise, offers two choices for lodging: 5 rooms in the main house and 22 cabanas dotting the grounds. The cabanas, especially those around the coconut tree–studded common, offer the most room and privacy. Each cabana has a small veranda, ceiling fan, a/c, satellite TV, phone, and fridge.

However, the Plantation House has seen better days and could use a face-lift—particularly the room furnishings. Our twin beds sagged, and the pillows were as fluffy as a sack of flour. At these rates, we expect to sleep comfortably. The main house has a wraparound arched veranda where meals are served. Fortunately the manicured grounds are lush and pleasant, so sipping a cocktail in the shade of a palm tree makes up for some of the hotel's deficiencies. There is a small but attractive raised kidney-shaped pool, along with the Greenflash Bar & Restaurant at the water's edge. A tiny beach with chaise lounges is tucked in front of the bar, but it's worth the five-minute walk over the point to HRH Maggie's Beach. The Plantation House hosts a popular barbecue night on Tuesdays at the Greenflash, replete with a reggae-soca band.

Julie's Guest House, P.O. Box 12, Port Elizabeth, Bequia, St. Vincent and the Grenadines, WI. © 784-458-3304, ✆ 784-458-3812, 🖳 julies@caribsurf.com

🛍 **Cheap** 🍴 **MAP (EP also available)** ⒸⒸ 19 rooms

Julie's is still one of the best deals in the Caribbean, and even though this guesthouse was undergoing a renovation as we went to press, we suspect that when the work is complete it will still be a bargain. For under $100 a night, you get a room with breakfast and dinner. The rooms are very simple, with firm platform double beds, mosquito nets, blond wood, bright wall colors, newly tiled floors, and private baths. All the rooms in the front building now have a/c. The food is good West Indian fare and, again, very simple. You really enjoy the meals here because the whole place is such a bargain that the food seems free.

Julie's is not on the beach; it's one block from the harbor in a residential neighborhood. You'll hear dogs barking and roosters crowing at all times (especially as you try to fall asleep). The "lullaby of Bequia" usually starts in the middle of the night with either an all-dog or an all-rooster chorus. The animals sing a duet that builds to a cacophony and then gradually winds down. You get used to it.

The people who stay here are an interesting bunch and are usually repeaters. This is not a place to be antisocial. There is a bar where a bunch of Julie's friends listen to the cricket matches. The staff is courteous and very friendly, especially when you introduce yourself.

Keegan's Guest House and Apartments, Lower Bay, Bequia, St. Vincent and the Grenadines, WI. © 784-458-3530, ✆ 784-457-3313, 🖳 www.keegansbequia.com (might be under construction), keegansbequia@yahoo.com

🛍 **Cheap** 🍴 **MAP (guesthouse), EP (apartments)** ⒸⒸ 12 units

Another great Bequia deal, this is your best bet if you want cheap accommodations at the beach with meals. Keegan's Guest House is less than 100 yards from a great and really fun beach, Lower Bay. Being a guesthouse, it has very simple rooms, but they do have private baths, ceiling fans, and mosquito nets, and you'll get breakfast and dinner with your room. The three apartments, located just across the street from the Lower Bay beach and De Reef Bar & Restaurant, are also a great value. These spacious one- and two-bedroom units are decently furnished and feature private baths and fully equipped kitchens. Keegan's restaurant serves good West Indian fare, and there are several other options right in Lower Bay.

Crescent Beach Inn, Industry, Bequia, St. Vincent and the Grenadines,
   WI. ℂ 784-458-3400

💲 **Cheap** 🍽 **BP** 3 rooms

We discovered this out-of-the-way place on a trip to Industry Bay. Set
right on a deserted beach and completely surrounded by coconut palms,
this is a spartan and very low-key kind of place. The three simple
rooms flank a large pavilion with a bar and a Ping-Pong table. Breakfast comes with the package, but don't expect much more. If Zen is
your style and hanging out on the beach, reading, or meditation is
what you're into, this might work for you. If you need a ride into
town, just ask Ricky (one of the owners) — he has a taxi business as
well. The inn also has a fun Full-Moon Barbecue with live music, held
on — you guessed it. No credit cards.

Burke House, P.O. Box 1, Bequia, St. Vincent and the Grenadines, WI.
   ℂ 784-457-3509, ✆ 784-458-3943, 🖳 www.burke-house.com,
   info@burke-house.com

💲 **$1,375** per week (includes accommodations for four and daily maid
service, cook, and laundress CC 2 bedrooms

This is a private home owned by John and Lusan Corbett (they live up
the path in another house). Situated 100 feet above sea level in the
famed (and restricted) Moonhole development, this very secluded
house was built in the 1960s by Tom Johnston. It's made of stone
and purple heartwood and resembles something out of Bedrock (no
glass in the windows). Vaulted stone ceilings enclose a living and din-
ing-kitchen area and two bedrooms, each with bath (the master bath
has one of the best views from the loo we've ever seen — talk about a
nice place to contemplate!). Other views are spectacular, too, especially from the upper roof deck. To the north is volcanic St. Vincent,
and to the south are fabulous Mustique and the Grenadine chain.
There are no phones here, and although there's 110-volt lighting and
electricity, you'll also find plenty of lanterns and candles for those romantic evenings. A hammock on the south terrace beckons, and a
whalebone throne chair is available for the royalty among us. The
maid will take care of cooking chores — stop by one of the island's
markets after your arrival to stock up the fridge. One of Bequia's prettiest and most deserted beaches is a two-minute walk from the house.

Where to Eat

If you're staying in town, avoid the hotel MAP plan because there are a
number of good restaurants to experience. Here are our dining choices.

$$$ **Coco's Place**, Lower Bay, 784-458-3463

Coco, a popular bartender, is the owner of this cool down-island pub and Bequian kitchen, with extensive à la carte and daily specials. He has satellite TV, live calypso on Friday, live string band on Tuesday, and happy hour from 6 to 7 p.m daily.

$$$ Dawn's Creole Bar and Restaurant, Lower Bay, 784-458-3154

Located on a hill at the far end of Lower Bay, Dawn's serves excellent West Indian Creole cuisine and seafood specialties. It's open for breakfast, lunch, and dinner, and a beach party is held on Sunday. Dinner reservations are a must.

$$ De Reef, Lower Bay, 784-458-3958

Since you're already on the beach, this is a convenient and casual place for lunch and cocktails. Dinners here are surprisingly good.

$$–$$$$ Devil's Table, Port Elizabeth, 784-458-3900

The Harpoon Saloon, at one time Bequia's most popular watering hole, has closed, but in 2005 this perky new Swedish-run restaurant opened its doors, so we'll stop complaining. Situated right at the water's edge and built into candle-adorned rocks—a lovely setting—the restaurant's menu has a seafaring theme. It actually has two menus: one called Pirate's Grub for those of us on a modest budget, the other called Admiral's Grub, with Black Angus steaks and the like. It's a little goofy, but we'll be back.

$$$ The Frangipani, Port Elizabeth, 784-458-3255

At the hub of the Belmont Walkway, the Frangi has consistently served good Caribbean cuisine at very fair prices for as long as we've been coming here. Reservations are suggested, especially for dinner.

$$$ The Gingerbread, Port Elizabeth, 784-458-3800

This is a Bequian institution, but the food is hardly institutional and is served in an airy second-floor dining room with views out onto the bay.

$$$$ Le Petit Jardin, Port Elizabeth, 784-458-3318

Probably Bequia's most expensive restaurant, Le Petit Jardin is located off the beaten track on Back Street. However, the cuisine, French with Creole flourishes, is excellent, and so is the service. Reservations are suggested. Closed Sunday.

$$$ ⊛ Mac's Pizzeria and Bake Shop, Port Elizabeth, 784-458-3474

Mac's is a must-stop when on Bequia, if only for Mac's mouthwatering lobster pizza. Perched on the Belmont Walkway with a breezy veranda, it is open for breakfast, lunch, and dinner. No stay on Bequia is complete without a pit stop here.

$$ **Theresa's**, Lower Bay Beach, 784-458-3802

Located at the base of the hill in Lower Bay, Theresa's will cook your own private Creole meal. You must call early in the day for a dinner reservation, because everything is bought and prepared to order. The Monday night international buffet is an island event not to be missed. No credit cards.

Don't Miss

Sailing the Grenadines

The nearby island of Mustique is a budget buster for most of us, but it's one of three enjoyable day trips available aboard the *Friendship Rose*, an 80-foot wooden schooner that formerly served as a Grenadine mail boat. The full day trip to Mustique, where you can bask on the beach in front of Mick Jagger's abode, costs just $100, including hot breakfast, lunch, afternoon tea, drinks, and snorkel equipment. Journey to the tropical coast of St. Vincent (to *Pirates of the Caribbean* shooting locations), or to the idyllic and uninhabited Tobago Cays, a 10-hour round-trip sail. Reservations: 784-495-0886; www.friendshiprose.com.

Also recommended by two of our readers—a honeymooning couple—is the sailing yacht *Myrick*, a 41-foot sloop that does multiday trips out of Bequia into the Grenadines. You can reach Captain Dwight Taylor at 784-458-3458; symyrick@yahoo.com.

Bequia Book Shop

Located on the waterfront across from the park, this features an excellent collection of West Indian writers and a good general selection. If it's maps and charts you're into, this is the place. Bequia Book Shop is owned by a very knowledgeable and polite ex-Bajan named Ian Gale, a good person to talk to about Caribbean authors. The store's logo T-shirt is a smart collector's item (as are the books). More information: 784-458-3905.

Mac's Pizzeria

On Tuesday night, Mac's throws a barbecue and jump-up with live bands.

Easter Regatta

This is a great time both on and off the racecourse. The racing is meant to be fun rather than competitive.

Industry Bay

Be sure to see this part of the island. It boasts lofty palm groves, a secluded beach, and a spectacular view of several nearby islands.

De Reef

For drinks in Lower Bay, go on Sunday afternoon.

The Frangipani

For drinks at the hub, go for the Thursday night jump-ups.

Canouan

WHEN WE FIRST STARTED TOOLING AROUND THE CARIBBEAN, Canouan was one of the more remote and undeveloped corners of the region. Not anymore. The island now ranks as one of the top luxury destinations in the Caribbean.

The multi-act story of Canouan's evolution began in 1991, when a group of Swiss and Italian investors created Canouan Resorts Development to acquire two-thirds of the island and adopt much of the Mustique model in developing the destination. Lavishing $160 million on Canouan, the company built desalination and electrical plants and a spiffy new airport. More than 100 multimillion-dollar villas — the key to Mustique's success — were drawn up, but the development's focal point was a 156-room resort, which debuted in 1999. Alas, on the road from sleepy backwater to tony resort, the project encountered a few potholes — problems large enough to force the operation into unexpected detours. When we visited in 2002, the resort had just closed. The management company, Rosewood Hotels & Resorts (of the fine Caneel Bay and Little Dix Bay operations in the Virgin Islands), had been fired, and lawsuits were filed. The problems weren't just with management, the original concept also had serious flaws, ranging from luxury rooms designed without air-conditioning to a golf course with only 13 holes.

So, two and a half years and another $39 million were spent reconceiving the resort and golf course, and Singapore-based Raffles International was brought in to manage the operation. The Trump Organization now runs the casino, golf course, and villa sales (more on that — and without any hairdo quips — in a moment). The resort celebrated a grand reopening in November 2004 and is now known as the Raffles Resort Canouan Island.

The island is physically beautiful, with a half-dozen fine beaches, a stunning, 3-mile-long reef protecting the east coast, and a tidy little village, built courtesy of the rising standard of living brought by the arrival of a $200 million resort. Canouan is a nonstarter for the backpacking set, but on the other side of the island from the resort, the Tamarind Beach Hotel is a moderately priced option for those who are a few greenbacks shy of a Trump-size billfold. At 3 square miles (about a third the size of St. Barth), Canouan offers plenty of entertainment for a few days, but if the travel bug bites mid-stay, you can always shuttle over to a neighboring islet. The 40-foot catamaran *Splendid Adventurer* does day trips to nearby Mayreau and the Tobago

Canouan

N

LEGEND

- ⊙ Capital City, Town
- ⑭ Route Number
- ■ Hotel / Point of Interest
- ⬛ Scenic View
- ⚓ Ferry / Cruise Ship Dock
- 🗼 Lighthouse
- 🏖 Beach
- ⛳ Golf Course

Point Moody

Point Jupiter

Mahault Bay

GOLF COURSE

RAFFLES RESORT
CANOUAN ISLAND

Mount Royal

TRUMP CLUB
PRIVEE

Rameau Bay

CARIBBEAN
SEA

TAMARIND BEACH
HOTEL & YACHT CLUB

Charlestown Bay

Charlestown

AIRPORT

Friendship Bay

South Glossy Bay

ATLANTIC OCEAN

Miles

0   1   2

Canouan: Key Facts

Location	13°N by 61°W
	18 miles/30 kilometers south of St. Vincent
	110 miles/177 kilometers west of Barbados
	2,060 miles/3,315 kilometers southeast of New York
Size	3 square miles/7.8 square kilometers
Highest point	877 feet/267 meters (Mt. Royal)
Population	1,165
Language	English
Time	Atlantic Standard Time (1 hour ahead of EST, same as EDT)
Area code	784
Electricity	220 volts AC, 50 cycles
Currency	The Eastern Caribbean dollar, EC$ (EC$2.68 = US$1)
Driving	On the left; U.S. and Canadian citizens must present a valid driver's license and pay $28 to obtain a temporary local driver's permit.
Documents	All U.S. and Canadian citizens must have a valid passport and a return or an ongoing ticket.
Departure tax	$15
Beer to drink	Hairoun
Rum to drink	Any Vincentian brand
Music to hear	Italian opera
Tourism info	www.canouan.com

Cayes, a quintet of uninhabited islets with grand snorkeling (and a shooting location for *Pirates of the Caribbean*).

The Briefest History

The Ciboney Indians first discovered Canouan, followed by the peaceful Arawaks, and then the island was settled by the fearsome Caribs. The Caribs were able to repel Europeans longer here than on almost any other Caribbean island, and eventually they bonded with escaped slaves from St. Vincent and became known as the Black Caribs (as on Bequia). The French finally built a settlement in 1719. Canouan traded hands between the French and British several times, until the Treaty of Versailles in 1783 deeded the land to the British. There was more fighting with the Black Caribs, but eventually the British won out and shipped the remaining 5,000 to Central America, where their descendants live today. In 1871 Canouan became part of the

British Windward Islands, and in 1979 St. Vincent and the Grenadines achieved independent statehood within the British Commonwealth.

Getting There

Believe it or not, Canouan's airport is the most advanced in the country, equipped for night landings and larger planes (though not jets), unlike the one on St. Vincent. A heavily subsidized (thank you, Carenage management) American Eagle flight arrives several days a week from San Juan, via St. Lucia. You can also reach Canouan on TIA, Mustique Airways, and SVG Air from Barbados and miscellaneous Grenadines, or on Air Caraïbes from Martinique. You can also take advantage of the Raffles' "flight concierge" program, with private Raffles jet service from Barbados or St. Lucia; the cost is $375 per person. There is also ferry service from St. Vincent and Union islands five times a week.

Getting Around

Since the island is so small (only 3 miles long by 1 mile wide), a rental car really isn't necessary. The hotels will meet you at the airport, and there is a shuttle service between the two hotels. Cars are available, however, for about $60 per day and can be arranged through the hotels.

Where to Stay

⊛ **Raffles Resort Canouan Island**, Canouan, St. Vincent and the Grenadines, WI. ℂ 877-226-6826 or 784-458-8000, ✉ 784-458-8885, ▭ www.raffles-canouanisland.com

💲 Stratospheric ⑪ BP ⒸⒸ 156 rooms

Construction of this resort forever changed the face of sleepy Canouan. Although we frown on the development of a once unspoiled place, it's a monumental achievement. Built by a consortium of Italian investors and a Swiss bank, the project encompasses most of the island. About half of the property is devoted to the resort and golf course (which opened in 1999, closed in 2002, and then reopened in 2004 after substantial modifications). The remainder will be sold off to investors for holiday homes (à la Mustique). The first three of these homes had been completed when we last visited, just as the resort was debuting under the Raffles banner.

We gasped the first time we saw the resort, set on the site of an old village, from a plane. Encompassing the northern two-thirds of Canouan, the resort's layout has not been altered, with the exception of a new road entrance that parallels the beautiful, 3-mile-long reef protecting the island's Atlantic coast. Alternately, a colonial-style wooden boat shuttles guests the 3 miles from the airport ($40 round-trip per person). Located in a broad amphitheatre facing a tranquil bay, it has more than 100 colorfully painted villas and buildings designed by the late Italian architect Luigi Vietti scattered about. Other highlights include a 12,900-square-foot free-form swimming pool (the longest we've seen in all the Caribbean), three lighted tennis courts, a health and fitness center, four restaurants, several bars, and all kinds of water sports, including scuba. A major focus is the 18-hole golf course, which surrounds the accommodations. There are two main beaches fronting the resort, and at least two more in an (as yet) undeveloped part of the property. At the center of the resort is the village's original church, which is still standing and has been restored.

The rooms are remarkably tasteful and well appointed. Amenities include lanais, a/c, ceiling fans, safes, minibars and minifridges, bathrobes, phones with data ports, and satellite TV. Some suites also have kitchenettes, and all have an espresso maker. The decor is a Tuscan-Sardinian fusion, with earth-tone walls and fabrics, natural woods, and terra-cotta tiles. The beds have Frette cotton sheets and feather pillows. The baths feature strikingly colorful glazed tiles, hand-painted sinks, large vanities (we love that), showers, and the requisite big tubs and bidets (for Europeans, that is). Laundry, dry cleaning, in-room catering, and babysitting services are available, too. We found the suites to be embarrassingly large—a junior suite would be more than sufficient for the average guest (if there is such a thing). News hounds will rejoice in the choice of more than two dozen newspapers from around the world, delivered to your room in full-size format —no mere *New York Times Fax* here!

This is a big property, and every room comes with its own golf cart for tooling around. The first place ours headed was the Amrita Spa. There are nine treatment *palapas* on the hillside overlooking the bay, each sheltered in thatch from Venezuela and reached via a funicular (!) that climbs a cliff. Two more *palapas* are perched on stilts over the lagoon and reached by boat. The treatments (which we enjoyed immensely) conclude with meditational time to admire billowing thatch against the azure lagoon. To us, this spa experience is probably the Caribbean's finest.

We think the resort's Euro-style casino is a white elephant, visually and otherwise. It sits isolated on a remote section of the property, and to seduce more high rollers the room has been spruced up with a scarlet paint job, a private members-only salon has been added, and Donald Trump was brought in to keep the tables busy (hence the new moniker, Trump Club Privee). On the other hand, following Jim Fazio's makeover, the 18-hole golf course (now known as the Trump

International Golf Club) boasts a spectacular layout. The front nine surround the resort, while the back nine are over the hill on the otherwise untouched north coast of the island.

The restaurants serve excellent food, most of it extravagantly priced — $60 veal sweetbreads, anyone? The service was exceedingly friendly, if exceedingly leisurely. But speaking of prices, Raffles is seeking another kind of high bar when it comes to the martini list, which is headlined by four $300 (yes, you read correctly) cocktails, each embracing a warrior theme and spiked with a 24-karat gold-plated miniature sword stirrer. We studied the menu and were briefly (very briefly) tempted to order the Knight of the Round Table — Bombay Sapphire, dry vermouth, *one* olive and an Excalibur replica. We passed. But we wondered: How many people have in their back pocket a cocktail-party conversation stopper like their encounter with a $300 martini?

Tamarind Beach Hotel & Yacht Club, Charlestown, Canouan, St. Vincent and the Grenadines, WI. ✆ 784-458-8044, ✆ 784-458-8851, 🖳 www.tamarind.us, reservations@tamarind.us

🛍 **Wicked Pricey** 🍴 **CP** ©© 40 rooms

Owned and managed by the Canouan Resorts Development (not Raffles) folks, the Tamarind sits on a pretty beach facing west and is at the edge of Charlestown, Canouan's only village. Strung along the beach in four two-story blue-roof buildings, the rooms have wood walls (whitewashed in lower units), louvered Jalousie windows, wicker furnishings, tile floors, ceiling fans (no a/c), bright fabrics, minibar, safe, good-size bathrooms, and twice-daily maid service. Downstairs units open right onto the sand; upper units have airy peaked ceilings. The Palapa Restaurant features surprisingly good Italian and Creole cuisine, and the Pirate Cove bar is a great place for a snack and sunset cocktails. All kinds of water sports are available or can be arranged by the hotel, including diving. The Moorings charter sail operation has established a Grenadines base next door.

Where to Eat

The resorts rule the dining scene on Canouan, which is basically a one-company island these days.

$$$$ Palapa Restaurant, Tamarind Beach Hotel, 784-458-8044

This is a good place to dine alfresco, overlooking the water. More informal than Raffles (but with reciprocity — guests can charge their meals to Raffles and vice versa), it has a mix of sailors and resort guests, which makes the atmosphere more interesting.

$$ **Pirate's Cove**, Tamarind Beach Hotel, 784-458-8044

Basically, this is a casual snack-bar where bathing suits are *de rigueur*.

$$$–$$$$$ Raffles Resort Canouan Island, 784-458-8000

There are four restaurants, serving meals that lean toward Italian, French, Asian, and island persuasions. Prices are about as high as they come in these parts, but the food we had was exemplary.

Carriacou

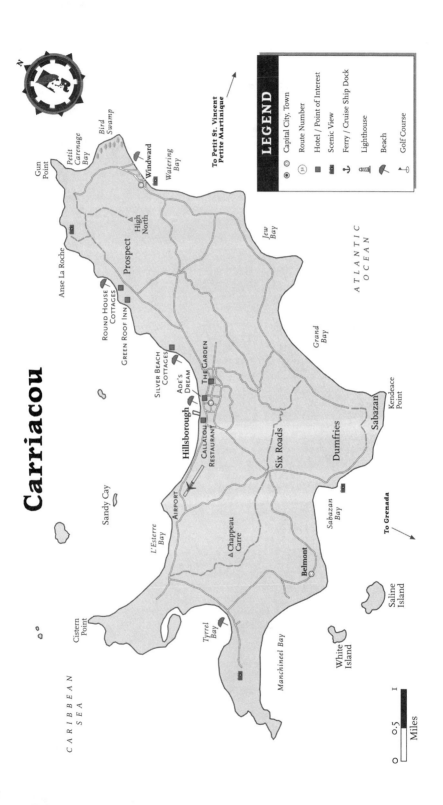

CARIBBEAN SEA

ATLANTIC OCEAN

Gun Point

Petit Carenage Bay

Bird Swamp

Windward

Watering Bay

To Petit St. Vincent
Petite Martinique

Anse La Roche

High North

Prospect

Jew Bay

Round House Cottages

Green Roof Inn

Grand Bay

Silver Beach Cottages

Ade's Dream

The Garden

Sandy Cay

Hillsborough

Callaloo Restaurant

Kendeace Point

Sabazan

Airport

L'Esterre Bay

Six Roads

Dumfries

Chappeau Carre

Sabazan Bay

To Grenada

Cistern Point

Tyrrel Bay

Belmont

Manchineel Bay

White Island

Saline Island

Miles
0   0.5   1

Carriacou

A FRIEND OF OURS ONCE TOLD US THAT JUST AS HER PLANE touched down on Carriacou (pronounced "KARRY-a-coo"), it suddenly lifted up with jarring swiftness. When she looked out the window, she saw a cow on the runway. That's Carriacou. It's on its own wavelength. Everyone — and everything — moves at its own pace (slow and slower), as did the runway keeper in this case. If you're an efficiency freak or one who's into deluxe accommodations, this island isn't for you. What makes Carriacou special is its sense of detachment and the resulting preservation of some unique African and Caribbean customs.

The first inhabited island north of Grenada, Carriacou is the largest of the Grenadine chain, but it's still pretty small, at 8 miles long and 5 miles wide. Most of its inhabitants live around the main village of Hillsborough. It gets extremely dry, and as the winter progresses, the island begins to look like autumn in New England — give or take a few palm trees and other tropical props. There are also several uninhabited "satellite islands" with gorgeous white-sand beaches.

After our first visit to Carriacou some years ago, we thought that an intrusion of tourism was around the corner, but that has not happened. There might be a few (small) cruise ships stopping here, taking advantage of idyllic Sandy Cay, but tourism on the island is mostly unchanged. As a matter of fact, things seem to have gone back in time. The only improvement in the last few years that we've noticed is that the airstrip is now fenced in, so there will be no more cows on the runway (and cars now have to make a long detour around the airstrip). Some of the roads have been repaired, although you'll still find stretches that are in abysmal shape. A few inns and guesthouses have popped up, but nothing out of the ordinary. There was talk of an Italian conglomerate building a 200-room condo-hotel complex. We'll believe it when we see it! However, we once were skeptical about plans to develop another Grenadine, Canouan, and it did happen. So who knows? However, at this writing you can still get away from it all on Carriacou. There are enough people around to keep your sensibilities alive, yet there is a mind-your-own-business philosophy — bred by the big business of smuggling — that allows you to socialize only when you want to do so. There are few formal activities designed for tourists.

Carriacou: Key Facts

Location	12°N by 61°W
	23 miles/37 kilometers northeast of Grenada
	2,175 miles/3,500 kilometers southeast of New York
Size	13 square miles/21 square kilometers
Highest point	High North, 955 feet/299 meters
Population	6,000
Language	English
Time	Atlantic Standard Time (1 hour ahead of EST, same as EDT)
Area code	473
Electricity	220/240 volts AC, 50 cycles
Currency	The Eastern Caribbean dollar, EC$ (EC$2.68 = US$1)
Driving	On the left; a local permit is required and will be provided for $12 with a valid driver's license.
Documents	All U.S. and Canadian citizens must have a valid passport and a return or an ongoing ticket.
Departure tax	$20
Beer to drink	Heineken
Rum to drink	Jack Iron
Music to hear	Dancehall
Tourism info	800-927-9554 or 473-443-7948 (in Carriacou)
	www.carriacoupetitemartinique.com

Although Carriacou was only minimally affected by the wrath of Hurricane Ivan, which hit Grenada hard in 2004, the island was trounced by Hurricane Emily in 2005. A number of homes were lost, and one hotel has not re-opened at the time of this writing. Although vegetation has sprung back to life and beaches have been restored, Carriacou is even sleepier than usual today.

The Briefest History

Carriacou is part of the country of Grenada, which achieved independence from Great Britain in 1974. During the 18th century the island was divided up into estates for raising sugarcane, and the lovely stone ruins of those plantations can be found around the island. The Kayaks (natives of Carriacou) are proud of their African heritage and take pains to preserve it. Both the English and the French colonialists left their marks in ways remarkable for such a small island. Most of the inhabitants of the town of Windward bear Scottish names, whereas those who live only a few miles away in L'Esterre have French names and still maintain a group (led by octogenarian artist Canute Caliste) that plays and dances the quadrille. Boat building is still a major occupation, and Carriacou's sloops are rated among the best in the Caribbean.

Getting There

The main route to Carriacou is via Grenada or St. Vincent, on SVG Air. The *Osprey Express* (473-440-8126), a high-speed motor-catamaran, makes the trip in less than 90 minutes. It departs from the Carenage in St. George's, Grenada, at 9 a.m. and 5:30 p.m., and departs the main dock in Hillsborough, Carriacou, for Grenada, at 6 a.m. and 3:30 p.m. Schedules are slightly different on weekends. Fare is $41 round-trip. Note that when the seas are remotely rough, the crossing inspires motion sickness among passengers. Check the schedule before you plan anything—times and dates change often and at will. There is also limited boat service between Carriacou and Union on Monday and Thursday—confirm the schedule with the tourist office in Carriacou (473-443-7948).

Getting Around

From early morning to sundown, buses (minivans, in reality) crisscross the island for $1. The drivers will be more than happy to throw out all the other passengers and charge you $5 to $10 for a "private taxi," although in the name of brotherhood, understanding, and good PR, we don't recommend doing this. Riding with the other passengers is lots of fun, too. For special or nighttime trips you will have to go private. You can rent a car on Carriacou for about $40 per day. You must provide a credit card and valid driver's license and obtain a temporary Grenada driver's license for $12. Try Quality Rentals at 473-407-2928. Remember, driving is on the left, which is easy here due to the minimal traffic, but you might feel (as we once did) as though you've entered a parallel universe and mistake the wiper arm for the turn signal. As we stated earlier, the roads were in bad shape when we visited, with promises of improvement soon—but in Caribbean time.

Focus on Carriacou: Walking

The northern and eastern sides of the island are almost entirely uninhabited and are traversed by an old plantation road. Spectacular views, 18th-century stone ruins, secluded beaches, and solitude will be your reward for braving the tropical sun and heat. Bring along plenty of water, some sandwiches, and pastries from the bakery in Hillsborough. Should you decide to bushwhack, follow the cow paths down the hillside and into the woods, where you might come upon a mysterious cultivated field of wacky weed (marijuana). It is definitely not a good idea to explore farther in that particular direction or to accost any mysterious passersby to inquire about local agricultural practices.

Walk 1: Anse La Roche (half to full day)

Take the road north out of Hillsborough to Bogles. At the end of Bogles take the dirt branch to the left, which climbs up past the former Caribbee Inn. Continue on this James Taylor country road shaded by manchineel trees (don't touch—the sap is poisonous—and never stand under them when it rains) until you come to a large tree on the right leaning out over the road. Take the cowpath to the left through the woods, past calabash trees to the ruins of an old plantation. In front is a huge sloping pasture that opens out onto a magnificent vista with Union Island looming in the distance. This view is so enjoyable that you might not want to proceed farther, but by all means do. Follow the trail down to the right until you reach a trail marker (when we were there it was a black rock with a shell on top), then take the steep path down the hill and into the woods again until you get to the beach. It is usually deserted, and snorkeling is good along the rocks on the north (far) end, but save some energy for the hot climb back up.

Walk 2: Windward (half to full day)

Follow the Walk 1 instructions past the old Caribbee Inn and past the cutoff to Anse La Roche. Continue on the same plantation road around High North to Gun Point and then to **Petit Carenage Bay**, where there is a nice deserted beach and a reef for snorkeling. At the right end of the beach is a mangrove swamp called the **Bird Swamp**. Directly across the bay is Petit St. Vincent, the *trôp chic et cher* resort on its own island, and on the right, Petite Martinique, often just called PM. Try to imagine an international frontier crossing between these two islands—to the north you're in the country called St. Vincent and the Grenadines, whereas everything from Petite Martinique south is part of Grenada. Islanders routinely cross this border without a thought!

As you continue your walk, the road leads into Windward. This is still a major boat-building center. Brightly colored wooden boats can be seen everywhere in the Grenadines, and they are particularly photogenic here on the beach, under construction or repair. As mentioned earlier, most of the residents of Windward are of mixed Scottish and West Indian descent—the Scots came here to build a merchant fleet when Britain ruled the islands.

There are several rum shops and minimarkets at which to get some refreshment (it can be very hot and dry in Windward). You can hire a boat here to take you to PM or to sail up the Grenadines to the Tobago Cays or Canouan. We had a very good experience sailing with Zev MacLaren on his hand-built boat, the *Sweetheart*. You can get back to Hillsborough by continuing to follow the road around across the island to Bogles.

Walk 3: Grand Bay–Kendeace Point–Sabazan–Six Roads (full day)

This is a serious walk for the more dedicated hiker, but it is well worth the effort. Take a bus or taxi over to Grand Bay — it is too steep and too far to walk. At the bus stop, walk down to the right until you discover the old plantation road that leads south and then west. You will reach Kendeace Point fairly quickly, but don't bother to bushwhack out onto the point. Instead, follow the cow patty trail down to the spectacular and totally deserted beach just to the north of the point. As you follow the road around to Sabazan, you won't see a single sign of human habitation, except some old stone ruins. Up on the hill at Sabazan, you'll see some fairly spectacular ruins peeking above the tree line. Getting to them is not as easy as it looks, and it is recommended only for the determined archaeologist or historian. At Sabazan Bay there is a beautiful beach, with a lovely little cove for swimming, on the north side and some weirdly wonderful wind-sculpted trees on the south side. At Dumfries make sure you take the cutoff up to the right, past the lime factory ruins, to Six Roads, or you'll be in for a very long hike indeed. There is a rum shop at Six Roads for refreshment, and at that point you'll be glad to know that it is only a short and easy walk back into Hillsborough.

Where to Stay

Unlike most Caribbean islands, there has been little growth in the range of accommodations offered on Carriacou. In fact, in the aftermath of Hurricane Emily in 2005, the Caribbee — our favorite place to stay — was closed, and its future is uncertain (call owners Robert and Wendy Cooper for an update: 473-443-7380). One other place, Cassada Bay, continues to have management and financial issues, so we can't recommend it for lodging. We'd love for some enterprising individual to take over these spectacular locations and bring them into the 21st century. Until then, here's the best of the rest.

Down Island Villas, Carriacou, Grenada, WI. ℂ 473-443-8182,
℡ 473-443-8290, ⌨ www.islandvillas.com

🖪 **Cheap** for apartments, **Not So Cheap** for villas ⑪ EP ⒸⒸ
20 apartments and villas

The villa rental option is surprisingly affordable in Carriacou, especially for families who need more space than a hotel room would provide. Down Island Villas rents homes in Craigston Estate or nearby. Simple apartments start at $60 per night in winter; villas range up to $200 per night for two for a new two-bedroom home with a private pool. A six-day minimum stay applies for most of the properties.

Round House Cottages, Bogles, Carriacou, Grenada, WI. ℂ and
℡ 473-443-7841, ⌨ roundhouse@grenadines.net

🖪 **Cheap** ⑪ CP ⒸⒸ 3 cottages

The three cute gingerbread-style efficiency cottages here come with fully equipped galley kitchens, private baths, ceiling fans, bedside tables, reading lamps, mosquito netting, and lanais. Well maintained and private, the inn is only 100 feet away from the beach. There is twice-weekly maid service. The Round House Restaurant & Bar is one of the island's best and serves lunch and dinner for guests.

Green Roof Inn, Bogles, Carriacou, Grenada, W.I. 🕐 and ✆ 473-443-6399, 🖥 www.greenroofinn.com, greenroof@caribsurf.com

🛍 **Cheap** 🍴 **CP** (CC) 5 rooms

Set on a hill overlooking Hillsborough Bay, the Green Roof Inn is a two-story guesthouse owned by a Swedish couple, Janas and Asa. The rooms are very simple but clean. Four have private baths; the compact shared-bath unit is usually rented as a single. There is a spacious restaurant and bar overlooking the bay—a great place for a sunset cocktail—and a tiny beach down below. Bicycles are available free of charge to guests.

Ade's Dream, Main Street, Hillsborough, Carriacou, Grenada, W.I. 🕐 473-443-7317, ✆ 473-443-8435, 🖥 adesdream@grenadines.net

🛍 **Dirt Cheap** 🍴 **EP** (CC) 23 rooms

In the heart of town, Ade's Dream is a hotel and guesthouse in one, located 100 yards from the ferry dock. The three-story building in front houses 16 hotel rooms, all with kitchen, private bathrooms, a/c, and a balcony; a large shared veranda in front offers street and sea views (the third-floor units are worth the few extra bucks). To the rear is another building with seven guesthouse rooms; these share a bathroom and cooking facilities and do not have air-conditioning.

Silver Beach Cottages, Silver Beach, Beausejour Bay, Carriacou, Grenada, W.I. 🕐 800-742-4276 or 473-443-7337, ✆ 473-443-7165, 🖥 silverbeach@caribsurf.com

🛍 **Cheap** 🍴 **EP** (CC) 16 rooms

This is a 16-room, West Indian–owned and –run hotel on the northern edge of Hillsborough. It is on the water, but since it is adjacent to the town wharf, it's not a great place for swimming, and the management strikes us as a bit out of touch. The rooms are comfortable and modern, with ceiling fans, private baths, and lanais. There are semidetached efficiency units out back. The food in the Shipwreck Restaurant is decent, and the bar is the place to meet locals.

Where to Eat

Basically, you eat at your hotel on Carriacou—especially dinner. What's on your plate largely depends on what was caught that day and/or what meat and produce came in on the boat recently—it's good to be flexible. For a little variety, we also recommend the following.

$ **Callaloo by the Sea**, Hillsborough, 473-443-8004

Serving West Indian fare from 10 a.m. to 10 p.m. daily in season, this pleasant spot sits on the water and has great callaloo soup as well as dependable Creole chicken and curried conch.

$$$ **Green Roof Inn**, Bogles, 473-443-6399

This Swedish-run restaurant serves European-style preparations of fish, lobster gratinée, and filet mignon. The sunset view is smashing from the open-air terrace. Reservations are required.

$$ **Round House Restaurant**, Bogles, 473-443-7841

The Round House is indeed in a curvy, round building made of stone; it features a tree in the center. We hope that the restaurant, which is under new management, will maintain its superb reputation. Open for lunch and dinner daily, with reservations.

Don't Miss

Sandy Cay

About a half mile offshore, this tiny island of creamy sand and palm trees offers a beautiful spot for a day's outing. There is also a fantastic reef for snorkeling off the northern end of the cay, with huge coral heads and a large variety of fish. Your hotel can arrange for a boat to get you there, or check with Silver Diving—it will arrange snorkel trips for $20 per person.

Carnival

Either because people got too rowdy for the tourists or because there was too much competition from Carnival in Trinidad, Carnival on Grenada was moved to August. However, on Carriacou it still takes place during the traditional week before Ash Wednesday. Here it is a lovely and charming small-town celebration with an intricate structure rooted in tradition. Each town spends the weeks leading up to Carnival making elaborate costumes for their queen (a young woman chosen for looks, talent, and style) and her court, called a band. Each queen and her band illustrate a theme, such as "the solar system" or "back to nature." On the Saturday a week and a half before Ash Wednesday, the festivities kick off with a parodistic competition —the choosing of a male "queen" and a female "king." The real competition occurs a week later when the genuine Carnival queen and her band of the year are chosen. Other features include a "dirty mas," when everybody gets totally tanked and smears everybody else (including you—dress accordingly!) with mud and ashes; a "clean mas," when everyone parades around in their Sunday best; a calypso contest; a parade on Shrove Tuesday; and an extraordinary custom peculiar to Carriacou — the "fighting mas," in which the men dress up as Pierrots and wander around reciting Shakespeare and beating each other with sticks (we're not kidding). If the thought of Carnival in Brazil or Trinidad intimidates, this is the one for you. The people are warm and welcoming, and should you get tired of celebrating, just get out of Hillsborough.

Big Drum

Another custom unique to Carriacou is Big Drum, also known as "nation dances." It is an all-night celebration featuring percussive music that stems from African tribal drumming. There are three drums made of rum kegs and goatskins, and the music is accompanied by a highly intricate and beautiful dance. Big Drum is played at most important island occasions — boat launchings, house blessings, and tombstone dedications, among them. You will be fortunate indeed to be invited.

Regatta

Featuring boat races and even more onshore fun, Carriacou's Regatta is the big hoo-ha of the Grenadines. The racing is really secondary to the drinking and other shenanigans characteristic of all Caribbean sailing regattas. It lasts four days (the first weekend of August) and features such frolicking summer-camp activities as greased-pole, tug-of-war, and donkey races. For more information, contact the island's tourism office.

Diving

The clear, calm waters around Carriacou provide some excellent dive sites. Call Max and Claudia at Carriacou Silver Diving (473-443-7882; www.scubamax.com), a family-run shop that does everything from Discover Scuba courses through Instructor Training; a two-tank dive runs $90, including all equipment.

Mustique

"DAH-LING, IT'S *FABOO*!" THOSE ARE THE WORDS WE OVER-heard about a gorgeous waterfront and pool-adorned stucco mansion, seen as we were landing at Mustique airport's tiny, sloping runway. We later learned it was for sale for millions (way beyond our budget). This made us recall our impression of Mustique on the first visit to this small, private island of the rich and famous. Arriving by boat (we weren't as well off in those days), we were overwhelmed by the vision of the huge Italianate mansion of Harding Lawrence and ad queen Mary Wells. It still sits on a hilltop like the House of Zeus on Mount Olympus, although the plantings surrounding it have matured and now partly shield it from view. Apparently things haven't changed much here, except that there are a lot more villas on the island and construction seems to be going on everywhere. The late HRH Princess Margaret and her son, Viscount Linley, used to come here every year to her villa. Schmatta king Tommy Hilfiger has built a very large, over-the-top mansion that screams "Look at me!" on L'Ansecoy Beach. Down the road is Mick Jagger's Japanese-style, six-bedroom beach house called Stargroves, a lesson in good taste—private, secluded, and unobtrusive, if a bit worn at the edges (it can be rented for $16,000 a week). Speaking of rock stars, David Bowie and Elton John once owned villas here, too. Welcome to Mustique, vacationland of the rich, famous, and even more rich.

Operated by the Mustique Company, Ltd., this is the Caribbean's small, private Martha's Vineyard without the New England quaintness and restraint. Many of the opulent villas resemble separate mini-resorts in the Victorian gingerbread mold, elevated to the appropriate grandness. Besides the Cotton House and Firefly Guest House, there are only about 85 houses on the island. A glance at the property titles would reveal a global representation of the fabulous and fortunate. No cruise ships come here; they and boats with more than 25 passengers are prohibited from visiting.

Don't know somebody with a villa? Well, you can easily rent one from the Mustique Company. At last count, there are about 60 available, at weekly prices from $6,000 (or $3,000 in low season) for a two-bedroom without pool to $35,000 for Toucan Hill, a spectacular four-bedroom Moroccan palace with lush mosaic tile fountains and 360-degree hilltop views (we're sworn to secrecy on the owner's name, but rest assured, it's one you'd

Mustique

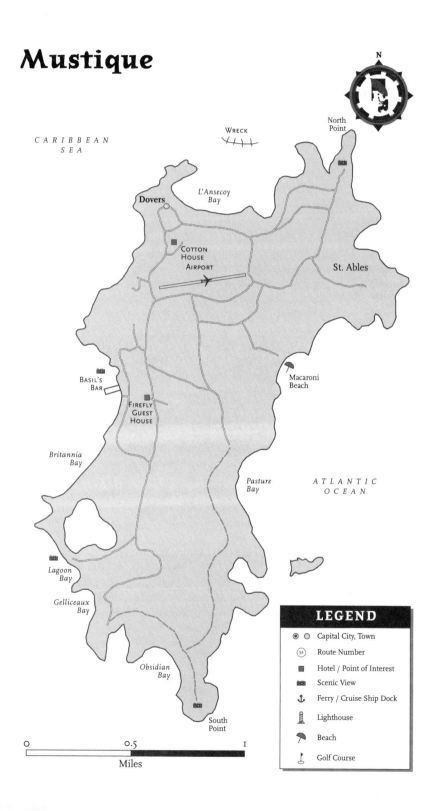

N

CARIBBEAN
SEA

WRECK

North
Point

L'Ansecoy
Bay

Dovers

COTTON
HOUSE
AIRPORT

St. Ables

BASIL'S
BAR

Macaroni
Beach

FIREFLY
GUEST
HOUSE

Britannia
Bay

Pasture
Bay

ATLANTIC
OCEAN

Lagoon
Bay

Gelliceaux
Bay

Obsidian
Bay

South
Point

LEGEND

◉	◎	Capital City, Town
	⑫	Route Number
	■	Hotel / Point of Interest
	📷	Scenic View
	⚓	Ferry / Cruise Ship Dock
	🗼	Lighthouse
	☂	Beach
	⛳	Golf Course

0   0.5   1

Miles

Mustique: Key Facts

Location	13°N by 61°W
	18 miles/30 kilometers south of St. Vincent
	110 miles/177 kilometers west of Barbados
	2,060 miles/3,315 kilometers southeast of New York
Size	2 square miles/5.2 square kilometers
Highest point	Fort Shandy, 496 feet/151 meters
Population	552
Language	English
Time	Atlantic Standard Time (1 hour ahead of EST, same as EDT)
Area code	784
Electricity	220 volts AC, 50 cycles
Currency	The Eastern Caribbean dollar, EC$ (EC$2.68 = US$1)
Driving	On the left; U.S. and Canadian citizens must present a valid driver's license and pay $28 to obtain a temporary local driver's permit.
Documents	All U.S. and Canadian citizens must have a valid passport and a return or an ongoing ticket.
Departure tax	$15
Beer to drink	Hairoun
Rum to drink	Any Vincentian brand
Music to hear	The Stones
Tourism info	784-458-8000
	www.mustique-island.com

recognize). You can also stay at the Cotton House, an inn on the northwest corner of the island. It's discreetly tasteful, with 20 rooms tucked into two plantation houses and three whitewashed, almost Swedish-looking cottages. All details are looked after, as is to be expected. The pool is small, but who swims, anyway? The main activity here is to have a drink, maybe a bite to eat, sit *by* the pool, and see who shows up. Visually, the pool ensemble is stunning. London stage, set, and costume designer Oliver Messel framed it with the remnants of an old sugar mill warehouse, its jagged edge outlined against the sky. The pool itself conjures up memories of the Clampetts' pool in *The Beverly Hillbillies*. Looking north from the pool, you can see the tennis courts and rooftops of a famous rock legend's compound giving him shelter. The beach in that direction, L'Ansecoy Bay, is very pretty and looks out on the wreck of the *Antilles*, a French cruise ship that ran a reef in 1971.

It used to be that if the Cotton House didn't fit your style or budget, there was an alternative: the modestly priced Firefly Guest House. Its old motto was "You don't have to be rich and famous to enjoy Mustique." That's not the case anymore. Since being acquired and reinvented by Brits Stan and Elizabeth Clayton, it's now "Not a hotel—an experience." Right. We think that "You don't have to be famous, but please leave your wallet at the door" is more appropriate, because the rates have skyrocketed (so much for the penny-pinching masses!). The Firefly's cozy bar and restaurant is where the island's *branché* residents and guests hang out when the sun sets (if they go out at all).

The hub of activity for Mustique's tourists is most certainly **Basil's Beach Bar**. Located on Britannia Bay along with Basil's Market, Boutique, and Water Sports Center, it's a favorite with both the yachting set and occasional celebutantes. His thatched-roof beach bar on stilts also serves lunch and dinner, featuring fresh lobster as well as beef, chicken, and veggie dishes. On Wednesday night during the winter season, there is a barbecue and jump-up with pan bands from Bequia or St. Vincent. It's very possible you'll recognize someone—the tip-off is the bodyguard. Basil's T-shirts are great collector's items and can be bought at Basil's Boutique. Neighboring Johanna Morris's Treasure Boutiques, set in two vividly colored gingerbread-style houses, also has souvenirs available. Tucked between the two houses is Johanna Banana, featuring Italian espresso, ice cream, breakfast, homemade pastries, and fresh fruit juices.

The Briefest History

Mustique was once inhabited by the Arawaks, then the Caribs, who were wiped out by England in the 18th century. In the 1700s, the island was used for sugarcane and was heavily guarded from the French (hence the remains of three forts still visible today). With the advent of the sugar beet and declining sugar prices, the island dwindled, with 100 or so fishermen and farmers living in a neglected settlement called Cheltenham. They eked out a meager existence that had little to do with the glimmering beaches curling around the island's perimeter. In 1958 Scotsman Colin Tennant (né Lord Glenconner) bought Mustique from the Hazell family. The purchase price was reportedly about $100,000! Tennant had a master's touch when he gifted England's Princess Margaret with a 10-acre (4.5 hectare) plot as a wedding present in 1960. The fanciful gift helped to put the island on the map as a potential playground for celebrities and royalty. Within a few years, Tennant built a new village for the islanders, and in 1968 he started the Mustique Company with the St. Vincent government to develop 140 high-end homes. An airstrip was built, and in 1969 famed British theatrical designer Oliver Messel helped to create Cotton House (on the grounds of the former Cheltenham) and the initial villas.

Getting There

Somehow Mustique's developers squeezed a runway onto the island. Since there are no landing lights, it can receive only small planes, and only until dusk. The easiest way to come here is via Barbados (see "Getting to the Grenadines" at the beginning of this section), connecting to Mustique Airways, TIA, or SVG Air. These airlines also provide scheduled flights from St. Vincent and charters from St. Lucia and Grenada. If you are on Bequia or another Grenadine, you can hire a boat to take you over for a day trip. From Bequia, it will cost around $250 (depending on your negotiating skills) for the round-trip hire of boat and crew. It makes sense to fill the boat with a group (usually up to 10), since the cost is the same for 1 or 10. This is a great way to see the island if you are staying on Bequia.

Focus on Mustique: Exploring the Island

The island is small, comprising only 1,400 acres (about 560 hectares). It can be seen fairly easily by renting a jeep, motorcycle, or a Mule (not an animal, it's a Kawasaki that resembles a rugged, souped-up golf cart). We rented a Mule for $60 per day. You can also hire a taxi for about $40 an hour, and an hour is sufficient for a cursory visit of the island. Starting the tour at the Cotton House, pick up a map at the office and have a drink by the pool. After a few refreshments, stop by the boutique in the windmill (it's cute, and you can buy a Cotton House T-shirt). Hop in your Mule or vehicle (the driver, of course, being sober) and proceed north to **L'Ansecoy Beach**. Here you'll pass Messrs. Jagger's and Hilfiger's villas, and even though we can't tell you exactly where they are (our lawyer's advice), most astute readers will figure it out (i.e., just ask a local). After passing the eastern end of the airport runway, turn right and pass the stables and tennis courts. At the second intersection, go straight up the hill and then screaming down a steep winding descent to the waterfront and Basil's. Time out for more refreshments.

When ready, follow the road along Britannia Bay until just past the jetty, and jog to the left. At the end, take a right, and within a short distance you'll be at the **Firefly**. Be sure to stop in and check it out (the bar opens around 4 p.m. and it's definitely a place to be seen). Continue on your drive and stay to the right at the fork, then go straight until you come to another intersection with a fork. The left fork goes uphill and the right one goes down. First go right. This will lead you to sheltered **Lagoon Bay**, which offers swimming possibilities for those of you who want to cool off. Returning to the fork, take a sharp right up the hill. This will take you past **Gelliceaux Bay** (the island's best snorkeling is found on the bay's northern end, and also on Lagoon Bay's southern end) and the late Princess Maggie's place. At the next major fork, bear left again or you'll end up in Obsidian Bay. The road here is rough in spots and mostly unpaved. Keep going until you see signs for **Pasture Bay**, Mustique's prettiest beach — but off-limits to swimming due to a fierce undertow.

Enjoy the scenery and at the first fork bear right. This will take you north until a sharp right and signs for **Macaroni Beach** — the island's most popular and the best for swimming. It's a curving beach of white sand and palm trees, with a few thatched-roof huts for shade. Time out for a swim. When you're ready, head back the same way and go to the end of the road, turn left, and then go right at the next intersection. The runway will be in front of you. A quick left and right will return you to the Cotton House. Time out for a swim in **Endeavour Bay** (good snorkeling on the northern side of the dock) and a cocktail (drivers included). You know where to go.

Where to Stay

If you really want to do Mustique with panache — and it's the best way to stay here if you are with a group or family — you can rent one of the 60 villas, in various sizes, degrees of luxury, and location. Prices start at $3,000 (low season) and $6,000 (high season) per week for a two-bedroom villa that sleeps four and has no pool; most are larger and much more expensive. Rates include airport transfers, household staff of at least three, vehicle rental, laundry service, and access to floodlit tennis courts. Contact the Mustique Company, P.O. Box 349, Mustique, St. Vincent and the Grenadines, WI.; local: 784-458-8000, fax: 784-488-9000, or if you want to save up for the villa, call Sanctuare, the stateside representative, on its toll-free line at 800-225-4255.

You can also stay at one of the following options.

The Cotton House, P.O. Box 349, Mustique, St. Vincent and the Grenadines, WI. ℂ 888-452-8380 or 784-456-4777, ✆ 784-456-5887, 🖳 www.cottonhouse.net, reservations@cottonhouse.net

🛍 **Stratospheric** 🍴 **BP (MAP** also available) 19 units
Situated on the private beach by Endeavour Bay, the Cotton House is the destination resort of celebrities and royalty. If you don't happen to be a celebrity or of real royal lineage, don't worry — you will be treated as if you are. A variety of guest cottages, suites, rooms, and even a two-bedroom villa make up this luxury hotel. Each has either a king-size bed or twin beds, a/c, ceiling fans, minibar, mosquito netting, telephone, and CD player with a CD menu (we love that touch, but bring your own music — the menu was geared toward a senior market). Several of the suites have their own plunge pool. They also come with a valet who will unpack your bags and press your clothes upon arrival (we love this, too!). We found some nice little touches that set the Cotton House apart from the rest — a bottle of rosewater spray to cool your face (one upon arrival and another when departing at the airport), Egyptian cotton linens and towels, and a personal pillow menu. We went gaga over the pillows and chose down ones of different firmnesses (you can even reserve one ahead of your arrival).

The Great House is spacious and airy. There is a bar inside, and lots of comfy chairs and couches for sitting, relaxing, having a drink, or reading a book — either in the main room or on the veranda. It also boasts a fabulous restaurant that serves breakfast, lunch, and dinner. The cuisine is a good mix of Caribbean and French, and the wine list is superb. We found the staff very accommodating. Room service is available. A variety of activities can be arranged, including tennis, horseback riding, and water sports, and there's a new spa. Upon your arrival, be sure to take advantage of the island tour they offer, conducted by the hotel's chauffeur, Bobsin. The hotel is closed in September and October.

Firefly Guest House, P.O. Box 349, Mustique, St. Vincent and the Grendadines, W.I. ℂ 784-456-3414, ✆ 784-456-3514, 🖥 www.mustiquefirefly.com, stan@mustiquefirefly.com

🅢 **Stratospheric**, including use of a Mule 🍴 **FAP** Ⓒ 4 rooms

Stan and Elizabeth Clayton have certainly changed things since taking over the Firefly in 1995. All four rooms have been completely redone, and although they're are on the small side, they are quite luxurious — from the four-poster king- or queen-size bed with Egyptian cotton linens to the unbleached cotton towels to the magnificent view of Britannia Bay. All have ceiling or regular fans (two have a/c), minibar, telephone, and room service; recent additions include wireless Internet and a loaded iPod for each room. Perched on a steep hillside, the Firefly has two freshwater swimming pools (connected by a rock waterfall and surrounded by lush tropical gardens), sundecks, private patios, a barbecue, and a garden bar.

The Firefly's bar and restaurant is the hot spot on the island, where the in crowd goes and where those in the know hang out. This is where you will see celebs as well as local homeowners and hotel guests eating dinner on the terrace or chatting over a Mustique Cocktail in the lounge area. There is a grand piano where a pianist provides entertainment every night from December to February. We particularly like the Mustique Martini Club. Drink all 14 martinis and get a free Martini Club polo shirt (now that is a collector's item!). There's also the Mustique Champagne Club. Drink all eight champagne cocktails and earn a Champagne Club polo.

The restaurant serves breakfast, lunch, picnics, and dinners, a fusion cuisine of international and Caribbean fare. After the candlelit dinner on the terrace, the lounge area heats up with the atmosphere of someone's living room rather than a bar. The Claytons do their best to make you feel at home (a very nice home, indeed, we might add!). They even throw in a Mule with the rates, so all in all it's still cheaper than Cotton House — but don't come to Mustique if you're even remotely thinking of watching your wallet. Hell, this place even has its own line of designer sarongs!

Where to Eat

There are four options: Your rented villa (have the cook whip up something light for you tonight) or the following three choices. Be sure to make reservations wherever you choose to dine.

$$$ **Basil's Bar**, Brittania Bay, 784-456-3350

Basil's is the island's closest approximation of a tourist attraction (besides celebrity-spotting), but since Mustique doesn't really have any tourists besides island guests and the occasional yacht, this "beach bar" on a pier is an institution on Mustique, as is Basil. Given its location, the emphasis is on fresh seafood. Speaking of yachties, Basil's is a favorite watering hole and is Mustique's "nightclub." Open daily for lunch, dinner, and, of course, sunset cocktails.

$$$$$ **The Cotton House**, Cotton House, 784-456-4777

Dining on the Great House veranda is an extraordinary experience indeed. We were impressed with the food, the service, the wine list, and the prices (but, then, this is Mustique, so who cares?). The cuisine is a French-Caribbean fusion by Chef Emmanuel Guemon. Open daily for breakfast, lunch, and dinner. Reservations required for dinner.

$$$$$ **Firefly**, Firefly Guest House, 784-456-3414

The other great (and celeb-heavy) restaurant on Mustique is the Firefly, where you'll find a fusion cuisine of international and Caribbean fare. Dinner is served on the candlelit terrace. The restaurant is open for breakfast, lunch, and dinner. Reservations are required for dinner.

Don't Miss

Drinks at Basil's and the Firefly

The island's two happening bars are both worth a visit after dinner. Basil's especially hops on Wednesday during the winter season, and it's anyone's guess who'll show up at the Firefly on a given night.

Mustique Blues Festival

First held in 1996, this brainchild of Basil Charles and Dana Gillespie is now an annual event and the Caribbean's only blues festival. It's held at Basil's Bar, usually at the end of January through early February, and the proceeds benefit the Basil Charles Educational Foundation, which provides scholarships for the children of St. Vincent. For more information, visit www.basilsmustique.com.

Mayreau

TALK ABOUT GETTING AWAY FROM IT ALL. NO ELECTRICITY. NO BANK. No phones. No cars. Hell, there are no roads. Well, we exaggerate. After all, this is the third millennium. The government installed a tiny power station on Mayreau in 2002, so electricity no longer comes from a half-dozen generators that putter through the night. The local establishments have phones, and there are two phone booths on the island where you can access an overseas operator for credit card calls (yes, contact with the outside world is possible). Until just a few years ago, donkeys were used to carry supplies from the bay up to the village. Now there are six cars, which transport goods to and from the ferries from St. Vincent and Union. There is also one concrete road that leads from **Saline Bay**—the port—up the hill to the village and down the hill on the other side to **Saltwhistle Bay**, one of the most picture-perfect beaches in all the Caribbean.

Still, despite all the "progress," Mayreau is a step back in time—peaceful, relaxed, and a perfect getaway from the chaos of the world. It's less than 2 square miles in size, so it's not hard to explore every corner of the island and get to know most of the locals (all 250 or so) in a few days.

Getting There

There's no airport on Mayreau—the nearest airpots are on Union Island and Canouan. From Barbados, Mustique Airways, SVG Air, and TIA fly to Union Island; SVG Air also flies from Grenada and Carriacou to Union. If you have prearranged a transfer with your Mayreau hotel, it is a short walk from the Union airport to the Anchorage Yacht Club dock, and a little farther to the Clifton docks. If your transfer is not prearranged, you'll need to walk into Clifton and hire a water taxi. The transfer should cost about $30 to $50, depending on your negotiating skills. American Eagle flies to Canouan from Barbados and San Juan. It's harder to hire a water taxi on the spot in Canouan, but there is a ferry four times a week.

These ferries, or "mail boats," make the trip up and down the Grenadines. The *MV Barracuda* leaves St. Vincent (southbound) on Monday, Thursday, and Saturday morning and takes about four hours to reach Mayreau (stopping at Bequia and Canouan, then Mayreau, en route to Union); the one-way fare is

Mayreau
Palm Island
Petit St. Vincent
Petite Martinique
Union Island

N

Petit Rameau
Petit Bateau
Baradel
Tobago Cays

Coral Reef

Saltwhistle Bay
SALTWHISTLE BAY CLUB
DENNIS' HIDEAWAY
ISLAND PARADISE
RIGHTEOUS
J & C BAR & RESTAURANT
Saline Bay

Mayreau

ATLANTIC OCEAN

Palm Island
PALM ISLAND RESORT

Petit St. Vincent
PETIT ST. VINCENT RESORT

Petite Martinique
DOCKS
MELODIES GUEST HOUSE

Union Island
Richmond Bay
Clifton
AIRPORT
CLIFTON BEACH HOTEL
ANCHORAGE YACHT CLUB & MARINA
Ashton

CARIBBEAN SEA

0   1   2
Miles

about $13. The *Barracuda* leaves Union (traveling north) on Tuesday and Friday mornings and Saturday afternoon, and the trip to Mayreau takes about 30 minutes (the ferry continues to St. Vincent). There's also the *MV Gem Star*, which travels south from St. Vincent on Tuesday and Friday, continuing to Union; it travels north from Mayreau on Wednesday and Saturday mornings. Before traveling, be sure to confirm ferry times and days with the St. Vincent tourist office (784-457-1502).

Where to Stay

There are only two real choices on Mayreau, so the decision is not difficult. They are dramatically different from each other in both luxury and cost, but each will allow you to experience the best of what the island has to offer.

Saltwhistle Bay Club, Mayreau, St. Vincent and the Grenadines, WI.
  ✆ 784-458-8444, ✎ 784-458-8944, ▱ www.saltwhistlebay.com,
  swbinfo@gmx.net

▪ 💲 **Ridiculous** 🍴 **MAP** CC 10 rooms

Located on what could be the most beautiful beach in the Grenadines, Saltwhistle Bay Club sits on 22 acres on the northern tip of the island. This is a private resort, enclosed by fences that help keep out the cows, donkeys, and other riffraff. There are 10 rooms in five double-unit cut stone cottages. Each has either a king-size bed or twin beds. The decor is a bit on the dark side, with stone walls and dark mahogany closets and desks. This helps to keep the rooms cool even in the heat of the day and very pleasant at night. Each unit has a large airy bedroom with a sitting area, a circular stone shower, wooden shutters, and ceiling fans. On top of each unit is an open-air terrace the size of the whole building, great for relaxing and enjoying the sea breeze. There are hammocks that are strung between palm trees right outside your door. All you need is a rum punch and a good book.

Saltwhistle has its own restaurant, which serves breakfast, lunch, and dinner. The dining area is made up of individual circular stone tables and booths with thatched roofs that can fit six people comfortably. The chef of the restaurant is local and has created a balanced menu of international and regional cuisine.

Since the hotel is situated on the most amazing beach, known not only for 3,000 feet of the most incredible sand but also for the island's best anchorage, there are usually 10 to 20 yachts floating in the bay. Most of those folks stay on their boats, coming ashore only to enjoy the restaurant or the beach for a bit. Unfortunately, though, this is also a great spot for those annoying day-trippers. Undine Potter, the manager, does a great job of keeping them at bay (in the bay). They usually stay for only about an hour, and it's only a couple dozen people at the most. The swimming is amazing, as there is no coral reef inside the bay. If you get a chance, go for a skinny dip at night (better yet if it's a full moon). It's a little secret of Saltwhistle you won't ever forget!

For entertainment at the Saltwhistle, there is a steel drum band that plays on Thursday. The band members come from another island in a boat on which most of us would never set foot. They pile in all their drums, and five or six people, and come over every week to entertain the "in town," but be prepared for a long walk up and down a hill. If you are going to go at night, ask Undine for a flashlight.

Saltwhistle offers snorkeling and fishing gear, windsurfing, and beach towels free to guests. There's good snorkeling at Saline Bay, around the wreck of the gunboat *Piruna* (kind of deep and a little rough). It can also arrange for other water sports, picnic trips to a small deserted islet, boat and yacht charters, and scuba diving. Closed September and October.

Dennis' Hideaway, Mayreau, St. Vincent and the Grenadines, WI.
© and ✆ 784-458-8594, 🖥 www.dennis-hideaway.com,
denhide@vincysurf.com

💲 **Cheap** 🍽 **CP** (CC) 5 rooms

Due to several rum punches offered at the bar by the ever friendly and gregarious Dennis, our memory about his place is a tad blurry (and we can't even read our notes). However, we will try our best. Dennis' is located in the little village up the hill from Saline Bay. It's just off the road, tucked away in a pretty garden of local plants and flowers. There are five twin rooms, each with a private bathroom and a balcony. The rooms are clean, light, and airy, and all have a nice view of Saline Bay, but the decor is minimal at best—a/c was added in 2005, which is a true sign that the island is entering the new century. There is a restaurant that serves breakfast, lunch, and dinner, with a Creole-style menu. Dennis's bar is frequented by locals as well as guests and visiting yachts.

Where to Eat

All the bars and restaurants are located in the village except for Saltwhistle Bay Club. With the exception of the latter, they are all within a few feet of each other. The night we last visited, which was a Thursday, Dennis' Hideaway bar was busy and Island Paradise was packed. There was a Windjammer sailboat in the harbor, and most of the 60 to 70 passengers and crew were up in the village whooping it up.

$$ **Dennis' Hideaway**, 784-458-8594

The Hideaway serves breakfast, lunch, and dinner. It has great food and is reasonably priced.

\$\$ Island Paradise, 784-458-8941

This seems to be the hot spot on the island. We didn't get to eat here, but we hear that the food is very good. The place was packed when we visited. There is a small dance floor with a jukebox playing a wide range of music, including reggae and island music. Everyone was dancing and drinking it up, including us! Note: The owner, James, has a cottage for rent. It is a self-contained two-bedroom unit, with running water, toilet, and kitchen, but no electricity. The rates are Dirt Cheap with a European Plan.

\$ J & C Bar & Restaurant, 784-458-8558

J & C serves a range of local and Creole foods along with cold drinks. The restaurant also has a small gift shop at Saltwhistle Bay, located right off the dock, where you can buy cold drinks. This is great if you take the walk from the village over the hill to the beach at Saltwhistle. The hike can be very hot during the day (the path is not shaded), so you will welcome that cold drink when you get to the beach. It's also a great place to pick up a souvenir T-shirt.

\$\$ Righteous, 784-458-8071

This restaurant serves a variety of local foods. We love the name.

\$\$\$\$ Saltwhistle Bay Club, 784-458-8444

The restaurant serves international and Creole cuisine. Open for breakfast, lunch, and dinner (see Where to Stay review above).

Palm Island

BAREFOOT VACATION FANTASIES MAY COME TO LIFE ON THIS
appealing outpost located just east of Union Island. The drawing card is gently rustling palms and a powdery white sand beach. A single resort gives the
all-inclusive experience a fresh spin. (For map, see p. 396.)

Getting There

From Barbados, Mustique Airways, SVG Air, and TIA fly to Union Island.
TIA flies to Union from Grenada, and TIA, Mustique Airways, and SVG Air
also have flights from the northern Grenadines and St. Vincent. Once you
are on Union, a Palm Island representative will escort you from the airport
to a nearby dock at the Anchorage Hotel and then on to the island via private
launch. The boat ride takes about 10 minutes.

Where to Stay and Eat

Palm Island, Palm Island, St. Vincent and the Grenadines, WI.
    $\textcircled{C}$ 800-858-4618 or 784-458-8824, $\textcircled{s}$ 784-458-8804,
    $\square$ www.palmislandresorts.com, res@eliteislandresorts.com

$\textbf{s}$ **Stratospheric** $\textcircled{¶}$ **All-Inclusive** (does not include any off-island
    activities) CC 37 rooms

Originally this was unappealingly named Prune Island, but entrepreneur John Caldwell purchased a 198-year lease to this 135-acre islet
back in the 1960s and renamed it Palm Island, planted a few thousand palms trees, and eventually built a beachfront resort by hand.
Over the years, Caldwell began to lease plots to individuals to build
private homes on the island, but eventually the hotel became run-down.
In 1999 the hotel was sold to Elite Island Resorts, a Florida-based operator of all-inclusive hotels. After \$4 million in renovations, Palm
Island was refashioned into a high-end, all-inclusive luxury operation.
A key difference between Palm and Petit St. Vincent (which follows
—the two are just a couple of miles from each other) is that two dozen
homeowners have villas on Palm Island. Palm's pretty beaches are also
visited by yachts and smaller cruise ships, whereas PSV manages to

keep most of these offshore. The villas are rarely occupied, so mostly you'll be sharing Palm with just the other guests of the 37-room resort. Fortunately, there are no cars, and just a few golf carts, not that you'll need any wheels to get across the island — nothing is farther than a 15-minute walk.

Overall, the renovations have done much to improve the experience. Four types of accommodations are available: Palm View rooms are the least expensive and have louvered windows, en suite bathrooms, walls of bluebitch stone, and ceilings made of attractive woven thatch. They may be at the bottom of the rate card, but they are perfectly fine. Beachfront rooms are similar, if a tad smaller, but with a beach view. Plantation Suites are in a two-story block of four, set back slightly from the beach, but with a huge lanai (second-floor units have views and slightly more privacy). Last, there are Island Lofts, which are perched on stilts about 5 feet off the ground and have huge bathrooms and cathedral ceilings. One kink that was still being worked out during our visit was air-conditioning — Palm has stand-alone units that sit on the floor. These have the advantage of keeping machine noise down outside the room (a big plus), but they don't do a great job of cooling down the room, and they aren't exactly quiet next to your bed. We turned ours off and opened the screened windows to let the island breezes do their trick, which worked just fine. Several guests during our visit made the a/c units their one and only complaint.

All rooms have ceiling fans, rattan and bamboo furniture, Egyptian cotton bed linens, room safes, bathrobes, and attractive original sea-theme artwork by Palm's resident artist, Patrick Chevailler, a French doctor who lives for much of the year on the island. Amenities include room service, coffeemaker, a stocked fridge (water, soft drinks, and beer only). There are no phones or TVs in the rooms. The island is wrapped by white-sand beaches, and there is excellent snorkeling available. An open-air fitness center, tennis, and croquet are available, and there's a tour desk that sets up day trips (at an additional cost). There are two restaurants, and the meals are better than we've experienced at most all-inclusive operations. The generous swimming pool looks a little awkward, what with its waterfall plunging from a faux summit, but it's also a good place to hang out if the beach gets busy (not that that happens often).

We think that Palm makes a good vacation for those who really want to get away from it all: TV, phones, traffic, noise. You'll find none of it here. You'll want to bring some reading material, and also don't forget to budget in some time for an excursion to the splendid Tobago Cays.

Petit St.Vincent

LOOKING FOR THE "PRIVATE ISLAND" EXPERIENCE, WHERE EVERY square inch of terra firma beneath your feet is "yours" — at least until checkout comes? Then check out Petit St. Vincent, perhaps the Caribbean's original private island resort, located just a stone's throw from the Grenada–St. Vincent border (St. Vincent side), but where border-crossing ministrations are a nonissue and barefoot informality is the rule. (For map, see p. 396.)

Getting There

From Barbados, Mustique Airways, SVG Air, and TIA fly to Union Island. TIA flies to Union from Grenada, and TIA, Mustique Airways, and SVG Air also have flights from the northern Grenadines and St. Vincent. Once you are on Union, a Petit St. Vincent representative will escort you from the airport to a nearby dock at the Anchorage Hotel and then on to the island via private launch. The boat ride takes about 30 minutes.

Where to Stay and Eat

Petit St. Vincent Resort, Petit St. Vincent, St. Vincent and the Grenadines, WI. ⓒ 800-654-9326 or 954-963-7401, ✆ 954-963-7402, 🖳 www.psvresort.com, info@psvresort.com

💲 Stratospheric ⑪ FAP ⒞⒞ 22 cottages

When *Hera*, the boat launch for PSV (as Petit St. Vincent is affectionately called) picked us up, we knew we were headed someplace special. Piloted by Maurice, a very friendly man dressed in a white uniform (which looked like formal military dress to us), the boat whisked us away to our very own private island. That is exactly what it is: a highly secluded resort nestled on a privately owned 113-acre island. It has just 22 cottages (three double units) sparsely dispersed around the island, each with its own discreet view of the ocean. Some of the cottages are right on the beach, some are tucked away on the hillside, and a couple are located on the far side of the island. All are extremely private. Each cut-stone and dark wood cottage has a living room with two sofas (which can be turned into daybeds), a bedroom (with two queen-size beds), a dressing room, a bathroom with shower, and a private patio with a hammock. All have ceiling fans, louvered windows, and terra-cotta tile floors. The stone walls (including the floor and walls of the shower) help to keep the rooms cool, even in the heat of the day. The fabrics are tropical pink and green (à la Gloria Upson and Bunny Bixley), exuding a faded elegance. We found the beds and pillows comfortable. There were soft cotton towels, plush robes, and upmarket toiletries, too. Conspicuously absent are TVs, a/c, and phones.

So how do you communicate with the resort? PSV has devised an ingenious system. Outside the cottage is a flagpole with two colored flags, red and yellow. If room service is desired, a written note is placed in the bamboo tube at the base of the pole and the yellow flag is raised. A member of the staff (who are constantly circling the island in minimokes) should be by within 20 minutes. If you do not want to be disturbed, raise the red flag. Trust us — and we tested this — if you raise the red one, you will not be disturbed for any reason. Privacy is valued on PSV (trysters take note)!

The service is excellent. There are more than 75 staff members to accommodate the needs of just 44 guests, so your needs will be met. The dining pavilion (if you don't opt for room service) is located in the main complex. We loved the open-air dining experience for all meals. Breakfast is standard fare, with nice touches of local fruits, vegetables, home-baked breads, and pastries. Lunch is served buffet style, with both hot and cold dishes such as seafood, pasta, sandwiches, fruit, and desserts. Dinner is informal, but men tend to wear trousers (not shorts) and women wear dresses (we sometimes get into dressing up a little, even on vacation). The dinner menu was a good fusion of international and Caribbean cuisine — using local seafood, fruits, and vegetables from St. Vincent — and other fine foods from the United States (like real Vermont maple syrup). PSV boasts its own bakery and pastry chef, and, we have to admit, the homemade stuff was great.

If swimming and sunbathing are the only things on your agenda, PSV will oblige, with almost 2 miles of white-sand beaches, all within a short walk or ride in a minimoke. The windward beaches have great snorkeling and stay relatively cool, thanks to the trade winds. The beach on the west side of the island has palapas (thatched-roof mini-pavilions), and the kitchen will pack a picnic lunch and arrange for a minimoke to give you a ride. There is now a yellow flagpole service on the west side beach. The resort has also added toilets and a shower — more time to spend lazing around, reading, snorkeling, or just sleeping. Chances are you won't find another soul within eyesight. The staff will check on you periodically for supplies (e.g., water, suntan lotion, food, or a ride back).

PSV also offers water sports, including Hobie Cats, Sunfish, windsurfers, and snorkeling equipment, and there is a 20-station fitness trail for those seeking some exercise. Just walking around the island is fun, too (the trip is about 2 miles and will take you about an hour). We started our walk late in the day, and as we came around the northern tip of the island into Conch Bay, we witnessed the most amazing sunset. There is a lighted tennis court (complete with rackets and balls at no charge), and we actually saw people using it. Scuba diving excursions to nearby islands can also be arranged.

Two things we will always remember about PSV are the sky at night—with its millions of stars shining brighter than anything we've seen up north—and the sound of the waves as they gently lulled us to sleep.

Closed September to October.

Petite Martinique

THIS ODD LITTLE OUTPOST IS PART OF GRENADA'S GRENADINES, although its residents hardly think so. Although we didn't exactly spot an independence movement during our visit to the island, there's definitely an autonomous streak running under the surface. Located 3 miles northeast of Carriacou, this 486-acre blip on the radar screen is inhabited by about 900 or so residents of predominantly French descent. They live at the base of a 738-foot extinct volcanic cone, and there are about two dozen cars on the island for tooling about the half mile or so of road. There are some odd looking tractors or dumpsters that ferry goods from the dock up to homes, and many people own a speedboat. It's safe to say they don't use them just for pleasure cruises.

Petite Martinique — also known as PM — has a much higher standard of living than its neighbors. This is largely due to its proudly held position as the smuggling capital of the West Indies, a decades-old tradition that was probably born from the lack of a customs official. Today it is common to see Carriacou-built trading boats laden with Sony Wega TVs, refrigerators, and Bordeaux wine coming from *gros* Martinique, St. Martin, and Guadeloupe. Need an outboard motor for your boat? One Grenadian priest told us how he saved hundreds of dollars by purchasing his on PM. Although the administration in Grenada cracks down on the contraband from time to time, they probably realize that if they were ever to really snuff out the trafficking, they'd have a bigger headache dealing with the hundreds of unemployed islanders.

There's a bank that's open for a few hours three days a week, there's a scruffy shell-laden beach that curls around the town (fair for swimming, but not for sunning), and you can hike to the summit of the island in about 30 minutes — the view is great. There's a disco at **Melodies** on weekends. Otherwise, that's about it. In short, we wouldn't spend the night here, but it's fine as a diversion for a few hours from PSV or Carriacou. For more information, visit www.petitemartinique.com. (For map, see p. 396.)

Getting There

There's no airport — the nearest is on Carriacou, which is served from Grenada (see the Carriacou chapter for details). The Osprey ferry travels to PM on Monday through Friday via Carriacou, leaving Grenada at 9 a.m. and 5:30

p.m., stopping at Carriacou at 10:30 a.m. and 7 p.m., and arriving on PM at 11 a.m. and 7:30 p.m., respectively. The return trip leaves PM at 5:30 a.m. and 3 p.m., arriving on Grenada two hours later. It's also possible to hire a water taxi in Windwardside on Carriacou.

Where to Stay

Melodies Guest House, Petite Martinique, Grenada, WI. ℃ 473-443-9052, ✆ 473-443-9093, 🖳 www.spiceisle.com/melodies, melodies@caribsurf.com

🗄 **Dirt Cheap** ⑪ **EP** ⓒⓒ 10 rooms

Although there are a couple of places to stay overnight, this is probably the best. The rooms are found on the second floor of a beachfront building. All are basic but clean and decent for the price. There's a restaurant and a dance hall downstairs.

Where to Eat

$$ **Palm Beach**, 473-443-9103

Located almost next to the boat dock, this serves an inviting menu of grilled fish, jerk chicken, rôti, and a variety of shrimp dishes.

Union Island

ONE OF THE SOUTHERNMOST OF ST. VINCENT'S GRENADINES, Union is perhaps the most topographically impressive island in the chain. Its profile of sheer peaks is unmistakable from a distance, rising dramatically to 999-foot Mt. Tobai. Coming in by plane is breathtaking as you swoop close to the mountains and then plunge to the short airstrip (sit on the left side for the best view). Alas, most of the island personality is owned by the Tahitian landscape. Otherwise, Union interacts with tourism primarily as a jumping-off point for Palm, Petit St. Vincent, and Mayreau. It also has a shady history as a transshipping axis for drugs, although we've never particularly observed this aspect. Our bags aroused more interest than usual when we arrived at the airport Customs counter — we have no idea why.

Originally a cotton plantation, then used for subsistence farming, today 14-square-mile Union Island thrives because of the yachting traffic and has a total population of about 1,900. The Anchorage Yacht Club (see below) is the social hub of most visiting sailors. There are two villages: **Ashton** is primarily residential, whereas **Clifton** has most of the businesses. In Clifton you'll find a bank, several restaurants, a couple of hotels, and **Captain Yannis**, who does day sails out of Union Island. Yannis does almost daily catamaran trips to the Tobago Cays, Mayreau, and Palm Island, and he is available for charters. Call for reservations, 784-458-8513, or check the Web site, www.captainyannis.com. Another day charter company is Wind and Sea, which can be reached at 784-458-8678; www.grenadines.net/union/windandsea.html.

It's a 20-minute walk from Ashton to Clifton. In fact, walking is a great way to explore the island — there are unpaved tracks on the west coast of the island that offer wonderful views, and Chatham Bay is beautiful and underdeveloped. There are usually a few yachts anchored in crescent-shaped Chatham, but the swimming is better at Big Sand (a.k.a. Belmont Bay), which has just a few buildings nearby. There is also a trail up to the striking Pinnacles, which offers the island's best view.

If you choose to stay a night or two, there's a tourist office in Clifton (784-458-8350), but they have little to offer beyond a few brochures. When we asked what activities there were to do on Union, the young woman behind the counter said, "Well, you can take a day sail to the Tobago Cays." When we explained that we had just come from there, she seemed stumped to offer something of interest on Union. Granted, the scene in Clifton is nothing terribly appealing, so don't plan on staying too long. However, if you are on a modest budget and want to sample several of the remote Grenadines, then Union is a good base for your explorations. (For map, see p. 396.)

Getting There

The gateway to Union is Barbados, and SVG Air, Mustique Airways, and TIA have daily flights. Mustique Airways and SVG Air also have flights from the northern Grenadines and St. Vincent, TIA connects Grenada and Carriacou to Union, and Air Caraïbes flies in from Martinique and Canouan. You can also take the mail boat from St. Vincent, the *MV Barracuda*. The ferry leaves St. Vincent on Monday, Thursday, and Saturday and takes about five hours to reach Union (stopping at Bequia, Canouan, and Mayreau en route); the one-way fare is $18. The Barracuda leaves Union (traveling north) on Tuesday and Friday mornings and Saturday afternoon. There's also the *MV Gem Star*, which travels south from St. Vincent on Tuesday and Friday, returning on Wednesday and Saturday mornings. Before traveling, be sure to confirm ferry times and days with the Union Island tourist office: 784-458-8350. There is also limited boat service between Carriacou and Union on Monday and Thursday — confirm with the tourist office.

Where to Stay

Anchorage Yacht Club Hotel & Marina, Union Island, St. Vincent and the Grenadines, WI. © 784-458-8221, ℘ 784-458-8365, 🖥 www.ayc-hotel-grenadines.com, ofc@ayc-hotel-grenadines.com or aycunion@caribsurf.com

🛍 **Cheap** for the standard rooms and **Not So Cheap** for the others
⑪ CP ㏄ 15 rooms

This outfit has a very "Don't Stop the Carnival" ambiance, with questionable service and less-than-primped rooms. Nonetheless, longtime manager Charlotte Honnart does her best to make your stay on Union memorable. There are three types of units, all of which boast sea views. Four cabanas in a low-slung block have a good amount of space and a/c; each has a semiprivate outdoor shower (more functional than exotic). There are six standard rooms in the main building above the restaurant; the upkeep is shoddy. There are five bungalows that are a short walk away from the main complex — these have a/c and a modicum of Robinson Crusoe escapist air, but little in the way of traditional polish (they feel a little forgotten). Along the waterfront is the restaurant, which is fronted by a pen containing nurse sharks. The dining is popular with visiting yachties, but we found breakfast to be overpriced and underwhelming—we threw our toast to the sharks.

Closed September through mid-October.

Clifton Beach Hotel, Union Island, St. Vincent and the Grenadines, WI. © 784-458-8235, ✆ 784-458-8313, 🖳 www.cliftonbeachhotel.com, cliftonbeachhotel@caribsurf.com

🛅 **Cheap** 🍴 **EP** ⓒⓒ 30 rooms

Anchorage may be the better known, slightly more polished operation, but this spot has one of our favorite rooms in the Grenadines: room 26, on the third floor. It is open to the breeze on three sides and looks directly out to the water and a scene of bobbing masts. It's really sweet. Other rooms are nowhere near as nice, but they're adequate if you're just passing through for the night. Expect little in the way of traditional hotel services, and note that there's no real beach here, despite the name.

Where to Eat

$$$ **Anchorage Yacht Club**, Clifton, 784-458-8221

The AYC offers pretty standard island fare, but it's pricey for what you get. There's a jump-up with a live steel band on Monday and Friday.

$$ **Captain Gourmet**, Clifton, 784-458-8918

This French-owned deli has fresh baked baguette and croissants, sandwiches, decent wine, and imported canned goods. There's no seating, but it is a little dollop of take-away refinement for the visiting boat crews.

$$ **Lambi's**, Clifton, 784-458-8549

This is a good spot at which to take in the local cuisine, particularly the titular item (a.k.a. conch), and other fresh seafood, all prepared Caribbean style.

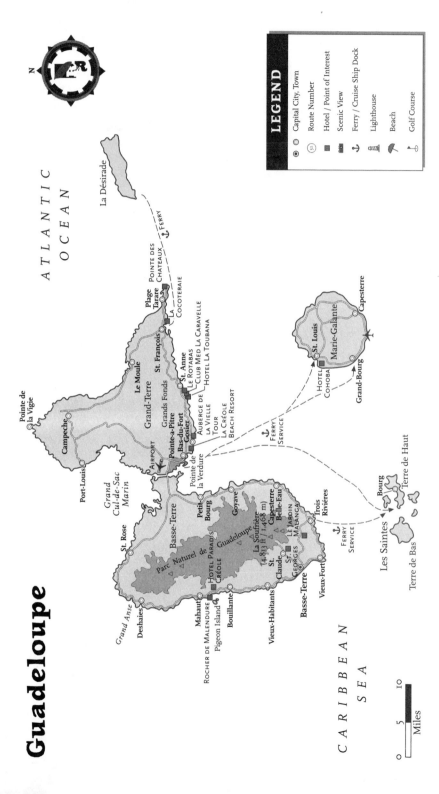

Guadeloupe
(with Les Saintes and Marie-Galante)

Guadeloupe

IT WAS AT GUADELOUPE'S GRAND ANSE, A LONG CARPET OF rose-colored sand, that we had one of those perfect moments that you know will stick to the recesses of your brain for a long time to come. We had opted to break up our round-island drive with lunch at Le Karacoli, a simple beach-side family-run restaurant at the edge of the sand. Chef Lucienne Salcede had taken our order, and then our gracious hostess urged us to go for a swim while our lunch was being prepared. We were each handed a glass of thick

Guadeloupe: Key Facts

Location	16°N by 62°W
	38 miles/61 kilometers south of Antigua
	30 miles/48 kilometers north of Dominica
	1,845 miles/2,989 kilometers southeast of New York
Size	530 square miles/1,373 square kilometers
	Basse-Terre: 312 square miles/808 square kilometers
	Grande-Terre: 218 square miles/565 square kilometers
Highest point	La Soufrière (4,813 feet/1,468 meters)
Population	426,496
Language	French and Creole
Time	Atlantic Standard Time (1 hour ahead of EST, same as EDT)
Area code	To call Guadeloupe from the U.S., dial 011 (the international dialing code), then 590-590 (the country code), followed by the six-digit local number.
Electricity	220 volts AC, 50 cycles; you'll need a transformer and an adapter for U.S.-made appliances.
Currency	Euro (€1 = US$1.25 at press time; check prior to departure)
Driving	On the right; your valid driver's license will suffice for up to 20 days; after that you'll need an international driver's license.
Documents	U.S. and Canadian citizens need proof of nationality (plus a photo ID) for up to three months; after that a passport is necessary; an ongoing or a return ticket is also necessary.
Departure tax	None
Beer to drink	Corsaire
Rum to drink	Damoiseau
Music to hear	Zouk
Tourism info	590-590-82-09-30, www.antilles-info-tourisme.com

punch coco — a rum-and-coconut concoction that tastes as though devised for the gods — and we wandered into the gently undulating sea to bob and dip. The only sounds were those of children playing down the beach and the ice tinkling in our glass. Fifteen minutes later, Lucienne was waving us in, and then we traded one exquisite moment for another as our plates were filled with traditional Creole items like boudin ("blood sausage"), blaff (fish poached in wine and spices), and colombo ("chicken curry"). The meal was delicious and not too expensive, and the afternoon seemed to encapsulate all that is perfect about the Caribbean — the French Caribbean, in particular.

Guadeloupe is *très français*, a full-fledged Région of France. Paris acts as the cultural and political capital of the island. Just off the coast of Guadeloupe is Marie-Galante and the archipelago known as the Iles des Saintes (a.k.a. Les Saintes) — smaller islands, and just as French, but less touristy (more on these in their separate chapters). Guadeloupe itself is actually two similar-size islands, Grande-Terre and Basse-Terre, separated by a narrow seawater channel, the Rivière Salée. These island monikers translate literally as "Big Land" and "Low Land," which are really misnomers — Basse-Terre is the mountainous volcanic part of the island, and Grande-Terre is fairly flat. There are several theories of why this is so. The most likely explanation is that they are named for the wind velocity that at one time powered sugar mills — the flatter island having stronger winds, thus being named Grande-Terre. Combined, Basse-Terre and Grande-Terre represent the sixth largest island in the Caribbean.

Although Martinique is somewhat more sophisticated and affluent, Guadeloupe is highly developed, with more than 5,000 hotel rooms. Often you will feel more as if you're in some part of continental France than in the Caribbean, especially in **Pointe-à-Pitre**, the island's commercial hub (the capital is the smaller city of **Basse-Terre**). There are high-rise apartment buildings, shopping centers, huge supermarkets, billboards galore, and freeways. There are wonderful Caribbean elements, too — like colorful open-air markets and quaint West Indian–style houses — and the contrast between the modern and the traditional is often striking. When you venture into the countryside, the balance tips more toward the Caribbean flavor, yet you have the great French road system to help you see the sights. The smaller islands are more rural still.

Most of the hotels and tourist areas are found on **Grande-Terre**, concentrated on its south coast from Pointe-à-Pitre east to the Pointe des Châteaux. This is also where most of the best beaches are located. Along this coast are three major resort towns: **Gosier**, **Ste-Anne**, and **St. François**, the last being the most desirable in terms of location but, of late, somewhat lacking in good hotels. It is a bit less developed and has the nicest beaches nearby, including **Plage Tarare**, the official nude beach. Ste-Anne is also on the radar and is the home of good windsurfing and the Club Med. Gosier is the most developed, with big resorts and lots of tourists, but also with some great restaurants and the best nightlife. The Basse-Terre side doesn't really have a tourist area per se, as its mostly black-sand and/or rocky beaches aren't a draw. But there are an increasing number of good lodging options here, including places near **Pigeon Island** — a popular snorkel and dive spot on the west coast — and the **Parc National**, a 74,100-acre preserve of waterfalls, rainforest, lakes, mountains, flora, and fauna. It's worth considering staying at two or even three different resorts in one Guadeloupe vacation to take in the various points of interest, including the offshore islands.

Americans make up only about 3 percent of the overnight visitors to Guadeloupe; the overwhelming majority of visitors are French or Québécois on package tours. If you are a Francophile, you'll love it, but you should note that English is not spoken widely—even less than in Martinique. As a matter of fact, you can generally count on it only at the major resorts. If you don't speak French, you will have a difficult time understanding and communicating—more so than in Paris, really. We consider our French to be passable, yet we had difficulty when something out of the ordinary occurred. For example, one bathroom didn't have a shower curtain, and we needed a voltage converter for a laptop. The front-desk staff didn't speak English. Trying to explain these problems in rudimentary French was hard enough. It would be quite an adventure trying to explain them without knowing the language at all. If you do speak a little French, however, you will have a ball; if not, a smile and *"Parlez-vous anglais?"* goes a long way toward opening doors.

Note: In recent years there has been trouble in this paradise. Labor unrest has been a recurring problem—travel agents in mainland France (where more than 85 percent of Guadeloupe's visitors come from) often discourage their clients from a Guadeloupe vacation. Air services have been cut, and tourism arrivals have fallen. In 2002, the world's largest hotel chain, the French-owned Accor Group, closed up shop on Guadeloupe (as well as on Martinique and St. Martin). In a letter to French President Jacques Chirac, Accor's co-president, Gérard Pélisson, cited a "hateful social climate" that prevented his company from operating profitably in the French West Indies; the high cost of employment is "five times less low" than on other Caribbean islands, he wrote. No doubt Accor has more profitable operations in Cuba and the Dominican Republic, where wages are a pittance and mainland French taxpayers aren't footing the bill for generous—by Caribbean standards—social provisions on par with their mainland counterparts. Unemployment pay and munificent welfare benefits simply aren't the norm on the neighboring (non-French) islands.

More to the point: Will these travails affect your Guadeloupe vacation? This is unlikely. We visit the island every few years and have not experienced any great decline in service standards, nor have we been inconvenienced by a strike (although they do occur). Living standards in the French West Indies are higher. Compared to most other Caribbean islands, health care is excellent, trash is picked up, mail is delivered in a timely fashion, and sanitation in restaurants is subjected to much closer scrutiny. Guadeloupe and Martinique's roads are the best maintained in all the Caribbean, and when a major hurricane storms through the region, the French army is called in to assist with cleanup and reconstruction, allowing these islands to bounce back more quickly than their neighbors. We can't find fault with any of that.

The Briefest History

Like almost all the other Caribbean islands, Guadeloupe was settled by the Caribs, who gave it its best name, Karukera, or "Island of Beautiful Waters." Columbus sighted the island on his second voyage, in 1493, and named it after Santa Maria de Guadelupe de Estremadura. The Caribs, fierce fighters that they were, kept the Spanish off the island, but the French landed a party in 1635 and eventually drove the Caribs away. Sugar became the major moneymaker, and the French imported lots of slaves from Guinea to make it work. The island was officially annexed by the king of France in 1674 and remained under French control except for the years 1759–1763, when the British occupied the island. It went back to France under the terms of the Treaty of Paris. The French Revolution brought instability to the island; there was a short reign of terror, and then slavery was abolished. The uncertainty was reversed with the advent of Napoleon, but slavery was reestablished in 1802 and remained in force until an Alsatian, Victor Schoelcher, was instrumental in abolishing it in 1848. To keep the plantations running, indentured labor (another form of slavery) was imported from the Comptoirs (French settlements in India). For a century Guadeloupe remained a backwater in French politics until it became an overseas Department of France in 1946, and finally a Région in 1974. Guadeloupe is governed by a prefect, who is appointed by the French minister of the interior, and by two locally elected legislative bodies, the Conseil Général and the Conseil Régional. There is a strong independence movement percolating in the background. Tourism and agriculture (bananas and sugar) are the primary engines driving the economy.

Getting There

Guadeloupe's Pôle Caraïbes International Airport, located a couple miles north of Pointe-à-Pitre, is one of the region's most modern facilities, and jumbo jets fly in daily from France. From North America, American Eagle flies nonstop from San Juan, allowing connections from most major U.S. cities; Air Canada has weekly nonstops from Montréal, and Air France has several flights weekly from Miami. From the French islands, plus Barbados, Santo Domingo, and St. Lucia, Air Caraïbes is the primary carrier; LIAT flies in from neighboring Antigua, Dominica, and Martinique.

The Express des Iles (590-590-83-12-45; www.express-des-iles.com), a high-speed catamaran, offers trips daily from Martinique (the passage from Martinique takes three and a half hours, and adult fare is about $80 one way, $125 round-trip) and several times a week from Dominica and St. Lucia. Other ferries making the link with Martinique include Brudey Frères (590-590-90-04-48) and Caribbean Ferries (590-590-82-05-05).

Getting Around

With the island's 1,225 miles of paved roads among the best in the Caribbean, you should definitely rent a car. The roads are clearly marked (a rarity in these latitudes), and the European sign system is helpful and easy to use. Note, however, that French drivers speed with merry abandon—an extreme example of joie de vivre (or should it be *joie de mort?*). All of the major international companies are here, including Avis (800-331-1084 or 590-590-21-13-54), Budget (800-527-0700 or 590-590-21-13-49), Hertz (800-654-3001 or 590-590-21-13-46; www.hertzantilles.com), Thrifty (800-367-2277 or 590-590-21-13-60), and National's affiliate, Europcar (800-227-3876 or 590-590-91-58-52). Be sure to reserve well in advance—the cheapest cars will be booked if you arrive without a reservation. You will also be able to lock in a better rate in advance.

If you don't want to drive, there are plenty of taxis (they're expensive), and there is the public bus system, which is excellent here and a great way to meet the locals. Look for the signs marked "Arrêt-Bus" and wave to the driver for a pickup. Taxis are also available but expensive; for radio dispatch call 590-590-20-74-74 or 590-590-82-96-69.

Day trips to Les Saintes and Marie-Galante, Guadeloupe's nearby siblings, are easy and worthwhile—for more info, see their respective chapters.

Focus on Guadeloupe: Exploring the National Park

Like Martinique, Guadeloupe possesses an outstanding and beautifully maintained trail system that ranges from easy walks approaching tall waterfalls to a fierce traverse of the island's volcanic spine. There is no shortage to keep the active visitor enthralled and busy.

The hikes center largely on Basse-Terre, where you'll find the Parc National, a 74,100-acre hinterland that occupies the higher slopes from north to south. The park is also home to the island's geologic hotspot, La Soufrière (4,813 feet/1,468 meters), the highest point in the Eastern Caribbean and one of the region's more troubled volcanoes—a series of eruptions in 1976–1977 were exciting enough to occasion the evacuation of the capital. Ironically, it's probably the Caribbean's most visited volcanic summit, and on a clear day you'll find dozens of people making their way to the top for spectacular views of Les Saintes and Dominica to the south (but do come prepared for the annual 400-plus inches of rain this mountain receives).

Even if you don't make the ascent, it's worth driving up to the end of the steep road that climbs up the western flanks from the capital, where you'll see ample evidence of the volcanic activity (and views down to the west). However, having tackled most of the volcanic summits in the region, we can report that Guadeloupe's Soufrière is one of the easier quests, and well worth the 90-minute climb on a well-defined path to the top. The Soufrière trailhead is high on the slopes, above the town of St. Claude, and from the large parking area the barren summit looks imposing. After circling from the green but treeless western slopes around to the eastern face, you'll enter a ravine where the path splits; take the right-hand passage to the top. You might expect a bowl-shaped crater at the summit, but instead you'll encounter a moist landscape that looks more like the moon—a series of small craters and ominous gray bulges provide topographical accents, and the smell of sulfur scents the crisp air. The ground is eerily warm to the touch, marked by moss and tufts of green grass. At the main vent, steam bellows from a gnarled gullet that leads deep into the island's belly. On the way down, turn right at the ravine junction; this takes you around the summit cone via its southern slopes and crosses the site of the most recent activity. A volcano museum at **Savane-a-Mulets**, a mile or so below the parking area, tells the geologic history of the area. It's a good stop on the way back.

Another of Guadeloupe's popular hiking areas lies in the rumpled valleys immediately east of the summit, above the village of **St. Sauveur**. The **Chutes du Carbet**, a three-tiered waterfall, pours down the slopes of La Soufrière. At the end of the road, a trail leads down 1.5 miles/2.4 kilometers to the lowest of the falls, which, at 70 feet/21 meters, are the shortest plunge but contain the greatest volume of water. From the same parking area, the 20-minute climb to the base of the 360-foot/110-meter second falls is reasonably easy, and when we arrived, a dozen bathers lolled in the spray of water at its base. The arduous, muddy trail to the premier Chute du Carbet, the most spectacular of the falls, is another matter, requiring about two hours to reach. At 370 feet/113 meters, this is possibly the tallest waterfall in the eastern Caribbean, and it offers a soaring view down the canyon. You can continue up the eastern slopes to the summit of La Soufrière (a very demanding trek) or return the way you came up. Take your time, it's a thigh-challenging descent.

The island's most ambitious hike is the **Victor Hugues Trail**, a spectacular traverse of the volcanic crest. Its length (allow eight hours, one way) and the rugged mountains make this an adventure for advanced hikers only. From Petit-Bourg, follow the N1 for 2 miles/3.2 kilometers south to a road leading to Montebello; stay to the left and proceed to the end, a banana plantation. The trail starts here and crosses through the bananas in a long, steep valley to a ridge, where it meets the Merwat trail. Follow the crest south, aiming for the summit of Soufrière, where the hike ends. Check with the National Park headquarters about trail conditions before embarking; they can also recommend local guides to accompany you.

Other, less rigorous goals in the National Park include the lush **Route de la Traversée**, a 16-mile passage through the center of Basse-Terre. Along the way you'll encounter the **Cascade aux Ecrevisses**, a waterfall just off the road, and just beyond is the **Parc Bras-David**, which offers easy strolls through the leafy canopy, and the **Parc Zoologique et Botanique**, a zoo and garden with a restaurant that provides great views from its perch, 1,500 feet/457 meters above sea level.

Where to Stay

As we noted earlier, most of the hotels and tourist developments are on Grande-Terre, concentrated on the south coast from Gosier to St. François. There is little in the way of hotels in Pointe-à-Pitre (and little reason to stay there, anyway) — the Gosier/Bas-du-Fort area is just a couple miles out of town. The Basse-Terre half of the island may have the best scenery, but it doesn't really have a tourist area per se. There are good places to stay that are close to both the diving on Pigeon Island and the Parc National.

A number of the smaller, nonchain hotels and villas are represented by the Santa Barbara–based French Caribbean International (800-322-2223; www.frenchcaribbean.com), which is a good source of up-to-date island info as well.

Grand-Terre

Auberge de la Vieille Tour, Montauban, Gosier, Guadeloupe, FWI.
 ℂ 800-221-4542 or 590-590-84-23-23, ✆ 590-590-84-33-43,
 🖳 www.sofitel.com

💲 **Wicked Pricey** 🍴 **CP** CC 180 rooms

Managed by Sofitel, this resort is the grande dame of the Gosier hotels, built around an 18th-century windmill and set on a 5-acre bluff, just steps away from town. The main building houses the (excellent) restaurant and bar; the latter offers a splendid view of Basse-Terre. Just below is a series of single-story buildings — the original rooms — stretched along the rock-lined shore. There are four categories of rooms; the middle two categories (Superior and Luxe) are represented in these older buildings and are by far the best choice. Both are beautifully decorated in colonial-style teak furnishings and tropical motifs. The Luxe rooms are like split-level junior suites and have gorgeous, glass-walled bathrooms that overlook the sea. They are among our favorite rooms to stay in throughout the West Indies. The less expensive standard (Mer) category and the more expensive Suites are found in a separate, newer wing located just past the pool. These aren't bad; they're just not as classy as the other categories. Note that two of the Mer rooms (Numbers 112 and 202) are located immediately above the sand — an unadvertised perk no other unit here has. All rooms are air-conditioned, and all overlook the sea with their own lanais. There is a small private beach, a pool, and tennis courts. One carp: During a recent visit, service hiccups at the front desk and in the restaurant were repeated and annoying. Otherwise, this is Guadeloupe's premier hotel.

Club Med La Caravelle, Ste-Anne, Guadeloupe, FWI. ℂ 800-258-2633 or 590-590-85-49-50, ✆ 590-590-85-49-70, 🖳 www.clubmed.com

💲 **Ridiculous** 🍴 **All-Inclusive** CC 329 rooms

This is an extensive complex with a wide variety of sports and activities, a Club Med hallmark. Originally opened in 1973, the hotel received an extensive remodel and upgrade in 2006 (probably to bring it somewhat up to par with the revitalized Club Med in Martinique). It's an all-inclusive resort — that is, your meals, drinks, and most on-site activities are packaged in one up-front price, which, on an island of superlative cuisine and restaurants, is a drawback (although the food here is surprisingly good). Compared to some other Club Meds, this is not much of a hopping singles scene—families and over-30 couples are the norm.

The place is big, with 44 acres of palm-dotted grounds and an attractive if somewhat crowded beach. Inside the resort there is a theater, a nightclub, several bars and restaurants, and billiards. Most of it buzzes morning, noon, and night. The rooms vary in size from modest to downright petite; not all have balconies, but the décor and amenities are greatly improved. Another recent addition is a good-size but busy pool. There are six tennis courts as well as volleyball, basketball, archery, trapeze, circus workshops, and every water sport you can imagine (most of them are included in the rates, including windsurfing, which is excellent in this area). Any organized excursions off-property are extra (Ste-Anne is just a 15-minute walk). This Club Med appeals to couples and families who are looking for a moderately priced Caribbean sojourn and who don't mind the occasional big-resort glitches the company is known for. Although there are plenty of French and French-speaking Canadians staying here, it's a good place for non-French-speaking Americans to land, because almost all the staff speaks some English.

La Créole Beach Resort, B.P. 61, Pointe de la Verdure, Gosier, Guadeloupe, FWI. ℂ 800-322-2223 or 590-590-90-46-46, ✆ 590-590-90-46-66, 🖳 www.deshotelsetdesiles.com

💲 **Very Pricey** at La Créole, Mahogany, and Les Palmes, and **Pricey** at Yucca 🍴 CP ⒸⒸ 384 rooms

For moderate-price rooms and a big-resort feel, this is your best bet in Gosier. Located just west of town on Pointe de la Verdure, it's a larger resort than its 384 units might indicate. That's because La Créole is one of four interconnected hotels that are operated by the same firm, spread out among several attractive Creole-style buildings. It has a large pool (good for laps), its own man-made beach, lots of water sports, and a poolside bar area that is a pleasant spot for a cocktail. The rooms are comfortable, furnished in what might be called tropical-French *moderne*, with a/c, balcony, TV, bath, and direct-dial phone. The staff is helpful, even if communicating takes some imagination.

La Créole's operation also encompasses the 64-room Mahogany Hotel, the 100-room Résidences Yucca, and a new fourth wing, the 66-room Les Palmes. The three share most facilities, the same address and phone number, and a maze of corridors and passageways that takes a few days to master. La Créole is nicest, Mahogany is a decent choice for those who desire a kitchenette, and the somewhat dog-eared

Yucca is the least expensive. There is also a new food court–style restaurant, La Route des Epices, which features different spice-oriented dining every night.

La Cocoteraie, St. François, Guadeloupe, FWI. ✆ 800-543-4300 or 590-590-88-79-81, ✆ 590-590-88-78-33, 🖳 www.la-cocoteraie.com

💲 **Beyond Belief** 🍴 **CP** [CC] 52 rooms

This is perhaps Guadeloupe's most indulgent address; in 1992 the Méridien folks supplemented their large St. François resort with this more intimate and upscale all-suite luxury wing. Although the two properties were physically joined at the hip, the other property has gone downhill (and is no longer a Méridien; rather, it is now known as Kalenda), while La Cocoteraie has a separate, discreet entrance. Two- and three-story bungalows house the colorful and delightfully designed rooms, each with a view of the sea, private balcony, minibar, and a round bathtub and separate shower in each bathroom. The two beachlets here are more or less segregated from the Kalenda "riffraff" next door (who, after all, are paying only a couple hundred a night for a room on the adjacent beach); La Cocoteraie also has two tennis courts and a gym. An overdue facelift is planned. Until then expect fading paint and worn and warped furnishings. The service is strong, and there is fine dining at the elegant restaurant, but what's with those big Chinese vases sitting in the immense swimming pool? The hotel is closed from late August through late October.

Hotel La Toubana, B.P. 63, Durivage, Ste-Anne, Guadeloupe, FWI. ✆ 590-590-88-25-78, ✆ 590-590-88-38-90, 🖳 www.deshotelsetdesiles.com

💲 **Pricey** 🍴 **CP** [CC] 32 rooms

Perched high up on a steep bluff overlooking the sea and the Club Med, this reasonably priced hotel is your best bet in Ste-Anne, although the vertigo-inclined might want to give it a second thought. Accommodations are scattered along the brink in bungalows in both standard (garden view) and superior classes (sea views and better furnishings). All have a kitchenette, a/c, phone, and a private garden and lanai; the rooms are nicely done in pastels. There is a spectacular cliff-edge pool and a deck with great breezes and views. At the bottom of the hill there is a small, rocky, man-made cove that is protected from the surf, but, alas, it is not protected from a fleet of Wave Runners that the hotel rents out. Other activities available are tennis, billiards, and Ping-Pong. The restaurant is quite good and English is spoken here — a plus. A car is a good idea since Ste-Anne and better beaches are a long walk — fortunately a Hertz office is on site.

Le Rotabas, B.P. 30, Durivage, Ste-Anne, Guadeloupe, FWI. ✆ 590-590-88-25-60, ✆ 590-590-88-26-87, 🖳 www.lerotabas.com

🛍 **Not So Cheap** 🍴 **CP** [CC] 44 rooms

Located right on the beach next to L.C.S. Funboard, between Club Med and Ste-Anne, this is a good, somewhat cheaper accommodation, especially appropriate for those who are here to windsurf. The air-conditioned rooms are found in several small buildings wedged around the property. There's a swimming pool, and the Club Med beach is a five-minute walk. It's a relaxed place and the rooms are pleasant, with phone, minifridge and (French) TV. The rooms are clean and are somewhat better than exterior appearance might indicate.

Basse-Terre

There are several accommodations here that we recommend. The first one is a great romantic hideaway; the last two are close to Pigeon Island and Guadeloupe's best diving. All provide easy access to hiking and the rainforest.

Le Jardin Malanga, L'Ermitage, Trois Rivières, Guadeloupe, FWI.
   ☎ 800-322-2223 or 590-590-92-67-57, ✎ 590-590-92-67-58,
   🖥 www.deshotelsetdesiles.com

🛍 **Very Pricey** 🍴 **CP** [CC] 9 rooms

You won't stumble across Malanga by accident—it's tucked into a quiet residential area above the town of Trois Rivières on the southern slopes of La Soufrière, but that's also its appeal. This is a 1927 home that was turned into a country inn, with smashing results. There is a trio of rooms in the main house and three newer, two-story, wood bungalows in the lush garden, each with two units. These six rooms have warm wood paneling and bathrooms that vaunt one-way picture windows overlooking the fruit tree–filled garden. Best of all is the small but peerless swimming pool, which has a horizon lip that spills into a view of Les Saintes in the distance—this is a panorama you could enjoy for hours. You'll want to do that, since there are few other on-site activities; it's less than an hour to the National Park, and five minutes down the hill is the ferry dock for Les Saintes (a great day trip). The restaurant is quite good (one complaint: quite limited menu choices), and the family management is attentive. It's a great romantic hideaway.

St. Georges, Rue Gratien Parize, St. Claude, Guadeloupe, FWI. ☎ 590-590-80-10-10, ✎ 590-590-80-30-50, 🖥 www.hotelstgeorges.com

🛍 **Not So Cheap** 🍴 **EP** [CC] 40 rooms

Located in the semi-fashionable hamlet of St. Claude, which is east of Basse-Terre (the capital) and up in the mountains, this hotel is a surprisingly modern addition to the Guadeloupe scene. Although it lacks island charm, the rooms are tastefully appointed with mahogany antique knockoffs, and there's a fine pool for lounging; you'll also find a squash court and fitness center. If you want to be near the Parc National, St. Georges is the closest hotel. La Soufrière volcano (and other hiking) is just a 20-minute drive up the hill, and fair beaches are 10 minutes away. Its perch in the hills affords great views, and the excellent restaurant serves cuisine *gastronomique*. The hotel draws mainly businesspeople headed to the capital, and weekend specials are not uncommon.

Hotel Paradis Créole, Route de Poirer-Pigeon, Bouillante, Guadeloupe, FWI. ✆ 590-590-98-71-62, 📧 590-590-98-72-08

💲 **Cheap** 🍴 **CP** ⓒⓒ 11 rooms

This small hotel, located a mile south of Malendure and almost a mile up a steep hill, features great sunset views. There are air-conditioned rooms with lanais, a pool, and a restaurant serving Creole cuisine. The hotel will help you arrange diving, waterskiing, hiking, deep-sea fishing, and other activities. It's a somewhat informal operation, but that's also its appeal.

Rocher de Malendure, Bouillante, Guadeloupe, FWI. ✆ 590-590-98-70-84, 📧 590-590-98-89-92, 🖥 www.rocher-de-malendure.com

💲 **Cheap** 🍴 **CP** ⓒⓒ 3 rooms

If you're looking for a seaside spot on the western coast of Basse-Terre, this is a good choice. Situated on a rocky bluff overlooking the sea, white-roofed bungalows (actually rondavels), containing just three units, are lined up on the hill in formation. The rooms are slightly rustic and worn but are freshly painted and air-conditioned and have a kitchenette on the terrace; the views are excellent for the price. There's a fine lobster restaurant, and one of the nicest black-sand beaches on the island is just down the road. Pigeon Island is just offshore (excursion boats run from the beach). The same family has another small inn, the **Jardin Tropical** (590-590-98-77-23; www.au-jardin-tropical.com), located up the hill and just below Paradis Créole, where you'll find 11 inexpensive rooms and a pool.

Where to Eat

This is the land of *cuisine gastronomique et Créole*, so eating out is a pleasure. There are hundreds of restaurants, from grand expensive affairs to little dives that serve great food. Part of the fun on Guadeloupe is discovering the latter, and we urge you to follow your nose and your instincts. We'll give you some suggestions, but if you discover other or better establishments, let us know. Be sure to pick up a copy of *Ti Gourmet*, a free restaurant guide, when you arrive. The following are among the best.

Grande-Terre

$ **food stands**, Caravelle, Ste-Anne

Wedged on the beach between the Club Med and Le Rotabas (and next to L.C.S. Funboard), these little lunch stands prepare heavenly sandwiches on fresh baguettes for about $5 — a steal on any French island.

$$$$ **Iguane Café**, St. François, 590-590-88-61-37

Located at the east end of the golf course, this pleasant establishment serves excellent French meals with Provençal touches. Closed Tuesday.

$$$$ **La Mandarine**, Rue Simon Radeguonde, Gosier, 590-590-84-30-28

Sylvette and Patrick run a fine French Creole restaurant in the heart of Gosier. Try the lobster profiteroles or the crayfish with passion fruit vinegar.

$ **L'Agouba Grill**, Gosier, 590-590-84-64-97

Here you'll find grilled chicken, ribs, fish, and beef brochette, served with freedom *frites* and lots of camaraderie.

$$$$ **Le Château de Feuilles**, Campêche, Anse Bertrand, 590-590-22-30-30

This is our favorite restaurant on Guadeloupe, well worth a special trip for lunch (it is not open for dinner). It is set out in the middle of nowhere (9 miles/15 kilometers from Le Moule on the Campêche road — nowhere, right?) in an old colonial house; you dine on a patio overlooking the pool. Specialties include sea egg pastries, kingfish pavé with garlic cream, and passion fruit crème brûlée. Reservations are a must; closed Monday.

$$ **Le Mareyeur**, St. François, 590-590-88-44-24

This is a nice spot in town, across the street from the water, with simpler Creole dishes that won't break the bank. Closed Tuesday.

$$$$$ **Le Zagaya**, St. François, 590-590-88-67-21

An expensive but excellent restaurant for lobster in St. François. The cuisine is Creole-Continental. Reservations are required.

$$$ **L'Endroit**, Face Ecotel, Gosier Montauban, 590-590-84-46-57

If you feel like eating pizza, there are more than 30 varieties served here in a garden setting, as well as fancier entrées like lobster au gratin. It's open until 1 a.m., closed Tuesday. A bar and pool table make this a fun late-night spot.

$$ **Les Pieds dans l'Eau**, St. François, 590-590-88-60-02

Literally "Feet in the Water," this is the place for modestly priced lobster in down-home surroundings that, you guessed it, hang over the shoreline.

$$ **Plage Tarare**, no phone

Situated at the end of a dirt road where you park your car for the nudie beach, this is a great place for wine and lunch (and after lunch you can step down to the beach and peel off your clothes).

Pointe-à-Pitre

$$$$$ Côté Jardin, La Marina, Pointe-à-Pitre, 590-590-90-91-28

If you're in the mood for haute cuisine and don't mind spending a few chips to have it, this restaurant provides delicious food and nice atmosphere. Open for lunch and dinner except Sunday. Reservations are advised.

$$$ **Le Plaisancier**, Pointe-à-Pitre, 590-590-90-71-53

Le Plaisancier serves French offerings with Creole touches, including crayfish sauté, duck with pineapple, and lobster in a pastry shell. Three-course meals are about $25. Closed Monday.

Basse-Terre

$$$ **Caprice des Iles**, Baillif, 590-590-81-74-97

Located just north of the capital city, near the foot of the airstrip, this is a great lunch spot if you're on a round-island tour. The dining terrace overlooks black sand, and the menu offers a nice array of seafood dishes. Closed mid-August through mid-September.

$$$ **La Touna**, Pigeon, Bouillante, 590-590-98-70-10

Right on the beach, with great views of Pigeon Island, this is where seafood (swordfish, kingfish, or dolphin) comes in fresh every day from the restaurant's own fisherman. It's open for lunch and dinner; closed Sunday evening and all day Monday. Reservations are suggested.

$$$ ⊛ **Le Karacoli**, Grande Anse, 590-590-28-41-17

Named for the jewel worn around the neck of Arawak and Carib Indians, this lovely spot sits right on the beach, with a menu embracing flavors typical of southern Basse-Terre. The three-course lobster feast for two is about $100.

$$$ **Le Rocher de Malendure**, Pigeon, Bouillante, 590-590-98-70-84

This long-popular restaurant sits on a perch overlooking the sea, with open-air huts built on the steep rock. The diverse menu focuses on seafood (ask to find out what was caught that morning), but most come for the reasonably priced lobster. Closed Wednesday and in September.

Don't Miss

Grande Anse

This is a long, beautiful strand of rose-hued sand; it is undeveloped except for a few restaurants and bars. It's worth a special trip.

Plage Tarare and Les Salines

A buff beach near Pointe des Châteaux and the pretty beach next to it are both local favorites.

Iles de la Petite-Terre

There is great snorkeling here — sail to Iles de la Petite-Terre via catamaran from St. François.

Les Saintes

An easy day trip, Terre-de-Haut is what St. Barth once was — unspoiled (see Les Saintes chapter).

Basse-Terre

Worth at least a day trip or two. Be sure to take the central road (Route de la Traversée) right through the lush Parc National. On the way, check out the atmospheric capital, Basse-Terre, and if you feel like it, go diving off Pigeon Island.

L.C.S. Funboard

With locations in Ste-Anne (for beginners and intermediates) and in Le Moule (for advanced and wave jumpers), this is Guadeloupe's best windsurfing school and facility, featuring Fanatic/Copello and Gaastra equipment (590-590-88-15-17, fax 590-590-88-15-21).

Parc National

Lots of great hiking opportunities are available here, including the trek to the summit of La Soufrière, or take the Route de la Traversée through the scenic center of the park.

Les Saintes

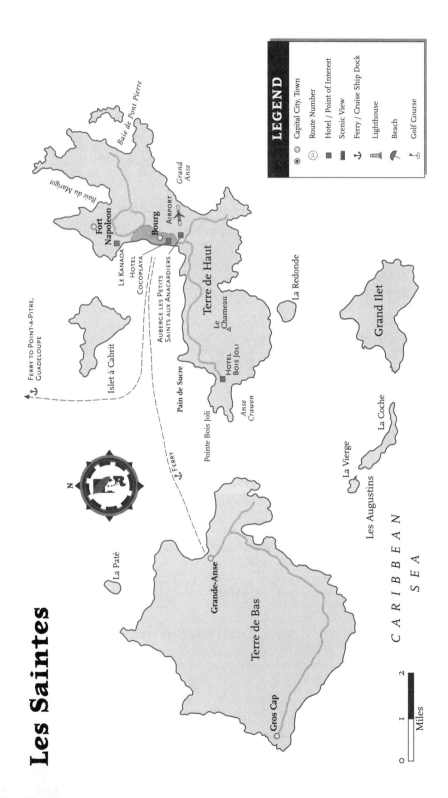

N

Miles
0   1   2

LEGEND

⊙ Capital City, Town
Ⓡ Route Number
■ Hotel / Point of Interest
⚓ Scenic View
⚓ Ferry / Cruise Ship Dock
🗼 Lighthouse
⛱ Beach
⛳ Golf Course

Baie de Pont Pierre

Baie du Margot

Fort Napoleon

Bourg

Grand Anse

Airport

Le Kanaoa
Hotel Cocoplaya

Auberge les Petits
Saints aux Anacardiers

Terre de Haut

Le Chameau

La Redonde

Grand Ilet

Hotel Bois Joli

Pain de Sucre

Pointe Bois Joli

Anse Crawen

La Vierge

La Coche

Les Augustins

Islet á Cabrit

Ferry to Point-a-Pitre, Guadeloupe

Ferry

La Paté

Grande-Anse

Terre de Bas

Gros Cap

CARIBBEAN SEA

Les Saintes

DO YOU LONG FOR THE OLD ST. BARTH, BEFORE THE ADVENT of super-luxury hotels and the influx of all those way-too-fabulous New Yorkers and Los Angelenos? If so, you will love Les Saintes (more formally, but less commonly referred to as Iles des Saintes), a diminutive cluster of islands located about 8 miles/13 kilometers south of Basse-Terre's southern coast. Just two are large enough to be settled (3,000 residents between them), and only one is developed for travelers: **Terre-de-Haut**. It's a picturesque and hilly island, with several good places to stay, nice restaurants, and attractive coves for sunning and swimming, including a nude beach. It boasts an appealingly dry and sunny climate. If fact, we think Terre-de-Haut is the single best reason for a Guadeloupe vacation. Barely a third the size of St. Barth, the island is quite petite, so it's easy to explore and discover. You can see it easily in a day, but if you stay longer you'll cultivate the sense of possessiveness that might be the key to why it stays intimate and quaint, and off the itinerary of the jet set, at least for now.

The Briefest History

Although most Americans have never heard of Les Saintes, Columbus thought the archipelago worthy enough to name (originally "Los Santos"). The islands were not thought to be suitable for sugarcane, however, so they escaped the slave trade that shaped most of the Caribbean (similar to what happened on St. Barth). The first inhabitants were fishermen from Breton, and the population today is still light-skinned and blue-eyed, and the salako hat (originating in Asia, but otherwise unique to Les Saintes) continues to be worn by fishermen. The British and French fought over the islands during several fierce naval battles, and the one in 1782, between Admirals George Rodney and Francois de Grasse, ended in three decades of British rule (the body count—2,000 French and 243 Brits—was especially severe for the French). Fishing remains the economic mainstay, particularly on Terre-de-Bas, where almost half the population lives, but Terre-de-Haut has a wonderfully low-key tourism infrastructure, catering largely to day-trippers from Guadeloupe (and a few smart overnight guests).

Terre-de-Haut: Key Facts

Location	16°N by 61°W
	8 miles/13 kilometers south of Basse-Terre
	20 miles/32 kilometers north of Dominica
	1,855 miles/2,987 kilometers southeast of New York
Size	3 square miles/8 square kilometers
Highest point	Le Chameau (1,014 feet/309 meters)
Population	1,729
Language	French and Creole
Time	Atlantic Standard Time (1 hour ahead of EST, same as EDT)
Area code	To call Terre-de-Haut from the U.S. dial 011 (the international dialing code), then 590-590 (the country code), followed by the six-digit local number.
Electricity	220 volts AC, 50 cycles; you'll need a transformer and an adapter for U.S.-made appliances.
Currency	Euro (€1 = US$1.25 at press time; check prior to departure)
Driving	On the right; car rentals not available
Documents	U.S. and Canadian citizens need proof of nationality (plus a photo ID) for up to three months; after that a passport is necessary; an ongoing or a return ticket is also necessary.
Departure tax	None
Beer to drink	Corsaire
Rum to drink	Rhum Père Labat
Music to hear	Zouk
Tourism info	590-590-99-58-60; www.antilles-info-tourisme.com; omt.lessaintes@wanadoo.fr

Getting There

Although there is a picayune airstrip with several flights a day to and from Pointe-à-Pitre, Guadeloupe, most people arrive by boat. If you are at all prone to seasickness, however, we strongly suggest flying in and out. The 20-minute Air Caraïbes flight from Pointe-à-Pitre is about $120 round-trip and operates three times daily (590-590-82-47-47; in the U.S., 877-772-1005); night landings are not permitted. Otherwise, take a heavy dose of Dramamine and find yourself a sunny spot on the outside deck. The one-hour voyage can be rough (and sometimes wet on the top deck); we've seen more than a few people hurl over the side. The well-steeled can ferry over with L'Express des Isles (590-590-83-12-45) or Brudey Frères (590-590-90-04-48), which leave the Pointe-à-Pitre harbor several times a day (about $45 round-trip). There are also two ferries daily to Terre-de-Haut from Trois Riviéres, Guadeloupe, through Compagnie Deher (590-590-99-50-68), which takes only about 30 minutes. There is limited service to Terre-de-Haut with L'Express des Isles from Fort-de-France, Martinique (an almost three-hour trip). Finally, be careful not to take the wrong ferry! (For information on getting to Guadeloupe from international destinations, see that chapter.)

Getting Around

There is no car-rental agency, nor any need for a car as long as you're comfortable riding a one- or two-passenger motor scooter (about $30 per day). There are several places to rent one, or you can arrange it through your hotel. There is limited taxi service available, and the Bois Joli and other hotels offer free minibus service for their guests. Either way, note that this is a small island; if you're on a budget you can walk to almost any point in less than an hour, and hitchhiking is safe and common. Do note that scooters are prohibited in town from 9 a.m. to noon and from 2 to 4 p.m.

Focus on Les Saintes: A Stay on Terre-de-Haut

Terre-de-Haut's main village, **Bourg**, is a symphony of red roofs and brightly colored West Indian houses and buildings. It is very clean and decidedly French (it was settled by immigrants from Brittany). Above all, it is picturesque — your camera will eat it up. The focal point of town is the ferry dock, and there is a small square at the foot of the dock that is fun for people-watching. When you disembark, you'll spot young women carrying baskets brimming with *tourment d'amour,* "the agony of love," delicious salty-sweet coconut tarts that are the specialty of these islands ($3 for a bagful).

You can explore the whole village on foot in an hour or two. Fortunately there are no major diversions to distract you from soaking in the ambiance. Bourg is also in the middle of the island, so all points are not far away (the airport and most of the hotels and restaurants are within a 10-minute walk from the dock). Ambitious types can walk to all the sights, but Terre-de-Haut is hilly enough that a Peugeot scooter is a welcome amenity (rental cars are not available). In addition to the fun means of transportation, note that the nicest beach, **Anse Crawen** (the nude beach), is at the southern end of the island — a long, hot walk from Bourg. The steep hills are particularly fun with scooters, especially the hairpin road across the flanks of **Le Chameau** (1,014 feet/309 meters), with the reward of great views and a hair-raising ride down awaiting you.

If you're just here on a day trip, get your scooter and head for **Fort Napoléon**, which sits on a hill overlooking the entrance to the harbor and bay and offers commanding views. It closes at noon, so this is a good first stop. The locals call Fort Napoléon the "Gibraltar of the Caribbean," which is not to be confused with Brimstone Hill on St. Kitts (the "Gibraltar of the West

Indies") or Haiti's Citadelle, which is truly the region's largest fortress. Exploring the fort is interesting for about 20 minutes, especially to note that it was never used in battle. Visit the historical museum, and the art gallery (none of the paintings features a war scene, but there's a reproduction of the Battle of the Saintes replete with little paper boats), see the botanical garden, take in the expansive view, and off you go to explore the various beaches. There aren't many roads, so it's easy, even without a map. We recommend finishing your tour by noon so you can have a leisurely lunch. Everything here closes for the midday meal; after lunch, hit the beach. Eat lunch at Bois Joli, then visit Anse Crawen, just over the hill. The best thing about this beach, besides being so remote, is that there are plenty of shade trees for relief from *le soleil*. It's also a clothing-optional cove, even though there are posted warnings to the contrary.

There are lots of day-trippers who come here from Guadeloupe, but if you've packed a bag, you can be one of the relative few who get to spend the night on this special isle.

Where to Stay

Anybody coming to Guadeloupe should still plan to stay here on Les Saintes (most specifically Terre-de-Haut) for several nights. Actually, we think a week here would be superb — quiet but truly relaxing. Be sure to make reservations well in advance, because this is a petite place. There are only a few places to stay, and here are the best.

Auberge Les Petits Saints aux Anacardiers, La Savane, Terre-de-Haut, Les Saintes, Guadeloupe, FWI. ℂ 800-322-2223 or 590-590-99-50-99, ✆ 590-590-99-54-51, ▢ www.petitssaints.com

🔳 **Not So Cheap** ⓣ CP ⒸⒸ 12 rooms

A few blocks up the hill from town sits the Anacardiers, a wonderfully eclectic and gay-friendly hotel set in a pretty Creole house (formerly the mayor's) and run by a local artist couple, Didier Spindler and Jean-Paul Colas. They travel the world in search of furnishings, so there's a birdcage from Java, statues from Bali, and old-fashioned lamps from France, and when the lobby starts to overflow with bric-a-brac (which is most of the time), you can make an offer on items you'd like to bring home. They also run a smart little shop in town near the ferry dock. Of course, all the rooms are individually decorated and have a/c, telephone, TV, and minibar. We'd recommend one or two specifically, except that Auberge operates to capacity most of the time, so instead try calling Didier and Jean-Paul and asking what's available when you want to visit (hint: the room upstairs above the pool made it to *Condé Nast Traveler*'s "Room with a View" page). A small terrace overlooking the bay is where breakfast and an excellent dinner are served, and the pool completes the picture. This place has a great spirit to it, and bringing along an empty steamer trunk for any treasures you come across isn't a bad idea.

Hotel Bois Joli, Terre-de-Haut, Les Saintes, Guadeloupe, FWI.
📞 800-322-2223 or 590-590-99-50-38, ✆ 590-590-99-55-05,
💻 bois.joli@wanadoo.fr

💲 **Pricey** for standard rooms, and **Very Pricey** for the cottages
🍴 MAP 🆑 40 rooms

Located in a small cove on the western end of the island, facing the Pain de Sucre, this is the biggest operation on Les Saintes. We wish we could get excited about it, but on each of our visits the reception has seemed a little chilly. Scattered out along the calm beach (fair, but others nearby are better), there are tastefully furnished, air-conditioned pink bungalows overlooking the sea, Ilet-à-Cabrit, Terre-de-Bas, and Guadeloupe's Soufrière in the distance, crowned with clouds. There are also standard rooms, which are less expensive. The hotel has a huge open-air dining pavilion with views of the water. A bridge straddles the pool, which seems to be more popular than the beach and in summer is filled with kids. The Bois Joli can be fun, depending on who's checked in; the food is generally very good. It's also probably the best place for active types — there are water sports available, including sailing, waterskiing, and *plongée* (scuba). Note that most of the staff prefers not to speak English.

Le Kanaoa, Anse Mire, Terre-de-Haut, Les Saintes, Guadeloupe, FWI.
📞 800-322-2223 or 590-590-99-51-94, ✆ 590-590-99-55-04

💲 **Not So Cheap** 🍴 CP 🆑 23 rooms

A compact hotel on the north end of the harbor, the Kanaoa is a good and moderately priced beachfront alternative if Bois Joli is booked or beyond your budget. It has its own very tiny sandbox as a beach, a boat dock, and a small but comfortable pool and patio. Fishing and waterskiing are available. The rooms, which have nice views of either the sea or garden, are simple and pleasant, featuring knotty pine furniture, private bath, and a/c; there are also four two-bedroom units. There is a central bar-restaurant area for meals and gathering, and Bourg is a short walk. Best of all, Le Kanaoa is run by some very nice people.

Hotel Cocoplaya, Terre-de-Haut, Les Saintes, Guadeloupe, FWI.
📞 590-590-92-40-00, ✆ 590-590-99-50-41,
💻 www.im-caraibes.com/cocoplaya, hotelcocoplaya@wanadoofr

💲 **Not So Cheap** 🍴 CP 🆑 12 rooms

One of the island's newest hotels, this is a 2001 revamping of the former Hotel Jeanne d'Arc situated at the southwest end of town in a nondescript two-story building on the water. It offers a series of charming, if small, rooms. All are air-conditioned, bright, and spare, but each has a different subtle design theme — one is the Japanese room (our fave), another is the African, and so on. Two are directly over the water and share a long balcony. Although the management has chosen to stop operating a restaurant, this is still a good, slightly cheaper waterfront alternative to Auberge Les Petits Saints aux Anacardiers.

Where to Eat

For such a *petite île*, there is a pretty good selection of restaurants. Among the best are the following.

$$$$ **Auberge Les Petits Saints aux Anacardiers**, Bourg, 590-590-99-50-99

This is the island's top bistro, with exotic meals prepared by Didier and Jean-Paul. Even if you're not staying here, this French Creole establishment is worth a visit, as much for the explosion of paintings and quirky antiques as for the tasty dinners. Reservations required.

$$$ **Hotel Bois Joli**, 590-590-99-50-38

Serving three meals a day, this is the island's full-service hotel venue. Specialties include fish pancakes, clams in Creole sauce, stuffed *burgots* (sea snails), and barbecued fish steaks. We do wish they would install screens to keep the flies at bay, but the French don't seem to mind them, so *c'est la vie*. Reservations are suggested.

$$ **La Saladerie**, 590-590-99-53-43

This is our favorite place for lunch, tucked just below the road, halfway between Bourg and Le Kanaoa. Salads, fish carpaccio, and pastas round out the menu. The view is splendid. Check for occasional live jazz combos.

Don't Miss

Anse Crawen

This beach is at the end of the road past Bois Joli — definitely worth an afternoon.

The View from Fort Napoleon

A few minutes here visually explains why Les Saintes was considered strategically important, even though the impressive fort didn't prevent the defeat of the French in a 1782 sea battle. The British Admiral Rodney foiled France's attempt to invade Jamaica by attacking them at Les Saintes (a small museum has models to illustrate the action). In the distance, on nearby Ilet-a-Cabrit, is Fort Josephine, named for Napoleon's wife, of Martinique.

A Scooter Ride up Le Chameau

The island's highest point can be reached by a precipitous cement road.

Coconuts

This is the bar to stop at on your way to the afternoon ferry, for a *planteur* or ti punch, perhaps. If you're spending the night, note that local fishermen show up on Friday night for informal jam sessions on congos and calabash, and the Beaver Bar upstairs gets peppy several nights a week. Closed Monday.

Diving and Snorkeling

Les Saintes has a number of good dive and snorkel sites, particularly Le Sec Pate, an undersea mountain rising to within 50 feet/15 meters of the surface, between Terre-de-Haut and Guadeloupe. It's an advanced dive, but you're likely to see large angelfish, wahoo, and friendly turtles. There are two dive shops—Pisquettes (590-590-99-88-80) and Dive Bouteille (590-590-99-54-25)—check with your hotel to see which it recommends. A one-tank dive runs about $60.

Terre-de-Bas

Located a half mile west of Terre-de-Haut, the lesser known of the two inhabited Saintes, is a 15-minute ferry ride from Bourg, offered five times a day aboard L'Inter ($8 round-trip). Terre-de-Bas hasn't been developed for tourism (mainly because there's less in the way of beaches), but it's worth a few hours' exploration, especially if you like to hike. The landscape is defined by a pair of peaks, topping out at Morne Abymes (962 feet/293 meters), and there are two villages on opposite sides of the islands—Grand Anse on the east (where there is a small tourist office just up from the dock), and the larger (in spite of the name) Petite Anse on the west. If you're up to it you can make a circuit of the island and visit both villages (about 6 miles), or there are cheap buses that make the trip back and forth. There are a couple decent restaurants and guesthouses. The tourist office has details.

Marie-Galante

ATLANTIC OCEAN

N
R

Grosse Pointe

St. Louis

LA COHUBA

FERRY SERVICE

FERRY TO GUADELOUPE

Grand-Bourg

Capesterre

Pointe des Basses

CARIBBEAN SEA

0   1   2
Miles

Marie-Galante

IN ADDITION TO LES LOVELY SAINTES, THE GUADELOUPE AR-
chipelago includes La Grande Galette — "the big pancake" — otherwise known
as Marie-Galante, a relatively untouristed and thoroughly French- and Creole-
speaking island located 18 miles south of Grand-Terre. Though still unknown by many non-French Caribbean regulars (we didn't make our first
visit until 2000), Marie-Galante is actually larger than many popular neighboring islands — almost twice the size of St. Martin/St. Maarten, for instance. The island is very rural, but what characterizes it best might be the
catchphrase we saw on the tourist map we received on the last visit: *Marie-
Galante, si vraie* — so genuine. Although we wouldn't dedicate an entire vacation to visiting Marie-Galante (unless our exclusive focus was beaches
— more on that in a minute), it makes an engaging side trip from busy
Guadeloupe and can easily be seen in a long day or two.

The Briefest History

The Arawak Indians first called the island Touloulou (after the feisty little orange and black crabs you'll see scampering everywhere), and then the Caribs
came, conquering the Arawaks. Columbus encountered Marie-Galante on
his second Caribbean cruise, in 1493, naming it after his flagship, the Santa
Marie la Galante, but it wasn't until 1648 that French colonialists arrived to
settle here, on the northwest coast. Five years later, the Caribs massacred the
few colonists, largely in retaliation for rapes committed by French sailors on
neighboring Dominica, but as throughout most of the West Indies, the native Carib population was soon obliterated. Tobacco, indigo, and cotton were
the first crops, then cattle and coffee; finally, sugarcane was planted, becoming the island's mainstay. Near the end of the 17th century, the Dutch invaded, and control of the island subsequently shifted between the French
and English (some of the English place-names, like Buckingham, still exist).
By the end of the 18th century, Marie-Galante's focus was sugar production,
and 106 windmills were built to replace animal and hydraulic mills. Emancipation took hold in 1848, but in the election the following year, there were
riots to protest ballot rigging by the white plantation owners; many blacks
were slaughtered. The last of the windmills was operating until 1941 (at

Marie-Galante: Key Facts

Location	16°N by 61°W
	18 miles/29 kilometers south of Grande-Terre, Guadeloupe
	20 miles/32 kilometers north of Dominica
	1,855 miles/2,987 kilometers southeast of New York
Size	63 square miles/163 square kilometers
Highest point	Morne Constant (670 feet/204 meters)
Population	12,410
Language	French and Creole
Time	Atlantic Standard Time (1 hour ahead of EST, same as EDT)
Area code	To call Marie-Galante from the U.S., dial 011 (the international dialing code), then 590-590 (the country code), followed by the six-digit local number.
Electricity	220 volts AC, 50 cycles; you'll need a transformer and an adapter for U.S.-made appliances.
Currency	Euro (€1 = US$1.25 at press time; check prior to departure)
Driving	On the right; your valid driver's license will suffice for up to 20 days; after that you'll need an international driver's license.
Documents	U.S. and Canadian citizens need proof of nationality (plus a photo ID) for up to three months; after that a passport is necessary. An ongoing or a return ticket is also necessary.
Departure tax	None
Beer to drink	Corsaire
Rum to drink	Rhum Père Labat
Music to hear	Zouk
Tourism info	590-590-97-56-51; www.ot-mariegalante.com

Grand-Pierre), and steam-powered factories took over the production and continue today. Most of the cane is still hauled to the factories by oxcart.

Getting There

You can reach Marie-Galante by ferry or plane from Guadeloupe. The ferry is cheaper, but flying is convenient if you're connecting to or from a flight in Guadeloupe's Pointe-à-Pitre. Note that the seas are often rough, and sea-sickness is not at all uncommon. From the Pointe-à-Pitre ferry dock (located just west of downtown), there are up to 12 ferries throughout the day on TMC Archipel (590-590-21-35-03), L'Express des Iles (590-590-83-12-45), and

Brudey Frères (590-590-90-04-48), for about $50 round-trip (note that half of the ferries dock on Marie-Galante at Grand-Bourg, and half at St. Louis). There is also limited service on L'Express des Iles from St. Francois, Guadeloupe. The trip takes under an hour either way. Air Caraïbes offers two or three flights a day out of Pointe-à-Pitre; the 20-minute crossing is about $120 round-trip (590-590-82-47-47; in the U.S., 877-772-1005). Marie-Galante's tiny airstrip is located midway between Grand-Bourg and Capesterre; it is not equipped for night landings. (For information on getting to Guadeloupe from international destinations, see that island's chapter.)

Getting Around

Once on the island, you can rent a car from Thrifty (800-367-2277 or 590-590-97-54-89) or Budget (800-472-3325 or 590-590-97-57-81); both are located in Grand-Bourg, and there are small local outfits near the ferry dock (it's worth shopping around, particularly in low season). Bike and scooter rentals are also possible; for motorbikes try Moto Location (590-590-97-12-42), or for bicycles try Location de Velos (590-590-97-99-09); the Grand-Bourg tourist office also had a few bikes for rent the last time we visited. You can get a taxi by calling 590-590-97-80-65 or 590-590-97-33-34, and minibuses travel regularly to and from the three main towns.

Focus on Marie-Galante: Rum & Relaxation

Unlike spiky and abrupt Terre-de-Haut, Marie-Galante is shaped in a near perfect circle, and the highest point is just a few hundred feet above sea level. In looks, it reminds us of Antigua's rolling fields of cane; there is little in the way of forests — Marie-Galante is fairly dry. The main town is **Grand-Bourg**, which holds little interest (it was destroyed by fire in 1901; subsequent rebuilding was uninspired), but the two smaller villages, St. Louis to the north and Capesterre to the east, have a little more appeal (and better beaches). The island's economy has been focused on farming, yielding a bucolic charm; tourism is a recent but growing notion. The dominant industry is sugarcane, still hauled by ox from the extensive fields of cane blanketing much of the island. About 95 percent of the crop is exported to foreign markets, and the remainder is used by three distilleries to produce Marie-Galante's increasingly famous rum.

The **local rum** is unique for two reasons. First, it is produced from fresh cane juice (common in the French islands) instead of molasses (as is standard in the non-French Caribbean). This creates a product similar to fine cognac, called *rhum agricole*. Second, Marie-Galante produces rum with an unusually strong 59 percent alcohol content — the *rhum agricole* of that strength is exclusive to this island (in the Caribbean, at least). Actually, the excellent rum of Marie-Galante is something we haven't seen for sale anywhere outside the French islands or in Parisian specialty shops. So while you're here, spend a couple hours touring the rum plants. The best for visitors is **Distillerie Bielle**, where you can watch the actual production process (usually spring and summer). There is also a gift shop selling the various Bielle products, including very tasty flavored rums, as well as a pottery shop. The second-largest rum producer is **Pere Labat**, which still has some of the ancient equipment used in the 1940s (like a wonderful copper pot still). Labat is not really set up for tours, but it has a tasting room and lots of ambiance. The third distillery, **Belleview**, was not in operation during our last visit, and it was unclear whether they would be resuming production anytime soon. At one time, Marie-Galante probably possessed more windmills per square mile than any other Caribbean island, leading to its nickname, "L'Ile aux Cent Moulins" (72 are still visible).

The other reason to come to Marie-Galante is its **beaches**, which are beautiful and sugar-white, dissolving into exquisite cerulean seas. The four best are found on the west and southeast coasts. North of St. Louis is **Anse du Vieux Fort**, which has picnic facilities, and immediately south is long **Folle Anse**, fronting the island's only resort. Even more idyllic and near Capesterre is **Petite Anse** and **La Feuillere**, and nearby **Anse Taliseronde** has the best snorkeling. If you visit Marie-Galante by ferry on a day trip, the beach immediately south of Grand-Bourg is also fine. Other things to see are the natural sea arch, **Gueule Grand Gouffre**, on the north coast; the **Moulin de Bezard**, a completely reconstructed and operational windmill; and **Habitation Murat**, a 17th-century plantation and distillery with a museum on sugar and rum production and exhibits of local crafts.

Riding around on a bike is an excellent way to tour the island (all of the hills are gentle), and there is a network of interesting trails. As we said, Marie-Galante is not an action-packed destination — nightlife is virtually nonexistent (although the **Discoteque Touloulou** in Petite Anse sometimes gets busy around midnight) — if you're content with very light sightseeing excursions or to curl up with a book on the beach, it might be just right for a few days of serious decompression.

Where to Stay

For years, there was little here in the way of tourist facilities, but the island's first resort opened in 1999, and there are a number of small inns and guesthouses now. La Cohoba (below) is far and away the best option. Some other places to check out are **Le Soleil Levant** (590-590-97-31-55), which is actually two facilities — a 6-room inn in Capesterre and a 13-unit facility just above town with a pool; **Jardin de Beausejour** (590-590-97-34-22) in Capesterre; **Au Village de Menard** (590-590-97-09-45) in Menard on the north coast; or the simpler **L'Arbre a Pain** (590-590-97-73-69) in the heart of Grand-Bourg. Rates for doubles for all of the above, except La Cohoba, are cheap. Finally, there's the new, and slightly more expensive, **Cap Reva** in Capesterre (590-590-97-50-00) — it fronts the beach, has 12 duplex apartments, 20 studio apartments, a pool, and a restaurant.

La Cohoba, Folle Anse, Grand-Bourg, Marie-Galante, FWI. 📞 800-322-2223 or 590-590-97-50-50, 📠 590-590-97-97-96, 💻 www.leader-hotels.gp

💲 **Not So Cheap** 🍴 **CP** CC 100 rooms

Located just south of the fishing village of St. Louis, the Cohoba is an abrupt, but not entirely unwelcome, addition to Marie-Galante. A series of one- and two-story buildings sprawls about sparse gardens — a fair-size pool is the focal point. The three categories of rooms are fairly simple but attractive in their minimalist design; the bungalows are nicest, with a semiprivate patio. Junior Suites have kitchenettes on the balconies. All have the basic modern conveniences: a/c, TV, hairdryer, minifridge, and safe. It's not necessary to tie yourself down to a meal plan, but the restaurant serves better food than you'd expect, in an open-air dining room with vaulted ceiling. Water sports and tennis are available. The hotel is set just behind (not on) lovely Folle Anse ("Crazy Bay"), and we think the word *cohoba* has something to do with smoking weed — hey, is there a theme going on here?

Where to Eat

There are a couple dozen restaurants to choose from on Marie-Galante, most of which serve Creole food, similar to that found on Guadeloupe. Still, a few unique dishes have developed, notably *bebele*, a soup of tripe, goat, green bananas, beans, and spices; and *matate touloulou*, the local bright orange and black crab served with breadfruit. Expect most of the restaurants here to be informal. Below are a few of the island's more respected dining options.

$$ Chez Henri, Avenue Caraïbe, St. Louis, 590-590-97-04-57

Serving Creole fare, the dining room opens up onto the beach. The food is good, but the real draw is the prickly tempered yet charming owner, Henri Vergorolle. Patrons flock to watch the unpredictable Henri in action.

$$ Le Footy, Rue de la Marine, Grand-Bourg, 590-590-97-99-19

This casual Creole restaurant sits just feet from the water. It offers both open-air dining and an enclosed air-conditioned space. Complementing the fine cuisine is a piano bar on Monday and a more upbeat music scene on Friday and Saturday nights. Open noon to 4 p.m., and 8 p.m. to 2 a.m.

$$ Le Neptune, Grand-Bourg, 590-590-97-96-90

This is a popular waterfront eatery, located just across from the center of town; Le Neptune serves Creole and French cuisine.

$$ Le Reflet de l'Ile, Rue de la Marine, Capesterre, 590-590-97-41-30

This casual place unfortunately sits across the street from the beach rather than on it. However, its Creole offerings are respectable, most notably the lamb ragout. Open Tuesday through Friday from 11:30 a.m. to 3 p.m. and 7 to 10 p.m. Open all day Sunday; closed Saturday midday and Monday night.

$$$ **Le Refuge**, St. Louis, 590-590-97-02-95

Le Refuge is a small bistro, situated within the hotel of the same name. It incorporates local ingredients to make traditional Creole and French cuisine in a cheerful and casual atmosphere. Open Monday through Sunday, 11:30 a.m. for lunch and 7:30 p.m. for dinner. Closing times for both meals are flexible.

Don't Miss

The Rum Distillery Tour

In a few hours you can see all three of the factories and sample their wares.

Notre Dame de Marie-Galante

This 1827 church of Grand-Bourg survived the town's 1901 fire; note the vaulted wooden ceiling and marble altar with a relief of the Last Supper.

Chateau Murat

In 1839, this 18th-century sugar estate was the largest sugar plantation of the Guadeloupe archipelago, with 207 slaves. Now restored, it is located just east of Grand-Bourg and still has its cane-crushing machinery posing for photos. A small museum, open sporadically, provides insight (in French) into the island's history and sugar, and guided tours are available.

Moulin de Bezard

Restored to its original working condition, this windmill has been converted into a small museum about sugar production and has a collection of slave cabins.

Hiking and Biking

The gentle landscapes and muted elevations of Marie-Galante make the island an excellent destination to explore on foot or by pedal. There are a variety of hiking trails and the tourist office has a brochure describing 11 in detail (in French), ranging from 2 to 14 miles in length; ask for Les Sentiers de Randonnee Pedestre. For guided hikes, mountain bike rides, and even oxcart excursions, call Pro Git Mag (590-590-97-97-86).

Jamaica

TOURISTO SCALE:

😀😀😀😀😀😀😀😀😀 (9)

I t was an island vacation that got started on the wrong foot. We were on our first trip to Jamaica, about 20 years ago, when we walked out of the Doctor's Cave Beach Hotel to start our day in Montego Bay. Waiting for us at the street was Sam. We didn't know Sam, but he seemed to know us. "First time to Jamaica?" he asked. Well, yes, it was. "I can show you around today." No, we don't really need a guide, especially since our first stop is the beach across the street. But before we could get to the water, it started to rain, so we decided to walk into town; Sam followed, making a lame attempt at telling us about the area, while we put on a show of uninterest. We didn't want to be rude, but we also didn't want a tagalong. We didn't know how to say no with the proper emphasis. To make a long story short, Sam ended up being our guide for the entire day, joining us for lunch (we bought), helping us negotiate for a souvenir we didn't need, and getting a $20 tip from us at the end of the day.

The next morning we breakfasted, exited the hotel, and guess who was waiting for us? Yes, *mon*, as we learned over the course of the week, "First time to Jamaica?" is a trick question. Answer in the affirmative and you'll have a friend, a salesperson, or a guide for the remainder of your stay. (Although living conditions have improved since our first visit, there is still a lack of gainful employment for many.) We learned instead to engage Jamaicans in

Jamaica

CARIBBEAN SEA

CARIBBEAN SEA

LEGEND
- ◉ Capital City, Town
- Ⓐ Route Number
- ▪ Hotel / Point of Interest
- ↘ Scenic View
- ⚓ Ferry / Cruise Ship Dock
- 🏛 Lighthouse
- 🏖 Beach
- ⛳ Golf Course

N

0   10   20
Miles

Negril Beach

Negril

Lucea

Round Hill Hotel & Villas
Coyaba Beach Resort & Club
Ironshore
Half Moon
Ritz-Carlton Rose Hall
Rose Hall Resort

The Tryall Club

Savanna-la-Mar

Montego Bay

Falmouth

Discovery Bay

Runaway Bay

Bluefields

Y's Falls

Mandeville

Santa Cruz Mountains

Dry Harbour Mountains

Jamaica Inn
Goldeneye
Hibiscus Lodge
Tamarind Great House

Ocho Rios

Dunne's River Falls

Firefly

May Pen

Spanishtown

Jake's

Long Bay

Macarry Bay

Ivanhoe's Guest House
The Jamaica Palace Hotel
Frenchman's Cove
Jamaica Hieghts Resort
Blue Lagoon Villas
Golden Hill Villas
Long Bay

Trident Villas & Hotel
Navy Island
Port Antonio
Hotel Mocking Bird Hill

Hope Bay

Buff Bay

Anotto Bay

Blue Mt. Peak
(7,402 ft / 2,257 m)

Strawberry Hill

Kingston

Jamaica Pegasus
Hilton Kingston Jamaica
The Courtleigh Hotel & Suites

Port Royal

Manley Airport

Morant Point

Jamaica: Key Facts

Location	18°N by 77°W
	90 miles/145 kilometers south of Cuba
	1,450 miles/2,335 kilometers south of New York
Size	4,411 square miles/11,424 square kilometers
	146 miles/235 kilometers long by 22 to 51 miles/35 to 82 kilometers wide
Highest point	Blue Mountain Peak (7,402 feet/2,257 meters)
Population	2.7 million
Language	English
Time	Eastern Standard Time all year
Area code	876
Electricity	110 volts AC, 50 cycles; 220 volts in some places; ask for a transformer and adapter if necessary
Currency	Jamaican dollar (J$65 = US$1)
Driving	On the left; a valid driver's license from back home is acceptable for short-term visits.
Documents	U.S. and Canadian citizens need proof of citizenship with a photo ID, plus an ongoing or a return ticket; other visitors need passports.
Departure tax	$27
Beer to drink	⊛ Red Stripe
Rum to drink	Wray & Nephew Overproof
Music to hear	Reggae/Dancehall — Yah, *mon*!
Tourism info	800-JAMAICA or 212-856-9727
	www.jamaicatravel.com

real conversation, to learn about their island. Sometimes what we heard was clichéd, sometimes it was fascinating. Jamaica is a place like no other in the world, and by showing some respect for the island and its people, we as visitors became something more than a tourist interchangeable with the next bloke walking down the street. Then, when services or wares were offered, a polite no was accepted and we all moved on with our day.

We've been back many times since, and each time, without fail, Jamaica kicks in again. We love this place, but we also understand how many first-time visitors are put off by the experience. Jamaica is an island equally awash in misconceptions and island clichés. In some ways, the land of rum and reggae (and Rasta!) represents the entire Caribbean, warts and all. Yet for all the visitors ruffled by the in-your-face attitude of Jamaicans, there are just as many who name this as their favorite island destination. Throughout the 1990s there was a concerted effort by the government to tone down the more assertive interactions that Jamaicans had with visitors; fortunately, the island hasn't lost its color, and we suspect that more foreigners are enjoying the island than ever before (1.5 million visitors a year, to be exact).

Jamaica is a big country—the island is the third largest in the Caribbean after Cuba and Hispaniola. There are many different destinations for the traveler, and your Jamaican experience will vary dramatically with each destination. You will be subjected to tourist hordes in Ocho Rios, especially if you're sequestered (really locked away) in a large resort, and there are more tourist swarms in Montego Bay. Although most of the hotel rooms are found along the long North Coast, with a few exceptions we recommend avoiding this area in general, with its tyranny of all-inclusive resorts (such as the Sandals, Couples, and the Superclub empires—Beaches, Breezes, Grand Lido, and the Hedonisms). The exceptions are places like Jamaica Inn, an old-time resort of character and style, and Goldeneye, a fabulous inn built around Ian Fleming's estate. We would also avoid Montego Bay (a.k.a. MoBay), except for Round Hill and Tryall and a few resorts to the east. Of course, we love Reggae SumFest, held in MoBay every summer. You should definitely go to Negril, which is fun, mellow, and what you think the Jamaican experience should be. You might also try Port Antonio, which is fairly quiet and incredibly verdant. Surrounding the seventh largest natural harbor in the world, Kingston is worth a trip for various cultural institutions, including the Bob Marley Museum (yeah, *mon*). The South Coast is just away from it all.

All kinds of people go to Jamaica, reflecting its size and diverse appeal. Package-tour groups go to the all-inclusive resorts, which we loathe (can you tell?) and which are bountiful in Jamaica. These are resorts where everything —room, meals, drinks, tips, and all kinds of activities—is included in one price. All-inclusives are, with a few exceptions, just a muddle of mediocrity, down to the last buffet dinner. Their clientele is generally not terribly sophisticated, but they are easily satisfied and very budget-conscious. Their attitude is, "Why should I go out for a lunch, dinner, or drinks when it's free here? "(It really isn't—they've already paid for it.) This thinking locks them in, however, and all-inclusive tourists rarely leave the front gates unless it's on a tour bus. We find this very sad. It also creates bad vibes with the locals, especially the merchants. The "let 'em out for two hours to shop" bus trip leaves local vendors and merchants little time to market their wares and increases the pressure on them to sell, because this is the way they make a living. The result is that they tend to aggressively hawk their goods, much to the terror of fear-fed tourists, who have heard all the negative stories about Jamaica. Thus a cycle of fear, resentment, and misunderstanding is perpetuated and exacerbated by these walled prisons called all-inclusives.

Even worse than the all-inclusive resorts are the couples-only all-inclusive resorts, like Couples (which used to use two fornicating lions as its logo —subtle, huh?). The very thought of staying at one of these places gives us hives! Can you imagine being stuck with hundreds of other couples gathered around the buffet table? We'd rather die. Then there is Hedonism II & III, which are trips in themselves. In sum, the all-inclusives are really just adult summer camps with double rooms instead of bunkhouses, and aerobics and crab races replacing arts and crafts. They are great for people for whom luxury is a fiberglass hot tub, an open bar with house brands, or "ethnic night" in the dining room.

The younger, more with-it crowd heads for **Negril**. This is where Jamaicans go to unwind, and unwound it is. Situated on the west coast of the island with a nearly 7-mile-long golden beach, Negril is a beehive of laid-back vibes. A good mood prevails here, probably because everyone is so high. The very relaxed atmosphere is reflected by the mildly laissez-faire attitude of the local government toward ganja (marijuana) and magic mushrooms (the ones that make you laugh hysterically and sometimes give you mild hallucinations). Although selling ganja is still illegal, and punishable with stiff fines and prison sentences, it and the mushrooms are easily available in Negril. At some local (i.e., Jamaican) restaurants, you can order a spliff for dessert or a steaming cup of mushroom tea — although you won't see them on the menu.

Those seeking a quiet and wonderfully lush setting can explore **Port Antonio**. This was Jamaica's first resort area, made famous by Errol Flynn, who had a residence here. There are some magnificent cove beaches here, hidden by really lush vegetation (it's the wettest part of the island, and rain can be very heavy in September and October). Port Antonio is known as Jamaica's "green" destination in another way: Environmentally friendly practices are the rule at a number of the establishments. Many films requiring an idyllic tropical location were shot here, including *Cocktail, Club Paradise, Lord of the Flies, Return to Treasure Island, Clara's Heart,* and *The Mighty Quinn.* Ironically, Port Antonio is now one of the least-touristy Jamaica destinations, which is why we like it. However, this area has rested too long on its glamorous-past laurels. Most of the lodgings here are in need of a face-lift or a shot of dollars, and their rates don't always equal the product delivered. The fact that the usual route to Port Antonio, along the B1 from Kingston, is riddled with landslides and potholes doesn't help (the routes through the mountains, on the A3, and straight along the north coast from MoBay are the alternates). However, Port Antonio is making an effort to join the 21st century with a spiffy new marina development. With Sandals acquiring the former Dragon Bay Beach Resort in 2002 (currently closed), real change might be around the corner. We view this with mixed emotions, however: Part of the town's appeal is its sheer time warp — a place where the clock seems to have stopped.

Finally, for reggae and art lovers, there is **Kingston**. Here you'll find the Bob Marley Museum — a must-stop — and numerous art galleries where you can buy Jamaican art. There is also the Institute of Jamaica and the National Gallery, the latter the best showcase for a lesson in Jamaican art, past and present. As the largest English-speaking city south of Miami, Kingston is big (population 750,000), so a day is all you'll need here, unless you like big cities.

Note: Many prospective visitors to Jamaica are alarmed by the island's reputation for violent crime—Kingston, in particular, is known for its appalling murder rate. However, it's important to stress that visitors touring Jamaica are unlikely to encounter any serious misfortune, particularly if they take the precautions one would exercise at home in an urban area. West Kingston is a dangerous neighborhood, and some parts of Montego Bay are not safe after dusk. Political unrest does occur from time to time, although the bulk of the conflict is usually acted out in the capital (if you do plan to spend time in Kingston, check with the U.S. State Department for the latest advisories: http://travel.state.gov). Otherwise, use common sense, keep your car doors locked when traveling at night through urban areas, and seek out the recommendations made by the hotels listed in this guide.

With high-rise hotels protruding from their shores, **Montego Bay** and Ocho Rios are Jamaican resort destinations brewed full-strength—seascapes buzzed by Jet Skis and punctuated by cruise ships and nightlife. MoBay is the island's main air hub and is served by flights from more U.S. cities than any other Caribbean destination, which makes MoBay popular for weekend escapes. Located two hours east via a new freeway, **Ocho Rios** (known as "Ochi" locally) was the country's first destination to be developed specifically for tourism, and it has one or two cruise-ship arrivals daily in high season, plus plentiful activities, three crafts markets, and a well-conceived shopping mall (Island Village). Most of it is geared to mass tourism, but there's also fine dining and art galleries catering to a cultured clientele. The dichotomies abound.

The Briefest History of a Complex Country

Jamaica was settled by the Arawaks, who had a peaceful agrarian society. The name Jamaica comes from the Arawak Xaymaca, which means "Land of Wood and Water." The fierce Caribs never made it here, but the Spanish did, beginning with Columbus's sighting of Jamaica on his second voyage, in 1494. They established a capital in 1509 near Ocho Rios and named it New Seville, which today is being excavated by archaeologists. The Spanish began sugarcane cultivation and introduced slavery, first with the Arawaks. It didn't take long for the Arawaks to be wiped out (there were about 100,000 when the Spaniards arrived), so the Spanish then imported Africans. Many of the slaves escaped into the mountains and later became known as the Maroons, from the Spanish word *cimarrones*, "runaways."

In 1655 the English drove out the Spaniards and proceeded to take the production of sugar and the importation of slaves to new heights. The English also encouraged pirates (Henry Morgan was one) to operate out of Port Royal, on the peninsula outside Kingston. They plundered Spanish and French ships and established Port Royal as "the richest, wickedest city in Christendom." The honeymoon ended in 1692, when a catastrophic earthquake caused much of the city literally to fall into the sea. Divine intervention, perhaps? Today there are still some buildings left, and Port Royal is an interesting stop if you are in the Kingston area.

Meanwhile, the Maroons were giving the British major headaches, periodically staging rebellions and attracting more runaway slaves. Frustrated, the British granted the Maroons autonomy in 1739, which they still have today, although the Maroons are also full-fledged Jamaican citizens. The planters, following the lead of the American revolutionaries, were getting restless. However, the towering presence of Lord Horatio Nelson and the British Navy in the West Indies squelched the discontent.

In 1834 slavery was abolished in the British Empire. Economic turmoil followed, but with the importation of Indians (from India) and Chinese as indentured servants, sugar and rum production continued in Jamaica, albeit with reduced success. Intermarriage created the mixed racial makeup you find on the island today; hence the national motto "Out of Many, One People." Other products were developed and exported, including bananas, ginger, allspice, coffee, and bauxite.

In the 20th century, the current political scene emerged with the creation of rival parties in the 1930s: the Jamaica Labor Party (JLP), founded by Alexander Bustamante, and the People's National Party (PNP), by Norman Manley (they were cousins, by the way). Jamaica was one of the first in the British West Indies to gain independence, which was granted in 1962 with these two parties in control of the government. Rivalries between the parties became very bitter and continue to this day, although elections aren't as violent as they used to be. At issue is patronage and jobs, and each party seems to control a large army of thugs who stir things up and occasionally get violent when intimidating the other side and the voting populace at large. The worst of this occurred in the late 1970s and in early 1980, when hundreds were killed prior to the elections held on October 30, 1980. This precipitated the historic Bob Marley "One Love" concert, held in Kingston in 1978, where he got the two rival leaders to hold hands on stage. Bob's song "One Love/People Get Ready" was written for that occasion. Today the PNP is in power, but Bob's legacy for harmony seems to have caught on. Yah, *mon*!

Tourism is a huge and fast-growing part of Jamaica's current scene, with about 1.5 million overnight visitors annually. Cruise ships are a smaller part of the picture, with a little more than half of the landings at Ocho Rios and the rest at MoBay (a few small ships occasionally dock at Port Antonio).

Getting There

There are two international gateways: Montego Bay's Sangster International Airport and Kingston's Norman Manley International Airport. The MoBay airport gets the bulk of the tourist arrivals with flights from most major cities in the eastern United States. (MoBay is equidistant between Negril and Ocho Rios; driving times within Jamaica are noted under Getting Around, below).

For Montego Bay: Air Canada flies in from Toronto; Air Jamaica from

Atlanta, Baltimore, Boston, Chicago, Fort Lauderdale, Houston, London-Heathrow, Los Angeles, Miami, Newark, New York–JFK, Orlando, Philadelphia, and Toronto; American Airlines from Dallas–Fort Worth, Miami, and New York–JFK; Continental from Houston and Newark; Delta from Atlanta and Cincinnati; Northwest Airlines from Detroit, Memphis, and Minneapolis (all seasonal); Spirit Airlines from Fort Lauderdale and Orlando; United Airlines from Chicago and Washington, D.C.; and US Airways from Boston, Charlotte, Fort Lauderdale, Philadelphia, and Pittsburgh. From within the Caribbean, Air Jamaica also serves Montego Bay from Barbados, Bonaire, Curaçao, Grand Cayman, Grenada, and Nassau, Bahamas; Cayman Airways flies in from Grand Cayman.

For Kingston: Air Jamaica flies in from London-Heathrow, Newark, New York–JFK, and Miami; American Airlines from Miami and New York–JFK; British Airways from London-Gatwick; Continental from Newark; Delta from Atlanta; Spirit Airlines and US Airways from Fort Lauderdale. From within the Caribbean, Air Jamaica and Cayman Airways fly from Grand Cayman; and BWIA from Antigua, Barbados, and Port of Spain, Trinidad.

Air Jamaica Express has small-plane service to and from Montego Bay, King-ston, Ocho Rios, and Havana, Cuba. The airports at Negril and Port Antonio are no longer served by commercial flights.

Getting Around

Since Jamaica is a big country, you'll want to rent a car if you plan to venture far. If you're based in Negril, you probably won't need a car if you plan to just stay there. There are plenty of cabs to take you around in Negril (average cab fare is $5). If you really want to explore the island, though, rent a car. The roads are in surprisingly good shape by Caribbean standards, but watch out for the local drivers — they go very fast, especially on the highway running from MoBay to Ocho Rios and Negril. Most of the major car-rental agencies have outposts here, including Budget (800-527-0700) and Hertz (800-654-3131); a local outfit we've used is Island Car Rentals, with offices at the Kingston and Montego Bay airports (866-978-5335 or 876-929-5875; www.islandcarrentals.com). Rental rates here are higher than in most places in the Caribbean, starting about $45 a day in low season. Also note that most American auto insurance policies *specifically* exclude coverage for driving in Jamaica — be sure to obtain insurance with your rental.

If you prefer not to rent a car and you're traveling beyond the two major airports, note that the one-way taxi fare from MoBay to Negril is $80 (for up to four persons), to Ocho Rios $100, to Treasure Beach (South Coast) $120, and to Port Antonio $250. The rate from Kingston to Port Antonio is $120. Licensed taxis all have red and white PP plates — if the vehicle you are getting into does not have these plates, it is not likely to be insured (they're known locally as "robots"), and you'll probably end up sharing it with others going your way. Once you spend a few days here, you'll see how some drivers seem to have a death wish, so be very cautious about using unlicensed taxis, and be sure to wear a seat belt. Always agree on the price before entering a taxi.

A cheaper alternative for Negril and Ocho Rios transfers is to use the scheduled bus service — the trip from the MoBay airport to Negril is $20 per person. MoBay to Ocho Rios is $22; to Treasure Beach is $25, and to Port Antonio is $60 via scheduled bus through JUTA (876-952-0813; www.jutatours.com) or JCAL (876-952-7574; www.jcaltours.com). Both outfits provide transportation for various activities islandwide.

You can also use the frequent minibus service that connects the island's major and minor destinations; MoBay to Negril or Ocho Rios is about $5. These minibuses will often be crammed with up to 20 people, which can create a real squeeze with your luggage, but they are a true Jamaican experience, speeding between major towns and with the bass boom of impressive sound systems pounding away. When you spot your destination, call out "One stop, driver!" and he'll pull over and collect your fare. Caution: Accidents involving speeding minibuses are not infrequent.

Since most people travel via road to their resort destination(s), here are driving times between the major points:

> Negril: 90 minutes from MoBay
>
> Ocho Rios: 2 hours from either MoBay or Kingston
>
> Port Antonio: 2.5 hours from Kingston, 4.5 hours from MoBay
>
> Treasure Beach: 90 minutes from MoBay, 3 hours from Kingston

There used to be a train from Montego Bay to Kingston, which was an amazing trip. We highly recommended it in the first edition of *Rum & Reggae's Caribbean*. However, it runs no more — a real shame.

Focus on Jamaica: **Sex and Drugs and Reggae, Mon!**

In our opinion (and we are very opinionated), there are only certain destinations in Jamaica worth visiting for the reasons we've described: Negril; Round Hill, Tryall, and Half Moon near Montego Bay; the Jamaica Inn in Ocho Rios; Port Antonio; the South Coast; and Kingston. These options offer plenty and are the best. One caveat: Jamaica is inundated with spring breakers during February and March, particularly MoBay and Negril. If a 24-hour frat-house scene and relentless thump of music into the wee hours isn't your style, don't visit these towns during this period.

Negril — All Your Brain and Body Needs

There is a resort in Negril called Hedonism II — one of the pervasive all-inclusives that are overwhelming Jamaica — that has established itself as the premier party place in the Caribbean. The tales emanating from here are mind-boggling, if they are indeed for real. Stories abound of people going at it in public — and not only in the usual places like hot tubs, but in the middle of the dining pavilion , while dinner is being served! Maybe it's the name that makes everyone feel naughty. Whatever, this is adult summer camp at its raunchiest.

There is also a place in Negril called **Miss Brown's**, where you can get magic mushroom tea and "special" cake (not unlike the brownies we used to make in college), as well as more down-to-earth fare. There are two strengths of tea, regular and double. May we suggest the regular-strength tea (about $3), as it will give you quite a buzz. For those of you who still don't get it (a reader told us she didn't know what "special" cake was, tried it, and was surprised and unhappy that she got high!), "special" cake is cake made with marijuana and magic mushrooms that will make you laugh hysterically and sometimes will be mildly hallucinogenic. Now you know. Anyway, Miss Brown's is really a must-stop. A visit here will definitely put a smile on your face. Located about a half mile east of the roundabout that separates the beach from the West End, it's a typical small, spartan Jamaican restaurant where you'll even find magic mushroom stir-fry on the menu. It is run by warm and modest country folk who are perfectly comfortable with inquisitive travelers who seek out their café. So it's somewhat surprising when Miss Brown hands out attractive business cards describing her place as world famous, although maybe by now it is. The logo on the card is, of course, mushrooms. She even sells T-shirts with the same logo. (We also hear good things about Ted's Shroom Boom nearby).

Sex and drugs — all that's missing is rock 'n' roll. As Ian Dury (of the Blockheads) once sang, "It's all me brain and body needs." If you replace rock 'n' roll with reggae, you should be very happy in Negril, the land of anything goes. Now don't get us wrong — Negril is not one huge bacchanalia (unless you stay at Hedonism II). It's just an extremely mellow place where rules and regulations seem to evaporate in the tropical heat. It's the quintessence of laid-back; the ambiance here is not some developer's contrivance but its own natural karma. We've never experienced anything quite like it. This is where Jamaicans go to relax, and they're already a helluva lot more relaxed than we are. So if you need to cool out at your own pace (without feeling programmed), this is the place to do it. If you're a believer in sunbathing in the buff, that's no problem here, either.

There are actually two parts to Negril, **Negril Beach** (a.k.a. Seven Mile Beach or just "the beach") and the West End. **Seven Mile Beach** is a 6.75-mile (close enough) arc of sand, calm turquoise water, and palm trees. It is highly developed, but in Negril fashion. Although the last few years have seen the development of several huge all-inclusive resorts, including the Grand Lido, Sandals, Beaches, Couples, one of the few rules in Negril that is followed is a strict building code that dictates that no building can rise higher than the trees. (However, we think a few crafty developers brought in very tall trees from elsewhere in order to build an extra story.) The beach itself is very public, making Negril one of the few destinations in Jamaica where tourists and

Jamaicans can mingle freely without security gates, guards, and the heightened ethnic fears that accompany such barriers. The beach is also a moving bazaar, with all kinds of goods and services brought to your beach towel or chaise for scrutiny. You will never really want for anything. Fresh fruit, sodas, beer, nuts, ganja—all the refreshments that make for a great beach day—are available cheap with a simple wave of the hand. If you are already taken care of, then a pleasant "no, thank you" will keep the traffic moving. Despite all of this human commotion, the beach's beauty is mostly intact. And the sand extends way out, creating a natural swimming pool of very clear water. The shoreline is shallow, which allows you to go far out before you're over your head. When the sun sets, the beach is home to the reggae party places: **Alfred's**, **Roots Bamboo**, **Bourbon Beach** (formerly DeBuss), and **Risky Business**.

The **West End** is a rocky peninsula that juts out from the southern end of the beach. It is the funkier, hippie-ish section of town. Here you'll find lots of Rasta vegetarian restaurants, bars and rum shops, local arts and crafts, some excellent accommodations, and some very popular hangouts. **Rick's Cafe**, located well down the West End Road, is very popular for sunset cocktails and is probably the biggest tourist attraction in Negril. It is also where local boys dive off the cliffs to the clicks of scores of cameras.

Kingston—Rastaman Vibrations, Yeah (Positive)

> *You're going to lively up yourself and*
> *don't be no drag,*
> *You're going to lively up yourself 'cause reggae is*
> *another bag.*
> *You lively up yourself and don't say no,*
> *You're gonna lively up yourself 'cause I said so.*

Thus spake **Bob Marley**. As the undisputed king of reggae, his 1974 song "Lively Up Yourself" was a call to action on behalf of Jamaica's biggest export—his music. At the peak of his career, his record sales accounted for about 10 percent of the country's gross national product. Even after his premature death in 1981, he is still considered the prime mover in popularizing reggae in North America and throughout the world.

Bob Marley is a national hero. His statue stands in the middle of a square across from the National Arena in Kingston, a tribute to his contribution not only to Jamaican music but to his country's cultural identity. As reggae music goes, he is certainly not the only Jamaican to leave his or her mark. There is Bob's son, Ziggy, with the Melody Makers, and Judy Mowatt—a former member of the Wailers' female backup singers, the I-Threes. Bunny Wailer and the late Peter Tosh, both former members of the Wailers, were known worldwide. So are Jimmy Cliff, Gregory Isaacs, Freddie "Toots" (of the Maytals), Sister Carol, Burning Spear, Nadine Sutherland, Terror Fabulous, Shabba

Ranks, Beenie Man, Buju Banton, General B, and the bands Third World, Black Uhuru, and Chalice. There are countless more. A visit to a Kingston record shop will reveal more artists you've never even heard of and a huge selection of 45s (from local talent and labels), which we haven't seen since the '60s. Surprisingly, two well-known reggae bands are not Jamaican—UB40 and Steel Pulse are British, although some of these groups' band members trace their roots to Jamaica.

Reggae now has a strong following around the world, and recent reggae bands like Ziggy Marley and the Melody Makers, Shabba Ranks, and UB40 have been hugely successful. Bob Marley's *Legend* album, a collection of his work first released in 1984, is still selling like crazy. Final proof of reggae's popularity is its offspring, dancehall—a reggae-rap hybrid—which has swept through the Caribbean, the United States, and Europe on the popularity of artists like Beenie Man.

It didn't used to be that way, even when Bob Marley was king (many say he still is). Reggae's success was a long time coming. The music first hit the charts in 1969, when Desmond Dekker reached number 12 on the Billboard chart with "The Israelites." Jimmy Cliff then had a hit in 1970 with "Wonderful World, Beautiful People." Bob Marley and the Wailers' 1976 album, *Rastaman Vibration*, reached number 8 on the Billboard album charts—which at the time was unprecedented for both Marley and reggae musicians in general.

On the other hand, mainstream musicians have made it big with reggae. Paul Simon led the way when he wrote "Mother and Child Reunion" back in 1972. About the same time, Johnny Nash took Bob Marley's song "Stir It Up," made it a hit, and followed shortly thereafter with the reggae-influenced "I Can See Clearly Now." Then came Eric Clapton's blockbuster version of "I Shot the Sheriff"—another Marley tune. After that, a number of musicians jumped on the reggae bandwagon, from The Police with songs like "Roxanne" to such all-time greats as Bonnie Raitt with "One Belief Away." Lauren Hill and Sugar Ray have had hits using the reggae or dancehall format.

Reggae's Roots

Reggae evolved from a variety of Jamaican musical styles. Its roots can be heard in the traditional Jamaican music called *mento*. It has a slow beat and rather lewd lyrics—much like the *beguine* of Martinique. Like the wine and calypso music, it is danced to very intimately, with two people joined at the hips simulating intercourse.

The advent of rhythm and blues in the United States, coupled with the spread of transistor radios, doomed *mento*. The powerful AM broadcasts out of Miami brought the R&B sound home to Jamaica. So did the growing popularity of sound systems—traveling DJs with PA systems and the hottest singles from the United States. American music soon influenced Jamaica's own, resulting in a fast-paced synthesis called ska.

Although ska was not tremendously popular elsewhere, Millie Small's 1964 song "My Boy Lollipop" was a worldwide hit. By the late '6os, ska gave way to yet another music called rock steady. It was much slower, with a more evenly paced beat — reggae's forerunner. Rock steady delivered an increasingly more serious message than its lighthearted predecessor. The music soon expressed the heightened sense of black pride brought on by the U.S. civil rights and Black Power movements.

It was rock steady's growing lyrical consciousness that gave birth to the slower, more powerful reggae. Reggae became the vehicle of discontent, rooted in the shantytowns of West Kingston and Trenchtown. Bob Marley and the Wailers became the stewards of this new music, formulating the now-familiar guitar rhythms and timing. In 1970 Marley founded the Tuff Gong Studios, and by 1971 he and his band were on their way with the hit "Trenchtown Rock." At the time of his death in 1981 at age 36 (of brain cancer), Marley had produced more than 20 albums and had made reggae a dynamic force worldwide.

Although reggae is still popular on the Jamaican scene, dancehall now reigns supreme. Beenie Man, Mr. Vegas, and Sean Paul are three of the most popular dancehall artists at the moment.

For reggae fans, there is one must-stop in Jamaica — the Bob Marley Museum.

The Bob Marley Museum, 56 Hope Road, Kingston, Jamaica, WI, 876-927-9152

Run by Rastas, the museum occupies the former Tuff Gong Studios, where most of Bob Marley and the Wailers' best music was recorded. It's located in a well-heeled neighborhood near Jamaica House (the official residence of the prime minister). When you pull up to the gate, you are greeted by a security guard who announces that the only pictures allowed are of the Marley statue inside. After that, all cameras and recording devices must be checked at the gatehouse. A guide will then take you inside to view an hour-long video presentation that shows Bob Marley in concert, recording at the studio (which is where you are sitting), and out and about. The rest of the tour includes the grounds, notably murals, herb gardens, Marley's statue, a beehive, and a real live ganja plant.

Back inside the museum, which originally was an old Victorian house, there are two floors of memorabilia. They include two rooms of news clippings pasted to the walls, a replica of Bob's first record shop in Trenchtown, called Wail 'n' Soul Records, his bedroom preserved intact (it looks like a hippie den — with pillows on the floor and a large smoking pipe), as well as a wax statue à la Madame Tussaud that one of these days will move to simulate him singing. When you finish the tour, you'll want to check out the souvenir shop for T-shirts and jewelry.

Admission is $10 for adults. Hours are 9:30 a.m. to 4:30 p.m. daily, except Wednesday and Saturday, 12:30 to 5:30 p.m., and closed on Sunday.

Also of interest to fans: Although Marley spent most of his life in Kingston, he was born — and now rests in his mausoleum — in Nine Miles, a remote village in the mountains above Ocho Rios that is especially lively on February 6, Marley's birthday. The island's big day-tour operator, **Chukka Adventure Tours** (876-972-2506; www.chukkacove.com) offers a five-hour Zion Bus Line excursion daily out of Ochi. You'll board a colorful authentic Jamaican country bus crested with fruits and vegetables that trundles along bumpy back roads pumping hearty reggae beats. It's a little Disneyish, but fun.

⊛ *Reggae SumFest*

Now here is an event for hard-core reggae and dancehall fans. Originally called Reggae Sunsplash and held each summer, this five-day festival always features the best talent in the field — a mini-Woodstock of reggae music. Held in Montego Bay, the Sunsplash venue was moved to Kingston in 1993, which proved very unpopular (no beaches and not enough tourist facilities) and led to the demise of Reggae Sunsplash. Now called Reggae SumFest (new producers and with Red Stripe chiming in as a sponsor), the festival returned to Montego Bay and is held at Catherine Hall in July. This event regularly draws more than 120,000 people during the course of the festival.

Daily admission to the events is $15 to $40, but weekly passes are also available, which include special entry and unlimited access to all SumFest events, a souvie 'zine, and access to the backstage hospitality area and parking. Many packages include these passes and lodging, airfare, and more. For info, call 800-JAMAICA or visit the official Web site at www.reggaesum fest.com, where you'll find tour operator packages, many including airfare from the United States. Arrive rested, 'cause once SumFest starts there'll be little break in the partying.

A somewhat lower-key Jazz-Blues Festival takes place each January on the grounds of Rose Hall's Cinnamon Hill golf course; individual tickets are $50 to $60. Information: www.airjamaicajazzandblues.com.

Other Cool Jamaican Stuff

Jamaican Art

There are few places in the Caribbean where the art scene is as dynamic or impressive as it is in Jamaica. This can readily be seen in Kingston, the island's capital. The average tourist might think that the crafts markets of Ocho Rios or Montego Bay, with their wood carvings and amateur paintings, encapsulate the Jamaican art scene, but this is hardly the case.

For a true perspective on Jamaican art, you must visit the **National Gallery**, Roy West Building, Kingston Mall (876-922-8540). Since 1982 the gallery has occupied two floors of this building—and it has already outgrown them. Its 18 galleries house various collections of paintings, prints, and sculptures from different eras and artists of Jamaica. The gallery also has an international collection that focuses on Caribbean works.

Of particular interest at the gallery is the magnificent sculpture collection of Edna Manley, one of the primary forces in modern Jamaican art. Her work is truly moving, from the reflection on political violence called *Ghetto Mother* (1982) to such timeless pieces as *Negro Aroused* (1935), *The Beadseller* (1922), *The Diggers* (1936), and *Horse of the Morning* (1943).

There are other prominent artists whose works should not be missed. These include Mallica Reynolds (known as Kapo), Barrington Watson, Christopher Gonzalez, Karl Parboosingh, and Albert Huie. Kapo is probably Jamaica's most prolific primitive sculptor, with evocative pieces like *All Women Are Five Women* (1965). He is also a renowned painter. Barrington Watson's neorealist oil paintings of the human form are outstanding, including *Conversation* (1981) and *Mother and Child* (1968). Christopher Gonzalez's mahogany sculpture *Man Arisen* (1966) explodes with emotion. *Ras Smoke I* (1972), by Karl Parboosingh, and *The Constant Spring Road* (1964), by Albert Huie, both oils, are powerful documentation of the lives and times of the Jamaican people. The gallery is open Tuesday through Friday, 10 a.m. to 4:30 p.m., Saturday from 10 a.m. to 3 p.m., and closed Sunday and Monday. Admission is $1. What a deal!

If you are in the mood to buy or browse, check out the **Contemporary Arts Centre** at 1 Liguanea Avenue (876-927-9958); **The Edna Manley School of the Visual Arts** at the Cultural Training Centre, 1 Arthur Wint Drive, with works in progress and a student exhibition during the last week in June and the first week of July (876-926-2800); the **Bolivar Bookshop and Gallery**, 1-D Grove Road (876-926-8799); **Chelsea Art Gallery**, 12 Chelsea Avenue (876-929-2231 or 876-929-0045); **Mutual Life Gallery**, 2 Oxford Road (876-929-4302); **Frame Centre Gallery**, 10 Tangerine Place (876-926-4644); **Art Gallery Ltd.**, the Hilton Hotel, 77 Knutsford Boulevard (876-960-8939); and finally the **Institute of Jamaica**, 12 East Street, (876-922-0620) with exhibitions by students of all ages.

No art adventure in Kingston would be complete without seeing the monumental wall murals on the campus of the **University of the West Indies**. While you're there, pick up a catalog. Who knows, the Jamaican art experience may arouse new interests that demand further study.

Montego Bay—Greens by the Sea

Montego Bay—a.k.a. MoBay—is Jamaica's second largest and least interesting city. It is the island's de facto tourism hub (the airport here is the region's second busiest, after San Juan), with lots of hotels, and Negril and Ocho Rios are less than two hours away by car. There is one reason to stay in MoBay, however: excellent **golf**. In fact, the island is home to the oldest golf course in the Western Hemipshere (Mandeville's nine-hole, Manchester Country Club, which was built in 1865), but of Jamaica's 12 courses, the most distinctive are in MoBay. There are five 18-hole courses in the area surrounding the city—at least three of them outstanding—making MoBay one of the Caribbean's top golf destinations. Here's an overview, starting with the headline attraction.

Named after Annee Palmer, the notorious mistress of Rose Hall Plantation in the 19th century, the **White Witch** course is considered by some to be the finest in the Caribbean—it's certainly one of the most beautiful. The fairway is designed by Robert van Hagge and Rick Baril, and it climbs up and down the abrupt hillsides overlooking the affiliated Ritz-Carlton resort—a fortune is spent keeping it up to snuff. The White Witch is 6,710 yards, and native stone inlaid walls shore up the greens and tees on many holes. However, it's a tough course, with dramatic elevation changes, and it can make the average player feel like a maladroit goon. But you can also count on breathtaking sea views and fresh, cool wind at this elevation. Being a Ritz-Carlton, the resort assigns a "golf concierge" (oh puh-leeze!) to every group to retrieve wayward shots, advise on club selection, and keep balls burnished and bright. That's called a caddie where we play golf, but the White Witch offers a difficult game, so a few tips from the resident experts are welcome (and most of them are quite engaging companions to have along).

Redesigned by Robert von Hagge and Rick Baril in 2003, the Rose Hall Resort's **Cinnamon Hill** course is full of twists, hills, dips, and water hazards, and the par-71 course benefits greatly from the significant infusion of money. Starting at an attractive English colonial–style clubhouse containing the requisite dining room and bar (and with the added flourish of a cannon in the courtyard), this uncompromising course of 6,637 yards is lined by historic ruins. The fourth hole, though short, requires you to place the ball over a pond about as big as the fairway; it ends only feet from the green. The eighth hole is a playable par 5 and one of the best birdie opportunities here, with plenty of room left off the tee. The back nine is full of obstacles and requires real skill to finesse the ball to several blind greens. The 14th was made more playable during the remodeling and features a slight dogleg down to the green, whereas the 15th hole is a toughie—it has water hazards, including a waterfall, both fore and aft of the green (used in the 007 film *Live and Let Die*). Rose Hall also has a great driving range up the hill behind the clubhouse.

Located about 20 minutes east of MoBay, near Round Hill, **Tryall** is one of the prettiest courses in the Caribbean. Indeed, one guest we talked to was on his 15th visit and preferred the Tryall course to Pebble Beach. A superbly maintained and scenic par 71, it has in the past accommodated the Johnny Walker World Championship and the Mazda Championship. The course is a hilly 6,221 yards and is full of water hazards on the last holes, especially the tricky 15th, a par 3. There are two par 5s that are each 500 yards or more. The course is tough and challenging, with wind from the sea and thick roughs, but it's also beautiful — signs of the property's glory days are everywhere, including the plantation's 200-year-old waterwheel. Views of the turquoise sea are a backdrop to every divot.

Designed by Robert Trent Jones in 1961, the **Half Moon** course is another well-maintained par 72, but it's easier and perhaps less dynamic than the previous three. With a more traditional links layout, it is long at 7,119 yards and consists mainly of deep, wide, straight fairways — it's a power hitter's dream. There are four par-5 holes that will keep your drivers very busy, and the greens are defended by all-embracing bunkers. Since our last play here, in 2005, the course has seen considerable upgrades, and there's a David Leadbetter Golf Academy at the resort to fine-tune your play.

A fifth MoBay course, **Ironshore**, is shorter, cheaper, and enveloped by villas and condos.

Where to Stay

More than any other island in the Caribbean, Jamaica has the greatest variety of accommodations, with options at all price levels and ranging from small mom-and-pop inns to huge all-inclusives. About three-quarters of Jamaica's visitors stay in MoBay, Ocho Rios, and Negril, split almost evenly among the three, that the remaining quarter is spread around the rest of the island. Our recommendations are organized starting with our favorite place to stay, Negril (at the western tip of the island) and continuing around clockwise to the South Coast.

Negril

In Negril there are more options for lodging, from rustic and funky to deluxe mega-resort, than in practically any other part of Jamaica. You can choose according to your style and budget, but the offbeat type of accommodation is still a Negril specialty. If you stay on the West End — the location of the first four hotels — there is no beach, but you get to dive into turquoise water from rock platforms — lots of fun and no sand to stick to your legs. For additional information, see www.negril.com.

The West End

Tensing Pen, P.O. Box 3013, West End Road, Negril, Jamaica, WI. ℂ 876-957-0387, ℘ 876-957-0161, ▢ www.tensingpen, tensingpen@cwjamaica.com

▮ **Pricey** ⑪ **CP** ⓒⓒ 17 rooms and cottages
Situated on a rocky bluff on the West End amid several acres of lushly landscaped grounds, Tensing Pen is our favorite place to stay in Negril.

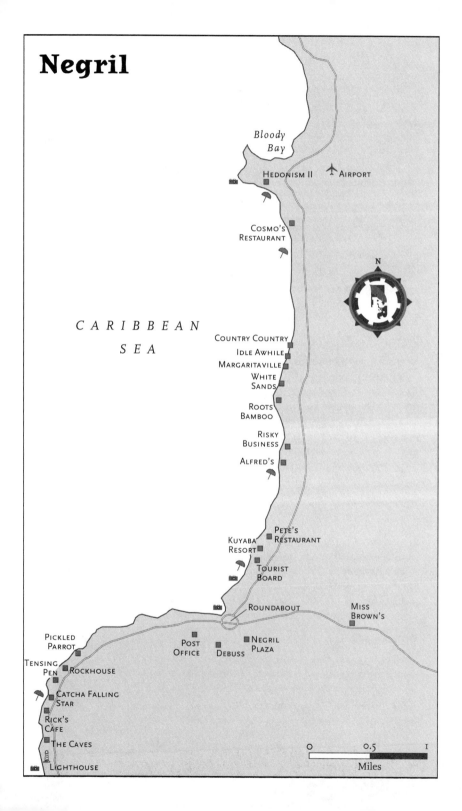

Negril

Bloody Bay

HEDONISM II ✈ AIRPORT

COSMO'S RESTAURANT

C A R I B B E A N

S E A

N

COUNTRY COUNTRY
IDLE AWHILE
MARGARITAVILLE
WHITE SANDS
ROOTS BAMBOO
RISKY BUSINESS
ALFRED'S

PETE'S RESTAURANT
KUYABA RESORT
TOURIST BOARD

ROUNDABOUT
MISS BROWN'S

PICKLED PARROT
POST OFFICE
DEBUSS
NEGRIL PLAZA

TENSING PEN
ROCKHOUSE
CATCHA FALLING STAR
RICK'S CAFE
THE CAVES
LIGHTHOUSE

0   0.5   1
Miles

The accommodations are truly fabulous for their uniqueness, privacy, and setting. Looking like primitive thatched huts, the wood, thatch, and cut-stone cottages are actually quite elegantly but simply furnished, with four-poster mosquito-netted beds, polished wood floors, and private bath. There are lanais with rocking chairs, most looking out over the water, facing west. We couldn't think of a better place in Negril to sit and read or watch for the green flash. Many of the huts are elevated and called the Pillars, giving the impression of a tree house. These also have outdoor showers—a fabulous touch in the tropics. Two favorites are Middle Pillar and Cove Cottage. All the units have privileges in a well-equipped communal kitchen attached to a very comfortable and pleasant dining and sitting area—delicious Jamaican-style dinners are now available nightly for guests of the inn. For large groups, there is a three-bedroom Great House with a huge living room; it is basically open to the sea and the views. The staff is very friendly and willing to help with any special needs.

Although Tensing Pen doesn't have a beach, it has a craggy coastline with all kinds of places to jump or dive into the crystal clear turquoise water and strategically placed ladders to get out easily. On most days the water is very calm, making it fun and safe. There are also sunning patios carved out of the rock, with chaises for your tanning pleasure. A cove bisects the property and a footbridge connects the two points, although it is not necessary to use the bridge. It doesn't have any railings and is sort of like walking a wide plank over the water —easy but a tad scary. Tensing Pen is not a place for small children.

⊛ **Rockhouse**, P.O. Box 3024, West End Road, Negril, Jamaica, WI. ℂ 876-957-4373, ✎ 876-957-0557, ⌨ www.rockhousehotel.com, info@rockhousehotel.com

💲 **Not So Cheap** 🍴 **EP** CC 34 rooms

This is Negril's original cliffside dwelling. The inn started in 1969, but it needed major refurbishing when a trio of Aussies took over in 1994. Today, the original thatched-roof bungalows remain, some with private outdoor showers, and you can still dive straight into the water from wooden bridges spanning the cliffs (the water here is clear and calm). Rockhouse now also claims the chic milieu of a rugged boutique resort, without the wallet wallop. A strikingly incongruous modern pool has been built at one end of the property, and the restaurant has been upgraded; room service is now available, and all the rooms have minibars and a/c. The least expensive rooms are in a two-story building back from the cliff—not much of a view, but these are a good buy. As with Tensing Pen, children under 12 are not permitted.

The Caves, P.O. Box 15, Lighthouse Road, West End, Negril, Jamaica, WI.
ⓒ 800-688-7678 or 876-960-8134, 📠 876-957-4930,
🖥 www.islandoutpost.com, thecaves@islandoutpost.com

💰 **Stratospheric** 🍴 **FAP**, including drinks, tax, and service charge ⓒⒸ
10 cottages

It was bound to happen. When The Caves opened, attitude arrived in
Negril. Located on the West End just south of the Negril Lighthouse,
this small property of 10 cottages caters to celebutants and their entourages. Chris Blackwell (of Island Records and Island Outpost, a
chain of chic hotels) knows what these people want in a vacation
hideaway — namely, luxury, hipness, design, and privacy. Keeping
these in mind, he gets his musician, model, and actor friends to pa-
tronize his establishments. They create a chichi buzz and welcome
publicity, lending his places an air of exclusivity and fabulousness
(the same thing happens in St. Barth). They also bring their "I'm,
like, way cool" attitude, which permeates right down to the staff (we
were scrutinized by the management to a degree that almost felt like
a strip search!). Shortly after The Caves opened, Jimmy Buffet paid a
visit in his seaplane. As he was landing, the local police opened fire
on the plane from the nearby Negril Lighthouse, thinking it was a drug
shipment from somewhere. Mr. B. wrote a song about the bullet-
dodging incident called "Jamaica Mistaka." Talk about an entrance!

For all this carping, you'd think The Caves would be our last resort
in Negril. Not at all. Island Outpost's boutique hotels (there are others in Jamaica, the Bahamas, and Miami's South Beach) are a welcome counterpoint to the depersonalized all-inclusive mega-resorts
that are swallowing up Jamaica and threatening the entire Caribbean.
Though technically an all-inclusive (meals, fruit juice and alcohol bar,
tax, and service charges are included in the room rates), The Caves
hardly has that atmosphere. Activities are kept to a minimum, except
for the Aveda spa, which has probably the most soothing massage
room in Jamaica. There are no pool aerobics here, only a gorgeous
saltwater pool built at cliff's edge (a hot tub seems to dangle over the
water). The mood is serene and discreet, with a staff chosen for its
looks and sophistication. Ambient music from the Island Records
catalog wafts through the grounds. A stairway of coral stone descends
into the huge cavern directly below the pool, where benches have
been carved in the rock and night lighting adds a sense of drama to
a midnight caress (the grotto can be reserved for a one-of-a-kind candlelight dinner). The cottages are groovy in décor (handmade furniture, batik fabrics, and bright colors), although some, like Moon-
shadow, seem to be a tad tight in the space department (we got the
feeling of being on a boat, down to the berthlike sofas and dinette).
Another, called Blue Hole, has polished concrete floors and an indoor

shower-and-bed combination as its focal point (very apropos for hot and heavy couples).

Catcha Falling Star, P.O. Box 22, West End Road, Negril, Jamaica, WI. ℂ 876-957-0390, ✆ 876-640-2546, 🖳 www.catchajamaica.com, stay@catchajamaica.com

💲 **Pricey** and up 🍽 **BP** [CC] 6 cottages

Located next door to Tensing Pen, Catcha Falling Star is a place to try if you can't get into Tensing Pen. It lacks Tensing Pen's charm and specialness, but Catcha Falling Star is still comfortable and pleasant. There are six attractive one- and two-bedroom cottages, with maid service and breakfast served on your veranda. As with its neighbor, you can swim off the rocks and sun on the specially built patios. Clothes-optional bathing is another plus.

Seven Mile Beach

Kuyaba Resort, P.O. Box 2635, Norman Manley Boulevard, Negril, Jamaica, WI. ℂ 876-957-4318, ✆ 876-957-9765, 🖳 www.kuyaba.com, kuyaba@cwjamaica.com

💲 **Cheap** 🍽 **EP** [CC] 22 rooms

If we were on a budget (and sometimes we have been), this is where we would stay. Located on the beach, this very charming smallish property (22 rooms) has several cute, simple wooden gingerbread units (called Rustic Cottages), Garden Rooms (across the street), and some new, more deluxe units. The Deluxe Rooms are truly a bargain for what you pay, and there's an upstairs honeymoon suite. These rooms have terra-cotta tile floors, comfortable furnishings, high ceilings, and a wonderful sense of spaciousness. Kuyaba is owned by the Williams family, and managers and sons Ralph and Marc are great guys who try to use as much local wood, brick, and stone as possible when renovating units. Many of the units have a/c—be sure to ask, if you want it. Ralph and Marc are constantly trying to make their place better for their guests. Ralph will negotiate a very fair price if you plan an extended stay.

Idle Awhile, Norman Manley Boulevard, Negril, Jamaica WI. ℂ 877-243-5352 or 876-957-9566, ✆ 876-957-9567, 🖳 www.idleawhile.com

💲 **Not So Cheap** 🍽 **EP** [CC] 15 rooms

Run by the couple that owns the nearby Swept Away all-inclusive, this is a charming inn with handsome, oversize rooms and swank Caribbean styling (by way of Miami, we'd say). Most units don't have beach views, but all are embraced by well-tended gardens. The restaurant specializes in Jamaican cuisine, and an *ital* (vegetarian) lunch special is offered daily. You can also book a one-bedroom suite and have a cook for $20 a day (plus groceries). Guests here also get free Wi-Fi and access to the 10-acre Swept Away sports and fitness complex. Idle Awhile also offers a trio of appealing villas on the West End, just past the lighthouse.

Country Country, Norman Manley Boulevard, Negril, Jamaica, WI.
℃ 888-790-5264 or 876-957-4273, 🖥 www.countrynegril.com

💼 **Pricey** 🍴 **BP** **CC** 20 rooms

Designed by acclaimed architect Ann Hodges and owned by the family that has Montego Bay's Coyaba Beach Resort, this spot is a cheery beachfront lodging, painted in bright Caribbean colors in patina, ringed by gingerbread and topped by tin roofs. Standard units have a minifridge, in-room safe, teakettle, and a/c. Superior rooms add a pull-out single bed and slightly more space; all herald minimalist appeal. There's a beachfront restaurant, Country Peppa's, serving Jamaican specialties.

White Sands, P.O. Box 60, Norman Manley Boulevard, Negril, Jamaica, WI. ℃ 876-957-4291, 📠 876-957-4674, 🖥 www.whitesandsjamaica.com, whitesands@cwjamaica.com

💲 **Cheap** 🍴 **EP** **CC** 46 rooms

A great beachfront value, White Sands is a casual but well-run, 40-unit property that sprawls over two sides of the road. The least expensive rooms are not on the beach side — they have simple appeal, and the upper units are preferable for their cathedral ceilings and balconies. Deluxe units on the beach side are just a few steps from the sand. There's a garden pool, screeching parrots and a beach bar and grill — no phones or TVs. One family has owned this spot since 1971, and though informal, glitz-free, and a terrific deal, it does have one absurd claim to fame: Cher and Gregg Allman stayed here on their honeymoon.

Hedonism II, P.O. Box 25, Negril Beach Road, Negril, Jamaica, WI.
℃ 800-467-8737 or 876-957-4200, 📠 876-957-4289, 🖥 www.superclubs.com/brand_hedonism

💼 **Stratospheric** 🍴 **All-Inclusive** **CC** 280 rooms

The name of this resort couldn't be more appropriate, although it's not too clear on what the "II" means (there was never a Hedonism I, but a Hedonism III opened at Runaway Bay — as if another one of these places is needed!). This resort was founded on the pleasure principle and has built its reputation on sophomoric play. Personally, you'd have to pay us to stay here. This is not because we disapprove of its philosophy. It fills a valid need for many people. We simply don't find the clientele terribly sophisticated or attractive. We felt this way the first time we visited and still do more than a decade later. Who needs culture and class when it comes to bodily pleasures, anyway? The management tries to sell Hedonism II with the line "Pleasure comes in many forms: the mind, the body, the spirit, and the soul." Judging from what we witnessed here, we'd say the overwhelming focus was a spirited and mindful effort to enhance the pleasures of the body to the point of selling one's soul.

The buildings and grounds are not very exciting. Frankly, the blocks of rooms look like a suburban medical center. The rooms themselves are sufficient in a contemporary sense, with lots of mirrors, including one over the bed (duh!), and have a private bath and a/c but no balcony, patio, or TV. Singles will be assigned a same-sex roommate unless they pay a supplement. There is a rather small free-form pool that adjoins the main bar and the entertainment and dining amphitheater. The bartenders there are kept very busy, often by shouting, drunken men and women who could easily be cast in *My Cousin Vinny*, down to the gold chains around their necks and the Ozone Park accents. At the other end of the pool is the disco roof on which is a see-through Jacuzzi (like, totally gross!). The throbbing beat of the music penetrates the poolside air. The disco bar has windows that look into the pool, much as you would find in a public aquarium. You'll see lots of dangling feet, legs, and torsos — the effect is quite provocative. There are stories of some very explicit happenings — a true exhibitionist and voyeur's dream.

Down the slope from the disco is the beach, which is nice if you want to get away from the main staging area. There is also a trampoline and trapeze (with safety net), for those with fantasies or fears of flying. Just about every conceivable land and water sport is available, including an ice-skating rink, a spa and fitness center, and a rock-climbing wall (clothes optional, of course). The management does pull in some superb entertainment, especially on Saturday night. The staff, in the mode of camp counselors, is very friendly and relentlessly "up." There is also a nude pool-Jacuzzi area (open 24 hours) near the beach and at the property line (a black screen has been erected — no pun intended — to shield the neighboring buildings from probably some of the most unattractive naked bodies you'll ever be subjected to). Get the picture!?!

There is a minimum two-night-stay requirement. Discounts abound most times of the year.

Montego Bay

We would avoid staying right in MoBay, a city of 110,000 with little appeal or charm. It's crowded and hot, with traffic jams at rush hour and bland all-inclusives along its fringes. However, if you want to golf, MoBay is your best base, and just a few miles out of town are better options, including four luxury resorts that are among the best on the island: Round Hill and Tryall are just west of the city, and Half Moon and the Ritz-Carlton are to the east. All of these hotels have relationships with the various golf courses in the area.

Round Hill Hotel & Villas, P.O. Box 64, Montego Bay, Jamaica, WI. ℭ 800-972-2159 or 876-956-7050, ❧ 876-956-7505, ⌨ www.roundhilljamaica.com, roundhill@cwjamaica.com

💲 **Beyond Belief** 🍽 **EP** [CC] 110 rooms and suites

Located 10 miles west of MoBay on a 98-acre peninsula, Round Hill is one of the grandes dames of Caribbean resorts. Since its inception in 1953, it has hosted more than its fair share of the Hollywood and jet set. There are pictures in the bar of Grace Kelly (in the buffet line) plus a score of other celebs, from Noël Coward and Queen Elizabeth to Rockefellers, Paleys, Kennedys, Andy Warhol, and Paul McCartney. This is an old-school resort, where flash is looked down on and understatement is the name of the game. Under the continued stewardship of Josef Forstmayr, Round Hill has maintained a standard of excellence and style unparalleled in Jamaica. Occasional resident Ralph Lauren, who has owned a villa here since 1979, helped to design the décor for much of the public space. His influence is apparent, especially in the bar, which would look right at home with the New York Yacht Club. There is a staff of 220 to attend to your needs; most have been with Round Hill for more than two decades — now that's loyalty.

There are 29 privately owned villas (really bungalows), painted white with green trim and nestled among the hibiscus and bougainvillea. Most of the villas have their own swimming pools, and all are fully staffed with maids (who cook your breakfast in your villa) and a gardener. All the villas are cut up into suites (two, three, or four units each — 74 in all). Each of the suites has its own entrance, which means that you will be sharing a house with someone else unless you rent the entire villa — our suggestion. Just put some friends together. That way, you won't have to share the pool or deck with anyone you don't know. Try to get villa 12 — it sits on the top of the hill and has two bedrooms, a great pool, and fab views.

There are also 36 rooms in the seaside building known as the Pineapple House, affectionately called "The Barracks" since its origin. The best rooms are on the second floor, with cathedral ceilings, large louvered windows overlooking the sea, and brightly colored walls; all are tastefully furnished. In front of The Barracks is a free-form pool for all guests and a (very) small beach with water sports. Guests can play golf at Tryall for a fee.

The Tryall Club, P.O. Box 1206, Montego Bay, Jamaica, WI. ℭ 800-238-5290 or 876-956-5660, ❧ 876-956-5673, ⌨ www.tryallclub.com, reservation@tryallclub.com

💰 **Ridiculous** for rooms in Great House; **Stratospheric** for villas ⑪ EP
(an **All-Inclusive** is also available) ⓒⓒ 69 villas and suites

Just 2 miles west and down the road from Round Hill, this sprawling
resort is really a huge, very deluxe country club. Situated on the site of
a 2,200-acre former sugar plantation and tumbling down to the sea from
a faraway hilltop, this is a magnificent property, especially for those
who love golf and tennis, the raison d'etre for staying at Tryall Club.

The resort itself is very grand. The U-shaped main building is a
lovingly restored 18th-century Georgian Great House — a symphony
of white, light blue, parquet, and chintz. Set atop a hill, it commands
expansive views of the grounds and the sea beyond. Connected to the
Great House are 13 one- and two-bedroom villa suites, all imaginatively
decorated, all one of a kind, and located close to the resort's restaurant,
bar, and main pool. The villa suites are actually a pretty good value
and even come with a housekeeper-cook. Then there are 56 privately
owned villas dappling the estate, ranging from one to six bedrooms.
Most are individually owned and showcase the taste of the owners.
Most are pretty lavish, but a few are admittedly kitschy. All have a private pool and a full-time staff (cook, chambermaid, laundress, and gardener); larger villas also come with a butler. To help you decide which
is right for you, the Club publishes brochures on all the villas, with photos and layouts for your perusal (also check the Web site). Down at the
beach there is a beach club and water-sports center. The tennis center
has nine nova-cushion courts (lit for night play), with ball machines, private lessons and clinics, and ball boys to hustle after your aberrant shots.

The all-inclusive plan includes greens fees, some water sports, and
tennis clinic.

Half Moon Resort, Rose Hall, Montego Bay, Jamaica, WI. ☏ 800-626-
0592 or 876-953-2211, ✆ 876-953-2558, 🖵 www.halfmoon.com

💰 **Wicked Pricey** and up ⑪ EP (**MAP**, golf, and **All-Inclusive** packages
are also available) ⓒⓒ 453 rooms

Located 6 miles east of the MoBay airport, this is one of Jamaica's
most deluxe resorts and was quite popular with the Japanese market
until the Asian market collapse. Though not quite as chichi as Round
Hill, it's just as expensive, and lots of celebrities land here (Barbra
Streisand, Queen Elizabeth II, George Bush Sr., and Whitney Houston,
for starters). The main difference with Round Hill is that this huge,
400-acre property is like a minicity, containing a shopping village
(home of the Bob Marley Experience Theatre), equestrian facility and
polo field, and a 24-hour medical office with dialysis center! It has a
pretty, mile-long crescent beach (and other beaches on either side), a
full-service spa and fitness center, 13 tennis courts for serve-and-volley
enthusiasts, and 4 squash courts. One swimming pool is Olympic

size, built for an Australian swimmer to train for her Jamaica-to-Cuba crossing, but there are others to explore, too.

The main building (rebuilt in 1996 following a fire), has an ante-bellum-style entry replete with fountains, white columns, black and gray marble tile floors, crystal chandeliers, Queen Anne mahogany antiques, Oriental rugs, and Jamaican art — what a combo! There are 453 rooms, which range from standard but attractive hotel rooms to four- and five-bedroom villas. The latter come with a maid, butler, and live-in cook, plus a private pool.

The Ritz-Carlton Rose Hall, 1 Ritz-Carlton Drive, Rose Hall, Jamaica, WI.
    ⓒ 800-241-3333 or 876-953-2800, ✆ 876-518-0110,
    🖳 www.ritzcarlton.com

💲 **Wicked Pricey** 🍴 **EP** Ⓒ🅲 427 rooms

A big source of local pride was the arrival of the Ritz-Carlton to Jamaica in 2000. The addition of this kind of monolith is not normally the kind of thing we applaud, but the Ritz-Carlton name is a big plus for Jamaica — it should help convince a number of Americans (the kind that need a big brand name to ensure peace of mind) to visit the island. The $125 million, five-story Ritz-Carlton was the first European Plan (non–all inclusive) resort to be built on the island since the 1970s. As such, it is a thoroughly state-of-the-art creation — even boasting its own power plant!

Located cheek by jowl with Half Moon, the hotel has 450-square-foot standard rooms, which are standard-issue Ritz-Carlton, with oversize sofas, framed bird and floral prints, faux antiques, and a minibar. On the downside, the five-story buildings are a bit soulless and feel hermetically sealed (to allow air-conditioning in the lobby and other common areas). The man-made beach is not particularly attractive, which is probably why Ritz-Carlton also bought a beach club 4 miles away (the same beach, incidentally, that Richard M. Nixon proclaimed as the finest on the island — for what it's worth, Dick, we've seen better in Jamaica). On the upside, the resort has an 8,000-square-foot full-service spa, the Lobby Lounge has a coffee bar to serve a variety of local blends along with some 150 types of island rums, and the impressive White Witch golf course is the best on the island. The addition of the Reggae Jerk Center on the beach — though not quite like the experience of going to Boston Bay — is a fun way to showcase authentic local food that ranges well beyond jerk fare.

Rose Hall Resort, P.O. Box 999, Montego Bay, Jamaica, WI. ⓒ 876-953-2650, ✆ 876-953-2617, 🖳 www.luxuryresorts.com

💲 **Wicked Pricey** 🍴 **EP** (an **All-Inclusive** plan is also available) 🅲🅲 485 rooms

This 400-acre, former Wyndham resort is best appreciated for its setting and excellent golf course (see the write-up on the Cinnamon Hill course earlier in this chapter). The hotel caters to the convention crowd, and it looks it. The property was renovated in 2000, but its architecture is big, bland, pink, and rectangular — none of these elements is exactly in harmony with the natural setting. The rooms are nicely decorated but not terribly large. There is a large main pool with swim-up bar, plus an elaborate, $7 million water park with slides through a sugar mill, channels, waterfalls, and faux plantation ruins, which seems to keep the children of the name-tag generation happy. For adults, there is a small shopping arcade and a casino.

Coyaba Beach Resort & Club, Mahoe Bay, St. James, Jamaica, WI. ℭ 877-232-3224 or 876-953-9150, ✆ 876-953-2244, 🖥 www.coyabaresortjamaica.com

💰 **Very Pricey** 🍽 **EP** (an **All-Inclusive** plan is also available) CC
50 rooms

Sitting on its own beach just west of Half Moon, this resort is a good spot for families with young children due to its size and various kids' programs. Owned and operated by a Jamaican family that lives on site, this is a truly Jamaican enterprise and a polished one at that. All furniture has been made on the island, and all produce is grown locally. The décor is island colonial style; the floors are Italian tile. French doors lead out to a lanai. All kinds of water sports are available, and there is a lighted tennis court. Golf is across the street.

Ocho Rios and Oracabessa

In past editions of *Rum & Reggae's Caribbean* we avoided sending readers to Ocho Rios, due to its crass embrace of cruise ships, high-rises, and all-inclusives. As megaboats take over an increasingly larger chunk of the Caribbean each year, however, and all-inclusives pepper every corner of this island, Ochi (as it's called locally) is starting to stand out less. There are a few special spots that manage to sequester guests well away from the hustle-bustle.

Jamaica Inn, P.O. Box 1, Ocho Rios, Jamaica, WI. ℭ 877-470-6975 or 876-974-2514, ✆ 876-974-2449, 🖥 www.jamaicainn.com, jaminn@cwjamaica.com

💰 **Ridiculous** (substantial discounts in summer) 🍽 **EP** CC 45 rooms and 6 cottages

Jamaica Inn is one of the classic resorts built on the island in the 1950s that drew notables like Winston Churchill and Alistair McLean. As newer, bigger, glitzier resorts were built during the last few decades, Jamaica Inn was sometimes knocked as old-fashioned or stuffy. Today, as the post–dot.com generation rediscovers glamour through the purity of a gin-clear martini, places like Jamaica Inn are back in style. Today's celebrity sightings might include I.M. Pei or Kate Moss, both of whom typify its eclectic but decidedly au courant clientele, yet all are welcomed by Eric and Peter Morrow, who grew up on the property as sons of the original owner. Ownership isn't the only thing that hasn't changed: The periwinkle blue and white color scheme remains, bullshots (bullion and vodka) are served on the beach, and upon checkout guests are still presented with a hand-written bill rather than a computer printout. Some of the staff were even here at the beginning (you'll quickly recognize which ones).

A few things have evolved. The resort broke with the jacket-and-tie policy recently and has gingerly improved the property by adding things like a fitness room and by sprucing up the rooms, but all of this has transpired without abandoning the unpretentious style of a bygone era. Every room has an ocean view, from a rise overlooking the beach. All have original tile floors and are oversize, with large balconies stocked with sofa, wing chair, lamp, and writing desk (this is a fabulous place to eat breakfast). Fabrics are cotton chintz, the four-poster beds are Jamaican antiques. There are other rooms right on the beach, as well as the White Suite, where Churchill stayed — the private pool for this room has a wheelchair access ramp, built long before anyone had heard of the Americans with Disabilities Act. The pretty, covelike beach is sequestered by peninsulas on each end that keep the riffraff out. Activities include kayaks, snorkeling equipment, tennis, and croquet. Meals are dressy affairs, but they are reliably good, served by candlelight, and accompanied by live music and dancing nightly.

⊛ **Goldeneye**, Oracabessa, St. Mary, Jamaica, WI., ✆ 800-OUTPOST, 305-531-8800, or 876-975-3354, ✎ 876-975-3620, 🖳 www.islandoutpost.com, goldeneye@islandoutpost.com

💲 **Stratospheric** 🍴 **FAP** including drinks ⒸⒸ 5 villas

We can never get enough of 007, and Goldeneye, the one-time estate of Ian Fleming, is the "birthplace" of James Bond. Thus it is a semi-shrine to us. Goldeneye is now part of the Island Outpost empire of Jamaica boutique hotels. As you may have noticed from reading this chapter, Island Outpost runs three other Jamaican properties: Strawberry Hill, the Caves, and Jake's. We love how owner Chris Blackwell (who started Island Records — the company that brought Bob Marley, and later U2, to the masses), imparts chic style without obliterating the distinctly Jamaican ambiance of these locales.

Located in Oracabessa, 10 miles east of Ocho Rios, Goldeneye is centered around the former home of Fleming, which is still adorned by many of the author's original furnishings — even including the desk where all the 007 novels were created. (Fleming owned the 15-acre property from 1946 until his death in 1964; Blackwell bought Goldeneye in 1977.) The three-bedroom home includes a high-tech media room, a splendid outdoor bathtub, and an elegant new pool. Original Goldeneye callers included Elizabeth Taylor and Errol Flynn; more recent guests include Martha Stewart, Jim Carrey, and Harrison Ford, most of whom have planted a tree bearing their name. (Ford's original tree didn't live long, so he planted another on his second visit. The trees also signify a $1,000 donation to a local charity.)

When Island Outpost converted Goldeneye into accommodations in 1997, a hamlet of four one-, two- and three-bedroom wooden cottages was added to the 15-acre estate. The cottages are beautifully decorated with batiks, outdoor tubs, and handcrafted sinks; each has a media room with plasma TV screen. Privacy is created with thick tropical vegetation and bamboo fences, and outdoor showers adjoin most of the bedrooms. A tiny private beach is located under the rooms, and water sports are also available. There is a private beach, Low Cay, that lies just a short swim from the rooms; Island Outpost has plans for a compound of "fractional ownership" villas here. We're not sure what this means for the personality of Goldeneye, but Blackwell seems to have the right touch when it comes to developing these kinds of projects, so we've got our fingers crossed.

Hibiscus Lodge, Ocho Rios, Jamaica, WI. ✆ 876-974-2676, ✆ 876-974-1874, 🖳 www.hibiscusjamaica.com

💲 **Not So Cheap** ⓨ **BP** ⓒⓒ 26 rooms

Perched atop the cliff that lines much of the town's shore, this charming older hotel is a find. Standard rooms are simply furnished in time-honored wicker and overlook tended gardens from a balcony or patio. Deluxe rooms were remodeled in 2005 with bamboo furnishings and new bathrooms and offer sea views for just $12 more. There's no beach, but stairs lead down to a seaside platform for sunning and swimming. The pool, bar, and restaurant are also set along the edge of the cliff. It's a 10-minute walk into town.

Tamarind Great House, Crescent Estate, Oracabessa, St. Mary, Jamaica, WI. ✆ and ✆ 876-995-3252, 🖳 www.jamaica-gleaner.com/gleaner/tamarind

💲 **Cheap** ⓨ **EP** ⓒⓒ 10 rooms

Located on a hilltop about 30 minutes east of Ocho Rios, inland from Oracabessa, this great house was rebuilt in 1995 by English ex-pats, from the bones of a 300-year-old plantation house once owned by Portuguese Jews. Today, the modern, immaculate home has lush hardwood floors of guango and soaring ceilings to absorb the heat; breezes flow through for natural cooling. There are 10 bedrooms, 8 of them upstairs, all which are adorned in fine furnishings, with four-poster beds and private bathrooms. Mango and other fruit trees ring the house, and a pool provides diversion, but you'll want a car at your disposal for exploring the countryside. There are no dining options within walking distance, but a full English breakfast or lunch is available on request for $12, and a four-course dinner is $35.

Port Antonio

Port Antonio was *the* Jamaican destination for visitors in the first half of the 20th century. Made famous by movie stars like Errol Flynn (who had a villa — actually an island and a plantation — here), Port Antonio today still seems stuck in the past, its glamour (and many of the resorts) faded like old color photographs. Most people today don't care about its famous past. All they want to know is if Madonna or Brad Pitt stayed there (not that we know of, but Tom Cruise filmed *Cocktail* here — whoopee!). For travel information specific to this region of the island, call the local tourist office, 876-993-3051, or go to www.portantoniotravel.com.

There aren't a helluva lot of good choices in this pretty and lush part of Jamaica. Three stand out as being well run and in good shape: Blue Lagoon, Dragon Bay, and the Mocking Bird Hill. Port Antonio is also the home of the Trident Villas and Hotel, once one of Jamaica's premier luxury destinations, which seems to be suffering from benign neglect. A German heiress has left a bizarre mark on the area with not only the creepy Jamaica Palace Hotel but also a new Bavarian-looking shopping center right in town. A few villa efficiency choices and a guesthouse or two round out the selection (for others, check with Jamaica Luxury Travel; 876-997-7874; www.stooshjamaica.com).

Blue Lagoon Villas, P.O. Box 2, Fairy Hill, Port Antonio, Jamaica, WI.
ⓒ 800-237-3237 or 876-993-8491, ✉ 876-993-8492,
🖥 www.bluelagoonvillas.com, reservations@bluelagoonvillas.com

💲 **Stratospheric** 🍴 **EP** including all drinks, transfers, and rental car
ⓒⓒ 13 villas

Port Antonio's "St. Barth by-the-Sea," these luxurious villas are about as waterfront as you can get in Jamaica. The two-, three-, and four-bedroom villas sit right on the water at the base of a lush hillside. Featured in *Vogue*, *Town and Country*, and others, these accommodations scream deluxe, as does the price tag. Rates start at $7,500 per week for a two-bedroom (high season) and can go well over $10,000. However, everything is included in the price. You get a car, chauffeured airport pickup, champagne on arrival, a stocked bar (Jamaican brands), a/c, a maid and chef service, a butler, a sound system, satellite TV, tennis, Internet access, and even a helicopter landing pad. That famous Blue Lagoon is just down the street.

Hotel Mocking Bird Hill, P.O. Box 254, Port Antonio, Jamaica, WI. ☏ 876-993-7267, ✎ 876-993-7133, 🖳 www.hotelmockingbirdhill.com, mockbrd@cwjamaica.com

🄢 **Very Pricey** 🍴 **EP** 🆑 10 rooms

Perched high on a hill overlooking sunsets and the coast, the eco-centric Hotel Mocking Bird Hill is set on 7 acres and is the dream of two women, one Jamaican and one Indian. Having met in Germany, Shireen and Barbara came to Jamaica and have toiled to make this 10-room inn one of the better places to stay in the Port Antonio area. Lots of thoughtful little touches, like hand-embroidered bathrobes, adorn the accommodations. The white-walled, white tile rooms are spacious and comfortable, with bamboo furniture, local art, ceiling fans, huge closets, safes, and coffeemakers. Mocking Bird Hill is Green Globe Certified, which means that it meets a new international standard of environmental sensitivity for hotels and attractions.

There is a pool below the inn, and the once-pristine Frenchman's Cove beach is 2 miles away. A restaurant, Mille Fleurs, serves commendable Jamaican and continental cuisine on the veranda, using local produce and seafood. Several large, friendly, but barky dogs roam the premises, which can be annoying to guests (especially at dinner), and they terrified our Jamaican guide. Suggestion: Exclude the dogs from the common areas. There is an art gallery, Gallery Carriacou, on the premises, and the hotel welcomes people of all persuasions.

Trident Villas & Hotel, P.O. Box 119, Port Antonio, Jamaica, WI. ☏ 876-993-2602, ✎ 876-993-2590, 🖳 www.tridentvillas.netfirms.com, tridenthotel@infochan.com

🄢 **Very Pricey** and up 🍴 **MAP** 🆑 30 rooms and suites

Situated just a few miles east of Port Antonio on 14 rocky waterfront acres, Trident is an institution not only in Port Antonio but also in Jamaica, having been one of its top deluxe hotels for eons. The atmosphere at Trident is decidedly British, one of quiet and reserve — very quiet, very reserved. There are no pool aerobics here. Rather, afternoon tea is served at 4:30 p.m. with sandwiches and teacakes. Croquet is set up on the lawn, and there are resident peacocks who will often fan their feathers and give you a real show (they are also quite noisy and make the strangest sounds, especially in the middle of the night). This resort is small, and staying here gives the impression of over-nighting at someone's seaside estate while the owners are out of town.

There are 30 guest accommodations ranging from Superior and Deluxe rooms to Villa Suites and the grand Imperial Suite. By far the best choice is one of the wonderfully designed (if somewhat frayed) villas, which have a spacious and airy living room, private patio (except for the security guards, who will walk in front of your villa at any time — hope you're not being naughty on your patio), and a huge bedroom with lots of closet space and a large bath. There is a breakfast gazebo where room service will set up your meal and where those peacocks will sometimes entertain you. (Warning: Don't feed them.) The sound of the surf crashing against the rocks is always present.

On the grounds is a free-form pool, a small beach in a protected lagoon, and two tennis courts. The hotel has a very tasteful parlor with a piano and a separate publike bar. There is a very formal dining room where the waiters wear red coats and white gloves and it feels like you can't speak above a whisper; the air-conditioning and closed windows unfortunately keep out the breezes and the sound of the sea. Jackets are required. Dinner is prix fixe at $40 per person (including the tip but not drinks), and the food is a pleasing mix of international and Jamaican cuisine. The service is excellent; so is their special drink, the Trident Rock.

Jamaica Heights Resort, Spring Bank Road, Port Antonio, Jamaica, WI.
℃ 876-993-3305, ✆ 876-993-3563, 🖳 www.jamaicaheights.net

💰 **Cheap** 🍴 **EP** ⓒⓒ 8 rooms

Occupying a prime, 8-acre summit perch, Jamaican Heights is a guesthouse with lush gardens and airy, comfortable rooms. The least expensive are two cramped units under the shady pool, with a minimum of view and circulation (fans on request). The best are four rooms at the top with four-poster beds and decks that survey Portland from 540 feet above sea level. The owners — a German-Jamaican family — make no pretense about being hoteliers, and some details get overlooked, but there is no better setting from which to enjoy the surrounding hillsides, waterfalls, and trails. Good meals are served at the informal restaurant on request.

The Jamaica Palace Hotel, P.O. Box 277, Port Antonio, Jamaica, WI.
℃ 876-993-7720, ✆ 876-993-7759, 🖳 www. jamaica-palacehotel .com, pal.hotel@cwjamaica.com

💰 **Not So Cheap** and up 🍴 **EP** ⓒⓒ 80 rooms

This is an unusual place. It looks very grand on approach, a stately and sprawling white Greek Revival building set on a hill (but not on the water). Built by a German heiress, Siglinde von Stephani-Fahmi, the Palace is geared to the European and especially the German market. A friend who was traveling with us said this place gave her nightmares. There is definitely something a tad creepy about it, à la the Overlook Hotel in *The Shining*. Maybe it is the eerie Baroque portrait of a woman (apparently Siglinde herself) in the lobby, or the painful-on-the-eyes black-and-white checkerboard painted concrete floors, or the asphalt tile pool deck that scorches your feet when you step out of the pool, or the rather odd décor in the rooms. Whatever, you get the picture.

The 80 rooms and suites are big, with high ceilings, spacious tile and marble baths, and an eclectic décor of antiques, platform beds, and chandeliers. There is a 114-foot swimming pool shaped like the island of Jamaica, and what seems like a football field of those dizzying checkerboards as a terrace (actually the roof of the building). With no shade or cover, the sun and the floor are blinding and very hot. If the décor is not a problem, or is actually appealing to you, the good rates might be a reason to stay here.

Goblin Hill Villas, San San, Port Antonio, Jamaica, W.I. ✆ 800-472-1148 or 876-925-8108, ✉ 876-925-6248, 🖥 www.goblinhillvillas.com, goblinhill@n5.com.jm

💼 **Not So Cheap** 🍴 **EP** (CC) 28 apartments

This villa resort sits high up on a hill on 12 nicely landscaped acres. There are great views of San San Bay and the Caribbean from the grounds. It is peaceful and breezy and well suited for families. There is a small pool, two lighted tennis courts, a pleasant lounge area, and the Tree Bar—a bar wrapped around the 12-foot trunk of a ficus tree.

Like most of the accommodations in the Port Antonio area, Goblin Hill could use an infusion of capital for cosmetic work, although the one- and two-bedroom villas—really more like apartments—are roomy and comfortable. Although a '70s-looking décor prevails, all the villas are individually decorated; some are better than others and have large picture windows that open to the sky—a nice flourish. All have fully equipped kitchens and come with a housekeeper and cook (you buy the food)—a definite plus. All in all, this is a good deal, especially for families.

Frenchman's Cove, Frenchman's Cove, Port Antonio, Jamaica, W.I. ✆ 876-933-7270, ✉ 876-993-8211, 🖥 www.frenchmanscove.com or www.frenchmans-cove-resort.com, info@frenchmanscove.com

💼 **Cheap** for rooms; **Pricey** for villas 🍴 **CP** (CC) 28 rooms and villas

A stylish and jet-setty destination in the 1950s and '60s, Frenchman's Cove reopened in the late 1990s after having been closed for years. For those dreaming of the resort's fabulous past (which included guests like Queen Elizabeth) and its idyllic cove, the results are disappointing. What could be an awesome place to renovate has, at the moment, a long, long way to go. There are 17 wonderful cut-stone villas spread out along the water, all fabulously retro in design, which ache for equally fabulous furnishings and décor (if only Island Outpost would buy and restore this property). Instead, you have the ragged bones of a wonderful resort, which means that the rates are surprisingly low. The villas' brown tile, wood-ceilinged interiors have faded wicker furniture and shabby upholstery; lighting is skimpy. Air conditioners and plastic outdoor furniture are the resort's nod to the '90s. The villas also don't have a phone, a TV, or a kitchen, and front-desk ministrations are at a minimum. Eleven simple but clean rooms and suites are also available in the main Great House, set back from the beach.

Although the grounds are spacious and lovely, the exploitation of the Frenchman's Cove beach is tragic. The owner has taken one of Jamaica's prettiest beaches and opened it up to day-trippers from the big resorts of Ocho Rios and environs. They arrive in buses, are served lunch on the beach, and overwhelm this rather intimate cove. As a result, the guests of the hotel become the big losers here!

Ivanhoe's Guest House, Port Antonio, Jamaica, WI. ✆ 876-993-3043

🛈 **Dirt Cheap** 🍽 **EP** (CC) 10 rooms

This is the best of several budget inns located in town on Titchfield Hill, a historic peninsula jutting from downtown into the old harbor. The rooms are spotless and bright, with fans and small TVs — air-conditioning was to be installed soon after our visit. There's an appealing breakfast terrace (meals served on request), and the upper-level rooms in the four-story building overlook a landscape of banana trees and corrugated tin roofs.

Kingston

If you are going to Kingston to see the Bob Marley Museum or the art scene, there are many lodging options. It's also the western end of the Jamaica-Trinidad cultural and commercial axis of the English Caribbean. By far the most spectacular and luxurious (and most expensive) accommodation is Strawberry Hill, set high up in the Blue Mountains. Although not terribly convenient to the sights and sounds of Kingston — it's about a 30-minute drive away — Strawberry Hill is a stylish place from which to sample the city. More convenient are the big hotels, which are conveniently located in a row, are safe, and have pools in which to refresh yourself. At the properties in town, be prepared to be asked for money by small but well-rehearsed barefoot children as soon as you step off the grounds. In addition, a number of street vendors will try to sell you many things, including audiotapes and ganja.

⊛ **Strawberry Hill**, Irish Town, Jamaica, WI. ✆ 800-688-7678 or 876-944-8400, ✉ 876-944-8408, 🖥 www.islandoutpost.com, strawberryhill@islandoutpost.com

🛈 **Stratospheric** 🍽 **FAP**, including drinks, tax, and service charges (CC) 12 rooms

Perched at 3,100 feet in the verdant hills above Kingston and 50 minutes from the airport (for those in a hurry, there is a helipad), this is one of Jamaica's premier luxury hotels and the only outstanding one on the eastern half of the island. Owned by Chris Blackwell, the founder of Island Records and the man who made Bob Marley Jamaica's most famous export, Strawberry Hill is truly a magical getaway for the high-pressured, stressed, and famous. The rooms are housed in Georgian-style villas that cling to the summit of the property, offering sweeping views of mountains, valleys, Kingston, and the Caribbean. In true Island Outpost form, details that we think are totally key are included, like CD-cassette players and a selection of Island CDs (of course), TV-VCRs, an intelligent library, room service, mosquito netting, and heated comfortable mattresses (remember the elevation). The décor is plantation-style, with mahogany four-poster beds. All rooms have kitchenettes and private verandas with hammocks. A wonderful Aveda concept spa is on the property for that aromatic massage, and there's a fabulous 60-foot infinity pool.

The hotel has an excellent restaurant serving both international and Jamaican cuisine, and the rates include all meals and drinks. Sunday brunch here has become an institution. There is also a cozy bar with a fireplace where you can toss down some mean rum punches and hobnob with whomever. In keeping with the colonial thing, high tea is served in the afternoon. A roster of mountain activities, including coffee plantation tours and hikes (at an additional price), is available through the hotel.

Jamaica Pegasus, P.O. Box 333, 81 Knutsford Boulevard, Kingston, Jamaica, WI. ℂ 876-926-3690, ℰ 876-929-5855, 🖥 www.jamaicapegasus.com, jmpegasus@cwjamaica.com

💲 **Not So Cheap** 🍴 **EP** ⓒⓒ 300 rooms

Formerly connected to the Meridien chain, this 17-floor high-rise — Kingston's tallest — sits in the middle of New Kingston, the tony area of the capital, and offers all the amenities of an American business hotel — including 24-hour room service. The rooms are standard big-hotel fare, and each has a coffeemaker, satellite TV, radio, a/c (of course), a safe, and a lanai. There is a large outdoor pool, two lighted tennis courts, a small health club, and a jogging track, plus two restaurants and a pub on the premises.

Hilton Kingston Jamaica, 77 Knutsford Boulevard, Kingston, Jamaica, WI. ℂ 800-445-8667 or 876-926-5430, ℰ 876-929-7439, 🖥 www.hilton.com

💲 **Pricey** 🍴 **EP** ⓒⓒ 303 rooms

Located just north of the Jamaica Pegasus, this hotel is set on more than 7 acres and is similar to the Pegasus, although we think it's a tad nicer. The rooms are either in the 15-story tower or in 2-story wings surrounding the pool — all are pleasant and comfortable, with satellite TV, a/c, and a lanai. Nonsmoking floors are also available. There is 24-hour room service, an Olympic-size pool and a pool bar, floodlit tennis courts, a small health club, two restaurants, and a nightclub on the property.

The Courtleigh Hotel & Suites, 85 Knutsford Boulevard, Kingston, Jamaica, WI. ⟡ 876-929-9000, ✎ 876-926-7744, 🖳 www.courtleigh.com, courtleigh@cwjamaica.com

💲 Not So Cheap ⟡ CP ⅭⅭ 129 rooms

Wedged between the Hilton and the Pegasus, this smaller hotel is a reasonably priced alternative to the behemoths on either side. The rooms and suites are furnished with four-poster beds and 18th-century mahogany reproductions. All rooms have satellite TV, a/c, and a safe, and nonsmoking rooms are available. There is a very small pool along with a restaurant, bar, fitness center, and business center.

The South Coast

The south coast of Jamaica is the least-toured part of the country. Partly due to a paucity of good beaches and extensive coral reefing, this region is largely ignored by most visitors to the island. However, some pockets of beauty are scheduled for mega all-inclusive development, like the pretty and lush Bluefields (there goes the neighborhood again!), but for the most part it's very unspoiled.

About 90 minutes out of Negril, or two hours from MoBay, is the tiny village of **Treasure Beach**. Reached through a maze of back roads where signage is virtually nonexistent, this totally local-style place with gray-sand beaches and scrubby vegetation is the home of a funky place called Jake's. A couple of days here would be refreshing from the hustle of, say, Negril.

Jake's, Calabash Bay, Treasure Beach, St. Elizabeth, Jamaica, WI. ⟡ 800-688-7678 or 876-965-0635, ✎ 876-965-0552, 🖳 www.islandoutpost.com, jakes@cwjamaica.com

💲 Not So Cheap (most are Very Pricey and up) ⟡ EP ⅭⅭ 18 rooms and cottages

Though not for everyone, Jake's will appeal to those who want to feel far away from tourism and who like the idea of a totally barefoot and casual existence — yet in a distinctly chic setting. This is "roughing it" for the *Architectural Digest* set. Situated on a rocky coastline and about a 10-minute walk to the village beach, Jake's has some of Jamaica's most interestingly designed accommodations. It's now connected to the Island Outpost chain of boutique inns. Owner Sally Henzell and her son, Jason, have built a hodgepodge of world architectural styles to beat the band, from Jamaican and Greek to Moorish and Mexican motifs. The cottages — individual rooms plus two-bedroom cottages — are all decorated with Sally's cool design sensibilities: concrete floors painted bright colors, green glass bottles embedded in the stucco walls, galvanized steel doors with punched-out designs, thatched awnings over terra-cotta tile terraces, outdoor showers, and very eclectic furnishings (colored bare-bulb lamps, for example). The best units are Seapuss (right on the water and great for romance) and the Abalone (especially the upstairs unit), and there are new two-, three- and four-bedroom villas scattered around. All have CD-cassette players and access to an excellent CD library. Mosquito nets are provided and indeed useful (the bugs, especially sand flies, can be fierce). There is an unusual saltwater pool (which could be a tad cleaner). A myriad of activities can be arranged for you, including crocodile-viewing excursions on the Black River, mountain-bike tours, fishing excursions, and a trip to YS (pronounced "WHY-ess") Falls. Jake's restaurant serves good Jamaican cuisine. Like the place it's at, service is slow.

Where to Eat

Negril

There are scores of restaurants in Negril, from small beach shacks to big hotel restaurants. Undoubtedly new ones will pop up, so be sure to ask around. But don't miss the ones below.

$ **Caribbean Delight**, Norman Manley Boulevard, 876-957-4687

This is a local-style restaurant, slightly fancier than Pete's (below). Located just south of Negril Gardens, it serves an excellent and very cheap breakfast. No credit cards.

$ **Chicken Lavish**, West End Road, 876-957-4410

Chicken Lavish is a simple but popular spot for tasty chicken dishes — fried, curried, etc. — plus delicious steamed fish.

$$ **Chill Awhile**, Norman Manley Boulevard, 876-957-3303

Tucked inside the small inn Idle Awhile, this beachfront spot serves the typical Jamaican dishes as well as a lunch menu of *ital*, or Rastafarian food. This means no salt, no meat, and no oil, and although some of it can taste a bit bland, you're welcome to spice it up with a little Scotch bonnet pepper sauce. Either side of the menu provides a nice diversion.

$$ **Cosmo's Seafood Restaurant and Bar**, Norman Manley Boulevard, 876-957-4784

This is a very popular restaurant with both locals and some way-too-cool-for-themselves tourists (we saw one table where everyone was wearing black — in the tropics!). It's fairly cheap and good, too, with a solid roster of local treats like mannish water (that would be goat stew) and bammy (pancake shaped, deep-fried cassava bread). Cosmos has expanded to become a restaurant-beach complex. Be sure to try the conch soup and get a T-shirt as a souvie.

$$$ **Kuyaba**, Norman Manley Boulevard, 876-957-4318

One of the best eateries in Negril, this on-the-beach restaurant serves superb seafood (as well as veggie, chicken, beef, and pasta) dishes with a definite Caribbean accent. Try the Cuban crab and pumpkin cakes or the coconut curried conch with mango and papaya chutney. There's live music nightly, ranging from jazz to classical.

$ **Pete's on the Beach**, Norman Manley Boulevard, no phone

Located just a little south of the Negril Gardens Hotel on the Beach, Pete's is the ultimate in very casual eating on the beach, local style. There are picnic tables set up about 20 feet from the water, and Pete, the chef, will grill up some mean red snapper, lobster, or chicken for you. The DJ/dub music will keep your feet tapping in the sand. For dessert there is some very strong ganja cake — just ask for the "special" cake.

$$$ **Rick's Cafe**, West End Road, 876-957-4335

This place is totally tourist and expensive to boot, so why bother? If you must, just go at sunset and have a drink. Or try the jerk burger specials from 2 to 4 p.m. No credit cards.

$$$ **Rockhouse**, West End Road, 876-957-4373

A romantic, cliff-edge dining terrace and reasonable prices for classy West Indian cuisine. Make a reservation to ensure a front-row seat for Negril's famous sunset.

$$ **Sweet Spice**, just inland, on the road to Mandeville, 876-957-4621

This is Negril's best institution for real Jamaican cuisine. Curried conch, oxtail in brown stew, and lobster in a variety of preparations are all available for under $20 each.

Other places worth checking out for eats are **Peewee's** (seafood), **Fudge Pastry** (fruit cakes), **Ossie's** and **Bourbon Beach** (jerk chicken and chips), **Jackie's on the Reef** (organic food and herbal body scrubs), **LTU Pub** (any and everything under the sun), **Serious Chicken** (jerk chicken), **Hungry Lion** (vegetarian Rasta fare), **Uprising** (Jamaican cuisine), **Norma's on the Beach** (upscale Jamaican), and **Erica's** (lunch).

Montego Bay

Besides the above hotels, where the food ranges from very good to excellent, here are a few places in town to try.

$$$$$ Georgian House, 2 Orange Street, 876-952-0632

> Probably the most elegant restaurant in MoBay, this is set in an old Georgian brick building in the heart of the old town. Beautiful mahogany floors and woodwork and big brass chandeliers create a very lovely, if somewhat formal, atmosphere. House specialties include tournedos Rossini, baked stuffed lobster, and pan-barbecued shrimp. The dessert of baked bananas in coconut cream is rich. Reservations required.

$$$$ Julia's, Bogue Hill, 876-952-1772

> Perched on a hill high above MoBay, Julia's offers Italian cuisine with an incredible view. Reservations required. It will provide transportation from your hotel.

$$$ The Pelican, Gloucester Avenue, 876-952-3171

> The Pelican specializes in Jamaican cuisine and also has malts and sundaes. This is a popular spot with the locals.

$$ The Pork Pit, 27 Gloucester Avenue, 876-952-1046

> Although the name is off-putting, this is a real MoBay institution and a must-stop for anyone in the area, especially if you're driving to Negril from the airport (or returning). Jerk pork or jerk chicken is the choice, with yummy side dishes like yams and sweet potatoes. Although the Pit has moved to bigger, more modern and less attractive digs (the old one had more of a parklike setting and felt like a backyard barbecue), everything is still fairly open-air and informal—you sit at tables and pig out. There are two jerk sauces, mild and hot (you can buy these to take home, too). The mild will be spicy enough for most non-Jamaicans. No credit cards.

Port Antonio

The pickings here are slim. Mille Fleurs at the Hotel Mocking Bird Hill is good; dining is on the veranda. The food at the Trident is very pricey and disappointing, and the atmosphere is much too formal. Your best bet is to hire a cook for the week—easily done if you have a villa. Here are a few other options.

$ Boston Bay jerk stands

> Right by the entrance to the beach in Boston Bay, several jerk stands, renowned throughout Jamaica, serve the best jerk in the country. Jerk was originated in Boston Bay, and there are a number of stands competing for your favor. Buses now arrive from Ocho Rios and other North Coast day trips, and all the locals have their favorite. Be careful, it is really hot—to the point of making you cry. A plate of jerk pork or chicken will cost you less than $5, lobster starts at about $10, and you can buy jars of sauce to take home.

$$ **DeMontevin Lodge Restaurant**, 21 Fort George Street, 876-993-2604

This is probably the best Jamaican local-style restaurant in town. Specialties include pepperpot and pumpkin soup, curried lobster or chicken, and flavorful desserts. Reservations are required. It's very casual and cheap.

$$ **Dickie's**, about a mile west of Port Antonio, just above the water on the main road; no sign, 876-809-6276

Suggested to us by our friends at Hotel Mocking Bird Hill, this is the place to come for lovely fruit and a sweet Jamaican vibe. The tiny roadside fruit shack looks at first glance like a hundred others. But Dickie, a gentle, former hotel chef turned Rastafarian, and his wife, Joy, also run a gracious and informal restaurant just behind the shack. The tree house–like setting has room for just a few tables that overlook the sea. Dickie also prepares candlelight dinner by reservation (great with a full moon), but we recommend a stop for breakfast (bring your own coffee) or lunch when you can go for swim at the nice beach next door and enjoy the dreamy view.

$$$$ **Mille Fleurs**, Hotel Mocking Bird Hill, 876-993-7267

This restaurant serves commendable Jamaican and continental cuisine on the veranda using local organic produce and seafood whenever possible. It's a bit pricey but a very pleasant experience. Vegetarian dishes are also featured. Reservations are suggested.

$$$ **Norma's**, Ken Wright Pier, 876-993-9510

Norma Shirley got her start in Kingston (see below) but has gradually branched out to other corners of the island. This venture, next to the new marina, is her latest. You'll find things like smoked double-cut pork chops and pan-fried butterfish in a more upscale setting than we thought possible in Port Antonio.

Kingston

Kingston is a big city with lots of possibilities. We've selected places that are either close to the recommended hotels, because it is a big city and tourists should be alert here, or a drive or courtesy van trip away. Both the Pegasus and the Hilton have two good restaurants each, and you may be happy just to stay put. Otherwise, consider these.

$$$$ **Blue Mountain Inn**, Gordon Town Road, 876-927-1700

This is a Kingston institution, perched up in the mountains about a 15-minute drive north of the city. The cuisine is continental and Caribbean and the menus change periodically. Jackets are required for men (ties optional), but the cool night air in the mountains makes it bearable. Women should bring a wrap. This is a definite Caribbean dining experience and well worth the trip, if just for the view. Reservations are required.

$ **Chelsea Jerk Centre**, 9 Chelsea Avenue, 876-926-6322

For a cheap and truly Jamaican meal—namely, jerk pork or chicken—within walking distance of the big hotels, this is the place. It's very popular with Kingstonians. No credit cards.

$$ **Gordon's Restaurant and Lounge**, 36 Trafalgar Road, 876-929-1390

If you're in the mood for cuisine from the Orient, Gordon's serves Chinese, Japanese, and Korean dishes.

$ **Hot Pot**, 2 Altamont Terrace, 876-929-3906

A favorite for Jamaican food and fresh juices, this is a must-stop for breakfast, lunch, or dinner when downtown. Ask for directions.

$ **Jam' Rock**, 69 Knutsford Boulevard, 876-754-4032

It's a sports bar; it's a steak and burger joint; it's a video bar; or whatever. It's always happening.

$$$ **Norma's on the Terrace**, Devon House, 26 Hope Road, 876-968-5488

Owned by famed Jamaican chef Norma Shirley, who was once dubbed the "Julia Child of the Caribbean" by *Vogue*, this hot spot is located on the magnificent grounds of Devon House, a restored great house. The menu features Caribbean fusion cuisine, with Italian and French influences, like jerk chicken penne pasta or *naje*-poached Chilean sea bass served on cappelini and callaloo. Closed Sunday.

$$$$$ **Strawberry Hill**, Irish Town, 876-944-8400

With views to die for, this hotel, a 30-minute drive from Kingston, has a superb restaurant serving both international and Jamaican cuisine. Sunday brunch is a must. There is also a chummy bar with a fireplace where you can rub elbows with the cognoscenti and sip a mean rum punch. Reservations are required.

Going Out

In addition to the Negril and Montego Bay nightlife options mentioned in the Don't Miss section below, consider some of the following spots in Ocho Rios and Port Antonio.

In Ocho Rios, two places deserve mention. **Acropolis** is a solid dance bar, whereas the club **Jamaica Me Crazy** offers live music a few nights a week and always seems populated by a cast of characters in addition to the usual tourists.

In Port Antonio, the place everyone goes to is the **Roof Club**—it sports an atmosphere that is hot, humid and dark, and it gets going well after midnight on Thursday through Sunday nights. A couple other spots worth checking out include **Crazy Fridays** and **Talk Town**.

Don't Miss

Overall

Ting
Jamaica's soft drink is made with grapefruit juice. We just can't get enough of a good Ting.

Red Stripe
It's Jamaica's beer, *mon.*

Negril

Miss Brown's, Sheffield Road
See description in Focus section.

Swept Away Sports Complex
This is an excellent health club and sports center. For $25 per day, anyone (you don't have to be staying at this couples-only resort) can work out with free weights and machines, do aerobics, play squash and racquetball, play tennis on 10 courts (half of which are clay), play basketball, swim laps in a superb lap pool, take yoga classes, play pool, or take a steam or sauna. This is a great place to keep those bis and tris in tone and to work off the hangover from the previous night. Norman Manley Boulevard, 876-957-4040.

YS Waterfall
What Dunn's River Falls used to be (that is, untouristy), YS (pronounced "WHY-ess") is, more or less, today. Located about two-thirds of the way from Negril to Mandeville and about 10 miles north of the town of Black River, this is a good day trip for waterfall lovers and will let you see the untrammeled part of Jamaica. The highlight for us was the jitney ride from the parking lot to the falls—you travel through pastures and vistas that are truly stunning. To get to YS, take the road to Savanna-la-Mar and then route A1 through Black River to YS (there are signs). Open from 9:30 a.m. to 3:30 p.m. Admission is $10. Closed on Monday and holidays (there are lots of the latter, so be sure to check before going, 876-634-2454).

Margaritaville
Located on Norman Manley Boulevard in the heart of the beach, this is daytime party central for the college and the *Real World* set (spring break is crazy here). With four open-air bars, big-screen TVs for sports and music videos,

CD jukeboxes, a dance floor, karaoke, a beach barbecue, basketball, beach volleyball, a 30-foot water trampoline, wet T-shirt and sexy bikini contests, nightly bonfires, and live entertainment — even a tattoo parlor — it's a mini-Daytona. There's one in MoBay, too. Call 876-957-4467.

Jammin'

For live reggae or dancehall music and partying on the beach with a real mix of Jamaicans and tourists from all over, Alfred's, Bourbon Beach, Roots Bamboo, and Risky Business alternate nights of hosting parties and shows. At press time, this was the schedule: Monday, Risky Business and Bourbon Beach; Tuesday, Alfred's (recommended); Wednesday; Roots Bamboo; Thursday, Risky Business and Bourbon Beach; Friday, Alfred's; Saturday, Risky Business and Bourbon Beach; Sunday, Alfred's and Roots Bamboo. This schedule might change, so be sure to check with your hotel or a local resident. Those who crave American dance music can head out any night to The Jungle, a slick new club, or on Saturday to Compulsion disco at 24 Plaza de Negril, although this spot is getting tired.

Famous Vincent

Vincent's trips to Sandy Cay Reef leave straight from the beach and offer great snorkeling for $35. He's a real character as a guide, escorting beginners through the various sights. He's a tad difficult to get hold of, but most hotels will know how to get in touch with him. Contact Tensing Pen, 876-957-0357 — they should know.

Jackie's on the Reef

Located on the West End, this spa offers day packages at reasonable rates that include lunch and massage. Yoga and meditation are also available. Appointments are suggested; call 876-957-4997.

Twin Star Market

This wonderful little superette is a must-stop for those staying in the West End and lacking orange juice, tonic water, or even booze for their cocktails.

Rusty's X-Cellent Adventures

Take a mountain-bike ride with Rusty, an American who has lived in Negril for two decades. The informal tours are suitable for all abilities and take in the rural area south of the lighthouse, usually concluding at a rum shack in Little Bay. Located on West End Road (near the lighthouse); call 876-957-0155.

Montego Bay

The Pork Pit

See the write-up in Where to Eat.

Margaritaville

Located on Gloucester Avenue (876-952-4777) and on the water right off Doctor's Cave beach, this club is a trip. Open day and night, you name it, it's here. It has 15 big-screen TVs featuring music videos and sports for the jocks among us, four open-air bars, a restaurant, CD jukeboxes, karaoke, an outdoor hot tub, a floating sundeck, and, the main attraction, a 110-foot water slide. There's also one in Negril. At night, a DJ spins. It offers free shuttles from your hotel. The cover on weekends is under $10.

Montego Bay's Nightlife

Gloucester Avenue is the hot strip, led by the Jimmy Buffett's aforementioned Margaritaville. Other Gloucester Avenue favorites are **Walter's** (876-952-9391), which is a sports bar and pub, and **PJ's**, which is a bar that's completely surrounded by trees — it offers great reggae and dancehall. Also, **Pier 1**, on Howard Cooke Boulevard (876-952-2452), is the place to be on Friday — it has a good mix of locals and tourists.

Port Antonio

Long Bay

Located about 10 miles east of Port Antonio and just a few miles east of the jerk stands at Boston Bay, this is one of the most beautiful (and undiscovered by the throngs) beaches in Jamaica. Twin mile-long crescents of uncrowded white sand, turquoise waters, and palm trees beckon. This is a really great place to spend the day, so you must stop here.

Boston Bay

There is a picturesque beach here, with small fishing boats. Try the jerk at the beach stands.

Blue Lagoon

This calm, protected cove is called the Blue Lagoon because the water is so deep (188 feet) that the water is cobalt blue. It's very scenic and fun to swim in, too. There is a dock and ladder for swimming at the Blue Lagoon Bar and Restaurant.

Rafting

Yes, Jamaica's bamboo raft rides are a touristy cliché, but they're still romantic — up there, in a way, with Venetian gondolas. In the 1950s, Errol Flynn would entice island girls aboard the two-person rafts; before that the rafts were used to ferry bananas down to the port for shipping. Today the rafts have been popularized for lovebirds, and hundreds of them ply three Jamaican rivers. The trip down the Rio Grande near Port Antonio is the classic route. Break the journey with a country lunch from Miss Betty, who serves informal meals under $10 at a pullout halfway down the river. Price: $52 per couple; information: 876-913-5434.

Firefly

Noel Coward's white stucco home in Port Maria, a village between Ocho Rios and Port Antonio, offers one of the most spectacular panoramas in all the Caribbean — and a history that includes visits by everyone from Queen Elizabeth to Elizabeth Taylor. Tours are $12 per person; call 876-725-0920.

Tea at the Trident

This is fun, relaxing, and reminiscent of the glory days of the Empire. Tea is served between 4:30 and 5:30 p.m. After tea, have Trident's special drink — a Trident Rock; call 876-993-2602.

Kingston

Port Royal

A 30-minute ferry ride will take you to this former "wickedest city on earth," located at the end of the airport peninsula, which was mostly swallowed up by the sea in the 1692 earthquake. The ferry ride is $1 round-trip. It departs Kingston five times daily, starting at 10 a.m.

Lime Cay

Kingston's best beach is on an islet off Port Royal and is a fun boat excursion. Avoid on weekends!

Bob Marley Museum

See the write-up earlier in the chapter.

The National Gallery

See write-up at beginning of this chapter.

South Coast

Pelican Bar

Located about half a mile off the shore at Treasure Beach, near Jake's, this is a shack built on stilts on a sandbar. Floyd is the character who created this one-of-a-kind bar that serves Red Stripe and Pelican Perfection (his house drink), plus fish and fresh-caught lobster on request. Call ahead to let Floyd know you're coming (876-354-4218). You'll need to get there via boat — ask one of the locals or the folks at Jake's to help with arrangements. It's a good stop after a trip to Black River.

Los Roques

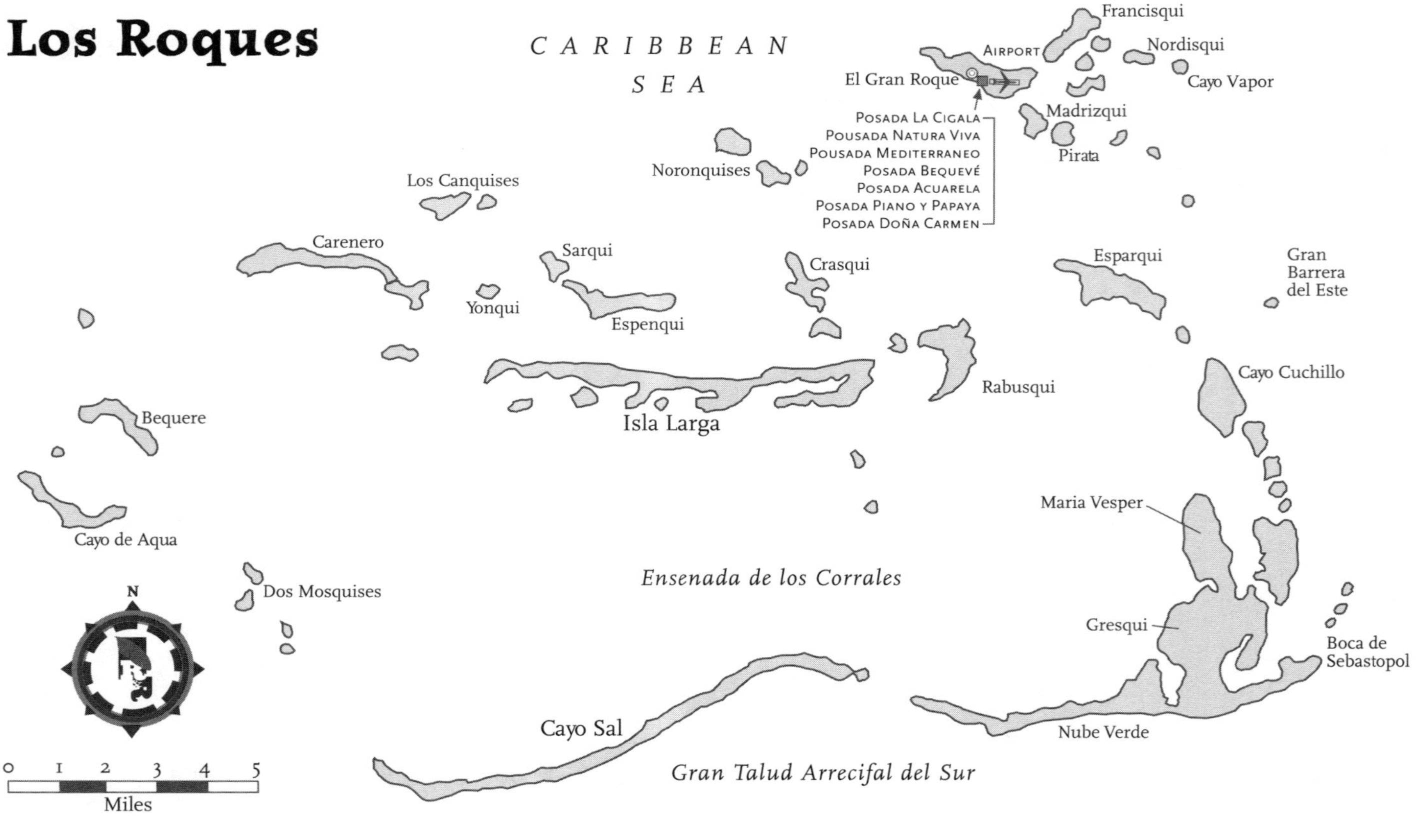

CARIBBEAN

SEA

Francisqui

Nordisqui

Cayo Vapor

AIRPORT

Madrizqui

Pirata

El Gran Roque

POSADA LA CIGALA
POUSADA NATURA VIVA
POUSADA MEDITERRANEO
POSADA BEQUEVÉ
POSADA ACUARELA
POSADA PIANO Y PAPAYA
POSADA DOÑA CARMEN

Esparqui

Cayo Cuchillo

Gran
Barrera
del Este

Boca de
Sebastopol

Maria Vesper

Gresqui

Nube Verde

Rabusqui

Gran Talud Arrecifal del Sur

Crasqui

Ensenada de los Corrales

Noronquises

Espenqui

Isla Larga

Sarqui

Cayo Sal

Yonqui

Los Canquises

Carenero

Dos Mosquises

Bequere

Cayo de Aqua

N

Miles

0 1 2 3 4 5

Los Roques

TOURISTO SCALE:

👤👤👤👤 (4)

Our last trip to Los Roques confirmed that this small archipelago has changed very little. It is still a place where you will absorb more sun than you want, move more slowly than you thought possible, and eat better than you have in a long time. Strict government concessions have limited growth on these islands, so there is little room for expansion and little capacity for more tourists. We are confident that Los Roques will remain a hidden nook in the Caribbean where just a relative handful of tourists will visit for years to come. There will never be high-rises, blaring discos, or roving bands of camera-toting tourist groups here. Nor will there be much more activity than applying buckets of sunblock and participating in the various activities on one of the islands that punctuate this archipelago of sandy coral islands located 84 miles north of the central coast of Venezuela. Of course, if all you want to do is sleep in the sun and then take a nap to recover sun-sapped energy, Los Roques is a perfect destination.

An unfortunate encounter with a self-righteous tour guide led us to discover that the dreaded Club Med has discovered it can drop anchor just off the southern coast of El Grand Roque. We suspect that in coming years, more cruise ships will return.

Despite Club Med attention, Los Roques is still a special place of countless beaches, sand roads, friendly people, great food and drink, inexpensive

Los Roques: Key Facts

Location	11°N by 66°W 84 miles north of Venezuela 95 miles north of Caracas 1,900 miles southeast of New York
Size	350 square miles (including the water), 42 islets plus hundreds of sandbars and reefs
Highest point	El Gran Roque (427 feet)
Population	1,500
Language	Spanish
Time	Atlantic Standard Time (1 hour ahead of EST, same as EDT)
Area code	From the U.S. dial 011, then 58 (the country code for Venezuela), then the number. From inside Venezuela, dial 0 first, then the number (do not dial 011-58); phones are few and most are cellular.
Electricity	110 volts AC, 60 cycles
Currency	The Venezuelan bolivar, B$, although most rates are quoted in U.S. dollars. (The official rate at press time was B$2,100 = US$1; the black-market rate is generally B$2,300–B$2,500 = US$1.)
Driving	There are no cars on Los Roques.
Documents	Valid passport for U.S. and Canadian citizens. (Note: You must keep it or a photocopy of it with you at all times — keep the copy in your wallet. This is especially true on the mainland.)
National park fee	B$30,000 (paid on arrival at El Gran Roque airport)
Departure tax	US$7.50 leaving Caracas for domestic destinations (Los Roques and Margarita)
Beer to drink	Polar Light, Solera Premium
Rum to drink	Pampero Aniversario
Music to hear	*Reggaetón*, salsa
Tourism info	www.venezuelatuya.com/losroques

lodgings, and no resorts, no cars, and few tourists. Officially called the Parque Nacional Archipiélago de Los Roques (The Rocks Archipelago National Park) and part of the Republic of Venezuela, the only rocks you'll see here are the rugged cliffs on the volcanic El Gran Roque — the highest and most populated of the 42-island archipelago. All the other islands are sandy, coral cays or islets, created from the rise and fall of sea level since the beginning of the Pleistocene period (about 15,000 to 19,000 years ago, for the scientifically deficient like us). These islets and the shallow bay that encompasses the archipelago sit on a volcanic "platform" that rises out of the deep. The only volcanic protrusion is the 427-foot summit on El Gran Roque.

Almost all of the population lives on **El Gran Roque**, and it's also where the guest accommodations and airstrip are located. The local population of 1,500 people and the 240 dwellings absorb about 80,000 visitors a year, many of them day-trippers from Caracas and the mainland. With this influx of visitors, many homes have been turned into guesthouses (*posadas*), which adds to a comfortable, anti-*touristo* feeling here. Doors are never locked. People don't cover their mouths while yawning, and the only security threat comes in the form of a hungry cat scraping for a piece of last night's meal.

Tourism has all but replaced fishing as the economic mainstay of Los Roques. Most visitors are from Venezuela or Italy, a surprising combination. Actually, we find Italians all over the Caribbean, especially in less traveled places like this—where there's an Italian market, there is good food (a prerequisite for them to visit any vacation spot).

Situated at just 11° north latitude and lacking mountains to catch clouds and rain, Los Roques is very sunny, hot, and dry. Fortunately, cooling trade winds blow consistently and vigorously most of the year. Because El Gran Roque lacks good beaches, speedboats zip guests around to various beaches on other islets. You will most likely visit Francisqui or Madrizqui; many *posadas* offer day trips to these nearby islands as part of a package deal. The coral sand on them is very white, so sunburn and sun protection are big factors here. There are few shade trees on most of the cays, but your *posada* will set up a canopy and beach chairs for shade. It will provide lunch and refreshments. Generally boat trips leave El Gran Roque starting around 9:30 a.m. and continue until 10:30, or sometimes as late as 11, and return around 4 p.m. Most ship captains will agree to pick you up sooner—a good idea if Los Roques is your first stop in the sun after a long stretch of winter bleakness. For the light-skinned folks among us, the sun here is definitely more than strong enough to scare the white away, and it will leave you looking like the lobster you ate last night if you're not careful!

The dry, hot climate keeps vegetation on the light side, with lots of cacti, mangroves, and succulents (and sand burrs—yee-ouch on bare feet!). There are palm trees, however, for palm tree–lovers like us—especially on El Gran Roque and other cays with vacation villas on them (no more of the latter have been built since 1972 due to the national-park status). Iguanas rule the dry land, and turtles nest on several of the protected cays, which represent some 50 percent of the archipelago. The only mammal besides the occasional lazy dog asleep in the middle of the road is the fishing bat. There are more than 92 species of birds, including the blue-eyed brown booby, pelicans, laughing gulls, frigate birds, terns, lapwings, plovers, and great blue and white-necked herons. Over half of these migrate to North America in the summer. Occasionally, pink flamingos find their way here from Bonaire and mainland Venezuela. Perhaps the most entertaining are the pelicans. Their bomb-diver strategy to gulp up a number of small fish in one swoop makes a huge splash, and they are not shy. Don't be surprised if while swimming off the coast of one of the cays you suddenly find yourself in the midst of two or three pelicans making depth-charge splashes in close proximity.

The Briefest History

Discovered in 1529 by the Spanish explorers and conquistadors, the islands were essentially uninhabited except for occasional encampments of Indians on fishing expeditions from the mainland and Aruba or Bonaire. For several centuries, the archipelago was a haven for English pirates. This accounts for the strange names of several of the islands, originally called cays and pronounced like the word *keys* by the English. Nationalistic Venezuelan linguists "Spanishized" the spellings, so many island names now end with *quí* instead of *cay* (e.g., Sand Cay is now Sandquí). Whatever. After the pirate age, pearl fishermen from Margarita eventually settled Los Roques, although the pearl industry never was very good here. Then lobster, turtle, and queen conch fishermen from Margarita came in the early 1900s; today they represent about 25 percent of the population (although conch and turtle fishing are now prohibited). The Parque Nacional Archipiélago de Los Roques was created by presidential decree in 1972. This put a moratorium on additional building but allows for conversion of existing homes to *posadas*, or guesthouses.

Getting There

Getting to Los Roques is actually quite easy because Caracas, Venezuela, is the major gateway. American, United, Delta, Continental, Servivensa, and Aeropostal all fly nonstop to Simón Bolívar International Airport from either New York or Miami. You then can connect with an Aerotuy, Aero Ejecutivo, or Sol de America flight to Los Roques (El Gran Roque) at the adjacent domestic terminal. Private charters are also available. Flying time from Caracas to El Gran Roque is a quick 45 minutes.

Getting Around

El Gran Roque is small and has sand streets, so walking around is easy — and you can go barefoot if you like. Your *posada* will take you by boat to outlying keys for the beach or other excursions, or it can easily arrange the trip for you.

Focus on Los Roques: El Sol, Agua Turquesa, Playas Arenas-Blancas

For those of you who *no entienden español* (don't understand the Spanish in the title), the focus of your trip to Los Roques should be the sun, the turquoise water, and the white-sand beaches. If a resort atmosphere is what you want, with pools, tennis, golf, and room service, this is not the place. But if you like being outside and barefoot, there's at least three days' worth of activities to enjoy under the sun, be it turtle- or bird-watching, bonefishing, windsurfing, scuba diving, snorkeling, going up in an ultralight, sunbathing, or just sipping a cocktail while watching the pelicans dive for fish as the sun sets in the distance.

Where to Stay

Almost all the accommodations for tourists are on El Gran Roque. A number of homes have been converted into guesthouses, or *posadas*, over the last decade, but there are seven that stand out: La Cigala, Natura Viva, Mediterreaneo, Bequevé, Acuarela, Piano y Papaya, and Doña Carmen. Many *posadas* are now owned by Aerotuy (the main airlink to Los Roques) or a business conglomerate in Caracas, and service and food at these places tend not to be as good as at the individually owned ones. Water is a precious commodity here, so don't expect your shower to be like Niagara Falls. *Most posadas are not able to accept credit cards because there are no fixed phone lines, so expect to pay in cash with bolivares.* For those places that do accept credit cards, expect a 10 percent service charge. Some *posadas* accept U.S. dollars and euros. For reservations, visit the very reliable and efficient Web site Discover Venezuela at www.discovervenezuela.com.

⊛ **Posada La Cigala**, El Gran Roque, Los Roques, Venezuela.

  ✆ 58-414-236-5721 or 58-414-318-2014, 🖳 www.lacigala.com

  💲 **Not So Cheap** and up 🍴 **All-Inclusive** CC 8 rooms

  The bright yellow building at the entrance to the town of El Gran Roque is the wonderful Posada La Cigala. Owners Liana and Enrique Ducournau spend their time between Caracas and a personal yacht moored off the coast of El Gran Roque. However, the couple always leaves the *posada* in the hands of a very capable management staff. Not only is the cuisine exquisitely delicious (Italian, of course), but the other amenities — daily boat excursions to various beaches and islets with lunch, a very friendly staff, a comfortable ambiance, an upstairs deck that offers views of the surrounding area as well as two enormous beanbags for lounging and napping — make La Cigala our first choice for accommodations on Los Roques. There is an impressive, high ceiling public space for dining and lounging, including an open courtyard with palm trees and the stars above.

  Eight simply decorated but comfortable guest rooms (some with double beds) come with private bath. Rooms that don't face the trade winds have fans for cooling. If you are a nut about privacy and quiet, request a room at the end of the hall and not on the courtyard. As mentioned, the food is fabulous and prepared by a cook trained by Liana personally. All meals are included in the price, but drinks will be billed—apart from the welcome *mojito* or *caipirinha*. Be sure to bring a CD of new music (Liana loves ambient groove, soulful stuff, and good dance music) to leave with the *posada*.

Note that La Cigala accepts credit cards only for reservations, but not for drinks or food once at the *posada*.

Posada Natura Viva, El Gran Roque, Los Roques, Venezuela. Ⓒ 58-237-221-1035 or 58-414-274-1231, ✆ 58-237-221-1473, 🖥 posadanaturaviva@hotmail.com

💲 **Pricey** and up 🍴 **All-Inclusive**, 16 rooms (one suite with ocean view)

Just over three years ago, a group of Italians purchased four homes on the island and converted them into one complex that includes a *posada*, a piano bar, an expansive upper deck, a restaurant, and a spa. All the room furniture and *posada* decorations have been imported from Italy. The richness of a distinctly Mediterranean style is well balanced with an attendant and unobtrusive local staff that caters to every whim. The rooms are larger than we would expect, impeccably clean, and with one of the best private bathroom designs we've seen on the island; the open shower, modern sink design, and a bidet have all been smoothly incorporated into what seems to be one large piece of labored rock. Attention to detail is apparent in every room, yet all are simply decorated with unique pieces of Italian furniture and distinct color themes that reflect the colors of nature found in the Caribbean. Besides the one suite with a stunning ocean view, there are rooms with single, double, and queen beds as well as a few rooms that have two levels to handle small families. The upper deck is a great place to catch the sunset. We recommend that you try the passion-fruit daiquiri! No credit cards accepted.

Posada Mediterraneo, El Gran Roque, Los Roques, Venezuela. Ⓒ 58-414-329-0621, ✆ 58-237-221-1130, 🖥 www.posadamediterraneo.com, posadamed@cantv.net

💲 **Pricey** and up 🍴 **All-Inclusive** 💳 6 rooms (one master suite)

Walking through the entrance of the Mediterraneo is taking a step out of the Caribbean and into Greece. The impeccably clean *posada* boasts white tiles from Athens, whitewashed walls, and stone-molded furniture. The common area is spacious and captures enough daylight to create a bright yet relaxing atmosphere. Elena, the Italian owner, is attentive and very charismatic. The rooms are simply decorated with a minimalist style that makes us think of Spartan living. Fortunately, the beds are very comfortable, and a remote-controlled air conditioner in every room assures a comfortable night's rest that's protected from bugs and sticky heat. All rooms are spacious and come with a safe. The one master suite boasts satellite TV. The private bathrooms are simple, with a clean-cut design and an obvious attention to detail. This *posada* caters to many Italians as well as guests who seek the thrill of bonefishing. An agreement with a local bonefishing guide guarantees easy access to fishing outings. This is the most technologically savvy *posada* on the island—both wireless Internet and international telephone calls are available.

Posada Bequevé, El Gran Roque, Los Roques, Venezuela. ℂ 58-212-264-7485 (in Caracas), ⌨ www.losroques-bequeve.com, info@losroques-bequeve.com

$ **Pricey** and up ⑨ **All-Inclusive** ©© 8 rooms

The most designed of the Los Roques *posadas* (by Fruto Bibas, a renowned Venezuelan architect) is Bequevé. Featuring a dramatic central courtyard with bright blue walls and terra-cotta tile floors, this eight-room (26-bed—there are two duplex double rooms) guesthouse is a good alternative to La Cigala. We were impressed with what appeared to be the efficiency of a luxury hotel squeezed into a small *posada*. Cleanliness and warmth radiate the place, and the friendly staff makes you feel welcome before you even clean the sand from your toes. Shades of blue permeate the comfortable guest rooms, which have cool concrete floors, fans, and spacious colorful tile baths. Bequevé has its own reverse-osmosis water machine (a big plus on an island of little rainfall and an overtaxed public seawater conversion system), cold-water bath and showers, and its own generators. For communication, radio contact is maintained with Caracas on a marine frequency. Bequevé also has its own "pavilion" on one of the Noronquíses (some nearby deserted cays), a 20-minute boat ride from El Gran Roque on its 30-foot speedboat.

Special rates are available for more than two nights' stay or for groups of six or more. Children under 12 are charged half price.

Posada Acuarela, 87 Calle Las Flores, El Gran Roque, Los Roques, Venezuela. ℂ 58-237-221-1456, ✎ 58-237-221-1008 (Caracas), ⌨ www.posadaacuarela.com, posadaacuarela@posadaacuarela.com

$ **Pricey** ⑨ **All-Inclusive**, 11 rooms

Newly restored, the Acuarela is one of the prettiest places to stay in Los Roques. An eclectic fusion of colonial Caribbean architecture and contemporary trends, the décor is accented with modern art pieces throughout. Stepping into the central courtyard of the Acuarela, the first thing we noticed were the forest-green marble tiles framed in sanded handmade brick. Touching your bare feet on marble tiles is a great way to cool off! The 12 rooms orbit the courtyard, providing a sense of space and light to most rooms. Five have a/c ($20 surcharge per night), and all rooms are different in design. There are single, double, and triple suites; all have mosquito netting. The most popular room is the Palma room with its own garden — and palm tree — in the bath. A faboo roof deck is great for lounging or stargazing. The Acuarela also offers dive packages with SCDR, a PADI-certified dive operation on Los Roques. The *posada*'s restaurant serves excellent Mediterranean cuisine with a menu that changes daily. Be advised that the Acuarela does not offer a boat shuttle service to other cays (a major disadvantage). And, no, it still hasn't corrected the English on its Web site. We've found toothless merchants in Caracas who could probably do a better translation! No credit cards accepted.

Posada Piano y Papaya, El Gran Roque, Los Roques, Venezuela. ℂ 58-414-281-0104 or 58-414-311-6467, 🖳 www.pianoypapaya.com, lucia@pianoypapya.com

💲 Not So Cheap 🍴 All-Inclusive, 5 rooms

Owner Alejandro speaks four languages (Spanish, English, Italian, and French), and with his wife, Lucia, runs a cheerful and comfortable *posada*. The central courtyard and attractive common area is airy and cool, with a hammock for those in need of a snooze. The modern look and Italian sounds in the background gave us the feeling of having departed a Caribbean island and landed in a small *posada* on the beach in Italy. A stairway leads up to a huge tile terrace with chaises, great for midnight stargazing (or whatever). All rooms have high ceilings, ceiling fans or a regular fan, sponge-painted walls, concrete floors, and white tile cold-water baths. Italians love this place and make up most of the clientele. Rates include all nonalcoholic drinks and, for $10 extra per person, a lobster for dinner (November through May). No credit cards accepted.

Posada Doña Carmen, Plaza Carmen, El Gran Roque, Venezuela. ℂ 58-414-262-7837, 58-237-221-1004, or 58-212-862-9618, 📧 58-237-221-1004 or 58-212-862-9618

💲 Cheap 🍴 MAP ©© 9 rooms

At the heart of El Gran Roque, this *posada* connects Plaza Bolivar with the beach. It is a modest and cheap *posada* typical of a local fisherman's home. The courtyard, on the plaza side, is decorated with furniture we're pretty sure Doña Carmen found in her own house — the wicker is split and coming loose and the cushions are threadbare and sun-bleached. All rooms have a private bath, with three (Rooms 4, 5, and 6) facing the water. The rooms are as simple and as homely as the courtyard, so don't expect a fabulous bed, high thread count sheets, or even a mosquito net. Opt for Room 6, which has a double and a single bed as well as its own seating area with tables and chairs on the beach.

Where to Eat

There are a limited number of restaurants on El Gran Roque due to the fact that most, if not all, *posadas* offer an all-inclusive meal package. There are, however, some exceptions. Here are a few that stand out.

$$ **Aquarena**, 414-320-2608

This is the best place for sandwiches, a cold coffee drink, or a sunset alcoholic beverage. A row of small beanbags on the beach blend with an organized display of small palms to complete a relaxing atmosphere — perfect for an hour or two off your feet.

$$$ **Crasquí**, no phone

The best lobster lunch in Los Roques is put on by local fishermen here, but don't expect their simple ways and smiling faces to make it onto your bill. Given the setting and relaxed atmosphere, it might be the best Caribbean lobster we've ever had, but it certainly isn't the cheapest! Before lunch, take some time to explore the reef just in front of the restaurant — it's worth a 15-minute swim. Your *posada* can arrange this trip for you. No credit cards.

$ **Nueva Cadiz La Querisse**, no phone

Located in the main plaza, across the way from the Pizza Pub, this locals' hangout serves the coldest Polar (beer) on the island. No credit cards.

$ **Pizza Pub**, no phone

A lively place on the plaza with a jukebox and sports video, the Pizza Pub serves great pizza (remember the Italians) and is also a good spot for hanging out and slamming down a few Polars. No credit cards.

Mainland Venezuela

If you're going to Venezuela, here are two places you should not miss.

Choroní

If you want to really experience the sensuality that is Venezuela, plan to spend a few days in Choroní. This colonial town has become famous for the colorful facades of its houses (renovated in the postmodern mode) and its unique combination of day and night entertainment. It is also one of the few places in the Caribbean where the beach is more fun at night than in the daytime. Here, in the early evening, suntanned bodies begin parading in various degrees of nudity. The famous Choroní drums, or El Tambor music, which is essentially percussion-based, manifest a pervasive erotic energy in the air. Drums are the best-known feature of Choroní (some of the drum groups are very much on demand at parties in Caracas) and are accompanied by dancing, naturally, which consists of nonstop spinning and hip movements. The tribal chants of sexual innuendo, the drinking of sweetened rum drinks, the trancelike rhythms of the drums, and the patina of sweat on tanned bodies all contribute to what people call the magic of Choroní. Be advised that Choroní can get very crowded, noisy, and rather littered during national holidays (which are quite often in this country), when nationals descend from surrounding states for sun, drinking, dance, drinking, sex, drinking — you get the picture! Playa Grande (the longest and most popular beach) can be overrun with tents and campers during this time, and the clientele isn't usually all that refined.

Getting to Choroní is part of the experience because of the lush tropical vegetation traversed on the very winding (and narrow) road that links it to Maracay (two hours by car from Caracas). There is no airport — Choroní is accessible only by car or bus. To get there from Simón Bolívar International Airport outside of Caracas, rent a car and take the Autopista Valencia to Maracay. Once in Maracay, get on Las Delicias Avenue (one of the most beautiful avenues in Venezuela) and follow it to its end. There you'll find plenty of road signs showing you the way to Choroní.

Choroní is just over a mile up the road from the water (built there to protect it from piracy) and from its seaside sister, Puerto Colombia, a fishing village set at the juncture of the Caribbean and the Río Choroní. Puerto Colombia is where the beaches, and boats to more secluded beaches, are located. Both places are full of *posadas* (many owned by Germans) in a range of styles. Among the best are the following: **Hostal Casagrande** (58-243-991-1251; www.hostalcasagrande.com) is a beautiful house with colonial-style architecture and period furniture. The open courtyard contains a swimming pool. We like this place! Rates are Not So Cheap (CP). **Posada Semeruco** (58-243-991-1050 or 58-243-991-1051) is another richly decorated colonial house with a fountain and garden in a central courtyard. Rates are Cheap (CP). **Posada Cataquero** (58-243-991-1120 or 58-243-991-1264) is a very quaint and neatly decorated *posada* with a fusion of old adobe and brick with various contemporary accents. There are 8 rooms with private baths and hot water. Rates are Cheap (CP).

During the day, if you're not sleeping off a rude hangover from the *guarapita* (the local specialty punch made of passion-fruit juice and *aguardiente*), there are options for both beach and river play. For beaches, there are only two choices: Playa Grande, a popular spot with sports and *hamacas* ("hammocks") in the morning and many tents at night, is a five-minute walk to the east from town around a point. Playa El Diario, a much smaller whiter beach, is approachable after a 40-minute walk over a hill. There is some nude bathing on this beach, and you have to bring drinks and food because there are no vendors here. Fishing boats can take you to more remote beaches for about $20 round-trip (a bargain — competition is fierce). Freshwater enthusiasts will love the river, which is as popular as the beach and has lots of natural pools and waterslides. The village of Chuao, one of the oldest cacao plantations in Venezuela and a short boat ride to the east from Choroní, is also worth visiting, especially during one of its many religious festivals. (Corpus Christi, the big one, occurs on the ninth Thursday after Samana Santa — check with your *posada*.)

In the early evening, young people begin crowding the Malecón, where tanned bodies are displayed, much drinking goes on, and everyone loosens everyone up. Around midnight, expect to see (or participate) in dancing that is blatantly erotic. This is a dance for one couple at a time, and someone from the surrounding crowd replaces one member of the couple from time to time. It is amazing to see how popular this is with foreigners who cannot dance salsa yet move like natives to these Afro-Caribbean rhythms. You might see some of the most sexual dancing this side of a XXX club. Talk about uninhibited! After the drums, people usually head for the local disco, called My God (and pronounced "my goo") for more conventional fare.

Hato Piñero

If you have some extra time while you're in Venezuela, we recommend visiting the Llanos, a vast area of grassy savannah and forested swamps that is one of the richest wildlife regions in all of South America. The Llanos is not a place for the casual visitor. Extreme climate conditions, insects, and heat see to that. During May through October, rain floods most of the 77,000-square-mile savannah. Many exotic creatures, like the capybara (the largest rodent in the world) and the cayman (a relative of the alligator), enjoy the lushness of this season. In November, the rain stops for six months, and the dramatic change in conditions is the key to the fantastic natural variety of the region.

Immense parts of these lowlands are owned by cattle ranchers who have opened their lands to conservationists and biologists from all over the world. Of this handful of ranches, none offers more diversity in both geography and wildlife than Hato Piñero. Pioneers in wildlife preservation, the Branger family, the owners of Hato Piñero, established a wildlife preserve in 1984 with the help of the World Wildlife Fund and opened it up to the public as an ecotourism enterprise that same year. Today, this ecotourism business supports most of the conservation and education initiatives. Experiencing the area through the lens of a place like Hato Piñero — the beauty of the low plains, the diversity of wildlife, the informal hospitality — provides the kind of unforgettable travel experience that will be treasured for many years.

With its expansive terrain and diverse habitats, Hato Piñero is one of the best bird-watching locations in the world. The place has become a must-visit resort for all who consider themselves serious birders. Close to 400 species have been catalogued in the area, and spotting 100 of these on your first day is not uncommon. On a typical day, you will observe numerous types of herons and egrets; white, scarlet, and glossy ibis; as well as osprey, macaws, parrots, various hawks, black vultures, and hummingbirds.

High season for Hato Piñero is the dry season — from November through April. This is when rivers shrink and ponds and lakes dry up, forcing the animals to congregate in smaller areas. However, at Hato Piñero, animals are easy to find no matter what time of year you visit. Whether seated high on a safari-style truck, in a boat, or on horseback with a biologist guide, you will encounter animals that run free and are surprisingly tame. Hunting has been banned here for more than five decades.

Throughout the open plains you will experience nature at its wildest and tamest. Giant anteaters and foxes will cross your path. Flocks of storks in full flight are seen overhead. Hawks perched above will look down and catch your eye, making you wonder who's the spectacle here. You will see and hear the howler monkey and be amazed by the agility of its cousin, the capuchin monkey. Deer are plentiful at sundown, carefully grazing, keeping a watchful eye for a preying jaguar or puma. There are more than a million animals living under protection at Hato Piñero.

Hato Piñero is also a working ranch, offering the visitor an ideal perspective and experience — mixing a lot of the old with some of the new. Important genetic research is done here to produce the ideal cattle breed to withstand the rigors of the climate. You might bump elbows with biologists from world-renowned universities and institutions. Equally important is the fact that the lodge is adjacent to the village and the quarters of the *llaneros* ("cowboys") who work at the ranch. This provides an insight into the culture and folklore of the region and of the people who were instrumental in the revolt against Spanish rule, winning independence for Venezuela in 1821.

The lodge at Hato Piñero offers eight double rooms, one quadruple room, one triple room, and a VIP suite. Of these, five have a/c and six are cooled by ceiling fans. If you are a nature lover, we recommend a room with a ceiling fan, because these don't drown out the wonderful wildlife sounds you will hear all around. All rooms feature rustic colonial architectural details.

Rates from December to April are $158 per person for a double room ($181 for a single), and from May to November are $118 per person for a double room ($141 for a single). All meals (an exquisite mix of indigenous and contemporary cuisine) are included, as is an open bar of soft drinks, beer, and rum. Also included are two tours (morning and evening), horseback riding, boat excursions (July to December), and a bilingual naturalist guide.

Hato Piñero is in the state of Cojedes, about five and a half hours from Caracas. One-way car transfers for up to four people can be arranged at a cost of $112 from Caracas or $135 from Simón Bolívar Airport. It is also possible to charter a small plane; the round-trip price for one to five passengers is $1,516 from Caracas's small airport or $2,220 from Simón Bolívar Airport.

For reservations and more information, call Biotours in Caracas (58-212-991-8935 or 58-212-991-0079; fax, 58-212-991-6668), or visit Hato Piñero's Web site at www.hatopinero.com.

Don't Miss

Cayo de Agua

This gorgeous deserted beach on the western end of the archipelago is one of the best in the Caribbean. A long, wet, and bumpy boat ride from El Gran Roque will get you there; beach lovers will think it's well worth the effort. Most *posadas* can arrange this excursion for you.

Bonefishing

Due to the lack of sportfishers and the newness of this sport to Los Roques, this is a bonefisher's paradise. Forget the Bahamas — this is the place to be. It's not uncommon to catch more than 15 bonefish on one outing. Now that is a lot of sport!

A Daiquiri at Natural Viva

Enjoying this common Caribbean drink on the upper deck at sunset is wonderful and a great way to mix and mingle. Be sure to ask for a list of the daiquiris in season. You may find a daiquiri fruit you've never tried. We particularly like the passion fruit.

Scuba Diving

SCDR is a PADI-certified dive operation that can provide opportunities for some fabulous dive experiences as well as instruction (www.scdr.com). Two-tank boat dives are about $80 (includes tanks and weights).

A Little Nooky on a Deserted Beach

If ever there was a place for a little "afternoon delight" (you know what we mean), a walk with that special someone on one of the outer keys should give you enough privacy for primal needs under the hot sun. (C'mon, how often do you get to do this in the great outdoors, anyway?!) Don't forget the beach blanket!

Margarita

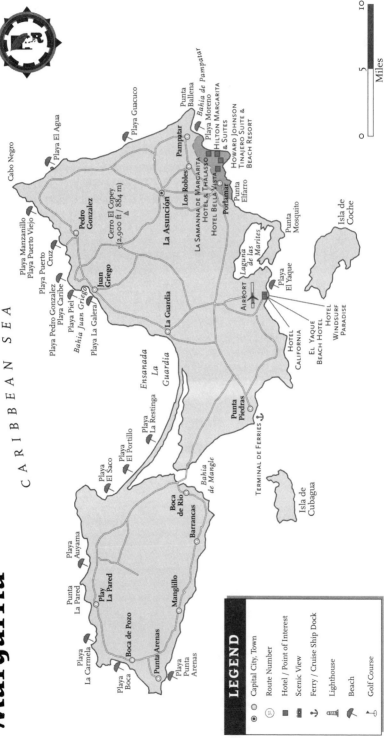

CARIBBEAN SEA

Cabo Negro

Playa El Agua
Playa Guacuco

Punta Ballena
Bahia de Pampatar
Pampatar
Playa Moreno
HILTON MARGARITA & SUITES
HOWARD JOHNSON TINAJERO SUITE & BEACH RESORT

Playa Manzanillo
Playa Puerto Viejo

Pedro Gonzalez

Cerro El Copey (2,900 ft / 884 m)

Los Robles
LA SAMANNA DE MARGARITA HOTEL & THALASSO
HOTEL BELLA VISTA
Porlamar

La Asunción

Playa Puerto Cruz

Juan Griego

Playa Pedro Gonzalez
Playa Caribe
Playa Piel
Bahia Juan Griego
Playa La Galera

Punta Elfarro

La Guardia

Punta Mosquito

Isla de Coche

Laguna de las Maries

AIRPORT
Playa El Yaque
Playa El Yaque

HOTEL CALIFORNIA
EL YAQUE BEACH HOTEL
HOTEL WINDSURF PARADISE

Ensanada La Guardia

Playa La Restinga

Playa El Portillo

Punta Piedras

TERMINAL DE FERRIES

Bahia de Mangle

Playa El Saco

Boca de Rio

Barrancas

Isla de Cubagua

Playa Auyama

Punta La Pared

Play La Pared

Mangllilo

Playa La Carmela

Boca de Pozo

Punta Arenas

Playa Boca

Playa Punta Arenas

LEGEND

⊙	Capital City, Town
(R)	Route Number
■	Hotel / Point of Interest
⌐	Scenic View
⚓	Ferry / Cruise Ship Dock
⚟	Lighthouse
☂	Beach
⚐	Golf Course

N

Miles
0   5   10

Margarita Island

You're more likely to find faded tattoos and leather-skinned retirees than nice beaches on Isla Margarita, but the people on this island continue to bring us back. A smiling waiter who will replace your beer on a moment's notice, a polite lady who will give you directions in Porlamar, a random reception clerk who is happy to lend an extra hand with luggage — this island is full of wonderful Venezuelans who are like a breath of fresh air on this sun-scorched rock. Like the other islands in the Lesser Antilles, such as Bonaire and Aruba, Margarita Island is very arid and scorched. Brown is much more prevalent here than green. The beaches are okay, but not great. The ocean is a greener hue here, due to the flow of the Rio Orinoco. It's not turquoise as it is in the latitudes a tad north. In addition, an unfortunately poor sewage system has begun to pollute some of the beaches around Porlamar and Palpatar.

The years have not been kind to the island's main town of Porlamar. It is still a dump. Development has stalled, leaving some projects half completed. Suburban sprawl has literally connected Porlamar with its neighbor Pampatar. What used to be two distinct towns is one widespread mess of concrete hovels, single-story commercial centers, and trash-lined sidewalks and

501

Margarita: Key Facts

Location	11°N by 64°W
	18 miles north of Cumana, Venezuela
	200 miles from Caracas
	2,100 miles southeast of New York
Size	414 square miles
Highest point	Cerro El Copey (2,900 feet)
Population	420,000
Language	Spanish
Time	Atlantic Standard Time (1 hour ahead of EST, same as EDT)
Area code	To call Margarita from the U.S. dial 011 (the international dialing code), then 58 (the country code for Venezuela), then 295 (the code for Margarita), followed by the seven-digit local number.
Electricity	110 volts AC, 60 cycles
Currency	The Venezuelan bolivar, Bs (B$2,100 = US$1 at press time)
Driving	On the right; a valid U.S. or Canadian driver's license is acceptable.
Documents	Valid passport (Note: You must keep it or a photocopy of it with you at all times — keep the copy in your wallet).
Departure tax	$21
Beer to drink	Polar Ice, Brahma Light
Rum to drink	Santa Teresa Gran Reserva
Music to hear	*Reggaetón*, salsa

roadways. Other areas in Porlamar have become home to squatters and low-rent ramshackle huts. There are even a few completely abandoned buildings, that give us a creepy, proletariat feeling, the kind you get from reading George Orwell's *1984.*

The locals here seem to have receded to forgotten corners of this island, whereas mainland Venezuelans and over-the-hill expatriates from Canada and Europe have swelled in ranks. The mixture of people here is still a healthy brew of fiesta, but we get the feeling that Isla Margarita has passed its peak. We can't get over the friendly Venezuelans, however. Their cheerfulness, charisma, and warm attitude transcend this island's relative lack of beauty and sense of passé.

The other reason we keep coming back is price. It is still cheap here because the U.S. dollar retains strong purchase power. A standard room at the top hotel on the island, the Hilton Margarita & Suites, is well under $200 a night (a rarity in the Caribbean), and a good meal will cost you around $25 per person. You can't beat the $1.50 daiquiri in El Yaque, and it costs less than $3 to fill a tank of gas.

Most of the visitors to Margarita are from Caracas — called Caraqueños — or from Europe (mostly Italians). There aren't a lot of North Americans here. The number of Canadians seems to be growing, but tourists from the United States are still few and far between. Package tours make it very affordable for couples and families. English is more widely spoken on Margarita than it used to be. Some places cater to tourists and so require their employees to be bilingual, but that is sometimes more in theory than reality, depending on the establishment. Don't expect spot-on American English presentation; nevertheless you're likely to get enough to get by. In most establishments below the pricey range, you'll get basic numbers and relevant words such as *rental*, *tour*, and *bathroom*, but not much else.

The island is divided into two distinct parts, east and west. Most of the activity is on the larger, eastern end. This is the location of Porlamar and the capital, La Asunción (Margarita is the biggest part of the state of Nueva Esparta), the windsurfing and kitesurfing center of El Yaque, and the most popular beaches. The western end, called the Peninsula de Macanao, is the most arid (read: desert) but does have some isolated beaches and a charming laguna.

The Briefest History

Amerindians inhabited the island when Columbus landed across the bay on the Venezuelan mainland in 1498 and claimed Margarita (along with Venezuela) for Spain. Pearls were then discovered on Cubagua, one of two islets just south of Venezuela (*Margarita* is the Latin name that's derived from the Greek word for "pearl," *margaron*). By the mid-1600s, however, the pearling industry was *finito*, because the oyster beds were depleted. The island was claimed by Spain and remained under its control, uncontested, until the War of Liberation led by Simón Bolívar in the early 1800s. Margarita was actually a hotbed of discontent and struggle in the war. After the war, it remained a sleepy island until the early 1980s, when the devalued bolivar (the Venezuelan currency) and duty-free status made Margarita an attractive and affordable destination for mainland Venezuelans, other South Americans, and Europeans.

Getting There

Caracas is a gateway to Margarita and a major international destination, with flights coming in from around the world. From the U.S., American, Delta, United, Continental, Avensa, Servivensa, and Aeropostal all have nonstop and direct flights, primarily from New York, Miami, and Orlando. Air Canada flies from Toronto. British Airways flies from London.

At the Simón Bolívar International Airport outside Caracas, there are tons of shuttle flights (at least 18 a day) to Porlamar on Avensa, Aeropostal,

Aserca, Aerotuy, Laser, and Rutaca. When booking your ticket, be sure to have this connection included; it will cost next to nothing. If you are already on the mainland, there is a car ferry from Puerto La Cruz to Margarita, which takes four to five hours.

Flights from nearby Los Roques can be found on a new airline, Conviasa.

Getting Around

The roads are good and the gas is so incredibly cheap—under $3 to fill a tank—that it makes sense to rent a car. Besides, you'll need one to get from Porlamar to Playa El Agua (about a 25-minute drive). All the major rental companies are here, including Avis (800-331-1084), Budget (800-527-0700), Hertz (800-654-3001), and National (800-227-3876). Check with your credit card company before you leave to make sure that your account covers collision here. If you aren't covered, by all means accept the CDW insurance when renting a vehicle. Make sure you reserve in advance—you'll get a better deal.

Note: When driving at night, Venezuelans rarely stop for red lights—they just slow down. So be advised. During the day, the Venezuelan recklessness on the road might make you nervous, but we haven't seen wrecks worse than a light scrape or a small fender bender!

Focus on Margarita: El Yaque

Known as the best windsurfing area on the island—and one of the best spots for the sport in the Caribbean—El Yaque (pronounced "el YAH-kay") has become the happening place to be on Margarita. Located south of the airport, this lively spot is a pocket of tourism that has only grown over the years. We consider it the best spot to visit on Margarita, regardless of your interest in water sports. It's the best place on the island to mingle, get active, dance, drink, and have fun.

El Yaque became famous for its large protected bay, which offers fantastic and reliable sailing conditions. A unique combination of shallow warm water, a protected inlet, and constant sunshine helps to create steady side-shore winds of 25 knots and higher year-round, with the best winds between January and June. Add air and water temps in the mid-80s (30° Celsius), the relatively calm and shallow waters, the fun and lively atmosphere on land, and enough English-speaking staff, and you have what makes El Yaque the windsurfer's destination in its own right.

The **windsurf** scene keeps growing here. An annual regatta called **Wild Wind** is held each June, and every year it attracts more racers and spectators from around the world. Several windsurfing schools and outfits are in evidence at El Yaque, including Club Mistral, Vela, Nathalie Simmons, and Happy Surf. With the increased commotion, El Yaque is it on Margarita. There is always something going on; many hotels take turns hosting events and live entertainment. At the hub of it all is a string of three bars located right on the bay behind El Yaque Beach Hotel. It all begins with the daily happy hour (from 5:30 to 7 p.m.), where you'll find either two-for-one or half-off deals. We're not sure which is better, but both will definitely take the serious look off your face quickly.

The latest windsurfing extreme, **kitesurfing**, has arrived in El Yaque. Kite-surfers share time and space with the windsurfers, so kitesurfers are able to use the full beach between 5:30 p.m. and 9:30 a.m. These minor restrictions are necessary to avoid accidents on crowded beaches; because the kite cables can be like guillotines. Wind conditions here, however, are ideal for the sport (and the airport is far enough away to prevent airspace issues). A separate beach, called Kitebeach, is about 1.5 miles windward of the main beach. Ask around — it's not hard to find.

The beach at El Yaque is a beehive of activity. Sunbathing couples lounge on towels while sipping beer and eating raw oysters. Children run around armed with floaties under mama's watchful eye. Pasty-white tourists struggle with sails, boons, and boards. There's always a handful of beginner wind-surfers who fall into the water with a smack and a nose full of water to boot. Their exasperated faces and fists pounding the surface have provided us with extra entertainment. We know it's not nice, but hey, everyone's a beginner sometime!

Overall, the beach is small, narrow, crowded, fun, and full of equipment. Those seeking peace and seclusion have some better options a short drive away or in the Internet café across the street. Even with the bustle, however, we'd rather stay here than in Porlamar. Only in low season (September–December) do the crowds — and the fun — diminish, but with more than 16 restaurants and bars on or near Playa El Yaque, there should be enough to do.

There are several rather low-key hotels in El Yaque. Don't expect spas and river pools here. Look at accommodations here as a place to sleep or perhaps for a "roll in zee hay." We suggest these hotels — and, remember, don't expect much.

Where to Stay

El Yaque

Hotel Windsurf Paradise, Playa El Yaque, Edo. Nueva Esparta, Venezuela.
       ☏ 58-295-263-8890 and 58-295-263-9760, ✆ 58-295-263-9003,
       🖳 www.windsurf-paradise.com,
       reservaciones@windsurf-paradise.com

  💲 **Cheap** and up ⑪ **CP** 🆑 55 rooms
      Only 150 feet from the beach, this hotel has simple air-conditioned standard and superior rooms. Go for the latter — they are bigger and have balconies with hammocks and ocean views. Tired of worn-out sheets that chafe your sensitive, sunburned skin? So are we! Thus, we

were pleasantly surprised to find that the sheets used by the WP have a higher thread count than any other hotel in El Yaque. Maybe it was our imagination, but we know it's a more comfortable sleep. The superior rooms on the bottom floor nestle right up to the pool; walk off your terrace and take one step into the refreshing cold water. We especially like the artificial waterfall—great for a free back massage!

Breakfast is included, but make sure to get a ticket from the receptionist on the way to breakfast, because the restaurant is independent of the hotel. The service there is spectacular, and the full-spread breakfast is the best we found in Margarita. All of this combines to make the WP our new favorite in El Yaque. It also has a completely equipped windsurf shop, small pool and hot tub, and a snack bar on the beach.

El Yaque Beach Hotel, Playa El Yaque, Edo. Nueva Esparta, Venezuela. ℂ 58-295-263-8441, ✆ 58-295-263-9851, 🖳 www.yaque-beach.com

💲 **Not So Cheap** and up 🍴 **CP** 🆑 24 rooms

The 24-unit pink palace of El Yaque sits right on the beach in the hub of the action. Rooms come in standard and deluxe versions. We like the deluxe rooms, which are on the top floor and have queen-size beds. Get one with a view of the sea (the standard rooms do not have views). There are also one-and two-bedroom apartments with fully equipped kitchenettes (the one-bedroom units have ocean views). The apartments are nice, but you're really just paying for more space, not comfort. All rooms come with a/c, satellite TV, phone, fridge, daily maid service, and mosquito nets on request.

The El Yaque Beach Hotel overlooks the bustling day and night scenes that are the center of the El Yaque social whirl. The hotel's restaurant, Terraza Tropical, is not our favorite, but it serves a decent breakfast with an entertaining twist—save your leftovers for the large macaw with enough personality to jump onto your table and give you an earful of Venezuelan charm. There is a Vela Windsurf Center at the hotel with F2, JP, and Neil Pryde Equipment. Windsurf-lodging packages are available. Check the Web site for last-minute deals.

Hotel California, Playa El Yaque, Edo. Nueva Esparta, Venezuela. ℂ 58-295-263-9494, ✆ 58-295-263-8536, 🖳 www.elyaque.com, contact@elyaque.com

💲 **Not So Cheap** and up 🍴 **CP** and **MAP** 🆑 47 rooms

The white, curvy, 47-room, five-story Hotel California looks like an Oscar Niemeyer takeoff design, but not quite as impressive. It used to be the new kid on the block but is now just part of the gang. Besides a well-known name, this hotel has little more to offer than the other, beachfront hotels. There are two pools (one for kids), a hot tub, two restaurants (one French and under new management) and a beach club. Rooms have a/c, terra-cotta tile floors, floral décor, and white rattan and wicker furnishings. In the lobby is a state-controlled exchange booth; use it only if you're in dire need of local currency. It will give you the official rate (robbery) and charge you a commission that we're sure just goes into the attendant's pocket. There is a hotel beach club with chaises and towels, but we think you'd rather hang out with the gang from the Windsurf Paradise or El Yaque Beach Hotel. Look for packages.

Porlamar

Most of the accommodations on Margarita are in Porlamar, but they are by far not the best places to spend a majority of your time on the island. This is where you'll want to stay if you want to spend some time shopping in town or lounging on the Mosquito Coast. Since the four hotels below are not very expensive, we recommend staying at one of them. They're big, they have great pools, and all are easy to get on a package deal — thus even cheaper.

Hilton Margarita & Suites, Calle Los Uveros, Urbanización Costa Azul, Porlamar, Margarita, Venezuela. ℂ Stateside and Canada: 800-HILTONS, UK: 800-HILTONS, local: 58-295-260-1700, ✆ 58-295-262-0810, 🖥 www.margarita.hilton.com

🏧 **Pricey** and up 🍴 **EP** CC 336 rooms, 11 suites

The Hilton is still the best place to stay on Margarita, now with all-suite accommodations in a beachfront wing and a river pool. Located on the edge of Porlamar on its own private beach, the hotel consists of two connected 10-story buildings that have everything you need: a friendly and attentive staff that speaks English, a fantastic pool, and a selection of bars and restaurants for those who are recovering from their hangovers or feel the need to get started on some drinking. There's live music three times a week. It has a decent beach with all water sports in front, comfortable rooms and deluxe suites with the Hilton standard of taste and cleanliness, a health club to keep up the muscle tone, two lighted tennis courts, three restaurants, two bars, and 24-hour room service. All rooms and suites have their own lanai overlooking the ocean and all the amenities. The suites even have Jacuzzis and sofa beds. An executive business center is open daily with full secretarial, telecommunication, and Internet services if you have some business needs while you're away. Look for packages and deals.

La Samanna de Margarita Hotel & Thalasso, Avenue Bolívar, Urbanización Costa Azul, Porlamar, Margarita, Venezuela. ℂ 58-295-262-2662 and 58-295-262-2222, ✆ 58-295-262-0989,

🖳 www.lasamannademargarita.com,
habitaciones@lasamannademargarita.com

💲 **Not So Cheap** and up 🍴 **EP** CC 69 rooms and suites

Across the boulevard from the Hilton is this pink stucco and thatched-roof hotel and spa. Though not on the beach, La Samanna offers Margarita's best spa facility, operated by the Parisian cosmetics house Thalgo. The spa includes a beautifully colonnaded seawater pool heated to 94°F, a 192-jet seawater whirlpool, and all kinds of wraps, scrubs, massages, and whatever else exists to pamper the body. There is a very pleasant covered terrace and an outdoor freshwater pool area with an unusual elbow-pipe fountain at one end. A good Japanese-Peruvian restaurant (an odd combo, but remember that Peruvian ex-President Alberto Fujimori is the same) is poolside, too.

Bright colors and terra-cotta tile rule at La Samanna. The rooms, though a little narrow, are beautifully decorated with mosquito-netted canopy beds, earth tones, balconies (most with ocean views), and extraordinary hand-painted tile baths. In European fashion, the bathroom has a bidet and a large tub. Spa charges are extra.

Howard Johnson Tinajero Suite & Beach Club, Calle Campos, Porlamar, Margarita, Venezuela. ℃ 58-295-263-8380 or 800-IGO-HOJO, 🖎 58-295-263-9163 🖳 www.hotelhowardjohnson.com, tinajeros@cantv.net

💲 **Cheap** and up 🍴 **EP** CC 72 rooms and suites

A Hojo's in Margarita? Who woulda thunk it? Well, this all-suite hotel is a far cry from the orange-roofed ice cream and restaurant rest stops of yore. Centrally located in Porlamar and only a stone's throw from the clubs and shopping galore, the Tinajero is a good value—especially for families or groups on a budget. All units have Jacuzzis, a/c, satellite TV, kitchenettes, microwaves, and room safes. There is a pool, bar, and restaurant on the premises and a beach club nearby. Don't expect to find too much peace and quiet here, however. Over the years, this Hojo has catered more to a young crowd. We were not surprised to see throngs of lounging youths, on vacation from Caracas, at the entrance, at the bar, in the pool, and hanging from the balconies. OK, maybe not that bad, but you get the picture.

Hotel Bella Vista Cumberland, Avenida Santiago Marino, Porlamar, Margarita, Venezuela. ℃ 58-295-261-7222, 🖎 58-295-261-2557, 🖳 www.hbellavista.com

💲 **Cheap** and up 🍴 **EP** CC 305 rooms and suites

The most centrally located accommodation in Porlamar, and virtually two steps away from the Mosquito Coast, this 305-room hotel is looking to bring in new clientele with its recent upgrade from four to five stars. Redecoration both inside and outside have given this hotel a much needed face-lift. The interior décor is still very 1970s, but we like the smooth wooden curves, plush shag carpet, and feeling of relaxed cool. Fortunately, the hotel is still not too pricey. It has a great pool area and is on the beach (although this beach gets crowded). The rooms here are standard big-hotel fare, but with new furniture, a/c, and larger beds. Look for packages.

Where to Eat

Porlamar

Due to the Italian invasion, that cuisine seems to predominate (things could be worse!). With the island's fishing industry, seafood — often à la Italiano — is also popular. Prices are lower here than elsewhere in the Caribbean, so why not feast? Here are some of our favorites.

$$ **Cheers**, Avenue Santiago Mariño (above Don Lolo), 261-0957

It's a busy, local favorite that serves an international menu. You won't hee-yah Boston accents hee-yah. It's also a great place for a cold bee-yah and a U.S. football game or two.

$$ **El Pescador de la Marina**, Avenue Raúl Leoni, turn at the marina, 261-6374

With a *muy romántico* setting on the bay overlooking Porlamar, this place is renowned for its lobster dishes as well as its international cuisine. The food is, well, excellent, to put it simply. Order anything — we're pretty damn sure you'll like it. There is an expansive deck, great for people-watching and checking out Venezuela's rich and famous who escape from Caracas to spend a weekend on their yacht. Stop by on Friday or Saturday for live salsa and an opportunity to meet someone local. Hey, you might get lucky and earn a free ride on one of those yachts!

$$$$ **Le Chateaubriand**, Hilton Margarita & Suites, Calle Los Uveros, 262-3333

As the name suggests, this is a French restaurant, and it's Margarita's best cuisine *française*. Guess what the house specialty is? Open daily. Reservations strongly advised.

$$$ **Mediterráneo Caffé Ristorante**, Calle Campo at Calle Patiño, 264-0503

This is one of our favorite Italian restaurants in the Caribbean. Owners Gaia and David Peri have created a menu so delicious that we now believe in food orgasms. Their shrimp sautéed in brandy with pistachio nuts sent us to heights we haven't been to in a long time. Gaia, originally from Italy, speaks English and puts the *v* in vivacious. She's also a wealth of information about Margarita. Open Monday through Friday for lunch and dinner, Saturday for dinner only. Reservations suggested.

$$ **Señor Frog's**, Avenue Bolivar at the Costa Azul shopping center, 295-262-0270

A typical Mexican restaurant and bar that also happens to be one of the nightclubs of the moment, this two-level spot is loud and young (the club is upstairs). This is not the place to go for a quiet, romantic dinner. A lively atmosphere reigns over the fare at the Señor; this is a fun place for a large group. Open 6 to 11 p.m.

Juan Griego

You may also want to try lunch and/or dinner in the scenic little harbor of Juan Griego (sunsets are spectacular). If you go, try **La Mamma** ($$), **El Viejo Muelle** ($$), or **El Sitio** ($$). All three are on the water and have tables outside. One block in from the water is the **Juan Griego Steak House**, offering a complete dinner, including wine, for about US$15.

Playa El Agua

There are more than 10 restaurants on the beach, so be sure to enjoy lunch and a few cocktails here. Try **El Pacifico** ($$), **Restaurant Jardin Tropical** ($$), **Golden Fish** ($$), or **La Dorada** ($$). Also try **Trattoria al Porto**, Calle La Marina, 264-8208; located in **El Tirano**, a beach town just south of Playa El Agua, this wonderful little restaurant run by an equally wonderful old woman features Italian-Peruvian cuisine.

Going Out

Porlamar hops at night, but a little less than it used to. The deteriorating economic situation in this town has put a stranglehold on most night spots we used to recommend. There are two clubs that are taking up the slack, Señor Frog's and Dady's Latino. Take note that not two blocks from these night clubs are some of Porlamar's less desirable neighborhoods. We strongly advise that you grab a cab and not wander around too much!

Dady's Latino, Avenue 4 de Mayo at the Jumbo shopping center, 295-265-9404

Dady's is a two-story dance club playing a mix of top 40, techno pop, and Latin faves. The crowd here is young, but it is diverse (a mix of locals and tourists — frequented by Americans and Europeans and some gay clientele), so things get pretty mixed up here. Special events and live entertainment on most nights make this a must-stop on the circuit.

Señor Frog's, Avenue Bolivar at the Costa Azul shopping center, 295-262-0270

This is a two-level Mexican restaurant and bar with a young (20ish), loud, and high-energy crowd; the action is on the second floor. Things get going around midnight with a music mix of hip-hop, salsa, merengue, and rock. The bar is open from 11 p.m. to 3 a.m.; the cover charge is about $14 (includes one drink).

Mainland Venezuela

Caracas

We used to recommend spending a couple of days in the capital of Venezuela, but the current tense political climate and its accompanying safety concerns make us much less enthused about a visit nowadays. Although it's a very exciting city of 3.5 million people set in a temperate valley about 3,000 feet above sea level (this altitude keeps the city surprisingly cool, especially at night), Caracas is a rather threatening place. It has replaced Rio de Janeiro and Sao Paulo as one of South America's most dangerous cities (although any city in Colombia still tops this list). If you want to visit Caracas (it can be fun), we would recommend that a savvy Caraqueño accompany you at all times.

That said, it's a surprisingly vertical city, due to a building craze from the OPEC 1970s oil money. Caracas has some fantastic neighborhoods (Alta Mira, Chacao, and the east side), restaurants, and nightlife to explore. It also has more than its share of Third World big-city issues like crime (particularly theft and robbery) because the economic situation in Venezuela is getting worse, despite its oil wealth and the swagger and promises of President Hugo Chávez. Use common sense when walking around, and dress down, especially regarding jewelry, expensive watches, and the like. Leave those in the hotel safe. With a career military man in power, a disturbing police presence is apparent. You might be stopped and randomly searched—ostensibly for weapons or drugs, but we think it's just harassment. There is no Bill of Rights here, so be cooperative. Be sure to have your passport with you and keep it in a pickpocket-proof place.

When there, stay at the centrally located **Caracas Hilton** (800-HILTONS or 58-212-503-5000; www.hilton.com). This full-service, luxury high-rise hotel has an English-speaking staff and very comfortable rooms—many with incredible views. A pool and health club keep you refreshed. Just beware of room service prices. A liter of Absolut costs $125! The location is convenient to Caracas's clean and efficient subway and to its various performing arts centers, theaters, and museums. Rates are Pricey and up (EP).

When considering a trip to Caracas, you should note that in January 2006, the bridge connecting Simón Bolívar International Airport to Caracas collapsed. Unfortunately, this has turned what was once an easy commute into quite a pain in the butt. Visitors must now choose between two other options, neither of which is appealing. One route is a rather sketchy ride through the slums and the surrounding hills that descend into Caracas. The second route is a circuitous voyage that can last from one and a half to three hours, depending upon traffic. Although the government has said that plans to build a new bridge could be completed by the end of 2007, that's not something we'd count on.

Don't Miss

Playa El Agua

This is the place to hit the beach and have lunch, although there is often an abundance of expats lounging around with a loose beer in one hand and an underage wife in the other.

Playa Manzanillo

This is a pretty fishing village and beach that offers a change of pace.

Playa Puerto Cruz

This is the local favorite with a big sand dune and point at the southern end of the beach.

Playa Piel

This is Margarita's nude beach, located around the rocks on the western end of Playa Caribe.

Juan Griego

This is a great place to watch the sunset while you enjoy a bottle of wine at one of several waterfront restaurants. The fort, La Galera, is also a good look-out post.

Pampatar

Just north of Porlamar, this is a very scenic fishing village and harbor with some great old buildings.

Macañao Peninsula

This is the desolate and dry western end of the island and worth the drive if you like deserts and deserted beaches.

Coche

This flat island south of El Yaque is another windsurfer's paradise and is a short speedboat ride from El Yaque (there's also a ferry from Punta de Piedras). Several tour companies offer daily excursions (ask your hotel to arrange this). If you want to stay here, try Coche Speed Paradise (214-995-2726).

The Francisco Narváez Museum

The Museo de Arte Contemporáneo Francisco Narváez, on Calle Igualdad in Porlamar (295-261-8668), is devoted to one of Venezuela's most important artists (paintings and sculpture), who was a native of Margarita. Open Tuesday through Friday, 9 a.m. to 5 p.m., and on the weekend, 10 a.m. to 3 p.m.

The Margarita Post

This free English-language newspaper lists current happenings on the island.

Los Roques

These beautiful, mostly deserted islets to the east of Margarita are part of Venezuela's national park system (see the Los Roques chapter). Aerotuy offers great day and overnight trips from Margarita. If you have the time, it's well worth it.

Martinique

LEGEND

- ◉ ◯ Capital City, Town
- ③² Route Number
- ■ Hotel / Point of Interest
- 📷 Scenic View
- ⚓ Ferry / Cruise Ship Dock
- 🗼 Lighthouse
- 🏖 Beach
- ⛳ Golf Course

ATLANTIC OCEAN

Grand-Rivière

Mt. Pelée
(4,584 ft / 1,398 m)
Prêcheur

Marigot

Sainte-Marie

St. Pierre

Carbet

La Trace

Robert

Le Jardin de Balata

Squash Hotel

Le Lafayette

Plein Soleil

Schoelcher
Hotel La Batelière
Fort-de-France
Hotel Sofitel Bakoua
Hotel Carayou
Village Créole
Anse a l'Ane

Lamentin

François

Frégate Bleue

Cap Est Lagoon Resort & Spa

Airport
Ferry

Pointe-du-Bout

Vauclin

Club des Trois-Ilets

Trois Ilets

Rivière Salée

Anse-d'Arlets

Diamant

Sainte-Luce

Marin

Hotel Diamant Les Bains

Diamond Rock

Mercure Diamant

Les Amandiers-Karibea

Club Med

Sainte-Anne

Domaine de l'Anse Caritan

Anse Trabaud

CARIBBEAN SEA

N

0   5

Miles

Martinique

Carib Indians called it Madinina — "isle of flowers." The French named it Martinique, exuding a Hollywood-style cachet most islands can only dream of, conjuring the tropics at their most exotic, tinged with a little intrigue for good measure. This is where Bogie and Bacall first seduced one another while assisting the French underground in *To Have and Have Not*; more recently, *The Thomas Crowne Affair* saw Pierce Brosnan cavorting with Rene Russo. The real-life drama includes the volcanic eruption of Mt. Pelée in 1902, when almost 30,000 residents of St. Pierre — then known as the "Paris of the West Indies" — were buried under hot ash in mere minutes. Of course, Napoleon's Josephine also hailed from here.

Today, the confluence of France and the Caribbean produces an equally sensual environment for travelers: Boutiques stock the latest Parisian haute couture, patisseries brim with robust cheeses fresh from the mainland, Martinique's distinct musical and dancing traditions percolate into resorts, and lively Creole cuisine dominates the menus of most restaurants. Although at night it is somewhat abandoned and quiet, by day the capital, Fort-de-France, maintains a measure of colonial charm.

Otherwise, spectacular scenery and an extensive network of paved roads make Martinique ideal for exploring by car — the *Route de la Trace* is particularly memorable, a spindly mountain road through the island's natural park. Few places are as steep, green, and moist — the rainforest canopy is

Martinique: Key Facts

Location	14°N by 61°W 21 miles/34 kilometers north of St. Lucia 26 miles/42 kilometers south of Dominica 1,965 miles/3,164 kilometers southeast of New York
Size	425 square miles/1,101 square kilometers 50 miles/80 kilometers long by 22 miles/35 kilometers wide
Highest point	Mount Pelée (4,584 feet/1,398 meters)
Population	429,510 (Fort-de-France is just over 100,000)
Language	French!
Time	Atlantic Standard Time (1 hour ahead of EST, same as EDT)
Area code	To call Martinique from the U.S., dial 011 (the international dialing code), then 596 (the country code), followed by the nine-digit local number.
Electricity	220 volts AC, 50 cycles; you'll need a transformer and an adapter for U.S.-made appliances.
Currency	Euro (€1 = US$1.25 at press time; check prior to departure)
Driving	On the right; a valid driver's license from the U.S. or Canada is valid for up to 20 days; after that, an international driver's license is required.
Documents	U.S. and Canadian citizens need proof of nationality (plus a photo ID) for up to three months; after that a passport is necessary; an ongoing or a return ticket is also necessary.
Departure tax	None
Beer to drink	Lorraine
Rum to drink	Neisson
Music to hear	Beguine, or Zouk
Tourism info	514-288-1904; on-island, 596-596-61-61-60; www.martinique.org

profuse with towering tree ferns and enormous mahogany, flush with bromeliads that burst from their flanks. Conical volcanic remnants thrust into the clouds, draped in a profusion of dewy green. Martinique is among the most beautiful of Caribbean isles, particularly its deep-green rainforests tucked between dramatic ridges and spires. There are brilliant white-sand beaches classically shaded by palm trees in the south, and seductive black-sand coves navigated by fishermen in the north. Lovingly tended gardens filled with tropical flora are found throughout the island, but especially at the exquisite Jardin de Balata, which overlooks the capital from the foot of the dramatic Pitons du Carbet.

Most English-speaking travelers to Martinique are Francophiles who want to indulge in the language and culture, eat great food, and get a tan while they're at it. As on Guadeloupe, most of the visitors are from France—some on package tours, some on business, and some vacationing at their villas. Like an American in Paris, if you don't speak French you might encounter some of the classic French brusqueness, but if you make even a small attempt to speak the language, the Martiniquais warm right up and are very helpful. With its surfeit of history, great food, and sightseeing that could fill a week or more, Martinique adds up to a well-rounded package that is one of the Caribbean's most appealing.

The Briefest History

Martinique was first settled by the Arawaks and then by Carib Indians, who called the island Madinina (which means "isle of flowers"). It was sighted by Columbus in 1493, but he did not come ashore until his last voyage, in 1502. The European influence really started in 1635, when Martinique was claimed by the French. A year later, King Louis XIII authorized the introduction of slavery into the French West Indies to work the sugar plantations, but the Caribs fought the French fiercely, which led to their elimination in the 1660s. King Louis XIV made the island the capital of France's Caribbean possessions, and in 1763 Marie-Josèphe Rose Tascher de la Pagerie was born in Martinique, the daughter of a plantation owner. She later became Napoleon's Empress Josephine. Throughout the latter part of the 18th century, the island was periodically occupied by the British, and it wasn't until 1814 that France regained permanent control of Martinique. Slavery continued unabated until 1848, when it was outlawed by the Republic.

In 1902 volcanic Mount Pelée erupted and in three minutes wiped out the capital, St. Pierre—at the time called "the Paris of the West Indies" —with an inferno of burning gas and ash that swept down the slopes, obliterating anything in its path. Thirty thousand people were killed. The lone survivor was a man in a dank jail cell. The capital was then moved to Fort-de-France. Forty-four years later Martinique became a Department of France and in 1974 was made a Région. The island is represented in the French Parliament by four MPs and two senators, and locally by the Conseil Régional and the Conseil Général.

The main economy of Martinique today is agriculture. Sugar, rum, bananas, pineapples, melons, avocados, limes, fruit juices, and canned fruits are the major products. Tourism is a growth industry, with more than 500,000 visitors a year staying in 6,000 hotel rooms. It's a big business.

Getting There

Martinique's sleek, modern Fort-de-France Lamentin Airport, located a few miles east of the capital, handles jumbo jets from France as well as smaller planes from within the Caribbean. After a six-year hiatus, American Eagle finally resumed service from San Juan in 2005, allowing same-day connections from major cities in the eastern United States. Air France provides flights from Miami, and Club Med operates a weekly charter in high season from New York–JFK on North American Airlines. Service within the Caribbean is provided by Air Antilles, which flies in from Guadeloupe; Air Caraïbes, from the French islands and Antigua, Barbados, St. Lucia, and Trinidad; and by LIAT, from Antigua, Barbados, Dominica, Guadeloupe, and St. Lucia.

You can also reach Martinique by ferry, on L'Express des Iles (596-596-91-52-15; www.express-des-iles.com), Brudey Frères (596-596-70-08-50), and Caribbean Ferries (596-596-63-68-68), high-speed catamarans that link Fort-de-France with Guadeloupe, St. Lucia, and Dominica. The passage from Guadeloupe takes three and a half hours, and adult fare is about $80 one way, $125 round-trip. The dock is just east of Fort, behind the large post office.

Getting Around

Although traffic congestion is becoming a dire problem (mostly on the road between Fort-de-France and Rivière-Salée), it makes sense to rent a car, especially if you want to hit the beaches, the best of which are in the southeast corner of the island. The roads in the northern half of the island are much less heavily traveled. With one of the best-maintained road systems in the region, replete with freeways and good signage, driving is on par with conditions in France. In addition to local companies, Avis (800-331-1084 or 596-596-42-11-00), Budget (800-527-0700 or 596-596-42-16-79), Hertz (800-654-3001 or 596-596-51-54-55; www.hertzantilles.com), Jumbo Car (596-596-42-22-26), and National affiliate Europcar (800-227-3876 or 596-596-42-42-42) all have airport and other island locations. Rates start as low as $40 per day; reserve in advance to obtain the cheapest and/or most desirable. There is a drop-off charge of $20 for picking up or returning the car to the airport; the agencies are located a couple miles from the terminal (van transfers are provided). Beware the breakneck pace of the drivers, which can make your head spin.

Due to the traffic congestion south of the airport, if you're traveling between the Trois-Ilets area (Pointe-du-Bout) and Fort-de-France, we highly recommend the *vedettes* (ferries) that shuttle back and forth once or twice an hour. The crossing takes 20 minutes (versus one to two hours most times of the day via road), runs between early morning and midnight daily, and costs $8 round-trip (for schedules and other info call 596-596-63-06-46). On the Trois-Ilets side, the docks are located at the marina in Pointe-du-Bout and at the pier at Anse-Mitan. On the Fort-de-France side, ferries land at Quai d'Esnambuc, near Fort St-Louis.

If you don't want to rent a car, and you're well-heeled, you can hire a taxi; most are swift Mercedeses. Rates for the trip between the airport and Pointe du Bout are about $55; between 8 p.m. and 6 a.m. there is a surcharge of 40 percent. For Radio Taxi, call 596-596-63-63-62. Most islanders use the collective taxis, eight-passenger limos with the sign "TC" — there are more than 400 on the island. The main terminal in Fort-de-France is at Pointe Simon, two blocks west of the Tourist Office on Boulevard Alfassa. Sample fare: Fort-de-France to Ste-Anne, about $7. Or use the public bus system, which is excellent and a great way to meet the locals.

Focus on Martinique: Parlez-Vous Français?

They are out there — a small but zealous group of Francophiles who can't get enough of Proust's mother tongue. Unfortunately for them, France is not the most inviting place to reside in the winter. There is, however, a tempting option that combines the challenge of speaking French with a wonderfully warm climate.

Where is this stimulating, sophisticated tropical oasis? It's right here in Martinique, and the focal point of it all is fashionable **Fort-de-France**. As its name implies, in appearance, style, and attitude, it is the most Gallic city in these latitudes. The beat here is tuned into Paris, not Kingston, and this is a city that looks decidedly tropical. Many find it to be a smaller, more casual, and more temperate version of Nice. It contains great restaurants, cafés, patisseries, lots of stores, and a central location. Although the temperature is warm to hot in the daytime, the evenings are delightful.

The Martiniquais may look like West Indians, but they act like the French. You're more likely to see Paris fashions than the Rasta liberation colors, although the latter certainly have made an impact here since our first visit. However, Fort-de-France is a stylish and well-dressed city for the West Indies. Expect a little of that infamous French attitude, imported straight from Paris, and don't expect much in the way of Americans to commiserate with — U.S. tourists make up less than 3 percent of the overnight visitors; Americans also stop here on cruise ships in the winter months, but most don't make it far beyond the capital. You will find a fair number of English-speakers in the primary tourist areas, but as you head north and east (and you really should), a French phrasebook will come in handy.

Fort-de-France is located in the center of the island's west coast, on the Baie des Flamands. It is surrounded by lush hills, and soaring volcanic cones rise up in the distance to the north. The center point of the compact city is **La Savane**, a 12.5-acre park with a statue of Empress Josephine (Martinique's Jackie O.) as its centerpiece. She has spent more than a decade beheaded and bloodied with drips of red paint — a pointed social commentary on her proslavery stance. Most of the city's sights are within walking distance of the statue. On the southeast corner of the park, lots of food vendors set up little cafés by their trucks at night. You can get all kinds of superb cuisine from them at prices that won't burn a hole in your wallet. They're especially popular because the movie multiplex is right across the street.

Adjacent is an open-air market where you'll find souvenirs and weavings.

Just west, on Rue Antoine Siger, the traditional fabric store run by Léontine Bucher offers bolts of vivid madras fabric, weavings from India in plaids that intermingle lines of saffron, curry, aqua, and lime colors — the prices average just $5 a yard. On Saturday morning a terrific spice market materializes at the corner of Rue Blenac and Rue Antoine — here you can buy madras-lined gift baskets of colorful spices (we bring these home to appreciative neighbors). The buys extend to jewelry, and at shops like Cadet Daniel you'll find beautifully crafted gold pieces in all price ranges (the duty-free savings amount to about 20 percent off typical U.S. prices). The city quiets down in the evening, but there are cafés, *salons de thé*, and nightclubs that will take you into the night. Start your exploration of Fort-de-France at the tourist office, where you can pick up brochures, maps, and a copy of the ever handy Choubouloute, a guide for visitors.

Note: Since our first visit here two decades ago, Fort-de-France has changed; its suburbs seem to have blossomed with modern (and often ugly) construction. The place has slipped — it's not as polished as when we first encountered it. The Savane is in need of some TLC, and the statue of Empress Josephine is still traumatized. Walking around town after dusk is not advised. McDonald's and Burger King have built block-long outlets — not a good sign in the midst of *le monde français*. We once suggested staying right in town, but some of the places we recommended then, like the Impératrice, are down at the heels now, so we've mostly chosen other places on the island. However, the city is worth at least a day's exploration because there is so much to see, and there is a concerted effort being made by the new mayor to return Fort-de-France to its past glory. There is discussion of a new Marriott Hotel for the capital, and on our last visit we were amused to see a new tourist police force on bicycles — present when cruise ships are in port — wearing T-shirts that read *Agents de Mediation Urbain*. If you want to avoid the cruise-ship masses, skip Fort-de-France on Tuesday in high season, when up to four ships dock at the capital.

Across the bay is Anse-Mitan and Pointe-du-Bout (collectively referred to as **Les Trois-Ilets**), the tourist area that sprang to life in the 1970s and is only a 20-minute ferry ride from the capital (much faster than driving). To the south is **Diamant**, where a 600-foot rock outcrop hovers just offshore, and **Ste-Anne**, which is close to the best beaches. To the north of Fort-de-France is a glorious mountain range, leading to spectacular **Mt. Pelée**. Fields of sugarcane and bananas blanket much of the land. These areas are discussed later in the chapter.

Where to Stay

There is no shortage of beds on Martinique, what with about 6,000 hotel rooms of various persuasions, but choosing your location is worth careful consideration. Accommodations are found throughout the island, but the primary resort landing is Anse-Mitan/Pointe-du-Bout. Although this area has the largest tourist infrastructure — not usually our cup of tea — there is a wealth of good restaurants plus a fair, if crowded, beach.

The other hotel areas (where there are beaches in front or nearby) are Diamant, Ste-Luce, and Ste-Anne. For cheaper digs, consider accommodations in Fort-de-France. However, in our quest to avoid the intense traffic congestion south of the airport, we have discovered a new favorite place to stay: the east coast around Le François. Although this area isn't exactly jumping with beaches, dining, or nightlife, it is centrally located for exploring the north, the capital, and the beaches to the south, and it will keep encounters with traffic jams to a minimum.

Note that the former Le Méridien has been sold to a local firm and is now called the Kalenda. Although we stayed here without a problem on our last visit, its future seems a little up in the air.

Fort-de-France

Le Lafayette, Place de la Savane, Fort-de-France, Martinique, FWI. ✆ 596-596-73-80-50, ✆ 596-596-60-97-75, 🖳 www.lelafayettehotel.com

💼 **Cheap** 🍴 **CP** [CC] 24 rooms

If you want to stay right in the center of town, across from La Savane, this is a relatively inexpensive hotel; it's kind of a dive but has lots of character. Built in 1957, and seemingly lacking in any modernization, it's a small, five-story, city hotel — that is, there's no pool. The rooms are fairly compact but clean; the ones in front share a broad terrace facing the Savane, but the ones in back are quieter (a few upper-floor rooms have a view of the harbor and Fort St. Louis). The restaurant serves cheap French Creole cuisine on the second floor, and breakfast is handled on the sunny top floor.

Squash Hotel, 3 Boulevard de la Marne, Fort-de-France, Martinique, FWI. ✆ 596-596-72-80-80, ✆ 596-596-63-00-74, 🖳 www.squashhotel.com

💼 **Not So Cheap** 🍴 **CP** [CC] 180 rooms

Located a stone's throw from downtown, this former PLM affiliate is a smart in-town accommodation for those who want to be near the action yet have some amenities — a pool, a sauna, a Jacuzzi, squash courts, and an elementary health club. With a view of the bay, the air-conditioned rooms come with phone, TV, and minibar; corner units are oversize. Businessmen primarily fill the rooms, none of which will win any awards for design, but at less than $150 a night in season, it's a very good buy.

Hotel La Batelière, Route 32, Schoelcher, Martinique, FWI. ✆ 596-596-61-49-49, ✆ 596-596-61-70-57, 🖳 Web site under construction at press time

⬛ Pricey ⑪ CP ⒸⒸ 199 rooms

Located a little over a mile from downtown on a steep bluff, this one-time Hilton was the place to stay in Martinique a decade or so ago, but the Batelière remains well run and reliable. You'll find large, if somewhat dated, rooms, and there are all the big-resort amenities, such as room service (for champagne cocktails) and a beauty salon (for the hair and nails). It has a small man-made beach with water sports, and a comfy pool to lounge around in and see what everyone else is doing. For more exercise, there are six lighted tennis courts, and you can exercise your wallet at the adjacent glitzy casino. The restaurant is reliable, and the views are nice. One problem: The management isn't interested in the Anglophone audience, having sold its soul to French tour groups.

Pointe-du-Bout and Anse-Mitan

Hotel Sofitel Bakoua, Pointe-du-Bout, Trois-Ilets, Martinique, FWI. ℭ 800-221-4542 or 596-596-66-02-02, ✆ 596-596-66-00-41, 💻 www.sofitel.com

⬛ Wicked Pricey ⑪ CP ⒸⒸ 140 rooms

For years, this was Martinique's premier establishment. Unfortunately, though managed by the Sofitel firm, the Bakoua operation has lapsed in recent years, and we can't give it the same recommendation we once did. However, it has a good location on the Pointe-du-Bout, with fab views of Fort-de-France and the volcanoes behind it that form the backdrop. The *chambres* are decorated in a Creole contempo style, and all are air-conditioned, with balcony or patio, phone, French TV, VCR, minibar, safe, and radio (so you can sing "Sous le Ciel de Paris") in the good-size bath. Most rooms are in a three-story wing that wraps around a garden, but the better (and considerably more expensive) units are directly on the compact, man-made beach, where the requisite water sports are located. A scallop-shaped pool is located up above, and we think there are few more pleasing places for a sunset ti punch than at this bar, drinking in the splendid panorama. The main restaurant is huge, with fairly good meals, although service can be perfunctory. When you step off the property there are more restaurants in Pointe-du-Bout, and lots of activity — an advantage if you suffer from cabin fever. If you want to *jouer au tennis*, there are two lighted courts, and Les Grands Ballets de Martinique, a troupe of talented singers and dancers, performs Friday night. Still, if it's a true luxury resort you want, by all means check into Cap Est instead.

Hotel Carayou, Pointe-du-Bout, Trois-Ilets, Martinique, FWI. ℭ 596-596-66-04-04, ✆ 596-596-66-00-57

💲 **Very Pricey** 🍴 **CP** CC 197 rooms

The Carayou offers lush grounds that surround an inviting decked pool area. Although it doesn't have the great views of Fort-de-France that its more expensive neighbor (the Bakoua) has, the views here are pleasant, as are the breezes that cool this rather large property. The grounds are spacious and converge on a diminutive man-made beach. All rooms have the standard resort amenities, including a/c, balconies, minibars, and phones. You'll find two restaurants and two bars on the property, and all water sports are available at the beach. There are two tennis courts, and Ping-Pong for the Gloria Upsons and Bunny Bixleys among you. You are also steps away from the marina (where the ferry will take you to Fort-de-France) and all the hubbub of the Pointe-du-Bout and Anse-Mitan area.

Village Créole, Pointe-du-Bout, Trois-Ilets, Martinique, FWI. ✆ 596-596-66-03-19, ✐ 596-596-66-07-06, 🖳 www.villagecreole.com

💲 **Not So Cheap** 🍴 **EP** CC 35 rooms

The apartments here occupy the second and third floors of a small but attractive shopping center fashioned in modern Creole style. Each unit has its own entrance, and inside are cute abodes with kitchenettes and simple furnishings; studios and one-bedroom versions are available. The beach is just two minutes away, and a half dozen restaurants are part of the complex.

Club des Trois-Ilets, Anse-à-l'Ane, Trois-Ilets, Martinique, FWI. ✆ 596-596-68-31-67, ✐ 596-596-68-37-65, 🖳 www.hotel-club3ilets.com

💲 **Very Pricey** 🍴 **CP** CC 77 rooms

Located a few miles southwest of Anse-Mitan, this resort sits on a lovely cove beach that is much quieter and prettier than Anse-Mitan. It is an attractive and well-landscaped medium-size hotel for those who want to be close to and yet removed from the hubbub. The rooms are all equipped with a/c, lanai, phone, French TV, mini-fridge, safe, and a dryer for your wet bathing suits.

The South

Hotel Diamant Les Bains, Le Diamant 97223, Martinique, FWI. ✆ 596-596-76-40-14, ✐ 596-596-76-27-00

💲 **Not So Cheap** 🍴 **CP** (a **MAP** option is available) CC 24 rooms

For the money, this cute abode offers the best beachfront value on Martinique. Situated right on the water at the edge of town, Les Bains is a compact mini-resort, with lots of character filling in where luxury is lacking. It sits on the eastern end of the 2.5-mile/4-kilometer-long Diamant Beach, with views of imposing Diamant Rock and St. Lucia in the distance, so you can stroll the beach to your heart's content. Half the rooms are in sweet little cottages, and the others are in the main building, offering sea views. All are air-conditioned, have private bath and a fridge, and are clean and simple in décor. There is a pool and a beloved restaurant and bar on the premises. Tennis and water sports can be found within five minutes of the hotel, and restaurants and town activity are but steps away. The English-speaking owners happily accommodate more Americans here than most other island properties do.

Club Med Buccaneer's Creek, Pointe du Marin, Ste-Anne, Martinique, FWI. ✆ 800-258-2633 or 596-596-767272, 🖂 596-596-767202, 🖳 www.clubmed.com

💲 Ridiculous 🍴 **All-Inclusive** CC 293 rooms

As the original Caribbean Club Med, Buccaneer's Creek was probably responsible for some of the wild stories about the (then) free-wheeling French all-inclusive operations. Built in 1969, the one-price-pays-all concept was fresh and original in the Caribbean back then, but of course, Sandals and others have since refined the all-inclusive arrangement—and hiked the rates as well. Although Club Med has gone through its changes and difficult periods, Buccaneer's Creek completed an 18-month $60 million overhaul in 2005 and now merits a recommendation. It delivers good value for the dollar, and U.S. visitors who are concerned about the mother tongue of Martinique will find an English-fluent staff and a quantity of American guests to play with them.

The hotel spreads over a 54-acre property graced by the shade of 3,500 coconut trees that dapple the grounds. The rooms, which were rebuilt from the ground up, are larger than before and offer a nice splash of Creole colors. They are equipped with TV, iron and board, minifridge, coffeemaker, and a/c, and they are still set well behind the beach. There are three restaurants, a brand new infinity-lipped swimming pool, and live music nightly. Club Med keeps the focus on activities, and there's a bounty to choose from: water skiing, tennis, windsurfing, and wakeboarding; all excursions off-property, including golf, diving, and 4 × 4 tours, plus spa treatments, are extra. Since the clientele includes many Americans (lots from New York and New Jersey), staying here is an atypical experience for Martinique.

Mercure Diamant, Pointe de la Chéry, Le Diamant, Martinique, FWI. ✆ 800-221-4542 or 596-596-76-46-00, 🖂 596-596-76-25-99, 🖳 www.accorhotels.com

💲 Pricey 🍴 CP CC 150 rooms

This is an agreeable efficiency hotel that slopes down to the sea just east of the town of Diamant. It's a full-service resort with most of the amenities of the bigger places and is good for families with small children—there are babysitting services and a laundry. The rooms come with a double bed and a smaller *canapé-lît* as well as kitchenette, a/c, safe, phone, and lanai. All rooms have views of the sea. There are two restaurants, a large pool with a water slide, and two lighted tennis courts, and a good swimming beach is 10 minutes away on foot (or by shuttle). Scuba is available nearby at Aqua Sud.

Les Amandiers–Karibea, Ste-Luce, Martinique, FWI. ☎ 596-596-62-32-32, ✆ 596-596-62-33-40, 🖳 www.hotellesamandiers.com

💼 **Pricey** 🍽 **CP** 🆑 117 rooms

This hotel is located just west of the lovely town of Ste-Luce, off a pretty, natural beach. Stretching from the road to the beach, the rooms are decorated in what could be called French contemporary Creole. Run by a friendly and helpful staff, the hotel caters predominantly to French and European tourists, so you may feel *une petite différence*. All rooms have a/c, a good-size lanai with hillside view (although it's a little too easy to see into your neighbor's room), French TV, and phone. There is a pool, a lighted tennis court, and beach facilities with water sports.

Domaine de l'Anse Caritan, B.P. 24, Ste-Anne, Martinique, FWI. ☎ 800-322-2223 or 596-596-76-74-12, ✆ 596-596-76-72-59, 🖳 www.leader-hotels.gp

💼 **Not So Cheap** 🍽 **CP** 🆑 228 rooms

Ideally situated near the charming village of Ste-Anne and just a few minutes' drive from Martinique's best beaches (Salines and Traubaud), this is a comfortable, unassuming efficiency resort that has more charisma and island personality than most others of its size. It still offers a decent array of resort amenities: a pool, a beach, and water sports, including kayaking and a dive shop. The rooms come with kitchenette, a/c, phone, safe, and private bath. All are pleasantly decorated, with the kitchenette on the large balcony, but they are minimally furnished. The hotel has two restaurants and a bar, and it's a short walk to others in town.

The East

⭐ **Cap Est Lagoon Resort & Spa**, Cap Est, Le François, Martinique, FWI. ☎ 800-735-2478 or 596-596-54-94-05, ✆ 596-596-54-96-00, 🖳 www.capest.com

💼 **Stratospheric** 🍽 **CP** 🆑 50 rooms

The first luxury resort to be built on Martinique in years picked a location we would not have expected: the lacy eastern coast, where sand is rare. Developer Geoffroy des Grottes had a different kind of escape in mind, and — with its nouveau Creole-meets-Asian design scheme — it reminds us less of the Caribbean than of that other Frenchish (and *très chic*) outpost, Mauritius, in the Indian Ocean. The result: Other than St. Martin's La Samanna and the top two or three addresses on St. Barth, this is easily the most exclusive hotel in the French West Indies. It was quickly accepted into the roster of Relais & Châteaux properties — one of only seven in the Caribbean.

The resort sits astride a tongue of ancient lava that almost made it to the sea, and the rooms are found in 18 cottages that (mostly) hover along the shimmering turquoise lagoon, with striking blood-red tin roofs. The landscaping is not tropical but native, highlighted by exotic cacti, including one that hugs the ground and produces pink flowers that unfurl with velvety allure, looking vaguely Martian (watch out — they're teeming with nearly invisible thorns). The rooms are extravagantly but very tastefully decorated, with low-slung furniture from Thailand and Burma and wonderful tactile materials like hemp cloth; the more expensive units are larger and have outdoor showers and private plunge pools. An infinity-edge pool reaches toward the shoreline; a beachfront restaurant, Le Campeche, serves superb light meals — the salmon we had there will be hard to top. There's a tiny beach in front, and kayaking, kitesurfing, and windsurfing in the reef-protected lagoon is excellent. Rounding out the facilities are a top-flight spa with all manor of seaweed and mud wraps, a Turkish hammam, a gym, and Le Belem, a restaurant that vies to be the island's best (and certainly Martinique's most expensive). In all, it is a superb addition to the French West Indies.

Plein Soleil, Pointe Thalémont, Le François, Martinique, FWI. © 596-596-38-07-77, @ 596-596-65-58-13, 🖥 www.pleinsoleil.mq

💲 **Not So Cheap** for upper units and **Pricey** for those downstairs
🍴 CP CC 12 rooms

Built by a caring but otherwise shy former art director from Paris, Jean-Christophe Yoyo, this friendly inn consists of three two-story cottages that wrap around a bucolic hillside a mile or so from the coast and are surrounded by banana farms. Each of the cottages has two smallish rooms upstairs with a balcony and two much larger rooms downstairs with a large (shared) veranda, all with their own private entrance and kitchenette. Each is perfectly decorated in a lean, handsome style; downstairs units have a/c, but no frills like TV or phone. There is a good-size pool down below on its own little point and, best of all, at the summit there is a very appealing restaurant, also beautifully decorated with treasures from Yoyo's travels — kilim pillows from Turkey, chairs from Africa, and so forth. Decent snorkeling and swimming is not far, but this is (obviously) not a beach resort. It is, however, a good place for young lovers seeking real solitude and for self-starters on a budget. Having a car at your disposal is a good idea.

Frégate Bleue, Quartier Frégate, Le François, Martinique, FWI. ✆ 596-596-54-54-66, ✎ 596-596-54-78-48, 💻 www.fregatebleue.com.

💲 **Pricey** 🍴 **CP** **CC** 9 rooms

This small inn is the brainchild of Charles and Yveline de Lucy de Fossarieu, the one-time owners of Leyritz Plantation, which they sold in 1988 and then converted this modern French country home into a small inn. There are five rooms on the second floor. All are well-appointed, with Asian rugs and antiques, and have a terrace with views of the nearby coast and offshore islets dotting a lagoon. There are three rooms downstairs (minus the terrace and view), and there's a charmingly rustic cottage behind the small pool that is mostly open to the breezes. Madame Fossarieu is quite personable and will happily tell the tale (with the weathered photos to prove it) of the day she hosted a 1974 mini-summit at Leyritz with President Gerald Ford, Henry Kissinger, and French President Giscard d'Estaing (the table they dined at is now at Frégate Bleue). *Petit dejeuner* is served on an idyllic balcony; dinners are prepared on request. Frégate Bleue is a proud member of the French organization called Relais du Silence, lodgings that celebrate the quiet moments. It's the only one in the Caribbean (though there are dozens in Europe). The setting is an upscale neighborhood, just off the main road between François and Vauclin.

Villa/Gîtes Rentals

Want a posh pad or a modest flat to call your own? Give the following a holler and see what they can do for you:

Villa Rental Service, Comité Martiniquais du Tourisme, Immeuble le Beaupré, Pointe de Jaham, Schoelcher, Martinique, FWI. ✆ 596-596-61-61-77, ✎ 596-596-61-22-72

Gîtes de France, Galerie de la Baie, 30 Rue Ernest Deproge, Fort-de-France, Martinique, FWI. ✆ 596-596-73-74-74, ✎ 596-596-63-55-92, 💻 www.gites-de-france.fr

Where to Eat

Like any French outpost, Martinique has lots of restaurants, and most of them would leave the majority of venues on other islands in the dust. Translation: It's pretty difficult to get a bad meal here. Expensive, yes, but remember, this is France and you're on vacation. The first *délicieuse* bite will soften the impact of the check (*l'addition, en français*) when it hits the table. Most restaurants feature what is termed cuisine *gastronomique*, or French food with Creole flair. Listed below are just a few of the highlights to be found on this gourmet island. For a complete listing, pick up a free copy of *Ti Gourmet* at your hotel. Try to be adventurous, and above all, *mange!*

Fort-de-France and Environs

$ **food stands**, southeast corner of La Savane

When the sun sets, you'll find tasty grilled food, great prices, alfresco dining, and a lively atmosphere. What more could you want?

$$$$$ **La Canne a Sucre**, Patio de Cluny, Schoelcher, 596-596-63-33-95

When we first visited Guadeloupe years ago, this was that island's finest restaurant, but chef-owner Gerard Virginius moved his operation to Martinique in 1999. Today it is one of the finest French restaurants in the Caribbean, and open for lunch and dinner. Though located in a decidedly unglam shopping center a couple miles north of downtown, the restaurant is decorated in an uber-colonial fashion. The menu courses through a litany of classic French cooking with island touches. The desserts are exotic and fruit-based, and the wine list is refined. Closed Sunday; reservations required.

$$$$$ **La Plantation**, Le Lamentin (near the airport), 596-596-50-16-08

Another class act—tucked in an unlikely suburban locale in a traditional colonial house, this has been one of the island's top draws for many years. The primped service and formal setting are equal stars to the sophisticated and rich cuisine, served on plates crowned with gleaming silver domes. Lunch is served Monday through Friday; dinner nightly, except Sunday; reservations are required.

Are you just in the mood for a nice cold beer or a café au lait? If so, here are the best spots for refreshment and people-watching.

El Raco, 23 rue Lazare-Carnot, 596-596-73-29-16

This is a wine bar for all of our oenophile readers, with specialties from Bordeaux.

L'Epi Soleil, 21 rue de la Liberté

In addition to this one, there are several tasty patisseries throughout the island and on just about every corner. They're all worth a visit. Some are open late.

Malmaison, rue de la Liberté

For daytime fun and pizza, this is worth checking out. It's opposite the Savane and the post office, so lots of foreigners stream in, including the crews from docked ships.

Tea Garden, 41 rue Victor-Hugo, 596-596-73-09-50

Open late, it serves great desserts and ice creams.

Pointe-du-Bout and Anse-Mitan

$$$ **Au Poisson d'Or**, Anse-Mitan, 596-596-66-01-80

Seafood is the specialty here, especially stuffed conch, fried sea eggs, and grilled lobster. The South Seas décor doesn't hurt. Closed Monday.

$$ **Chez Fanny**, Anse-Mitan, 596-596-66-04-34

Crowds can make service sporadic, but this is a great joint for inexpensive lunch or dinner with huge portions, starring an excellent couscous. Closed Wednesday

$$$ **La Grange Inn**, Village Créole, 596-596-66-01-66

This is the place for grilled steaks and seafood that are competently prepared. It's also one of the better spots for cold beer. Open daily 8:30 a.m. to midnight.

$$$ **La Langouste**, Anse-Mitan, 596-596-66-04-99

As the name implies, spiny lobster is this restaurant's specialty. Eating here is a pleasure — you are on the beach with great views of the bay and Fort-de-France. Reservations are suggested.

$$ **La Marine**, Pointe-du-Bout Marina, 596-596-66-02-32

La Marine offers passable dining for sailors and others on shore leave — pizzas, grilled meats, grillled fish, and salads. The service can be slow, but it's inexpensive and a good place to meet the transient yachtie crowd. Two others with similar menus and ambiance in the same vicinity are Le Yacht and L'Embarcadere (the latter is especially convenient for hanging out while waiting for the Fort-de-France ferry; happy hour runs daily 6 to 7 p.m.). Open daily 8 a.m. to midnight.

$$$$ **La Matadore**, Anse-Mitan, 596-596-66-16-46

This is a highly regarded restaurant, despite its lousy view. Cuisine is *gastronomique*, with an emphasis on local specialties.

$$ **Le Barbaroc**, Anse-Mitan, 596-596-66-02-07

For lunch and dinner, this is a casual joint serving Creole cuisine — just the ticket if you want lighter fare or don't want to spend a fortune for a meal. Open daily.

$$ **Ti Calebasse**, Anse-à-l'Ane, 596-596-68-38-77

Ginette is the chef here, and she specializes in tasty Creole dishes. Taste her homemade black pudding. On Friday, there's a barbeque with live zouk and merengue, but make reservations. Closed Sunday evening and all day Wednesday.

The South

$$$ Chez Gracieuse, Cap Chevalier, 596-596-76-93-10

Open for lunch only, this beachside institution serves simple but delicious Creole to the adoring masses. Closed Monday; reservations are suggested.

$$$ Diamant Les Bains, Le Diamant, 596-596-76-40-14

The chef whips up a seafood storm at this delightful, family-owned restaurant. Try the squash stuffed with crab au gratin, or sweet peppers with sea eggs. In season, there are weekly lobster parties, complete with a band and, you guessed it, limbo.

$ food trucks, Pointe des Salines

As at the Savane at night, all kinds of portable restaurants arrive at the beach, especially on weekends. The food is good and cheap, and you can eat in your bathing suit. They park mostly in a spot past the entrance to the dirt road that goes along the beach in both directions.

$$$ Le Diam's, Place de l'Eglise, 596-596-76-44-46

This is a fun place, a sea of color, flowers, and *objets d'art*. The menu is quite diverse, from salads, pizzas, and pastas to full-course meals (the Creole paella is a favorite). The price is right as well, which is why this place gets so busy. Reservations are always recommended, and note that Le Diam's will provide transportation for guests staying in the Diamant area.

The East and North

$$$$ La Decouverte, St. Jacques (just north of Ste-Marie), 596-596-69-44-04

This is perhaps the island's top haunt for authentic Creole dishes, the specialty being cous-cous royal fruits *de mer*. Walk off your lunch on the trail through the Foret La Philippe next door. Open for lunch only; closed Wednesday. Reservations are recommended.

$$$$$ ⊛ Le Belem, Cap Est, 596-596-54-80-80

This is the outstanding restaurant at Cap Est Resort, with a staff imported from three-star Michelins back in Paris; Executive Chef Herve Rameau hails from La Samanna. It has an outstanding all-French wine cellar (all the top Bordeaux are present), plus a collection of fine rums ranging from a 1929 Depaz to 1875 bottles from St. James, before the St. Pierre factory was buried by the 1902 eruption of Mt. Pelée (now that's a sip of history!). Reservations are essential.

$$ **Le Ruisseau**, Plantation Leyritz, 596-596-78-53-92

Although, sadly, we no longer recommend the Leyritz as a place for an overnight, it's still a good place for lunch, where vanilla-scented fish and other Creole dishes are served at tables sitting next to free-flowing streams. Try to arrive around 2 p.m., when the tour bus contingent starts to clear out.

$$ **Le St. James**, Ste-Marie, 596-596-69-07-33

This is a good spot for a Creole lunch, particularly if you're visiting the St. James distillery next door. Closed Saturday.

Going Out

Unlike much of the West Indies, where nightlife consists of little more than a hotel disco and the occasional skeletal steel band, Fort-de-France has some great clubs that feature both current French and English-American hits. Note that like almost everything else on a French island, most are closed on Sunday. Check ahead of time and ask your hotel concierge about which is the best place to go on a given night (he or she may even give you the scoop on something new), or check *Choubouloute*, the visitor's guide (available from the tourist office). The following are among the best.

Le Calebasse Café, 19 Boulevard Allegre, Marin, 596-596-74-69-27

Calebasse is located just down the street from Zanzibar (below). It's a hot spot for live entertainment.

Le Yucca Bar, Rivière Roche, Fort-de-France, 596-596-60-48-36

This restaurant serves meals early in the evening, but later the disco revs up with an international bent, luring a friendly mix of all types for dancing and pool (as in tables). It's popular, but watch the iffy neighborhood.

Le Zanzibar, 11 Boulevard Allègre, Marin, 596-596-74-08-46

At this spot, you'll find jazz, soul, R&B, and Caribbean music, accompanied by an equally international menu.

Don't Miss

The Beaches

Le tout Martinique goes to the beach on the weekend, with families and major picnics in tow. They park their Mercedeses, set up the tarp and table, and *voilà*. Expect incredible traffic from Ste-Anne to Le Marin returning from the beaches on weekends—a stoplight at Le Marin backs up traffic for miles. We strongly suggest having dinner in Ste-Anne to wait it out. Although there are other smaller beaches sprinkled throughout the island (primarily on the west coast), as well as numerous man-made coves fronting the resorts, the following are the three beauties for which Martinique is best known.

Anse Traubaud. Located on the southeastern corner of the island just past the better known beaches of Les Salines, this is actually part of the Baie des Anglais. It's Martinique's prettiest beach — a long stretch of sand bordered by groves of palm trees. Topless usually (as is the French custom), during the week, it can veer unofficially to "clothes optional." To get there, drive past Aux Delices de la Mer and follow the dirt road until you can go no farther. Park; you are at Anse Traubaud. If you cross the footbridge and follow the path through the brush (there are cliffs to your right), you'll come to another series of beaches — a 25-minute walk. You can also access these beaches by car by heading north from Ste-Anne. About .5 mile/1 kilometer north of the entrance for Club Med, take the dirt road that forks to the right off the main road. Go about 3 miles/5 kilometers and look for the parked cars (you might have to pay an access fee — about $3 — to a farmer who owns the land the road passes through). Tourists are encouraged to visit Les Salines next door, but you'll notice that most of the locals don't talk about Traubaud — this is their beach.

Les Salines. This most famous of Martinique's beaches can get crowded and busy on weekends. This is where the food trucks set up, and if you keep driving to the right past the entrance, over a road you might think your car cannot negotiate (it can), you come to some quieter beaches. If you go to the left after the entrance, you'll eventually hit Aux Delices de la Mer and then Anse-Traubaud. At the far right end of the parking area is a sign for Petite Anse des Salines, and a footpath that leads through the woods and to the island's unofficial nude (and mostly gay) beach. Feel free to park the car and set up wherever you want along the whole stretch.

Diamant. If you don't feel like hassling with the drive and traffic of the Ste-Anne beaches, Diamant is a 2.5-mile-long strand of salt-and-pepper sand with stunning views of Diamant Rock. A swim here can be included with a pleasant "ooh-cruise" around the southwestern tip of the island. After a day at the beach, visit Anses-d'Arlet, a scenic fishing village that inspired Gauguin and should inspire the photographer in you as well. The late-afternoon light is superb on the brightly painted fishing boats.

The Rum Distilleries

Martinique is arguably the world's foremost producer of fine rum, or actually, *rhum agricole*, which is made from a fresh cane juice rather than molasses (as is standard in neighboring non-French islands). In fact, the French government awarded Martinique the prestigious label *Appellation d'Origine Controlée*, putting the island's rums on a par with French cheese and wine, like Camembert or Bordeaux. There are 11 distilleries open to the public for tastings, and all of them make respected rums; at least two offer tours of the plant: **St. James** (in Ste-Marie; 596-596-69-30-02) and **Clement** (Le François;

596-596-54-62-07). As long as you're here, it's worth springing for a really good bottle (the fine rums can be hard to find in the United States). An aged rum, or *rhum vieux*, has been sitting in barrels for 3, 5, or 10 years (or even longer), acquiring an aroma not unlike a fine cognac. The really noteworthy bottles can cost $50 or more and ideally should be enjoyed neat, after a fine meal, or perhaps preprandial, in a ti punch (but please, not in a piña colada or other mixed drink!). The distilleries usually have the best selection of their product, but you'll find a very good selection from all of Martinique's producers at **La Route du Rhum** in the Village Créole shopping complex (Pointe-du-Bout) or **La Case à Rhum**, opposite the Savane (Fort-de-France). Note that most island supermarkets carry a decent selection at cheaper prices.

Yacht Charters

Martinique is one of the major ports for those interested in cruising to St. Lucia and the Grenadines. Most of the charter operators are located in Le Marin (a few are also in Pointe du Bout). If you are interested in multiday rentals, try **Stardust Marine** (Le Marin, 596-596-74-98-17, fax 596-596-74-88-12), **Star Voyage** (Trois-Ilets and Le François, 596-596-66-00-72, fax 596-596-66-02-11), or **The Moorings** (Le Marin, 596-596-74-75-39, fax 596-596-74-76-44; or from the U.S. 800-334-2435). For additional referrals, contact the **Capitainerie of Le Marin** (596-596-74-83-83, or fax 596-596-74-92-02).

Biking

Martinique's excellent road system makes the island a favorite winter training ground for French racers. It's also a popular weekend activity for Martiniquaise. The **Parc Naturel Regional de la Martinique** (9 boulevard Général de Gaulle, Fort-de-France, 596-596-64-42-59) has developed biking itineraries in conjunction with local bike clubs. For rentals, try these outlets: **Locabikes** (Fort-de-France, 596-596-63-33-05), **Sud Loisirs** (Ste-Anne, 596-596-76-81-82), and **Blue Monday** (Diamant, 596-596-76-18-80). If you want to go on mountain bike excursions, contact **VT Tilt** (Trois-Ilets, 596-596-66-01-01); tours cost about $55, including a guide and a meal.

Touring the North

The island's excellent road system invites exploration, and Martinique has a number of worthwhile places to visit on day trips. Some of our favorites include the following.

   St. Pierre. This city, once acclaimed as the Paris of the West Indies, was wiped out by the eruption of Mont Pelée in 1902. The city never recovered its prominence, which was usurped by Fort-de-France. There's a little Pompeii ambiance, and you can easily see the town aboard the Cyparis Express, a one-hour tour aboard a rubber-sole train ($9). Of supreme interest to natural disaster buffs is the **Musée Vulcanologique** (Volcanological Museum, 596-596-78-15-16). Here you'll find photos, melted glass, warped musical instruments from the once-grand city theater, and other lurid paraphernalia. It's open daily from 9 a.m. to 12:30 p.m. and 3 to 5 p.m., and admission is $2. Another small museum focusing on volcanoes of the world is the **Maison des Volcans** (596-596-52-45-45), located higher on the slopes in the town of Le Morne Rouge.

Mt. Pelée. The volcano might have conquered St. Pierre a century ago, but you can occupy its summit today. Three separate trails ascend the 4,584-foot/1,398-meter peak. The most popular is the shortest and steepest, which starts from a point above the village of Le Morne Rouge. The hike takes about four hours round-trip, and on clear days the northernmost peak yields excellent views of Dominica.

Grand' Rivière Trail. The ambitious will also enjoy this six-hour, 13-mile/21-kilometer walk around Martinique's undeveloped north coast. The trail explores both lush rainforest and striking volcanic topography, and starts in Grand' Rivière and ends in Prêcheur. Once there, you can haggle (in French) and hire a fishing boat to bring you back—or arrange to be picked up in Prêcheur. For more info on this and the island's extensive network of marked trails, contact the **Parc Naturel Regional de la Martinique** (9 Boulevard Général de Gaulle, Fort-de-France, 596-596-73-19-30).

Route de la Trace. This is easily one of the Caribbean's most stunning drives. The road leads up the slopes from Fort-de-France suburbs and into the island's greenest, wettest rain forest. Along the way you'll pass by Sacre Coeur, or Martinique's version of the Parisian landmark. The asphalt snakes and winds along the base of the dramatic Pitons du Carbet at the center of the island before crossing a high plateau to the village of Le Morne Rouge. Here the flanks of Mont Pelée soar into the clouds to the north. For your return to the south, you can drive down to St. Pierre on the west coast or take the longer route via the equally scenic east coast. There is another spectacular road between the Route de la Trace and St. Pierre, via Fonds-St. Denis, and although signs advised that this road was blocked halfway down, we used this on our last visit and were able to navigate around the rockfalls without a problem (we wouldn't advise it during inclement weather).

Canyoning. Aventures Tropicales offers half-day trips down the narrow and lush Rivière Case-Navire. The descent involves a rappel over a cliff into the gorge and several plunges over waterfalls, so this isn't a trip for anyone with a fear of heights. However, you will be immersed in a gorgeous rainforest with soaring tree ferns and ancient mahogany trees. Reservations: 596-596-75-24-24; www.aventures-tropicales.com.

Jardin de Balata. Martinique is called "the isle of flowers," and here's where you can revel in more than 1,000 species of plants, including a bamboo forest and dozens of different palm trees. The setting, above Fort-de-France and at the foot of the Pitons du Carbet, is sensational. Open daily from 9 a.m. to 6 p.m.

Anse Caffard Memorial

Located on the point facing Diamant, this is a monument marking where hundreds of slaves drowned when their ship crashed on the rocks in 1830. Although that kind of incident presumably happened often during the terrible slave-trading days, what happened after was unusual: Because slave trading was illegal in France after 1815 (although slaves were still used on Martinique until 1848), the 86 survivors had no legal rights and were subsequently deported to Guyana. The memorial is a somber collection of featureless statues facing Guyana, "in memory of the unknown victims."

Art Galleries

There are a number of art galleries in Fort-de-France that are worth visiting. Of particular interest is the painter Cathérine Théodose's **Villa Métisse** (6 rue Paulo-Rosine, Ravine Vilaine, 596-596-79-61-89). You can find excellent (as opposed to roadside) Haitian art at **Galerie Bleu Vert** (25 rue Victor Hugo, Fort-de-France, 596-596-60-55-34). Also worth visiting in Fort-de-France are **Galerie Art Pluriel** (596-596-63-10-48) and **Galerie Raymond Honorien** (596-596-60-48-77).

The Schoelcher Library (Bibliothèque Schoelcher)

Located on the rue de la Liberté across from the Savane in Fort-de-France, this is a marvelous piece of Romanesque-Byzantine architecture, named after Victor Schoelcher, the Parisian-born deputy who helped facilitate the liberation of Martinique's slaves in 1848. The elaborate structure, first displayed at the 1889 Paris Exposition, now houses the capital's library.

Montserrat

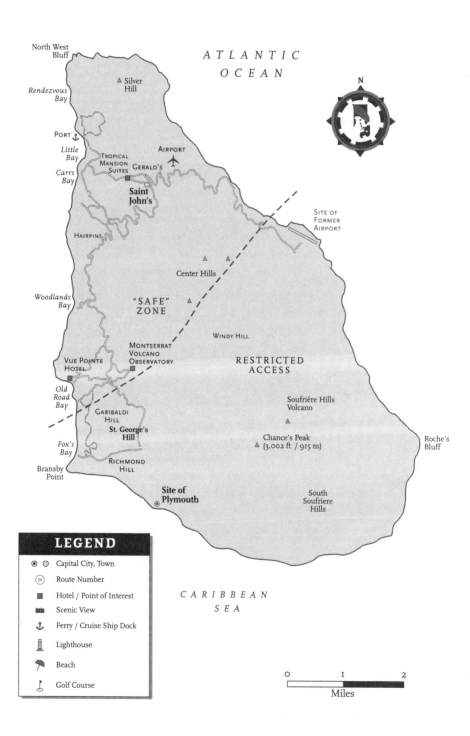

ATLANTIC
OCEAN

N

North West
Bluff

△ Silver
Hill

Rendezvous
Bay

PORT ⚓

Little
Bay

Carrs
Bay

TROPICAL
MANSION   GERALD'S
SUITES ■

AIRPORT ✈

Saint
John's

SITE OF
FORMER
AIRPORT

HAIRPINS

△   △

Center Hills

Woodlands
Bay

"SAFE"
ZONE

△

WINDY HILL

RESTRICTED
ACCESS

MONTSERRAT
VOLCANO
OBSERVATORY ■

VUE POINTE
HOTEL ■

Old
Road
Bay

GARIBALDI
HILL

Soufriére Hills
Volcano

△

Fox's
Bay

St. George's
Hill

Chance's Peak
△ (3,002 ft / 915 m)

Roche's
Bluff

Bransby
Point

RICHMOND
HILL

Site of
Plymouth
◉

South
Soufriere
Hills

LEGEND

◉ ◎ Capital City, Town

(32) Route Number

■ Hotel / Point of Interest

📷 Scenic View

⚓ Ferry / Cruise Ship Dock

🗼 Lighthouse

🏖 Beach

⛳ Golf Course

CARIBBEAN
SEA

0   1   2
Miles

Montserrat

TOURISTO SCALE:

👤👤👤 (3)

Montserrat is one island that has never lived in the fast lane and has been all the better for it. It was known as "the Emerald Isle," for both its lush hillsides and its Irish heritage, and visitors discovered true peace and quiet here—not the fleeting kind of relaxation promised in glossy travel brochures. The people are wonderful, as we discovered when we stepped off the plane on our first visit. The immigration officer was actually welcoming, telling us to enjoy our stay. So was the Customs man. Yikes, are they tripping, or are we? Bracing for the usual cabbie rush as we walked through the doors, we were pleased to find that even the cabbies were courteous. Incredible. It was then that the calm, which seems to be the raison d'être of this island, began to take hold of us.

Of course, Montserrat then is not Montserrat now. In 1995 a fissure opened in the long-dormant **Soufriere Hills** volcano and signaled the start of what would become a multiyear ordeal for this formerly tranquil spot. Although the volcanic eruption was taken seriously from the very beginning by scientists from the United States, England, and Trinidad, it wasn't until 1996 that they recommended that the capital, Plymouth, be evacuated. Many residents resettled to the northern third of the island (which was deemed safe), and thousands more left Montserrat to pursue their lives—temporarily or otherwise—in England or elsewhere in the Caribbean. Inside the crater, a

Montserrat: Key Facts

Location	16°N by 62°W
	27 miles/43 kilometers southwest of Antigua
	1,800 miles/2,898 kilometers southeast of New York
Size	39 square miles/101 square miles (and growing!)
	11 miles/18 kilometers long by 7 miles/11 kilometers wide
Highest point	Chance's Peak (3,002 feet/915 meters; the summit of the volcano's dome has sometimes been as much as 300 feet/91 meters taller since the start of the volcanic eruption).
Population	4,700 at publication (11,000 in 1996)
Language	English
Time	Atlantic Standard Time (1 hour ahead of EST, same as EDT)
Area code	664
Electricity	220 volts AC, 60 cycles; you will need a transformer and an adaptor for U.S.-made appliances.
Currency	The Eastern Caribbean dollar, EC$ (EC$2.68 = US$1)
Driving	On the left; a temporary driving permit is necessary; you'll need to present a valid U.S. or Canadian license and pay $19.
Documents	For U.S., Canadian, and British citizens, proof of nationality with a photo ID is acceptable; all others need a passport; everyone must have an ongoing or a return ticket.
Departure tax	$21
Beer to drink	Red Stripe
Rum to drink	Mount Gay
Music to hear	Dancehall
Tourism info	664-491-2230
	www.visitmontserrat.com

lava dome began to build, eventually growing taller than Chance's Peak, Montserrat's highest point. Soufriere Hills entered a more volatile phase, and scientists urged residents to stay out of the exclusion zone, which included fields of crops on the slopes of the volcano. Then, at midday on June 25, 1997, the dome collapsed and superheated clouds of ash, gas, and rock exploded down the mountain, vaporizing everything in their path (in much the same manner that Mount Pelée destroyed St. Pierre on Martinique in 1902). Nineteen people were killed in the space of a few minutes, and eight villages were severely damaged or destroyed that day. Over the next few months, similar eruptions wiped out Plymouth and other villages, and deposited a delta of volcanic debris on the east coast of the island.

An eruption on Boxing Day (the day after Christmas) 1997 produced a massive nighttime explosion — thought to have been as big as the 1902 outburst of Mt. Pelée. Amazingly, residents were so used to the behavior by now that everyone on the island slept through the blast — everyone but the scientists, that is, who could only witness it on the banks of computer screens displaying seismograph readouts. Although Soufriere Hills entered a period of repose, the island's tourist-dependent economy was decimated. All of Montserrat's hotels and restaurants were either buried in ash or closed. Islanders opened up guesthouses to accommodate the influx of journalists, insurance agents, and emissaries from England (the Duke of York, a.k.a. Prince Andrew, has toured the devastation on at least two occasions). This lasted a little over a year, and then in 1999 the lava dome began growing again. As Howard Fergus sang: "The volcano is boss, man... only one in its class, man."

Soufriere Hills entered another period of relative quiet in 2004, which was followed by a tourism push and the construction of a new airport. However, eventually the familiar cycle of dome growth restarted and resulted in another big collapse in May 2006. Ash clouds rising 55,000 feet shut down Caribbean flights for the day, and mini-tsunamis were reported in Antigua and Guadeloupe. Today, the island's team of resident scientists will predict that the current activity might last months, years, or even decades. Fortunately, most of the action is fairly benign, but the volcano continues to steam, and eruptions of ash occur as the unstable lava dome builds, cools, and collapses, rendering the slopes of the volcano — the southern half of Montserrat — uninhabitable for some time to come. Although the island's population narrowed to less than 2,500 at the height of the crisis, Montserratians and others have been moving back, and the population today is about 4,700 (about half what it was pre-eruption). These islanders are slowly rebuilding the infrastructure in the northern "safe" zone, aided by the new airport that has been built above Little Bay.

The Briefest History

Montserrat was "discovered" by Christopher Columbus on November 11, 1493, during his second voyage to the New World. Ciboney, Arawak, and Carib Indians had already lived on the island for centuries. It is named after a Spanish abbey where Loyola received his inspiration for future fame. A few centuries after Columbus's find, the British settled it as a unique Irish-Catholic colony in the Caribbean (there are many Irish surnames here, and St. Patty's Day is a big deal). The French wrestled with the Brits over ownership in the ensuing centuries until it was clearly established as a British colony in 1783 by the Treaty of Paris. Slavery ended in 1834. The last sugar mill shut down in the 1960s, and tourism slowly bubbled to the forefront as the economic turbine.

Hurricane Hugo hit the island in 1989 with incredible fury, but within a few years the island's infrastructure had staged a rebound. However, the eruption of Soufriere Hills has been a more maleficent force to contend with, as much for the difficult questions it leaves about Montserrat's economic future as for its widespread devastation. The old airport on the east side of the island and the capital on the west were inundated by pyroclastic flows, and most businesses and government offices have moved north, to Salem, St. Peter's, and St. John's, areas which scientists say are safe for habitation. Previously undeveloped Little Bay now serves as the island's official port of entry for sea arrivals and Montserrat's capital. Also, an $18.5 million new airport opened on the hillside above in 2005, linking the island to Antigua and St. Martin/ St. Maarten once again. European aid grant has provided funds to promote tourism on the island.

Getting There

Flights to Montserrat's original airport ended in 1997, not long before an ash flow swept over the runway and engulfed the terminal in flames. An audacious new airport was completed in 2005 at Gerald's Bottom, above Little Bay. It has a 2,000-foot runway that bisects a ridge. WinAir offers several flights daily from Antigua and St. Maarten.

The ferry system that connected Montserrat with Antigua was discontinued when the new airport debuted.

Getting Around

There are quite a few car- and jeep-rental agencies on the island, most with a small fleet of fewer than a dozen vehicles. Check at the airport on arrival. You'll need to obtain a local driver's license ($19). Taxis are plentiful and are available at the airport or through your hotel. During the day, you can also get around using the local minibus service, which is unscheduled but covers the main roads; fares are just a dollar or two.

Focus on Montserrat: Life under the Volcano

A trip to Montserrat is an excursion into Mother Nature's kitchen. As the most significant volcanic eruption in the region for more than a century, the activity at Soufriere Hills has provided scientists with a greater understanding of the geologic forces at work in the Caribbean. Visiting Montserrat is not going to be everyone's cup of tea, and we can offer only a skeleton outline today since things on the island are still evolving. More than half of the island is off-limits due to the eruption, although some of this area is open for daytime visitation if the volcano is quiet. There are hundreds of undamaged homes and businesses located on the fringes of the exclusion zone. England has been cautious about doling out assistance, and the mother country has been roundly criticized for not providing proper housing for islanders during the crisis. Some of the activities that were formerly available to tourists are not (notably the golf course). If you visited Montserrat pre-1996, don't look for Galways Soufriere, the Great Alps Falls, the trek through the Bamboo Forest —these are no more. A few activities, like hiking and diving, continue unabated. In fact, the diving is reportedly quite good, having benefited from the minimized human interference over the last decade.

What you will also find is the wonderful Montserratians, as before; those who have stayed behind have a spirit and determination that is admirable. They have provided an invaluable link to Montserrat's history and culture for generations to come. There are a few decent black-sand beaches (Woodlands is the nicest), and a pretty gold-sand cove, Rendezvous Bay, which is reached only by a 30-minute trail over a bluff or via a short boat ride from Little Bay. The tourist board has prepared a list of trails that are safe for hikers.

The main thing to see is the volcano, and on clear days, excellent views can be had from several vantage points. At this writing, the closest view is from the top of **St. George's Hill**, which is reached by a rutted road lined with abandoned houses and mango trees. When you crest the hill, the summit of the volcano looms before you less than 2 miles away, and steam and gas exhale from the rim; broad frozen rivers of ash sweep down the slopes into Plymouth. It's a breathtaking sight, but it's open only when the volcano is relatively quiet, and not after dusk. To reach St. George's, take the winding west coast road south to the Belham Valley, where you'll cross the former golf course (now inundated with mud and ash). The road continues to the village of Cork Hill—St. George's Hill is right in front of you, with a road winding up to the summit. Another excellent position is on the east coast, on the road to the old airport. From the last ridge (before the road drops down to the airstrip), you get an excellent view of the huge expanse of pyroclastic flows that have reached the sea on this side of the island. Caution: Do not walk over these innocent-looking fields of ash without a guide. It is almost impossible to tell how deep the flow is at any given point, and where the ash is more than a few feet thick, there's a good chance the flow is still cooling inside—and might be for years. (Some of the ash deposits are well over 100 feet deep!) The danger here is either sinking into quicksand-like ash or being vaporized in lava—not our idea of a fun vacation. Plan to stop by the **Montserrat Volcano Observatory** (www.mvo.ms), which usually has scientists on hand who can help explain the various stages of activity so far and their prognosis for the future. In fact, the MVO also has a fabulous view, from a distance of about 3 miles.

You can tour Plymouth, but as of this writing, one can do it only with a police escort. You can arrange this through the tourist board (or the hotels): The police department asks for 48 hours' notice and charges $56 per person for a police escort. Needless to say, walking through this contemporary Pompeii is fascinating.

It's possible to see most of the island on a day trip from Antigua or St.

Maarten/St. Martin—try to come on a clear day for the best volcano views. You can easily arrange for a driver once you arrive; just ask around at the airport. The going rate for a full-day tour is $100.

Where to Stay

In addition to the two hotels, there are a number of guesthouses available; check the tourist board Web site for details: www.visitmontserrat.com. You can also rent an attractive villa for considerably less than you'll pay on most Caribbean islands—a three-bedroom house with pool, housekeeper, and more rents for under $2,000 per week in high season and about 30 percent less in low season. There are several agencies on the island; one we have worked with and like is **Tradewinds Real Estate** (664-491-2004; www.tradewindsmontserrat.com).

Vue Pointe Hotel, P.O. Box 65, Salem, Montserrat, WI. ⓒ 664-491-5210, ⓦ 664-491-4813, ⌨ www.vuepointe.com, vuepointe@candw.ms

$ Not So Cheap ⓨ **EP** ⓒⓒ 22 rooms

Located on a sunny western point at Old Road Bay, this inn sits on a 5-acre bluff above a black-sand beach. The beach, in fact, is much larger now due to the ash flows that swept down the Belham Valley and buried the hotel's former golf course. If this sounds like a dire setting, it's not, and the cottage-style Vue Pointe—which closed twice due to the proximity of the eruption—is back open for its fans (the area was deemed safe by the Montserrat Volcano Observatory). It's wonderfully managed by Cedric and Carol Osborne (he helped his father build it in 1961), and the hotel's rooms are arranged in hexagonal cottages sprinkled on the hillside. Each unit has TV and phone and a small seating area with rattan furnishings; some have kitchenettes. There are two tennis courts, a gift shop, and a beach bar, and the pool offers resplendent views of the steaming volcano.

Also on the Vue Pointe premises now is the **Sea Wolf Diving School** (664-496-7807; www.seawolfdivingschool.com), which offers diving and snorkeling trips around the island.

Tropical Mansion Suites, P.O. Box 404. Sweeney's, Montserrat, WI. ⓒ 664-491-8767, ⓦ 664-491-8275, ⌨ www.tropicalmansion.com, hotel@candw.com

$ Not So Cheap ⓨ **CP** ⓒⓒ 18 rooms

The hotel was the first to open post-eruption and was the source of enormous local pride. It has oversize apartment-style rooms, each with cable TV, ceiling fans, and telephone, and a few feature kitchenettes. There is a restaurant and small pool, but you're about a 15-minute drive from the volcano. Although the location is conveniently close to the airport (about a half mile away), and there are nice views, this area of Montserrat was quickly and sloppily developed in the first bout of construction after the eruption started. There are often good discounts for singles.

Where to Eat

In addition to restaurants at the two hotels, there are a surprising number of choices on Montserrat. Be sure to sample the national dishes, such as goat water, which is a tasty stew, and "mountain chicken" (a.k.a. frog's legs).

$ **The Attic**, 664-491-2008

Located in Ovelston, this is still a good choice for lunch, with roti (like a Trinidadian burrito), quesadillas, and fresh local juices.

$$ **Gourmet Garden**, 664-491-7859

It reopened in 2001 and continues to be a good spot for lunch (salads and sandwiches) and dinner (garlic shrimp or the beef stroganoff).

$$ **Jumpin' Jack's**, 664-491-5645

This is a lively expat hangout for lunch on the beach below the Vue Pointe — come here for grilled fish, burgers, and chicken and mushroom pie. It's also open for dinner, but only on Friday.

$ **Morgan's Spotlight Bar**, 664-491-5419

Mrs. Morgan continues to serve her renowned goat water on weekends in St. John's.

$$$ **Ziggy's**, 664-491-8282

A beacon of civilization among the turmoil of the last few years, Ziggy's is now located in Woodlands. Lobster quadrille, jerk pork, and a divine chocolate sludge dessert are on the menu. Reservations are required.

There are others worth checking out, but the restaurant scene is evolving as the volcano settles into a more predictable pattern, so new choices will have opened by the time you visit; the tourist board will have the latest.

Puerto Rico

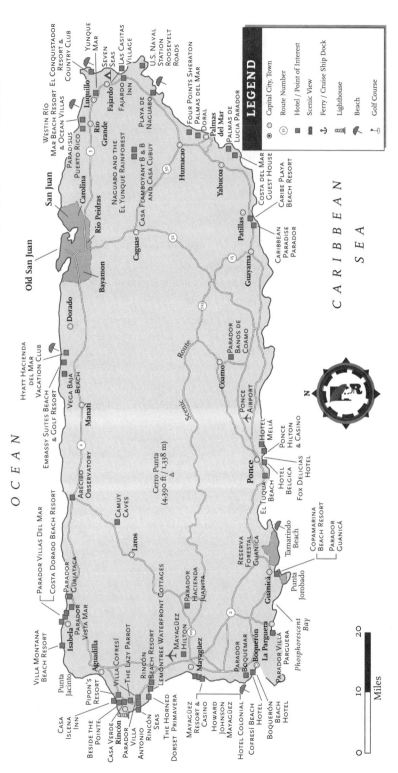

LEGEND

- ◉ Capital City, Town
- ⑭ Route Number
- ■ Hotel / Point of Interest
- ♦ Scenic View
- ♪ Ferry / Cruise Ship Dock
- ♨ Lighthouse
- 🏖 Beach
- ⛳ Golf Course

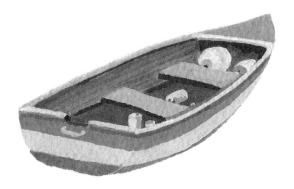

Puerto Rico

TOURISTO SCALE

🐷🐷🐷🐷🐷🐷🐷🐷🐷 (9)

We have now come to expect it. Just after we hear the screech of the jet's wheels touching down at San Juan's Luis Muñoz Marín International Airport, there is a burst of applause. For the most part, the applause does not come from the tourists, but from the Puerto Ricans. Their trip has ended safely and they are happy to be home. This ritual always causes us to chuckle; it's so genuine that even our jaded cynicism melts away. And hell, we're also pleased to be here 'cuz we just *love* Puerto Rico. Why? Well, not just because this is a beautiful and diverse island, but because of the people. Puerto Ricans, also called Boriquas (the Taíno or Indian name), are very happy, warm people who appear to always be up and wanting to have a good time. *Party* seems to be their collective middle name.

Puerto Rico is a big island, roughly the size of Connecticut. It is home to more than 3.9 million people, a major metropolis with a diverse economy, mountains, a rainforest, miles of beautiful beaches, the hip swaying beat of salsa, and the "she bang" hip thrusts of Ricky Martin. Because Puerto Rico is a commonwealth of the United States, the American influence is very pervasive—from every conceivable fast-food and convenience chain (there are more than 50 Burger Kings on the island) to the huge pharmaceutical and high-tech companies. This is unfortunate but inevitable. The culture is still Latino and the language is still Spanish, but most Puerto Ricans speak English

Puerto Rico: Key Facts

Location	18°N by 65°W
	70 miles east of Hispaniola (Dominican Republic)
	1,040 miles southeast of Miami
	1,662 miles southeast of New York
Size	3,423 square miles
	110 miles long by 35 miles wide
Highest point	Cerro de Punta (4,390 feet)
Population	3.95 million
Language	Spanish; English is officially the second language and is widely spoken in San Juan.
Time	Atlantic Standard Time (1 hour ahead of EST, same as EDT)
Area code	787 (must be dialed before all local numbers as well)
Electricity	110 volts AC, same as U.S. and Canada
Currency	The U.S. dollar
Driving	On the right
Documents	None for Americans and no Customs hassles, either; Canadians need proof of nationality (birth certificate, certificate of citizenship) or a passport (recommended); Brits need a passport. (A visa is required for some British citizens. Check with the U.S. Consulate or your travel agent.)
Departure tax	None
Beer to drink	Medalla
Rum to drink	Don Q or Bacardi
Music to hear	Salsa or *reggaetón*!
Tourism info	787-721-2400 or 800-223-6530, www.prtourism.com, www.puertoricowow.com or www.gotopuertorico.com

or at least understand it to a degree. Former Governor Pedro Roselló reinstated the policy that Puerto Rico has two official languages — Spanish and English — to encourage bilingualism among the populace and inch the island toward statehood. More often than not, however, you'll hear and marvel at the hybrid, commonly known as Spanglish.

Most visitors who come to Puerto Rico see only San Juan (or its airport). San Juan is a city of about 450,000 residents, or Sanjuaneros, as the locals are called. There are more than 1.3 million inhabitants, when you include the surrounding metropolitan area. San Juan is where most of the big hotels and casinos are located. It is also the second largest cruise ship port after Miami. The combination ensures lots of tourists, especially in places like Old San Juan and Isla Verde. But San Juan is a big city, and with it comes the best nightlife (both straight and gay) in the Caribbean. If you want great restaurants, big and lively casinos (without the Las Vegas tackiness), pulsating nightclubs, and some of the hottest men and women you'll ever mix with — look no farther for your next vacation spot. If you're single, you're crazy not to go here.

There is much more to Puerto Rico than the throbbing beat of San Juan, however. There are beautiful mountains and lush valleys, and small seaside towns with lots of character, like Boquerón and Guánica. There is Puerto Rico's second city, Ponce, which has undergone a restoration similar to Old San Juan. There is some of the best golf in the Caribbean at the Dorado Beach area. There are the extraordinary Camuy Caves — huge natural caverns several hundred feet in the earth. There is great windsurfing off Rincón on the west coast. There are the unspoiled out-islands of Culebra and Vieques (detailed in their own chapters). There is the Caribbean National Forest, El Yunque, which is an easily accessed rainforest. There are deserted beaches on all sides of the island. Even so, you're never more than a two-hour drive from San Juan or very far from an ATM and a Big Gulp from 7-Eleven.

Puerto Rico gets all kinds of tourists and travelers. There are the convention and tour groups who come for a purpose as well as to play in the big casinos and on the beach. There is that element of middle America that always seems to find its way here via the cruise ships that flood Old San Juan. There are lots of European tourists, especially Germans, and rich South Americans up on shopping sprees. Of course, most of the visitors here are American. Then there are the independent travelers who dive into the culture and countryside in search of the real Puerto Rico, and the long-weekenders down for a dose of sun and fun because San Juan is so easy (and cheap) to reach.

The Briefest History

Puerto Rico was first settled by Taíno Amerindians who ventured up the chain of the West Indies from the Amazon and South America. They had been on the island for thousands of years when Columbus landed here on his second voyage, in 1493. He discovered about 60,000 Taíno Amerindians, living off the land and sea, who had named the island Boriquen. Spain claimed the island, and Columbus called it San Juan. With Columbus was Juan Ponce de León, Mr. Fountain of Youth himself, who sensed gold in "them-thar hills" and received permission to colonize the island. It was Ponce de Léon who, in 1508, renamed this "rich port" Puerto Rico upon becoming governor of its first Spanish settlement at Caparra. That site became disease-ridden, so in 1521 the settlement was moved to what is now Old San Juan. It became a fortress with El Morro fort at its entrance.

The Spanish never lost control of Puerto Rico for more than 400 years, despite repeated attempts by the British, French, and Dutch to dislodge them. It wasn't until the Spanish-American War in 1898, when Teddy Roosevelt led the charge up that hill in Havana shouting "Remember the Maine" and defeated the Spanish, that control ceded to another power: the United States. In 1917 Puerto Ricans became full-fledged U.S. citizens, and in 1952 Puerto Rico became a commonwealth of the United States.

It remains so today. There is an ongoing drive for statehood, which is being spearheaded by the current governor. The most recent plebiscite was to keep the status quo. Under commonwealth status, Puerto Ricans have a U.S. passport and can live anywhere in the United States. They have local representation in a commonwealth government and pay no federal income tax as residents of Puerto Rico (however, they do pay Puerto Rican government income taxes). The drawback to commonwealth status is that Puerto Ricans have no representation in Congress (nor can they vote for president). However, they do have a nonvoting Interests Section in Congress. No federal taxes and no sales tax—what a deal. We're moving to Puerto Rico!

Getting There

Of all the Caribbean islands, Puerto Rico is the easiest to reach. San Juan has a huge international airport (Luis Muñoz Marín), which is the hub of American Airlines' Caribbean operation, has more than 30 airlines serving it, and receives more than 400 nonstops weekly from the United States. Most major eastern and southern cities have nonstop service to San Juan on American, Jet Blue, Continental, Delta, Northwest, United, US Airways, and American Trans Air. From Canada, connections can be made on several U.S. carriers from Montreal and Toronto; there is service on Canadian Airlines. From Europe, British Airways, Ibéria, and Air France all have nonstop service. American Eagle and LIAT fly to neighboring islands.

Getting Around

With just about every major rental-car player here offering great weekly (and daily) rates, and with so much to see, it makes perfect sense to rent a car. Avis (800-331-1084 or 787-253-5963), Budget (800-527-0700 or 787-791-2311), Hertz (800-654-3131), National (800-227-3876), and Thrifty (253-2680) are all here. We found the best rates with Thrifty—plus, for those headed to Vieques or Culebra, Thrifty is the only major company with a drop-off office in Fajardo. In addition, several local companies might offer you a better rate; try Charlie Car Rental (787-728-2418) and L&M Car Rental (800-666-0807 or 787-791-1160). Check with your credit card company to see what your coverage includes before you rent.

The Puerto Rican Tourism Company has instituted a welcome and easy-to-use taxi system at the airport and in the major tourist areas. Outside the baggage claim, there is a taxi stand with several representatives of the P.R.T.C. (they have the "Puerto Rico Does It Better" buttons on as well as IDs). The cabs are painted white, with "Taxi Touristicos" and the official logo on the front doors. Fixed rates apply to the major tourist zones. Longer trips are metered.

A cab ride from the airport to Isla Verde is $10, to the Condado area is $14, and to Old San Juan is $16 (not including tip).

Within San Juan, there is a good bus system run by the Metropolitan Bus Authority, 787-250-6064. The buses (called guaguas) pick up passengers at upright yellow post stops (called paradas), and the fare is 25¢ or 50¢.

Públicos (public cars) are cars or minivans that provide low-cost transportation to the main towns in Puerto Rico. Their rates are set by the Public Service Commission. For information call 787-756-1919.

Some words about driving in Puerto Rico: Puerto Rican drivers are pretty crazy behind the wheel, so be alert. On the freeways (called *autopistas*), particularly Route 52 from San Juan to Ponce, the left lane is often much smoother because trucks don't drive on it. Actually, the left lane often seems to be the de facto travel lane, and the right lane the passing lane. However, cars pass on both left and right, depending on what is open. In addition, don't be confused when you see highway mileage signs in kilometers and speed signs in miles. Finally, Puerto Rico is the land of more than a million cars — too many for the current infrastructure. It often seems that everyone who owns a car here is on the road at the same time, especially in the cities. Due to the effects of traffic lights on multilane roads, there are often traffic jams on secondary roads. East of San Juan, on Route 3, traffic can be heavy all the way to Fajardo. Traffic on roads around Ponce (Routes 1 and 2) can also jam up, although a bypass road has alleviated that problem a bit. Of course, all major roads in and around San Juan will be very busy during rush hours, so plan accordingly. Be sure to ask your rental car company for road sign translations (most are in Spanish), or bring your own Spanish-English dictionary.

Focus on Puerto Rico: San Juan — The Long Weekend Destination

Where to go for a long or extended weekend in the sun? South Beach, in Miami? Forget it! That place is so 10 years ago. The rest of Florida? Nah, it's just not very exotic or exciting. Havana is not yet easily accessible and is technically off-limits to Americans; a quick jaunt there is neither easy nor convenient. Where, then, does one go for a quick tropical getaway? Well, we think it's a no-brainer. There aren't many other choices where the weather is guaranteed hot, the destination is easy to reach for weekends or longer, and there are great choices of restaurants and nightlife. Now the in-the-know are heading to San Juan.

What used to be San Juan's glittering and main tourist destination — the **Condado** area — is still a tad seedy but is showing signs of a comeback. Anchored by the San Juan Marriott (the old Dupont Plaza), the Condado resembles a cross between Waikiki and Miami Beach. There are some art deco buildings, lots of high-rises, many hotel rooms, and a nice beach here. The water is clean and there is surf, so it's fun; and then there are the restaurants

Old San Juan

San Juan

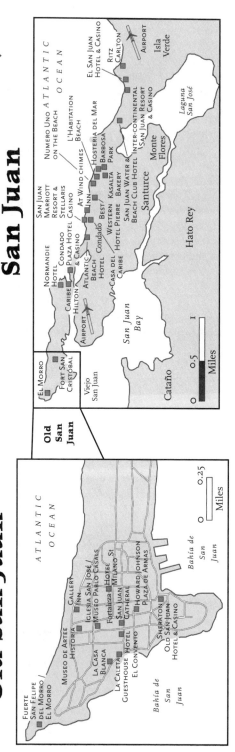

and nightlife. **Old San Juan**, home of some of the Caribbean's most valuable Spanish colonial architecture, has also experienced a boom, primarily due to the thriving cruise-ship industry. Though not directly on the beach (but on a rocky point at the entrance to the harbor), this pretty part of the city has some very cool places to stay. There is Ocean Park, east of the Condado, with the city's best beach and a string of charming and cheap guesthouses. At the eastern end of the city and very near the airport is Isla Verde, where most of San Juan's big and luxury properties are located.

San Juan is reasonably priced (especially with package deals) and now on par with South Beach (the latter's prices have escalated dramatically in the last few years). Although you can go to Miami and taste its nightlife, restaurants, and beaches, here you get all that *and* you're in the tropics. You won't experience a chilling winter cold front in Puerto Rico. The weather is pretty much the same year-round (as in Florida, the summer has more rain), and the summer in San Juan is actually much cooler than in Florida because of the trade winds. Another bonus is that you can drive an hour out of San Juan and be in the mountains, or two hours and be in a beautiful Caribbean beach town. In Miami, where do you go for diversion — Ocala? Finally, Puerto Rico is 100 percent Latin, not semi-Latin like Miami.

Besides nightlife and beaches, San Juan also has lots of historical sights to see, almost all of them in Old San Juan. You could easily spend at least a half day exploring or just hanging out in this beautifully restored part of the city. Our favorite site here is the ⊛ **Castillo de San Felipe del Morro**, 501 Calle Norzagaray, 787-729-6754, which is one of the best-preserved Spanish forts in the New World. Located at the mouth of the bay, this six-level fort was the main line of defense for the Spanish. It's open from 9 a.m. until 5 p.m.

Not to be missed are **Fuerte San Felipe del Morro (El Morro)**, Calle del Morro, 787-729-6960, open daily from 9 a.m. to 5 p.m., English tours at 10 a.m. and 3 p.m., admission $3, children under 12 go free; **Casa Blanca**, 787-724-4102, open from 9 a.m. to noon and from 1 to 4:30 p.m., closed Monday, admission $2 for adults, $1 for seniors; **Catedral de San Juan**, 787-722-0861, open daily from 8 a.m. to 4 p.m. (it houses the remains of Ponce de León); **Iglesia San José**, 787-725-7501, open daily from 8:30 a.m. to 4 p.m. and for Sunday Mass at noon; **Museo Pablo Casals**, 787-723-9185, open Tuesday through Saturday from 9:30 a.m. to 5:30 p.m., admission $1; **Museo de Arte e Historia de San Juan**, 787-724-1875, open Tuesday through Sunday from 10. a.m. to 4 p.m., free admission; **Plaza de Armas** (the main square of Old San Juan, where San Juan's city hall has been located since 1789); and **La Fortaleza** (which has been the governor's mansion since 1540), 787-721-7000, open Monday through Friday (except holidays) from 9 a.m. to 4 p.m., with tours in English on the hour.

There's a lot more to see — the above are just highlights. Stop in at **La Casita**, 787-722-1709, open Saturday through Wednesday from 9 a.m. to 8 p.m., and Thursday and Friday until 5:30 p.m. Located on the Plaza de la Dársena by the cruise-ship docks, it's operated by the Puerto Rican Tourism Company and has a wealth of information, walking tours, and maps available.

SAN JUAN

Where to Stay

¡Caramba! There are so many hotels, inns, resorts, guesthouses, and *paradores* in Puerto Rico that the choices are staggering. However, after doing some weeding and sifting, which is our job, here are some suggestions. Most of the accommodations are in San Juan, but there are certainly great alternatives, like Dorado, Rincón, Guánica, and Boquerón.

The Puerto Rico Tourism Company operates Paradores Puertorriqueños, a grouping of small hotels and inns scattered about the island, often in great locations. Don't expect cute little Vermont-style B&Bs or inns. The *paradores* are simple, motelish accommodations that are well under $100 a night and clean. Some are in the mountains, some are on or near a beach, but they all provide an inexpensive and comfy place to hang your hat while you explore the island. All have basic amenities, like air-conditioning, TV, and phones, and many have pools. For a complete listing, visit www.gotopuertorico.com or call 800-866-7827 or 787-721-2400 (in San Juan).

There are four different parts of San Juan in which you can stay. The primary area is Isla Verde, a newer big-hotel strip near the airport. This is where most of the large hotels are located. We do not recommend staying in Isla Verde if the roar of jets landing and taking off will bother you (it is especially loud once you're east of El San Juan Hotel). Another major area is the more centrally located Condado, once the primary place for hotels and experiencing a renaissance of sorts. Between the Condado and Isla Verde is Ocean Park. This is one of our personal favorites; it's a residential neighborhood of charming two-story homes and some big old stucco houses on the beach. The beach itself is the best in the city (and a pretty beach in its own right). The accommodations here are guesthouses, which are casual, relaxed, beachy, and cheap. We like this combination. The last area is Old San Juan, which is full of colonial architecture and character, although it is inconvenient to nightlife and the beach (everything is a cab ride away), and during the day the cruise ship–tourbus circuit swarms the area. Still, it's unique, and the two places we recommend there, El Convento and the Gallery Inn, are superb.

With all that in mind, here are our favorites.

Condado

San Juan Marriott Resort & Stellaris Casino, 1309 Ashford Avenue, San Juan, PR. © 800-464-5005 or 787-722-7000, ✆ 787-722-6800, 🖥 www.marriott.com

🛈 **Ridiculous** and up ⓘ EP ⒸⒸ 525 rooms, 17 suites

For years, this has been our favorite place to stay in the Condado, and now that the Marriott has poured another $16 million into a massive renovation project, this hotel is leagues above the competition. The rooms have been revamped in keeping with the "Marriott room" template, with new plumbing, plasma TVs, and plush bedding. The restaurants and lobby have been revamped as well, and sparkle with glamour. As a matter of fact, we now prefer the Marriott to all the big hotels in San Juan. Its location is perfect, the beach in front is wide and spacious, the pool area is comfortable and private, the staff is friendly and helpful, and the lobby bar is a magnet for good musical talent and Sanjuaneros out for a dressy good time. Best of all, the size of the hotel doesn't overwhelm, and travel time from pool to room is less than five minutes — a major convenience. We also appreciate the fact that the Marriott was key in the renaissance of this part of the Condado, renovating the old Dupont Plaza (closed in 1987 after a tragic fire), putting millions into the 21-story building and compact grounds, and reopening in 1995.

The rooms are comfortable and tasteful, with details like two-line speaker phones, data ports, voicemail, safe, and even an iron and ironing board. We have our own spiritual beliefs and guide, so we find the replacement of the standard Gideon's Bible in the bedside table with that of the Church of Latter-Day Saints (Marriott is based in Utah) to be a bit pushy. However, our bed was firm, and the air-conditioning worked well. The baths are a tad small, but the hotel was built in the days when bathrooms weren't meant to be lounges. All rooms have a lanai. If you get an oceanfront room, the sound of the surf will fill your room, even up to the 20th floor. We like the 24-hour room service, too. After a night on the town, we need something to absorb the alcohol.

Because the Marriott is centrally located, you can walk almost everywhere (except Old San Juan). Even the best nightclubs are an easy walk or cab ride (recommended) away. The resort has a spa, an excellent small gym, two lighted tennis courts, and the Stellaris Casino (which is fortunately located to the side of the lobby and thus not too intrusive). There are a few restaurants here as well, the best being the Italian Tuscany. Late-night diners (and hungry gamblers) will enjoy the Wan Chai Noodle Bar inside the casino. Look for corporate rates and package deals — they can reduce the rates by 30 percent or more.

Note that in the summer and fall of 2006, the Marriott will be undergoing a $35 million renovation of the Tower Wing. During this renovation, guests will be able to stay in the poolside cabana rooms without construction interference. Construction should be finished by the time you read this.

At Wind Chimes Inn, 1750 McLeary Avenue, Condado, PR. © 800-946-3244 or 787-727-4153, ✆ 787-728-0671, 🖳 www.atwindchimesinn.com, reservations@atwindchimesinn.com

💲 **Not So Cheap** ⑪ **BP** Ⓒ 22 rooms

This quaint inn, set in a charming well-preserved Spanish villa that dates back to the Roaring '20s, is the perfect place for anyone seeking solace from the row of high-rise hotels here in the Condado. Just walking through the white arch that separates this tranquil inn from the busy San Juan streets, we felt right at home. Although we have never had a home like this, the phrase seems to work here, as a laid-back air pervades. After all, how hectic can life be in a place named after its wind chimes? The old house retains its colonial feel, embellished by the colorful artwork of the owner's mother, along with period pieces throughout. The different wings have ceramic tile sundecks and Spanish-style patios shaded by bougainvillea and palm trees. Although it's been open for more than 20 years, recent improvements have lifted the Wind Chimes to a new level of comfort. The quaint pool, replete with Jacuzzi-bay, provides the perfect cool-off spot for sun lovers. The brand-new tiki boat bar is a great place to check out the murals, enjoy a tropical drink, and dream of the open seas. Also, being just a block from the beach, guests are within range of the Condado's fine sands. The rooms are tastefully decorated with vibrant colors, terra-cotta floors, cable TV, a/c, and a fan. The junior suites, which include balconies and kitchenettes, are especially comfortable. After our enjoyable stay in this picturesque inn, we realized that the Wind Chimes is San Juan's ideal urban oasis.

Caribe Hilton, P.O. Box 9021872, Calle Los Rosales, San Gerónimo Grounds, San Juan, PR. 📞 800-468-8585 or 787-721-0303, 🖂 787-725-8849, 🖳 www.hiltoncaribbean.com/sanjuan

💲 **Wicked Pricey** and up 🍴 **EP** CC 645 rooms

Opened in 1949, the Caribe Hilton is an institution on the island and a focal point of activity in the city. Business, government, and cultural meetings and events happen here regularly. The hotel was extensively renovated in 1999, with a total redesign of the lobby and public areas, a new swimming complex, and a huge health club. Sitting in the breezy lobby of the hotel, you will see people from all walks of life and from everywhere—always a hubbub of activity. The hotel is the biggest in San Juan and a huge property, for being in the midst of a city. Nestled on 17 acres on the other end of the Condado Bridge in an area called Puerto de Tierra, it consists of two multistory buildings and a tower, all of which house 645 rooms and suites (it's a big hotel). There are gardens with fish ponds, a new pool area centering the airy Terrace Bar (where the piña colada was invented in 1957), and the beach, which is man-made but still attractive and protected by a lagoon.

On the grounds are three lighted tennis courts and a new health club and spa. The gym is the largest we've seen at a hotel, period. The size of a school gymnasium, it features lots of free weights, machines, treadmills, and a stadium ceiling. The spa with sauna and Jacuzzi costs extra. There is also a small snack bar. Water sports can be arranged by the hotel. The recently redone rooms are a mix of pastel and dark green, with wall-to-wall carpeting and marble baths. Most rooms have lanais and all the amenities you would expect from a major international hotel. There are five restaurants, two bars, and a newly renovated casino. We love the fact that the hotel often has great Latino bands at the Oasis Bar, which has always been well attended by dressed-up locals. Also available is the Executive Business Center, which is free for use by hotel guests. For a fee, it will also provide secretarial and translation services, fax and photocopy service, the use of PCs with high-speed Internet, and binding. Check for corporate rates or package deals.

Condado Plaza Hotel & Casino, P.O. Box 1270, 999 Ashford Avenue, San Juan, PR. Ⓒ 800-468-8588 or 797-721-1000, 🖂 787-722-7955, 🖥 www.condadoplaza.com

⑤ Wicked Pricey ⑨ **EP** Ⓒ 575 rooms

The Condado Plaza is another large hotel and is on the other side of the bridge from the Caribe Hilton. Although it doesn't have an impressive lobby, it does have a fairly airy manageable casino with windows, so you know when the sun is coming up and when it's time for bed. The best thing about the hotel is the spacious and fun pool area (there are three declared pools — one is salt water). The hotel is on a small, calm public beach, anchoring one end of the bridge that spans the lagoon. Condado spent $40 million for a much-needed refurbishing in 1998. The rooms are attractive and comfortably furnished and have all the standard amenities, including 24-hour room service and an iron and ironing board. The hotel consists of two buildings connected by a bridge over the road (we prefer the oceanside one). There are six very different restaurants as well as the La Fiesta Lounge, which has live Latin bands (we like that). We like Max's Grill, a 24-hour spot with great steaks and pizza. Keep an eye out for the new restaurant (being built at press time) overlooking the lagoon. There are two lighted tennis courts, a water sports complex offering kayaks and windsurfing (extra charge), and a fitness center with sauna and steam (extra charge). Look for package deals.

Normandie Hotel, P.O. Box 50059, Riviera Avenue at the New Millennium Park, San Juan, PR. Ⓒ 877-987-2929 or 787-729-2929, 🖂 787-729-3083, 🖥 www.normandiepr.com

⑤ Very Pricey ⑨ **EP** Ⓒ 177 rooms

The stylish Normandie was severely damaged by 1998's Hurricane Georges and reopened in January 2000. The hotel recently completed an $8 million renovation that included 7,000 square feet of meeting space, wireless access throughout the property, a couple of

800-gallon fish tanks that adorn the lobby, a spa, two restaurants, and a lounge.

Located next to the Caribe Hilton complex and on a slice of beach, this is San Juan's only real art deco hotel. It looks like it's right out of South Beach. Architecturally, it's very interesting on the outside. The new lobby is on the small side, giving the hotel the feeling of being a small inn. The décor, though warm, isn't carried out throughout the hotel. There is a large atrium inside with the usual glass elevator and a restaurant and the sleek N Bar. But the place screams for a decorator and some foliage. The redecorated rooms are more a melange than art deco. We want to warm this place up. The pool is small, missing landscaping (you must walk from the hotel across the asphalt driveway to reach it — a missed opportunity). The management says the pool is slated to be renovated. The Jacuzzi, however, is no longer open. There is a small beach, but seriously, folks, if you want art deco, go to South Beach.

Best Western Hotel Pierre, 105 Avenida de Diego, Santurce, San Juan, PR. ✆ 800-528-1234 or 787-721-1200, ✎ 787-721-3118, 🖥 www.bestwestern.com

🛍 **Pricey** and up 🍽 **CP** CC 184 rooms

Although it's not anywhere close to the beach (it's a 10-minute walk), the Hotel Pierre is a very attractive property and an excellent value for a full-service hotel in the Condado area. It's very popular with the business set, which is always a good sign. The lobby features marble floors and plenty of places to sit, chat on your cell phone, and plan your day or evening. There's even a small gym with sauna. The hallways have attractive dropped ceilings of wooden slats, and all the rooms have new bathrooms, refrigerators, and microwave ovens. All rooms have a/c, phones, and cable TV. There are three restaurants, a bar, and a pool on the grounds. Look for packages or corporate rates.

Atlantic Beach Hotel, 1 Calle Vendig, Condado, San Juan, PR. ✆ 787-721-6900, ✎ 787-721-6917, 🖥 www.atlanticbeachhotel.com, reservations@atlanticbeachhotel.net

🛍 **Not So Cheap** 🍽 **EP** CC 36 rooms

This is the Condado's gay hotel and the site of a daily happy hour (4 to 6 p.m.) that is popular with both tourists and locals. This place needs not only a face-lift but some lipo and major tucking, too. To quote the late great Bette Davis, "What a dump!" If you want to stay in a gay-friendly environment, stay at one of the guesthouses in Ocean Park (see below). The bar, however, is definitely fun for happy hour, especially on Sunday. There is a restaurant adjoining the bar. Given the orientation of the hotel's guests, the beach in front is Condado's gay beach (the hotel provides chaises).

Casa del Caribe, 57 Caribe Street, Condado, San Juan, PR. ℂ 877-722-7139
or 787-722-7139, ✎ 787-728-2575, 💻 www.casadelcaribe.net,
reservations@casadelcaribe.net

💲 **Cheap** 🍴 **CP** CC 13 rooms

The title "tropical bed and breakfast" might be a bit of a stretch — the
conditions are far from tropical, and the breakfast is not much to
speak of, either, but we cannot deny that this cute inn is a suitable alternative for those who are seeking a cheap stay in the otherwise
pricey Condado. We had no problem taking advantage of the fancy
pools, beach, and bars of the "conveniently located" Marriott, just a
block away. Housed in a 70-year-old building on a relatively quiet side
street, its rooms are simple but comfortable, equipped with pumping
a/c and cable TV. Under new management, the Casa del Caribe has
a super-friendly staff ready to assist guests in their San Juan endeav-
ors. Parking is available for $5. The breakfast is nothing special, unless
you're a lover of white toast and generic orange juice.

Isla Verde

Isla Verde is a strip of large condos and hotels on the beach side, and every
conceivable fast-food joint known to humanity is on the other. The beach
here is nice, and some people seem to love staying in this part of San Juan.
Our biggest gripe is that the airport is down the street; we loathe the sound
of screaming jet engines while we're reading Jane Austen (very incongruous,
indeed!). Incredibly, hotel chains keep building here, including the fairly
new Ritz-Carlton, which is literally across the street from the end of the
runway where the jumbo jets rev their engines to take off. Hello? Anybody
home? Fortunately, El San Juan and the San Juan Grand (née The Sands), are
far enough away so that the noise is only a dull roar. We also find it rather removed from the nightlife and restaurant scene — a car or significant taxi ride
is necessary. But the airport is close!

San Juan Water & Beach Club Hotel, 2 Tartak Street, Isla Verde, PR.
ℂ 888-265-6699 or 787-728-3666, ✎ 787-728-3610,
💻 ww.waterclubsanjuan.com

💲 **Wicked Pricey** 🍴 **EP** CC 84 rooms

This boutique hotel, formerly just The Water Club, has *sexy* written
all over it. Not literally, of course, but with its chic ambiance and array of
sensual restaurants and bars, some couples never make it out the
front door. The Water Club debuted in late 2001, and the intent was
to create an environment that has more in common with a Manhattan boutique hotel than with a typical beach resort. The recent name
change was meant only to clear up confusion that it was a members-
only property (which it's not) — the style and vibe remain the same.

Although the hotel sits across the street from a good beach, the focus is on the modern, wallpaper-worthy interiors — no generic tropical print bedspreads here.

Falling water is a key element of the concept: There's a waterfall over corrugated metal behind the main bar, glass-enclosed waterfalls tumble inside the elevators (quite a head rush when the elevator zips up and down), and a hall mirror on each floor is drizzled with trickling water. The central lighting scheme throughout is dark and neon blue — votive candles glow in the lobby and hallways 24/7. By day, the rooms are stylish and bright, with blond wood floors (faux, but attractive) and king-size beds angled toward the water; all rooms have at least a partial ocean view. All of the au courant furnishings were designed to order. The recently renovated sexy bathrooms include double-head showers with glass doors and stainless steel pedestal sinks. There are special touches, like the CD and TV stand on a floor-to-ceiling swivel, clock radios with MP3 player connections, in-room Wi-Fi access, and the "desires" board — a glass notepad and pen for guests to make maid requests. There are a few annoyances: The rooms don't have a real closet, just a recess in the wall with a hanger, and, at the prices charged here, isn't collecting a rental fee for the front desk's library of CDs a little much?

There is a tiny yet very chic rooftop pool, where Sunday afternoon champagne parties are staged, and a bar with a terrific view just below with sushi and a fireplace. On the ground floor is another bar, and the restaurant, Tangerine, breaks with the blue-light intrigue — the small dining room is white and orange with smooth curves and sharp lines. Room service is 24 hours, and the food is delicious, if somewhat skimpy in the portion department. The Water Club is located about a half mile west of El San Juan, on a dead-end street that becomes jammed with traffic on Friday and Saturday nights. Yes, San Juan's cogniscetti discovered this spot instantly, and as long as the hotel stays in favor with that crowd, this will be the scene to beat.

El San Juan Hotel & Casino, P.O. Box 9022872, 6063 Avenida Isla Verde, San Juan, PR. © 800-468-2818 or 787-791-1000, 🖂 787-791-0390, 🖳 www.luxuryresort.com

💲 **Wicked Pricey** and up 🍴 **EP** CC 385 rooms, 21 suites

El San Juan is the largest deluxe hotel-resort-casino property in Isla Verde, located on more than 15 acres. Its entrance — through a dim carved-mahogany lobby with a massive crystal chandelier hovering over the bar like the cloud shadow in a Magritte painting — is impressively different from most tropical hotels. The floors are dark marble. To the right is the best looking and most spacious casino in San Juan. To the left is the reception area, and beyond it the pools and beach. The outside area is fantastic. There are several pools, including a

nice-size lap pool and the requisite resort pool with waterfalls and islands. Around it are a Jacuzzi and some very comfortable chaises with
cushions (which we love). Pool bars seem to be everywhere, and overall it is a very attractive setting. There are ocean premier suites (*casitas*),
which can be rented, that border one of the best big-hotel beaches in
San Juan. Two lighted tennis courts and water sports round out the
outdoor activities. The rooms are decorated in shades of yellow and
green and have dark wood colonial-style furnishings. Though on the
smallish side, they are fully loaded with such items as VCR, stereo, a
tiny TV in the bathroom, tile bath, an iron and ironing board, a
hairdryer, and three phones. A new three-story structure on the
grounds houses 21 luxury suites with the same amenities but with
more space and privacy. On the roof of the main building is the
Rooftop Spa and Fitness Center with steam and sauna. Downstairs
there are seven dinner restaurants, two snack bars, eight cocktail
lounges (including the Tequila Bar on the 10th floor and a cigar bar),
and the Babylon disco (a dressy club where locals take their dates to
impress them). Look for packages.

Inter-Continental San Juan Resort & Casino, 5961 Avenida Isla Verde, Isla
Verde, San Juan, PR (mailing address: P.O. Box 6676, Loíza
Station, Santurce, PR 00914-6676). ✆ 800-443-2009 or 787-982-
4329, ✆ 787-791-7091, 🖳 www.interconti.com,
sanjuan@interconti.com

💲 **Wicked Pricey** and up 🍴 **EP** 🆑 402 rooms

Formerly the San Juan Grand, the Inter-Continental San Juan received a $15 million face-lift when it was the San Juan Grand, and its
rooms and halls will undergo another renovation in 2007. It still has
that fabulous early '60s look — but now it's yellow instead of white.
The lobby's marble floors are more colorful now, and the mirror-and-
chrome motif is gone. There is a good-size casino; when we were there,
someone was gambling away thousands of dollars at the craps table
(and enjoying every minute, strangely enough). Outside, there is a
large free-form pool (reportedly the largest free-form pool in the
Caribbean with Jacuzzi and swim-up bar) with the standard tropical
resort feature of an island in the middle with bridges. There is a spacious beach in front with chaises. The rooms all have little lanais with
soundproof sliders. The new décor features modern furnishings, gold-
tone carpeting, yellow walls, artwork with dark woodwork, and a distinctly international or European feel. The renovated hallways feature
dark mahogany woodwork and gold striated wallpaper. There are also
five well-frequented restaurants on the premises, including Ruth's
Chris Steak House (San Juan's best steak house). The Italian joint
here, Passaggio, offers "creative Italian" cuisine in an intimate setting
and gets rave reviews. Look for packages.

The Ritz-Carlton San Juan Hotel & Casino, 6961 Avenue of the Governors, Isla Verde, Carolina, PR. ✆ 800-241-3333 or 787-253-1700, ✉ 787-253-0777, 🖳 www.ritzcarlton.com

💲 **Wicked Pricey** and up 🍴 **EP** CC 414 rooms

Although this hotel is a Ritz—down to the crystal chandeliers, oriental rugs, dark heavy furniture (which we found rather out of place in tropical Puerto Rico), afternoon tea, and its renowned service—we couldn't grasp why it would build this resort (opened in 1997) adjacent to the runway of the international airport. The noise, especially on the entrance side, is horrendous when the jumbo jets rev their engines to take off. Even on the ocean side, where the very pretty and well-designed pool area is located, the roar of the jets could be heard through our iPod headphones (we were playing Beyoncé—Joni Mitchell couldn't compete with the planes). The windows of this oversize hotel are double-paned for noise insulation and do not open. Of the hundreds of rooms available, only 21 offer lanais, and they are on the ocean side. Our room was on the airport side, and we heard what sounded like muffed screams every time a plane took off. If this will bother you (as it did us), then look elsewhere.

Otherwise, this is a fine hotel, and it features the largest casino in Puerto Rico. All the amenities that make the Ritz famous are available, including twice-daily maid service and those sumptuous terry-cloth bathrobes. There is 24-hour room service, served with silver and china on a wheeled-in table—wonderful to enjoy while wearing those robes, a Ritz experience. Our standard room was on the smallish side, with dark wall-to-wall carpeting, mahogany furniture, and brightly colored upholstery. The baths are a symphony of marble.

Besides the pool (between jets) and the robes, we loved the Ritz's spa and fitness center, contained in a wing of the hotel. A 12,000-square-foot space, the gym is one of the best of any hotel on the island and includes a fabulous aerobics room with nine spinners, treadmills, and stationary bikes. All kinds of body pampering is available, as well as fitness and aerobics classes. There are two lighted tennis courts, a pretty beach (for a city beach) in front, and all kinds of water sports available through the hotel. There are three restaurants, two bars, and the only casino in the Ritz chain. Check for corporate rates or packages.

Ocean Park

This is a wonderful residential neighborhood without high-rise hotels and with the best beach in San Juan. There are several guesthouses, four of which we recommend. All are mixed gay and straight, with the Ocean Walk and L'Habitation Beach Guest House being the gayest, but everyone of any persuasion is welcome.

⊛ **Numero Uno on the Beach**, 1 Calle Santa Ana, Ocean Park, Santurce, PR. ℂ 787-728-3379, ✆ 787-727-5482, 🖳 www.numero1guesthouse .com, info@numero1guesthouse.com

💲 **Not So Cheap** and up 🍽 CP 🆑 11 rooms, 2 suites

Numero Uno is one of our favorite places to stay in Puerto Rico and the best accommodation of its kind in San Juan. Located on the beach about halfway between Hostería del Mar and the Ocean Walk, this 11-room, two suite, three-story guesthouse is beautifully relaxed, friendly, and comfortable. Owners Chris and Ester Laube (ex–New Jerseyans — he's American and she's Puerto Rican) know their business well, having completely renovated a dilapidated old house on the beach and built it into a solid business of repeat customers, all in a decade. Like all other guesthouses in Ocean Park, the clientele here is mixed straight and gay, American and European. Numero Uno's restaurant, Pamela's, is one of the best in San Juan.

The rooms are comfortable and clean — all have a/c, double or king-size beds, white tile floors, private baths, and no TVs. The downstairs has a plunge pool and lots of shady places where you can sit and sip a cocktail while you reread *Valley of the Dolls*. The beach in front is never crowded and is sort of the gay section of the beach. Numero Uno provides chaises and beach towels for its guests.

Hostería del Mar, 1 Calle Tapia, Ocean Park, Santurce, PR. ℂ 877-727-3302 or 787-727-3302, ✆ 787-268-0772, 🖳 www.hosteriadel marpr.com, hosteria@caribe.net

💲 **Cheap** and up 🍽 EP 🆑 23 rooms

Situated right on the beach, there is a very tranquil air at Hostería del Mar, apparent as you enter through a gate, pass a goldfish pool, and step into a breezy lounge attractively decorated in light woods, rattans, and tropical plants. To your left is one of our favorite places to have lunch in San Juan (see Where to Eat). The restaurant's setting is extraordinary, especially since it's in a city. Sitting inside, you definitely wouldn't know you were in San Juan — the sound of the surf is omnipresent. The rooms are simply but nicely decorated, with terra-cotta tile floors, rattan furnishings, a/c, cable TV, phones, and private baths. Many rooms have lanais and ocean views, and some have kitchenettes. The beach out front is never crowded.

L'Habitation Beach Guest House, 1957 Calle Italia, Ocean Park, Santurce, PR. ℂ 787-727-2499, ✆ 787-727-2599, 🖳 www.habitationbeach .com, habitationbeach@msn.com

💲 **Cheap** 🍽 CP 🆑 10 rooms

This beachside gay guesthouse sits next door to Numero Uno and is now owned by Marie and Michel Barrabes, so don't be surprised to hear some French in the halls. Known years ago as the Beach House, L'Habitation Beach Guest House is a simple and casual place to stay, with a sand patio and bar in front for guests. Thankfully, the owners have made good on their promise to give this hotel a spiffing up, and everything has been nicely remodeled. The rooms are basic, clean but comfortable, with cable TV and a/c. The price is right, so don't expect too much. All rooms have ceiling fans and private baths but no room phones. The best and most spacious rooms front the beach (ask for Room 8 or 9). Windows are louvered—there is no glass. There are beach chairs outside and there is free parking for guests.

The beach bar serves burgers and sandwiches for lunch. A complimentary continental breakfast is also served at the beach bar. The guesthouse provides chaises for its guests. People with children are discouraged from staying at L'Habitation Beach.

Old San Juan

Old San Juan now has more lodging possibilities, partly due to the cruise-ship impact on this part of the city, but also due to the beautiful Spanish colonial architecture of the oldest part of the city. Two small hotels, the fabulous Convento and the art-filled Gallery Inn, are great choices for those seeking something different. The Sheraton Old San Juan is a larger chain hotel that caters to the cruise-ship industry. Although there is no beach in Old San Juan (the closest one is in the Condado), it is surrounded by water on three sides. Water views abound from rooftops, from between buildings, and from the steep, narrow streets.

Hotel El Convento, 100 Calle Cristo, Old San Juan, PR. ✆ 800-468-2779 or 787-723-9020, ✎ 787-721-2877, 🖥 www.elconvento.com, elconvento@aol.com

🛍 **Wicked Pricey** and up 🍴 **CP** 🆑 58 rooms

Probably the finest small hotel in San Juan (it's the only "Small Luxury Hotels of the World" member property in Puerto Rico), El Convento resides in a 350-year old building across from the Cathedral of Old San Juan. Occupied for 250 years by Carmelite nuns, the building was abandoned in 1903 due to neglect. Many uses followed until it was finally purchased in 1995 and experienced a much-needed $16 million face-lift, completed in 1997 and fully utilizing the architectural distinctiveness of the building and its stunning multistoried, arched interior courtyard.

We loved the whole ambiance, look, and energy of this place (maybe all that past praying rubbed off on us a little). The courtyard features several restaurants, including El Picoteo Tapas Bar—the best place for drinks in Old San Juan. (Be careful with the olives in your martini. Savoring that final martini treat, we bit down to discover that it wasn't pitted and consequently cracked a crown. Now that was an expensive drink!) The courtyard also has a shopping arcade on the ground level.

The hotel occupies the top four floors of the building (the lobby is located on the third floor). Access is controlled by an elevator passkey. Guests are met by a porter at the front gate and are escorted to the reception desk. The rooms are all different, in both size and décor. Standard rooms are on the small side — an upgrade might be desired. The walls are brightly colored and hand-painted. The furniture is a mélange of restored mahogany antiques and hand-crafted wrought-iron pieces. All rooms have a/c, CD players, TV-VCRs, two-line phones, data ports, fridges, irons and ironing boards, and bathrobes. El Convento also has suites, including the spectacular and intriguing Gloria Vanderbuilt Suite, with marble floors, parlor, hand-painted and stenciled walls, Spanish colonial antiques, high-beamed ceilings painted blue, vintage art, and black marble bath with Jacuzzi — all for $1,200 a day. There is a new fitness center with treadmills and free weights, a small pool, and a Jacuzzi on a terrace with fab views of the Fortaleza, the Cathedral, and the harbor. Look for packages.

The Gallery Inn, 204 Calle Norzagaray, Old San Juan, PR. ✆ 787-722-1808, 787-977-3929, 🖳 www.thegalleryinn.com, reservations@thegalleryinn.com

💲 **Very Pricey** and up ⑪ **CP** (CC) 22 rooms

Now this is an unusual place. Packed floor to ceiling with the art of Jan D'Esopo (mostly watercolors and sculptures), the Gallery Inn has the ambiance of a small museum. Indeed, the inn's lobby could easily be mistaken for a cramped art gallery (we weren't even sure we were in the right place). However, the lobby leads to an inner courtyard and working studio with a more comfortable sense of space. We were fascinated by the artwork, which made us a tad dizzy after a while from constantly changing focus. Seated with a cocktail, we regained our composure.

Set in a rambling 350-year-old building at the crest of Old San Juan, this inn has become a popular gathering spot for the young, up-and-coming bohemian crowd. The views from the Inn's roof terrace, called the Wine Deck, are breathtaking. Begun in 1984, the Inn has grown over time, and the rooms reflect the owners' constant collecting of interesting furnishings and art. Some might complain that the rooms are not kept up so well, which could be a valid point, but the ambiance seems to make up for it. There are many quiet nooks, crannies, patios, and gardens for repose or reading. There's even an air-conditioned music room with a Steinway grand piano for the pianists among us. Several caged birds also live here, as do the owners, Jan D'Esopo and Manuco Gandía. Twenty-two suites and rooms, primarily named after children and grandchildren of Jan and Manuco, are scattered throughout the Inn. All are individually decorated and have phones (no TVs), private baths, and central a/c. The staff here is especially warm and helpful, and an honor bar in the lobby makes an afternoon glass of wine a perfect opportunity to chat with the owners, other guests, or just the parrots.

Sheraton Old San Juan Hotel & Casino, 100 Brumbaugh, Old San Juan, PR. ✆ 866-653-7577 or 787-721-5100, ✆ 787-721-1111, 🖥 www.sheratonoldsanjuan.com

💲 **Very Pricey** and up ⑪ EP Ⓒ 240 rooms

Opened in 1997 by Wyndham and recently taken over by Sheraton, this nine-story hotel gets most of its business from cruise-ship customers who stay at the beginning or end of their trips. The hotel has a very small lobby that is dominated by the cacophony of slot-machine bells from the adjoining casino. A rehab by Sheraton has made a difference—the rooms are now more comfortable, especially with the Sheraton Sweet Sleeper beds. Deluxe rooms face outside and have stucco walls, blond wood furnishings, wall-to-wall carpeting, and earth-tone fabrics, which were a refreshing change from the omnipresent pastels. We found the rooms and windows smallish, but the baths were comfortable, with good showerheads and Italian tiles. Other amenities include two-line speakerphones with data ports and voicemail, a safe, satellite TV, and an iron and ironing board. We also liked that feather pillows were available, as well as 24-hour room service. The suites have balconies and views of the bay and old city. There is a small rooftop pool with tile deck and a great view of the harbor. A tiny fitness center is adjacent. Look for packages or corporate rates.

Hotel Milano, 307 Calle Fortaleza, Old San Juan, PR. ✆ 787-729-9050, ✆ 787-722-3379, 🖥 www.hotelmilanopr.com, hmilano@coqui.net

💲 **Not So Cheap** ⑪ CP Ⓒ 30 rooms

Willing to trade style for location? The Milano is housed in a restored colonial building right in the heart of San Juan, which means that guests are steps from shops and restaurants, but there is street noise to deal with as a result. Unfortunately, the Milano does not retain any of the colonial charm of some of our more favored hotels here in the old city. The motel-style rooms have cable TV, minibar, and a/c. There is no Puerto Rican flair to speak of, but the rooftop restaurant, though not renowned for its cuisine, does offer great panoramic views of Old San Juan. Ask for a room in the back to cut down on street noise.

Howard Johnson Hotel Plaza de Armas, 202 Calle San José, Old San Juan, PR. ✆ 787-722-9191, ✆ 787-725-3091, 🖥 www.hojo.com, plazadearmas@hotmail.com

💼 **Not So Cheap** 🍴 **CP** 🆑 51 rooms

What was once the funky Plaza de Armas has now been taken over and spruced up a bit by Howard Johnson. Being right on the plaza of the same name, this hotel is perfectly located. Rooms are not elegant, but all have a/c, cable TV, and Wi-Fi hookups. The dark lobby is being re-modeled and a wine bar is opening in the atrium, so hopefully this hotel will see brighter days.

La Caleta Guesthouse, Calle de las Monjas, Old San Juan, PR. ✆ 787-725-5347, ✉ 787-977-5642, 🖥 www.caletarealty.com, reservations@thecaleta.com

💼 **Not So Cheap** 🍴 **EP** 🆑 15 rooms

We have listed La Caleta for those who are looking to spend a little more time in Old San Juan. Though billed as a guesthouse, La Caleta is much more of a short-term vacation rental. The rooms are housed in a colonial three-story building on a quiet street close to the bay. All of the apartments have kitchenettes, but they vary greatly in the range of amenities offered—some have TV, phone, and a/c, whereas others are much more basic. The two top-floor rooms are appealing—their bedrooms have a/c and the balconies have choice views. Keep in mind that this is not a hotel—there is no maid service, restaurant, or sem-blance of a front desk. However, for those looking to find their way and live like a true resident, La Caleta offers some great apartments, with rates from three nights to a month. The Sunshine Suite on the top floor has themed rooms with brushed pastel walls, a small sofa bed, and a TV. The bedroom is very simple, with a small bed and a/c.

Where to Eat

San Juan is a big city, and there are restaurants galore—from very expensive chichi bistros to the little snack bar on the street. By all means leave your hotel and sample and experience. We've tried to weed through the myriad of choices and to provide a good cross-section of the San Juan dining scene. Old San Juan seems to be the happening place in dining and should definitely be explored, but other parts of the city also hold their own, so you will never be far from a good restaurant.

Keep in mind that all the large hotels and resorts now have several restau-rants that offer a variety of international cuisine. Although the food at many of these resorts is good, the one thing they all have in common is that they are very expensive, even overpriced. However, if you're staying in Dorado, for ex-ample, which is a 45-minute drive from town, you might have to bite the bul-let and eat at your hotel for sheer convenience, but if you're staying right in San Juan, why sit home? Get thee out and about!

Here are our suggestions.

Old San Juan

$$$$ Aguaviva, 363 Calle Fortaleza, 722-0665

Ever wonder what it would be like to eat in an underwater restaurant? Well, in this ultra-chic spot featuring seaside Latino cuisine, the fantasy comes to life. The style is impeccable, with turquoise floors, tables, and walls, accented by white trim and hanging neon *aguavivas* ("jellyfish"). The food is even better than the décor. The seviches are fantastic — try the mahi mango lime or tuna and salmon sashimi duo. The seared halibut medallions with crabmeat fondue and spinach is quite savory, as are the wide array of oysters and special seafood towers. Open for lunch from 11:30 a.m. to 4 p.m. and for dinner from 6 to 11 p.m. No reservations are accepted, so expect a wait.

$$$ Amadeus, 106 Calle San Sebastian, 722-8635

Right in the heart of Old San Juan, this famous intellectual meeting spot serves all kinds of Puerto Rican and Caribbean cuisine with a nouvelle flair. We adore the romantic candlelit dining room in back and love the food, especially its delicacies like risotto de mar with salmon and calamari. Open from noon to 1 a.m.; no lunch on Monday. Reservations are suggested.

$$$$ Barú, 150 Calle San Sebastian, 977-5442

Set in a building dating back 250 years, Barú is a great place to soak up some atmosphere along with some tasty fare. Signore Bignami, Barú's Italian chef, offers exciting Caribbean-Mediterranean fusion cuisine, such as pork ribs with a ginger-tamarindo glaze or our favorite — crab cakes topped with seared scallops and a coconut curry sauce. There is an elegant art-filled dining room, although we prefer the romantic courtyard. The bar, complete with soothing lounge music, is a well-frequented spot for the local young professional crowd. Open for dinner from 5 p.m. to midnight and on Sunday from 4 to 10 p.m.

$$ ⊛ Café Berlin, 407 Calle San Francisco, 722-5205

If you're looking for vegetarian or lighter and healthier fare, this is a fine and hip place for breakfast, lunch, and dinner. It's not at all expensive, and the Caribbean and international offerings include great breads, salads, and desserts. Vegetarians can try the tofu steak. If you just want coffee or herbal tea, this is the place. Open until 10 p.m. daily.

$$$ Casa Borinquen, 109 Calle San Sebastian, 722-7070

This quietly elegant nouvelle Latino restaurant on a peaceful side street is a pleasant, unassuming spot with a varied menu and an alfresco bar. The cream of yautia is a local specialty, served with chorizo bruschetta. For cheeseheads, the fried Puerto Rican cheese with guava rum sauce is worth a try. Entrees range from pasta (roasted pumpkin and macadamia ravioli) to meat and seafood (ahi tuna with garlic spinach). With candlelit tables, smooth jazz, and chandeliers, the small dining room is intimate, and the outdoor bar in back is a great place for an open-air cocktail. Open 6 p.m. until 1 a.m.; closed on Sunday.

$$$$ Dragonfly, 364 Fortaleza, Old San Juan, 977-3886

This hot must-visit Asian eatery is across the street from the Parrot Club, and it's owned by the same entrepreneur, Robert Trevino. There are only seven tables, and no reservations are taken (expect a wait). It offers a community table option, or patrons can dine at the bar. The room is painted deep red and appointed in assorted chinoiserie. The music is from the Buddha Bar, and the gorgeous waitresses wear long silk dresses slit up the leg. It's got sex appeal to spare, but the food is also indelible: Peking duck nachos, rock shrimp tempura tacos, quesadilla spring rolls, seviche in coconut milk and ginger, and — well, you get the idea. The sake martinis are wicked good, and the chocolate pot de crème is our favorite dessert in all of Puerto Rico — indulge! Open 6 p.m. until midnight; closed on Sunday.

$$ El Picoteo, Hotel El Convento, 100 Calle Cristo, 723-9202

The best place for drinks in Old San Juan, El Picoteo serves tapas and light fare and is a symphony of connecting arches and tones of burnt sienna. We recommend its renowned grilled mushrooms and the baby eels (which were quite pricey). For those who don't want to take the tapas route, the mixed paella is a heftier selection. Open for lunch and dinner; closed on Monday.

$$$$ Il Perugino, 105 Calle Cristo, 722-5481

Old San Juan's best Italian cuisine is served in this old colonial building that dates back more than two centuries. Specialties include carpaccios, homemade pastas, and a superb wine cellar. Come see why this is an award-winner. Open for lunch and dinner until 11 p.m.; closed Sunday.

$$$$ Kudetá, 314 Calle Fortaleza, 721-3548

This stylish new restaurant is a chic spot in Old San Juan that offers an eclectic cuisine. We love this place on weekends — there is an energetic young crowd and a mélange of loungy rooms upstairs in which to enjoy a postdinner cocktail, as well as the nightclub on the third floor. The Peking duck pancake appetizer is a favorite, and we love the snapper with risotto and the mashed potatoes with edamame. Open 6 to 11 p.m. (and midnight on the weekend).

$$ La Bombonera, 259 Calle San Francisco, 722-0658

An institution in Old San Juan — it has been open for over a century

—this is a great place for cheap Puerto Rican food when you're in the historic district. It's packed at lunchtime. It's also reputed to have the best Puerto Rican coffee in town. Open daily from 7:30 a.m. to 8:30 p.m.

$$$$$ La Chaumiére, 367 Calle Tetuán, 722-3330

Right at the entrance to Old San Juan, Chef Didier welcomes guests from the world over. If you want French Provençal cuisine, this is San Juan's best. It's also one of San Juan's most elegant and most expensive restaurants. The scallops provençale will not disappoint. Reservations are advised. Open for dinner only; closed Sunday.

$$ La Fonda del Jibarto, 280 Calle del Sol, 725-8375

Once we visited this local favorite, we learned that thousands of San-juaneros can't be wrong! With its fun atmosphere and hearty tasty *criollo* cuisine, this laid-back family-run spot has been packing them in for years. When you ask what is best on the menu, they will say, "*Todo!*" We can't argue. Open 10 a.m. to 9 p.m. daily.

$$$ La Mallorquina, 207 Calle San Justo, 722-3261

This is a fine old-style restaurant that serves Puerto Rican and Spanish specialties (try the *asopao*—a Puerto Rican rice dish). Set in an old building with murals and ceiling fans, this is a very pleasant place for lunch. It is San Juan's oldest restaurant and has been owned and operated by the same family since 1848. It's open for lunch and dinner, but is most popular as a lunch spot. Closed Sunday.

$$$ Makario's, 361 Calle Tetuan, 723-8653

Arab chef Oliver Makario offers contemporary Arab Mediterranean cuisine in this Egyptian-owned eatery. For an authentic taster, we recommend the vegetarian platter—a hearty mix of falafel, baba ghanoush, and tabouli served with pita bread. The grilled halibut filet with mango sauce is a good bet for those who aren't into the traditional Arab options (such as stuffed grape leaves, shish kebabs, or falafel). We recommend this place on weekends, when the cozy upstairs den features a belly dancer. Open noon until 11 p.m.

$$$$ The Parrot Club, 363 Calle Fortaleza, 725-7370

One of the hottest restaurants in town is chef Robert Trevino's Parrot Club, featuring *nuevo latino* cuisine—best described as a mélange of Puerto Rican and other Latino dishes. Colorful and lively, the restaurant and its popular bar are always packed. The *bocalitos* with spicy crab salad make a wonderful appetizer, and the seared sea bass with lobster and scallop confit will satisfy any seafood lover. Meat eaters will love the roast pork served with cranberry salsa. One of the sides offered is a *torta* made with goat cheese, grilled portabellos, and sweet plantains—gotta try it to believe it. With live music, the Parrot Club is ideal for those seeking a taste of Puerto Rican flair. Open for lunch and dinner every day, and open until midnight Thursday through Saturday.

$$$ ⊛ **Sake**, 305 Recinto Sur, Viejo San Juan, 977-1082

San Juan continues to go upscale, as this stylish sushi restaurant proves. The design here is simply sensational, with three different ambiances. The front room (the Lotus Room) is more of a lounge, although we wish we could hang out on the circular couches all night. The main dining room is a little chilly, but the back room, the actual sushi bar, is more laid back and fun. The menu includes imaginative twists on hot apps and sushi rolls. The impressive drink menu includes special sushi wine from France. For groups, the Japanese-style VIP table is a must—it has great style and fabulous presentation. Open from 6 to 11 p.m.; closed Monday and Tuesday.

$$$ **Sofia**, 355 Calle San Francisco, 721-0396

The latest of Robert Trevino's creations, this Italian restaurant has won over stomachs in a short time. The Latino Bellini (mango juice and prosecco) whets any appetite, as does the grilled shrimp and eggplant appetizer. The pastas here are the specialty—baked ziti with four cheese sauce, or our favorite, linguini with clams, pancetta, and pepperocini. Open 6 p.m. to midnight.

$$$$ **Tantra**, 356 Calle la Fortaleza, 978-8141

Old San Juan finally has an Indian restaurant, but judging from the menu and its Indo-Latino vibe, this is not pure Indian cuisine. The East Indian pork with yogurt risotto is a perfect marriage between the two, as are many of the tasty appetizers. Open for lunch and dinner, with a belly dancer Thursday through Saturday.

Condado

$$$ **Ajili Mójili**, 1006 Ashford Avenue, 725-9195

This is the best place in San Juan to sample authentic Puerto Rican cuisine. The restaurant, in a new, larger location, is very attractive and full of locals, so you know it's good. There's great service, too. Try the *mofongo* or the salmon skewers wrapped with bacon. The *tostones*, another Puerto Rican specialty, are excellent. Keep your eyes open for celebs. Open for lunch and dinner (on Saturday for dinner only). Reservations are suggested.

$$$$ **Cherry Blossom**, 1309 Ashford Avenue, 723-7300

This Japanese steak and seafood restaurant offers teppanyaki dining, with the chef at the table slicing and dicing his way through three courses. Choose shrimp, steak, or scallop, and watch him go to work.

It also offers a great selection of sushi. Open daily for lunch and dinner; no lunch on Saturday.

$$$$$ Ramiro's, 1106 Avenida Magdalena, 721-9049

Serving delicious international cuisine with Spanish Castilian flourishes (dubbed "New Creole"), the Ramiro brothers create food that is as pretty to look at as it is good to eat. Closed for lunch on Saturday. Reservations are suggested.

$$ Vía Appia, 1350 Ashford Avenue, 725-8711

If you want southern Italian cuisine (lasagna, baked ziti, spaghetti, eggplant parmesan) and pizza, this is a pleasant place to sit and eat under the awning in front. Although the service can be slow and at times indifferent, the food is hearty and the price is right. Open daily for lunch and dinner.

$ Waikiki, 1025 Ashford Avenue, 977-2267

This super-casual place looks like nothing special from the street, but those in the know pass through to the picturesque deck overlooking the Caribbean Sea. We love to come here and nosh on some marlin nuggets and have a rum and Coke. Though enjoyable in the sun, this place is even better on those humid nights, as the sea breeze provides natural air-conditioning. Open from 11 a.m. to midnight Monday through Friday and 8 a.m. to midnight on the weekend.

$$$ Yerba Buena, 1350 Ashford Avenue, 721-5700

With creative Caribbean cuisine and streetside dining right on the main drag, this bistro-style spot offers up a tasty blend of entrées. Try the rack of lamb in guava rum sauce. Yerba Buena also has live Cuban music on Thursday and Sunday. Open from 6 p.m. to midnight and until 2 a.m. on the weekend; open Sunday from 5 to 11 p.m.

Isla Verde

$$$ Caribbean Grill, in Ritz-Carlton Hotel, 253-1700

This casual restaurant in the Ritz-Carlton is a consistent spot for well-prepared food using regional recipes and spices. It offers indoor or alfresco dining. We prefer the Caribbean buffets offered for breakfast and lunch, and we warn readers that the Friday night Seafood Extravaganza is in fact extravagant! For an à la carte option, try the surf 'n' turf of the red snapper in a banana leaf and served with *fufu* and *criollo* sauce. The guava crème brûlée is divine. Open daily for lunch and dinner.

$$ Casa Dante, 39 Calle Loíza, 726-7310

This bustling family spot on the main drag specializes in *mofongos*.

For those who don't know, *mofongo* is a famous *boriqua* dish. Casa Dante is the perfect place to sample these mashed plantains, which are stuffed with meat or seafood and topped with red sauce.

$$$ Pescadería Atlántica, 2475 Calle Loíza, Punta Las Marías, 726-6654

In a new and bigger location, this is the place to go if you want really fresh seafood at reasonable prices. This is a popular spot with locals at lunch and dinner. Don't expect a fancy restaurant, just fresh fish. Closed Sunday.

$$$ Ruth's Chris Steak House, Inter-Continental San Juan Resort and Casino, 791-6100

Even with such a difficult name to pronounce, Ruth's Chris is renowned as the best steak joint in the city. If you crave beef, this is the place. Its steaks are cooked in its signature 1800°F oven. The New Orleans–inspired appetizers like barbequed shrimp are a great start. Open for dinner.

$$$$ Tangerine, in San Juan Water & Beach Club Hotel, 728-3666

Searching for chic dining? Look no farther. Local chef Nelson Rosado welcomes you to the sexy San Juan Water & Beach Club Hotel for a sensuous dining experience where even the menu is loaded with sexual innuendos. The cuisine is a Caribbean-Asian fusion, with succulent appetizers such as the geisha seviche with lobster and green onion. The entrees are just as good—we loved the rack of lamb with tamarindo sauce, as well as the red snapper. And who can pass up the orgasm cheesecake, which is fried and topped with homemade vanilla bean ice cream and ginger marmalade? With water-filled glass walls and sleek design, the décor fits into the seduction theme of the hotel, and the food is fantastic as well. Open for dinner until 11 p.m.

Ocean Park

$–$$$ Hostería del Mar, 1 Calle Tapia, 727-3302

This is one of the best spots for lunch in San Juan. You dine in a wooden pavilion with windows open to the beach and the trade winds. The service is lacking but the menu is rich, from macrobiotic and vegetarian to *criollo* and chicken and fish dishes. There are also great sandwiches. It's good for breakfast ($), lunch ($$), and dinner ($$$).

$ Kasalta Bakery, 1966 Calle McLeary, 727-7340

An institution in Ocean Park, this very popular local bakery and cafeteria eatery for breakfast, lunch, and dinner serves the best café con leche in town. The prices are really cheap here, too. Lunch and dinner specials include Puerto Rican dishes (*caldo gallego*, for instance) that are completely unknown to non-Latinos. Also popular are the Cuban sandwiches — a meal in themselves. Open daily from 6 a.m. till 10 p.m. A definite must-stop!

$$$$ Pamela's Caribbean Cuisine, Numero Uno on the Beach, 1 Calle Santa Ana, 728-3379

Executive chef Esteban Torres continues the excellent cuisine of this beachside restaurant, which has created quite a stir in restaurant-rich San Juan. Pamela's also now has air-conditioning, more space, and a view of the beach from every table (the wall on the beach has been opened up). Service may be a tad slow, but the fusion of Caribbean and international cuisine and the use of fresh island produce and seafood make for a wonderful dining experience. ¡*Sabroso*! Open daily for lunch (noon to 3 p.m.) and dinner (7 to 10:30 p.m.). It now offers tapas from 3 to 7 p.m. Reservations suggested.

$$$$ Ristorante Casa di Legno, 1130 Avenida Roosevelt, 273-1584

This is a wonderful Italian restaurant in the old Mona's space. Chef Pierre St. Hubert has created one of San Juan's best-kept secrets, with more than 40 choices of pasta, seafood, and meat dishes. Closed Monday.

Miramar

$$$$ Augosto's Cuisine, Excelsior Hotel, 801 Avenida Ponce de León, 725-7700

A favorite restaurant of well-to-do locals, Augosto's features one of the finest chefs on the island. The cuisine is classic European, and the menu changes frequently. The dining room is an elegant setting with plenty of flowers. Reservations are suggested.

$$$$ Chayote, Olimpo Court Hotel, 603 Avenida Miramar, 722-9385

This is consistently rated one of San Juan's best dining experiences. Chef Alfredo Ayala merges Caribbean, Puerto Rican, and international cuisine in such a delicious way that Chayote is the delight of in-the-know locals. Be sure to save room for dessert here. Reservations are a must. Open Tuesday through Saturday for lunch and dinner, but no lunch is served on Saturday.

Puerto Nuevo

$$ Aurorita's, 303 Avenida de Diego, 783-2899

Good Mexican food, live mariachi music (Thursday through Sunday), and an out-of-the-way location (take a cab) make this a fun excursion. Closed Monday.

Santurce

$$ **Bebos Café**, 1600 Calle Loíza, 268-5087

If you're seeking an authentic Puerto Rican meal, head to this hot-spot in Santurce. Renowned for its *criollo* cuisine, Bebos is busy from morning to midnight. For those who haven't tried *mofongos,* this is another good spot to give it a go! Open daily from 7:30 a.m. until 12:30 a.m.

$$$ **La Casona**, 609 Calle San Jorge, 727-2717

Set within a colonial-period house, this restaurant is authentic in ambiance and cuisine. Traditional Spanish fare keeps customers coming back to this popular spot. Lunches cater to businesspeople looking for a hearty meal, whereas dinners are romantic affairs. The meats are exceptionally seasoned, especially the rack of lamb, which is a local favorite. Open for lunch and dinner; closed on Sunday.

$$$ **Las Tablas**, 166 Ponce de Léon, 977-5601

Located next to the Luis A. Ferre Performing Arts Center, this stylish spot combines flavors from the Indians, Spanish conquistadors, and Africans. The result is delectable. We like to start with a drink on the patio and then enter the softly lit restaurant for dinner. It often has dancing later. For an unusual surf 'n' turf, we recommend the lamb chops in red wine sauce, complemented by langostinos in cilantro sauce.

$$$$ **Pikayo**, Museum of Art, 299 Avenida de Diego, 721-6194

Housed in the Art Museum, this is an elegant yet relaxing place to sample celebrity chef Wilo Benet's "exotic Caribbean" cuisine (although we also saw traces of Chinese, Middle Eastern, French, and Thai, to name just a few). The creative dishes are presented so beautifully that it seems a shame to eat them — but we got over that feeling quickly! The menu changes frequently. We sampled the spicy tuna tartar with peanut sauce and the sea bass with Hawaiian purple mashed potatoes — they were both excellent. We love watching the action in the kitchen on the big TV screen placed over the bar. Come see why this place was named one of the world's top 100 restaurants by *Condé Nast.* Open for dinner Monday through Saturday and for lunch on Tuesday through Friday; closed Sunday.

Going Out

Get out those cha-cha heels! With the best and greatest variety in the Caribbean, nightlife is why you stay in San Juan. There are lots of bars and clubs of all persuasions, and there is no set closing time. Most places close when the last person spins off the dance floor and stumbles onto the street. As in any city, weekend nights will be the busiest and most crowded in the clubs.

Also, all clubs will usually have a cover charge of between $5 and $15 (especially on weekends), which usually includes at least one free drink. For those who like to gamble, all the big hotels in Condado and Isla Verde have casinos (the most glittering is the one at El San Juan in Isla Verde). So take your disco nap, strap on those sling-backs or put on those Pradas, and off you go into the night.

Straight Bars and Clubs

For years, two of the hottest clubs in San Juan have been Stargate and Club Lazer. But there is a new generation of clubs springing up, such as Teatro and Kudetá, which are nightclubs that could easily be in Miami or New York. We've also listed some other choices in case you get tired of them and want a change of pace. Note that when going to the straight clubs here, people tend to get dressed up — that means no shorts, T-shirts, athletic shoes, or sandals for men (jeans are iffy; best to wear dressier pants); for women, dresses are preferred (the tighter and more leg showing, the better — remember, this is macho and sexist Latin America).

Blend, 309 Calle Fortaleza, Old San Juan, 977-7777

On Thursday through Sunday, this bar turns into a thumping scene with electronica pulsing through the two rooms. There is never a cover, but dress elegantly. This gets crowded, but the dance energy is infectious. Open 11 p.m. until 4 a.m.

Brava, El San Juan Hotel, Isla Verde, 791-2781

This is actually two clubs in one, with *reggaetón* and hip-hop on the first floor and electronic music on the top floor. For those looking for the big club experience in San Juan, Brava is it.

Club Babylon, El San Juan Hotel, Isla Verde, 791-2781

This is dressy disco for good date impressions. It gets the Euro-trashy element as well as local flashy types. Open Thursday through Saturday. This is a popular spot for singles.

Club Lazer, 251 Calle Cruz, Old San Juan, 725-7581

This is San Juan's premier disco. For those who want to experience the *reggaetón* craze firsthand, head to Club Lazer. In this three-floor club, you'll hear all the current dance hits with all the high-tech accoutrements you expect in a hot club; there is also a roof-deck garden jungle. It's stylish, it's fun, and it gets packed.

Dunbar's, 1954 Calle McLedary, Ocean Park, 728-2920

This is a casual, popular landmark in Ocean Park, packed with locals. It has live music on weekends and pool tables as well. Best of all, it's beachside.

Houlihan's, 1309 Ashford Avenue, Condado, 723-8600

This is always packed, somewhat dressy, and featuring live music on weekends. Just look for the line out front.

⊛ **Ku Lounge/Kudetá**, 314 Calle Fortaleza, Old San Juan, 721-3548

Places like this make it clear that San Juan is coming into its own on the nightclub scene. The top two floors of Kudetá Restaurant make up the lounge and club here. There is a variety of ambiances: a Library Room, a Moroccan Room, and even a Chandelier Room. The top floor is best and includes a VIP room with bottle service. The supermodern nightclub features top-notch DJs spinning pure house music, and the state-of-the-art Kriogenyx cooling system keeps things dry and comfy. There is a cover charge, but restaurant clients get free admission until midnight. Open on the weekend until 5 a.m.

Liquid and **Wet,** in San Juan Water & Beach Club Hotel, Isla Verde, 728-3666

The hotel offers two nocturnal options: downstairs there's Liquid, a pulsing and stylish nightclub with a fantasy nautical theme—imagine walls made of water. The sexy little lounge on the top floor is Wet. It offers sushi for late diners, but many come to enjoy the intimate setting, plush furniture, and smooth tunes. The two clubs combine into a sultry setting for late-night forays. Open every night after 10 p.m.

Maria's Bar, 204 Calle de Cristo, Old San Juan, no phone

One of the oldest bars in San Juan, this institution offers an authentic look at Old San Juan's nightlife. Open from 10:30 a.m. until early morning.

Marriott Condado, 1309 Ashford Avenue, Condado, 722-7000

The lobby bar of the Marriott attracts a stylish crowd, especially on Thursday through Saturday, with live salsa and merengue music —there is lots of dancing here.

⊛ **Nuyorican Café**, 312 Calle San Francisco, Old San Juan, 977-1276

This authentic spot is our favorite place for live music in San Juan. Located on a little side street, it has a great mixed crowd and a supercool ambiance. There is live music every night and simple food, such as pizza and appetizers. Open from 7 p.m. until late.

Parrot Club, 363 Calle Fortaleza, Old San Juan, 725-7370

This restaurant gets very lively and crowded after the dinner crowd leaves (if it ever does). It often features fantastic live music. Open until 1 a.m.

Pool Palace, Calle Comercio, Old San Juan, 725-8487

Designed to lure the cruise-ship clientele, this brand-new spot offers Americans the chance to sample "exotic" American culture: 16 pool tables, projection TVs for sports games, and bar grub. Sure, it's well-designed and pretty plush for a pool hall, but it's hardly Old San Juan. There is a bar and adjoining disco as well. Open daily from 11 a.m. to 4 a.m.

Stargate, 1 Avenida Roberto H. Todd, Santurce, 725-4664

Located just south of Condado and the expressway, across the street from the fast-food plaza, this has for years been one of San Juan's premier clubs. The clientele here is mostly Puerto Rican young professionals.

Teatro, 1420 Avenida Ponce de León, Santurce, 723-3416

This is a dressy dance club that is popular with the local crowd. It was once the ever popular Asylum, but it has since been converted into a hot *reggaetón* club. It's open Thursday through Saturday.

Ventana al Mar, Ashford Avenue, Condado

This little complex of bars on the coast looks out over a cute park and fountain and provides perfect vistas of the sea. These chic little bars are a great place to grab a cocktail in the fresh air. The action builds on weekends. It's good for those who are not interested in the club scene.

Gay and Lesbian Bars and Clubs

San Juan has the best, and pretty much only, gay and lesbian nightlife in the Caribbean. Although there is a little nightlife scene in Santo Domingo in the Dominican Republic, San Juan is it until you get as far south as Caracas, Venezuela. There is even a gay newspaper published here, *Puerto Rico Breeze*, available at most newsstands or online at www.puertoricobreeze.com. Many of the gay clubs in Puerto Rico are mixed gay and lesbian, especially outside San Juan. And everyone, it seems, is dropping the "gay" and "straight" labels altogether. You'll find many of both, no matter where you go dancing in San Juan. There are frequently gay nights at many of the straight clubs (which change constantly, so be sure to check the *Breeze*). Here are the best spots.

Atlantic Beach Bar, 1 Calle Vendig, Condado, 721-6900

This is the happy-hour spot from 4 to 6 p.m. Monday through Saturday. Sunday is dance night and features a show.

The Bar, 2688 Acenida Jesus Pinero, Hato Rey, 751-9067

Located right next to the Galeria Soto, this bar has a great atmosphere and is open Thursday through Sunday.

Cups at the Barn, 1708 Calle San Mateo, Santurce, 268-3570

Where the girls are. Cups has been open for 15 years now and is still the place to be. It also has pool tables. Very popular on Wednesday and Friday and very busy.

⭐ **Eros**, 1257 Avenida Ponce de Léon, Santurce, 722-1131

> The hottest gay club in San Juan (and the best dance club in the city) is located next to the Metro Theater and just around the corner from Stargate. The DJ spins world-class house music, and there are often shows starting around 1 a.m. Wednesday is hip-hop and *reggaetón*; Thursday and Friday are house or tribal; Saturday is mixed '70s to '90s tunes; Sunday is hip-hop and Latin. Many lesbian couples come here to dance, and you'll also see cool straight couples.

Junior's Bar, 613 Calle Condado, Santurce, 723-9477

> There are actually two bars in one here: Junior's Bar and **The Latin Music Place**. This bar and club duo is open seven days a week. Junior's has strippers every night.

Nuestro Ambiente, 1412 Avenida Ponce de Léon, Santurce, 724-9093

> Another of the popular newer gay bars in San Juan, Nuestro Ambiente is recognized as the best late-night spot in town.

Starz, 365 Avenida de Diego & Ponce de Léon, Santurce, 721-8645

> This new club is a popular weekend spot and includes a pulsing club and lounge area. There is no shortage of scantily clad dancers. Dress to impress.

Station d'Club, Casablanca Shopping Center, Hormigueros, 613-4852

> Located outside the city, this big, gay-owned and -operated club is open Wednesday through Sunday and features strippers and transvestites.

Steamworks, 205 Calle Luna, Old San Juan, 725-4993

> This gay gym and sauna, a.k.a. bathhouse, is well equipped with sauna, steam room, "hot tub lockers," and video area. It is open 24 hours a day and has all kinds of themed parties throughout the month, so call ahead for details.

THE NORTH COAST

Dorado

The name *Dorado*, or "Golden," might come from the name of an influential family from the 1500s or from the golden sand beaches here. Whatever the origin, Dorado is regarded today as one of the premier golf resorts in the Caribbean. Since this was developed as a resort town, there is not much to do here besides golf and hang out at the beach (although there is a pleasant plaza with a statue paying homage to the Taíno Indians, the Spanish conquistador, and the African slaves). Two sister resorts, built by the Rockefellers' RockResorts company in 1958 (Dorado Beach) and 1972 (Cerromar Beach) and purchased by the Hyatt in 1985, share a 1,000-acre former grapefruit and coconut plantation just west of the town of Dorado and 22 miles west of San Juan. Unfortunately, the Cerromar has been converted into a time-share called Hyatt Hacienda del Mar Vacation Club Resort, and the Hyatt Dorado Beach ceased operations in May 2006. The Hyatt Hacienda del Mar will accept some bookings like a regular hotel, but only on a limited basis. As for the Hyatt Dorado Beach, the Puerto Rico Tourism Company has hopes that a new owner will step forward and renovate the outdated facility, but there is nothing in the works to suggest that this will happen in the near future.

Despite the aforementioned changes, the four 18-hole Championship golf courses (some of the best in the Caribbean) remain open. Thus, Dorado Beach is still a golfer's paradise. The four 18-hole Robert Trent Jones II Championship courses (called East, West, Pineapple, and Sugarcane) are on flat and rolling terrain that will challenge all golfers. They have been the site of numerous golf tournaments. All feature Mr. Jones's trademarks: huge greens, lots of bunkers and water hazards, and long fairways. Probably the toughest links are the East and West courses. The **East**, at 6,985 yards, has the super-tough 13th hole, a double-dogleg, 540-yard, two-pond nightmare. The **West**, at 6,913 yards, has the toughest par-3s at the resort, spiting you with sloping greens and *muchos* bunkers. Both the Pineapple and Sugarcane courses were redesigned in 2004. The **Pineapple** (formerly known as North) course is a 6,620-yard links-style course, and the **Sugarcane** (formerly known as South), at 6,571 yards, is a challenge of winds and mega water hazards. Greens fees are $195 (but only $105 after 1 p.m.) and include carts. Club rentals are $55. For tee times, call 797-796-1234.

Where to Stay

Hyatt Hacienda del Mar Vacation Club Resort, 301 Highway 693, Dorado, PR. © 787-796-3000, ✎ 787-796-3610, 🖥 www.hyatthaciendadelmar.hyatt.com

🛄 **Ridiculous** and up 🍴 **EP** CC 160 rooms

Hacienda del Mar is a multiwinged seven-story building with a big-resort feel (the lobby looks much like an airline terminal). Now that its primary function is as a time-share, it has very limited availability and doesn't quite have the energy that the Cerromar once had. However, families still love this place, with its huge River Pool complex, expansive beach (beware the often strong undertow), and activities geared for adults and kids of all ages. One of Hacienda del Mar's unique features is the River Pool—at 1,776 feet long, it's said to be the longest current-propelled pool in the world (but who's checking on those things?). It moves water at 22,600 gallons per minute and has 14 waterfalls and 4 water slides. The slide, at its conclusion, is three stories high and requires stairs to climb, but it is a blast. Be prepared to get a noseful of water from the splashdown (we did). Although the whole River Pool idea is contrived (it was added in the '80s to attract families and vacationers who like the mega-resorts), it is different and fun, and both adults and kids will enjoy it (there is a bar with barstools in the water about halfway down, for a quick piña colada). There are five restaurants and bars, a casino, eight tennis courts, and a business center on the property.

All rooms at Hacienda del Mar face the ocean. Most are very comfortable studio apartments with well-equipped kitchens or kitchenettes. They are attractively furnished, with marble baths, a/c, voicemail, cable TV, VCR, stereo, room safes (and safe deposit boxes at the front desk), minibars, irons, and ironing boards. Some rooms have data ports.

Unfortunately, the once-popular kids club, Camp Hyatt, has been nixed, and, gasp, there is no longer any room service—a definite negative.

Embassy Suites Beach & Golf Resort, 201 Dorado del Mar Boulevard, Dorado, PR. 📞 800-EMBASSY or 787-796-6125, 🖨 787-796-6145 🖳 www.embassysuites.hilton.com

💼 **Very Pricey** 🍴 **BP** CC 210 rooms

It seems that the Hilton has successfully muscled in on what was once the Hyatt's territory, as this new Embassy Suites suggests. Although this hotel complex looks enormous, one of the huge buildings is a time-share associated with the hotel. As usual, all rooms here are suites and include a big living room with cable TV. The bedrooms resemble an Embassy Suites in Louisville or elsewhere. The kitchenette has microwave, coffeemaker, and fridge. The lagoon pool is built over the ocean and is home to the Blue Seahorse Bar and Grill. There is also the run-of-the-mill, always open, casual Paradise Restaurant, which is hardly paradisiacal. The hotel's Italian restaurant offering is called Oregano—it overlooks a golf course. Speaking of golf (and who isn't, when it comes to Dorado?), there is a putting green and a driving range, as well as access to the courses here in Dorado. We like the cook-to-order breakfast, but this resort is a bit of a cookie-cutter variety.

THE NORTHEAST COAST
Río Grande and Río Mar

Located 19 traffic-prone miles east of San Juan's international airport and just west of the pretty and popular (with locals) Luquillo beaches are Río Grande and its Río Mar development. Río Grande was once full of sugar and coffee plantations, but now it is known for its imports—rich tourists. In this once sleepy part of Puerto Rico, the mid-1990s saw the rapid development of the 451-acre Río Mar Resort, swallowing up a mile of pristine beach with a big resort hotel, two golf courses, and condo developments. However, we weren't terribly impressed with the look and design of the resort.

Río Mar is very close to El Yunque National Forest (see the Don't Miss section at the end of this chapter) and the Fajardo marina mecca on the east coast. Minutes away is Luquillo Beach, one of the best in all of Puerto Rico. Once a coconut plantation, and now a still majestic beach shaded by palms, it is a fun place at which to hang out and commune with Puertorriqueños. For a little adventure, we recommend a kayak trip with Aqua Frenzy (741-0913). It has both single and double kayaks and runs guided trips.

Luquillo also has Puerto Rico's first wheelchair-accessible beach recreational facility. There is a ramp system from the parking lot right into the water, as well as wheelchair-accessible restrooms. For more information on Luquillo wheelchair facilities, call Compania Parque Nacional at 787-622-5200.

Where to Stay

Westin Río Mar Beach Resort & Ocean Villas, 6000 Río Mar Boulevard, Río Grande, PR. ℂ 800-237-8129 or 787-888-6000, ✆ 787-888-6600, ☐ www.westinriomar.com

🛍 **Ridiculous** and up 🅿 **EP** ⒸⒸ 600 rooms

The Westin Río Mar Beach Resort & Casino sprawls along the beach in a very long, multistoried, and rather architecturally bland building. Fifty-eight ocean villa suites were built next to the main hotel and opened in 2000. It's popular for its convention facilities (with a whopping 48,000 square feet available) as well as its two Championship 18-hole golf courses (designed by the Fazio Brothers and Greg Norman) that spread out behind and around the hotel, but we find this to be just another big, expensive, and boring place to stay. True, golfers and expense-accounters will love it, and there are a slew of other activities. These include 13 Har-Tru tennis courts (four lighted), a spa and fitness facility, water sports and a dive center, three beachfront pools, a kids' club, a daily activities calendar, and (yawn) the requisite casino. Far more appealing to us is its proximity to El Yunque and San Juan (but we'd rather stay in San Juan—that's just our personal preference). The palm-lined beach is pretty, but it can get a tad rough. The sand here is coarse and a light shade of brown (i.e., it is not a white-sand beach).

Things get better on the inside. The rooms are new and close to the sea. We like that oceanside guests can open their slider and hear the surf. The golf course side has very pretty views of the almost perpetually cloud-topped El Yunque summit and the mountains around it. The room décor is attractive and colorful. All have lanais; a/c, phones with voicemail, data port, and conference-calling ability; minibars and coffeemakers; TVs with in-room movies; Nintendo; video account re-view and checkout; and irons and ironing boards. We like that the Westin has 24-hour room service, since we'll be hungry after a night out in San Juan. The hotel also has a business center and, count 'em, 12 restaurants, as well as a slew of bar possibilities. Look for packages and corporate discounts.

Paradisus Puerto Rico, P.O. Box 43006, Playa Coco, Río Grande, PR.
 ℂ 888-95-MELIA or 787-809-1770, ✎ 787-809-1785,
 🖳 www.paradisus.com, paradisus.puerto.rico@solmelia.com

💲 **Beyond Belief** 🍽 **All-Inclusive** ⓒⓒ 486 rooms
 The latest addition to the Paradisus chain, owned by Spanish giant Meliá Hotels, is this monstrous resort built on the Miquillo Penín-sula. Although it's billed as a "tropical oasis of elegance and fun," we don't see much more than a super-pricey all-inclusive resort, but beauty is in the eye of the beholder. For those who seek pampering at a high level of comfort — and are prepared to pay for it — this chic re-sort fits the bill. The lagoon-style swimming pool is perched next to a beautiful beach close to Río Grande. The pool has a swim-up bar and is especially beautiful when illuminated at night. The resort fea-tures all the typical amenities. Paradisus is known for casino, water sports, nightly entertainment, "daily activities," two golf courses, tennis courts, spa, and health club. There are different classes of rooms, but all have 25-inch cable TV, alarm clock, minibar, hairdryer, coffeemaker, and room service. We prefer the suites here, which are housed in in-dividual two-story bungalows and include separate living rooms and veranda. The Royal Service — including personal butler service, breakfast and snacks in a private area, and newspaper service — is a bit over-the-top and not worth the hefty price of an upgrade. Besides El Mirador buffet on the beach, the Paradisus offers five à la carte restaurants with cuisine options such as Californian, sushi, or Italian. Be warned — this place is expensive!

Fajardo

The northeast corner of Puerto Rico has the huge Roosevelt Roads U.S. Naval Station, El Yunque National Forest, and the bustling town of Fajardo — a major marina area for boats due to its proximity to the marine playground of several Puerto Rican islands, cays, and the Virgin Islands. There is not much in Fajardo itself, which is why we find it quite humorous that locals of-ten refer to it as the Metropolis of the East. In fact, it seems that most peo-ple come to Fajardo in order to leave, because this is where ferries and most scheduled air services depart for Culebra and Vieques. Due to traffic, the drive from San Juan can take an hour to an hour and a half. Just north of Fajardo, on the bluffs of Las Croabas, is the gigantic El Conquistador Resort & Country Club. Fajardo is a great place from which to take day trips—there are great spots for scuba diving as well as snorkeling. For those who are into aquatic sports, **Island Kayaking Adventure** (462-7204) runs great trips from Fajardo.

Where to Stay

In addition to the hotels listed below, Fajardo has one of Puerto Rico's best camp sites, **Seven Seas** (787-863-8180), which has room for 500 tents and basic facilities, as well as a restaurant.

Fajardo Inn, P.O. Box 4309, 52 Parcelas Beltran, Puerto Real, PR. ☏ 787-860-6000, ✆ 787-860-5063, 💻 www.fajardoinn.com, info@fajardoinn.com

💲 **Not So Cheap** 🍽 **EP** CC 100 rooms

Since so many tourists pass through Fajardo on their way to and from Vieques and Culebra, we were eager to find a hotel more suited to our readers' taste than the over-the-top El Conquistador. Luckily, we found a hidden gem. The Fajardo Inn is located on a hilltop minutes outside town, offering exquisite views of the ocean and of El Yunque National Rainforest. Visitors who aren't planning on visiting the forest can at least take a good look from here. The hotel has been vastly improved with the recent addition of Coco's Park water park, a sprawling complex of pools, complete with a waterslide, Jacuzzi, swim-up bar, tennis court, and, yes, the highlight of anybody's trip to Puerto Rico—a miniature golf course. The inn is housed in a plantation-style stucco building, replete with an elegant spiral staircase. There are three on-site restaurants to choose from, the best of which is the award-winning Starfish Restaurant—it offers a fusion of *criollo* cuisine specializing in seafood.

The rooms are equipped with a/c, cable TV, and queen-size beds. This inn has the amenities of a resort but still retains the ambiance of an inn. We still prefer to stay along the coast, but for those looking to break up a trip to or from one of the islands off the coast, a layover at the Fajardo Inn may be just the solution.

El Conquistador Resort & Country Club, 1000 El Conquistador Avenue, Fajardo, PR. ☏ 800-468-5228 or 787-863-1000, ✆ 787-863-6500, 💻 www.elconresort.com

💲 **Wicked Pricey** and up 🍽 **EP** CC 919 rooms

With more than 500 acres, nearly a thousand rooms and suites, an acclaimed Arthur Hill 18-hole golf course, seven tennis courts (four lighted), six swimming pools, a marina, all kinds of water sports (including a dive shop), its own private island with beaches, two restaurants and bars, chaises, horseback riding, a fitness center, nine restaurants, eight bars, a shopping arcade, a casino, and even a funicular to climb part of the 300-foot bluff over which the hotel is sprawled, El Conquistador Resort & Country Club is the biggest hotel in Puerto Rico. Indeed, it can take 20 minutes just to walk from top to bottom. The hotel has four distinct guest wings or buildings. At the top of the hill is the La Vista Wing, midway down the hill is the Las Brisas Wing (where we stayed), and at the bottom of the hill near or on the water are Las Olas and La Marina Villages. Adjacent to the La Vista Wing is Las Casitas, which has 90 luxury villas with a price tag to match. The first Golden Door Spa in the Caribbean is also located there.

Although it is a tad large for our taste (bigger isn't always better), El Conquistador will appeal to those who want a self-contained resort with lots of options and activities. Most of the hotel's activities are on the top of the hill, including the soaring lobby and the casino. Also on top is the striking main pool area featuring several levels, three pools (including a lap pool), columns, palm trees, and fab views. Those who want to be near them should consider staying in La Vista or Las Brisas. The yellow-toned décor of the rooms is quite nice and a refreshing change from pastels. All rooms have lanais, a/c, three multilined phones with voicemail, two TVs with movie channels and VCR, bars, safes, fridges, irons and ironing boards, and good-size baths. But what we really loved was the stereo system with three-disc CD and dual-cassette player — a rarity in any big resort.

We didn't like three things about the resort. We found the dining experience to be unexceptional and very expensive — even with nine choices. Given the location, going out to dine in Fajardo is inconvenient. We also did not like having to schlep to Palomino Island by scheduled water taxi (it leaves every 30 minutes between 9 a.m. and 4 p.m. — the last taxi returns at 6 p.m.). It's bad enough just getting to the bottom of the hill! Though exclusively used by hotel guests, the 100-acre island has a small swimming beach that can get crowded. It had lots of seaweed in the water when we were there. Look for packages and corporate discounts.

Las Casitas Village, 1000 El Conquistador Avenue, Fajardo, PR.
ⓒ 800-468-8635 or 787-863-1000, ✆ 787-863-6758,
🖥 www.lascasitasvillage.com

💲 **Beyond Belief** 🍴 **CP** CC 155 rooms
Prices here start at around $800 a night for a one-bedroom villa without a water view, so we'd rather go to St. Barth — even if there is a personal butler who is assigned to each villa! There are limits. One of two "Five Diamond AAA Award" recipients in the Caribbean (the other is the Four Seasons on Nevis), Las Casitas offers one-, two-, and three-bedroom *casitas* and the Golden Door Spa. Designed to resemble a Spanish colonial village, the villas have a lot of the same amenities as

its next-door neighbor, plus the aforementioned butler, 24-hour room service, private pool, fully equipped kitchen, and your favorite refreshments and reading materials stocked in your villa before you arrive. (No, they're not psychic, and they don't have access to your supermarket scanner card records. The reservations people ask lots of questions.) Needless to say, the villas are nicely done and quite luxurious. The villas are perched on a bluff that's 300 feet high, but you still have to take that damn water taxi to get to the beach! There are packages, but the rate category doesn't even come close to changing!

Naguabo and El Yunque Rainforest

Naguabo happens to be the closest town to the rainforest, although the town does not offer much to the visitor. Instead, we recommend driving to one of the inns listed below, which are located in the hills leading into El Yunque. Both places offer comfortable rooms with awe-inspiring views of the jungle. As we began twisting our way up the winding mountain roads, we understood why the Indians named Naguabo "the place where the mountains start." For camping enthusiasts, although there is no official campsite within the park, it is legal to pitch a tent. Simply stop at the National Forest's Palo Colorado Information Center (888-1810) on Road 191 any day before 4 p.m. to make a reservation.

Where to Stay

Casa Flamboyant B&B, P.O. Box 175, Naguabo, PR. ☎ 787-874-6074 or 787-613-3454, 🖷 787-874-6135, 🖳 www.casaflamboyant.com,
💲 **Not So Cheap** ⑪ **BP** ⒸⒸ 8 rooms

Perched up in the mountains at the southern cusp of El Yunque Rainforest, this petite B&B sits on 25 lush and landscaped acres with more than 200 kinds of trees, 50 species of orchids, and at least 100 exotic ferns. Nearby waterfalls of the Cubuy River provide natural ambient sound. The tile deck of the small but attractive and heated swimming pool has distant views of the Caribbean to the southeast. Maybe that is why so many artists, from painters to ballet dancers, have spent so much time here. Even though this is a B&B, Chicago native Shirley has added artistic details and the amenities of luxury lodging, such as 350-thread-count sheets and a variety of massages. The eclectic décor runs from pink and frilly with painted angelic statuary to more sedate yellow tones and wood paneling. One guest room and the villa have terraces, and all rooms have private baths. We love the Rainbow Room with its own sitting room, complete with big art books. Casa

Flamboyant is off the beaten path (roughly between Fajardo and Palmas de Mar) and thus a good choice for those seeking peace and quiet. Activities can be arranged, however. An easy hike down the hill leads to the natural pools at the river below. There are several local-style seafood restaurants in Playa Punta Santiago (about a 20-minute drive down the mountain). No children under 12 are allowed during the winter season.

Yunque Mar, Playa Fortuna, Luquillo, PR. © 787-889-5555, ✆ 787-889-8048, ▢ www.yunquemar.com, hotel@yunquemar.com

  💲 **Cheap** 🍽 **EP** CC 15 rooms

If you're wondering where the name of this hotel originated, imagine a cross between jungle and sea. Yes, this small hotel is ideally located between El Yunque Rainforest and the beautiful Luquillo Beach. It's also very close to Fajardo, making it a great location for those who are on their way to Vieques and Culebra. Standard rooms in this two-story white hotel overlooking the ocean have a/c and cable TV, but we recommend the upgrade to the sea view rooms, which have a balcony with great vistas. The beds are small — even the VIP suite has only a double bed — but the rooms are clean and airy. The price is right, especially considering the outrageous prices many pay for a sea view room here in Puerto Rico.

Casa Cubuy, P.O. Box 721, Rio Blanco, PR. © 787-874-6221, ▢ www.casacubuy.com, info@casacubuy.com

  💲 **Not So Cheap** 🍽 **BP** CC 10 rooms

We are always looking for hotels that allow us to live within the attraction. Instead of packing up and leaving our hotel in order to "see the sights," we have always preferred to have it all in our backyard. That is why we love Casa Cubuy, a small eco-lodge on the edge of El Yunque National Rainforest. Located high in the mountains, up a winding (paved) road from Naguabo, is this "healthy mountain retreat," which is run by ex-Floridian Marianne and her son Matthew. Although she has lived here since 1972, she decided to expand her house into a B&B just eight years ago. Each of the 10 rooms includes fans and huge sliding doors that open right onto the forest. Be sure to request one of the five upper-level rooms with spacious verandas over the forest. Those visitors arriving at night (like us) will be delighted to wake up to the unbelievable spread of green that greets them from their room. To sleep here is especially enjoyable — there are no mosquitoes at this altitude, and the quiet surroundings make sleeping a cinch. Best of all, the owners have built some leisurely trails that lead to the cascading river below. After an easy 10-minute walk, hikers are rewarded with a natural swimming pool in the crisp, clean river. There are also prehistoric rock carvings nearby—ask Matthew for more information. For those who are seeking more excitement, Marianne can arrange everything from massage to horseback riding. For sunny days, there is a sundeck; for rainy days—well, there is a library! There isn't a ton of style emanating from this inn, but the accommodations are quite comfortable and the staff is very helpful.

THE EAST COAST

Yabucoa

Yabucoa first earned its stripes as a cassava town but rose to prominence as Sugarcane City. There were once six sugar mills here, the most important being the granddaddy Central Riog that was in business for more than 70 years, closing in 1981. Today, Yabucoa draws people for its beaches, but with the exception of the *parador* listed below, there are hardly any dining options.

Palmas de Lucia Parador, Roads 901 & 9911, Playa Lucía, Yabucoa, PR.
℗ 787-893-4423, 🖳 www.palmasdelucia.com, palmasdelucia@direcway.com

💲 Cheap 🍴 BP ⒸⒸ 34 rooms

For those who are craving more tranquillity and less fanfare than the over-the-top Sheraton, this local-owned *parador* is a pleasant option. The three-story hotel has its own pool and is steps from the Playa de Lucía, which gets crowded on weekends but is often quite desolate during the week. The rooms have sea views and either a king or two double beds and come equipped with TV, a/c, minibar, and microwave. The pool area includes a terrace with sun chairs, although we could do without the "Kodak Spot" sign that tells us this is a good photo spot (especially because the beach that's located just a few steps away is 10 times more picturesque). There is also a small restaurant and the always important basketball court for guests who need to work on their jump-shot. For a low-key beach experience at affordable prices, this *parador* doesn't offer much in terms of style, but it can be a pleasant getaway from the big resorts.

Costa del Mar Guest House, Carretera 901, km 5.6, Yabucoa, PR.
℗ 787-266-2868, [web] www.costadelmargh.com

💲 Cheap 🍴 EP ⒸⒸ 16 rooms

There are a few reasons we cannot give this guesthouse a ringing endorsement. First and foremost, we felt like Tantalus at this place. So close to the ocean, yet no beach access—it killed us! We learned that we had to go all the way to Palmas de Lucía Parador (same owners) just to swim. Sure, there is a pool here, but we crave the salty sea. This hotel is quite antiseptic, all the way down to the overwhelming aroma of cleaner we noticed upon first entry. The rooms are basic, with a/c, sliding glass door, and a tiny terrace without any furniture for enjoying the view. Since it's located out of the way, we expected a restaurant, but there is no food offered. We found it to be a bit of a pain to be forced to "hunt" for food in our rental car.

Palmas del Mar

Located on the southeast coast near the town of Humacao on almost 2,800 acres, this is a condo-resort development of mammoth, sprawling, haphazard, and sometimes not-so-pretty proportions. Popular as a weekend haven for Sanjuaneros (it's less than an hour from San Juan) and snowbirds North America, Palmas del Mar boasts more than 3 miles of beaches (including one with lifeguards, bar, and cafe); two 18-hole golf courses (designed by Gary Player and Rees Jones); 20 tennis courts (7 lighted); an equestrian center; 7 pools; a fitness center; a large boat basin with several marinas and Coral Head Divers; the rather stark and behemoth Palmanova Plaza shopping center; more than 15 restaurants, cafes, and pizza joints; several bars, and a casino. Sheraton has a resort here, and several of the condo clusters have all kinds of rental units available. Although we prefer other parts of Puerto Rico (Palmas is not our style), Palmas del Mar might be a good and affordable alternative for families who go the condo rental route. Contact Coldwell Banker or Diane Marsters (800-835-0199 or 787-850-3030; www.marstersrealty.com), Palmas del Mar Real Estate (787-852-8888), or RE/MAX de Palmas (787-850-7069).

Where to Stay

Four Points Sheraton Palmas del Mar, 170 Candelero Drive, Humacao, PR. ✆ 787-850-6000, ✎ 787-850-6001, ⌨ www.sheraton.com

💲 **Not So Cheap** ⓨ **EP** ⓒⓒ 126 rooms

We see this as more of a country club than a resort. Located on a grandiose 2,750-acre resort, this Sheraton estate has recently been upgraded after a major renovation in 2004. We aren't a big fan of the setup here, though; the hotel is located in a sprawling subdevelopment that has an extremely non–Puerto Rican feel. With all of the houses being built here, it seems that the hotel is a bit of an afterthought. The rooms do have all the amenities, as well as the patented Sheraton Four Comfort Bed, which is extremely comfortable, if that is any consolation. The golf course is great for those who crave hitting the links. There is an infinity pool, a wine bar, and restaurants on site.

THE SOUTH COAST

Patillas

On our most recent visit to Puerto Rico, we discovered this relaxed minicity, which retains an authentic small-town Puerto Rican feel. Patillas was named after the watermelon, but its claim to fame is the juicy grapes that are harvested here and sold to American winemakers. Patillas is also called "The Emerald of the South" — one look at the sparkling water of the beaches will explain why. Patillas is the perfect place to relax and kick back — especially if, like us, you spent too much time in the clubs while visiting San Juan.

Caribe Playa Beach Resort, HC 764, P.O. Box 8490, Patillas, PR. Ⓒ local: 787-839-6339, ✆ 787-839-1817, 💻 www.caribeplaya.com, engel@caribeplaya.com

💲 **Not So Cheap** Ⓨ **EP** CC 32 rooms

Tucked within a secluded cove on the southeastern coast is this little gem. Sure, nobody has ever heard of Patillas, but that is half the fun. This is where the rainforest descends to the crescent-shaped beach, which is testimony to the natural beauty of this less-traveled corner of Puerto Rico. If you're looking for the comfort of a resort without the extravagance (or stratospheric prices), this unassuming hotel is the perfect option. This family-run establishment has recently come under a new management that is intent on catering to its guests' every need.

The hotel is an ochre and white two-story structure, and each of the rooms has direct sea views. Unlike at some resorts that are built way off the shore, the balconies here are right over the beach — a private beach, at that, complete with sun chairs to soak up the Puerto Rican sun. There is also a sundeck, a relaxing pool area, a barbecue grill, and hammocks. The grounds are nicely landscaped with plenty of palms and plants. The stretch of beach here is beautiful, with tall palms hanging right over the sea. Each room has either two double beds or a queen and includes a/c, fan, cable TV, minibar, and coffeemaker. There is also Internet access, a library, and a TV room for those non-nature types. The restaurant is quite tasty as well; they have recently switched over to Latino-Caribbean fusion cuisine.

It's no surprise that many of the resort's clientele are repeat guests — after our stay, we were aching to return, too. Sure, the hotel is not located in one of the island's main tourist zones, but that is a blessing, not a curse. Right in front of the beach, there is surfing, swimming, and snorkeling (dolphin and manta rays are commonly sighted), so be sure to bring your snorkel gear. The picturesque town of Patillas is just five minutes by foot, providing an authentic glimpse of the real Puerto Rico — more than any super-resort will ever offer.

Caribbean Paradise Parador, Road 3, km 114, Barrio Guadarraya, Patillas,
PR. ✆ 787-839-5885, ✉ 787-271-0069,
🖥 www.caribbeanparadisepr.com, caribbean@isla.net

💲 **Cheap** 🍴 **EP** CC 23 rooms

For a 10-year-old who doesn't like the beach, this hotel may be a
"Caribbean Paradise," but for us, it's a nightmare. First of all, it's not
on the beach, which causes it to automatically lose its "paradise" tag. It's
only about a block and a half off the shore, but it gets quite hot without the sea breeze. The hotel has little to brag about except the array of
video games and playground equipment for toddlers. The rooms have
a/c, coffeemaker, and cable TV but are boxy. Without a fan, it is impossible to keep the windows open, making for a bit of a claustrophobic experience. There are two pools, one of which is designated for kids. We
are starting to think that this hotel was opened by kids, as they seem to
enjoy all the amenities. This place has no flair or local flavor—just a
lot of kids' toys.

Ponce

Known as "The Pearl of the South," Ponce is a wonderful mélange of Spanish
and Caribbean architecture, with other styles thrown in for the hell of it. The
city was founded by Ponce de León's great-grandson, who proceeded to name
it after, who else, his great-granddaddy. In downtown Ponce, the Spanish
colonial influence is still very pronounced. Most of the central district around
Plaza Las Delicias has been or is in the process of being restored and is definitely worth seeing. In the plaza are the **Catedral Nuestra Señora de
Guadalupe** and the very colorful old firehouse, the **Parque de Bombas**, which
sparkles after its recent renovation. Other must-stops while in Ponce are the
Museo de la Música Puertorriqueña, (848-7016, at the corner of Calles Isabel
and Salud and open Tuesday through Sunday, 8:30 a.m. to 4:30 p.m.), which
provides a great perspective on Puerto Rican music from *bomba* and *plena* to
danza and *salsa*; the neoclassical and colorful facade of **Teatro La Perla** (Calle
Mayor); the **Museum of the History of Ponce** (Casa Salazar), 844-7071, open
every day except Tuesday from 9 a.m. to 5 p.m., admission $3 for adults and
$1.50 for children; and the world-class **Ponce Museum of Art**, 848-0505,
open daily from 10 a.m. to 5 p.m., admission $4 for adults and $2 for children.
Note that once you leave the center of town, there are very few street signs,
so be sure to have a good map and a sense of humor.

Just south of town, past the Ponce Hilton at the end of Route 14 (Avenida
Malecón), is **La Guancha Paseo Tablado**, a happening boardwalk on the water that is lined with bars, cafes, and restaurants. It's a hangout spot for both
young and old Ponceños. We like having a cold Medalla or piña colada and
watching the crowd, boats (it's a marina, too), and water. The trade winds

keep things cool. There is also a pier where you can catch a boat to **Caja de Muertos** (Coffin Island). On the island there is a gorgeous beach for swimming, excellent snorkeling, and an old lighthouse built in 1880. **Aventuras Puerto Rico** (380-8481) leads trips here and all over Puerto Rico.

Where to Stay

Hotel Meliá, P.O. Box 1431, 75 Calle Cristina, Ponce, PR. ✆ 787-842-0260, ✆ 787-841-3602, ⌨ www.hotelmeliapr.com

💲 **Cheap** and up ⑪ EP ⒸⒸ 73 rooms

Located adjacent to the Parque de Bombas, this family-owned and -operated hotel is very affordable and within walking distance of all the historic sites of central Ponce. The clean, simple (and somewhat retro-funky) rooms all include a/c, private bath, phone, and cable TV. The rooms on the high floors offer some nice views, especially those facing west and the Plaza Las Delicias. There is a wonderful rooftop terrace where breakfast is served — it is also a great place for evening cocktails. The recent completion of a swimming pool has elevated the Meliá above the competition. There is a restaurant and bar at the hotel, and you are steps away from countless others. We loved the lobby's Spanish charm — tile floors, high ceilings, faded décor — and the last time we visited, there were plastic covers on the lampshades (so anti-chic!). A newly added Executive Center (a room with two computers) offers free Internet access for guests.

Ponce Hilton & Casino, P.O. Box 7419, 1150 Avenida Caribe, Ponce, PR. ✆ 800-HILTONS or 787-259-7676, ✆ 787-259-7674, ⌨ www.hilton.com

💲 **Very Pricey** and up ⑪ EP ⒸⒸ 153 rooms

Geared to the business traveler, the blue and white Ponce Hilton is the city's biggest hotel and the largest resort on Puerto Rico's south coast. Located about 10 minutes south of the Plaza Las Delicias (depending on traffic), this hotel is lacking in warmth and charm. Indeed, the lobby has the feel of a suburban mall. The property has 80 acres, is on the waterfront (although the beach in front is not very pretty), and sea views are decent only from the top (fourth) floor. It does have a putting green and driving range, four lighted tennis courts, a pool, a fitness center, a basketball court, a playground, and a pool table (we love eight-ball). There are two restaurants, three bars (including the Pavilion Discotheque), and, of course, the casino. The rooms, furnished in rattan and tropical colors, are loaded with amenities, including a/c, lanai, cable TV with video games, speakerphone with voicemail and data port, safe, minibar, and iron and ironing board. Look for packages or corporate discounts.

Hotel Belgica, 122-C Villa, Ponce, PR. ✆ and ✉ 787-844-3255, 💻 www.hotelbelgica.com, hotelbelgica@yahoo.com

💲 **Cheap** 🍴 **EP** CC 20 rooms

The cheapest of the three hotels located in the heart of Ponce is this old-fashioned spot. Right off the plaza, the Belgica offers easy access to the city and features rooms with high ceilings, comfortable beds, and Spanish-style balconies. The sheets are a bit starched and the towels not much softer than sandpaper, but the rates are cheap and the rooms pleasant. For those who don't mind street noise, the rooms with a balcony are recommended.

Fox Delicias Hotel, 6963 Calle Isabel, Ponce, PR. ✆ 787-290-5050, ✉ 787-259-6413, 💻 www.foxdeliciashotel.com

💲 **Not So Cheap** 🍴 **EP** CC 30 rooms

Hey, all you mall lovers, we have found your paradise! The Fox Delicias bills itself as "your downtown getaway," but we have deemed it "the mall rat's Eden." What was once Ponce's mall has recently been converted to a hotel and, best of all, it has retained the feel of a shopping mall! Upon entering, we couldn't help but notice that the layout has remained the same. What were once small shops have been equipped with beds and bathrooms, and even the beauty salon has survived the makeover (excuse the pun). This place is so tacky that we found ourselves running for the exits! We are not mall haters, but who would build a hotel with 30 rooms without windows? Excuse us, only 28 of the 30 are self-enclosed. It's great for those who have always fantasized about staying in the mall after closing time, but it's a nightmare for those of us who like a little fresh air or at least a window to remind us that we aren't in prison. Sure, the rooms have cable TV, a/c, and a phone, but the ceilings are low and the atmosphere is as stuffy as a tiny gift shop (coincidence?). The mall's escalators remain, although the kiosk with the "You are here" sign has mercifully been dismantled. Can we use the word *tacky* again? The owners have even held on to that mall mainstay, the food court. Guests emerge from their windowless rooms on the ground floor to be greeted by a slew of people seated right in front of their door, chowing down on one of the five cheap daily specials. High class it's not. For those searching for the sleep-in-the-mall experience, call the number above. If not, steer clear of the Fox Mall, we mean Hotel.

Where to Eat

$$$ **El Ancla**, 805 Avenida Hostos, 840-2450

We love sitting at this seaside restaurant, where the waves caress the shore as we dine on great *criollo* cuisine, such as the famous seafood stew. El Ancla is located on the docks just south of the city. It's very popular, so directions are easy to come by. Open 11:30 a.m. to 9:30 p.m. and later on weekends.

$$$$ La Terraza, in Ponce Hilton, 259-7676

Although housed in a big hotel, La Terraza has an ambiance that is quite conducive to a great dining experience. The colonial décor and New World charm, coupled with the acclaimed cuisine, keep tourists and locals coming back for more. The menu changes every few months, but expect Caribbean specialties with a creative flair and excellent presentation. Open for dinner from 6 to 10 p.m. Reservations recommended.

$$ Lupita's, off the plaza, 848-8808

This is as close to bona fide Mexican food as we have found here in Puerto Rico. The open courtyard, decorated in authentic Mexican tile work, is a great place to sample the chimichangas, fajitas, or whatever Mexican delicacy you crave. The margaritas are spot-on. Open 11 a.m. to 11 p.m.

$$$ Pito's Seafood, Road 2, 841-4977

This is one of our favorite seafood spots. It offers three floors of open-air seaside dining. Pito's has its fancy side, such as its wine cellar, but the mood here is casual and comfortable. Seafood abounds — dig in. It also has a "Wine Oysters Espresso" Bar, but we urge readers not to mix all three in the same glass. With live music on the weekends and endless ocean breezes, Pito's is a great spot from which to enjoy the scenery. Open from 11 a.m. to 11 p.m. Sunday through Thursday; Friday and Saturday until midnight.

Guánica and La Parguera

Located on the southern coast of the island, west of Ponce and near three great natural sites — the Guánica Forest Reserve, the Phosphorescent Bay, and Gilligan's Island — Guánica is an example of the "real" Puerto Rico. There are few fast-food chains, 7-Elevens, or Blockbuster Videos — just lots of *bodegas* and *panaderías*. Guánica has a cool-looking waterfront (camera, please), and just outside of town, the **Guánica Forest Reserve** has some gorgeous and deserted beaches. To get to the Reserve, just follow Route 333 until you can go no farther. You'll see places to stop along the way. Guánica also has some of the best dive sites in Puerto Rico. **Gilligan's Island** is a small, uninhabited, mile-offshore cay with a secluded beach and excellent snorkeling. The folks at Copamarina, 821-0505, can arrange an excursion there.

About 10 miles/16 kilometers west of Guánica is **La Parguera** and **Phosphorescent Bay** (Route 324 — watch for signs). La Parguera is a fishing town with a handful of restaurants and a few bars where we like to play pool with the locals. Most go there for the "bio bay," as it's called — in the dark of a calm night, phosphorescent plankton (dinoflagellates, to be precise) create sparks when there's any movement in the water, which disturbs their nesting. La Parguera's coastline is filled with mangrove islands and is not a beach destination. However, the harbor is a haven for fishing charters, especially the deep-sea variety. Call **Parguera Fishing Charters** (787-899-4698) for more info. **Aleli Tours** (390-6086) runs sailing, snorkeling, and kayaking tours. Its catamaran is available for charter. Our favorite dive shop in town is **Paradise Scuba** (899-7611), which leads dives to the bio-luminescent bay.

Where to Stay

Copamarina Beach Resort, P.O. Box 805, Route 333, km 6.5, Caña Gorda, Guánica, PR. ✆ 800-468-4553, 800-981-467, or 787-821-0505, ✉ 787-821-0070, 🖳 www.copamarina.com, info@copamarina.com

💲 **Pricey** and up ⑴ **EP** ⓒⓒ 106 rooms

Copamarina is a reasonably priced resort situated on the Bahía de Guánica in a quiet part of the island. It has recently expanded and now has 106 rooms and suites spread out over 16 acres. The rooms are attractive — with wall-to-wall carpeting or tile floors, bamboo and light wood furnishings, a/c, cable TV, fridges, safes, hairdryers, coffeemakers, and phones — and they sport little lanais. The main lobby has a very pleasant veranda on which to sit and read.

This is a great place to go if you want to be somewhere tranquil and be near the extensive Guánica Forest Reserve (where you can take long walks or bike rides). Copamarina is very popular with weekenders from San Juan who want a secluded getaway. The grounds are well tended and the beach is pretty. The seas here are calm because the bay is sheltered. However, sometimes after storms, the water contains lots of seaweed. (If only we could control the weather.) There are more beaches close by in the Forest Reserve. The beach area here has recently been spruced up and embellished by big raised beds that are ideal for relaxing in the sun, sipping piña coladas, or sunbathing topless. There are two pools, a kids' pool, full water sports — including a full-service PADI Dive Center — a small fitness center, and two lighted tennis courts. For dining, there is the open-air Las Palmas Café and the new Alaxandra Restaurant, which offers gourmet Caribbean dining in an elegant dining room or out on the terrace and has a live guitarist most nights.

Parador Guánica 1929, Avenida Los Veteranos, km 2.5 & Road 3116, Guánica, PR. ✆ 787-821-0099, ✉ 787-821-1842, 🖳 www.guanica1929.com

💲 **Cheap** 🍽 **EP** or **All-Inclusive** CC 27 rooms

Back in the days when this region was prime sugar-growing territory, there were lots of investors, "sugar daddies," and bigwigs passing through these parts. In 1929, the stately Hotel Americano was built on this site to accommodate these important guests. Today the sugar industry is no longer king, but thankfully this historic hotel has recently been reopened. With experience running *paradores,* Juan and Maria have done a fine job here as well. They have completely renovated the property and have geared it toward families, Puerto Rican and foreign alike, who are looking for an affordable vacation spot. The rooms within the peach-colored, two-story hotel include verandas with views of Ensenada Bay. Below is an appealing pool area with sun chairs. It offers an all-inclusive plan that is quite affordable — the food from the à la carte *criollo* restaurant is good, but we like the freedom to try new spots in town or at the Copamarina. Legend has it that Teddy Roosevelt stayed here, but we don't think he had a/c or cable TV, as we did. A note to drinkers: Due to a family-friendly policy, no alcohol is served at the Guánica.

Parador Villa Parguera, P.O. Box 3400, Lajas, PR. ✆ 787-899-7777, ✆ 787-899-6040, 🖳 www.villaparguera.net, pvparguera@prtc.net

💲 **Not So Cheap** 🍽 **EP** CC 74 rooms

Perched right on the seafront in downtown La Parguera, this three-story hotel is not overflowing with style, by any means, but the rooms are well-equipped, clean, and affordable. Each has cable TV and a/c, but no fan. One reason we prefer staying in the Guánica is that there is no beach here to speak of (although sun chairs are set out on the grass along the rocky sea front). The swinging palms provide some shade, and there is a small pool. The on-site restaurant is a bit bleak — hardly the *Méson Gastronomico* it's billed to be. On weekends, the hotel puts on small-scale floor shows. The dock for the bioluminescent bay trips is located just a few steps away — quite convenient if you're up for a nighttime algae show.

THE WEST COAST

Boquerón

Located in an area called Cabo Rojo in the southwestern corner of the island, Boquerón used to be a charming little village, but over the past decade it has grown tremendously. Boquerón has a beautiful long beach and calm bay and is considered one of Puerto Rico's best bathing beaches. For this reason, it has become a very popular weekend getaway spot for Sanjuaneros (just over a two-hour drive). The bay is very scenic, with mountains at the southern end. Actually, the entire area is quite wonderful. It's rural, with pastures and herds of cattle reaching up to green hills and mountains.

It's also a boat town — lots of cruising boats stop here, bringing with them those weathered and boozy "boat rats." Now, we're not one to bitch about a few cocktails. After all, Nick and Nora Charles (and, of course, Patsy Stone) are our idols. But these people start early, hang out at the bar for hours, get totally blotto, and by a miracle of gravitation and balance, somehow manage to get back to their boats intact. They're always in their berths early because they get so trashed. We're amused as long as they don't start talking to us in an advanced state of inebriation. If they do, we excuse ourselves to go to the loo and never return.

The center of activity in Boquerón is the main intersection in town, by the bay, where there are two prominent bars on opposite corners. The one with the action and a very competitive pool table is called **Shamar**. You know it's a yachty favorite from all the tattered burgees and ensigns donated to the bar by boaters from yacht clubs and countries around the world. Although this place used to get quite rowdy on weekends, recent ordinances have put an end to the mayhem. Weekend nights are still fun — the streets are blocked off and the town bustles with a young crowd. The public beach is great, but if you're aching to get off the beaten track, check out Playa Buyó, which is about 2 miles north of town. **Mona Aquatics** (851-2185) has a full range of activities, from scuba to snorkeling in bio bay — it is right next to the marina. We also recommend renting kayaks to explore the waters here — **Boquerón Kayak Rental** (255-1849) can arrange everything. We have listed our favorite hotels, but for those looking for apartment rentals, contact **Centro Vacacional Boquerón** at 787-851-1900; it has access to more than 150 beachside apartments with kitchens (although many apartments have those often-annoying bunk beds).

Where to Stay

Parador Boquemar, P.O. Box 133, Route 101, Boquerón, Cabo Rojo, PR.
ⓒ 787-851-2158, 📠 787-851-7600, 🖳 www.boquemar.com

💲 **Cheap** 🍴 **EP** 🆑 75 rooms

This pink *parador* in Boquerón resembles a motel but is clean, efficient, and cheap. Recently renovated, this three-story hotel's rooms are equipped with a/c, fridge, phone, cable TV, and private bath. There is a swimming pool, a restaurant (La Cascada), and a bar. The rooms on the second and third floors have lanais. The town junction (where all the activity happens) and the beach are just around the corner and down the street. Be sure to make reservations well in advance — the Boquemar is popular with folks from San Juan on weekends. It's not glamorous, but it's more modern than many *paradores*.

Cofresí Beach Hotel, 57 Calle Munoz Rivera, Boquerón, Cabo Rojo, PR.
Ⓒ 787-254-3000, 🖂 787-254-1048, 🖳 www.cofresibeach.com

📓 **Not So Cheap** 🍴 EP ⒸⒸ 16 rooms

This art deco–like hotel offers one-, two-, and three-bedroom apartments, all of which are equipped with fully functioning kitchens. The bedrooms include queen-size beds and a/c. For television buffs, each apartment includes cable TV and a DVD player. The hotel also has a small rectangular pool and views of the sea. The beach is a hop, skip, and a jump away, and the prices are reasonable as well. It's a good spot for the simple traveler craving a cheap spot close to the action and the beach.

Boquerón Beach Hotel, Boquerón, Cabo Rojo, PR. Ⓒ and 🖂 787-851-7110, 🖳 www.boqueronbeachhotel.com

📓 **Cheap** 🍴 EP ⒸⒸ 193 rooms

Though not right in town, this older hotel is blessed with original Spanish tile work and colonial-style wrought-iron balconies. Recent renovations have also given some of the rooms a well-needed sprucing up. The rooms have TV, a/c, and minibar. Request one of the rooms in front — these are the best. For those who don't mind being right out of town, this quiet old hotel is a good bet. It is located by the entrance to the public beach (Balneario de Boquerón).

Where to Eat

In Boquerón, there are options within town and on the outlying beaches. Of the restaurants in town, our favorites are listed below. In the morning, there are several little cheap and simple breakfast spots next to the happening bars. Some of the nearby beaches are ideal for a visit and a seaside meal. This is perhaps the best place on the island to sample the fresh oysters and clams. They are available along Calle de Diego (the beach road) from vendors who crack them open upon demand. **El Combate** is one of the best beaches in the region, and most of the nearby restaurants are quite similar, so make a visit and take a look around. Just up the coast, **Joyuda** is known for its seafood and has several good restaurants, including **Perichi's** (851-3131), **Tino's** (851-2976), and **Annie's** (851-0021), which has the best food.

$$$ **El Bohío**, Carretera 102, km 13.9, Joyuda, 851-2755

This is our favorite restaurant here. We love to sit on the deck over the water. The menu is Caribbean and seafood — the cold conch salad is a perfect light lunch option.

$$$ **Fishnet**, Calle Jose de Diego, 254-3163

It is only fitting that this centrally located restaurant has a marine theme, because Boquerón's best seafood is cooked here. The owner has another restaurant a few steps away called **Roberto's Villa Playera**, which has the same quality food with better views. Either one is a solid bet for fresh fish and more.

$$$ **Galloway's**, 12 Calle José de San Diego, 254-3302

We love the location, perched above the sea. Beautiful sunsets (and of course, happy-hour specials) make this a popular hangout spot. Food is well-prepared, with a focus on seafood and pasta. All the seafood is extremely fresh. Daily lunch specials are quite affordable and the American owners, Dan and Gladys, are good conversationalists as well.

$$$ **Pika-Pika**, 244 Calle Estacion, 851-2440

Though a little pricey, this Mexican restaurant warrants a few extra bucks. Its specialties are meat plates, served with all the fixings. It has a varied cocktail menu and offers weekend lunches.

$$ **Pizzeria Lykken**, Calle Jose de Diego, 851-6335

For the best pizza around, Lykken is the way to go. We like the outdoor terrace and the big selection of pies.

Going Out

Galloway's is a popular spot for drinks, catering to the Irish pub crowd. Rock music predominates. Another good spot on Calle de Diego is **La Bahía** (851-5003), which is especially lively on weekends and is known for Latin music. Most action centers around **Shamar** (851-0542), which has happy-hour specials, pool tables, and a lively atmosphere. Beers are cheap, and live bands play salsa music on the weekend.

Mayagüez

After San Juan and Ponce, this is Puerto Rico's largest city. Mayagüez is one of the island's major ports, but it is hardly a metropolis. Much of the city was destroyed in an earthquake in 1918, but the central square, **Plaza Colón**, is attractive, as is the City Hall that flanks it. **Teatro Yagüez** has a lot of history and now stands as the cultural nexus for western Puerto Rico. Mayagüez is also the site of the island's major university and zoo, which has been recently renovated to provide more living space for the animals.

Where to Stay

Mayagüez Resort & Casino, Route 104, km. 0.3, Mayagüez, PR. ℂ 787-832-3030, 🖳 787-265-3020, 🖳 www.mayaguezresort.com

🔳 **Very Pricey** 🅨 **All-Inclusive** ©© 140 rooms

Fifteen minutes out of Mayagüez, this hilltop resort is set on 25 acres and offers beautiful bay views. The problem is that it's not much of a resort. Sure, there is a pool, a few tennis courts, and a small gym, but besides that there is not much offered. The rooms are housed in a five-story boxy building overlooking a nonspectacular pool. It does offer 24-hour room service and a big casino that is a popular hangout. There are restaurants on site and a pool bar as well. We do like the tropical grounds here—there are beautiful trees and flowers, but it seems that everyone else was too busy tossing quarters into the slot machines to notice.

Howard Johnson Mayagüez, 70 Calle Mendez Vigo, Mayagüez, PR.
🕿 866-668-4577, 🖂 787-832-9122, 🖳 www.hojo.com,
hjsales@coqui.net

🛅 **Not So Cheap** 🍴 **EP** ⒸⒸ 39 rooms

This brand-new member of the once illustrious Howard Johnson hotel chain has at least a tad of local flavor—it was built in the town's old convent. We find it kind of strange to stay in a penthouse in the priests' house, but for those seeking layman luxury, there are four of these top-floor suites. Each of the rooms has exactly what one would expect from HoJo's—cable TV, a/c, hairdryer, iron and ironing board, coffeemaker, and tacky comforters. There is a teeny-weeny pool in the enclosed courtyard—apparently the men of the cloth were not big poolgoers. Located right in the heart of town, HoJo's is a good spot from which to tour the city or act out any converted convent fantasies.

Hotel Colonial, 14 Calle Iglesia Sur, Mayagüez, PR. 🕿 and 🖂 787-833-2150, 🖳 www.hotelcolonial.com, colonial@hotel-colonial.com

🛅 **Cheap** 🍴 **CP** ⒸⒸ 20 rooms

This old-fashioned hotel has been lodging visitors for at least 90 years—that's a lot of dirty sheets! Not surprisingly, the Colonial is a little aged. The original ceramic floor tiles are still found in some rooms, which is a welcome bridge to the past, but the tacky furniture within brings back memories of the late 1970s—which was a great era for disco parties, but not for hotel furnishings. There are not enough windows for our liking, either—many rooms do not have any at all. Rooms have a/c, cable TV, and a minibar, but not much in the style department.

Where to Eat and Go Out

$$ **El Castillo**, in Mayagüez Resort, 832-3030

This is the best place in town for a hearty meal. The lunch buffet on weekdays is chock full of local dishes—a great opportunity to sample everything under the Puerto Rican sun. The breakfast buffet is plentiful, although it is usually devoured by the hotel guests. The weekend brunch is, well, a combination of the two, which makes sense. Dinners are à la carte—we recommend the sea bass. Open 6:30 a.m. to midnight.

$$$ **Restaurant El Estoril**, 100 E. Calle Mendez Vigo, 834-2288

By far the best restaurant in town, El Estoril offers a wonderful selection of sophisticated fare. The appetizers, such as escargot, seviche, and Galician soup, are fantastic, and the entrées are no disappointment, either. The fish is served in a variety of ways: with capers, port sauce, or, our favorite, creole sauce. The scallop-stuffed crepes are also worth a try. Open Monday through Saturday from 5:30 to 10:30 p.m.

Note that the bar next door, **La Galeria**, is a great place to get a drink and enjoy jazz and blues music. It opens after 10 p.m. every day (although it's closed on Sunday) and usually has live bands on the weekend. There is also a popular sports bar, **Red Corner** (313-6943), also on Calle Mendez Vigo, that has plenty of action.

Rincón

This corner of Puerto Rico is a surfer's mecca. Actually, some of the best surfing in the Caribbean is found here during the winter months. There are more than 20 surf spots in the Rincón-Aguadilla area, with names like Dogman's, Domes, and Shithouse, and several surf shops. A visit to the local post office will turn up as many bleached-out surfer dudes as Puerto Ricans. Rincón is also one of the most anglicized parts of the island. Being on the west coast, sunsets are fantastic, whether viewed from a beachside bar, hotel balcony, or the ocean surf. During the winter months (January until March) the whales migrate to Rincón—they are visible from the lighthouse park or from private boats available for excursions. **Punta Higuero** is where the lighthouse stands—north of the lighthouse are the best surf spots and popular hangouts; to the south are deserted beaches such as the beautiful Playa Córcega. Pick up a copy of the tourist map for $1 at many locations or visit the **Tourist Information Center** (787-823-5024) at the intersection of Routes 413 and 115. A rental car is a must if you stay in the area. There is an airport in Aguadilla (about a 30-minute drive). Most people fly into San Juan (about 95 miles away and more than a two-hour drive). **West Coast Surf Shop** is right in downtown Rincón (823-3935). It rents out boogie and surf boards for $15 a day (weekly rates are also available). There are other nearby surf shops that rent out boards—try **Desecho Inn Surf Shop** near the lighthouse (823-0390).

Taino Divers (823-6429) is the most reputable dive shop in Rincón, specializing in two-tank dive trips to Desecho Island. There is often 100-foot visibility, and the wealth of marine life is astounding. U.S. Coast Guard Captain Tim runs **Cactus Fishing Charters** (833-0308), which offers great full-day trips. **Oceans Unlimited** (823-2340) charters boats from Puerto Real to Mona Island and beyond.

Where to Stay

⊛ **Casa Isleña Inn**, P.O. Box 1484, Road 413, km 4.8, Barrio Puntas, Rincón, PR. ℂ 888-289-7750 or 787-823-1525, ✆ 787-823-1530, 🖳 www.casa-islena.com, reservations@casa-islena.com

   💲 **Not So Cheap** ⑪ **EP** (cc) 9 rooms

Ah, this is the life! That's how we would sum up our experience at the Casa Isleña, our favorite spot in Rincón. It's not nearly as sophisticated as the Horned Dorset, but it's the ideal beach house. Located smack dab on the beautiful beach, close to the action, this sexy Mediterranean-style house has just nine rooms, which limits the number of guests. In 2002, Colombian owner Dario renovated what was a private residence into this beachfront inn, injecting his easygoing style and friendly nature. Vibrant colors run throughout. Regardless of the season, the inn is usually full, which comes as no surprise to us. Each of the rooms has one or two queen-size beds as well as fan, a/c, cable TV, and terra-cotta floors. The Mexican tiles and well-crafted hand-made wooden furniture (also imported from Mexico) add a stylistic flair. We prefer the upstairs rooms with a view, especially Room 254, which has a king-size bed and a Jacuzzi in the bathroom. The small on-site restaurant serves fresh foods, such as salads and seafood. With a limited number of guests and an attractive beachside pool, the Casa Isleña maintains a friendly atmosphere and is our favorite Island House for miles.

The Horned Dorset Primavera, P.O. Box 1132, Route 429, km 3.0, Rincón, PR. ℂ 800-633-1857 or 787-823-4030, ✆ 787-823-5580, 🖳 www.horneddorset.com, info@horneddorset.com

   💲 **Ridiculous** ⑪ **EP** and **MAP** (cc) 22 suites; 17 villas to come

Fine food, tranquillity, and service seem to be the mantra here at this sophisticated inn. Cheers to that! We love the Horned Dorset Primavera, a small and lovely four-acre property, tucked away on the coast south of Rincón (so tucked away that we have driven by it on two separate occasions). It's a symphony of taste with a touch of attitude (the management still requests that guests refrain from cell phone use in the lobby), and owners Harold Davies, Wilhelm Sack, and Kingsley Wratten have gone to great pains to make the property a tranquil and comfortable hideaway. Named after Davies and Wratten's first inn in upstate New York, it is well appointed, nicely decorated, has a very attractive staff, and features a fantastic library. Readers will be thrilled. You can sink into a big comfy chair, order a drink, check out the spectacular western view of the water (or the staff), and occasionally look up to see who might be passing through the lobby—a piece of heaven to some, including us. Breakfast is served on the veranda of the main building or in your room (we had it on our lanai in our bathrobes —it is a great touch). Lunch is on the veranda or by the main pool. The hotel's prix fixe dining room, which we found a tad stuffy, features delicious French cuisine with Caribbean accents by chef Aaron Wratten. There is also a casual bistro, a gym, and massage services. The hotel can arrange activities such as tennis, horseback riding, and diving.

The 22 two-story suites have no phones or Internet, which is uniquely welcome. They are, however, stylish, comfortable, and tasteful, with four-poster mahogany king-size beds and antiques. They also have lanais with a full or partial ocean view, a/c, and a ceiling fan. Some have private plunge pools. The very large bathrooms have brass claw-foot tubs, large vanities and mirrors (we love that—room for everyone's toiletries), and lots of white marble.

As if it were possible, this elegant inn is being upgraded to "become the most exclusive beachfront property on the island," according to Sack. In addition to expected enhancements to the 22 suites, there are 17 new villas that are in the works for completion by Christmas 2006. These villas will (unfortunately, in our opinion) become super-exclusive condos that will be selling in the million-dollar-plus range. Each residence will retain the Horned Dorset's Mozarabic style and will include a private dipping pool and ocean view. The interiors will be ultra-fancy, with marble floors, oversize tubs, Kohler surround showers, plasma TV with DVD, wine cooler, and a fully equipped Dwyer kitchen. Although the units will be sold as condos, many will still be rented out to visitors—at least that's the plan. Nobody can be sure how participatory the individual condo owners will be when it comes to renting out their villas. Either way, we do hope that this new condo conversion will not spoil the special ambiance of the Horned Dorset. If the currently discussed plan for an on-site heliport is any indication, the days of no cell phone use in the lobby will be long gone.

That being said, we won't argue with the expected arrival of valet parking and spa services (who would complain about a spa?). Rounding out the amenities on the well-manicured grounds are a medium-size pool, a smaller pool on the top of the hill by the Mesa Suites, and a tiny beach for sunning and swimming. However, we'd say the main reason to come here (at least, for now) is to read, be quiet, spend time with your companion, and enjoy great food, or maybe have that secret tryst with that certain someone. The hotel does not have facilities for children, and no one under 12 is accepted as a guest. We say hooray for the HDP! No crying babies, strollers, or whining kids to distract us from the latest Danielle Steele novel.

We recommend the MAP upgrade for an additional $160 per couple per day.

Lemontree Waterfront Cottages, P.O. Box 200, Route 429, Rincón, PR.
🕾 787-823-6452, 📠 787-823-5821, 💻 www.lemontreepr.com, info@lemontreepr.com

💲 **Not So Cheap** and up 🍴 **EP** CC 6 cottages

Just down the road from the ultra-fancy Horned Dorset is this sort of funky place. Located so close to the water that a misstep will virtually put you in the drink, the Lemontree is two houses linked together by a patio. The property has a seawall, steps down to the water, and a sliver of sand (and we mean *sliver*). Owned and operated by Lov and Lora Carabello, there are six efficiency units — two studios, two one-bedroom cottages, one two-bedroom apartment and one three-bedroom apartment. All have simple rattan furnishings, some custom woodwork, lanais that face west and toward the Mona Passage (we love the views), fully equipped kitchens (with blender, coffeemaker, and microwave), tile floors, cable TV, and a/c. The three-bedroom Papaya unit has a wet bar on the lanai. Maid service and linen change occurs halfway through your stay. Laundry service is available for a small fee. There is a three-night minimum.

Pipon's Resort, P.O. Box 4468, HC-01, Route 413, km 3, Barrio Puntas, Rincón, PR. 🕾 787-823-7154, 💻 www.piponsresort.com, pipons@coqui.net

💲 **Not So Cheap** 🍴 **EP** CC 6 rooms

Run by Harry and Marthy, a friendly Puerto Rican–New Jersey couple, Pipon's is an ideal option for those travelers seeking more tranquillity and/or a chance to cook their own food. Think of it as a sea-view apartment with daily maid service. All rooms have a/c and fans, and there are fully stocked kitchens, including full stoves and refrigerators. There is a bedroom with a queen-size bed (and a/c) as well as a sitting room with wicker cushioned furniture and cable TV. Our favorite feature, however, is the private lanai, with its expansive and refreshing sea views. (The beach is 1,000 feet away, and accessed by a newly laid path.) An adequate pool with a sundeck sits just below the rooms. Pipon's is a perfect spot for those who want to get away from the typical resort experience. Its homey setting is great for families — cots and cribs are available upon request. Since there are not many culinary options around Rincón, access to a kitchen is quite a plus.

Rincón of the Seas, P.O. Box 1850, Route 115, km 12.2, Rincón, PR. 🕾 787-823-7500, 📠 787-823-7503, 💻 www.rinconoftheseas.com

💲 **Very Pricey** 🍴 **BP** CC 111 rooms

The owners of this new resort aimed to incorporate an eclectic yet classy swirl of styles. Judging from the lobby containing marble columns imported from Oman and the art deco décor that's peppered with furniture and artwork from India, Pakistan, and Indonesia, their creation was a success. Although many places are more effective at sticking to one theme, the Rincón of the Seas is a wonderful resort, highlighted by an expansive pool area and wonderful beach. Despite the Asian and art deco influences, there is still a tropical feel here, thanks to the flowers and hand-painted murals. The rooms are located in three wings that overlook the pool and the sea. There are a few classes of accommodations. We prefer the Deluxe Ocean View rooms (on the upper three floors) — they are equipped with king-size bed, a/c, cable TV, coffeemaker, iron, and hairdryer. The Art Deco Suite includes a sofa bed and DVD player. Each room has a private lanai with sliding glass doors and comfy furniture for enjoying the view. There is a small video arcade and gym, but our favorite feature is the clean expanse of beach with its overhanging palms and great sunsets. The 4,000-square-foot free-form pool has a swim-up bar and café, but the fine dining takes place in the Deco. Rain is the name of the trendy wine bar — it presents a jungle theme and super-comfortable chairs. With an injection of style into a resort mold, Rincón of the Seas offers an exuberant getaway for sun-loving guests.

Rincón Beach Resort, Route 115, km 5.8, Añasco, PR. ℂ 866-589-0009, ℘ 787-589-9010, ⌨ www.rinconbeach.com, reservations@rinconbeach.com

🛍 **Wicked Pricey** ⑨ **EP** (CC) 118 rooms

Located on its own desolate beach, this Puerto Rican–owned resort is a pleasant place at which to take a time-out. The rooms are housed in one of three buildings, and many have views overlooking the beach. The resort also offers villas, which include a dining room, kitchen, and living room — best for families or larger groups. The rooms come equipped with phone, cable TV, iron, hairdryers, and a/c, although they also have fans for those of us who crave fresh sea breezes. The layout of the resort is well designed, with a wide-open lobby that offers guests a place to grab a drink and relax. Through the arch is a path leading to the horizon pool and beach area, which is fully equipped with sun chairs. There is no dearth of food or drink at the Rincón Beach Resort — in addition to a swim-up pool bar and boutique wine bar, the casual Pelican Bar & Grill serves lunch, and Las Brasas Restaurant offers a great selection of Latino fusion cuisine for dinner. We recommend the lamb chops with mint sauce or the local favorite, mashed fried plantains stuffed with fresh seafood and topped with creole sauce. Another plus is the oversize chess board with two-foot tall pieces — it gives new meaning to the expression "Get in the game!"

Villa Cofresí, P.O. Box 874, Route 115, km 12.0, Rincón, PR. ☎ 787-823-2450, ✆ 787-823-1770, 🖳 www.villacofresi.com, info@villacofresi.com

💲 **Not So Cheap** 🍴 **EP** CC 69 rooms

Villa Cofresí sits right on a great swimming beach. Motelish in look with no visual or ambient appeal, the clean and simple rooms all include a/c, cable TV, and fridges. The large rooms have tile floors, dropped ceilings, and all-tile baths with new fixtures. All of the recently added rooms face the ocean. A restaurant, a bar, a pool, and kayaking round out the facilities. Don't expect a groovy crowd here, but it's reasonably priced and right smack dab on the beach. Anti-chic seekers (or beach bums) might like this place. The hotel's restaurant, Ana de Cofresí, serves seafood, steaks, and traditional Puerto Rican cuisine from 5 to 10 p.m.

The Lazy Parrot, P.O. Box 430, Route 413, km 4.1, Rincón, PR. ☎ 787-823-5654, ✆ 787-823-0224, 🖳 www.lazyparrot.com, lzparrot@lazyparrot.com

💲 **Not So Cheap** 🍴 **CP** CC 11 rooms

For those looking to sacrifice beachside location for cheaper prices, the Lazy Parrot is a decent option. Located up in La Cadena hills, this 12-year-old Puerto Rican–owned inn offers great panoramic views and has a refreshing pool area to help you escape the heat. The beach is half a mile down the hill. The rooms are unique, though not overflowing with flavor. We prefer the four upstairs, due to their panoramic view of the sea and green hills behind. The rooms have terra-cotta tile floors, cable TV, and a/c, but the double beds aren't exactly like floating on a cloud (don't say we didn't warn you). Room 10 is our favorite — next time we will bring our own mattress! With its well-proportioned pool, small number of rooms, tiki garden, and cute bar, the Lazy Parrot can be a fun spot to stay.

Parador Villa Antonio, P.O. Box 68, Route 115, km 12.3, Rincón, PR. ☎ 800-443-0266 or 787-823-2645, ✆ 787-823-3380, 🖳 www.villa-antonio.com, pva@villa-antonio.com

💲 **Cheap** and up 🍴 **EP** CC 61 rooms

One of the *paradores* of Puerto Rico, Villa Antonio is next door to Villa Cofresí. What it lacks in ambiance — its low, squat, pink buildings aren't very visually appealing — it makes up for with a wonderful swimming beach. All units are air-conditioned and have kitchenettes. The rooms are basic motel fare and have phones, cable TV, daily maid service, and lanais. There are two pools, a children's play area, a game room, and two tennis courts. It's a good budget choice for families.

Beside the Pointe, P.O. Box 4430, HC-01, Route 413, km 4, Rincón, PR.
© and ✆ 787-823-8550, 🖥 www.besidethepointe.com,
info@besidethepointe.com

💰 **Not So Cheap** 🍴 **EP** CC 8 Rooms

Located right on Punta Higuero Beach (or Sandy Beach, as it is called by non-Spanish speakers), this is a surfer's mecca. The downstairs is the popular Tamboo bar and restaurant, so there is never a lack of social life here. In fact, this is the cultural nexus of the beach, so if you want to jump into the scene, look no farther. For those who crave tranquillity, some of the aforementioned options might be better suited. This was once just a surfer's spot but has recently been spruced up to attract a more moneyed crowd. As a result, the eight rooms are not too fancy, but they are a step up from the Casa Verde. Each has a/c and cable TV, and three feature a small kitchen. We prefer the upstairs rooms, which have their own lanais with sea views. Room 8 is the best — it has not one but two balconies — perfect for those sea-loving couples who aren't talking to each other.

Casa Verde, P.O. Box 1102, Route 413, Barrio Puntas, Rincón, PR. © 787-605-5351, 🖥 www.enrincon.com, enrincon@caribe.net

💰 **Dirt Cheap** 🍴 **EP** CC 5 rooms

This no-frills guesthouse has been one of Rincón's cheapest and most popular places to stay for years. In other words, it's a good party spot. Frequented by lots of surfers who are attracted to the rock-bottom prices and easy beach access, Casa Verde has never needed to do much publicity. The rooms are on the first or second floor of a concrete block–like structure and won't be featured in any fancy magazines. However, they are clean and comfortable. It's run as part of the Rock Bottom Bar & Grill, and there is always a mix of interesting people passing through. Casa Verde has a studio, equipped with a kitchen, as well as one- or two-bedroom suites with a/c, TV, fan, arched doorways, and terra-cotta tile floors. Some rooms open onto a shared veranda with hammocks. The rooms are just steps from the beach and are even closer to the bar that churns out tropical drinks well into the night.

Where to Eat

$$$ **El Molino del Quijote**, Route 429, km 3.3, 823-4010

Virtually next door to the Horned Dorset, this restaurant is open Friday through Sunday and serves Puerto Rican and Spanish cuisine. We have heard only good things about the food here.

$$$$$ **Horned Dorset**, Route 429, km 3, 823-4030

The Horned Dorset offers superb French dining along the Caribbean coast. The food is extremely expensive but impeccably prepared, with a menu that changes daily. We had Peruvian seviche, sauteed foie gras, and lobster tail with pineapple relish — and those were just three of the seven courses! Meals are well over $100 a person, but they are exquisitely presented in the elegant dining room. Expect only the best. Dress is formal.

$$$ **Las Colinas**, at Parador J. B. Hidden Village, Route 4416, km 2.5, Sector Villa Rubia in neighboring Aguada, 868-8686

For a real Puerto Rican dining experience, check out this place — it's famous for its *churrasco* (grilled meats) and *mofongo* (mashed green plantains). Open Sunday through Thursday from 5 to 11 p.m. and Friday and Saturday from 3 to 11 p.m.

$$ **Lazy Parrot**, Route 413, km 4.1, 823-5654

This hilltop perch (get it?) has great views and pretty good food as well. Its menu is mixed, including good vegetarian options.

$$ **Rock Bottom Bar & Grill**, on Sandy Beach, 605-5351

This is another popular eatery that features happy-hour specials and tasty dinners, specializing in fresh fish. It churns out a lot of tropical drinks well into the night.

$$ ⊛ **Tamboo**, on Sandy Beach next to Beside the Pointe, 823-8550

This surf spot offers alfresco lunch and dinner, with views of the sea and its surfers. We were told to steer clear of the burgers, so we opted for a shrimp salad. At night, the activity pulses with DJs and cheap drinks. This place also happens to be the biggest party spot in Rincón, although there is also plenty of action at the bar above Casa Verde as well.

$$ **The Spot @ Black Eagle**, Route 413, km 1, 823-3510

This a good weekend hangout, offering happy-hour specials and sophisticated snacks like grilled snapper with lemon sofrito sauce and hummus with grilled eggplant, goat cheese, and mint served with pita bread.

⊛ Isabela

Isabela, located in the northwest corner of the island, is a new feature in our Puerto Rico chapter. Thanks to its beautiful beaches, this region (including the nearby settlements of Aguada and Aguadilla) is undergoing a tourism boom. In short, it's an ideal beach retreat — the shore here is much less developed than in other parts of Puerto Rico. For centuries, Isabela was a tobacco-growing town, but today people come for its smokin' coastline (we couldn't resist). Desolate beaches give way to rolling sand dunes and limestone cliffs. The natural beauty here provides the perfect backdrop for

nature-oriented activities such as kayaking or horseback riding. For eques-
trians, **Tropical Trails** (872-9256) offers amazing two-hour $35 guided rides
through the almond forest and along the beach. Shacks Beach is perhaps the
best spot on Puerto Rico for windsurfing or kitesurfing, and the waves at Jobos Beach are ideal for surfers. **Hang Loose Surf Shop** (872-2490) can help
arrange gear for any of these activities.

What makes this place so special (and an undiscovered gem) is the fact
that there is so much coastline that has yet to be developed. With a rental car,
it's easy to cruise along and stake out your own little slice of paradise at which
to spend the day. We love Montones, Bajuras, and Sardinera Beach as well.
In Jobos, ask for **El Pozo de Jacinto** — it is a blowhole in the rocks that looms
over a swirl of oceanic turbulence. The nearby **Guajataca Forest** is noteworthy for its geological formations of limestone. *Karst* is the word used to describe this inland terrain, which is quite rugged and surreal-looking at times.
Route 446 rings through the forest and is a beautiful drive; there is a lookout
tower as well. Close by is Lake Guajataca, formed by a dam, which is a popular fishing site. Although there is still not much in terms of restaurants or
nightlife, the allure of Isabela is starting to turn heads, and it definitely caught
our attention — this is one of our favorite places on the island. The best dive
shop in town is **Aquatica** (890-6071).

Where to Stay

Villa Montaña Beach Resort, Road 4446, km 1.9, Barrio Bajuras, Isabela,
PR. ✆ 888-780-9195 or 787-872-9554, ✉ 787-872-9553,
🖥 www.villamontana.com, sales@villamontana.com

💲 **Ridiculous** 🍴 **EP** CC 75 rooms

How do we love thee, Villa Montaña? Let us count the ways. Sorry for
the romantic interlude and the perversion of Elizabeth Barrett Brown-
ing's fine verse, but we are really high on this beach resort. The mantra
here seems to be that good taste need not equal extravagance. Unlike
many resorts that boast hundreds of rooms and an unlimited number of amenities, the French and Spanish owners here have focused
instead on creating a more intimate sense of luxury. Set on 26 acres
along a pristine beach, the resort is spread out among its manicured
grounds. Instead of being a blocklike hotel right on the beach, it has
preserved harmony with nature. The beach naturally gives way to a
beautiful lawn peppered with palms and tropical plants.

Guests can choose hotel rooms or villas that range from one to
three bedrooms. The villas are exquisite: Brushed pastel stucco walls
adjoin cathedral-style ceilings. We love the Jacuzzis in the bathrooms
(be sure to request one when making reservations) and the open-air
showers. The villas also come with climate-control a/c, ceiling fans,
and digital cable TV. They vary in size, but all have kitchens and

queen-size sofa beds in the living room. The one-bedroom villa is ideal for four people. We prefer the Ocean Villas, which are right on the beach. The hotel's rooms (as opposed to its villas) are built into a cliff that's situated a bit off the beach, but they are blessed with sea views and an endless ocean breeze. Each is equipped with a queen-size bed and a terrace with chairs.

The stylish pool is embellished with Asian elevated sofas and wide sun chairs, all topped with plush purple cushions. The Eclipse Restaurant is an open-air experience that is classy yet casual. Due to its new Puerto Rican chef's experience in France and California, the Eclipse now specializes in French-Asian-Latino fusion. After a dinner here on the torch-lit terrace overlooking the sea, readers will understand our romantic prologue. The beach out front is an untouched gem of barren beauty, but for those who seek more activities, there is an open-air spa, horseback riding, bikes, kayaks, a rock-climbing wall, and two tennis courts. With tropical plants, birds, and an easygoing atmosphere, the Villa Montaña is an ideal resort at which to enjoy the beauty of Puerto Rico in a naturally harmonious setting.

Parador Villas del Mar Hau, P.O. Box 510, Road 466, km 8.3, Isabela, PR. © 787-830-8315, 🖳 www.paradorvillasdelmarhau.com, villahau@prtc.net

🔳 **Not So Cheap** ⑪ **EP** ⒸⒸ 42 rooms

With a setting as splendid as this, it didn't take much to wow us. Located right on the picturesque bay of Playa Montones—one of the most beautiful little beaches in all of Puerto Rico—this unassuming collection of wooden *cabañas* provides just enough comfort for a very relaxing and unpretentious vacation spot. We cannot boast enough about this beach. Palms and pines compete for space on the shores of this horseshoe bay, whose serene waters are perfect for swimming. For those looking to enjoy a gorgeous beach without the pomp and circumstance of a big resort, the brightly colored cottages here are ideal and very affordable. The cottages come equipped with cable TV and a/c, but they also have fans and screen doors that allow for a sea breeze. Each has a full kitchen, a sitting room with a sofa bed, and a bedroom. The porches are huge, complete with table, chairs, and barbeque grill. There are also studios, which are more traditional hotel rooms housed in two-story wooden huts—they have their own terrace, cable TV, a/c, and fan. With fewer than 50 units, there is never a big crowd here.

The hotel grounds include tennis courts, a sand volleyball court, and a small pool out back, and with a beach like this, we were in heaven. The seaside Olas y Arena Restaurant is a great spot at which to enjoy the sea breeze over a tropical dinner. The Villas del Mar Hau has traded silly amenities for pure, natural beauty, which suits true beach lovers like us just fine.

Costa Dorada Beach Resort, 900 Calle Emilio, Road 466, km 0.1, González, Isabela, PR. ℂ 800-981-5693 or 787-872-7255, ✆ 787-872-7595, 💻 www.costadoradabeach.com, info@costadoradabeach.com

💲 **Pricey** ⑨ **EP** [CC] 52 rooms

Judging from the brochure or Web site, this place looks like a Caribbean jewel. However, the Costa Dorada is in fact a very tacky, run-of-the-mill resort. Our main gripe here is the layout—the rooms are crammed together tightly in tall concrete blocks, which takes away from the relaxing seaside experience we crave. Many don't have sea views but instead face the measly pool area. Although it's billed as a "beach resort," guests have to walk through a gate and across a street to get to the beach, which seems to have been treated as an afterthought. We have no problem walking a few paces to the beach, but a few chairs out front would be nice. It appears that the pool (which was drained when we stayed here) is the resort's centerpiece, which isn't saying a lot —it is very small and completely lacking in style. It's just a pool and a few chairs—not what we would expect for a resort in this price range.

The rooms have the normal amenities, but the whole place is completely devoid of style or sophistication. We recommend that you save some money and enjoy the natural beauty of the Villas de Mar Hau or drop a few more dollars and upgrade to the Villa Montaña. The resort also offers one- to three-bedroom villas next door, but we were equally unenthused.

Where to Eat

$$$ **Eclipse Restaurant**, Villa Montaña Beach Resort, 872-9554

Sure, it is set within a resort, but we love this romantic spot where the waves caress the shore. The restaurant fits gracefully into the natural setting, and the food is excellent, too. Dinners are candlelit, and the cuisine is a fusion of European and Caribbean.

$$ **Happy Belly's**, Jobos Beach, 872-6566

This beachside sports bar and grill is good fun. The food is basic but tasty. It has great views and happy-hour specials, too.

$$$ **Mesón Gastronómico El Pescador**, 872-1343

Don't call it a restaurant—it's a Mesón Gastronómico, which is the Puerto Rican connotation for exceptional cuisine. If a kitchen cooks up creole food this delicious, we don't care what it's called. It's set right on the beach. The seafood is the best option here, and the weekday lunch buffet is quite a spread as well.

$$ **Mi Casita Tropical**, Jobos Beach, 872-5510

This is a great bet day or night; the sunny lunches are just as enjoyable as the romantic dinners. Seafood is the way to go here, especially the catch of the day. Beware of the karaoke nights.

Don't Miss

El Yunque

You can't visit Puerto Rico without a visit to El Yunque (officially the Caribbean National Forest and part of the U.S. National Forest system). It is a great example of a rainforest for those who have never seen one before, although it was ravaged by 1998's Hurricane Georges. Evidence of the deadly storm is apparent everywhere, but in the tropics recovery is remarkably quick.

El Yunque is only about an hour's drive east of San Juan, and it is almost impossible to drive to the summit (which was possible before Hurricanes Hugo and Georges). The drive up to the visitors' center takes you past towering banks of green ferns and canopies of trees and vines. The forest itself consists of 28,000 acres and is the largest and wettest in the U.S. National Forest system (240 inches, or 100 billion gallons, of water fall on the forest every year). Note that there are no poisonous snakes in Puerto Rico. Be sure to stop at the **Sierra Palma**, an interpretive center located at km 11.6 on Route 91, just before the parking area, for information on the hiking trails; open daily from 9:30 a.m. to 5 p.m., except on Christmas Day (787-888-1880).

If you decide to hike (you should), the first section of the trail to the summit of El Yunque is a well-worn concrete path. Though a steady climb, it is fairly easy but very humid (remember — *rain*forest). The second section turns into a path, which, though a little muddy, is rather easy to walk. If you walk at a steady pace, you can make it to the summit in one hour (we did). For the length of the trail, you will be walking through forest. Some people might be over the whole concept in 15 minutes and will turn around. The few vista points you come to, including the towers, are more often than not shrouded in clouds, so don't expect spectacular vistas; expect the forest and its hundreds of varieties of foliage and birds (which you hear more often than see). In this age of sound bites and short attention spans, if you don't like the forest you will be bored fairly quickly. Once you get near the top, there is a choice — you'll reach a fork in the road. We recommend going to the tower, which is just a few hundred yards away. The temptation is to go to the peak of El Yunque, because it is the summit. However, when you get to the peak, there are at least seven huge microwave transmission towers to thoroughly radiate you (or at least there were before Hurricane Georges). Since the clouds usually block the view, these lovely structures will be what you see. The only advantage to going to the peak is that you can take the road down (open to official vehicles only), which is a faster route.

Bioluminescent Bays

On moonless nights, some of Puerto Rico's bays come alive with incredible "underwater fireworks" caused by millions of bioluminescent organisms that light up the sea. It is an amazing sight to behold. In addition to Vieques's well-known bioluminescent bay, there are two on the main island that also merit checking out. One is in Fajardo and the other is at La Parguera, the fishing village near Guánica. There are plenty of local tour agencies that offer cheap excursions to witness this natural spectacle.

Scenic Drives

There are several nice drives on this very scenic island. The two we would recommend are a half-day and an overnight journey from San Juan, respectively.

Trip 1 takes you east on **Route 3 to Luquillo**, the location of a great local beach (the drive between San Juan and Luquillo is pretty hideous), and south past Fajardo and the very pretty Playa de Naguabo. It continues on Route 3 past industrial Humacao and into sugarcane territory. When you get to Yabucoa, you start to climb through some very winding mountain roads with great vistas of the valley and the sea (watch out for the cane trucks — don't worry, you'll hear their horns). The road descends to Maunabo and eventually follows the sea along the Caribbean. When you get to Guayama, take Route 15 north to Cayey. This is incredibly scenic — lots of mountain vistas and lush foliage and vegetation. At Cayey, get on Route 52 and head north back to San Juan.

Trip 2 takes you through the **Cordillera Central**, the mountainous spine of Puerto Rico. This is a long, twist-and-turn drive, so leave early in the morning for a relaxing pace. Arrange to stay in Boquerón or Rincón at the other end of the road. Take Route 52 south from San Juan, get off in Cayey, and take Route 14 to Coamo and the **Baños de Coamo** (hot springs), where you can enjoy a natural hot tub. From Coamo, take Route 150 west past Lago Tao Vaga, through the tiny town of Villalba. At Villalba, head north on Route 149 until you reach the junction of Route 143. Turn left (west) to enjoy this stretch of majestic scenery. This road will take you past the biggest mountains in Puerto Rico, including Cerro de Punta, Puerto Rico's highest peak at 4,390 feet. At the junction of Route 10 (not the highway under construction, but the secondary road just beyond), head north until you get to Route 518. If you've had enough and there is enough daylight left for you to head back to San Juan (you'll need at least three hours), continue on Route 10 (it will eventually meet the completed part of Highway 10, which you should take) until you reach the junction of Route 22, then go east on 22. If you want to continue, take Route 518 to Route 525. About 3 miles/5 kilometers later is the junction of Route 135. Turn left (west) on Route 135 until the junction of Route 128. Turn left (south) again on Route 128 and follow to Route 365. Take Route 365, which will merge with Route 366. At the junction of Route 120, turn right (north) onto Route 120 and continue until you come to Route 106. Turn left (west) onto Route 106 and follow this all the way to Mayagüez. Once you are in Mayagüez, Route 2 North takes you to the Rincón area and Route 2 South takes you to Route 100 to Boquerón.

Río Camuy Cave Park

Everyone raves about these "oh, you've got to see them" caves. Personally, the last thing we want to do in the tropics is go subterranean. However, they are a wonder, and kids will love them. They are located near Lares, and tours are usually conducted via trolley. However, we prefer the more adventurous option, which includes rappelling or hiking to the center of the Cueva Catedral, which was recently opened to the public. This cave contains 14th-century petroglyphs as well. Tours run two hours. Open Wednesday from 8 a.m. to 3 p.m. You must call ahead to reserve a space on the tour (787-898-3100 or 787-763-0568). The cost is $10 for adults, $7 for children.

Arecibo Observatory

Home of the world's largest radio telescope (the radar dish is over 1,000 feet in diameter, 565 feet deep, and covers 20 acres), the observatory and its scientists listen for signs of life in the universe. It is part of the National Astronomy and Ionosphere Center and is operated by Cornell University in conjunction with the National Science Foundation. Viewers of several movies, including *Contact* and an early *007* movie whose name we can't remember, will recognize the dish. A new visitors' center has a cool "More Than Meets the Eye" interactive exhibit and a great view of the observatory. Open Wednesday through Friday from noon to 4 p.m., weekends and holidays from 9 a.m. to 4 p.m. Admission is $5 for adults and $3 for kids and seniors. Call 787-878-2612 for more information.

Casa Bacardi Visitor Center

Any place that churns out 100,000 gallons of liquor per day can spare a few samples here and there, and that is just the way it is at this famous rum distillery. Opened in 2000, the visitors' center offers an informative 45-minute tour of the distillery, and, of course, the gift shop—funny how that always seems to happen. Come see why Bacardi has made Puerto Rico the rum capital of the world (or so it claims). It's located at Bay View Industrial Park, Road 888, km 2.6, Cataño; phone 788-8400. Tours are offered Monday through Saturday from 8:30 a.m. to 5:30 p.m. (last tour at 4:15 p.m.) and Sunday from 10 a.m. to 3 p.m. (last tour at 3:45 p.m.), free of charge.

Nature Resort

Although we have not been here, the buzz is interesting enough about this place that we will mention it. In a jungle-like mountain setting in Utuado (near the Camuy Caves) is **Hotel La Casa Grande** (888-343-2272 or 787-894-3939/3900, www.hotelcasagrande.com). Once the hacienda for a 5,000-acre ranch, the old house and its surroundings have been turned into a 20-room inn and restaurant by ex–New Yorkers Steven and Marlene Weingarten.

Windsurfing and Surfing in Rincón

If you're a windsurfer or surfer, this is one of the best places to do both in the

Caribbean. Many championships in both sports are held at Surfer and Wilderness Beaches, and there is a growing California-style surfer community.

Guánica

This is a wonderful and scenic town for those in search of the real Puerto Rico (see Guánica section).

Lunch at Hostería del Mar and Dinner at Pamela's

Our favorite spots for lunch and dinner in San Juan are in Ocean Park (see Where to Eat).

Culebra and Vieques

These two small islands off the east coast of Puerto Rico offer a fun day trip, overnight excursion, or entire holiday. See the Culebra and Vieques chapters.

Que Pasa?

Published by the Puerto Rico Tourism Company, this is a great free publication to peruse for events and the latest info. It also has an ample listing of hotels and restaurants in Puerto Rico. For a free copy, call 800-223-6530 from the United States or 721-2400 in Puerto Rico, or visit the Web site: www.prtourism.com.

Ponce Museum of Art

Designed by famous architect Edward Durrel Stone, the design of this building alone, reminiscent of the Greek Parthenon, is worth the visit. With more than 850 paintings, 800 sculptures, and 500 prints highlighting 500 years of Western art, this museum is a must-see for art enthusiasts. Look for featured exhibitions of Latin American artists. Open daily from 10 a.m. to 5 p.m.; phone 848-0505.

Museo de Arte de Puerto Rico

Opened in 2000, the museum incorporates part of the old San Juan Municipal Hospital designed in the neoclassical style by William Shimmelphening with a brand new modern architectural five-story gem designed by Otto Reyes and Luis Guiterrez. The museum has more than 130,000 square feet of exhibition space and a three-story atrium called the Great Hall. Puerto Rican art throughout the island's history is on display here. Finally, Puerto Rico has a world-class art exhibition space! Located on Avenida de Diego 299 in Santurce, it's open Tuesday through Saturday from 10 a.m. to 5 p.m., Wednesday until 8 p.m., and Sunday from 11 a.m. to 6 p.m. Admission is $5 for adults and $3 for kids and seniors. Call 787-977-6277 or go to www.mapr.org for more info.

Surf

Puerto Rico is home to excellent surf breaks all year round. In the winter, the waves at Rincón are sensational. This is the premier surf location on the xisland — surfers are drawn to breaks such as The Landing, Punta Higuero, and Sandy Beach. Around the lighthouse are even more gnarly waves, sometimes up to 20 feet high. For those interested in seeking out these giant waves, just ask for Tres Palmas. But Rincón is not the only surf spot. Even San Juan itself has great surf from November through February — this is evident from all the high school kids playing hooky. In the city, our favorite surf spots are Isla Verde Beach (just east of the Ritz-Carlton Hotel) and Aviones, which is in Piñones. On the east coast, check out La Pared in Luquillo or El Convento in Fajardo. Those staying at the Four Points Sheraton in Palmas del Mar (Humacao) will find great breaks as well. Some of the best spots, though, are along less traveled beaches. The stretch between Hatillo and Arecibo along the northern coast has some great breaks, in particular Hollows and La Marina. Isabela's surf scene is being discovered as we speak — there are already surf schools popping up, and for good reason. Jobos Beach here is perhaps the best break on the island, which is why international competitions are held here. Farther west toward Aguadilla are several other great surf spots, such as Gas Chambers and the aptly named Surfer's Beach.

Saba and St. Eustatius (Statia)

TOURISTO SCALE:

SABA (3)

STATIA (2)

Saba and Statia are like stepsisters. Located south of St. Martin/St. Maarten, they are two of the Caribbean's smallest and least known islands. They are both politically connected to the Netherlands, and they share a similarly concise population count and an eccentric local scene that is minimally impacted by tourism. They can be reached only from St. Maarten. A scenic volcano provides a visual anchor for each island, but from the visitor's standpoint, that is where the resemblance between the two islands ends. These two outposts have vastly different appeal. To us, Saba is like a charming and lush alpine village that somehow got airlifted and plopped into the Caribbean, where it is surrounded by spectacular diving. St. Eustatius (better known as Statia) has its fans, but it's quite the backwater and lacks some of Saba's charm and appeal. To some, the lack of appeal, which keeps most tourists away, provides its own kind of attraction.

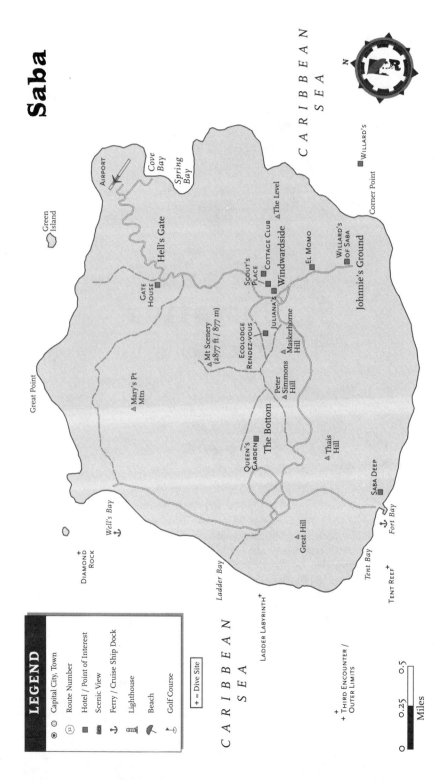

Saba

LEGEND

- ◉ ⊙ Capital City, Town
- ⑫ Route Number
- ■ Hotel / Point of Interest
- ⚓ Scenic View
- 🚢 Ferry / Cruise Ship Dock
- 🗼 Lighthouse
- 🏖 Beach
- ⛳ Golf Course

+ = Dive Site

N

CARIBBEAN SEA

CARIBBEAN SEA

Green Island

AIRPORT

Cove Bay
Spring Bay

Hell's Gate

GATE HOUSE

Scout's Place
COTTAGE CLUB ▲The Level
Windwardside
JULIANA'S
EL MOMO
WILLARD'S OF SABA

WILLARD'S

Corner Point

Johnnie's Ground

▲Mt Scenery (2877 ft / 877 m)
ECOLODGE RENDEZ-VOUS
▲Maskerhorne Hill
Peter ▲Simmons Hill

▲Mary's Pt Mtn

Great Point

QUEEN'S GARDEN
The Bottom

▲Thais Hill

Great Hill

SABA DEEP

Well's Bay
⚓

DIAMOND + ROCK

Ladder Bay

LADDER LABYRINTH +

+ THIRD ENCOUNTER / OUTER LIMITS

Tent Bay

TENT REEF +

🚢 Fort Bay

0   0.25   0.5
Miles

Saba

SABA'S BIGGEST CLAIM TO FAME WILL GRAB YOUR GUT BEFORE you even arrive. The island's airstrip is not only reputed to be the shortest commercial runway in the world (1,312 feet) but is also a landing strip clearly defined on three sides by precipitous cliffs that plunge into the crashing surf below. Be sure to have a few cocktails (or Valium) in St. Maarten before making the 12-minute flight. Watching the landing approach from the DeHavilland Twin Otter aircraft will remind you of an old movie filmed in Cinerama — only you're in the plane heading directly for the rocky cliff, when at the last possible moment the aircraft banks to avert disaster. Fortunately, you are on the ground before you can let out a scream. The plane seems to land on a dime.

Just 5 square miles in size, Saba is refreshingly distinct from other islands in the West Indies. There are no permanent beaches — only a wandering one of ruddy black sand that barely exists at all for a few summer months at Wells Bay. The island is basically one big mountain with roads and villages clinging to its sides. Mount Scenery is the highest point, 2,877 feet above sea level and usually with its head in the clouds. There are four villages — Hell's Gate, Windwardside, St. John's, and The Bottom (the capital) — that are home to Saba's 1,200 residents. The 5-mile-long road that connects the villages has been in existence only since 1943, built by hand over a period of 18 years. When Dutch engineers declared the steep and mountainous terrain unfit for construction, a local man designed and built the roads with knowledge culled from a correspondence course.

It sounds pretty bleak, but the island is surprisingly green and beautiful — it's nicknamed "The Unspoiled Queen," and with good reason. The climate is ideal — the elevation of the villages keeps it comfortably cool and breezy in the evening, just right for sleeping. The days are warm but not hot; the temperature of both air and water is around 80°F all year round. The vegetation is tropical and verdant — this is not a dry island. The villages have the charm and appeal of small towns in coastal Maine (minus the clapboard). By tradition, most of the tidy houses are white with green trim and red roofs. It's very picturesque. It's also probably one of the cleanest islands in the Caribbean. If it had a beach and a decent harbor, Saba would quickly become the next St. Barth. Thank God it doesn't!

There are three reasons to come to Saba. The first is for solitude and quiet: The deadline for your latest novel or screenplay is swiftly approaching,

Saba: Key Facts

Location	17°N by 63°W
	28 miles/45 kilometers south of St. Martin/St. Maarten
	200 miles/322 kilometers east of Puerto Rico
	1,680 miles/2,704 kilometers southeast of New York
Size	5 square miles/13 square kilometers
Highest point	Mount Scenery (2,877 feet/877 meters)
Population	1,200 (plus 500 students at the medical university)
Language	English, although the official one is Dutch
Time	Atlantic Standard Time (1 hour ahead of EST, same as EDT)
Area code	To call Saba from the U.S., dial 011 (the international access code), then 599 (the country code), plus the seven-digit local number.
Electricity	110 volts AC, 60 cycles — same as the U.S.
Currency	The Netherlands Antilles guilder, also called the florin, NAf, (1.78 NAf = US$1), but U.S. dollars are accepted everywhere.
Driving	On the right; a valid driver's license from your own country is acceptable.
Documents	U.S. and Canadian citizens must show proof of citizenship and have a return or an ongoing ticket.
Departure tax	$5 if continuing to the Netherlands Antilles, or $20 if heading home
Beer to drink	Heineken
Rum to drink	Mt. Gay
Music to hear	Dancehall, reggae, calypso
Tourism info	599-416-2231
	www.sabatourism.com

and you need a place with few distractions and no one to call. The second is that you hate beaches, are scared of the sun, or just want a pleasant climate without boatloads of tourists and the hassle of Third World politics — it's a vacation away from the Caribbean conventional. The last is by far the best reason to come here: the diving and hiking. It is one of the last "virgin" dive locales and has probably some of the finest sites you'll find in the Lesser Antilles (i.e., Puerto Rico all the way down to Trinidad). And although Saba is small, there are hiking trails offering resplendent views that lace the island's lush slopes.

Beyond diving and hiking, the island of Saba offers a quiet calm that is very soothing and is best appreciated on foot. You can hike up Mount Scenery (1,064 steps that just won't quit!) from the village of Windwardside. Queen Beatrix of the Netherlands did it in 45 minutes — a very steady clip indeed. Legend has it that she arrived on top (in high heels, no less) and proclaimed, "This is the highest and smallest point in my kingdom!" Some guidebooks claim that you can hike up and down in an hour. Ha! Running up and down with a five-minute break at the top took us an hour and five minutes. Down on the shoreline, the Ladder is another series of steps that at one time was how goods—even pianos—were hand-carried up to The Bottom, the island's capital, which is actually 820 feet above sea level (it took 12 hours to carry a Steinway). Just walking around the various villages is appealing, though. Be sure to stroll through the especially appealing hamlet of Hell's Gate (located above the airport).

As on any small island, nightlife consists of the local bars. The local student population (500 or so at the medical school) ensures that there's a bit of partying on weekends or on "Black Monday"—the night of an exam—but don't set your sights on anything exciting. Wednesday is Ladies Night at a number of bars. Otherwise, ask if something special is happening during the time you are here, or come the last week of July for Carnival (a.k.a. the Saba Summer Festival), which is the island's big annual event, with steel bands, costume parades, competitions, speeches, and the national anthem.

The Briefest History

Saba was uninhabited when Columbus sighted this rock in the sea on his second voyage, in 1493. Since the island has no harbor and is basically all mountain, it wasn't settled until the 1640s, when some Dutch colonists built the communities of Tent Bay and The Bottom. The island then changed hands 12 times among the Dutch, British, French, and Spanish. In 1816 a treaty gave the island permanently to the Netherlands, but it remains today a part of the Dutch West Indies, a self-governing and verdant gumdrop in the Kingdom of the Netherlands.

Getting There

Winair (Windward Islands Airways) makes the flight from St. Maarten's Juliana Airport several times a day as well as from Statia. Round-trip fare from St. Maarten averages about $125. Juliana is a major gateway to the Caribbean, with nonstops from the United States on American, Continental, Delta, United and US Airways; American Eagle flies to St. Maarten from San Juan. US Airways offers connecting baggage service with Winair, which can be helpful. Note that the Saba runway does not operate after sundown.

If the idea of savoring Saba's abbreviated landing experience is too much, you can also ferry over from St. Maarten. The trade-off is that the 75-minute crossing can be rough, and seasickness is not uncommon. *The Edge* (besides being a member of the band U2) is a high-speed, 60-passenger catamaran that leaves from Pelican Marina (near the Juliana Airport) at 9 a.m. Wednesday through Sunday, leaving Saba for the return trip at 3:45 p.m. The trip is $45 each way; note that an overnight in St. Martin/St. Maarten is required at both ends of your Saba visit to connect to international flights. If you're visiting Saba as a day trip from St. Maarten, the round-trip fare is $65 (but only for a same-day return). Be sure to verify the current schedule: 599-544-2640; aquamania@sintmaarten.net.

Another ferry based in French St. Martin, *Voyager*, discontinued service to Saba, but it might come back—check with the Saba Tourist Office.

Getting Around

Given the hair-raising nature of the mountain-clinging road, don't rent a car —take a taxi, or hitch a ride (passing up hitchhikers is decidedly disrespectful here), or walk. You'll find there really aren't that many places you can drive to, anyway, and this way you can enjoy the view rather than worry about plunging off the cliff.

If you must drive, rental cars can be arranged through Caja's Car Rental: 599-416-2388.

Focus on Saba: Diving

Saba is renowned for its world-class diving. Until recently it has been kept fairly quiet, largely because of the island's uniqueness (there are no postcard-perfect beaches to lounge on between excursions) and its inability to accommodate a large number of divers (there are well under 100 hotel rooms on the entire island). Fortunately, the government has declared the entire shoreline, out to the 200-foot depth, to be the Saba Marine Park. This prevents the reef destruction and souvenir hunting that have ravaged popular dive sites elsewhere in the Caribbean.

There are three dive operations on the island. **Saba Deep Dive Center** (866-416-3347 or 599-416-3347; www.sabadeep.com), owned by Mike Meyers (and not to be confused with *Austin Powers*'s "oh behave" Mike Myers), is conveniently located in Fort Bay, right on the water. Mike has been on Saba more than two decades, making him the island's longest-running operator. His shop has three decent-size boats (25 to 30 feet) and a compressor. Typically, the outfit does a deep dive at 9 a.m., followed by an intermediate dive and then an early afternoon shallow dive. A two-tank dive (the norm) costs $110. Mike offers resort courses ($95) and with advance notice will conduct a PADI open water certification course ($450). He also has package arrangements with various hotels.

The second shop, **Sea Saba Dive Center** (599-416-2246; www.seasaba .com), another fine dive operator, is based in Windwardside. It is owned by John Magor and Lynn Costenaro, who run a modern, attractive shop with new and well-maintained equipment and a complete roster of packages worked out with the various hotels. Packages include dives, equipment taxis (which can cost a lot when negotiated separately), all meals, accommodations, taxes, and service. John and Lynn sponsor slide shows, marine biology seminars, and lessons in underwater photography, all on request. If the above is not enough to lure you to their operation, they offer a nice package for groups of eight or more. Sea Saba has two covered dive boats (40 feet each). A two-tank dive costs $90, not including mask, fins, regulator, and BC. A resort course is $80 for a group of three or more ($100 for one), and certification is $350 to $450 depending on the group size; both of these prices include all gear. Sea Saba will also take snorkelers out on the afternoon dive—usually a shallower site —for $25, including gear.

The island's third dive shop, also located in Windwardside, **Saba Divers** (866-656-7222 or 599-416-2740; www.sabadivers.com), is run by a German couple, Barbara and Wolfgang Tooten. They also own the hotel Scout's Place (see Where to Stay), so the outfit offers competitive dive and hotel packages but caters somewhat more to the European market—instructors and staff speak English, German, French, and Spanish. They have two dive boats, DAN oxygen equipment, and a Nitrox blender.

Fort Bay is the center of all boating activity on the island. Unfortunately, the "harbor" is just plain ugly. There is no village here, just a rock and concrete pier that also serves as a breakwater. An upwind gravel crusher (which grinds rocks into sand for other islands' beaches and cement) sends clouds of grayish-white powder into the air, coating everything in sight with layers of dust—what a blight on this otherwise beautiful isle. That aside, there is a cafe called In Two Deep that is a fun place to hang out with a Heineken and play dominoes or study dive tables. Located next to Saba Deep is the island's recompression chamber, which makes the sport safer for all.

There are 28 official dive sites that rim the Saba coastline and probably a few more yet to be discovered. However, the current spots are so good that the incentive to find more is minimal. Of particular interest are the deep dives, where you really feel that you've entered another realm. **Shark Shoal** and the **Pinnacles** are the most spectacular and are located just a 5- or 10-minute boat ride from Fort Bay. Unlike with many islands, deeper water is quite close; around much of Saba the depth reaches 1,000 feet only a half mile from shore. The shallow dives, while not quite as profound, are exceptional and longer. On our first shallow dive we saw a shark swimming right at us. Trying to stay calm, we turned to our diving instructor, who wrote on his tablet, "Nurse shark—not dangerous." Somehow we already knew that, especially when the shark swam right by without showing the slightest interest (we later swam within 3 feet of it while it was resting on the bottom, then it decided we were too close and swam away).

There are so many great dives on Saba that it's hard to pick a favorite. If we must, it would have to be ✹ **Third Encounter**, one of four sites at a formation known as the Pinnacles, a submerged volcanic outcrop located a mile west of Ladder Bay. This very open-water dive takes you down 100 feet to a plateau about the size of a football field. As you descend, it doesn't seem that you've gone very far until a check of your depth gauge tells you otherwise. Because of the depth, you can stay down only 20 minutes before you need decompression—the time passes much too quickly. Once there, however, you feel as if perhaps you've found nirvana. Big groupers and bar jacks swim close — out of curiosity (and possibly hoping for a handout). A sea turtle swoops by giant sponges, oblivious to the bubbling intruders. Then the guide motions you to swim off the plateau into the blue water, to the surprise of all. As you follow him you think, "Maybe he's got nitrogen narcosis" or rapture of the deep (caused by breathing compressed air, which is mostly nitrogen, at very high atmospheric-pressure levels).

Then you see why he is luring you into the open water. It seems like an apparition at first, a fuzzy spire of darkness against a light blue background. Images of Devil's Tower in Wyoming come to mind. Close up, you can see that the pinnacle, called Eye of the Needle, is covered with brilliantly colored coral. Keeping a watchful eye on the depth (if you go deeper it will alter your available bottom time), it's exciting to explore this wonder of nature. Unfortunately, the beeps you suddenly hear are the signal from the guide's watch indicating that 20 minutes are up and it's time to surface, but the memory of this experience will stay with you forever.

Other favorite sites include those surrounding **Diamond Rock**, another pinnacle, but one that juts about 100 feet out of the water. From a distance the rock seems translucent, a grayish mass that lives up to its name. The illusion is shattered when you arrive to see that what you thought was beautiful is really just a rock covered with bird droppings. However, you won't be disappointed with what's 80 feet below the surface. Circumnavigating this large structure reveals schools of all kinds of fish; here we encountered the biggest barracuda (about 6 feet) we've ever seen. The currents can be swift here, making it one of Saba's most advanced dives.

Two other superb shallow sites are Tent Reef Wall and Ladder Labyrinth, which are found at a 40- and 50-foot depth, respectively. **Tent Reef Wall** is a long overhang of coral that harbors all kinds of marine life, including spotted moray eel. This is also a preferred spot for night dives, as it's close to port and in the dark has a dreamlike quality. **Ladder Labyrinth** has the look of a J.R.R. Tolkien or Lewis Carroll fantasy. The coral heads resemble giant mushrooms, and the barrel sponges would be a perfect home for the White Rabbit. There is actually a mazelike network of sandy-floored passages between the Middle Earth–looking mounds of coral.

Where to Stay

There are several inns on the island, but you can also rent an efficiency apartment from Juliana's or the Gate House, or check the listings for homes and cottages managed by Glenn Holm at the **Tourist Bureau** (599-416-2231). We prefer staying in Windwardside; it's prettier, cooler, and livelier (if liveliness is possible on Saba!), although the queen — Queen Beatrix of the Netherlands that is — chose Queen's Garden Resort for her 2001 visit to the island. Note that no accommodations are found lower than 1,000 feet above sea level — fittingly, none have air-conditioning. Beth Jansen runs **Dive Saba-Statia** out of

Seattle — she can help U.S. residents with reservations for hotels, dive shops and airfare: 800-883-7222; www.divesaba.com.

Juliana's Hotel, Windwardside, Saba, NA. 𝄯 888-289-5708, 599-416-2269, ✆ 599-416-2389, 💻 www.julianas-hotel.com, info@julianashotel.com

  💰 **Not So Cheap** 🍴 **BP** CC 12 units

Our favorite option on Saba is this inn, located just below the crest of Windwardside. The inn was taken over in 2001 by Wim and Johanna, an enthusiastic young couple who devote hands-on attention to useful details, like adding Wi-Fi to the property. Each of the nine rooms has a minifridge and coffeemaker, private bath, and balcony, and although they are small, they're sufficient for people who plan to spend most of their Saba visit outdoors. There are three additional units — two charming Saba-style cottages loaded with real island character, and an efficiency apartment — for anyone desiring a little more space (or a private Jacuzzi!). Across the road is the inn's small pool, along with the Tropics Café, where your breakfast is served.

The Gate House, Hell's Gate, Saba, NA. 𝄯 599-416-2416, ✆ 599-416-2550, 💻 www.sabagatehouse.com, info@sabagatehouse.com

  💰 **Not So Cheap** 🍴 **BP** CC 7 units

Offering a sweeping panorama of St. Martin/St. Maarten, St. Barth, and Statia, plus Saba's puny airstrip, the Gate House is now run by a very friendly French couple who retired to Saba in 2001. There are five rooms in the main lodge, all with bright tropical art and long views; upper units have airy cathedral ceilings. There is also a cute one-bedroom cottage and spacious four-bedroom villa with a private pool. It's a bit isolated here — a 20-minute walk up the hill to Windwardside — but there's a terrific restaurant on site and a pool with those great vistas.

Ecolodge Rendez-Vous, Windwardside, Saba, NA. 𝄯 599-416-3348, ✆ 599-416-3299, 💻 www.ecolodge-saba.com

  💰 **Cheap** 🍴 **EP** CC 12 cabins

The new Ecolodge promises a genuine back-to-nature experience, 1,800 feet above sea level. Located close to the Mt. Scenery trailhead, the cabins are constructed from recycled materials and boast solar power and composting toilets; be prepared for coolish showers. In keeping with the self-sustaining theme, many of the fruits and vegetables served at the restaurant are grown on site (the restaurant is beautifully illuminated by lanterns — it's quite romantic). The lodge is actually a 2-minute walk from the road and a 15-minute hike from Windwardside. Bring a small flashlight; there's little ambient light on the property after dark (and definitely none along the trail into town). The hotel was conceived and is overseen by Tom Van-Hof, founder of the pacesetting marine parks in Saba, Bonaire, and Curacao.

El Momo, Booby Hill, Saba, NA. ✆ 599-416-2265, 🖥 www.elmomo.com, info@elmomo.com

💲 **Cheap** 🍽 **EP** Ⓒ🅒 7 rooms

Located just outside Windwardside and at the top of a long flight of stairs that leads past a tiny pool, this sweet little guesthouse is a series of wooden cottages, trimmed in gingerbread and perched on the steep hillside. Two share a bathroom; the others have private bathrooms with sun-heated showers. The owners serve dinner a few times a week, family style around a large table. It's simple but usually convivial, and you get superb views of Mt. Scenery.

Willard's of Saba, Booby Hill, Saba, NA. ✆ 800-504-9861 or 599-416-2498, ✎ 599-416-2482, 🖥 www.willardsofsaba.com, willards@unspoiledqueen.com

💲 **Wicked Pricey** 🍽 **EP** Ⓒ🅒 7 rooms

You'll find no better view on Saba (except, perhaps, from the summit of Mt. Scenery) than here at Willard's, Saba's fanciest property. Although it's somewhat overstated and definitely overpriced, the guesthouse sits on a cliff top, 2,000 feet above sea level, overlooking Windwardside and the sea, making it the highest hotel in the Netherlands. A Jacuzzi sits at the cliff edge (with a glass railing, thankfully). The pool is almost big enough for laps, and Saba's only tennis court is well maintained. There are three different types of rooms: Best are the four bungalows that climb the cliff above the pool (they offer more privacy than the three rooms inside the main building). All are decorated in bright tropical colors and offer spacious living arrangements. There's a low-key but very pricey restaurant serving good meals, but it's just a 10-minute walk to Windwardside.

Scout's Place, Windwardside, Saba, NA. ✆ 599-416-2740, ✎ 599-416-2641, 🖥 www.sabadivers.com, sabadivers@unspoiledqueen.com

💲 **Cheap** 🍽 **CP** Ⓒ🅒 13 rooms

Scout's motto used to be "Bed and Board, Cheap and Cheerful," but that was before a crew of German divers took over the spot and spruced it up with fresh paint and four-poster beds. The rooms are now genuinely clean and cheerful, comfortable and adequate — and the rates still haven't crested the $100 mark in the least expensive units. Virtually all of the guests are divers, and a good number are European — the enchanting clatter of tanks being refilled permeates the inn most afternoons.

Queen's Garden Resort, The Bottom, Saba, NA. ✆ 599-416-3494, ✎ 599-416-3495, 🖥 www.queensaba.com, info@queensaba.com

💲 **Very Pricey** 🍽 **EP** Ⓒ🅒 12 rooms

Tucked into a hillside above the medical school, this all-suite hotel, which opened in the mid-'90s, had several years of ups and downs but seems finally to have come into its own as a recommendable upscale option for Saba. It's overpriced (discounts are often available), but the suites are quite attractive, with East and West Indies furniture, king-size four-poster beds, full kitchens, and superb views of The Bottom. Royal suites have a Jacuzzi built into an outdoor nook facing the view. There's a big pool and a restaurant, and the young couple from Holland that arrived in 2005 to manage the hotel seems dedicated.

The Cottage Club, Windwardside, Saba, NA. ℂ 599-416-2486, 🖳 www.cottage-club.com, cottageclubsaba@yahoo.com

💲 **Not So Cheap** 🍴 **EP** 🆑 10 rooms

A collection of quaint and clean duplex cottages, each has a fully equipped kitchen, living room, balcony, TV, and phone. Compared to some of Saba's other spots, these are due for a spruce-up, but the prices are reasonable. There's a nice garden-wrapped pool, but no restaurant (several are a short walk away). Units 1 and 2 have the best views. This is a good spot for families.

Where to Eat

Dining on Saba used to be pretty uninspired, but the food scene has improved in the last few years, and satisfying meals are easier to find.

$$$$ The Gate House, Hell's Gate, 599-416-2416

This spot—probably Saba's best for a gourmet menu—is located on the steep hillside above the airport. The French food can be very satisfying, and there's a *Wine Spectator*–commended wine list. Reservations are recommended for dinner; lunch is available on request.

$ In Two Deep, Fort Bay, 599-416-3438

We wouldn't normally recommend restaurants owned by dive shops, but this one is a fun hangout between dives, with tasty burgers and sandwiches. It serves breakfast and lunch daily.

$$ My Place, Windwardside, 599-416-2539

This is the newest spot on the island, with a dependable selection of steaks and seafood, continental style, plus a yummy bakery that can provide pastries for the hike up Mt. Scenery (the restaurant is located next to the trailhead).

$$ Scout's Place, Windwardside, 599-416-2205

This is a decent spot for lunch, when you can best appreciate its airy patio that juts over one side of the village like the prow of a ship. Most of the menu is simpler fare, but check out the curried goat. Because of its pirate-themed ambiance at night, we find it a bit suspect for dinner.

$$ **Tropics Café**, Windwardside, 599-416-2469

Tropics serves lighter, more health-conscious fare, bolstered by mango daiquiris and the occasional fish 'n' chips special. The covered terrace here has a view with a pool — take a dip between courses.

$$$$ **Willard's of Saba**, Booby Hill, 599-416-2498

It's overpriced, but the Asian-accented food here is very good, and the sunset view from this perch above Windwardside is spectacular. It has a good wine list, too. Reservations are required.

Don't Miss

Saba Marine Park

The underwater scene is steep and fast, but moderately experienced divers will be exhilarated.

Mt. Scenery

The hike to the summit of this dormant volcano takes some stamina but rewards it with a rainforest at the top and splendid views on clear days. It starts from a roadside trailhead just beyond Windwardside. Nearby, the Trail Shop (599-416-2630; www.sabapark.org) — run by James "Crocodile" Johnson (despite an absence of crocs on Saba) — is a good spot for info on the island's other wonderful treks. We especially like the Sandy Cruz Trail, which winds from Hell's Gate around the uninhabited northwest side of the island to the Bottom (allow about two hours one way). A $3 hiking donation has been established to help fund trail maintenance; Crocodile does guided hikes for $10 per person.

The Bottom

This is the place of Saba's seat of government — it's oddly named (it's actually 820 feet above sea level), but it's a charming village to wander through.

Jo Bean Glass

Staking a claim as the only flame-working glass workshop in the Caribbean, Jo Bean Chambers creates and sells ornaments, mantel creatures, and jewelry; she also does classes for visitors, sharing the talents she learned from masters in Venice, Italy. Info: 599-416-2490; www.jobeanglass.com.

Croquet

Matches are held on the museum grounds in Windwardside on the first and third Sunday of each month. All are welcome, free of charge, but beware the blasphemy tariff — a guilder for every curse word you utter (guilderless Americans can deposit 55 cents in the till).

St. Eustatius (Statia)

JUST 12 SQUARE MILES IN SIZE, THIS ODD LITTLE OUTPOST was once the most important trading center and slave depot in the West Indies. Merchandise from Europe and raw goods from the Americas made their way to St. Eustatius's port, and the island itself was fiercely traded — 22 times — among the Dutch, English, Spanish, and French. As the riches poured in, the island became known as The Golden Rock. However, you're excused if the name St. Eustatius (which refers to an obscure second-century martyr) isn't on your radar. Affectionately called Statia today, the island is one of the Caribbean's least known tourism frontiers — a dry plain weighted on either end by extinct volcanoes. There is a tiny town, Oranjestad, and the ruins of a fort and other historical sites are found in Lower Bay, on the water and just offshore. With fewer than 3,000 residents, the island is one of the three Dutch Windwards (along with Saba and St. Martin/St. Maarten), and English is commonly spoken (but you'll also hear Dutch and some Spanish). Still, tourism is a pretty low-key affair — it's several notches below the local medical school and a mammoth oil shipping facility in terms of economic importance for the island government. Since there's little in the way of conventional Caribbean attributes, whom is this island for?

Statia is a place for those who want to explore life well off the beaten track. You won't find nightlife, shopping, or resorts, and the most attractive beaches (on the east coast) are too rough for swimming, but the absence of traffic jams, discos, and strip malls is a nice antidote for anyone overdosed on civilization. The arid island has a nicely sculpted landscape, dominated in the south by The Quill, a graceful volcano that rises to 1,968 feet. Moderate trails lead up the gentle slopes, and a rainforest is found in the deep crater bowl. There is very good diving and snorkeling, and in 2003 a 50-year-old cable repair ship, the 327-foot *Charles Brown*, was sunk as an artificial reef, boosting the appeal of this largely undiscovered dive destination. The historical museum is worth an hour, and you can tour most of Fort Oranje and Oranjestad, the capital, in another hour or two. Most people will find enough to explore for two or three days, but beyond that, you'll need to have a real taste for Statia's uniquely quirky and quiet lifestyle. If you combine a stay here with a visit to Saba, you'll have all the makings of an enjoyable adventure to places your friends have never heard of. One big plus: Statia is inexpensive by Caribbean standards.

St. Eustatius

LEGEND

- ◉ ◎   Capital City, Town
- (12)   Route Number
- ■   Hotel / Point of Interest
- Scenic View
- ⚓   Ferry / Cruise Ship Dock
- 🗼   Lighthouse
- Beach
- Golf Course

Cocluch Bay

Boven Bay

Fontaan Bay

Venus Bay

Boven (965 ft / 294 m)

Jenkins Bay

Little Mountain (656 ft / 200 m)

Zeelandia

Zeelandia Beach

Concordia Bay

Great Bay

Lynch Beach

Signal Hill (768 ft / 234 m)

Tumble-Down Dick Bay

Compagnie Bay

AIRPORT

Concordia

COUNTRY INN

Corre Corre Bay

Golden Rock

KING'S WELL

THE OLD GIN HOUSE

GOLDEN ERA HOTEL

Oranjestad

The Quill

Gallows Bay

Mazinga Peak (1,968 ft / 600 m)

Kay Bay

Fort de Windt

Bucaneers Bay

Back-Off Bay

CARIBBEAN SEA

0   1

Miles

N

St. Eustatius: Key Facts

Location	17°N by 63°W
	38 miles/61 kilometers south of St. Maarten
	150 miles/241 kilometers east of San Juan
	1,680 miles/2,704 kilometers southeast of New York
Size	12 square miles/31 square kilometers
Highest point	The Quill/Mazinga Peak (1,968 feet/600 meters)
Population	3,000
Language	Dutch, although English, Spanish, and Papiamento is spoken by everyone
Time	Atlantic Standard Time (1 hour ahead of EST, same as EDT)
Area code	To call Statia from the U.S., dial 011 (the international access code), then 599 (the country code), plus the seven-digit local number.
Electricity	110 volts AC, 60 cycles — same as the U.S.
Currency	The Netherlands Antilles guilder, also called the florin, NAf (1.78 NAf = US$1), but U.S. dollars are accepted everywhere.
Driving	On the right; a valid driver's license from your own country is acceptable.
Documents	U.S. and Canadian citizens must show proof of citizenship (passport, or photo ID and birth certificate) and have a return or an ongoing ticket.
Departure tax	$5 to the Netherlands Antilles, or $12 when heading home
Beer to drink	Heineken
Rum to drink	Mt. Gay
Music to hear	Calypso and reggae
Tourism info	599-318-2433
	www. statiatourism.com

The Briefest History

The first inhabitants were Saladoid Indians, who were originally from Venezuela — their pottery shards and other remnants date back to 500 B.C. Columbus sailed close to the island on his second voyage but apparently didn't see it; almost a 100 years later, the first record to mention "Estazia" was that of Sir Francis Drake in 1595. In 1629 the French built a small fort, which was followed by a Dutch settlement, and the island's economy grew rapidly shortly thereafter when the first of its tobacco was shipped overseas.

Statia quickly developed, and it peaked economically in the 1700s, when some 8,000 inhabitants lived here and its port was the Caribbean's richest

— a major slave depot and trading center that helped channel gunpowder and other supplies to the American colonies during the War of Independence. As many as 3,500 ships visited Statia annually back then, trading everything from African slaves to silk from the Far East. But the island had an unfortunate hiccup, according to legend: In 1776 Statia fired an 11-gun salute to the *Andrew Doria*, a war brig flying the Stars and Stripes, and thus became the first foreign port to pay tribute to the just-declared United States of America. The gesture provoked retaliation by the British, who plundered the port and town, causing the economy to collapse. Historians say that beyond the salute, changing trade routes, nasty hurricanes, and the Emancipation Proclamation of 1863 (freeing U.S. slaves) really caused the island's downfall. Statia became a Dutch colony for good in 1816, and today the island's major employer is a port of a different sort: Statia Terminals, a huge oil transshipping facility located out of eyesight on the northeast coast of the island, at Jenkins Bay (the terminal is off-limits to visitors).

Getting There

To get to Statia's Franklin Delano Roosevelt Airport, you'll need to fly in from St. Maarten, 20 minutes away — there are four or more flights daily on Winair, as well as flights from Saba. St. Maarten is served by American, Continental, Delta, United, and US Airways, as well as American Eagle from San Juan. A new service on Caribbean Sun provides several flights a week from San Juan. There is no interisland ferry service to Statia.

Getting Around

Most of the sights and restaurants are concentrated around Oranjestad, so you can see a fair amount on foot. Besides, Statia's roads are potholed and often navigated by cows and goats. But should you want to rent a car for your stay, there are several firms based at the airport. Andy Harris rents bicycles for $20 a day: 599-318-2697. To get a taxi, call the dispatcher at the airport: 599-318-2620. A three-hour island tour can be arranged for about $40.

Where to Stay

Tourism has slowly bubbled in low gear for years, but there are no resorts or major hotels, nor any of the amenities or activities that they would offer. There are several cheap guesthouses available through the tourist board (599-318-2433), or you can work with Seattle-based Dive Saba-Statia, which puts together air, hotel, and dive packages (800-883-7222; www.divesaba.com). Otherwise check into one of the following.

The Old Gin House, 1 Orange Bay, St. Eustatius, NA. 🕐 599-318-2319,
 🖂 599-318-2135, 🖳 www.oldginhouse.com,
 reservations@oldginhouse.com

💲 **Not So Cheap** 🍴 **CP** ⒸⒸ 18 rooms

A one-time cotton refinery converted to an inn, this is Statia's best place to stay. The death of the original owners caused the hotel to go into disrepair and eventually it closed, but the inn is now owned by the folks behind Holland House in St. Maarten. They took it over and refurbished the facility with attractive furnishings and amenities like cable TV and air-conditioning. They also added four waterfront rooms that are surprisingly well appointed. There's a by-reservation restaurant (we didn't have one, so it didn't open on the night of our visit), and a decent waterfront grill. Service hiccups can be a factor to contend with (they were during our visit), but otherwise this is a place with lots of island character.

King's Well, Bay Road, Lower Town, St. Eustatius, NA. 🕐 599-318-2538,
 🖂 599-318-2538, 🖳 www.kingswellstatia.com

💲 **Not So Cheap**, including tax and service 🍴 **BP** ⒸⒸ 12 units

This is a nice spot that overlooks Lower Town and the island's main swimmable beach. There are spacious rooms in the house, with simple furnishings and balconies — all the units have a minifridge, and a few have air-conditioning. There's also a well-liked restaurant (perhaps the island's best). Win and Laura Piechutzki are the friendly husband-and-wife manager-owners (there are also some iguanas and a crew of canines roaming the property). A good base for divers since the water is only five minutes away; town is slightly farther.

Two other lodging possibilities are available but are not comparable to the above two. Golden Era Hotel is located near the Old Gin House down on the water and has a swimming pool (599-318-2345); the cheap Country Inn is close to the airport and has six tiny rooms (599-318-2484).

Where to Eat

The culinary scene here is one of the Caribbean's less dynamic, but there are a few places for decent food.

$$ **The Blue Bead**, Lower Town, 599-318-2873

Everyone winds up at this pretty blue-and-yellow-trimmed house sooner or later — it's the island's unofficial hangout. The kitchen serves up tasty steaks, grilled chicken, and fish. Sunday brunch is a must.

$$ **King's Well**, on a bluff overlooking Lower Town, 599-318-2538

Win and Laura Piechutzki serve nice steaks and seafood with a German flair (schnitzel and rostbraten) from their small hotel dining room.

$$ Ocean View Terrace, Oranjestad, 599-318-2934
This is a cute lunch spot next to the tourist office. It offers burgers, fish, and steaks.

Don't Miss

The Hike to The Quill

You can climb to the summit and back in a couple of hours, but it's worth adding a scramble down inside the crater to see the rainforest and maybe catch a glimpse of the monkeys that live there. From the crater rim you can usually spot six neighboring islands: St. Kitts, Nevis, Antigua, St. Barth, St. Martin/St. Maarten and Saba — what a panorama!

Diving

Statia is known for historical diving — that is, sites littered with anchors, cannons, pottery shards and bottles, and the remains of the old warehouses that were once lined with trading ships. Because the diving is low-key, the sites are in good shape, and marine life is relatively abundant; there's even a hyperbaric chamber on the island. Most dives are at a depth of less than 75 feet and range from shallow reefs on volcanic fingers to a graveyard of intertwined shipwrecks. There are also two newer wrecks put down in the last few years as attractions for divers, including the Charles Brown, a 327-foot AT&T cable repair ship scuttled in 2003. Check with **Dive Statia** (866-614-3491 or 599-318-2435; www.divestatia.com), **Golden Rock Dive Center** (800-311-6658 or 599-318-2964; www.goldenrockdive.com), or — catering to the Euro crowd — **Scubaqua Dive Center** (599-318-2345; www.scubaqua.com).

Sunrise Walk at Zeelandia

This beach is usually too rough for swimming, but it's quite striking in the morning, particularly from the north end with The Quill rising up in the background.

St. Barthélemy
(St. Barth)

People say they come to St. Barth to get away from it all. Hah! One of the main pastimes on this island is running into other people you know, with the most points for those who have acquaintances with the highest Q Factor. A prime example of this is the Christmas–New Year's extreme peak season, when St. Barth becomes the hottest ticket in the Caribbean and the island struggles to keep from sinking under the weight of excess affectation. Everyone who is anyone is on the island, preferably at someone's house or on someone's yacht (the more famous the host, the better). Life consists of house hopping, yacht yo-yoing, and dinner parties. Coyly detached celebrity name dropping is the name of the game. By day, many hang out at their pools, whereas the more adventurous go to Nikki Beach or La Plage beach clubs or to the naturist (and natural) Salines Beach — a fave of ours, too.

When we first came here in 1987, we were put off by all the attitude and sheer fabulousness. It was just too much. Now, on subsequent visits, we like the island a whole lot more. Maybe it's changed (it doesn't seem quite so ul-trachic, attitudinal, and fabulous as it used to be), or maybe we've changed (we're older and fussier), but whatever happened, it's a great island to visit

St. Barth

N

ATLANTIC OCEAN

CARIBBEAN SEA

LEGEND

- Capital City, Town
- Route Number
- Hotel / Point of Interest
- Scenic View
- Ferry / Cruise Ship Dock
- Lighthouse
- Beach
- Golf Course

La Tortue

Ile Frégate

Ile Chevreaux ou Bonhomme

Anse de Flamands

FRANÇOIS PLANTATION

HOTEL SAINT BARTH ISLE DE FRANCE

HOTEL MANAPANY

Baie de St. Jean

Pointe Milou

Pointe Mangin

GUANAHANI

St. BARTH's BEACH HOTEL

HOTEL LE TOINY

Point à Toiny

Anse à Toiny

Anse de Grand Fond

Fourmis

Roches Roubes

Ile Coco

SOFITEL CHRISTOPHER ST. BARTHÉLEMY

LA BANANE

EDEN ROCK

VILLAGE ST. JEAN

LA NORMANDIE

HOSTELLERIE DES TROIS FORCES

Morne de Vitet (938 ft. / 286 m)

Morne de Grand Fond

Le Tamarin

Anse de Grand Saline

Anse de Gouverneur

St. Jean

AIRPORT

Gistavoa

SUNSET HOTEL

HOTEL CARL GUSTAF

Pain de Sucre

Anse de Colombier

FERRY TO St. MARTIN

CARIBBEAN SEA

0 1
Miles

St. Barth: Key Facts

Location	17°N by 62°W 15 miles/24 kilometers southeast of St. Martin/St. Maarten 1,693 miles/2,742 kilometers southeast of New York
Size	8 square miles/21 square kilometers
Highest point	Morne du Vitet (938 feet/286 meters)
Population	About 8,200
Language	French, but English is widely spoken; native islanders speak French with a vague Norman dialect.
Time	Atlantic Standard Time (1 hour ahead of EST, same as EDT)
Area code	To call St. Barth from the U.S., dial 011 (the international dialing code), then 590-590 (the country code), followed by the six-digit local number.
Electricity	220 volts AC, 60 cycles, so you'll need a transformer and an adapter for U.S.-made appliances (most hotels and villa agencies can provide one).
Currency	The euro (€1 = US$1.25 at press time; check before departure). Most hotels, restaurants, and stores accept U.S. dollars, but the exchange rate will not be favorable. Use a credit card for the best exchange rate.
Driving	On the right; a valid U.S. or Canadian driver's license is acceptable. There are just two gas stations on the island and both are closed evenings, Sunday, and holidays.
Documents	U.S. and Canadian citizens need proof of nationality (plus photo ID) for stays up to 3 months; after that a passport is necessary. An ongoing or a return ticket is also necessary.
Departure tax	About $4.50, usually included in the cost of your airline ticket
Beer to drink	Presidente
Rum to drink	Um, excuse me? Rum? What's that? Is that, like, Cristal, Grey Goose, or something?
Music to hear	Any version of "La Vie en Rose" (we prefer Grace Jones's)
Tourism info	www.saint-barths.com; 590-590-27-87-27

— if you can afford it. It still takes a chunk of change to visit St. Barth properly. That has not changed.

Speaking of change, once upon a time in another century, St. Barthélemy, pronounced "Saint bar-TEL-leh-mee," was just an island — a picturesque, beach-girded outpost flying the French flag, but still pretty much an unknown entity. The only bar in town was Le Sélect — a one-room affair jammed with memorabilia and the crews of visiting yachts. A cheap cheeseburger could be had at the stand next to it (named after Jimmy Buffet's "Cheeseburger in Paradise"). There was no pretense to this joint, and not much to the island, either. That was then.

Today, St. Barthélemy epitomizes the Caribbean lifestyles of the very rich, famous, and very, very beautiful. Remarkably, Le Sélect and its cheeseburger stand are still intact, a pocket of low-key sanity on this isle of vanity. But step outside and you're in the Caribbean version of the Hamptons times 10, the West Indies by way of St. Tropez.

It's called St. Barts by everyone now (but if you're really in the know, you'll spell it St. Barth, as the French do), and it is proudly, smugly, heart-stoppingly expensive — the priciest destination in the Caribbean. Some resorts are more exclusive than others, but you can't pay more for what you get than here, especially when the dollar is down versus the euro. Going out to eat on St. Barth — the major evening pastime — almost requires an armored truck. What was once a sleepy hideaway for the Rockefellers and other elite families has become the glitz capital of the New York and Los Angeles creative celeb-elite.

St. Barth is also the most un-Caribbean of Caribbean islands. It's almost as though your 10-minute flight from St. Maarten traveled at Warp One and landed in Cap d'Antibes in the Med. Most shocking, particularly after you've spent some time on the other islands, is the population, which is almost totally white. There is also no poverty — no one-room houses with water from a public tap. The French themselves find St. Barth too pricey, although when hotel rates go down after Easter, and there's an influx of Parisians in July–August, it lends the requisite air of authenticity to the Euro-decadence.

The hilly island is tiny — just 8 square miles. Most of the terrain is fairly dry and developed. St. Barth is not a place for enthusiasts of the wild kingdom. Most activity centers on the water, the stomach, and the right side of the brain. There are 22 or so beaches — 6 are quite fine, 1 is clothing-optional. There are well over 80 restaurants, most specializing in *cuisine gastronomique*, which is basically French food with Créole flourishes. There are several fun bars and cafés, places to see and be seen, and many restaurants turn into free-spirited clubs after the last entrée is served, including the legendary Le Ti St. Barth. The island also has a few nooks for shimmying the night away, including Le Petit Club, Le Feeling, and the New York–owned Luna.

The Briefest History

St. Barthelémy was first settled by the Ciboney about 1000 B.C., then the Arawaks around A.D. 200. The Caribs invaded and conquered in the 10th century and called the island Ouanalao, which roughly means "Bird Sanctuary." Columbus sighted the island on his second voyage, in 1493, and named it after his brother, Bartolomeo. The island wasn't settled by Europeans until 1648, when French colonists from St. Kitts set up shop, hence St. Barthélemy. They were wiped out by the Caribs five years later. The second attempt to colonize, in 1678, took hold, when French men and women arrived from Normandy and Brittany. Their influence is still present on St. Barth today. Many of these settlers were pirates preying on Spanish galleons, the most infamous of whom was Monbars the Exterminator. The island remained in French hands, except for a period in 1758 when the British briefly took control. Then the ill-fated Louis XVI, to get trading rights in Gothenburg, Sweden, sold the island to Sweden in 1784. Again the British occupied, in 1801–1802 (it's the same old story), and finally, after the abolition of slavery in 1848, St. Barth was returned by plebiscite to France in 1878.

For the last six decades St. Barth has been a dependency of Guadeloupe. However, in 2003, the island voted overwhelmingly to become an Overseas Collectivity of France, making St. Barth financially and politically independent of Guadeloupe. New regulations pertaining to matters as minuscule as garbage collection fees and as large as customs policies, plus new port duties and capital gains taxes, are in St. Barth's future—all prickly subjects for an island that has always treasured its duty free, tax-free status.

Getting There

Landing at the aptly named St. Barthelémy Aérodrome la Tourmente is one of the most thrilling aerial experiences in the Caribbean, matched only by the approach to neighboring Saba's cliff-wrapped runway. The 19-seater STOL aircraft (usually a deHavilland Twin Otter) flies stomach-wrenchingly low over a notch in the mountains, then plummets to the runway. With trees, cars, and an anxiety-inducing cross rushing past your window, the plane seems to bounce on the runway as the pilot hits the brakes so hard that you lurch forward in your seat. Fortunately, the runway was "renewed" in 2004, ensuring a smoother landing for all.

There are several airlines that will share this tranq-popping ride with you, the most common connecting point being St. Maarten's Juliana Airport (reached from the U.S. by American, Continental, Delta, United, and US Airways). Air Caraïbes, St. Barth Commuter, and WINAIR have flights to St. Barth throughout the day, usually timed to meet the jets as they come into St. Maarten. Since landing on St. Barth after dark is prohibited, the last flight from Juliana is around 5 p.m. You can also fly in from San Juan, Puerto Rico, or Guadeloupe using Air Caraïbes. Of course, private charters are available and often used, and they are always a stylish entrance and exit. Your villa broker or hotel will make the necessary arrangements.

If you have a fear of flying, or a love of the open sea, another route to consider is via high-speed catamaran or ferry from St. Martin/St. Maarten. Newest and fastest is *Rapid Explorer*, which makes the trip in a swift 40 minutes at a round-trip price of about $115. The ferry leaves from Dock Maarten in Philipsburg three times daily; call 599-542-9762 or 590-590-27-60-33 for schedule and reservations. *MV Voyager* is a 125-passenger ferry that makes the trip in 75 minutes, twice a day, five days a week from Marigot and two days a week from Oyster Pond; call 590-590-87-10-68 in Marigot or 590-590-27-54-10 in St. Barth; www.voyager-st-barths.com. *The Edge* (not of U2 fame) is a smaller catamaran leaving from Pelican Marina in Simpson Bay several times a week; call 599-544-2640. Fares for *Voyager* and *The Edge* are about $81 round-trip; a port fee of $9 applies for all. There are discounts available for kids under 12 and for same-day round-trips on all of these ferries.

Getting Around

Le car to rent is a Smart. St. Barth was the location of our first encounter with the Smart, and the moment we saw one, we wanted one. Looking like a bauble from a Pixar animated film, these tiny, two-door autos resemble a child's toy. They are simple vehicles, and convertibles are available, too. This is such a small island and the roads are fairly good — if often steep and winding — so why not have some fun? You must be able to drive a stick shift, but fortunately the speed limit is 45 km (about 28 mph) so you don't need to worry about being run down by those impatient francophones. The car doesn't have a trunk, per se, but theft is not a major occurrence. Get Smart through Smart of Saint Barth: 590-590-29-71-31. The vehicles might not look like much, but the rates are as high as $60 per day in winter (and as low as $40 in the summer months).

Of course, there are other cars and jeeps for rent. There are several international rental-car branches, including Hertz (800-654-3001 or 590-590-27-71-14), Avis (800-331-1084 or 590-590-27-71-43), Budget (800-527-0700 or 590-590-27-66-30), and Europcar (590-590-27-73-33), as well as smaller local companies, such as Turbo; most or all of them also rent Smarts. Be sure to call ahead to ensure availability and to get the best possible rates.

If you just can't deal with driving, there are taxis, but they can get expensive if you plan to move around a lot. Trips of up to five minutes are about $4, plus $3 for each additional three minutes. Note that fares are higher at night (but many drivers don't work at night) and on Sunday and holidays. For a taxi call 590-590-27-75-81 or 590-590-27-66-31.

Tailgating

This seems to be the unofficial island sport. Due to the confluence of narrow, twisting two-lane roads; vacationers in rental cars; and very impatient, lead-footed French locals, tailgating is de rigueur on this most de rigueur of islands. Don't be surprised if you look in the rearview mirror and see nothing behind you, then 10 seconds later, another glance in the rearview mirror reveals a car right on your ass (with a driver glaring at you). Our advice, let him pass at the nearest opportunity.

Focus on St. Barth: Exploring Its Fabulousness

Even by Caribbean standards, St. Barth is very small—only about a quarter the size of St. Thomas—and it is severed in two by the airport. On the smaller, western side there are two nice beaches: **Anse des Flamands** and **Anse de Colombier**. Flamands is a beautiful beach despite its steep rake and the presence of several hotels. Colombier, once known as Rockefeller's beach, is more remote, about a half-mile walk from La Petite Anse. This one is a favorite of visiting yachts. Besides these beaches, there's not a lot to see on this side, except hills, vistas, and valleys.

East of the airport is where you'll find most of the action. **St. Jean**, with its beach, is the focal point of the island (even more so than Gustavia, the capital). Everyone passes through St. Jean at some point or other during the day. The beach features several hotels and restaurants as well as water sports and a number of stores. If you're staying in a house, the beach here is good for meeting people. You'll find them especially to the west of Eden Rock, the notable promontory in the middle of the bay. Off the beach, the major social spot is the shopping center at the east end. Plan on having a café au lait at the ice cream shop up the street just past La Louisiane (skip the ice cream—that's one dish the French have yet to master).

If you head east out of St. Jean, a pleasant drive takes you around a loop that winds through the hills to the windward side. There's a pretty, small beach on the right end of Anse de Marigot. The stretch of road that hugs the Anse à Toiny is very scenic, with hilly pastures rising up on the opposite side. Here you may spot some expert surfers at the "Washing Machine" break. Once you pass through Grand Fond, take a left at the sign for **Salines**. Go all the way to the end of the road (a salt pond will be on your right, and dunes in front of you) and park where you can. Follow the path and you'll quickly arrive at St. Barth's de facto nude beach. Most everyone here is either topless or naked, so you may feel uncomfortable if you don't remove something—even if it's just to swim (otherwise your neighbors will think you came to gawk at them). Around the point to the west is another great beach, Gouverneur, a smaller version of Salines. Pretty **Gustavia** (on the other side from St. Jean and the airport) is the capital, where the banks are located. The harbor is U-shaped, with the shops and restaurants clustered tightly around the basin. Stroll around, browse the galleries and shops, and be sure to head up the hill and have a pricey sunset cocktail at the Carl Gustaf. Then head to Le Sélect for a Heineken and welcome yourself to the "real" St. Barth.

Where to Stay

The Villa Option

Those in the know will tell you the thing to do is to rent a villa for your St. Barth holiday. This will allow you to throw your own cocktail or dinner parties and also provide an added level of privacy for your vacation. Renting a house can also save you a considerable amount of money on food; you won't have to go out to eat all the time — but you shouldn't tell anyone this, because spending money is very much in vogue here. Most of all, by renting a home, you will in effect have a patch of St. Barth all to yourself — a villa that is unlike anyone else's, your own piece of paradise.

To get the villa you want, you'll have to book as early as possible, especially for the Christmas season, when most units are grabbed six months or more in advance. The best boast *Architectural Digest*–worthy interiors, sweeping views, and sky-high price tags. On our last visit we ogled **La Fleur Sur la Mer**, a five-bedroom residence roosting atop the hill in Colombier, where a 360-degree view avails both sunrise and sunset. Amenities include Kenzo-appointed bedrooms, a mirrored fitness room, a screening room, a formal dining room, an infinity-edge pool, and a lily pond. The price: $30,000 per week in season.

Most of the villas are not nearly so dear. Weekly rates for a basic one-bedroom bungalow in the winter start at about $1,600 (or $1,100 and up in the off-season). Rates are higher, of course, for units with three or four bedrooms, a pool, and a stellar view. The economy of scale works for those who bring a posse of favorite friends. For instance, eight can share a four-bedroom with private pool in high season for under $175 per night, per person — less than the price of four comparable hotel rooms for eight in winter. In fact, because the villas are priced in dollars (whereas hotels are priced in euros), villas are currently a much better deal than most hotels now that the dollar is languishing.

There are several firms that handle villas, the largest being **Sibarth Real Estate** (590-590-29-88-90, fax 590-590-27-60-52). The woman to speak to here is Brook Lacour — the power broker of rental properties on St. Barth. She handles a majority of the available villas, more than 200 islandwide, and offers a full-color catalog with photos of many of their units. She and her Guadeloupean husband, Roger, also started a stateside office that handles villa and hotel rentals on St. Barth (and around the world) called **WIMCO**. Although they represent the largest selection, both firms tack on a 10 percent service charge. WIMCO does not accept Visa or Master Card, and the agency adds a 5 percent surcharge for the luxury of using American Express. Sibarth accepts all three credit cards, yet due to French law it is restricted from adding the 5 percent surcharge. Regardless of the extra fees, this is St. Barth, so what's a few hundred extra for a convenience fee? Reach WIMCO at 800-932-3222 or 401-849-8012; fax 401-847-6290. The mailing address is: P.O. Box 1461, Newport, RI 02840; e-mail: wimco@well.com; Web site: www.wimco.com.

French Caribbean International in Santa Barbara, California, is a smaller company that handles a variety of villas on St. Barth (as well as the other French islands). It represents more than 100 units on St. Barth, starting at $1,600 a week ($1,000 in low season), and it doesn't add a service charge or credit

card fee. Call 800-322-2223 or 805-967-9850; fax 805-967-7798; www
.frenchcaribbean.com.

Another stateside representative is **St. Barth Properties**, based in Massachusetts. Rates start at about $1,500 a week ($1,000 in low season) for a one-
bedroom cottage in Anse des Cayes without a pool; the company charges
an administration fee of 12.5 percent (discounted to 10 percent if you pay with
check or cash). Call 800-421-3396 or 508-528-7727; fax 508-528-7789; www
.stbarth.com.

Country Village Rentals, based in Nantucket, is not quite the St. Barth
specialist that the above outfits are, but it does represent more than 150
properties on St. Barth, starting from $1,500 per week ($1,000 in low season). Like WIMCO, it adds a service charge — 10 percent — to all rentals. Call
800-599-7368 or 508-228-8840; fax 508-228-8804; www.cvrandr.com.

Note that all of these agencies work from more or less the same rental
pool, so if you have a particular place in mind, it doesn't hurt to call each
agency and compare rates and services.

The Hotel Option

If you're not fortunate enough to have wrangled an invitation or secured a
private home, fear not — there are a number of hotels that are intimate, chic,
and expensive. There is also a smattering of less expensive accommodations,
some of them with a modicum of charm; yet all but the cheapest will cost
more than $300 a night during high season (remember, this is St. Barth,
where the motto is "Why pay less?"). Note that most hotels (and villas)
charge a higher price still during the Christmas–New Year's period. There
are some good values, however, that won't break the bank. Keep in mind that
many hotels (and restaurants) close for a few weeks in September and/or
October, the island's true low season, when St. Barth catches 40 winks.

⊛ **Hotel Le Toiny**, Anse de Toiny, St. Barthélemy, FWI. ℂ 800-27-TOINY
or 590-590-27-88-88, ✆ 590-590-27-89-30, 🖳 www.letoiny.com,
letoiny@wanadoo.fr

🛍 **Stratospheric** 🍴 **CP** CC 15 villas

Le Toiny is quite tony and tops all others as the poshest hotel on St.
Barth. In fact, it's one of the most smashing accommodations anywhere in the Caribbean and, at just shy of $2,000 per night (in win-
ter), probably the region's single most expensive place. While Toiny
bills itself as a hotel, it actually looks more like a private club, with
one-bedroom villas — each with its own pool, 10 by 20 feet — dappled
on a sunny hillside below the main building (there's also a two- or
three-bedroom villa). Lying naked on the sprawling terrace of your
villa is the best way to appreciate Le Toiny, but note that this is where
Brad Pitt got caught in the buff (courtesy of a paparazzo endowed
with a hefty telephoto). In fact, when we stopped for lunch on one

visit and innocently peered from the cocktail area toward the villas, we got an eyeful — a couple not only free of bathing costumes but quite involved in a different sort of diving (i.e., a few of these terraces are not as private as they appear to be!).

The spacious villas are totally loaded and furnished in mahogany period pieces, including four-poster beds. There's enough land here that from inside the room or out on your terrace you might feel like you're the only guest. Everything is beautifully manicured, and the whole place looks like a photo shoot for *Architectural Digest*. One guest told us that after years of going to Taiwana, he'll never go back now that there is Le Toiny.

There is a superb restaurant, Le Gaïac, and a bar on the premises, and the most attractive staff we've seen in some time. The two flaws are that the beach (a 10-minute walk down the hill) is not ideal for swimming, and the resort overlooks a somewhat unsightly coffee-colored pond; however, the turquoise Caribbean is in the distance. And some might carp that it's a bit out of the way, but for lovers with big bucks and something besides cocktail parties in mind, Le Toiny is it. Closed September through mid-October.

Eden Rock, St. Jean, St. Barthélemy, FWI. ℂ 877-563-7105 or 590-590-29-79-99, ✆ 590-590-27-88-37, 🖳 www.edenrockhotel.com

💲 **Stratospheric** 🍽 **BP** CC 32 rooms and suites

Claiming one of the most prime settings in all the Caribbean, Eden Rock is also one of the few island hotels that is accurately described by the term *legendary*. The onetime home of Dutch wartime entrepreneur Remy de Haenen, Eden Rock sits on a perch in the middle of St. Jean Bay, surrounded by sea and sand on all sides. It became the island's first hotel in the 1950s, with six rooms hugging the granite, and soon racked up an impressive guest list: Greta Garbo, Montgomery Clift, and the like. In the 1980s the Rock slipped well into the background as increasingly swank resorts were built on the island. Then, in 1995, David and Jane Matthews, an English couple with a knack for renovations and antiques, bought it and began a careful upgrade of the property, eventually crafting one of the Caribbean's fiercest inns, filled with quirky nuances and a dreamer's caprice.

The rooms on the rock — already unique and wickedly plush, with antiques and paintings, choice views, and deluxe amenities — now include the Greta Garbo Suite, decorated in 1930s Hollywood style, and the Howard Hughes Loft Suite, built atop de Haenen's original house at the rock's apex. There are two new shops, and the Sand Bar and On the Rocks restaurants have been rebuilt with open kitchens. In addition to the rooms on the rock, there are beach cottages (less expensive than those on the rock but without beach views). In 2004, the Matthewses acquired the Filao Beach Hotel next door, and they have integrated the two properties into one spectacular resort, adding unique villas to the mix. Water sports and other activities can be easily arranged.

Hotel Saint Barth Isle de France, B.P. 612, Baie des Flamands, St. Barthélemy, FWI. 🕾 800-810-4691 or 590-590-27-61-81, 🖂 590-590-27-86-83, 🖵 www.isle-de-france.com, isledefr@saintbarths.com

🏷 **Stratospheric** (with good discounts for garden rooms in summer) 🍽 CP ⓒⓒ 33 rooms

Located on Baie des Flamands, St. Barth's choicest hotel beach, the rooms at this *très chic* establishment are a notch below Le Toiny and Eden Rock, but they have the advantage of a prime beach setting. The plantation-style building and accommodations are very tasteful, as you would expect, with mahogany furniture draped in billowy mosquito netting, framed historical prints, plush marble baths, and all the appropriate amenities. There is a pretty pool at beachside, as well as tennis and a small but fully equipped gym and fitness center; water sports and horseback riding can be arranged. In 2003 an exquisite spa was added, featuring Molton Brown treatments, like the Corporeal Cocoon Bodywrap and Mirror of Life Facials — ooh-la-la (no wonder Elle MacPherson is a regular).

Besides being attractive inside and out, the big plus about the Isle de France is the superb beach, but you pay through the nose for beach-view rooms; the more reasonable garden-view rooms are 100 to 200 feet from the sand across the road and offer greener settings and a second pool. The restaurant, La Case de l'Isle, serves excellent French cuisine on the beach. Twenty-four-hour room service is a recent addition. Closed September through mid-October.

Hotel Carl Gustaf, B.P. 700, Rue des Normands, Gustavia, St. Barthélemy, FWI. 🕾 590-590-29-79-00, 🖂 590-590-27-82-37, 🖵 www.carlgustaf.com

🏷 **Stratospheric** 🍽 CP ⓒⓒ 14 rooms

Now, this place is truly royal deluxe — after all, the hotel is named after a Swedish king. With a commanding view of Gustavia's harbor, one of the prettiest sights in the Caribbean, this is an impressively expensive place to stay (upwards of $1,300 a night in winter), but why pay less? The rooms are plush and elegant, decked out with their own plunge pools and open-air parlors with oh-so-tasteful and comfortable furniture and, of course, totally loaded (including a small but fully equipped kitchen, two phone lines — one for your fax, which is provided — a stereo system, and TVs in both the living room and the bedroom). Beautiful lanais with dramatically columned removable canopies frame your view. Needless to say (but we'll say it anyway), the sunset views here are awesome, and room service is available 24 hours. There is a bar and restaurant (live music most nights) and a small fitness center, and there's a nice beach just down the hill, as well as shopping and dining for days in town. Got the money and want to be in a hotel? Go for it. Closed September through early-October.

Village St. Jean, St. Jean, St. Barthélemy, FWI. ℂ 800-651-8366 or 590-590-27-61-39, 📧 590-590-27-77-96, 🖥 www.villagestjeanhotel.com

💲 **Very Pricey** 🍽 **CP** ⓒ 25 rooms

Okay. You've basked long enough in the glamour of St. Barth's posh and primped — you just want a place you can stash your bags without breaking the bank that won't be too *déclassé*. Check into Village St. Jean, one of St. Barth's most endearing hotels. Actually, these are stone and wood cottages — each with one or two bedrooms, a full kitchen, and a private terrace — they almost replicate the island's villa lifestyle on a small scale. You'll also find six standard hotel rooms with twin beds and a small refrigerator that are a good value in peak season. There's a very satisfying Italian restaurant on the premises, a pool, and a Jacuzzi, and the beach is a 10-minute walk down the hill. This friendly, unpretentious, family-run operation has a loyal repeat clientele and books up weeks in advance each winter.

François Plantation, Colombier, St. Barthélemy, FWI. ℂ 590-590-29-80-22, 📧 590-590-27-61-26, 🖥 www.francois-plantation.com

💲 **Beyond Belief** 🍽 **CP** ⓒ 12 bungalows

Perched on a peak in Colombier, this is an expensive but low-key place offering great views, with beautiful gardens and landscaping, and it is one of St. Barth's finest accommodations. There are 12 charming bungalows, which are tastefully done and have everything you need. Perhaps the best thing about the François is its feeling of informality. The public areas are comfortable and quiet — good places for reading a book or havng a conversation. This is not a pretentious or slick establishment, but it's well run and the restaurant and wine cellar are among of the island's best. There is a small pool with a dizzying view at the top of a steep hill. Climbing hills is de rigueur here, so be advised. Low season rates are under $300 a night and include a car. Closed September and October.

La Banane, Lorient, St. Barthélemy, FWI. ℂ 590-590-52-03-00, 📧 590-590-27-68-44, 🖥 www.labanane.com

💲 **Beyond Belief** 🍽 **CP** ⓒ 9 rooms

This groovy Belgian-owned inn is the latest dose of panache to the island. With just nine bungalows, each named after a different exotic fruit and with its own color scheme, La Banane is intimate and sexy. Rooms have clapboard walls adorned with black-and-white photos, swank Casa Milano four-poster beds with Belgian linens, and bathrooms that open onto patios or gardens (room 9 even has an outdoor tub!). Other amenities include DVD player, minibar, and library. The common area had a two-tiered swimming pool shaded by palms (the effect is that of a little hothouse). Though not on a beach, you're just 300 feet from one, and although there's no restaurant on the premises, room service from K'Fé Massaï next door is available. There is a bar at La Banane, and breakfast comes with the room. The compromises are easy to live with for such a chic hideaway.

Hostellerie des Trois Forces, Vitet, St. Barthélemy, FWI. ℭ 590-590-27-61-25, ✆ 590-590-27-81-38, 🖳 www.3forces.net

💲 **Very Pricey** (noteworthy discounts for singles) 🍽 **CP** ⒸⒸ 8 rooms

This is a quirky place, a New Age accommodation designed to take care of body, mind, and spirit. Set high up in the windward mountains with views of the water to the east, this is St. Barth's most cosmic lodging option. Owner Hubert Delamotte, an astrologer in a big way, has designed rooms to match the signs of the zodiac. Each room is in a separate or shared bungalow, with nice detail using gingerbread trim and special touches to complement the personality traits of each sign. The Aquarius Room, for example, is water-focused (yes, we know Aquarius is actually an air sign) with little color (because Aquarians don't need color, especially in the bathroom, according to Hubert). Most of the rooms have four-poster beds and double hammocks on the porches; all have air-conditioning. Currently there are rooms for eight signs; the remaining four might come in the future (but then we've been hearing that for years now).

There is a pool, a comfortable bar, and an excellent restaurant (with organic veggies). The whole place is homey, not at all pretentious (like a number of other St. Barth establishments). Mr. Delamotte is also into yoga and meditation, and he welcomes all lifestyles to his holistic retreat. He encourages spiritual and self-help groups to stay at his place, and if you give him your birth date, time, and place, he'll do your astrological chart.

La Normandie, Lorient, St. Barthélemy, FWI. ℭ 590-590-27-73-78, ✆ 590-590-27-58-32

💲 **Cheap** 🍽 **EP** ⒸⒸ 8 rooms

One of the rarest of birds on St. Barth is a cheap hotel. La Normandie is a decent choice for those on a budget (who can't spend more than $100 a night for accommodations). It's simple, clean, and run by a French family—a true old-fashioned Antillean guest house. It's set in a verdant valley, and there are eight small rooms, all with private bath and ceiling fans (most have air-conditioning, too). There is a restaurant and bar on the premises and a tiny pool with sundeck. Lorient Beach is about 150 yards away.

Sunset Hotel, Gustavia, St. Barthélemy, FWI. ℰ 590-590-27-77-21, ✆ 590-590-27-81-59, 🖥 www.st-barths.com/sunset-hotel/

💲 **Not So Cheap** 🍽 **EP** ⓒⓒ 10 rooms

St. Barth's other budget spot is located right in Gustavia, facing the harbor and sunset. Although parking can be problematic, Shell Beach is a 10-minute walk, and you'll have more than two dozen restaurants just as close, plus plenty of shopping. This older inn has smallish rooms, each with a/c, satellite TV, minibar, hairdryer, and phone. Breakfast on the terrace is available for $8 per person. Be sure to get one of the rooms yielding harbor views — others have only transom windows onto the hall. Otherwise, it's a great deal for this island.

Guanahani, B.P. 609, Anse de Grand Cul-de-Sac, St. Barthélemy, FWI. ℰ 800-223-6800 or 590-590-27-66-60, ✆ 590-590-27-70-70, 🖥 www.leguanahani.com

💲 **Stratospheric** 🍽 **BP** ⓒⓒ 69 rooms

This 69-room resort sits on 16 acres at the end of the western peninsula encasing Anse du Grand Cul-de-Sac. Renovated in 2004, Guanahani is the largest hotel on the island, and it lacks some of the cherished intimacy provided at most St. Barth properties; it also draws a larger contingent of American guests. Yet it has a modicum of big-resort amenities, like 24-hour room service, a variety of water sports, and a fitness room. The best units are the oceanfront cottages on the bluff to the right. Each has a tile terrace, a vaulted ceiling with fan, a/c, a queen-size bed, wood and canvas furnishings, and a terrific double-sinked bathroom. You can also get units with their own pools. All of the cottages are gingerbread-trimmed and are painted bright modern lime and lavender colors.

There is a beach-level pool, backed by a fine restaurant, a cabana bar, and a spa — the island's most comprehensive, which debuted in 2005. A reef keeps the water calm for swimming and snorkeling. The water sports center (sailing, windsurfing, waterskiing, scuba, and fishing) is located on the beach. The beach itself is adequate — better ones are nearby. Two hard-surface, lighted tennis courts round out the recreational facilities.

We think the rack rates here are mighty steep for what you get (then again, what isn't, on this island?), but the Guanahani offers good summer packages that are worth looking into.

Sofitel Christopher St. Barthélemy, 9 Point Milou, St. Barthélemy, FWI. ℰ 800-221-4542 or 590-590-27-63-63, ✆ 590-590-27-92-92, 🖥 www.accorhotels.com, H1599@accor.com

💲 **Stratospheric** 🍽 **BP** ⓒⓒ 42 rooms

Once again, the Sofitel has gotten it right — if only it had gotten it right on the beach! Located on a bluff in breezy Pointe Milou, on the island's northern tip, the Christopher is the island's second largest hotel. The array of rooms in white, two-story structures have fabulous ocean vistas. Unfortunately, you can look, but you can't touch—the closest worthwhile beach requires at least a 10-minute commute by car (as do most shops, bars, and restaurants). The sloping grounds of the resort feature Creole décor with a mega-size swimming pool (the island's largest) as its centerpiece. With its super views and full-service bar serving meals throughout the day, the pool really is the place to hang. For breakfast and evening dining, the waterfront L'Orchidée restaurant is quite good. There is also a fully equipped gym offering fitness classes. All leisure activities such as diving, fishing, tennis, and other water sports can be arranged through the concierge.

The oceanfront and ocean-view rooms are spacious, with an attractive décor of light-colored walls, beige tile, colorful print curtains, and a furnished veranda. All contain twin beds or a king-size bed, a ceiling fan, a/c, and a minibar. The hotel can arrange for a direct phone line into your room, Internet access, and all the other electronic amenities that you really shouldn't be using on your vacation. Basically, we think the Christopher is a stylish, professionally run operation, but we do find the rates to be a bit hefty for a hotel that's not on the beach (we'd opt for a villa).

St. Barth's Beach Hotel, B.P. 580, Grand Cul-de-Sac, St. Barthélemy, FWI. ℂ 888-790-5264 or 590-590-27-60-70, ✆ 590-590-27-75-57 🖳 www.saintbarthbeachhotel.com

💲 **Wicked Pricey** (with good discounts for singles) 🍴 **CP** ⓒⓒ 36 rooms This two-story motel — er, we mean hotel — is located right on the decent beach at Cul-de-Sac, which makes it a worthwhile choice if you seek beachfront lodging without emptying your trust fund. Served by a friendly and low-key staff, it has 36 rooms with straightforward tropical furnishings, plus eight one- and two-bedroom villas with full kitchens. There's a swimming pool, the St. Barth's Gym, and a respectable, not-too-pricey restaurant, Le Rivage, which is popular with locals. The beach fronts what is the island's prime windsurfing and kitesurfing spot. Although several restaurants are within walking distance, the location is a bit isolated, so a car is a good idea.

Hotel Manapany, B.P. 114, Anse des Cayes, St. Barthélemy, FWI. ℂ 590-590-27-66-55, ✆ 590-590-27-75-28, 🖳 www.lemanapany.com

💲 **Beyond Belief** (with good discounts for singles) 🍴 **CP** ⓒⓒ 52 rooms The first of the luxury resorts on St. Barth, Manapany sweeps up a hill from the beach at Anse des Cayes. For many years, this was the island's only upscale hotel, but time has not served Manapany well. Today the island has more than a half-dozen full-service resorts, and Manapany looks a bit long in the tooth by comparison. On the other hand, the hotel's maturity is favorably displayed in its landscaping and gardens; it looks established. There are cottages perched on the slope, and while the ones at the top have the best views, you have to climb a fairly steep hill and stairs if you forgot something (there are golf carts available). If you don't want to climb, there are also bungalows on the beach. The rooms and suites themselves are not extraordinary, but they are spacious and pleasant. All have the amenities one would expect from a luxury resort with a stiff price tag. Manapany's strongest point is its service, which is friendly, very helpful, and efficient. There is a nice poolside restaurant, the Fellini, serving Italian cuisine. Facilities include a pool, a Jacuzzi, a lighted tennis court, and a small, fair beach.

⊛ Where to Eat

With more than 80 restaurants to choose from, you'll never go wanting, particularly because the food here is so good — and so expensive (remember, virtually all the food has to be imported from faraway places). Although French cuisine is king, you'll also find Creole, Vietnamese, Italian, and other tastes to tantalize your palate. All of the luxury hotels have excellent restaurants, including the Carl Gustaf, Le Toiny (Le Gaïac), Hotel Manapany (Fellini), Eden Rock (the Sand Bar and On the Rocks), the Isle de France (La Case de l'Isle), Christopher (L'Orchidée), the Guanahani (Bartoloméo), and the François Plantation — see the write-ups above for the various phone numbers. They are all *très cher* in cost, as are most restaurants on St. Barth, although you can always grab a Cheeseburger in Paradise at the stand next to Le Sélect for about $6. Other recommendations are below.

$$$$ Do Brazil, Shell Beach, 590-590-29-06-66

Jet-set Parisian Boubou has operated a number of restaurants on St. Barth, but he's no Ray Kroc and instead manages to anticipate dining trends to import to this tiny isle. Do Brazil is a co-venture with tennis star Yannick Noah, located on the beach just outside the Gustavia harbor (below the Carl Gustaf). The cuisine is Brazilian with French embellishments, the room is open-air, with wonderful sea views — ideally, come for sunset cocktails and pupus. The other Boubou of the moment is La Mandada (590-590-27-96-96) which overlooks the Gustavia harbor for Thai curries and other spice-happy dishes. At both, the food is hit-and-miss, the scene is often better.

$$$$ Eddy's, rue du Centenaire, Gustavia, 590-590-27-54-17

Eddy Stakelborough used to run the famed and much-loved Eddy's Ghetto, but he turned his attention to this more upscale establishment, decked out in Balinese teak and bamboo. It's a gem and still not too expensive or pretentious. Creole cuisine is the focus, with

Asian and classic French twists. Closed on Sunday. No reservations, so get there early.

$$$ **The Hideaway (Chez Andy)**, St. Jean, 590-590-27-63-62

This is the place for delicious pizzas and salads that won't break the bank. Closed Sunday for lunch and all day Monday.

$$$ **K'Fé Massaï**, Lorient, 590-590-29-76-78

Fashionably appointed in African sculpture and fabrics, K'Fé has a menu that embraces Asian and Caribbean accents prepared with nouveau French style. It's exceedingly popular, and a relatively good value. Open nightly.

$ **Kiki-é Mo**, opposite Eden Rock, 590-590-27-90-65

This is a positively indispensable island institution—a cheap place for delicious panini built on fresh focaccia. Also, stock your villa fridge from the excellent selection of antipastos, pasta, cold cuts, cheese, and wine.

$$ **La Cantina**, rue du Bord de Mer, Gustavia, 590-590-27-55-66

We love this groovy, popular, and *petit* place on the harbor for late-afternoon cocktails. La Cantina plays great music (we heard great groove when we were there) and serves up faboo sandwiches and salads for lunch and dinner. Closed on Sunday.

$$$ **La Gloriette**, Grand Cul de Sac, 590-590-27-75-66

We adore this very romantic restaurant (especially at night), what with its great food, attentive yet informal service, reasonable (for St. Barth, that is) prices, and lovely setting facing the caressing trade winds. The menu is more casual than most, which allows the lagoon views to take their proper place in your memories. Lunch and dinner are served daily, except Wednesday.

$$$$ **La Langouste**, Anse des Flamands, 590-590-27-63-61

This informal spot, set on the magnificent beach at Anse des Flamands, is the smart choice for moderately priced lobster dishes, along with codfish fritters, court bouillon, spicy fish soup, and other Creole specialties. Annie Ange, the owner of this favorite, is an island original. It serves lunch and dinner daily, except Monday.

$$$$$ **Le Gaïac**, Toiny, 590-590-29-77-50

Named after the rare Gaïac trees of the island, this intimate 30-seat terrace prepares superb French cuisine with Creole accents, all under the eye of *cuisinier* Maxime des Champs, who who has been at this property since 1994. The views are across an infinity pool down a deserted hillside to a windswept beach. Lunch and dinner are rewarding, but the Sunday brunch has become an island institution; make reservations well in advance. Closed Monday in the summer.

$$$ **Le Grain de Sel**, Salines, 590-590-52-46-05

This is a convenient spot for lunch or refreshment when beaching at Les Salines. The Mediterranean-style menu includes excellent sandwiches and salads, dusted with grains of salt harvested from the nearby salt ponds. Open daily for lunch and dinner.

$$$ **Le Rivage**, Grand Cul-de-Sac, 590-590-27-82-42

This is another helpful lunch and dinner spot for its reasonably priced offerings. Le Rivage has a relaxed atmosphere and a pleasing French Creole menu. Closed on Tuesday.

$$$$$ **Le Sapotillier**, rue de Centenaire, Gustavia, 590-590-27-60-28

Serving dinner only, this is an excellent in-town restaurant serving classic French cuisine in a *très romantique* outdoor garden, under a *sapotillier* ("sarsaparilla") tree. Closed most of the off-season, and on Monday. Reservations are required.

$$$ **Le Tamarin**, Route des Salines, 590-590-27-72-12

On the road to Anse des Salines, this is a great place to take a break from the sun, surf, and sand for a little sit-down. It has good French Creole cuisine in a garden setting. Le Tamarin is open for lunch daily from 12:30 to 4 p.m., and sometimes for dinner in season.

$$$$ **Le Ti St. Barth**, Pointe Milou, 590-590-27-97-71

This spot is less known for its food than for its crazy, decadent shows. We haven't seen the new remodel, which abandons the old pirates of the Caribbean ambiance in favor of a setting described as "very theatrical" (perhaps Elton John circa 1978?) by a friend. However, this is sure to remain an in-spot for a certain crowd. Open from 7 p.m., with dancing until late; closed on Sunday.

$$$ **L'Entracte**, rue du Bord de Mer, Gustavia 590-590-27-70-11

Known for its pizzas, this is a locally popular, lively, and well-priced eatery on the harbor in Gustavia that won't break the bank. Closed on Sunday.

$$$$$ **L'Esprit Salines**, Salines, 590-590-52-46-10

This place, opened by the former staff of Maya's (below) and located next to the salt flats just off the wonderful beach at Salines, continues to win raves from a loyal following. It's closed Tuesday and Wednesday and in September and October.

$$$$$ **Maya's**, on the waterfront in Public, 590-590-27-75-73

With gorgeous views of the harbor and sunsets, this restaurant just west of Gustavia has great Creole food, atmosphere, and service — and frequent celebrity sightings. We think Maya's is somewhat overrated, but it's another essential St. Barth scene. It serves dinner only, Monday through Saturday; closed in September. Reservations are essential in high season. Also check out Maya's to Go (590-590-29-83-70), located opposite the airport and offering great takeout, catering, and survival kits for the flight home.

Going Out

In addition to the previously mentioned Do Brazil (for sunset cocktails) and Ti St. Barth (for absolute craziness), there are a few venues for light nightlife. Of course, villa and yacht parties are de rigueur. **Le Petit Club** is the dinosaur, and it's so small it has to be exclusive. Located behind L'Ananas in Gustavia, it is no doubt the smallest disco we have ever seen, but it has a disco ball, and owners Veronique Boëte and Marc de Bono keep this place open nightly (weekends are best); it gets going late. Other nighttime possibilities are the presumptuously named (but sometimes percolating) **Le Feeling**, a disco with a roomy outdoor patio and bar, high above Gustavia in Lurin (just past the Santa Fe Restaurant), and **La Licorne** in Lorient, a hot dance club open only on Saturday night, with a very local crowd. **Nikki Beach** in St. Jean is just W.T.M. (Way Too Much). It's ostensibly a restaurant, but the mediocre food is totally overwhelmed by the delicious afternoon scene, featuring a DJ in the evening and a symphony of white bed-lounges or banquettes, upholstery, and canopies. **La Plage**, located at Tom Beach Club, offers another variation of attitude, but in sari colors, awful food, and a better, breezier beach. There's also **Luna**, which is owned by New Yorkers with New York accents and serves pricey drinks in a lovely harborside setting. Why not? Finally, there's **Le Sélect**, on Rue de la France — it's the island's oldest bar and has a comfortable, laid-back atmosphere.

Don't Miss

Anse des Salines and Anse du Gouverneur

On an island of great beaches, these two are the best; the former is nude, the latter is drop-dead gorgeous.

The Hike to Colombier

Another outstanding beach, this one is undeveloped (save for an old house built by David Rockefeller, reached only by boat). The trail is reached via the road that passes Anse des Flamands; continue west to the end of the road. From here, an obvious trail continues along the coast, over a ridge and down to the beach (allow 20 minutes). Be sure to bring sunblock; there's no shade once you leave the road.

Diving

For certified divers, the underwater scene off St. Barth offers bountiful marine life and an interesting wreck dive. Our fave is Marine Service, Quai du Yacht Club (PADI certified) (590-590-27-70-34); there is also Scuba Club la Bulle (590-590-27-68-93) and St. Barth Plongée (590-590-27-54-44). One-tank dives are about $50.

Windsurfing and Kitesurfing

There are excellent places for all levels to boardsail around the island. Call the Eden Rock Sea Sport Club (590-590-27-74-77) or Wind Wave Power, St. Barth's Beach Hotel (590-590-27-62-73).

The Golf Driving Range

Enthusiasts should not pass up this opportunity to belt golf balls into the lagoon. Distance markers are placed in the water.

Gym

Need a well-equipped free-weight gym to keep those pecs pulsating? If you must, try Forma Form Fitness (590-590-27-51-23), located in Gustavia. Like everything else on this island, it's expensive for a day's pass.

Match!

Located across the street from the airport terminal, this is the best supermarket on the island. Here you can stock up on fine cheese, pâté, bread, and wine for your picnics.

Radio St. Barth

At 98 MHz on your FM dial, this station plays great music, and we enjoy listening to it even on neighboring islands. Call 590-590-27-74-74 for requests.

Le Sélect

As stated above, this is the island's oldest bar, and it's a quaint little package of history and authentic ambiance. The bar across the street, **Au Bar de l'Oubli**, is also a fun hangout.

St. Kitts
and Nevis

TOURISTO SCALE:

ST. KITTS 👤👤👤👤👤👤 (6)

NEVIS 👤👤👤👤👤 (5)

On our first trip to St. Kitts some years back, we drove around and couldn't help but be surprised at how much sugarcane was still being cultivated. There was just miles and miles of it. We commented on this to Mr. Brown, our taxi driver, and after saying, "Uh-huh" (he said this a lot, with emphasis on the second syllable), he told us that on St. Kitts, you are always in sight of "the cane" — that, and the towering mountains, which the clouds surround like a set of the Queen Mother's choker pearls. Just across the channel, Nevis (pronounced "*nee*-vis"), which hasn't produced cane since the 1950s, is like a miniversion of St. Kitts. Both limbs of this two-island nation — the smallest country in the Western Hemisphere — are beautiful, especially if you love mountains and plantation ruins that run down to the azure sea. We fondly recall the sensory experience of driving on the rutted back roads through St. Kitts's cane fields — terrain that waved like a flag in the breeze, the gusts creating whispery patterns visible across the endless panoply of green. So it is with mixed emotions that we tell you how the cane fields that ring St. Kitts are becoming history.

St. Kitts and Nevis: Key Facts

Location	17°N by 62°W
	1,750 miles/2,817 kilometers southeast of New York
Size	St. Kitts — 68 square miles/176 square kilometers
	Nevis — 36 square miles/93 square kilometers
Highest point	St. Kitts: Mount Liamuiga (3,792 feet/1,156 meters)
	Nevis: Nevis Peak (3,232 feet/986 meters)
Population	St. Kitts: 35,217
	Nevis: 11,108
Language	English
Time	Atlantic Standard Time (1 hour ahead of EST, same as EDT)
Area code	869 for both
Electricity	230 volts AC, 60 cycles, so you may need an adapter and a transformer for U.S.-made appliances; some big resorts have 110 volts.
Currency	The Eastern Caribbean dollar, EC$ (EC$2.68 = US$1)
Driving	On the left; you'll need a local permit to drive ($25); present your valid U.S. or Canadian driver's license and pay the fee.
Documents	U.S. and Canadian citizens can enter with proof of citizenship and a photo ID; other nationalities need a passport; all need an ongoing or a return ticket.
Departure tax	$22 from St Kitts, $20.50 from Nevis
Beer to drink	Carib
Rum to drink	Cane Spirit Rothschild
Music to hear	Dancehall
Tourism info	800-582-6208 (St. Kitts), 866-556-3847 (Nevis)
	www.stkitts-tourism.com
	www.nevisisland.com

Sugar production in the Caribbean has always been a blessing and curse. In addition to the slave industry that sugar nourished, fields of cane have been an environmental disaster for many islands. A look at the denuded landscape of Antigua — now sugar-free — tells the sad story. In recent years, cane has become another kind of problem: With the advent of beet sugar in the early 1900s, it became an unprofitable crop for most Caribbean islands. The St. Kitts–Nevis government subsidized sugar to the tune of $11 million annually to keep cane in production on St. Kitts. That figure was a bit ironic, considering that much of the muscle toiling in these fields in recent years was not Kittitian, but workers imported from the Dominican Republic and

Guyana—places where the low standard of living still lured some to labor in these fields, despite meager wages and arduous harvest conditions. So in many ways, the decision to abandon sugar in 2005 was a positive development for St. Kitts. Nevertheless, we get wistful thinking about the loss of those long, eloquent vistas.

Fortunately, since the island doesn't have the money to convert these thousands of acres to their original forested slopes, the cane will linger on for a few years while various proposals for developing lands—some good, some bad—are evaluated. We hope they take their time, for this plantation bucolia also gives St. Kitts (née St. Christopher) and Nevis an appealing sense of peace and quiet and history. With only one large resort on St. Kitts and some midsize ones, all of which are concentrated in one area near the best beaches, and only one on Nevis—the super-deluxe Four Seasons—there is no tourists-on-the-loose frenzy here (which can be so tedious). Our favorite places to stay are the small plantation-style inns found on both islands—hotels that deliver personal service and style. Hence the pace is slow, especially on Nevis and throughout the northern two-thirds of St. Kitts.

These dual lures of plantation settings and peace and quiet attract a well-heeled and sophisticated crowd. It's perfect for those frazzled corporate managers who want a week to be "out to lunch and cannot be reached." You can stay sequestered here on your estate—stroll the grounds, loll in the pool, sip rum punches to oblivion, catch up on all your Peter Mayle and Frances Mayes books, and muse about how much longer you can maintain the staff (what with the price of sugar these days). You might even feel strong enough to hit the beach or try a round of golf at the superb Four Seasons course.

Both islands are volcanic, and each has a 3,000-foot-plus dormant volcano, usually topped with a halo of clouds. Nicknamed "The Sisters of the Caribbean," they are separated by a 2-mile-wide channel. Each has beautiful golden-sand beaches that are concentrated in one area. On St. Kitts, they are at the southern tip of the island. On Nevis, they are on the northeast side of the island. Each also has monkeys, the green vervet monkey to be exact, which —other than in Barbados—is an oddity in the West Indies. The monkeys were introduced by the British, or maybe the French, in the 17th century and have proliferated to the point that you'll probably see some during your visit. Monkeys, it is said, outnumber people on these islands, although nobody knows for sure. Really, who cares? It's not as if you're here to hang out with the monkeys or as if you're competing with them for restaurant reservations or beach chairs.

A Brief History

St. Kitts and Nevis were first settled by the Arawaks and then the Caribs. Columbus sighted the islands on his second voyage, in 1493, and named St. Kitts after his patron saint and the patron saint of travelers, St. Christopher (you've seen him—or used to see him—on the dashboards of many cars).

Nevis was named Nuestro Señora del las Nieves, or "Our Lady of the Snows," because the clouds around the volcano reminded him of snow. Snow—in the tropics! Chris, you were on that boat too long. The Caribs, who were fierce fighters, held off the Europeans until 1623, when England established its first colony in the West Indies on St. Kitts. The French came a year later, and, as you can imagine, there were problems between the two. Nevis was settled five years later, in 1628. Sugar production became a big business, along with the slave trade, and St. Kitts became known as Sugar City, providing huge wealth for the absentee plantation owners. After a century and a half of battling and squabbling, the Treaty of Paris finally deeded all rights to Britain in 1783. In 1967 the islands achieved self-government as an Associated State of Great Britain, and in 1983 St. Kitts and Nevis became a fully independent nation. Under the constitution, Nevis is allowed to secede, but in the 1998 vote it lacked the two-thirds majority needed for secession—by a mere few dozen!

Focus on St. Kitts and Nevis:
Peace and Quiet on the Plantation

Once upon a time, before Nutrasweet, Diet Coke, and The Zone, sugar was king. A glimpse into the life of the Caribbean sugar plantation during the last few centuries makes this point very clear: big manor houses, a sprawling sugar-mill complex, fields and fields of cane, and presumably overworked, underpaid, or slave labor scurrying around. Indeed, vestiges of the once opulent plantations remain today. Windmill towers, mill foundations, and ruins of warehouses that once housed a fortune still stand on practically every island. Fortunately, the manor houses have fared much better, kept intact by the remnants of the plantation wealth that once was.

Interest in the glory days of the distant past has created a wave of acquisitions and restorations of these places. Many of the interested are refugees from the north, pouring money into the Taras of yesteryear and turning them into gilded resorts for the unlanded aristocracy of the urban and suburban elite. And nowhere is this trend more prevalent than in St. Kitts and Nevis.

St. Kitts

ST. KITTS IS THE BIG SISTER TO NEVIS — IT'S ALMOST TWICE the size of Nevis and is home to about four times as many people. About half of the population of St. Kitts resides in the capital, Basseterre. North of the capital, the island is wonderfully scenic as three mountains soar into the clouds. Their steep slopes gradually fade into the fields of sugarcane as they get close to the sea. Yes, this is a beautiful place, but in the last decade little Nevis has somewhat stolen the show with the introduction of the Four Seasons. We can't argue with the seductiveness of the Four Seasons, but there's no need for St. Kitts to be jealous of her younger sister — we'd be equally happy to spend time with either sibling.

Getting There

St. Kitts's Bradford International Airport can handle jets, and with the advent of the Marriott, it is starting to see a few. To get here, American and American Eagle fly via San Juan and Miami; US Airways comes in from Philadelphia. LIAT and Caribbean Star fly here direct from Antigua and other neighboring islands; Winair flies in from St. Maarten and neighboring islands; Caribbean Sun flies in from San Juan. There is also usually a charter company that flies from Toronto in the winter — check with your travel agent.

If you're on Nevis, it's easy to get to St. Kitts on one of the six public ferries that run between Charlestown and the St. Kitts ferry dock in Basseterre. There are as many as five daily crossings in each direction. The trip takes about 45 minutes, and the round-trip price is $8. For ferry schedules, which change weekly, call 869-466-4636.

Getting Around

St. Kitts has plenty of taxi drivers to take you around the island. Allow a full day for the drive around the north coast of St. Kitts and down to the southeast peninsula, and be sure to include a lunch stop at one of the plantation inns. You can negotiate for an island tour at a reasonable price, depending on the

St. Kitts

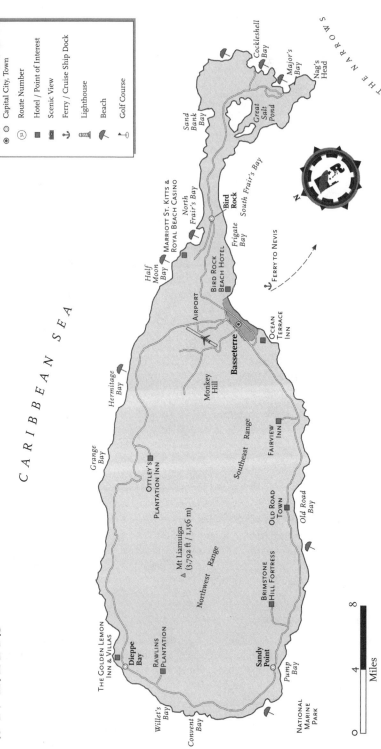

CARIBBEAN SEA

THE NARROWS

LEGEND

- Capital City, Town
- Route Number
- Hotel / Point of Interest
- Scenic View
- Ferry / Cruise Ship Dock
- Lighthouse
- Beach
- Golf Course

Cockleshell Bay

Major's Bay

Nag's Head

Great Salt Pond

Sand Bank Bay

MARRIOTT ST. KITTS &
ROYAL BEACH CASINO

North Frair's Bay

Bird Rock

South Frair's Bay

Half Moon Bay

BIRD ROCK BEACH HOTEL

Frigate Bay

FERRY TO NEVIS

AIRPORT

Basseterre

OCEAN TERRACE INN

Hermitage Bay

Monkey Hill

Grange Bay

OTTLEY'S PLANTATION INN

Southeast Range

FAIRVIEW INN

△ Mt Liamuiga
(3,792 ft / 1,156 m)

OLD ROAD TOWN

Old Road Bay

Northwest Range

THE GOLDEN LEMON INN & VILLAS

Dieppe Bay

RAWLINS PLANTATION

BRIMSTONE HILL FORTRESS

Sandy Point

Willet's Bay

Convent Bay

Pump Bay

NATIONAL MARINE PARK

Miles

0   4   8

time involved. Always negotiate up front, and you should be able to get an agreeable fare. Rates to and from hotels are posted at the airport.

Rental cars are in ample supply and run about $40 to $50 per day. Avis (800-331-1084 or 869-465-6507) has an outpost here, and there are also some local outfits. We had good luck with TDC Rentals, which has offices on both islands and allows you to substitute cars when you go from one island to the other. Call 869-465-2991 if on St. Kitts, or book cars stateside through Thrifty Car Rentals (800-847-4389), which partners with TDC. Roads are in good shape here, so driving, though on the left, is neither complicated nor difficult.

There are also privately owned minibuses that circle each island. They aren't on a schedule, but fares top out at just a couple bucks for the longest trips. The main hub for the St. Kitts minibuses is located at Basseterre, next to the ferry dock.

For ferry day trips between St. Kitts and Nevis, see Getting There.

Where to Stay

There are several good "plantation-style" accommodations on St. Kitts. Although they vary in degrees of luxury, amenities, and cost, almost all will give you the feeling of space, Old World charm, and relaxation. Note that several of them close for a few weeks around September. For those who are interested in splurging, consider heading over to Nevis and staying in the luxurious Four Seasons. Otherwise, there are more economical options on St. Kitts, where the addition of the mammoth Marriott has kept room rates depressed for a lot of smaller hotels around Frigate Bay.

The Plantation Inns

Ottley's Plantation Inn, P.O. Box 345, Basseterre, St. Kitts, W I. ☎ 800-772-3039 or 869-465-7234, ✆ 869-465-4760, 🖳 www.ottleys.com, ottleys@caribsurf.com

💲 **Very Pricey** 🍴 **EP** CC 23 rooms

This is the best place to stay on St. Kitts — one of our favorites in the Caribbean and certainly one of the most romantic. It has one of the most stunning settings for this type of accommodation we've ever seen. Located on 35 acres at the foot of the mountains, where the rainforest spills down the slopes to the fields, it has beautifully maintained grounds that provide sweeping views down to the sea. The restoration of the white 18th-century Great House is excellent, retaining its charm but providing modern amenities, like great bathrooms. Down the slope, set in the ruins of a mill, there's a 65-foot spring-fed pool alongside a patio and restaurant. It's very pretty and tasteful, especially when lit up at night.

There are 15 guest rooms in the two-story Great House, with a wraparound veranda on each floor. Each room is simply but effectively decorated and has louvered doors and windows that open to the trades (there is also a/c for those who want it). All rooms have private baths. There is also a series of lavish new stone cottages just below the Great House that have beautiful furnishings and private plunge pools — these are a great spot for a honeymoon. In fact, the immaculate grounds would be a great site for a wedding, and many have been performed here. There is a comfortable sitting area in the Great House, and a library and video room for those who want to watch CNN or a movie. The inn has our favorite restaurant on the island, too, the Royal Palm, serving a nouvelle Caribbean continental cuisine (the Sunday brunch is quite popular). The four-course dinner is priced at $68, but à la carte options are available.

The inn offers a daily shuttle to the beaches on the southern tip of the island, and a charming new spa room, open on one side to the rainforest, delivers coddling to the weary.

Rawlins Plantation Inn, P.O. Box 340, Mount Pleasant, St. Kitts, WI. ℂ 869-465-6221, ✆ 869-465-4954, 🖳 www.rawlinsplantation .com, rawplant@caribsurf.com

💲 **Ridiculous** ⑪ **MAP,** including afternoon tea and laundry service 🆒 10 rooms

The original plantation inn on St. Kitts, the Rawlins occupies a stunning setting on the north coast of the island. Situated about 350 feet above sea level amid the cane fields on the slopes of Mt. Liamuiga, the views to the sea and Statia in the distance are magnificent. As at Ottley's, the grounds here are wonderfully maintained, with ample room to stroll and muse. There is a comfortable veranda from which to watch the sunset while sipping the omnipresent rum punch. There is a small spring-fed pool, a croquet lawn, and a grass tennis court for those inclined to get out of their chairs.

The guest rooms are tastefully furnished, mostly with antiques (none have a/c, but the Rawlins's perch guarantees steady trade breezes). One of the rooms is in an old windmill, and there are several more private stone cottages with rooms. The Rawlins restaurant is the best on St. Kitts for traditional West Indian lunch, although four-course dinners are now Cordon Bleu style ($65 per person). Meals are served on the veranda, and there is a comfortable library-lounge where you can catch up on your reading. The nice beaches are far away, so if beaches are key, you might want to consider alternate options. Rawlins changed hands in 2005 and is now owned and managed by a spirited Trinidadian lady, Zai Karim-Mohammed. She has upgraded the property nicely and has plans to add 10 duplex cottages to the 13-acre property.

The Golden Lemon Inn & Villas, Dieppe Bay, St. Kitts, WI. © 800-633-7411 or 869-465-7260, ✆ 869-465-4019, 🖳 www.goldenlemon.com, info@goldenlemon.com

💰 **Very Pricey** for Great House; **Ridiculous** for villas 🍴 BP ꜾꜾ
26 rooms

Another institution on St. Kitts, and a formidable one at that, is the Golden Lemon. It's been around for more than 40 years, under the close scrutiny of Arthur Leaman, its owner and manager. Mr. Leaman is a former decorating editor at *House & Garden*, so you can imagine that the Golden Lemon was tastefully conceived — to within an inch of its life! Unlike the other plantation inns on St. Kitts, the Golden Lemon is on the water, on the northernmost tip of the island, and surrounded by a fishing village. It has a windy black-sand beach, which is just okay as far as beaches go (the best are on the southern tip of the island, 30 minutes away). What is nice about the location is the sound of the waves breaking over the coral reef and the steady trade winds. The grounds are rather small, so strolling the lower 40 is limited here. But the villas more than make up for any deficiency in space, especially since they have their own pools.

The Great House has tons of character, bathed in a white and lemon yellow paint scheme, and with a big veranda on each floor. The spacious rooms are comfortable, furnished with antiques and decorated to a tee. Beds are four-posters or wrought-iron bedsteads, and there are antique armoires. Room 1 is highly recommended if you want to stay in the Great House (these rooms are also cheaper than the villas). On the other hand, the one-and two-bedroom villas are more private and more contemporary but still creatively decorated (there is real — not repro — art on the walls). Furnishings here are comfortable, tasteful, and eclectic — an African floor vase might sit next to a chintz-upholstered wicker armchair. All of the villas have plunge pools, and all are walled for maximum privacy. If you want the best, the Lemon Grove Villa 7 is spacious, has a great pool, sits behind a wall on the beach, and has a wonderful veranda with a table for alfresco dining. All the villas have fully equipped kitchens, and a few have a/c (with a $15 per night surcharge). Nice touches like fresh flowers daily add to Arthur's statement.

Besides the beach and the private plunge pools of the villas, there is a 40-foot pool for guests set within a walled courtyard with lots of tropical foliage. Adjacent is the very appealing Brimstone Bar and another of the island's best restaurants, where you can dine on the veranda or in the ornate dining room.

Fairview Inn, P.O. Box 212, Basseterre, St. Kitts, WI. © 800-223-9815 or 869-465-2472, ✆ 869-465-1056, 🖳 wall@caribsurf.com

🛍 **Not So Cheap** 🍴 **EP** (CC) 20 rooms

The Fairview Inn is also considered a "plantation-style" accommodation, although it seems more like a motel to us and hardly stands up to the other choices on the island. It is, however, less than half the price. There is a Great House, but it lacks any sense of décor, just like the cottages; the furnishings are merely functional. The grounds also don't have that manicured look about them, and service is spotty, at best. If you're watching your dollars, however, the Fairview's prices are reasonable and you will see great sunsets because the accommodations face west. Note that the size, condition, and upkeep of the rooms varies quite a bit. Some have a/c, others fans. A pool and restaurant-bar are on the premises. The beaches are a 20-minute drive away.

Other Options

Ocean Terrace Inn, P.O. Box 65, Fortlands, St. Kitts, WI. ℂ 800-524-0512 or 869-465-2754, ✉ 869-465-1057, 🖥 www.oceanterraceinn.net, otistkitts@caribsurf.com

🛍 **Pricey** 🍴 **EP** (CC) 78 rooms

A far better choice than the Fairview is the Ocean Terrace Inn, located at the edge of Basseterre on the water; it draws a number of local businessmen but is fine for vacationers on a modest budget. The OTI sits on a terraced hill and affords good views of the harbor and Nevis. There are three pools, a Jacuzzi, two bars, and a restaurant, Fisherman's Wharf, which is quite popular. All rooms are comfortably furnished and have a/c, private bath, and terrace. The pool is a rock-lined multilevel beauty.

Marriott St. Kitts Resort and Royal Beach Casino, Frigate Bay, St. Kitts, WI. ℂ 800-228-9290 or 869-466-1200, ✉ 869-466-1201 🖥 www.stkittsmarriott.com

🛍 **Very Pricey** 🍴 **EP** (CC) 648 rooms

Absurdly large for an island of St. Kitts's size, this monstrous hotel landed here in 2003, and Frigate Bay will never be the same. The resort's opening more than doubled the number of rooms on the island overnight, and that was before the Jack Tar resort across the street closed, because it couldn't compete. No big loss there, but most other hotels on the island are also having a tough time keeping their rooms full; the Marriott folks have been known to drop their rates to $99 just to get the rooms full when there's no big convention tying up a bunch of the bunks. Intimate and subdued it's not, but if you're looking for a big meeting-oriented American chain resort, the Marriott will suffice nicely.

The main building is a seven-story structure that is open to the breezes and contains about half of the guest rooms, several restaurants, two gyms, a vast and posh spa facility, a cigar bar, and more. Actually, the rooms are pretty appealing, primped with colorful fabrics, coffeemakers, and high-speed Internet access. More rooms are found in blocks of three-story wings that cluster around the three swimming pools. There's a decent Marriott-run golf course across the street, and the beach can be pleasant but sometimes rough or windy. Dining was sub-par during our visit, with a steakhouse staff that knew little about the cuts of meat they were selling (at $40 and up) or about the short, overpriced wine list. Our advice: If you snag a room for cheap, don't hesitate to investigate dining options off-property.

Bird Rock Beach Hotel, P.O. Box 227, Bird Rock, St. Kitts, WI. ✆ 888-358-6870 or 869-465-8914, ✉ 869-465-1675, 🖳 www.birdrockbeach.com, brbh@caribsurf.com

💰 **Cheap** ⑲ **EP** [CC] 46 rooms

There are a lot of accommodations in the Frigate Bay area, just southeast of Basseterre — most of them no better than ordinary. Bird Rock is a small hotel on a bluff facing Basseterre that offers simple but clean rooms, all with a sea view. Some have kitchenettes, but there's also a decent restaurant on site. Many of Bird Rock's guests are here for the diving — the hotel has a number of scuba packages available with St. Kitts Scuba, a PADI/NAUI facility on the property. Note that the man-made beach here is tiny and surrounded by concrete walkways, but all in all this is a very good value.

Where to Eat

St. Kitts has solid dining options, but you'll pay through the nose for what is usually good but not quite great food. Among the best (and most expensive) are the plantation inns, including Ottley's, Golden Lemon, and Rawlins. At all of these, budget about $60 per person for a set, three-course dinner without drinks, and not including service charge and tax. If you elect to stay at one of these inns, you might choose to be on the MAP plan anyway; note that there's a revolving West Indian Barbecue night that occupies one place or another every night of the week. Thus, all of the above options should keep you happy for a week. Other choices include the following.

$$ **The Ballahoo**, The Circus, Basseterre, 869-465-4197

Ballahoo offers good West Indian–Caribbean food in the middle of town at reasonable prices. Closed on Sunday.

$$ **Fisherman's Wharf**, Ocean Terrace Inn, Basseterre, 869-465-2754
This is an island institution for seafood and other meats, with live music on some nights.

$$ **PJ's**, Frigate Bay, 869-465-8373
The Caribbean isn't the place to come for great pizza and pasta, but PJ's is a decent and cheap option for an emergency pie fix. They'll deliver to hotels in the Frigate Bay area. Closed on Monday.

$ **Sprat Net**, Old Road Town, 869-466-7535
This is the local hot spot, where Kittitians come to party. The place serves truly fresh fish and lobster (it's a fishing village) plus ribs and chicken. It can get very busy. Closed on Monday.

$$$ **StoneWalls**, Basseterre, 869-465-5248
Here you'll find a short but varied menu of good island-accented cooking in a small tin-roofed courtyard. The bar plays good music and is sometimes a lively social scene, but meals are a bit overpriced for the informal setting.

Don't Miss

Brimstone Hill

Now a historic park, this is a massive fortress built by the British that earned the title "Gibraltar of the West Indies" and is now a UNESCO World Heritage Site. Built entirely by slave labor, Brimstone Hill sits spectacularly on 40 acres of steep hilltop, 800 feet above sea level, 9 miles northwest of Basseterre.

The St. Kitts Scenic Railway

Starting in 1912, St. Kitts's sugarcane used to be hauled by rail to a factory near the airport. With the demise of sugar, a group of North American investors introduced a tourist attraction along the same route, using newly built double-deck passenger cars. The three-hour trip travels from the Needsmust Station (near the airport) to a turnaround near Sandy Point, from which you'll take a van back to Basseterre. Although it's oriented toward cruise-ship passengers, and steeply priced ($89, including drinks), we think this is a terrific addition to the island, and it allows visitors a chance to see the remnants of a bygone industry. For reservations and more info: 869-465-7263; www.stkitts scenicrailway.com.

Major's, Friar's, Sand Bank, and Cockleshell Bays

Located on the southern tip of the island, these are the best and least crowded beaches. Unfortunately, hotels are slated to materialize on several beaches down here, but otherwise, for now, the southeastern peninsula of the island remains mostly undeveloped. At the end, there's Turtle Beach Bar and Restaurant, which is a good place for a drink, tasty roti, and views of St. Kitts. Note that it can be quite busy on cruise-ship days.

Mount Liamuiga

The hike to the crater rim of St. Kitts's sleepy volcano is a terrific immersion into the rainforest environment. You'll climb through groves of mango, mahogany, and tree ferns, eventually entering the island's "original" forest, a dense rainforest of ancient hardwood trees that tower 80 feet above the trail. After two to three hours of steady hiking you'll reach the lip of the crater—an immense bowl with sulfur vents inside the northern wall and a towering peak on the opposite ridge. Fifth-generation Kittitian Greg Pereira of **Greg's Safaris** (869-465-4121) has been doing the volcano climb and other great hikes for more than a decade—he knows his stuff. On your way down from the peak, be sure to stop by.

Kate Design

We love the work of English artist Kate Spencer, who has been painting on St. Kitts since the 1980s. Her home and studio is next to Rawlins Plantation, where you can see her paintings, serigraphs, note cards, and more, in a pleasing variety of styles. She has another showplace in Basseterre, on Bank Street. For more info: 869-465-5265; www.katedesign.com.

Scuba Diving

St. Kitts offers plenty of dive shops that can lead divers to interesting sites. We like Dive St. Kitts, situated at the Bird Rock Beach Hotel (869-465-1189). A number of dives are located in the Narrows, the channel between the two islands—they can be reached through dive tours from either St. Kitts or Nevis.

Golf

If you need to quench your golf thirst, try the Royal St. Kitts Golf Club, located next to the Marriott. It's an 18-hole, par-71 layout designed by Canadian Thomas McBroom. The course stretches from the Atlantic across Frigate Bay to the Caribbean. Call 869-466-2700 for more info and tee times.

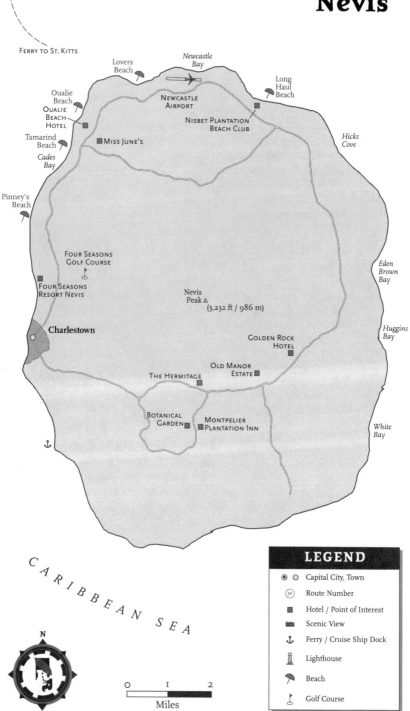

Nevis

FERRY TO ST. KITTS

Newcastle Bay

Lovers Beach

Long Haul Beach

Oualie Beach
OUALIE BEACH HOTEL

NEWCASTLE AIRPORT

NISBET PLANTATION BEACH CLUB

Tamarind Beach

Hicks Cove

MISS JUNE'S

Cades Bay

Pinney's Beach

FOUR SEASONS GOLF COURSE

Eden Brown Bay

FOUR SEASONS RESORT NEVIS

Nevis Peak △
(3,232 ft / 986 m)

Huggins Bay

Charlestown

GOLDEN ROCK HOTEL

OLD MANOR ESTATE

THE HERMITAGE

BOTANICAL GARDEN

MONTPELIER PLANTATION INN

White Bay

C A R I B B E A N   S E A

N

O   1   2
Miles

LEGEND

- ◉ ◎ Capital City, Town
- (32) Route Number
- ■ Hotel / Point of Interest
- 📷 Scenic View
- ⚓ Ferry / Cruise Ship Dock
- 🏮 Lighthouse
- ☂ Beach
- ⛳ Golf Course

Nevis

WITH SPLENDID MOUNTAINS AND STELLAR BEACHES, NEVIS IS seen as the baby sister to St. Kitts. It's basically a smaller version (half the size) of St. Kitts, except that sugarcane is no longer farmed here. Of the two islands, Nevis has traditionally been known as the quiet one, but with the arrival of the Four Seasons Resort in 1991 and the vacationing of numerous celebrities and royalty, the island has been discovered as a kind of rustic alternative to St. Barth. This change in Nevis's status was brought to a head in the late 1990s when the two islands spent some time quarreling over a possible secession. There was a hue and cry on Nevis about "controlling our own destiny" (hmm... sounds typical of a kid sister). The bottom line was that Nevisians were starting to feel that too much of the tax revenue generated by tourism on Nevis was winding up on St. Kitts. However, a resolution to split the islands into two separate governments was narrowly defeated by the populace. Because blood runs thicker than the sea channel between them—and there are many Nevisions with relatives on St. Kitts and vice versa—the secession forces have quieted for the moment.

Getting There

Unlike St. Kitts's Bradford International Airport, which can handle jets, Nevis's Newcastle Airport can handle only smaller-size prop planes. To get to Nevis by air, the easiest route is to connect through San Juan on American Eagle, which has two flights daily. Note that the airline (perhaps cued by the rate cards at the Four Seasons) often charges exorbitant fares, well above those for flying into St. Kitts. So if you can't find a good fare, use LIAT or Winair, which handle the 10-minute hop from St. Kitts, as well as the short flights from their hubs in Antigua and St. Maarten.

Another option is to take one of the six public ferries that run between Basseterre in St. Kitts and Charlestown in Nevis. (It's just a 10-minute taxi ride from the St. Kitts airport to the ferry dock in Basseterre). There are five daily crossings that run in each direction. The trip takes about 45 minutes, and the round-trip price is $8. For ferry schedules—which change weekly—call 869-466-4636. Lastly, the Four Seasons Resort has zippy private launches for its guests; the fare is $90 round-trip per person and will take you from the St. Kitts airport direct to the hotel. The schedule is based on air arrivals and departures in St. Kitts.

Getting Around

A driving tour of Nevis takes little more than three or four hours, and there are lots of taxi drivers who are willing to show you around. Taxi stands are located at the airport and in Charlestown. We particularly enjoyed exploring with "TC" — the saucy Brit says the name stands for "tough cookie," and who are we to doubt her (call 869-469-2911). You can negotiate for an island tour at a reasonable price, depending on the time involved. Always negotiate up front, and you should be able to get an agreeable fare. Rates to and from hotels are posted at the airport.

Rental cars are in ample supply and run about $40 to $50 per day. There are local outfits on both islands. We like TDC Rentals because it has offices on both islands and allows you to substitute cars when you go from one island to the other. Call 869-469-1005 if on Nevis, or book cars stateside through Thrifty Car Rentals (800-847-4389), which partners with TDC. Roads are in good shape on both islands, so driving, though on the left, is neither complicated nor difficult.

There are also privately owned minibuses that circle each island. They aren't on a schedule, but fares top out at just a couple bucks for the longest trips. The main hub for the Nevis minibuses is located at Charlestown, next to the ferry dock.

For ferry day trips between St. Kitts and Nevis, see Getting There.

Where to Stay

As with St. Kitts, Nevis has several "plantation-style" accommodations that offer comfort and charm with various levels of cost and luxury. Note that some of them close for a few weeks around September. However, if it's a luxury resort you want, the plush Four Seasons is one of the best-run hotels in the Caribbean.

The Plantation Inns

⊛ **Montpelier Plantation Inn**, P.O. Box 474, St. Johns, Nevis, WI. Ⓒ 869-469-3462, ✎ 869-469-2932, ▯ www.montpeliernevis.com, info@montpeliernevis.com

　　💰 **Ridiculous** 🍴 **BP** including afternoon tea ⒸⒸ 17 rooms
　　One of our favorites, Montpelier provides a wonderful sense of privacy and intimacy. If we were famous movie stars traveling incognito, we might stay here — a few have. The late Princess Di came here with the kids after her separation from Charles. There are lots of gardens

and secluded spots in which to lose oneself and evade the snooping pa-parazzi. The Hoffman family, which acquired Montpelier in 2001 and has done a grand job upgrading the property, is always here to attend to their guests' needs.

Yes, an air of grandeur still permeates the Montpelier. The Great House is a magnificent structure of stone with black-and-white trim. In-side, there are twin mahogany bars and four sumptuous chintz-covered sitting areas. Handsome antique furniture dominates the interior, and vintage paintings adorn the stone and wood walls, which are capped by a high vaulted ceiling. Off to one side there is a library and card room, and a terrace ideal for viewing sunsets through the tall coconut trees as well as for candlelight dining. Through the doors to the left of the great hall is an arched stone loggia leading to a covered terrace where breakfast and lunch are served. Adjacent to the terrace is a lap-size swimming pool distinguished by its wall murals. There are com-fortable chaise longues and a great pool cabana-bar. We were surprised to learn that the entire complex is less than 50 years old, built on the ruins of the old estate — it looks authentic even to old hacks like us. They did use the original stones from the ruins, so it's sort of real, and of course there is the requisite windmill tastefully landscaped with hibiscus and bougainvillea.

The guest rooms — in one- and two-room cottages — are well ap-pointed, with king-size four-poster beds, individual reading lights (very thoughtful), fresh flowers daily, and oversize bathrooms. The rooms themselves are not huge, but they're comfortable enough, and there is a veranda with lounge chairs and views of the ocean; all now have a/c. A small family suite can be rented for larger groups. Combined with the rest of the package, you will be very happy here for a week.

There are 60 hillside acres on which to meander. For exercise, there is a tennis court near the great house and a private beach club on the northernmost and prettiest end of Pinney's Beach. A shuttle will take you there and pick you up and you can arrange for a picnic lunch. Save room for the other meals, though: Breakfasts start with a huge bowl of chilled fresh fruit accompanied by yogurt and cereal, fol-lowed by a delicious hot selection. The afternoon tea features freshly baked scones. Dinners are elegant and slightly formal without being stuffy. They feature local produce and seafood on a terrace overlook-ing the lights of St. Kitts in the distance or in the stone mill (three-course meals are $57). All of this befits the inn's 2005 incorporation onto the Relais and Chateaux list of esteemed hotels and restaurants. It makes for a place we look forward to returning to again and again.

Nisbet Plantation Beach Club, Newcastle, Nevis, WI. © 800-742-6008 or 869-469-9325, 869-469-9864, www.nisbetplantation.com, nisbetbc@caribsurf.com

💲 **Ridiculous** ⑨ MAP, including afternoon tea and laundry service ⓒⓒ 36 rooms

The overwhelming impression you get when seeing Nisbet for the first time is that of a fairway on the sea. The grounds are so spacious and well manicured that you almost expect a golf ball to land at your feet at any time. Tall coconut trees form an airy canopy for the eclectic mix of cottages that are comfortably spaced across the lawn. A dramatic planting of palm trees creates a Champs Elysées effect from the Great House to the sea — very regal indeed.

The plantation house itself is attractive and charming. Wide stone steps lead to a screened-in sunny veranda with very comfortable sitting areas where you can stretch out with a book and spend hours undisturbed. The bar is within finger-snapping distance for that occasional libation. There is a fine library, if you forgot your Jane Austen. The air-conditioned dining veranda commands that majestic Champs Elysées vista, lending a regal air to the dramatic setting. We enjoyed our last meal here (three-course dinners for nonguests are $57), but when the hotel is full, it's busier than the other plantation inns.

Scattered about the grounds are cottages of various styles, some octagonal, some in the Victorian gingerbread mold. Each has two units, with veranda, twin or king-size beds, vaulted ceiling with fan, vanity, bookcase, rattan furnishings, and modern bath. The newer Premier rooms are in four-unit, two-story buildings closer to the beach — very sumptuous, with a/c and huge baths.

Nisbet's big advantage is that it has its own beach. It's not the nicest on the island, but it is white sand and salt water and you don't have to hop in a van to get there. An outlying reef keeps the water fairly calm for swimming and provides the best snorkeling on the island. There is a beach bar, a pool by the beach, and an outdoor restaurant for lunch. Horseback riding is available nearby, and there are tennis and croquet courts with rackets, mallets, and balls provided.

The Hermitage, Hermitage Village, Nevis, WI. ℂ 800-682-4025 or 869-469-3477, ✆ 869-469-2481, 🖥 www.hermitagenevis.com, nevherm@caribsurf.com

💲 **Wicked Pricey** ⑨ BP, including afternoon tea ⓒⓒ 15 rooms

Sitting high up on a hill overlooking Montpelier and the Caribbean beyond, this delightful property of shingled gingerbread cottages is very relaxed and casual, and a must if you're into horses. The Hermitage maintains thoroughbred stables for those who want to ride among the palm trees and bougainvillea, and the owners participate in the monthly races at the bantam Nevis racetrack. The focal point is a comfortable and quaint 1740 Great House — purportedly the oldest wooden plantation home still standing in the islands. In it there is a very good library, a comfy sitting room and bar, and a terrace restaurant serving delicious food under the eyes of a longtime chef named Lovey Body. Around and up from the Great House are cottages containing rooms in three levels of style, comfort, and price: hillside, deluxe, and luxury. For those who want to cook their own meals, the luxury cottages have full kitchens. Three great choices are Pasture House (hillside), Twin Gables (deluxe), and the White House (luxury). There is also a two-bedroom villa called the Manor House, with its own ceramic tile pool, which sits at the crest of the property and is very private. All units are nicely and tastefully furnished with antiques, four-poster canopy beds, and ceiling fans; most have a veranda with a hammock.

In addition to the stables, there's a pool and a tennis court; there is no beach or beach club, but transportation to Pinney's can be arranged. Richard and Maureen Lupinacci and their grown children are your hosts and look after guests kindly.

Golden Rock Hotel, P.O. Box 493, Gingerland, Nevis, WI. ℂ 869-469-3346, ☏ 869-469-2113, 🖳 www.golden-rock.com, info@goldenrock.com

🛆 **Very Pricey** 🍴 **EP** CC 15 rooms

The drive up to the Golden Rock is stunning—you pass stone walls and bougainvillea that set the stage for a truly magnificent Great House to loom in front of the car at any moment. So it's a letdown when you arrive and see only several rather plain-looking buildings surrounding a restored windmill. What it lacks in grandiosity, however, is made up for in the warmth and wealth of knowledge of its manager, Pam Barry. She's a great person and a direct descendant of the original owner of this estate.

This is not to say the place isn't special—in its own low-key, disheveled sort of way it's actually exquisite. The grounds, on 96 acres, are lush and verdant, with fantastic views of the windward side from 1,000 feet above sea level. The low stone buildings are attractive and overgrown with vegetation, particularly the bougainvillea-covered, 200-year-old Estate Long House—where a courtyard serves as the alfresco daytime dining area and is the place for afternoon tea. The interior of the Long House contains a neat bar and game room with nets and ivy on the ceiling. The old stone walls of the dining room once housed the plantation's kitchens. What we enjoy most here is lunch on the terrace, starting with bartender Rolston Hobson's deliciously tart ✪ rum punch, probably our favorite on all the islands, and followed by the best lobster sandwich we've ever sunk our teeth into.

There are decent rooms for guests in a cluster of cottages with verandas, handmade king-size (or twin) bamboo four-poster beds, dressing rooms, and baths. There is also a duplex suite in the old windmill that the management promotes as the "honeymoon suite." It consists of an upstairs "playpen" with a king-size four-poster bed as its centerpiece ("Oh sweet mystery of life, at last I've found you"). The bathroom throne has a stupendous view out over the water to Montserrat. A circular staircase follows the stone walls around to the lower level, where two more double four-posters can accommodate whoever else wants to join the party.

There is a tennis court and a large, spring-fed, somewhat industrial-looking swimming pool on the grounds. The hotel has facilities at Pinney's Beach (with restaurant and water sports) and at its own beach down on the rough-and-tumble windward side — watch the undertow.

Old Manor Estate & Hotel, P.O. Box 70, Gingerland, Nevis, WI. ☎ 800-892-7093 or 869-469-3445, ✆ 869-469-3388, 🖳 www.oldmanor nevis.com, oldmanor@caribsurf.com

💲 **Very Pricey** ⑪ **BP** ⓒⓒ 13 rooms

This compact plantation on a shoulder of Nevis Peak will appeal to character seekers. It's unusual because this plantation was operated by steam power instead of a windmill, and the rusting machinery poses quaintly near the entrance. Alas, the property has had management hiccups for some years, and in low season guests are sporadic. There are restored buildings next to the dilapidated original ones, the combination of which is marvelous. Renovations first began in the mid-1960s, when the place looked like London in 1945.

The accommodations are built into restored original structures, like the blacksmith's shop and carriage house, so each is unique in shape and style. There are rooms with touches of excellent wood craftsmanship, marble terrazzo floors, vaulted ceilings with fans, wide-board floors with carpeting, stone walls, and Jacuzzis in their own gardens. The 44-foot-wide round pool is also unique, built out of volcanic stone that was originally the water-collection cistern for the mill boiler and steamer. There is a cabana with a hammock and a view of Mt. Nevis.

The popular restaurant has a patio grill and bar, where on Friday night a steak and lobster buffet is spread out to the tunes of pan (steel band) music — this is when the property is at its liveliest. The bar and grill room is actually the old plantation kitchen — the ovens are still intact. The card and piano room was originally the birthing room for the slaves. The dining room is in the old cooperage room, the library was the old disco (just kidding), and so on. Old Manor is the least polished of the five plantation inns on Nevis, but it's still a lovely property.

Other Options

⊛ **Four Seasons Resort Nevis**, P.O. Box 565, Pinney's Beach, Charlestown, Nevis, WI. ☎ 800-332-3442 or 869-469-1111, ✆ 869-469- 1040, 🖳 www.fourseasons.com/nevis

$ **Stratospheric** Ⓨ **EP** Ⓒⓒ 196 rooms

It all became clear to us in an instant. We were calling Trinidad from our room at the Four Seasons and had dialed the wrong number, which in the Caribbean costs at least five bucks. So we rang the hotel operator to get credit, as anyone would. She laughed at us—she laughed! In that laugh was the definite insinuation, "You're forking over $600 a night for a room, and you want a refund for a phone call. What a schmuck!" We were briefly humiliated. Then that age-old credo dawned on us, "If you have to ask, you don't belong." Welcome to the Four Seasons, where you'll happily pay through the nose for everything, or else someone like the hotel operator will make you feel insignificant.

This is the option on St. Kitts and Nevis for those who want a full fledged, high-amenity resort: 24-hour room service, sports facilities galore, excellent restaurants, and great service (aside from the hotel operator). On the last attribute (not the hotel operator), we particularly applaud the Four Seasons. The Caribbean is not known as the capital of hotel service, but somehow this 196-room resort has managed to attain five-star pampering on a mellow island like Nevis. How much service? Well, when you lie on the resort's attractive beach, the attendants bring you cool spritz bottles and iced towels to beat the heat! All of this luxury comes with a whopping price tag and just a touch of attitude, especially from many of the guests who stay here. The Four Seasons is not an old-money place, if you get our drift. Instead you get a younger crowd than is common at many of the Caribbean grande dame resorts, including quite a few honeymooners.

Built on the best stretch of Pinney's Beach, the resort is 350 acres big. The rooms and suites spread out among two-story, architecturally tame buildings (the resort reminds us of a '90s version of the Dorado Beach in Puerto Rico). The rooms, however, are truly fab and show off the resort's attention to detail. Let's begin with the huge marble baths, all with double sinks, separate shower and bath, separate head, and tons of big fluffy towels. The rooms are large and tastefully furnished, including carved mahogany headboards and armoires to house the cable TV and VCR. There is a wet bar with an icemaker (a big plus), an attractive rattan and chintz seating area, and cushioned armchairs with hassocks on your screened-in veranda or terrace. Of course all the rooms have a/c, which shuts off when you open the sliding glass door (smart idea). Finally, there is a complimentary washer and dryer in every building—a thoughtful touch, especially for schleppers like us, who encounter a laundry crisis every seven days.

The sporting life here is as good as it comes. Wrapping around the resort is an 18-hole Robert Trent Jones II course that winds up the volcanic slopes (see Don't Miss). The tennis facility, with 10 all-weather and red clay courts, is superb, with a program run by Peter Burwash.

All water sports are available, and there are three free-form "infinity" pools and Jacuzzis. A full-service spa was added in 2002 that is as good as they come in this neck of the woods. There are three restaurants: the informal beach terrace Mango; Neve, which features an Italian menu; and the fancier Dining Room for a dressy and decadent dinner only. Dress codes in the main great house are in effect in the evening; jackets and ties aren't required, but ladies, no capris, please.

To accommodate arriving passengers in St. Kitts, the resort runs a launch service from Basseterre for $90 per person, round-trip. It's a nice way to arrive; you check in at the airport in St. Kitts and then the waiters pump you with rum punch—we had so many we could have landed in China and wouldn't have known it. We sobered up enough to note a couple of caveats: For all the attention and service, the ministrations struck us as slightly impersonal, like the general architecture—characteristics not typical of either St. Kitts–Nevis or other Four Seasons properties. Still, if you're looking for a big, full-service, chain-managed resort, you probably won't find a better one in the islands than this.

Note that golf, tennis, and romance packages are available; check into hefty off-season discounts.

Oualie Beach Hotel, Oualie Beach, Nevis, WI. ✆ 800-682-5431 or 869-469-9735, ✉ 869-469-9176, 🖳 www.oualiebeach.com, gm@oualie.com

🔳 **Very Pricey** 🍽 **EP** ⓒⓒ 32 rooms

Oualie Beach is a small, unpretentious place on a nice little beach that won't cost you an arm and a leg. It's not cheap, but it's casual and has a friendly staff. The informal atmosphere attracts a local following who mingle at the bar, and the beach is also a hub for a number of activities on the island: diving and snorkeling trips, bicycling, kayaking, and so on.

The rooms are situated in gingerbread cottages and two-story buildings along the beach, with your choice of studio rooms (double bed with bath and kitchen and optional connecting doors to form two- and three-bedroom suites); honeymoon rooms with a four-poster mahogany canopy bed and bath; and standard rooms with two double beds and a bath. Most have screened-in lanais facing west (for sunsets), minibars, phones, and ceiling fans; cable TV is available. The furnishings are simple and tasteful. There is a decent West Indian restaurant on the premises.

Where to Eat

Nevis, like St. Kitts, offers good (but generally not great) dining options, most of which are overpriced. Some of the best cuisine can be found at the plantation inns, including Montpelier, Nisbet, Golden Rock, Old Manor Estate, and Hermitage. All are expensive—expect to pay $55 to $65 per person for a set, three-course dinner without drinks, and not including service charge and tax. If you are staying at one of these inns, it might be cost-effective to choose the MAP plan. Note that there's a rotating West Indian Barbecue night that can be found at one place or another on almost every night of the week. Let's also not forget the Four Seasons, where there is both a fine dining restaurant, and Mango, a new waterside venue next to the 18th hole. The following is a list of some other options.

$$$$ Coconut Grove, Nelson's Spring, 869-469-1020

Just north of the Four Seasons, this restaurant arrived in 2005 and quickly became the hot new food destination—it doesn't hurt that the kitchen stays open until 10:30 every night and the bar till midnight (with a happy hour that kicks off at 11 p.m.). The food, though inventive and beautifully presented, was a bit hit-and-miss for us—a fusion of French, Asian, and Caribbean—but the seafood Napoleon and the duck and risotto were crowd pleasers. The setting is the real appeal, under a huge thatched roof, next to the surf; a smart wine cellar and the only draught beer on the island doesn't hurt, either.

$$ Eddie's Restaurant, Main Street, Charlestown, 869-469-5958

A casual restaurant for lunch and dinner, Eddie's features West Indian cuisine with American twists. Closed Saturday and Sunday.

$$$$$ Miss June's, Stoney Grove Plantation, 869-469-5330

Miss June Mestier, originally from Trinidad, has been living here for more than 40 years but retains her Trinidadian sense of cuisine, combining Indian, Chinese, Arab, French, Spanish, and Creole cooking styles into her own blend. For $86, you get an evening of food and drink, from cocktails in the bar lounge and sit-down dinner to brandy and crystallized grapefruit on the front porch—about two dozen dishes in all. Seating is limited, and dinners are just once or twice a week, so reservations are a must. This should be a definite stop when you're on Nevis.

$$$ Sunshine's, Pinney's Beach, 869-469-5817

A Nevisian institution, Sunshine set up his beach bar at the south end of the Four Seasons Resort and created a memorable drink, the Killer Bee—he's been cleaning up ever since. This ramshackle bar is the primary target of the few small cruise ships that land on Nevis (mostly Windjammers), and by late afternoon the scene gets as festive as you'll find on the island. Sunshine also serves up grilled meals, with some downright tasty shrimp on offer during our last visit, but don't miss his licentious libation.

Don't Miss

Golf at the Four Seasons

This is one of the finest golf courses in the Caribbean. Designed by Robert Trent Jones II, the 6,766-yard championship course undulates over the slopes between the resort and Nevis Peak. It's a par 71, with lots of water hazards and hilly terrain to maneuver, all beautifully tended. The tough holes include the fourth, a 394-yard par 4 with a long water hazard running parallel to the fairway; the eighth, a tough 511-yard uphill dogleg par 5 (the course's hardest); the tenth, another uphill dogleg par 5; the 13th, a par 4 with a hidden flag; and the 15th, a long 663-yard downhill dogleg, with the tee at the highest point on the course (and great views, too). The golf-cart access to the 15th tee is as exciting as any hole, with hairpin turns and a steep grade through a ravine. Greens fees aren't cheap, but the pro shop does have some great hats and visors for sale that won't break the bank. For tee times, call 869-469-1111.

Horseback Riding

The Hermitage plantation is a great place to go riding if you want to hop in the saddle. A 90-minute ride, escorted, and English style, is $45 (869-469-3477). Near Pinney's Beach is the Nevis Equestrian Centre, which offers rides along the shore: 869-469-8118.

The Botanical Garden

This new attraction has quickly become the island's top tourist site. It's located close to Montpelier and offers wonderful views of Nevis Peak. The 7-acre garden has an enviable collection of palms from around the world, plus orchids, cacti, fruit trees, and a rainforest conservatory with an awkward Mayan (!) temple. For more info, call 869-469-3509. Closed on Sunday.

Hiking

Biologists Jim and Nikki Johnson run Top to Bottom, an education-oriented hiking outfit. They do trips to the top of Nevis Peak (a hard four to five hours, round-trip), hikes into the rainforest, and even a Starlight and Storytime beach campfire. Call 869-469-9080 for more info. We actually did the Nevis Peak hike with Lynell Liburd of Sunrise Tours; he's an enjoyable Nevisian who has taken hundreds of groups to the summit. For more info, he can be reached at 869-469-2758.

Scuba Diving

There are several dive shops that offer worthwhile excursions. For starters, try Scuba Safaris on Oualie Beach (869-469-9518). Inquire about the many dive sites that are located in the Narrows, the channel between the two islands.

St. Lucia

The Marquee Stars of St. Lucia are Gros Piton and Petit Piton, a pair of massive volcanic cones that soar up from the sea on the southwest coast of the island. The sight of them is truly breathtaking. They inspire — well, at least enough to make you get your camera out and figure out a way to somehow squeeze them into the frame. There is nothing else quite like them in the Caribbean, and they are just part of the beauty of this lush and scenic island.

St. Lucia (pronounced "LOO-sha") is also interesting in that it seems to be going in two different directions at once. On the one hand, its scenery makes it seem so serene and peaceful — as though nothing discordant or worrisome would ever happen here. On the other hand, there's a restiveness among the population, which is agitating for better economic conditions. This can be seen in the animosity of the island's political parties toward each other and in the increased hostility of some residents toward visitors.

Tourism is important here, having eclipsed agriculture in the last few years as the island's biggest industry. Major new resorts are under construction, cruise ships are now a daily blight in high season, and St. Lucia's government has approved building casinos. Not everyone is cashing in on the tourist bonanza, however. As on some neighboring islands, there is high unemployment here, especially in the village of Soufrière, where the Pitons are located. In all our travels throughout the Caribbean, Soufrière is the only

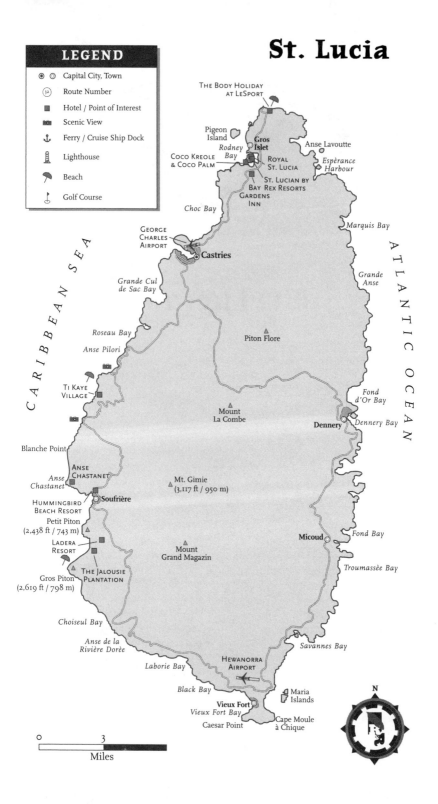

St. Lucia

LEGEND

- ◉ ◎ Capital City, Town
- ③ Route Number
- ■ Hotel / Point of Interest
- ▣ Scenic View
- ⚓ Ferry / Cruise Ship Dock
- ⛲ Lighthouse
- ⚑ Beach
- ⛳ Golf Course

THE BODY HOLIDAY AT LESPORT

Pigeon Island
Anse Lavoutte
Rodney Bay
Gros Islet
COCO KREOLE & COCO PALM
ROYAL ST. LUCIA
Espérance Harbour
ST. LUCIAN BY BAY REX RESORTS
GARDENS INN

Choc Bay

Marquis Bay

GEORGE CHARLES AIRPORT

Castries

Grande Cul de Sac Bay

Grande Anse

CARIBBEAN SEA

Roseau Bay

Anse Pilori

Piton Flore

TI KAYE VILLAGE

Fond d'Or Bay

Mount La Combe

Dennery

Dennery Bay

Blanche Point

ANSE CHASTANET

Anse Chastanet

Mt. Gimie
(3,117 ft / 950 m)

HUMMINGBIRD BEACH RESORT

Soufrière

Petit Piton
(2,438 ft / 743 m)

LADERA RESORT

Micoud

Fond Bay

Mount Grand Magazin

Gros Piton
(2,619 ft / 798 m)

THE JALOUSIE PLANTATION

Troumassée Bay

ATLANTIC OCEAN

Choiseul Bay

Anse de la Rivière Dorée

Savannes Bay

Laborie Bay

HEWANORRA AIRPORT

Black Bay

Maria Islands

Vieux Fort

Vieux Fort Bay

Cape Moule à Chique

Caesar Point

0   3
Miles

N

St. Lucia: Key Facts

Location	14°N by 61°W
	21 miles/34 kilometers south of Martinique
	24 miles/39 kilometers north of St. Vincent
	2,020 miles/3,250 southeast of New York
Size	238 square miles/612 square kilometers
	27 miles/42 kilometers long by 14 miles/23 kilometers wide
Highest point	Mt. Gimie (3,117 feet/950 meters)
Population	156,000
Language	English
Time	Atlantic Standard Time year round (1 hour ahead of EST, same as EDT)
Area code	758
Currency	The Eastern Caribbean dollar, EC$ (EC$2.68 = US$1)
Electricity	220 to 230 volts AC, 50 cycles, you'll need an adapter and transformer.
Driving	On the left; you'll need a local permit — present your valid driver's license and pay a fee of $12 for a one-day license, or $20 for three months.
Documents	Proof of nationality and an ongoing ticket
Departure tax	$21
Beer to drink	Piton
Rum to drink	Bounty
Music to hear	Dancehall
Tourism info	888-478-5824
	www.stlucia.org

place besides St. Thomas where we have experienced outright unprovoked rage. The crowning incident happened on our first trip to St. Lucia in 1987, when someone started chasing our Jeep after we declined to use him as a guide. He screamed a series of nasty things at us. On a subsequent trip we had an encounter with a belligerent Soufrière teen who insisted we owed him money for taking a photo of "his" boat sitting empty in the water; he berated us and then followed us on foot for 25 minutes. The latest gimmick is that when you drive into Soufrière, young men are likely to run into the road in front of you, shouting, "wrong way, wrong way," regardless of where you are headed. This is simply a diversion to offer you guide services or directions and then ask for a handout (it happened to us twice within five minutes during our last visit). So enjoy the view, carry a map, ask politely before you take an islander's picture, and be prepared to move along quickly — and beware those picturesque fishing boats. This shouldn't prevent you from visiting Soufrière, but you should know up front what you might encounter when visiting the island's most scenic region.

That said, St. Lucia is a wonderful experience, and most islanders (particularly in the more-developed north) welcome visitors to their beautiful country. There are lots of options here in both activities and accommodations. There is plenty to see and explore in a week, as well as a fun yachty scene, good hiking, and some great diving as well. With this depth, St. Lucia attracts a diverse crowd — a mix of Brits, Germans, and, increasingly, Americans. There are large tour groups, adventurers who do things like climb the Pitons or sail to the Grenadines, and the sophisticated, content-to-read-a-book traveler. The island has something for everyone, but don't expect it to be undiscovered. As we said before, tourism is a well-developed industry here.

The Briefest History

The Arawaks were the first people to settle St. Lucia. They prospered until about A.D. 800, when the Caribs invaded and killed them off. The Caribs called the island Hiwanarau. Columbus first sighted the island on his fourth journey, in 1502 (this is disputed), but it wasn't settled by Europeans until 1605, when English settlers from St. Kitts arrived. The Caribs drove them off soon after, and again after a second attempt in 1639. The French came 12 years later and claimed the island. Of course the British did not agree, and consequently the island changed hands 14 times, with many battles and burnings. In 1746, during one of their occupations, the French managed to set up shop successfully in Soufrière. Sugarcane production was also started by them, along with slavery. Finally, after Napoleon's defeat, the island went to Britain for keeps in 1814. With all the squabbling, the sugar industry never grew enough to compete with the other islands. Slavery was abolished in 1838, soon after peace was established, and without free labor a sugar industry wasn't going to happen. Coaling steamships sustained the economy in the latter part of the 19th century and also led to the importation of indentured Indian labor (that influence can be seen here today). Coaling eventually failed in the early 1900s, and the island fell into a sustained slump until the advent of bananas in the 1950s, followed later by tourism. In 1979 St. Lucia became an independent state within the Commonwealth of Nations. For the latter part of the 20th century, bananas were the island's biggest industry, but with increasing competition from banana producers in Central America, tourism is now St. Lucia's top earner.

Getting There

There are two airports on St. Lucia. If you're staying in the north, where most of the hotels are located, the most convenient is George Charles Airport, which is on the edge of downtown Castries. However, only smaller planes fly here: American Eagle and Caribbean Sun from San Juan; plus Air Caraïbes, Caribbean Star, and LIAT from neighboring islands.

Jets land at Hewanorra International Airport, located at the southern tip of the island and about an hour from Castries or Soufrière by car. This includes Air Jamaica from New York–JFK; American from Miami; Delta from Atlanta; United from Chicago-O'Hare; and US Airways from Charlotte, North Carolina, and Philadelphia. Also flying into Hewanorra are British Airways, Virgin Atlantic, and BWIA from London; Air Canada from Toronto; BWIA from Barbados and Trinidad; and Caribbean Star and LIAT from neighboring islands.

Taxi fares from the two airports to the main tourist areas are as follows:

> George Charles to Rodney Bay, $16
> George Charles to Soufrière, $80
> Hewanorra to Rodney Bay, $80
> Hewanorra to Soufrière, $65

Finally, L'Express des Iles (758-452-2211) is a hydrofoil service that runs several times weekly between Martinique and Castries; round-trips are about $103.

Getting Around

This is a big island, and in order to really see it you should rent a car. The roads have been much improved during the last few years, but the less traveled routes can still be horrendous, depending on how bad the rainy season has been. By all means, when you're renting your car be sure to ask where the rough spots are (on our last visit, the road between Hewanorra and Soufrière was the pits). Two of the major car-rental players are here: Avis (800-331-1084 or 758-452-2700) and Hertz (800-654-3001 or 758-452-0679); rates start at about $45 a day. Note that neither of these firms has a location in the Soufrière area—for rentals there, contact Cool Breeze (758-459-7729). You'll have to purchase a temporary local driver's license, and driving is on the left.

If you don't want to drive, there are taxis galore (they're expensive), particularly for shuttling between the Rodney Bay–Castries area and Soufrière or Hewanorra. A taxi from the Castries area to Soufrière is $80 for up to four persons (confirm that the driver is quoting the rate in U.S. dollars). There are also efficient and cheap minivans with colorful names that ply the major roads and blast dancehall. It's a great way to meet the locals, and fares are just a few bucks to almost anywhere.

Focus on St. Lucia: Gros Islet Jump-Up; Walking and Hiking

Gros Islet Jump-Up

The town of Gros Islet is a fishing village that borders Rodney Bay on the north. Every Friday night, Gros Islet hosts a jump-up, or street jam—what amounts to a minicarnival on the main street. You can't miss it—just head for the music.

An impressive PA system is set up in the middle of the town's major intersection, playing calypso mixed with dance hall and disco. The street is lined with food and beer vendors. Smoke swirls around the crowd, making the scene look rather tribal. For about $2 you can buy barbecued chicken with pepper sauce or *lambi* ("conch") on a skewer. Heineken and Piton, both brewed on St. Lucia, are sold in buckets, and there are roadside carts selling rum punch.

There are several fun bars. One is **Hector's Café**, recognized by the Cockspur sign hanging in front. The two-story building has the look and air of a western saloon. The upstairs porch provides a great vantage point for watching the action. Across from Hector's is the **Golden Apple**, but you'll find there's as much or more action taking place in the street as in the bars.

The crowd is primarily St. Lucians, who are friendly, although the young males will try to hustle your money for almost any reason (except sex). There are quite a few tourists—the bulk of whom are boat people—but otherwise this is a local scene. The town heats up around 10:30 p.m., and the action goes on until the wee hours.

You can reach the jump-up by taxi or via local bus, which is really cheap and a lot more fun. The buses are actually minivans with names painted on the front (e.g. "Xterminator"). They leave for Gros Islet (be sure to ask) from Paynier Street near the market in Castries and will stop for anyone who flags them down on the main road. It's remarkable how many people they can hold. Calypso or reggae resounds from the formidable stereo, creating a convivial atmosphere. All types ride the bus, from Rastas to old ladies with baskets on their heads. One time, the bus we were riding had a flat and it was fixed within five minutes—uncharacteristic efficiency for the islands. The buses run until very late on weekends and leave from the eastern end of the main street in Gros Islet.

Walking and Hiking

For those who love the outdoors but think camping is slumming it with nature, welcome to St. Lucia. This island—wonderfully diversified in vegetation, climate, and geography—has excellent and accessible trails that are both beautiful and invigorating. Yet it also has available all the creature comforts to keep the fussiest travelers pampered.

These amenities are concentrated in St. Lucia's northwest corner, where you'll find the rather unattractive capital, Castries. The majority of the island's hotels are located north of the capital, on a calm and attractive, though certainly not pristine, series of beaches. There are also accommodations and resorts around the island's other major town, Soufrière. These have much more West Indian character and ambiance than those in the north, as well as far more dramatic natural settings.

The beauty of St. Lucia lies in the countryside, the villages, and its rugged coast and interior. Here the feeling is reminiscent of a more tranquil, unhurried era — a marked contrast to the bustle of Castries. Yet it's all easily accessible by car, and the visuals are truly phenomenal. The lush green expanse of the banana plantations, a cricket game on the east coast, the incredible Pitons, and the center's tropical wilds can all be experienced in a day's drive.

Although you can see a lot of St. Lucia by car, driving doesn't allow you to get very close. Fortunately there is a well-developed system of walks and hikes that enable you to do so. These access much of the island and can be reached by rental car, tours, and in a few instances, public minibus.

The Short Walks

For those who desire minimal exertion, there are three short walks that are nicely cooled by breezes or the shade of the forest. Any of these can be done in a leisurely couple of hours.

In the north, above Gros Islet, there is **Pigeon Island**, connected to the mainland by a causeway built in the early 1970s and now home to a huge resort. There are several short marked trails around the point and leading up to the ruins of a fort, which offers fine views. There is an entrance fee for the National Trust, which maintains the park (about $4). The island will appeal to history buffs. It was first used as a pirate's ambush point, then it weathered hundreds of years of English-French squabbles and also served as a whaling station and later as the retreat of an obscure English actress, Josset Agnes Huchinson. The visitors' center provides all the gory details. Pigeon Island will also appeal to bird-watchers, who, if they happen to be around after a heavy storm, might see a large number of exotic seabirds blown in from all over the Caribbean.

The second walk is right on the main west-to-east-coast highway, between Castries and Dennery. From the roadside viewpoint, there is a very short loop called Barre de L'Iles (about a quarter mile long). It's not very interesting, but another trail, which branches off by the picnic table gazebo, leads to **Mt. LaCombe** (not a climb; the peak is 1,442 feet). It's a pleasant 2.5-mile round-trip walk that takes you along a ridge with some nice north and south views. This trail is also noteworthy because it is by far the easiest forest walk to access. Crime has been a problem here, however, so be sure to leave valuables at your hotel before embarking.

The third walk is an excursion to the **Maria Islands**, off the southeast corner of St. Lucia. This is the only place in the world where the Maria Islands ground lizard and the Couresse snake can be found. Tours can be arranged through the **National Trust** (758-452-5005) or the **Maria Islands Interpretive Centre** (on the highway near the Hewanorra Airport). The price is $40 per person (minimum four), and both request 24 hours' notice for tours. While you're in this area, there is a short walk offering fantastic views of the southern end of the island on **Cap Moule à Chique**. To get there, drive through Vieux Fort up to the lighthouse and walk behind it until you reach a cliff and the vista point.

The Long Walks

Muddy shoes are the vogue here. These walks are for those who really enjoy getting into more remote areas. Each hike will require at least three to four hours, exclusive of travel time to the trailhead. Plan to carry some refreshment, wear cool clothes you can sweat in, and bring your camera.

In the north, there is a good walk around the northern tip of St. Lucia from Cap Estates. The resort here, **The Body Holiday at LeSport** (758-450-8551), organizes tours for its guests, but otherwise these are not marked routes or itineraries. The headlands to the east can also be interesting, but in almost all cases you'll need a four-wheel-drive vehicle to get close enough. If you do try this, don't leave any valuables in your Jeep and don't carry any — practically all the trails are in uninhabited areas.

Moving farther south to the north-central part of the island, there is an excellent walk at Forestière called **Piton Flore** (not to be confused with the Pitons of Soufrière). It is located within the Forest Reserve, so you must get permission and request a guide from the **Forestry Department** (758-450-2231) before embarking. This trail, actually a loop in and out of Forestière, used to be highly traveled, but Hurricane Allen toppled trees to make passage more interesting. Begin by parking your car at the Forestière school (just after the town — you can't miss it); your vehicle is safer there. Directly in front, on your left, will be a Caribbean pine plantation. Keep going down the road, and you'll pass several houses on the right. Eventually you'll come to a flatter area where you will see a house on the left, a Forestry Department rest house. Next to the house you'll see and hear a pumping station. If you take the steps down to the pumping station, you'll find yourself on a trail that will bring you back to the top of the stairs. It will take about two hours to walk the loop, which provides superb glimpses into the rainforest habitat. An alternative to walking the entire loop is to walk past the pumping station (do not go down the steps). This will put you on the upper part of the loop. Follow this path for about a half hour until you come upon an old concrete-block house on the right. Behind this, there are steps that lead up to Piton Flore and a TV tower, elevation 1,871 feet. The ascent, about a half hour, is quite strenuous. The top, however, offers some terrific views of the east and northern coasts. The walk from the summit back to your car will take you a little over an hour.

The **main rainforest** is down in the south-central part of the island. There is a trail (originally the major trading route for the Arawak and Carib Indians) that traverses the island from east to west, linking the Fond St. Jacques road, west of Soufrière, with the Mahaut road, above Micoud. It makes for a very interesting walk — about three and a half hours from end to end. By law you must enter the rainforest with a guide from the Forestry Department, although exceptions can be made if you work it out in advance; in any event, check in with them to verify that the trails are passable.

The most enjoyable way to get to the rainforest and this walk is from the west. The drive down from Castries through Anse La Raye, Canaries, and Soufrière is wonderfully scenic. From the road you can see the Pitons, which have become the symbol of St. Lucia. When you get to Soufrière, don't be surprised if young men insist on guiding you to the volcano or shout "wrong way" — ignore them. Your best bet is to ask an older resident how to get to the Still Restaurant. On the way to the Still, you'll pass a cathedral on your left. Follow the road until you arrive at the restaurant, which features local cuisine and is a great spot for lunch. You'll also pass the sulfur springs — actually part of a dormant volcano called Qualibou, whose waters were cherished by Louis XVI. Today it's billed as the world's only drive-in volcano. You can tell you're near it when you start smelling rotten eggs. If you've seen a sulfur spring at a national park out West, don't bother with this one. If you do choose to go, be prepared to be surrounded by Rastas selling trinkets or their services as trail guides for the springs (which is a rip-off — you don't need one, but the government allows this).

Continue inland on the road past the Still. On the entire stretch, there are only two turnoffs. At the first fork (after about 2 miles), bear right (or down) and keep driving for another 2 miles, where the road forks again. Bear left (or uphill), which brings you to the village of Fond St. Jacques — you'll know you're there when you see an enormous church. To reach the heart of the rainforest, keep going. The road will get progressively worse, but your rental car will make it. Soon you'll come upon some fabulous views of Mt. Gimie, St. Lucia's highest peak, and the scenery continues to get better as you climb. Eventually you'll come to a farm that grows anthurium lilies. Ahead the road becomes a track, but you can still drive it. Go straight down until you come across a clearing with a sign that reads "Designated a Nature Reserve" and a small hut on the right. This is the Forest Reserve house and might be occupied. Park the car in the clearing ahead of you. This is the beginning of the rainforest walk.

If you walk this trail for about three and a half hours, you'll come to the road on the other side (where there is another clearing and a "Designated" sign). That's the end of the walk. However, it's probably a good idea to walk to the halfway point and then turn back — the entire end-to-end round-trip takes seven hours, and you still have the long drive back. (You'll know you're halfway when you come across the Quilesse Forest Reserve, a clearing with rest houses.) The exception is if you've arranged for someone to meet you on the other side, or if you switch car keys with another party at the midway point to rendezvous back at the hotel — great if you can do it.

If you aren't up for this ambitious trail, there is the **Edmund Forest Reserve**, located on the edge of Fond St. Jacques, where you will see much of the same vegetation and views. This trail is actively maintained by the Forestry Department. There is also the **Des Cartiers Rainforest Trail**, which accesses the mountains from the eastern side, above the village of Mahout. To reach Des Cartiers, drive down the east coast highway. Just before you get to Micoud, there is a turnoff for Mahaut. Drive straight inland on what looks like the main road; pay no attention to several turnoffs along the way. Keep on driving until you can drive no farther and you arrive at the "Designated" sign at Edmund Forest.

In the rainforest you will see both natural and planted forestation. The planted part, consisting mostly of blue mahoe (a tree hibiscus from Jamaica) and Honduras mahogany (from Belize), is basically a strip about 100 feet wide on either side of the trail. You can tell it's planted because there is usually only one species per grouping. Beyond that is indigenous vegetation. There are scattered strips of natural forestation along the trail, recognizable by the denser and varied species.

Quilesse, midway on the Rainforest Trail, is a bird-watcher's heaven, especially at dawn or dusk. If you're quiet and patient you may see 30 to 40 species of birds. With luck you may spot the rare green St. Lucian parrot —or jacquot—recognizable by its loud squawking. There are only about 500 left in the wild, but they numbered fewer than 100 only a few decades ago. They are on the rebound thanks to the diligence and dedication of the Forestry Department and to an education program introduced by Paul Butler. There are also three varieties of hummingbirds: the very small Antillean crested hummingbird (the male has a green crest), the green-throated Carib, and the purple-throated Carib. You'll also see the broad-winged hawk—a smaller predator—and various species of doves. If you're really lucky, you might spot the St. Lucia oriole, readily distinguishable by its black and orange markings. The small bird with a bright reddish tail that flits out to snag moths and flying insects is the stolid flycatcher. Other species winging about include Adelaid's warbler, the St. Lucia peewee, and the mangrove cuckoo. There are more that your guide or a good birding book will point out. If you're fortunate, you might even spot a boa constrictor. Fortunately, you needn't worry about the deadly pit viper—it's mostly found in the island's drier scrub areas and is nocturnal.

The best way to experience the rainforest is through the Forestry Department. It will arrange for a guide for the reasonable fee of $10 per person (you'll need to provide transportation and lunch). Call 758-450-2231 at least 24 hours prior to your trek. There are several tour operators on the island that organize hikes, and there are also private individuals who provide tours, but you might want to check with your hotel directly for its recommendation; the folks at Anse Chastanet, Ladera, and Jalousie are very familiar with the guides in the Soufrière area.

The Big Hikes

These last two vigorous hikes are exhilarating climbs that will give you a real sense of accomplishment. The first is the grueling hike up **Mt. Gimie**, the tallest mountain on the island at 3,117 feet. It can be arranged through the Forestry Department if several days' notice is given. This is a very long, hard hike — it will take you one hour just to reach the base, and the summit is four hours after that. It should be attempted only in the dry season (the summit is surrounded by clouds otherwise). Because there is a maze of unmarked trails crisscrossing the slopes of Mt. Gimie and it is easy to get lost, a guide is strongly recommended.

The other hike, not under the jurisdiction of the Forestry Department, is up the face of **Petit Piton**, the smaller (and steeper) of the two dramatic volcanic cones outside Soufrière. This is a serious bordering-on-dangerous climb, about two and a half hours up (the summit is 2,438 feet) and one and a half hours down. You won't need rope, but a guide is a prerequisite, and don't try it if you suffer from any degree of acrophobia. There are two difficult stretches where you must use handholds and walk across a narrow rock ledge. It can be scary. Get up there before it gets hot (before noon), and carry water. Don't attempt the climb when the ground is very wet or very dry — both make the ascent more slippery. Bring very little else except maybe your camera, and wear good walking shoes. Officially, due to an accident some years ago, Petit Piton is off-limits, and guides are not permitted to take visitors up. However, **Gros Piton** (2,619 feet), which is less steep, is not discouraged. Go to the Tourism Office in Soufrière and ask it to help you find a guide for the Pitons; alternatively, call the Gros Piton Guides Association, which charges $25 per person (758-459-3833 or 758-489-0136, or e-mail ahead of your visit: grospitontours@candw .lc). Negotiate your fee before you start, and tell your guide that the fee is for the group, not per person — repeat it at least two or three times. Invariably, when you leave town, the guide will ask if you want to tackle Petit or Gros Piton (the guides prefer Petit because it takes less time and they charge the same price either way). If you elect Gros Piton, allow most of a day for the ascent, which tackles the summit from the south, above the village of L'Ivrogne.

It should be stressed that all hikes into the Forest Reserve must be sanctioned by the Forestry Department for several reasons. The first is that the Department lacks the manpower and facilities for large-scale manhunts, and it's very easy to get lost in the dense vegetation. Second, there is illicit marijuana farming going on, and woe to the hiker or tourist who stumbles upon that (harvest times in July and December are particularly uptight periods).

Where to Stay

St. Lucia offers a wide range of accommodations, catering to all budgets. As of late 2006 there are more than 5,200 hotel rooms on the island, a majority of which are found in all-inclusive resorts, which we usually don't recommend. There is one all-inclusive (The Body Holiday at Le Sport) that is worth looking into for its nifty spa facility. Here are our recommendations.

Rodney Bay and Castries

From Castries to the north there is a series of ivory-colored beaches that run all the way to the northernmost point of the island. Most of the hotels and resorts are in the northwest quarter of the island, especially around Rodney Bay. This area was sloppily developed in the early 1980s but in the last few years has been a focus of redevelopment that is aiming to solve some of the traffic, congestion, and trash issues. A surfeit of moderate- and budget-priced hotels provides lots of options, especially if you don't mind a short walk to (rather than a location on) the beach.

Royal St. Lucia, P.O. Box 512, Reduit Beach, Castries, St. Lucia, WI.
ⓒ 800-255-5859 or 758-452-9999, ✆ 758-452-9639,
🖥 www.rexresorts.com

💲 **Wicked Pricey** ⑪ EP ⓒⓒ 96 suites

Situated on pretty Reduit Beach and only steps away from the bustle of Rodney Bay, this all-suite resort has a modern, spacious, airy feel to it. You enter through a stucco, white marble, and bleached wood lobby with a fountain. Outside, four three-story buildings surround a huge courtyard where there's a curvy pool complex, replete with islands and a pool bar with seats in the water. There is little shade out here except for the pool umbrellas, but it's a nice place to hang out when you've had your fill of the beach. Inside, all the suites have a separate bedroom and sitting room. The off-white rooms are attractive and decorated in tropical pastels and rattan, if slightly dowdy. Baths are ample and feature lots of marble, and there are plenty of other deluxe amenities, including a small, intimate spa. There are two restaurants in the resort, and guests are welcome to use the tennis and water-sports facilities next door at the St. Lucian (they're owned by the same company, London-based Rex Resorts). The physical property has a somewhat stark, impersonal feel, but the staff and management are friendly.

Coco Palm, Rodney Bay, St. Lucia, WI. ⓒ 758-456-2800, ✆ 758-452-0774,
🖥 www.coco-resorts.com

💲 **Pricey** ⑪ EP ⓒⓒ 83 rooms

Allen Chastanet, who helped Chris Blackwell launch his chain of Island Outpost boutique resorts in Jamaica, returned to his native St. Lucia and created this hotel where the focus is on value, but not at the expense of service. Opened in 2005, there's no impersonal registration desk; instead you're greeted by a host who handles check-in at your leisure and then familiarizes you with St. Lucia, its culture, and attractions, performing the duties of a concierge. The four-story hotel comes with amenities found in American boutique hotels:

rain shower heads in bathrooms, minifridge, coffeemaker, cordless phones, flat-screen TVs, and free Wi-Fi access throughout the property. There's a free-form swimming pool (six of the rooms have swim-up access to the pool), a pair of restaurants (one is open 24 hours), and live music nightly. There's even a small spa—almost unheard of for a hotel in this price range. What Coco Palm's rooms do not have is a beach view, but it's located 200 yards from Reduit Beach, St. Lucia's best white-sand bay, and water sports and picnic baskets can be arranged through your host.

Coco Kreole, Rodney Bay, St. Lucia, WI. ℂ 758-452-0712, ✆ 758-452-0774, 🖥 www.coco-resorts.com

💲 **Not So Cheap** 🍽 CP ⒸⒸ 20 rooms

A revamp of the former Candyo Inn, this is Allen Chastanet's fore-runner to Coco Palm, with rooms that are simple and well kept, if small. All have nice extras like cordless phone, minifridge, coffeemaker, and iron. The cheapest rooms face the street; poolside rooms are a little extra. Facilities include a bar area (used for breakfast), a pool, a free Internet station, and Wi-Fi access; the beach is a five-minute walk. You'll have signing and lounging privileges at the slightly more expensive Coco Palm next door.

The Body Holiday at LeSport, P.O. Box 437, St. Lucia, WI. ℂ 800-544-2883 or 758-457-7800, ✆ 758-450-0368, 🖥 www.thebodyholiday.com

💲 **Stratospheric** 🍽 **All-Inclusive** ⒸⒸ 155 rooms

We don't normally recommend all-inclusive resorts. However, LeSport, located at the northern tip of the island, is pretty swank, as these things go. This is largely because of The Oasis, a Moorish-style spa that features all kinds of ooh-ahh things to do with your body—in-cluding massage, reflexology, hydro massage, salt loofah rubs, algae baths, eucalyptus inhalations, seaweed nutrient wraps, facials, and hair treatments. The beachfront resort also offers a daily program of aerobics, stretching, yoga, and stress management; there's even a re-laxation temple. Guests at the hotel get one daily treatment included in their all-inclusive rate. The cuisine at LeSport is meant to be lighter and health-aware—all of this is part of its theme to "free your mind and body." Just about every conceivable sport is available to you here, too, including tennis, biking, scuba, fencing, archery, an 18-hole golf course, and a gym. Guests are also encouraged to venture beyond the resort and into the backcountry for climbing the Pitons, river walks, turtle-watching and more—these all carry a surcharge, however.

The rooms and suites were renovated in 2006 and are more at-tractive and comfortable. There are also 29 "singles" rooms—slightly

smaller units that allow the resort to do away with single supple-
ments that are standard at other all-inclusive properties (the price for
one is half the price of a double). Food is also greatly improved with
the addition of Tao, a restaurant featuring East-West fusion cuisine,
although there is a surcharge for many of the items on the menu. Another plus (for some of us): LeSport is an adults-oriented property;
children under 16 aren't allowed (except in summer, when teens are
permitted).

Bay Gardens Inn, P.O. Box 1892, Rodney Bay, St. Lucia, WI. ✆ 758-452-
8200, ✆ 758-452-8002, 🖳 www.bargardensinn.com

💲 Not So Cheap 🍴 **EP** ℅ 33 rooms

Renovated in 2004, this (now) well-run inn is an offshoot of the popular Bay Gardens Hotel, which sits just across the street. Located near
(but not on) Rodney Bay, standard rooms have a minifridge, a/c, in-
room safe, coffeemaker, cable TV, and a balcony or patio with a pool
view. There's a pool, a restaurant and bar, and an Internet café; the
hotel is a ten-minute walk from Reduit Beach and plentiful dining
and nightlife options. Rooms at the 71-room **Bay Gardens Hotel** (758-
452-8060; www.baygardenshotel.com) have a few extra amenities
and slightly higher rates, drawing a lot of Caribbean business travelers.

St. Lucian by Rex Resorts, P.O. Box 512, Reduit Beach, Castries, St. Lucia,
WI. ✆ 800-255-5859 or 758-452-8351, ✆ 758-452-8331,
🖳 www.rexresorts.com

💲 Very Pricey 🍴 **EP** ℅ 120 rooms

If you want the amenities of a big hotel at more moderate prices, the
Rex St. Lucian should work for you. A one-time Holiday Inn, the
rooms are standard in décor and size. All are air-conditioned and
have phones and radios. The beach is great, and a variety of water
sports is available. There are lighted tennis courts, two restaurants,
and lots to do within walking distance. You can also use the facilities
of the somewhat fancier Royal resort next door.

Soufrière and the West Coast

South of Castries, the beaches are more of the gray or silvery black variety,
and the jungle creeps from the mountains right down to the sea. There are
few accommodations outside Soufrière, but a series of developments are set
to debut around Marigot Bay in late 2006, including the 124-room resort
Discovery at Marigot Bay (www.discoverystlucia.com), run by the Sonesta
chain. In late 2007, there are plans for a 232-room **Westin Le Paradis** resort
(www.leparadisstlucia.com) to open at Praslin Bay, on the island's east coast.
It will include an 18-hole Greg Norman golf course and a 25-room spa.

Anse Chastanet, P.O. Box 7000, Soufrière, St. Lucia, WI. ℭ 800-223-1108 or 758-459-7000, ✆ 758-459-7700, 🖳 www.ansechastanet.com, ansechastanet@candw.lc

💲 **Ridiculous** ⑪ **MAP**; a much lower **EP** rate is available in the offseason 🆑 49 rooms

With great views of the Pitons, this is St. Lucia's most unique beach resort, created by Nick and Karolin Troubetzkoy. Tucked away in foliage on a hilly point just outside Soufrière, Anse Chastanet is reached by one of the more horrendous roads on the island. Once there, however, the resort (sequestered within a 600-acre property) offers a superb retreat. There are two black-sand beaches, and wonderful water sports are offered, including the best scuba diving on the island, right off the beach. The accommodations range from Deluxe Beachside rooms just off the sand to Premium Hillside suites at the top of the crest. The latter are large, from 900 to 1,600 square feet, and offer great things like soaring cathedral ceilings, spacious lanais, and open-air showers with views of the Pitons (ask for 7A or 7B). Unit 14B of the Deluxe Hillside suites has a full-grown tree in its open-air shower. All the units are unique, however, and are furnished with local woods, fabrics, rugs, and crafts. Amenities include fridges, coffeemakers, ceiling fans, and real privacy. These rooms are the kind that you could stay in all day and not want to leave, especially if there with the right someone. There is no pool, but that wouldn't be the style of this place—the beach and nature is.

In keeping with that theme, you won't find any elevators, so take note that the resort is located on a steep hill, with about 100 steps from the beach to the main building (and more climbing if you're in a Premium unit up above). Most people don't mind the little workout every time they leave their room—just don't forget your sunblock or reading material!

Opt for one of the beachside rooms, which are beautiful and positioned just a few steps from the sand but lack the splendid views found up above. Incidentally, all of the rooms have original artwork—much of it quite good. The ultimate way to remember your stay here is to negotiate for the painting hanging in your room, or you can visit the new art gallery on the beach. There's also a discreet new spa here, which has some unusual treatments on offer. Another feature worth noting is the mountain-bike facility built at Anse Mamin next door—there are bike trails at all levels through the grounds of a crumbling plantation. If and when you can tear yourself away from Anse Chastanet, the hotel will help you arrange hikes in the rainforest and other sightseeing options. For dinner, Piton is the tree house–like restaurant halfway up the hill, and Trou au Diable is the moderately priced beach bar-restaurant for lunch.

Anse Chastanet doesn't have TVs, phones, a/c, and maybe a few other luxuries some guests demand. However, in a region where cookie-cutter resorts increasingly litter the touristed landscape, this place is a one-of-a-kind experience that seems to us almost the essence of the perfect barefoot island fantasy we dream of when we're back home. A resort-within-the-resort is being developed to open on the hill above the highest rooms — Anse Chastanet's Jade Mountain Infinity Suites will add another level of luxury to the existing facility.

⊛ **Ladera Resort**, P.O. Box 225, Soufrière, St. Lucia, WI. ℂ 800-738-4752 or 758-459-7323, 🖹 758-459-5156, 💻 www.ladera.com

💰 **Ridiculous** 🍽 **BP** plus afternoon tea **CC** 25 suites and villas

We think Ladera has, hands down, the best view of any resort or hotel in the Caribbean. From a perch 1,100 feet above sea level and within spitting distance of Petit Piton, you just cannot get a better panorama. The 16 suites and 9 villas feature a completely open western wall, so there is nothing obstructing your view, which plunges dramatically to the sea below. The effect is spectacular. If you ever wanted a place where you could live outdoors in privacy yet total luxury (with your own plunge pool; some are fed by your own waterfall), this is it. The happiest guests here are those who want to romp and read, all with the magnificence and power of the Pitons right there before their eyes. The rooms are romantic and comfortably furnished in local woods and fabrics. We would be very happy here for a tranquil week with a companion. There is a very good restaurant, Dasheene, on the premises (highly recommended for nonguests for a great lunch, or for a sunset cocktail at the accompanying bar Tcholit) and a common spring-fed pool. Ladera calls itself a resort, but it's really a small hotel — the ultimate room with a view. There is no beach, no tennis, no water sports — just a great space and heavenly vistas. The rates include a beach shuttle and snorkel equipment. Closed in September.

Ti Kaye Village, Anse Cochon, St. Lucia, WI. ℂ 758-456-8101, 🖹 758-456-9105, 💻 www.tikaye.com

💰 **Very Pricey** 🍽 **BP** **CC** 33 rooms

Sequestered at the intersection of sea and jungle and about halfway between Castries and Soufrière, Ti Kaye is a great addition to St. Lucia's lodging options. Opened in 2003, the hotel offers wonderful Creole-style wooden cottages that dapple a hillside overlooking the sea. These have a/c, private outdoor showers, and broad verandas, with rocking chairs and hammocks for two; the more expensive ones have a plunge pool. The restaurant here is surprisingly good, and a wooden staircase leads down 166 steps to gray sand Anse Cochon, with its beach bar and dive shop. The island's best wreck dive, the *Lesleen M*, a 170-foot cargo boat that sunk in 1985, slumbers right in front of the hotel — it's ideal for diving or snorkeling. The location is St. Lucia's most isolated — plan on a rental car, or leave room in the budget for island touring by taxi. The resort is an 80-minute drive from Hewanorra and 40 minutes from George Charles, a $130 and $90 transfer each way respectively.

The Jalousie Plantation, P.O. Box 251, Soufrière, St. Lucia, WI.
℡ 800-544-2883 or 758-459-7666, ✆ 758-459-7667,
🖳 www.thejalousieplantation.com

💲 **Ridiculous** 🍴 **EP** CC 112 rooms

The former plantation of Lord Glenconner is set on the hillside between the two Pitons. You could not ask for a more tranquil yet majestic setting, so much so that local opposition was fierce when the government approved construction of the property in 1989. The resort's initial incarnation was plagued with difficulties, and then Hilton International took over in 1997, making various improvements, including adding a shipload of brilliant white sand (incongruously) at the base of the black-rock Piton. In 2005 Sunswept Resorts, the locally owned company responsible for The Body Holiday at LeSport, acquired Jalousie and set about rebranding and refurbishing the hotel and adding a new spa to open in 2007.

There are 102 cottages scattered about the hillside, connected to the Great House (restaurants and other facilities), and a beach and pool by a shuttle system. All are loaded with amenities and feature their own semiprivate plunge pools. There are also a few units in a building just above the beach that lack the personal charm of the cottages; however, these Sugar Mill rooms require less shuttling about the expansive property. That shuttle service is decidedly problematic: Getting around the logistically challenged grounds requires some fortitude (and maybe a little luck). When we stayed here (during Hilton's tenure), calls for pickups took as long as 25 minutes. There are four restaurants, tennis, squash, a voluptuous pool, all water sports, and a spa with gym, aerobics, massage, and saunas. The beach, garish as it looks, is quite nice, and the snorkeling and diving around the base of Petit Piton is spectacular. It's just not as tranquil as we'd like, for there's a landing pad and transfers to the resort are available by helicopter (the airports are at least an hour away by car). So your stay is occasionally marred by the whacka-whacka of chopper blades cutting through the edenic setting from dawn till dusk. This brings us back where we started — this is a magnificent spot for a resort, but shouldn't it engender a little reverence?

Hummingbird Beach Resort, P.O. Box 280, Soufrière, St. Lucia, WI.
℡ 758-459-7232, ✆ 758-459-7033, 🖳 hbr@candw.lc

💰 **Not So Cheap** for the superior units, and **Very Pricey** for the cottage
🍴 EP Ⓒ 10 rooms

Not all of the Soufrière-area hotels charge prices to match the luxuriant setting. This classic inn is located at the north end of town, facing Petit Piton and overlooking a black-sand beach. The trio of Superior rooms is best, with stone walls, canopied four-poster beds, and Piton views from their small balconies. There is also a pair of cozy Standard rooms that share a bathroom (fine for budget-minded folks), and a cute two-bedroom cottage across the street. The beach isn't great, and the word *resort* in the title strains credulity, but Hummingbird's pool is a splendid place to spend the afternoon, and the restaurant is pretty good too, if overpriced.

Where to Eat

There are lots of restaurants to choose from on St. Lucia, and although the island is not a culinary standard-bearer, there are certainly enough good ones to keep you happy for a week. Many of the hotels and resorts have strong restaurants.

Rodney Bay and Castries

$$ **Café Claude**, Rodney Bay, 758-458-0847

This is a great place to hang out pretty much any time of day — from morning, when full English breakfasts and local dishes (salt fish and bakes) are served, to lunch and dinner when the reasonably priced catch of the day and sweet-and-sour spare ribs come out of the hopping kitchen. There's hip music, and you can survey the Rodney Bay street scene from the tables in front. The artsy boutique next door is also worth checking out. Open daily.

$$$ **The Charthouse**, Rodney Bay, 758-452-8115

Need a steak? It's a Charthouse, like all the rest, which means no surprises. It also serves lobster in season. Open for dinner only; closed Sunday. Make reservations.

$$$$ **Green Parrot**, Red Tape Lane, Morne Fortune, 758-452-3399

Overlooking Castries Harbour, this is a Lucian institution with wild Chef Harry at the helm. The menu features West Indian dishes served with a Creole flair — try the Stuffed Pussy (avocado stuffed with codfish); no joke, it's on the menu, but it's only available from July to December. The food is good, not great; people come here for the entertainment. There are floor shows on Wednesday (Princess Tina belly-dances) and Saturday (Chef Harry entertains with limbo). On Monday, ladies dine free when they wear a flower in their hair and their dates wear a jacket and tie (but what about two women wearing flowers or two men wearing jackets and ties?). Reservations are a must; open daily.

$$ **Key Largo**, Rodney Bay, 758-452-0282

This is a fun and lively place featuring California-style brick-oven pizzas, pastas, and great salads. This is also where you come for your afternoon cappuccinos and espressos.

$$ **The Lime**, Rodney Bay, 758-452-0761

A Rodney Bay staple, The Lime serves good West Indian food and is especially popular at lunch. The bar is one of the mainstays of Rodney Bay nightlife. Closed Tuesday.

$$ **Razmataz Tandoori Restaurant**, Rodney Bay, 758-452-9800

Looking for an alternative from Creole? Under the guidance of a Nepalese chef, this is a pleasant place for decent, inexpensive Indian meals, including tandoori oven preparations. Open daily.

$$$$$ **Tao**, Anse Galet, 758-450-8551

LeSport's signature restaurant has a Filipino chef creating excellent East-West fusion cuisine in a striking black-and-white setting. Some of the delectables include wok-seared lobster, basil-infused tomato tea, and a Kashmiri pork tenderloin. Dishes are on the small side—remember, you're at a spa resort. Reservations are essential.

The West Coast, Soufrière, and Vieux Fort

$$ **Anse La Raye Fish Fry**, Anse La Raye

If you're staying in the south and don't want to face the long, winding drive to Gros Islet for the weekly jump-up (see Focus on St. Lucia), a reasonable alternative is the Friday night fish fry in the village of Anse La Raye, located halfway between Castries and Soufrière. Though considerably more low-key than Gros Islet, it's more homespun, and since this is a fishing community, you know the catch is as fresh as it gets (and might include octopus, whelks, shrimp, and lobster). The evening starts earlier, too, around 6:30 p.m. If you miss Friday here, you can head to the east coast village of Dennery, where an even smaller-scale fish fry is held on Saturday.

$$ **Chak Chak**, Vieux Fort, 758-454-6260

This is a popular local favorite on the beach just south of the airport, handy if you arrive early for your flight out of Hewanorra. West Indian–style steaks and chops are a specialty, but check into the catch of the day. Usually open daily until midnight.

$$$$ Dasheene, Ladera Resort, Soufrière, 758-459-7850

This is the best place for lunch on St. Lucia. The food is reliable (if unspectacular), but the views are fabulous (see the write-up in the Where to Stay section). It's also open for dinner.

$$$ Hummingbird, Anse Chastanet Road, Soufrière, 758-459-7232

A pleasant local restaurant, Hummingbird features West Indian cuisine and a dining terrace overlooking the sea and Petit Piton. It's a little expensive, but if you're lucky, it might have some freshwater mountain crayfish, which is delicious. Open for lunch and dinner daily.

$$$ Kai Manje, Anse Cochon, 758-456-8101

This restaurant at Ti Kaye resort, located halfway between Castries and Soufrière, is a good place to break up a round-island tour. We love lunch next to the sea, and the dinners are really worthwhile, supplanted by a surprisingly good wine selection.

$$$$$ Piton, Anse Chastanet, 758-459-7000

If you can survive the road to Anse Chastanet (your car will make it), the reward is this delightful restaurant in a tree house–like setting with views of the Pitons, fine sunsets, and a friendly staff. The cuisine is Creole and continental.

$$ The Still, La Perle Estate, Soufrière, 758-459-7224

Located on a 300-acre working plantation owned by the DuBoulay family for five generations, this lunch-only establishment serves excellent Creole food. Virtually all the food prepared here is grown on the estate. Reservations are suggested, and be sure to verify that it doesn't have a large group (usually cruise-ship tours) on the day you want to visit.

Don't Miss

The Pitons

It would be unthinkable not to see them while on St. Lucia.

A Drive Around the Island

A must-do — you won't grasp the beauty of the island any other way, and you'll see the Pitons, too.

Spa Treatments

St. Lucia has bloomed with spa facilities in the last few years, led by the comprehensive Oasis at LeSport, an all-inclusive resort. There are 36 rooms featuring Thalassotherapy treatments, body tonic baths, wraps, reflexology, and more. Other places with spa facilities include the Royal St. Lucian, Jalousie, and even one on the beach at Anse Chastanet.

Lunch at Dasheene

With Dasheene's breathtaking view of the Pitons and good food to boot, this will be a meal to remember.

Gros Islet on Friday

You can't leave St. Lucia without experiencing this Friday street jump-up (see Focus on St. Lucia).

Scuba at Anse Chastanet

If you're a diver, the underwater scenery and dive shop here (a five-star PADI facility) are excellent. Call Scuba St. Lucia at 758-459-7000.

The Walks and Hikes

See up close the beauty with which Mom Nature has blessed the island. Check out the Focus on St. Lucia section.

Choisel Scenic Drive

This is a beautiful drive through the lovely seaside village of Choisel and continuing along the coast to La Pointe Beach on the island's southwest corner. Also in the area is the "St. Lucian Stonehenge," man-made stone formations that have been tentatively carbon-dated at 2500 B.C.

The Drive-Through Volcano

If you haven't been to a volcano before, the still-simmering **Qualibou Crater** can be interesting. There are guides galore, but good luck finding one who actually knows the geology.

St. Martin/ St. Maarten

LEGEND

- ◉ ◎ Capital City, Town
- ⑬ Route Number
- ■ Hotel / Point of Interest
- ■ Scenic View
- ⚓ Ferry / Cruise Ship Dock
- 🕯 Lighthouse
- 🌂 Beach
- ⛳ Golf Course

N

ATLANTIC OCEAN

Île Tintamarre

FERRY TO ST. BARTH

Red Rock

Cap Caraïbes Hotel/ Caribbean Princess
Friar's Beach
Cay Verte
Club Orient

Raddison St. Martin Resort and Spa.

French Cul de Sac
AIRPORT

Grand Case
Grand Case Beach Club
Hotel L'Esplanade Caraïbes
Le Petit Hotel

Green Cay Villas

Orleans

French Side

△ Paradise Peak (1,391 ft / 424 m)

Guana Bay

Guana Key

Williams Hill

Great Salt Pond

Point Blanche

Point Blanche

Friar's Beach
La Batterie

Marigot

Golfe

Dutch Side

Philipsburg

Great Bay

Pasanggrahan Royal Guest House

FERRY TO SABA

FERRY TO ANGUILLA

Pointe de Bluff

Mercure Simson Beach Coralia
Baie Nettle

Le Flamboyant

Simpson Bay Lagoon

Mary's Boon

Simpson Bay

AIRPORT

Mullet Bay

Terres Basses

Pointe Plum

Long Beach
La Samanna

Wyndham Sapphire Beach Club & Resort
The Inn at Cupecoy

CARIBBEAN SEA

0   1.5   3

Miles

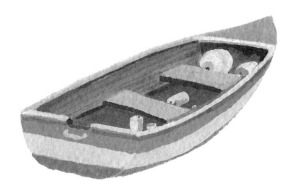

St. Martin/
St. Maarten

Looking for a beach-girdled slice of Europe in the Caribbean? A place where a border crossing is as effortless as travel in the European Union, and where the croissant from the corner bakery is as reliable as the best in Paris? You've come to the right chapter: St. Martin/St. Maarten, which is the smallest territory in the world to be shared by two sovereign states, France and the Netherlands. Because this is a European island, as much as if not more than it is a Caribbean island, the food here is superb—in part because jumbo jets from Europe arrive almost daily in the winter months, delivering a fresh cargo of epicurean supplies. The island's cultural flotsam and jetsam also allow for a surprisingly diverse selection of cuisines; Indian, Italian, and Indonesian are among the many non-French tastes to be found here. Although food on the French side is to die for (the prices could kill you, too), there are good meals to be found on the Dutch side as well.

Sometimes our timing is a little off. On our most recent visit to this taste bud paradise, one of our party was on the South Beach diet. French food and the South Beach diet are not a match made in heaven (it's a baguette–*pain au chocolat*–croissant conspiracy). This diet kept us from indulging in the puff pastry topping that came with escargot dripping in mouth-watering

St. Martin/St. Maarten: Key Facts

Location	18°N by 63°W
	195 miles/314 kilometers east of San Juan
	1,690 miles/2,719 kilometers southeast of New York
Size	37 square miles/96 square kilometers
	St. Martin — 21 square miles/54 square kilometers
	St. Maarten — 16 square miles/41 square kilometers
Highest point	Paradise Peak (1,391 feet/424 meters)
Population	90,000 (officially, St. Maarten 48,000, St. Martin 42,000, but illegal, uncounted immigrants are estimated to number well into five digits)
Language	English is primarily spoken, although you will hear a little Dutch on the Dutch side and French on the French side.
Time	Atlantic Standard Time (1 hour ahead of EST, same as EDT)
Area codes	To call French St. Martin from the U.S., dial 011 (the international access code), then 590-590 (the country code), then the six-digit local number; to call Dutch St. Maarten, dial 011, then 599, then the seven-digit local number.
Electricity	St. Martin — 220 volts AC, 50 cycles; adapters and transformers often necessary.
	St. Maarten — 110 volts AC, 60 cycles, same as U.S. Bad planning by both sides!
Currency	St. Martin: the euro (€1 = US$1.25 at press time; check before departure). Most hotels, restaurants, and stores accept U.S. dollars, but the exchange rate will not be favorable. Use a credit card for the best exchange rate.
	St. Maarten: the Netherlands Antilles guilder, NAf (1.78 NAf = US$1). Because this is a fixed rate, U.S. dollars are accepted everywhere at the current exchange rate; most restaurant menus and all hotel rate cards are published in U.S. dollars.
Driving	On the right; a valid U.S. or Canadian driver's license is acceptable.
Documents	U.S. citizens need proof of nationality (plus photo ID) for stays up to three months; after that a passport is necessary. An ongoing or a return ticket is also necessary. Canadian citizens will need a passport.
Departure tax	$30 (usually added to the price of your airline ticket)
Beer to drink	Presidente
Rum to drink	Wild Sint Maarten Guavaberry, a liqueur
Music to hear	Chill-Out Lounge
Tourism info	French St. Martin: www.st-martin.org, 877-956-1234
	Dutch St. Maarten: www.st-maarten.com, 800-786-2278

melted garlic butter—the flaky crust just begging to be dipped. This was sheer torture and elicited a shaking of heads from the staff. We could just hear them saying under their breath: "Those crazy Americans. First they call *pomme frites* from Belgium 'french fries,' then rename them 'freedom fries' when they get irked with French politics, and now this thing called the South Beach diet? Puh!" (That would be a Gallic expression of disgust.) Hey, *c'est la vie, mes amis!*

The island, co-governed by France and the Netherlands, has no immigration or customs posts between the two sides, just road markers indicating the boundaries. (It's also the most populous island per square mile in the Caribbean.) We've always had a knack for the French side, which has dozens of truly gourmet restaurants and a smidgen of French haute couture. The beaches are pretty nice, too. Even Orient Beach, with its beach bars and crowds, is just a fun place to hang out and people-watch. Of course, there is also shopping in the French capital, Marigot.

In addition to a plethora of hotels and time-share developments, Dutch St. Maarten is also home to gnarly-looking casinos, the huge, newly rebuilt Juliana International Airport, and the island's main cruise-ship port. Philipsburg, the Dutch capital, is similar to Charlotte Amalie in St. Thomas—avoidable, except for shopping. Still, on our last visit, a fresher-looking Philipsburg looked better than it has in many years. The town is cleaned up, the beach lining it has been dredged back in place, and a boardwalk now runs along the sand. Although both sides have made questionable decisions on development, the Dutch have really gone overboard in recent years. For example: Cupecoy Beach, a unique if evanescent strand, is being ruined with a series of charmless condo projects that cling to the ruddy cliffs (perhaps Mother Nature can plunder what environmentalists could not prevent). Dawn Beach has been foolishly sullied with a resort that is set to become a Westin when it opens in 2007. Long-time islanders on both sides of the island are appalled by the wanton development. Furthermore, traffic jams in and out of the two capitals are a growing problem, and the strip between the airport and Simson Bay is a royal pain to navigate each afternoon as the international flights start to land.

Why come to St. Martin/St. Maarten at all when there are other, more *Caribbean* choices? Certainly there are many Americans who love this cluttered little isle and wing down to their condo or time-share once or twice each winter. Probably the best reason to come here is to get a literal taste of France: St. Martin has excellent restaurants. English is also spoken everywhere (this is not the case on Martinique or Guadeloupe). You can get air or land packages and charter flights that are very reasonable. Both sides are duty-free ports, so shopping frenzies are a daily event—it's the place to snag that Rolex or Tag Heuer you always wanted. The other reason to come here is that it's easy to get to—connections on small planes, which eat up precious time, are not necessary from major East Coast cities. The island is also the principal gateway for a collection of smaller satellite islands—St. Barth, Saba, St. Eustatius,

Anguilla—which makes this a good base for sampling two or three choice islands on one trip.

The Briefest History

All right, how the hell did this small island get split in half politically in the first place? Patience, readers, we will enlighten. First, let us note that as with most of the islands in the region, it was settled by the Ciboney around 1000 B.C., then the Arawaks around A.D. 300, and finally the Caribs about 600 years later. Columbus sighted the island on his second voyage, in 1493, on the feast day of St. Martin of Tours—hence the moniker. The Dutch were the first to battle the Caribs and set up shop on the salt ponds (salt was the major industry before sugarcane). Then came the Spanish and French. The Spanish lost interest in the island in the mid-17th century, and a group of French and Dutch settlers established separate communities. Of course, the two groups fought like cats and dogs until a treaty was signed in 1648 on the summit of Mt. Concordia, establishing boundaries between France and Holland. The French got the bigger slice of the pie because their navy was a stronger force in the region, but the Dutch got the best port, Philipsburg.

With the advent of sugar and tobacco plantations, and with them slavery, the British became interested. The island became a battleground again and changed hands 16 times between 1648 and 1816, when a final settlement was reached. Relations between the two countries settled into a groove and have remained stable to the present day. However, the fortunate demise of slavery (in 1848 on the French side and in 1863 on the Dutch) brought the economy to a standstill. Things didn't start looking up until 1939, when the island was made a duty-free port. That brought in all kinds of business and commerce. Juliana Airport, built during World War II and far larger than any other airstrip in the neighborhood, started the tourist boom, which is in full force today.

Getting There

Queen Juliana International Airport, on the Dutch side, handles jumbo jets from all over, and a spiffy new terminal was nearing completion as we went to press. American, Continental, Delta, United and US Airways fly nonstop from their hubs in the United States. It's also worth checking with your travel agent for charter flights, especially in winter months. From Canada, Air Transat has nonstops from Toronto and other cities, and Conquest and Air Canada offer them from Toronto.

Caribbean Star, LIAT, and Winair (partnered with US Airways) fly from islands in the Eastern Caribbean. BWIA flies in from Barbados, Jamaica, and Trinidad. American Eagle and Caribbean Sun fly from San Juan. Air Caraïbes has daily flights from the French and other neighboring islands, and Dutch Caribbean Airways has flights from Aruba, Curaçao, and Bonaire. There is a small airport on the French side in Grand Case, L'Espérance, but this is used only for flights to the French islands.

Getting Around

Taxis are expensive and the roads are good throughout, so there is no reason not to obtain a car from one of the many major rental-car agencies, including Avis, Hertz, Budget, Dollar, National, Thrifty, and Alamo, plus a host of local outfits renting slightly more worn cars for slightly better rates. Reservations are a good idea in high season. Prices are more reasonable here than on other Caribbean islands. If you're visiting in low season, you should be able to get a car for under $25 a day; high-season rates start around $40 a day but can go higher. The advantage of negotiating for a car at the airport on arrival is that you can bargain hard — competition is just a few feet away; the disadvantage is you'll pay a $7 surcharge (they've got to pay for that trim new airport somehow!). Driving is on the right.

Alternatively, there is frequent minibus service that circles the island's main roads between 6 a.m. and midnight, connecting Philipsburg, Marigot, and major residential areas. Most destinations cost under $3.

Traffic congestion can be worse here than on many other islands in the Caribbean, so it pays to time your trips carefully. Traffic heading in and out of Marigot and Philipsburg at the start and end of the business day is bad. The

Petty Theft and More

Crime is a serious problem on St. Martin/St. Maarten. Although recent years have seen incidents of violence increase, most of the crime is of the petty variety. However, even petty crime can make a serious dent in the enjoyment of your vacation or wallet (or both). Places to be particularly aware include the somewhat isolated French beaches Happy Bay and Friar's Bay, just west of Grand Case. We have heard numerous reports of beachgoers carefully hiding their valuables in the bushes and going for a swim only to find that thieves were watching all the time. Car break-ins at Cupecoy seem to be a regular occurrence. Several islanders have warned that walking through the Mullet Bay area after dark is not advised. Our suggestions: Never leave valuables in your car, even locked; do not leave anything unattended on a beach if you are not prepared to lose it, even if it's "hidden" from view; and, most important, avoid poorly lighted areas after dark, especially when you're alone. In sum, treat a visit to St. Martin/St. Maarten as you would any big, unfamiliar city.

jams on the road between the airport and Cole Bay are even worse — they start at around 2 p.m., as the day's flights start to arrive, and last until about 6 p.m.

There are ferries to neighboring St. Barth, Saba, and Anguilla; information on these is detailed in those respective chapters.

Focus on St. Martin/St. Maarten:
⊛ Duty-Free Shopping

If you ever wanted to buy a good Swiss watch or any kind of jewelry, you should do it here; the prices are great. With electronics and cameras, there are some deals to be had, but you're better off shopping for these items on the mainland or ordering from discount houses or on the Internet, because warranties can be a bugaboo. Both **Philipsburg** and **Marigot** have major duty-free stores. Of the two, Marigot is more civilized, and you can go out for a wonderful lunch, too. The prices are very similar on both sides. You can and should negotiate; the price should come down a tad (although we had no luck at the Lacoste store). If you pay cash, you may get a small discount on top. Bon shopping!

Where to Stay

There are thousands of hotel rooms on both the French and Dutch sides of the island. We strongly suggest staying on the French side, although there are a few places on the Dutch side worth recommending. Note that a 5 percent tax is added to rates on the French side; sometimes a service charge is also added. A 5 percent tax plus 15 percent service charge is typical on the Dutch side. Look for package deals — you'll save a lot of money, and there are many from which to choose. Note that many establishments close for a few weeks in September and/or October — check with the individual property before blocking your vacation time at the office.

French Side

Le Petit Hotel, 248 Boulevard de Grand Case, Grand Case, St. Martin,
  FWI. ℂ 590-590-29-09-65, ✆ 590-590-87-09-19,
  🖥 www.lepetithotel.com, info@lepetithotel.com.
  💲 Wicked Pricey ⑪ CP ©© 10 units

We adore this small (as its name implies) three-story hotel on the beach in Grand Case. Located at the southern end of town, it is a short five-minute walk along the beach until the beginning of Restaurant Row (Rue des Restaurants *en français*, Rue de Grand Case on the map). Owned by Marc and Kristin Petrelluzzi, the same wonderful couple who owns L'Esplanade (below), this has become one of our favorite *petit* hotels in the Caribbean.

All the rooms face the water — a big advantage — and come with fully equipped kitchens (another plus). Each floor presents different options for accommodation style. The ground floor has a studio and a one-bedroom suite with lanais that step down to the beach, great for quick dips in the water at any time of day or night (midnight dip, anybody?). The second-floor studios have lanais with see-through railings for optimal aqua views from the room and lanai. The third-floor studios have cathedral ceilings for that haut, airy feeling, but the lanai railing is solid, blocking views of the water while seated. We were happy in a second-floor studio, because we like to keep the door open at night to hear the waves (which are actually quite loud) and optimize our view of the water. The rooms are attractively furnished, with white walls, tile floors, dark wood trim, and Brazilian wood ceilings in the first- and second-floor units; and rattan furniture, attractive fabrics, king-size bed, safe, dining area, cable TV, CD/cassette player, a/c, ceiling fan, and direct-dial phone. The marble and Brazil wood baths are a good size and feature walk-in showers and large mirrors.

Guests at Le Petit Hotel have privileges at its nearby sister resort, L'Esplanade, which has a bar and a pool for those looking for a drink and a freshwater dip. With the ocean at our feet, we are happy just to stay put or to venture down the beach to Calmos Café to take in the sunset. We hope that someday they'll be able to squeeze a bar in at Le Petit, to serve as the social focal point of this great little place.

Hotel L'Esplanade Caraïbes, B.P. 5007, Grand Case, St. Martin, FWI. ℭ 866-596-8365 or 590-590-87-06-55, ✆ 590-590-87-29-15, 🖳 www.lesplanade.com, info@lesplanade.com

💰 **Wicked Pricey** 🍴 EP Ⓒ 24 units

The big sister of Le Petit Hotel, this pretty lodging is set on the hillside with commanding views overlooking Grand Case and the bay. L'Esplanade is a great find for spacious living, and prices are somewhat less than at Le Petit (the trade-off for not being on the beach). Designed by an Argentine, the recently spruced-up décor uses lots of dark woods, and we love the rooms with lofts. The 24 units are huge for a hotel and would be a wonderful space to live in, let alone stay in for a few days. Families will appreciate the leg room, the quiet hillside location, and the pool.

Each space has a large lanai with a view of the town and the sea, a fully equipped kitchen with new Balinese furnishings, Corian countertops, direct-dial phone, cable TV, CD/cassette stereo, a/c, king-size bed, safe, and ceiling fans. There is a pool with a swim-up bar on the property, and the beach is a five-minute walk down the hill. A great advantage of L'Esplanade is that dozens of fine restaurants in Grand Case are no more than 15 minutes away on foot. As with Le Petit, the management here is very friendly and helpful and will arrange for any other activities that you desire.

Grand Case Beach Club, Grand Case, St. Martin, FWI. ✆ 800-344-3016 or 590-590-87-51-87, 📠 590-590-87-59-93, 🖳 www.grandcasebeachclub.com, info@gcbc.com

💲 **Very Pricey** (look for promotional specials on the Web) 🍴 **EP** ㏄ 71 rooms

Another of our favorites on this side of the island, Grand Case Beach Club sits by itself on the northern end of the beach in Grand Case. Its location is one of its greatest assets, away from traffic noise and with calm lagoon-like water—excellent for swimming—yet it's only a 10-minute walk to town and faboo food.

The resort is strung along the beach, with a small bluff in the middle hosting the minuscule pool, the superb dive shop, and its restaurant, the Sunset Café. The Beach Club has a loyal clientele (mostly American) that just seems to like the laid-back style and atmosphere, and it returns year after year. The resort is well-maintained and clean, although we think the pastel décor looked dated and uninspired. The rooms come in studio, one-, and two-bedroom configurations, with either garden or ocean views. All have a/c, white tile floor, lanai, tropical rattan furnishings, small bath, kitchenette, satellite TV, direct-dial phone, safe, and CD/stereo.

Besides the dive shop and water sports center, there are two very good beaches (one of which is quite secluded, though a bit narrow at times) and a lighted tennis court with artificial turf (something different!). This is a good place for families with small children—the calm beaches, swimming, and location should make for a carefree vacation. In summer, the rates drop by more than 50 percent, which makes this resort a *really* sweet deal.

La Samanna, B.P. 4077, Baie Longue, St. Martin, FWI. ✆ 800-854-2252 or 590-590-87-64-00, 📠 590-590-87-87-86, 🖳 www.lasamanna.com

💲 **Stratospheric** 🍴 **BP** ㏄ 81 rooms

When we first came to St. Martin on spring break in the time-warp year of 1977, La Samanna was one of the "it" places in the Caribbean (Jackie O was a regular then). The hotel was a trendsetter that greatly influenced the design and style of resorts built on other islands. La Samanna sort of lost its sparkle in the early 1990s as it changed hands a couple of times, but the property has been operated by Orient-Express Hotels since 1996, and the chain has spent lots of money to bring it back to its former glory. From past to present, it is still far and away the most luxurious and expensive resort on this island.

Catering to a well-heeled, international clientele, it has 81 rooms and apartments spread over 55 secluded acres in the nicest and ritziest part of the island (ironically named Lowlands, despite the gently undulating landscape). The rooms come in two principal categories:

deluxe—which were renovated in 2005—and premium. The latter are larger and have added perks like oversize baths with dual showers, soaking tubs, walk-in closets, and CD players. Quite honestly, considering the deluxe room rates start around $900 a night in winter, all rooms should have CD players; expect to pay a large premium (read: double) for the premium rooms. Some units are in the main building; they command a stunning view of the whole Baie Longue beach and the sea beyond. The rest of the rooms are found in small buildings along the beach, each with a spacious semiprivate patio. The décor throughout has a stucco, Moorish accent, with shades of yellow as the unifying color scheme, and Spanish tile floors. You'll find all the amenities of a European-style luxury hotel here: gorgeous hand-painted bedspreads, chintz curtains, sumptuous rattan furnishings, attractive prints on the walls, lavish bathrooms with hand-painted tiles and L'Occitaine bath products, and high-tech TVs that elevate out of a cabinet. All rooms have a ceiling fan, a/c, a small library, fresh flowers and fruit, 24-hour room service, a minibar with customized bar menu, and puka shells on the door as your "Do Not Disturb" signal.

The incredible beach is never crowded, although the sand seems to ebb and flow depending on the severity of summer storms and currents, exposing coral shelves at the waterline (a dock and raft help alleviate this situation). There are three lighted tennis courts; a full-service spa; a well-equipped fitness center with treadmills, elliptical machines, free weights, Cybex machines, and Pilates; and yoga studios. All types of water sports can be arranged. Sunset cocktails by the attractive pool and bar are a must-do, even if you don't stay here, and dinners are outstanding, coddled by a deep, rich wine cellar containing 380 varieties of Bordeaux alone. Closed September to October.

Radisson St. Martin Resort and Spa, Anse Marcel, St. Martin, FWI.
ⓒ 800-333-3333 or 590-590-87-67-00, ✉ 590-590-87-67-88,
💻 www.radisson.com

💲 **Very Pricey** 🍽 **CP** CC 253 rooms
Nestled in a mountainous cove on the northern tip of St. Martin, this former Le Méridien property is about as remote as one can be on this populous island. If you like both an isolated setting and lots of resort amenities, this is as good as it gets on St. Martin. The pretty, 1,600-foot-long beach here is usually calm, and those into boating will appreciate the adjacent marina—one of the few between Marigot and Philipsburg. For those seeking signs of life, it's a 15-minute drive over the hill to Grand Case or Orient Beach.

However, with Radisson acquiring and injecting $60 million in renovations into the property in 2006, it could become the French side's premier resort, after La Samanna. Radisson's newly redesigned rooms feature flat-screen TVs, oversize bathrooms, and premium amenities. A lavish new spa has also been created. The resort has four restaurants, three bars, a pool, a fitness room, tennis courts, squash courts, racquetball courts, and tons of water sports, including a new "lazy river" pool that is sure to be a hit with the kids.

Green Cay Villas, Parc de la Baie Orientale, St. Martin, FWI. Ⓒ 886-592-4213 or 590-590-87-38-63, ✆ 590-590-87-39-27, 🖥 www.greencayvillas.com

💲 **Stratospheric** (for three bedrooms) 🍴 **BP** ⒸⒸ 16 villas

Perched above pretty, breezy Orient Beach and caressed by steady trade winds, Green Cay is a collection of spacious and fully equipped villas, each with its own private pool and ample private deck. Sweeping views and privacy abound, especially from the villas on the top of the hill (which we recommend, although they're priced a few euros more). Even if there is only one of you, you have the pool to yourself. The 4,500-square-foot villas have complete kitchens (including blenders for those frozen daiquiris and margaritas), big living rooms with comfy sofas and chairs to flop around in, and up to three bedrooms with marble baths and bidets. Studios are also available.

The décor is a pastel palette with bright tropical accents and white tile floors. Amenities include a/c, CD/tape player, TV/VCR, and an outside dining patio. There is daily maid service, and breakfast is served by your pool. Green Cay is part of the Orient Bay development; room service is available from several of the resort's restaurants, and guests have charge privileges at all the beach restaurants and water sports–tennis facilities. The beach itself is a 10-minute walk down the hill. This is a good choice for families or small groups.

Club Orient, 1 Baie Orientale, St. Martin, FWI. Ⓒ 800-690-0199 or 590-590-87-33-85, ✆ 590-590-87-33-76, 🖥 www.cluborient.com

💲 **Very Pricey** 🍴 **EP** ⒸⒸ 137 rooms

There is an old song by the B-52s called "Theme for a Nude Beach," which immediately popped into our heads as we first strolled into the Club Orient's beach restaurant and took a seat at the bar next to two buck-naked patrons. This is the original naturist (nudist, but they prefer *naturist*) colony in the Caribbean. It is without a doubt the premier clothes-optional resort in the Caribbean, and everyone except the employees lounge naked. Located on the southern end of Orient Beach, the red-pine chalets are scattered about the somewhat barren property and come in chalet, minisuite, and studio configurations. Wiped out by Hurricane Luis in 1995, the entire resort had to be rebuilt, and it reopened a year later with all new structures. All rooms are furnished in simple yet comfortable summer-cabin-retreat style (the wood and tile-accented interiors make us think of a large sauna with furniture), and all units have fully equipped kitchens, lanais, and ceiling fans (Orient is on the northeast corner of the island and thus faces the trade winds). There's also a new three-bedroom villa that sleeps seven. Note that there are no phones or TVs in any of the rooms. You'll find two tennis courts (nudie tennis, anyone?) and all water sports, including a nude cruise to Tintamarre Island across the bay. Although the resort welcomes singles, most guests are couples or families, many of whom return year after year.

Cap Caraïbes Hotel, B.P. 5100, Parc de la Baie Orientale, St. Martin, FWI. 🕿 590-590-52-94-94, ✆ 590-590-52-95-00, 💻 www.cap-caraibes.com

💲 **Very Pricey** 🍽 EP 💳 35 rooms

We like this hotel, which is located right on the beach in Orient. Just walk through the palm trees and sea grapes and *voilà*, you're at Waikiki, one of the five "star" restaurants on the beach with padded chaise — waitron service included in the room ticket. Now who can beat that? Those who love the action-oriented Orient and the constant cooling trade winds should opt for this choice. The emphasis here is the beach, so don't expect a vast array of services and palatial hotel lobbies and public rooms. The staff is very friendly and adds to the wonderful, laid-back beach ambiance. There is a small, kidney-shaped pool and the Waikiki beach bar in front (as well as others strung out along the beach). The hotel also offers Internet access, room service, a small gym, and an activities desk.

The 35 rooms at the Cap are actually studios with fully equipped kitchenettes. All have terra-cotta tile floors, tropical furnishings, and a distinctly French Caribbean look, both inside and out. The bathrooms have a walk-in shower and are an adequate size. All rooms come with phone, satellite TV, minisafe, a/c, and ceiling fans (the trade winds here are among the strongest on the island).

Caribbean Princess, B.P. 5100, Parc de la Baie Orientale, St. Martin, FW.I. 🕿 590-590-52-94-94, ✆ 590-590-52-95-00, 💻 www.cap-caraibes.com

💲 **Wicked Pricey** 🍽 EP 💳 12 units

This is the the pricier sister hotel of Cap Caraïbes. In fact, these two hotels share the same ownership, style, and reservation line. The difference is that the Princess offers all one- to three-bedroom condo units featuring comfortable living rooms with overstuffed sofas and armchairs. The Princess is right on the sand, and all units come with phone, satellite TV, minisafe, a/c, and ceiling fan.

Le Flamboyant, Route de Terres Basses, Baie Nettlé, St. Martin, FWI. 🕿 800-221-5333 or 590-590-87-60-00, ✆ 590-590-87-60-57, 💻 www.hmc-hotels.fr

💲 **Very Pricey** 🍽 EP 💳 271 rooms

Located on the calm, lake-like Simpson Lagoon (great for small children), Le Flamboyant is the best of the hotels and resorts in Baie Nettlé. It's a big but well-maintained resort, with rooms spread out among 23 buildings and attractive landscaping. Along with a breezy and handsome marble and mosaic lobby, there are two swimming pools, two restaurants, a bar, a gym, a lighted tennis court, a pool table and practice golf, Internet access, and all kinds of water sports on the lagoon (water skiers, take note).

As with other hotels in Nettlé, the design is a colorful mix of Creole influences — three-story, red-roofed, tan buildings with large lanais. Unlike many of the hotels in Nettlé, which were built with tax incentives from the French government and have reached their full depreciation value (and have been sold off as condo units, or as time-share or vacation apartments), Le Flamboyant has remained a hotel.

The room décor is typically *caraïbes francaise* and features dark wood and rattan furnishings with bright fabric and tile floors. The standard rooms have small baths with tub and dual vanity (an odd visual). The deluxe rooms have larger baths, bigger beds, and a better view (hence the deluxe label). All rooms have fully equipped kitchenette (fridge, two-burner stove, sink, china, and utensils) on the outside lanai (watch your step with the slider), a/c, satellite TV, direct-dial phone, and safe.

Mercure Simson Beach Coralia, B.P. 172, Baie Nettlé, St. Martin, FWI. ⒸÀ 800-MERCURE or 590-590-87-54-54, 🖥 590-590-87-92-11, 💻 www.accorhotels.com

🟥 **Very Pricey** 🍽 **CP** 🆑 168 rooms

This is a cheaper and more basic alternative to Le Flamboyant for those who desire the calm waters of the lagoon. We think it's a little on the Spartan side and reminds us of the Club Med school of basic décor, with terra-cotta tile floors, white wicker and rattan furnishings, and precious little artwork on the walls. Actually, the Mercure could use a little sprucing up (bring in the Fab Five), but the prices are generally reasonable (especially when purchased on the Web). All rooms have a/c, satellite TV, radio, safe, lanai, and kitchenette. Baths feature walk-in showers and marble and tile and pastels throughout. There is a restaurant and a beach bar, plus a pool, Ping-Pong, volleyball, tennis, and all water sports. The beach here is very calm because it is on the lagoon, so this place would be great for small children.

Golfe, B.P. 974, Marigot, St. Martin, FWI. ⒸÀ 590-590-87-92-08, 🖥 590-590-87-83-92, 💻 golfe.hotel.saint.martin@wanadoo.fr

🟥 **Cheap** 🍽 **EP** 🆑 24 rooms

The location isn't much — this modern three-story inn is on the outskirts of bustling Marigot — but the prices here can't be beat. The lobby is decorated in bright blues and yellows, and a smallish pool is in back. The rooms upstairs are simple and cozy (request a lagoon view, which has a balcony and a little more space). If you're headed onto a yacht or to another island, Golfe is also a good spot for in-transit visitors — it's located 15 minutes from the airport and just a few hundred yards from the marina.

Dutch Side

Wyndham Sapphire Beach Club & Resort, 147 Lowlands, Cupecoy, St. Maarten, NA., ℂ 800-WYNDHAM or 599-545-2179, ✆ 599-545-2178, ☐ www.sbcwi.com

💲 **Very Pricey** 🍴 **EP** ⒸⒸ 180 rooms

Yes, this is a time-share resort that rents hotel rooms depending on availability (in our experience, any establishment that has "Beach Club & Resort" in its moniker screams time-share). So expect some form of sales pitch during your stay and use Nancy R.'s famous dictum, "Just Say No." That said, the rooms aren't all that bad. A symphony of white (from the floors to the ceiling), all units sport the same blinding and somewhat cold décor, feature granite-countered kitchens, and are fully equipped right down to the standard-size side-by-side refrigerators (a bit of overkill, in our opinion). Oceanside rooms have Jacuzzis on the teak-decked lanais. The bathrooms are marble-lined, ample in size, and have soaking tubs. Furnishings are of the wicker and rattan genre, in, you guessed it, white. Some relief to the absence of color is achieved in the form of bright tropical prints and accents. Deluxe units have living rooms, two baths, and a double-size lanai. Rooms also feature a/c, satellite TV, VCR, iron and board, high-speed Internet access, coffeemaker and coffee, safe, and room service.

There is a decent-size pool in the middle of the property, which is essential since the beach in front is often underwater. For sand, Mullet Bay is a short walk to the east, and the clothing-optional Cupecoy is about a half mile to the west. A poolside café offers an international menu.

The Inn at Cupecoy, 130 Lowlands, Cupecoy, St. Maarten, NA. ℂ 599-545-4333, ✆ 599-545-4334, ☐ www.theinnatcupecoy.com

💲 **Very Pricey** 🍴 **CP** ⒸⒸ 5 units

Surrounding a central pool and lounge space, these five eclectically and interestingly decorated rooms provide a different option from standard hotel fare. Although we are a tad trepid about sharing such an *intimé* common space with unknowns, who knows, it could be interesting. We think the Inn is overpriced, however, given its roadside location and busy restaurant and market downstairs (which some might consider a convenience). Also, during our visit, a new 120-unit, four-story condominium resort, called the Rainbow Beach Club, was nearing completion across the street smack dab in the sight lines of the sea and Saba on the horizon. Boo, hiss!

We do like the tumbled marble baths, the Rolex fixtures (Do they tell time, too?), and the large walk-in showers with rain-soak shower-heads—a curious effect on this rain-parched island. We also like some of the decorating flourishes (a zebra-skin rug stands out in our minds). Vaulted ceilings create a nice illusion of space, and the mos-quito-netted metal-framed beds (à la Crate & Barrel) are an interesting touch. So is the original art and paintings on the walls—always wel-come, in our book. Rooms feature a/c, ceiling fan, direct-dial phone, satellite TV, CD/DVD player (with available library), safe, and—are you ready for this—590-thread-count Linea Casa sheets. During high season, guests have the use of an open bar (we like that!).

Downstairs, as we mentioned, is Citrus, one of the Dutch side's best restaurants (and the other, Temptation, is just down the street). Also downstairs is the Market at Cupecoy, a groovy gourmet food store that is open daily. Closed late August to late October.

Mary's Boon, 117 Simpson Bay Road, St. Maarten, NA. ℭ 599-545-7000, ✆ 599-545-3403, 🖳 www.marysboon.com, info@marysboon.com

💲 **Pricey** ⓨ **EP** 🆑 36 rooms

Sandwiched between a terrific, 2-mile-long beach and the island's main runway, Mary's Boon is a unique inn catering to a loyal follow-ing that doesn't seem to mind the occasional thunder of jumbo jets overhead and next door on the runway (the owners seem impervious to the disruption). Even though the beach here is stunning, we're not so sure we wouldn't mind.

The hotel has a storied history. It was built by the legendary Mary Pomeroy, a true island character who owned Nisbet Plantation Inn on nearby Nevis, guarding her property from government interlopers with a shotgun. After she was run off of Nevis, Pomeroy headed to St. Maarten in 1970 and built Mary's Boon, running this beachcomber inn for more than a decade until she finally disappeared in her self-piloted plane (oh, Amelia). In 1999, Hurricane Lenny swept the place off the face of the earth, leaving little more than foundation in its wake. The new owners rebuilt, and they managed to revive the inn's former homey ambiance.

Although some might find this place charming, we find all the signs, statuettes, and fountains a bit too cute. In addition, does the term *time-share* scare you? As you know, it scares us, and Mary's Boon has been a time-share—excuse us, vacation-ownership—property since 1997. You are forewarned. That said, this place ranks highly in the Reader's Choice Awards from *Condé Nast Traveler*. The rooms are decorated in tropical colors and four-poster beds and furniture from

Bali, with tile floor, a/c, direct-dial phone, ceiling fan, kitchenette, and satellite TV. Beachfront units have fabulous views up and down the beach, and a quartet of rooms in the basement—yes, the basement!—offers budget options for those who don't need a window on life. Okay, they're not as bad as we make them sound, and they're a decent value if you're looking for a cheap crash-pad while connecting through Juliana to another isle. The barefoot ambiance is well countered by the attentive Texan owner-managers, and the restaurant has featured food by the same chef for three decades. The inn's honor bar is a treasured long-standing asset.

Pasanggrahan Royal Guest House, P.O. Box 151, Philipsburg, St. Maarten, NA. 📞 599-542-3588, 📠 599-542-2885, 🖥 www.pasanhotel.com

💲 **Not So Cheap** 🍴 **EP** CC 28 rooms

We sort of love the Pasanggrahan Royal Inn, a classic West Indian guesthouse and the oldest lodging on the island, located at the east end (the best part) of Philipsburg and right on the beach at Great Bay. The Pasanggrahan is kinda funky, so don't expect too much. In fact, why anyone would want to stay in Philipsburg, except maybe to meet a boat or ship (the main pier is within walking distance), is beyond us—as they say, "different strokes for different folks." It was originally a 19th-century governor's house, and accommodations were built for Queen Wilhelmina on one of her periodic tours through the Dutch Caribbean. The least expensive rooms are decorated in wicker and have a balcony or patio; all are air-conditioned. Deluxe and "specialty" rooms are worth the few dollars extra and add kitchenettes and four-poster beds trimmed in lace from Saba. Spring for the Queen's Room, an irresistible glimpse into turn-of-the-century elegance. Afternoon tea and beach service is available; the restaurant is disappointing, but there are plenty of other options nearby.

⊛ Where to Eat

Mon Dieu! So many choices! St. Martin has become the foodie capital of the Caribbean. The restaurant scene here surpasses even that of St. Barth in quantity and variety. Gourmands should consider St. Martin the ultimate tropical vacation. It has really come into its own, with the focus being ⊛ Grand Case on the French side. Here's a smattering of favorites, but note that with more than 300 restaurants in business, it doesn't hurt to ask around when you arrive to find out what's new and hot.

Note that due to the recent spike in the value of the euro to the dollar, going out to eat at finer restaurants will push most dinners to well over $50 per person. During our last visit—when the euro was worth $1.21—some restaurants were offering a 1-to-1 euro-to-dollar exchange rate. This is no guarantee of better food than the next joint, but the price may be cheaper. This is the island where splurging on food is warranted and rewarded, so you're better off if you come prepared to pay for it.

French Side – Grand Case

$$$ **Bombay Brasserie**, 147 Boulevard de Grand Case, 590-590-29-67-20

This is a very good Indian restaurant, for those in curry *tabanca* (*tabanca* is West Indian for "jones"). An authentic charcoal-fired Tandoor oven keeps the tastes and aromas savory. Open nightly.

$$ **The Bounty**, next to the pharmacy on road to Orient, Grand Case, 590-590-87-16-11

A terrific gourmet food, cheese, and wine store (also booze) that has delicious takeout prepared foods, pizzas (local delivery in the evening), sandwiches, fresh baguettes, and croissants. If you don't feel like cooking and don't feel like dining out, this is the place to go. We wish we had The Bounty in our neighborhood back home.

$$ **Calmos Café**, 40 Boulevard de Grand Case, 590-590-29-01-85

Our favorite place on St. Martin to watch the sunset, this ultra-cool shack-cum-café of sand floors, chaises, and bistro and picnic tables is located literally feet from the water and serves up great sandwiches, salads, and burgers to accompany requisite sunset libations. Calmos also plays wicked music (sometimes live in winter), and has a barefoot *branché* that's missing from most places on this crowded island. Open for lunch and dinner.

$$$$$ **Fish Pot**, 82 Boulevard de Grand Case, Grand Case, 590-590-87-50-88

An old Grand Case institution with an oddly un-French name, the Fish Pot serves up very good French cuisine in a seaside setting. Some say this is more tourist-oriented than other Grand Case restaurants, but the chefs still have it down. Open for lunch and dinner daily.

$$$ **La California**, 134 Boulevard de Grand Case, 590-590-87-55-57

Situated right on the beach, this is a fun and very affordable pizza and pasta place featuring wood-fired ovens. The traditional buckwheat crepes are well-known, and there's a great choice of salads, too. Fair prices make the restaurant popular. Open daily for lunch and dinner (recommended for lunch).

$$$$$ **Le Cottage**, 97 Boulevard de Grand Case, 590-590-29-03-30

Another of our favorites, Bruno Lemoine's French eatery boasts one of the most extensive wine lists on the island; quite a few wines are available by the glass. Not to be missed is the house specialty: homemade foie gras served on toast, or as a tart with cocoa and mango (it's as extraordinary as it sounds). The Grand Case lobster raviolis in a basil and ginger sauce and the crispy veal sweetbread in a puff pastry and porcini mushroom sauce is also delectable. Totally evil is *le guet-apen*, the "chocolate dessert." Open nightly during high season (closed early October and Sunday in low season). Reservations are a must.

$$$$$ Le Pressoir, 30 Boulevard de Grand Case, Grand Case, 590-590-87-76-62

Superb traditional French cuisine is served in this adorable restaurant. Try the cold cream of pumpkin soup, the sliced foie gras with port, or the grilled snapper in a fresh vanilla sauce. Open for dinner only, closed Sunday during low season. Reservations are a must.

$$$$$ Le Tastevin, 86 Boulevard de Grand Case, 590-590-87-55-45

Look for the blue awning of this delightful restaurant on the beach, with an excellent wine list and delicious French repasts. Try the iced cucumber and chives cream soup and the fresh fish in licorice butter. Open daily for lunch and dinner. Reservations are a must for dinner.

$$$ Le Ti' Coin Créole, Boulevard de Grand Case (Route de Petite Plage), 590-590-87-92-09

This is a cute little place on the road to the Grand Case Beach Club. Owner and chef Carl serves up *delicieuse* local Creole fare of conch, fish, goat, and chicken — and a fab pecan torte — at *marveleuse* prices. Open daily for lunch and dinner.

$$$$$ L'Escapade, 94 Boulevard de Grand Case, Grand Case, 590-590-87-75-04

This is an established, family-run restaurant with wonderful French food and excellent fish. The intimate setting, on the water in the town's oldest house, is quite lovely. Open daily for lunch and dinner; closed Saturday night in low season.

$-$$ lolos (Talk of the Town, Germain's, Rib Palace), Grand Case, no phone

One of the most popular ways to eat in St. Martin is the *lolo* — basically a food stand with barbecue and bar — several of which are clustered on the beachfront in the center of Grand Case. There are tables and service under a canopy, and the whole atmosphere, despite a recent government effort to spiff up (and sanitize) these *lolos*, still has a semblance of beach-shack, open-air casual (because they are open-air stands, albeit newer ones). You can get grilled lobster, chicken, and ribs for next to nothing. Well, the lobster's not cheap, but it's affordable (around $20). Always busy and open for lunch and dinner daily.

$$$$$ Rainbow Café, 176 Boulevard de Grand Case, Grand Case, 590-590-87-55-80

Long one of the most popular restaurants on the island, Rainbow offers casual elegant dining right above the beach (cleverly lighted to highlight the gentle surf—talk about *très romantique*); this is still one of our favorites. The view of Anguilla over the rolling sea is wonderful, and the French food with Italian and Creole accents is always delicious. Try the superb red snapper with a parmesan-onion crust. Reservations are a must.

$$$$$ Spiga, 4 Route de l'Espérance, Grande Case, 590-590-52-47-83

This Italian spot is a refreshing and superb change of cuisine from the tyranny of French restaurants in Grand Case (not that we're complaining). Located on the Espérance airport road near the entrance of Hotel L'Esplanade, Lara and Ciro Russo's small trattoria serves fab fresh pastas and excellent risottos. Try the Chilean sea bass with lobster crust and carrot sauce. Open nightly. Reservations are a must.

$$–$$$ Sunset Café, Grand Case, 590-590-87-51-87

The restaurant at Grand Case Beach Club is a scenic spot *sur la mer pour petit dejeuner* (for breakfast by the sea). The lunch and dinner menus are quite good, too—the mussels in white wine are a specialty. Open daily.

French Side—Marigot, Sandy Ground, and Baie Nettlé

$$$$ Don Camillo, 68 Marina Port la Royale, Marigot, 590-590-87-52-88

If you are in the mood for Italian in a pretty setting and with great service, this little charmer is the place. Open nightly except Sunday.

$$ La Main à la Pâte, Marina Port la Royale, Marigot, 590-590-87-71-19

Our friend Dorothy raves about this place, especially for lunch. It's delightful and serves excellent pizzas and salads. Closed Sunday.

$$ L'Arhawak, Front de Mer, Marigot, 590-590-87-99-67

We like this place primarily to sit at the outside bar and watch both the characters sitting at the bar (there are always a few) and the passersby. It's open for lunch and dinner; the food is OK (and provides something for the alcohol to land on) and is reasonably priced, with a streetside barbeque à la Bar de la Mer (which closed in 2005).

$$$$ Le Bistro Nu, Allée de l'Ancienne Geôle, Marigot, 590-590-87-97-09

Pricier than it used to be, this petite one-room restaurant still serves good French bistro food, but we think there are better alternatives elsewhere. Open daily except Sunday for lunch and dinner.

$$$$$ Le Chanticler, 19 Marina Port la Royale, Marigot, 590-590-87-94-60

With excellent French haute cuisine and wonderful desserts, this

10-year-old spot in the marina is a romantic treat. Open nightly. Reservations are suggested.

$$$$ **Le Tropicana**, Marina Port la Royale, Marigot, 590-590-87-79-07

This typical and small French brasserie has a nice view of the boats in the marina. The food here is quite good and the prices are decent. Seafood dishes are a specialty, and be sure to order the yummy *frites*. Open for lunch and dinner. Reservations suggested.

$$$ **Maï**, 161 Rue de Hollande, Marigot, 590-590-77-18-74

The island's best Vietnamese cuisine (there aren't too many of this option on St. Martin) is surprisingly good. Situated on the second floor with terrace dining, Maï is actually an extension of the hostess and owner's home, in more ways than one. This place, and Maï herself, is unique and an experience. We were ushered into her living area (just off the terrace) to wait for her. Sitting on the settee, we were riveted by all the paintings and portraits of her, as we were with the woman herself (and the motion-sensing croaking frog). It is a beauty of unknown years (we don't dare guess), and dining here is an unforgettable experience.

$$$$$ **Mario's Bistro**, Route des Terres Basses (just east of the bridge), Sandy Ground, 590-590-87-06-36

This is among the hardest places on the island to get a reservation. Quebec-born Mario helmed the kitchens at Rainbow, Fish Pot, and Chez Martine before establishing this romantic canalside bistro in 1995. You can't go wrong with its French and Indonesian flair — *if* you can get in (and good luck securing a waterside table). The ingredients used in this totally delicious cuisine are among the freshest on the island. Reservations are a must (two seatings). Closed Sunday and mid-June through August.

$$$ **O Plongoire**, Marina Fort-Louis, 590-590-87-94-71

This is a reasonably priced place by the West Indies Mall, with a funky-chic casual atmosphere. A good place for a break from shopping, it's open for breakfast, lunch, and dinner.

$$ **Zee Best**, Marina Port la Royale, Marigot, 590-590-87-27-51

Pastries, fresh-squeezed juices, coffee — what more do you need? This is the best breakfast spot in Marigot. Open daily for breakfast and lunch.

French Side — Orient, Mont Vernon

$$$ **Bikini Beach**, Baie Orientale, 590-590-87-43-25

A tapas bar and grill, Bikini is marked by a glowing white Buddha statue and has fabulous fried calamari. The Oasis Bar, in front, is as nice a place as any to hang out with a cocktail and soak up the refreshing trade winds while listening to great music.

$$$ Kontiki, Baie Orientale, 590-590-87-43-27

In the heart of topless (as opposed to totally nude) Orient Beach, Kontiki is a South Seas beach bar with a decent menu of salads, grilled fish and chicken, and excellent sushi. It can be quite a scene. Closed in September.

$$ Le P'tit Cul de Sac, Route de Cul de Sac (across from the Texaco station), 590-590-87-40-41

This is the best to-go pizza joint, and it delivers in the Grand Case area for free. Open for lunch and dinner, or until they feel like closing; closed Saturday and on Sunday afternoon.

$$$$$ Sol é Luna, Mont Vernon, 590-590-29-08-56

This beautifully decorated eatery has a distinctly Provençal atmosphere and a satisfying Italian menu. The wraparound lanai with views of Orient Bay and soothing trade winds makes this a very romantic place to dine. Open nightly; closed September.

French Side – Pic Paradis

$$$ The Hidden Forest Café at Loterie Farm, Route de Pic Paradis, 590-590-87-86-16

Run by a transplanted Canadian couple on the grounds of an old sugar plantation, this is the other St. Martin of long ago — quiet and serene. It is situated in a fabulous and magical spot, especially at night (it's in a valley surrounded by darkness and the sounds of tree frogs — no traffic noise here. Try Julia's curry spinach chicken — it's delicious — or the beef with onion-garlic relish. Prices are very reasonable for St. Martin. Open for lunch and dinner from Tuesday through Saturday and for brunch on Sunday from noon to 6 p.m. Reservations suggested. No credit cards accepted.

Dutch Side

$$ Au Petit Café, 120 Old Street, Philipsburg, 599-552-7070

We adore this oasis among the shopping hordes, tucked away on a quiet side street off the "good part" (the east end) of Front Street. There are tables inside and out, and daily specials, fresh salads, omelettes, crepes, panini, and homemade ice cream. Cold beer and frozen drinks will cool you off, and delicious coffees and teas will wake you up. Open daily.

$$$$ Captain Oliver's, Oyster Pond, 599-525-0240

Part of a resort complex, the restaurant at Captain Oliver's is known for its Saturday night lobster buffet; it's also great for families. It can be a bit hokey, but there is lots to do and see here. Part of the restaurant has a glass floor, so you can look down at the marine life in the sea below (the restaurant mercifully does not play the theme music to *Jaws*), or you can watch swimmers in the "people aquarium." There is also a mini-zoo, with toucans, parrots, iguanas, an alligator, and sea turtles (Captain Oliver's is a designated rehab center for injured — not drunk or high — sea turtles). Reservations are advised.

$$$$ Citrus, 130 Lowlands, Cupecoy, 599-545-4333

One of the two best restaurants on the Dutch side (the other is Temptation), Citrus is known for its imaginative, French-inspired cuisine and is set in a pretty space of earthy red and gold tones. Chef Jeffrey Kipp's creative use of fresh ingredients is worth the trip (although we've heard comments that the service could be improved). Open nightly. Reservations are a must.

$ La Casa del Habano, 24 Front Street, Philipsburg, 599-543-1001

This is the place for Great Cuban coffee (and, of course, Cuban cigars). A few tables on Front Street are perfect for those who are averse to smoke. For those who aren't, a walk-in humidor keeps the cigars at the ready. Enjoy! Open daily.

$$$ La Gondola, Lowlands, 599-595-3938

Formerly located in Sandy Ground, now based at the Atlantis Casino, this is the best place on the island for homemade pasta. Its very involved chef-owner cooks a long list of delicious, fresh pasta dishes and delectable fish and meat entrees; you won't go wrong. Open nightly.

$$ Lal's Indian Cuisine, Airport Road, Simpson Bay, 599-557-9059

This curry bar, located on the water across from Juliana International Airport, is a great place to stop for those in curry *tabanca* (the curry "jones"), when you have time to kill at the airport or need some nutrition from the Simpson Bay area pub crawl. Try Lal's drinks, named after rock stars, and don't miss Lal's fun happy-hour. Open till 11 daily.

$$ Mark's Place, Food Center Shopping Mall, Philipsburg, 599-543-2625

We like this place for its reasonably priced West Indian food, and so do all the locals who come here in droves. Most visitors skip it because it's in the most unglamorous of locations, and few tourists even see it (as you head west out of Philipsburg toward the airport, it's located where you make the left turn to go over Cole Bay Hill, in the shopping center on the left). Try the octopus stew or curried goat for a real taste of the West Indies.

$$ **Paris Bistro**, Maho Plaza, Maho Bay, 599-545-5677

Set amid casinos and clubs, this brasserie is a welcome alternative to the hubbub around it. A diverse French menu should satisfy most palates, and the outdoor terrace dining can be a fun spot from which to watch the surrounding commotion. There's live solo jazz on Sunday, Tuesday, and Wednesday. Open nightly.

$$$$$ Saratoga, Simpson Bay Lagoon, 599-544-2421

This pretty dining spot at the Simpson Bay Yacht Club on the Dutch side is a good choice when you're on this part of the island. The fish is always fresh and is prepared in a variety of contemporary ways. Open nightly except Sunday.

$$ **Saveurs de France**, 114 Old Street, Philipsburg, 599-542-3916

Another oasis next to Au Petit Café, it serves delicious croissants, pastries, cafés, quiches, patés, and sandwiches. It's also a great little market for wine, cheese, and baguettes. Open daily.

$$$$$ Temptation, Atlantis Casino, 599-545-2254

The most highly acclaimed restaurant on the Dutch side, Temptation brings the big-city groovy dining experience to the Caribbean. The nouveau Caribbean-international fusion menu is simply to die for. For starters, try the grilled peach salad, then segue to the grilled yellowfin tuna in an Asian barbeque sauce with wasabi mashed potatoes and spicy arugula salad. This is a perfect special occasion place and a great spot to pop the question (ask the pianist to "Play It Again, Sam"). Open nightly.

$$ **Top Carrot**, Airport Road (next to the Royal Village Complex), Simpson Bay, 599-544-3381

Situated near Juliana Airport at the junction of the Philipsburg-Marigot roads, this is a good choice for vegetarians and is also a health food store. Open for breakfast, and lunch is served until 6 p.m. Closed Sunday.

Going Out

Aside from the casinos on the Dutch side (we're not too keen on them — we've never even been to Foxwoods!), there are some fun places to go out and kick it up on both the French side and the Dutch side. The key to good times is the weekly K-PASA guides, with up-to-the-minute info on where to boogie-oogie-oogie. It's available almost everywhere you look (pick one up at the airport when you arrive). Usually there is a rotating schedule of which bar or club is the place to go on a given night, as well as a comprehensive list of happy hours.

On the French side, **Boo Boo Jam** (590-590-29-42-20), on Orient Beach, is a hopping spot on Friday and Saturday evenings, often with live music. **L'Alibi** (590-590-87-08-39) is the island's gay bar, located in Marigot, and it revs up late (well after midnight), with a plugged-in DJ keeping the dance floor happy. In Grand Case, **Bye Bar Brazil** (590-590-87-76-49) also kicks up later — check out the great selection of single malt whiskeys. The Monday night hot spot is **Le Cohibar** (590-590-40-59-00) in Baie Nettlé. On Tuesday night, Grand Case becomes a street scene when the main boulevard is closed to vehicular traffic and opened for vendors, crafts sellers, and live music.

On the Dutch side, the **Sunset Beach Bar** (599-545-3998) is an afternoon scene — how many other places can you loll in translucent water and watch a jumbo coming in for a landing about 50 feet overhead? Sunday is the big day, but there's a surfboard/blackboard with landing times for the afternoon jets, so you'll never need to worry about missing a KLM 747. The Tuesday night scene is dominated by the **Green House Café** (599-542-2941), located at Bobby's Marina. **Bamboo Bernie's** (599-545-3622) at the Caravanserai Resort is good on Wednesday, but the open-air **Bliss** (599-545-3996), also located at Caravanserai, takes the honors as the coolest scene. It has four-poster beds, tents ringed with throw pillows, and evocative lanterns — sort of a South Beach–meets–Morocco cocktail lounge. Bliss is especially fun (post-midnight) on Thursday with DJ and live music. The **Lady C Floating Bar** (599-544-4710) is very popular with crew members from visiting yachts, especially on Friday. Also although we didn't do it, the **Lagoon Pub Crawl** on board the 40-foot catamaran *Celine* (599-545-3961) looks like a blotto time (let us know). A couple other Dutch-side places worth investigating are **Cheri's Café** (599-545-3361), across from the Maho complex, an immensely popular burger and steak place with good live music nightly except Tuesday; and **Indiana Beach** (599-544-2797), an Indiana Jones–theme joint that draws a lot of Americans and other visitors for dancing. Located above the Casino Royale in Maho is **The Q Club** (599-523-7157), which has a busy dance floor on weekends.

Don't Miss

Orient Beach

This is the island's official nude beach, and although it's not the best beach on the island, it's certainly the most famous. There is, of course, the nudie resort Club Orient (see Where to Stay, above), and next door are concessions that sell crafts, T-shirts, and food (including crêpes). It's a reasonably long strand, and even though most sunbathers are no more than top-free, the funny thing is that there are people who are totally naked browsing next to people who are totally clothed. In addition to ample water toys rented on the beach — kite boards, windsurf gear, and parasailing boats, just for starters — Orient has grown quite a few beach bars and restaurants during the 1990s, and it has become *the* place to hang out during the day.

Cupecoy Beach

The most unique beach on the island is suffering from development, and the unofficial nudie section at the north end might be inaccessible by the time you read this, due to a pair of building projects. However, the unique rose-colored bluffs are still there, as well as the nooks and caves carved out by the sea (note that the sand comes and goes seasonally—it's widest from about Christmas until May or so). The Cliffhanger Bar, a great spot for sunset libations, is reached by a walkway next to the Cupecoy Beach Club, but don't leave valuables in your car—we hear stories of car break-ins here all the time. Cupecoy is also the island's gay beach, but lots of families share the sand, too.

St. Maarten's 12-Meter Challenge

Though geared to cruise-ship visitors, this is still a pretty nifty attraction—a chance to crew aboard a genuine America's Cup racing yacht. The fleet of five vessels were built for the 1987 event in Australia, and one is Dennis Conner's winner, *Stars and Stripes*. Once on board you'll be assigned a position to man, and your yacht will race one or more of the other vessels, tacking and jibing along the island's south coast. The three-hour tours are based out of Philipsburg, and reservations are advised; the cost is $70 to $90 per person. Information: 599-542-0045; www.12metre.com.

Spa

The spa at La Samanna is fabulous (so is the resort). Treat yourself and have a drink at the pool bar. Jackie O stayed here in the '70s.

Gym

If you need to amp-up the bis, tris, and pecs for the beach, the Princess Port de Plaisance complex has the best health club on the island. It also has a spa.

Vinissimo

When in France, one must indulge in wine, and when in St. Martin, stop by this wonderful wine store located in an industrial park on the south side of Marigot. You'll find lots of bottles that are not typically imported into the United States. There are wine tastings on Thursday.

Club 241

This is the infamous "exchangist" club (read: sex and party) in the Lowlands. People fly in from all over for it. To find out more, call 590-590-87-10-66, or visit www.4swinging.com/DESTINATIONS/club241.htm. It's quite a conversation item!

St. Vincent

Other islands claim to preserve the Caribbean the way it used to be; St. Vincent actually lives it. The island's somewhat ramshackle capital, Kingstown (not to be confused with Jamaica's Kingston), has weathered wooden guesthouses and a colorful marketplace with gaping fish and colorful fruit for sale; cruise ships and their passengers are not part of the scene. An agricultural economy predominates, and large portions of St. Vincent remain undeveloped. There are no real white-sand beaches, so the island has minimal tourism infrastructure. Visitors are usually steered to the nearby Grenadines, an idyllic archipelago to the south — most of these islands are linked to St. Vincent politically (and the nation is properly referred to as St. Vincent and the Grenadines, as most islanders will cheerfully point out). Covered in separate chapters, the Grenadines have more conventional tourist appeal, the government reasons, so the main island is left relatively untouched. When producers of the movie *White Squall* were looking for a spot that could represent the West Indies of the 1960s, they chose St. Vincent for much of their location shooting.

The flip side of this seeming bucolia is that the island is struggling under the weight of its banana-based economy. The World Trade Organization took the side of the United States (and American banana-exporting companies) in its "banana war" with the European Union (which tried to protect the more

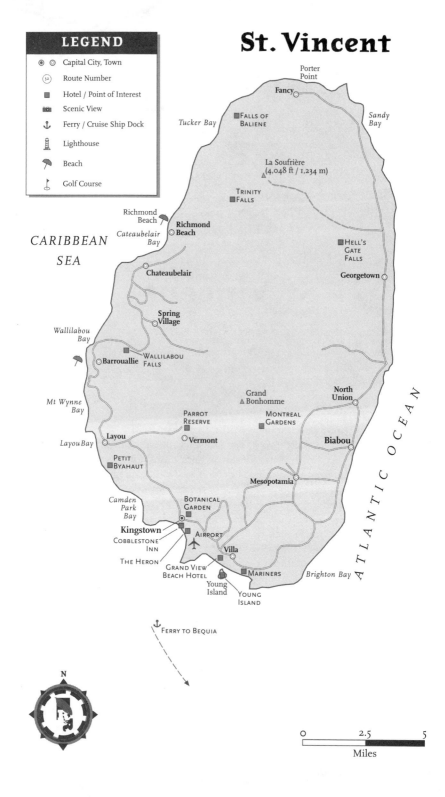

St. Vincent

LEGEND

◉ ○ Capital City, Town

⬡ Route Number

■ Hotel / Point of Interest

▦ Scenic View

⚓ Ferry / Cruise Ship Dock

🗼 Lighthouse

🏖 Beach

🚩 Golf Course

Porter
Point

Fancy

Tucker Bay

■ FALLS OF
BALIENE

Sandy
Bay

La Soufrière
▲ (4,048 ft / 1,234 m)

CARIBBEAN
SEA

TRINITY
■ FALLS

Richmond
Beach

Cateaubelair
Bay

Richmond
○ Beach

■ HELL'S
GATE
FALLS

○ Chateaubelair

Georgetown

Spring
○ Village

Wallilabou
Bay

WALLILABOU
○ Barrouallie FALLS

Mt Wynne
Bay

Grand
▲ Bonhomme

North
Union

PARROT
■ RESERVE

MONTREAL
■ GARDENS

Layou Bay

○ Layou

○ Vermont

Biabou

PETIT
■ BYAHAUT

Mesopotamia

Camden
Park
Bay

BOTANICAL
■ GARDEN

Kingstown
COBBLESTONE
INN

AIRPORT

THE HERON

GRAND VIEW
BEACH HOTEL

✈

Villa

■ MARINERS

Brighton Bay

Young
Island

YOUNG
ISLAND

ATLANTIC OCEAN

⚓ FERRY TO BEQUIA

N

0   2.5   5
Miles

St. Vincent: Key Facts

Location	13°N by 61°W 2,040 miles/3,283 kilometers southeast of New York 100 miles/161 kilometers west of Barbados 75 miles/121 kilometers north of Grenada
Size	133 square miles/344 square kilometers
Highest point	La Soufrière, 4,048 feet/1,234 meters
Population	97,486
Language	English
Time	Atlantic Standard Time (1 hour ahead of EST, same as EDT)
Area code	784
Electricity	220 volts AC, 50 cycles, so you'll need to bring an adapter and transformer for laptops and electric shavers.
Currency	The Eastern Caribbean dollar, EC$ (EC$2.68 = US$1)
Driving	On the left; you'll need a temporary permit. Just present your valid U.S. or Canadian driver's license and pay the $28 fee (!) for a local license.
Documents	U.S. and Canadian citizens must have a passport; all visitors must hold a return or an ongoing ticket.
Departure tax	$15
Beer to drink	Hairoun
Rum to drink	Any Vincentian brand
Music to hear	Dancehall
Tourism info	800-729-1726 www.svgtourism.com

expensive banana exports of its members' former colonies). Furthermore, the United States has devoted plenty of manpower toward eradicating a certain leafy herb (canonized by Cheech & Chong and a popular export to the United States) from Vincentian soil. Luckily (for St. Vincent, at least) the efforts to quash marijuana appear to have been put on hold. However, considering that these two items have been the number one and number two cash crops on the island for decades, this double whammy did not endear Americans to locals, and it can be felt in the somewhat brusque interactions that have become commonplace.

That said, adventurous travelers who head off the beaten track will find dramatic scenery, great hiking, a good array of less expensive hotels, and real West Indian charm. All of this adds up to a pretty special package: an island that shows few of the scars of modern tourism that some of its neighbors wear.

It might be one of the last West Indian islands to be stepping into the 21st century, but St. Vincent has an irresistible backwater appeal that is getting hard to find in the increasingly packaged-for-the-masses Caribbean.

The Briefest History

St. Vincent's first residents were the Ciboney Indians, who arrived by canoe from South America and were followed by the Arawaks and then the Caribs. The latter were a tenacious bunch and overwhelmed their predecessors. Columbus cruised by St. Vincent in 1498, although historians are unsure whether he actually saw the island, let alone came ashore. Legend has it that the Caribs were ferocious enough to keep subsequent explorers away for almost two centuries (those who visited the island did not find a red carpet rolled out). In the late 1700s, the Caribs, British, and French battled for control of St. Vincent; in fact, as the Caribs were defeated on neighboring islands, survivors made their way to St. Vincent, swelling the Indian ranks. Then escaped slaves from Barbados sailed to St. Vincent and mixed with the Indians to form a fierce tribe known as the Black Caribs. The Europeans and Indians fought for control of the island for decades, until 1797, when the British successfully dominated the Black Caribs and deported 5,000 of their ranks to the island of Roatan (near Honduras) — not a very PC maneuver. The remaining Caribs retreated to the northeast shore of the island. (A few descendants of the Caribs still live around Sandy Town, and the Caribbean Organization of Indigenous People is based on St. Vincent.)

By the 19th century, a plantation economy thrived, and sugar, cotton, cocoa, and coffee were the primary products. In 1812 La Soufrière erupted and damaged much of the island; an eruption in 1902 caused even more devastation, killing 2,000 people. After the emancipation of the slaves, East Indians and Portuguese indentured servants came in to work the plantations, and their descendants are part of the island's multicultural makeup today. Britain granted St. Vincent and the Grenadines statehood in 1979; today it is an independent state within the British Commonwealth, with 8 percent of the population living on the Grenadines.

Getting There

Although American Eagle flies to Canouan in the Grenadines, St. Vincent's small E.T. Joshua Airport can be reached only on small prop planes. Caribbean Sun has a daily flight from San Juan; LIAT and Caribbean Star fly to St. Vincent from Antigua, Barbados, and other neighboring islands. SVG Air, TIA, and Mustique Airways fly in from the Grenadines and Barbados. St. Vincent's airport is conveniently located between Kingstown, the capital, and Villa, the primary hotel area — within a ten-minute drive of each.

Getting Around

The good news is that almost all of St. Vincent's hotels and restaurants are concentrated around the island's southern tip. The bad news is that the roads are rough and driving is on the left. However, there are a few small car-rental firms on the island; in Kingstown try David's Auto Clinic (784-456-4026); near the airport and handling Jeeps is Ben's Auto Rental (784-456-2907); and Avis Rent-a-Car is at the airport (800-331-1212 or 784-456-4389). Prices are high, starting at about $48 per day, or about $70 for a jeep. A taxi ride from the airport to any of the hotels in Kingstown or Villa is about $7.

If you just want to spend a day sightseeing, it might be easier to hire a taxi. We've had good luck with Sam's Taxi Tours (784-456-4338). Alternatively, you can use the local minibus service, particularly for trips between the Villa area and Kingstown. Fares are rarely higher than $2; note that service to the north, beyond Barrouallie on the west coast and Georgetown on the east, is rare. For travel into the Grenadines by speedboat, contact Fantasea Tours, located in Villa opposite Young Island (784-457-4477).

Day trips to Bequia are easy using the ferries that depart from St. Vincent — there are as many as eight daily departures (service is more limited on weekends). The crossing takes one hour, and the first ferry leaves Kingstown at 8 a.m.; the last one leaves Bequia at 5 p.m. One-way fare is $6; same-day round-trip fare is $10. There are also ferries to the southern islands, discussed in the Grenadines chapters, but day trips are not possible.

Focus on St. Vincent: The Hike to La Soufrière

This is a day trip that will both please and exhaust the most energetic: a hike up the Soufrière volcano on the northern end of the island. Other than Montserrat's English Crater, St. Vincent's Soufrière has been the region's most actively monitored volcano in recent years; an eruption in 1902 caused 2,000 deaths, and in 1979, 20,000 were evacuated when the crater rumbled to life and deposited a layer of ash across the northern half of the island (everyone returned home safe and sound that time). The flip side of this is that La Soufrière keeps St. Vincent lush, green, and fertile (the ash makes for great soil). The volcano has been relatively quiet for the last couple of decades, so pack your good walking shoes, water, an energy snack, and a windbreaker or sweatshirt. It's cool and windy at the top, and after the sweaty hike it will make your teeth chatter.

The traditional route to the summit climbs the eastern slope above Georgetown, about an hour's drive from Kingstown (another trail ascends the slopes from Richmond on the west side, but it is more arduous). From the Rabacca Dry River just beyond Georgetown, watch for the road that leads up through banana and coconut plantations. After about 2 miles on this rutted road, you'll reach the trailhead. From here it is a two-and-a-half-hour, moderately strenuous hike through bamboo forests and along misty ridges to the main crater rim — about 3,100 feet in elevation. The term *rim* is no exaggeration — you actually crawl up to the edge of the crater and peer over a sheer lip that drops hundreds of feet to the floor of the volcano. There used to be a rather large lake in the crater, but it is now only a semblance of its former self.

If you walk carefully along the rim to the right from the top of the path, you will find a rope pegged into the ground. It was put here by scientists who go down to take measurements on the activity deep inside the mountain. You can climb down on the rope (with some sort of protection for your hands) to roam around the crater floor. Before doing this, examine it carefully to make sure it's in good shape, and avoid putting your full weight on the rope (otherwise you might end up as a postscript on the hometown 11 o'clock news). Obviously, the climb back up to the crater rim is very tiring; before heading down, you should definitely think about whether you have the energy for the return trip up. After you've taken your pictures and refueled, the trip back down the main trail will be easier, and if you've been lucky enough to tackle the trek on a clear day, you'll come home with great pictures, too. La Soufrière actually comprises several overlapping craters, and the largest, horseshoe-shaped outer one rises to the right (north) and encompasses the volcano's highest point, but most people don't head up to this spot.

It is possible to hike La Soufrière on your own (the trail is relatively easy to follow), but a well-versed guide will provide valuable insight into the lush flora and fauna on the way up. Clint and Mildred Hazell at **HazECO Tours** (784-457-8634; www.hazecotours.com) are your best bet, offering several different versions of the trip at prices ranging from $70 to $140 per person, including lunch and transportation. They also offer bird-watching trips, excursions to the waterfalls, jeep safaris, and more (see below).

What Else to See

Less strenuous hiking trips visit other interesting sights on St. Vincent. The **Vermont Forest Nature Trail** climbs through the Buccament Valley, home to the endangered and beautiful St. Vincent parrot, a dazzling brown-and-gold bird with a white head and tail feathers sporting a rainbow of colors. There are only about 800 in the wild, but conservation efforts are beginning to pay off. The trailhead is just above the town of Vermont and leads to a 1.5-mile loop that traverses the serene tropical rainforest on the slopes of 3,000-foot Grand Bonhomme. There's a viewing area halfway around the loop, and at dawn or just before sunset you have a good chance of spotting the parrots winging through.

Another worthwhile hike visits **Trinity Falls**, set deep in a lush canyon below La Soufrière's western flank. The trailhead is found by driving the leeward coast road through Chateaubelair to the Richmond Vale Academy, where a side road leads about a mile farther, eventually to become a four-wheel-drive track. Follow this path into the valley to the falls, about a 45-minute trek. A hot spring, which emerged after the 1979 eruption of La Soufrière, is a recent addition to the remote canyon. Another waterfall that's even more isolated is the **Falls of Baleine**, located on the north coast of the island and reachable only by boat. The 60-foot falls aren't as impressive as Trinity, but on a clear day the boat trip along these undeveloped shores can be quite invigorating.

Kingstown is worth at least a half-day of exploration. Of particular note is the **Botanical Gardens**, which are located on a hillside just north of town. This 20-acre garden is the oldest in the Western Hemisphere, dating back to 1762. You'll find teak, mahogany, and cannonball trees, as well as breadfruit trees descended from the seedlings brought over by Captain Bligh. About three dozen St. Vincent parrots are found here in an aviary toward the back of the garden; the up-close scrutiny of these stunning birds is a rare privilege. Also check out **St. Mary's Catholic Cathedral**, an unexpected blend of Romanesque, Moorish, and Georgian architecture that was built in 1823. Market Square, right next to the harbor, bustles with activity on Friday and Saturday — it's quite photogenic, but remember to ask permission before snapping photos.

St. Vincent isn't known for its beaches, and the best ones are those of black sand. There are a number along the west coast, and the one at **Wallilabou** (used as the setting for Port Royal in the *Pirates of the Caribbean* movies) is particularly attractive; also try Cumberland Bay and remote Richmond Beach. Around Villa there are slivers of gray-brown beaches. Although these are sufficient for swimming, they aren't much to get excited about. If white-sand beaches are a prerequisite, head to Bequia or the other Grenadines.

Where to Stay

Accommodations on St. Vincent are concentrated between Kingstown and Villa, the mostly residential area facing Young Island.

Young Island, P.O. Box 211, Young Island, St. Vincent, WI. ✆ 800-223-1108 or 784-458-4826, ✆ 784-457-4567, 🖳 www.youngisland.com, youngisland@caribsurf.com

💲 **Wicked Pricey** 🍴 EP ⓒⓒ 28 rooms

If it's luxury you want, there's Young Island, the closest thing to a real resort "on" St. Vincent. Calling it a private island resort is a bit of an exaggeration: a Chappaquiddick-size swim, and you're practically in downtown Kingstown. Nevertheless, it is one of those service-and-sunshine places that are à la mode for some. In fact, Young's prices are a fair notch below those of other private island resorts in the Caribbean, so it does represent good value, especially considering the resort recently converted from its long-established MAP-only rate structure to one that allows for no meals. Since you won't save much (if any) money adding the meal plan to your package, we recommend the EP structure and sampling a few other Vincy restaurants during your stay.

The hotel sits on a 35-acre rock outcrop located about 200 yards off St. Vincent's Villa area. There's a trifling, some would say charming, boat that chugs back and forth across the channel all day. The rooms are in rock-walled cottages cooled by trade winds and ceiling fans; the decor has been spruced up, and the rooms are spacious and fairly private, with outdoor showers wrapped in volcanic stone and vines. Some are just above the water, others clamber over the rock, and four have private plunge pools. Diversions include tennis, a tropical pool, hammocks, a smallish white-sand beach with a swim-up bar floating just offshore, nonmotorized water sports, and a new spa. There is also a pair of 44-foot yachts available for overnight trips into the Grenadines — a good way to combine a resort and sailing vacation. The food is reliably good, if unspectacular, and service is attentive.

Grand View Beach Hotel, Villa Point, St. Vincent, WI. 📞 800-223-6510 or 784-458-4811, 📠 784-457-4174, 🖥 www.grandviewhotel.com, grandview@caribsurf.com

💲 **Pricey** 🍴 **EP** CC 19 rooms

This former cotton plantation house sits on a dramatic lava bluff overlooking Young Island and the beach at Villa — the setting lives up to the hotel's name, although the beach is pretty marginal. The rooms are not dressy but are decent, and some have nice views from their balconies. There's a very good restaurant serving island fare (Friday night is jerk night), tennis and squash courts, a well-appointed fitness center, and a small pool, and we love the contemporary art collection that has started to materialize on the walls. Open since 1964, the Grand View is well connected to the local political scene and is mainland St. Vincent's best-run property. Rates are higher than most in St. Vincent, but we've always found the welcome of owners Tony and Heather Sardine and their staff to be the most hospitable.

Mariner's, Villa Bay, St. Vincent, WI. 📞 800-223-1108 or 784-457-4000, 📠 784-457-4333, 🖥 www.marinershotel.com, marinershotel@caribsurf.com

💲 **Not So Cheap** 🍴 **EP** CC 20 rooms

Also facing Young Island, this inn packs quite a lot of style into its small property and has reasonable rates to boot. All rooms are bright and spacious, with a/c, cable TV, and a balcony; an Internet café is complimentary. Water sports and excursions are nearby. There is no beach, but the small shoreside swimming pool offers nice views, and French cuisine is served on the restaurant's delightful terrace.

Cobblestone Inn, P.O. Box 867, Kingstown, St. Vincent, WI. 📞 784-456-1937, 📠 784-456-1938, 🖥 www.thecobblestoneinn.com

💲 **Cheap** 🍴 **EP** CC 19 rooms

An easy walk from the ferry dock, this is a great spot to stay at if you want to catch the early boat to Bequia. The Cobblestone Inn is a classic

West Indian guesthouse, in a Georgian building that dates to 1814 or earlier — the cobblestone walkways and arches ooze history. The three-story building surrounds a small courtyard, and the rooms come in various sizes and design, most of which have been tastefully updated for today's travelers and feature Asian rugs and rattan furniture; two of the rooms have a/c. There's a rooftop bar, and downstairs is Basil's Restaurant, a Vincentian institution.

Also in Kingstown is **The Heron** (784-457-1631), another old guesthouse that was undergoing a major rebuilding project during our last visit.

Petit Byahaut, Petit Byahaut, St. Vincent, WI. *C* and ☏ 784-457-7008, 💻 outahere.com/petitbyahaut, petitbyahaut@caribsurf.com

💲 **Wicked Pricey** (includes water sports, guided hikes, airport transfer; three-night minimum required) **⑨ FAP** CC 5 tents

If you want to stay in a pristine 50-acre valley that is accessible only by boat, try this solar-powered establishment, where your room is a 10-by-13-foot floored tent with screened windows, queen-size bed, outdoor shower and flush toilet, and hammock. All rooms overlook the sea, fronted by a 500-foot black-sand beach. The rates include all meals and activities (including scuba and snorkeling equipment, kayaks, and Sunfish sailboats). There's a safari-style atmosphere (minus the big game), but this is a love-it-or-hate-it spot that seems overpriced to us. On the other hand, pairing it with a stint on Young Island would be a dream escape for some. Closed September and October.

Where to Eat

Despite the setting, St. Vincent is not a culinary paradise (although things are improving). Here's the best of a mediocre bunch.

$ **Aggie's**, Kingstown, 784-456-2110

Aggies is an informal lunch spot with a good West Indian selection, including roti, conch souse, curried beef or mutton, and pumpkin or callaloo soup.

$$$ **Basil's Bar and Restaurant**, Kingstown, 784-457-2597

The name of Mustique fame, this is a colorful island hangout with an all-you-can-eat buffet at lunch, and lobster, filet mignon, and grilled red snapper at dinner.

$$$$ **Lime Restaurant**, Villa, 784-458-4227

This is probably the island's most popular hangout, though a bit overpriced. The dinner menu includes grilled steaks, fish, and lobster (live in season, September to April). The local yachties tell us to try the African black pepper steak. There's also a cheaper pub menu available for lunch and dinner.

$ **Nice Food**, Kingstown, 784-456-1391

Situated beneath the Heron, a classic guesthouse near the ferry dock, this spot serves a full English breakfast and buffet Creole lunches.

$$$ **Pebbles**, Ra-wa-cou, 784-458-0190

Noel Frasier runs this unexpected find on the east coast of the island, above a small beach at Mount Pleasant. Frasier used to cook at American resorts and maintains an organic veggie garden for much of his produce. You'll find international dishes. Reservations are required.

$ **Vee Jay's**, Kingstown, 784-457-2845

This is a good place for an inexpensive West Indian lunch while you're touring the capital. It's located on Upper Bay Street.

$$$$ **Young Island**, Villa, 784-458-4826

The food is not stellar, but this is the place for a special meal (assuming you're not ensconced at Young Island already). The West Indian buffet on Wednesday and barbecue on Saturday are popular ($50 per person). Other nights, look for a limited entrée selection, served in a pretty open-air setting just off the beach.

Don't Miss

La Soufrière

The trek to the summit is one of the Caribbean's top hikes. The volcano has a major blowout about once a century, so catch it while it's still sleeping.

Vermont Nature Trails

This is a beautiful valley that is the most likely place you'll see the St. Vincent parrot in the wild (or even an iguana or armadillo).

The Botanical Gardens

The gardens are fair, but this is your best bet for viewing the St. Vincent parrot up close.

Bequia

Even if you only take a day trip, this is one of the region's most appealing islands at which to hang out, and it's easy to reach on the regular ferry from Kingstown. Be sure to bring along your bathing suit.

Trinidad
and Tobago

Like night and day and Jekyll and Hyde, the two-island nation of Trinidad and Tobago couldn't be more different. Trinidad is a major industrial and petroleum force in the Caribbean basin, with a dynamic energy level and a fast pace. Tobago is the sleepy cousin and much more typical of a West Indian island. Somehow they got stuck together in a political marriage, but each benefits from the other. Tobago gets the wealthier Trinidad to fund government services and build roads, schools, and bridges. Trinidadians use beautiful Tobago for weekend and holiday escapes. The relationship seems to work.

The islands are 21 miles apart and are located just off the coast of Venezuela. Only 7 miles separate Trinidad from Venezuela, and in fact both islands were once geographically connected to South America. Yet they are very West Indian in orientation. Trinidadian influences can be seen all over the Caribbean, both economically and culturally. Although there is diverse wildlife and an attractive cultural scene, for most travelers, Trinidad is interesting primarily for Carnival—the biggest in the Caribbean and the world's third largest after Rio de Janeiro and New Orleans. It will appeal to the adventurous party lover who revels in mass celebrations, calypso and pan music, and rubbing sweaty elbows with the local populace. By contrast, Tobago is a year-round destination that will appeal to the lover of quiet, very friendly, and rather undeveloped islands where few Americans roam. Both are located outside the hurricane belt, which makes them a good vacation option at the height of hurricane season (August through October).

The Briefest History

Trinidad was first settled by Amerindians thousands of years ago. When Columbus landed on the island on his third voyage, in 1498, he found several tribes living on Trinidad, including the familiar Arawaks and Caribs. The latter, who lived in the north, warded off colonization attempts until the late 1500s. Spain ruled Trinidad until 1797, when the British seized control. It was formally deeded to England in 1802. After the emancipation of the slaves in 1834, when labor opportunities developed, massive immigration from Europe and even the United States occurred. Then, there still being a demand for cheap labor, waves of indentured servants from India and China arrived. These immigration waves account for the unique racial and cultural makeup of Trinidad. Indeed, Trinidadians are among the most beautiful people we have ever seen.

Tobago was also sighted in 1498 by Columbus, who found Caribs inhabiting the island. They were observed growing tobacco, hence the name. No settlements were attempted until the mid-17th century. The island was contested for the next 100 years by the British, French, and Dutch. The British were deeded control in the Treaty of Paris in 1763.

Both islands were united under one government in 1888 as a Crown Colony of Britain. In 1962 Trinidad and Tobago gained their independence within the British Commonwealth, finally becoming a republic in 1976.

Trinidad

AS WE'VE MENTIONED ABOVE AND AS WE'LL MENTION BELOW, Trinidad is primarily about Carnival. In fact, the word *Carnival* is mentioned 52 times in the Trinidad section alone (feel free to count, but we've saved that task for our editor). So although there is culture and nature on this large island, if you're here, you're most likely here to spend a wild week jumping in the streets of Port of Spain. As you'll quickly learn, you *will* be jumping.

Getting There

Trinidad's Piarco International Airport is a major Caribbean gateway, located 17 miles east of Port of Spain. American flies to Trinidad from Miami; American Eagle and Caribbean Sun fly from San Juan; BWIA (which is based in Trinidad) flies nonstop from Miami, Toronto, and Washington, D.C.–Dulles; and Continental flies from Houston and Newark. Air Canada also flies in from Toronto. BWIA and British Airways fly nonstop from London. BWIA, Caribbean Star, and LIAT fly in from other Caribbean islands. Note that airline seats are at a premium during Carnival—ideally, make air arrangements several months in advance.

Getting Around

Most people come to Trinidad for Carnival, and taking a cab makes the most sense. Port of Spain is a 45-minute taxi ride from the airport, which will cost you about $25. You'll be in the city and walking everywhere, so there's no need for a car during Carnival. If you're coming at another time of year, a car is a worthwhile investment for exploring the spectacular north coast or the mountains. Rentals start at about $40 per day for a well-worn set of wheels. Avis (800-230-4898 or 868-628-8996), Hertz (800-654-3131 or 868-669-4332), and Thrifty's (800-847-4389 or 868-669-0602) have offices here, or check with one of the local firms at the airport, like Econo-Car Rentals (868-669-2342 or 868-669-1119), Kalloo's Auto Rental (868-669-5673) or Singh's Auto Rentals (868-669-5417 or 868-623-0150).

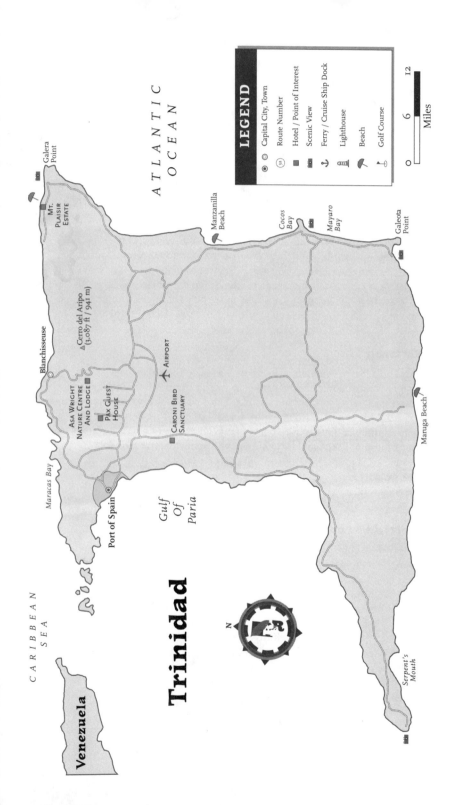

Trinidad: Key Facts

Location	10°N by 61°W 7 miles/11 kilometers east of Venezuela 2,250 miles/3,620 kilometers southeast of New York
Size	1,864 square miles/4,828 square kilometers 50 miles/80 kilometers long by 37 miles/60 kilometers wide
Highest point	Cerro del Aripo (3,087 feet/941 meters)
Population	1.25 million
Language	English, with many different accents
Time	Atlantic Standard Time year-round (1 hour ahead of EST, same as EDT)
Area code	868
Electricity	110 volts AC, 60 cycles
Currency	The Trinidad and Tobago dollar (TT$6.3 = US$1)
Driving	On the left; valid driver's license okay
Documents	A valid passport or proof of citizenship, plus an ongoing or a return ticket
Departure tax	$17
More taxes!	10% hotel, 10% service charge, 15% VAT on all goods and services
Beer to drink	Carib
Rum to drink	Vat 19
Music to hear	Calypso, pan, soca
Tourism info	800-816-7541 www.visitTNT.com

Focus on Trinidad: Boom-Boom Time — ⊛ Carnival in Port of Spain

Wine de boom-boom. It's the motto of Carnival. The "wine" is a wonderfully lewd grind of gyrating hips that would shame Elvis. It's usually — but not always — done in duos with both participants pressed together in any number of lascivious ways. The slower and more exaggerated, the better. *Boom-boom* is local slang for one's rear end — and Carnival, in the words of at least one past calypso hit, is boom-boom time. There are more pelvises pushed, shoved, and slammed in the last 48 hours of Carnival than in a million reruns of *Deep Throat.* Sex is in the air — you can feel it everywhere. This is hedonism at its finest.

Where does this bacchanalia happen? Carnival takes place in **Port of Spain**, a relatively large metro area wedged between the Gulf of Paria and the mountain range that extends along Trinidad's 50-mile north coast. The focal point of the celebration is the **Queen's Park Savannah**—an open expanse right in the middle of the city; most recommended hotels are within easy walking distance. Carnival concludes on Ash Wednesday, in February or early March, which is the dry season, although Port of Spain is still rather humid and very hot (you're only 10 degrees above the equator). This is wilt weather.

Carnival is really a street scene. That's where most of the jumping takes place. *Jump-up* is the West Indian term for a party or a good time, and often you *are* literally jumping up and down. Most of the downtown area south of the Savannah is packed, particularly on Frederick Street and Independence Square. Music blares from the largest collection of PA systems in the Caribbean. Each road march has about 50 life-size speakers precariously balanced on large flatbed trucks, and every corner seems to have a system suitable for a concert in New York's Central Park. These provide the amperage for the calypso. Perhaps it is the decibel level that makes one learn the songs so quickly. (Pack a few swabs of cotton to protect sensitive eardrums.)

Carnival is not for everyone. It's not Mardi Gras in New Orleans or *Carnaval* in Rio. The former is a real drunk and the latter more of a spectator event. Trinidad's Carnival is truly a people celebration. To enjoy it, you must participate, get down, lose your inhibitions, and join the boom-boom spirit. It used to be that those who didn't participate would stand out, looking like misplaced tourists who took the wrong exit for Disney World, but there are plenty of spectators these days. They stay on the fringes, avoiding the hot and steamy downtown streets—where the action is.

What does it mean to participate? It means throwing yourself into the sweaty crowd, giving in to the calypso beat, and having a good sense of humor. Carnival is meant to be R-rated fun. In 14th-century France, the celebration was a public orgy. In Trinidad the experience is raunchy—a bit rude, perhaps—but rarely obscene or X-rated. Although we never saw anybody doing it in the street, it's likely that female visitors—particularly if they are pretty and white (a novelty on these streets)—will get wined a lot. Be forewarned that you will be treated like a sex object. Of course, you can turn the tables and surprise the winers, but please don't take offense—it's all in harmless fun and you won't be taken advantage of. Undoubtedly you'll hear lots of "pssssts" and lip-smacking. These are meant as compliments, and the appropriate response is to play along. As we said, it's not for everyone.

The people of T&T make Carnival the celebration that it is. There are rarely brawls or drunken fights—people don't get "ugly" drunk, just silly and happy. You won't see this in Times Square on New Year's Eve.

Why is everyone so up? It's the music. **Calypso** has a contagious rhythm that makes the body move almost involuntarily. The lyrics are pretty much incomprehensible to the inhabitants of middle latitudes, but the constant repetition will make at least the refrains familiar. Often the lyrics are biting political commentaries, but just as often sex is the topic. By the last three days, you should have a repertoire of about 10 songs you just can't live without (and maybe one or two that you've heard enough to last the rest of your life). Several of the smaller record shops sell mix CDs of your favorite calypsos for about $20. You can also buy one of the lyric books sold at record stores or by vendors on the Savannah.

Sharing the music scene is steel-band music — or *pan*, as it is called in the West Indies. Both calypso and pan were born in Trinidad, and they have avid fans. Pan in particular has become a high art form. Listening to a pan orchestra, purists can tell if just one of almost 100 drums is out of sync. What's really amazing is that many pan musicians can't read music; they learn each song in pattern segments. For the Panorama competition (the main pan event of Carnival), new songs are often rehearsed on paper patterns so that no other band will hear the practice sessions and lift the tune. Even the band members won't have heard the song until it is played in the competition.

Although Carnival itself lasts just two days, the season begins right after Christmas, when Trinis become feverish in anticipation. Actually, preparations start immediately after the previous Carnival, and it's a local joke that if Trinis put as much effort into work as they do into preparing for Carnival, they'd be a major power. The fact is, Carnival is big business, employing thousands in such cottage industries as costume making, and of course there are thousands more (unpaid) in calypso and pan entourages. The last three days are the climax, but there are scores of *fêtes* from New Year's on. Each road march, or "mas" camp (short for *masquerade*), has several of these parties, and the rounds of eliminations for Calypso Monarch take weeks throughout Port of Spain and Trinidad.

If you have only a week, the best way to do Carnival is to fly in on the Friday or Saturday before Ash Wednesday, stay in Port of Spain until Wednesday, and then fly to Tobago to recuperate for a few days and fly out the following Saturday or Sunday. This allows you to see the best of both islands. The week before Dimanche Gras (the start of the major festivities on Sunday night) is packed with activities, but its primary attraction is the music eliminations and the **Kings and Queens Competition**, when prizes are given out for the best of the immense costumes that lead the bands. Some of these tower 20 feet or more and weigh several hundred pounds, the weight resting on little wheels. If you are in one of the mas camps, you'll be plugged into all the fêtes going on about town. Thus, arriving on Saturday will place you right in peak Carnival time. You'll be able to see the Panorama finals, join in some of the big fêtes around the Savannah (you'll hear them, everyone is welcome, and some have small cover charges if they're inside a tent), and sleep in on Sunday — a major requirement for survival during the next three days. If you come in on Friday, you'll also have time for a relaxing drive up to the Asa Wright Nature Centre, or to the beach at Maracas Bay, before the real party begins. So put on your dancing shoes, it's time to *j-u-m-p!*

Dimanche Gras

This is the big windup. Eat a good dinner on Sunday night. It will probably be the last relaxed, balanced meal you will have until Wednesday. Then head toward the Savannah to catch the finalists for the Calypso Monarch. This event can look like a set for a Cecil B. DeMille biblical epic. People are literally hanging from the rafters. There is a continuous roar from the crowd, and the ever-present dust cloud shimmering in the spotlights casts a surreal glow over the whole scene. Don't miss it. It is an unforgettable experience to be wedged among thousands chanting "burn he" or "burn she" when the name of some Third World oppressor is mentioned in a song. Once the Monarch is crowned, it's best to head down to Frederick Street for the beginning of a 24-hour nonstop jump. Around midnight, you might want to return to your hotel to freshen up. Then, around 3 a.m., listen for the nearest road march — its distance detected by the volume of the calypso — and join in the band. J'ouvert has begun.

J'ouvert

Heralding daybreak or sunrise, J'ouvert (pronounced "joo-vay," a contraction of the French *jour ouvert*) is our favorite part — and the most free-spirited and silly day — of Carnival. It begins with the road march bands assembling at bars and other locations throughout Port of Spain. At 3 a.m. Monday morning, they begin a slow procession through the neighborhoods and toward the Savannah. Bands can number anywhere from 100 to more than 5,000 people. As a visitor you can buy a pass to join one of the J'ouvert bands on the spot. For J'ouvert they usually have a theme (often different from their costume on Tuesday), which can be outrageous. One that played the last Carnival we visited was the Zulu Warriors. Members of this troop would cast spells on spectators' private parts (one of the female warriors even had a retractable penis — and boy, was she having fun with that!).

Once you hear the march, grab a Carib — the Trini beer of choice — and start "chipping" with them. *Chipping* can best be described as a pouty walk where you slide the balls of your feet ahead in small steps to the beat of the music. You can put as much or as little energy into it as you want. Soon, dawn breaks, but with a twist. Usually you would be heading home after a night of partying. Here, the fun is just beginning.

After chipping with the march for a while, step out and head for downtown. As the road marches approach the central streets, it becomes more fun to party-hop, or party-jump. Allow yourself to wander and explore the streets to see what might turn up. With a crowd on virtually every corner, there is no shortage of possibilities. Pickup trucks piled high with fresh coconuts provide refreshment; a man wielding a huge and intimidating machete will adroitly split one open for you. The milk is tasty and nourishing. A piece of the shell is used to scoop out the meat. There are also vendors selling peeled oranges if you don't want coconut milk dripping down your chin. Of course, you can always have another beer, rum punch, or soft drink — they are on sale about every 100 feet.

As you wander, you'll notice lots of bodies smeared with mud, paint, chocolate, or even pitch (a Trinidadian natural resource). Some of the marches will have buckets of "home-brewed" mud in various colors — white T-shirts are a favorite target for smearing. At that point there's not much you can do. The mud does keep you cool, and it's a look. Just don't wear your favorite clothes (the stains still haven't come out of ours!). Some of the revelers will carefully paint your face with the colorful mud.

Around noon you'll begin to fade. The combination of heat, jumping, and a walking hangover will have taken its toll. Time to take refuge in your hotel pool. The swim will feel marvelous, and lunch may quell your throbbing temples. You might want to sneak in a quick nap, but plan to be back on the streets soon because many road marches will already be in partial costume. Jump until about 7 p.m. and retire for a simple repast. Chances are you'll crash around 10. But for those with more energy to burn, the party goes on all night.

Carnival Tuesday

Rise and shine by 8 a.m., as the grand finale is ahead and you shouldn't miss any of it. Eat a good breakfast and once more head downtown or to the Savannah. The road marches are in full regalia, and seemingly there's one on every street. Bring your camera, for today anyone who's not a tourist is in costume — better yet, bring a camcorder because the music and movement are so much a part of what you are seeing. The mas camps will be winding their way swiftly through the streets to get in good position to cross the Savannah stage for the final judging (judges are posted throughout the city). The grandstand, for which you will need tickets (about $20; contact the Trinidad & Tobago Tourist Board), is a good place to be to watch Tuesday's parade, especially if it's your first time. It is not necessary to purchase the tickets in advance. It's a long, hot show, and sitting down in the shade will help you deal with the heat, but drink lots of water. Keep an eye out for the mas camps of **Peter Minshall** and **Edmond Hart** — they are the best (Hart's kids have split off to form a new camp that is even bigger). Minshall, the enfant terrible of Carnival bandleaders, is the most creative and visionary (he was principal artistic director of the 1996 Olympic ceremonies in Atlanta). His large-scale spectacles are tight, dazzlingly conceived, and well organized, but he's controversial for pushing the envelope. One year his concept was Red, and every costume was the same color, but with imaginative flourishes in dozens of variations. In 2004 and 2005, Minshall didn't participate — it was said he was protesting the oversexed bacchanalia that Carnival has become (he also wasn't happy with the paving over of some of the Savannah in 2003). If you want to join a Minshall Mas Camp for the next Carnival, write to the Callaloo

Company, Building C-22, Western Main Road, Chaguaramas, Trinidad, West Indies. Minshall's Web site is www.callaloo.co.tt.

If you take a break and peer down the Savannah, you'll see an endless sea of bands — the longer ones can take a full hour to cross the stage. The show goes on until after dusk. If you get itchy, take a walk past the bands, still jumping, chipping, and having fun.

Once you've had your fill of mas, head back to the hotel, have a swim, grab a bite to eat (maybe some *pelau*, which is a combination of rice, beans, and peas with either chicken or beef) and be back out on the streets by 9 p.m. for **Las Lap** — the final hours of partying before the ax falls at midnight and Ash Wednesday arrives. There's a sort of sentimental air about Las Lap. It's almost like graduation — everyone is trying to make the most of their last few hours together. In reality, Lent doesn't stop Trinidadians from partying as it used to. There are several big parties the following weekend (they say it's for the tourists, but we're no fools). However, Lent does mark Carnival's symbolic end, which is what makes Carnival so much fun and so intense.

The music will be going strong and then suddenly stop at midnight sharp — right in the middle of a song. The dancing and jumping will cease and people will momentarily mill around, then gradually disperse. You'll walk home incredulous, planning Carnival for next year, not wanting the fun to end. By dawn Wednesday morning, the streets will miraculously have been cleaned up, and life will be slowly crawling back to normal. Now is a good time to sit by the pool, mellow out with some cold Caribs (stored in the fridge of your room), and recap this truly wonderful experience. For more information on Carnival in Trinidad, see www.carnivalondenet.com.

Where to Stay

Here are a few hotels that work well with Carnival. They're nothing quaint or cozy — these are city accommodations designed primarily for business travelers. Keep in mind that Port of Spain rates increase dramatically during Carnival (as much as double in some cases, often with five-day minimum stays), and rooms book up weeks in advance. The first few hotels listed are all within walking distance of the Savannah and downtown. Also of note: A new Hyatt is slated to open in 2007 as part of Port of Spain's International Waterfront Project.

Hilton Trinidad, Lady Young Road, Port of Spain, Trinidad, WI. ℭ 800-HILTONS or 868-624-3211, ✆ 868-624-4485, 🖳 www.hilton.com, hiltonpos@wow.net

🔳 **Very Pricey**; rates are about double during Carnival ⑨ **EP** Ⓒ©
    394 rooms
    This has been Port of Spain's longstanding top business hotel, set on a steep bluff overlooking the Savannah. It's close to the Carnival action and has essential services, a great deep pool, and overpriced

restaurants. After a few days of jump-up, the Hilton can seem like an oasis — that is, when the staff shows up (understaffing is a serious problem during Carnival). All 394 rooms have balconies, and most face the Savannah — a plus when you want to join a road march on J'ouvert. However, this Hilton has been resting in its laurels for too long, and the rooms are in serious need of attention (we suspect the Hyatt opening will force Hilton to invest in this property). Another disadvantage: The hill you climb to reach the Hilton can feel like Everest when you're tired.

Kapok Hotel, 16–18 Cotton Hill, St. Clair, Port of Spain, Trinidad, WI.
Ⓒ 868-622-5765, ✆ 868-622-9677, 🖥 www.kapokhotel.com, stay@kapokhotel.com

💲 **Pricey**; higher during Carnival 🍴 **CP** Ⓒ🄲 94 rooms

This is a good, locally owned alternative to the Hilton, a 10-story business hotel also near the Savannah in a nice residential area. It has rooms and suites with views, a pool, an exercise room, two restaurants, and a coffee bar. It's a very professional outfit and was nicely refurbished in 2005.

Hotel Normandie, 10 Nook Avenue, St. Ann's, Port of Spain, Trinidad, WI.
Ⓒ 868-624-1181, ✆ 868-624-1184, 🖥 www.normandiett.com

💲 **Not So Cheap**; higher during Carnival 🍴 **BP** Ⓒ🄲 53 rooms

A smaller, less impersonal alternative to the Hilton and just as close to Carnival grounds, this place looks like it belongs in Santa Fe. An artsy pool and courtyard are the focal points of the 53-room hotel, which was renovated in 2005. There is also a good nouvelle West Indian-cum-Italian restaurant (everything goes nouvelle eventually) called Ciao Vidalia, but don't go there during Carnival days — service will take forever. Four galleries featuring local artists round out the complex. It's about half the price of the Hilton.

Crowne Plaza Hotel, Wrightston Road, Port of Spain, Trinidad, WI.
Ⓒ 877-227-6963 or 868-625-3366, ✆ 868-625-4166,
🖥 www.crowneplaza.com

💲 **Not So Cheap**; higher during Carnival 🍴 **EP** Ⓒ🄲 223 rooms

This 14-story business hotel, a mid-priced offshoot of the Intercontinental chain, is located on the harbor, right downtown and relatively near the party. There is an array of business amenities like dry cleaning, a newsstand, and secretarial services, plus a gym and a pool. It's nothing spectacular, and service doesn't always come with a smile, but it's functional and relatively glitch-free. The Hyatt that's opening across the street will give this place a run for its money.

Alicia's House, 7 Coblentz Gardens, St. Ann's, Port of Spain, Trinidad, WI. ℂ 868-623-2802, ✉ 868-623-8560, 🖳 www.aliciashouse.com

💲 **Cheap**; higher during Carnival 🅟 **BP** ⓒⓒ 17 rooms

This nice, informal inn located just below the Hilton and a few hundred feet from the Savannah is like a guesthouse but very clean and well run. The small pool in back will provide some respite, but the noise level here during Carnival is high (serious partying goes on next door). The owner was about to open another inn as we went to press: **Alicia's Palace** (868-624-8553).

Other Options

Carnival isn't the only time to come to Trinidad, but it's the only time to spend more than a day in Port of Spain. The following two places are special alternatives for seeing the natural Trinidad.

⊛ **Asa Wright Nature Centre and Lodge**, P.O. Box 4710, Blanchisseuse Road, Arima, Trinidad, WI. ℂ 800-426-7781 or 868-667-4655, ✉ 868-667-4540, 🖳 www.asawright.org

💲 **Very Pricey** 🅟 **FAP**, plus afternoon tea and cocktail ⓒⓒ 24 rooms

Bird-watchers will be in heaven at this rustic mountain lodge, located about 90 minutes from Port of Spain. Formerly a plantation for various high-altitude crops, it was converted into a 730-acre wildlife sanctuary in 1967, well before the term *ecotourism* had been thought up by some marketing genius. The rooms are in a dozen duplex cottages on a densely forested hillside. Two additional rooms are in the original Great House and have wonderful character but can be a bit noisy. Throughout the day hummingbirds, honeycreepers, and more than 100 other species wing through. Of special note are the nearby caves that are home to the exotic oilbird. A three-night minimum stay is required for this tour. The food is decent, but there's no entertainment or nightlife nearby — this is an unusually secluded retreat.

Mt. Plaisir Estate, Grande Rivière, Trinidad, WI. ℂ 868-670-2216, ✉ 868-670-0057, 🖳 www.mtplaisir.com

💲 **Cheap** 🅟 **EP** (we recommend upgrading to the **MAP**) ⓒⓒ 13 rooms

Farther still from "civilization" is this guesthouse located on the remote north coast past the town of Toco, in a hardscrabble fishing village (population 300). This is not a place for anyone who needs modern conveniences close at hand — minibars and Internet access are probably unknown concepts to most of Grande Rivière's residents. The beach here is home to more than 2,000 nesting leatherback sea turtles, who return year after year to perform their egg-laying ritual. Nesting season is mid-March through mid-July, with the hatchlings appearing two months later. The swimming, in the ocean or in nearby rivers, is good, and there are hikes and canoeing nearby. The rooms are basic but sweetly adorned in local, African, and Asian crafts; there's a restaurant that serves locally grown food and a spa that specializes in natural treatments. Allow three hours for the 75-mile drive to Grande Rivière from Port of Spain. Transfers from the airport run $95 each way.

Where To Eat

Going out to eat at a restaurant during Carnival is a bad idea because no one wants to work. Thus restaurants are understaffed, with service arriving by the next century. So why bother? Your best bet is to eat on the street. Don't be scared—it's good stuff and it's cheap. Here are some of the most popular selections.

Pelau

This is a national dish of T&T, composed mainly of rice with pigeon peas or black beans. There are chicken or beef chunks mixed in, too. It's tasty, nutritious, and not too spicy for tender tummies.

Roti

This is the Caribbean version of a burrito, minus the rice and beans. Instead, you get curried potatoes and chunks of meat. If you get chicken, make sure you ask for boneless or you'll be biting into the more esoteric parts, like the neck or the pope's nose. A safer bet is beef.

Buss Up Shut

This is the mock-pasta dish of T&T. It tastes like shredded flour tortillas with meat, curry, and spices. Its name is *so* compelling (it means "busted up shirt") that you've got to try it.

On the other hand, if you're visiting Trinidad when Carnival hasn't taken over, try these:

$$$$ A la Bastille, Ariapita Avenue, Port of Spain, 868-622-1789

This is classic French with island accents. Entrées include Moroccan vegetable *tajine*, or rabbit terrine with prunes and rosemary. On Saturday the restaurant becomes a *creperie*. Inquire about live performances. Breakfast is served Tuesday through Saturday; lunch and dinner are served Monday through Saturday; closed Sunday.

$$$$ Battimamzelle, Coblentz Inn, Cascade, 868-621-0591

The name means *dragonfly*. Situated in an unassuming small business hotel, this is the current shining star of the island's restaurant scene. Chef Mohammed marries French technique and Trinidad flair with dishes like Black Angus ribeye doused in spicy hollandaise, and kingfish barbecued in guava sauce. Reservations are recommended.

$$$ **Joseph's**, Rookery Nook, Maraval, 868-622-5557

Joseph's specializes in Lebanese *mezza* and eastern Mediterranean dishes, like kebabs, tabouleh and hummus. Entrées include red snapper baked in tahini sauce, pine nuts, and garlic, and lamb stewed with eggplant and tomatoes.

$$$$ **Solimar**, 6 Nook Avenue, St. Ann's, 868-624-6267

Solimar serves an international menu with indoor and outdoor dining, located behind the President's House. Chef and patron Joe Brown has worked in 10 countries around the globe, which gives him license to prepare pork loin in an Oriental style, with a ginger-chili-garlic sauce on stir-fried noodles, or the classic Indian curry, chicken *vindaloo*. Closed Sunday; reservations are recommended.

$$ **Tiki Village**, Kapok Hotel, Port of Spain, 868-622-5765

This spot, found on the 10th floor of a business hotel, is exceedingly popular with locals for its Chinese-Polynesian blend and for its traditional dim sum brunch on Sunday.

$$ **Veni Mangé**, 67A Ariapita Avenue, Port of Spain, 868-624-4597

Marked by colorful local art, a friendly reception, and a devoted clientele, this place serves a small but vibrant selection of Trinidad favorites. West Indian stewed chicken and dumplings are a specialty, but the vegetarian black-eyed pea croquettes in tamarind sauce is another winner. Open for lunch Monday to Friday, dinner on Wednesday and Friday or whenever the busy Trini sisters (who run the joint) feel like opening. Call ahead.

Don't Miss

Maracas Beach

This is where everyone goes, especially after Carnival. When there's no traffic it's a 30-minute drive over a very scenic road, good for a swim and general oooh-cruise. Las Cuevas, about 5 miles to the east, is a less crowded alternative. Around sundown, the drive back to Port of Spain can take well over an hour.

Pax Guest House, Mt. St. Benedict

This is a 600-acre monastery in the hills above the airport. Afternoon tea here is an island tradition, taken by such notables as Fidel Castro and the Dalai Lama. Tours of the monastery are available, hiking and bird-watching nearby are good, and it's also an inexpensive place to stay overnight. Reservations: 868-662-4084; www.paxguesthouse.com.

Caroni Bird Sanctuary

Caroni Bird Sanctuary is a 40-square-mile mangrove swamp located just outside Port of Spain, home to two-toed sloths, crab-eating raccoons, and scarlet ibises that roost at sunset nightly. Winston Nanen provides boat tours for $10 per person (868-645-1305).

Tobago

N

CARIBBEAN SEA

ATLANTIC OCEAN

Melville Island

Bird of Paradise

Little Tobago

North Point

Blue Waters Inn

Charlotteville

Manta Lodge

Goat Island

Speyside Inn

Speyside

Emma's

Man o' War Bay

Pirate's Bay

Pedro Point

King's Bay

Batteaux Bay Lookout

King's Bay Falls

Richmond Island

Prince's Bay

Bloody Bay

Parlatuvier Road

Roxborough

Goldsborough Bay

Englishman's Bay

Leeward Road

Study Park Beach

Smith's Island

Castara Bay

Cuffie River Retreat

Moriah

Granby Point

Footprints Eco Resort

Ft. George

Half Moon Blue

Arnos Vale Hotel

Scarborough

Amos Vale Rd

The Mount Irvine Bay Hotel & Golf Club

Rockley Bay

Milford Road

Hampden Inn

Grafton Beach Resort

Le Grand Courlan Spa Resort

Grafton Rd

Mt. Irvine Bay

Claude Noel Hwy

Shirvan Rd

Kariwak Village

Holistic Haven and Hotel

Hilton Tobago Golf & Spa Resort

Buccoo Bay

Bon Accord

Airport

Crown Point

Pigeon Point

Coco Reef Resort

Miles

0 1 2 3 4 5

Tobago

ALTHOUGH IT HAS EXPERIENCED TOURIST GROWTH AND development, Tobago is still a relative backwater compared to some of the other more popular Caribbean destinations. Tobagonians are wonderfully friendly, the pace is very laid-back, and the scenery is beautiful. See Tobago soon, before "progress" changes it too much.

Getting There

Tobago is not the easiest place to reach. At this writing, the only flights from North America are a weekly BWIA flight from Washington D.C. and a weekly Air Canada flight from Toronto. Otherwise, the most direct route is flying to Trinidad's Piarco International Airport on Air Canada, American, BWIA, or Continental, and then making the 20-minute hop on BWIA, Caribbean Star, LIAT, or Tobago Express to Tobago. Caribbean Star and LIAT also fly to Tobago from neighboring islands, including Barbados and Grenada, offering another routing option. British Airways, ExcelAir, and Virgin Atlantic provide service from London.

Another option is to take the new high-speed ferry service that offers two daily departures between Port of Spain and Scarborough. The two-and-a-half-hour trip (depending upon whether or not the seas are favorable) costs $50 for adults ($25 for children) each way. If you're not in a rush, if you happen to *really* like boats, *and* you're visiting both islands, you can sail on the Port Authority's 700-passenger ("slow-speed") ferry. The six-hour journey is made daily (except Saturday); note that the trip from Scarborough to Port of Spain is overnight. Cabins are a bargain at $13 each way; tourist class (reclining seats) and steerage are cheaper. For additional information on all ferry options, contact the Port Authority at 868-639-2668 or visit www.patnt.com.

Getting Around

Tobago is an island that begs for exploration (see below). By all means rent a car when you arrive at the airport. In addition to Hertz (800-654-3131), Econo-Car (868-660-8728), Peter Gremli (868-639-8400), and Rattan's (868-639-8271)

Tobago: Key Facts

Location	11°N by 60°W
	22 miles/35 kilometers northeast of Trinidad
	2,300 miles/3,700 kilometers southeast of New York
Size	116 square miles/300 square kilometers
	26 miles/42 kilometers long by 7 miles/11 kilometers wide
Highest point	Pigeon Peak (1,890 feet/576 meters)
Population	45,000
Language	English, with a West Indian lilt
Time	Atlantic Standard Time year-round (1 hour ahead of EST, same as EDT)
Area code	868
Electricity	110 or 220 volts AC, 60 cycles — always ask before you plug in.
Currency	The Trinidad and Tobago dollar (TT$6.3 = US$1)
Driving	On the left; valid driver's license okay
Documents	A valid passport or proof of citizenship, plus an ongoing or a return ticket
Departure tax	$17
More taxes!	10% hotel, 10% service charge, 15% VAT on all goods and services
Beer to drink	Carib
Rum to drink	Vat 19
Music to hear	Calypso, pan
Tourism info	800-816-7541
	Web site: www.visittobago.gov.tt

are some other rental shops at the airport. The roads are in fairly good shape, so driving is not an unpleasant experience.

Focus on Tobago: Exploring

Tobago's slow pace and mellow atmosphere doesn't mean that there is nothing to do. *Au contraire*. Besides snorkeling, diving, golf, and other recreational activities, the best way to spend time on Tobago is to explore it. Although the island's western end at times resembles standard tourist fare found elsewhere in the Caribbean, the center and eastern end can be magical.

There are several excursions that will take you all over the island. They are detailed in the following pages and are best done early in your visit so that the places you really adore can be revisited.

Hitchhiking Tobagonians

Here is one annoyance you should be aware of: Although we'll pick up the occasional hitchhiker when we're not in a rush, it's not uncommon on Tobago — particularly on the main road heading out toward Speyside — for young men to jump into the back seat of your car, uninvited! On one occasion, a golf cap that the local tourist board had given us disappeared from the back seat upon a hitchhiker's exit. The golf cap was no big loss, but we thought of other valuables (like a passport or camera) that could just as easily have disappeared. Our advice: Keep your back doors locked and, if an uninvited passenger does enter your car, *insist* on his getting out — no need to encourage such ruffian behavior.

Excursion 1: The Windward Road

Starting from Crown Point, head east on the Claude Nöel Highway to Scarborough, the island capital. Turn right on Wilson Road, then left on Darrell Spring West (the only route — Wilson turns into a one-way street). Follow the traffic onto Gardenside. At Carrington, turn left. Just before Castries Street, there is a parking lot on the right. You should be able to find a space there. This is a good, central location and will allow you to walk everywhere. Keep in mind that Scarborough can get hot, so plan to visit in the early morning or late afternoon. On the waterfront, there is a cruise-ship complex and such American export abominations as KFC. Across the street from the cinema, on Wilson Road, is a great roti place called Jat's Roti Shop. Roti is a delicious soft Indian bread (*paratha*) roll-up or wrap with curried meats and/or veggies. Be sure to ask if the meat is deboned, or your teeth and fillings are in for a hard and potentially damaging shock. Heading up the hill on Castries Street, check out Arcadia Records (tell owner Walter that Rum & Reggae sent you), where you can buy premixed calypso, pan, and dancehall CDs of your favorite hits (they do a brisk business right after Carnival). Then go up the hill to **Fort George**. Here you'll find beautifully landscaped grounds and some old buildings that are just screaming to be photographed. When you're ready, proceed on the Windward Road — there is little else to see in Scarborough.

Windward Road will be your course for the remainder of the day. There are many points along the way that are worth stopping for. Note that there is a gas station in Roxborough in case you need to fill up. Here are the possibilities.

Granby Point, Mt. St. George
This is a high-up vista of Hillsborough Bay and Smith's Island.

Studley Park Beach, Studley Park

This is a very pretty palm-lined, brown-sand beach, just beyond the bridge.

Richmond House, Belle Garden

This Great House on a breezy hilltop has a beautiful view. The dark wood interior is definitely worth checking out.

King's Bay Waterfall, Rosenwald Estate, Delaford

This is a good place for a freshwater swim. Turn into the cocoa plantation at the 20-mile post and proceed to the car park.

Batteaux Bay Lookout, above Speyside

After a twisting and turning ascent through a landslide area and gorge, there is a lookout at the top of the road on your left. Extraordinary views of Little Tobago Island and the blue Atlantic are beyond.

Speyside

Have lunch at now-famous Jemma's Sea View Kitchen and check out the beach at Blue Waters Inn.

Charlotteville

The end of the road belongs to this very interesting fishing village. There are good beaches on both Pirate's and Man o' War Bays. Tobago's best diving is here.

Excursion 2: The Leeward Side

This outing will be slower, more laid-back, and beach-oriented. There will be many occasions when you will pass a road or path that leads to a beach not even mentioned here. By all means investigate (but mind the "No Trespassing" signs!). It might be just the secluded cove for an unscheduled tryst.

Beginning at Crown Point again, follow the signs for **Pigeon Point**. It's acclaimed as the nicest beach on the island—forget it! It's crowded and small, but it is a good place to people-watch. There is a $2 admission fee that the government (which recently took over the beach from private hands) is considering dropping. You can also arrange snorkel trips to Buccoo Bay, Tobago's famous reef. For about $15 you get gear, instruction if you need it, and a ride in a vessel about as stable as a canoe.

If you skip Pigeon Point (which sits at the western tip of the island), or if you've visited and want to see more, simply head east on the Claude Nöel Highway and turn left (the first major left) at the Milford-Shirvan Road. Follow Shirvan Road to Grafton Road to Arnos Vale Road. It sounds complicated, but keep in mind that all you are doing is following the north coast road. Once you reach Bloody Bay you will probably want to turn around; the road beyond to Charlotteville is in bad shape and requires a four-wheel drive (unless the government has finished the long-overdue paving and road improvement). On the way to Bloody Bay, there are lots of points of interest and many deserted or secluded beaches. Half the fun is discovering your own. Here are a few suggestions.

Mt. Irvine Golf Course, Grafton Road

This is an above-average course for the Caribbean (868-639-8871). You can't miss it, as you drive by several fairways and greens before you get to the clubhouse. The pro shop sells Tobago Golf Club T-shirts and hats.

Mt. Irvine Beach, Grafton Road

With public facilities set up by the Tourist Board, this beach is noteworthy as Tobago's only surfing beach. On some days the surf can break quite nicely. The best waves (especially in July and August) are found on the reef just to the right of the beach.

Mt. Irvine Back Bay, Grafton Road

After you pass Mt. Irvine Beach heading east, you'll notice Gleneagles Drive on your right. On your left will be a track through a field. Follow this to the end, park, and take the footpath down to one of the best beaches on Tobago.

Grafton Beach, Grafton Road

When you pass Gleneagles Drive, follow the first road (not track) on the left. This will take you to Grafton Beach.

Turtle Beach, Grafton Road

Before you get to the Turtle Beach resort, you'll notice a small dirt road with black-and-white striped posts. Follow this road to this lovely beach. You'll be the only ones there.

Arnos Vale Hotel, Arnos Vale Road

From Grafton Road, turn onto Arnos Vale Road and follow it to the Arnos Vale Hotel for a rum punch at the beach bar (868-639-2881; description follows).

Castara Bay, Leeward Road

Castara is a small fishing village with a public beach and some local lunch spots, on the beach, for fresh fish.

Englishman's Bay, Leeward Road

This is the nicest beach on Tobago and one of the best in the Caribbean. A crescent of golden sand with a greenish hue is framed by craggy rocks on each end of the bay, like natural sentinels guarding this special place. There is also great snorkeling on the east (right) side of the bay. All this beauty might not last long, however, because a large parcel of land (possibly including this beach) could be developed soon.

A few miles east of Castara Bay, look for a handmade sign for English-man's Bay in the middle of a pasture at sea level. Follow the short dirt road and park. There are a few refreshment and crafts stands at the entrance to the beach.

Where to Stay

Tobago has numerous accommodations, from deluxe resorts to very funky and rundown guesthouses. There are basically four areas of tourist accommodations: Crown Point, the North Coast, Scarborough, and the East End. The airport sits at the very western end of the island in Crown Point, so a destination like the Blue Waters Inn, which is at the eastern end of Tobago in Speyside, will take about 90 minutes to reach by car or taxi. Be prepared for a surcharge of more than 20 percent when service and tax are added to your hotel bill.

Crown Point

Kariwak Village Holistic Haven and Hotel, P.O. Box 27, Crown Point, Scarborough, Tobago, WI. © 868-639-8442, ✎ 868-639-8441, 🖥 www.kariwak.com, kariwak@tstt.net.tt

💲 **Not So Cheap** 🍴 EP CC 24 rooms

Over the years, Kariwak Village has subtly transformed itself into a holistic retreat, with owners Cynthia and Allan Clovis offering instruction in Hatha Yoga, Qi Gong, and stretching and relaxation. Classes are conducted in an open-air *ajouba* (a huge octagonal, wood-floored yoga pavilion) and are complimentary for guests. Massage — including ayurvedic marma, deep tissue, lymphatic drainage, reflexology, and shiatsu — is also available from two resident massage therapists. A wonderful Jacuzzi and waterfall ensemble at the back of the property offers even more relaxation opportunities.

Although its location next to the airport might make one ponder the soothing sounds of jet engines, the airport isn't O'Hare, and the takeoff revs happen at the far end of the runway, downwind from the hotel (and, actually, the island currently receives fewer than seven jets a week). This doesn't deter repeat guests (more than half return), mostly from Britain. The rooms are arranged around an attractive pool or garden, are all at ground level, and are decorated with lots of natural wood and white tile floors. All come with a queen and single bed, reading lights (we love these!), a/c, phones, and maid service. A thatched-roof loggia or hut arrangement houses the bar and restaurant — one of the best on Tobago. Breakfast here is the best on the island, and the dinners are great, with special attention paid to vegetarians. Live bands make this a festive place on weekends. The beach and airport are a five-minute walk away.

Coco Reef Resort, P.O. Box 434, Coconut Bay, Scarborough, Tobago, WI.
ⓒ 800-221-1294 or 868-639-8571, ✆ 868-639-8574,
🖥 www.cocoreef.com, cocoreef-tobago@trinidad.net

💲 **Very Pricey** ⓨ **BP** Ⓒ 150 rooms

Coco Reef Resort opened in 1995 and quickly established itself as one of the premier luxury resorts on Tobago. Less than a mile from the airport (you could easily walk it if you have a carry-on with wheels), the two-story hotel is the brainchild of Bermudian John Jefferis, and an attitude of pretension permeates the facility. Although there are other deluxe properties on Tobago, most noticeably the Grand Courlan, the Coco Reef is more tastefully done (the green-and-white Natuzzi leather sofas in the Grand Courlan lobby are atrocious). Although Mr. Jefferis's cream-colored Rolls Royce parked in front of Coco Reef is a close taste faux pas runner-up (this is an island where many live in poverty), the rest of the resort is thankfully less ostentatious. The lobby is open and airy, with bamboo palms and fountains framing the view of the resort's own man-made beach and lagoon. The rooms are lathered in pastels, with terra-cotta tile floors, bleached-wood ceilings, wicker furnishings, and very spacious and clean bathrooms.

There are two restaurants and a spa, and the jettied lagoon and man-made beach provides glasslike water, perfect for morning laps. Two Har-Tru lighted tennis courts provide other recreational opportunities. If you want resort-style accommodations, this is the place, and the rates (like the Hilton's) won't gouge you.

The North Coast

The Mount Irvine Bay Hotel and Golf Club, P.O. Box 222, Mount Irvine, Tobago, WI. ⓒ 868-639-8871, ✆ 868-639-8800,
🖥 www.mtirvine.com, mtirvine@tstt.net.tt

💲 **Pricey** ⓨ **CP** Ⓒ 105 rooms

Once *the* luxury resort on Tobago, Mount Irvine Bay has the appearance of a resort from a different era, like a RockResort from the 1960s. Renowned for its Championship golf course, the rooms have lots of dark wood, wall-to-wall carpeting, colonial furniture, and brightly colored upholstery. There are two lighted tennis courts, but the raison d'être here is golf, golf, and more golf. The Mount Irvine only overlooks the water — no beachfront villas here — although there is a beach club down the street and a large pool with a swim-up bar. The rates aren't bad, especially for golfers.

Footprints Eco Resort, Culloden Bay Road via Golden Lane, Tobago, WI. ℂ 868-660-0118, ✆ 868-660-0027, 🖥 www.footprintseco-resort.com, info@footprintseco-resort.com

💲 **Not So Cheap** 🍽 **EP** CC 10 rooms

Set on 62 acres on Culloden Bay and designated as a nature preserve, Footprints was Tobago's first eco-resort. The emphasis of this place is preservation and protection of the environment. Judging from the hair-raising ride down the access road in our non–four-wheel-drive rental car (we thought the car would not make it, either getting stuck in a hole or falling off a precipice), there's no doubt in our minds that the environment is number one here (and we've been told that road improvements have been done when conditions got really bad). Renewable energy sources are used here whenever possible. All buildings have thatched roofs and sit on columns. Boardwalks connect the buildings and protect the ground from erosion. There are lots of trails for hiking, a multilevel saltwater pool (pumped from the beach — the water is greenish), and a small sandy beach with some good coral reefs for snorkeling.

The rooms are surprisingly nice and interesting, with canvas ceilings, dark recycled wood, wainscoting cut from telephone poles, a garden shower open to the outside, ceiling fans, all-natural untreated fabrics, Adirondack chairs, and simple double beds. The sound of the breakers can be heard from all five guest rooms. There are also one- and two-bedroom villas available (some have their own swimming pool or Jacuzzi). A health-food-oriented restaurant and bar pavilion has a retractable roof for dining alfresco when the stars are out.

Cuffie River Nature Retreat, P.O. Box 461, Scarborough, Tobago, WI. ℂ 868-660-0505, ✆ 868-660-0606, 🖥 www.cuffie-river.com, cuffiriv@tstt.net.tt

💲 **Not So Cheap** 🍽 **BP** CC 10 rooms

This is a wonderful inn built at the junction of the Cuffie and Prarie rivers, on a former cocoa estate located high in the mountains. The locale is excellent for bird-watching — more than 50 species of tropical birds, including 8 of the top 10 sought-after exotics like the blue-backed mannakin and the collared trogan. Standard rooms have clay tile floors and simple but appealing furnishings; there are also two "executive" rooms, which are large corner units. There is no air-conditioning, but the breeze wafts through quite adequately. There's a decent restaurant serving indigenous fare, a swimming pool, and lots of forest to explore on foot. Note that the nearest beach is a 20-minute drive.

Arnos Vale Hotel, P.O. Box 208, Arnos Vale, Scarborough, Tobago, WI. ℂ 868-639-2881, ✆ 868-639-4629, 🖥 www.arnosvalehotel.com

💲 **Pricey** 🍽 **CP** CC 30 rooms

Once an old plantation estate, the 30-room Arnos Vale Hotel has been through the ringer for the last decade — this once grand hotel even served as an all-inclusive resort for Italians for several years. It finally received a much-needed face-lift, and now thrives as a sleepy, 450-acre retreat for bird lovers and nature enthusiasts. Situated on a steep hill (with many steps) are a main house and cottages cooled by ceiling fans and air conditioners. The bulk of the accommodations are in more modern and rather bland rooms near the beach (these are more expensive). There is a smallish pool and a tennis court, as well as nicely landscaped grounds. The restaurant gets complaints for being overpriced, and few options are nearby. The "private" beach is small, but the surrounding reefs offer decent snorkeling.

Le Grand Courlan Spa Resort, Black Rock, Tobago, W.I. ☎ 868-639-9667, ✆ 868-639-9292, 🖥 www.legrandcourlan-resort.com

💰 **Beyond Belief** 🍴 **All-Inclusive** CC 78 rooms

This place calls itself "the most luxurious spa resort in the Southern Caribbean," but one would have to be open to different interpretations of what luxury is. Certainly a lack of taste causes a drop in the standards for luxury. In other words, this is luxury meant for the Mob. Opened in 1995, the first telltale sign was — literally — the sign: an etched resort logo in the reception window that was crooked. This is followed by green-and-white leather sofas. Leatha? In the tropics? Is this a fee-ancy nightclub in Queens? Built on a hillside overlooking Great Courlan Bay (why the pretentious French name on this most *un*pretentious of islands?), the multilevel hotel has various rooms and suites that descend to the beach. The ponds in the various gardens look brown and murky. The rooms feature all the amenities, including pine furniture, beige marble floors, remote a/c, and a pastel color scheme. Most of the suites have rattan furniture and Jacuzzis. Appealing to a large English and German clientele, some of the baths have bidets. Furnishings, however, seem rather spartan for the price.

On a more positive note, the health club is quite good and will satisfy even die-hard gym bunnies. The spa has all kinds of body-indulging opportunities, from sauna and steam to wet massage rooms for seaweed treatments. There is a good-size pool with a swim-up bar, although shade is somewhat lacking. The greenish-tan beach in front is very nice, and there is a dive shop. Golf is nearby at Mt. Irvine, and two lighted tennis courts are on the premises.

Note that the all-inclusive rates limit spa treatments to one per day, and motorized water sports are not included.

Grafton Beach Resort, Black Rock, Tobago, W.I. ☎ 888-790-5264 or 868-639-0191, ✆ 868-639-0030, 🖥 www.grafton-resort.com

💰 **Wicked Pricey** 🍴 **All-Inclusive** CC 108 rooms

Literally a few feet from sister property Le Grand Courlan and sharing many of the amenities and the same beach, the Grafton Beach is a cheaper alternative with the look and feel of a standard medium-size hotel. The rooms and suites offer décor and furnishings that are neither remarkable nor offensive. This hotel caters to lots of Europeans on package tours, so don't expect glamour here. However, this is a better buy than Le Grand Courlan, and you do get access to the rich neighbor's facilities (it's not a bad choice for families or those on a budget). Two air-conditioned squash courts add a unique touch. There is also a windsurfing center with all levels of instruction.

Scarborough and Environs

Hilton Tobago Golf and Spa Resort, P.O. Box 633, Lowlands, Tobago, WI. ⓒ 800-HILTONS or 868-660-8500, ✉ 868-660-8503, 💻 www.hilton.com, reservations.tobago@hilton.com

💲 **Pricey** 🍴 **EP** CC 200 rooms

This 20-acre, $35 million resort sits on a long Atlantic-facing beach a couple miles east of the airport—the beach is often too rough for swimming, and garbage (presumably floating over from Africa) washes up daily. Adjoining the site is a 90-acre natural lagoon and a 60-acre mangrove forest. The 200 rooms are located in three-story buildings—all offer ocean views, minibar, coffeemakers, and cable TV. There are two restaurants and four bars, including a swim-up pool bar; tennis courts, a fitness and spa facility, a dive center, and a tough 18-hole championship golf course round out the amenities. This resort delivers the expected Hilton package, and though not in the most ideal of locations (beach lovers will want a car at their disposal), the room rates are pretty reasonable for what you get.

Hampden Inn, LP171 Milford Road, Lowlands, Tobago, WI. ⓒ and ✉ 868-639-7522, 💻 www.hampden-inn.com, thorb@tstt.net.tt

💲 **Cheap** 🍴 **CP** CC 12 rooms

This 12-room guesthouse, across the street from the mammoth Hilton development, is a find for budget travelers. Located eight minutes from the airport and five minutes from Scarborough, the simple yet clean and comfortable rooms have stone floors, wood ceilings, large tile baths, a/c, TV, and verandas with hammocks. There is a smallish pool on the premises, a dining pavilion called D'Carat Shed, and a bar. The management is very friendly and helpful. The beach is 400 yards away, and public transit is at the end of the street. It's popular with Europeans. Even with the cheap rates, packages are sometimes available. Such a deal!

Half Moon Blue, 73 Bacolet Street, Scarborough, Tobago, WI. ℂ 868-639-
3551, 🖂 868-639-6124, 💻 www.halfmoonblue.com

📑 **Pricey** ⑪ **CP** (CC) 10 apartments

Formerly called the Old Donkey Cart House, this charming spot started
out in 1980 as a restaurant in a 150-year-old house and expanded to
include apartments. Set on a hill in Bacolet, a suburb of Scarborough,
and located 100 steps above Bacolet Beach (once you cross the street),
this lodging is the dream of Gloria Jones Schoen, a Tobagonian who
used to model in Germany. Renovated and updated in 2004, the apartments have king-size four-poster beds with mosquito netting, ceiling
fans and a/c, phone and TV, fridge, dark wood floors, rattan furnishings,
and lanais with ocean views. The baths are rather plain but are large
and clean. There is an unusual pool, with a tile "beach" sloping into
the pool—great for sunbathing and staying cool underwater (midnight swims encouraged). La Belle Creole restaurant serves dinner in
the garden each evening.

The East End

Blue Waters Inn, Batteaux Bay, Speyside, Tobago, WI. ℂ 868-660-4341,
🖂 868-660-5195, 💻 www.bluewatersinn.com,
bwi@bluewatersinn.com

📑 **Pricey** ⑪ **EP** (CC) 38 rooms

Probably the best thing about the Blue Waters Inn is its stunning location, seemingly at the end of the world. With its own private arc of
greenish sand set on 46 acres at the bottom of plunging verdant hills,
this is an ideal place for a romantic tryst or a reconciliation holiday. The
trades blow onshore, keeping the air cool and the palm fronds and sea
grape trees swaying. Framed between the two rocky points of the beach
are Goat and Bird of Paradise islands. The latter is a bird-watcher's
haven (the hotel can arrange excursions). The BWI has a pier that juts
out from the beach and provides a place to dock for the resort's dive
operation (Aquamarine Dive, Ltd.) and various excursion boats. It is
also a wonderful place to sit on a chaise and enjoy the view, the breezes,
and a good book. You can swim off the dock, too. People who are
sand-phobic will love this option.

The accommodations consist of simple two-story buildings with
standard rooms, efficiency apartments, and deluxe bungalows. The
standard rooms are only steps away from the beach, and the sound
of the waves will lull you to sleep. The décor of the rooms is basic,
with terra-cotta tile floors, white walls, and wicker furniture. The
baths are also on the basic side and could use an upgrade. In 2005,
air-conditioning was added to the rooms; ceiling fans and the trade
winds provide additional ventilation. The apartments and bungalows

are on the hill above the main hotel building. A restaurant, the Fish Pot, is decent for dinner and obviously features fresh seafood; breakfast is just okay. There is a very comfy beachside bar and an air-conditioned video-satellite TV room with a library (mostly German books). The inn has a tennis court, and there are several hiking possibilities from the property. We've had good experiences here, but we've also heard complaints about slow service and the lackadaisical dive operation.

Manta Lodge, P.O. Box 433, Windward Road, Speyside, Scarborough, Tobago, WI. ℂ 800-544-7631 or 868-660-5268, ✇ 868-660-5030, 🖥 www.mantalodge.com, info@mantalodge.com

🛍 **Not So Cheap** ⑪ **BP** ⓒⓒ 22 rooms

Oriented toward divers (it's the home of the Tobago Dive Experience operation), this small hotel, across the road from a coral beach, is a friendly and relaxed place to hang out after a day of diving, hiking, or bird-watching. The rooms are spacious and comfortable, with green tile floors, wicker furnishings, lanais with canvas chairs, and such amenities as cotton linens and a comforter (a rarity in this clime and price range). All rooms have a beach or ocean view; most have a/c. Only eight of the rooms have queen-size beds — the rest are twins (à la Rob and Laura Petrie). The baths are on the smallish side but are tile, clean, and certainly adequate. There are no telephones or TVs in the rooms. A small pool off the restaurant-bar area provides a place for a dip.

The Speyside Inn, 189 Windward Road, Speyside, Tobago, WI. ℂ and ✇ 868-660-4852, 🖥 www.speysideinn.com

🛍 **Not So Cheap** ⑪ **BP** ⓒⓒ 18 rooms

Set in a converted old house across the street from the beach, the Speyside Inn is a friendly, family-run inn comprising 6 rooms in the old house plus 12 rooms in a newer building overlooking the bay. The rooms are big and, though spare (they could use some comfy seating), are airy with high ceilings, terra-cotta tile floors, and decks facing the bay and the cooling trade winds. The baths are white tile and perfectly adequate. The traditional Demerara (push-out) louvered windows and French doors add a tropically elegant touch to the place. The inn's location is close to the Manta Lodge's dive shop and several hiking opportunities.

Where to Eat

There are several places we recommend for your dining pleasure.

$$ Jemma's Sea View Kitchen, Speyside, 868-660-4066

Situated in an expanded two-story structure on the beach at Speyside,

Jemma's has become famous on Tobago, especially with tourists. It feels a bit like dining in a treehouse — the big almond tree leans out over the beach with a built-in loveseat. The food is mostly simple seafood — Jemma's fish and chips are just great.

$$$ **Kariwak Village**, Crown Point, 868-639-8442

Owner Cynthia Clovis plans and supervises a menu that concentrates on West Indian cuisine with a liberal use of Kariwak's own herbs and spices. A holistic point of view toward food is embraced. Canned and frozen foods are not used (quite a feat on a tropical island!). The four-course dinner at Kariwak Village has consistently been one of our best dining experiences on Tobago. Reservations are suggested.

$$$$ **La Belle Creole**, Bacolet Street, Scarborough, 868-639-3551

This is owned and operated by a local woman who used to model in Germany, which explains the fine collection of somewhat overpriced German wines. The food is good — a panoply of Caribbean dishes served from an open kitchen. Most of the dining is alfresco, by candlelight, and the staff is friendly and efficient. Reservations are advised. Check on the days of operation — it's often closed Sunday and Monday.

$$$ **La Tartaruga**, Buccoo Bay, 868-639-0940

We don't normally steer people to Italian in the Caribbean, but this is a wonderful, friendly spot. The Italian owner, Gabriele de Gaetano, and his chef know their stuff, and they prepare fresh pastas daily. Some are embellished with garden-grown herbs, and fish is delivered daily from a reliable source. The service is warm and as quick as it gets on this island. Closed Sunday and Thursday.

$ **Store Bay food shacks**, no phone

If you really want good local food fast and cheap, this is where you'll find it, right next to the island's busiest beach. There's Miss Jean's shack, and Miss Trim's and Miss Alma's, but probably the most celebrated is Miss Esmay's (no one, including Miss E., is sure of the spelling). The dish to get is crab and dumplings, although these land crabs look more like a very large tarantula — big and hairy. Still, everyone loves 'em. Moving down the road a bit, there's a shack that sells Buss Up Shut (T&T's idea of pasta) with curried beef and *chana* (chickpeas). To drink, there's *mauby* — a spiced drink that's made from tree bark, looks like swamp water, and is definitely an acquired taste. You can also try sea moss (a seaweed milkshake that's supposed to put lead in your pencil) and tamarind nectar (a very tart juice made from the coating of the tamarind seed). Other favorites are roti (the Caribbean burrito), *pelau* (a seasoned rice dish), and fresh coconut. The latter is macheteed open for you as you cringe, terrified that the man will chop off his hand as well. The coconut milk is very tasty, and the meat is scooped out with a piece of the shell.

Don't Miss

Golf on Tobago   *

You wouldn't think that one of the best courses in the Caribbean would be tucked away on this relatively remote island. The Tobago Golf Club (868-639-8871), part of the Mount Irvine Bay Hotel, is a Caribbean links-style course that is 6,793 yards long (Championship) and a par 72. It's a tough course all around, despite the lulling landscape of gentle rolling hills and turquoise Caribbean. Especially infamous on these coconut-tree-studded fairways is the ninth hole, with a hook right past a water hazard and a green that seems the size of a postage stamp. There's no relief until the "19th" hole, as number 18 will torment you with a sharp hook left, a water hazard, and a humiliating finish by the golf club. A round is just $48, plus cart rental.

Arcadia Records

Located on Castries Street in Scarborough (868-635-1424), Arcadia Records has great CDs of the latest Carnival hits.

The U.S. Virgin Islands

TOURISTO SCALE:

ST. JOHN 👤👤👤👤👤👤 (6)

ST. THOMAS 👤👤👤👤👤👤👤👤👤👤 (10)

ST. CROIX 👤👤👤👤👤👤 (6)

A trio of time-honored vacation havens with the Stars and Stripes flying overhead, the U.S. Virgin Islands offer the best and worst of the West Indies, and a good deal in between. You can find perfect hidden beaches where you might be the first to plant your feet one morning, as well as overdeveloped coves where too many bags of cement have been sacrificed in the name of condo and time-share developments. There is some of the Caribbean's best dining, and then there's a Wendy's for the cruise-ship masses who (seemingly) need to provide their taste buds a vacation from McDonald's. There are miles of idyllic and peaceful hiking trails in one of America's most beautiful national parks, but you'll also find a rush-hour commute in and out of the capital, where traffic slows to a snarled crawl.

If it sounds schizophrenic, it is, but despite these extremes, you can have a great vacation in the USVI—you just have to know where to go and what to avoid. There are 50 islands in all, most of which are little more than

ATLANTIC OCEAN

Prickly Pear Island
Necker Island
VIRGIN GORDA
North Sound
Mosquito Island
Scrub Island
The Dogs
Spanish Town
THE BATHS
Fallen Jerusalem
Ginger Island
Beef Island
Cooper Island
Salt Island
BRITISH VIRGIN ISLANDS
Great Camanoe Island
Marina Cay
R.M.S. RHONE
Peter Island
Guana Island
TORTOLA
Road Town
SIR FRANCES DRAKE CHANNEL
Deadman's Bay
Norman Island
Cane Garden Bay
Sandy Cay
Long Bay
The Bight
JOST VAN DYKE
Coral Bay
Great Tobago
Little Tobago
Great Thatch Island
ST. JOHN
Cinnamon Bay
Cruz Bay
Red Hook
ST. THOMAS
Charlotte Amalie
Buck Island
Water Island

U.S. Virgin Islands

CARIBBEAN SEA

ST. CROIX

Christianstead
ST. CROIX

N

Miles
0 5

U.S. Virgin Islands: Key Facts

Location	18°N by 64° W 68 miles/109 kilometers east of San Juan 1,600 miles/2,575 kilometers southeast of New York St. Croix is 40 miles/64 kilometers south of St. Thomas St. John is 3 miles/5 kilometers east of St. Thomas
Size	St. Thomas: 32 square miles/83 square kilometers St. Croix: 82 square miles/212 square kilometers St. John: 19 square miles/49 square kilometers
Highest point	St. Thomas: Crown Mountain (1,556 feet/474 meters) St. Croix: Blue Mountain (1,096 feet/334 meters) St. John: Bordeaux Mountain (1,277 feet/389 meters)
Population	St. Thomas: 51,181 St. Croix: 53,234 St. John: 4,197
Language	English
Time	Atlantic Standard Time all year (1 hour ahead of EST, same as EDT)
Area code	340
Electricity	110 AC, 60 cycles — same as the mainland U.S. and Canada
Currency	U.S. dollar
Driving	On the left; your valid U.S. or Canadian driver's license is acceptable.
Documents	None for U.S. citizens (a passport is a good idea for U.S. and Canadian citizens if there is a possibility for travel to the B.V.I.); proof of nationality for Canadians; passport and visa for U.K. visitors.
Departure tax	None
Beer to drink	Corona
Rum to drink	Cruzan Gold
Music to hear	Soca, reggae, quelbe (Quelbe is similar to the BVI's fungi but with origins in St. Croix. Its percussive "scratch" sound comes from corrugated gourds.)
Tourism info	800-372-USVI, www.usvitourism.vi

uninhabited rock outcrops, but all add greatly to the backdrop of outposts dotting the horizon in every direction. There are three islands on offer for vacationers, and each has a unique personality and individual attributes. It won't take a rocket scientist to figure out which one we prefer (pssst... St. John).

Of the territory's total population (officially about 109,000), more than 95 percent live on the two primary islands, St. Thomas and St. Croix. These islands aren't large by Caribbean standards, but they have been well established as vacation destinations for decades, drawing about two million visitors annually to their shores. The jewel of the U.S. Virgins, however, is St. John. Almost two-thirds of the island is part of the National Park Service, and most of the rest is not heavily developed—there isn't even an airport. Because the remaining land is exceedingly expensive (and there has never been a large population here), the relatively few homes are usually very tasteful and restrained. There are just two resorts and a handful of smaller inns, thriving villa-rental businesses, and three unique campgrounds that helped create the region's burgeoning ecotourism industry. Consequently, St. John is one of the most unspoiled and handsome islands in the West Indies. There are incredible snorkeling and swimming areas within an easy swim of shore, trails to hike, ruins of the old Annaberg sugar plantation to explore, and a variety of programs conducted by the park and outside vendors. In short, St. John is the closest thing to virgin territory in the USVI, and it's one of our favorite places to relax in all the Caribbean.

The Briefest History

The Virgin Islands were first settled around A.D. 700 by Amerindians (Arawaks) migrating north from South America. The Caribs soon followed and replaced the Arawaks. On Columbus's second voyage, in 1493, he landed on St. Croix and laid claim to all the islands for Spain. Nothing much happened until the 1600s, when St. Croix was settled by the Dutch, then the English and the French, and sugar plantations and slavery took root. The Danes eventually took control of the islands (St. John was uninhabited at the time), and in 1754 the Danish West Indies became a prosperous colony. The 19th century was a hard period for the islands because of declining sugar prices and changing trade routes, followed by the abolition of slavery by Danish decree in 1848 (anticipating Lincoln's Emancipation Proclamation by 15 years). With the lack of a labor force and the low cost of sugar beets on the mainland, sugar production dropped dramatically, and most of the land went fallow. In 1917, the United States purchased St. Thomas, St. Croix, and St. John for $25 million. Although the larger islands were welcoming visitors at least as early as the 1930s, it was the American trade embargo with Cuba that helped launch a tourist boom in the 1960s. Creation of the Hess Oil Refinery on St. Croix further strengthened the economy. Today, the USVI are an unincorporated territory with a nonvoting delegate to the U.S. House of Representatives. Despite prosperous tourism, major hurricanes in 1989 and 1995, along with budget shortfalls and a heavily overstaffed government, have contributed to a long-running financial crisis in the USVI.

Getting There

There is an airport on each of the two larger islands (St. John is reached only by boat). St. Thomas is served by American from New York–JFK and Miami, American Eagle from San Juan, Continental from Newark, Delta from Atlanta, Spirit from Ft. Lauderdale, United from Chicago and Washington-Dulles, and US Airways from Charlotte. St. Croix is served by American from Miami, American Eagle from San Juan, Delta from Atlanta, and US Airways from Charlotte. Charter services fly to the USVI from cities in the U.S. northeast during the winter; check with your travel agent. There are now also weekly charters from Gatwick-London to St. Thomas via First Choice Holidays.

There are smaller airlines connecting the USVI with San Juan and the BVI, including Air St. Thomas, Cape Air, Caribbean Sun, and LIAT. American Eagle and Cape Air fly between St. Thomas and St. Croix, but a better (and often cheaper) route between the two is the Seaborne Seaplane (888-359-8687 or 340-773-6442; www.seaborneairlines.com), which flies to and from the harbors of Charlotte Amalie, Christiansted, and Old San Juan throughout the day. There is also a ferry between St. Croix and St. Thomas via Island Lynx (340-713-LYNX); the crossing takes about an hour, costs $44 each way, and runs twice a day except Tuesday.

Since there is no airport on St. John, you'll have to fly into St. Thomas and take a ferry. There are two routes, one from Charlotte Amalie and one from Red Hook, at the eastern tip of the island. The route most convenient to the St. Thomas airport is the one from Charlotte Amalie, which leaves about every two hours from the downtown waterfront from 9 a.m. to 5:30 p.m. The trip takes 45 minutes and is $8 each way. The Red Hook ferry leaves every hour from 6 a.m. to midnight and takes about 20 minutes, priced $4 each way for passengers. There is also a car ferry between Red Hook and St. John, but this is *not advised* for day-trippers—there are more cars than ferry slots, and competition is fierce. You are better off leaving your car on St. Thomas and taking taxis on St. John. (Be further advised: Parking at Red Hook and Charlotte Amalie is severely constrained.) The ferry dock on St. John is right in Cruz Bay, the island's only real town. For more details, call Transportation Services (340-776-6282) or Varlack Ventures (340-776-6412), or visit www.st-thomas .com. Also note that St. John's Caneel Bay and Westin resorts have their own ferry service for guests (at a considerably higher cost, of course).

Getting Around

Transportation can be problematic in the U.S. Virgin Islands. There is very little in the way of public transportation, so your options are pretty much limited to renting a car or taking a taxi (you can thank the local taxi drivers for the lack of options—they wield enormous political clout). Driving is on the left, but most cars are American models with left-hand drive—this can

Service and Energy Surcharges

In most Caribbean hotels a service charge of 10 percent is added to your room rate at checkout. This is in lieu of leaving a tip in your room or on the hotel bill, and although we prefer being able to leave a tip based on the service actually received, the system is pretty well ingrained. A notable exception is the French islands, which don't add a service charge. In the USVI, there's no standardized policy. In general, hotels do *not* add a service charge to room or restaurant bills, but a few of the bigger facilities — perhaps sensing that there were a few extra bucks in the wallets of guests checking out — do add a surcharge. Confirm this when making your reservation. Sometimes hidden charges in the USVI take the form of an "energy surcharge" of a few dollars (or more) per day. Why these hotels aren't capable of analyzing their energy costs and factoring it into their rates is beyond us, but you've been warned.

take some getting used to. Another obstacle is traffic on St. Thomas, which can be very slow at rush hour (which coincides with when passengers are traveling to and from cruise ships).

On all three islands there are plenty of taxis to take you from your hotel to beaches, shopping, and dining, but the costs add up when you want to go sightseeing. If you are on a budget, our recommendation is to rent a car for most or all of your visit to St. Croix (which is a larger island to explore) and to rent a car only for a day or two of sightseeing on St. Thomas and St. John. Car rental prices on the two primary USVI fluctuate seasonally; expect to pay $40 to $50 per day. St. John rates are $60 and up per day. If you are renting a remote villa on St. John, you will find that a car is a must for your entire visit.

Avis (800-331-1212) and Hertz (800-654-3131) are represented on all three islands, but their rates are usually higher than the local outfits. On St. Thomas, try Anchorage E-Z Car (800-524-2027 or 340-775-6255) or Dependable (800-522-3076 or 340-774-2253). On St. Croix, there's Olympic-Ace (888-878-4227 or 340-773-8000) or Centerline (888-288-8755 or 340-778-0450). On St. John, call St. John Car Rental (340-776-6103), O'Connor (340-776-6343), or Cool Breeze Jeep Rental (340-776-6588).

You can ferry to Tortola and Virgin Gorda from Charlotte Amalie and Cruz Bay, St. John. Remember, this is an international trip, so a passport (or other form of photo ID and birth certificate) is required. Arrive 30 minutes prior to departure for international formalities. More information on ferries to the BVI is contained in that chapter.

Focus on the USVI:
St. John and the Virgin Islands National Park

At some point the Rockefeller family probably owned a chunk of all of America's most beautiful property, including 30,000 acres in upper Jackson Hole that became part of Grand Teton National Park in Wyoming, and 2,700 acres of Mount Desert Island, which became part of Acadia National Park in Maine. Can you imagine being that wealthy? Fortunately, the family gave the land to the government for everyone's enjoyment (and, we imagine, a sizable tax write-off). Legend has it Laurance Rockefeller first sailed to St. John in 1952, when there were just 400 residents and few businesses besides a fishing camp. Rockefeller bought the camp and an initial 600 acres for $350,000 and set about developing an upscale resort called Caneel Bay. He wound up buying nearly a third of the island. On the same day that the hotel opened its doors for business — December 1, 1956 — Rockefeller handed over 4,666 acres of prime St. John real estate to the director of the National Park Service. The following year President Dwight Eisenhower signed the bill creating the Virgin Islands National Park. Subsequent purchases and gifts brought the park size to its current 12,000 acres (two-thirds of the island), plus another 5,650 acres of submerged land. The result: Some of the most beautiful beaches and last stretches of undeveloped coves, hills, and vistas in the Caribbean are preserved for us, the above-average public.

St. John is definitely a must-see, thanks to the largesse of Laurance Rockefeller, who continued to visit his resort (and Little Dix Bay, in the British Virgin Islands) each year, right up until his death in 2004.

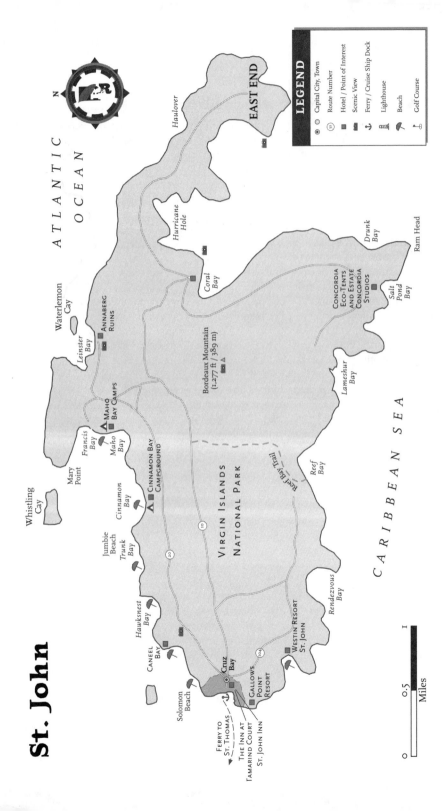

St. John

YOU COULD SAY ST. JOHN IS THE ST. BARTH OF THE VIRGIN Islands. It's pretty, it's expensive, it has cachet, and it takes a little extra effort to reach — but it's not, thankfully, St. Barth. People come here not to be *français* pretenders, eat French cuisine, or see and be seen, but to swim, snorkel, and enjoy the park. It has some of the loveliest beaches anywhere and terrific reefs for snorkeling. As with any beautiful and scenic public property, there will also be plenty of people, but many of them are day-trippers from nearby St. Thomas. The more renowned beaches (such as Trunk and Cinnamon) are gorgeous, but they can be crowded — at least popular enough to squelch your idea of a deserted Caribbean beach — but there are smaller and little-known beaches where you still might fulfill your fantasy. These include Jumby Bay, Salomon, and Honeymoon Beach on the north coast, and Salt Pond Bay on the south coast. Finding these beaches might take a little patience and determination, but they're worth the effort. The reefs are easily accessed and not hard to find (you can see them in the water from the beach). There is a marked underwater trail at Trunk Bay, but this is exciting only for beginners. If you are a snorkeling neophyte, Trunk Bay is a good place to learn — come first thing in the morning or late afternoon to avoid the crowds. Once you've earned your stripes, better snorkeling will be found off Hawksnest Beach, Cinnamon Bay, and Waterlemon Cay in Leinster Bay.

Beyond the National Park, St. John is lightly developed and includes the town of Cruz Bay and a ramshackle village at Coral Bay, on the western and eastern ends of the island, respectively. To explore the whole island, it's a good idea to rent a jeep: Some of the less-traveled roads are rough. If you don't want to deal with a vehicle (car rental is expensive, and driving is on the left), most of your shopping, dining, and bar needs will be met in Cruz Bay, and taxis are easy to procure on the west end of St. John. Just north of town is Caneel Bay, the original Rockefeller resort. The veranda bar here is a super spot for a cocktail. The seven beaches at Caneel are perfect, but access by land is restricted to use by hotel guests (you can visit them by boat without being a guest, however). Do stop by for a drink.

Besides the locals (who are much friendlier here than on the other U.S. Virgins), there are four types of visitors to St. John: (1) the villa owner or renter — the elite who come for weeks or months (country music's Kenny

Chesney shot a video here and then built a mega-manse to house his old blue chair); (2) the resort and honeymooner type — they stay at either Caneel (establishment) or the Westin (dot-com/pink lounge/mileage redeemer types); (3) the camper or guesthouser — naturalist and/or budget-minded types; and (4) the cruise-ship day-trippers from St. Thomas — the tourist hordes. Fortunately, the latter leave by early afternoon (large cruise ships don't dock here); during the day you'll find them camped out on the prime beaches. Although Trunk and Cinnamon are beautiful, they become fairly crowded by late morning with the type of people we are trying to escape.

Where to Stay

For such a small island, there is a wide variety of accommodations. The resort of note has long been Caneel Bay, the island's original hotel, but rapid development of the southwestern part of the island over the last two decades has added lots of private villas and condos, plus a 285-room Westin Resort. There are also relatively inexpensive guest houses in Cruz Bay and, of course, there are villas to rent at all levels of luxury. One other St. John option not commonly found in the Caribbean is camping. Now, camping on St. John is not your typical "roughing it" experience. First of all, the weather is about as perfect as can be — no cold, gloomy days to put a damper on your fun. Next, there is the warm, clear water and palm trees right at your doorstep. Finally, you don't have to drag along your tent, sleeping bag, and lantern; you can choose accommodations that allow you to be outdoors without the usual aggravations (remember, though, mosquitoes go hand in hand with island life). So, in keeping with the back-to-nature theme of St. John, we'll start with three picks that make the campground lifestyle easy — don't forget your flashlight and towel!

Campgrounds

Cinnamon Bay Campground, P.O. Box 720, Cruz Bay, St. John, USVI.
🄲 800-539-9998 or 340-776-6330, 🖂 340-776-6458,
🖳 www.cinnamonbay.com

🏧 **Not So Cheap** for the cottages and **Cheap** for tents 🍴 **EP** ⒸⒸ 40 cottages and 86 tents and bare sites

Now you can say you stayed at Rockefeller's place without spending a fortune. Located on the north coast on one of St. John's "big three" beaches, this well-managed campground was established by the oil tycoon and occupies prime national park land. There are cottages, tents, and bare sites available, all within a few hundred feet of the water. Our preference is to stay in one of the cottages, clustered in 10 blocks of four. The best (i.e., right on the water) are situated in the number

8, 9, and 10 blocks, which also cost a few bucks extra. The cottage is really just a 15-by-15-foot room, with two of the walls consisting only of screens with adjustable shades for privacy (the walls that separate each cottage are made of concrete, as is the floor). Though basic (remember, you are camping), it is actually not bad for two people. The furnishings, though sparse, are comfortable. There are twin trundle beds (with linens), a table, and four canvas captain's chairs under spotlighting. Cooking is done on a propane stove or charcoal grill outside, and there is a cooler, a water container, and utensils. Outside, there is a backyard patio and picnic table. The bathrooms are nearby and communal, with unheated showers. It's rustic but functional, and it's rewarding to fall asleep to the sounds of the forest and water.

There are also tents with beds (avoid tent clusters A, B, and C—there is little privacy), and bare sites can be rented for $27 a night. The campground has a commissary and an attractive outdoor dining pavilion called the Tree Lizard, where meals are available three times a day. There is a water-sports center on the beach, with windsurfing, sailing, scuba, and snorkel gear available; a dive package is also available. The park rangers conduct a weekly program of slide presentations, hikes, and snorkeling trips.

Maho Bay Camps and Harmony Studios, P.O. Box 310, Cruz Bay, St. John.
ⓒ 800-392-9004 or 340-776-6226, ✉ 340-776-6504,
🖥 www.maho.org, reservations@maho.org

💲 **Not So Cheap** for tent cottages; **Very Pricey** for studios 🍴 EP ⓒⓒ
114 cottages and 12 studios

Maho Bay is more intimate and slightly more deluxe than Cinnamon Bay. It's also the place we would land. Situated about 8 miles out of Cruz Bay and a few miles past Cinnamon, it consists of tented cottages connected by a series of wood walkways (à la Fire Island). Although none are located on the beach, each has a view of the bay (the best views are on the Skyline Trail, but they're a hike from the beach) or of the dense vegetation, which provides privacy. There are double beds (or twins) with linens, electricity, reading lights, a convertible couch, table and chairs, a cooler, utensils, a porch with deck chairs, and a Coleman stove. As at Cinnamon Bay, the bathrooms are communal (unheated showers—remember, you're camping). Privacy, view, and other factors vary considerably among the units. The tents closest to the beach tend to be popular with families and noisier, whereas units out on the tip sit atop a small cliff, with only the lapping water below for a soundtrack; some of the tents are above the dining area in the forest, which can be peaceful, but it's a long walk down to the sand.

The friendly management here is very eco-minded—hence the boardwalks, so as to not disturb the ground growth; the organic toilets, to save water; and the help-yourself herb garden. The clientele is very nature-oriented — most guests hang out in bathing suits throughout the day. Male employees wear bandannas on their heads, female employees wear Indian print dresses, and self-help groups often hold retreats here. The campground is surrounded by the National Park, so there's lots of breathing room and ample opportunity to commune with nature. There is an open-air dining pavilion, and breakfast and dinner are available daily. A small, expensive commissary is on the grounds for that quart of milk you forgot to buy at the supermarket in Cruz Bay. Maho Bay has its own beach and a fully equipped water-sports and activities center.

If the tents seem a little too rustic for you, there is also an adjacent 12-unit complex of studios called **Harmony** (part of the Maho Bay complex) with tasteful furnishings, full kitchens, and fully private bathrooms, and it's constructed almost entirely out of recycled materials. It's located high on the hill above Maho (a five-minute walk down to the beach) and utilizes the same facilities.

⊛ **Concordia Eco-Tents and Estate Concordia Studios,** 20–27 Estate Concordia, St. John, USVI. ℂ 800-392-9004 or 340-693-5855, ✆ 340-693-5960, ▯ www.concordia-eco-tents.com

🔒 **Not So Cheap** for eco-tents and studios ⑪ EP ⒸⒸ 18 tents and 9 studios

Also part of the Maho organization but located on the remote south coast, Concordia is perhaps the epitome of ecologically sensitive vacationing. Like Maho, this has wood-frame tent cabins, built on stilts, on a dry, scrubby hillside overlooking beautiful Salt Pond Bay. The cabins are somewhat more deluxe: Each has a minifridge, a flush toilet (of the composting kind), a solar-heated shower, and three double beds (although sleeping six would be very crowded). Four are wheelchair accessible. There's more privacy than at Maho, and every unit has a great view, but the isolation doesn't work for some guests. It's a 10-minute walk down to the beach, but there is absolutely nothing else within walking distance, so you really need a rental car (it's a 10-minute drive to Coral Bay; 40 minutes to Cruz Bay).

There are also free-standing cottages, the **Estate Concordia Studios,** which are attractive alternatives for those who want something more like four walls. These are spacious, with Mexican tile floors, wraparound decks, open-air showers, and fully equipped kitchens. The complex shares a good-size pool, a yoga pavilion, and a café — a restaurant is in the works to open in 2007. Note that this part of the island is exposed to direct sun all day, so it can get very hot (and there's no forest canopy for shade).

Villa Rentals

Private villas are a great way to experience St. John, and there is a wide variety on the island. Rates for a one-bedroom villa start at about $2,400 a week in the winter, but you can get an apartment for much less.

Caribbean Villas, P.O. Box 458, Cruz Bay, St. John, USVI. © 800-338-0987 or 340-776-6152, ✆ 340-779-4044, 🖥 www.caribbeanvilla.com

This organization rents more than 100 homes, villas, and condos. Some are very sought after, so reserve early.

Catered To, 522 Mongoose Junction, Cruz Bay, St. John, USVI. © 800-424-6641 or 340-776-6641, ✆ 340-693-8191, 🖥 www.cateredto.com

Eileen Sundra rents about 30 two- to five-bedroom homes and villas, most of which have pools, and at all levels of luxury.

McLaughlin Anderson Luxury Villas, 1000 Blackbeard's Hill, Charlotte Amalie, St. Thomas, USVI. © 800-666-6246 or 340-776-0635, ✆ 340-777-4737, 🖥 www.mclaughlinanderson.com

This outfit rents more than 50 villas throughout the U.S. and British Virgins. It even has properties on Anegada.

St. John Properties, P.O. Box 700, St. John, USVI. © 800-283-1746 or 340-693-8485, ✆ 340-776-6192, 🖥 www.stjohnproperties.com

This is a full-service real estate office that offers short- and long-term rentals. Apartments start at about $900 a week.

Resorts and Inns

Caneel Bay, P.O. Box 720, Cruz Bay, St. John, USVI. © 888-767-3966 or 340-776-6111, ✆ 340-693-8280, 🖥 www.caneelbay.com, caneelres@rosewoodhotels.com

💲 **Ridiculous** in the Courtside wing, other categories are **Stratospheric**; a 10 percent service charge is added 🍴 CP ⓒⓒ 166 rooms

This is the original RockResort, developed by Laurance Rockefeller in 1956. Although it is now managed by Rosewood Resorts, Caneel remains one of the grandes dames of luxury escapes in the Caribbean. The ambiance here is low-key, the clientele sophisticated and moneyed. You'll find a number of guests who have been visiting annually since the Rockefeller days, as well as younger arrivals (particularly honeymooners). Ensconced on a 171-acre peninsula of the primest of St. John real estate, the resort is spaciously and subtly laid out. There are seven beautiful beaches on the property, three of which are reserved for hotel guests. A variety of water sports is available. Most rooms are in two-story buildings, with two opposing walls composed of just screened louvers, allowing the trade winds to blow through, which we always thought was just fine. Alas, enough guests complained of the heat in these tropics (can you imagine!) that Rosewood installed air conditioners for all the rooms. The grounds are no longer quite as peaceful as they once were, what with all the a/c units whirring through the night now. The rooms have tile floors, attractive décor in shades of khaki, and brightly colored upholstery. There are also single-story cottages with similar interiors and a little more privacy. Three restaurants, 11 tennis courts, a small pool, and several bars round out the amenities. Note that nightlife is in short supply here; the place pretty well shuts down around 9 p.m., but Cruz Bay is just a 10-minute drive. The resort ferry from Charlotte Amalie is $85 round-trip.

Gallows Point Resort, Gallows Point Road, Cruz Bay, St. John, USVI.
© 800-323-7229 or 340-776-6434, ✆ 340-776-6520,
🖳 www.gallowspointresort.com,
information@gallowspointresort.com

💲 **Ridiculous** 🍴 **EP** 🆑 60 units

If you want to rent a condo on the water with a sunset view, this place offers fab views of either the Cruz Bay harbor or St. Thomas from the lanai, with the loft units being the best and most spacious. Units come with VCRs, a bartender-style stainless steel blender (the best for making pina coladas), and quarry tile floors. They are generally attractively decorated (since many are individually owned, décor varies from unit to unit). Most have phone and/or cable TV and all the units have air-conditioning. There's no beach, but there is a sunny pool and great snorkeling in front. A gourmet shop and decent dinner restaurant is on the property, and Cruz Bay is just a five-minute walk.

Westin Resort St. John, P.O. Box 8310, Cruz Bay, St. John, USVI.
© 888-627-7206 or 340-693-8000, ✆ 340-779-4985,
🖳 www.westinresortstjohn.com.

💲 **Stratospheric**, but watch for hefty discounts when rooms aren't full; a $20 per day service charge is added to the bill. 🍴 **EP** 🆑 349 rooms

This attractive modern property is the obvious resort alternative to Caneel Bay, although the two are quite different in style and appeal. It originally opened in 1987 but has gone through a few management changes en route to its current incarnation as a Westin. Our main complaint is its size—at 349 rooms it simply overwhelms the intimate, back-to-nature style of this island and requires the Westin to lure group-and-meeting business to keep it occupied. That said, it sits on a leeward and thus less breezy hillside that leads down to a decent beach, where you'll find a full complement of water sports; there's a huge pool lined with rainbow-colored neon (striking, but also not very St. John). The rooms are dark but nicely appointed, with all the standard Westin amenities, including Westin's trademark "heavenly" beds; all have air-conditioning, but only a few have lanais. There are four restaurants, room service, and two bars. Kids have the Westin Kids Club program, which gets them out of their parents' hair — a definite plus.

The Inn at Tamarind Court, P.O. Box 350, Cruz Bay, St. John, USVI. 🄲 800-221-1637 or 340-776-6378, 📠 340-776-6722, 🖳 www.innattamarindcourt.com

💲 **Cheap** for singles in the six economy units, **Not So Cheap** for the remaining doubles 🍴 **CP** ⒸⒸ 20 rooms

This is a funky but decent guesthouse — much improved since a family of new owners took over in 2004 and renovated inside and out. There is a variety of clean, simple rooms, six of which are tiny single units with a shared bath. The best rooms are on the second floor — they have high ceilings and are more airy and spacious, all have a/c, and one has a full kitchen. There is a courtyard bar and a surprisingly good restaurant, often filled with the backpacker set, and occasional live music. It is, however, right on a busy street, so it can get noisy.

St. John Inn, P.O. Box 37, Cruz Bay, St. John, USVI. 🄲 stateside: 800-666-7688, Local: 340-693-8688, 📠 340-693-9900, 🖳 www.stjohninn.com, info@stjohninn.com

💲 **Pricey** 🍴 **EP** ⒸⒸ 12 rooms

This is a cute little guesthouse just up from the town center, with simple, clean rooms and a bar and patio for hanging out. The rooms have air-conditioning, and the cheapest units share a bath (housekeeping units have private bathrooms). Its location is on a hill at the edge of Cruz Bay and within walking distance of the Paradise Gym; there is also a small dipping pool. It's a bit overpriced for what you get, but you do get St. John.

Where to Eat

The last few years have brought some very good restaurants to the island. In addition to the resort restaurants, which are good but overpriced, here are our suggestions.

$$$$$ Chateaux Bordeaux, Centerline Road, Bordeaux Mountain, 340-776-6611

This intimate little nook is tucked in a cleft near the highest point on the island, overlooking Coral Bay — it's a great spot to watch the moonrise. Inside you'll find atmospheric oil lanterns and chandeliers, and a great menu of French cuisine, including wild game specials. Reservations required.

$$$ **The Fish Trap**, Cruz Bay, 340-693-9994

A good variety of surf, turf, and shellfish make this the best place on the island for moderately priced seafood. The conch fritters and the coconut rum cake are renowned. Closed on Monday.

$$$ **Lime Inn**, Lemon Tree Mall, Cruz Bay, 340-776-6425

Wednesday night is Shrimp Feast, all the shrimp you can eat for $20. Fresh Caribbean lobster for $26 a pound is another attention-getter. Closed Sunday.

$$ **Luscious Licks**, Cruz Bay, St. John, 340-693-8400

Before heading out for a hike, stop by this vegetarian snack bar to stock up on pita sandwiches, smoothies, or the house specialties: the stroller (a tortilla stuffed with hummus, sprouts, veggies, yogurt, and tahini) or split-pea soup. Open for lunch only; closed on Sunday; no credit cards.

$$$ **Morgan's Mango**, North Shore Road, Cruz Bay, 340-693-8141

This is good neo-Caribbean cuisine with very reasonable prices. For that reason, it's always packed and fun. Reservations are suggested.

$$$$ **Paradiso**, Mongoose Junction, Cruz Bay, 340-776-8806

Set on the second floor with tables on a wraparound veranda, this spot serves steak, seafood, and designer Italian, with an excellent wine list. Thursday from 4 to 6 p.m. is two-for-one Cuervo margaritas time. Reservations for dinner are suggested. Closed on Sunday.

$$$ **Shipwreck Landing**, Coral Bay, 340-693-5640

This breezy patio overlooks the bay south of town and is a refuge for anyone staying at Concordia, a mile or so down the road. There are decent beer specials, and on Wednesday there is live music.

$ **Skinny Legs**, Coral Bay, 340-779-4982

This burger joint looks like a shack next to the road, but devoted locals would prefer to think of it as their local dive. The burgers are mighty tasty, and this is also the island's most reliable place to see a major sporting event on TV.

$$$$$ **Stone Terrace**, Cruz Bay, 340-693-9370

Overlooking the harbor and with great ambiance, this is a local favorite, especially for oysters Rockefeller (how appropriate!) and a macadamia-tamarind encrusted pork tenderloin. It offers a smart wine list. Dinner is served every night.

$$ **Woody's Seafood Saloon**, Cruz Bay, 340-779-4625

A hole-in-the-wall frequented by famous local Kenny Chesney, this is the place to be for happy hour on St. John — it's also the only dining spot on the island open past 10 p.m. Most people come for the libations ($1 beer from 3 to 6 p.m.), but there is also a decent seafood menu (the blackened fish sandwich is a highlight) and a big bad cheeseburger. This is probably Cruz Bay's liveliest spot — the party rages till 1 a.m. on weekday nights, or till 2 a.m. on Friday and Saturday.

$ **Vie's Snack Shack**, East End, 340-693-5033

Satiate your hankering for West Indian cuisine at this East End spot: conch fritters, beef and fish patties, and garlic fried chicken legs. There's a tiny, little-used beach across the street that is a good place for a dip. Lunch only; closed Sunday and Monday.

Don't Miss

⊛ Snorkeling

You won't find a better island in the Caribbean for snorkeling than St. John. Our favorite spot includes Waterlemon Cay, a tiny islet located a couple hundred feet off Leinster Bay, where you'll find starfish sprinkled through the turtle grass beds, and the shallow, healthy reef growing between Salomon and Honeymoon Bays. Check in with the Park Service for its recommendations, or take Captain Bob Conn's snorkeling trip aboard his charming motor yacht *Cinnamon Bay*. Conn has been on the island for a couple decades and knows the better snorkeling sites around St. John, as well as on neighboring islets. On our last trip we visited Congo Cay, where we saw turtles and swam over a staggering drop-off where sea pinnacles soared to within 15 feet of the surface. The cost is $65 per person — well worth it. Conn also does full-day excursions to the BVI for $95. Reservations (strongly advised): 340-776-6462; www.motoryachtcinnamonbay.com.

The Beaches

The best and least crowded are Salomon (nude, but rangers sometimes issue citations, so be forewarned), Honeymoon, Little Hawksnest, Francis, Salt Pond, Lameshur, and Waterlemon Cay. The most scenic and crowded are Hawksnest, Trunk Bay, and Cinnamon Bay.

Hiking

The national park has 22 marked, maintained trails. The most popular is the Reef Bay Trail, a 2.2-mile downhill hike (one way) from Centerline Road to the south side of the island, passing sugar mill ruins and ancient petroglyphs en route to a pretty beach (accessible by trail only). The park service offers a guided trip that avoids the uphill return; a boat takes you back to Cruz Bay. For reservations (required) call 340-776-6201, ext. 238. The Ram Head Trail is another worthwhile hike that affords dramatic ocean views (1 mile each way) and little-visited coves. Stop by the Park Headquarters in Cruz Bay for info and a free trail map; the waterproof Trails Unlimited topography map is detailed and worth purchasing.

Diving

Both Low Key Watersports (800-835-7718 or 340-693-8999; www.divelowkey .com) and Cruz Bay Watersports (340-776-6234; www.divestjohn.com) offer full-service dive facilities and all kinds of scuba instruction, from resort (intro) dives to night dives and advance certification programs. Don't miss diving in the Virgins.

Sunset Drinks at Asolare

Getting a table at this French/Asian restaurant timed to watch the sunset over Pillsbury Sound can be an exercise in frustration. A drink at the bar is easier, and the view is almost always a winner. The food is excellent. For reservations, call 340-779-4747.

A T-shirt from Woody's Seafood Saloon

St. Thomas

WITH ITS STRIKING HARBOR SURROUNDED BY SPINDLY, ABRUPT mountains, St. Thomas boasts one of the Caribbean's most dramatic backdrops. There are at least a half dozen fine beaches and tucked-away coves, and the view of the neighboring Virgins never disappoints. However, islands cannot be judged by physical assets alone, and the savvy traveler should be aware of some of the island's disagreeable features.

Long one of the Caribbean's busiest resort destinations, St. Thomas is also its top cruise-ship port—as many as 10 vessels dock in the harbor at Charlotte Amalie on some winter days (the year-round average is 20-plus a week). On an island that already boasts one of the highest population densities in the region, the daily cruise-ship infestation is a major contributing factor to St. Thomas's congestion and blight. There are condominium developments, massive resorts, and shopping malls framing the view in almost every direction; little traditional Caribbean personality survives. If you pick up the daily newspaper, you'll discover that crime—in the form of muggings, robberies, and an astonishingly high per capita murder rate—makes New York City look like a country village.

Why come here at all? First of all, St. Thomas is more accessible than most Caribbean destinations, making it ideal for a quick weekend escape from the East Coast. Package deals that combine airfare and accommodations often provide worthwhile savings. You will also find excellent dining and great shopping, starting with 300 or so jewelry shops (note that the USVI has the highest duty-free limit in the Caribbean: $1,600 per person, and no sales tax). Finally, just about any activity that might be associated with the Caribbean (with the exception of gambling, found on St. Croix) is available here: parasailing, golf, diving, game fishing, sailing, and much more. Of course, to get to our favorite Virgin, St. John, you will probably have to travel via St. Thomas, and the pair makes a good two-island vacation if you don't want to commit an entire sojourn to the languid pace of St. John.

Where to Stay

With more than 4,000 hotel rooms on this relatively small island, there are plenty to choose from, but oversize mega-resorts dominate the scene. If you

St. Thomas

ATLANTIC OCEAN

CARIBBEAN SEA

Outer Brass

Inner Brass

Thatch Cay

Hendrick Bay

Stumpy Point

Bordeaux Bay

Fortuna Bay

Brewers Bay

Magen's Bay

Signal Hill (1,480 ft / 451 m)

Crown Mountain (1,556 ft / 474 m)

Crown Mtn Rd

University of the Virgin Islands

Cyril E. King Airport

Lindbergh Bay

Flat Cays

Mahogany Run Golf Course

Fairchild Park

Hotel 1829

Crystal Palace

Galleon House

Charlotte Amalie

Hospital

Havensight

Paradise Point

Fort Mylner

Tutu

Nadir

Frenchman Bay Rd

Morning Star Beach Resorts

Marriott Frenchman's Reef

Hassel Island

Water Island

Gregerie Channel

East Gregerie Channel

Pineapple Village Villas

Wyndham Sugar Bay Resort

Pavilions and Pools

Sapphire Beach Resort

Red Hook

Red Hook Rd

Cowpet Bay

Great Bay

The Ritz Carlton

Great James Island

Pillsbury Sound

Leeward Passage

Ferry to St. John

Ferry to St. John

LEGEND

- ◉ Capital City, Town
- ⑭ Route Number
- ■ Hotel / Point of Interest
- ▲ Scenic View
- ⚓ Ferry / Cruise Ship Dock
- 🗼 Lighthouse
- ⛱ Beach
- ⛳ Golf Course

Miles
0   1   2

want a beach scene with umbrella-garnished drinks close at hand, choose a resort; if a more intimate ambiance with a modicum of island atmosphere is your preference, head for one of the small inns.

Resorts

The Ritz-Carlton, St. Thomas, 6900 Great Bay, St. Thomas, USVI.
  📞 800-241-3333 or 340-775-3333, ✎ 340-775-4444,
  🖥 www.ritzcarlton.com

💰 **Stratospheric** plus $35 per day "resort fee" 🍴 **EP** ᴄᴄ 200 rooms

As you might expect from the name alone, this is St. Thomas's premier hotel. It had a $75 million expansion and renovation in 2002. Also, between August and November 2006 it had plans for a $35 million renovation that would add 24 luxury suites, 6 spa treatment rooms, and a huge lounge, as well as improvements to three of its restaurants. Originally opened as the Grand Palazzo and lavished with Italian Renaissance touches, this resort sits on a 30-acre site on the island's east end, facing St. John. In the original wing, all rooms are identical in size and layout, with tropical, if somewhat excessively tasteful, furnishings. We know that the Ritz-Carlton is supposed to be stuffy and sophisticated, but this is the Caribbean, after all. So the tropical touches seem to be a nose up to its location. We have to admit that we didn't mind hanging out in the marble baths or on the elegant balconies.

The only difference in room price is based on view, and since all face the sea, extracting extra bucks for the elevation of your terrace is a bit of a stretch, in our opinion. The 48 rooms in the newer wing are the same size as the original rooms but slightly closer to the water, and they have a club level for noshing throughout the day. These rooms are part of the property's "fractional ownership" program.

The overall property is quite attractive, with bougainvillea draped around the peach-colored buildings and lush gardens dividing them. There's a sweeping free-form pool with an infinity edge, a beautiful beach, three tennis courts, a well-maintained health club, a dive shop with an array of watersports, and a 53-foot luxury catamaran — the *Lady Lynsey* — for sunset sails. Views across Turquoise Bay to St. John are splendid. There is also an over-the-top, marble-lined lobby and fine dining in the main restaurant.

Marriott Frenchman's Reef and Morning Star Beach Resorts, P.O. Box 7100, St. Thomas, USVI. 📞 800-570-4423 or 340-776-8500, ✎ 340-715-6193, 🖥 www.marriottfrenchmansreef.com, resorts@marriott.vi

💲 **Wicked Pricey** at Frenchman's Reef, **Beyond Belief** at Morning Star, but check into package deals. 🍴 **EP** Ⓒ© 483 rooms

On our first visit some years ago to Frenchman's Reef, the larger of two adjacent Marriott hotels, we thought it was an ugly mishap — a bit like a mammoth cruise ship that accidentally veered on its way into the St. Thomas harbor and beached on the rocks. It's still immense, but a major makeover in 1997 did much to improve the luster of the USVI's largest hotel. It now has a rich color scheme and West Indian touches, redesigned rooms, and the addition of a ninth floor to create two-story suites. A health club and spa were added, offering a variety of cardiovascular and Paramount muscle training equipment, along with sauna and steam room. Both resorts share these amenities, plus tennis courts, two pools, a water-sports center, aerobic sessions, 11 restaurants, and a bevy of bars.

It's all one Marriott property, but there are separate front desks for the two very different wings. The majority of the rooms are found at Frenchman's Reef (which sits on a choice bluff above the water). All have ocean views — there are two-story suites on the top floor, with loft bedrooms. Down below, the 96-room Morning Star Beach has the more traditional Caribbean ambiance, with clusters of two-story buildings lining a fine beach. All of the rooms here were renovated in late 2006 and, except for the view, all are identical, oversize, and luxurious. Some step right out onto the sand (you'll pay a ridiculous premium for the beach view). Since the combined hotels contain the region's largest meeting and convention space outside Puerto Rico, you are almost bound to be sharing this property with corporate types garnished in name tags. On the positive side, if a full-amenity resort appeals to you — one with 24-hour room service, WiFi throughout, a multitude of restaurants and bars to choose from, and plentiful activities, then this is probably a good place to camp out. A water taxi connects the property with downtown Charlotte Amalie, passing the new Marriott Vacation Club (i.e., time-share wing) en route.

Sapphire Beach Resort, Route 6, Smith Bay, St. Thomas, USVI.
📞 800-524-2090 or 340-775-6100, 📠 340-775-2403,
🖥 www.antillesresorts.com

💲 **Wicked Pricey** plus 10 percent service charge 🍴 **EP** Ⓒ© 171 rooms

This is an agreeable beachfront property that caters to families. Each of the rooms is on or close to the sand, where hammocks are strung between the palm trees and the views are of Virgin Islands trailing into the distance. The rooms are actually villa-style suites, with full kitchens, spacious balconies, and attractive furnishings. The resort has a full water-sports center, a large pool, tennis courts, two restaurants and bars, and a 67-slip marina. There's a well-regarded, complimentary kids program to provide parents with a little relaxation of their own. The Sunday afternoon beach party is a huge scene with a live band, and the snorkeling on the reef on the point to the right of the resort is superb.

Smaller Inns

Pavilions and Pools, 6400 Estate Smith Bay, St. Thomas, USVI. ℂ 800-524-2001 or 340-775-6110, ✆ 340-775-0374 ▭ www.pavilionsand pools.com, info@pavilionsandpools.com

⬛ **Very Pricey** ⑪ **CP** ⓒⓒ 25 units

The apartments here are a good bet for anyone who wants seclusion from the hubbub of St. Thomas and the amenities of a villa without the wallet wallop. Each unit is a one-bedroom bungalow with a totally private pool on a terrace. There is a full kitchen and dining area, a living room and a bedroom, and an oversize bathroom with an open-air shower. The hotel has seen better days, but most of the wear and tear is superficial (e.g., sun-faded soft goods and chipped tile). Also, some rooms suffer from road noise during the day, and there's no view, really. The (good) beach is a five-minute walk, and there's a small café on site with a limited menu. This is a good place for self-starters who want to see St. Thomas independently and at a reasonable cost. The privacy can't be beat.

Hotel 1829, P.O. Box 1567, St. Thomas, USVI. ℂ 800-524-2002 or 340-776-1829, ✆ 340-776-4313, ▭ www.hotel1829.com, hotel1829@islands.vi

⬛ **Not So Cheap** for the smallest units, and **Pricey** for the larger rooms, plus a 10 percent service charge ⑪ **CP** ⓒⓒ 14 rooms

This home was built by a French sea captain for his new bride in 1829, and despite clunky additions that crawl up the steep hill, it still has lots of atmosphere and charm. The rooms vary in size and décor; the least expensive are too cozy and dark, whereas the rooms in the original house are bigger and have the lion's share of antiques, with brick walls and four-poster beds providing additional ambiance. There's a plunge pool and an appealing bar. Note that there are lots of stairs to deal with, but the location in the heart of Charlotte Amalie is convenient for shopping. It is a National Historic Site.

Galleon House, 31 Kongens Gade, St. Thomas, USVI. ℂ 800-524-2052 or 340-774-6952, ✆ same as local number, ▭ www.galleonhouse.com, info@galleonhouse.com

⬛ **Cheap** in the shared bath units, and **Not So Cheap** in the newer apartments ⑪ **CP** ⓒⓒ 12 units

This is a homey guesthouse located on a hill overlooking Charlotte Amalie. The four original rooms are small and rustic but have character. Two of these units share a bathroom. Newer accommodations are found just up the hill in a pair of apartment buildings. These have kitchenettes, a/c, and nice views. There's a small pool and a sundeck, and iguanas lope about the garden.

Crystal Palace, 12 Crystal Gade, St. Thomas, USVI. ℂ 866-502-2277 or 340-777-2277, ✎ 340-776-2797, ▭ www.crystalpalaceusvi.com

　💲 **Not So Cheap** ⑪ **CP** (CC) 5 rooms

Situated in St. Thomas's historic district, on Synagogue Hill, this is a newer bed and breakfast in a classic colonial mansion. There are five rooms, two of which have private bathrooms; all have a/c. The communal living area is beautifully appointed in original and reproduction antiques, and a terrace faces the town and harbor. An honor bar is available, and more than a dozen restaurants are within a 10-minute walk.

Where to Eat

$$$$$ Craig and Sally's, Frenchtown, Charlotte Amalie, 340-777-9949

Perhaps our favorite spot on the island, this restaurant has a revolving menu highlighted by always-fresh fish and an enviable wine list. Dinner is served Wednesday through Sunday; lunch is served Wednesday through Saturday.

$$　Duffy's Love Shack, Red Hook, 340-779-2080

At the opposite end of the spectrum from The Ritz-Carlton is the Love Shack, a very friendly bar scene with the added attraction of basic grill items like burgers and mahimahi. Note that a drink known as the Shark Tank contains five different rums and no less than three liqueurs. Tin roof... rusted! (You were thinkin' it, so we had to say it.)

$$$　Epernay Champagne Bar, 24-B Honduras Street, Frenchtown, 340-774-5348

This is more bar than restaurant, although a bistro-style menu of entrées, salads, and caviar is on offer. You'll also find a nice selection of wines and champagnes by the glass — great for before or after dinner.

$$　Gladys' Café, 17 Main Street, Charlotte Amalie, 340-774-6604

Informal and unpretentious, this café has tasty local food for breakfast and lunch. It's a good spot for a break from a shopping expedition, although it's a bit hidden in an alley within the Royal Dane Mall.

$$$$$ The Great Bay Grill, The Ritz-Carlton, Red Hook, 340-775-3333

Sign up for a luxurious meal at the island's premier hotel. The focus is on grilled meat and seafood, of course. This is a great place to be on moonlit nights, gazing across the channel at St. John, which is cast in various shades of gray and black. Dinner is served Tuesday through Saturday, with a champagne brunch on Sunday ($69 per person). Smart casual attire is requested.

$$$$$ Havana Blue, Morning Star Beach Resort, Frenchman's Reef, 340-715-2583

Overlooking a beautiful beach, this is St. Thomas's current trendsetter, occupying a terrific venue that has always been home to lesser resort restaurants. Havana Blue offers a tantalizing blend of Cuban and Pacific Rim flavors, served with showy panache (don't worry—the tastes live up to the theatrics). The spacious room is wrapped in billowy curtains and primped with an aquatic lighting scheme. It's definitely worth a splurge.

$$$$ Hervé Restaurant and Wine Bar, Government Hill, Charlotte Amalie, 340-777-9703

Positioned on a prime perch next door to Hotel 1829, this is a long-standing favorite for French continental (with the requisite splash of Caribbean, of course), served with twinkling views of Charlotte Amalie and the harbor. It's surprisingly reasonable. Open for lunch and dinner daily.

$$$$ Oceana Restaurant and Wine Bar, Villa Olga, Frenchtown, 340-774-4262

Housed in the one-time home of a 19th-century Russian diplomat, the new Oceana has pretty harbor views. More important, it has very good seafood and excels at unusual preparations. Our two favorite dishes were the smoked oyster-crab-avocado salad and a delicious bouillabaisse that was brimming with mussels, Manila clams, and lobster. Don't overlook the decadent desserts.

$$$$ Room With a View, Bluebeard's Castle, Charlotte Amalie, 340-774-2377

Start your evening with a passion fruit mimosa, then move on to a rewarding menu that fuses Mediterranean dishes with Caribbean ingredients like mango. It's a little hard to locate, but well worth the effort—the sparkling views from the top of Bluebeard's Castle are endless. Closed on Sunday.

$$$$ Virgilio's, Charlotte Amalie, 340-776-4920

Don't be put off by the dressy, semiformal atmosphere. This often quiet spot hiding on a side street has lots of colonial atmosphere and great homemade pastas. The artwork is fun and the staff is all-pro —very seductive.

Don't Miss

Udder Delight

The name makes us groan, but this place — on the road to Magens Bay — makes great milk shakes from the Trans-Caribbean Dairy. Try one with a shot of crème de menthe or amaretto.

Paradise Point

This is one of the choicest viewpoints in the Caribbean, 700 feet above sea level and overlooking Charlotte Amalie and the harbor. There is an expensive ($15), three-and-a-half minute tram ride to this point, but there's also a steep road that winds to the top, where a gift shop and bar await. It's a great spot for a sunset cocktail, and there's a quarter-mile nature trail that reveals other choice viewpoints.

St. Thomas Synagogue

This is the second oldest synagogue in the Western Hemisphere, founded in 1796 and used by more than 100 Jewish families on the island today. The current building, built in 1833, is a beautiful temple with sand floors and unique relics, including an 850-year-old menorah. It's located on Synagogue Hill in Charlotte Amalie and open to the public daily; 340-774-4312.

Virgin Islands Ecotours

This kayak outfit offers two-and-a-half-hour tours through a marine sanctuary and mangrove lagoon (the last stand on the island). After paddling out to the edge of the lagoon, you can snorkel along with the baby reef fish. It's a bit pricey, at $65 per person, but well run; 340-779-2155; www.viecotours.com.

Mahogany Run Golf Course

This is a scenic and challenging 6,022-yard, par-70 course designed by George and Tom Fazio that sits on a bluff on the north coast. The cliffside Devil's Triangle — holes 13, 14, and 15 — is quite memorable. Rates fluctuate seasonally, but there are discounts after 2 p.m. and in summer. Reservations: 800-253-7103 or 340-777-6006; www.mahoganyrungolf.com.

Diving

There are a number of dive operators on the island; just make sure you don't join up with one of the cattle-drive operations that caters to the cruise ships en masse. **Chris Sawyer Dive** in Red Hook (and with a store at Wyndham Sugar Bay Resort) is a good choice, and it does regular trips to the wreck of the RMS *Rhone* in the BVI: 877-929-3483 or 340-775-7320; www.sawyerdive.vi.

Night Snorkeling

Homer Calloway, a former instructor at Chris Sawyer Dive, offers this unusual experience, typically working out of Hull Bay. This is a trippy, sci-fi-like excursion: Each snorkeler is equipped with a wet suit and a submersible flashlight, and a lime green glow stick is attached to snorkels so that Homer can keep track of where everyone is in the dark. We kept thinking about how it looked from shore — this group of alien blobs hovering in the black sea with green-glowing antennae and landing lights surveying the sea floor. Typically, you'll spot some of the creatures that normally stay hidden during the day, like sea slugs and octopi (Homer brings up the more intriguing specimens for topside viewing). Priced at just $38, the night snorkel is recommended for people who have some snorkeling experience, not because it's difficult but because its appeal is more refined. Homer also does snorkel tours by kayak and even kayak and dive trips during the day. To reserve a tour call 866-719-1856; www.nightsnorkel.com.

Water Island

Located a half mile out in the harbor of Charlotte Amalie, 492-acre Water Island is sometimes called the fourth Virgin. Legend has it that this spot was the inspiration for Herman Wouk's classic novel *Don't Stop the Carnival* (the fabled Water Isle Hotel ruins can still be spotted today). There are 161 inhabitants, a lovely beach, and a terrific snack stand called **Heidi's Honeymoon Grill**, where you can snare a half-pound Black Angus burger grilled perfectly to order. A ferry leaves from Tickles Restaurant at Crown Bay Marina (between the airport and Charlotte Amalie) about every hour between 6 a.m. and 6 p.m.; the fare is $9 round-trip. The beach and Heidi's are just a 10-minute walk from the ferry dock; the hotel ruins are just southwest of the beach, on the point. Another option for visiting is to come over with **Water Island Adventures**, a bike-tour operation that caters to cruise-ship passengers. Since there are few cars, here the island is ideal for leisurely touring, and you get to swim at the beautiful beach after riding around. The half-day tours are priced at $60 and leave at 9 a.m. and 1 p.m. daily. Reservations: 340-714-2186; www.waterislandadventures.com.

Magens Bay

This is unquestionably the island's most scenic beach, but it's crowded with cruise-ship passengers throughout the day. You can avoid them by coming at dawn or dusk (there are no hotels on the beach), or by viewing Magen's from Mountain Top, the highest point on the island. On the other hand, Mountain Top is also a tourist trap that sells overpriced banana daiquiris and tchotchkes. Other beaches worth visiting include Morningstar, Coki, and Lindberg. The latter is right near the airport, but it's very good for swimming and not too noisy early in the morning or late in the afternoon.

Charlotte Amalie

Named after a Danish princess, this was once undoubtedly a lovely Caribbean port, and you can probably get a great deal on some rose-colored glasses to help you filter out today's clutter and commercialism. Wednesday is the busiest, and Saturday is usually the lightest, cruise-ship day, and a glimmer of history and romance sometimes peeks out between the T-shirt shops and liquor stores. Quite a few good deals can be found, particularly in jewelry, fine china, crystal, perfume, and, of course, rum; gems, watches, and electronic products (verify the service warranty) can offer other bargains. The main savings come from the lack of sales tax and duty-free rules: U.S. residents can bring home $1,600 worth of goods free of duty, and the next $1,000 is subject to just 5 percent duty. Also, items produced in the USVI don't count toward the exemption — they're completely duty-free. Stores are generally open 9 a.m. to 5 p.m. Monday through Saturday (and Sunday when cruise-ship business warrants).

The British Virgin Islands

If you've "done" St. John and want to get away from the hustle of St. Thomas, **New Horizons Charters**, which operates out of the Sapphire Resort Marina, does day trips to four of the BVI via a 44-foot powerboat. You'll visit The Baths on Virgin Gorda, have lunch at Marina Cay, snorkel at Guana Island, and wrap things up with a Painkiller in a hammock on Jost Van Dyke. The nine-hour trip sounds decadent, but we think the cost, $135 per person, is quite reasonable (lunch and customs fees are not included). Reservations are essential: 800-808-7604 or 340-775-1171; www.newhorizonscharters.com.

St. Croix

ST. CROIX ALWAYS SEEMS TO DRAW THE SHORT STRAW OF the three U.S. Virgins. Nightlife and shopping activities are eclipsed by those on busy St. Thomas, and St. John's National Park hogs the limelight when it comes to outdoor pursuits. As a result, the island still awaits discovery, even among many Caribbean regulars. What they'll find, however, is some of the best of the Virgins: an appealing capital (Christiansted) with historic buildings and shopping, an undeveloped forest, decent beaches, tantalizing golf courses, excellent diving, and the only casino in the Virgin Islands.

St. Croix is more than twice the physical size of St. Thomas, but it has a much smaller tourism infrastructure—1,000 hotel rooms compared to St. Thomas's 4,000. It wasn't always this way: For the middle part of the 20th century, the two islands were a roughly comparable draw. St. Thomas expanded its airport to accommodate jets in 1968, however, and soon after embraced mass tourism with the opening of the Frenchman's Reef and other big convention hotels. Meanwhile, on St. Croix, a notorious robbery-turned-murder spree in 1972 and major damage from Hurricane Hugo in 1989 conspired to propel the two islands into separate destinies. In fact, even today, tourism plays second fiddle to St. Croix's primary breadwinner, the Hess Corporation Oil Refinery, the largest such operation in the Western Hemisphere. Crime has been a problem on and off through the years, and Crucians always grumble about the preferential treatment that St. Thomas seems to get from politicians, businesspeople, and cruise-ship operators. (Charlotte Amalie is the USVI seat of government.) The good news is that St. Croix offers a well-rounded menu of vacation activities and less expensive hotel rates than its siblings, and it is set to a more relaxed pace than you'll find on St. Thomas. Also, crime is less a problem here than on St. Thomas, and we like the low-key infrastructure of St. Croix. Expect your welcome at local hotels to be warmer than usual.

Although there is a cruise-ship pier in Frederiksted (the island's second town), in 2002 St. Croix experienced a devastating blow from the cruise industry when four major lines cut the island from their Caribbean itineraries. Various reasons for the pullout were cited, including concerns about passenger safety and the distance between the port in Frederiksted and shopping in Christiansted (cruise ships and shopping are attached to each other at the

St. Croix

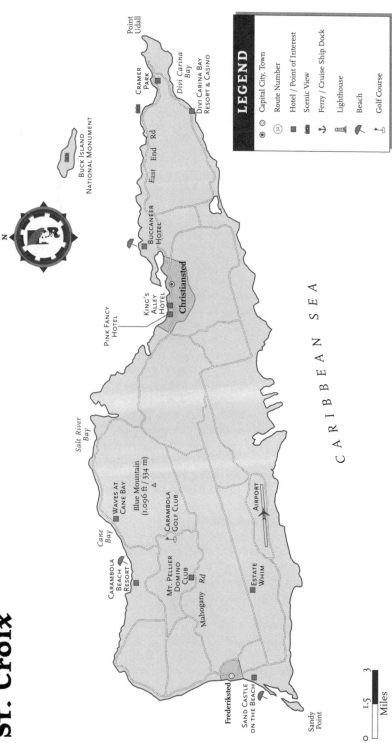

N

CARIBBEAN SEA

Point Udall

CRAMER PARK

Divi Carina Bay

DIVI CARINA BAY RESORT & CASINO

East End Rd

BUCK ISLAND NATIONAL MONUMENT

BUCCANEER HOTEL

Christiansted

KING'S ALLEY HOTEL

PINK FANCY HOTEL

Salt River Bay

WAVES AT CANE BAY

Cane Bay

Blue Mountain (1,096 ft / 334 m)

CARAMBOLA GOLF CLUB

CARAMBOLA BEACH RESORT

Mt. PELLIER DOMINO CLUB

Mahogany Rd

ESTATE WHIM

AIRPORT

Frederiksted

SAND CASTLE ON THE BEACH

Sandy Point

LEGEND

- ◉ Capital City, Town
- ⊙ Route Number
- ■ Hotel / Point of Interest
- ■ Scenic View
- ⚓ Ferry / Cruise Ship Dock
- 🏛 Lighthouse
- ☂ Beach
- ⛳ Golf Course

0   1.5   3

Miles

wrists and ankles). However, the real reason is that the VI government was playing hardball with the cruise industry over the costs for a new development on St. Thomas. The major cruise players called the governor's bluff, and St. Croix paid the price. In the last couple of years the number of cruise calls has increased somewhat, but it's still nothing like the intense cruise traffic St. Thomas experiences every day. There is talk of a new 2,500-acre, $500 million resort to start construction in 2007 at Annaly Bay, at the west end of the island, with up to 1,000 hotel rooms in three hotels. Although this is projected to raise the number of hotel rooms on St. Croix back to 1980s levels, there are a lot of plans that never quite materialize on this island — we'll believe it when we see it.

Where to Stay

Most accommodations are centered in and around the towns of Christiansted and Fredericksted, with a smattering along the north and east coasts.

Resorts

Buccaneer Hotel, P.O. Box 25200, Gallows Bay, St. Croix, USVI. 📞 800-255-3881 or 340-712-2100, 🖂 340-712-2104, 💻 www.thebuccaneer.com, mango@thebuccaneer.com

💲 **Wicked Pricey** plus a 4 percent energy surcharge 🍴 **BP** ⒸⒸ
138 rooms

If you're looking for a full-amenity resort, the Buccaneer is one of the all-around best values in the Caribbean. Located a couple miles east of Christiansted, the 60-year-old Buccaneer has a wide variety of rooms from which to choose. There are the original units in the Great House, which are nicely furnished and comfortable but are a five-minute walk from the water. Other rooms include family cottages, suites with private terraces overlooking the sea, and, best of all, the (very expensive) Doubloon Rooms. The latter encompass more than 800 square feet and have window seats with day beds, marble and brass bathrooms, and walk-in closets, all in tasteful, muted pastels (if pastels can ever be considered tasteful).

The resort sits on a 340-acre landscaped peninsula and includes two pools and three beaches of varying appeal, with all the accompanying water sports. Activities aren't limited to the water: You'll also find an 18-hole golf course, a 2-mile jogging trail, a fitness room with spa, and eight lighted tennis courts (the tennis program is a key asset — co-owner Elizabeth Armstrong was a top tennis pro a few years back). So despite the fact that the resort continues to draw an older clientele that has visited for years, there is plenty on offer for a younger generation of Caribbean travelers.

Carambola Beach Resort, Estate Davis Bay, St. Croix, USVI. © 888-503-8760 or 340-778-3800, ✆ 340-778-1682, 🖳 www.carambolabeach.com, info@carambolabeach.com

💲 **Wicked Pricey** 🍴 EP ⒸⒸ 151 rooms

Carambola boasts one of the most generous and attractive "standard" room layouts in the West Indies. Alas, the hotel has been plagued by hurricanes, management changes (and their shifting priorities), a location that is too secluded for some vacationers, and a beach that is sometimes a bit rough. A U.S.-based group of investors purchased the property in 2002, and they hired New Hamphire–based Ocean Properties to run it. In 2006 they embarked on a $5 million renovation, and although we haven't seen the results, we've got our fingers crossed that Carambola's future is better secured.

The resort sits in a stunning cove called Davis Bay, about 30 minutes west of Christiansted. There is an excellent golf course in the hills that rise behind the 28-acre property, but otherwise the surrounding mountains are undeveloped and lush. The rooms are found in two-story villas along the beach and are basically identical in size, layout, and amenities (prices are based on view). All are essentially suites (though without a dividing door) and feature lots of dark woods, with sitting areas, spacious bathrooms, and screened porches. Second-floor units, which are recommended, have soaring cathedral ceilings. Each room has a pullout queen bed, and there is no additional charge for a third or fourth person, making this a very good deal for families. The renovation is adding a full kitchen to each unit, with granite counters, distressed marble floors, and two flat screen TVs. There are tennis courts, a pool, an exercise room, and three restaurants. Water sports are found on the beach, including excellent diving on the nearby Cane Bay Drop-Off.

Divi Carina Bay Resort & Casino, 25 Estate Turner Hole, Christiansted, St. Croix, USVI. © 877-773-9700 or 340-773-9700, ✆ 340-773-6802, 🖳 www.divicarina.com

💲 **Very Pricey**, plus 4 percent service charge 🍴 EP ⒸⒸ 200 rooms

St. Croix's newest hotel is also one of its oldest. The Divi Carina Bay lies on the grounds of an old Divi property that was all but flattened by Hurricane Hugo in 1989. Surely one reason the rebuilding took a decade to begin is the Divi's location. It is near the island's remote eastern tip—too isolated from town, restaurants, and that duty-free addiction, shopping. It's a full 30-minute drive back to Christiansted. However, the hotel finally reopened in 2000, and the USVI's first casino was added, in a garish building that looks as Vegas as they come. The guest rooms are trendy-chic—the fun décor will be dated in a heartbeat (like, it already is). However, they have good amenities, like a VCR, wet bar, minifridge, and coffeemaker. There's a decent beach with water sports, tennis, and an attractive pool area; the snorkeling off the beach to a diverse fringing reef is excellent (the hotel has an on-site dive shop). A spa and two restaurants are on the property—a good thing, since any other dining is a 10- to 30-minute drive away. The 10,000-square-foot casino is sleek and above average, as these things come in the Caribbean, but it's discouraging to see that the only people using it are island residents.

Smaller Inns

King's Alley Hotel, 57 King Street, Cristiansted, St. Croix, USVI. ☎ 800-843-3574 or 340-773-0103, ✆ 340-773-4431, 🖳 harbourwalk@ vipowernet.com

🛍 **Not So Cheap** 🍽 **EP** CC 33 rooms

This is a good bet for anyone who wants a location in the heart of Christiansted, on the water. The hotel's 21 original rooms are in a three-story building with ocean-facing balconies—these were renovated in 2006. Next door are 12 rooms located on the second floor overlooking a shopping courtyard—they are handsomely decorated with Indonesian furniture, batik prints, and king-size four-poster beds. There's no beach in town, but you can ferry over to one on the tiny island across the channel for a dollar.

The Waves at Cane Bay, 112-C Estate Cane Bay, St. Croix, USVI. ☎ 800-545-0603 or 340-778-1805, ✆ 340-778-4945, 🖳 www.canebayst croix.com, info@canebaystcroix.com

🛍 **Not So Cheap** 🍽 **EP** CC 12 rooms

This spot has just a dozen rooms, trimmed in wicker and floral themes, and with a full kitchen and balcony. All rooms face the roiled ocean, and the beach is just a couple minutes away on foot. The hotel's two chief assets are a small but inviting restaurant and a dive shop that caters only to hotel guests and is within a short swim of the Cane Bay Wall. On the other hand, the out-of-the-way location (20 minutes from either town) is appealing if you want an easy, get-away-from-it-all vacation.

Sand Castle on the Beach, 127 Smithfield, Frederiksted, St. Croix, USVI. ☎ 800-524-2018 or 340-772-1205, ✆ 340-772-1757, 🖳 www.sandcastleonthebeach.com, info@sandcastleonthebeach.com

🛍 **Not So Cheap** 🍽 **CP** 21 rooms

As the name suggests, this hotel is situated right on the beach, just south of Frederiksted. The inexpensive, gay-owned operation offers accommodations that are nothing elaborate, but they come with TV, VCR, kitchenette, and balcony, and all were renovated in 2005. An attractive garden surrounds the small pool, and a low-key, amiable atmosphere dominates throughout the day, enticing gay, lesbian, and straight visitors. There's a mini–fitness room and a restaurant that is open five days a week. The beach is narrow, but mostly undeveloped, and we loved watching an armada of glowing squid while snorkeling not far from the shoreline.

Pink Fancy Hotel, 27 Prince Street, Christiansted, St. Croix, USVI. 🕻 800-524-2045 or 340-773-8460, 📠 340-773-6448, 🖥 www.pinkfancy .com, info@pinkfancy.com

🔹 **Cheap** in the street-level rooms, **Pricey** for all others, plus 8 percent energy tax ⑪ **CP** 🆑 12 rooms

Opened as a hotel (and named!) in 1948 by an ex–Ziegfield Follies girl, this charming spot is listed on the National Register of Historic Places — it dates to the 1780s. Since 1999 the inn has been owned by Motasem and David and represents another good gay-friendly landing on St. Croix, but (owing to its location) it's frequented by plenty of nongay business travelers. The rooms are spread out in four buildings surrounding a small tile pool on a hillside, each lavishly decorated in antiques, Oriental carpets, and tasteful artwork, and all featuring a kitchenette. Four street-level rooms are not as fancy and are priced less, but bright cheery colors abound throughout. Downtown Christiansted is just a few blocks away.

Where to Eat

$$$ **Blue Moon**, 17 Strand Street, Frederiksted, 340-772-2222

This is a waterfront favorite, with live jazz on Friday and a Sunday jazz brunch. The chalkboard menu offers Cajun-accented steak, seafood, osso bucco, vegetarian dishes, and occasional Mexican food. Lunch is served Tuesday through Friday; dinner Tuesday through Sunday.

$$ **Bombay Club**, Christiansted, 340-773-1838

A cavelike passage leads to a dungeonlike dining room. Despite the surroundings, you'll find decent burgers and sandwiches for lunch and filet mignon and fettucini Alfredo for dinner.

$$ **Harvey's**, Christiansted, 340-773-3433

This is a family-run spot serving West Indian fare (Montserratian, to be specific). Typical offerings are barbecued chicken, ribs, stewed goat, and kingfish.

$$$$ **Kendrick's**, 51 ABC Company Street, Christiansted, 340-773-9199
The former slave quarters of a restored West Indian Great House is the setting for satisfying French continental. Closed Sunday and Monday.

$$ **No Bones Café**, Gallows Bay, Christiansted, 340-773-2128
Tamas Janda, the son of Gypsies, serves up a tasty drunken chicken and great salads, all lovingly presented. If you're feeling adventurous, order the "Feed Me" and see what arrives.

Don't Miss

Diving the St. Croix Wall

Along the north coast of the island, between Christiansted and the western tip of St. Croix, is a 13,000-foot-deep underwater canyon that yields spectacular sightseeing. The best areas are at Cane Bay and Salt River Canyon, and there are several outfits that will take you out. Try Anchor Dive Center (800-532-3484 or 340-778-1522; www.anchordivestcroix.com) or Dive Experience (800-235-9047 or 340-773-3307; www.divexp.com).

Buck Island

This 850-acre national monument—designated as "one of the finest marine gardens in the Caribbean sea" by JFK—is located 1.5 miles north of St. Croix. It has a picture-perfect beach curling around its western side, hiking trails, and an underwater snorkeling trail through a forest of elkhorn coral populated by 250 species of fish and 3 types of sea turtles. Various outfits do half-day and full-day trips to the unpopulated island; try Mile Mark Watersports (340-773-2628; www.milemarkwatersports.com) or Big Beard's Adventure Tours (866-773-4482; www.bigbeards.com). Note that the snorkeling trail is sometimes bumper-to-bumper with fins, but the reduction in cruise ships has probably eased congestion.

Snorkeling on the Eastern Beaches

St. Croix's undeveloped eastern tip has several untrammeled coves with reefs for sightseeing, but be alert for bumpy surf. To reach them, drive out the East End Road to Cramer Park and follow the dirt road to Pt. Udall, the easternmost tip of the United States East End Bay can be a bit rough for safe swimming, but just around the tip you'll come to Isaac's Bay, an often-deserted beach protected by a splendid reef. Word to the wise: Don't leave any valuables in your car!

St. Croix Heritage Trail

If you prefer to tour on your own, try this trail. It's a 72-mile-long driving route from one end of the island to the other, and it contains 200 historic and natural attractions. Detailed maps are available at most hotels, or for more information; call 340-713-8563, or go to www.stcroixheritagetrail.com.

The Beaches

St. Croix doesn't have the dramatic coves of St. John, but its beaches aren't as heavily developed as those on St. Thomas. Prime sunbathing is found on the west coast between Frederiksted and Sandy Point, on the southwest tip (not open during turtle-nesting season), and on several strands along the north coast. Also of note is the pretty beach on Buck Island.

Estate Whim Plantation Museum

This is an elegant, restored sugar plantation with an unusual oblong great house (built European style rather than West Indian). A tour of the site is $5, and there's a well-stocked gift shop; located between Frederiksted and the airport. Call 340-772-0598.

Carambola Golf Course

One of the Caribbean's better courses is this Robert Trent Jones par-72 set amid rolling hills on the west end of the island. A round is $95, including cart in high season, $79 in low. Reservations: 340-778-5638; www.golf-carambola.com. Down a notch is the 18-hole course at the Buccaneer Resort, but it's a little cheaper, too.

A Drive Along Mahogany Road

This road winds along the north coast between Frederiksted and Christiansted and through the island's lushest scenery and views. On the way, stop by to visit the next item.

Beer Drinking Pigs at Mt. Pellier Domino Club

For those who think they've seen it all, check this out. Buster passed away several years back, but his wife, Miss Piggy, and assorted relatives will gulp down an O'Doul's (OK, so they're nonalcoholic beer–drinking pigs) for the bargain price of $2 a can. Why not?

Off the Wall Beach Bar

This is where live music (most nights) and sunset views are combined with a cheery, hammocks-and-sand setting. There are free shooters at sunset, but watch those strong drinks, especially if you're the one driving that windy road back to your hotel. Also open for breakfast, lunch, and dinner.

A Day Trip to St. Thomas on the Seaborne Seaplane

We don't get very excited about St. Thomas, but the shopping and dining are excellent, so why not visit on a day trip using the Seaborne Seaplane? You won't have to mess with pesky airport security checks or terminals as the 18-seat Twin Otter floatplanes commute between the harbors of Christiansted and Charlotte Amalie throughout the day, making the 15-minute crossing a breeze. Reservations: 888-359-8687 or 340-777-4491; www.seaborneairlines.com.

Vieques

TOURISTO SCALE:

👤👤👤👤 (4)

There was a time when Vieques was an outpost of sorts. With a limited selection of hotels and the presence of a huge U.S. naval base, the island was not known for drawing crowds. In the last few years, however, this beach-studded island has experienced a boom — well, at least in Vieques terms. Today, more and more travelers are discovering the range of activities and incredible array of paradisiacal beaches here. As a result, more specialized hotels and restaurants are springing up to cater to the new influx of tourists. Although the island still retains its laid-back charm, change is on the way. There is even a new airport terminal under construction that will allow travelers to fly right into Vieques without changing planes (or airports) in San Juan. There is no need to panic, however — the island is still as charming as ever.

One of the Spanish Virgin Islands, Vieques lies 7 miles east of Puerto Rico and is considered a municipality within the Commonwealth of Puerto Rico. Viequenses, as the almost 10,000 residents are called, are also U.S. citizens. About one-third of the island was owned by the U.S. Navy, which for years used the island for live bombing practice (this means real bombs). Military maneuvers were executed from the huge Roosevelt Roads Naval Station, on the other side of the Pasaje de Vieques in Puerto Rico. Even napalm was dropped on the island. The military presence, and particularly the continued live bombing, infuriated many locals (it would us, too!) because it upset the

Vieques

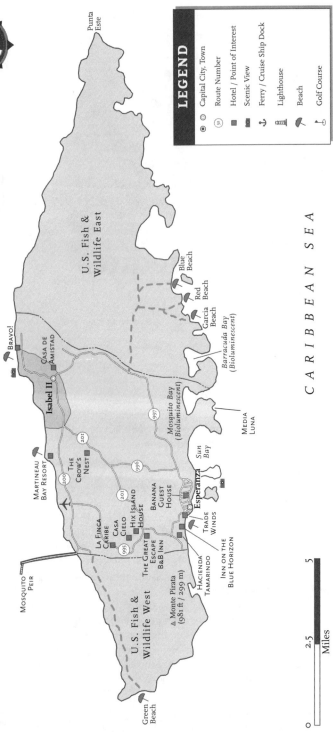

ATLANTIC OCEAN

CARIBBEAN SEA

Punta Este

LEGEND
- Capital City, Town
- Route Number
- Hotel / Point of Interest
- Scenic View
- Ferry / Cruise Ship Dock
- Lighthouse
- Beach
- Golf Course

U.S. Fish & Wildlife East

Blue Beach

Red Beach

Garcia Beach

Barracuda Bay (Bioluminescent)

Mosquito Bay (Bioluminescent)

Media Luna

Sun Bay

Bravol

Casa de Amistad

Isabel II

997

Martineau Bay Resort

The Crow's Nest

200

201

201

996

995

La Finca Caribe

Casa Cielo

Hix Island House

Banana Guest House

The Great Escape B&B Inn

Esperanza

Trade Winds

Hacienda Tamarindo

Inn on the Blue Horizon

△ Monte Pirata (981 ft / 299 m)

U.S. Fish & Wildlife West

Green Beach

Mosquito Peir

0   2.5   5
Miles

Vieques: Key Facts

Location	18°N by 65°W 7 miles east of Puerto Rico 1,660 miles southeast of New York
Size	55 square miles 21 miles long by 5 miles wide
Highest point	Mt. Pirata (981 feet/299 meters)
Population	Approximately 10,000
Language	Spanish (but most Viequenses speak English)
Time	Atlantic Standard Time (1 hour ahead of EST, same as EDT)
Area code	787 (must be dialed before all local numbers as well)
Electricity	110 volts AC, 60 cycles, same as U.S. and Canada
Currency	The U.S. dollar
Driving	On the right
Documents	None for Americans and no Customs hassles, either; Canadians need proof of nationality or a passport; Brits need a passport and visa.
Departure tax	None
Beer to drink	Medalla
Rum to drink	Don Q or Bacardi
Music to hear	Reggae, rock, and *reggaetón*
Tourism info	787-741-0800 www.vieques-island.com www.enchanted-isle.com/enchanted/Vieques.htm

wonderful ambiance of the island. Who wants to live in a bombing range? Tensions heightened in April 1999, when a civilian was killed and four were injured by two stray 500-pound bombs. This incident made the U.S. military presence a hot-button issue, not only in Vieques but in all of Puerto Rico. After the bombing accident, President Clinton commissioned a study to determine the need for a continued U.S. military presence in Vieques and Puerto Rico. As a result, the Navy gave up control of its former base on the west end of the island in May 2001. Encompassing approximately 15,000 acres, the base was primarily used for support, ammunition storage, and housing for Navy personnel. Under the agreement, approximately 4,200 acres will be made available for local housing and other development. The remaining acreage, except for 100 acres still used by the Navy for its radar installation, is preserved as conservation land administered by the U.S. Fish and Wildlife Service and the Puerto Rican Conservation Trust. The conservation lands, including the popular Green Beach, are open to the public. Many of the beautiful beaches along the coast are now open to the public.

There are two towns on Vieques: **Isabel II** on the north side, the island's port and commercial center, and **Esperanza**, a smaller, mellower town on the south side geared more toward tourism. Of a total of about 55 square miles, only 17 are available for residential and commercial use. Even so, this part of Vieques seems uncrowded, unspoiled (no mega-resorts, fast-food chains, or traffic lights), and often very pretty. The island is hilly but lacks the big peaks to capture rain clouds (the highest summit is Mt. Pirata at 981 feet). Hence it is an arid island (about 40 inches of rain fall annually) and a marked contrast to the El Yunque rainforest just 16 miles away in Puerto Rico. Vegetation here is similar to other Caribbean islands like Antigua and many of the Grenadines. Fortunately, water is piped in from the El Yunque watershed, so shower water pressure is good.

After a few days on the island, we noticed that an inordinate number of New Englanders, especially from Massachusetts and particularly the Boston area, have moved here. Perhaps the no-frills air of Vieques appeals to our Yankee mentality, or maybe it was just that real estate was cheap. (Prices have risen considerably but are still cheaper than on many other islands.) We also noticed that besides some outdoor activities like going to the beach, reading, exploring the island, and maybe diving or snorkeling, there's not a helluva lot to do here. It's fine if that is your intention. Another thing we noticed (we're so observant) is that none of the hotels are on a swimmable beach. It is necessary to rent a car and drive. This might be an inconvenience for some. Finally, we noticed a lot of couples, which makes sense given the paucity of nightlife. It's definitely B.Y.O.B. (Bring Your Own Bedmate).

The Briefest History

The Taíno (Arawak) Indians first settled the island about 2500 B.C. and prospered until the arrival of Columbus in 1493. He named the island Vieques after its Taíno name Bieques ("Small Island") and claimed it for Spain. A series of rebellions and disease epidemics ensued, and by 1514 the Taínos were gone from the island, either enslaved on Puerto Rico or dead. Between 1514 and 1843, the island remained uninhabited and under the control of Spain's command post in Puerto Rico. As happened with most Caribbean islands, the European powers all tried to get their hands on it. Colonization attempts were made by the English, Danish, and French, and all were repelled by the Spanish forces in Puerto Rico. During this period of skirmishes over Vieques, many pirates, sustained by seafood, shellfish, and fowl, called the island home.

Annoyed with other nations trying to capture the flag of Vieques, Spain finally made the island a Spanish municipality in 1843, and a fort was built and a colony begun. Prosperity followed in the form of sugar plantations worked by African slaves brought over from neighboring English islands (slavery was abolished in the English colonies in 1834 but not in Puerto Rico until 1873). In 1898 the Spanish-American War ceded the island to the United States, which absorbed Vieques into the Commonwealth of Puerto Rico. At that time there were four *centrales* ("sugar mills") in operation, owned by just a few families who didn't share their wealth. Worker conditions were deplorable and remained so until a general strike in 1915 improved the workers' situation significantly. Sugar and fishing sustained the island's economy until World War II.

With American involvement in the war inevitable, the U.S. Navy initiated a search for a training and maneuvers area that would be similar to the climate and conditions of the Japanese-occupied South Pacific. They found it on the east coast of Puerto Rico (Roosevelt Roads) and on Vieques. In 1941 70 percent of Vieques was expropriated, much to the chagrin of its 10,000-plus residents. The Navy land grab shut down the *centrales* (the last one closed in 1942). Construction jobs for the bases provided employment for a few years, but by 1945, about 3,000 Viequenses had been relocated to St. Croix. The rest were left in the middle section of the island with little or no employment opportunities. Thus the seeds of the anti-Navy movement were sown. The live bombing and use of other lethal weapons on the island from World War II to the present accelerated the momentum. With the April 1999 incident, when a civilian was killed by a stray bomb, that movement gained momentum and was fueled by public outrage. This ultimately resulted in the full withdrawal of U.S. military forces.

While many Viequenses sought economic opportunity in Puerto Rico or the United States, the Puerto Rican government tried and failed several times to reestablish agriculture. Finally realizing that that wasn't the way to go, it shifted the emphasis toward industry in the 1960s. With the added boost of Federal Tax Code 936, which gave U.S. companies huge tax breaks if they invested in and established plants or companies in Puerto Rico, the economic picture brightened in Vieques. The 1969 opening of the General Electric plant anchored the effort; it is still in operation today. Tourism on the island is a relatively recent phenomenon. In its infancy in the 1980s, tourism accelerated into the 1990s as Vieques was discovered by both independent travelers and the media.

Getting There

Travel to Vieques will soon be much easier — there is a new American Eagle terminal under construction, which will allow flights from the United States to land here without the usual connection in San Juan. This will cut down travel time and provide a huge boost for tourism. Until then however, the most convenient way to get to Vieques is to fly from San Juan's Luis Muñoz Marín International Airport. Vieques Air Link (stateside: 888-901-9247, 787-741-8331 in Isla Verde and San Juan) has three round-trip flights daily to

Vieques's fairly new, modern terminal. Round-trip airfare is $167 for adults and children. Planes are of the small propeller variety, so early reservations are advised. The trip takes about 30 minutes. Isla Nena Air Service (787-791-0413) also flies to Vieques from Marín International Airport. In addition, Vieques Air Link has scheduled service from San Juan's smaller, domestic Isla Grande Airport (just to the west of the Miramar section of San Juan and very convenient for anyone staying in the Condado or Old San Juan). Both airlines offer charter service. Air Flamenco (787-741-8811 in Vieques or 787-724-6464 in San Juan) also offers flights from the Isla Grande airport in San Juan.

Another option is to fly from Fajardo, which is an hour to an hour and a half east of San Juan (depending on traffic). This small airport has a lot more daily flights, and they take only 10 minutes. Both Vieques Air Link and Isla Nena Air Service (787-741-1535) offer scheduled and charter service here. Finding the airport is a tad tricky, so pay attention to the airport signs and don't be afraid to ask for directions (it happens often here).

The **Fajardo Port Authority** also provides passenger and car ferry service three times daily to Vieques (787-863-0705 in Fajardo and 787-741-4761 in Vieques). Passengers do not need reservations; the fare is $4 round-trip. Reservations are necessary for cars; fares are $26 round-trip for the car plus $4 for each passenger. The trip takes an hour.

Finally, there is a seasonal Fast Ferry service available from Old San Juan to Vieques that takes under two hours. The one-way cost is $47; the roundtrip fare is $73. Contact Island Hi-Speed Ferry at 877-899-3993 or www.islandhispeed ferry.com more information.

Getting Around

Since you have to drive to get to a swimming beach in Vieques (especially the good ones), renting a car is a must. While the island roads are in good shape and are well marked, the naval base roads can get bumpy. We suggest renting a jeep for this reason — and because it's fun. Be sure to request one with a removable soft top (even more fun). Rentals range between $35 and $50 a day for jeeps and cars. Minivans are about $60. All rental companies are local, and most will arrange for airport pickup and drop-off (or will let you leave the car at the airport). Our favorite is Maritza's Car Rentals (787-741-0078); it features great vehicles, such as soft-top 4 × 4 Jeeps, and it offers drop-off service to hotels. Or try Island Car Rentals (787-741-1666; islandcar@aol.com) or Steve's Car Rentals (787-741-8135). For moto rental, try Extreme Scooter Rental (787-435-2121) — its scooters are about $55 per day.

Focus on Vieques: Mellowing Out on the Beaches

We know that's a very '70s expression — "mellow out" — and we really have tried to erase that decade from our collective memory, but the term is really what Vieques is all about. How does one mellow out? Well, just staying here will automatically start you on the path. Reading, sleeping, and maybe a few cocktails will help. Lying or walking on the beach and swimming in the clear turquoise water won't hurt, either.

There are a lot of undeveloped beaches to explore. Although Vieques lacks the truly stunning beaches of its sister Culebra, or of St. John or Anguilla, most visitors will be very pleased with the more than 50 options available (we're more than a little jaded, so it takes a lot to impress us). Our favorite are Sun Bay, Media Luna, and Navio Beach. All hotels provide directions to the island's beaches, which, with one exception (Green Beach), are on the south side of the island.

Sun Bay is just east of the center of Esperanza and wins the prize for best beach on Vieques. A long, palm-fringed crescent of white sand with good swimming areas (many of the island's beaches have shallow coral reefs close to the water's edge), Sun Bay also has picnic tables, bathroom facilities, and a sandy road that runs parallel to it. The best part is on the left (eastern) end of the beach, where it's calmer and there is good snorkeling. The beach is "open" from 7 a.m. until 5 p.m. and requires a $2 parking fee; call 787-741-8198 for more information. Media Luna and Navio Beach are accessed from the bumpy, sandy road at Sun Bay. **Media Luna** is fairly secluded and has shade trees, shallow calm water, and good snorkeling (again on the eastern side). **Navio Beach** is small, very secluded, and framed by rocky bluffs; it is only a half-hour walk from Sun Bay, has the most-turquoise water, and often has body-surfable waves. Some bathers take it all off here. Be advised that there is no shade, so bring an umbrella.

On the east end of the island is **Camp García**. Here, on the south coast, are Red, Blue, and García Beaches, which are now all open to the public.

Also on the east end is **Green Beach**. This faces Puerto Rico and has great views of El Yunque. However, stick to weekdays here; on weekends boaters from Fajardo anchor at Green Beach, and it gets crowded. Sheltered from the trade winds, the beach can get buggy by mid-afternoon if it has rained recently. Blue and Red Beaches have become popular spots now that the military base is closed. They are easily accessed by road — a taxi from Esperanza runs about $10.

Where to Stay

Since the 136-room and 20-suite deluxe Martineau Bay Resort will soon be renovated and opened as a W Hotel, it is obvious Vieques is undergoing a step up in style. There is even talk that the resort will be building a golf course, which has sparked debate among the locals. We were surprised to see that the level of sophistication has risen here in the few years since our last visit; more swanky inns and fine restaurants are popping up on this little island. Our new favorite hotel on the island, Bravo!, is one prime example. For those seeking the small and serene, have no worries — the island is still a place of tiny inns, guesthouses, and villa rentals.

⭐ **Bravo!**, P.O. Box 1374, North Shore Road, Vieques, PR. ℂ 787-741-1128,
📠 787-741-3918, 🖳 www.bravobeachhotel.com

💲 **Very Pricey** 🍴 **BP** **CC** 11 rooms

This sensual oceanside boutique hotel takes accommodation in
Vieques to a whole new level. Owned by a trio of style-minded New
Yorkers who transformed an old hacienda into an ultra-stylish hotel,
Bravo! retains some traditional style in its architecture, most specifically
in the design of its central plaza and fountain and in the restaurant
that is shaped like a passing ship. However, the rooms evoke a much
more modern appeal. Everything here is done to the max. The rooms
are super-modern, with white throughout and sleek glass doors opening onto private lanais. The queen-size mahogany beds are draped
with gauzy mosquito nets and outfitted with Frette linens, and the
bathrooms are stocked with Aveda bath products. All rooms come
equipped with satellite TV, DVD players, and Playstations for rainy days.
Original art and photography adorn the rooms, which also have ceiling fans, a/c, and dehumidifiers. Our favorite rooms are 3 through 7,
which are oceanfront studios with the best views. Although there are
only 11 rooms, there are two pools for guests to enjoy, one right over
the ocean and the other in the garden, replete with cushions and an
honor bar. An upstairs sea-view deck is perfect for special events and
massages. Hanging at the pool with its red lights and chill tunes
would be our ideal "night out." After one night here, we were seduced
by the comfortable style of Bravo and were not surprised to learn of
the accolades this boutique hotel is quickly garnering. Here's another:
the renowned Rum & Reggae Sexiest Hotel in Puerto Rico Award.

Hacienda Tamarindo, P.O. Box 1569, Route 996, km 4.5, Vieques, PR.
ℂ 787-741-8525, 📠 787-741-3215, 🖳 www.haciendatamarindo.com,
hactam@aol.com

💲 **Pricey** and up 🍴 **BP** **CC** 16 rooms

We adore the Hacienda Tamarindo, a Spanish-style inn opened in
1997, set on breezy rising grounds with sweeping views of sloping
pastures and the Caribbean. Ex-Vermonters Linda and Burr Vail built
and opened the inn in an amazingly short time, considering the difficulties of building and running a business in the Caribbean and on
a small island. With it they've created an extraordinarily comfortable
and warm environment. They are a very amiable and hospitable couple, and their friendly and helpful style as innkeepers is one of the great
things about the Hacienda. So is the 40-something-foot tamarind tree
growing smack dab in the middle of the inn (it graces the Hacienda's
atrium and dining terrace). The Vails' collection of art, collectibles,
and antiques acquired during years in Vermont adorn both the public spaces and the guest rooms. An honor bar in the lobby provides

refreshment, and there is an air-conditioned lounge with TV-VCR and a library. Outside, at a pretty pool with chaises, you can take a dip and get some sun. Be sure to say hello to the talking parrot. He'll give you an earful!

Each of the rooms has its own style and décor (Linda was a commercial interior designer), and all feature mahogany louvered doors and windows, terra-cotta tile floors, ceiling fans, and baths with tile showers. A suite comes with a Jacuzzi tub and private lanai. The Hacienda is also wheelchair accessible. A full American breakfast is served on the second-floor dining terrace (we loved the real Vermont maple syrup on the table). We hope the new condos being built by the hotel's owners don't compromise the intimate setting here, but we are confident that the Hacienda will retain its tranquillity, as these units will be located slightly down the hill.

No children under 15 are allowed (that means no screaming kids and stroller obstacles—we like that!).

Inn on the Blue Horizon, P.O. Box 1556, Route 996, km 4.5, Vieques, PR. ℂ 787-741-3318, ✎ 787-741-0522, 🖳 www.innonthebluehorizon .com, blue_inn@compuserve.com

💲 **Very Pricey** and up 🍴 **CP** 🆑 9 rooms

The first time we visited the Inn on the Blue Horizon in 1996, there were only three rooms, and Café Blu was the island's best restaurant. Now there are nine rooms at this wonderful place, and the restaurant is in the process of being rebuilt after a recent kitchen fire. The inn, set on 20 acres, is under new ownership but is still beautifully decorated —to within an inch of its life. Common areas have big overstuffed sofas and chairs; antiques, art, and open space abound. Books and magazines are placed just so, and dramatic flower arrangements are strategically located throughout the inn. It's like a page out of *Architectural Digest*. There is a library crammed with books. A pretty pool surrounded by a tile deck faces the sea and is bordered by a hibiscus hedge. There's even a tiny gym for the gym bunnies among us. With all this studied stylishness comes a slight attitude, but since we can give it, too (only when deserved, of course), it didn't bother us a bit.

Not surprisingly, the guest rooms (three in the main house and the other six sharing three cottages) are extremely tasteful. Most have four-poster beds; all rooms have queen- or king-size beds, except one, which has an antique double four-poster. All rooms except for the suite in the main house are air-conditioned and are also cooled by the steady trade winds and ceiling fans. All have antiques, terra-cotta tile floors, a color scheme of warm muted tones, bright upholstery and fabrics, all-cotton linens, cut flowers, glass-block showers, and spacious lanais with white wooden chairs (in the cottage units). Our favorite rooms are called Mariana and Esperanza. The Joseph and Judith rooms in the back cottage, though very pretty, did not have as good a view of the sea as the other cottage rooms. The original three main-house rooms have high ceilings, four-poster beds, and very dramatic drapes. Thoughtful touches in the rooms include a beach umbrella and chairs, a cooler and thermos, beach towels, a flashlight, and bug spray.

No children under 14 are allowed.

The Crow's Nest, P.O. Box 1521, Route 201, km 1.6, Vieques, PR. ℂ 877-CROWS-NEST or 787-741-0033, ✆ 787-741-1294, 💻 www.crows nestvieques.com, thenest@coqui.net

💲 **Cheap** 🍴 **CP** ㏄ 17 units

This is the epitome of what Vieques used to be; very casual, no-frill, laid-back, and inexpensive. Seven of the Crow's Nest's units are rented as condos, and 10 as hotel rooms—which are actually condos rented out by the inn. With new owners Scott Bowie and Eli Belendez, this 5-acre inland property sits on a hillside with sweeping views to the north of Vieques Sound and Culebra. The units, all freshly painted, are studios with TVs, kitchenettes, phones, ceiling fans, a/c, coolers, and beach towels and chairs. Some units have a balcony or private terrace. Best of all, it won't break the bank to stay here. The Crow's Nest boasts one of Vieques's best restaurants, Island Steakhouse, and a friendly bar, too. It also recently opened a new garden grill restaurant. There is a comfortable pool and a lounge area as well.

No children under 12 are allowed from May through mid-November.

The Great Escape B&B Inn, Box 14501, HC-02, Vieques, PR. ℂ 787-741-2927, 💻 www.enchanted-isle.com/greatescape, jonssch@coqui.net

💲 **Not So Cheap** 🍴 **CP** ㏄ 11 rooms

Nestled up in the hills is this remote bed & breakfast, ideal for those who want a time-out from flashy hotels and big crowds. Though quite a distance from the beach and devoid of sea views, the house is located on a spacious plot of open land with pleasant green views. The rooms are housed in a two-story house, and each has a green vistas. Activity is centered around the tile pool deck, which has an honor bar with some chairs in the sun and others under shelter for those sunburn victims. We like that there is a stereo for guests to use, as well as comfy chairs and a little cactus garden with figurines. Hammocks add a pleasant touch. All rooms have poster beds and a/c. Sure, it's a bit out of the way and best for those with a rental car, but as the name indicates, it's a Great Escape. The funky mirrored Mickey Mouse outhouse near the pool is most unusual!

Casa de Amistad, 27 Benitez Castaño, Vieques, PR. ℂ 787-741-3758, 💻 www.casadeamistad.com, viequesamistad@aol.com

💰 **Cheap** 🍴 **EP** (CC) 7 rooms

This cozy guesthouse is a great place to unwind. The rooms are simple but equipped with a/c and minibar. What we like most about the "Friendship House" is the intimacy. We felt very comfortable staying here, and we found plenty of hangout spots, from the wicker furniture on the front porch to the library with satellite TV, to the "freshwater" plunge pool and the garden in the backyard. The honor bar in the lobby is a nice addition, especially for those sitting by the pool or in the library. The rooftop deck is an added bonus. The guesthouse is not right on the ocean, but for those who desire a seaside accommodation, it is also possible to rent out the Becker Room, two blocks away, which looks right over the sea.

La Finca Caribe, P.O. Box 1332, Route 995, km 2.5, Vieques, PR. ✆ 787-741-0495, 📠 787-741-3584, 🖥 www.lafinca.com

💰 **Cheap** and up 🍴 **EP** (CC) 6 rooms and 2 cabins

Formerly the very funky women's retreat known as New Dawn, La Finca Caribe is definitely a different kind of lodging experience. Though no longer just a women's retreat, La Finca is still funky. Think Indian print bedspreads, summer camp, Birkenstocks, pajama parties, rustic communal living, hammocks, and the music of Jimmy Buffet all rolled into one, and you have an image of what this place is like. With the addition of some paint and a much-needed swimming pool (curiously saltwater despite the fact that La Finca is way up in the hills and 3 miles from the beach), it's certainly in better shape than the New Dawn ever was. However, if you have an aversion to plywood, you won't like it here—the exterior and the floors are just that. Nevertheless, there is a good-size porch with hammocks, and all showers are outdoors (and enclosed, of course).

The six rooms in the main house share two baths. All have mosquito nets, white walls and whitewashed floors, wall hangings, Indian print upholstery, and not a lot of privacy. There are two separate cabañas: one with a separate bedroom and private bath and the other a studio with sleeping loft. There are no TVs or phones in the rooms and cabañas. There is a communal kitchen in the main house. The entire place can be rented to a group and sleeps 20.

Hix Island House, P.O. Box 14902, HC-02, Vieques, PR. ✆ 787-741-2302, 📠 787-741-2797, 🖥 www.hixislandhouse.com, info@hixislandhouse.com

💰 **Wicked Pricey** 🍴 **CP** (CC) 13 rooms

This ultra-modern spot may be featured in architectural and fashion magazines, but we didn't enjoy our stay here. The inn is the creation of Canadian architect John Hix, who has created a stunning concrete collection of loft apartments in the middle of the forest. Yes, indeed, it is definitely a strange mix. We aren't turned off by the idea of super-mod design in the woods—in fact, we love that style. Our gripe is that as guests, we just weren't very comfortable. Perhaps the biggest problem is the fact the inn is located high in the woods, without sweeping vistas (except one at the pool). In these parts, this means that there are a whole lot of mosquitoes, which become quite a pain when the rooms have no screens. The beds have mosquito nets, but we have heard some guests complain that they don't always offer sufficient protection. The rooms are ultra-minimalist, with rough unfinished concrete, which may be great for a gallery in Berlin, but it just doesn't work for us in a tropical setting like Vieques. To be honest, the gray concrete makes the whole place look unfinished. Each apartment has a veranda and full kitchen. If we have to choose, Room 1 is our favorite, although the Matisse Room has a great rooftop deck. One feature we do really like (and wish was more common) is that the inn stocks the refrigerators with fresh bread, fruit, and juice, so guests can make breakfast at their leisure. Oh, and of course, we love the open-air showers. We must admit that the pool design is divine. No children under 12 allowed. Yoga is offered three days a week.

Trade Winds Guest House and Restaurant, P.O. Box 1012, 107 Calle Flamboyan, Malecón, Esperanza, Vieques, PR . © 787-741-8666, 🖉 787-741-2964, 🖳 www.enchanted-isle.com/tradewinds, tradewns@coqui.net

💲 **Cheap** 🍴 **EP** (CC) 11 rooms

Located right in Esperanza on the western end of the Malecón, this is a fairly modern, motelish lodging with an affordable price tag and a convenient location. Its shortage of ambiance and direct location on the malecón make it a less desirable place to stay, although we did notice some renovation since our last visit. All rooms include private bath and ceiling fans. Some rooms also have a/c, kitchenettes, and lanais.

Casa Cielo, P.O. Box 310, Route 995, km 1.1, Vieques, PR. © 787-741-2403, 🖉 787-741-2403, 🖳 www.enchanted-isle.com/casacielo, cielo@coqui.net

💲 **Pricey** and up 🍴 **CP** (CC) 9 rooms

We weren't kidding about former New Englanders living on Vieques. This nine-room inn with commanding views of the Vieques coastline to the south has two new owners from the Bay State: JoAnne Hamilton and Jim Ducharme. *Architectural Digest* from the 1960s is the simplest way to describe the inn's contemporary design. Once a private home, it was converted into an inn by an architect who knocked down the outside walls facing the water and built extended, wraparound decks on the ground and second levels. They provide room for a large pool and plenty of open-air seating for taking in the sweeping views —and do we mean sweeping. This adults-only inn may just have the best views on the island. The architecture includes lots of glass, so there's plenty to see from the inside, too. The design includes a common room with an atrium on the second level and a full kitchen available to the guests. Standard rooms come with balcony and are simply furnished, with white walls. Some are air-conditioned. All have ceiling fans. One room is wheelchair accessible. We only wish the driveway were more accessible, as well, and we recommend a 4WD vehicle or intrepid driver for the trip up.

Villa Rentals

For groups or families, a villa rental is probably your best bet, and there is a good selection from which to choose. These reputable companies can find the right place for you and can help with other island details as well.

Connections / Jane Sabin Real Estate, P.O. Box 358, 117 Calle Munoz Rivera, Vieques, PR. T 787-741-0023, F 787-741-2022, N www.enchanted-isle.com/Connections

Crow's Nest Realty, P.O. Box 1409, Vieques, PR. T 787-741-2843, F 787-741-1294, N www.crowsnestrealty.com, sheilevin@aol.com, elimelindez@coqui.net

Rainbow Realty, www.enchanted-isle.com/rainbow. Contact Lin Wetherby at 787-741-4312 or rainbowrealty@hotmail.com

Where to Eat

For such a small place, there are a surprising number of restaurants. Here are our picks.

$$ **Bananas**, Calle Flamboyán, Malecón, Esperanza, 741-8700

This fun, casual open-air restaurant (of course there's a roof) is a local gathering spot and a great place to hang out and work on some margaritas. It looks out on the Malecón and the sea beyond. The menu is pub fare: steaks, grilled seafood, and its famous burgers. Open daily for lunch and dinner until 10 or 11 p.m. (depending on business).

$$$ **Bilí**, Malecón, Esperanza, 741-1382

This well-designed restaurant right on the Malecón is a little pricey but tasty. We love the coco martinis and also recommend the rigatoni with crabmeat ragu. Open Wednesday through Sunday for lunch and dinner.

$$$ Café Media Luna, 351 A. G. Mellado, Isabel II, 741-2594

Located in downtown Isabel II, this restaurant in a restored house offers a creative international menu by chef Monica Chitnis. The café is one of Vieques cultural meccas, so keep an eye open for live music. Open Wednesday to Sunday, 7 to 10:30 p.m. in-season; off-season Friday through Sunday.

$$$ Chez Shack, Route 995, Km 8.6, 741-2175

This funky collection of brightly painted tin shacks was originally built around 1910. Just down the road from La Finca Caribe, Chez Shack offers a great menu of local dishes and seafood and has a very popular barbecue on Monday night — a mesquite grill featuring lobster, shrimp, steak, lamb, and fish, along with a salad bar. Eat in the sun or in the shade. Open daily, 6 until 11 p.m. or so.

$$$ Island Steakhouse, Route 201, km 1.6, 741-0011

The popular restaurant at the Crow's Nest has made a few changes. Hurricane Georges took off the restaurant's back roof, which has been replaced, and a new open deck has been added to the front. The new chefs have done a great job. They do lunch during the high season as well. Happy hour is from 5 until 7 p.m. Closed Monday. There is a new restaurant under construction here — it will offer burgers and *pinchos* ("snacks") by the pool.

$$ La Campesina, Barrio La Hueca, Route 201, Esperanza, 741-1239

This small restaurant, nestled beneath a roofed patio at the side of the road, is an island tradition of more than 20 years. The tree-house-like setting is intimate and unpretentious. The menu features pork, steak, and seafood. The bar is set around an enormous boulder. Open daily, 6 to 10 p.m.

$$$ M Bar, Isabela, 741-4000

The anticipated second restaurant of Puerto Rican chef Juan Camacho should now be open here in Isabela next to Uva. His nouvelle cuisine places an emphasis on the freshest ingredients. The style of the restaurant, with its raw wood and cement, adds to the ambiance. Look right into the kitchen and watch him do his thing.

$$ Tradewinds, Malecón, Esperanza, 741-8666

We simply love this seaside restaurant that is elevated to take in the fresh breezes. There is a varied array of cuisine options, but all are consistently delicious. The Caribbean fish cakes are a popular starter, but we favor the warmed goat cheese with sun-dried tomatoes and crostini. For those not ready for pricey lobster, try the guava chicken with sherry-guava glaze or the Thai coco-curry pasta with shrimp. Open Thursday through Monday for breakfast (homemade corned beef hash is a favorite) and lunch, and daily for dinner.

$$$ Uva, Isabela, 741-2050

This stylish rustic eatery is a member of the latest generation of upscale restaurants to hit Vieques in recent years. The Argentine chef offers a range of specialties, from meats to pasta. Cool tunes pervade throughout, and the bar is a great place to relax with a drink. Open from 7 to 10:30 p.m.; closed Tuesday.

Going Out

Not quite a nocturnal mecca, Vieques is still more of a day-lover's place. But some of the restaurants along the Malecón (such as Bananas, Bilí, and Tradewinds) and in Isabela (Uva and M Bar) are great places to relax at night.

Al's Mar Azul, Calle Plinio Peterson, 741-3400

Located steps from the ferry terminal, this laid-back bar is pure Caribbean. Its outdoor deck offers wonderful sunset views that are well-timed for happy-hour dollar beers. The pool table and darts add activities, and the crowd here runs the whole Vieques spectrum. Closed on Tuesday during the low season.

The Palms, Isabela, 741-1128

The Palms is a part of the Bravo Hotel — in fact, it's the second pool, which the hotel opens to the public on weekend nights. We love sitting along the red-lit pool here, enjoying a cocktail as the DJ spins loungelike house music. There are cushions laid out along the edge of the elevated pool, which is in tune with the easygoing sexy vibe. This is a very romantic setting and an ideal spot for a late-night swim, so dress accordingly. Open weekends until late.

Don't Miss

Bioluminescence Bay

Mosquito and Barracuda are two of the few bioluminescent bays in the world. There was also one in La Parguera, Puerto Rico, but failure to protect its fragile ecosystem led to a fading of its bioluminescence. In the dark of a calm night, phosphorescent plankton (dinoflagellates, to be precise) create "sparks" with any vigorous movement in the water that disturbs their nesting. Island Adventures (787-741-0720, www.biobay.com), which is recently under new ownership, offers popular tours of the bay. The one-and-a-half-hour tour on the pontoon boat includes swimming and stargazing. Departure time is around 6:30 p.m., and rates are about $30 per person. To truly appreciate the serene beauty of the bio bay, we recommend going via kayak. Blue Caribe Kayak (741-2522) is the best bet here.

Snorkeling and Diving

Vieques has some great dive sites and a full-service dive operation. Call the Blue Caribe Dive Center (741-2522) in Esperanza. Captain Richard Barone of Vieques Nature Tours has a glass-bottom boat and offers snorkeling and education tours (787-741-1980). For water-sports addicts, Extreme (435-2121) rents jet skis from the Malecón in Esperanza for $100 an hour (yeah, pricey).

Fuerte Conde de Mirasol

The fort in Isabel II was the last to be built by a colonial power in the western hemisphere (it was built in the 1840s). It has been restored and houses interesting island exhibits, art, and the Vieques Historic Archives. Open Wednesday to Sunday from 10 a.m. to 4 p.m. or by special appointment. Call 787-741-1717.

INDEX

ABOUT THE AUTHOR

JONATHAN RUNGE is the author of 16 other travel books: *Rum & Reggae's Costa Rica*, co-authored with Adam Carter (2006); *Rum & Reggae's Brazil* (2005); *Rum & Reggae's French Caribbean* (2005); *Rum & Reggae's Grenadines, Including St. Vincent and Grenada* (2003); *Rum & Reggae's Virgin Islands* (2003); *Rum & Reggae's Caribbean* (2002); *Rum & Reggae's Jamaica* (2002); *Rum & Reggae's Puerto Rico* (2002); *Rum & Reggae's Dominican Republic* (2002); *Rum & Reggae's Cuba* (2002); *Rum & Reggae's Hawai'i* (2001); *Rum & Reggae's Caribbean 2000* (2000); *Rum & Reggae: The Insider's Guide to the Caribbean* (Villard Books, 1993); *Hot on Hawai'i: The Definitive Guide to the Aloha State* (St. Martin's Press, 1989); *Rum & Reggae: What's Hot and What's Not in the Caribbean* (St. Martin's Press, 1988); and *Ski Party!: The Skier's Guide to the Good Life*, co-authored with Steve Deschenes (St. Martin's Press, 1985). Jonathan has also written for *Men's Journal, Outside, National Geographic Traveler, Out, Skiing, Boston*, and other magazines. He is the publisher and a partner of Rum & Reggae Guidebooks, Inc., which is based in Boston.

RUM & REGGAE'S
TOURISTO SCALE

1. What century is this?

2. Still sort of a secret; this place is practically empty.

3. A nice, unspoiled yet civilized place.

4. Still unspoiled, but getting popular.

5. A popular place, but still not mentioned in every travel article.

6. The secret is out; everybody is starting to go here.

7. Well-developed tourism and lots of tourists;
fast-food outlets conspicuous.

8. Highly developed tourism and tons of tourists.

9. Mega-tourists and tour groups;
fast-food outlets outnumber restaurants.

10. Swarms of tourists.
Run for cover!